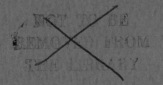

abnormal
psychology

abnormal psychology

henry e. adams
university of georgia

wcb

Wm. C. Brown Company Publishers
Dubuque, Iowa

wcb
group

Wm. C. Brown Chairman of the Board
Mark C. Falb Corporate Vice President/Operations

Book Team

James L. Romig Editor
Julia A. Scannell Designer
Mary M. Monner Production Editor
Mary M. Heller Visual Research Editor
Mavis M. Oeth Permissions Editor

wcb

Wm. C. Brown Company Publishers, College Division

Lawrence E. Cremer President
Raymond C. Deveaux Vice President/Product Development
David Wm. Smith Assistant Vice President/National Sales Manager
David A. Corona Director of Production Development and Design
Matthew T. Coghlan National Marketing Manager
Janis Machala Director of Marketing Research
Marilyn A. Phelps Manager of Design
William A. Moss Production Editorial Manager
Mary M. Heller Visual Research Manager

Cover photo by Bob Coyle.

Cover mannequin from Decter Mannikin Company.

All text and visual credits start on page 619.

Copyright © 1981 by Wm. C. Brown Company Publishers

Library of Congress Catalog Card Number: 80-68349
ISBN 0-697-06636-3 (Cloth)
ISBN 0-697-06641-X (Paper)

Printed in the United States of America

For
Irwin A. Berg,
Donald J. Lewis,
and Brendan A. Maher,
my professors

contents

unit 2 neuroses, personality disorders, and special symptoms 195

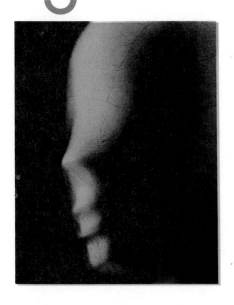

preface

Abnormal Psychology was written to guide students in applying the principles of psychology to the study of abnormal behavior. It is especially designed for students, majors or nonmajors, who want a scientific introduction to the field and who are interested in research-based, practical, applicable information.

The emphasis of the text is on broad topical coverage followed by a study of the appropriate theory and research. Although no research endeavor has been deliberately neglected, a behavioral emphasis has evolved. This emphasis is conducive to the comprehension of abnormal behavior as a variation of normal behavior, distinguishable in many instances only by degree. Knowledge of perception, motivation, learning, biopsychology, and social psychology, all of which is based on normally functioning individuals, is directly related to the understanding and modification of deviant behavior. Consistent with this assumption, this text stresses that labels of deviance and normality should be used to categorize behavior patterns and not individuals. Throughout the book the preference for classifying abnormal behaviors and not stereotyping individuals is stressed.

Organization

Familiarizing the student with the tools of diagnosis and assessment is essential to understanding specific disorders. Thus, basic concepts, such as historical models, the scientific approach to abnormal behavior, classification methods, causal factors, assessment, and modification procedures, are presented in Unit 1. This organization allows each disorder discussed in Units 2 through 5 to be examined in terms of specific methods of assessment and also in terms of modification. Each chapter in these sections uses a similar organizational pattern, discussing clinical characteristics, research, assessment, and treatment. Throughout, an emphasis is placed on clinical concerns.

The presentation of the disorders is similar to other abnormal psychology texts with a few notable exceptions. Psychophysiological problems are placed in the section on behavioral disorders associated with biological factors. Since psychophysiological disorders are diagnosed by dysfunction of biological systems, this placement seems appropriate. Material on social, moral, and political aspects of abnormal behavior is integrated throughout the relevant sections of the book. Eating disorders, stuttering, personality disorders, tics, and sleeping disorders are covered, despite their frequent omission from abnormal psychology textbooks.

Pedagogical Aids

Because of the amount and diversity of material in *Abnormal Psychology,* much attention has been paid to pedagogical aids. Unit introductions, key topics and key concepts lists, marginal notes, highlighting of key points in the text proper, chapter review questions, glossary, and extensive reference list—all have been professionally prepared to reinforce the student's understanding of text material.

The numerous case histories presented throughout the text give students the opportunity to see how text material and research can be applied to the assessment and modification of real-life disorders. In addition, the case histories help students to appreciate the human aspects of dealing with abnormal behavior.

The scholarship is current and thorough and should satisfy the most curious of graduate students. However, the text is primarily designed as an undergraduate text. The writing level as well as the content rigor has undergone three major revisions by professional writers and consultants.

Instructor's Manual

The instructor's manual, written by Jean Hanebury, provides many suggestions for organization of the abnormal psychology course, including course outlines and assignment schedules. Lecture outlines have been prepared, as have detailed answers to the review questions at the end of each text chapter. Appropriate films, transparencies, suggested term papers, and possible guest lecturers are listed. In addition, two sets of examination questions are supplied for each chapter.

acknowledgments

I would like to express my gratitude to many individuals at William C. Brown Company Publishers, including Ed Bowers, David Smith, and Mary Monner for their technical and emotional support throughout this project. The editorial assistance of William Fitzgerald, Dr. Mary Baine, Lionel Gambill, Perrie Lou Bryant, and Jean Hanebury is gratefully acknowledged.

The manuscript benefited greatly from the comments and critiques of numerous scholars in the field, including:

Don C. Fowles, Ph.D.
The University of Iowa

Herbert E. Howe, Jr., Ph.D.
University of Nebraska

Daniel S. Kirschenbaum, Ph.D.
University of Wisconsin—Madison

Victor L. Ryan, Ph.D.
University of Colorado

W. Larry Ventis, Ph.D.
College of William and Mary

I am especially grateful to the many talented graduate students who assisted me in writing this book, particularly Phillip Brantley, Tracey Potts Carson, Elizabeth P. Lamson, Betsy Lyons, Lois Smith, Ellie T. Sturgis, C. David Tollison, Ira Turkat, Carolyn Williams, and Mary Warner.

Additionally, the support and sacrifice provided by my family—June, Eddie, Kim, and Karen Adams—made this textbook a reality.

Henry E. Adams

abnormal psychology

scientific approaches to the study of abnormal behavior

Attempts to understand and modify abnormal behavior have taken a variety of forms over the years. As we shall see in Chapter 1, those forms are dictated largely by the beliefs and assumptions already held by the scientists and therapists themselves. Those beliefs and assumptions take the form of scientific **models,** or **paradigms,** and they serve to focus inquiry in such a way that ideas can be tested against experience. A system of *classification* is necessary to organize the data yielded by that process; we shall discuss such systems in Chapter 2. Furthermore, the data cannot be meaningful or verifiable unless certain rules are observed in their gathering and interpretation. We shall discuss those rules in Chapter 3. And in Chapter 4 we shall discuss one of the primary objectives of science, the discovery of *cause-and-effect relationships.*

As interesting as they might be, such scientific inquiries achieve no practical realization until we are face to face with someone who needs help. Then, the task is *assessment*—deciding whether the person's behavior does indeed warrant intervention and finding out exactly how and to what degree there is a deficiency, excess, or inappropriateness of behavior. This kind of information forms the basis for deciding what kind of treatment is most likely to be effective in modifying the behavior. Such treatments, or *therapies,* are of four general types. We shall discuss three of these types—*psychodynamic, humanistic,* and *medical* approaches—in Chapter 6, and the fourth type—*behavior* therapy—in Chapter 7.

emergence of the major models of abnormal behavior 1

Key Topics

Five major models of abnormal
behavior

Treatments related to the models

Historical perspectives from the
primitive to the contemporary
Impact of the discovery of the
cause of paresis
Experimentation with hypnosis
Impact of the medical model and
psychoanalysis

Development of behaviorism

Respondent conditioning and
learning

Existential and humanistic
psychologies

Viewpoint and organization of this
text

Imagine that you and another person—someone you have just met for the first time—have been assigned a task that demands your combined skill and concentration. Imagine further that you have been tipped off by a third person that your partner in this task is "mentally ill." How would this information affect your perception of, and your behavior toward, that partner? A situation exactly like that was created in a series of experiments (Farina and Ring 1965; Farina, Holland, and Ring 1966). If you claimed your partner behaved "unpredictably," you would be responding like the majority of the participants. Most partners were judged solely on the basis of the "mentally ill" *label,* as their "normal" partners tended to recognize only those actions that confirmed the label. In other words, on hearsay, they *stigmatized* their partner and acted accordingly, *regardless* of how their partner acted during the experiment.

"Mental illness" as a stigma

Now what if you had been the labeled partner—the one thought to be mentally ill by others? Like the majority of the labeled partners in similar experiments (Bord 1971; Snyder, Tanke, and Berscheid 1977; Snyder and Swann 1978), you would have behaved more and more in ways that confirmed the label! Even if you were not informed of the labeling, even if you had behaved "normally" in the past, you would start to behave according to the way you were treated.

This exercise should suggest several questions to you that are fundamental to the study of abnormal psychology: Why do people stereotype and stigmatize others? Why should we study abnormal behavior? What causes abnormal behavior? What qualifies behavior as abnormal, or a person as mentally ill? We shall examine each of these questions in turn.

Why Do People Stereotype and Stigmatize Others?

The less we know about another person, the more likely we are to apply stereotypes so that we can make predictions and exercise control in our interactions. R. J. Grandison (1980) reasons that "It may be that the most threatening characteristic of those labeled mentally ill is their presumed unpredictability." The basis for this threat, according to Nunnally (1961), is the fear

Unpredictability seen as threatening

that "because of their erratic behavior, [they] may suddenly embarrass or endanger others. . . . Consequently, most people are very uncomfortable in the presence of someone who is, or is purported to be, mentally ill." Ross (1977) adds:

Individuals must, for the most part, share a common understanding of the social actions and outcomes that affect them, for without such consensus, social interaction would be chaotic, unpredictable, and *beyond the control of the participants.* [Emphasis added.]

And Berscheid and Graziano (1980) observe:

In terms of the perceiver's exertion of control over his social environment, it seems reasonable to assume that, other things being equal, novel or unfamiliar people are more likely to represent potential problems of control than are familiar (and predictable) others.

In short, a mentally ill person is viewed as a threat to our control over our social interactions.

Ironically, the experiments we have cited seem to suggest that stigmatizing does increase predictability and control, though in counterproductive ways. Stigmatizing apparently can create "symptoms" where none had existed, and can intensify and prolong symptoms that already exist. This is, as we shall see, a serious problem in modifying abnormal behavior. On the positive side, when abnormally behaving people are expected by those around them to recover, their recovery rate is much higher (Waxler 1974).

Why Should We Study Abnormal Behavior?

As we shall see in Chapter 3, *predictability* and *control* are the objectives of the scientific study of abnormal behavior. The hope is, of course, that the control will be exercised in a positive, therapeutic direction, as opposed to the "sick-making" effects of stigmatizing. The obvious question is, "Does studying abnormal psychology reduce stigmatizing?" Some studies suggest that such change, when it does occur, results more from the teacher's attitude or the student's ability and belief system than from the content of the course. Nevertheless, positive changes do occur. Students who have completed abnormal psychology courses are likely to be less authoritarian

scientific approaches to the study of abnormal behavior

When he was thirteen, Henry Mercer was committed to Rockland State Mental Hospital for four years. The doctors recognized that he was not psychotic, but there was no other place for him to live. (No foster home placement was available.) When he was finally released to the custody of his brother, Mercer settled down, earning his high school diploma in night school and working his way up from nurse's aide to trusted ambulance attendant at a local hospital. Fifteen years after his commitment, Mercer was refused a license to drive a taxi in New York City because he had been in a mental institution. During the year-long court battle that ensued, six psychiatrists unanimously agreed that Mercer showed no signs of current disturbance and was completely capable of holding a hack license. Indeed, he had never evidenced any psychotic behavior. After three court appearances, numerous letters and petitions, and numbers of recommendations unqualifiedly testifying to Mercer's stability and competence, the Hack Bureau offered to settle out of court. In short, there was no favorable court decision and, consequently, no precedent established for prohibiting discrimination against former mental patients. Henry Mercer was granted a hack license with the provision that he furnish psychiatric evaluations every six months. The Hack Bureau's assumption seemed to be "once a mental patient, always untrustworthy."

or socially restrictive in their attitudes toward abnormal behavior, and to believe that such behavior is caused by interpersonal factors (Costin and Kerr 1962; Graham 1968; Gulo and Fraser 1967; Dixon 1967).

Another frequent outcome of studying abnormal psychology is the realization that abnormal behavior occurs in everyone. We shall make this point repeatedly. Even the most severe disturbances in behavior are generally different only in degree, not in kind, from behavior that is common to everyone's responses to life. Realizing this is the first step toward a greater understanding of others and perhaps a greater predictability and control in one's own life.

What Causes Abnormal Behavior?

Abnormal behavior can result from genetic disorders, physical illness or injury, maturation factors, aging, deprivations and deficiencies, stress, emotional trauma, learning, or a combination of any of these factors. As we shall see in Chapter 4, abnormal behavior is commonly acquired in the same ways as normal behavior.

What Qualifies Behavior As Abnormal, or a Person As Mentally Ill?

We have already seen, in the exercise at the beginning of this chapter, two important criteria of abnormality—*labeled deviance* and *maladaptive behavior*. In general, abnormal behavior is any behavior that differs from the expected or the customary. Every human being behaves abnormally at some point. When such behavior results in labeling, either the behavior or the person is called abnormal, mentally ill, deviant, maladjusted, emotionally disturbed, or crazy. Our position in this book is that labeling the person is more likely to be part of the problem than part of the solution. Labeling the behavior has its drawbacks too, but without it, classification is difficult if not impossible, and without classification, research and modification could not occur.

To answer with purpose and satisfaction the four questions raised in the preceding paragraphs, we need a structure to organize our study. The most appropriate structure is one that is common to most sciences—*models,* or *paradigms.*

Models of Abnormal Behavior

Imagine again that someone has labeled your behavior abnormal. To do so, that person had to perceive your behavior as either deviating from some preconceived idea of normality or matching some preconceived idea of abnormality. However, these preconceptions are different at different times

Effects of studying abnormal psychology

Two criteria of abnormality

Edmund Emil Kemper III, a shy and ungainly boy with an I.Q. of 131, was about eight years old when he first thought of murdering his mother. She was described in subsequent accounts as "a strict disciplinarian," who often banished her son to the basement. She also sent him to live for a time with grandparents in North Fork, California. There, on an August afternoon in 1964, when he was fifteen, Kemper shot his grandmother to death with two bullets in the head. When his grandfather returned from the grocery store, Kemper shot him too. Then he telephoned his mother to confess. "I just wondered how it would feel to shoot Grandma," he said.

Kemper spent five years in the Atascadero State Mental Hospital, where, among other things, he apparently memorized twenty-eight different psychological tests and the answers that the psychiatrists considered appropriate. In 1970, when he was twenty-one, he was set free. By now, he was a huge, blubbery figure, six feet nine inches, 280 pounds, but still oddly babyish, with steel-rimmed glasses and a droopy mustache. He found work on a highway construction crew and seemed to live in a state of respectable obscurity. In September of 1972, he went back to court to ask that his record as a juvenile offender be permanently sealed. The court ordered two psychiatrists to examine him. They had no way of knowing, of course, that just four days before their examination, Kemper had picked up a fifteen-year-old girl named

Aiko Koo, on her way to a ballet class, and dismembered her. "He has made an excellent response to the years of treatment," one of the psychiatrists declared. "I see no psychiatric reason to consider him a threat to himself or any other member of society."

The following May, the court records having been appropriately sealed, Kemper achieved his lifelong ambition. During an argument with his mother, an administrative assistant at the University of California at Santa Cruz, Kemper hit her on the head with a hammer. Then he cut off her head and her right hand. He also strangled a friend of hers, another employee at the university. After stuffing the bodies into two bedroom closets, he drove east as far as Pueblo, Colorado, and then telephoned back to the Santa Cruz sheriff's office to confess. He also confessed that he had killed Miss Koo and five other girls during the previous year. He said that he was afraid his mother would find out about these murders, and therefore he had decided to "bear the burden of killing her as well, to avoid her suffering any embarrassment."

Why, under the circumstances, had Kemper been repeatedly examined and found harmless? "Kemper is a marvelous example of the fact that psychiatrists don't know everything," observed Dr. Herbert McGraw, a staff psychiatrist at California's Napa State Hospital. "If you're right 75 percent of the time, you're doing pretty well."

*Models are
belief systems . . .*

and in different cultures, since they are derived from *models,* which are part of the culture itself. Some of these models are part of the broad culture of an entire society; others are part of the tradition of a scientific discipline. If you mutilated yourself, you would be perceived as abnormal in our society. Yet, in the Middle Ages, your behavior might have been accepted as evidence of your piety and spiritual devotion.

On the island of Mangaia a man whose women friends did not consistently have multiple orgasms when he made love to them would be ridiculed for his "impotence" (and as a result might become impotent). In Inis Beag, Ireland, a woman who had an orgasm would be considered strange. All of these and countless other differences in the way people see and evaluate the behavior of others reflect different models.

scientific approaches to the study of abnormal behavior

What Is a Model?

A model, or *paradigm,* as it is often called, is a belief or system of beliefs about the structure and workings of reality. Newtonian dynamics, relativity, and quantum mechanics are models in physics. Ptolemaic and Copernican systems in astronomy are models, and so are communism, socialism, and capitalism in sociology.

Science historian T. S. Kuhn (1962) is a popular observer of models in science and sees models, or paradigms, as achievements that "define the legitimate problems and methods of a research field for succeeding generations of practitioners." He points out that a model both guides and limits observation—a scientist looks at what the model points to, and—at first—does not see the anomalies (events that fail to fit the model), but the more exhaustively the scientist uses the model to solve puzzles, the more it forces him or her to recognize those anomalies. Eventually, this recognition points out the need for a different model, through a process Kuhn calls a **paradigm clash.** We shall encounter many paradigm clashes in our study of abnormal psychology.

For our purposes, we see models as complex hypotheses, derived from other fields of knowledge, that attempt to explain phenomena—in our case, abnormal behavior. These models may come from philosophical positions such as religion or from other scientific fields such as medicine, biology, or sociology. In a sense, a model is like a game. Certain assumptions are made; rules of the game are followed; and then attempts are made to control, explain, describe accurately, or make useful predictions about behavior. If the model appears to predict what actually occurs, then the model is useful; if it does not, a newer, more accurate model must be developed.

In abnormal psychology, there have been a variety of models to account for deviant behaviors. These models have greatly influenced our opinion regarding deviant behavior, especially in terms of assessment, treatment, and further investigations of abnormal behavior. For this reason, it is useful to understand these models of abnormal behavior and their history. In general, there are five major models of abnormal behavior: *animism, moral models, phenomenological models, medical models,* and *environmental models.*

Animism

Animism is the belief that spirits, gods, or demons animate natural forces, objects, animals, and humans. The two major tenets of animism are belief in the *supernatural* and belief in *free will.* This primitive model of the universe assumes both good spirits and bad spirits. If an individual behaves inappropriately or is unlucky, the gods may punish him by allowing a demon to possess him and rob him of his own free will. Or an individual may voluntarily enter into a pact with an evil spirit and exchange her soul for certain supernatural powers. Treatment of an individual usually consists of *exorcism,* which in its extreme form can be quite traumatic for the individual.

Abnormality as demon possession

Moral Models

If you had lived in the late eighteenth or early nineteenth century and worked with abnormally behaving people, you might have seen them as normal people who had been overwhelmed by their problems, an approach not unlike some present-day ones. These approaches are called **moral models.** Their presupposition is that abnormal people were once normal but have "lost their reason" due to exposure to psychologically or socially stressful environments that they could not manage because they had deviated from contemporary moral or social standards, such as Christianity. These conditions were once called the "moral causes of insanity" (Rees 1957). Treatment consists of purposeful activity in an atmosphere of kindness, firmness, and reason.

as a problem caused by stress

A Humanistic Model
The humanistic position is a type of moral model that focuses on our individual uniqueness—our values, dignity, and worth as individuals—and other human attributes that contribute to self-actualization (the

realization of the full potential of one's capabilities). In this particular approach, our uniqueness and dignity, personal growth, meaning, positive self-regard, creativity, self-actualization, and authenticity are key concepts. The concept of self is a unifying concept among humanistic theorists, who focus on values, personal growth, and a positive view of human nature and human potential.

Phenomenological Models

If you tried to understand a person's abnormal behavior by trying to find out from that person what the behavior felt like to him or her, how it looked "from inside," from the context of that person's life experience, you would be using a **phenomenological model.** Phenomenological models are based on the belief that a person's behavior is best understood in terms of that person's *consciousness.* Abnormal behavior is explained largely in terms of blocked feelings, negative self-image, and loss of authenticity. (Authenticity is the capacity to respond naturally and spontaneously, as opposed to censoring feelings and thoughts and controlling behavior carefully to manage the impression one makes on others.) Treatment can be through individual psychotherapy in which the therapist reflects and clarifies what the client says, or it can make use of group interaction or the enactment of the conflicting parts of the self. The aims are increased awareness, openness, authenticity, personal growth, and self-actualization.

as blocked feelings

as disease

An Existential Model
The existential approach developed from the philosophy of Kierkegaard, Heidegger, Jaspers, and Sarte. It is very similar to the humanistic model but focuses on the nature of humans and the meaning of existence to the individual. People are viewed as being in a continual state of transition, and this process of becoming is their "being." While individuals are able to make free choices and decisions in the process of becoming, they must assume the responsibility that comes with this freedom. If we choose the

proper values in life and find a set of creative, experiential, and attitudinal values that are consistent with our individuality, we are well adjusted. If not, we may be alienated and suffer feelings of isolation, depersonalization, and loneliness, which result in frustration and neuroses.

Medical Models

Currently, the most popular models of abnormal behavior are the **medical models,** which define deviant behavior as *mental illness.* Each disease has a specific cluster of *symptoms,* which are called a *syndrome.* Symptoms are fevers, skin rashes, or similar observable external physiological phenomena that are often caused by infectious diseases, such as the common cold, pneumonia, and hepatitis. A second origin or etiological source of symptoms is the *systemic disease,* which is a disorder usually due to an inherited condition that may be influenced by environmental factors. Diabetes and Huntington's Chorea are two examples. The third type of etiological source is the *traumatic diseases,* which are produced by external agents, such as ingestion of toxic substances, accidents, or similar events causing physiological damage. In the medical models, each condition has a specific prognosis and a specific treatment method, such as medication, surgery, or rest.

Perhaps the major reason that the medical models have been applied to abnormal behavior was the discovery that **paresis,** a disorder associated with gross behavioral and physiological deterioration, is caused by syphilitic infections. This discovery facilitated the assumption that abnormal behavior represents symptoms that indicate an underlying cause. Mental disorders have since been associated with a specific prognosis and require medical treatment. Typically, there are two major types of medical models.

Biogenic Models
The first type, the **biogenic approach,** assumes that mental illness is caused by *systemic* diseases. Behavioral disorders "run in the family"; they are caused by the in-

dividual's genetic endowment. Typical biogenic models, such as the biochemical and genetic theories of schizophrenia, will be discussed throughout the book. The psychiatrists who favor this model are often called *organic psychiatrists.* Typical medical treatment techniques include chemotherapy, psychosurgery, and electroconvulsive shock.

Psychogenic Models

The **psychogenic approach** is the second major type of medical model. The supporters of this approach assume that the causes of mental illness involve **psychic trauma,** such as Oedipal conflicts or sibling rivalry. Abnormal behaviors are seen as symptoms of these underlying, usually unconscious, conflicts that have been repressed. The treatment is to awaken the individual to the unconscious determinants of his or her behavior so that the conflicts can be consciously resolved. The process is called psychotherapy, and it will be discussed in Chapter 5.

Certainly, medical models are vulnerable to a variety of criticisms, but they are credited with being the first to apply modern research methods to the study of abnormal behavior. The researchers assume that behavior is determined, that all abnormal behaviors have common or similar elements, and that the crucial events, or at least their symptoms, are observable.

Environmental Models

Other scientists have reasoned that abnormal behavior is a malfunction of an individual's socialization. Environmental events are seen as primary causes, while physiological factors are regarded as secondary. These **environmental models** are similar to moral models in that both are concerned about the influence of social conditions on one's psychological adjustment. Environmental models differ, however, by assuming that behavior is *learned,* that it is determined by environmental factors, and that scientific laws require observable demonstration. Environmental models emphasize similarity rather than the uniqueness of individuals. They are, like the medical ones, scientific models since the assumption of

determinism and public demonstration make the claims amenable to scientific proof.

The first proposition of environmental models is **cultural relativism**—that what constitutes acceptable or abnormal behavior *varies* from culture to culture. For example, Benedict (1934) noted the marked differences between the Plains Indians and the Pueblo Indians of North America. Plains Indians were hunters whose culture encouraged dangerous living, emotional excesses, and violence. Their children were deliberately provoked to have temper tantrums and were exposed to traumatic situations, such as hunger, thirst, and pain. The ideal person among the Plains Indians was brave, reckless, and cruel. Most Sioux and Crow warriors acquired these traits. In contrast, the Pueblo Indians of the Southwest, such as the Hopis and Zunis, cultivated the traits of moderation, restraint, and mildness. Their children were taught to be cooperative, flexible, and kind. An orderly, even-tempered life, free of excess, excitement, and violence constituted their cultural ideal. Hence, normal behavior in one culture was viewed as abnormal in the other. Other examples of relativism are shown in Table 1–1.

A Social-Cultural Model

The second proposition of environmental models is that any culture's success in creating *conformity* to its standard of normal behavior is limited. Thus the "normal" members of a culture behave, most of the time, in conformity to the norms of the specific culture. However, a certain amount of culturally determined deviant behavior does occur. In addition, some deviant behavior usually exists for which the culture has neither a name nor a solution (Scheff 1966). An example of this *social-cultural* model would be giggling at the funeral of one's mother, an unusual reaction to stress. Such behavior is usually transitory and, according to Scheff, is considered normal. If the behavior is not transitory, however, the person may be labeled "mentally ill" and cast into the role of a "mental patient," a role that the individual is then expected to seriously adopt.

Table 1–1 Exotic Patterns of Abnormal Behavior in Other Cultures

Type	Cultural group	Description
Amok	Malaya	This disorder generally appears among males and is typically precipitated by a frustrating event. Usually, the patient goes through several stages: an initial withdrawal, a meditation period, and then the amok proper. When the subject "runs amok," he may commit multiple homicides, mutilate himself and others, and is likely to be killed by frightened neighbors. If he survives the amok period, he may be depressed after regaining consciousness. Most often the subject has amnesia for the amok period.
Koro	China	A patient with this syndrome believes that his penis will withdraw into his abdomen, causing his death. Sufferers of this disorder often clamp the penis in a box to prevent the withdrawal.
Lattah	Malaya	Women in middle or older age typically display this syndrome. An attack is usually precipitated by sudden fright or tickling. This is followed by a short period in which the woman imitates the behavior of others, automatically obeys commands, and utters obscenities.
Miryachit	Siberia	The victim has an irresistible urge to imitate the behavior of others and repeat everything that is said.
Susto	Peru	This syndrome is an acute anxiety reaction that generally occurs in children or adolescents. Susto, or magic fright, is the belief that the soul has been stolen from the patient's body.
Windigo	Ojibwa, Cree	The victim of this disorder suffers from a morbid craving for human flesh and the delusion that he or she is a Wiikitiko, a supernatural being feared by the tribe.
Pibloktog	Eskimo of western Greenland	This occurs primarily in women. Onset is marked by singing that increases in intensity until loss of consciousness ensues. Often the patient will tear off her clothing, throw objects, and imitate birdcalls. Any opposition she encounters is resisted violently.

A Social Psychological Model

as learned habits

A similar environmental model, the *social psychological* model of Ullmann and Krasner (1975), begins with the assumption that no intrinsic difference exists between normal and abnormal behavior. Behavior is labeled abnormal, according to this model, if three factors exist: (1) the behavior, (2) a social context in which the behavior is inappropriate, and (3) an observer in authority. Thus, a person can be nude at home without being labeled abnormal, but if he or she is nude in the street in the presence of a police officer, the behavior will be labeled abnormal. Both the behavior labeled abnormal and the act of labeling are viewed, in this model, as *learned* behaviors.

The Behaviorist Position

A more purely psychological type of environmental model is the *behaviorist* position. Unlike the medical models, the behaviorist position assumes that symptoms are *learned habits*. This model has been most clearly formulated by Eysenck (1959), who maintains that the same principles govern the acquisition of both normal and abnormal behavior. Furthermore, according to Eysenck, abnormal behavior has no underlying causes. Once the symptoms are eliminated, the disorder also is eliminated.

The behaviorist position assumes that some behavior patterns may be intrinsically abnormal. For example, if a person reacts to a stress-filled environment by acquiring a peptic ulcer, the behavior is life threatening and therefore intrinsically abnormal and independent of social norms. Behaviorism regards psychological factors as primary and cultural ones as secondary. It also assumes that behavior is determined and that biological factors are important since they often have profound effects on learning and behavior. Finally, in contrast to some of the other models we have discussed, the behavioral position insists on *public verification* of research results—research reports must contain enough information

scientific approaches to the study of abnormal behavior

about methodology to permit other investigators to replicate the study. *The behaviorist position is the viewpoint of this book.* The following section will help us see how it evolved.

The Historical Perspective

An historical overview of the development of the study of abnormal psychology will help further define the importance of these models and explain how they have shaped our perceptions and treatment methods.

Primitive Times

Though our knowledge of primitive beliefs and behavior is limited, archaeological evidence and studies of present-day nontechnological cultures indicate that the central concepts in early beliefs about abnormal behavior were *animistic*. Natural phenomena were explained as the work of gods or spirits, both good and bad, that inhabited trees, rocks, rivers, animals, and occasionally humans. Lightning and thunder, for example, might be perceived as the angry outburst of a god, physical illness or misfortune might be interpreted as punishment dealt out by a supernatural being, and abnormal behavior was attributed not to the person but to some spirit entity that possessed the person.

References to possession abound in early Chinese, Egyptian, Hebrew, and Greek literature. In the Old Testament, for example, we read that David took advantage of this popular myth and simulated madness to escape from Achish, the king of Gath (1 Samuel 21: 12–14). And the New Testament tells how Jesus cured a man by casting out the devils that possessed the man into a herd of swine (Mark 5: 1–13). The persistence of animistic ideas, even in our own time, is demonstrated by the recent rash of horror movies in which some demon-possessed character (often a child) terrorizes everyone.

Demon possession was evidently treated by exorcism, which could take various forms. One of these forms, trephining, was a primitive kind of brain surgery. Its existence is inferred from the condition of skulls recovered at archaeological sites. Evidently,

the surgeon chipped away a circular or triangular piece of the patient's skull, which permitted the evil spirits to escape. Ironically, this may have incidentally reduced physiological pressure on the brain, resulting in an apparent cure.

Exorcism could involve anything from prayer, incantations, and noise making to the use of concoctions made, for example, from sheep dung and wine. In extreme instances, flogging, starving, and other methods of torture to make life in the possessed person intolerable for the possessing demon, was not unheard of.

The Golden Age

Modern thinking about abnormal behavior is generally attributed to the Golden Age of Greece, although similar enlightened thought appeared in other parts of the world. Hippocrates (460–377 B.C.), who has been called the father of medicine, rejected the concept of possession. He believed instead that abnormal behavior was due to natural causes and that it required humane treatment. His theories were, in fact, the first clear statement of the *medical model*. Since he assumed that the brain was the center of cognitive activity, he reasoned that brain pathology caused abnormal behavior. He also stressed the importance of heredity and of head injuries as determinants of sensory and motor disorders.

Hippocrates was a good clinician and observer of behavior. He gave detailed clinical descriptions of such specific disorders as alcoholism, epilepsy, and hysteria. (He was sometimes wrong, however. For example, he thought hysteria occurred only in women and was due to the wandering of the uterus to various parts of the body, motivated by a craving to bear children. Male hysteria was not recognized until the present century.) Hippocrates classified abnormal behavior into three general categories: *mania,* a form of extreme excitement; *melancholia,* a disabling depression; and *phrenitis,* or brain fever and thought disorders.

Hippocrates believed that abnormal behavior was caused by an imbalance of the *four humors*: *blood,* which was associated with a sanguine, or cheerful, temperament;

Primitive animism

The medical model of Hippocrates

The bringing up of Dakota children was such that they grew up to feel that they were part of nature, or relatives of all things, to feel that "there was no complete solitude," because, wherever they were, they were with their relatives—the rocks, the trees, the wind. They grew to feel, as Standing Bear put it, ". . . that we are of the soil and the soil is of us. We love the birds and beasts that grew with us on this soil. They drank the same water and breathed the same air. We are all one in nature." Responsibility toward the buffalo, reluctance to kill wantonly, to waste any of the products of nature, stemmed from this feeling of relatedness and mutuality.

Lee, 1959

Dakota Indian children were taught that they were related to all things.

black bile, which identified a melancholy temperament; *yellow bile,* which was associated with a choleric or irascible temperament; and *phlegm,* which indicated sluggishness and apathy. Generally, his methods of treatment were ingenious for his time. For depression, he recommended a regular and tranquil life; for sobriety, avoidance of all excesses, and proper exercise and diet. For many mental disorders he administered *hellebore,* a plant with purgative properties, and his remedy for hysteria was marriage. His notions may seem "humor"-ous today, but he is credited with laying the foundation for the scientific study of abnormal behavior.

Plato (429–347 B.C.) maintained that the causes of abnormal behavior were partly organic, partly moral, and partly divine. He believed that emotionally disturbed individuals were not responsible for criminal acts, that they should be cared for by relatives or by the community, and that treatment should be humane. Aristotle (384–322 B.C.) agreed with the *humor* theory of Hippocrates but also extensively discussed abnormal behavior that he attributed to such psychological factors as *frustration* and *conflict.*

Aristotle's thinking about abnormal behavior was similar to Chinese thought during the same period. As early as the seventh century B.C. Chinese medicine viewed abnormal behavior as due to natural rather than supernatural forces (Tseng 1973). The human body, like the entire cosmos, was seen in terms of the mutual interaction of two complementary principles, *yin* and *yang,* which embraced all polarities. Thus yin is feminine, yang masculine; yin is passive, yang active; yin is dark, yang light; yin is wet, yang dry; yin is cold, yang hot; and yin is expanded, yang contracted. As long as yin and yang are in balance, the organism is healthy, but any excess or deficiency of either can lead to mental or physical illness.

About 200 A.D. Chung Ching wrote two well-known medical works in which he set forth views that were similar to Hippocrates' in the sense that he saw organ-pathology as the cause of both physical and mental disorders. He also believed that stressful psychological conditions could cause organ-pathology and recommended treatment with drugs and appropriate physical activity to restore the yin/yang balance. The yin/yang model eventually reemerged and is still part of oriental medical practice. It has recently been imported as the guiding principle of such practices as the macrobiotic diet (Kushi 1977).

In China, as in the West, medical opinion degenerated into beliefs in supernatural forces as causative agents, but those beliefs

Abnormality as maladaption to the environment

scientific approaches to the study of abnormal behavior

did not last as long as they did in the West, nor was the treatment of abnormal behavior as punitive.

In later Greek and early Roman periods, Hippocrates' views prevailed. Emotionally disturbed individuals were treated with dieting, massage, hydrotherapy, hypnosis, education, and recreation. In the first century B.C., Asclepiades differentiated between *illusions, delusions,* and *hallucinations.* He also noted a difference between *acute* and *chronic* conditions. Although he recommended bleeding and restraint as treatments for abnormal behavior, he also suggested relaxation and humane treatment. Aretaeus, in the first century A.D., described abnormal behavior as an extreme form of normal behavior. In other words, mania was an extreme form of joy and depression an extreme form of seriousness. Aretaeus also emphasized the role of *emotional* factors in abnormal behavior.

Not long after Aretaeus, Galen (A.D. 129–199) divided the causes of abnormal behavior into physical and mental ones and suggested that many disorders were caused by head injury, alcohol, shock, fear, economic problems, and similar physical and environmental factors (Guthrie 1946).

The roots of *constitutional* (body type or body build—thin, fat, muscular) psychology can be traced to Alexander Trallianus (A.D. 526–605), who emphasized constitutional factors and claimed that certain body types were likely to be associated with specific abnormal behavior patterns (Whitwell 1936).

In Arabia the more scientific aspects of Greek and Roman medicine survived during the Medieval period. One of the first mental hospitals was established in Baghdad in A.D. 792, followed by others in Damascus and Aleppo. Abnormally behaving

individuals received much more humane treatment in these places than in Christian lands (Polvan 1969). During this period Avicenna (A.D. 980–1037) was discussing *hysteria, epilepsy, manic reactions,* and *melancholia* (Campbell 1926).

The Medieval Period

With the fall of Rome and the rise of Christianity, Greek and Roman civilization collapsed and *superstition* and *demonology* returned. As Rosen (1967) has noted, this deterioration apparently continued to its culmination in the fourteenth century. Fundamental changes occurred in institutions, social structures, beliefs, and outlooks. This was a time of peasant revolt, urban uprisings, wars, plagues, and barbaric practices. Diagnosis and treatment of abnormal behavior were dominated by the clergy because physicians and the clergy were one and the same. Often, the monastery served as church, university, and mental hospital.

At the beginning of the Medieval era abnormally behaving individuals were treated humanely, but these practices deteriorated as belief in the natural causes of abnormal behavior declined and, though modified by the religious beliefs of the time, superstition and demonology revived. One belief was that the body and mind contained a battleground for devils and angels. A person who lost his or her reason was possessed by the devil and was therefore treated as a beast, not as a human being. Deviant behavior was evaluated in terms of whether it was a service to Christ or to Satan (Kroll 1973), and if a person appeared to be possessed by the devil, *exorcism* was warranted. The *animistic* model had returned.

Humane treatment in Greece, Rome, Arabia

Animism revived

box 1–5
An Example
of Avicenna's
Treatment

A certain prince . . . was afflicted with melancholia, and suffered from the delusion that he was a cow . . . he would low like a cow, causing annoyance to everyone, . . . crying, "Kill me so that a good stew may be made of my flesh," finally . . . he would eat nothing. . . . Avicenna was persuaded to take the case. . . . First of all he sent a message to the patient bidding him be of good cheer because the butcher was coming to slaughter him, whereat . . . the sick man rejoiced. Some time afterwards Avicenna, holding a knife in his hand, entered the sickroom saying, "Where is this cow that I may kill it?" The patient lowed like a cow to indicate where he was. By Avicenna's orders he was laid on the ground, bound hand and foot. Avicenna then felt him all over and said, "He is too lean, and not ready to be killed; he must be fattened." Then they offered him suitable food of which he now partook eagerly, and gradually he gained strength, got rid of his delusion, and was completely cured.

Browne, 1921

Avicenna with his students.

Witch hunting

Possession was due, according to accepted theological belief, either to Satan's seizure of the individual as a punishment by God for past sins or to a voluntary pact between Satan and the individual. By entering into such a pact, people supposedly acquired supernatural power to cause pestilence, storms, and floods; to inflict injury and impotence on their enemies; and to turn themselves into animals or work such mischief as causing milk to sour.

In keeping with their supposed capacity for supernatural mischief, people who behaved abnormally were commonly regarded as witches. That view became official church policy when Pope Innocent VIII issued a Papal Bull decreeing that the clergy must let "no stone go unturned" in the search for witches. Two northern German Dominican monks, Sprenger and Kraemer, published, in 1487, the *Malleus Malleficarum* (The Witch's Hammer), a manual for witch hunters, giving detailed instruc-

tions on how to identify, examine, and judge witches. It contained clinical descriptions of various signs by which witches could be detected—for example, "devil's claws," which were red spots or anesthetized areas on the skin supposedly left by the devil to signify the sealing of the pact.

The prescribed method of obtaining proof was to torture the suspect. If a confession did not result, the suspect was often burned at the stake. Witches were blamed for any misfortune that occurred, from poor crops to illness, famine, plague, and pestilence. Many people who would now be classified as mentally ill thus became victims of the Inquisition and were tortured and executed. Some, especially if they were depressed, readily confessed to their alleged crimes, even elaborating on their sins. If they were convicted of witchcraft, their souls were freed from the devil's power by the more extreme forms of exorcism—beheading, strangulation, or burning at the stake, sometimes preceded by mutilation.

"There is a flock of yellow birds around her head!" a woman cried out at this Salem witchcraft trial.

Persecution of alleged witches persisted for hundreds of years, and in the sixteenth and seventeenth centuries spread to the American colonies. In one such episode (Veith 1965) the daughter and the niece of a Calvinist minister were seized by fits in which they claimed they were suffocating because the devil had put steel balls in their throats to choke them. They claimed also that they were being stuck with needles, and one of them said she had vomited needles. Soon these seizures spread to other women in the community, who subsequently named some 200 people as agents of the devil. The suspects were imprisoned and tried, and at least nineteen of them, including a five-year-old child, were executed.

The Renaissance: The Dissenters

By the sixteenth century, resistance to demonology and more humane concerns regarding the victims of witch hunts began to appear. Paracelsus (1490–1541) rejected the theory of demonology and argued that

Dissent is the forerunner . . .

emergence of the major models of abnormal behavior

abnormal behavior was a *natural* disease. The keenness of his insight is revealed in his view of *tarantism,* a form of mass hysteria that originated in Taranto, Italy, and was sweeping southern Europe at the time. It consisted of a wild dance, the *tarantella,* performed to the point of exhaustion, and was sometimes accompanied by the tearing off of one's clothes or by other unconventional behavior. Tarantism was variously believed to be either a disease caused by a tarantula bite or the only cure for a state of extreme agitation caused by such a bite. Paracelsus saw tarantism instead as a disorder resulting from conflict between the instinctual and spiritual natures of people. He maintained that deviant behavior had psychic causes and suggested treatment by *body magnetism,* a form of hypnosis (Mora 1967). He also believed people were subject to *astral* influences and that the influence of the moon could produce abnormal behavior (people so influenced being, of course, *lunatics*). Paracelsus was persecuted until his death for his beliefs.

Other important dissenters included physicians Johann Weyer (1515–1588) and Reginald Scott (1538–1599), who is referred to as the "father of psychiatry." Both protested that burning and torturing witches was inhumane because these people were mentally ill. Weyer even urged the punishment of the monks who were persecuting the mentally ill. His works were banned by the church, and he was accused of having a pact with Satan. Scott devoted his life to attacking the prevailing belief in witchcraft and demonology. His book, *The Discovery of Witchcraft,* was an outspoken denunciation of the demonology theory. He denounced, as well, the belief in *incubi,* male demons who visited women at night and forced them into sexual relationships, and *succubi,* female demons who visited men for sexual purposes. Like Paracelsus, Scott considered these beings pure fiction and claimed that they were excuses for lechery and attempts at cuckoldry concocted by an overzealous clergy. King James I rejected Scott's thesis and had his books burned.

Dissenters soon appeared among the clergy too. Saint Vincent de Paul (1576–1660) believed that abnormal behavior was a natural phenomenon and that abnormally behaving individuals should be given humane treatment. Finally, the views of the dissenters, coupled with the development of modern scientific thought, gradually brought about a return to more humanitarian practices and beliefs.

The Modern Perspective: The Eighteenth, Nineteenth, and Twentieth Centuries

With the decline of demonology, five major trends emerged that have resulted in modern approaches to abnormal behavior. These were the development of *asylums,* the emergence of *psychogenic* and *biogenic* approaches based on the medical model, the formulation of *environmental* models, and the development of *humanistic* and *existential* approaches.

Reemergence of the Moral Model: Asylums

The influence of the moral model on the establishment of insane asylums is reflected in the word *asylum,* which literally means an inviolable place, a haven, shelter, or refuge. As we saw earlier, the practice of institutionalizing people who behaved abnormally originated in Greek and Roman civilization and continued during the Middle Ages. A *Dollhaus* (madhouse) was erected as part of the Georgetown Hospital at Elbing in 1326 (Kroll 1973), and in Valencia, an institution for the treatment of the mentally ill was started in 1410 by a friar, Father Juan Gelabert Jofre (Rumbaut 1972). The monastery of St. Mary's of Bethlehem in London was converted into a hospital for the insane in 1547. Eventually, conditions deteriorated so badly here that *Bedlam* (the popular name for the hospital) came to symbolize maltreatment of the mentally ill, and today the word is a synonym for an uproarious or confusing situation. Similar hospitals were established in Paris (1641), Moscow (1765), Vienna (1784), and Mexico (1565). Although treatment in these places was an improvement over Medieval practices, it can best be described as inhumane, involving neglect, physical restraints, and other cruel and dehumanizing practices.

scientific approaches to the study of abnormal behavior

An artist's representation of Bedlam, the famous English hospital for the insane.

Phillippe Pinel

Benjamin Rush

The fortunes of the mentally ill took a turn for the better when Phillippe Pinel (1745–1826) became director of La Bicêtre Hospital in Paris and ordered the patients released from their chains. During the same period William H. Tuke (1732–1822), an English Quaker, started the York Retreat and introduced humane treatment of mental patients into England.

In America, Benjamin Rush (1745–1813) effected a similar improvement in the Pennsylvania Hospital. Almost from the moment of its introduction, however, the *moral* model, as applied by Rush, was challenged, and in many instances supplanted by, the *medical* model. Rush was both a physician and a politician, and as the father of American psychiatry, he initiated the mental health movement here by writing the first American textbook in psychiatry, *Medical Inquiries and Observations upon Diseases of the Mind*. He also organized the first course in psychiatry at Pennsylvania Hospital.

Rush believed that mental illness was due to a stress-induced deluge of blood in the brain. Therefore he used and taught such techniques as *bleeding, cold baths,* and the use of the *tranquilizing chair.* At the same time, he insisted that physicians be kind to patients, be fit companions to them, and share in their activities, all of which was very much in keeping with the assumptions of the moral model. Abnormally behaving individuals were simply people who had severe problems that they were unable to handle, but with compassion and understanding from their caretakers they could resume their roles in society (Bockoven 1963).

Moral therapy emphasized a therapeutic environment. The physical setting of the hospital was cheerful and homelike, and the patient was expected to participate in meaningful recreational activities. As we shall see in Chapter 6, this approach anticipated and laid the groundwork for milieu therapy. Bockover claims that moral treatment was as successful as present-day hospitalization; nearly 70 percent of the

Moral treatment was both humane and effective

Pinel ordering that the patients be released from their chains.

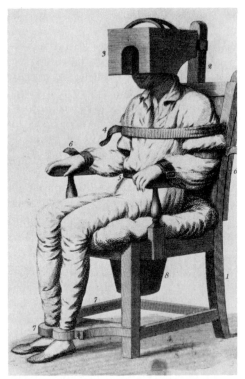

Rush's "tranquilizing chair" to treat a stress-induced deluge of blood in the brain.

Dorothea Dix

patients were discharged within a year and many were reintegrated into society. However, as the moral model gave way to the medical model and mental hospitals replaced asylums, much of this momentum was lost.

Dorothea Dix (1802–1887) contributed to the growth of the *medical* model by campaigning vigorously to have the mentally ill

scientific approaches to the study of abnormal behavior

removed from almshouses, jails, and prisons and placed in mental hospitals. Unfortunately, her work, more than that of any other individual, led to the spread of large state hospitals, which were worse than many prisons, and to the decline of moral treatment. Dix founded thirty-two of these mental hospitals. They, and the others like them, became overcrowded almost immediately. They lacked both an adequate professional staff and sufficient funds to operate in a productive way.

Furthermore, Dix's insistence that these places be directed and operated by physicians resulted in forcing the person with a behavior problem into assuming the role of a physically sick person. Great emphasis was placed on rest, diet, and other aspects of treatment associated with physical illness. Interest in *diagnosis* replaced interest in *rehabilitation* (Ullmann and Krasner 1975). Once admitted, people were expected to behave as good patients; to wait patiently until a cure for their illnesses was found; and to be passive, submissive, and quiet. In these circumstances, the moral model's assumption that the person could recover gave way to the medical model's assumption that behavior would deteriorate as the disease progressed. Not surprisingly, the recovery rate began to drop.

Because of the shortage of professional personnel, these hospitals were soon being operated by psychiatric aides, people who were paid low wages and who were usually untrained and uneducated. Their approach to patients was almost a caricature of the medical model. Restraints, isolation, and other harsh medical procedures were used. Only in recent years has the development of *milieu therapy, token economies,* and *community mental health centers* reversed these trends.

The Reemergence of Biogenic Approaches

Although many people had for centuries associated abnormal behavior with disease, the medical model was by no means universally accepted. What precipitated its widespread acceptance was the discovery that some forms of abnormal behavior were due to central nervous system disease or injury. Emil Kraepelin (1865–1926), in his textbook on psychiatry, published in 1883, argued that brain pathology was always the cause of deviant behavior. He believed that mental diseases, like physical diseases, could be differentiated on the basis of different organic causes that resulted in clusters of symptoms called *syndromes*. On the basis of this hypothesis, Kraepelin developed the first comprehensive *classification* of abnormal behavior. Once a physician using this system had classified a patient's disorder, he or she could predict its course (*prognosis*) and recommend treatment, just as would be done for a case of measles. Richard von Krafft-Ebbing (1840–1902) extended the work of classification with the publication of *Psychopathia Sexualis* (1892), a comprehensive description of deviant sexual practices. The work of these two individuals, as well as that of many others, resulted in the identification of toxic psychosis, cerebral atherosclerosis, and many other types of organic disorders, mental retardation, and abnormal behavior.

The biggest success of the biogenic movement was associating *paresis* with syphilis. This discovery, more than any other, sparked the research in organic bases of abnormal behavior.

Emergence of Psychogenic Approaches

Today abnormal behavior is most commonly conceptualized in terms of *psychodynamic* sources and treated with psychodynamic therapy. Although the orientation of psychodynamic approaches is definitely based on the medical model, the roots of psychodynamic approaches are in the practice of hypnosis and the phenomenon of conversion hysteria (a pattern of abnormal behavior that mimics physical illness). The psychodynamic approaches are so thoroughly accepted that we can easily forget that they grew out of a radical movement whose initiators almost always believed they were dealing with physiological events. The initial stimulus for that movement came from Franz Anton Mesmer (1734–1815), a man largely disowned by the scientific and medical community for his use of a technique similar to hypnosis.

Mental hospitals and medical model expectations . . .

lowered the recovery rate

Abnormality as a disease

Franz Anton Mesmer

Mesmer treating a patient with steel magnets. This treatment often had dramatic effects.

Mesmer's "magnetic" appeal

Mesmer, who was trained as a physician, believed that behavior could be explained in terms of *magnetic fluids* that filled the universe. Consequently, he began to treat all forms of disease by a method that employed steel magnets and a great deal of suggestion. Patients in Mesmer's Paris clinic sat in a circle around a *baquet*, an oval vessel containing bottles of magnetized water covered with a mixture of water and iron filings, on top of which was an iron cover with many holes. Long movable iron rods protruding from the holes were applied to the afflicted parts of the patients' bodies. While the patients sat with hands joined and knees pressed together to facilitate the flow of magnetic force, the assistant magnetizers, generally handsome young men, entered the room and "magnetized" the patients by rubbing gently up and down their spines and applying gentle pressure to the breasts of the female patients, all the while maintaining strict silence. Soon patients would begin to sob, tear their hair, and go into fits. Mesmer then entered the room and, staring into each patient's eyes, stroked the patient with his hand and touched him or her with his wand until the patient regained consciousness. Typically,

Early psychogenic explanations

the patient then became calm, and readily acknowledged Mesmer's power. Many reported feeling streams of cold or burning "vapors" passing through their bodies while Mesmer waved his wand or hand in front of them. This "animal magnetism" often had dramatic effects, and, not infrequently, alleviated the symptoms of hysterical disorders.

Declaring that Mesmer's dramatic cures were based on imagination, a committee appointed by the faculty of medicine in Vienna expelled him from the local medical profession. Mesmer's success was probably due to his charismatic personality and his flair for showmanship; the same qualities were probably responsible for his expulsion from the medical profession (Zilboorg and Henry 1941).

James Braid (1795–1860), the first person to use the term **hypnosis,** proposed that the effects of this procedure were due to the arousal of ideas in the patient by the *suggestions* of the hypnotist (1843). Liebeault (1823–1904), who with Bernheim founded the *Nancy School* for treating abnormal behavior, was the first to suggest that *hypnosis* and *hysteria* were both due to states of suggestibility. In essence, Liebeault and Bernheim claimed that hysteria was induced by self-hypnosis or *autosuggestion.*

scientific approaches to the study of abnormal behavior

An organic explanation of hysteria and hypnosis was then advanced by Jean Martin Charcot (1825–1892) at the Salpêtrière Hospital. Charcot argued that generative brain changes occurred in hysteria that rendered the person susceptible to hypnosis. This theory led to a major debate between the Nancy School and the Salpêtrière Hospital, which spurred research into the psychological basis of abnormal behavior. Eventually, Charcot himself came to accept the psychological point of view and did much to promote interest in the study of psychological factors in mental disorders. Pierre Janet (1859–1947), a student of Charcot, believed that susceptibility to hypnosis was due to a constitutional weakness of the nervous system. Janet was the first to refer to the role of the unconscious in hysteria, but did not pursue this original insight.

Freud and Psychoanalysis

The most famous of Charcot's students in Paris was Sigmund Freud (1856–1939), a young Viennese physician. Before returning to Vienna, Freud also became acquainted with the methods of Liebault and Bernheim. He then worked with an older physician, Joseph Breuer (1842–1925), who was also experimenting with hypnosis. Breuer was working with a classic case of hysteria, Anna O., who suffered from hysterical paralysis, inability to eat, and various disturbances of sight and speech. Breuer discovered that under hypnosis Anna O. would freely discuss the origin of her symptoms and was therefore able to effect a remission of those symptoms. He recognized the apparent therapeutic value of this emotional purging and labeled it the **catharsis** method or the *talking cure*. Actually, there is reason to doubt that Anna O. was cured; records indicate she later relapsed and continued to seek medical care throughout her life (Ellenberger 1972).

Nevertheless, Freud, collaborating with Breuer, became convinced that hysteria and other disorders were caused by *unconscious* conflicts that could be made conscious under hypnosis. Once these conflicts were discussed, the individual would develop *insight* into their causes, and the result would be *symptom remission*. Breuer and Freud published this theory of the unconscious in a book called *Studies in Hysteria* in 1895. Subsequently, however, Freud found that he was unable to hypnotize some of his patients and that some patients he had treated successfully later had a recurrence of symptoms. These relapses were apparently the basis for Freud's belief that symptomatic treatments such as hypnosis led to *symptom substitution* (the appearance of other, related symptoms) unless the cause of the disorder was treated directly.

Freud later discarded hypnosis for conversation, which eventually evolved into **free association:** The patient relaxed on a couch and said whatever came to mind, especially dreams and memories of childhood. The analyst then interpreted this information via the psychoanalytic theory, leading the patient to insights and, consequently, to eliminating the basic conflicts.

Freud has had such a profound influence on abnormal psychology and psychiatry that his theory still dominates many aspects of assessment, treatment, and research. *Psychoanalysis* was the first comprehensive theory of personality to cover the course and development of specific personality traits, normal and abnormal, and to suggest methods of assessing and modifying personality disturbances. Since much of abnormal psychology cannot be understood without a knowledge of at least the basic concepts of psychoanalysis, we shall summarize the theory here. For further details, see Chapter 6.

A major premise of psychoanalysis is **psychic determinism,** the belief that every aspect of human behavior has a cause and that even seemingly trivial events, such as slips of the tongue, forgetting, jokes, fantasies, and dreams, are significant in understanding the individual and his or her behavior. Freud suggested that the reason we often do not understand our own behavior is that the mind functions on three levels: the *conscious,* the *preconscious,* and the *unconscious.*

The conscious consists of whatever we are aware of at the moment. The preconscious consists of information we are not currently aware of but can recall in response to a relevant *cue*. The unconscious consists of material we were once aware of but can now recall only with great diffi-

Psychoanalysis was based on psychic determinism

Sigmund Freud with the "Committee" in Berlin (standing, left to right: Otto Rank, Karl Abraham, Max Eitingen, Ernest Jones; seated: Freud, Sandor Ferenczi, Hanns Sachs).

culty. This material has been forced out of consciousness because it causes us distress; it expresses itself only in disguised or *symbolic* form because our active mental processes censor it. The unconscious is the principal determinant of behavior, both normal and abnormal. It is the basis for Freud's hypothesis that behavior is caused by *intrapsychic* or **unconscious conflicts** and that the symptoms of mental illnesses are the symbolic expressions of these conflicts.

Freud assumed that the personality also has three parts: the **id,** the **ego,** and the **superego.** The id is the only structure present at birth and is the reservoir of psychic energy or *libido,* the sexual and aggressive instincts or drives that cause undesirable inner states of tension.

At birth the mechanism for satisfying these drives is the *pleasure principle,* which operates via the **primary process,** the thinking that consists largely of unrestrained sexual and aggressive fantasies. The id operates to gratify these basic and instinctual drives without regard to reality. But since fantasies fail to gratify basic needs, the need for transaction with the external world arises, and the ego develops from the id.

The ego mediates between the id and the outside world and operates on the **reality principle,** which consists of the reality-testing functions of the ego—problem solving, thinking, memory, and other higher level cognitive processes, which Freud called *secondary process thinking.* The superego, the last of the three major components of personality to develop, arises as a function of *rewards* and *punishments* and is the moral arm of the personality, making us feel proud when we adhere to the moral standards we have been taught and guilty when we transgress.

Freud believed that the formation of the superego is related to the resolution of the Oedipal situation: The child at age four or five experiences an intense but fantasy love relationship with the parent of the opposite sex and consequent hostility toward the parent of the same sex. The male child wants to assume his father's role (the Oedipus complex), and the female child wants to assume her mother's role (the Electra complex). Freud assumed that fear of retaliation by the same-sex parent and guilt over death wishes resolves the Oedipal and Electra situations and results in identification with the same-sex parent. The Oed-

Id, pleasure principle, primary process

Ego, reality principle, secondary process

scientific approaches to the study of abnormal behavior

ipal and Electra situations are responsible for *castration anxiety* in the male and *penis envy* in the female.

Socialization, according to Freud, proceeds through a sequence of **psychosexual stages** linked to the body's erogenous zones. Difficulty at any stage leads to *fixation,* which is the failure of the personality components to continue developing beyond that stage because the individual anticipates even greater conflicts. Thus, failure to develop beyond the *oral* stage (birth to two years) can result in an oral-dependent (passive) or oral-aggressive (biting) personality. Failure to develop beyond the *anal* stage (concurrent with toilet training) can result in an anal-expulsive (pushy, disorderly, messy) or anal-retentive (obstinate, frugal, meticulous) personality. During the *phallic* stage (three to five years) the child's erotic focus shifts to the genitals, and future sexual adjustment depends on how well the child resolves the Oedipal conflict. During the *latent* period (six to twelve years) the child's sexual impulses are repressed, and his or her attention is turned toward mastery of developmental skills. At *puberty,* sexual feelings are reactivated, and sexual energy is directed toward other people, in what Freud called the *genital* stage. Throughout puberty and adolescence, *altruistic* love and libidinal energies merge to produce mature sexuality.

Intrapsychic conflicts, according to Freud, develop in the interplay between id, ego, and superego. The greater the conflict, the greater the likelihood that impulses, desires, fantasies, or memories will be repressed—forced into the unconscious. Repressed material evokes anxiety, and the individual tries to reduce or prevent that anxiety by employing **defense mechanisms.** Because defense mechanisms are frequently referred to, they are briefly introduced here:

1. **Repression**   Responding to anxiety by forcing unacceptable impulses or desires into the unconscious. For example, if a boy has an unacceptable incestuous desire for his mother and a fear of retaliatory castration by his father, he may reduce anxiety by repressing the offending ideas and thoughts.

2. **Displacement**   Shifting emotions or ideas to a substitute; it is based on a gradient of similarity and fear. For example, a student irritated by a poor grade in abnormal psychology may yell at a friend instead of the instructor, who is the real object of hostility.

3. **Denial**   Refusing to acknowledge relevant aspects of a situation. This denial may be obvious to most but is unrecognized by the individual.

4. **Intellectualization**   Here an individual describes the self or the situation in a coherent, reasonable manner, but does not accept the description emotionally.

5. **Projection**   Internal threats are denied and transformed into external threats. The woman with a fear about her own feminine identification may, for example, accuse other women of homosexual impulses toward her.

6. **Fixation**   In development, an individual might experience anxiety and refuse to progress beyond that stage for fear that even greater conflicts may occur. Technically, this is not always considered a defense mechanism.

7. **Regression**   Under extreme internal or external pressure, the return of the ego to an earlier stage of development to avoid conflict at the higher stage. For example, schizophrenia, a severe psychotic disorder, is viewed by many psychoanalysts as regression to the early oral stages of development where the ego has not been formed. A consequent loss of reality testing occurs, which results in bizarre, primary-process thinking and behavior.

8. **Sublimation**   The use of socially acceptable substitutes to obtain gratification when more direct forms of impulse gratification are blocked. For example, Freud saw Leonardo da Vinci's paintings of women or madonnas as a sublimation of da Vinci's incestuous desires toward his mother.

The psychosexual stages of development

9. **Reaction formation** Unacceptable impulses transformed into their opposites. If individuals have strong, unacceptable sexual impulses, they may, through the process of reaction formation, engage in very moralistic behavior and attempt to suppress unacceptable sexual behavior in both self and others.

Neo-Freudians

Neo-Freudians rejected Freud's emphasis on early sexual conflict

During the 1920s and 1930s several of Freud's disciples and contemporaries rejected several of his theoretical beliefs and founded their own schools of psychoanalytic thought. Typically, such disputes were over the nature of the causal factors involved in abnormal behavior. These *neo-Freudians* generally either rejected Freud's emphasis on libido as the driving energy in normal and abnormal behavior, or reinterpreted libido.

Carl Jung (1875–1961), one of the most influential of these contemporaries, defined libido as a *life energy* produced by body processes that could force the person toward *introversion* or *extraversion.* Jung also introduced the concept of the **collective unconscious** or *objective psyche,* a shared unconscious that contains memories retained from previous generations and the *archetypes* of myths, dreams, and symbols.

Alfred Adler (1870–1937) substituted *social drives* for the sexual drives of Freudian theory. He encouraged conscious efforts in his patients to overcome inferiority complexes, as well as the conscious development of a life-style congruent with that goal. Another neo-Freudian, Otto Rank (1884–1939), focused on the profound shock of birth, the *birth trauma,* as the driving force behind human striving to regain control and achieve self-development.

Harry Stack Sullivan (1891–1949) saw the origins of abnormal behavior in disturbed interpersonal relationships, especially within the family. Sullivan emphasized the role of *reflected appraisals*—the responses of others to one's behavior—as the key factors in the formation of a person's self-concept. Sullivan's focus on communication problems served as a stimulus for much later work, especially by Gregory Bateson and R. D. Laing.

Despite their rejection of concepts that Freud considered indispensable to psychoanalysis, the neo-Freudians generally retained most of the theory's basic notions—the foundations of abnormal behavior in underlying conflicts, the origin of those conflicts in the developmental process, the belief that abnormal behavior is mental "illness," and the belief that insight into one's problem is necessary to change.

Carl Jung, Alfred Adler, and Harry Stack Sullivan

scientific approaches to the study of abnormal behavior

The Emergence of Environmental Models: Behaviorism

At the time that the biogenic and the psychogenic hypotheses of abnormal behavior were being formed, a similar development resulted in the hypothesis that abnormal behavior is a function of *environmental* conditions. Ivan Pavlov (1849–1936), a physiologist working on the chemical regulation of digestion, serendipitously observed laboratory dogs salivating before food reached their mouths. He then noted that even the presence of the person who brought the food or the sound of his footsteps or other stimuli associated with feeding eventually elicited the salivatory response. Pavlov originally called this phenomenon *psychic secretion,* then later coined the psychological term *conditioned reflex.* The originally neutral *stimulus,* such as the sight of the experimenter, was called the *conditioned stimulus (CS),* the food was called the *unconditioned stimulus (UCS),* which would initially evoke salivation, or the *unconditioned response (UCR),* and the response of salivation that came before receiving the food powder was called the *conditioned response (CR).* These studies were the foundation for the development of *classical* or **respondent conditioning.**

Notably, Pavlov also demonstrated that neuroses could be induced in animals. He found that a dog, given the task of discriminating between a circle and an ellipse that was being gradually modified to a circle, became excited, began to whine, and to bite and tear at the restraining harness. This discovery led to the use of *animal analogues* of neurotic behavior to investigate the principles that operate in similar human conditions.

In 1913 John B. Watson (1878–1958), inspired by Pavlov's work, defined psychology as the *science of behavior.* Watson was especially dissatisfied with the then common practice of relying on introspection for information about psychological processes. Such information was not publicly verifiable and therefore, in Watson's view, of no value in a scientific study of psychology. Watson urged psychologists to exclude from their studies all internal and therefore unverifiable processes—thoughts, feelings, sensations, perceptions, and consciousness. Watson argued that everything we call personality can be explained as behavior conditioned by the social environment (Watson 1919).

In 1920 Watson and Rayner demonstrated the relevance of behaviorism to abnormal behavior by showing that a phobia

Pavlov's conditioning experiments

Watson defines behaviorism

Pavlov and his staff demonstrating conditioned reflex.

(an irrational fear) can be rapidly produced by associating a neutral stimulus with an aversive one. The experimenter, holding a steel bar and a hammer, stood behind a small boy, Albert. When Albert reached for a white rat (UCS), the experimenter would hit the steel bar with the hammer (CS), and the loud noise would elicit a fear response (UCR) from Albert. After several repetitions of this process, Albert began to fear the rat (CR), and his fear then generalized to other furry animals and objects. The implication of this experiment was that phobias and other types of abnormal behavior may be the result of *learning.* Thus, if learning can induce abnormal behavior, it seems logical to assume that learning can modify abnormal behavior.

A further demonstration that learning could be useful in the modifications of abnormal behavior was conducted by Mary Cover Jones (1924a). With the advice of Watson, Jones was successful in eliminating the fear of a white rabbit in a child named Peter. Little Peter, a 2½-year-old, exhibited less fear when he observed other children handling a rabbit. Jones was thus the first to demonstrate the behavior modification technique of **modeling.** In addition, she progressively exposed the child to the white rabbit by a series of gradual steps that brought the child closer and closer in contact with the animal. In time, Peter was able to fondle the rabbit calmly. This procedure was the forerunner of a behavioral treatment procedure called *systematic desensitization* (Wolpe 1958).

Operant conditioning and the Law of Effect

A few years earlier, Edward Lee Thorndike (1874–1949) had formulated the **Law of Effect,** which was the basis of *instrumental learning,* later to be called **operant conditioning** (Skinner 1953). Thorndike asserted that responses that are followed by positive consequences are more likely to recur when the stimulus patterns that elicited them are repeated. Also, any act that in a given situation produces discomfort is less likely to recur when that situation is again presented. Skinner (1953) extended and refined these ideas, noting that these basic principles of learning could be beneficially applied to problems of behavior, including abnormal behavior.

Husserl's search for a science grounded in direct experience

During the thirties, Liddell (1956) and Gantt (1944) continued to explore how pathological behaviors could be conditioned in animals. In 1943, Masserman reported the first of a long series of animal studies employing behavioral methods in overcoming experimentally produced pathology. Meanwhile, Max (1935) had already paired mild electric shock to erotic stimuli as a method of extinguishing homosexual thoughts. Mowrer and Mowrer (1938) utilized a similar procedure to control enuresis (bedwetting). Dunlap (1932), another forerunner of modern behavior theory, introduced a behavioral treatment procedure termed *Negative Practice,* which involves a person repeating an undesirable behavior, such as a tic, hundreds of times until it is extinguished. The work of these individuals prepared the way for such modern behavior therapists as Wolpe (1958), Eysenck (1960), Ullmann and Krasner (1975), Bandura (1969), and numerous others.

The Emergence of Phenomenological Models: Humanistic-Existential Approach

Behaviorism's emphasis on public verification is a logical outgrowth of its roots in the philosophy of *positivism,* which rejects metaphysical speculation and asserts that the only real knowledge is **empirical** knowledge—that obtained by rigorous scientific observation and experimentation. This emphasis on verification by experience is turned in a different direction by *existential* psychology, an approach whose rise has paralleled that of behaviorism and which grew largely out of the philosophy of *phenomenology,* as formulated by Edmund Husserl (1859–1938).

Husserl noted that every existing science rests on presuppositions that are not clarified within that science. In his own field, he believed philosophy ought to be a science of ultimate grounds—a superscience that would cut through all those presuppositions, not to another level of abstraction, but to an absolutely valid knowledge of *things,* a science grounded in direct experience. Like most existentialists, Husserl had a deep distrust of purely rational and analytical approaches to knowledge. He sought to replace this intellectualization

scientific approaches to the study of abnormal behavior

box 1–6
Maslow on a
Psychology
of Being

Another preoccupation of existentialist writers can be phrased very simply, I think. It is the dimension of seriousness and profundity of living (or perhaps the "tragic sense of life") contrasted with the shallow and superficial life, which is a kind of diminished living, a defense against the ultimate problems of life. This is not just a literary concept. It has real operational meaning, for instance, in psychotherapy. I (and others) have been increasingly impressed with the fact that tragedy can sometimes be therapeutic, and that therapy often seems to work best when people are *driven* into it by pain. It is when the shallow life doesn't work that there occurs a call to fundamentals.

Maslow, 1968

---

with an intuitive grasp of the thing-in-itself, and to ground philosophy in quantitative experience. This insistence on returning to the immediate and direct data of consciousness is a major theme in existential and humanistic approaches in psychology; for example, Gestalt therapists often turn aside attempts at intellectualizing and encourage "here-and-now awareness."

Husserl himself was deeply interested in psychology, which he defined in 1913 as a *science of experience*. Jaspers (1913), one of the first psychologists to use Husserl's emphasis on consciousness, concentrated on describing his patients' subjective experience and on empathizing with them. Instead of probing beneath the surface as a psychoanalyst would, he focused on the patients' conscious self-descriptions, feelings, and sensations, on the theory that the best source of information about abnormal behavior is precisely the individual who is behaving abnormally.

Binswanger (1963), another influential therapist, asserted that a person's growth depends on maintaining a balance between three modes of experience: the *unwelt,* the world of biological energy and physical reality; the *mitwelt,* the world of other people; and the *eigenwelt,* the inner world of phenomenological experience.

These early phenomenological approaches continue to be reflected in the views of Viktor Frankl, Rollo May, Carl Rogers, Abraham Maslow, Fritz Perls, and R. D. Laing. Frankl (1962) stresses our responsibility to choose our own values in life. His theories draw extensively on his own experiences as a prisoner in a Nazi concentration camp, and so he sees the *will to meaning* as the basic human motivation.

Maslow (1968) took issue with the psychodynamic approach for its emphasis on disease, which he believed had fostered a one-sided picture of the human organism by failing to present a clear image of health as something more than the mere absence of symptoms. To try to fill in that gap, he studied the lives of people he considered *self-actualized* (Lincoln, Jefferson, Einstein, Eleanor Roosevelt, William James, Spinoza, Pablo Casals, Martin Buber, Fritz Kreisler, Adlai Stevenson) and listed the qualities they had in common.

Perls (et al. 1951) saw abnormal behavior as a failure of awareness due to a fragmenting of the personality that splits thought, feeling, and action apart. Through *Gestalt* therapy he tried to help the individual to get in touch with all the alienated parts of personality and recover the *authenticity* that the socialization process had crippled.

The idea that modern societies produce alienated people is a common thread in the work of many existentialists, especially R. D. Laing (1967). Laing believes that most people are *neurotic*; that is, they are divided into two selves, a false *outer self* calculated to win acceptance and approval and a real *inner self* that contains their natural impulses and strivings. The split occurs in early childhood when the child's spontaneous expressions provoke parental disapproval. To win the desperately needed approval of parents, the child becomes false and takes on the role defined by parental expectations.

Rogers (1959) believes people are born with a *valuing process* that enables them to sense whether an experience feels right.

Self-actualization and authenticity as goals of humanists and existentialists

If the environment nurtures that valuing process, the person's drive to become self-actualized will result in a healthy, well-integrated person. But if the person is coerced or manipulated into adopting the values of others, conflict with the inner criteria will lead to anxiety and threat. We shall discuss some of these theories in greater detail in Chapter 6.

This reemergence of the existential and humanistic approaches to behavior reflects an increased interest in the moral models in reaction to the medical and environmental models. Many humanistic and existential theorists feel that the scientific models dehumanize and degrade the individual. These phenomenological approaches represent an alternative by emphasizing our subjective experiences, free will, innate goodness, and the importance of our values.

This Book's Viewpoint

Our purpose in this textbook is twofold: (1) to explain the principles of abnormal psychology and (2) to assist the student in understanding and accepting people who have problems in living. Despite the great strides that have been made in recent years, a stigma is still attached to mental disease, and one of our objectives here is to eliminate the assumptions that sustain that stigma. A basic premise of our own that we have already touched on and that we hope to illuminate throughout the book is that abnormal behavior occurs on a continuum. Even its most bizarre or maladaptive forms are different only in degree from responses we all make to the stresses and conflicts in our daily lives. Therefore, the first step toward understanding the abnormal behavior of others is to understand our own behavior.

We have organized the book to give first an overview of the issues in classification, assessment, treatment, and research. This is then followed by discussion of specific behavior disorders. That discussion is organized by a system of classification according to the functional behavioral system involved—emotion, perception, cognition, motor behavior, biological needs, and social behavior.

This way of organizing the book serves three major purposes. First, it helps to illustrate our premise that abnormal behavior can best be understood as a variation of behavior observed in everyone. For example, to understand a disorder that involves loss of memory, such as a *fugue* state, we need basic information about memory as it occurs in all humans, whether they are behaving normally or abnormally.

Second, this organization encourages us to see behavior disorders as disruptions in the life of a human being and to refrain from *labeling* that individual as psychotic or neurotic, or implying that the total personality is diseased. Labeling people rather than response patterns is a form of stereotyping. Like racial or sexual stereotyping, it can be damaging to the individual, as we shall see in Chapter 2.

Third, traditional categories of abnormal behavior are based largely on the medical model and on psychoanalytic theory. As we shall show in Chapter 2, that system has been severely criticized. Unfortunately, it is extensively used, and no alternative system is available. Our solution to this problem is to organize the material first in terms of *response patterns* of normal behavior and then discuss the disorders under their traditional labels as they relate to those response patterns. An exception to this rule is our discussion of psychotic disorders, which involve many aspects of an individual's life and thus cannot be classified, for example, as strictly cognitive or strictly perceptual.

The orientation of this book can best be described as broadly *behavioral*. We shall try to explain abnormal behavior in terms of basic psychological principles, including—but not limited to—learning. We shall thus use, where they are appropriate, principles drawn from perception, memory, cognition, and physiological and social psychology. We assume that the reader's ability to understand and help people with problems in living will increase as he or she learns the basic facts and principles of human behavior and how to apply them in making life less stressful and more meaningful.

scientific approaches to the study of abnormal behavior

Summary

Five major models have dominated the study of abnormal behavior. Animism attributes abnormal behavior to possession of the individual by supernatural beings. Moral models begin with the assumption that people who behave abnormally are normal people who have "lost their reason" because of stress. Phenomenological models involve a belief that a person's abnormal behavior can best be understood in the context of his or her consciousness. The medical model views abnormal behavior as symptomatic of disease, either biological or psychological in origin. And environmental models emphasize the role of socialization in the development of both normal and abnormal behavior.

Primitive people apparently have generally assumed that abnormal behavior was due to supernatural forces. During the Golden Age of Greece, however, treatment and conceptualization of abnormal behavior were humane.

During the last 200 years, after vigorous opposition to supernatural concepts, modern approaches to abnormal behavior have developed. Asylums for the insane were established, and for a short time during the nineteenth century were dominated by the moral model and moral treatment, which was generally humane and effective.

During the late nineteenth century, the medical model became dominant, following the discovery that many patterns of abnormal behavior were due to infections, genetic factors, or brain trauma. During the same period, the psychogenic approach developed, mainly through the clinical work of a succession of theorists, from Mesmer to Freud.

On the basis of his work with hypnosis and free association, as well as his belief that mental disorders are the result of unconscious conflicts that can be resolved through insight, Freud developed the method called psychoanalysis. Freud postulated three divisions of the mind—the conscious, the preconscious, and the unconscious. Of these, the unconscious is the most important for psychoanalysis, since it is, according to Freud, the repository of all the threatening and unacceptable impulses, wishes, and memories that are kept out of the conscious by repression. They nevertheless find expression in symbolic form as dreams, slips of the tongue, and other involuntary or supposedly accidental behaviors. For Freud these seemingly trivial events were significant for understanding people and their behavior, and his concern with them gave rise to the principle of psychic determinism.

According to Freud, conflicts arise between three parts of the personality—the id, the ego, and the superego. The id is the reservoir of libido, or psychic energy, and expresses itself mainly in sexual and aggressive fantasies. The ego, which mediates between instinctual needs and the external world, constrains impulses emanating from the id. The superego, the last of these structures to develop, is the moral arm of the personality. Its formation, Freud assumed, is due to the resolution of the Oedipal conflict. During socialization a person goes through five stages of psychosexual development. These are the oral stage, the anal stage, the phallic stage, the latency period, and the genital stage. Conflict may occur at any stage, and if it is severe enough, the individual may become fixated at that stage. Conflict triggers anxiety, and the individual defends against anxiety through various defense mechanisms, repression being the most basic. During the 1920s and 1930s several of Freud's contemporaries broke with him over theoretical questions, mostly involving the causes of abnormal behavior, and founded their own psychoanalytical schools. The best known of these neo-Freudians were Carl Jung, Alfred Adler, Otto Rank, and Harry Stack Sullivan.

Behaviorism developed concurrently with psychoanalysis, beginning with the animal experiments of Ivan Pavlov. Pavlov found that a dog would salivate in response to any stimulus associated with feeding, and postulated that the dog was conditioned by the pairing of an unconditioned stimulus (US), in this case the food, with a conditioned stimulus (CS), in this case an environmental cue such as the presence of the person who brought the food. The dog's salivation in response to the food was the unconditioned response (UR), and its salivation in response to other cues was the conditioned response (CR). This process is called classical or respondent conditioning.

John B. Watson demonstrated that abnormal behavior, such as a phobia, could be conditioned by pairing a neutral stimulus with an aversive one. He also proposed that psychology exclude from its study all events not subject to public verification, such as thoughts, feelings, sensations, perceptions, and consciousness. Mary Cover Jones later showed that a phobia could be extinguished by having the phobic person observe others handling the feared object, a process now called modeling. She also showed that a phobia could be reduced by gradual exposure to the feared object, foreshadowing the form of therapy called systematic desensitization.

Edward Lee Thorndike observed that learning also occurs when an organism acts on the environment and that act has favorable consequences. He called this the Law of Effect; this is the basis for operant conditioning, a method further extended and refined by B. F. Skinner.

During the same period, phenomenological models evolved, stimulated originally by Edmund Husserl's proposal that philosophy should ground its knowledge in direct experience to avoid the untestable presuppositions that most existing sciences are based on. Following his lead, humanistic and existential psychologists have generally stressed the value of direct experience and the data of consciousness as opposed to abstract thoughts about reality. Viktor Frankl has emphasized the will-to-meaning as the essential human motive. Abraham Maslow argued for the formation of a more complete and balanced picture of humanity through the study of positive health as opposed to the psychodynamic emphasis on pathology. Fritz Perls saw abnormal behavior as a split between thought, feeling, and action. R. D. Laing sees neurosis as a division between a false outer self and a real inner self. And Carl Rogers defines abnormal behavior in terms of conflict between a natural, intuitive valuing process and the internalized values of others.

One of the premises of this book's viewpoint is that abnormal behavior differs only in degree from responses all of us make in dealing with the stresses and conflicts of everyday life.

Key Concepts

animism

biogenic approach

catharsis

collective unconscious

cultural relativism

defense mechanisms

ego

empiricism

environmental models

free association

hypnosis

id

law of effect

medical models

modeling

moral models

operant conditioning

paradigm clash

phenomenological models

primary process

psychic determinism

psychic trauma

psychogenic approach

reality principle

respondent conditioning

stages of psychosexual development

superego

unconscious conflicts

Review Questions

1. Describe the five major models of abnormal behavior.

2. What treatment method developed from each of these five models?

3. During which historical periods would acquiring the label "abnormal" have been most hazardous to life and limb?

4. During what historical periods would a person labeled abnormal have had the best chance of returning to a normal, productive life?

5. How did the discovery of the cause of paresis affect beliefs about abnormal behavior in general?

6. What role did hypnosis play in the development of psychoanalysis?

7. How does operant conditioning differ from respondent conditioning?

8. What was Husserl's chief complaint about existing science?

9. Describe the viewpoint of this textbook.

scientific approaches to the study of abnormal behavior

classification 2

Sorting out and labeling behavior is an activity people engage in every day without giving it much thought. We are usually not conscious of the classification process implied in such statements as, "I'm feeling uptight today" or "You were pretty abrupt with me" or "She has an amazingly cheerful outlook." Sometimes, just as unconsciously, we label people: "What a loser!" "Charlie belongs in the cracker factory." "I'm too easy." "She's not wrapped too tight." In science, the same thought processes go on, but the scientist has to pay close attention to what he or she is doing in classifying events, and must be aware of the role of *classification*.

Classification organizes facts

Classification systems organize and integrate the facts in a particular field in a way that allows scientists to communicate in a common language. This integration of facts is a prerequisite for the development of scientific principles and laws. In other words, development of a useful classification system paves the way for the development of a science.

The Principles of Classification

Unlike psychology in general, which has no classification system, abnormal psychology has had several. The current system is known as the *Diagnostic and Statistical Manual of Mental Disorders* (**DSM II**). It has been formulated and revised over the years by the American Psychiatric Association (APA) and is now in its third revision, **DSM III** (APA 1980).

Medical model assumptions in DSM II

The DSM has been traditionally based on the medical model assumptions that abnormal behavior is a form of illness and that specific behaviors are labeled as symptoms (such as depression or anxiety), that cluster in patterns that form syndromes (such as schizophrenia or alcoholism).

Conjunctive categories make for homogeneity

Classifying behavior into one of these diagnostic categories suggests a certain *etiology* (cause), a *therapy* (treatment), and a *prognosis* (probable course and outcome). In DSM III, the medical model bias is somewhat ameliorated but not eliminated. We shall compare both DSM II and DSM III, as well as suggest an alternative system that will serve as an organizing principle for our discussion of abnormal behaviors. First, we shall examine the principles used in organizing data into categories.

Scientific Terminology

Taxonomies (classification systems) require a proper **scientific terminology**. Such a terminology should define measurable qualities—in our case, of behavior—that are *necessary* and *sufficient* for "membership" in a specific category, for example, schizophrenia or psychosis. It should also differentiate between observations and inferences.

Conjunctive and Disjunctive Categories

Additionally, categories should be mutually exclusive. The more distinct the categories are, the less likelihood there is of confusing different items, such as schizophrenia and depression.

In defining categories, Hempel (1959) has recommended that **operational definitions** be used. (An operational definition is formulated in terms of the way the behavior is measured or assessed; that is, the behavior is defined in the words of the measurement *operations*.)

In **conjunctive categories,** the attributes (the symptoms or behavior patterns) "necessary and sufficient for membership" are defined or specified through operational definitions. The absence of one or more of these symptoms disqualifies a behavior from that category. For example, if a phobia is seen as anxiety toward and avoidance of a specific stimuli, and if an individual responds to a stimulus situation with anxiety but *not* avoidance, or vice versa, the behavior cannot be categorized as phobic. Thus, conjunctive categories tend to create more clearly defined, homogeneous groups.

Disjunctive categories are those in which any of a number of symptoms defines the category, and the condition for inclusion is the appearance of some or even one of the designated symptoms. Disjunctive categories create difficulties as there is no absolute criteria for deciding which symptom or combination of symptoms is *necessary* for membership and so, the *sufficient* con-

scientific approaches to the study of abnormal behavior

An operational definition of "a student" is an individual who engages in studying behavior.

ditions cannot be clearly defined. For this reason, as Bruner (1965) has shown, the use of specific attributes (symptoms) in disjunctive categories often becomes debatable and leads to questions of **reliability** (consistency of diagnosis and agreement among classifiers) and **validity** (assurance that labels describe what they are supposed to describe).

Use of a Single Classification Principle

To avoid confusion, a **single classification principle** should be used. If possible, the system used should base all its categories either on behavior or on etiology, but not one on behavior and another on etiology. Furthermore, categories should be based on essential attributes and not on **extraclassificatory attributes** (Zigler and Phillips 1961), symptoms or behaviors that empirically correlate with the essential attributes. For example, while numerous personality traits correlate with various behavioral disorders, the significant but small correlations observed do not warrant including personality traits as definitions of these disorders.

Evaluation of Abnormal Behavior: Two Criteria

Any attempt to classify behavior as normal or abnormal presupposes, as we suggested in Chapter 1, some criteria of abnormality, either explicit or implicit. Two such criteria—the **criterion of labeling** and the **criterion of adjustment**—have most commonly been used, and as we shall see, have often been confused. Deviant behavior is behavior that violates social norms and for that reason causes the person to be labeled mentally ill, deviant, abnormal, emotionally disturbed, or for that matter, a genius (Ullmann and Krasner 1969; Scheff 1963). *Labeling* solves a social problem, since the individual can then be hospitalized, or other treatment measures can be taken that are believed to be justified by the label.

Criterion of Labeled Deviance

What constitutes abnormal behavior under this criterion is thus a function of local conventions, which can vary considerably from

Switching classification principles causes confusion

Is abnormality labeled deviance . . .

society to society, from time to time, and even from place to place. For example, the normal sexual behavior of people in the Trobriand Islands, where children are sexually active and often observe adults having sex, would be classed as pathological in any scheme based on the sexual conventions of the Aran Islands, where almost all forms of sexual expression are considered deviant or immoral. Likewise, sexual practices prescribed by sex therapists in America today, such as masturbation training, would have been seen by many American physicians in the nineteenth century as symptomatic of severe mental disease. To a degree, the use of deviance as a criterion of abnormality undermines confidence in the entire clinical field, since it leaves clinicians vulnerable to the charge of ethnocentrism (treating current values as if they were universal absolutes).

or is it maladaptive behavior?

Multiple classification principles in DSM II

Criterion of Adjustment

In contrast, the criterion of *adjustment* (how well an individual copes with his or her environment) is, within limits, culture-free, since it is keyed only to the satisfaction of one's biological and social needs and one's ability to survive.

Acute and chronic syndromes

Frequently, conflict may arise between these two criteria. For example, the hard-driving executive may meet all the deviance-criteria of normality but qualify as abnormal in terms of adjustment criteria because her hard driving has earned her a peptic ulcer. And the person whose draft resistance during the Vietnam War qualified him as deviant may be alive and well in Canada, and therefore normal by the adjustment criterion. Obviously, because what we perceive as "normal" behavior depends on the criterion we use, we need to keep these two criteria distinct.

With the importance of a functional classification system in mind, let us examine the most recent system (DSM II) and then its latest revision (DSM III), paying special attention to the ways in which these taxonomies meet—or fail to meet—the requirements we have outlined above: scien-tific terminology, operational definitions, conjunctive and disjunctive categories, and the single classification principle.

Classification of Abnormal Behavior: DSM II

DSM II (APA 1968) has ten major categories and numerous subcategories of abnormal behavior (see Table 2–1). It classifies behavior disorders on the basis of either *physiological malfunctions, developmental processes, etiological factors,* or *behavioral patterns.*

Physiological Malfunctions

Disruption of the central nervous system is usually associated with changes in behavior, such as impairment of memory, judgment, orientation, and other cognitive functions. *Organic brain syndromes* (damage to the brain) may also be associated with changes in emotional response, such as lability (emotional instability) or shallowness of affect. If behavior impairment is severe, the individual may be labeled *psychotic.*

The distinction between acute and chronic brain syndromes is important because of differences in the disorder's course, prognosis, and treatment. A syndrome is *acute* if the brain pathology and disorganized behavior are reversible, and *chronic* if they are permanent. Since the same factors may produce either temporary or permanent brain injury, a brain disorder may appear reversible but later prove permanent. We shall discuss organic brain disorders in Chapter 18, and mental retardation associated with physiological handicaps in Chapter 17.

While behavior disorders are sometimes caused by physiological impairments, the reverse also may be true as physiological disorders can be caused by psychological factors. These are the *psychophysiological disorders,* disturbances in biological functions regulated by the autonomic nervous system: for example, ulcers, hives, and asthma. These disorders will be discussed in Chapter 16.

Table 2–1 DSM II Diagnostic Nomenclature*

I. Mental retardation

Borderline
Mild
Moderate
Severe
Profound
Unspecified
With each: Following or associated with
Infection or intoxication
Trauma or physical agent
Disorders of metabolism, growth, or nutrition
Gross brain disease (postnatal)
Unknown prenatal influence
Chromosomal abnormality
Prematurity
†Major psychiatric disorder
†Psychosocial (environmental) deprivation
Other condition

II. Organic Brain Syndromes (OBS)

A. Psychoses

Senile and presenile dementia
Senile dementia
Presenile dementia

Alcoholic psychosis
†Delirium tremens
†Korsakoff's psychosis
†Other alcoholic hallucinosis
†Alcohol paranoid state
†Acute alcohol intoxication
†Alcoholic deterioration
†Pathological intoxication
Other alcoholic psychosis

Psychosis associated with intracranial infection
General paralysis
Syphilis of CNS
Epidemic encephalitis
Other and unspecified encephalitis
Other intracranial infection

Psychosis associated with other cerebral condition
Cerebral arteriosclerosis
Other cerebrovascular disturbance
Epilepsy
Intracranial neoplasm
Degenerative disease of the CNS
Brain trauma
Other cerebral condition

Psychosis associated with other physical condition
Endocrine disorder
Metabolic and nutritional disorder
Systemic infection
Drug or poison intoxication (other than alcohol)
†Childbirth
Other and unspecified physical condition

B. Nonpsychotic OBS

Intracranial infection
†Alcohol (simple drunkenness)
†Other drug, poison, or systemic intoxication
Brain trauma
Circulatory disturbance
Epilepsy
Disturbance of metabolism, growth, or nutrition
Senile or presenile brain disease
Intracranial neoplasm
Degenerative disease of the CNS
Other physical conditioner physical condition

III. Psychoses not attributed to physical conditions listed previously

Schizophrenia
Simple
Hebephrenic
Catatonic
†Catatonic type, excited
†Catatonic type, withdrawn
Paranoid
†Acute schizophrenic episode
†Latent
Residual
Schizo-affective
†Schizo-affective, excited
†Schizo-affective, depressed
Childhood
Chronic undifferentiated
Other schizophrenia

Major affective disorders
Involutional melancholia
Manic-depressive illness, manic
Manic-depressive illness, depressed
Manic-depressive illness, circular
†Manic-depressive, circular, manic
†Manic-depressive, circular, depressed
Other major affective disorder

Paranoid states
Paranoia
†Involutional paranoid state
Other paranoid state

Other psychoses
Psychotic depressive reaction

*Many of the titles listed here are in abbreviated form.
†These diagnoses are new and do not appear in DSM I.

Table 2-1 (continued)

IV. Neuroses

Anxiety
Hysterical
†Hysterical, conversion type
†Hysterical, dissociative type
Phobic
Obsessive-compulsive
Depressive
†Neurasthenic
†Depersonalization
†Hypochondriacal
Other neurosis

V. Personality disorders and certain other nonpsychotic mental disorders

Personality disorders
Paranoid
Cyclothymic
Schizoid
†Explosive
Obsessive-compulsive
†Hysterical
†Asthenic
Antisocial
Passive-aggressive
Inadequate
Other specified types

Sexual deviation
†Homosexuality
†Fetishism
†Pedophilia
†Transvestism
†Exhibitionism
†Voyeurism
†Sadism
†Masochism
Other sexual deviation

Alcoholism
†Episodic excessive drinking
†Habitual excessive drinking
†Alcohol addiction
Other alcoholism

Drug dependence
†Opium, opium alkaloids and their derivatives
†Synthetic analgesics with morphinelike effects
†Barbiturates
†Other hypnotics and sedatives or "tranquilizers"
†Cocaine
†Cannabis sativa (hashish, marihuana)
†Other psychostimulants
†Hallucinogens
Other drug dependence

VI. Psychophysiologic disorders

Skin
Musculoskeletal
Respiratory
Cardiovascular
Hemic and lymphatic
Gastrointestinal
Genitourinary
Endocrine
Organ of special sense
Other type

VII. Special symptoms

Speech disturbance
Specific learning disturbance
†Tic
†Other psychomotor disorder
†Disorders of sleep
†Feeding disturbance
Enuresis
†Encopresis
†Cephalalgia
Other special symptom

VIII. Transient situational disturbances

Adjustment reaction of infancy
Adjustment reaction of childhood
Adjustment reaction of adolescence
Adjustment reaction of adult life
Adjustment reaction of late life

IX. Behavior disorders of childhood and adolescence

†Hyperkinetic reaction
†Withdrawing reaction
†Overanxious reaction
†Runaway reaction
†Unsocialized aggressive reaction
†Group delinquent reaction
Other reaction

X. Conditions without manifest psychiatric disorder and nonspecific conditions

Social maladjustment without manifest psychiatric disorder
†Marital maladjustment
†Social maladjustment
†Occupational maladjustment
Dyssocial behavior
†Other social maladjustment

Nonspecific conditions
†Nonspecific conditions

No mental disorder
†No mental disorder

XI. Nondiagnostic terms for administrative use

Diagnosis deferred
Boarder
Experiment only
Other

scientific approaches to the study of abnormal behavior

Developmental Processes

DSM II also classifies some behavior disorders in terms of *developmental processes,* establishing a category for behavior disorders of childhood and adolescence, which often differ from adult disorders only in the age of the person. These disorders are considered more serious than transient situational disorders but less serious than psychoses, neuroses, and personality disorders. Since most of these disorders seem to differ from adult disorders mainly in terms of age, we shall cover them in our discussions of like disorders in adults.

Etiology

Some disorders are classified in DSM II according to the events that *caused* the behavior disorder. These are the transient situational disturbances, which are caused by life stresses, and they include the *adjustment* reactions of infancy, childhood, adolescence, and later life. These life stresses may result from combat, pregnancy, separation from a parent, failure, or other serious environmental stressors. This is a classification of the *causes* of abnormal behavior rather than of the behavior itself, and we shall discuss these causes in Chapter 4.

Behavior Patterns

Conditions classified according to behavior patterns include: psychoses not attributable to physical conditions, neuroses, personality disorders, and special symptoms.

Psychoses

Psychoses are deviant behavior patterns of such intensity as to interfere grossly with an individual's ability to contend with the stresses of everyday life. These handicaps usually result from severe thought distortions that affect a person's perception of reality. The person may have hallucinations, delusions, and severe mood disturbances, or may be disoriented in time, place, or situation. We shall discuss psychotic disorders in Chapters 14 and 15.

Neuroses

The medical model assumes that *anxiety* is the chief characteristic of *neuroses* and that this anxiety may be felt directly or it may be removed from the person's consciousness by repression or other defense mechanisms. It also assumes that the anxiety, or its derivatives (that is, defenses against anxiety), produce symptoms that cause subjective distress (shame, disgust) from which the individual desires relief. We note, however, that this definition of neurosis is weakened by the *hypothetical (untested)* nature of the proposed causes and explanations—that is, in many neuroses extreme anxiety is not evident. For our purposes, we shall define neuroses, as behavior patterns characterized by *anxiety* or by *other behaviors the individual considers undesirable,* where these is no gross misrepresentation of external reality. We shall discuss these disorders in Chapters 8 and 9.

Age as a factor

Personality Disorders

Personality disorders (antisocial, passive-aggressive, hysterical, or similar personalities) are characterized by maladaptive behavior patterns that seem quite different from psychotic or neurotic symptoms. These lifelong behavior patterns, which are often obvious as early as adolescence, involve the person's manner or style of interacting with others. No obvious bizarre behavior is present, and the behavior is not usually distressing to the person emitting it. We shall discuss traditional personality disorders in Chapter 10.

Classifying by causes

Also included in the original DSM II list of personality disorders are sexual deviations, alcoholism, and drug dependence. The category labeled Sexual Deviations (APA 1968, p. 44) is for:

Psychosis and neurosis

individuals whose sexual interests are directed primarily towards objects other than people of the opposite sex, toward sexual acts not usually associated with coitus, or toward coitus performed under bizarre circumstances as in necrophilia, pedophilia, sexual sadism, and fetishism. Even though many find their practices distasteful, they remain unable to substitute normal sexual behavior for them. This diagnosis is not appropriate for individuals who perform deviant sexual acts because normal sexual objects are not available to them.

An alcoholic. Alcohol intake can be great enough to damage physical health and personal and social functioning.

DSM II was amended in 1973 to exclude homosexuality from the sexual deviations. We shall discuss sexual deviations in Chapter 12.

Individuals are labeled alcoholic when their alcohol intake is great enough to damage their physical health, their personal and social functioning, or when it becomes a prerequisite to normal functioning. These patterns can be defined in terms of episodic excessive drinking, habitual episodic drinking, or addiction to alcohol. We shall cover alcoholism in Chapter 13.

Deviance and dependency

Drug dependency involves addiction to or dependence upon drugs other than alcohol, tobacco, and ordinary caffeine-containing beverages. The diagnosis of drug dependency requires evidence of habitual use or a clear sense of need for the drug. Withdrawal symptoms are *not* the only evidence of dependence. They are always present when opium derivatives are withdrawn, but may be entirely absent when cocaine or marijuana is withdrawn. We shall discuss drug dependency in Chapter 13.

Inconsistencies of DSM II

Special Symptoms

The special symptoms include speech and psychomotor disorders, disorders of eating and elimination, tics, learning disorders, and sleep disorders. We shall cover most of these disorders in Chapters 9 and 11.

Evaluation of DSM II

The predominant use of the medical model in constructing the classification system of DSM II has caused many problems and has been the subject of controversy for several years. Some of those problems that precipitated its revision are discussed here.

Application of Classification Principles

DSM II fails to meet the classification principles we described earlier in a number of ways.

Medical Model Assumptions

First, it assumes without proof that abnormal behavior is a disease, thereby sidestepping the issue of whether a given abnormal behavior pattern is a variation of normal behavior or is qualitatively different, an issue that ought to be empirically determined rather than arbitrarily prejudged. For example, anxiety obviously is a continuous variable, present at some time in all of us, and certainly a familiar experience to almost every student who ever took an exam. Yet the anxiety reaction is presented as a category in the medical classification system. Whether an individual whose behavior is deviant is totally different from one whose behavior is not should be a research concern, not a matter of definition.

Inadequate Terminology

Another problem is that the classification scheme of DSM II lacks an adequate scientific terminology. Too many of the terms used as defining attributes of a category can be neither observed nor operationally defined. Consequently, obtaining reliability, or agreement among classifiers, is difficult. For example, the definition of *schizophrenia* states that "Disturbances in thinking are marked by alterations of concept formation which may lead to misinterpretation of reality and sometimes to delusions and hallucinations, which frequently appear psychologically self-protective" (p. 33). Terms such as "concept formation" and "psychologically self-protective" are inferences rather than observations. Therefore, it is possible that each clinician will develop a personal idea of what constitutes a concept formation or a psychologically self-protective mechanism. It would be more useful if the classifiers could agree on the definitions of basic terms and if the system clearly distinguished between what is observed and what is inferred.

Complex Classification Units

A third problem is that persons rather than responses are used as the basic classification units. This approach does not promote the principle that units of classification should be as simple as possible. In defense of that approach, one could argue that the clinician observes the individual's responses and then places the person in the appropriate category. Nevertheless, a common practice is to place people in categories on the basis of impressions *and then* search for behavior to justify such placement. Many studies of clinical judgment have shown that after a clinical decision has been made, further information—even if it contradicts the original judgment—has the effect of increasing the clinician's confidence that the original judgment was correct (Goldberg 1968).

Disjunctive Categories

Perhaps the most serious problem the DSM II encounters is the use of disjunctive categories. For instance, schizophrenia may be classified on the basis of any of a wide va-

riety of behaviors, a number of them extra-classificatory attributes, such as disturbances in thinking, mood disorders, withdrawn behavior, delusions, or hallucinations. As a result, one individual may be classified as schizophrenic *solely* on the basis of inappropriate emotional responses and another placed in the same category *solely* on the basis of delusional behavior. Consequently, the use of disjunctive categories can lead to heterogeneous, rather than the desirable homogeneous, groupings of people.

A further risk of disjunctive categorizing allows the same behavior to be classified into several different categories. For example, depressive behavior might be labeled as a psychotic depressive reaction, a manic-depressive illness, a depressed type, an involutional melancholia, a depressive neurosis, or a schizo-affective schizophrenia. Ideally, a given response pattern such as depression should impel the clinician to seek other data to complete the classification procedure, but as we noted earlier, the search for other relevant data may be used to justify a decision rather than to increase understanding.

Lack of Single Classifying Principle

Finally, DSM II fails the requirement of a single classifying principle. A classification system has the option of sorting disorders on the basis of observed behavior (symptoms), causes (etiology), development over time (prognosis), or response to treatment, but only one of these should be used to empirically determine the other aspects of the disorder. In other words, if a behavior disorder is classified on the basis of symptoms, then etiology, prognosis, and response to treatment can be determined empirically. Instead, DSM II determines all of these aspects by definition. The result is a self-fulfilling prophecy. Any data that would motivate the clinician to modify his or her beliefs about the disorder are ignored. The end result is not a set of descriptive labels but a set of stereotypes.

Reliability

Can the APA classification scheme be used to reliably place individuals in the correct categories, and can clinicians agree on the

DSM II categories are not homogeneous

sorting? In a review of classification studies, Zubin (1967) found moderate agreement among raters (rarely over 80 percent) in diagnosing broad classes of disorders, such as organic brain syndromes, functional psychoses, and neuroses, but less than 50 percent agreement on the average when specific categories were used. While the violation of several basic classification principles is responsible for this low reliability, the most common cause is the use of disjunctive categories. As evidence of this, one need only note that an individual's symptoms are not highly related to the diagnosis—certainly, a curious situation.

Validity

The discrepancy noted in the previous section also implies that the categories have low validity. In fact, diagnosis within the classification system seems to be highly dependent on local customs and conventions. Temerlin (1968) demonstrated how this problem most likely occurs. He developed a tape recording of a "supernormal" man: An actor played the role of a man who had effective work habits; related well to the interviewer; was self-confident and secure without being arrogant, guarded, or grandiose; was heterosexual, married, and in love with his wife; and consistently enjoyed sexual intercourse. Temerlin played this tape for a number of psychiatrists, clinical psychologists, and clinical psychology graduate students, who were then asked to rate the person as psychotic, neurotic, or mentally healthy. The raters were divided into six groups as follows: the first group were

told they were listening to an employment interview; the second were given no suggestion about the tape; the third were given a suggestion by a prestigious person that the person was mentally healthy; and the fourth, fifth, and sixth groups were given the suggestion by an M.D., a Ph.D., or a clinical psychology graduate student, respectively, that the person was psychotic. The results, shown in Table 2–2, reveal that the supernormal individual on the tape was consistently evaluated as neurotic or psychotic when a suggestion of psychosis had been made. The clear implication is that diagnosis is frequently determined by the bias the clinician has before seeing the individual. Thus, as Chapman and Chapman (1967) note, agreement among clinicians may be a function of systematic biases rather than accurate evaluation of behavior. They call this type of error *illusory correlations*.

Another way of evaluating validity is to ask whether the diagnosis determines the selection of a treatment program. In medical practice, for example, a diagnosis of severe appendicitis determines the treatment, usually surgery. Does a diagnosis of paranoid schizophrenia determine the treatment method? According to Bannister, Salmon, and Leiberman (1964), the answer is no. Since determination of the appropriate treatment program is one of the main objectives of a classification system, the success of the current system is obviously questionable.

The proneness of many clinicians to seeing the label rather than the person is further illuminated by a study (Rosenhan

Table 2–2 Suggestion Effects in Psychiatric Diagnosis: Percentages of Ratings As Psychotic, Neurotic, or Mentally Healthy

Group	N	Psychotic	Neurotic	Healthy
Employment interview	24	0	29	71
No prestige suggestion	21	0	43	57
Suggestion of mental health	20	0	0	100
Suggestion psychosis, psychiatrist (M.D.)	25	60	40	0
Suggestion psychosis, clinical psychologists (Ph.D.)	25	28	60	12
Suggestion psychosis, graduate students in clinical psychology	45	11	78	11

scientific approaches to the study of abnormal behavior

1973) in which eight normal "pseudopatients" gained admission to twelve different hospitals. Among these pseudopatients were three psychologists, a pediatrician, a psychiatrist, a painter, and a housewife, all of whom complained to the various admissions offices that they were hearing voices. When asked in the *intake* interview what the voices said, they replied that the voices were unclear but sounded "empty" or "hollow."

Once admitted, the pseudopatients behaved normally. All but one were admitted with the diagnosis of schizophrenia and discharged shortly afterward with a diagnosis of schizophrenia in remission (schizophrenia with no symptoms). At no point was the deception detected by the professional staff, though the other patients' suspicions were aroused by the fact that the pseudopatients took notes.

Rosenhan drew two major conclusions from his study: (1) Many professionals are unable to distinguish between sane and insane people, and (2) hospitalization can have drastic consequences. The first conclusion rests on the failure of professionals to detect the pseudopatients. The second is supported by considerable evidence that the professionals' perceptions of the pseudopatients' behavior were distorted by the assumptions and expectations associated with the label. Once applied, the label was so powerful that many of the pseudopatients' normal behaviors were either overlooked entirely or profoundly misinterpreted. The impact of labeling was especially well illustrated by the responses to attempts to obtain information. In several instances a pseudopatient approached a staff member with questions such as, "Could you tell me when I will be eligible for privileges?" or "When am I likely to be discharged?" To supply control data for this portion of the study, a student approached faculty members in a large university and in a university medical center and asked similar questions. As shown in Table 2–3, the responses were quite different. If the pseudopatient in the psychiatric hospital asked the question, the staff responded less than 5 percent of the time. Other data in the study also support Rosenhan's contention that patients were treated as powerless and nonhuman.

Rosenhan's study has been severely criticized, and these criticisms run the gamut, from emotional tirades to compelling logical analyses of the study's weak points (Farber 1975; Millon 1975; Spitzer 1975; Weiner 1975). All things considered, Rosenhan has raised serious questions about the need for a better diagnostic system. In particular he has underscored the need to observe behavior to determine whether it is

Rosenhan's pseudopatients went undetected

Table 2–3 **Self-Initiated Contact by Pseudopatients with Psychiatrists and Nurses and Attendants, Compared to Contact with Other Groups**

Contact	Psychiatric hospitals		University campus (nonmedical)	University medical center Physicians		
	(1) Psychiatrists	(2) Nurses and attendants	(3) Faculty	(4) "Looking for a psychiatrist"	(5) "Looking for an internist"	(6) No additional comment
Responses						
Moves on, head averted (%)	71	88	0	0	0	0
Makes eye contact (%)	23	10	0	11	0	0
Pauses and chats (%)	2	2	0	11	0	10
Stops and talks (%)	4	0.5	100	78	100	90
Mean number of questions answered (out of 6)	•	•	6	3.8	4.8	4.5
Respondents (No.)	13	47	14	18	15	10
Attempts (No.)	185	1283	14	18	15	10

*Not applicable.

box 2–1
I Was a Teenage
Incorrigible

Dallas County Hospital District
Psychiatric Division

To the Staff of Woodlawn Hospital:

I wish to give my consent for the use of Electroshock Therapy on _____

_____

I fully understand the dangers accompanying the use of this form of treatment.

Patient signature _____

Signed _____

Relationship _____

Witness: _____

Date: _____

The above is an excerpt from a form that was casually handed to me in the early morning hours some nine years ago upon being admitted to Woodlawn Psychiatric Hospital. I was told that my signature on this piece of paper was a necessary and routine part of the admission procedure. My signature on this form would, in essence, turn custody of my brain over to the local electric company at the "discretion" of student psychiatrists and petty bureaucrats with psychiatric degrees. I refused to sign.

After much argument—attempts of bribery and intimidation (reward and punishment)—they finally relented. But only after one psychiatrist, who had been called away from his home in the middle of the night, informed my mother that, "We don't believe we will have to use this treatment, *but we can get the signature if necessary.*" So without further ado I was admitted to Woodlawn, sent to the women's ward, assigned a room, given a pill, and told to go to sleep.

During my stay I was spared the unpleasantness (understatement!) of electro-shock therapy. However, I encountered many individuals who were not so fortunate. While all of them were not quite on top of things and some of them were close to the vegetable stage,

they all had one thing in common . . . they were easily controlled. And the very presence of these people was threatening enough to control me also.

At this point in my life I was sixteen years old, frightened, unable to take control of my life and being punished at every attempt to do so. My "incorrigible" conduct consisted of running away from home after being severely beaten, grounded and expelled for skipping school. I was sent to a juvenile home for two weeks then transferred to Woodlawn for further evaluation. My parents and the school labelled my behavior "trouble making"—the hospital labelled it "incorrigible" and "unable to accept authority." In retrospect, I regard my behavior as being healthy adolescent rebellion against repressive systems: an authoritarian public school and a domineering and overprotective family used as tools in my overall socialization. I mention this only to establish that I was not a felon nor a criminal, but was sixteen and female and therefore guilty of not being submissive . . . sixteen and female.

Most of my memories concerning the hospital have disappeared over the last nine years. However, there is one that remains vivid. It was a particularly intimate conversation with a patient who was later to kill herself. She made the following statement to me with such bitterness and resentfulness that I never forgot it. "Oh you'll find out what's going on here. You'll learn the ropes. If you wanna get out of here, all ya gotta do is play their games. Fix your hair up nice, put on some makeup, dress up, and above all be a good girl."

At the time I was incapable of fully understanding the implications of her statement. I only knew if I wasn't a "good girl," I wouldn't get out and, carried a bit further, that if I did get out and I didn't stay a "good girl," I might be right back. Now I realize this expensive public hospital was using reward and punishment as treatment and the cure was, in many cases, sexist resocialization and control of individuals whose only crimes were attempts at self-determination.

While writing this article I ran into incredible difficulties with Woodlawn Hospital in an attempt to acquire my own hospital records. It seems they feel a patient has no right to have their records because "they might not understand them." I have managed, however, to obtain my release statement from another source. The following are direct quotes from the two-page analysis. I feel no further explanation will be necessary.

Presenting Complaint [nothing deleted]: The patient has been a management problem both at home and school with recent expulsion from the tenth grade because of excessive truancy from school. There have been several episodes of running away, staying out late at night, a questionable episode of being raped about two months prior to admission while staying away from home all night, and severe difficulty with impulse control in general.

[My note: the man who raped me was later convicted of raping his little sister and two other young girls within a period of several weeks.]

Present Illness: The patient was referred to the Child Service for re-evaluation in early November, 1965,

because of having become increasingly more of a management problem for the mother. The mother found it increasingly difficult to set limits on the patient's behavior, and there had evolved a very angry interaction between the patient and her mother in which any attempt of the mother to set limits was answered with outbursts of hostility and verbal aggression on the part of the patient.

There was a clear-cut MMPI profile of a personality disorder involving impulsive acting out and insufficient inhibition and control of impulses. The patient was seen to be self-centered and emotionally unstable. In addition to her reckless disregard of the consequences of her behavior and inability to plan ahead, she is quite angry and hostile toward authority and society, and does not closely identify with recognized conventions. Though superficially pleasant, she is quite moody and resentful and feels rather victimized by others. . . . . It was felt that the patient could benefit significantly only from a much longer term hospitalization than could be provided her here at this time.

Diagnostic Impression: Emotionally unstable personality.

Within the last week I have spoken with the man who was my physician during my hospitalization. He has obviously gone through some very drastic and positive changes over these years. In closing I would like to enter a more recent quote from our phone conversation. . . . "Debbie, I want you to know I cringe every time I read that paper!"

I cringe too, knowing that city and federal employees have access to this diagnosis and that it will follow me for the rest of my life, and there is not a damn thing I can do about it at this time. I strongly urge that all ex-patients do everything in their power to get ahold of their own records (they might be quite surprised) and work for changes that will destroy whatever perpetuates the myth of the almighty white healers who are above questioning by anyone.

unusual compared to normative behavior; in other words, the perception of behavior should determine the assessment of abnormality, rather than the assessment of abnormality determining the perception of behavior.

The Impact of Labeling— Other Criticisms

The disastrous consequences of *psychiatric labeling* have been a target of numerous criticisms. Laing (1960) argues that diagnostic labeling is antitherapeutic, that it dehumanizes and invalidates the labeled person, and that it functions as a self-fulfilling prophecy. Sarbin (1967) calls it a transformation of social identity associated with social degradation and loss of status. Szasz (1966) calls it an illegal exercise of social power over individuals. And Ullmann and Krasner (1969) suggest that labeling an individual "mentally ill" is a way of maintaining social control; that once labeled, the individual is expected to behave

Labeling dehumanizes individuals and casts them into a sick role

in accordance with the diagnosis. Psychiatric diagnosis, in short, is a process that tends to stereotype individuals and then coerce them into behaving in accordance with the stereotype.

A Revision System—DSM III

The latest revision of the *Diagnostic and Statistical Manual of Mental Disorders* (1980), outlined in Table 2–4, seems to have corrected many of the faults of DSM II. One major improvement is the fact that DSM III seems not to be heavily influenced by one theoretical position. Another advantage is that the language appears to be more *operational,* with specific criteria that must be met before an individual can be diagnosed. This practice produces more *homogeneous* categories and tends to eliminate disjunctive categories, all of which should greatly improve the reliability of the diagnostic system.

Table 2–4   DSM-III Classification: Axes I and II Categories and Codes

Disorders usually first evident in infancy, childhood, or adolescence

Mental retardation
Mild mental retardation
Moderate mental retardation
Severe mental retardation
Profound mental retardation
Unspecified mental retardation

Attention deficit disorder
With hyperactivity
Without hyperactivity
Residual type

Conduct disorder
Undersocialized, aggressive
Undersocialized, nonaggressive
Socialized, aggressive
Socialized, nonaggressive
Atypical

Anxiety disorders of childhood or adolescence
Separation anxiety disorder
Avoidant disorder of childhood or adolescence
Overanxious disorder

Other disorders of infancy, childhood, or adolescence
Reactive attachment disorder of infancy
Schizoid disorder of childhood or adolescence
Elective mutism

Oppositional disorder
Identity disorder

Eating disorders
Anorexia nervosa
Bulimia
Pica
Rumination disorder of infancy
Atypical eating disorder

Stereotyped movement disorders
Transient tic disorder
Chronic motor tic disorder
Tourette's disorder
Atypical tic disorder
Atypical stereotyped movement disorder

Other disorders with physical manifestations
Stuttering
Functional enuresis
Functional encopresis
Sleepwalking disorder
Sleep terror disorder

Pervasive developmental disorders
Infantile autism
Childhood onset pervasive developmental disorder
Atypical

Specific developmental disorders
Note: These are coded on Axis II.
Developmental reading disorder
Developmental arithmetic disorder

scientific approaches to the study of abnormal behavior

Developmental language disorder
Developmental articulation disorder
Mixed specific developmental disorder
Atypical specific developmental disorder

Organic mental disorders

Section 1. Organic mental disorders whose etiology or pathophysiological process is listed below (taken from the mental disorders section of ICD-9-CM).

Dementias arising in the senium and presenium

Primary degenerative dementia, senile onset,
 with delirium
 with delusions
 with depression
 uncomplicated
Primary degenerative dementia, presenile onset
Multi-infarct dementia

Substance-induced

Alcohol
 intoxication
 Idiosyncratic intoxication
 withdrawal
 withdrawal delirium
 hallucinosis
 amnestic disorder
Dementia associated with alcoholism
Barbiturate or similarly acting sedative or hypnotic
 intoxication
 withdrawal
 withdrawal delirium
 amnestic disorder
Opioid
 intoxication
 withdrawal
Cocaine
 intoxication
Amphetamine or similarly acting sympathomimetic
 intoxication
 delirium
 delusional disorder
 withdrawal
Phencyclidine (PCP) or similarly acting arylcyclohexylamine
 intoxication
 delirium
 mixed organic mental disorder
Hallucinogen
 hallucinosis
 delusional disorder
 affective disorder
Cannabis
 intoxication
 delusional disorder
Tobacco
 withdrawal
Caffeine
 intoxication
Other or unspecified substance
 intoxication
 withdrawal
 delirium
 dementia
 amnestic disorder
 delusional disorder
 hallucinosis

 affective disorder
 personality disorder
 atypical or mixed organic mental disorder

Section 2. Organic brain syndromes whose etiology or pathophysiological process is either noted as an additional diagnosis from outside the mental disorders section of ICD-9-CM or is unknown.

Delirium
Dementia
Amnestic syndrome
Organic delusional syndrome
Organic hallucinosis
Organic affective syndrome
Organic personality syndrome
Atypical or mixed organic brain syndrome

Substance use disorders

Alcohol abuse
Alcohol dependence (alcoholism)
Barbiturate or similarly acting sedative or hypnotic abuse
Barbiturate or similarly acting sedative or hypnotic dependence
Opioid abuse
Opioid dependence
Cocaine abuse
Amphetamine or similarly acting sympathomimetic abuse
Amphetamine or similarly acting sympathomimetic dependence
Phencyclidine (PCP) or similarly acting arylcyclohexylamine abuse
Hallucinogen abuse
Cannabis abuse
Cannabis dependence
Tobacco dependence
Other, mixed or unspecified substance abuse
Other specified substance dependence
Unspecified substance dependence
Dependence on combination of opioid and other nonalcoholic substance
Dependence on combination of substances, excluding opioids and alcohol

Schizophrenic disorders

Schizophrenia
 disorganized
 catatonic
 paranoid
 undifferentiated
 residual

Paranoid disorders

Paranoia
Shared paranoid disorder
Acute paranoid disorder
Atypical paranoid disorder

Psychotic disorders not elsewhere classified

Schizophreniform disorder
Brief reactive psychosis
Schizoaffective disorder
Atypical psychosis

Table 2-4 (continued)

Neurotic disorders: These are included in Affective, Anxiety, Somatoform, Dissociative, and Psychosexual Disorders. In order to facilitate the identification of the categories that in DSM-II were grouped together in the class of Neuroses, the DSM-II terms are included separately in parentheses after the corresponding categories. These DSM-II terms are included in ICD-9-CM and therefore are acceptable as alternatives to the recommended DSM-III terms that precede them.

Affective disorders

Major affective disorders

Bipolar disorder,
  mixed
  manic
  depressed
Major depression
  single episode
  recurrent

Other specific affective disorders

Cyclothymic disorder
Dysthymic disorder
(or Depressive neurosis)

Atypical affective disorders

Atypical bipolar disorder
Atypical depression

Anxiety disorders

Phobic disorders (or Phobic neuroses)

Agoraphobia with panic attacks
Agoraphobia without panic attacks
Social phobia
Simple phobia

Anxiety states (or Anxiety neuroses)

Panic disorder
Generalized anxiety disorder
Obsessive compulsive disorder
(or Obsessive compulsive neurosis)

Post-traumatic stress disorder

Acute
Chronic or delayed
Atypical anxiety disorder

Somatoform disorders

Somatization disorder
Conversion disorder
(or Hysterical neurosis, conversion type)
Psychogenic pain disorder
Hypochondriasis
(or Hypochondriacal neurosis)
Atypical somatoform disorder

Dissociative disorders (or hysterical neuroses, dissociative type)

Psychogenic amnesia
Psychogenic fugue
Multiple personality
Depersonalization disorder
(or Depersonalization neurosis)
Atypical dissociative disorder

Psychosexual disorders

Gender identity disorders

Transsexualism
Gender identity disorder of childhood
Atypical gender identity disorder

Paraphilias

Fetishism
Transvestism
Zoophilia
Pedophilia
Exhibitionism
Voyeurism
Sexual masochism
Sexual sadism
Atypical paraphilia

Psychosexual dysfunctions

Inhibited sexual desire
Inhibited sexual excitement
Inhibited female orgasm
Inhibited male orgasm
Premature ejaculation
Functional dyspareunia
Functional vaginismus
Atypical psychosexual dysfunction

Other psychosexual disorders

Ego-dystonic homosexuality
Psychosexual disorder not elsewhere classified

Factitious disorders

Factitious disorder with psychological symptoms
Chronic factitious disorder with physical symptoms
Atypical factitious disorder with physical symptoms

Disorders of impulse control not elsewhere classified

Pathological gambling
Kleptomania
Pyromania
Intermittent explosive disorder
Isolated explosive disorder
Atypical impulse control disorder

Adjustment disorder

With depressed mood
With anxious mood
With mixed emotional features
With disturbance of conduct
With mixed disturbance of emotions and conduct
With work (or academic) inhibition
With withdrawal
With atypical features

Psychological factors affecting physical condition

Specify physical condition on Axis III.
Psychological factors affecting physical condition

Personality disorders
Note: These are coded on Axis II.

Paranoid
Schizoid
Schizotypal

scientific approaches to the study of abnormal behavior

Histrionic
Narcissistic
Antisocial
Borderline
Avoidant
Dependent
Compulsive
Passive-Aggressive
Atypical, mixed or other personality disorder

V codes for conditions not attributable to a mental disorder that are a focus of attention or treatment

Malingering
Borderline intellectual functioning
Adult antisocial behavior
Childhood or adolescent antisocial behavior
Academic problem

Occupational problem
Uncomplicated bereavement
Noncompliance with medical treatment
Phase of life problem or other life circumstance problem
Marital problem
Parent-child problem
Other specified family circumstances
Other interpersonal problem

Additional codes

Unspecified mental disorder (nonpsychotic)
No diagnosis or condition on Axis I
Diagnosis or condition deferred on Axis I

No diagnosis on Axis II
Diagnosis deferred on Axis II

Table 2–5 Ratings of Psychosocial Stressors from APA DSM III

Code	Term	Adult examples	Child or adolescent examples
1	None	No apparent psychosocial stressor	No apparent psychosocial stressor
2	Minimal	Minor violation of the law; small bank loan	Vacation with family
3	Mild	Argument with neighbor; change in work hours	Change in schoolteacher; new school year
4	Moderate	New career; death of close friend; pregnancy	Chronic parental fighting; change to new school; illness of close relative; birth of sibling
5	Severe	Serious illness in self or family; major financial loss; marital separation; birth of child	Death of peer; divorce of parents; arrest; hospitalization; persistent and harsh parental discipline
6	Extreme	Death of close relative; divorce	Death of parent or sibling; repeated physical or sexual abuse
7	Catastrophic	Concentration camp experience; devastating natural disaster	Multiple family deaths
0	Unspecified	No information, or not applicable	No information, or not applicable

Multiaxial Classification

The major innovation is the use of a **multiaxial classification** scheme that allows classification of an individual along five different axes, as follows:

Axis I Clinical Psychiatric Syndrome and Other Conditions This axis is used to designate behavior patterns associated with abnormal states, such as depression or schizophrenia.

Axis II Personality Disorders and Specific Developmental Disorders This axis is used to designate personality disorders in adults and specific developmental disorders, such as learning disabilities, in children and adolescents.

Axis III Physical Disorders If an individual has a physical illness, it is recorded on this axis.

Axis IV Severity of Psychological Stressors This axis is used to rate the severity of stressors that might elicit or provide for the appearance of an abnormal behavior pattern. These include parenting, marital, occupational, legal, or developmental stressors, natural or other environmental disasters, family pressures, physical illnesses or injuries, and similar distressing events that could disrupt behavior. These stressors are rated in terms of severity, as shown in Table 2–5

DSM III's five axes are an improvement . . .

classification   49

Pregnancy, the death of a spouse, and incarceration are all psychologically stressing situations in terms of personal and family adjustments.

Axis V Highest Level of Adaptive Functioning (in the Past Year) This axis can be used by the clinician to assess the degree of change in the individual's life in the past year. The individual's adaptive functioning is gauged in terms of his or her social relationships, occupational functioning, and use of leisure time. The levels of adaptive functioning are shown in Table 2–6.

The use of these axes' partially eliminates the confusion between etiology and description of behavior. For example, Axes I and II comprise the entire classification of mental disorders, while Axes III and IV are etiological factors in terms of either environmental or physical causes. An additional advantage is that Axis III allows a determination of whether the deviant behavior is associated with a physical disor-

scientific approaches to the study of abnormal behavior

Table 2–6   Highest Level of Adaptive Functioning in Past Year

Levels	Adult examples	Child or adolescent examples
1 Superior—Unusually effective functioning in social relations, occupational functioning, and use of leisure time.	Single parent living in deteriorating neighborhood takes excellent care of children and home, has warm relations with friends, and finds time for pursuit of hobby.	A twelve-year-old girl gets superior grades in school, is extremely popular among her peers, and excels in many sports. She does all of this with apparent ease and comfort.
2 Very good—Better than average functioning in social relations, occupational functioning, and use of leisure time.	A sixty-five-year-old retired widower does some volunteer work, often sees old friends, and pursues hobbies.	An adolescent boy gets excellent grades, works part-time, has several close friends, and plays banjo in a jazz band. He admits to some distress in "keeping up with everything."
3 Good—No more than slight impairment in either social or occupational functioning.	A woman with many friends functions extremely well at a difficult job, but says "the strain is too much."	An eight-year-old boy does well in school, has several friends, but bullies younger children.
4 Fair—Moderate impairment in either social relations or occupational functioning, or some impairment in both.	A lawyer has trouble carrying through assignments; has several acquaintances, but hardly any close friends.	A ten-year-old girl does poorly in school, but has adequate peer and family relations.
5 Poor—Marked impairment in either social relations or occupational functioning, *or* moderate impairment in both.	A man with one or two friends has trouble keeping a job for more than a few weeks.	A fourteen-year-old boy almost fails in school and has trouble getting along with his peers.
6 Very poor—Marked impairment in both social relations and occupational functioning.	A woman is unable to do any of her housework and has violent outbursts toward family and neighbors.	A six-year-old girl needs special help in all subjects and has virtually no peer relationships.
7 Grossly impaired—Gross impairment in virtually all areas of functioning.	An elderly man needs supervision to maintain minimal personal hygiene and is usually incoherent.	A four-year-old boy needs constant restraint to avoid hurting himself and is almost totally lacking in skills.
0 Unspecified	No information.	No information.

der. Axis V allows the classifiers to determine how much deterioration of adjustment has occurred.

Evaluation of DSM III

Although it is a huge improvement over DSM II, DSM III presents a number of unresolved problems. For example, some confusion could arise in the use of Axis II, on which specific developmental disorders (such as reading disability) are diagnosed for children but personality disorders (such as the antisocial personality) are diagnosed for adults. Personality disorders do occur in adolescence, and learning disorders often continue into adulthood. Labeling an individual on Axis II before and on Axis I after he or she reaches the age of eighteen is likely to cause confusion. In fact, using either age or developmental periods as a factor in diagnosis is a source of real confusion. It ignores the recommendation that a taxonomy use a single principle of clas-

sification by using etiologies or behavioral descriptions as principles of classification. The multi-axis approach came close. The chances for confusion could have been reduced if the behavior had been included on Axis I (clinical syndromes) or Axis II (stable behavior patterns), and stress in the developmental period on Axis IV (Psychosocial stressors).

An interesting sidelight of DSM III is that the continuing struggle to find appropriate terminology has evidently led to a decision to abandon some terms, such as *psychophysiologic disorder*. Psychophysiologic disorders, which were earlier defined as psychosomatic disorders, are now called "psychological factors affecting physical disorder." We shall retain the old terminology partly because it is in common usage and partly because "psychophysiological disorder," as bulky a label as it is, is not nearly as unwieldy as "psychological factors affecting physical disorder."

but some problems remain

Overall, the multiaxial classification system of DSM III is a significant advance beyond DSM II, and it adheres better to our list of classification principles. Because it uses operational criteria for placing an individual in a category, it should greatly improve the reliability of diagnosis. Many problems remain, however, including the use of multiple principles of classification and some illogical groupings of disorders. Nevertheless, DSM III is compatible, to some extent, with the preferred system we shall present below. Since no data are available yet on the usefulness of DSM III, and since the categories of DSM II are familiar, we shall refer to both in our discussions of specific disorders.

A Behavioral Classification System

One approach that would reduce the errors and the stereotyping produced by DSM II and DSM III would be a classification system based on *normal* behavior. Such a system would provide a standard for evaluating psychological malfunctioning in the same way that a physician evaluates physiological malfunctioning in terms of normal physiology. This is the approach we shall use in this book: *classifying on the basis of responses that are overt, measurable, and based on current behavior,* rather than on the basis of theoretical constructs.

Using this approach, the clinician who must decide whether a certain pattern of behavior is abnormal can ask, "How does this behavior compare with the behavior of typical individuals under the circumstances or to this individual's past behavior in similar circumstances?" On the basis of this comparison, the clinician may then determine whether the behavior in question is atypical and whether a DSM III diagnostic label is appropriate. This would also involve an evaluation in terms of the two criteria discussed earlier (adjustment and labeled deviance) to decide whether the deviation is pathological or constructive.

Basing a classification system on normal behavior is hardly a new idea, since such a system has been used for many years to classify psychologists' areas of applied and research interests. We call this system the **behavioral classification system** (Adams, Doster, and Calhoun 1977) because it uses observed behavior as the units of classification. It is not a system based on the theoretical position labeled behaviorism.

Advantages of the Behavioral System

Using overt behavior as the basis for classification has several advantages. First, theoretical notions about causes, modification of behavior, and the development and maintenance of behavior are quite primitive at this stage in the development of psychology. As Kety (1965) has stated, theoretical inferences stimulate research but are not a sound basis for a classification system.

Second, basing classification on all behavior rather than on abnormal behavior alone avoids prejudging the continuity-discontinuity controversy. Since the issue of whether abnormal behavior differs in kind or only in degree from normal behavior has not been resolved, it would be more prudent to view abnormal behavior as a deviation from normal behavior even when labels from DSM II or DSM III are used.

Third, a behavioral classification system distinguishes classification (which concerns the philosophy of the science and the identification and definition of phenomena) from research (which involves the methodology of information gathering). These are two quite different activities, and to confuse them compromises the usefulness and validity of both.

Fourth, this approach unifies basic and abnormal psychology under a common classification system. At present, abnormal psychology is so dominated by the concepts and terminology of the medical model and psychodynamic theory that there is little transfer from such basic psychology topics as sensation, perception, motivation, emotions, and even learning. The premise here is that abnormal behaviors are disorders of a person's basic response systems and that the basic theory and data of psychology are relevant to these disorders. For example, hallucinations should not be discussed without some knowledge of perception and sensation, nor should delusions be discussed without some knowledge of cognitive psychology.

Behavioral classification relates abnormal behavior to normal behavior

Classification of Response Systems

Units of classification should be simple and easy to define. In a behavioral classification system these units are the individual's *responses*. In contrast, the common practice in DSM II or DSM III has been to classify *people* into categories, such as schizophrenics, or to place individuals on some continuum, such as degree of anxiety, and to otherwise rank or order their placement.

The whole person is a complex phenomenon, and use of persons as classification units results in poor reliability and validity. Such an approach always presupposes, explicitly or implicitly, stable personality characteristics or stable abnormal behavior. Those presuppositions are questionable, as we shall see in Chapter 5. Furthermore, as we noted earlier, classifying people rather than behavior encourages stereotyping.

Response systems are derived, as far as possible, by subdividing all behavior into distinct and nonoverlapping classes (see Table 2–7), with each class representing one response system. This is not intended as a denial of the interaction between response systems. Obviously, response systems do interact with each other. For example, the emotional and sensory systems interact to a great extent. This situation is also found in physiological classification schemes, where, for example, the cardiovascular and respiratory systems interact greatly. We shall briefly describe each of these response systems and show how it corresponds to disorders classified in DSM II and DSM III.

Emotional Response System

The emotional response system includes the activity of tissues and organs affected by the autonomic nervous system, and is usually expressed in specific behavior patterns or subjective experiences, such as anxiety, anger, or imagined fear. Clinicians and researchers have investigated the emotional response system extensively and have divided it into three response categories: (1) *anxiety/tranquility,* (2) *dysphoria/euphoria,* and (3) *anger/affection.* These categories are by no means exhaustive, but they do include such behavior as embarrassment, anxiety, pleasure, joy, elation, euphoria, anger, disgust, rage, jealousy, sadness, depression, and melancholia. In many cases, different adjectives have been used to describe behaviors that may differ only in intensity or duration. For example, irritation and rage may differ only in intensity, and anger and hatred may differ only in duration.

Extremes of anxiety could be labeled as anxiety disorders or phobic disorders in DSM III. Variations along the elation/depression continuum correspond to any of a variety of labels from DSM II and III, such as depressive disorder, manic disorder, or cyclothymic personality.

Sensory/Perceptual Response System

This system is designed to include the activities of detecting, discriminating, and interpreting *environmental* stimuli. Since differentiating between sensation and perception on an empirical basis is not possible, we shall define *sensation* as the simple detection of a signal and *perception* as the interpretation of more complex signals. The response categories of this system include auditory (hearing), visual (seeing), gustatory (tasting), olfactory (smelling), pain, and proprioceptive reception (reception of stimuli arising within the organism).

Responsiveness to sensory inputs can be greatly diminished or augmented, causing an individual to become functionally blind or deaf, to lose or increase sensitivity to painful stimuli, or to suffer other sensory disorders labeled in DSM II as hysterical neuroses or in DSM III as somatoform disorders.

Cognitive Response System

Cognitive response system behaviors include the evaluation, processing, retention, and retrieval of *information.* Subcategories include attention, memory, reasoning, and concept formation. Many response patterns labeled as abnormal reflect variations in this response system. For example, a delusion could be considered an unusual way of processing information. Fugue and multiple personality states are disorders of memory. Schizophrenia has often been called a disorder of the associative processes or of attention (Ullmann and Krasner 1975).

The whole person is complex; units of classification should be simple

Emotions vary qualitatively and quantitatively

To sense is to detect; to perceive is to interpret

Unusual ways of handling information are often labeled abnormal

Table 2-7 Response Systems in a Behavioral Classification System

Response systems	Definition	Response categories	Examples of variations as diagnosed by DSM II and DSM III
Emotional	Activity of tissues and organs innervated by the autonomic nervous system that is associated with specific behavior patterns and subjective experience of an individual	Anxiety Euphoria/Dysphoria Anger/Affection	DSM II—Anxiety neuroses; phobic neuroses; depressive neuroses; explosive personality DSM III—Affective disorders; anxiety disorders; impulse disorders (anger); anxiety disorders of childhood or adolescence; intermittent explosive disorder
Sensory/Perceptual	Activities involving detection, discrimination, and recognition of environmental stimuli	Visual Auditory Gustatory Vestibular Visceral Olfactory Kinesthetic Cutaneous	DSM II—Hysterial neuroses, conversion type (sensory) DSM III—Somatoform disorders (sensory)
Cognitive	Behaviors involving the processing of information	Information selection Information retrieval Conceptualization Reasoning	DSM II—Hysterical neuroses, dissociative type; depersonalization neuroses; obsessive-compulsive neuroses (obsessions); hypochondriacal neuroses DSM III—Dissociative disorders
Motor	Activity of the muscles and glands involved in physical activities but exclusive of the meaning or content of those activities	Oculo-Motor Facial Throat Head Limb Trunk	DSM II—Hysterial neuroses, conversion type (motor); obsessive-compulsive neuroses (motor rituals); tic; psychomotor disorders; speech disorders DSM III—Somatoform disorders (motor); obsessive-compulsive disorders (motor rituals); speech disorders; stereotyped movement disorders
Biological Needs	Behaviors associated with basic body needs arising from specific biochemical conditions or unusually strong peripheral stimulation that can impair the well-being or health of the individual if not satisfied	Hunger Thirst Elimination Sex Sleep Respiration Harm-Avoidance	DSM II—Neurasthenic neuroses; asthenic personality; sexual deviations; disorders of sleep; feeding disturbances; enuresis; encopresis DSM III—Psychosexual dysfunctions; paraphilias; other sexual disorders; sleep disorders; eating disorders; enuresis; encopresis
Acquired biological needs	Acquired physical dependencies (intake of substances into the body that change the biochemistry of the physiological systems so that the presence of these substances is required to avoid physiological or psychological distress)		DSM II—Alcoholism; drug dependence DSM III—Substance use disorders
Social	Reciprocal actions of two or more individuals	Aggression/Submission Dependency/Independency Altruism/Selfishness Conformity/Deviations	DSM II and DSM III—Personality disorders in adults and children
Complex variations	Functional interaction of two or more response systems		DSM II and DSM III—Mental retardation (functional); schizophrenia; paranoid states; pervasive developmental disorders including infantile autism; major affective disorders

Motor Response System

Motor response determines an act's form, but not its meaning

Motor response behaviors are physical actions that involve *movement* in time and space. Subcategories include locomotion, posture, speech, and other instrumental motor behavior. The motor response system determines the structure or form of physical acts rather than their content or meaning. For example, verbal behavior can be viewed either in terms of communication of cognitive or emotional content or in terms of such variables as loudness, fluency, or other physical parameters of sound production. Motor response variations labeled abnormal in DSM II or DSM III include compulsive rituals, tics, stuttering, stammering, and loss of the motor function without cause (conversion hysteria).

Biological Needs Response System

The behaviors associated with the biological needs response system are responses to basic body needs arising either from specific

Obesity and anorexia nervosa (self-starvation) are both disorders of the biological needs response system.

biochemical conditions within the body or from strong peripheral stimuli that must be satisfied or reduced to protect the individual's (and ultimately the species') health or well-being. They are the behaviors associated with hunger, thirst, sleep, elimination, harm-avoidance, and sex. Biological needs give rise to *drives,* which motivate behavior, and to *wants,* which connect needs with goals.

Behavioral variations between individuals and within an individual in satisfying biological needs are dependent on two variables: (1) the *range* of different environmental events that will satisfy the need, and (2) the *maximum duration* of deprivation without harm to the organism. For example, behavior variation in satisfying the need for oxygen is slight, since the maximum safe deprivation schedule is short and the need can be met only by breathing oxygen. In contrast, a variety of events can satisfy sexual needs, and the possible deprivation schedule can be extremely long.

Consequently, behavior arising out of sexual needs varies over a very wide range.

Many of the variations of behavior associated with the biological needs response system have been labeled abnormal, including obesity, anorexia nervosa (loss of appetite due to nervousness), insomnia, and sexual deviations.

Acquired Biological Needs Response System

Acquired biological needs result from the intake of substances that change the body's chemistry in such a way that the presence of those substances is necessary to avoid physiological or psychological distress (Solomon 1977). The behavior patterns involved are those associated with physical or psychological habituation (addiction) to any of a variety of substances, including alcohol, nicotine, opiates, amphetamines, and barbiturates.

Biological needs differ in the diversity of satisfying stimuli and the maximum possible duration of deprivation

Substances can create biological needs

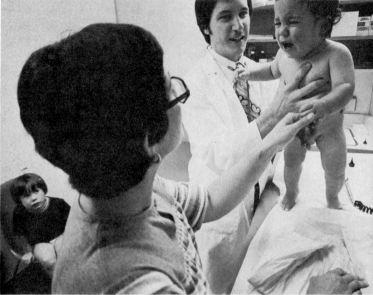

The chauffer and his employer have a social relationship that is dictated by the social class system. A baby's relationship with its mother is one of dependence. Because this baby is frightened of the doctor, he looks to his mother for reassurance and comfort.

Social Behavior Response System

Social behavior is interaction between two or more people that influences the nature of the relationship between them. In general, the aspects of behavior involved in this system are the ones commonly referred to as *personality*. Personality, in this sense, includes the types and degrees of skill with which an individual interacts with others; it can be specified in terms of such bipolar coordinates as conformity/deviation, aggression/submission, dependence/independence, and altruism/selfishness. For example, a person's behavior could be specified on an altruism/selfishness scale by counting the frequency of his or her "giving behaviors." Variations in the social response system have been labeled in DSM II and DSM III with terms such as antisocial personality, dependent, passive/aggressive, and paranoid.

Individuals interact
to varying degrees
and with varying skill

Accounting for Complex Variations in Behavior

Complex variations in behavior are responses that involve two or more of the response systems described in the preceding section. A good example of such complex variations is *intelligence,* which is most di-

rectly manifested in the cognitive response system but also involves the sensory/perceptual response system, the motor response system, and others.

The distinction between a complex variation in behavior and a variation in a response system is that the complex variation involves attributes (symptoms) that are intrinsically related and not independent of one another. Thus, we could call intelligence a complex variation, since it embraces reasoning, judgment, memory, perception, and sensitivity to social cues, but we would also have to demonstrate that these attributes are highly correlated with one another in *all* individuals. If they are not, we can consider each attribute independently in a less complex response system, and we would have no need for a complex category.

A more complicated case is that in which two or more behavioral attributes interrelate in some people but are independent in others. Suppose, for example, that lack of emotional responsiveness (emotional response system) is associated with thought disorders (cognitive response system) in 5 percent of the population. We could call this category "schizophrenia" and use it as an independent category (rather than a simple variation of typical behavior) if we could show that the association between

scientific approaches to the study of abnormal behavior

these two response variations is not random but is due to distinct pathological processes. In the long run, establishing the existence of a phenomenon such as schizophrenia requires a demonstration not only that these attributes of behavior are associated but also that they are causally related in a meaningful fashion, which are the requirements for a secondary or *beta* classification.

Before we could consider such a category meaningful, we would have to demonstrate empirically that these individuals share a common set of conditions, either physiological or environmental (for example, genetic predisposition or "schizogenic mothers") that consistently produce schizophrenic behavior. As it stands, schizophrenia is a hypothesis, not an entity, and until its existence as an event in the real world can be demonstrated, it should not be used as a classification category. (This is an important concept. The word schizophrenia and the idea of schizophrenia as a disease were *made up* to try to explain some behavior seen in the real world. We cannot say yet that such a disease exists in the real world. Schizophrenia exists in people's minds as an idea, but does not necessarily exist "out there" as a disease, though people commonly mistake an idea for a fact.) The same caution should be observed for other complex variations in behavior. They should not be treated as diagnostic categories until relations between causes and response categories have been established empirically. No one has yet demonstrated that such complex concepts as schizophrenia are distinct processes and not simply exaggerations of behavior patterns observable in everyone.

Summary

Psychology has no formal system for classifying normal behavior, but a number of schemes have been used to classify abnormal behavior. The most widely used classification system at present is the *Diagnostic and Statistical Manual of Mental Disorders* (DSM II and DSM III), which is based on a number of medical model assumptions about abnormal behavior.

Taxonomies (classifications systems) should be constructed according to certain principles of classification: use of proper scientific terminology, conjunctive rather than disjunctive categories, and single classification principle. Extraclassificatory attributes should not be used as defining attributes, and classification units should be as simple as possible.

Both labeled deviance and adjustment have been used as criteria in evaluating abnormal behavior, and this has caused some confusion and conflict.

DSM II is based on several classification principles—physiological malfunctions, developmental processes, etiology, behavior patterns, and special symptoms. It violates the principles of classification in several ways: It confuses observation and theory. It uses persons as the basic units of classification, thereby violating the principle that classification units should be as simple as possible. And it uses disjunctive categories. These violations of classification principles, as shown by several studies, have led to serious problems of validity, reliability, and usefulness. By using a multiaxial approach, DSM III has eliminated much of the confusion caused by DSM II but continues some of its confusing practices.

One way to reduce the confusion that surrounds the present approach would be to use normal behavior as a standard for evaluating abnormal behavior. By classifying responses rather than persons, such a system would reduce the tendency to stereotype. It would treat abnormal behavior as a variation of the normal behavior of the system affected, and the major categories would be the organism's response systems—the emotional response system, the sensory/perceptual response system, the cognitive response system, the biological needs response system, the acquired biological needs response system, and the social behavior response system. Complex variations of behavior could be examined in terms of the relation between various response systems. If a meaningful causal relationship could be empirically established, the complex variation could be established as an independent category.

Schizophrenia is an idea about *the real world, but* not necessarily an event in *the real world*

Key Concepts

behavioral classification system

conjunctive categories

criterion of adjustment

criterion of labeling

disjunctive categories

DSM II

DSM III

extraclassificatory attributes

multiaxial classification

operational definitions

reliability

response systems

single classification principle

taxonomy

scientific terminology

validity

Review Questions

1. What qualities should a classification system have?

2. What are the two main criteria of evaluating abnormality? Give examples of behavior that would be normal according to one criterion but abnormal according to the other.

3. List four classifying principles used in DSM II.

4. What are the four major criticisms of DSM II?

5. How is DSM III better than DSM II? How is it still inadequate? (Give one example of each.)

6. How is a behavioral classification system better?

7. What are the response systems used as units of classification in this book? What would be an abnormal response of each system?

scientific approaches to the study of abnormal behavior

science and the study of human behavior 3

Key Topics

Role of determinism in science

Difference between self-control and social control

Public verification and science

Intervening variables and hypothetical constructs

Importance of causality and correlation

Rationalistic and empirical methods in scientific inquiry

Research methods: naturalistic observation, correlational studies, and experimental methods

Controls and their functions in experimental research

Practicality of group comparison designs and single case designs

If a friend treated you rudely, you would probably try to find out why. You might go to your friend and ask if something was wrong, or you might look for changes or clues in your friend's past and present behavior. **Scientific inquiry** does the same; the key difference is the degree to which a *methodology* is defined and emphasized. Similarly, if someone else offered an explanation for your friend's behavior, you might want proof and ask, "How do you know?" The attempt to devise methods that can provide answers to the question "How do you know?" has been an integral part of the development of modern science.

The Science of Abnormal Behavior

Science is a search for order in the universe

Determinism is a belief in cause and effect

Behavior is already controlled

Science has emerged as an organized human activity only in the last few centuries, and only in this century as a full-time occupation. Comparatively, the behavioral sciences—psychology, sociology, and anthropology—have been slower to develop than the physical and biological sciences, largely because of the complex nature of humans. The development of these sciences has been further hampered by the traditional Western belief that the human species stands apart from all others and therefore cannot be scrutinized in many of the same ways. In particular, the suggestion that human behavior is *determined* has been resisted and viewed as contradictory to common sense. The further suggestion that human behavior can be *controlled* has been perceived as a threat to individual freedom.

Many of these negative reactions to a "science of behavior" are due to misconceptions about science. A behavioral science is neither a denial of *religion* (of a concept of ultimate truth based on faith) nor a denial of *metaphysics* (a rational approach to discovering the ultimate nature of reality). Science is a system developed in an attempt to find order in the universe.

It has its own limits with natural and logical boundaries that, because of the nature of science, do not permit final answers or ultimate truths.

Essentially, science is a game in which certain assumptions are made and certain rules followed. We *predict* events on the basis of **hypotheses** suggested by observed phenomena and then apply the rules in finding out whether the predictions are borne out by experience. This process is guided by three basic assumptions: (1) that events are *determined;* (2) that research results are *publicly verifiable;* and (3) that *cause-and-effect* relationships can be discovered.

Determinism

Determinism is the belief that the universe is orderly and that all events occur within a framework of *cause and effect*. This assumption differs from the religious concept of predestination in that it does not necessarily mean that an event was preordained from the beginning of time. It simply means that each behavioral event is caused by events that precede it. It is not a denial of choice or responsibility in human affairs; in fact, if there were no way to understand the causes or predict the consequences of our acts, the concept of choice would be meaningless.

The assumption of determinism, that each event (behavior) has a cause, is implicit in the purpose of a *science of behavior,* the *prediction* and *control* of behavior. To say this, however, is to call up images of the mind-controllers from George Orwell's *1984* or Anthony Burgess's *A Clockwork Orange*. Yet, as B. F. Skinner (1971) has pointed out, behavior control is nothing new. Behavior is already under the control of social and environmental contingencies. In fact, behavior control is the purpose of socialization; it is the objective of most parents, most religions, and most government agencies, especially law enforcement agencies. The question is not whether behavior can or should be controlled but what the **locus of control** should be, what type of control should be used, and how effective it can be.

Because of his arrest, this man's locus of control has shifted from himself to the law enforcement system. The two joggers, however, are exhibiting an internal locus of control over their health.

Locus of Control

Control of behavior can come from within the person (self-control) or from others (social control) or both. The purpose of socialization is to teach self-control. When socialization is successful, the locus (source or position) of control lies within individuals, and they can make responsible choices between alternatives. Thus, control is not a one-way street (Craighead, Kazdin, and Mahoney 1976), a **reciprocal determinism** operates between the individual and society; if it did not, there would be many fewer avenues of social change. Nothing in the concept of determinism denies the possibility of individuals changing their environment.

Type of Control

Control of behavior can be accomplished by either *pleasant* or *aversive* events that are made contingent on specific behaviors. Aversive control using pain, fear, or distressing emotions is rarely warranted but often employed because it is easy to use and many people believe in its effectiveness. Positive, pleasant reinforcement applied with real concern for the individual is not only more humane but in the long run more effective. Furthermore, aversive control often has unfortunate side effects for the person under treatment as well as the person or agency administering the treatment. The effects of positive and negative reinforcement are discussed in Chapter 4.

Effectiveness of Control

To assume determinism we need not assume that all the factors determining behavior are discoverable or that all behavior can be controlled. Scientific principles are, by their nature, statements of *probability* at the present time. Given a set of known causal conditions, we can predict, with varying degrees of confidence, how most individuals will respond most of the time. We can never know all the factors, nor can we rule out the possibility that some behavior may be inherently unpredictable. How actually effective behavior control has been will be discussed in more detail in Chapters 6 and 7.

Behavior control is not always effective

box 3-1
Watts on
"Scientific Truth"

Although the phrase "scientific truth" has for our age almost the same ring of ultimate authority as the phrase "Catholic truth" had for the past, the honest and strict scientist is the last person to claim such authority. As a human being, every scientist is a philosopher; but he is not a philosopher as a scientist. As a scientist, he is vividly aware of the limitations of his branch of knowledge. He knows that science is the measurement, description, and classification of natural processes; it is the study of *how* things behave. It cannot tell *what* things are, nor *why* they behave. It describes life in operation, but does not presume to say what life is for. The scientist has somewhat the same relation to the philosopher as the grammarian to the poet. The grammarian classifies the various words in a poem; identifies them as nouns, verbs, or adjectives; and describes their syntactical relation to one another. He judges the poem grammatical or ungrammatical, but he does not presume to say whether it is good or bad poetry either in respect to the beauty of the words employed or in respect to the sense conveyed. It is therefore a most serious abuse of science to attempt to make it produce a philosophy of life. This it can no more provide than the study of grammar can supply meanings to be expressed in words.

Watts, 1972

A scientist measures, describes, and classifies a natural process.

Public Verification

Research that can be replicated is an answer to "How do you know?"

One of the central ideas of modern science is that scientific data should be **publicly verifiable.** This means that a scientist who announces or publishes a discovery, a principle, or a set of results ought to be able to provide enough information to allow other researchers to use the same methods to *replicate,* or check, the results. This implies use of a *scientific terminology, empirical observation,* and *systematic probes* or checks on the observations.

An abstraction is not a thing . . .

Psychologists, perhaps because they deal with *processes* rather than tangible *objects,* are often guilty of poor communications, and the lack of an adequate scientific terminology aggravates this problem. For example, does personality or intelligence exist in the real world, or are they concepts that we project into the real world? Is schizophrenia a disease process that produces certain behavior, or is it an abstract category that psychologists and psychiatrists use as a way to organize their perceptions of what their patients are doing? This is a complaint common to critics from all of the major theoretical camps of modern psychology—that many of the *abstractions* of psychology have been **reified,** that they have been treated as if they were tangible and observable events in the natural world.

scientific approaches to the study of abnormal behavior

Reification

One way to reduce **reification** is to define behaviors exclusively in terms of operations, intervening variables, and hypothetical constructs. For example, we could measure or **operationally define** anxiety as the number of psychogalvanic skin responses (GSR)—a measure of palm sweating—in a given time period. Or we could operationally define intelligence as the measurable score on a specified intelligence test.

An **intervening variable** is scientific shorthand for the relation between two or more operationally defined variables (any measurable quantity or value subject to change). For example, a fugue state (a temporary amnesia) is an intervening variable describing the state that exists when one is asked about his or her past history (stimulus) but is unable to give correct answers (response). Intervening variables can be defined as *response-response* relationships as well as *stimulus-response* relationships.

A **hypothetical construct** is an intervening variable that is assumed to have meaning beyond its function as scientific shorthand. In the example in the preceding paragraph, the intervening variable simply provides a noun (fugue) to describe an event (this person cannot remember how he or she got to this place). The hypothetical construct, on the other hand, describes a definite process or thing that is believed to exist. A hypothetical construct is not directly observable, but the assumption is that with more refined methods of observation it might be. In genetics research, chromosomes were and genes are excellent examples of hypothetical constructs.

Most experimental psychologists believe that such concepts as personality, intelligence, and mental illness are neither observable events nor hypothetical constructs but must be considered as intervening variables. When the researcher refuses to acknowledge or fails to recognize these concepts as intervening variables, reification—the belief or assumption that they exist in the real world—results.

Another fallacy closely related to reification that is also a major problem in psychology is **circular reasoning:**

Q. Why is Joseph so shy?
A. He is a schizoid personality.
Q. How do you know he is schizoid?
A. That's obvious. He doesn't interact with people, he doesn't talk to them, and he is very shy.

"Schizoid personality" is used here first as a description of Joe's behavior and then as an explanation for it. This fallacy often occurs when a descriptive adjective becomes so familiar it begins to be used as a noun to represent an entity. Another example is the term "unconscious." Freud originally used the term to describe psychological activity that one cannot observe, even in oneself. Originally, he used the term "unconscious activity." Later, however, Freud used the term as a noun and began to treat it as an entity. Such poor language habits are a major problem in psychoanalytic and other personality theories.

A definition is not a cause, but is often mistaken for one

Establishing Cause-and-Effect Relationships

A major purpose of science is to demonstrate **cause-and-effect relationships**. One step in establishing causality is called the **method of agreement**—the principle that states that when condition X is present, condition Y will be also. For example, if Jason does not talk when females are present, we might infer that he has a heterosocial phobia. However, method of agreement does not alone establish causality. In our example we have no way of knowing, on the basis of the information presented so far, that Jason's silence is not a general state, rather than a sex-specific response. To conclusively establish causality, we must use the **method of difference** in conjunction with the method of agreement. The method of difference infers that there is a *conditional* relationship between two events: if not X, then not Y. If we observe that Jason becomes extremely verbal in the absence of females, then we have established both areas of agreement and difference and can conclude that he has a heterosocial phobia.

Method of agreement: if X, then Y

Method of difference: if not X, then not Y

Empirical Versus Rational Investigation

The rationalist: I believe my reason

The empiricist: I believe my senses

Behavior can be observed as it occurs in the real world

Rationalism is the belief that humans can understand and explain the universe solely by applying correct logic—that is, without any direct examination of the natural world. During the Middle Ages rationalism was the only approved and recognized method of inquiry. A typical story of the time tells of a group of monks who sat for several days debating the number of teeth in a horse's mouth. When a young novice suggested that they settle the argument by counting the teeth of a nearby horse, the monks became incensed. The novice's suggestion is an example of **empiricism,** which is the attempt to understand the universe by examining it.

Both rationalism and empiricism were practiced in ancient Greece and in many Eastern civilizations, but rationalism is most closely associated with Plato and Aristotle, who were often cited as authorities by the rationalists of the Middle Ages. Galileo contributed much to the swing toward empiricism by his insistence on testing belief through observation of actual events. Scientific discovery has accelerated rapidly since Galileo's time, and rationalism and empiricism have been integrated into the scientific inquiry process in which theory is based on logical inference and tested by observation. In today's typical story the novice would have been the hero. For example, when a yoga teacher described a certain posture to a physician, the physician replied, "It is physically impossible for the human body to assume such a posture." The yoga teacher thereupon demonstrated the posture. And Pier Luigi Nervi, the engineer and architect who pioneered in the use of reinforced concrete, tells about a letter his engineering professor read to a class, in which a group of German engineering students proved mathematically that the Risorgimento Bridge in Rome could not possibly stand. The joke, of course, was that it was standing and had been for some time.

Methods of Investigating Abnormal Behavior

In investigating abnormal behavior, the method is usually determined by the problem to be solved and by the resources available. Different approaches have different goals and vary considerably in their determination of cause and effect. The three major approaches are naturalistic observation, correlational studies, and experimental methods.

Naturalistic Observation

Naturalistic observation is the collection of behavioral data in *real-life* situations with as little interference from the researcher as possible. For example, an investigator interested in the effects of psychotherapy on depressed patients would simply observe the therapeutic sessions, interfering as little as possible. An investigator interested in the role of the family in abnormal behavior would try to observe family interactions as closely as possible without intruding into the life of the family. The major advantage of naturalistic observation is that it is the least artificial method—the behavior observed is real-life behavior.

The major disadvantage of naturalistic observation is that, of all the methods we are considering here, it provides the least control over the variables that might be affecting the behavior. Unfortunately, ruling out alternative explanations for observed behavior is especially difficult. The chief value of naturalistic observation then is not in explaining the cause of the behavior observed but rather in describing it accurately and generating hypotheses (suppositions regarding the cause of behaviors) that can be tested by experimental methods.

Correlational Studies

The object of a **correlational study** is to measure the degree of *relationship* between two or more variables: does changing one variable in a given direction have a positive, negative, or neutral effect on the other variable? This method is more artificial than naturalistic observation, but the results it yields permit more accurate predictions of responses. Studies of this type will be discussed frequently throughout the rest of this book. An excellent example is the application of psychological tests to measure such traits as anxiety in order to predict other behavior.

The primary purpose of correlational studies is to determine relationships between events, but like naturalistic observation, correlational studies are not very useful for determining cause-and-effect relationships. In fact, a basic and oft-repeated axiom of psychological research is that "correlation does not establish causality." Like naturalistic observation, correlational studies are useful in generating hypotheses that can be tested by experimental methods.

Experimental Methods

In contrast to naturalistic observation, **experimental methods** provide maximum control and maximum artificiality. Their main advantage, as we shall see, is that they significantly reduce the likelihood of unknown variables influencing the results. Their major disadvantage is that, because of their great artificiality, the chances are sometimes high that the experimental situation itself influences the results obtained.

In its simplest form, an experiment compares two conditions, a *treatment condition* and a *control condition,* that are identical in all respects except the presence or absence of the **independent variable.** If the effect being studied (the **dependent variable**) occurs when the independent variable is present (treatment condition) but not when the independent variable is absent (control condition), then causality is assumed: If *X,* then *Y;* if not *X,* then not *Y.* Table 3–1 summarizes the basic concepts applied in scientific research, with emphasis on those used in experimental methods.

For our purposes, we shall consider two main types of *experimental methods:* group comparison designs and single case designs.

Group Comparison Designs
In **group comparison designs,** two or more groups are treated identically in all respects except one. Experimenters try to control for variables that might arise in the selection of subjects by matching subjects in one group to those in the other in all possibly relevant respects, by randomly assigning subjects to different groups, by **counterbalancing** so that control and treatment conditions are presented in counterbalance order, or by using statistical procedures to try to remove initial differences between groups.

Experimenters also try to control other possible influences, such as noise level or temperature in the experimental setting. Once successful in controlling possible error-causing variables, experimenters have a strong case for asserting that differences between groups in the dependent variable are functions of the treatment.

To see how this might work in practice, consider a hypothetical study of the effects of psychotherapy with depressed patients. Experimenters might randomly assign these patients to two equal-sized groups. One group would receive psychotherapy and would therefore be the *experimental group.* The other group would not receive psychotherapy and would therefore be the *control group.* We could designate length of hospitalization as the *dependent variable,* assuming that remission of depression is the "necessary and sufficient" requirement for discharge. If the average length of hospitalization is shorter for the experimental group than for the control group, we can conclude that psychotherapy was effective in reducing depression.

The type of group comparison study described above is called the **equivalent groups method**—the groups are selected in advance to be as alike as possible and then treated differently. Another research strategy is the **ex post facto study,** in which the groups are selected "after the fact" or without direct experimental manipulation. This is also called the **different groups method,** since the experimenter begins with groups that are initially different in some respects and then treats them identically. Numerous examples of this design are found in the study of abnormal psychology. Such studies commonly compare a normal group with an abnormal group in the performance of some task. For example, an experimenter might

One variable can be manipulated to determine its effect on another variable

A difference between the groups in the remission rate is assumed to be due to treatment

Groups having known differences can also be compared in an identical situation

Table 3–1   Review of Basic Concepts in Scientific Research

Independent variable	The condition or stimulus the experimenter manipulates or has under control; that which the experimenter is investigating.
Dependent variable	The aspect of a subject's behavior that is measured after manipulation of the independent variable.
Controlled variables	The factors in an experiment that are prevented from influencing the dependent variable. Methods of controlling these extraneous variables include the following: 1. **Matching** This insures that the experimental and control groups are equal on variables such as age, race, sex, education, and others that could influence results. 2. **Counterbalancing** Administering the conditions of the experiment to different subjects in varying orders so that order effects are controlled. 3. **Randomizing** Subjects are randomly assigned to the treatment and control groups on the assumption that any differences in the subjects will be evenly distributed throughout all conditions. 4. **Statistical controls** Various statistical procedures are used in an attempt to remove the initial differences between the groups in the experiment. The analysis of covariance is one of these procedures.
Error variables	Sources of error that may bias the results of an experiment. The following are examples of common error variables: 1. **Experimenter bias** This occurs when the experimenter has a preconceived idea about the outcome of an experiment and unintentionally influences the results. 2. **Subject expectancy** This is any preconceived notion the subject brings into the experiment that may influence the results. 3. **Demand characteristics** Subjects occasionally believe that they have to change or show improvement simply because they are in a psychological study. This makes it difficult to determine whether any change observed is due to treatment.
Double blind	A procedure that is often used to control experimenter bias and subject expectancy. In this procedure neither the experimenter nor the subject knows the status of the groups (for example, which is a control and which is the treatment group).
Placebo	Subjects in the control group receive a "treatment" that is known to have no effect (such as a harmless, inert drug) to control for demand characteristics. After the experimental phase, the subjects are given an effective treatment.
Analogue study	This is often used when not enough subjects from a clinical population are easily available for an effective study. For example, college students with small-animal phobias are often used to study various treatment techniques for phobia. Several authors have commented on problems of generalization from analogue studies.
Hypothesis	A statement based on observed data that an investigator seeks to prove or disprove through experimentation.
Theory	A general principle that attempts to explain observed facts.
Model	A complex set of hypotheses derived from other fields of knowledge and used in psychology to attempt to explain behavioral phenomena.

compare reaction times of normal and depressed people. After matching the two groups in terms of intellectual level, age, sex, socioeconomic status, and other factors, the experimenter might measure the time required for each person to push a key after seeing a light go on. If the normal group showed a faster reaction time, the experimenter could conclude that depression decreases reaction time.

Such conclusions ought to be viewed with extreme caution, however, since in the study described there would be no assurance that depression is the only difference between the two groups. In other words, such experiments are subject to the same kinds of explanatory problems as correlational strategies. The different groups design is weak in establishing causality, although it may allow accurate description of the groups due to its control of extraneous variables.

Results obtained with group experimental designs show how a particular treatment variable, on the average, affects the group. They do not indicate how a particular treatment variable affects a given member of the group. For example, our hypothetical experiment with the effect of psychotherapy on depressed patients might indicate that depressed people, on the average, can be expected to be discharged more rapidly if they receive psychotherapy. But if we look beyond the statistics at individual cases, we

scientific approaches to the study of abnormal behavior

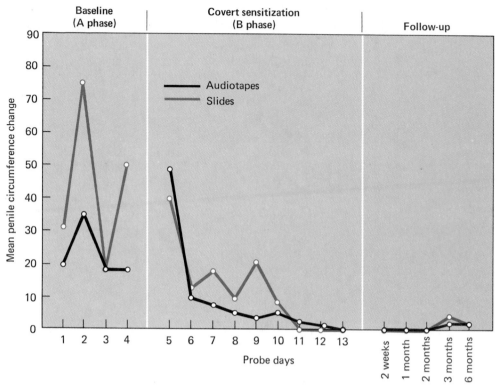

Figure 3–1 Mean penile circumference change to audiotapes and slides during baseline, covert sensitization, and follow-up.

might find that out of ten patients in the treatment group, four were discharged before any in the control group, four more at about the same time as most members of the control group, and the remaining two later than any member of the control group. In other words, the study has some value for predicting the probability that psychotherapy will reduce the length of hospitalization, on the average, but cannot be used to predict with any accuracy the effect of psychotherapy on an individual depressed patient. For that purpose, single case designs are more appropriate.

Single Case Designs

Until early in the twentieth century most knowledge in psychology was acquired through research with single organisms. Pavlov worked with individual dogs rather than with groups of dogs. Ebbinghaus, in his classic work on memory, used himself as the subject. Freud's development of psychoanalysis was stimulated partially by Breuer's classic description of Anna O. and her hysterical symptoms. The **single case design** is now a sophisticated investigation of the individual in which interest centers on how a particular variable affects that individual. There are three major types of single case designs: the case history (AB design), the withdrawal design (ABA or ABAB), and the multiple baseline design.

In the **case history design** an individual's behavior is observed, and then a treatment is applied. In general, the *A* phase involves a series of baseline observations of the natural frequency of some type of behavior, and in the *B* phase a specific treatment is introduced. The specific dependent variable, the target behavior (the behavior to be modified), is continuously monitored. An example of such a study is one conducted by Harbert et al. (1974), who examined the effects of covert sensitization, a type of behavior therapy (see Chapter 7), on the incestuous behavior of a 52-year-old male who had a long history of incestuous episodes with an adolescent daughter. The major dependent variable was changes in penile circumference (degree of penile erection as measured by a strain gauge) in response to audio-taped descriptions of incestuous activities and to slides of the daughter, presented while the patient had incestuous fantasies. As shown in Figure 3–1, baseline (A phase) measures were

The effect of changing an independent variable can be studied in the case history of an individual

science and the study of human behavior   67

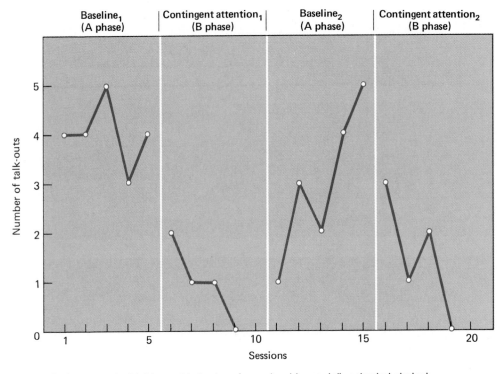

Figure 3–2 A record of talking-out behavior of an educable mentally retarded student.

The independent variable may be introduced and then withdrawn to determine its effects

taken for four days. Covert sensitization (B phase) consisted of approximately three weeks of daily sessions during which descriptions of incestuous activities were paired with descriptions of scenes designed to elicit nausea or, in the latter phases, a guilt scene in which the patient's current wife and a respected priest were depicted as discovering the patient in a sexual act with his daughter. As Figure 3–1 shows, covert sensitization was effective, presumably, in eliminating sexual arousal in response to slides and descriptions of sexual activity with the daughter. The father was apparently no longer being sexually aroused by the daughter, and no relapse occurred during a six-month follow-up period.

Nevertheless, we cannot conclude from the results of this experiment that covert sensitization alone eliminated incestuous behavior; we can only conclude that a correlation existed between the two events.

The possibility of determining cause-and-effect relationships is greatly increased in the **withdrawal design** (sometimes called a *reversal* design). This is an equivalent-time design in which experimenters intro-

duce and withdraw the independent variable. In this design, individuals serve as their own controls. Baseline measures are taken (A phase), treatment is introduced (B phase) and later withdrawn (A again). This design permits statements of both agreement (when X is present, Y is present) and difference (when X is not present, Y is not present) and meets all the requirements for the demonstration of cause-and-effect relationships.

An example of the ABAB strategy is given by Hall et al. (1972). In this study the dependent variable was a ten-year-old retarded boy's "talking out" during special education classes, a behavior that distracted other children and encouraged them to emulate it. Under normal circumstances (baseline), episodes of talking out caused the teacher to pay attention to the child (A phase). In the next five sessions the teacher was instructed to ignore "talk-outs" and pay greatest attention to the child's productive behavior (B phase). During the third series of five sessions the baseline condition was restored (A phase again), and the last series of five sessions was a second B phase. Figure 3–2 shows the results of the study. As we can readily see, when contingent attention was paid to productive behavior and talk-outs ignored, the number of talk-outs decreased. Now we have a case for cause-and-effect.

The withdrawal design poses two major problems. The first is a practical consideration: If the effects of the treatment are irreversible and the behavior does not return to baseline condition, establishing a cause-and-effect relationship is impossible. The second is an ethical consideration. If we have eliminated disruptive behavior in the retarded boy, do we have the right to allow these abnormal behaviors to recur simply to establish a cause-and-effect relationship? Because of these problems, the ABAB design is preferred to the ABA design.

Another alternative that is frequently used when either of these considerations is important is the **multiple baseline design.** In the multiple baseline design another response, another situation, or another subject serves as the control. For our purposes, we shall illustrate the multiple baseline design across *responses,* which is the most frequently used design of this type. In this design a number of responses are identified and measured over time to provide a baseline (phase A) against which change can be evaluated. Once the baseline is established, the experimenter applies a treatment (phase B) to one of the responses and produces a change in it. Ideally, little or no change occurs in the other responses. The experimenter can then apply the same treatment to a second response and note the rate of change in that behavior. The treatment is thus worked across the different responses and is systematically applied to all the target behaviors.

A basic requirement of this design is that target behaviors be independent of one another. Although the argument is somewhat weaker than in the withdrawal or reversal design, we can draw cause-and-effect conclusions from the multiple baseline design by stating that when the treatment variable is introduced with a given behavior, the behavior changes (Hersen and Barlow 1976). Change occurs in a target response when treatment is present (X present, Y present) but not in other independent behaviors where it is not presented (X absent, Y absent).

An example of a multiple baseline design across *behaviors* is given in a study by Liberman and Smith (1972), who studied the effects of systematic desensitization on a 28-year-old woman with multiple phobias. Four specific unrealistic fears (phobias) were identified: being alone, menstruating, chewing hard food, and going to the dentist. The patient made self-reports of each of these phobias for four weeks. Both *in vivo* (in actual life situations) and standard (in artificial situations) systematic desensitization (a treatment consisting of relaxation training coupled with a step-by-step confrontation with the phobias—see Chapter 7 for more details) were used. Systematic desensitization was then applied sequentially to each of the phobic behaviors over a period of weeks. Figure 3–3 shows the results of this study. No evidence of generalization to the untreated phobias appeared when a specific phobia was treated, indicating that the four target behaviors were independent. As systematic desensitization was applied to each phobia, the phobia was eliminated. A strong case can thus be made for the premise that systematic desensitization eliminated the phobias.

This procedure can also be used when a number of independent *situations* are identified and a particular behavior can be modified sequentially across situations. It can also be used when a specific behavior can be identified in a number of *subjects* and modified sequentially across subjects. In the multiple baseline across subjects, the design is almost identical to a group comparison design except that individual differences are considered as a source of investigation rather than as error.

Whether a single case or a group approach should be used depends on the purpose of the research. The single case design is appropriate to the study of individual responses, and group designs are more appropriate to the study of population parameters. It should not be (but often is) necessary to point out that one ought not to make generalizations about groups on the basis of individual data or assumptions about individuals on the basis of group data.

Another response, another situation, or another subject can serve as a control

The purpose of the research determines the choice of experimental design

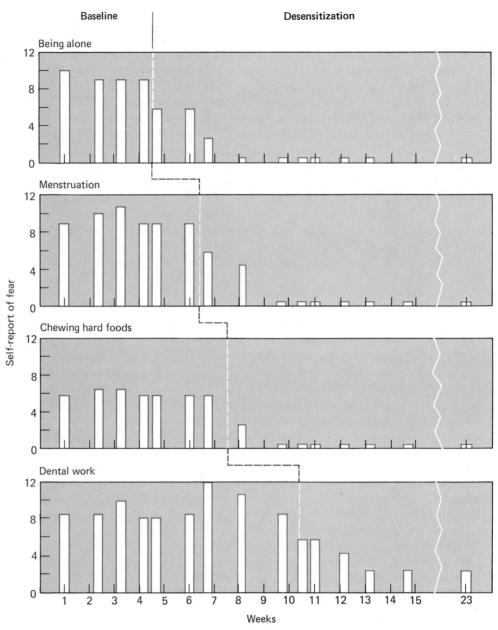

Figure 3–3 Multiple baseline evaluation of desensitization in a patient with four phobias.

Summary

One of the basic assumptions of the scientific approach is that events are determined. This assumption is implicit in the purpose of science, which is prediction and control. For many people talk of behavior control raises a specter of totalitarian mind-manipulators, but the fact is that behavior is controlled now, especially through the process of socialization. The real questions are where the locus of control should be (self-control versus social control), what type of control should be used (pleasant or aversive), and how effective that control is.

A second basic assumption of modern science is that scientific data should be publicly verifiable. This requires the use of a scientific terminology, empirical observation, and systematic probes (replication of observations). A scientific terminology in turn requires the use of

scientific approaches to the study of abnormal behavior

operational definitions, intervening variables, and hypothetical constructs. Properly used, these should help to avoid reification (treating abstractions as if they were tangible realities) and circular reasoning (such as labeling someone's behavior and then citing the label as the explanation of that behavior).

Causality can be demonstrated in various ways. The method of agreement (if X, then Y) does not establish causality because it does not rule out the possible influence of other variables. Causality is more clearly established by using the method of difference (if not X, then not Y) in conjunction with the method of agreement.

Scientific investigation can be pursued by either rational or empirical methods. Rational methods are attempts to understand nature by the use of correct logic. Empirical methods are attempts to understand nature by examining nature. Modern science combines both methods, subjecting its logically derived theories to the empirical test—does the theory fit observed events? Can it be used to predict observable events?

The three major methods of investigating abnormal behavior are naturalistic observation, correlational studies, and experimental methods. Naturalistic observation is the observation of the behavior under study as it occurs in real life. It is the least artificial method, but because it affords the least control over possibly significant variables, it is the least effective way to establish causality. Correlational methods are attempts to determine the relationship between two or more variables, but like naturalistic observation, they do not establish causality. Experimental methods combine maximum control with maximum artificiality and are the most effective way to establish causality, although their artificiality requires caution in generalizing their results. The two major types of experimental designs used to study abnormal behavior are group designs and single case designs. In group designs at least two groups are treated identically in all respects except one (the independent or treatment variable). In single case designs individuals serve as their own controls. Three types of single case designs are used: the case history, the withdrawal or reversal design, and the multiple baseline design.

Key Concepts

case history design

cause-and-effect relationships

circular reasoning

correlational studies

counterbalancing

dependent variable

determinism

different groups method

empiricism

equivalent groups method

experimental methods

ex post facto study

group comparison designs

hypothesis

hypothetical construct

independent variable

intervening variable

locus of control

method of agreement

method of difference

multiple baseline design

naturalistic observation

operational definition

public verification

rationalism

reciprocal determinism

reification

scientific inquiry

single case design

withdrawal design

Review Questions

1. What is determinism? Why is it important in science?

2. How does self-control differ from social control?

3. What is public verification? Why is it important in science?

4. How does a hypothetical construct differ from an intervening variable?

5. Does correlation prove causality? Why or why not?

6. How do naturalistic observation, correlational studies, and experimental methods differ?

7. What purpose do controls serve in an experiment?

8. What kind of information could best be obtained from (a) a group comparison design; (b) a single case design?

factors in the development of abnormal behavior 4

Key Topics

Necessary, sufficient, and
    modulating conditions

Predisposing and precipitating
    factors

Effects of dominant and recessive
    genes

Methods of studying heredity in
    human behavior

Role of maturation in human
    behavior

Effects of social and sensory
    deprivation

Influence of learning and
    socialization on human
    behavior

Processes of respondent, operant,
    and avoidance conditioning and
    modeling

Influence of traumatic experiences
    on behavior

We use the term *abnormal behavior* to refer to an extremely diverse assortment of behavior patterns that perhaps have nothing in common beyond that label. The obvious implication of this diversity is that abnormal behavior has multiple causes, which is borne out by the evidence. Some disorders are apparently due to environmental factors, some to genetic factors, and some to the interaction of the two. Furthermore, causes are almost never present in pure form; in any condition, a variety of factors are likely to interact and so encourage, inhibit, or otherwise modulate the behavior. To understand the causes of abnormal behavior, we need to understand the roles of different conditions and factors involved in establishing and maintaining such behavior.

Necessary, Sufficient, and Modulating Conditions

The first step is to distinguish between *necessary, sufficient,* and *modulating* conditions. A necessary condition for a certain behavior pattern is one without which the behavior would not occur. For example, a highly reactive autonomic nervous system (high excitability) may be a necessary condition for the development of a pervasive anxiety disorder. The disorder will not develop, however, unless a sufficient condition also occurs, such as a traumatic experience. To cite another example, a single dominant gene for Huntington's chorea is a sufficient condition for that disorder (a rapid deterioration of the central nervous system that usually results in death when the individual reaches middle age). If the gene is present, the disorder will develop.

A modulating condition is one that either enhances or inhibits the development or the severity of a disorder. For example, locale would be a modulating condition for a person with a snake phobia. That disorder would present little difficulty in midtown Manhattan, where there are not very many snakes, but could seriously impede a phobic person's functioning in the Okefenokee swamp.

Predisposing and Precipitating Factors

The second important distinction is between *predisposing* factors and *precipitating* factors. A predisposing factor is

Without a necessary condition, the behavior does not occur; with it, the behavior may occur; with a sufficient condition, the behavior will occur

A predisposing factor increases the likelihood that the behavior will develop; a precipitating factor triggers the disorder

somewhat similar to a necessary condition, in that it also increases the likelihood that the disorder will develop. The difference between them is that the disorder can also develop in the absence of a predisposing factor—the predisposing factor is not a necessary one. A precipitating factor is one that triggers the disorder. For example, the loss of a spouse might trigger a depressive disorder. It differs from a sufficient condition only in the sense that a precipitating factor for one person might not be a precipitating factor for someone else, whereas a sufficient condition will produce the disorder in every instance.

Causal and Maintaining Factors

The third major distinction is between *causal* factors and *maintaining* factors. A causal factor is one that contributes to the development of a disorder, while a maintaining factor is one that keeps it going. For example, a person may receive a head injury that causes pain, but the pain persists after the injury is healed. The pain is kept going by maintenance factors—possibly attention from others, disability insurance, or other reinforcers. Maintaining factors are sometimes called **secondary gains** or *compensations.*

The main concerns for our study are the *causative factors* in abnormal behavior, which we have sorted into six main categories—*genetic inheritance, constitution, maturation, learning, socialization,* and *traumatic experiences.* This arrangement approximates the spectrum extending from purely physiological to purely environmental factors. It is misleading, however, to take that spectrum too seriously. We shall see, for example, that some physiological maturation processes are affected by environmental factors and that learning is the vehicle for socialization, as well as for some other forms of environmental inputs.

Genetic Inheritance

Every human cell contains 46 chromosomes—23 contributed by each parent—and these chromosomes contain 40,000 to 80,000 genes. The genes exist in pairs, one member of the pair from each parent, and they carry all of the person's *hereditary characteristics.* They determine the individual's **genetic inheritance,** which involves

scientific approaches to the study of abnormal behavior

not only the person's body structure but also many aspects of physiological functioning that profoundly influence the development of specific behavior patterns.

Dominant and Recessive Genes

Genes may be either *dominant* or *recessive*. If the dominant gene is present, the dominant trait is expressed. A recessive trait is expressed only if both members of a pair are recessive genes. For example, three types of genes determine blood type: Type A, Type B, and Type O. If an individual receives Type A from one parent and Type O from the other, the **genotype** (the actual genetic constitution) will be Type AO, and the **phenotype** (the physical expression of the genotype) will be Type A, since Type O is recessive. Only if both parents contribute a Type O gene will their children have Type O blood. Pairing of identical genes (for example, an AA pair for blood type) is called a *homozygous* condition, and a nonidentical pair (for example, AO) is a *heterozygous* condition. If two dominant genes (for example, blood types A and B) are present in the genotype, the phenotype will have both characteristics (Type AB in our example).

Sex Chromosomes

Sex is usually determined at the moment of conception by the **sex chromosomes.** Every egg cell contains an X-chromosome, and every sperm cell contains either an X-chromosome or a Y-chromosome. If the egg is fertilized by a Y-bearing sperm, the fertilized egg will divide into cells so that each contain an XY pair, and the person will be male. If the egg is fertilized by an X-bearing sperm, the fertilized egg will divide into cells so that each contain an XX pair, and the person will be female. A trait that appears only in one sex is called a "sex-linked trait."

Thus far we have presented a highly simplified account of Mendelian genetics for purposes of illustration; the actual picture is considerably more complicated. Few traits are "either/or" matters. Height, skin color, autonomic reactivity, and many other physiological and psychological traits vary by degrees from individual to individual.

A recessive trait is expressed only if both parents have the recessive gene

Genetic factors determine such things as height and skin color. Notice the family resemblance between father and daughter.

Most traits are determined by multiple genes rather than a single pair as in our examples, and a single gene may also influence many traits. Furthermore, genetic factors interact with other factors. For example, both genetic and nutritional factors influence height. Obviously, simplistic explanations of complex human behavior in terms of simple genetic determinism ought to be approached with a good deal of caution. Nevertheless, genetic factors appear to be involved in both normal and abnormal behavior, so we shall now look at some of the ways of evaluating the influence of those factors.

Methods of Evaluating Genetic Contribution

How can we find out what role genetic inheritance plays in behavior? Several methods have been used: chromosomal analysis, twin studies, pedigrees and kindreds, animal studies, and human population studies. We shall consider the advantages and disadvantages of each of those methods in turn.

Chromosomal Analysis

Through **chromosomal analysis** (examining photomicrographs of chromosomes), geneticists have been able to associate certain physical abnormalities with certain chromosomal aberrations—either a surplus or a deficit in the standard number of chromosomes. For example, **Down's syndrome** (mongolism), one of the causes of mental retardation (see Chapter 17), has been linked to a *trisomy* (three chromosomes instead of two) in the set numbered 21; see Figure 4–1. Geneticists have not yet discovered the mechanism by which the chromosomal aberration causes the disorder, but the evidence of its role is fairly conclusive (Lejeune, Turpin, and Gautier 1963).

Several genotypes with extra sex chromosomes have been discovered. The majority of these involve extra female chromosomes (XXY, XXXY, XXXXY) and are called **Klinefelter's syndrome.** People with Klinefelter's syndrome have the superficial appearance of a male and usually a normal-size penis but very small testicles. They also have many female characteristics, such as developed breasts and little

Female   Male

Figure 4–1 Karyotype of a patient with Down's syndrome. The set numbered 21 contains three chromosomes instead of two.

body hair. They are always sterile. People with **Turner's syndrome,** a similar disorder, have the superficial appearance of a female but immature sexual development and physical abnormalities such as polydactyly (more than ten fingers).

The presence of an extra Y-chromosome (XYY) was for a time believed to be a factor in highly aggressive, violent behavior. Richard Speck, who was convicted of the murder of eight nurses in Chicago in 1966, was at first thought to have an extra Y-chromosome. The hyperaggressive XYY male hypothesis later gained momentum from a study indicating that this aberration, which occurs in 0.10 to 0.40 percent of the general population, is found more frequently in penal and mental institutions (Hook 1973). Many behavioral scientists are skeptical of that hypothesis, however, since XYY males are an insignificant portion of the individuals who commit violent crimes, and since many nonviolent XYY males can be found in the general population (Fox 1971; Jarvik, Klodin, and Matsuyama 1973). Owens (1972) claims, in fact, that no consistent pattern of behavioral characteristics exists that will predict the presence of the XYY disorder. Chromosomal analysis, although it has been used successfully to identify the causes of a limited number of physical disorders often associated with mental retardation, has been relatively unhelpful in investigating the causes of abnormal behavior.

For a time XXY males were believed to be hyperaggressive

scientific approaches to the study of abnormal behavior

Table 4–1 Concordance Rates for Abnormal Behavior in Monozygotic and Dizygotic Twins

Form of Illness	Monozygotic Twins		Dizygotic Twins	
	Rate	N	Rate	N
Schizophrenia	86.2%	268	14.5%	685
Childhood schizophrenia	70.6%	17	17.1%	35
Manic-depression	95.7%	23	26.3%	52
Senile psychosis	42.8%	33	8.0%	75
Involutional melancholia	60.9%	29	6.0%	67

Twin Studies

One method of investigating the influence of genetics on behavior is to study *monozygotic* (identical) twins. Because monozygotic twins result from the separation into two embryos of the two cells into which the fertilized egg (zygote) divides, they have exactly the same genetic endowment. (Dizygotic, or fraternal, twins result from the simultaneous fertilization of two eggs by two sperms and are therefore no more alike genetically than siblings born at different times.)

The rationale of twin studies is that since twins have the same genetic endowment, any condition caused by a gene or set of genes should, if it is present in one member of a pair, also be present in the other. The first step in a twin study is to define the characteristic (for example, depression) to be studied, and the next is to find an individual with that characteristic—called the **proband** or *index case*—who has a monozygotic twin. The final step is to find out whether the twin also has the characteristic. After several pairs of twins have been examined, a **concordance rate** can be established. Monozygotic twins are concordant if both members have the characteristic under study. Concordance rates can fall anywhere in the range from zero to one hundred percent. Low concordance rates presumably indicate that genetic factors play only a small role in the characteristic under study. Table 4–1 gives an example of the concordance rates for abnormal behavior in monozygotic and dizygotic twins.

Twin studies are plagued by a number of methodological problems. In the first place, most monozygotic twins enjoy not only identical genetic endowments, but also highly similar environments. Consequently, researchers are faced with the problem of sorting out genetic from environmental factors. The preferred way to do this is to study two sets of twins, one set reared together and one set reared apart. Unfortunately, identical twins reared apart are not that easily found.

A second methodological problem is the uncertain rigor with which abnormal behavior is classified and assessed. For example, schizophrenia—a favorite target of genetic investigators—is diagnosed much more frequently in the United States than in the British Isles, largely because the British use much more rigorous criteria (Pope and Lipinsky 1978). When schizophrenia is defined so loosely that an individual who seems shy and withdrawn can be labeled schizophrenic (or "within the schizophrenic spectrum"), the concordance rate is high, but when schizophrenia is rigorously defined, the concordance rate is low. This fact goes a long way toward accounting for the rather wide range of concordance rates found for schizophrenia—from zero to over ninety percent (Fischer, Hanald, and Hauge 1969). We shall discuss these studies further in Chapter 15.

A third major methodological problem in twin studies is that a blind analysis is seldom used. The researcher who identifies the disorder in one twin also diagnoses it in the other, and is likely to be looking for clues that would indicate a high concordance.

Experimenter bias of this sort can be controlled only by using two different sets of investigators to examine the twins, one for each member of the pair, and denying each investigator access to information about the other twin. A further control for experimenter bias is to select the sample so that it has the same relative prevalence of the disorder as the general population. Obviously, if the researcher knew, say, that the entire set of proband cases had the disorder, any attempt at a blind analysis would

A high concordance rate points to genetic factors

Concordance rates rise as the definition is broadened

be futile. Controls such as these are rarely used in genetic investigations of abnormal behavior; these and other methodological flaws make the drawing of conclusions about genetic contributions to abnormal behavior extremely difficult.

Pedigrees and Kindreds

The role of genetic factors can be examined in a family history by pedigree and kindred studies

The **pedigree** is a method for determining, by the use of a single family history, whether heredity influences a given characteristic. The pedigree extended to **kindreds** is a method for determining the influence of heredity on a specific characteristic by assuming that as the degree of kinship, or blood relationship, decreases, the similarity of genetic endowment also decreases. For example, if a proband case is identified with a certain abnormal behavior, the risk of a relative having this disorder should increase in proportion to the degree of genetic similarity. Thus, the incidence should be highest among identical twins; next highest among fraternal twins; full siblings, parents, and children; and next highest among half-siblings, aunts, uncles, grandparents, and grandchildren. It should be lowest for nonrelatives.

The pedigree is useful for providing evidence about genetic endowment, particularly if a trait is due to a single gene, which can then be traced through various generations. However, when multiple genes are involved, the situation is much more complicated. Pedigree and kindred studies both suffer from the same kinds of methodological flaws as twin studies.

Animal Studies

Animal studies can make use of selective breeding

Another method of investigating the influence of genetics on specified behavior patterns is **selective breeding.** In selective breeding, individuals who possess a particular trait are inbred, and their offspring are compared with the offspring of individuals who do not possess the characteristic or who have not been inbred. This method is restricted to animal studies, since such studies with human subjects would violate strongly held cultural values. In addition, animals usually have shorter life spans and generate more offspring than humans do;

Tryon bred bright rats and dull rats

Hall bred fearful rats

thus, geneticists can more easily observe a number of cases in a number of generations.

Perhaps the most famous behavior study of this type was conducted by Tryon (1940). He took a random group of rats and tested their ability in maze learning. Those who performed very well he labeled "brights," and those who performed poorly he labeled "dulls." He then bred brights with brights and dulls with dulls. Each generation was similarly evaluated, segregated, and inbred. By the ninth generation, as Figure 4–2 shows, the descendants of the original bright parents were far superior in maze learning ability to rats with dull ancestors. If we operationally define intelligence as maze-learning ability, then genetic factors are extremely important in determining the intelligence of rats.

A similar study by Hall (1934) illustrated the role of genetics in causing anxiety or fearfulness in rats. Hall placed his animals in an open field-test situation, which elicited emotional responses in naive rats. Emotionality was measured by an animal's refusal to eat and incontinence, both good indications of fear or anxiety, even in humans. His results were similar to Tryon's. The unselected animals showed a mean emotionality score of 4, while the ninth-generation offspring of timid or fearful parents showed an average score of 10. The ninth generation of the fearless strain had an average emotionality score of 1.4.

Exactly how emotionality was being influenced in these animals is not clear, although autonomic reactivity would be a good guess. As later chapters will show, similar data suggest that humans also show wide differences in reactivity of the autonomic nervous system (that is, how rapidly and strongly the individual responds to stimuli that elicit a "flight or fight" reaction) at birth (Richmond and Lustman 1955). Overreactivity of the autonomic nervous system is assumed to be a major factor in several behavioral disorders.

Human Population Studies

An indirect method of investigating selective inbreeding in humans is the study of an **isolated population** that has had a high degree of inbreeding. For example, the Hutterites, a religious sect whose members believe marrying outsiders is sinful, are direct

scientific approaches to the study of abnormal behavior

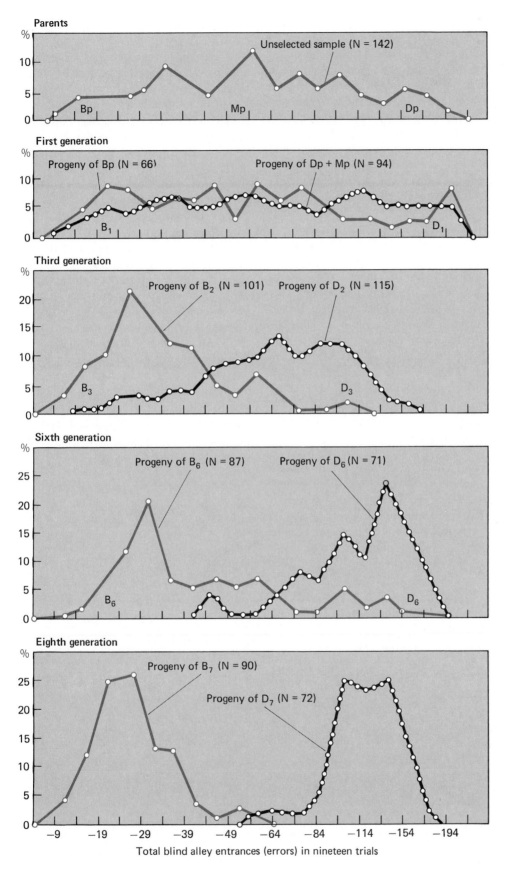

Parents

% — Unselected sample (N = 142)

Bp   Mp   Dp

First generation

% — Progeny of Bp (N = 66)   Progeny of Dp + Mp (N = 94)

B₁   D₁

Third generation

% — Progeny of B₂ (N = 101)   Progeny of D₂ (N = 115)

B₃   D₃

Sixth generation

% — Progeny of B₆ (N = 87)   Progeny of D₆ (N = 71)

B₆   D₆

Eighth generation

% — Progeny of B₇ (N = 90)

Progeny of D₇ (N = 72)

−9   −19   −29   −39   −49   −64   −84   −114   −154   −194

Total blind alley entrances (errors) in nineteen trials

Figure 4-2 Differences between maze-bright and maze-dull animals in successive generations. (B_p = Bright parents, M_p = Average parents, D_p = Dull parents; B_1 = Bright parents' first generation of offspring, D_1 = Dull parents' first generation of offspring, etc.)

factors in the development of abnormal behavior 79

descendants of 101 married couples who settled in South Dakota in the 1870s. This group has a rigid and stable social order. When the prevalence of mental illness in this group was studied, manic-depressive psychosis was found to be the most common form of psychosis, whereas schizophrenia was more prevalent in the general population. One might argue that these studies suggest a genetic basis for manic-depressive psychosis, because of the isolation from outside genetic influence, but the likelihood is at least as great that the type of social order prevailing in this subculture plays a major role in the type of psychosis that develops (Eaton and Weil 1955).

The genetic isolation of the Hutterites suggests a genetic basis for differences between them and other populations but environment cannot be entirely ruled out

Although genetic inheritance clearly plays a major role in the development of a number of abnormal behavioral patterns, the exact nature of this role is not clear. In most cases, genetic factors appear to be *predisposing* or *modulating* factors. In other words, having a particular genotype may make an individual more likely to develop a certain type of abnormal behavior if exposed to factors in the environment that precipitate the behavior disorder. Genetic factors may also play modulating roles in that an individual with a certain genetic background could be either more or less vulnerable to the development of a specific pattern of abnormal behavior. In later chapters we shall see examples of genetic hypotheses and evidence of the role of genetics in abnormal behavior.

Constitutional psychology as folklore

Constitution

The hypothesis that behavior patterns or personality characteristics can be determined from physical appearance and physiological characteristics (**constitution**) is as old as human history. Doubtless, the physical appearance of other people has influenced our perception of them, particularly on initial contact. We "know," for example, that people with "beady" eyes are not to be trusted, that fat people are jolly, that muscular people are aggressive, and that thin people are intellectual.

Only slightly more sophisticated were the "sciences" of *phrenology* and *physiognomy* that flourished in the eighteenth and early nineteenth centuries. According to phrenologists like Gall (1825), one could determine an individual's personality from the location and size of the bumps on the individual's head. According to Gall, a person with a large bump behind the ear is amorous. Physiognomists, such as Laveter (1775), claimed they could predict a person's behavior pattern from facial features. And Lombroso tried to prove that criminals could be identified by the size and shape of their heads. Facial expressions do indicate mood (Schwartz 1975), but their usefulness in predicting stable behavior patterns is doubtful. Table 4–2 lists various constitutional categories that have developed throughout history.

Table 4–2 Classification of Body Types

Nationality of School	Name of Main Investigator	Name of Constitutional Types Type I	Type II	Type III	Type IV
Roman	Hippocrates Galen	Apoplecticus Sanguine	Phthisicus Melancholic	— Phlegmatic	— Choleric
French	Rostan	Digestive	Respiratory-Cerebral	Muscular	
Italian	De Giovanni Viola	Megalosplanchnic Brachymorphic	Microsplanchnic Dolichomorphic	Normosplanchnic Eumorphic	
German	Gall-Beneke Kretschmer Stockard	Hyperplastic Pyknic Lateral	Hypoplastic Asthenic Linear	Athletic	Dysplastic
Anglo-American	Rees-Eysenck Sheldon	Eurymorphic Endomorphic (viscerotonic)	Leptomorphic Ectomorphic (cerebrotonic)	Mesomorphic Mesomorphic (somatotonic)	Dysplastic

scientific approaches to the study of abnormal behavior

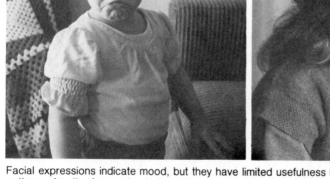

Facial expressions indicate mood, but they have limited usefulness in predicting stable behavior patterns. Are the fans going to leave the game in disgust? Will the child have a temper tantrum or be smiling in a few minutes? Is the woman a depressive or has she just gotten some bad news?

Somatotypes and Personality

Perhaps the most popular constitutional approach is the classification of people according to body type, and the most comprehensive of these is Sheldon's theory of **somatotypes.** Sheldon associated his three types—*endomorph, mesomorph,* and *ectomorph*—with the body's three primary layers of skin: the endoderm, which forms the digestive system; the mesoderm, which forms the blood vessels, bones, muscles, and connective tissues; and the ectoderm, which forms the outer layers of the skin and the nervous system. He also proposed an association between somatotypes and specific temperaments or traits. Using photographs, he rated an individual's physique on a seven-point scale. For example, an extreme ectomorph would have a rating of 1–1–7, and an extreme endomorph would have a rating of 7–1–1. Figure 4–3 shows the three

factors in the development of abnormal behavior

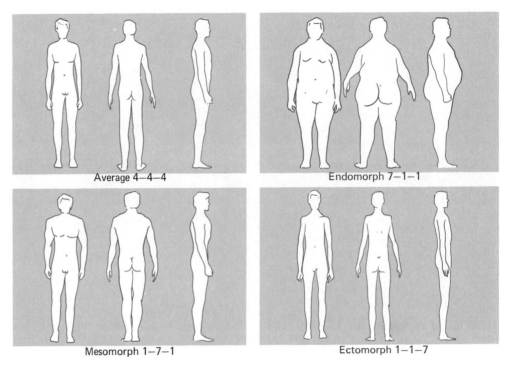

Figure 4–3 Sheldon's three body types and an average combination of the three extremes.

Average 4—4—4

Endomorph 7—1—1

Mesomorph 1—7—1

Ectomorph 1—1—7

Endomorphy/viscerotonia; mesomorphy/somatotonia; ectomorphy/cerebrotonia

somatotypes and the average combination of the three extremes. Sheldon defined these somatotypes and their assumed temperaments as follows:

1. **Endomorph** The endomorphic physique is predominantly soft and round. The digestive viscera (organs) are massive and dominate the body. Sheldon labeled the temperament associated with this dominance as *viscerotonia*. The viscerotonic loves physical comfort, good food, and good company, and desires approval and affection.[1]

2. **Mesomorph** The mesomorphic physique has a predominance of muscle, bone, and connective tissue, and the mesomorph's skin is thick because of heavy underlying tissue. Sheldon labeled the temperament associated with this dominance as *somatotonia*. The somatotonic loves physical excitement, exertion, and adventure. As a result, this outgoing person is often athletic, reckless, callous, and socially insensitive.

3. **Ectomorph** The ectomorphic physique has a predominance of linearity and fragility, with the largest areas consisting of skin, brain, and central nervous system. Sheldon labeled the temperament associated with this dominance as *cerebrotonia*. The cerebrotonic displays mental attentiveness, emotional control, restraint, and tenseness. He or she also loves privacy and tends to be introverted.

Although Sheldon reported significant associations between physique and temperament, later study has shown that these relationships are much less significant than Sheldon claimed (Child 1950).

Somatotypes and Abnormal Behavior

A relationship between somatotypes and abnormal behavior has been demonstrated. For example, Rees (1957, 1961) noted a relationship between ectomorphy and schizophrenia, a severe cognitive disorder

[1]The obvious fact that most of us do want approval and affection illustrates one of the theoretical shortcomings of the constitutional approach.

scientific approaches to the study of abnormal behavior

associated with social withdrawal and fantasy activity. He also associated endomorphy with manic-depressive disorders, which are marked by extreme variation in mood. Glueck and Glueck (1962), in their longitudinal studies of delinquent youngsters, found that most delinquents were mesomorphs, a finding that is consistent with Sheldon's hypotheses.

However, interest in *constitution* as a factor in abnormal behavior has declined for a number of reasons. In the first place, even though the relationship between body type and abnormal behavior may sometimes be statistically significant, it is nevertheless a weak relationship. In the second place, the body type of an individual is related not only to genetic endowment but also to a number of other factors, including the prenatal and the postnatal environments in which maturation occurred. As so often happens in correlational studies, the question then becomes whether the relationship between body types and patterns of behavior is causal or whether a third factor produces both. The cultural stereotypes that label fat people jolly, muscular people aggressive, and thin people intellectual may result in individuals being reinforced for behavior consistent with their body types. These stereotypes may also bias observers so that they "perceive" such behavior in these individuals. Thus, the role of somatotypes in predicting abnormal behavior appears to be minor at best.

A variation of the constitutional approach examines individual differences in physiology as well as in behavior patterns. From the moment of birth, infants exhibit wide individual differences in levels of activity, intensity of reaction, adaptability, quality of mood, and other patterns of behavior (Escalona 1968). These functional differences in behavior may predispose an individual to develop specific behavioral disorders in later life. For example, an individual may be born with a highly reactive autonomic nervous system, which may produce a quicker or more intense startle response, increased muscle tension, and other indices of the "fight or flight" reaction to environmental stress. If exposed to an adverse life situation, this individual may be more likely to develop a pervasive anxiety disorder than others.

Maturation

Biological contributions to behavior do not cease at birth. The brain and other organs continue **maturation** through infancy and childhood. Some of these processes are continuous; others appear at certain times, as if in response to an internal timetable (such as puberty). Aging is another maturational process, although its effects may have been overrated.

Both constitution and behavior are associated with numerous other factors

Impact of Early Experience

Both the nature and the quantity of an infant's sensory experiences are crucial for the development of appropriate behavior patterns. Spitz (1945) claimed that infants in a foundling nursery who were not cuddled, fondled, or involved in the usual mother-child caring relationship showed serious behavioral and developmental abnormalities, which he called **hospitalism**. The mortality rate among these infants was extremely high, although disease was not a primary factor. Goldfarb (1945) and Bowlby (1951) have advanced similar views on the drastic and permanent effects of *maternal deprivation*. They both believed that early separation from the mother resulted in anxiety, excessive need for love, vengefulness, guilt, and other maladaptive emotional and social behavior.

Differences in biological functioning may affect behavior more than differences in biological structure

Spitz found a high mortality rate in infants who were not handled

Sensory and Social Deprivation
Although little doubt exists that early deprivation produces abnormal behavior, some researchers question whether this effect is due to maternal deprivation or to institutionalization or even whether the effect is permanent. Casler (1968) suggested that **sensory deprivation** may be the reason for the damaging effects of institutionalization. Spitz's clinical data would support this hypothesis as his motherless children were so poorly cared for that they developed deep hollows in their mattresses that restricted their motor activity. This restriction resulted in a lack of tactile stimulation and an overall decrease in cutaneous, kinesthetic, and vestibular stimulation, all of which seem to be crucial in the development of normal behavior patterns.

Development of normal behavior patterns requires touching and movement

Moore (1968) has shown that filtering out of irrelevant stimuli is a function of past experience or learning. Thus, infants deprived of sensory input have not learned to discriminate between signals that require a response and those that should be ignored. Consequently, they either ignore the environment completely or they are at the mercy of all environmental stimuli.

Schapiro (1968) has further suggested that the quality and complexity of stimulation in early experience may exert a direct influence upon growing neurons, which may determine the later functional capacity of the brain and limit the organism's future behavioral repertoire. Supporting this view is the work of Rosenzweig et al. (1968), who found that when rats are placed in a sensory-enriched environment, positive changes take place in brain chemistry and anatomy, such as weight increase in the cerebral cortex, which is associated with increased learning ability. In addition, evidence suggests that sensory stimulation early in life contributes to the maturation of the *hypothalamus*, a structure that plays a vital role in emotions (Gellhorn and Loofbourrow 1963).

Maternal deprivation resulted in abnormal behavior in Harlow's monkeys

Apparently, the developing child needs sensory stimulation for normal psychological and physiological development. Zigler (1971) noted that, for mentally retarded children, these experiences may be present in some institutions but not in others as they vary considerably in the amount of stimulation they provide for a child.

In any event, the deprivation effects of separating a child from its family may not be permanent. In a sample of 500 children separated from their families within the first three years of life, Lewis (1954) found two or three years later that, with few exceptions, no significant difference existed between separated children and normal children.

Harlow's work with monkeys casts some light on this problem (Harlow 1958). Harlow separated infant monkeys from their mothers and reared half of them with a "cloth" mother surrogate, a soft terrycloth doll containing a nursing bottle in its chest; the other half had a "wire" mother surrogate, a bare wire mesh figure with a bottle in its chest. The monkeys raised with the cloth mother were normal, friendly, playful monkeys who interacted quite well socially

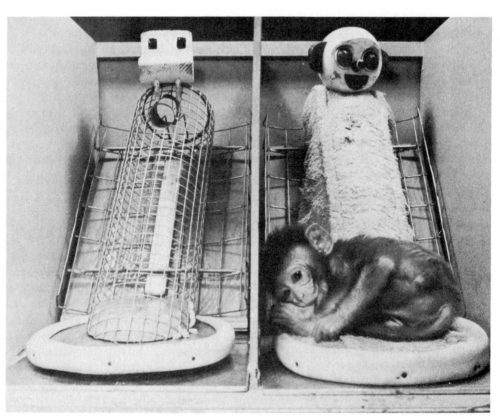

One of Harlow's monkeys resting with the "cloth" mother surrogate. The "wire" mother surrogate is in the adjoining cage.

scientific approaches to the study of abnormal behavior

and sexually with other monkeys. The monkeys raised by the wire mother, on the other hand, became hyperactive, disorganized, hostile, and fearful. They spent much time rocking and sitting, and exhibited deviant social and sexual behavior (Harlow and Harlow 1962). If these monkeys had not been raised in a laboratory, their survival rate would probably have been no better than that of Spitz's infants.

Maccoby and Masters (1970) have shown that **social deprivation** elicits later dependent clinging behavior in humans as well. Sensory deprivation and social deprivation also have an effect later in life. Suomi et al. (1975) have shown that when adolescent monkeys were separated from a family unit, they showed depressive reactions when housed by themselves in a vertical chamber apparatus (see Figure 4–4), but not when they were housed with friends. Moreover, as Heron (1957) has shown, an adult deprived of sensory input, as in a sensory deprivation study, exhibits confusion, inability to concentrate, hallucinations, and other abnormal behavior patterns. "Brainwashing," as practiced during the Korean conflict, also shows the dependence of hu-

mans on stimulation from the external environment for the maintenance of normal thinking (Brownfield 1965). The success of the Chinese in altering and controlling the beliefs of American prisoners of war is ample evidence that restriction and alteration of the sensory environment can disrupt behavior. McReynolds (1960) asserts that a low rate of sensory input, whether due to lack of environmental events or to an individual's difficulty in assimilating them, leads to problems in distinguishing between real and unreal experiences. Moreover, it facilitates hallucinations and illusions. In summary, a certain degree of sensory input and social interaction appears to be necessary for the development and maintenance of normal behavior patterns. Alterations, reductions, and deprivations in the sensory or social environment can and do produce abnormal patterns of behavior.

Impact of Aging

As individuals reach their later years, they encounter circumstances that can precipitate adjustment problems. This period is marked by declining health through bodily deterioration. Whether the **aging process** is accelerated by environmental conditions, such as toxins, faulty nutrition, harsh climates, or psychological stress it is certain that numerous neurological and circulatory changes do take place as an individual ages. A reduction of brain weight is measurable and is associated with a decrease in the number of cells, especially in the cortex. Both large and small blood vessels lose their elasticity and fatty deposits block normal blood flow, all of which retard the delivery of oxygen and reduce the metabolic rate. These changes are associated with failing memory, increasing intellectual rigidity, declining capacity for new learning, and declining ability to solve problems that require reflection and imagination.

While some of these changes may not hold true in specific cases (Schaie and Gribbin 1975), specific problems have been related to this stage of life and are assumed to be due to the aging process. Examples are senile dementia and cerebral atherosclerosis. These disorders will be discussed in Chapter 18.

The physiological effects of aging may have been overrated

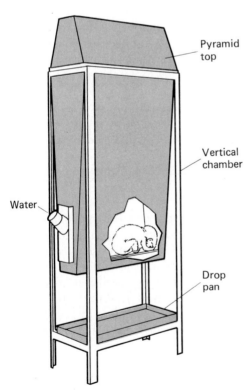

Pyramid top

Vertical chamber

Water

Drop pan

Figure 4–4 The vertical chamber apparatus used by Suomi et al. to induce depression in monkeys.

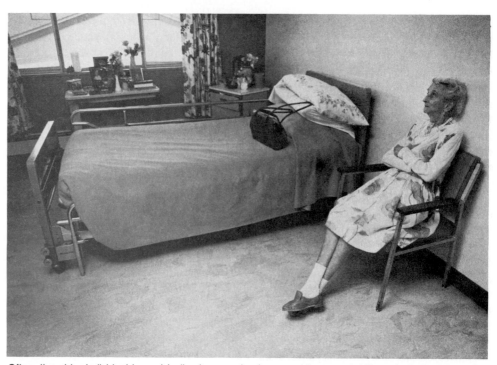

Often, the older individual is sent to live in a nursing home not because of the actual physiological effects of age but because of the cultural stereotype of our "youth-oriented" society.

On the other hand, many of the behavior problems of old age are not due to the physiological changes associated with aging. Different individuals age at different rates, and when individuals who are chronologically aged but physiologically young are forced to deal with cultural stereotypes and negative societal sanctions, they may well suffer stress. Being unemployed because of biases against older job candidates, being forced to retire at 65 or 70, and living in a society that believes "youth is everything," are not pleasant conditions for the elderly to contend with. Add to those the reality of death of one's friends, the eroding of traditional ideas on religion, and sex roles and behavior, and the breakdown of interpersonal relationships, and many older persons find themselves caught in a "generation gap." Such a situation increases their isolation and they soon find themselves belonging to minority groups with opinions, attitudes, and beliefs that are incongruent with those of a youth-oriented society. This situation frequently results in withdrawal, disengagement from society, and severe adjustment problems.

Social change increases the isolation of older people

Learning by respondent conditioning: a neutral stimulus (CS) paired with a stimulus (UCS) that evokes a specific response (UCR) subsequently evokes that response (CR)

Learning

From the moment of birth every human being is exposed to a wide range of stimuli that effect behavior change through a variety of processes. We call this **learning**. A very large part of our behavioral repertoire, normal and abnormal, is acquired through these processes. And though the distinctions may be arbitrary, for our purposes we shall separate learning into three types: *classical* or *respondent conditioning, operant conditioning,* and *modeling.*

Classical or Respondent Conditioning

In **respondent** or **classical conditioning**, behavior falls into two categories, *learned* and *unlearned*. Unlearned responses are reflexes—innate and simple physiological responses elicited by specific stimuli. If a certain stimulus is present, it will automatically evoke a specific response, such as coughing, sneezing, automatic withdrawal from painful stimuli, or—in an infant—sucking to receive nutrition. One form of respondent conditioning simply pairs a neutral stimulus (**conditioned stimuli: CS**) with

scientific approaches to the study of abnormal behavior

specific stimuli (**unconditioned stimuli: UCS**) that evoke a simple reflex (**unconditioned response: UCR**). If the CS occurs simultaneously with or before the UCS, the CS, after a number of pairings, begins to function like and even acquire the properties of a UCS. In other words, the CS now elicits the reflex, which can now be labeled a **conditioned response (CR)**. This process is called **acquisition.** Consequently, we can conclude that any neutral stimulus paired with a stimulus that regularly evokes the response will acquire the properties of that stimulus. This process is often called **stimulus substitution**, since the CS is substituted for the UCS in evoking the response.

If, in a second phase, the CS is no longer paired with the UCS, the probability that it will evoke the response decreases. This process is called **extinction.** If the subject is allowed to rest and then placed back in the conditioning situation after extinction has occurred, the CS will recover its ability to elicit the response. This phenomenon is called *spontaneous recovery.* The CS can then be reassociated with the UCS, and conditioning again rapidly occurs (*reconditioning*). In the next step, the previous CS can be used as a UCS and paired with yet another neutral response, that is, a second CS, and the whole phenomenon will be repeated. This process is called *higher order conditioning.*

The probability that a stimulus different from the CS will evoke a CR depends on the similarity of the two. If leg lifting is conditioned in a dog to a 500 Hz (cycle per second) tone, an 800 Hz tone may also elicit the response. This is called **stimulus generalization.** If the UCS is paired only with a tone of 1,000 Hz but not when it is set at 800 Hz, the reverse of stimulus generalization occurs. This process is called **stimulus discrimination.** Stimulus discrimination is crucial because one must be able to differentiate between such things as five and ten dollar bills, poisonous and edible mushrooms, and different facial expressions.

The importance of respondent conditioning in human behavior can be illustrated with the development of affection in an infant. When hungry, an infant feels uncomfortable. But when the child is given a bottle or breast (UCS), the food produces a sensation of satisfaction, relieves hunger pains, and eliminates crying (UCR). This warm state of satisfaction can be arbitrarily called affection. The neutral stimulus is the mother, whose appearance precedes feeding (CS). After a number of pairings, the sight of the mother alone will stop the infant's crying and produce a pleasurable state (CR).

Sometimes the mother is associated with another individual, the father, who also on occasions may feed the infant; therefore, through higher order conditioning, the father may eventually evoke affection too (higher order conditioning). Individuals such as aunts and uncles who resemble the mother and the father may also, through the process of stimulus generalization, evoke affection. However, the child soon learns that he or she cannot respond to every male as "dada," since this response is not reinforced and sometimes upsets the mother, a reaction that in turn aids stimulus discrimination.

Operant or Instrumental Conditioning

In **operant** or **instrumental conditioning** the individual emits responses, and particular responses are followed by a **reinforcing stimulus (S^r)**—any stimulus that increases the probability of a response. A study by Cook and Adams (1966) illustrates this type of conditioning. When a retarded and disturbed child entered the experiment room, he would run about wildly and create chaos. The first goal was to have the child sit in a chair. After measuring the baseline or operant level of time spent sitting in the chair, the researchers gave the child candy (S^r) when he sat in the chair. Conditioning had occurred when it was noted that the length of time the child spent sitting in a chair during the experimental sessions had significantly increased; see Figure 4–5.

Reinforcers can be either *positive* or *negative.* A positive reinforcer is a pleasant addition to a situation, such as food, water, sexual contact, candy, social approval, or

Learning by operant conditioning: behavior followed by a reinforcing stimulus (S) is more likely to be repeated

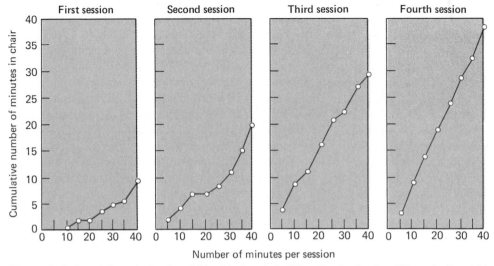

Figure 4-5 Cumulative minutes the child sat in the chair. When the line is at a 45° angle, the child was sitting all of the time.

other rewards. A negative reinforcer is the withdrawal or removal of noxious stimuli, such as electric shock, loud noise, extreme heat or cold, or social disapproval. Both negative and positive reinforcers increase the probability that the response on which they are made contingent will recur.

Punishment is either the presentation of negative events or the removal of positive events (Skinner 1953). Examples are slapping a child's hand for stealing from the cookie jar or sending the child to a quiet room. The latter procedure is a withdrawal of or a **"time out"** from reinforcement, a technique often used in shaping the behavior of children. Punishment decreases the rate of response but does not necessarily eliminate it. On the other hand, if a response is no longer followed by reinforcement, *extinction* occurs.

Extinction or punishment in behavioral treatment programs is frequently paired with the reinforcement of competing or other responses, a process that helps insure the permanence of the behavior change. This procedure is called a **differential reinforcement for other behavior (DRO)**. In addition, the individual may be placed on various schedules of reinforcement such as a *continuous reinforcement schedule (CRF schedule)* or a *partial reinforcement schedule (PRF schedule—also called an intermittent schedule)* based either on time or on a number of responses. Reinforcement can be given for a correct response after either a fixed or a variable number of responses (*ratio* schedules) or a fixed or a variable time interval (*interval* schedules). Behavior under these schedules frequently differs in terms of acquisition, maintenance, and the extinction of responses. Consequently, a particular schedule may be more useful than others for producing and maintaining a certain type of behavior (Ferester and Skinner 1957). Reinforcement schedules are usually abbreviated *FR* or *VR* (*fixed or variable ratio*) and *FI* or *VI* (*fixed or variable interval*). The number that follows these abbreviations indicates either the number of responses or the length of the interval. For example, a FI 5″ indicates that the individual received reinforcement every five seconds.

The major advantage of operant conditioning is that it can be used to teach very complex behavior by breaking the behavior pattern into simple, easily learned components and by teaching a sequence of responses so that the individual can gradually approximate or acquire the desired behavior. A good example would be the following hypothesis on language acquisition. Early in an infant's life almost any sound is reinforced. The child is later reinforced only for sounds that approximate the desired verbalizations. This method is called **successive approximation** or **shaping**. As the child becomes more proficient, the criterion for an appropriate response is raised. Later, the child receives stimulus discrimination

scientific approaches to the study of abnormal behavior

training. In other words, the child receives reinforcement only when an appropriate verbalization occurs on a proper occasion. The child may be reinforced for saying "daddy" only to the proper male.

Responses may also be **chained**. For example, during toilet training, the child may be first taught to sit on the pot, then to signal when he or she feels the urge to eliminate, and then to undress. Finally, these responses are put together so that the child can go through the proper sequence of behavior and master toilet training.

Modeling

Another type of learning has been called no trial learning, imitation, identification, vicarious learning, observational learning, or most commonly, **modeling**. Most socialization occurs through this process. It occurs when one individual observes another individual (the model) engaged in behavior that is rewarded, ignored, or punished. Then, in a similar situation, the observer will imitate the model's behavior. Significantly, the observer has not engaged in any overt responding but has only duplicated behavior, and multiple observational trials may be needed before the behavior can be reproduced accurately.

Modeling stimuli come not only from direct observation but also from verbal instructions, reading, television, and almost any source of information. The only conditions necessary for modeling to occur are that an individual attentively observe the original behavior, remember the sequence of responses, and finally reproduce the motor act.

In general, modeling can have four basic effects (Bandura 1969):

1. It can lead to the acquisition of new or novel behavior. Also, an individual may observe a model and learn, yet not exhibit the behavior. Performance of a vicariously learned response depends upon appropriate *incentives* for such behavior.
2. Observation of a model's actions may have an inhibiting effect on the subject. An individual is not likely to behave in a certain way if the model is observed being punished for the same responses.
3. Modeling behavior may also have a disinhibiting effect. If an individual sees a model behave in a way that may not be socially sanctioned and then sees either that the model is rewarded for such behavior or that no negative consequences follow, the individual may then exhibit the behavior. Or the observer may have learned the behavioral pattern but will not exhibit it because of fear of the consequences.
4. The behavior of others may serve as a discriminating stimulus that will facilitate the emission of a previously learned response from the observer. This response facilitation is different from the other three effects in that no new response is acquired and disinhibiting processes are not involved.

The emotional responses of other people, as conveyed through vocal, facial, or other cues, may arouse similar emotional reactions in observers. This is also a form of modeling. On the basis of exposure alone, individuals can adopt intense emotional attitudes and reactions toward persons, events, or situations with which they have had little previous association. A good example of this phenomenon is racial prejudice, which may be acquired with little or no contact with the individuals who are the objects of the prejudice. Another example is empathy. Empathy is an emotional response in a person due to another person's emotional experience. The fact that emotional response patterns can be extinguished as well as acquired plays an important part in developing behavioral techniques for modifying emotional disturbances.

Avoidance Conditioning

Avoidance conditioning involves both respondent and operant conditioning. In the initial stages of learning, a novel stimulus is paired with a painful or uncomfortable stimulus. Eventually, the CS elicits a fear or anxiety response just as the UCS does, even though the CS is not intrinsically noxious. This is simple respondent conditioning. However, the CS or the UCS or both

Learning by modeling: behavior that is observed in others is imitated

may also elicit attempts to escape or avoid the painful or uncomfortable stimulus. Thus, any response that succeeds in avoiding, escaping, or decreasing the aversive stimulus is strengthened. This process is operant conditioning. The individual may also try to minimize or avoid the aversive situation by becoming immobile or otherwise restricting activity. This is called *passive avoidance conditioning*. If the individual cannot completely avoid the CS or the UCS, the behavior exhibited is called a **conditioned emotional response (CER)**. The CER is important in the acquisition of maladaptive emotional behavior such as that seen in depression and pervasive anxiety states. If the individual can escape or avoid the CS or UCS by motor or other activity, the procedure is labeled *active avoidance conditioning*, and the behavior exhibited is called a **conditioned avoidance response (CAR)**. Many types of maladaptive behavior patterns, including phobias, are examples of CAR.

Punishment follows the response rather than preceding it as in avoidance conditioning, and is a method of suppressing or eliminating behavior. Punishment is most effective when given consistently after every response and when highly aversive stimuli are used (Azrin 1960). Although punishment has been applied to undesirable behavior for many centuries, there is little evidence that it is effective or efficient. Furthermore, the effects of punishment are usually temporary.

Avoidance conditioning and punishment are often similar in many ways. The major difference between them is that avoidance conditioning develops new responses while punishment merely suppresses old responses. Because punishment and avoidance conditioning often involve emotional behavior and procedures that are considered inhumane, these techniques should be used only as a last resort.

Abnormal behavior is often a function of aversive circumstances in an individual's life, but it is not necessarily so. There is little doubt that irrational, noncontingent use of punishment does facilitate or instigate patterns of abnormal behavior. However, contingent positive reinforcement has shaped many deviant behavior patterns, such as temper tantrums, which increase in frequency if they produce the desired effect.

Learning deficits can also cause abnormal behavior patterns. The individual who withdraws, avoids social situations, and seems shy may not be fearful of social contacts but may simply lack the social skills necessary for interacting with others. Training an individual in appropriate living skills constitutes a major effort in behavior modification.

Early Learning

Behavior patterns learned in the first few years of life do seem to persist even though they often have limited usefulness in later life (Babladeris and Adams 1967). Although most patterns of behavior are modifiable, the strength and persistence of early acquired habits are well documented. At least three major characteristics of early learning behavior account for this persistence:

1. The infant is completely dependent on others for the satisfaction of its needs. This survival dependency of the young guarantees that their behavior will be susceptible to reinforcement contingencies that exist in their small social world. As the social world expands, most of the previously rewarded behavior of the young is at least intermittently rewarded. Thus, the behavior resists extinction even when the behavior pattern is undesirable.

2. In the very early years when the child's world consists largely of the family, new instrumental behaviors acquired through learning have little interference from competing responses. The child's repertoire is small, and the child has few alternative ways of handling situations. Furthermore, the novelty of new stimulus situations may well evoke an alertness and an emotional arousal that may intensify the reinforcing event. The parents support only a limited range of responses and may be intolerant of responses outside this range. Thus, a premium is placed on early stability of response patterns.

Learning by avoidance conditioning: a person is rewarded or reinforced (operant conditioning) for avoiding a novel stimulus that has been paired (respondent conditioning) with an aversive stimulus

Abnormal behavior can result from aversive (punishing) circumstances, from the reinforcement (rewarding) of undesirable behavior, or from inadequate learning of social skills

Behavior learned early in life is especially persistent, even when it is not useful or appropriate

scientific approaches to the study of abnormal behavior

3. In early learning the situations, responses, and reinforcement contingencies, particularly those of an interpersonal sort, are repeated literally thousands of times. This repetition results in an extreme degree of over-learning, which firmly "stamps in" behavior patterns.

Behavior patterns acquired early in life, either normal or abnormal, can be modified, but the three factors just described increase the persistence of these early behavioral strategies. When these early patterns of behavior are maladaptive, serious adjustment problems arise for the individual in later life.

Socialization

The objective of **socialization** is to produce uniform patterns of behavior, beliefs, and attitudes in a society's members. The type of behavior produced is determined by the *socializing agents*, principally family and peers. The method by which socialization is accomplished is *learning*.

Learning insures cultural transmission of behavior patterns and is responsible for most of a person's complex behavior: language, beliefs, and similar behavior patterns that show almost infinite variation from culture to culture and individual to individual. Learning shapes the individual much as a sculptor shapes marble.

Acquisition of Self- and Social Controls

The acquisition of norms and values is enforced by group pressures and laws. However, the principal method of behavior control in society is *self-control*. Self-control is ultimately another form of social control, since it develops through the process of socialization, during which one eventually views and evaluates the self from the standpoint of the group (Goslin 1969). Conscience, values, self-restraint, adherence to one's beliefs, and similar prosocial behaviors are largely mediated and regulated by self-regulatory processes.

A reward of cookies and milk for being a "good girl" is one way of shaping a child's behavior.

In early life, a child's behavior is usually shaped by physical rewards and punishment. Standards, set by the parents, are established for a variety of behaviors, and the child is given a variety of tangible rewards for achieving, or punishments for falling below the expected standards. As motor and language behavior are acquired, social reward and disapproval replace tangible reinforcement. With repetition of these situations, the child soon begins to anticipate reward or punishment, depending on whether the act is forbidden, falls below a certain standard, or is behavior that is desirable by the parent.

Socialization is the learning, early in life, of the language, beliefs, and attitudes of one's culture

Guilt and Shame

When an individual experiences temptation, emotional arousal and anticipation of punishment may lead the individual to avoid the response or resist the temptation. If the individual transgresses, shame or guilt may result. *Shame* is the fear of being caught and punished for an act; *guilt* is distress that may be present even if detection of a wrongful act is not likely. Thus, shame is external while guilt is internal

(Dienstbier et al. 1975). Whether the individual experiences shame or guilt or attempts to avoid the act or avoid detection appears to be related to the training procedure used by the parent. As Dienstbier and his colleagues note, if the child is physically punished for a transgression, the child is likely to fear the parents rather than the act because the punishment itself may draw attention away from the transgression. The more severe the punishment, the more emotionally arousing the situation is and the less likely an individual is to learn to avoid temptation. Consequently, the child tends to feel anger toward the parent and avoids detection rather than avoiding the act (Hoffman 1970). On the other hand, when love-oriented procedures, including withdrawal of love, are used, the parent's comments about the transgression draw the child's attention to the nature of the transgression, facilitating emotional arousal to the act rather than to the parent. Moreover, the child is likely to attribute the unpleasantness to his or her own behavior, apologize, and feel anger toward the self (guilt) rather than toward the parent.

The child observes and imitates the behavior of parents and thereby learns to apply their standards to his or her own behavior

Modeling

Modeling plays an important role in the acquisition of standards and values as well as in direct learning (Bandura 1976). A child observes the parents' behavior and models his or her behavior on theirs. Furthermore, as the child observes the parental models reinforcing themselves positively or negatively for maintaining or falling below standards, the child is likely to acquire the standards the parents exhibit as well as the ones they reinforce. The child then attempts to apply these standards to his or her own behavior. If the child succeeds, the behavior is reinforced, and the child's *self-esteem* increases. On the other hand, if the child's behavior does not come up to certain standards, or if the child violates norms, the child will engage in self-criticism and suffer from poor self-esteem.

Conflict between intrinsic motivation and external rewards can lead to abnormal behavior

After the child learns self-regulation, a given act may receive internal reinforcement or external reinforcement, or both

(Kanfer and Phillips 1970). External regulation of behavior instigates internal or self-regulation. Self-esteem now comes from social reward associated with behaving in accordance with social expectations and self-reinforcement associated with internal values. Although these two systems of behavior control usually complement or facilitate each other, they may eventually conflict and compete when social expectations conflict with internal standards.

As social sanctions replace tangible reinforcement, standards are established and changed first by parents, then by peers, and then by abstract ideas. An example of how cognitive behavior standards are changed might be as follows: When one is given an external reward for a task one would perform without payment, one will act as if less intrinsically motivated than before the external reward. In other words, external reward has inhibited self-reinforcement. As Dienstbier and his colleagues noted, this inhibition occurs because the external reward has shifted the focus of attention from the act to the reward. The result is a change of the standard for performance. If severe conflict arises between internal control and external control of behavior, and one's value system conflicts with the external reinforcement for a certain type of behavior, maladaptive behavior can result.

Self-Concept

Self-regulatory processes are also related to what phenomenologists call *self-concept* (Bandura 1977). If during the process of socialization an individual develops a dysfunctional evaluative system, it can cause severe disruptions of behavior. For example, if the standards of self-evaluation are too high because of lack of potential, unrealistic standards, comparison of oneself with more talented peers, or failure to contribute as much to a collective enterprise as other members of the group do, then depression, discouragement, feelings of worthlessness, lack of purpose, and a negative self-concept may occur. On the other hand, if the individual's standards of conduct are extremely low and positive self-reinforcement is frequent, the individual is likely to engage in asocial, unprincipled behavior.

scientific approaches to the study of abnormal behavior

The Family

The *family* is the social agency responsible for socializing the individual early in life. The family, particularly the parents, determine the individual's values, beliefs, and social behavior almost from the instant of birth. Adequate parenting also requires that the parents teach the young the *basic ecology* of their environment (Kaufman 1970). This basic ecology consists of physical and cultural facts about the environment.

The interaction between child and parent is reciprocal. As the child matures and the behavioral repertoire increases, parental behaviors also change. For example, Bandura (1977) has noted that a mother's verbalization to her child during infancy is shorter when the child tends to imitate and repeat phrases; but, as the child develops proficiency in language, the length and the complexity of the mother's verbalization increases until, during the child's middle years, the mother is verbalizing to the child as she would to another adult. Chess (1967) has noted that mothers developed a quicker and stronger emotional attachment to children whose temperament made them easier to care for than they did to children whose temperament was more difficult. Ferguson (1970) has also shown that newborns influence the interaction with their degree of responsiveness and emotional behavior. However, children often influence their parents' choice of residence and restrict their life space. Dependency training in the child may also depend on the child's behavior, and the parents' use of discipline may be determined by the size of the family and the child's location within it (Harper 1975). The presence of children may require major adjustments in parental behavior because parenthood itself may cause stress in terms of the identity of the new parents and the nature of their marriage.

Society

As previously noted, some aspects of abnormal behavior can be viewed as a *social role* assumed by an individual in distress (Scheff 1966). Social roles are defined by the consensus of the group or by authority and consist of our views of ourselves, our behavior in conforming to those views, the reactions of others to our roles, and our reactions to the roles of others. Socialization is the learning of various roles that shape the behavior of individuals in various situations. Roles determine the relationship between mother and child, husband and wife, male and female, teacher and student, and many other human interactions.

The importance and value of roles vary significantly in terms of rewards and punishment. Many roles are arranged in a hierarchy called **social stratification**. The level or location of individuals' roles in this organization determines their social status. Members of society are deeply affected by their status or social class, since social class limits and defines social contact, attitudes toward self, values, interests, motivation, and behavior. Since social class determines the methods of socialization and the opportunities, beliefs, values, and other events available to individuals, it is directly related to the frequency of various types of abnormal behavior. Individuals from the lower classes are more frequently labeled as severely disturbed and are more likely to receive less expensive treatments for their abnormal behavior than individuals from the upper classes (Hollingshead and Redlich 1958).

The degree of social mobility in a society is often assumed to be associated with the frequency of abnormal behavior. For example, Merton (1957) states that abnormal behavior is a function of the lack of opportunity to achieve success as defined by one's culture. Success is usually measured by change in social class and in the opportunity to achieve, which is directly related to social mobility. On the other hand, some psychologists have argued that individuals whose adjustment is borderline tend to drift into the lower classes. This is the **social drift hypothesis,** which would account for more frequent and severe behavioral disorders in lower classes. Hollingshead and Redlich have demonstrated, however, that 91 percent of the mental patients they investigated were still in the same social class as their parents and only 1.3 percent were in a lower class.

The family is the primary agent of socialization

Abnormal behavior can be conformity to a social role

The idea that abnormal people drift to the lower economic class is not supported by available evidence

Leighton (1959) has shown that the more a society fits the needs of its members, the lower is the incidence of abnormal behavior. This hypothesis implies that societies, like individuals, vary in their degree of adjustment and that societies themselves can be labeled abnormal. The degree of adequate functioning of a society can be determined by epidemiological studies that investigate factors influencing the incidence, origin, frequency, and types of abnormal behavior in various cultures. Incidents of crime, suicide, and similar forms of maladaptive behavior are indications of the stability of a society. Because whole societies can be maladaptive, *social engineering* as a method of insuring human rights and the functioning of members of society becomes increasingly important as the assessment of social malfunction becomes more precise.

Traumatic Experiences

The events that lead to abnormal behavior are not confined to infancy

Highly *aversive* or highly *traumatic* situations have a profound effect on the organization of behavior patterns. In general, there are two major types of traumatic events, those which cause physiological injury and those which cause emotional injury to the person. The first type, of course, also involves emotional reactions. These events may be experiences common to everyone, such as sibling rivalry, strict toilet training, repressive sexual indoctrination, and faulty relationship with parents. Early life experiences have been a favorite area for speculation about the causes of abnormal behavior, especially among psychodynamic theorists. Freud, as we have seen, was convinced of the importance of the Oedipal and Electra situations in the formation of a variety of symptoms. Obviously, experiences early in life can cause later disorders, but the role of the usual developmental events in causing adult disorders has been overrated. Abnormal behavior patterns can and do develop at any stage of the individual's life, and they may or may not have antecedents in childhood. As Vinokur and Selzer (1973) have noted, any changes in any age of life may be related to stress and emotional disturbances.

Combat stress can evoke abnormal behavior

What constitutes stress varies from person to person, and what is viewed as neutral or positive by some individuals may be perceived by others as highly repulsive. In life-threatening situations, however, individuals do undergo similar extreme reactions. In these aversive situations the individual demonstrates an increase in perspiration, tremors, increased heart rate, quick breathing, and other common "flight or fight" reactions. If the stress event is of long duration or of high intensity, the individual may have nightmares and sleep problems, become highly irritable, have difficulty in controlling temper outbursts, be unable to concentrate, and show startle reactions to minimal stimuli. Such disordered behavior may appear after a number of different civilian disasters, such as fires, floods, accidents, and earthquakes. In these situations the individual may show a *panic reaction*, manifested in flight and a loss of self-control. Panic reactions do usually occur when individuals are extremely fearful and if they have only limited access to an escape route. However, if escape is impossible, as in mine or submarine disasters, panic reactions do not occur (Mintz 1951).

In combat zones during war, many participants show extreme disorganization of behavior, which in World War I was called "shell-shock"; in World War II, "war neuroses"; and during the Korean War and the Vietnam Conflict, "combat fatigue." These reactions occur particularly after prolonged exposure to combat situations during which the individual begins to manifest extreme fear, an increase in irritability, sleep disturbances, recurring nightmares, and difficulty in concentrating. If the individual is exposed to the death of friends, the initial reaction may be, "I'm glad it was him rather than me"—a reaction common in civilian disasters as well and one that may later elicit feelings of guilt. Brill (1967) has indicated that the best method of treating combat fatigue is to detect the condition early, treat it immediately and as close to the combat zone as possible, and return the individual to duty as rapidly as possible. Under these conditions 80 to 90 percent of the patients can be returned to duty. A common method of treatment is *catharsis,* during which the individual can discuss the traumatic event, respond emotionally to it, and recall it and react to it if he is amnesic

scientific approaches to the study of abnormal behavior

A prime candidate for "combat fatigue": A squad leader after a mission near Saigon in which one man in his squad was killed and three were missing.

to the experience. If the individual is not treated immediately and if he is given a service discharge with a disability compensation, the emotional disability can persist and resist modification because of secondary gains (maintaining factors or compensations).

Other highly aversive life circumstances, such as being a prisoner of war, facing major surgery, and similar traumatic experiences can disrupt well-integrated patterns of behavior. How rapidly or severely an individual will cease to function properly is related to various personal characteristics and to how the individual perceives the situation. DSM III diagnoses these conditions as posttraumatic stress disorders, or as adjustment disorders where the behavioral manifestation of the problem, such as anxiety, is specified.

A major variable is the individual's *perception of control* over the traumatic event. In other words, if a person believes he or she can in some manner reduce or eliminate the threat, the degree of stress diminishes (Averill 1973). There seem to be three major types of personal control: (1) *behavioral control* or direct action on the environment, (2) *cognitive control* or the way the individual interprets the events, and (3) *decisional control* or the individual's ability to choose among alternative courses of action. If an individual can modify stress in some way, understand it, and choose between acts, stress decreases. If these variables are not present because of the nature of the situation or the characteristics of the individual, either apathy or a panic reaction is likely to ensue.

Stress inoculation is a procedure now being used by the military, civil defense, and other agencies to prevent extreme disorganization of behavior that may be encountered in personal, civilian, or war disasters. During stress inoculation, the individual receives as much information and as many methods as possible of handling stress situations and reactions to them.

The more control people believe they have, the more capable they are of withstanding stressful situations

factors in the development of abnormal behavior

Summary

A number of different factors cause, or contribute to, the development and maintenance of abnormal behavior. One such factor is the genetic constitution of the individual. Genes, located in chromosomes, affect the individual's morphological structure and physiological functioning, which in turn profoundly influence the development of behavior patterns. Methods of studying the effects of genetics in abnormal behavior include chromosomal analysis, twin studies, pedigrees, animal studies, and human population studies.

The interaction of genetics and environmental factors also plays a role in causing abnormal behavior. Body types or constitutional factors have been assumed to play an important role in abnormal behavior. Three main body types—endomorphic, mesomorphic, and ectomorphic—are associated with three temperaments: viserotonic, somatotonic, and cerebrotonic, respectively. The relationship between body types and abnormal behavior, however, appears to be slight. More important is maturation, which may also cause stress and produce abnormal behavior, especially when there is either early or late maturation. In the later stages of life, declining health and cultural stereotypes may impair an older individual's adjustment.

The nature and the quality of sensory experiences in the young organisms are crucial for the development of appropriate behavior patterns. If an individual is deprived of sensory and social experiences at an early age, problems of adjustment may occur later. This fact has been demonstrated in the study of social and sensory deprivation in lower organisms, in "brainwashing," and in clinical studies of humans.

The purpose of socialization is to produce uniform patterns of behavior, through its principal mechanism, learning. Essentially, there are three kinds of learning: classical conditioning, instrumental conditioning, and modeling. Avoidance conditioning is a combination of classical and instrumental conditioning. The effects of early learning tend to be more resistant to extinction and change than those of later learning. During early socialization, norms and values are acquired that are enforced by group pressures. Subsequently, self-regulatory systems are developed in which internal standards are established for a variety of behaviors. The individuals then reward or punish themselves. Two mechanisms of behavior control then exist, and they are external and internal regulation.

The family is the social agency responsible for the socialization of the individual in early life, in terms of the acquisition of values, beliefs, and social behavior. The family's role is also to teach the young the basic ecology of the environment. The interaction between child and family is, however, reciprocal, since the child can also influence its parents. Society sets the standards for behavior and designates what behavior is appropriate in given situations. Such designation produces social roles. The organization of social roles, in turn, determines patterns of reward and punishment. Some social roles are arranged in a hierarchy called social stratification. Social stratification influences the development of types of abnormal behavior and determines how the behavior may be viewed and modified as well.

A major source of abnormal behavior is traumatic experience. Many experiences, such as civilian disasters, combat, and similar life-threatening events, are traumatic for everyone. However, what constitutes a traumatic event may vary with the individual's perception, and events common to all individuals—such as developmental tasks—may be viewed as threatening to some. How stressful a particular event is depends on the amount of control individuals believe that they have over the stressor. Stress caused by developmental tasks has been the basis for hypotheses about abnormal behavior for many traditional psychologists. Stress that occurs at certain ages and that has been assumed to cause disorganized patterns of behavior has also been used as a basis for diagnosing disorders such as adjustment reaction in infancy, childhood, adolescence, adult life, and late life.

Key Concepts

acquisition

aging process

chaining

chromosomal analysis

concordance rate

conditioned avoidance response (CAR)

constitution

conditioned emotional response (CER)

conditioned responses (CR)

conditioned stimuli (CS)

differential reinforcement for other behavior (DRO)

Down's syndrome

experimenter bias

extinction

genetic inheritance

genotype

hospitalism

isolated populations

kindreds

Klinefelter's syndrome

learning

maturation

modeling

operant conditioning (instrumental conditioning)

pedigrees

phenotype

proband

reinforcing stimulus (Sr)

respondent conditioning (classical conditioning)

secondary gains

selective breeding

sensory deprivation

sex chromosomes

social deprivation

social drift hypothesis

socialization

social stratification

somatotypes

successive approximation (shaping)

stimulus discrimination

stimulus generalization

stimulus substitution

time out

Tumer's syndrome

unconditioned responses (UCR)

unconditioned stimuli (UCS)

Review Questions

1. How is a necessary condition different from a sufficient condition or a modulating condition?

2. What is the difference between a predisposing and a precipitating factor?

3. How do dominant and recessive genes affect genetic inheritance?

4. How are twin studies, family studies, and pedigrees used to study genetic factors in abnormal behavior?

5. Describe one possible maturational factor in abnormal behavior.

6. How does sensory deprivation early in life affect behavior?

7. Describe one way that socialization or learning can result in abnormal behavior.

8. How does modeling differ from respondent or operant conditioning?

9. How do traumatic experiences play a part in abnormal behavior?

assessment of abnormal behavior 5

Key Topics

Operational definitions of reliability, validity, standardization, and norms

Error variables that interfere with the assessment of human behavior

Four main methods of assessing personality

Stanford-Binet and Wechsler intelligence tests—usefulness and effectiveness

The main assumption of behavioral assessment

Four main methods for behavioral assessment

Ethical issues in the assessment of personality or behavior

Before we can describe, explain, or understand abnormal behavior, we must first assess, or measure, that behavior. Our assessment should be as precise as possible because it determines our ability to classify and differentiate between different types of behavior disorders, to choose between different hypotheses about and models of abnormal behavior, to conduct effective research into the causes and parameters of such behavior, and to select appropriate treatment techniques to modify it. Because assessment provides the basis for all our work with abnormal behavior, it will always be present in our work in some form, whether as a gross description of a person's behavior or as a set of highly sophisticated laboratory measurements of physiological responses.

Reliability: how stable and consistent?

The first part of this chapter will be a review of some of the basic parameters of psychological measurement. These parameters are important regardless of the psychologist's approach to assessment. We shall then discuss personality testing, intelligence testing, and behavioral assessment, all of which proceed from different assumptions and employ different techniques.[1]

Basic Parameters

To assess abnormal behavior accurately, clinical psychologists must use techniques that meet four important requirements. First, they must be *reliable*; that is, they must consistently give identical readings on different occasions and for different raters. Second, they must be *valid*; that is, they must provide the information about a person's behavior that they are designed to provide. For example, a test that is called an intelligence test ought to measure some ability that can reasonably be called intelligence, such as academic achievement. Third, these techniques must be standardized so that an assessment can be duplicated by other examiners. And finally, they must be applied to a number of individuals to establish norms against which an individual score can be compared.

Reliability

The **reliability** of an assessment procedure is the degree to which it gives the same reading at different times and with different examiners. In measuring physical dimensions such as height, reliability is a relatively minor problem. Small measurement errors occur, but the results are generally consistent. The reliability problem can become serious, however, when the quality being measured is a less tangible one, such as a person's assertiveness.

Three types of reliability are important in assessment—*internal consistency, stability over time*, and *agreement* among raters or examiners. Internal consistency is a function of the homogeneity of the technique's parts: Does the first half of a test yield the same results as the second half? The internal consistency of any assessment instrument can be checked by dividing the instrument in half and correlating the results of the two halves.

Stability over time is the ability of a test to yield the same results at different times. It can be checked by correlating the results obtained at two different times.

Agreement among raters, as we noted in Chapter 2, is a major problem in classifying abnormal behavior. If two different examiners using the same measurement techniques are unable to agree, their measurements are meaningless.

Validity

Validity is the degree to which a measurement is meaningful—that is, the degree to which the information obtained is the information sought. For example, phrenologists claimed they could assess personality by measuring the size and location of bumps on a person's head. Bumps can be measured pretty accurately and reliably, but they tell us nothing about personality; consequently, phrenology has very low validity. Validity and reliability are related in the sense that reliability is a prerequisite for, and sets an upper limit on, validity.

[1] Reading this chapter does not qualify the student to conduct psychological measurements.

scientific approaches to the study of abnormal behavior

Psychologists are concerned with four types of validity: *concurrent validity, construct validity, predictive validity,* and *content validity.* A measuring instrument has **concurrent validity** if it yields results consistent with other measurements of the same behavior. Examples of concurrent validity would be agreement between results of two intelligence tests or two scales of depression.

Construct validity is the fit between a hypothetical notion or theory and actual behavior in a test situation. For example, a personality theory might predict that if a number of individuals were placed in a stressful situation and asked to perform some task, those labeled dependent as a result of their personality test scores would give up sooner than those labeled independent. If actual behavior confirmed that prediction, the personality test would have construct validity.

Predictive validity is the degree to which a testing or assessment technique predicts future performance. For example, a scale of suicidal tendencies would have predictive validity if high ratings on the scale were eventually found to correlate significantly with actual suicide attempts.

Content validity is the degree to which a test or assessment technique samples the behavior it is designed to measure. For example, a final exam would have low content validity if it did not test the student's grasp of the material covered in the course. In general, an assessment instrument or technique has content validity if it accurately samples behavior as it would occur in real-life situations.

Validity: how accurately does it sample the real situation?

Standardization

Standardization of test procedures allows different examiners to administer a test in the same manner and thereby, presumably, achieve the same results. When such factors as examiner behavior, measurement instruments, and environmental conditions are not standardized, reliability and validity cannot be achieved.

Standardization of test procedures allows different examiners to administer a test in the same manner.

Norms

If the purpose of the psychological measurement is to determine how the examinee performs relative to some population, then **norms** for the standard examination must be established. To establish adequate norms, it is necessary to administer the examination to a random sample of the population in which the test constructor is interested—for example, high school graduates for the SATs. This random sample should be representative of the population in terms of age, sex, socioeconomic status, race, and similar variables. Only if the normative sample is representative will examiners be able to describe accurately how the examinee performs in comparison with the general population. Unfortunately, if the population is large and heterogeneous, the norms are not likely to be representative of a more homogeneous segment of that population. An excellent example of this problem is the charge that intelligence tests discriminate against blacks (Williams 1970). One could also argue that intelligence tests discriminate against lower-class people, since the tests are constructed by white middle-class psychologists and therefore may measure not intelligence so much as a type of knowledge typical of white middle-class culture (Mischel 1968). This problem is especially vexing when intelligence is assumed to be a trait or an entity based on genetic endowment rather than behavior shaped by environment. We shall discuss this problem in greater detail when we discuss intelligence tests.

Error Variables

A number of *error variables* interfere with accurate and objective assessment of human behavior. Because these error variables grossly distort the results of a psychological examination, the examiner, the test constructor, and the designer of analogue measurement situations must devise strategies that eliminate them. Furthermore, evaluation of test results should involve careful consideration of the possibility that these variables may have contaminated the results.

A major difficulty is *examiner bias*, a form of experimenter bias. A friendly, alert, and informative examiner establishes rapport and facilitates the examinee's performance. In contrast, a distant or negative attitude of the examiner can adversely affect the examinee's performance. A similar problem arises when the examiner expects a subject to behave in a certain manner and thereby facilitates that behavior. For example, an examiner who assumes that the examinee is bright may unintentionally give clues to the correct answers on an intelligence test. Similarly, an assumption that something is wrong with the examinee can function as a self-fulfilling prophesy. In a study of court-appointed psychiatric examiners conducting interviews to determine sanity, Scheff (1966b) found that examiners often assumed mental illness or incompetence in examinees and tended to "see" behavior that confirmed the assumption. Examiner biases are typically a function of the examiner's behavior and preconceived notions about how an examinee should behave in a given situation.

Examinee bias is also an important error variable. People tend to behave according to their perception of what the situation demands (demand characteristics). In a clinic, a person may strive to describe a presenting complaint accurately or even exaggerate its severity, whereas in an experiment they may try to minimize their psychological problems. A common error variable of this type is *social desirability*, the tendency of some individuals to try to portray themselves in the most socially acceptable light when being interviewed (Edwards 1957). This variable influences the behavior of most people in most examining situations.

Another examinee error variable is *response set*, the tendency of some individuals to behave consistently in spite of changing cues (Jackson and Messick 1958). For example, a person may have a tendency to answer "yes" or "true" on personality inventories. This tendency to acquiesce distorts the findings of most personality inventories and must be counterbalanced by using both true and false answers to indicate the same tendency on any given scale.

An error variable that arises in situational assessment is the *reactivity* of measuring procedures (Kent and Foster 1977).

Unrepresentative norms bias tests

Error variables contaminate test results

Examiner bias can affect results

Demand characteristics, response set, and reactivity can affect the examinee's responses

The awareness of being observed may cause a person to alter his or her behavior, grossly affecting the evaluation. This variable is an especially difficult one to control in behavioral assessment.

Other kinds of measurement errors also contribute to the distortion of the evaluation process. Most of these error variables are associated with specific assessment techniques and shall be described when we discuss the techniques. Measurement errors also arise in research and modification procedures.

Assessment of Personality

Personality assessment developed from psychodynamic and trait theories of behavior. One of the assumptions of these approaches is that personality traits are characteristic of an individual and are expressed in most of the individual's life situations. Behavior in a given situation is assumed to be a function of traits rather than situations, and these traits are assumed to be fairly stable across situations.

Because of this assumption, situational or stimulus factors in trait approaches to personality assessment are given a relatively minor role. Instead, interest centers on static behavior. Responses to the test or the test situation are considered indirect signs of underlying processes, which personality tests are designed to tap (Mischel 1972).

A major goal of personality assessment is prediction and classification of behavior. As a result, personality assessment is discrete, usually occurring only once or twice, perhaps when the individual is hospitalized, before entering psychotherapy, or when released from the hospital. It is assumed that the trait or underlying conflict exhibited in the testing situation indicates the type of disorder the individual has, the way in which the individual will respond to treatment, and similar predictive data. Although a variety of tests are used in personality assessment, all individuals seeing a given clinician are usually given the same tests, regardless of their behavior problem.

The major emphasis of personality assessment is on the assessment of verbal behavior, although nonverbal behavior, such as mannerisms, gestures, or other gross motor behavior during the examination, or behavior in a specific situation, such as a ward of disturbed individuals, may be rated. Four major types of personality assessment procedures are used: interviews, rating scales, self-report inventories, and projective techniques.

The Interview

The **interview** is a verbal interaction between two or more people in order to gather firsthand information about the concerned individual. How the interview is used depends on the purpose and theoretical assumptions of the interviewer. While clinicians using humanistic and existential approaches are typically skeptical of any type of measurement, they do rely heavily on the interview for assessment as well as therapeutic purposes.

The belief that behavior is a manifestation of underlying traits imposes a specific structure on the interview. In the typical initial clinical interview (the *intake* interview) an attempt is made to establish rapport with individuals so that the information they give will be as accurate as possible. The interview usually covers the *presenting* problem; the individual's mood; relationships with other people including family; biological functions, such as sexual behavior, sleeping, and eating; and similar information. The clinician may also ask about other behaviors, such as dreams and fantasies, that are believed to reveal unconscious processes and presumably yield information about the individual's problem.

The individual's developmental history is also part of the interview and includes development of motor and verbal skills; ability to function in an educational setting; relationship with parents, siblings, and peers; type of family background; sexual development; early memories; early traumatic events; and similar aspects of the individual's case history. The interviewee's behavior, gestures, and other nonverbal communications during the interview may give additional clues to the individual's personality assessment. The clinical interview is the primary method used by psychiatrists to diagnose abnormal patterns of behavior.

Personality assessment assumes a major role for traits rather than situations

All individuals are given the same test

Theoretical assumptions determine the structure of the interview

A clinical interview. The clinician is establishing rapport with his client by the relaxed atmosphere in his office.

Rating Scales

Rating scales focus on symptoms

Another way to assess individuals is by rating them on scales or other indices of personality after observing their behavior. These ratings are conducted by professionals, by paraprofessionals, or by family and peers trained or instructed in the procedures. The **rating scales** are designed to sample certain aspects of the individual's behavior and to focus on symptoms rather than traits. They are commonly used in institutions by nurses, psychiatric aides, or other hospital personnel. One such rating scale is the Wittenborn Psychiatric Rating Scale (Wittenborn 1955), which has a number of different scales representing different behavior disorders. The patient is rated on such symptoms as difficulty in sleeping, delusions, hallucinations, and so on. These symptoms are then translated into such psychiatric terms as "acute anxiety," "conversion hysteria," "manic states," and "depression." The purpose of this scale and others like it is to define in terms of actual behavior, an individual's psychological functioning at a given time.

Self-Report Inventories

Self-report inventories or *objective personality tests,* are similar to standardized interviews. In these inventories individuals are asked specific questions such as "Do you believe people are following you?" or "Do you lose your temper rapidly?" or they are presented with statements such as "I read mechanics magazines" and are asked to respond with a number of fixed alternative responses, such as "Yes," "No," "Cannot say," or "True," "False." The items presented to all examinees are identical, and administration and scoring procedures are the same for all subjects in order to facilitate comparison with other individuals. These inventories are usually printed in booklet form and can be administered to a number of people simultaneously.

Two major types of self-report inventories exist, and they differ mainly in their methods of construction. In the first type the clinical psychologist assumes understanding of the behavior to be assessed and devises items on the basis of information about the condition. For example, the psychologist assumes that individuals who are depressed typically have difficulties in sleeping, eating, and interacting with other people, as well as in mood. On this basis the psychologist can construct test items such as "I sleep very well," "My appetite is very poor," "I am frequently depressed," "I have difficulty relating to other people," or similar statements calling for a true or false response. This is the rational method of personality construction and relies on the clinical psychologist's knowledge about the personality traits or types of abnormal behavior to be assessed.

scientific approaches to the study of abnormal behavior

This interview was conducted by a therapist (Victor Meyer) with a depressed 71-year-old inpatient at a London teaching hospital, who was referred for assessment. The interview was carried out in the presence of twelve clinical psychologists for teaching purposes.

Therapist Sit down, I prefer to have you on my left hand side. Well, these are all professional people; it is confidential.

Patient You need not worry about that.

Therapist I would like you to talk about your problems and then see whether there is any way we could help you. In fact, your doctor was coming to see me about you because, as you probably know, there are various schools of thought in this field and they were thinking about coming to me to see if my tricks can help you.

Patient What are your tricks?

Therapist I'll explain to you. First of all, we have to find out what your problem is. You have been on this ward how long now?

Patient Since the end of January.

Therapist End of January. All right, and you came with what problem? What was your original complaint?

Patient The thing is it came on so suddenly, I just do not know.

Therapist You know what came suddenly?

Patient The depression.

Therapist Can you tell me what you mean by depression?

Patient Just one day I did not want to get up and go to work.

Therapist You did not want to go to work.

Patient I am a retired pensioner.

Therapist I see, and you stay in bed and what do you feel there?

Patient I feel that things are getting worse and worse, everything is an effort.

Therapist Let us go through it. Are you interested in anything at the moment?

Patient Unfortunately, I have got no emotional feelings at the moment.

Therapist No interest, what do you enjoy?

Patient If I could enjoy something, I would be a happy man, enjoy something for ten minutes a day. I enjoy nothing at all, unfortunately.

Therapist Do you eat?

Patient Very little.

Therapist Weight loss?

Patient I have not really troubled . . .

Therapist Has there been any loss of weight?

Patient I could not say.

Therapist Eating, does it mean anything to you?

Patient No.

Therapist How do you sleep?

Patient Now that is the amazing thing, I can sleep and sleep and sleep.

Therapist Is the problem getting up, waking up?

Patient Yes.

Therapist So that is one thing that you can enjoy?

Patient Sleeping, yes, because I am unconscious, I do not know what is going on.

Therapist But in that period before you go to sleep, when are you drowsy?

Patient That is the unfortunate thing, there is no period when I am awake nor asleep.

Therapist You mean to say you put your head on the pillow and what happens in that period of time before you fall asleep, what are you thinking about?

Patient How I am going to feel tomorrow.

Therapist So looking at any day there is nothing in front?

Patient Nothing.

Therapist You are not looking forward to anything at all?

Patient Nothing at all.

Therapist Would you take your life?

Patient If I had the opportunity.

Therapist Have you seriously considered it?

Patient I certainly have.

Therapist Do you sometimes weep when you are on your own?

Patient I have done the last couple of times.

Therapist Okay. So how long have you been depressed like that?

Patient Since March of this year. Depressed about my life, I mean.

Box 5-1
Transcript of a
Behavioral Interview

Therapist You said that you came here first in January of this year?

Patient I noticed it getting worse.

Therapist Is it the first time in your life that you noticed this depression?

Patient No.

Therapist Then the first time in your life, how long ago?

Patient Going back 25 years, just after the war.

Therapist Okay. Just after the war. You have no idea why you feel like that?

Patient None at all.

Therapist You seem to have no energy either?

Patient That is correct.

Therapist Are you very slow in your movements?

Patient Painfully slow.

Therapist What about thinking, is it an effort to think?

Patient No, I am clear in my head, I know white is white and black is black.

Therapist So your thought processes are as clear and as fast as ever, but do you still daydream?

Patient I like to.

Therapist What do you daydream about?

Patient Being well again.

Therapist Do you blame yourself for the way that you are?

Patient No, because I do not know why it has happened, how it has come about.

Therapist Do you think that you deserve it?

Patient No, I do not think that I deserve it.

Therapist Do you sometimes think that you are a worthless man?

Patient I know I am a worthless man.

Therapist Why?

Patient Because I have got a sick wife at home and I went home yesterday and could only help her with very, very little.

Therapist So you are married?

Patient Yes.

Therapist Got any children?

Patient Yes, you see I married twice and the second time that I married, I married a young person not half my age.

Therapist How old are you?

Patient Seventy-one.

Therapist Your wife?

Patient Thirty-four.

Therapist You are retired, so you do not work?

Patient I had to work to sort of supplement my income. I had a little pension from work. We could manage quite nicely and now this lot has cropped up. Why it has cropped up, I do not know.

Therapist Could you give me an idea of how you spent your time before you came here?

Patient Got up in the morning, got my breakfast, couple of days work a week.

Therapist Half days?

Patient Full days.

Therapist Enjoyed it?

Patient Very much.

Therapist What did you do?

Patient Two days as a serviceman.

Therapist And on those days that you did not work?

Patient Used to help the wife very, very much indeed. Unfortunately, she has had a very severe illness.

Therapist What is it?

Patient Well, woman trouble, you know.

Therapist Did she have a hysterectomy?

Patient That is the next thing they are talking about; that is taking the womb away is it not?

Therapist Have you got any emotional feeling toward your wife?

Patient Let us say responsibility.

Therapist Here is the problem in a nutshell: nothing interests you?

Patient Correct.

Therapist You might as well stay in bed?

Patient Exactly.

Therapist Let us go back, when you enjoyed life, you can recall that? What did you particularly enjoy?

Patient Music.

Therapist Now does it mean anything to you?

Patient Nothing means anything to me.

scientific approaches to the study of abnormal behavior

Therapist Let's go back soon after the war started. What did you enjoy doing during the war? I remember that period very well; I enjoyed myself very much indeed.

Patient I was in the Air Force.

Therapist So was I. Which part? Bomber Command? Fighter Command?

Patient A little command called *X*.

Therapist Where were you stationed?

Patient (Town) for a time.

Therapist In the forces did you enjoy life?

Patient Yes.

Therapist What did you particularly enjoy?

Patient It is difficult to say, just life in general.

Therapist I am trying to see you as a youngster in the Air Force. What sort of bloke were you, can you recall?

Patient Happy-go-lucky sort of person.

Therapist Happy-go-lucky sort of person. Lots of friends or a few close friends?

Patient A fair amount of friends.

Therapist Girl friends?

Patient Eh . . . no.

Therapist You were not a ladies' man, were you? What about drink, did you like to have a pint?

Patient Oh, yes.

Therapist Good sense of humor?

Patient Pretty good.

Therapist You see, when you talk about it, you begin to smile; when you think about it, you begin to cheer up a bit. Just think about, what suddenly stopped you enjoying life?

Patient That I would like to know myself.

Therapist Shall we try to find out?

Patient Yes.

Therapist Will you help me?

Patient I certainly will.

These inventories can be restricted to one type of behavior, as are the Beck Depression Inventories (Beck 1972) shown in Figure 5–1. In most cases, however, the test has a number of scales designed to measure a variety of personality attributes or traits.

An example of this type is the California Psychological Inventory (Gough 1957). This type of scale relies heavily on the content of the item to indicate a particular psychological maladjustment or trait.

The rational method relies on the content of the item to indicate a particular trait or maladjustment

General instructions: Read the group of statements and check the ONE statement that best describes how you feel right now.

A. ____ I make decisions about as well as ever.
   ____ I try to put off making decisions.
   ____ I have great difficulty in making decisions.
   ____ I can't make decisions at all any more.

B. ____ I don't cry any more than usual.
   ____ I cry more now than I used to.
   ____ I cry all the time now. I can't stop it.
   ____ I used to be able to cry, but now I can't cry at all, even though I want to.

C. ____ I don't have any thoughts of harming myself.
   ____ I have thoughts of harming myself, but I would not carry them out.
   ____ I feel I would be better off dead.
   ____ I feel my family would be better off if I were dead.
   ____ I have definite plans about committing suicide.
   ____ I would kill myself if I could.

Figure 5–1 Sample items from the Beck Depression Inventory.

assessment of abnormal behavior

Table 5-1 Interpretations of Scales of the MMPI

Scale		Sample similar item	Interpretation of the scale
Can't say	(?)	No sample. It is merely the number of items marked in the "cannot say" category.	This is one of four validity scales, and a high score indicates evasiveness.
Lie	(L)	I have borrowed objects without returning them. (FALSE)	This is the second validity scale. Persons trying to present themselves in a favorable light (e.g., good, wholesome, honest) obtain high L scale elevations.
Validity	(F)	My voices sometimes guide my actions. (TRUE)	F is the third validity scale. High scores suggest carelessness, confusion, or "fake bad."
Correction	(K)	I do not always tell the truth. (FALSE)	An elevation on the last validity scale, K, suggests a defensive test-taking attitude. Exceedingly low scores may indicate a lack of ability to deny symptomatology.
Hypochondriasis	(Hs)	I never get low back pains. (FALSE)	High scorers have been described as cynical, defeatist, and "crabby."
Depression	(D)	Friends have said that I am overactive. (FALSE)	High scorers usually are shy, dependent, and distressed.
Hysteria	(Hy)	Headaches are rare occurrences for me. (FALSE)	High scorers tend to complain of multiple symptoms.
Psychopathic deviant	(Pd)	My parents and I get along fine. (FALSE)	Adjectives used to describe some high scorers are adventurous, courageous, and generous.
Masculinity-Femininity	(Mf)	I am interested in automobiles. (FALSE)	Among males, high scorers have been described as aesthetic and sensitive. High-scoring women have been described as rebellious, unrealistic, and generous.
Paranoia	(Pa)	People tend to mind their own business. (FALSE)	High scorers on this scale were characterized as shrewd, guarded, and worrisome.
Psychoasthenia	(Pt)	I have trouble starting projects. (TRUE)	Fearful, rigid, anxious, and worrisome are some of the adjectives used to describe high Pt scorers.
Schizophrenia	(Sc)	Everyone hates me. (TRUE)	Adjectives such as withdrawn and unusual describe Sc high scorers.
Hypomania	(Ma)	Lots of things interest me. (TRUE)	High scorers are called sociable, energetic, and impulsive.
Social introversion	(Si)	I get along well with others. (FALSE)	High scorers are described as modest, shy, and self-effacing. Low scorers are described as sociable, colorful, and ambitious.

Note: The TRUE or FALSE responses within parentheses indicate the scored direction of each of the items.

The criterion group method is based on responses to the test items by a group of abnormally behaving people

The second type of test construction relies less on the content of specific items and more on the criterion group method, which involves the use of test items that have evoked a certain response from people with behavior disorders but not from a control group of "normals." Of these, the most frequently used is the Minnesota Multiphasic Personality Inventory (MMPI) (Hathaway and McKinley 1951).

There are three control scales on the MMPI. The *L* or lie scale was devised to measure tendency to attribute socially desirable characteristics to oneself. For example, one L-score item is "I never tell a

Control scales are an attempt to control for various error variables

lie." The *F* scale was included to reflect the subject's carelessness or confusion in taking the inventory. The *K* scale, a more subtle scale, was designed to take into account the fact that some people are highly self-disclosing while others are not. Consequently, a K-scale correction is made on a number of clinical scales to compensate for this tendency. Table 5-1 gives further information on these scales.

An individual's raw score for each scale is converted into a *T* score. A *T* score of fifty on a scale equals the average score of a normal group. For each scale the standard deviation is 10. (The standard deviation indicates what percentage of the population scores below a given score. For example, 84 percent of the normal population scored below a T score of 60, while 98 percent of the population scored below a T score of 70.)

The various scales of the MMPI are plotted on a profile. Although the MMPI Scales were designed to differentiate between diagnostic groups and normal subjects, in actual clinical practice the MMPI is rarely used as originally designed. For example, a score above 70 on Scale 2 (D) should indicate that an individual is depressed. However, empirically and clinically, this is not always the case. For this reason, profile analysis or a study of the configuration of peaks and valleys on the profile is more commonly used. If elevations occur on Scales 1 and 3 (Hs and Hy) and a low score occurs on Scale 2 (D), the diagnosis of conversion hysteria (having disease symptoms without an organic basis) is warranted. These configurations not only provide the basis for applying diagnostic labels but also help describe individuals and their personality dynamics on the basis of clinical judgment.

Because of the practice of using clinical judgment, often based on the clinician's theoretical biases about the MMPI, the label "objective personality test" is somewhat factitious. The administration, standardization, and scoring of the MMPI are objective, but the interpretation of the profiles usually is not, although empirically derived code atlases or "cookbooks" are available for profile analysis (Dahlstrom, Welsh, and Dahlstrom 1972).

An additional problem is that the rational method of devising personality tests makes two extremely questionable assumptions. The first assumption is that examinees understand their behavior and personality and respond truthfully. The second is that the psychologist has sufficient information about the trait and its parameters to construct items to test for it. Unfortunately, a clinician's knowledge is usually based on theoretical bias rather than objective data. Consequently, most of the instruments devised by this method have acceptable reliability but little validity.

Personality inventories have been shown to be contaminated by response sets such as acquiescence and social desirability. It has been claimed that the MMPI measures the tendency to answer "true" or to answer "false" and that the tendency to give negative responses is associated with neuroticism, while the tendency to give positive responses is associated with psychoticism (Barnes 1956). However, Block (1965) has argued that these response sets represent important aspects of the personality factors being measured rather than simply error. When clinical and computer interpretations of profiles are used, the objective tests are similar to projective techniques, which also rely on clinical judgment and experience. Problems with these interpretations will be discussed in the next section.

Projective Techniques

Freud defined projection as the process of ascribing one's unacceptable drives, feelings, or sentiments to other people or objects in an effort to defend against becoming aware of those aspects of oneself. To elicit such projections, **projective techniques** minimize stimulus factors or make use of ambiguous stimuli. Usually, the examiner gives a minimum of instruction and requires the examinee to interpret the stimuli by using imagination.

Lindzey (1959) described the following five types of projective techniques whose common characteristic is that the subject has a wide latitude in responding: (1) *association techniques* require the individual to react to words, ink blots, or other stimuli with the first thought that comes to mind. The Rorschach test and word association tests exemplify this kind of technique; (2) *construction techniques* require the individual to create something like a story or a drawing; (3) *completion techniques* require the subject to complete some incomplete item, such as a sentence fragment like "I am . . . "; or "I feel . . . "; (4) *choice* or *ordering techniques* require the subject to choose from or establish order among a group of stimuli. The subject might, for example, be asked to sort a group of objects into categories; and (5) *expressive techniques* require the subject to express him or herself freely in some manner such as finger painting.

How objective are "objective personality tests"?

Response sets can contaminate personality inventories

Projective techniques permit a wide range of responses

The Minnesota Multiphasic Personality Inventory

Starke R. Hathaway and J. Charnley McKinley

Scorer's Initials _____

Name _____

Address _____

Occupation _Housekeeper_   **Date Tested** _____

Education _College_   **Age** _26_

Marital Status _M_   **Referred by** _____

NOTES

F
Female

Brief History:

This 26-year-old, married (to a graduate ministerial student) woman was admitted to the psychiatric unit of a general hospital with complaints of marked withdrawal, anhedonia, fatigue and general loss of interest. The MMPI was routinely administered on admission. Initially, the diagnostic picture was unclear on clinical evaluation. Eventually she revealed to her therapist a fully developed "other life" in which, in fantasy, she spent most of her time, having concluded that the real world was too painful to engage. She successfully suicided by surreptitious hoarding of sleep medication approximately one month following completion of the MMPI.

—RCC

	L	F	K	1 Hs+.5K	2 D	3 Hy	4 Pd+.4K	5 Mf	6 Pa	7 Pt+1K	8 Sc+1K	9 Ma+2K	0 Si
Raw Score	14	2	15	11	7	32	16	24	34	13	21	33	18	48
K to be added				6			4			11	11	2	
Raw Score with K	13					28	28	32	44	20	

Female

MMPI profile and case summary.

Signature _____   Date _____

box 5-2
MMPI Interpretation

While the "2–7" type of profile (significant elevations on the Depression and Psychasthenia scales) is the most frequently occurring one in a psychiatric population, the basic pattern seen here is also not uncommon. It would be described as an "8–2–4"—significantly elevated Schizophrenia, Depression, and Psychopathic deviate scales—with the usually accompanying elevations on "F" and Social introversion. Individuals with this type of profile virtually always show marked distrust, cynicism, and disidentification with the social environment. As a group, they tend to be overtly angry, although in a withdrawn and distance-maintaining way. The social feedback they receive tends to confirm their apparent view of the world as a hateful, loathesome place in which to be, a place in which sincere affection and love is not to be found.

Unconventional or frankly peculiar ideation (F and Sc elevations) is likely to be an accompanying feature, as is occasional impulsiveness (Pd), where the latter is most likely to produce self-defeating outcomes (D, Sc) and often a transfer of blame to the external environment (Pd and moderately elevated Pa). The relative absence of "neurotic" defenses (low Hs and Hy) suggests that the person is somewhat lacking in cognitive and emotional controls, and may be capable of extreme or even bizarre experience (Sc). The basic personality type is distinctly schizoid (F, D, Pd, Sc, Si), and the zone of overall elevation renders it likely that a psychotic process of the schizophrenic variety is present. The latter would be this interpreter's "most favored" blind diagnosis.

Suicide attempts of a serious and lethal variety are relatively common with this group of persons. Treatment efforts are likely to founder on the issue of trust and the related problem of therapist anger and counter-aggression.

Robert C. Carson, Duke University

The two most commonly used projective techniques are the Thematic Apperception Test (TAT) and the Rorschach Inkblot Test. In the TAT, the individual is presented with pictures showing people engaged in various activities. The individual is then asked to describe each picture and the events that led up to the scene, as well as the events that will develop from it. The examinee is also asked to describe both the feelings and the thoughts of the people in the picture (Murray 1943). Interpretations of TAT stories are content-oriented and rely heavily on the quality and the characteristics of the stories. There are methods for objectively scoring this test, but more often the TAT serves as a probe of unconscious processes.

In the Rorschach, a series of ten cards, five in color and five in black and white, are presented one at a time to the subject. The subject is then asked to describe what he or she sees in the cards. There are no right or wrong answers: what is important is what each individual perceives in the cards.

A large number of studies have evaluated the validity of projective techniques, most of them with negative results (Fisher 1967). In spite of these findings, however, projective techniques continue to be used widely in psychological assessment, largely because many clinicians believe that their experience and talent in using these tests have not been adequately evaluated by the research evidence.

Chapman and his colleagues gave one of the reasons for the continuing use of these techniques in their discussion of *illusory correlations* (Chapman 1971; Chapman and Chapman 1969). Illusory correlations are based on *associative connections* of the test data with clinical interpretations rather than with valid

Projective tests remain popular despite negative results of validity tests

box 5–3
Response and
Interpretation of
Response to a
TAT Picture

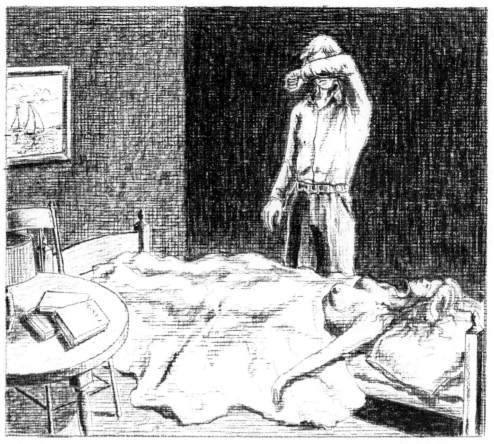

This illustration is similar to the TAT picture on which the response and interpretation are based.

The following is a response and an interpretation of that response to the TAT picture on which the above illustration is based. The client was a twenty-two-year-old Protestant woman who was hospitalized at the time of testing.

Response

Reaction Time: 3″   Total Time: 1′27″

Uh, this man is the husband of the woman. She's been very sick for many years and uh—suffering quite bad, in part, you know, terribly. And so he has just killed her—mercy killing, so to speak. And he is quite horrified by what he has done. He doesn't know if it's the right thing or the wrong thing. However, he decided that it is the right thing. And—uh—[sighs] he—no dramatic ending. He just continues to go along his merry way. He's given her an overdose of something, so as to make it look accidental—[sighs]. That's it.

Inquiry: [When you say he just goes on his merry way—] Well, that's just a phrase. Uh—uh—he continues through his life. I mean, he doesn't jump out a window or anything. He's not sent to prison [sighs]. He just keeps on existing [sighs]. [What do you think he might do?] Might do. Well, he'll probably remarry. You mean at the moment what he might—oh, he'll probably remarry and build a—another life for himself—never, of course, forget his wife—first wife. But I think he'll feel that he did the right thing eventually.

Interpretation

She goes to great lengths to try to minimize and deny the dysphoric—depressive and aggressive—implications of the story. The major expressions of her use of denial are seen in the benevolent quality of the killing, in his somewhat

The Thematic Apperception Test (TAT) is a projective technique in which the individual is asked to describe the situation depicted in various pictures.

inappropriately "going on his merry way," and in the emphasis on what he does not do as a result of his feelings (e.g., jump out of the window), and what does *not* happen to him (e.g., go to prison). The instability of her use of denial, however, is made apparent by the breakthrough of the horrified feelings which follow his action, by the theme of futility, "He just keeps on existing," which has now appeared several times, and by the inappropriateness and incongruity of the affects in the story (he is horrified but goes on his merry way). The antecedents of her feelings of futility are specified in this story (the second in which one person is responsible for the death of another) as representing guilt and its concomitant self-blame. It seems almost superfluous to point out that in this story another death occurs, which by now is almost commonplace for her TAT. Previously, death was due to violence (auto accident, jumping out of a window, mutual destruction); in this story, however, it is caused by oral means. In questioning why this change has occurred here, serious consideration must be given to the fact that a sexual scene is often depicted

in this card. One might speculate that orality and sex are closely intertwined, that is, that sexual activity is accompanied by oral fantasies (being fed and nurtured), and is generally thought of in oral terms, or consists directly of oral activity. We will have to await further data to elaborate on this speculation.

From a structural point of view of particular note is the suggestion of a mild distortion in the perception of the generation of the figures. Usually they are seen as relatively young, but the implication here is that they have been married for many years. It would seem then that she is considering them to be older than they are customarily perceived. This mild misperception is similar to her unsureness on the previous card (#7; Picasso's "La Vie") about her own maturity and about the distinctness of boundaries between generations, thereby suggesting a lack of definition between parental and child roles and a fuzzy and unclear differentiation between parent (mother) and child.

Allison, Blatt, and Zimet, 1968

box 5-4
Response and
Interpretation
of Response
to an Inkblot

The following is a response and an interpretation of that response to the inkblot shown. The inkblot is similar to Card V of the Rorschach Inkblot Test. The client was a twenty-two-year-old male college student who was reportedly at the beginning stage of an acute psychotic episode at the time of testing. (W = whole blot was used in percept; F+ = percept fit inkblot very well; AP peculiar = animal percept but peculiar)

Response

Reaction Time: 8″   Total Time: 1′ 15″

(W F+ A P Peculiar) An insect of some sort, possibly a bat—another bat. It could be an insect or a bat, I suppose. The wings seem to be pointing slightly inward, toward you.

Interpretation

His repetition of the response in his second sentence indicates a ruminative proclivity that could be the obsessive counterpart of the compulsive meticulousness suggested in I-1. The stimulation of special ruminativeness at this point may derive from anxiety associated with his need to choose between a potentially threatening bat and an essentially innocuous insect.

The three-dimensional quality and the wings pointing specifically toward the tester have the same malignant, paranoid implications elaborated in connection with the reaching hands. This response is particularly paranoid in that the card was flat on the desk at the time the verbalization was delivered, so that, if anything, the wings were pointing toward the floor.

The patient's experiencing the wings as pointing toward the tester indicates an interpersonal significance in the response—in particular, the possibility that the bat is an externalization of himself and that something of his relationship to the tester is stated through this image. Whereas the implications of reaching hands were ambiguous, here the bat probably partakes of such threatening qualities usually associated with bats as *eerie, dirty, vampirish, grasping, enveloping,* and *evil.* If this line of reasoning is correct, the patient is preoccupied with and feels threatened by as well as guilty about his hostile, demanding impulses toward the tester and the real life figure(s) for whom the tester stands.

Illusory correlations— different raters may be biased by the same stereotype

observations. For example, an individual instructed to draw a person may draw a person with a small head. The associative connection might go like this: head → mind → intelligence; small → little → inferior. Therefore, the clinician may interpret the drawing as indicating that the examinee feels intellectually inferior. Such associative norms operate in all individuals.

Consequently, when the clinician asks a professional colleague to interpret the test material, the same verbal association process is quite likely to occur, and consensual validation (subjective agreement) of the interpretation results. A study by Chapman and Chapman (1969) compared Rorschach responses that clinicians erroneously be-

Art therapy can be used to evaluate how patients feel about themselves. This approach is being used more frequently with institutionalized patients.

Table 5-2   Valid and Invalid Signs of Male Homosexuality on the Rorschach

Popular but invalid signs	Mean rated strength of association between sign and homosexuality*
Rectum and buttocks	4.38
Part man—part woman (sexual confusion)	3.53
Feminine clothing	3.12
Sexual organs	4.47
Unpopular but valid signs	
Part animal—Part human	1.93
Monsters	1.68

*Association with male homosexuality: 6 = very strong; 5 = strong; 4 = moderate; 3 = slight; 2 = very slight; 1 = no association at all.

lieved to be valid signs of homosexuality with valid signs of homosexuality not commonly used by clinicians (see table 5–2). When students were asked to rate which responses indicated homosexuality, they too gave much higher ratings to the popular but invalid signs than to other responses. This agreement of students with clinicians indicates that similar associative norms were operating in both groups.

An attempt was made to eliminate this bias by giving the students several stacks of Rorschach protocols (that is, examinations of individuals). They were told that one stack was composed of responses from heterosexual individuals. This stack included many of the popular but invalid responses or signs of homosexuality, such as perceptions of rectums, buttocks, and sexual organs. The students were also given a stack of protocols of homosexual individuals that had valid signs of homosexuality, the purpose being to eliminate illusory correlation by experience. Upon completion of the experiment, the students were asked to list the signs of homosexuality. They still listed the popular but invalid signs as indicators of homosexuality. Apparently, this bias is very difficult to eliminate, and a clinician's experience does not help. As this study shows, an individual's response to a projective technique allows one to predict how *clinicians* will behave (how they will interpret the data), but does not always provide the basis for an accurate prediction of the examinee's behavior. In other words, these tests often detect only consensual agreement among clinicians, which may not be related to the examinee's behavior.

Assessment of Intelligence

Intelligence is usually viewed as an inherent attribute of the individual molded by life experiences and biophysical endowment (Wesman 1968), and disorders of intellectual behavior are labeled as mental deficiency, mental retardation, or the like (see Chapter 17). The assessment of intellectual behavior is similar to personality assessment because it assumes that intelligence is an aspect of the individual that is stable across time and situations. Consequently, assessment occurs on discrete occasions by means of standardized tests. The assessment of intelligence is also similar to behavioral assessment because **intelligence tests** rely heavily on content validity: They make a systematic attempt to sample behaviors that are indices of intellectual performance in an individual's life.

A variety of intelligence tests exist. They vary from those designed to be administered rapidly to large groups by minimally trained examiners to highly sophisticated indices of intelligence individually administered by well-trained professionals. In comparison to other methods of assessing behavior, intelligence tests have been more carefully produced: More attention has been paid to test construction, norms, standardization, reliability, and validity. Consequently, as compared to other assessment techniques, intelligence tests tend to be highly reliable and valid. We shall describe two different tests.

Stanford-Binet Scales

Modern-day intelligence testing is largely based on the work of (French psychologist) Alfred Binet (1857–1911), who believed that sensory motor tasks were given too much emphasis in the assessment of intellectual functioning. Binet designed tests to assess reasoning (the ability to understand and follow directions) and the exercise of judgment (Pollack and Brenner 1969). Consequently, in the 1916 version of the Binet scales Binet and Simmons included such tasks as the recognition of objects, sentence completion, visual memory, definition of simple words, and digit repetition. In the United States, Lewis Terman of Stanford University developed English versions of the Binet test (Stanford-Binet) and over the years he revised and improved both the test items and the procedures for gathering normative data (Terman and Merrill 1960).

Binet conceptualized intelligence as an ability that grew with maturation, and his tests consisted of tasks that were appropriate for the average child at a given age. The tests for young children involved relatively simple discriminations and recall, whereas those for middle childhood and adolescence required much more complex reasoning, as may be seen in Table 5–3. How far a child could go up the ladder of tests before failing determined the quality of intellectual functioning. For example, if a child passed all of the tests for children of age 6, two of four tests at age 7, one of four tests for age 8, and none at age 9, his or her *mental age* would be 6 years (the age for which the child passed all tests, called the *basal* age) plus six months (for passing two of four tests at age level 7), plus three months (for passing one of four tests at age level 8) for a total of 6 years, 9 months—which is called the child's mental age (MA). To determine the **intelligence quotient** (IQ), the mental age is divided by the child's chronological age (CA) and multiplied by 100. If the child is 6 years of age and has an MA of 6 years, 9 months, his or her IQ will be approximately 112 (81 months divided by 72 months multiplied by 100). Thus, the formula is $IQ = \dfrac{MA}{CA} \times 100$. In the later versions of the Stanford-Binet, the MA is converted to an IQ by referring to a table. The highest mental age obtainable on the Stanford-Binet Scales is 22 years, 10 months. For this reason the Stanford-Binet Scales are not suitable for adult testing because they have an insufficient ceiling for superior adults and adolescents.

scientific approaches to the study of abnormal behavior

Table 5-3 Representative Items of the Stanford-Binet

Year level	Task
II	Identifying parts of the body: Show the child a picture of a person and ask the child to point to the various parts of the body, e.g., "Show me his eyes."
III	Copying a design: Show the child a simple picture and say, "Make one just like this."
IV	Opposite analogies: "Aunt is a woman, uncle is a _____."
V	Picture completion: Present the child with an incomplete picture of a person and ask the child to complete it.
VI	Differences: "What is the difference between a cat and a fish?"

Picture arrangement

Digit symbol   Object assembly   Picture completion

Figure 5-2 Items similar to those found on the WAIS and WISC Performance Subtests.

Wechsler Intelligence Scales

The major competitor to the Stanford-Binet are the scales developed by David Wechsler (1958) who believed that the **deviation IQ** was a better approach to intelligence testing than the mental age concept. In the deviation IQ approach individuals are compared to other individuals of their own age group in terms of how they perform on intellectual tasks rather than to individuals older or younger, as they are on the Binet Scales. Wechsler regarded the Binet Scales as deficient because they produced only a single score, and he believed intelligence could be better measured as an aggregate of abilities. Consequently, Wechsler designed his tests to obtain three types of IQ: (1) *verbal IQ,* which reflects levels of attainment on subtests dealing with general information, comprehension, ability to think in abstract terms, immediate memory, and arithmetic; (2) *performance IQ* (shown in figure 5-2), which reflects levels of attainment on tasks requiring the solution of puzzles, the substitution of symbols for digits, the reproduction of designs, the detection of sequences of events, and the location of missing details;

Table 5–4   Sample Similar Items from the Two Subtests of the WAIS

Subtest	Verbal subtests Representative item
Information	Where is Argentina?
Comprehension	Why do children go to school?
Arithmetic	How many inches are there in three and one-half feet?
Similarities	In what way are peaches and apples alike?
Digit span	Say the following numbers after me: 7-4-9-3. Now say these numbers backwards: 4-6-5-2.
Vocabulary	The subject is required to define several words, e.g., What does tooth mean?

Subtest	Performance subtests Description
Digit symbol	These items contain boxes with symbols in them matched with numbers. The subject is instructed to draw the correct symbol for each number in a timed test.
Picture completion	The subject is shown pictures in which an important part is missing. He/she is instructed to name that part.
Block design	The subject is instructed to put colored blocks together to form a design like a picture shown to them.
Picture arrangement	In this subtest the subject arranges pictures so they tell a meaningful story.
Object assembly	The subject is given parts of a puzzle and told to make something.

Table 5–5   Distribution of IQs: Descriptive Adjectives and Percentage in Each Category

IQ	Classification	Percent included
130 and above	Very superior	2.2
120–129	Superior	6.7
110–119	Bright normal	16.1
90–109	Average	50.0
80–89	Dull normal	16.1
70–79	Borderline	6.7
69 and below	Mental defective	2.2

and (3) the *total score.* Examples of the verbal and performance subtests are given in Table 5–4.

Wechsler designed three major tests: (1) the Wechsler Adult Intelligence Scale (WAIS) for individuals over 16, (2) the Wechsler Intelligence Scales for Children (WISC) for individuals from 5 to 16 years of age, and (3) the Wechsler Preschool and Primary Scales (WPPSI) for younger children. Each test is scored in terms of the individual's performance as compared to other individuals of the same age group. The individual's total score is then converted to a deviation score, the average IQ being 100 and the standard deviation being 10. Table 5–5 shows the distribution and

classifications of intelligence scores in the normal population.

In recent years a storm of controversy has arisen around intelligence testing and their significance. Some individuals view intelligence tests as measuring innate, biologically given intellect; others see them as reflecting the values and achievement of white middle-class culture. The norms for intelligence tests were originally standardized on white populations and thus penalized members of minority groups as well as individuals from lower socioeconomic backgrounds. However, as Wechsler has noted, intelligence is not a tangible thing but a construct or intervening variable and therefore *is* culturally biased. A discussion of the

Intelligence is an abstraction, not a thing, and is culturally biased

scientific approaches to the study of abnormal behavior

heredity-environment controversy of intelligence is beyond the scope of this book but should be carefully considered in evaluating intelligence tests (Mischel 1968; Williams 1970).

Assessment of Behavior

In personality assessment, whose main purpose is prediction and diagnosis, group designs provide the basis for construction of tests. Consequently, many psychodynamically oriented psychotherapists rely very little on traditional assessment procedures, which they see as having little relevance to treatment. Some plainly doubt the validity of those instruments (Meehl 1960). Moreover, since these therapists commonly use the same treatment procedures with all behavior disorders, personality assessment is obviously meaningless for treatment planning.

In behavior therapy, assessment plays a major role in selecting, devising, and evaluating modification procedures. Consequently, single-case designs are the principal methods used to devise behavioral assessment techniques, and group designs are used only when behavior therapists have to decide whether an individual's behavior is appropriate or inappropriate compared to that of other individuals or when they are used to develop norms.

The major assumption in **behavioral assessment** is that behavior is a function of stimulus variables, including stimuli that precede or follow responses. In other words, behavior is elicited by discriminate stimuli in the environment and, in turn, is maintained as a consequence of the stimuli (that is, positive and negative reward, punishment, and extinction). This approach to assessment can be abbreviated as the *S-R-C* approach, in which S = stimulus, R = response, and C = consequences of behavior. When behavior therapists are interested in organismic variables, they use an *S-O-R-C* approach, in which O = organismic variables such as the individual's cognitions (Kanfer and Phillips 1970). This is a *situational approach* to the assessment of behavior. Since a situational approach to behavior demands clear definition and measurement of stimulus cues,

the behavior therapist must assess eliciting stimuli (those that evoke response from an individual) and discriminative stimuli (those that set the occasion for the response). In most cases, the therapist manipulates or observes stimulus cues and evaluates the consequential changes in the responses. This procedure also allows the therapist to determine whether there is a deficit in stimulus control (that is, the individual does not respond to appropriate stimulus cues).

The situational approach also demands that the means of measuring response variables be clearly specified. In other words, because interest focuses on the continuous monitoring of behavior, a targeted response has to be clearly defined. Behavioral assessment thus has *high fidelity* and *narrow bandwidth,* that is, a very specific response that is usually very accurately assessed. Personality assessment, on the other hand, has low fidelity and wide bandwidth because it seeks to obtain a great deal of information about a number of the responses of an individual.

Because behavior therapists focus on specific problems, they have been accused of inadequately describing underlying causes of an individual's behavior or other aspects of behavior presumed to be associated with its causes. Such accusation, however, results from a misunderstanding of the behavioral approach. Behavior therapists do not define the individual's presenting problems in terms of hypothetical constructs, such as defense mechanisms or complexes, and do not assume that behavior is a function of unconscious mechanisms. They assume, on the contrary, that the cause of a specific behavior pattern should be determined empirically.

Because the usual purpose of behavioral assessment is the modification of behavior, the therapist must also assess the consequences of behavior. If a problem behavior occurs because it is followed by reward or punishment, an accurate assessment of these consequences is crucial for devising modification programs to decrease or eliminate the deviant behavior pattern. An individual who exhibits depression, for example, may receive so much attention from others that the depressive behavior is

Behavioral assessment relies more on single case designs, less on group comparison designs

Behavior as a function of stimulus variables

Behavior therapists do not assume "underlying causes"

Table 5–6   A Comparison of Traditional and Behavioral Assessment Strategies

	Behavioral assessment	Traditional assessment
Assumptions		
1. Personality concept	Behavior (f) environment	Behavior (f) underlying causes
2. "Test" interpretation	Behavior as sample	Behavior as sign
3. Situations sampled	Varied and specific	Limited and ambiguous
Primary functions	Description in behavioral-analytic terms	Description in psychodynamic terms
	Treatment selection	Diagnostic labeling
	Treatment evaluation	
Practical aspects		
1. Relation to treatment	Direct	Indirect
2. Time of assessment	Continuous with treatment	Prior to treatment

reinforced and maintained. On occasion, particularly with avoidance behavior, the payoff is difficult to see, but consequences must always be assessed in order to understand accurately the behavior being exhibited.

Behaviorists are also frequently interested in *organismic variables*. These variables are characteristic of an individual and may include activity level, physiological and constitutional factors, and internal mediating cognitive responses such as expectations or sets (Goldfried and Davison 1976). Although early behavior therapists often ignored these variables, many behavior therapists are now interested in how an individual's physiological and cognitive processes influence behavior. However, behaviorists do insist that these variables be operationally defined and specified before they can be meaningfully considered in an assessment procedure or a treatment program.

The usefulness of a given behavioral assessment technique is usually determined by content validity. In other words, the behavioral approach attempts to reproduce or sample behavior as it actually occurs in the environment (Goldfried and Sprafkin 1973). While some procedures, such as interviews and ratings, used in behavioral assessment are similar to procedures used in personality assessment, they are likely to be used in quite different ways, as may be seen in Table 5–6. A major difference is that behavioral assessment describes behavior without attempting to interpret it.

Physiological and cognitive factors considered too

Attempt to sample behavior as it occurs in real life

Functional analysis— assessment determines modification procedure

This is a direct approach to the measurement of behavior in which the assessor attempts to secure a sample of the individual's behavior that is relevant to the presenting problem.

Behavioral Interviews

The usual purpose of **behavioral interviews** is to obtain information for devising an assessment program that will establish the optimal modification procedure. This method is called a *functional analysis* of behavior. Kanfer and Saslow (1965) describe in detail the steps in functional analysis and thus provide a good guide for conducting behavioral interviews:

1. **Analysis of the problem situation** The individual's presenting complaints are first categorized into classes of behavior excesses and deficits. The client describes the form, frequency, intensity, duration, and appropriateness of the problem responses, as well as their stimulus conditions. These response classes will constitute the target of the therapeutic intervention. Kanfer and Saslow also emphasize that the individual's behavioral assets should be determined so that they can play a role in the behavior therapy program.

2. **Clarification of the problem situation** Attempts are then made to determine what individuals or circumstances maintain the target behavior and what are the consequences of these

scientific approaches to the study of abnormal behavior

target behaviors to the individual and others in the environment. To determine the positive and negative side effects of a modification program, attempts are also made to ascertain the possible consequences of changing these behaviors.

3. **Motivational analysis** Attention is next paid to the hierarchy of persons, events, and objects that serve as reinforcers for the individual. These include reinforcing events that facilitate approach behavior as well as those that prompt avoidance responses. One purpose of obtaining this information is to permit the therapist and others in the individual's social environment to use the appropriate reinforcers.

4. **Developmental analysis** The individual is now asked about biological characteristics, social-cultural experiences, and physical and behavioral development. These questions are designed to (1) evoke description of habitual behavior in various chronological stages of life, (2) relate specific new stimulus conditions to noticeable changes from this habitual behavior, and (3) relate such altered behavior to the present problem.

5. **Analysis of self-control** Because deficits or excesses of self-control are important to successful planning of therapeutic programs, an attempt is also made to examine both the methods and the degree of self-control the person exercises in one's daily routines. Persons, events, or institutions that have successfully reinforced self-control are also considered.

6. **Analysis of social relations** Inquiries about the individual's social interaction are also made to evaluate the significance of people in the individual's environment who influence the problem behavior or who are influenced by the individual for the individual's own satisfaction. In particular, social skills are evaluated. This information also allows planning for the participation of significant others in the assessment and treatment program.

7. **Analysis of the cultural and physical environment** The norms of the individual's social environment must be considered. The discrepancies between the person's idiosyncratic life pattern and the norms or standards of behavior in the environment are defined so that the importance of these factors can also be evaluated. The interviewer must be able to understand the social environment of the interviewee in order to understand adequately the individual's problem behavior.

In the behavioral interview, the clinician should attempt to acquire sufficient information to form a clear understanding of the individual's problems. However, detailed delving into areas that may be irrelevant to the problem behavior is inappropriate and raises ethical questions (Morganstein 1976). For example, we are all interested in sexual behavior, but a detailed inquiry into the sexual activities of someone who has "hand washing" rituals is clearly inappropriate. A cursory probe into such activities to determine whether they are related to the presenting problem is sufficient.

The major purpose of the behavioral interview is to set the stage for more comprehensive assessment of the target behavior. In contrast to personality assessment, behavioral assessment often involves all three channels of responses: subjective or verbal reports, motor behavior, and indices of physiological responses.

Aims at assessing target behavior

Subjective Reports

Behavioral assessment of subjective reports can be divided into two major types. The first type requires the client to complete various questionnaires that report the status of his current problem behaviors. An example of such a **behavioral questionnaire** is the Behavioral Analysis History Questionnaire, which samples possible problem areas in an individual's life, such as fears, marital relations, relationships with family and others, employment satisfaction, and sexual behavior (Cautela and Upper 1976). Whereas this type of questionnaire gives a general indication of specific problems

What would you do in the following situation? Indicate by circling 1, 2 or 3.

A. You have been waiting in line for a ticket. Someone gets in front of you.
1. You say it is your turn and get in front of the person.
2. You say it is your turn, but you let the person go before you.
3. You say nothing.

Figure 5–3 Item similar to those found on the Assertive Behavior Survey Schedule.

Self-monitoring records frequency, duration, and intensity of responses, as well as situations and consequences

in the individual's life, the other kind of questionnaire focuses in detail on specific problems. For example, assertiveness questionnaires like the Assertive Behavior Survey Schedule (Cautela and Upper 1976) might have items such as the one shown in Figure 5–3.

Other questionnaires include the Rathus Assertiveness Schedule (Rathus 1973), the Social Avoidance Distress Scale (Watson and Friend 1969), the Fear of Negative Evaluation Scale (Watson and Friend 1969), and the Fear Survey Schedule (Wolpe and Lang 1964). These scales have the individual rate a specific response in a variety of situations. For example, in the Wolpe-Lang Fear Survey Schedule, the individual rates the degree of fear felt toward objects and events in the environment. This rating gives an indication of one's phobic behavior. Still other questionnaires, like the Reinforcement Surveys Schedule (Cautela and Kastenbaum 1967) and the Pleasant Events Schedule (MacPhillamy and Lewinsohn 1971), attempt to determine the number and type of reinforcing events in an individual's life. These questionnaires aid in determining what reinforcers may be used in modification procedures.

The second major type of verbal report is **self-monitoring** (Ciminero, Nelson, and Lipinski 1977). In self-monitoring, individuals and behavior therapists first clearly define the target behavior; then individuals observe their own behavior, keeping a record of the frequency, duration, or intensity of their responses. They also note the situations in which the behavior occurs and the consequences of the responses. For example, individuals with pervasive anxiety would keep a daily record of their anxiety

Reactivity in self-monitoring: monitoring of the target behavior may in itself modify the behavior

level in different situations. An individual with unacceptable sexual impulses would be asked to count them and describe the stimulus situations that elicit them.

Besides being used to track behavior in the natural environment, self-monitoring is also used in conjunction with other assessment procedures or in treatment analogues. For example, during assessment of deviant sexual behavior an individual may observe or imagine erotic stimuli related to various sexual preferences and estimate the degree of sexual arousal in a laboratory setting while physiological indices of sexual arousal are being monitored. Or an individual receiving behavior therapy for fear of flying could be asked to imagine various scenes related to flying while self-monitoring signs of tension and reporting these signs to the therapist.

Self-monitoring presents several problems. A major problem is that the responses that are monitored are often unobservable, a situation that creates difficulties in determining the reliability and the validity of the assessment procedure. If the self-monitored behavior is an observable response such as smoking, for example, other individuals can help establish reliability. But if the behavior is not observable, the procedure has all the difficulty associated with introspective reports. A second major problem is that self-monitoring procedures are often reactive (Ciminero, Nelson, and Lipinski 1977). When an individual observes a targeted response, the frequency, duration, and intensity of that response may change as a function of the individual's observation of his or her own behavior. An example of reactivity in self-monitoring is demonstrated in a study by Lipinski and Nelson (1974), who found that self-monitoring of face-touching reduced this behavior. If a target behavior is reactive to self-monitoring, there may be a therapeutic effect, but accurate assessment is difficult.

Behavioral Observation

The most frequently used method of behavioral assessment is **behavioral observation.** For behavioral observation to be successful, the response or responses to be observed must be clearly defined, the observers must be trained in observation techniques, and "calibrating observers" must be

scientific approaches to the study of abnormal behavior

Table 5-7 Response Code for Studying Children in a Classroom

Symbols	Classes	Class definitions
X	Gross motor behaviors	Getting out of seat; standing up; running; hopping; skipping; jumping; walking around; rocking in chair; disruptive movement without noise; moves chair to neighbor; kneels on chair.
N	Disruptive noise	Tapping pencil or other objects; clapping; tapping feet; rattling or tearing paper; throwing book on desk; slamming desk. (Be conservative, only rate if could hear noise when eyes closed. Do not include accidental dropping of objects or if noise made while performing X above.)
∧	Disturbing others directly	Grabbing objects or work; knocking neighbor's books off desk; destroying another's property; pushing with desk.
⟶	Aggression (contact)	Hitting, kicking; shoving; pinching; slapping; striking with object; throwing object at another person; poking with object; biting; pulling hair.
⌐	Orienting responses	Turning head or head and body to look at another person; showing objects to another child; orienting toward another child. (Must be of 4 sec. duration, not rated unless seated; or more than 90° using the desk as a reference.)
V	Verbalizations	Carrying on conversations with other children when it is not permitted. Answers teacher without raising hand or without being called on; making comments or calling out remarks when no question has been asked; calling teacher's name to get her attention; crying; screaming; singing; whistling; laughing loudly; coughing or blowing loudly. (May be directed to teacher or children.)
/ /	Other tasks	Ignores teacher's question or command; does something different from that directed to do; includes minor motor behavior such as playing with pencil eraser when supposed to be writing; coloring while the record is on; doing spelling during arithmetic lesson; playing with objects; eating; chewing gum. *The child involves himself in a task that is not appropriate.*
—	Relevant behavior	Time on task; e.g., answers question, looking at teacher when she is talking; raises hand; writing assignment. (Must include whole 20-sec. interval except for orienting responses of less than 4-sec. duration.)

used to determine the reliability of the procedure. Observers may be behavior therapists, peers, family members, or almost anyone who is willing to help and who can be taught to observe and record behavior. When more than one target response is to be observed, the training of the observers must be meticulous because coding systems must be used to allow the recording of the various behaviors as they occur. Table 5–7 gives an example of such a coding system.

Monitoring of responses may be continuous, or *time sampling techniques,* such as observing for five minutes out of each hour the disruptive behavior of a child in a classroom, may be used. Another useful tool, the observation checklist (the Timed Behavioral Checklist for Performance Anxiety—Paul 1966), can be used in monitoring in-

dividuals with speech anxiety. This checklist is shown in Figure 5–4.

Directly monitoring an individual's behavior in the natural environment seems accurate but poses three major problems (Nay 1977). First, the observer's presence may contaminate the behavioral sample. For instance, a family may not behave as they normally would in the home if observers are present (although they apparently often do). Second, the natural environment may have to be restricted in some way if the assessment is to be accurate. For example, while it may be impossible to observe a group of teenagers while they are playing records, prohibiting the music would greatly distort the environment in which subjects are being observed. Third,

Problems of observing behavior in the natural environment

Behavior observed	Time period									
	1	2	3	4	5	6	7	8	Σ
1. Paces									
2. Sways									
3. Shuffles feet									
4. Knees tremble									
5. Extraneous arm and hand movement (swings, scratches, etc.)									
6. Arms rigid									
7. Hands restrained (in pockets behind back, clasped)									
8. Hands tremor									
9. No eye contact									
10. Face muscles tense (drawn, tics, grimaces)									
11. Face "deadpan"									
12. Face pale									
13. Face flushed (blushes)									
14. Moistens lips									
15. Swallows									
16. Clears throat									
17. Breathes heavily									
18. Perspires (face, hands, armpits)									
19. Voice quivers									
20. Speech blocks or stammers									

Figure 5–4 Timed behavioral checklist for performance anxiety.

Behavior can often be more easily observed in a simulated environment

direct observation in the natural environment may be quite costly and impractical for the practicing behavior therapist.

One solution to this problem is to use analogue situations. The *assessment analogue* is an attempt to construct a situation as similar to real life as possible, yet still allow the behavior therapist to accurately assess the individual's target behavior. A real advantage of observation in simulated environments is that one-way mirrors, recording devices such as audio and video tapes, and other equipment can be readily used.

An excellent example of the use of **behavior analogues** is the Behavior Avoidance Test or BAT. If a therapist wished to observe an individual who reported a fear of snakes, he could place the individual in a room with a harmless snake and ask the individual to approach the snake. The therapist could then observe how close the individual came to the snake and note various behavioral indications of fear. If the individual does not approach or handle the snake, trembles, expresses fear, and shows other indices of fear, the observer can conclude that the individual has a snake phobia, and has some indication of the severity of the problem. Other phobias and fears can be assessed in a similar manner by the BAT.

Another example of analogue assessment is the determination of obedience in a child. A therapist who wanted to observe how a child obeys a parent could place child and parent in a room and observe them through a one-way mirror. The therapist could then give the parent a list of commands to relay to the child and observe how often the child complied with the commands. Almost any behavior can be assessed with a behavioral analogue. A therapist who needed to assess an individual's social skills could contrive a situation

scientific approaches to the study of abnormal behavior

in which the client had to interact with another individual and then observe the client's behavior to determine proficiency in getting acquainted, carrying on a conversation, and similar social skills.

Behavioral observations present a number of problems. Research has demonstrated that the reliability of the observers may decrease without continuous monitoring (Reid 1970). Consequently, calibrating observers have to make periodic reliability checks to counter this effect. Moreover, the behavioral sample itself presents a problem. In naturalistic observations, the observer's presence may distort the situation so much that the sample of behavior is no longer valid. On the other hand, in analogue assessment there is always the problem of obtaining a behavior sample that is truly representative of the behavior as it occurs in the natural environment.

In behavioral observation, the demand characteristics of the situation also create a perplexing problem (Bernstein 1973). That is, the person being observed may behave as he assumes the behavior therapist expects him to behave rather than as he actually behaves in his environment. For example, Bernstein found that in a behavioral assessment task evaluating fear of rodents, individuals who were supposedly afraid of these animals would pick up rats when instructed to do so and put them in cages before starting the behavior avoidance test. However, the same subjects showed fear and avoidance during the behavioral test. Are such individuals really afraid of rats or are they behaving as they think they are expected to behave in the situation? An accurate behavioral assessment must include controls for demand characteristics.

Another problem in behavioral assessment is the fact that most assessment situations are designed for a particular individual; therefore, norms are not always available, and standardization of procedure is difficult to achieve. These and other difficulties often make behavioral assessment as unreliable as personality assessment.

Physiological Indices

Measuring physiological responses as a method of clinical assessment is a relatively new procedure. In essence, the purpose of **physiological assessment** is the quantification of physiological events as they are related to psychological variables (Kallman and Feuerstein 1977). For example, a clinician interested in assessing anxiety in social interactions could not only take a subjective report and observe the behavior, but also monitor the individual's skin resistance, heart rate, or other physiological responses indicating arousal of the autonomic nervous system. Because of technological advancement in electronic monitoring devices for biological events, the assessment of physiological responses has become more popular. Table 5–8 lists some of the biological signals most frequently used in behavior assessment.

In some cases, physiological indices are crucial. For example, a therapist who is interested in assessing an individual's sexual preferences must know what stimulus cues cause sexual arousal. Consequently, in the assessment analog the individual may watch slides of heterosexual, homosexual, pedophiliac, and other sexual cues in a darkened chamber and estimate verbally his sexual arousal. In males, a strain gauge (plethysiometer) may also be attached to the penis to measure the individual's erection in response to certain types of stimuli. In females, a photoplethysiometer may be used to measure vaginal lubrication in response to specific stimuli. This type of assessment provides the therapist with both verbal and physiological indices of sexual preference.

Since many biological signals can be converted into radio waves and transmitted to a centrally located receiver, an assessment of the individual's physiological reactivity to various situations in the natural environment can be obtained. A response such as heart rate can be monitored while the individual actually performs in familiar surroundings.

A case reported by Kallman and Feuerstein (1977) illustrates the usefulness of assessing physiological responses in clinical cases. The client was a 45-year-old male with chronic anxiety. Initially, he complained of severe reactions to sudden noises that prevented him from driving a car or working regularly at his job in construction.

The observer's presence may distort the situation and weaken the validity of the behavior sample

Demand characteristics may also affect validity

Physiological indices are valuable in assessing sexual preferences

Table 5-8 Characteristics of Biological Response Systems and Appropriate Psychophysiological Instrumentation

Response system	Psychophysiological response	Physiological basis of response
Somatic	Electromyogram (EMG)	Muscle action potentials
Cardiovascular	Electrocardiogram (EKG)	Action potentials of cardiac muscle during contraction
	Blood Pressure (BP)	Systolic: Force of blood leaving the heart
		Diastolic: Residual pressure in the vascular system
	Blood Volume (BV)	Tonic level of blood in the tissue
	Blood Volume Pulse (BVP)	Phasic level of blood with each cardiac contraction
Electrodermal	Skin Resistance Level (SRL) and Response (SRR)	Source of signal is uncertain; current theories favor sweat gland activity
	Skin Conductance Level (SCL) and Response (SCR)	Reciprocal of SRR and SRL
	Skin Potential Response (SPR)	Unclear; probably represents changes in membrane potentials
Central nervous system	Electroencephalogram (EEG)	Electrical activity of cortical neurons
	Average Evoked Response (AER)	Same as EEG in response to identifiable stimulus
	Contingent Negative Variation (CNV)	Same as EEG, appears during preparatory responses
Gastric	Stomach motility	Peristaltic movement of stomach
	Stomach pH	Level of acidity of stomach contents
Specialized responses	Sexual Male (penile circumference)	Engorgement of penis with blood
	Female (vaginal blood volume or pulse)	Engorgement of vagina with blood
	Temperature	Probably vasomotor and sweat gland activity
	Respiration	Inhalation and exhalation of air

However, when he was hospitalized, the problem appeared to be more global. The information from an intake interview suggested that the client's problem dated to a work incident involving an explosion and the death of a friend that had occurred twenty years before the assessment. Specific stimuli evoking the anxiety could not be identified from the client's response to the Fear Survey Schedule because he ranked all items very fearful. Originally, the global nature of the client's problem suggested a *free-floating* or *pervasive anxiety reaction,* a difficult disorder to modify.

In the initial assessment the client watched numerous audiotaped scenes depicting specific events or objects in the environment, such as blood, automobiles, sports, and other common events, as well as social interaction with family and peers. The client was then asked to rate the level of anxiety associated with each scene on a scale from one to ten, with ten indicating maximum anxiety. In addition, his blood pressure, respiration, and heart rate were measured. From this initial assessment it appeared that three types of stimuli evoked an anxiety response. The phobic stimuli were (1) blood, (2) being confined in a small room, and (3) exposure to noises. As Figure 5–5 shows, the individual's heart rate increased greatly when these stimuli were presented.

scientific approaches to the study of abnormal behavior

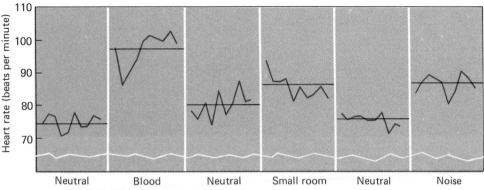

Figure 5–5 Beat-by-beat heart-rate activity in a client with multiple phobias.

As is quite common in behavioral assessment, these initial results were used to design a specific assessment program for this individual. In this next phase of assessment, behavioral avoidance tests were developed for each stimuli. For the blood stimulus the client was asked to stand in a room with a blood-stained (actually vegetable-dyed) sheet. For the fear of the small room, the subject was asked to stay in a three foot by three foot closet lit by a 75-watt overhead bulb. In the noise task, the client listened to a tape of random noise presented at a fixed volume. The time the individual spent in the presence of each of these stimuli was used as an inverse measure of fear. After each behavioral test, the client was also asked to rate his level of anxiety in these situations on a scale of one to ten. Heart rate was also monitored. As shown in Figure 5–6, this subject had a highly stable response pattern across sessions. He was clearly most fearful of the blood stimulus, loud noise being intermediate, and small rooms being the least distressing stimuli.

The value of using all three channels of assessment, particularly the psychophysiological assessment, in this case is clear. This person had been suffering from severe anxiety for twenty years without getting any professional help. He was reluctant to discuss his past experiences and lied about his functioning from the time of the war incident to his hospital admission. His avoidance of the fearful stimuli was so complete that verbal reports and self-rating devices were of little use in identifying the relevant stimuli. Use of all three channels of measurement led to the identification of specific stimulus events that could be used in designing a treatment program and avoided

the mistake of labeling this individual as a pervasive or free-floating anxiety case, when in fact he had multiple phobias. This finding is important, since even multiple phobias are much easier to modify than pervasive anxiety reactions (anxiety neuroses).

Unfortunately, assessing all three channels of behavior is not always possible. For example, very little is known about the physiological characteristics of some response systems, such as social behavior or cognition. Consequently, physiological assessment of these behavioral systems is not presently possible. Still, as our knowledge of the physiological correlates of behavior advances, the precision of our clinical assessment of such behaviors will be greatly enhanced.

Ethical Issues in Personality and Behavioral Assessment

Personality and behavioral assessment raise a number of ethical issues, particularly with regard to human rights and the invasion of privacy. Psychological tests are used for a number of purposes, such as screening individuals for employment, predicting job performance, and assessing behavior for clinical purposes. The question is how much information should employers, government, law enforcement agents, or even clinicians be allowed to obtain about an individual? The answer to this question is that the examiner is entitled only to information that is directly relevant to the presenting problem. If an individual is applying for a job as a clerk, the employer is entitled to know about his clerical skills but not about his

Behavioral avoidance tests were used to measure fear

Danger of invasion of privacy

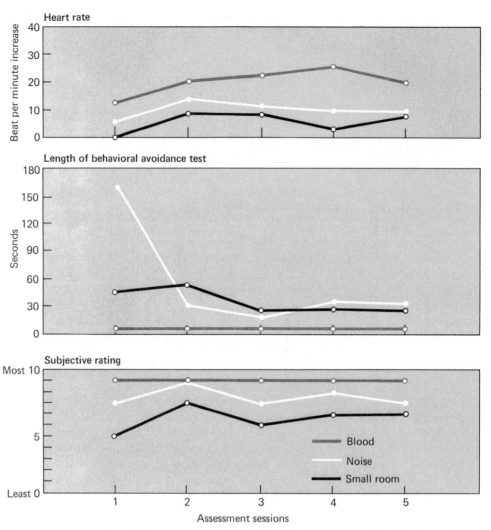

Figure 5–6 Comparison of three response patterns (physiological, behavioral, and self-report) in a client with multiple phobias.

Doubtful validity of lie-detector results

relationship with his mother. Even in the clinical context, therapists should restrict themselves to aspects of the individual's life that directly relate to the problem behavior. For example, intensive inquiry into an individual's sex life is probably not legitimate if the individual has a presenting problem of stuttering (Morganstern 1976).

A similar questionable practice is predicting or describing with assessment instruments that are not reliable or that do not produce valid results. An excellent example of this kind of practice is the use of the so-called "lie detector" test to determine the truthfulness of an individual's replies. The lie detector test is based on an individual's galvanic skin responses (GSR), respiration, and heart rate as the individual answers certain questions. As Lykken (1974) has noted, the validity of this procedure is highly debatable even though those who use the device, including law enforcement agencies, believe it is highly accurate. Unfortunately, conclusions about an individual's innocence or guilt that are drawn from this procedure may have a profound impact on his or her life. Moreover, the lie detector is a psychological test but most examiners have had little or no training in test construction, test evaluation, or psychophysiology. The situation is even more grotesque when this device is used as a method of screening individuals for employment.

scientific approaches to the study of abnormal behavior

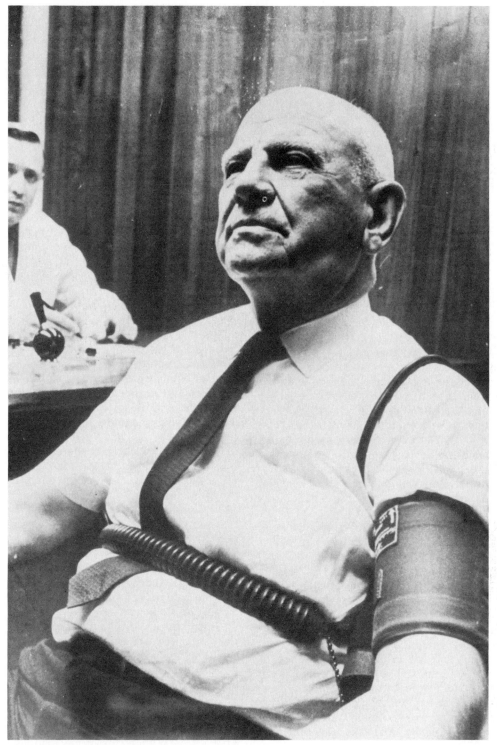

The lie detector test is based on the individual's galvanic skin responses, respiration, and heart rate as certain questions are answered.

A similar problem is the confidentiality of records. The use of computers for personality tests is an example. The potential for invasion of privacy grows when computers are used for large-scale storage and rapid retrieval. Obviously, this situation requires special attention to insure that the confidentiality of these records is not compromised.

Summary

The measurement of behavior is a necessary prerequisite for describing, explaining, predicting, and controlling abnormal behavior. To be accurate, measuring instruments must be reliable and valid. The three major types of reliability are internal consistency, stability over time, and agreement among raters. The four types of validity are concurrent, construct, predictive, and content validity. If the purpose of psychological measurement is to compare how the examinee performs relative to other members of the population, norms must be established. Moreover, the administration of assessment techniques must be standardized.

There are two major approaches to the measurement of behavior: personality assessment and behavioral assessment. Personality assessment developed from psychodynamic and trait theories of behavior. The major assumption of this approach is that individuals have stable traits that will be manifested in a variety of situations. Because of this assumption, stimulus factors are given a relatively minor role in assessment. The major goals of personality assessment are prediction and classification of behavior. Behavior is evaluated on only one or two occasions, and the emphasis is on the individual's verbal report. There are four major types of personality assessment procedures: interviews, rating scales, self-report inventories, and projective tests. The interview is usually centered around the theoretical assumptions of the clinician. Some attempt is made to determine the existence of unconscious conflicts or underlying traits. Rating scales are usually attempts to determine the presence or absence of certain personality traits or symptoms.

Objective tests take the form of self-report inventories, which are similar to standardized interviews. The individual is asked specific questions and responds with one of a fixed number of alternative responses, such as "True," "False," or "Do not know." One type of personality test relies on the content of the item to predict how individuals will behave or how they should be classified. The second type of personality test uses the criterion group method in which response patterns of a given individual are compared to the response patterns of certain abnormal groups. The Minnesota Multiphasic Personality Inventory is an example of such a test. Various response sets such as social desirability often bias or contaminate objective personality tests.

In projective techniques the individual is presented with ambiguous stimuli, such as ink blots, and requested to make a response. Presumably, the individual will project his or her unconscious conflicts onto the stimulus materials. The two most popular projective techniques are the Thematic Apperception Test and the Rorschach Inkblot Test. Because of the nature of these techniques, determining reliability and validity is difficult. They are particularly susceptible to illusory correlations, which occur when two clinicians agree about a personality description or a behavior prediction because of associative norms. The accuracy of such descriptions and predictions is highly questionable.

The major purpose of behavioral assessment is to devise and assess treatment programs. In behavioral assessment, responses are assumed to be functions of situational variables; therefore, attempts are made to manipulate stimulus situations, observe the effect on given responses, and note the consequences of the behavior. The major technique in behavioral assessment is the observation of behavior by trained observers. This may occur in a natural environment or in an assessment analogue. Usually, responses are described in terms of their frequency, duration, and intensity. The stimulus conditions that evoke, reinforce, or set the occasion for occurrence of target responses are also assessed.

Other techniques of behavioral assessment include behavioral interviews, subjective indices, and the monitoring of physiological responses. Behavioral interviewing emphasizes an assessment of what stimuli elicit certain behavior and what the consequences of the response pattern are. The usual purpose of the behavioral interview is to obtain enough information to devise an assessment program. Subjective indices of behavior consist of questionnaires and self-monitoring techniques in which the individual observes his or her own behavior. The monitoring of physiological functions provides clues to such responses as fear or sexual arousal.

Because of the risk of invading privacy and violating human rights, psychological assessment of individuals must be restricted to aspects of behavior that are relevant to the presenting problem. The confidentiality of reports must be strictly maintained.

Key Concepts

behavior
    analogues

behavioral
    assessment

behavioral
    interviews

behavioral
    observation

behavioral
    questionnaires

concurrent
    validity

construct validity

content validity

deviation IQ

intelligence
    quotients

intelligence tests

interview

norms

physiological
    assessment

predictive validity

projective
    techniques

rating scales

reliability

self-monitoring

self-report
    inventories

standardization

validity

Review Questions

1. What is the difference between reliability and validity?

2. What may happen when a population segment is given a test based on norms that are not representative of that population segment?

3. What are two kinds of error variables that could contaminate the results of an assessment of human behavior?

4. What are the four main methods of assessing personality?

5. What is the main difference between the approaches of the Stanford-Binet and the Wechsler intelligence tests?

6. What is the main assumption made in behavioral assessment?

7. What are the four main methods of obtaining information for behavioral assessment?

8. What are two of the ethical issues that arise in the assessment of personality or behavior?

psychodynamic, humanistic, and medical therapies 6

Key Topics

Four major criteria for evaluating treatment methods

Four basic techniques of psychoanalysis

Three goals of psychoanalysis

Difference between Jungian analysis and Freudian psychoanalysis

Major tenets of Adlerian therapy

Sullivan's explanation of abnormal behavior

Transactional analysis and its concept of abnormal behavior

Goals of family therapy

Four major assumptions of the humanistic-existential therapies

Goals of client-centered therapy

Aims of Gestalt therapy

Original aim of humanistic group therapy

Consequences of lobotomy

Effects of shock therapy

Four main types of chemotherapy

Ethical issues in hospitalizing people with abnormal behavior

The major responsibility for changing people's behavior has shifted in the last century from the clergy, family physicians, or friends to the professional clinicians (therapists or counselors). Psychotherapy is now a business—one in which a therapist and a client actually enter into a contract that commits both to changing the client's distressing or problematical behavior. One large group of therapists pay a great deal of attention to current values and philosophies and then try to either restructure the client's personality or character accordingly or help the client find meaning or become self-actualized. Others, including behavior therapists, avoid questions of value and philosophy, but work instead to change specific behavior problems. All therapists, regardless of their orientation, try to help clients gain more control over their lives.

Each of the three approaches to therapy discussed in this chapter involves different assumptions about the nature of abnormal behavior, different therapeutic goals, and different methods of treatment. We shall therefore discuss each approach in a separate section. Clinicians using behavior therapy, which we shall discuss in Chapter 7, are less likely to differ in their assumptions about the nature of abnormal behavior or in their goals. Chapter 7 will therefore focus on treatment techniques rather than theoretical stances.

A Variety of Therapists

Therapists are usually clinical psychologists, psychiatrists, or psychiatric social workers

The three major professional groups engaged in the modification of abnormal behavior are *clinical psychologists, psychiatrists,* and *psychiatric social workers.* Clinical psychologists specialize in experimental and clinical analysis and modification of abnormal behavior. They usually study for four to six years in graduate school, which includes a year of internship in a medical school, community mental health center, or hospital. Psychiatrists are physicians who specialize in psychiatry by taking a residency of three to four years at a medical school or other medical facility. Psychiatric social workers achieve a master's degree in social work (MSW) and specialize in casework and treatment of abnormal behavior. A major adjunct profession is *psychiatric nursing.* Psychiatric nurses are nurses, many of whom have a master's degree in psychiatric nursing, who specialize in the care of abnormally behaving people.

In recent years a number of other professionals, primarily from education, have entered the mental health field. These include school psychologists, counseling psychologists, vocational counselors, rehabilitation counselors, guidance counselors, pastoral counselors, sex therapists, marital therapists, and a number of other types of counselors, therapists, and paraprofessionals. School counselors and school psychologists may receive their formal training in psychology, education, or sometimes a combination of both. Generally, these therapists are trained to handle specific problems often found in normal individuals. The other therapists vary considerably in their qualifications.

Evaluating Techniques of Behavior Change

Techniques for behavior change have developed in various branches of philosophy, medicine, and psychology. As a result, the types of psychotherapy available today are numerous (see Table 6–1). The range of these approaches extends from the reasonable to the ludicrous. Thus, a major endeavor in the science of abnormal psychology is the appraising and evaluating of therapeutic approaches and methods. This is not a particularly easy task, since therapeutic goals may vary widely from one form of treatment to another. Therapeutic methods can be evaluated by either a rational or an empirical method. While a rational appraisal of these approaches may have its merits, we believe that an empirical evaluation of these techniques must be conducted to develop a science of abnormal behavior that will be effective in preventing, identifying, and eliminating problems in living.

Generally, treatment methods should be evaluated according to four major criteria (Adams and Calhoun 1974):

scientific approaches to the study of abnormal behavior

Table 6-1 Varieties of Psychotherapeutic Approaches

Supportive methods

1. Bibliotherapy
2. Color therapy
3. Conditioned-reflex therapy
4. Correction of physical defects
5. Dance therapy
6. Desensitization
7. Environmental manipulation
8. Hypnotherapy
9. Inspirational group therapy
10. Motivational procedures (such as reward and punishment)
11. Music therapy
12. Narcotherapy
13. Negative practice
14. Occupational therapy
15. Persuasion and reasoning
16. Physiotherapy
17. Placebos
18. Pressure and coercion
19. Progressive relaxation
20. Reassurance
21. Recreation
22. Reeducation
23. Religious approaches
24. Rest
25. Suggestion and advice
26. Selected types of group therapy
27. Verbal catharis and abreaction

Reconstructive methods

1. Adlerian individual psychology
2. Alexander's psychoanalytic therapy
3. Analytical group therapies
4. Art therapy
5. Classical psychoanalysis
6. Client centered therapy
7. Deutsch's sector analysis
8. Federn's ego psychology
9. Ferenczi's active methods
10. General semantics
11. Gestalt therapy
12. Herzberg's activity psychotherapy
13. Horney's approach
14. Hypnoanalysis
15. Jungian analytical psychology
16. Karpman's objective psychotherapy
17. Levy's relase therapy
18. Meyer's psychobiology
19. Mowrer's retraining approach
20. Narcoanalysis and narcosynthesis
21. Play therapies
22. Psychodrama
23. Puppetry psychotherapy
24. Rankian will therapy
25. Reich's character analysis
26. Rosen's direct analysis
27. Stekel's active analysis
28. Sullivan's interpersonal relationship therapy
29. Whitaker and Malone's experiential therapy

1. A treatment method should be *clearly defined* and described so that its evaluation is possible. Unfortunately, most psychotherapeutic methods do not meet even this minimal requirement.

2. It ought to be demonstrated that the method in question is more *effective* than no treatment, placebo, or competing treatment methods. Evaluation on this criterion requires not only administering the treatment and a competing treatment to random samples of the population for which the treatment was designed, but also establishing necessary control groups to account for factors such as placebo and spontaneous recovery. What is needed, then, is an *outcome* paradigm as opposed to a process paradigm, which investigates factors in behavior change during treatment. In an outcome paradigm, the question is how effective a given technique is for the majority of individuals with a specific disorder, irrespective of individual differences. If large individual differences occur and if the characteristics that are responsible for these differences can be identified, the use of the modification procedure can be restricted to the subpopulation for which it is most effective.

One technique may be very effective against one type of abnormal behavior, but relatively ineffective against others. For example, *systematic desensitization* is highly effective with phobias, but not particularly effective for treating personality disorders.

3. A technique should be efficient. Although a technique may be effective with a given pattern of abnormal behavior, it may be so complex, expensive, or time consuming that it is useless. A good example is classic psychoanalysis, in which the client is usually seen four or five times a week for three or four years: approximately 500 hours of treatment at $75 an hour. The cost of such treatment can total over $35,000.

To be evaluated positively a treatment method should be clearly defined, . . .

effective, . . .

and efficient . . .

To aggravate the problem further, psychoanalysis is a complex verbal interaction in which the client must have at least average intelligence, an adequate amount of education, and other qualifications—all of which tend to restrict the population for which this technique can be effective. Moreover, the therapist in psychoanalysis requires years of training. Obviously, this form of treatment is extremely limited, regardless of its effectiveness, by its high cost and restricted population, as well as the paucity of qualified personnel.

If a treatment is fairly simple and effective, it can be taught to teachers, parents, technicians, and other individuals who do not have extensive backgrounds in psychology or medicine. The professional is then free to focus on assessing the problem, developing a treatment program, and teaching various behavioral engineers who can then execute the treatment. The ratio of individuals who can implement the treatment to the number who need the treatment is increased, and the procedure becomes available to a larger number of people.

and should not have unacceptable side effects

4. The *side effects* of the method should be within acceptable limits. While side effects have been emphasized in chemotherapy, they have often been neglected in psychological treatment techniques. These side effects do exist, however, and are well documented in the literature. For example, an individual treated by aversion therapy for a fetish may become impotent with his wife because he was able to engage in heterosexual intercourse only by using deviant sexual fantasies. Similarly, if an individual is taught to be more assertive, this new social skill may actually disrupt relationships with others who prefer that the client be more modest.

Emphasis on unconscious processes and client-therapist relationship

Psychodynamic Approaches

Psychodynamic approaches to personality change have developed largely from the psychoanalytic theory of Sigmund Freud. While these theories differ in terms of what they view as the critical incidents that produce psychopathology in the individual and, in some cases, in the techniques for handling abnormal behavior, they have many similarities. *Psychodynamic theories* assume that patterns of abnormal behavior are formed early in childhood, although they may not be manifest for many years. These abnormalities are assumed to involve the whole individual and are evident, often in subtle ways, in most of the individual's personal and social activities. Consequently, the goal of psychodynamic therapies is usually a restructuring of the personality.

These theories also assume that unconscious processes are important in the production of behavior patterns or symptoms. They further assume that the relationship between the client and the therapist is crucial and that it may be, by itself, a sufficient condition for behavior change. Finally, all of these theories stress the necessity for the client to develop insight into his or her problems as a prerequisite for eliminating abnormal patterns of behavior.

Psychoanalysis

Freud believed that *early childhood experiences* common to all individuals are crucial in the development of psychopathology. If these early experiences are difficult for the individual, they can cause conflict and thus evoke anxiety. The major defense mechanism against this anxiety is repression—the removal of the conflict from conscious awareness to the unconscious, a process that may reduce anxiety but not completely eliminate it. Because Freud viewed almost any pleasant activity as sexual, he believed that unconscious conflicts originate in the difficulties encountered during the *oral, anal,* or *phallic* stages of infant sexuality. Since the conflicts are unconscious, the individual is unable to resolve the problem and, thus, is susceptible

A traditional psychoanalytic therapy session.

to expressing the conflicts through disturbing symptoms or in seemingly meaningless disguises, such as dreams, fantasies, or slips of the tongue.

To reduce the anxiety produced by unconscious conflicts, the individual develops other ego-defense mechanisms, which may also manifest themselves in symptoms. In the psychoanalytic framework, treatment techniques that eliminate symptoms are undesirable because they do nothing to resolve the basic conflicts that are assumed to underlie the symptoms. If the basic conflicts are not resolved, the psychoanalyst assumes other symptoms will develop in some cases. This process is called **symptom substitution**.

In the traditional form of **psychoanalysis** the patient reclines on a couch while the therapist (the psychoanalyst) sits behind.

The therapist has at his or her disposal four basic techniques for uncovering the patient's unconscious material: free association, dream interpretation, analysis of resistance, and analysis of transference.

The principal method is **free association**, in which the "basic rule" is that the patient must say anything that comes to mind, no matter how personal, painful, or trivial it appears, on the theory that such apparently aimless mental wandering will facilitate the recall of repressed material or give clues to the nature of unconscious material. The therapist, or psychoanalyst, can then deduce the symbolic meanings from these verbalizations and interpret the patient's remarks. Through interpretation, the analyst shows the client the possible connection between behavior and unconscious material.

The psychoanalyst uses free association, dream interpretation, analysis of resistance, and analysis of transference

box 6-1
An Example of
Psychoanalytic
Therapy

The following example of free association demonstrates how a female patient of thirty-eight with a phobic disorder gains an understanding of certain unconscious conflicts.

Patient   So I started walking, and walking, and decided to go behind the museum and walk through Central Park. So I walked and went through a back field and felt very excited and wonderful. I saw a park bench next to a clump of bushes and sat down. There was a rustle behind me and I got frightened. I thought of men concealing themselves in the bushes. I thought of the sex perverts I read about in Central Park. I wondered if there was someone behind me exposing himself. The idea is repulsive, but exciting too. I think of father now and feel excited. I think of an erect penis. This is connected with my father. There is something about this pushing in my mind. I don't know what it is, like on the border of my memory. (*Pause.*)

Therapist   Mm hmm. (*Pause.*) On the border of your memory?

Patient   (*The patient breathes rapidly and seems to be under great tension.*) As a little girl, I slept with my father. I get a funny feeling. I get a funny feeling over my skin, tingly-like. It's a strange feeling, like a blindness, like not seeing something. My mind blurs and spreads over anything I look at. I've had this feeling off and on since I walked in the park. My mind seems to blank off like I can't think or absorb anything. [*This sounds like a manifestation of repression, with inhibition of intellectual functioning, perhaps as a way of coping with the anxiety produced by a return of the repressed.*]

Therapist   The blurring of your mind may be a way of pushing something out you don't want there. [*Interpreting her symptoms as resistance.*]

Patient   I just thought of something. When father died, he was nude. I looked at him, but I couldn't see anything, I couldn't think clearly. I was brought up not to be aware of the difference between a man and a woman. I feared my father, and yet I loved him. I slept with him when I was very little, on Saturdays and Sundays. A wonderful sense of warmth and security. There was nothing warmer or more secure. A lot of pleasure. I tingle all over now. It was a wonderful holiday when I was allowed to sleep with father. I can't seem to remember anything now. There's a blur in my mind. I feel tense and afraid.

Therapist   That blur contaminates your life. You are afraid of something or afraid of remembering something. [*Focusing on her resistance.*]

Patient   Yes, yes, but I can't. How can I? How can I?

Therapist   What comes to your mind?

Patient   Sunday I got stomach pains. I was depressed and frightened. I started crying. I wanted to hold onto mother. What is the use of becoming aware of needs if you can't satisfy them. I had a dream that night. A group of army officers in my sister's room. I felt jealous. They weren't interested in me. Then I was on the water. One man was walking on water with no legs. He walked confidently. I asked him where his legs were, and he said that when he had legs he felt strong and masculine. Then I see flowers and I feel lost. Then I am on a ruined street. I see an old horse, emaciated, wating to be slaughtered. I'm horrified, sick, upset. I have flowers, but everybody criticizes them. I felt they weren't good. And that's all.

Therapist   What do you associate to the dream?

Patient   I felt the officers kissed my sister and mother and not me. I feel father gave my sister and mother everything and not me. I wanted to look into the room where the officers were with my sister, but my mother wouldn't let me. I was mad. I remember a part of the dream where I saw condoms in a box. I felt my sister could have it and not I. I feel deprived and helpless, like a mutilated person. That must be me walking on the water. I walk, but like a cripple. I want to be strong and not weak. Men are strong. My father wouldn't let me grow up. My sister has a husband and I don't have one. She has everything. I have nothing. Not anything that is worth while. What I have is not much. I always wanted to be strong. I used to fantasize being a boy and having a penis. I suppose the flowers in the dream are my femininity. I put little value on myself. I realize now how bitter I feel toward father for not devoting himself to me. [*The patient goes on to correlate her incestuous wishes, her castration fears, and her penis envy.*]

The second major technique in psychoanalysis is **dream interpretation**. According to Freud, dreams are an important source of clues to the unconscious processes because people lower their defense mechanisms when asleep and allow unconscious material to surface in dreams. This material is expressed in symbols, which the analyst must interpret. For example, a long protruding object may represent a phallus, while a dark tunnel may represent a vagina. Dreams have both *manifest* content (the material the individual reports) and *latent* content (unconscious material being expressed in a disguised fashion in the dream symbols). Other seemingly trivial aspects of behavior, such as slips of the tongue, may also reveal unconscious material and may be interpreted in a similar way.

A third major technique is the analysis of **resistance**. As the client undergoes psychoanalysis and becomes increasingly aware of unconscious motivation, he or she begins to manifest resistance to change by using ego-defense mechanisms to avoid confronting certain memories or impulses. Resistance may show itself in a number of ways. The patient may be late for appointments, miss appointments, pick quarrels with the analyst, disrupt the session by subtle maneuvers such as telling jokes, discuss the analyst's fee, or engage in other such ploys to avoid the task at hand. By attending to these manifestations of resistance, the psychoanalyst may pick up clues to unconscious conflicts, which can then be interpreted for the client.

A fourth method is analysis of the **transference**. This technique emphasizes the relationship between the analyst and the client, and many psychoanalysts view it as a major means of producing personality change. During analysis, the client may develop either an extremely positive or an extremely negative reaction to the analyst. Such reactions are interpreted as a transference to the analyst of the client's childhood relationships with important people in his or her life, particularly parents. During this stage of treatment, called the *transference neurosis*, the client reenacts childhood conflicts, including dependency, anger, hostility, and other emotions that have been repressed. Working through the transference relationship allows the client to confront the emotional conflicts of childhood and to evaluate them realistically.

The goals of psychoanalysis are (1) to replace the unconscious with conscious motivation, (2) to eliminate personality conflicts generated during the infantile stages of sexual development, and (3) to overcome imbalances between the ego and the superego by strengthening the ego processes that deal with reality. These goals are to be achieved when, through the analyst's interpretation, the client gains insight into troublesome unconscious conflicts. The client can then eliminate or modify the ego's defense mechanisms and, in doing so, eliminate the symptoms produced by childhood conflicts. If treatment is successful, the final outcome is a restructuring of the client's personality.

Psychoanalytic goals: replace unconscious with conscious motivation, eliminate infantile sexual conflicts, strengthen ego processes

Neo-Freudians and Other Psychodynamic Approaches

Only a few psychodynamic therapists practice orthodox psychoanalysis. While retaining the Freudian vocabulary, the majority practice a modified form of psychoanalysis based partly on Freud's theories and partly on those of his followers who deviated from classic psychoanalysis. Through their efforts, psychoanalysis has been modified in a number of ways, in terms of both theoretical issues and the modification of unwieldy and time-consuming methods of treatment. While the role of unconscious processes, the developmental aspect of abnormal behavior, the production of insight through interpretation, and the analysis of the relationship between therapist and client are still vital concerns in all these approaches, the major theoretical difference appears to be the view of what constitutes the significant factor for the development of psychopathology. Most theorists have differed with Freud on the role of early infantile sexuality as the major causal factor in neuroses and have emphasized other factors.

One of the best known of these neo-Freudians was Carl Jung (1875–1961). In his system, called **analytic psychology**, Jung differed sharply with Freud on several basic theoretical issues. Freud had defined *libido* as sexual energy; Jung defined it as undifferentiated energy, a universal life force. Freud believed that human behavior was caused by unconscious forces set in motion early in childhood; Jung stressed both conscious and unconscious motivation, and believed that human behavior resulted partly from events in the individual's past, partly from events in the evolutionary past of the human species, and partly from aims or goals. Freud divided the human psyche into three structures—id, ego, and super-ego; Jung divided it into three systems—*ego* (conscious mind), *personal unconscious* (akin to Freud's preconscious), and *collective unconscious,* or objective psyche.

Jung's three systems—ego, personal unconscious, collective unconscious

Jung believed that the personal unconscious contained *complexes*—constellations of thoughts, feelings, images, and meanings—and that the collective unconscious contained **archetypes**—universal and primordial ideas or images so basic that they find expression in every culture. These archetypes include, for example, the mother, the child, the hero, the demon, the earth mother, the wise old man, and God. Jung's belief in the universality of archetypes came out of a lifelong study of the human imagination in such areas as art, ritual, religion, mythology, alchemy, astrology, and anthropology. He explained archetypes as products of repeated experiences occurring throughout the evolution of humankind and added that the collective unconscious has the capability of reviving experiences from the distant past.

Persona, anima, animus, and shadow—the Jungian personality systems

Some archetypes, according to Jung, have evolved into systems of personality. These include the *persona*, the *anima*, the *animus*, and the *shadow*. The persona is the mask a person adopts in response to social demands and expectations, the apparent self one presents to others in the attempt to manage the impressions one makes on them. The anima is the feminine side of the male, and the animus is the masculine side of the female. The shadow is the side of the personality that is hidden from the view of others and that contains one's animal instincts.

Origin of abnormal behavior in neglect of the unconscious

Jung also described two attitudes, *extraversion* and *introversion*, that he believed were present in every personality.

Jung adapted therapy to the client

One or the other may be dominant and conscious, while the other is subordinate and unconscious. He went on to describe four functions, *thinking, feeling, sensing,* and *intuiting,* which develop to different degrees in all of us.

Abnormal behavior, in Jung's view, resulted from neglect of the unconscious regions in the mind, which react to such neglect by distorting our conscious rational processes, producing delusions, phobias, and other similar symptoms. Other factors include the failure to achieve a compromise between the demands of the collective unconscious and the realities of the external world, or between such polarities of the personality as extraversion and introversion.

Because Jung was interested more in a purposive, goal-seeking interpretation of behavior than in its causes, his therapy emphasized current difficulties and future strivings rather than past unconscious sources of present behavior. Jung, furthermore, did not limit himself to the life purposes of specific individuals but further hypothesized collective life purposes, related to the collective unconscious. He also made free association secondary to therapist-directed conversation and contended that the therapist's interpretations should vary with the personality type of the patient: introverts should receive more extensive and detailed interpretations of dynamic causes while extroverts would be satisfied with more practical suggestions for behavior changes.

Jung's mysticism has been a major stumbling block to general acceptance of his theories. Many psychologists have found such concepts as the collective unconscious and collective life purposes especially vague and untestable. Consequently, Jungian psychology has not attracted many followers in the United States, although Jung has influenced the work of Karen Horney, Erich Fromm, and Fritz Perls, among others.

Alfred Adler (1870–1937) also believed that Freud had greatly overestimated the role of biological and sexual drives as determinants of human behavior (Adler 1964). He contended that the social context within which an individual lives can be more important in determining behavior. He also argued that sexuality is merely an available tool for individuals in their struggle for power over others, the real determiner of human behavior.

Because Adler saw individuals as constantly striving toward *goals* and seeking *power, self-actualization*, and *fulfillment*, he believed that human functioning could best be interpreted in terms of aims and goals, rather than the infantile sexual past. If individuals do not realize their ideals of superiority or attain their goals, which indeed may be grossly distorted in disturbed individuals, they develop inferiority complexes. Consequently, their styles of life or their active adjustments to the social milieu may be maladaptive. The major aim of the Adlerian therapist is to understand the client's particular *life style* or *life plan* so that the client may be re-educated or redirected toward healthier patterns and goals. Like Jung, Adler focused on the present and the future rather than the past. Past events were to be considered only when they helped the client develop insight into present problems. He also did away with the couch and substituted face-to-face, therapist-directed interviews. Moreover, he de-emphasized transference in favor of the social relation between therapist and client on the theory that disturbed individuals interpret life in a way that stops short of deep and positive feelings for others.

A number of psychodynamic theories emphasize socialization and the social context of behavior as opposed to instinctual sexual drives. This approach, broadly described as ego psychology, stresses the ego functions, such as memory, judgment, perception, and planning instead of dwelling on the id and unconscious processes.

One of the foremost ego theorists was Harry Stack Sullivan (1892–1949), who thought that abnormal behavior stemmed from disturbed interpersonal relationships (Sullivan, 1953). Sullivan stressed the basic conflict that occurs between individuals and their environment and argued that anxiety and pathology develop from social relationships such as that with an anxious or malevolent mother, and, later, from social ostracism, ridicule, or punishment. In time, a complex pattern of self-protective ideas and behavior develops, which Sullivan called the *self-system*. The self-system produces the rewards of security and avoids the anxiety of insecurity. Thus, to eliminate abnormal behavior, the therapist must concentrate upon modifying the client's self-system.

Numerous other deviations from classic psychoanalytic theory have been proposed by Karen Horney, Erich Fromm, Erik Erikson, and other neo-Freudians who differed with Freud primarily over the causes of abnormal behavior. Even though they rejected some aspects of psychoanalysis, most of these theorists accepted the structure of the theory in terms of *unconscious processes, psychic determinism*, and the role of *early experiences* in forming personality.

Transactional Analysis

In recent years a number of therapists have formulated an approach to psychotherapy based on psychoanalysis, communication theory, and social role theory, and they call this combination **transactional analysis**. According to Eric Berne (1964), the best known of these therapists, everyone has three ego states that he or she exhibits at different times and on different occasions: the *adult*, the *parent*, and the *child*. The adult is objective, realistic, and adaptive. The parent is moralistic, controlling, and critical, but also, on occasion, nourishing and sympathetic. The child feels, acts, and responds as one might expect a two- to five-year-old to do. In this role the individual is spontaneous, emotional, funloving, dependent, frightened, and sometimes rebellious.

Since everyone has these ego states, interpersonal encounters may be complicated. Transactions between people are favorable when they are complementary—for example, when a husband acts as a parent toward his wife and she responds as a child. The situation grows difficult, however, if the wife responds as an adult, which is an appropriate response for her. These are the games people play, but they are not always fun. Often, a player exploits some weakness in another person to get that person to participate in some other activity. After the "marked" victim is "hooked," the player makes a sudden switch to end the game, and so wins a psychological payoff.

Emphasis on life style

Ego psychology emphasizes socialization

Dr. Eric Berne, transactional analyst.

Sullivan focused on disturbed interpersonal relationships and tried to modify the self-system

Adult, parent, child as ego states in transactional analysis

Table 6-2 Eric Berne: Games People Play

Let's You and Him Fight

A woman sets up a competition between two men, and while they are fighting, she goes off with a third.

Blemish

A player is not comfortable with a stranger until he finds some weakness or defect in him, in order to avoid responsibility for his own blemishes.

Why Don't You—But

A person solicits help from another, but knocks down all suggestions, in order to prove that others, not the player, are inadequate.

Uproar

Two persons, accused and defendant, start a fight in order to avoid intimacy.

Cops and Robbers

A game played by losers; a player gets a payoff by acting chagrined when caught although he plans to get caught.

Kick Me

A player provokes a situation in which another person puts him down to prove that "I'm not O.K."

See What You Made Me Do

A player responds to an irritating interruption by dropping something or making a mistake; the punch line gets rid of the intruder. A modification is projecting blame by saying "You got me into this."

Wooden Leg

Handicaps are used as excuses for failure or for avoidance of responsibility for actions.

Stupid

Others are manipulated into calling the player stupid or acting toward him as if he were which gives the player an excuse to do little or nothing.

Games people play

The game "Nigysob" illustrates such hiding of motives or "one-upmanship." A wife playing this game might convey the covert message to her husband that she would be willing for him to have extramarital sexual affairs if he would leave her alone. The husband proceeds to do so, since he seems to have the tacit approval of his wife. The wife, in turn, appears to ignore his infidelity until she has sufficient evidence; then she angrily confronts him with her proof and triumphantly announces the payoff line, "Now I've got you, you son of a bitch." Table 6–2 describes several other games people play.

Client-therapist contract specifies goals

Individuals appraise themselves and others. The well-adjusted individual might say, "I'm O.K. with myself, and you're O.K. with me"; the paranoid individual might admit, "I'm O.K., but you're not O.K."; a depressed person might say, "I'm not O.K. but you're O.K."; and the schizophrenic would probably argue, "No one is O.K."

According to Berne, the interaction between the therapist and the client generates insight into the client's characteristic interpersonal maneuvers and reveals several varieties of his or her everyday social behavior. These behavior patterns are usually modified in group settings in which members meet once a week for about a year. Berne believed that the group provides a natural setting for the transactions between people and that feedback from the therapist in the group setting contributes to increased self-awareness and insight. Emphasis is thus on intellectual awareness rather than emotional catharsis. A useful innovation of transactional analysis is a behavioral contract between the therapist and client that states explicitly the goals of treatment (usually the alleviation of a particular symptom or the correction of some undesirable behavior). This contractual arrangement gives structure and direction to the treatment process.

scientific approaches to the study of abnormal behavior

Group therapy sessions employ techniques of various therapeutic approaches in a group setting. They are more economical than one-to-one psychotherapy, and interpersonal skills learned during these sessions may transfer more easily to other social settings.

Group Approaches

Group therapies have been used principally as a means of broadening the application of psychotherapeutic procedures. These therapies offer a number of advantages. First, group methods are more economical than individual treatment and have the added advantage of allowing the solution of personal problems within a social context. That group members interact with each other as well as with the therapist sometimes makes group therapy more effective than individual therapy. When an individual interacts with others in a setting similar to the natural interpersonal and social world, skills learned in therapy sessions may transfer more easily to other social settings. Moreover, group members learn vicariously by watching each other behave and may acquire a range of adaptive and interpersonal skills. These new skills can then be tested in the relatively safe atmosphere of the group. Further, behavior change may be much more rapid. Social pressure can be surprisingly strong in a cohesive group where individuals must learn to accept criticism as well as praise and to develop a more realistic appraisal of social strengths and weaknesses. Distortions in social judgments are rapidly detected and corrected. Finally, passive and withdrawn people often derive comfort and support from their relationships with others in the group.

Almost any orientation in psychodynamic psychotherapy can be and has been used in groups. In psychoanalytically oriented groups the therapist may ask each member of the group to respond in terms of specific thoughts, feelings, behavior patterns, topics, or themes, introduced either by a patient or by the therapist. This procedure is called the *go-around*. Other techniques of psychodynamic psychotherapy are also used, including dream analysis, free association, and the analysis of various transference relationships within the group. Occasionally, co-therapists, one male and one female, will participate and serve as parental surrogates for the group. Issues such as whether new members will be allowed into the group, who can be a member, and when the group terminates are usually determined by the orientation of the group therapist.

One form of psychodynamic group psychotherapy is **psychodrama**, developed by J. L. Moreno (Moreno & Kipper, 1968). In this form of group therapy the participants are asked to act out their feelings as if they were in a play, with members of the group taking various roles in the drama. An actual stage is used, and the drama is performed in the presence of an audience, composed of the group members. If an individual has difficulties with his or her mother, another group member may play

Group provides a setting for learning social skills

Cotherapists may assume parental roles

During family therapy, the family is considered the patient, and family members are treated conjointly.

Feelings and conflicts are acted out in psychodrama

the role of the mother and the individual will be asked to act out a childhood scene with her. Other members may enter the play as father, brothers, or sisters. A mirroring, or doubling technique is also used, in which another person portrays the patient and thereby furnishes the client with concrete information about how others view him or her. The aim of psychodrama is not only to encourage a person to confront and act out feelings but also to reveal the unconscious roots of these feelings, which are then interpreted in the usual psychodynamic manner.

Marriage therapy focuses on improving the interaction between partners

As the name implies, *marriage therapy* is specifically designed to assist people with marital problems. Because of their intense emotional involvement, couples with marital problems often do not perceive the realities of their relationship. For this reason, the partners are seen together, and therapy usually focuses on improving their interaction. Marriage therapies can have a number of different orientations, but by and large, they all emphasize mutual need, gratification, social role expectations, communication patterns, and other interpersonal factors. In psychodynamic approaches to marital therapy, these problems are viewed in terms of unconscious conflicts, defense mechanisms, and transference.

Family therapy treats the entire family structure rather than one individual

Another type of group therapy that developed largely from psychodynamic theory is **family therapy**. This procedure views the family as the patient and treats family members conjointly. The usual premise is that psychopathology in the individual is the product of family structures and interactions and that changes in the individual can therefore occur only if the family system changes (Haley 1962). Family therapy is used extensively in the treatment of marital problems, family crises, parent-child conflicts, neuroses, and other abnormal behavior patterns of children and adults. How many and which family members are seen in treatment sessions vary according to the situation and the preferences of the therapist. Most family therapists have a co-therapist, preferably one of the opposite sex.

Family therapists resist assigning traditional diagnostic labels to individuals. Instead, they attempt to formulate a general description of the family on the basis of information about the parents, the marital relationship, family origins, the use of authority within the family, the personality structure of individual members, family values, and patterns of interaction. The usual goal of family therapy is not necessarily to bring the family closer together, since the members of a disturbed family may be too emotionally involved with one

scientific approaches to the study of abnormal behavior

another. Instead, the goal is more often to promote the differentiation, individuation, and growth of each family member (Bowen 1966). It is believed that each family builds up patterns of relating, sets up roles, and unconsciously enforces expectations. These roles include the scapegoat, the disciplinarian, the one who needs looking after, the strong one, and similar demeaning roles. Therapy is aimed at clarifying role expectations and increasing communication among members. Encouraging family members to examine their roles and the roles they impose on each other, and emphasizing better communication so that families can become less restrictive, more sympathetic, and more mutually reinforcing are typical goals of family therapy (Satir 1967).

Evaluation of Psychodynamic Approaches

In the evaluation of individual and group psychodynamic approaches to behavior change, two distinct but interwoven issues are pertinent: the scientific value of the theoretical propositions and the effectiveness of the therapeutic procedures. While most aspects of psychodynamic theory have been criticized, the concept that unconscious processes or underlying conflicts produce symptoms has received the closest scrutiny. Levy (1963) has claimed that the existence of the unconscious as an entity is, in principle, not testable, and thus the assertion of its existence is meaningless. Insight, which the psychodynamic psychotherapist views as the client's recognition of some important historical connection or the relationship between present behavior and earlier crises may be only the patient's acceptance of the therapist's belief system (London 1964). Marmor (1962) has suggested that insight means different things to different psychodynamic schools. For example, Freudians tend to elicit insights into Oedipal complexes, Sullivanians produce insights into interpersonal relationships, and various other clinicians elicit insights from their clients that are consistent with their theoretical orientation. These problems are well-known to psychodynamic clinicians, who usually question the validity or relevance of these criticisms. However, in re-

cent years attempts have been made to develop a more scientific approach in psychoanalysis (Rapaport, 1959).

Another drawback of psychodynamic approaches is their apparent inefficiency. Extensive treatment is required over a long period of time, a problem only partially alleviated by using group processes. Additional difficulties involve prerequisite client characteristics. For example, if the client is too old, brain damaged, or psychotic, he or she is not a proper candidate for most forms of psychodynamic psychotherapy (Bernstein 1965). This problem has concerned some psychodynamic psychotherapists, and they have attempted to modify these approaches to make them briefer and more applicable to a wider variety of cases (Albin 1977). Transactional analysis also developed as a response to the complexity of psychoanalysis.

Perhaps the major difficulty with psychoanalytic treatment involves the effectiveness of its method. After surveying a number of studies, Eysenck (1952, 1966) argued that the effects of psychodynamic psychotherapy are about the same as *spontaneous remission*. In other words, if an individual receives no formal psychotherapeutic treatment, his or her chances of improvement may be as good as those of the individual who has had psychodynamic psychotherapy. Specifically, Eysenck claims that his survey indicates a 44 percent improvement or cure rate for classic psychoanalysis, 64 percent for ecletic forms of psychotherapy, and 72 percent for spontaneous remission. Needless to say, Eysenck's position was sharply criticized, sometimes emotionally and sometimes objectively (see Eysenck 1966).

Two important issues arise in evaluating this controversy. First, are the figures for psychotherapeutic effectiveness accurate? Bergin's (1971) survey of outcome studies in psychotherapy also noted a two-thirds improvement rate, as did Levitt (1977) in his evaluation of psychotherapy with children. Evidence from a meeting of the Society of Psychotherapy Research cited similar figures (Albin 1977). However, after modifying the criterion for evaluating improvement (placing "slightly improved" in the "improved" category, eliminating

Differentiation, individuation, and growth of each family member as goals of family therapy

Different therapies may provide different insights

Psychoanalysis is costly, but is it effective?

cases of "drop-out," and eliminating non-neurotics), Bergin (1971) recalculated the studies cited by Eysenck and found an 83 percent improvement rate for psychoanalysis. His method of calculating improvement with other forms of psychotherapy yielded results similar to those of Eysenck. Nevertheless, Bergin's estimate of the effects of psychoanalysis was probably over-inflated, as other studies have indicated only minor differences between the various forms of psychotherapy (Luborsky, Singer, and Luborsky 1975). In short, the two-thirds improvement rate originally cited by Eysenck (1952) appears to be accurate.

Methodological problems complicate evaluation

The second major issue is whether 72 percent of all neurotic cases spontaneously recover. On a rational basis, this figure seems highly inflated, since Eysenck used a discharge rate for untreated hospitalized neurotics and an improvement rate for medically treated life insurance claimants. A more careful survey of the spontaneous recovery rate for neuroses by Bergin (1971) indicates about 30 percent improvement over time. This rate is probably much higher in children (Levitt 1977), since many of their problems are developmental in nature. Thus, the research concludes that about two-thirds of clients with neurotic symptoms improve with various modes of psychotherapy as compared to about one-third without psychotherapy. We should note, however, that this is a difficult issue and that spontaneous recovery rates vary with a number of factors, particularly the type of behavior disorder involved.

Does psychoanalysis have undesirable side effects?

A major problem is deciding what constitutes clinical improvement. Is it a change in behavior, in personality structure, in cognition, or in feelings? The answer is relatively unclear, and it is obvious that different approaches would emphasize different concepts. For psychodynamic therapists, a change in personality structure would be the desirable goal. Questions arise, however, as to what this indicated. Thus, the issue remains unresolved.

Focus on the now

A related issue is the negative side effects of psychotherapy. Bergin (1966, 1971) has shown that some individuals' problems are aggravated by psychotherapy, and their adjustment declines (about 10 percent for psychotherapy cases and less than 5 percent for controls). This *deterio-*

Encouraging the client to take responsibility

ration appears to occur in fragile individuals already showing a decline in psychological functioning and in cases in which the psychotherapist disrupts the individual's emotional equilibrium (Korchin 1976). An inept psychotherapist can aggravate an individual's problems. This and other issues clearly emphasize the need to determine which treatment or therapist is best for what problem with each individual (Kiesler 1966).

Humanistic-Existential Psychotherapies

Humanistic and existential approaches to psychotherapy are based on phenomenological models (see Chapter 1). The therapist seeks explanations for a client's behavior, not in external facts, but in the phenomena of experience, since he or she assumes that each individual's unique perception of reality determines that individual's public or observable behavior. For example, a person's behavior may be a response to a hallucination. Though the object of his or her perception cannot be observed or measured by the clinician, it is part of the client's experience and a factor in his or her behavior. The therapist further assumes that his or her perception of the client is unique and subjective, and therefore is an element in the therapeutic interaction. Humanistic and existential psychotherapists make these four major assumptions:

1. *Present events* should be the center of focus in changing the individual's behavior. Consequently, the therapist concentrates on what the client is doing and feeling in the here and now, as well as on his or her future goals.
2. People *choose* to act as they do on the basis of their perceptions of the world. This is essentially a rejection of determinism, especially of what humanists see as mechanistic descriptions of humans driven by forces they cannot control and are not aware of. Therapy is therefore aimed at encouraging clients to take *responsibility* for their feelings and actions and to see themselves as being in *control* of their own destinies.

scientific approaches to the study of abnormal behavior

3. An individual's *subjective experience* is the key to understanding his or her behavior. Since subjective experience is difficult to measure, this aspect of phenomenological approaches makes them difficult to evaluate in a scientific manner. Many humanistic and existential therapists believe that evaluation of therapeutic approaches by publicly verifiable means is neither necessary nor relevant; hence, they see this fact as no problem.

4. *Conscious processes* are important in determining an individual's unique perception of the world. In other words, the individual is not motivated solely by unconscious forces. In this sense, phenomenologists reject the proposition of psychodynamic theorists that unconscious motivations determine behavior, but they share with those theorists the belief that the principal determinants of a person's behavior are to be found within the person. They also resemble psychodynamic theorists in one other important respect—their treatment techniques are likely to depend on the therapist's orientation rather than on the client's presenting complaint.

We shall now examine two major phenomenological approaches—Carl Rogers's *client-centered therapy* and Fritz Perl's *Gestalt therapy*—as well as several group approaches that have grown out of phenomenological theory.

Client-Centered Therapy

Carl Rogers assumes that every individual is the center of a changing world of experience, which can only be understood in terms of the individual's perception of life (Rogers 1951, 1959). Behavior, furthermore, can be understood as an interaction of two forces: the *organism* and the *self*. The organism is the individual's total perception of his or her experience, both internal and external, while the self is the individual's image of the self. Rogers defines the *self-concept* as the organized, consistent, conceptual image of the individual. This image is composed of the perceived characteristics of the *I* or *me*, along with

the individual's perception of the relationship between the *I* or *me* and others, and with the various life values associated with these perceptions.

Rogers believes that the tendency to grow and to realize one's potential is innate. **Self-actualization** is thus the key concept in Rogers's theory. The actualizing tendency motivates the individual to seek ways to enhance and maintain the self. It includes drives to reduce tension and satisfy biological demands, as well as to attain higher goals, such as exposing the self to new experiences, mastering new skills, and similar experiences that enhance the self-concept. The tendency toward self-actualization is guided by an innate valuing process, an inborn capacity to judge which experiences feel right for the individual and which do not. If the individual is exposed to conditions that allow development of the inherent self-actualizing tendencies, he or she will become a mature, healthy, and well-integrated adult.

The development of abnormal behavior is associated with acquisition of the self-concept. As the child becomes aware of self, he or she develops a need for *positive regard*, and the perceived source of positive regard is the affection and approval of important people in the child's life. However, positive regard from significant others usually requires that the individual behave in a prescribed manner. The values of the socializing agents dictate to the child which experiences are "good" and which are "bad"; if the child accepts them, they are incorporated into his or her conditions of self-worth. If these conditions are reasonable, the child can develop a self that is flexible enough to allow him or her to entertain a variety of experiences and determine which of these experiences are self-enhancing and which are not. However, if the conditions of worth are severely limited or restrictive, they will screen out a large portion of the significant experiences of the organism and impede self-actualization. Consequently, the individual cannot judge personal experience in terms of the innate valuing process but, because of the need for self-regard, must judge in terms of a set of socially learned criteria. This conflict between external criteria and the individual's

Subjective experience as the key to understanding behavior

Conscious processes also have a role

Behavior as interaction of organism and self

An innate valuing process guides self-actualization

Self-concept involves a need for positive regard; positive regard comes from the affection and approval of others; affection and approval may be given only when one behaves in prescribed ways

Conflict between external (socially learned) and internal (innate) criteria may produce abnormal behavior

The socialization process involves young children being taught behavior that is socially acceptable.

Attempts to harmonize the conflicting values by denial and falsification can lead to psychotic behavior

Goal of client-centered therapy: harmony between self and experience

innate criteria causes a distortion of the self and leads to the development of anxiety, defensiveness, and other patterns of abnormal behavior.

If there is conflict between the innate valuing process and the self, the individual will attempt to resolve this incongruence by denial or by ignoring the contradiction between the self and the social judgments. This distortion occurs when contradictions between innate and social values are misinterpreted or falsified in order to make them appear in harmony. If the condition is severe enough, the individual's self-structure will break down and become disorganized. The result is behavior that could be labeled psychotic.

To ameliorate these abnormal conditions, Rogers developed client-centered or *nondirective* therapy (also called Rogerian therapy). Client-centered therapy focuses directly on individuals and their unique experiences rather than on general theories or laws of human behavior. It also focuses on the relationship between therapist and client, the conditions of therapy, and the development of insight. The goal is to bring the self back into harmony with experience. Presumably, in a warm, accepting environment with a therapist who shows concern for the client's welfare and accepts the client as he or she is, the client's self-actualizing tendencies will manifest themselves, and behavior change will occur. For the accomplishment of this end, the characteristics of the therapist are important. The three key characteristics are *warmth, genuineness,* and *unconditional positive regard* (or empathy). The client must feel that the therapist accepts him or her and empathizes with his or her problems. The therapist must also be genuine and express personal feelings without distorting them. And the therapist must have unconditional positive regard for the client, since the client is best able to evaluate his or her own behavior and contribute to the enhancement of the self if he or she is not brought under judgmental scrutiny.

In terms of the actual process of psychotherapy, client-centered therapists avoid interpretations. They believe interpretations are judgmental and impose arbitrary values on the patient. The therapist listens to the client, attempts to understand the client's feelings and messages, and then tries to express acceptance of the individual and communicate understanding of the client by making simple acceptance statements like, "Yes, I see" or "I understand," rephrasing what the patient said, or clarifying the patient's feelings. If silences occur, the therapist might say, "I guess you don't feel like talking today" or "You seem to be enjoying just sitting." Thus, the main therapeutic ingredients of client-centered therapy are *acceptance, recognition*, and *clarification* of feeling used within the context of a warm therapeutic relationship. This therapeutic environment combined with the mirroring of feelings back to the client facilitates the removal of emotional conflicts that are blocking self-actualization.

In fairness, however, we should note that Truax and Mitchell (1971) have demonstrated that genuineness is negatively related to warmth and empathy, a proposition that seems obvious. How can one be warm and accepting, and at the same time completely candid, with an individual whose behavior often seems inappropriate? Whether the qualities described by Rogers are actually necessary in a therapist is another question, and the evidence has been mixed (Garfield and Bergin 1971). It has been shown, in fact, that Rogers may have shaped his client's verbal behavior by selectively attending to desirable verbalizations (Truax 1963).

Rogers was one of the pioneers in stimulating research into the process and outcome of psychotherapy (Rogers and Dymond 1954). Much of his research and that of his students has centered on variables operating in the psychotherapeutic situation.

Nevertheless, as far as the effectiveness of client-centered therapy is concerned, it compares favorably to psychodynamic approaches to personality change (Cartwright 1956; Luborsky, Singer, and Luborsky 1975). More recent evidence in a study by Gomes-Schwartz (reported by Albin 1977)

has not altered this conclusion. However, client-centered therapy has tended to be used with college students in counseling centers and with other individuals with less severe disorders as compared to the more severe psychiatric disorders usually treated by psychodynamic approaches. As far as efficiency is concerned, client-centered therapy compares very favorably with other approaches to therapeutic change, since it is brief (usually fewer than twenty sessions) and does not require extensive training of therapists.

Gestalt Therapy

Gestalt therapy is a mixture of psychoanalytic theory, humanism, and Gestalt psychology. The founder of the school, Frederick (Fritz) Perls (1951–1970), was trained in Europe as an orthodox Freudian psychoanalyst. However, Perls repudiated many of the basic beliefs of psychoanalysis. Like other humanists, he believed in the innate goodness of people and in their ability to determine their own destiny.

Gestalt therapy assumes that abnormal behavior patterns are the result of *unresolved conflicts* left over from the past, which must be located and worked through. The main premise is that individuals are unaware of, or unwilling to accept, the undesirable or painful parts of their personalities because of "unfinished business" in the past. The aim of therapy is to help individuals expand self-awareness, digest and assimilate previously ignored or denied parts of the self, and reclaim and integrate the fragmented parts so that they can become whole persons. Presumably, the individual will then become a more self-reliant, confident, and authentic person.

Perls explained abnormal behavior by the Gestalt concept of figure and ground. For example, for you, the reader of this text, the *figure* in *the Gestalt* is this book while other events occurring in the environment can be considered *ground*. Similarly, people need to focus on certain needs, and the failure to do so causes psychological distress. Though these needs may vary at different times, they must be satisfied. Thus, if a need is prevented from assuming

Therapists strive to be nonjudgmental

The therapist may sometimes have to choose between being supportive and being real

Gestalt focuses on "unfinished business"

box 6-2

A Session with
Carl Rogers

Third Interview

October Twenty-First

Nondirective Lead

C56.[1] Well—how do you want to use the time today?

Answer   *Insight*

S56.[2] Well—I don't quite know. A . . . . . (*Long pause.*) I was just wondering, I was reading a book the other day. It was called, uh—*Your Life as a Woman*, and in this book—and the subtitle was "How to make the most of it." In this book it showed different types of people and their work, and it didn't go into the causes of it or anything—but—uh—it showed how that person is not living a full life, and it sort of shows why—I mean, uh—it shows why there are different responses to people and it defines for you the reasons why people didn't like them—I mean, uh—it went into how, uh—they thought too much of themselves when they were in a group. They didn't give anything and it explains very carefully that that person was just lazy—and didn't make the effort to do those things. Well, I thought the book was very good, and it said that the person who doesn't grasp those things isn't necessarily crazy, he just hasn't made the effort to do those things, and it's a constant effort to improve—to change. Well, when I read it, it gave me a sort of clear insight into the thing.

[1]C56. This is a very good beginning for an interview. It emphasizes the idea that the client is free to make use of the time as she sees fit, and that it is not the counselor who will direct the interview.
[2]S56. The client has been making an effort to learn something about behavior; although she is unsure about what she has learned, the sign of positive effort on her part is a good one.

Problem

But still—I didn't know where to start. When I read it I realized that people do go

Miscellaneous

through those things—I don't even know why I brought that up—it just seemed to be sort of a good start.

Simple Acceptance

Clarification of Feeling

C57.[3] M-hm. You felt that you gained something from reading that book that indicated that not getting along with a group wasn't necessarily abnormal, but that it might be a constant effort to keep building an association with a group. Is that it? But it still leaves you feeling "where do I start?" Is that right?

Agreement

S57.[4] That's right. (*Long pause.*) Well,

Problem—Negative Attitude toward Self

in the first place, if I *were* to take a job right now I don't think that it would be fair to the employer, I mean, I really don't think that it would be—when I'm in a rut like

Insight—Ambivalent Attitude toward Self

this. The point is, am I just raising that as

[3]C57. The counselor avoids evaluating the material read, responding instead to the feelings that the client has about what it has done for her. If he had criticized the book, as he might justifiably have done, an intellectual discussion of the book and probably a defense of it by the client would have ensued. Such a discussion would not have been very profitable in helping the client to a better understanding of her own feelings.
[4]S57. The client has shown some sophistication regarding psychological concepts; her question about whether her thinking is a defense mechanism gives some estimate of her fairly high level of intelligence, and her sophistication regarding behavioral mechanisms.

the appropriate center of attention (figure) because of various pressures from the surrounding environment (ground), the proper figure-ground relationship is not achieved. Consequently, the individual's experience is distorted, and he or she may be unable to move freely from one figure to another. For example, if an individual denies his or her sexual needs, which are a part of the personality, he or she will not be able to achieve a proper Gestalt and be a whole person.

Gestalt therapy is usually done in groups, but the focus of attention is on an individual who is willing to work on his or her problem and takes a turn sitting in the "hot seat." Like Freud, Perls believed that past conflicts were significant causes in blocking awareness. The difference was Perls insistence that these difficulties must be handled by focusing on the "now."

a defense mechanism for not getting out? Or am I really thinking that it just wouldn't be fair? That's an important question to me.

Clarification of Feeling

C58. You feel that it wouldn't be fair, and at the same time there rises in your mind a question, are you just putting that up to keep from undertaking what would be a hard thing to do.

Agreement

S58.[5] That's right. (*Pause. Laughs.*) You

Asking for Information

shake your head. Is that all?

Clarification of Feeling

C59. You feel perhaps I should know the answers, then.

Agreement   *Asking for Information*

S59. That's right. Is it fair to an employer to go out and take a job that you feel, well, it may help you but it may not do very much for him? (*Pause.*) Is it justifiable?

Clarification of Feeling

C60. You feel you might really be cheating the employer by doing that.

Agreement

S60. That's right. I've said that before. I know we've covered that once before.

[5]S58, S59, S60. The client attempts here to force the counselor to give her an answer to her questions. First, she asks, can she work this thing out by herself, and secondly, why can't the counselor give her some suggestions such as telling her whether she is justified in not going to work. She alternates between a feeling that such a solution is not feasible and one that the counselor may be niggardly about the help he offers.

Carl Rogers, founder of nondirective therapy.

Asking for Information—

Uhuh. (*Long pause. Laughs.*) Well, what's

Negative Attitude toward Counselor

the answer? Am I supposed to get the answers?

Clarification of Feeling

C61. You are wondering that, too, aren't you, whether maybe the answer is in you?

Insight

S61. In other words, I'd have to make a radical change . . .

Gestalt therapy is extremely active and uses a number of techniques to accomplish its goals. One method is the emphasis on changing "*it* language" into "*I* language" so that individuals assume responsibility for what they are and what they become. Rather than saying, "it is blocking me," the individual is encouraged to say, "I am blocking myself." In this way the individual takes responsibility for alienated portions of the self. Gestalt therapy also uses direct confrontation, acting out, and role-playing techniques. Occasionally, the therapist engages in provocative behavior toward the client in the form of explanation, encouragement, and suggestions for new ways to get in touch with the self and others. The client is encouraged to act, talk, fight, swear, and take stands.

Emphasis on "I" language and taking responsibility

box 6–3
An Example of
Gestalt Therapy

Client *(Assertively, to the therapist.)* I want to get held in the right way. *(Her partner moved over, and I held her, with my arms around her and her head on my shoulder.)*

Therapist Say, "It's my turn to be held."

Client It's my turn to be held, I want to be held!

Therapist Say "I need to be held."

Client I need to be held! *(Tears.)* I need to be held when I feel all that pain!

Therapist Say "It's too much pain without being held!"

Client It's too much pain to feel all alone!!!! *(Sobbing so hard she cannot talk.)*

Therapist "Too much pain to feel all alone! TOO MUCH PAIN TO FEEL ALL ALONE!! IT'S SOOO PAINFUL!!! *(I continued repeating this with intense feeling about a dozen more times, while she sobbed hard. Gradually the sobbing subsided.)*

Client It's nice being held. I feel better. Now I can go on with that pain. *(She continued on, talking about the painful situation, crying and getting subsequent relief. She had previously discussed the same material, but without discharge of emotion, and with much less resolution.)*

In *role playing*, unresolved past conflicts are worked through. For example, if the client has an unresolved conflict with his or her father, the therapist might play the father and the client him- or herself, or, in a role reversal, they might switch and play the opposite roles. More often, the client plays both roles, switching back and forth. Another technique is to have the individual talk to a projection of a feeling, object, subject, or situation. For example, if the client is feeling depressed, the therapist might ask the client to imagine the "depression" sitting in a chair opposite and then speak to it. The most common and basic role play is between parts of the self, which is where the conflict ultimately operates.

Role-playing the alienated parts of the self to recover wholeness

As in psychoanalysis, the interpretation of dreams is an important technique, although the Gestalt analysis of dreams is quite different from Freudian dream analysis. Dreams are seen as alienated portions of the self. By reexamining and retelling the dream in the present tense, and taking the part of each character or image in it, the individual can reclaim these alienated fragments of the self. Gestalt therapists also use a variety of breathing techniques (derived largely from Reichian therapy), fantasy methods, and relaxation exercises to teach the client to get in touch with both mind and body.

Gestalt therapy teaches a set of values

While Perls emphasized "doing your own thing" and that therapists should not "lay their trips" on the clients, Naranjo (1970) has indicated that a major aspect of Gestalt therapy is the philosophy that the therapist conveys to the patient. This includes focusing on the present, experiencing events rather than imagining them, feeling rather than thinking, expressing one's feelings rather than justifying or explaining them, being aware of pain as well as pleasure, and taking responsibility for one's own actions and feelings.

However, Gestalt therapy is not unique among humanistic, existential, or psychodynamic approaches in teaching the patient a system of values. Any method of behavior change in which the emphasis is on the whole individual and the restructuring of the personality cannot accomplish its goal without also influencing an individual's value system. Even in behavioral approaches, which focus on limited aspects of an individual's life, the same phenomenon usually occurs. As Rosenthal (1955) has noted, most individuals adopt the values of their therapists. Therapists should be honest about this risk and inform their clients of it.

At present, the effectiveness of the Gestalt approach to behavior change has not been determined. Unfortunately, some Gestalt therapists, like many humanistic-existential theorists, regard effectiveness studies as irrelevant. They claim that the scientific approach violates their basic assumptions about the nature of human behavior, especially the concepts of free will, the uniqueness of the person, and the validity of subjective experience (Korchin 1976). Nevertheless, additional data are needed

In T-groups, attention is focused on the ways in which members interact with and affect one another and the reactions they elicit from each other.

before the issue of effectiveness can be settled. Gestalt therapy, like psychodynamic and client-centered therapy, is probably most effective with intellectual, well-educated individuals who have relatively mild adjustment problems.

Group Approaches

Humanistic group therapy had its origins in client-centered therapy and originally aimed at facilitating self-awareness within a social context, but the aim has changed greatly in more recent years, as can be seen in later encounter groups (Rogers 1970). T-groups, or sensitivity training groups, on the other hand, were originally designed to deal with normal individuals in business organizations.

Sensitivity Training

The **T-group** or training group was originally conceived at the National Training Laboratories in Bethel, Maine, and utilized the principles of group dynamics. In the T-group, people who were interested in developing self-awareness and interpersonal skills would meet for a specific time period, usually a week or two. The participants were typically business executives, school

principals, parents, or similar homogeneous groups. Sensitivity training was intended to increase social sensitivity and behavioral flexibility, but could generally be viewed as educational. The purpose of learning in the T-group was usually to gain information about oneself—one's reactions to and relationship with others. The general goal of the T-group was to help participants become more creative, more fully functional, less defensive, better able to consider the feelings of others, and more innovative (Aronson 1972).

There have been a number of variations on sensitivity groups, particularly in industry. These have varied from *team-building* groups, designed to develop more closely knit and effective working teams, to *task-oriented* groups, which emphasize the task of a group in its interpersonal context, to *organizational development* groups, which focus primarily on growth of ability and leadership, and to *creativity workshops,* which emphasize creative expression. In T-groups, attention is generally given to the ways in which members interact with one another, the ways in which they affect one another, and what reactions they elicit from

T-groups are mainly educational

T-groups and sensitivity groups focus on growth

others. The group leader, or *facilitator*, is usually a well-trained psychologist. The group members limit themselves to verbal interchanges, and the purposes of the group are well defined. These groups were essentially designed for normal people.

Encounter Groups

The major goal of humanistically oriented group therapy is personal growth through understanding of and experimentation with one's own behavior. This personal growth should increase openness and honesty and foster better personal relationships. While **encounter groups** focus on fostering increased effectiveness or the growth of essentially normal individuals, there is no doubt that many people with problems of abnormal behavior also see these groups as a solution to their problems.

Emphasis on honest expression of feelings

Encounter groups allow a great deal of flexibility and experimentation, and a variety of different types of groups have been used: sensory awareness groups, body awareness groups, body movement groups, Gestalt groups, nude encounter groups, groups designed for people with particular problems, and groups designed for particular community problems. Typically, encounter groups consist of six to twelve participants and one or two group leaders in a setting that encourages maximum freedom of movement and activity. The emphasis is on the removal of inhibitions, the free and honest expression of feelings, the resolution of confrontation, and other interactions that occur within the group. Verbal techniques are used to facilitate group interaction, to provide feedback, and to focus on particular problems.

Awareness exercises

These groups are of two general types— the *process* group, in which the interaction consists mainly of a more or less continuous attempt at an honest encounter among all group members, or groups in which the interaction consists mainly of work by one member sitting on the *hot seat* and coached by the therapist, while the other members either remain silent, serve as a sounding board, or contribute support or challenge. The second technique is used in Gestalt groups, as we have already noted, and in *attack* therapy and Synanon *square games*.

The marathon as "pressure cooker"

Both verbal and nonverbal exercises are also used, sometimes as a central part of the group interaction and sometimes as warmup exercises to facilitate awareness. One such exercise is the *now* continuum, used in Gestalt groups, in which each person describes his or her feelings and sensations for a few minutes, beginning each sentence with "Now, I'm aware of. . . ." Other games and exercises include guided fantasies; "eyeball to eyeball," in which two participants gaze into each other's eyes for two or three minutes; the blind mill, in which group members walk around with their eyes closed, learning to communicate by touch; and trust exercises, in which—for example—participants take turns being lifted and passed around a circle formed by other group members. Partial or total disrobing is also sometimes used, not for sexual excitement but to enhance spontaneity and confidence. Table 6–3 describes several encounter group exercises.

The encounter group may be intensified by the use of the *marathon* encounter, in which the group meets for a live-in weekend or a period of two or three days with only a brief break for sleep. The premise is that this continuous contact, coupled with fatigue, lowers the inhibitions of the group members and hastens the "opening-up" process. The marathon encounter has been called a "pressure cooker" because of the emotional tension it builds up. The group leader or leader participant, whose function is not highly directive, is responsible only for establishing a climate of psychological safety in which all members feel free to express themselves, drop their guard, and try out new ways of interacting with one another. The leader also serves as a model by expressing feelings openly and honestly and by accepting expressions of affection or hostility from group members. The leader encourages members to give honest, direct, and responsible feedback—for example, "I feel threatened by your attempt to make eye contact with me," rather than "Some people don't seem to know that it's impolite to stare." The group leader is also responsible for seeing that confrontations between members are resolved in a satisfactory manner. In general, group leaders serve as resource people when the group needs guidance or comes to an impasse.

scientific approaches to the study of abnormal behavior

Table 6-3 Encounter Group Exercises

Blind milling

In this exercise the members of the group walk around the room with their eyes closed and are told to engage in nonverbal contact with any other member of the group they bump into, doing whatever they wish.

Breaking out/breaking in

Here the group forms a tight circle around an individual, preventing him/her from breaking through the circle.

Falling back

The individual falls backward, putting complete trust in the person behind him/her to catch him/her.

High noon

Two men go to opposite sides of a room and face each other. They very slowly approach each other while remaining silent. Once they meet they are to spontaneously follow their impulses. The other group members watch in silence.

Fantasy game

Group members are asked to tell which part of the body they would try to cover if they found themselves suddenly nude. Then they are told to imagine that part of their body sitting in an "empty chair" and are instructed to have a conversation with it. As an example, one woman asked her breasts why they were so small. Speaking for her breasts she replied, "Because you don't deserve any better!"

Most sensitivity-training groups have specific goals, a specific audience for which the group is designed, specific requirements for entrance to the group, and a well-trained leader. Moreover, most *T*-groups do not represent themselves as appropriate methods for handling abnormal patterns of behavior. Some encounter groups, on the other hand, have much lower standards. There may be little or no attempt to screen group members, and leaders may be untrained. Such encounter groups can even aggravate personal problems. As Yalom and Lieberman (1971) have demonstrated, encounter group casualties can occur when subjects are unable to handle the intense emotional stimulation and feedback about unrecognized aspects of themselves and the pressure to open up. Before an encounter group is used in treating abnormal behavior, qualified people should be obtained to lead the group, members should be carefully screened, and the guidelines established by the American Psychological Association and other mental health associations should be met.

Medical Therapies

Medical therapies are physical techniques that change the *physiological* functioning or structure of the individual to eliminate or cure behavior pathology.

There are a number of theoretical reasons for using physiological intervention to modify behavioral disorders:

1. Some behavior patterns have physiological substrates that can be manipulated by physiological techniques to modify the behavior patterns. For example, the central nervous system operates via chemically coded synaptic transmissions, which can be selectively influenced by drugs.
2. Because of evolutionary influences on behavior and the process of natural selection, individuals differ widely in genetic endowment. Although these individual differences reflect normal genetic variations, a particular characteristic, such as an overreactive autonomic nervous system, may handicap an individual and require physiological as well as psychological intervention.
3. In some disorders, such as the psychophysiological disorders, psychological events do cause physiological malfunctions. In many of these cases it is more feasible and useful to intervene—initially, at least—at a physiological level.
4. Some behavior scientists believe that abnormal behavior is mental illness and should be treated by the same principles used in treating physical illnesses.

Encounter group casualties

While theoretical reasons for the use of physical (medical) intervention may vary on a pragmatic basis, medical intervention is often a useful alternative or adjunct to psychological methods, particularly with severely disturbed individuals.

There are four major types of medical interventions in behavioral disorders: psycho-surgery, shock therapies, chemotherapy, and institutionalization.

Psychosurgery

After Antonìo Egas Monìz had noted that one of the behavioral effects of frontal lobe damage in monkeys was a marked difference in response to stimuli that had previously elicited intense agitation, he and a colleague, Almeida Lima, began to use brain surgery to alleviate psychiatric symptoms, particularly agitated behavior. Psychosurgery was introduced into the United States by Freeman and Watts (1942) during the thirties. They used two types of lobotomy: *prefrontal* and *transorbital*. Prefrontal lobotomy involves drilling two "burr" holes in either the top side or the front of the skull and inserting an instrument through these holes to reach and sever sections of the frontal lobes (see Figure 6–1). Transorbital lobotomy involves inserting underneath the eyelid and over the eyeball an instrument that is then usually tapped with a mallet through the bony cav-

ity over the eye and thus inserted into the brain. Fibers at the base of the frontal lobes are severed by swinging the instrument toward the middle and then toward the side of the head. Freeman practiced this technique with an ice pick and claimed that the surgical procedure was so simple that it could be performed in a doctor's office (Valenstein 1973).

During the forties and fifties, **psychosurgery** became quite popular and was used not only on severely disturbed psychotic patients, but also on psychoneurotics or individuals with psychophysiological complaints. These surgical procedures not only calmed patients but also rendered them apathetic, irresponsible, and asocial. Usually a blunting of intellectual functioning, impaired judgment, and reduced creativity also occurred (Chorover 1974). In addition, a high incidence of epileptic seizures followed these procedures. Consequently, these techniques are rarely used today.

With the development of methods for implanting electrodes in the central nervous system, new forms of psychosurgery have been developed. At the present time, an electrode can be placed almost anywhere in the brain, and once the tip of the electrode is in the desired location, it can serve three functions: (1) recording of electrical activity of the local brain area; (2) electrical stimulation of the area with a weak current; and (3) coagulation or destruction of the

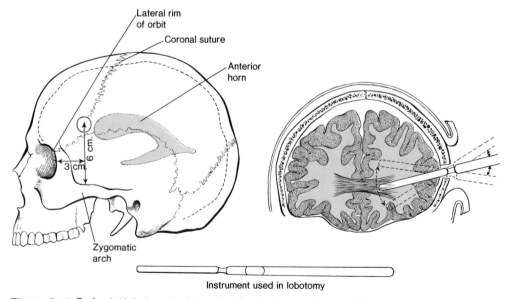

Instrument used in lobotomy

Figure 6–1 Prefrontal lobotomy technique for the treatment of severe disturbances.

　　　scientific approaches to the study of abnormal behavior

brain tissue surrounding the tip of the electrode (Dunner and Somerville 1977). The newer forms of psychosurgery usually involve restricted lesions in various structures in the limbic system, which is assumed to control emotional behavior. Three types of psychosurgery are performed: cingulumotomy, thalamotomy, and amygdalatomy.

Cingulumotomy

This procedure, consisting of lesions placed in the cingulate gyrus (see Figure 6–2), is performed on individuals who have behavior disorders but do not have any apparent brain pathology (Holden 1973). These operations have been conducted by H. T. Ballatine, professor of neurosurgery at Harvard Medical School, who considers them a safe and effective treatment for affective disorders (manic-depressive psychosis, obsessive-compulsive neuroses, anorexia nervosa, and even severe anxiety neuroses) that do not respond to other forms of treatment. Ballatine claims that this procedure produces no severe side effects, but this is highly unlikely (Valenstein 1973).

Thalamotomy

This procedure, once a common surgical procedure in severe cases of Parkinson's disease, consists of placing lesions in the thalamus (see Figure 6–2). It has also been performed to modify aggressiveness and

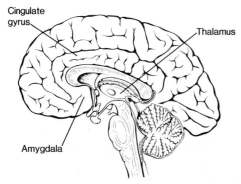

Figure 6–2 The newer forms of psychosurgery involve placing lesions in the cingulate gyrus, the thalamus, or the amygdala.

overactivity among hyperactive children. Orlando J. Andy, at the University of Mississippi Medical School, has performed thirteen or fourteen of these operations on hyperactive children from six to nineteen years of age and claims that it is a reasonable procedure (Chorover 1974).

Amygdalatomy

This operation has been performed to control violent behavior that is presumably associated with abnormalities of the amygdala (see Figure 6–2), a limbic system structure that is surgically removed or lesioned. This operation is usually performed only when there are signs of abnormal neurological activity, in behavior patterns such as hyperactivity, violent aggressiveness, or assault behavior. Unfortunately, in many of these cases the evidence for brain abnormality is minimal (Holden 1973).

The tremendous controversy over psychosurgery is well-documented in a book called *Violence in the Brain* (Mark and Ervin 1970). The critics of psychosurgery maintain that the procedures cause the patient to become a "vegetable." Since little is known about how the brain functions and since the effects of these procedures are irreversible, their use is a serious risk to the individual. Particularly with the advent of tranquilizers, serious doubts have arisen over whether these procedures are ever warranted.

Shock Therapies

Shock therapy has two major forms, *chemical* and *electrical*. **Chemical shock therapy** was introduced in the early 1930s by Sakel (1937) whose *insulin coma* therapy relied on a hypoglycemic coma induced through the reduction of blood sugar content by large dosages of insulin. The claim, made at various times, that insulin shock therapy was effective in 90 percent of schizophrenics has never been confirmed. In fact, the evaluations of insulin coma therapy have indicated that the method is not much better than no treatment at all (Staudt and Zubin 1957). Other convulsive drugs, such as Metrazol, were introduced by Meduna (1938). However, the mortality rate and other side effects of chemically induced convulsions have been so high that they have generally been discontinued.

Electrodes can be inserted in the brain to record activity, stimulate areas, or destroy tissue

Does psychosurgery produce human vegetables?

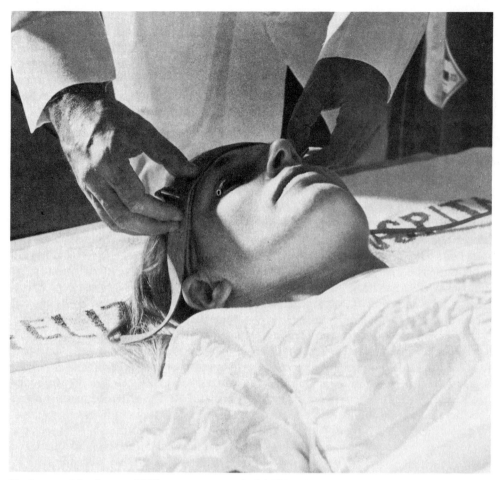

Electroconvulsive therapy (ECT) passes a current of 1,600 milliamps through the brain. The tonic-clonic seizure that results can cause broken bones, so a sedative or neuromuscular depolarizer is administered to minimize jerky movements.

ECT induces a grand mal epileptic seizure

Electroconvulsive therapy (ECT), introduced by Cerletti and Bini (1938), works by passing a current of approximately 1600 milliamps through the brain by means of electrodes attached to the head. The current induces a *grand mal* seizure. This procedure, which at one time was used for a variety of behavioral disorders, is now used primarily for the treatment of depressions, typically those that occur during middle and late life. ECT is also assumed to be effective in treating mania and certain schizophrenic states involving immobility or very aggressive behavior (Kline and Davis 1969). ECT treatments can be given in the hospital or administered on an outpatient basis. The number of ECT treatments varies with the orientation of the psychiatrist and may consist of seven, ten, or up to fifty treatments over a short period

Use of ECT to treat depression

of time. Since the *tonic-clonic* seizure can cause the individual to break bones during the convulsion, the usual procedure is to administer a sedative or a neuromuscular depolarizer such as succinylcholine, which largely eliminates the usual clonic or jerky movements seen in the seizure. After ten or fifteen minutes the patient usually wakens in a confused state. This confusion clears shortly but may last longer after a series of treatments. ECT also causes temporary memory losses. However, clinicians claim that when unilateral ECT (in which the electrodes are placed on one temple over the nondominant side of the brain) is used, less confusion results.

The use of ECT has almost completely replaced chemical methods of inducing convulsions. It is particularly useful with agitated or stuporous states. Mendels (1973) claims that ECT is the quickest sure method of returning the individual with severe depression to social functioning. Furthermore, ECT appears to be effective and superior to antidepressive drugs with refractory or chronic depression (Davison et al. 1978). ECT is not particularly effective with mild or neurotic depression (Mendels 1967). For less severe types of abnormal behavior psychological or drug therapies are more effective. At present, no one knows why or how ECT works.

Chemotherapy

The introduction of drug therapies during the 1950s, particularly the use of the major tranquilizers, largely eliminated the more drastic forms of medical treatment. It has been known for many years that chemicals influence behavior. For example, narcotics reduce pain; sedatives, such as the barbiturates, lessen anxiety and induce sleep; stimulants, such as caffeine, reduce depression. However, only in recent years have chemicals been used extensively in treating maladaptive behavior.

Four major types of drugs are used in treating abnormal behavior: antianxiety, antidepressive, antimanic, and antipsychotic drugs.

Antianxiety Drugs

Antianxiety drugs are routinely dispensed, not only by psychiatrists but also by general practitioners. Consequently, over 15 percent of Americans between the ages of eighteen and seventy-four use antianxiety tranquilizing drugs (*Behavior Today* 1974). Meprobamate (Miltown, Equanil) has strong antianxiety effects but has been largely replaced by chlordiazepoxide or diazepam (Librium, Valium). Table 6–4 lists the common antianxiety agents.

In general, antianxiety drugs are used for anxiety, nervousness, or neurotic disorders. Of all the psychotropic drugs, the antianxiety drugs seem to be the least effective. There is no real evidence that they reduce anxiety more than the sedatives, such as phenobarbital (Greenblatt and Shader 1971), and some clinicians believe these drugs are no more effective than placebos (Kramer, Ornstein, and Whitman 1964). Furthermore, risks of addiction and dependency are increased with higher doses (Dunner and Somervill 1977).

Antidepressant Drugs

Two major classes of **antidepressant drugs** are used: the tricyclic compounds and the monoamine oxidase (MAO) inhibitors. The tricyclic compounds are called tricyclic because they are chemically structured in three rings. The most frequently used are amltriptyline (Elavil), which is frequently prescribed for depressed patients who have insomnia, and imipramine (Tofranil), which is often used with depressed patients who have psychomotor retardation, as it is an activating drug. The side effects of the tricyclics include dry mouth, increased sweating, constipation, and orthostatic hypotension, a condition in which the blood pressure falls when the patient rises from a prone position, resulting in fainting and dizziness.

Tranquilizers to reduce anxiety

The monoamine oxidase (MAO) inhibitors were taken off the market a few years ago because of severe side effects associated with the ingestion of certain food. Monoamine oxidase is an enzyme that normally metabolizes certain agents that raise blood pressure. The inhibition of the enzyme results in sudden increases in blood pressure if food containing the chemical tyramine is eaten. This sudden increase can lead to headache or even cerebral stroke. Behaviorally, antidepressant drugs can increase tension or intensify psychotic symptoms (Kline and Davis 1973).

Side effects of MAO inhibitors

The effects of antidepressants do not become evident until two or three weeks have passed. Since depression is often an episodic disorder, the dosage of the antidepressant drug is faded and eventually discontinued after the symptoms begin to disappear.

Tricyclic drugs appear to be most effective in treating severe depression (LaPolla and Jones 1970), while MAO inhibitors are more effective with depression that is secondary to other disorders (Akiskal and McKinney 1973). The tricyclic drugs appear to be particularly effective with depression involving a slow, insidious onset, weight loss, insomnia, and psychomotor disturbances (Bielski and Friedel 1976). One of the major contributions of antidepressives has been the reduced use of ECT in severe depression.

Tricyclic drugs and depression

The relative effectiveness of cognitive psychotherapy and imipramine therapy in treating moderately to severely depressed outpatients has been studied by Hollon et al. (reported by Albin 1977). After twelve weeks of treatment, 79 percent of the psychotherapy groups and 20 percent of the groups receiving imipramine showed improvement. These gains persisted at a six-month follow-up. Moreover, antidepressive drugs can be usefully combined with psychological techniques. For example, Gittelman-Klein and Klein (1973) combined persuasion and desensitization, a behavior therapy technique, with either placebo or imipramine to treat children with school phobias. After six weeks, the school attendance rate was 81 percent for the imipramine groups and 47 percent for the placebo group.

Antimanic Drugs

Lithium used to treat manic behavior

The symptoms of *mania*—highly agitated, confused, and hyperactive behavior—are often treated with an **antimanic drug** such as lithium carbonate (lithium salts). Lithium has only recently been approved by the Food and Drug Administration because of the possibility of severe side effects. How it affects hyperactive behavior is not known, and it usually requires five to fourteen days to become effective. The blood level of lithium during drug treatment must be carefully monitored because high blood levels of lithium produce toxic symptoms and even death. Potential side effects, even at the appropriate levels of administration, include fatigue, muscular weakness, tremor, slurred speech, nausea, increased thirst, and increased urination.

Side effects of antipsychotic drugs

Two studies by Prien, Caffey, and Klett (1973) and by Stallone et al. (1973) have shown that lithium is highly effective in controlling manic behavior compared to placebos. It also appears to be more effective than other antipsychotic drugs in controlling manic episodes. Good evidence also exists that, in acute psychosis or reactive schizophrenia, lithium may be superior to, or at least as effective as, antipsychotic drugs (Pope and Lipinski 1978). However, it appears to be ineffective with chronic schizophrenia.

Antipsychotic Drugs

The use of the **antipsychotic drugs,** sometimes called the major tranquilizers, is viewed by many as one of the most important advances in psychiatry and has revolutionized the treatment of seriously disturbed mental patients (Gellhorn and Kiely 1973). These drugs are listed in Table 6–4. Probably the most frequently prescribed of these is chlorpromazine (Thorazine), a type of phenothiazine. These drugs are assumed to be effective in the treatment of various types of psychotic disorders by eliminating agitation, hallucinations, hyperactivity, and delusions. Side effects associated with high doses of antipsychotic drugs include orthostatic hypertension. Extrapyramidal symptoms, similar to those of Parkinson's disease and including "pill-rolling," tremors of the fingers, drooling, muscular rigidity, and stiffness of posture can occur. These symptoms can be controlled with anti-Parkinsonian drugs such as benztropine mesylate (Cogentin). Another side effect is tardive dyskinesia, which is characterized by movement of the lips, tongue, and jaw, and by jerky movements of the extremities. Symptoms may become worse with the withdrawal of the antipsychotic agent.

A multitude of studies have evaluated the effects of the antipsychotic drugs. In the initial or acute phase of psychotic disorders, antipsychotic drugs appear to be highly effective. Klerman, Davidson, and Kayce (1964), in a double-blind study comparing chlorpromazine (Thorazine) and two other phenothiazines with placebo pills, found that 95 percent of these patients improved in six weeks on phenothiazines, a much higher rate than occurred in patients treated with placebos. Antipsychotic medication decreases anxiety, agitation, aggressive behavior, hallucinations, and, to a lesser extent, delusions. The patient becomes docile, calm, and easy to manage.

The effectiveness of these drugs for maintenance of chronic psychotic patients in mental hospitals is less clear. Paul, Tobias, and Holly (1972) conducted a well-controlled triple-blind study in which neither the patients who were severely disturbed hospitalized psychotics, the treatment

scientific approaches to the study of abnormal behavior

Table 6-4 Common Antianxiety, Antidepressant, and Antipsychotic Agents

Antianxiety agents

Generic name	Trade name
Chlordiazepoxide	Librium
Diazepam	Valium
Oxazepam	Serax
Clorazepate dipotassium	Tranxene
Tybamate	Solacen
Hydroxyzine	Vistaril, Atarax
Meprobamate	Miltown, Equanil

Antidepressant agents

Chemical basis	Generic name	Brand name
Tricyclic	Amitriptyline	Elavil
	Nortriptyline	Aventyl
	Protriptyline	Vivactil
	Imipramine	Tofranil, Presamine
	Desipramine	Norpramin, Pertofrane
	Amitriptyline—perphenazine	Triavil, Etrafon
Monoamine oxidase inhibitors	Isocarboxazid	Marplan
	Phenelzine	Nardil
	Tranylcypromine	Parnate

Antipsychotic agents

Chemical basis	Generic name	Brand name
Phenothiazines		
Dimethylamine	Chlorpromazine	Thorazine
Piperazine	Trifluoperazine	Stelazine
	Perphenazine	Trilafon
	Fluphenazine	Prolixin, Permitil
Piperadine	Thioridazine	Mellaril
	Mesoridazine	Serentil
Butyiophenones	Haloperidol	Haldol, Serenace
Thioxanthines	Chlorprothixine	Taractan, Solatran
	Thiowuxene	Navane

staff, nor the researcher knew who was receiving the drug and who was receiving placebo. One-half of the subjects were placed in a social learning program and the other half in a milieu treatment program. While one subgroup in each program continued to receive the drug, the other group had the drug substituted with a placebo that appeared identical. After seventeen weeks, a comparison of the patients on active medication with those on placebos indicated no differences in the two groups. Paul and his colleagues suggested that the strong tranquilizers may be effective in acute psychotic episodes, but their effectiveness in controlling symptoms in chronic psychotics who have been hospitalized many years may be due only to the expectations of patients and staff. However, their population could have

consisted of individuals who did not respond well to strong tranquilizers. Further evidence is needed on this question.

It has been demonstrated that, of schizophrenic patients discharged from the hospital and maintained on either chlorpromazine or placebo, 31 percent of those receiving chlorpromazine and 72 percent of those receiving placebo relapse within one year (Crane 1973; Hogarty and Goldberg 1973). It may be that psychotic patients benefit most from phenothiazines in unstructured environments such as custodial hospitals without social learning or milieu programs (as in the Paul, Tobias, and Holly study, 1972) or in discharged status.

Staff expectations may influence results

psychodynamic, humanistic, and medical therapies

A related question is how antipsychotic medication compares with other forms of treatment for psychotic disorders. Five

Drugs vs. psychotherapy

studies comparing psychotherapy and drugs in treating schizophrenia have been evaluated by Feinsilver and Gunderson (1972). They concluded that while the drugs were effective in the treatment of schizophrenia, there was no evidence that psychotherapy was helpful. A representative study of this type with a five-year follow-up was conducted by May (1968, 1975). He assessed the effects of individual psychotherapy alone, antipsychotic drugs alone, individual psychotherapy plus antipsychotic drugs, ECT, and the usual hospital custodial treatment without drugs in 228 schizophrenic patients randomly assigned to these groups. They were evaluated on ratings of their symptoms, length of hospital stay, cost of treatment, and ratings of improvement by the patients themselves or by their therapists. Generally, he found that antipsychotic drugs and ECT were superior to psychotherapy and routine hos-

Uses of drugs

pital treatment, while combined treatment of psychotherapy and drugs offered no greater benefits than drugs alone. The five-year follow-up of these patients did not alter these conclusions. Furthermore, the cost of treatment was lowest for the group treated with antipsychotic drugs.

In conclusion, chemotherapy appears to be more effective than psychotherapy with psychotic individuals, but this is not the case with neuroses or other less severe types of abnormal behavior (May 1971). The evidence for psychological therapies versus chemotherapy is not yet clear, but there is little reason to suspect different conclusions. However, psychological therapies and chemotherapy may be complementary in many cases and may be usefully combined. In other words, chemotherapy may reduce agitation, confusion, and extreme autonomic nervous system responses to a

Consequences of hospitalization

level at which problem solving and acquisition of more appropriate social skills (or personality change) can be facilitated by psychotherapy or behavior therapy, or both. Nevertheless, drug therapies have many advantages: (1) they are useful with a wide range of disorders and populations; (2) they are effective with severe, acute disorders; (3) they can be used with severely disturbed, psychotic populations not amenable to psychological therapies; and (4) they are relatively inexpensive.

Institutionalization

If the clinician believes that an individual is so severely disturbed as to be unable to function in the community, he or she may recommend hospitalization. Typically, hospitalization is recommended for individuals who are assumed to have acute or chronic psychotic episodes or who are unable to function in the community, such as severely retarded individuals. Individuals can voluntarily commit themselves, or they may be involuntarily committed by family members or a legal guardian. Legal commitment involves examination by a physician or a psychologist, or both, in some states, after a complaint from the family and subsequent commitment by the courts. Although the criteria for involuntary commitment vary from state to state, the usual legal requirement is that individuals, as well as being mentally ill, be dangerous to themselves or others or unable to function in society. Commitment may be for a specific time for observation, or it may be indefinite. If there is, at the same time, a legal judgment that the individual is insane, the individual may lose his or her civil rights and a legal guardian may be appointed. Unfortunately, because of the confusion surrounding the definition of mental illness, the laws are so vague that an individual's civil rights can easily be violated. For example, if a man's wife caught him in an extramarital affair and began to cause difficulty, he could have her committed. If she protested that he was involved with another woman and was threatening her, he could maintain that she was paranoid and exhibiting delusions of persecution. After having her committed, he could continue his infidelity uninterrupted. Similar but less dramatic situations have occurred.

If legally committed, the individual cannot leave the institution without the court or the hospital's permission. While hospitalized, the individual is usually treated with rest and recreational, occupational, musical, or individual psychotherapy. Unfortunately, in many state hospitals in the past the only treatment has been custodial care. The individual is expected to play the

A building at the mental hospital complex in Belmont, Massachusetts. Many such mental hospitals are unmodernized and forbidding.

An Ohio mental hospital in 1967. This is a typical day hall or recreational area where the institutionalized spend most of their time while hospitalized.

sick role assigned to him or her by being clean, quiet, and passive, and waiting for a cure. Because of the shortage of professional personnel, the institution is often operated by psychiatric aides whose goals in organization are often to benefit the aides, not the patients (Dunham and Weinberg 1960). Frequently, the results of this operation are to train the patients in more bizarre behavior, which appears to confirm the staff's expectations and further aggravates the problem. We shall cover the effects of institutionalization in greater detail in the chapters on psychotic behavior.

In recent years various treatment innovations have been introduced into mental hospitals. One example is the *therapeutic community* or milieu therapy (Jones 1953). Under this arrangement the ward is a warm, supportive environment that serves as a small community. Patients are expected to participate in patient government, be responsible for their own behavior, and prepare themselves for functioning in the community.

Although it is generally assumed that the reason for hospitalization is the severity of the abnormal behavior, this is not always the case. For example, social workers are less likely to hospitalize individuals than psychiatrists or psychologists, while psy-

chiatry residents are the likeliest to place the individual in an institution (Mendel and Rapport 1969). If individuals are seen during working hours, 32 percent are hospitalized, while 61 percent of those seen after working hours are hospitalized. These clinicians claim that they would have chosen not to hospitalize 84 percent of the cases if someone had taken the responsibility for the individuals. Appell and Tisdall (1968) say that retarded individuals are often hospitalized because they have no other place to go.

Further aggravating this problem is the fact that the goals of hospitalization are often different for patients and hospital staff. The staff often want patients to undergo changes in perception and behavior while in the hospital, but the patients' goals are usually readjustment to the outside environment (Polak 1970). The recent emphasis on treating an individual in community mental health centers on an outpatient basis is a positive one that is counteracting many of the negative side effects of hospitalization. In addition, recent court decisions have required that institutions provide more than custodial care and must provide the least restrictive treatment possible in terms of the individual's civil rights.

The therapeutic community

Institutions must now provide more than custodial care

Summary

A variety of approaches to behavior change or psychotherapy have been developed. In general, these techniques can best be evaluated in terms of four criteria: (1) clarity of definition, (2) effectiveness, (3) efficiency, and (4) potential side effects.

Psychodynamic approaches developed from the psychoanalytic theory of Sigmund Freud, which assumes that the roots of abnormal behavior are formed in childhood. Unconscious conflicts produce symptoms, and insight into these symptoms is a prerequisite for eliminating the disorder. In traditional Freudian psychoanalysis the analyst uses four basic techniques: free association, dream interpretation, analysis of resistance, and analysis of transference. The goals of psychoanalysis are to replace unconscious with conscious motivation; to eliminate conflicts generated in early stages of development; and to overcome imbalances between the ego, the id, and the superego by strengthening ego processes.

Only a few psychodynamic therapists practice orthodox Freudian psychoanalysis. Most theorists have differed with Freud on the role of early infantile sexuality in neuroses. Carl Jung believed that the libido consists of undifferentiated energy, a universal life force. Jung also believed that people's instinctual forces contained social tendencies and reflected the group psyche or collective unconscious. Dreams, fantasies, association, and other symbolic processes reflect archetypes, including the ego, the animus or male force, the anima or female force, the persona, and the shadow. He also stressed two attitudes—extraversion and introversion. Jung's therapy dealt with current difficulties and future strivings.

Alfred Adler believed that the social context is more important than biological factors in determining behavior and emphasized the struggle for power. Individuals constantly strive toward goals, seeking power, self-actualization, and fulfillment. If these goals are not attained, individuals develop inferiority complexes. Consequently, their behavior can become maladaptive. A number of other neo-Freudians, such as Harry Stack Sullivan, also emphasized disturbed interpersonal relationships as the source of psychopathology.

Transactional analysis is based on psychoanalysis, communication theory, and social role theory. Eric Berne theorized that everyone has three ego states, the adult, the parent, and the child. In interaction among people these ego states may be complementary or conflicting. As a result, people play "games," which may lead to conflict and abnormal behavior.

Group approaches have been used to increase the application of psychotherapeutic processes, as well as to provide a chance for the individual to exhibit behavior and change within a social situation. These groups include the traditional psychodynamic groups, psychodrama groups, marriage counseling, and family therapy.

In humanistic and existential psychotherapies, the focus is on the individual's unique perception of the world. These approaches emphasize the individual's freedom, concern with the future, and choice of personal destiny. They also reject certain concepts of the psychodynamic approach, such as unconscious motivation.

Client-centered therapy emphasizes the self-concept. In a warm, accepting environment, the innate tendency to grow and realize the potential for self-actualization manifests itself. However, in a hostile environment, the development of the self is distorted, and conflict occurs between external and internal values. This conflict leads in turn to the development of anxiety, defensiveness, and other patterns of abnormal behavior. To eliminate abnormal behavior, client-centered therapists respond with warmth, empathy, and genuineness, allowing the individual to grow or self-actualize.

Gestalt therapy is a mixture of psychoanalytic theory, humanism, and Gestalt psychology. Gestalt therapy assumes that abnormal behavior is the result of unresolved conflicts left over from the past, and the main purpose of the therapy is to take care of this "unfinished business." The aim is to help the individual expand self-awareness by becoming aware of and accepting alienated or hidden parts of the self.

scientific approaches to the study of abnormal behavior

Humanistic group approaches include sensitivity training, which increases social sensitivity and behavioral flexibility, and encounter groups, which emphasize personal growth through experimentation with one's own behavior to increase openness and honesty. Encounter groups have had few positive or negative effects on behavior, probably because of the lack of training of many group leaders and the lack of screening of individuals for admission to the group.

Biological approaches to behavior change are based on a variety of assumptions. Psychosurgery is a method that was first designed to eliminate violent and psychotic behavior in individuals. Critics claim it has been indiscriminately applied to many disorders for which it is not appropriate. Because of psychosurgery's adverse side effects, it is rarely used now. The chemical forms of shock therapy, including insulin and metrazol induction of seizures, are rarely used and have been replaced by electroconvulsive shock (ECT), which is effective in severe cases of depression or psychosis.

In chemotherapy, four major types of drugs are used: antianxiety, antidepressive, antimanic, and antipsychotic. The effectiveness of antianxiety drugs is questionable. The antidepressive drugs appear effective with severe depression and have reduced the use of ECT. Lithium, the major antimanic drug, appears to be effective in controlling manic states. The major tranquilizers, or antipsychotic drugs, have been among the effective chemotherapies for chronic psychotic disorders.

Institutionalization is a technique whose major purpose is to provide care for disturbed or retarded individuals who cannot function without supervision.

Key Concepts

analytic psychology
antianxiety drugs
antidepressant drugs
antimanic drugs
antipsychotic drugs
archetypes
chemical shock therapy
dream interpretation
electroconvulsive therapy (ECT)
encounter groups
family therapy
free association
medical therapies
psychoanalysis
psychodrama
psychosurgery
resistance
self-actualization
symptom substitution
T-groups
transference
transactional analysis

Review Questions

1. What are the four main criteria for evaluating treatment methods?
2. What are the four basic techniques of psychoanalysis?
3. List three goals of psychoanalysis.
4. How does Jungian analysis differ from Freudian psychoanalysis?
5. What is the major aim of Adlerian therapy?
6. How did Sullivan explain abnormal behavior?
7. How do unfavorable transactions occur between the ego states of two people, according to transactional analysis?
8. What is the goal of family therapy?
9. What are the four major assumptions of humanistic-existential therapies?
10. What is the goal of client-centered therapy?
11. Explain the *figure* and *ground* concept in Gestalt therapy.
12. What was the original aim of humanistic group therapy?
13. What are the effects of lobotomy?
14. What are the benefits of electroconvulsive therapy over insulin or metrazol shock?
15. What four main types of drugs are used to treat abnormal behavior?
16. What is the main ethical issue in the hospitalization of abnormally behaving people?

behavior therapy 7

Key Topics

Four major assumptions behavior therapists make about abnormal behavior

Five major phases of behavioral intervention

Operant conditioning techniques

Respondent conditioning techniques

Modeling techniques

Cognitive techniques

Biofeedback and behavior change

Advantages and risks of aversion techniques

Token economies in institutions

B. F. Skinner

Behavior therapy, or **behavior modification,** is the application of certain principles of psychology aimed at changing undesired behavior. It developed largely from the theoretical concepts of John B. Watson (1919), and its usefulness was first demonstrated over fifty years ago in Mary Cover Jones's work (1924) on children's fears. Nevertheless, except for a few psychologists such as Dunlap (1932), this approach was largely ignored until the 1950s, when *behaviorism* began to emerge as a major orientation in psychiatry and clinical psychology. Its growth within the last two decades has been phenomenal.

One major cause of this growth has been a disenchantment with the medical model of abnormal behavior and with psychoanalytic theory (Ullmann and Krasner 1965). From the beginning, behavior therapists have questioned the scientific basis of those models and have based their own work on the learning theories of Pavlov, Watson, Hull, Tolman, and Skinner.

Foundations of learning theories

A second major reason was the development of psychological theories and principles, especially in the field of learning, that could be directly applied to the modification of abnormal behavior. The research of B. F. Skinner (1953), in particular, suggested many such applications.

The *early* behavior therapists, such as Wolpe (1958) and Eysenck (1960), often took radical positions on the scientific and philosophical merits of other theoretical approaches and treatment methods (Bellack and Hersen 1977). However, the *radical* behaviorism of Watson and Skinner, in which humans were often viewed as *empty* organisms responding mechanically to stimuli, is rapidly being replaced by more complete, sophisticated approaches, such as *social learning* theory (Bandura 1969). These developments in behavior therapy occurred as it became obvious that social, developmental, and physiological psychology also had contributions to make to the theory, research, and clinical applications of behavior therapy. Consequently, there has been a resurgence of interest among behavioral clinicians in the internal functioning of the individual, including cognitive processes (Mahoney 1974) and control of physiological responses through biofeed-

Broad spectrum behavior therapy includes internal processes

Abnormal behavior as a variation of normal behavior

Emphasis on observable events

back (Yates 1975). Many behavior therapists are now also using techniques first developed in psychodynamic and humanistic psychotherapy in what Lazarus (1971) calls *broad spectrum* behavior therapy.

We shall provide a general summary in this chapter of the many techniques used by behavior therapists, and throughout the book we shall describe applications of these techniques to specific disorders.

Assumptions of Behavior Therapy

Behavior therapists make four major assumptions about the nature of abnormal behavior:

1. Abnormal behavior is acquired in the same manner as normal behavior. What this implies is that, until it is demonstrated otherwise, *abnormal behavior is a variation of normal behavior*. This is not a denial that some individuals—because of their genetic or physiological characteristics—are more susceptible to acquiring deviant behavior.

   The principal mechanism for acquiring abnormal behavior patterns is learning. While much attention has been paid to the fact that deviant behavior is usually acquired under stressful conditions, it is also true that a significant number of abnormal response patterns are acquired through positive reinforcement (Sandler and Davidson 1973). Furthermore, some abnormal behavior patterns are learning deficits. The shy, socially inept individual who is labeled a schizoid personality may be a person who has never learned how to interact appropriately with other people.

2. *A scientific approach* to abnormal behavior is both feasible and productive. For behavior therapists this means either dealing with observable behavior or—when investigating or modifying unobservable events such as cognitive processes—defining and measuring these events in terms of observable references. Behavioral clinicians must

scientific approaches to the study of abnormal behavior

also pay close attention to the fact that they deal with processes rather than objects and not fall into the trap of treating their ideas about the real world as if the ideas alone were real.

3. *Insight is not a necessary prerequisite* for behavior change for two reasons. First, it is well known that some people understand their deviant behavior very clearly but are unable to change it. It is also well documented that even after individuals understand what causes their behavior, the behavior often does not change. As a matter of fact, insight is often a product rather than an instigator of behavior change. Second, the clinician may never know exactly what causes a particular client to behave in a particular way. Logically, knowing exactly what caused a particular behavior pattern is impossible; in fact, people only rarely are able to explain their behavior accurately (Nisbett and Wilson 1977). Thus, it is not always necessary to know the cause of the behavior in order to modify it.

Cognitive behavior therapists, it should be noted, have approached insight in a different manner (Beck 1976; Ellis 1962; Mahoney 1974). They assume that if an individual's abnormal behavior is a function of irrational beliefs, then alternating these cognitions is an effective technique for changing behavior. Their emphasis is on an accurate perception of situations and oneself, or the elimination of irrational thinking.

4. The goal of behavior therapy is to *change a specific pattern of behavior* that is considered problematic. Behavior therapists do not assume that abnormal behavior is always an intrinsic aspect of an individual's personality, or that a change in personality structure is necessary for effective treatment. Many behavior therapists question the traditional concept that implies persistent and consistent stable personality traits. Rather, they assume that an individual's behavior is a function of specific stimulus situations and that

the systematic use of environmental contingencies can alter these responses (Mischel 1968). However, recent evidence on the stability of personality characteristics in some individuals, to be discussed in Chapter 10, has altered this assumption to some degree (Bowers 1973; Mischel 1973). Nevertheless, a major benefit of this type of approach is that the necessity for changing the individual's value system, which often occurs with the reconstruction of personality, is minimal in most behavior therapy cases. As a rule, behavior therapy alters specific *target behaviors* (the behavior therapist's term for symptoms) rather than value systems. This, of course, limits the types of problems behavior therapy addresses.

Deemphasis of insight

Process of Behavior Therapy

Behavior therapy is characterized by a highly active interaction between therapist and client. The nature of the client-therapist interaction and the techniques used vary with the individual's problem. For example, some individuals may be seen once or twice a week for hourly sessions as in classic psychotherapy, but in other cases they may be seen for three or four hours daily. Contact with the client may occur in the behavior therapist's office, in the client's house, or in other situations in the client's environment where the problem is occurring. This tailoring of the treatment technique to the individual's problems makes it difficult to characterize the exact process of all behavior therapy, but there should be five major phases in the *therapeutic intervention:*

Goal is to change problematic behavior

1. During the initial contact there is usually a careful *definition and assessment* of the problem behavior. As mentioned in Chapter 5, the focus is on clearly delineating the problem, identifying aspects of the individual's behavior and environment that contribute to the difficulty, and

Definition and assessment

In behavior therapy, the treatment is tailored to the individual's problems. In this initial contact, the child's problem behavior is carefully defined and assessed.

carefully assessing the whole situation so that the behavior therapist has as much information about the pattern of abnormal behavior as possible.

Formulation

2. When all the data have been collected, there is a careful consideration of the factors leading to the development and maintenance of the behavior pattern, or a *formulation* of the problem behavior. In recent years, behavior therapists have been interested in theoretical and clinical explanations of problem behaviors as well as in the techniques of modification. A knowledge of how the problem behavior developed and why it continues to occur is helpful for effective therapeutic intervention.

Selecting treatment technique

Discussion with client

3. Once the behavior therapist has reasonable hypotheses about the specific pattern of abnormal behavior, he or she is in a position to *select a suitable treatment technique* for the problem. The initial stages of assessment, formulation of problem behavior, and selection of one or two feasible treatment plans are the most difficult aspects of behavior therapy and require a great deal of clinical skill.

Implementation

The modification techniques selected are often tailored to the individual's specific problem. Personal adjustments in technique are necessary because no two cases are ever exactly the same, even if they have the same diagnostic label.

4. After the initial phases have been completed, the behavior therapist *discusses the formulation with the client* or, in some cases, with a child's guardians. Most behavior therapists emphasize that during this stage the client is entitled to all the information about the case, including the therapist's hypotheses. A good general rule is that therapists should discuss with the client all aspects of the case in the same way they would discuss it with a colleague. This approach ensures that the client has an opportunity to correct misconceptions that the behavior therapist may have about the case and thereby avoid therapeutic blunders.

Now the behavior therapist presents one or, preferably, several treatment possibilities. These techniques are usually discussed in detail with the client: the client is told how they work, how much time they require, their possible positive and negative side effects, the chances that they will be effective, and any other information that will help the client select one of the treatment alternatives or even decline therapy. In most cases, clients are given time to consider the alternatives before they make a decision. If the client then decides to try one of the treatment plans, he or she may be required to sign a *treatment contract* with the therapist, which specifies that the client understands the nature of treatment, the potential risks involved, and other aspects of the treatment plan.

5. The final phase of the intervention process is the *implementation of the treatment plan*. During the treatment phase the problem behavior is usually monitored directly so that the therapist can determine whether the behavioral technique being used is

scientific approaches to the study of abnormal behavior

effective. Most behavior therapists expect behavior change in a short period of time, and if it does not occur, its absence may indicate an inadequate formulation of the case or an ineffective treatment plan. With continuous monitoring of the behavior, these errors become immediately evident, and the behavior therapist can take steps to correct the techniques.

Techniques of Behavior Therapy

A large variety of behavioral techniques are currently used, and the list is growing. Many of these techniques are quite effective in most cases; some are effective with specific kinds of disorders; and some are relatively ineffective.

Operant Conditioning Techniques

These procedures were developed from *operant* psychology described by B. F. Skinner (1953). In general, the techniques employ systematic environmental contingencies to directly alter the subject's response to specific situations. The individual's responses are referred to as *operants,* a term that implies that the organism is operating on the environment by emitting responses that generate reinforcement reward. The probability (frequency) of these responses can be altered by making positive or negative experiences contingent (dependent) upon particular behaviors. If a behavior is rewarded or punished in the presence of a particular stimulus situation (that is, a discriminative stimulus) the probability of that response occurring is altered when the situation is presented again. A number of strategies are then possible.

Contingent Reinforcement

Contingent reinforcement is employed to increase the probability of a specific behavior pattern by making a positive reinforcement contingent on a desired response. For example, if an individual has poor social skills, such as lack of eye contact with other people, the person could be encouraged through reinforcement to increase the duration as well as the frequency of eye contact at each social interaction. Later in training the individual might be given only intermittent reinforcement so that reinforcement occurs only for a fixed or variable number of responses or intervals of time. This procedure makes the desirable behavior more resistant to extinction.

Feedback

Feedback provides an individual with information about the performance of a well-defined and measurable behavior. For example, an individual afraid of small enclosed spaces might be put in a small room with a timer that would indicate the amount of time spent in the room. This type of feedback is viewed as positive. Feedback intended to extinguish behavior can be labeled negative. If providing feedback is seen as a form of reinforcement, then feedback itself can be used as a specific type of reinforcement procedure. Feedback is more effective when instructions are used as stimuli to occasion a specific response (that is, as *discriminative stimuli*). The client is instructed in how to execute a behavior and then informed about how accurate the performance is.

Extinction

Extinction is a procedure through which the probability of a response is decreased by withdrawal of reinforcement. For example, if an individual were engaging in delusional or nonsense talk, one method of eliminating this behavior would be to have people ignore it or leave the client's presence when the behavior begins to occur. Extinction is a very powerful technique and often is the principal ingredient in more complex behavioral techniques such as *systematic desensitization,* which we shall describe later in this chapter.

Shaping

Shaping is a procedure by which a complex response pattern not in the individual's repertoire can be produced. This is the technique used by animal trainers to teach unusual tricks. Pigeons have even been taught to play tennis this way. The procedure essentially involves breaking down a

Operant conditioning: organism operates on environment and is reinforced

Reinforcement is contingent on response

Performance feedback as reinforcement

Extinction is withdrawal of reinforcement

Shaping is reinforcing successive approximations of target behavior

complex response into simple components. Each segment of the complex pattern is then taught as a successive approximation of the final desired target behavior. For example, Cook and Adams (1966) shaped verbal behavior in a retarded mute adolescent. The first step was to teach the individual to sit in a chair, next to maintain eye contact, then to verbalize and approximate the sounds of specific words. Finally, the client was taught to produce words and simple sentences. Each step was reinforced with M&Ms and social approval. Similar procedures were used by Sherman (1965) to teach verbal behavior to mute psychotic adults.

Fading and Prompting

Prompts are faded when no longer needed

Prompts are cues, instructions, gestures, directions, examples, and models of responses that facilitate the probability or development of a desired behavior. When a prompt initiates behavior that is reinforced, the prompt becomes a discriminative stimulus. When the behavior is performed consistently, the prompt can be gradually reduced and finally removed from the situation. This procedure is called **fading**. An example of the use of these techniques is given in a case by Barlow and Agras (1973). The client, who desired to alter his homosexual behavior, was twenty-

nine years old and had a fourteen-year history of exclusive homosexual behavior, although he occasionally dated women. In the treatment procedure he was shown slides of male and female nudes, while his sexual arousal was measured with a penile strain gauge. Two slides, one male and one female, were projected on a screen by separate projectors so that the pictures were superimposed. Brightness of each slide could be decreased or increased. During the initial phases the male slide was shown at 100 percent brightness, and the female slide at zero percent brightness to prompt a sexual arousal. Then the male slide was gradually decreased in brightness while the female slide was increased in brightness. To fade from one step to the next, a 75 percent criterion of full erection was required. The final step was 100 percent female illumination and zero percent male illumination. This technique of prompts and fading was successful in shaping sexual arousal to females in this individual (see Figure 7–1).

The Premack Principle

The **Premack principle** states that a behavior of low probability can be reinforced and thus increased by making the privilege of engaging in another preferred or more probable behavior contingent upon its occurrence. If the goal were to increase studying behavior in students (usually a low-

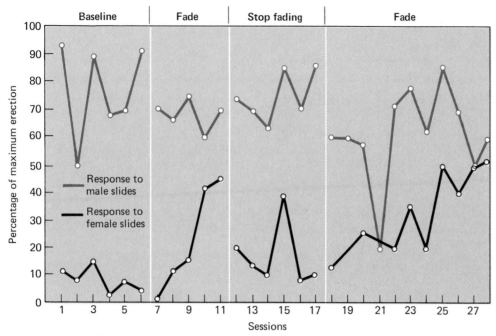

Figure 7-1 Mean penile circumference as a percentage of full erection for a homosexual subject.

probability behavior), it might be accomplished by making television viewing dependent upon a certain amount of studying time.

Contingency Contracting

A *contingency* or *behavioral contract* is a negotiated agreement between two people and identifies the conditions under which each will reinforce the other. Contracts explicitly define the relationship between each individual's behavior and the consequences, positive or negative, for that behavior. Built into this contract is the notion of *reciprocity* or mutually reinforcing consequences for the purpose of improving the quality of the relationship. *Contingency contracting* has been used as a treatment strategy to remedy marital problems, to improve relationships between parents and children, and to improve almost any type of social, interactional problem.

Respondent Conditioning Techniques

The monumental work of Ivan Pavlov formed the basis for a number of important behavior therapy techniques developed by individuals such as Mary Cover Jones, Andrew Salter, Joseph Wolpe, and Martin Shapiro. These techniques are most frequently used for *counterconditioning* and

extinction of conditioned emotional responses, although they are applicable to many other problem behaviors. The most common techniques are systematic desensitization, assertiveness training, and flooding.

Systematic Desensitization

Systematic desensitization is a technique developed by Joseph Wolpe (1958) to deal with maladaptive anxiety responses elicited by specific stimuli in the environment. The technique is based on the assumption that if a response that counters or is antagonistic to anxiety can be made to appear in the presence of the anxiety-provoking stimuli, a complete or partial reduction of the anxiety response will occur.

The first step is to identify responses that are antagonistic to anxiety. These include sexual arousal, eating, drinking, and various other responses. The antagonistic response most frequently used is progressive or *deep muscular relaxation,* a technique specifically developed by Jacobson (1938) to combat anxiety and tension. Deep muscular relaxation involves focused attention on the major voluntary muscle groups. The client is usually placed in a very quiet, undisturbed environment and instructed to close the eyes and relax as much as possible.

Contracts define consequences of behavior

Systematic desensitization pairs an anxiety-provoking response with one that is antagonistic to anxiety (e.g., relaxation)

The undersigned, Frank and Wilma B., enter into the following agreement with each other. The terms of this agreement include the following:

1. During this weekend Wilma agrees not to mention any of Frank's past drinking episodes or possible drinking in the future.

2. Wilma will be allowed one infringement of this agreement per day provided that she immediately terminates her alcohol-related conversation contingent upon Frank's reminding her of this agreement.

3. On Friday, Saturday, and Sunday afternoons or evenings Frank agrees to take Wilma out of the house for the purpose of a shopping trip, dinner, movie, or a drive depending on her choice.

4. Wilma's agreement to refrain from alcohol-related conversation is binding only if Frank fulfills his agreement stated under term number 3.

5. Frank's agreement to take Wilma out each day of the weekend is binding only if Wilma fulfills her agreement stated under term number 1.

6. The terms of the contract are renewable at the beginning of each day so that failure of one partner to fulfill his or her part of the agreement on any one day breaks the contract for that day only.

_____
Frank B.

_____
Wilma B.

_____
Witness

The therapist then instructs the client to first tense and then relax a specific group of muscles. The initial tension serves to acquaint the individual with muscle activity in one specific muscle group, while the relaxation sensitizes the client to feelings of overall calm. A typical session might proceed as follows:

Now, I want you to be completely calm and relaxed, get a very pleasant relaxing scene in your mind, and let your body go completely limp. Breathe deeply and slowly and continue to relax. Now, I want you to focus your attention on your right hand. Make a fist with your right hand. That's it. Pull it tighter, tighter. Feel the tension across your fingers, arms, and wrist. Now, I want you to let your hand relax, let your muscles completely relax as your hand falls in the chair. Don't force it, just let the muscles go limp rather than forcing them to go limp. Feel the relaxing, feel the warmth; note how it is different from the tension. Now, let's do it again and notice the difference in relaxation and tension.

The progress of the procedure is usually: right hand/right arm, left hand/left arm, forehead, eyelids, nose and cheeks, mouth and jaw, neck and shoulders, left leg/left calf, right leg/right calf, right side of the chest, left side of the chest, stomach, lower back, and then the entire body. The client is also instructed in breathing exercises. If the client goes into a semi-trance, so much the better. The client is also instructed to practice this procedure several times a day at home.

Next, the anxiety stimuli must be presented in such a way that they will not override the competing positive response. This is done by breaking down the phobic stimuli into a gradient of responses. The client and the therapist develop a number of aspects or approaches to the anxiety-provoking situation that are arranged in a hierarchy of the amount of anxiety they provoke. For example, as shown in Table 7–1, an individual may suffer anxiety while taking examinations. Just thinking about the exam may cause some degree of discomfort, while being in the room when the examination is passed out may provoke maximal anxiety. When a hierarchy of ten to fifteen of these items is listed, the therapist can move to the final step.

The individual is placed in a comfortable chair and relaxes completely through progressive muscular relaxation; then the therapist presents the lowest item on the

scientific approaches to the study of abnormal behavior

Table 7–1 Examples of Temporal and Thematic Hierarchies

Item	Percentage of maximal anxiety
Temporal hierarchy (examination anxiety)	
Teacher passes out exams	100
Sit down in exam room	90
Enter exam room	80
Standing in hall, waiting to enter the exam room	70
Walking to school on day of exam	60
At home on the morning of an exam	50
Studying on the night before an exam	40
1 week before an exam	30
Teacher announces that an exam will be upcoming in 2 weeks	20
Teacher announces he will give a midterm and a final	10
Thematic hierarchy (heterosexual dating anxiety)	
Ringing a date's doorbell	100
Calling a prospective date on the telephone	90
Asking a girl to dance	80
Asking a girl for her phone number	70
Leaving to pick up a date	60
Asking a girl for a date	50
Dressing for a date	40
Talking to a girl in class	30
Being introduced to an attractive girl	20
Thinking about next Saturday night	10

hierarchy, and the client imagines the scene as vividly as possible. If any anxiety is felt, the client signals the therapist, who instructs the client to stop imagining the scene. The therapist again gets the client completely relaxed and on the next presentation either gives the imaginary scene for a shorter length of time or presents an item lower on the hierarchy. After each item is successfully mastered, the next item on the ladder is presented. Gradually, the whole hierarchy is mastered. With mastery of the situation in imagination, a reduction of fear in the actual anxiety-provoking situation should occur.

For a number of reasons the typical method of presenting the hierarchy of anxiety responses in imagination may not be feasible. For example, the individual's imagination may be poor, and there may be little generalization from the imaginary scenes to the actual situation. In these cases the hierarchy may be presented *in vivo*; that is, the individual may be gradually exposed to the hierarchy in actual situations. When **in vivo desensitization** is possible, it is usually much more effective than the classic method of systematic desensitization.

Assertiveness Training

In **assertiveness training,** the aim is to improve one's ability to express appropriate feelings and to insist on one's legitimate rights. This includes the expression of socially appropriate irritation and anger as well as the expression of positive feelings, such as affection and excitement (Lazarus 1971). The need arises when the inability to assert themselves leads individuals to perceive themselves as weak or incompetent. This inability may also manifest itself in inappropriate rage or temper tantrums. A deficit in assertiveness may be due to failure to learn the skill, inadequate stimulus discrimination, an inability to detect the situations in which assertiveness is appropriate, or the inhibition of assertiveness by anxiety. In assertiveness training the therapist arranges a series of tasks that gradually approximate the desired social response. The client is then confronted with these tasks and taught appropriate assertive skills in progressively more difficult situations. The therapist may use prompts, fading, reinforcement, role playing, modeling, or reasoning to get the client to emit the desired behavior. Once the response is mastered in the analogue training situation, the individual is gradually exposed to an actual situation. As clients become more successful in handling people in a confident manner, their self-esteem and self-confidence increase. This procedure is appropriate for dealing with both anxiety responses and social skill deficits.

Feared stimuli in imagination...

... and in vivo

Assertiveness training teaches the expression of socially appropriate feelings

box 7-2
Assertiveness
Training with
a Timid Child

Therapist Let's play a game with these blocks; we'll build a house. I'll be the worker, and you be the person in charge. (*Role playing.*) OK now, where shall I put these blocks?

Client (*Softly.*) Uh . . . they can go over there.

Therapist [*Although her response is somewhat tentative, I'll go along with it so as to provide some initial positive reinforcement for what is an approximation to an assertive response.*] (*Placing blocks where indicated.*) OK, I'll put them right here then. How about these?

Client (*Softly.*) You can put them there also.

Therapist [*Let's see if I can get her to show some initiative by deciding what we should be doing next.*] What shall I do now?

Client (*Pause.*) Get some more blocks and put them in the same pile.

Therapist OK. Now what?

Client Put more there.

Therapist [*She seems to be handling that fairly well. Let's see what she can do if I throw a mild obstacle in her path.*] (*Softly.*) No, I want to put them in a different pile.

Therapist [*She needs some encouragement. Perhaps I can coach her on a more appropriate way of responding.*] (*Stepping out of role.*) Wait a minute. Remember that *you* are the one that's in charge, and you have to tell *me* what to do, even if I don't want to do it. (*Back in role.*) I want to put these blocks in a new pile.

Client No, I'm sorry, but you can't. We have to build up that section first.

Therapist All right. But can I knock over the blocks and start again?

Client (*Hesitantly.*) No. Let's finish it first.

Therapist [*She seems to be holding her ground fairly well. Some reinforcement is in order at this point. Also, I'd like to change the situation somewhat so as to focus on how softly she's been speaking. Let's see if I can come up with a game that's more likely to elicit a louder response.*] (*Stepping out of role and putting his arm around client.*) That was real good. Let's make believe now that you're on top of this high building, and I'm working below. You can stand up on the chair and make believe you're at the top of the building. (*Back in role.*) How many more blocks do we need here?

Client (*Standing on chair.*) Five more.

Therapist What? I can't hear you. I'm all the way down here.

Client (*A little louder.*) Five more.

Therapist What was that?

Client (*Much louder.*) I SAID WE NEED FIVE MORE!

Flooding arouses maximum anxiety to produce habituation

Flooding

Flooding is a procedure for extinguishing anxiety by over-exposing the individual, usually in imagination, to stimuli that evoke the maximum anxiety response. Flooding arouses the maximum amount of anxiety in order to habituate or to extinguish anxiety responses to fearful situations. In flooding, anxiety is evoked by *cues* associated with the disorder. This overexposure to or flooding with stimuli that evoke a high degree of arousal sometimes continues for hours until the individual no longer emotionally responds. An example of the use of this technique with an individual who had a snake phobia is given by Hogan (1968).

A variation of flooding is **implosive therapy.** Developed by Thomas Stampfl, implosive therapy combines psychodynamic and learning approaches. It is based on the theory that neurotic behavior consists of *avoidance responses* that are learned and perpetuated because they reduce anxiety. Such defensive responses are usually learned in childhood when the individual is punished, rejected, or deprived in some way. These early experiences produce fears related to feelings and impulses commonly believed to involve conflict, such as infantile rejection, sexuality, or aggression (Stampfl and Levis 1967). These fears later manifest themselves in behavioral symptoms. Because anxiety perpetuates neurotic symptoms, Stampfl reasons, elimination of anxiety will result in a disappearance of the neurotic symptoms. In this therapy, the individual is forced to experience intense anxiety in the absence of any real aversive consequences. Again, emphasis is on imaginative rather than actual experience of the feared stimuli, and the therapist must

scientific approaches to the study of abnormal behavior

box 7–3
An Example of
Flooding with a
Snake Phobia

[*Imagine that the snakes are*] touching you, biting you, try to get that helpless feeling like you can't win, and just give up and let them crawl all over you. Don't even fight them anymore. Let them crawl as much as they want. And now there is a big giant snake, it is as big as a man and it is staring at you and it is looking at you; it's ugly and it's black and it has got horrible eyes and long fangs, and it is coming towards you. It is standing on its tail and it is looking down at you, looking down on you. I want you to get that feeling, like you are a helpless little rabbit, and it's coming toward you, closer and closer; feel it coming toward you. Horrible, evil, ugly, slimy, and it's looking down on you, ready to strike at you. Feel it in your stomach, feel it coming, oooh, it is getting closer and closer and it snaps out at you. Feel it biting at your head now, it is biting at your head; it opens its giant mouth and it has your whole head inside of its mouth. And it is biting your head right off. Feel it; feel it biting, the fangs going right through your neck. Feel it, and now it is starting to swallow you whole. It is pulling you right inside its body, feel yourself being pulled and dragged into its body. Feel yourself inside, helpless, lost, and now you are starting to turn into a snake. Feel yourself turning into a slimy snake. And you are crawling out of its mouth. All the other snakes see you. And they start to attack you. Feel them; they are coming to bite and rip you apart. Do you know how animals attack each other? Look at the snakes attacking you, feel them biting you, ripping you to shreds.

Hogan, 1968

box 7–4
Implosion in a
Case of Fear
of Rejection

Shut your eyes and imagine that you are a baby in your crib. You are in a dark, shabby, dirty room. You are alone and afraid. You are hungry and wet. You call for your mother, but no one comes. If only someone would change you; if only they would feed you and wrap you in a warm blanket. You look out the window of your room into the house next door, where a mother and father are giving another baby love, warmth and affection. Look how they love the baby. You are crying for your mother now. "Please mother, please come and love me." But no one comes. Finally, you hear some steps. They come closer, and closer, and closer. You hear someone outside your door. The door slowly opens. Your heart beats with excitement. There is your mother coming to love you. She is unbuttoning her blouse. She takes out her breast to feed you. Then she squirts your warm milk on the floor and steps in it. Look, see her dirty heel mark in your milk. She shouts, "I would rather waste my milk than to give it to you. I wish you were never born; I never wanted you."

Hogan, 1969

make sure that the client does nothing during the therapy session to avoid experiencing the full intensity of the anxiety.

In summary, several points should be made about flooding. First, the more similar the cues used for flooding are to the cues eliciting the anxiety response, the more effective the treatment procedure will be. For this reason, flooding is probably more effective than implosion. In addition, flooding can be conducted *in vivo* (in the actual situation), a procedure that is probably more effective than flooding in imagination. For example, an individual might be forced to ride in an elevator if he or she has a fear of elevators. The second point is that flooding must be continued until the individual is no longer responding to the cues (McCutcheon and Adams 1975). Thus, it is often desirable to have autonomic indices of the decrease in anxiety response. If the session is terminated while the individual is still responding to the cues, the person may still be sensitized and the problem aggravated, as can be seen in Figure 7–2 (McCutcheon and Adams 1975). Third, flooding may be more effective than system-

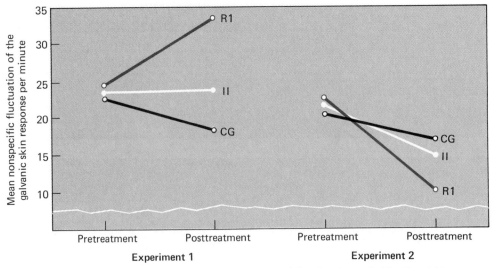

Figure 7–2 The first experiment involved a short period of flooding for a phobia of watching surgical operations (RI), flooding for an irrelevant phobia of snakes (II), and no flooding (CG or Control Group). In the second experiment a longer period of flooding was used. Anxiety as measured by galvanic skin response (GSR) increased with short periods but decreased with longer exposure.

Flooding is a difficult technique

atic desensitization with pervasive "free-floating" anxiety, while systematic desensitization may be more effective with specific phobias (Boulougouris, Marks, and Marset 1971). In any case, flooding is a difficult technique whose administration requires considerable clinical sophistication since, if it is misused, potential side effects may be tragic. In most situations, systematic desensitization is preferred to flooding.

Other Respondent Conditioning Techniques

A number of other techniques are used less frequently than the ones described thus far. *Response prevention* is a method of controlling *stereotyped high-frequency behaviors* often associated with compulsive behaviors. In this procedure the stereotyped response is clearly defined, and the client agrees to allowing the therapist and others to prevent the response. In treatment, the individual is prevented from engaging in the response by persuasion, diversion, mild restraint, and other techniques. Response prevention is usually continued for a week or two, at which time supervision is *faded.*

Negative practice is repeated emitting of the undesired behavior

Negative Practice

Negative practice is a procedure wherein an individual is required to repeat an undesirable behavior, such as a tic, stammer, or other motor response, hundreds of times

Modeling is imitative learning

in mass trials in order to extinguish the behavior. This technique was introduced by Dunlap (1932) and has been described extensively by Yates (1958). The efficiency of negative practice has been questioned, and it is no longer used frequently.

Thought Stopping

Thought stopping is a technique often used with obsessive thinking. The individual is instructed to engage in the undesirable thought, and while the cognitive response is occurring, the therapist loudly yells "STOP!" The *startle response* stops the cognitive activity. The individual is then trained to use the technique, first to yell "stop" out loud to halt the undesirable behavior, and later to "yell" it covertly. This technique is most effective when used in combination with other procedures, such as contingent reinforcement.

Modeling Techniques

In general, *modeling* is a procedure by which the client observes another individual, usually the therapist, engaging in some behavior and then imitates this behavior. The goal here is to control undesirable responses or to acquire desirable responses through imitation. Modeling stimuli can come from other individuals, reading, instructions, television, and many other such sources. While modeling may be present in

scientific approaches to the study of abnormal behavior

some form in many behavior therapies, it is the major ingredient in the following procedures:

Behavioral Rehearsal

In **behavioral rehearsal** the client is asked to describe a difficult situation for which the client and therapist together can then determine the appropriate behavior. Once the situation is delineated, the therapist may play the role of another individual, and the client has to handle the situation. Behavioral rehearsal is a strategy that many of us use when we go into a difficult situation and say, "Well, if he says this, then I will say this," "If she does A, then I will do B." By rehearsing a situation, an individual is prepared to respond to most events that may occur. This technique is frequently used in assertiveness training.

Participant Modeling

Participant modeling involves watching a skillful individual perform a response and then imitating this model. The components of the skill are learned by observation, and by enacting the sequence of responses, feedback on the accuracy can be obtained, resulting in skill improvement. Suppose an individual who had difficulty obtaining dates observed a highly skilled person interact with a member of the opposite sex. After this observation the individual would then attempt to reproduce these skills, and the therapist would provide feedback on the accuracy.

Vicarious Extinction

If a behavior is followed by noxious consequences, the behavior will be suppressed, and the stimuli associated with the aversive consequences will, in the future, evoke a conditioned fear response. This conditioned fear response may continue to occur even though punishment for the behavior no longer occurs. *Vicarious extinction* occurs when one individual observes another engage in the anxiety-producing behavior with no undue consequences, and anxiety is thereby eliminated in the observer. The term "vicarious" is used because the subject is not directly exposed to the extinction trials. Bandura and Menlove (1968) used this technique with children who were fearful of dogs. These children observed other children interacting with dogs in a fearless

This child is learning through vicarious extinction that the dog is friendly.

manner. As a result of their observations, the fearful children showed a reduction in fear and avoidance behavior towards dogs. O'Conner (1969) also used this method with socially withdrawn children, who observed a film of children interacting with others. As a consequence, the withdrawn children showed a marked increase in their own interaction with other children. At present, the full range of possible treatment techniques derived from modeling has not been explored; however, the possibilities for useful modification techniques are limitless (Bandura 1976).

Cognitive Techniques

In the past few years behavior therapists have begun to focus their attention on treatment techniques developed from cognitive psychology and to use these procedures to modify overt behavior as well as internal mediating responses, including reasoning, thinking, and believing (Mahoney 1974). We shall describe a few of these techniques.

Vicarious extinction is watching someone engage in the anxiety-producing behavior with no undue consequences

Cognitive Restructuring

Cognitive restructuring is based on the assumption that people behave in self-defeat-

box 7–5
An Example of
Rational-Emotive
Therapy

Patient But why shouldn't I want things to go my way? Why *shouldn't* I try to get what I want?

Therapist No reason at all. To want what you want when you want it is perfectly legitimate. But you, unfortunately, are doing one additional thing—and that's perfectly illegitimate.

Patient What's that? What's the illegitimate thing?

Therapist You're not only *wanting* what you want, but *demanding* it. You're taking a perfectly sane desire—to be able to avoid standing trial for your crimes, in this instance—and asininely turning it into an absolute *necessity*.

Patient Why is that so crazy?

Therapist For the simple reason that, first of all, *any* demand or necessity is crazy. Wanting a thing, wanting any damned thing you happen to crave, is fine—as long as you admit the possibility of your not being able to get it. But as soon as you demand something, turn it into a necessity, you simply won't be able to *stand* your not getting it. In that event, either you'll do something desperate to get it—as you usually have done in your long history of antisocial behavior—or else you'll keep making yourself angry, excep-

tionally frustrated, or anxious about not getting it. Either way, *you* lose.

Patient But suppose I *can* get what I want?

Therapist Fine—as long as you don't subsequently defeat your own ends by getting it. As in this case. Even assuming that you could skip bail successfully—which is very doubtful, except for a short while—would you *eventually* gain by having to live in terror of arrest for the remainder of your life or by having to give up everything and everyone you love here to run, let us say, to South America?

Patient Perhaps not.

Therapist Perhaps? Besides, let's assume, for a moment, that you really could get away with it—you really could skip bail and that you wouldn't get caught and wouldn't live in perpetual fear. Even then, would you be doing yourself such a great favor?

Patient It seems to me I would! What more could I ask?

Therapist A lot more. And it is just your *not* asking for a lot more that proves, to me at least, that you are a pretty sick guy.

Patient In what way? What kind of crap are you giving me? Bullshit!

Cognitive restructuring is a direct attack on an irrational belief

Self-control

ing ways because they have false, misguided, or irrational beliefs. The purpose of cognitive restructuring is to identify and eliminate these beliefs through reasoning. For example, a client may have learned to believe that "I must be loved and approved of by everyone." During therapy, this belief is challenged directly in the hope that it can be revealed as irrational and thus eliminated. The best-known example of cognitive restructuring is the *rational-emotive therapy* of Albert Ellis (1962), which Ellis himself has variously referred to as a "psychoanalytically derived" therapy, a form of behavior therapy, and, lately, a type of humanistic therapy.

Self-Control Procedures
Self-control procedures are often used by behaviorists whose goal in any behavioral intervention is to increase the control individuals have over their own behavior. Some

techniques attempt to directly modify self-regulation or self-management. This implies that individuals can learn to resist contingency in the external environment by reinforcing themselves covertly. For example, individuals on a diet may resist the offer of a piece of candy by otherwise rewarding themselves for their restraint. Kanfer (1975) has described three stages of the *self-regulatory process.* The first stage is *self-monitoring,* in which individuals observe their performance and its context. The second stage is *self-evaluation,* during which individuals compare their performance with some standard criterion to assess its adequacy. These criteria may be internal, external, or both. The final stage is *self-reinforcement,* in which individuals self-administer rewarding or punishing stimuli, contingent upon good or poor performance. Self-reinforcement, as noted earlier, is presumed to operate in the same manner as external reinforcement.

Therapist Well, I could get highly "ethical" and say that if you get away with things like that, with rifling vending machines, jumping bail, and such things, that you are then helping to create the kind of a world that you yourself would not want to live in, or certainly wouldn't want your friends or relatives to live in. For if you can get away with such acts, of course, others can too; and in such a pilfering, bail-jumping world, who would want to live?

Patient But suppose I said that I didn't mind living in that kind of world—kind of liked it, in fact?

Therapist Right. You might very well say that. And even mean it—though I wonder whether, if you really gave the matter careful thought, you would. But let us suppose you would. So I won't use that "ethical" argument with a presumably "unethical" and guiltless person like you. But there is still another, and better argument, and one that you and people like you generally overlook.

Patient And that is?

Therapist That is—your own skin.

Patient My own skin?

Therapist Yes, your own thick and impenetrable skin. Your guiltless, ever so guiltless skin.

Patient I don't get it. What the hell are you talking about?

Therapist Simply this. Suppose, as we have been saying, you are truly guiltless. Suppose you, like Lucky Luciano and a few other guys who really seem to have got away scot-free with a life of crime, really do have a thick skin and don't give a good goddamn what happens to others who may suffer from your deeds, don't care what kind of a world you are helping to create. How, may I ask, can you—you personally, that is—manufacture and maintain that lovely, rugged, impenetrable skin?

Patient What difference does it make how I got it, as long as it's there?

Therapist Ah, but it does!—it does make a difference.

Patient How the hell does it?

Therapist Simply like this. The only practical way that you can get guiltless, can maintain an impenetrable skin under conditions such as we are describing, where you keep getting away with doing in others and reaping criminal rewards, is by hostility—by resenting, hating, loathing the world against which you are criminally behaving.

Ellis, 1962

In the clinical application of self-control procedures two major strategies are used. The first strategy is *environmental planning,* wherein the individual attempts to modify the environment so as to maximize desired behavior or minimize undesired behavior. For example, suppose an individual wanted to modify eating behavior to control weight. The client might restrict the situations in which he or she eats, establish a routine in which eating occurs only at fixed times, or decrease the rate of eating. Such attempts at stimulus control of behavior are shown in Table 7–2.

The second major self-control procedure is *behavioral programming* (Thoresen and Mahoney 1974), which is the self-administration of the consequences of desired behavior changes. Two major strategies are used in behavioral programming: *self-monitoring* and *self-reinforcement.* In self-monitoring, individuals define and describe their behavior, and keep a record of it, either in simple frequency counts or elaborate diaries. Such self-monitoring is a necessary precursor to self-evaluation and self-reinforcement. As observed earlier, the process of self-observation is often reactive, and behavior change may occur simply as a function of self-observation (Kazdin 1974). As the frequency of the target behavior is determined, the individual may then begin to administer self-reinforcement for each change in the frequency of behavior in the desired direction. Self-reinforcement may be internal when the individual either praises or criticizes him or herself, or external when, if a certain criterion is met, the individual engages in some pleasurable activity, such as smoking or watching TV.

Changing environment to change behavior

Self-observation alone may change behavior

Table 7–2 Procedures to Reduce Stimulus Control of Eating

Modification of meal quantity

1. Eat slowly; gradually increase minimal time allowed for each meal.
2. Take small bites.
3. Put eating utensil for food items down while chewing.
4. Take one helping at a time.
5. Leave table for a brief period between helpings.
6. Eat one food item at a time (e.g., finish meat, before taking vegetable).
7. Serve food from kitchen rather than placing platter on table.
8. Use small cups and plates.
9. Leave some food on plate at end of meal.

Modification of meal frequency

1. Do nothing else while eating.
2. Eat in only one place, sitting down (preferably not in kitchen and not where you engage in other activities).
3. Eat only at specified times.
4. Set the table with a complete place setting whenever eating.
5. Wait a fixed period after urge to eat before actually eating.
6. Engage in an activity incompatible with eating when urge to eat appears.
7. Plan a highly liked activity for periods when the urge to eat can be anticipated (e.g., read evening newspaper before bedtime).

Modification of types of food eaten

1. Do not buy prepared foods or snack foods.
2. Prepare lunch after eating breakfast and dinner after lunch (to avoid nibbling).
3. Do grocery shopping soon after eating.
4. Shop from a list.
5. Eat a low calorie meal before leaving for a party.
6. Do not eat while drinking coffee or alcohol.

Other Cognitive Techniques

Cautela (1970, 1971) has taken a similar approach to covert events as a technique for altering response frequency. One procedure is *covert reinforcement:* the person imagines a low-rate response and then imagines a positively reinforcing event. Cautela suggests that, like overt reinforcement, covert reinforcement increases the probability of the response after repeated covert conditioning trials. A similar procedure is *covert extinction:* the client repeatedly imagines engaging in a target behavior and receiving no reinforcement. Covert negative reinforcement uses an escape conditioning paradigm in which the client first imagines aversive stimulus and then terminates that image while simultaneously initiating an image of the target response.

Biofeedback

Biofeedback teaches conscious control of bodily processes

Biofeedback training is an operant conditioning technique in which an individual monitors biological signals from the central nervous system, the autonomic nervous system, the musculoskeletal system, and the cardiovascular system in order to acquire control of those responses. The initial step in the procedure is learning to discriminate these internal cues or sensations (Brener 1974). Voluntary control is accomplished when the individual can, upon instructions, change a response. The procedure is actually quite simple. A physiological response such as heart rate, blood pressure, skin temperature, muscle tension, or electrical activity of the brain is monitored. The client is presented with an ongoing auditory or visual signal that reflects the level of activity in that system. The individual is then instructed to try to change the biological activity in whatever manner imaginable. If a change occurs in the response, it is immediately *fed back* as an external auditory or visual cue. After a number of sessions, depending on the system, the individual can usually acquire control of the response. For example, an individual may greatly decrease the level of frontalis muscle activity, a response associated with tension headaches. The second major step is then to test for voluntary control when the individual is instructed to change the response but no feedback is given (Sturgis, Tollison, and Adams 1978). If the individual can demonstrate this voluntary control without the

scientific approaches to the study of abnormal behavior

aid of external stimuli, the purpose of biofeedback training has been accomplished.

As we shall see later, biofeedback techniques have been used with some success to treat psychophysiological as well as behavioral disorders. The success of these techniques appears to depend on which physiological response system is involved. For example, people have been quite successful in learning to control their muscle tension level and their heart rate, but learning to control high blood pressure in treating hypertension is much more difficult.

Aversion Techniques

Aversion techniques are used primarily to modify behavioral excesses, such as self-injury, drug and alcohol abuse, or disorders that are considered socially reprehensible. In most cases, **aversion therapy** is a last resort. Nevertheless, chemical aversion with alcoholics has been used for decades with literally thousands of patients (Lemere and Voegtlin 1950). There are two major types of aversion therapy. In the first type, noxious stimulation is presented either before or after a response, and in the second type positive reinforcement is withdrawn after a response has occurred.

Noxious Stimulation

Although a variety of environmental stimuli have noxious properties, the two major types used in aversive therapy have been *electrical shock* and *chemical aversion.* (It should be noted that electric shock used in behavior therapy is not electrical convulsive therapy (ECT) and involves a low but nevertheless painful level of shock administered to the forearm, fingertips, or calves.) Chemical aversion, usually used with alcoholism, involves the injection of an emetic, which induces nausea and vomiting.

In general, electric shock is preferable to chemical aversion because in electric shock the intensity of the stimulus and the length of application are much more easily controlled. The four major types of *aversive conditioning* with noxious stimuli are *punishment, classical conditioning, avoidance training,* and *escape training.*

Punishment

In *punishment,* aversive stimuli immediately follow the occurrence of the undesir-

able behavior. An example is the use of response-contingent shock used to treat persistent vomiting that had reached life-threatening proportions in an infant (Cunningham and Linscheid 1976). In this case, a 9½-month-old male infant had to be hospitalized for malnutrition and weight loss due to ruminative vomiting. The infant's symptoms first occurred at age six months and had required hospitalization within two weeks. The disorder was diagnosed as being of psychogenic origin, but over the next 3½ months a variety of medical and psychological approaches failed to control the rumination. In light of the patient's deteriorating condition, it was decided to try aversion procedures. The punishment procedure consisted of shocking the patient with electrodes attached to the calf whenever vomiting occurred. These shocks were of 0.5-second duration, were given at 1.0-second intervals, and were no greater than 4.5 milliamperes in intensity. These shocks were administered to the child in several settings, including a simulated home environment with a variety of observers present. Rumination episodes went from a baseline level of thirty-six per day to four in the first day. Within two weeks, vomiting had ceased, and there was a marked improvement in the child's social behavior (see Figure 7–3). At a six-month follow-up, the child weighed thirty pounds and showed no evidence of behavioral abnormalities. Punishment may have saved the child's life.

Respondent Conditioning

In aversive *respondent conditioning,* the stimulus that elicits maladaptive behavior is repeatedly paired with an aversive stimulus. For example, in alcoholism, the stimulus may be a glass of whiskey; the maladaptive response, abusive drinking; and the aversive stimuli may be electrical shock, chemically induced nausea, or verbal abuse. After repeated pairings, the sight or smell of alcohol acquires noxious properties that lead to the avoidance or cessation of drinking. At the physiological level, actual conditioning of autonomic nervous system responses such as increased heart rate may develop and may then appear upon presentation of the whiskey.

Avoidance Training

In *avoidance training,* the individual learns to escape or avoid aversive stimulation by

Aversion therapy is a last resort

Repeated pairing of alcohol and nausea makes alcohol a noxious stimulus

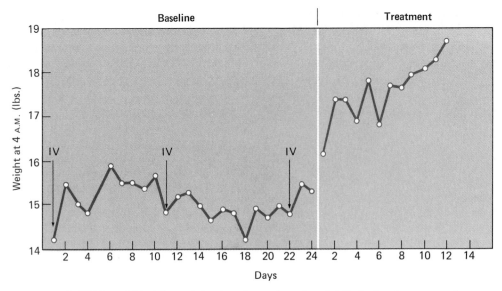

Figure 7-3 Child's weight at 4 A.M. during baseline and treatment. *IV* indicates days on which intravenous feedings were required.

emitting an instrumental response that removes the stimuli from the environment. For example, while being shown slides of attractive male nudes, males desiring to extinguish their homosexual responses may avoid receiving a painful electrical shock by pressing a switch that turns off the slide (Feldman and MacCulloch 1965). Alcoholics may similarly avoid an electrical shock by refusing a drink or pushing it away.

Escape Training

The desired behavior can be presented as the only escape from a noxious stimulus

In *escape training,* the individual is able to terminate the aversive stimuli by engaging in behavior that is more adaptive. In this method the individual always receives the noxious stimulus. For example, an alcoholic takes a sip of beer, and an electric shock is administered contingent upon this sip. The shock is terminated only when the individual spits out the alcohol and thus *escapes* (Miller and Hersen 1972).

Time Out

Forcing individuals to take *time out* from positive reinforcement is a highly effective technique that has been used largely with children. The procedure is fairly simple: When undesirable behavior occurs, access to positive reinforcement is withdrawn for a given amount of time. For example, a child who is engaging in disruptive behavior in a classroom may be taken out of the classroom and placed for a short period of

Positive reinforcement is withdrawn when the undesired behavior occurs

time (say, fifteen minutes) in a "time out" room, which is usually a small room with no furnishing. As Bellack and Hersen (1977) have suggested, time out is probably an effective treatment strategy for three reasons: (1) it removes the individual from the situation in which the undesirable behavior is being reinforced; (2) the individual is being placed in a situation in which access to positive reinforcement is withdrawn; and (3) time out prevents possible physical harm to the individual in question, to others in the environment, and to the physical environment itself.

Response Cost

Response cost is essentially a fine or loss of privilege contingent upon inappropriate or undesirable behavior. This is the technique utilized by law enforcement agencies when they give fines for parking, traffic violations, smoking marijuana, or other illegal behavior. Response cost is frequently used in token economies (to be discussed later) but is also used in a variety of laboratory, educational, and clinical settings with both children and adults.

Cognitive Techniques of Aversion

Because of the unpopular reaction to the use of noxious stimuli in modifying behavior, techniques that evoke a negative cognitive state have been developed as a means of suppressing undesirable behavior. Discussions of some of the more successful techniques follow.

scientific approaches to the study of abnormal behavior

This person's speeding behavior has led to a traffic violation.

Covert Sensitization

The most popular of these techniques is *covert sensitization,* developed by Cautela (1967) and used in a variety of disorders. In Cautela's version, the client is first taught relaxation, a procedure that usually requires three to four sessions. Then the individual is given a rationale for the technique and is instructed in scene visualization. The therapist then describes the deviant approach behavior, which is paired with a noxious scene. For example, if the patient is an alcoholic, the therapist may describe a scene in which the patient is about to take a drink, but becomes nauseous and vomits, then leaves the barroom (this is the escape aspect). The patient is also instructed to practice imagining this scene at home once or twice a day.

You are walking into a bar. You decide to have a glass of beer. You are now walking toward the bar. As you are approaching the bar you have a funny feeling in the pit of your stomach. Your stomach feels all queasy and nauseous. Some liquid comes up your throat and it is very sour. You try to swallow it back down, but as you do this, food particles start coming up your throat to your mouth. You are now reaching the bar and you order a beer. As the bartender is pouring the beer, puke comes up into your mouth. You try to keep your mouth closed and swallow it down. You reach for the glass of beer to wash it down. As soon as your hand touches the glass, you can't hold it down any longer. You have to open your mouth and you puke. It goes all over your hand, all over the glass and the beer. You can see it floating around in the beer. Snots and mucous come out of your nose. Your shirt and pants are full of vomit. The bartender has some on his shirt. You notice people looking at you. You get sick again and vomit some more and more. You turn away from the beer and immediately start to feel better and better. When you get out into clean fresh air you feel wonderful. You go home and clean yourself up.

Cautela, 1967

Shame Aversion Therapy

Shame aversion therapy used to treat exhibitionism

Another cognitive technique, *shame aversion therapy,* has been used to treat sexual exhibitionists (Serber 1970). During treatment patients are asked to expose themselves under controlled conditions in the clinic, and an effort is made to evoke shame and embarrassment. The resulting negative cognition apparently suppresses the undesired behavior.

Ethical Problems of Aversive Techniques

Aversion therapy may be warranted in life-threatening situations . . .

or when no alternatives are available

Token economies reinforce appropriate social and self-care behavior

In contrast to the fairly widespread endorsement and practice of some behavioral techniques (notably assertiveness training, systematic desensitization, and biofeedback training), a good deal of criticism has been aroused concerning the ethical use of aversion techniques. However, these issues cannot generally be resolved in categorical, black-and-white terms. The real issue may be not whether to use aversion therapy, but under what circumstances and with what behaviors. It seems clear that aversive techniques are warranted when the target behavior is threatening the safety of the individual or others. In the case of the baby whose vomiting was a life-threatening response, the use of electric shock—as repugnant as it might have seemed—probably saved the baby's life.

A more complex ethical question arises when the target behavior is not life-threatening but no other techniques are available. For example, is aversion therapy justifiable when it is requested by a married homosexual male whose homosexual activity is threatening to disrupt his marriage and is causing him to be depressed? Davison (1976, 1977) answers no; Sturgis and Adams (1978) answer yes. Nevertheless, it is an important question, and one which will come up frequently in this book, since aversive techniques are often the only effective ones available for treating certain disorders. When aversion therapy is called for, it should be practiced but only by the most experienced and professionally qualified behavior therapists, and the ethical and legal guidelines of society, as well as those of professional organizations, should be scrupulously observed.

Token Economies

The **token economy** has had extensive application in a large variety of treatment and educational institutions (Kazdin 1975). Token economies have been used in psychiatric hospitals, prisons, the military, institutions for the delinquent, institutions for the retarded, classrooms, and halfway houses. The major purpose of the token economy is to reinforce appropriate social and self-care behavior in an institutional setting. More specifically, the goals are the development of behaviors that will lead to reinforcement by others, the enhancement of skills necessary for responsible behavior

scientific approaches to the study of abnormal behavior

in the hospital, and eventually the acquisition of behavior necessary to live successfully outside the institution (Atthowe and Krasner 1968).

The token economy has three major components. First, the desired behavior must be *specified*. Desirable behaviors may include simple activities, such as bathing, brushing teeth, making up beds, attending meals promptly, responding to questions, and engaging in work activity and similar social skills. Undesired behaviors may also be specified in some cases, and a system of either ignoring them or applying negative reinforcement such as response cost may be used.

Second, there must be some method of reinforcing desired behavior and suppressing undesired behavior. In the token economy this is usually accomplished by a system of *tokens* or *points* dispensed contingently for desired behavior. These tokens may come in a wide variety of colors, shapes, forms, and materials. Figure 7–4 shows a token card specifying the desired behaviors and the number of points they earn.

Third, the token economy must provide *backup reinforcers*—various privileges such as commissary items, recreational opportunities, leave, and similar pleasant events that can be bought with the tokens.

In a sense the token economy operates very much like the outside environment. To obtain privileges and avoid penalties, an individual must engage in appropriate social and work behavior. Unfortunately, these contingencies do not always prevail in institutions. As Gelfand, Gelfand, and Dobson (1967) have demonstrated, psychiatric aides tend to ignore appropriate behavior and reinforce inappropriate behavior. This study also demonstrated that nurses tended to emit noncontingent warm behavior regardless of patient behavior. Consequently, the institution may have shaped crazy behavior, a problem that will be discussed more extensively in a later chapter.

Like any economic system, token economies present a number of problems that tax the ingenuity of behavior therapists. For example, patients may hoard tokens and then, when a sufficient supply is saved, take a "vacation" from work or appropriate behavior. Theft and even counterfeiting of

M	T	W	T		Behavioral assessment card		F	S	Su
					Weekly evaluation/Vocational training/Academics				
1	1	1	1	am	Attendance	am	X	X	X
1	1	1	1	pm		pm	X	X	X
1	1	1	1	am	Interaction	am	X	X	X
1	1	1	1	pm		pm	X	X	X
1	1	1	1	am	Participation	am	X	X	X
1	1	1	1	pm		pm	X	X	X
1	1	1	1	am	Behavior	am	X	X	X
1	1	1	1	pm		pm	X	X	X
3	3	3	3		Occupational therapy		3	3	3
3	3	3	3		Music therapy		3	3	3
3	3	3	3		Ward officer		3	3	3
3	3	3	3		Group therapy		3	3	3
2	2	2	2		Special earnings		2	2	2
2	2	2	2		Laundry		2	2	2
					Self-care skills				
1	1	1	1	1	Up on time		1	1	1
1	1	1	1	2	Bed area clean		1	1	1
1	1	1	1	3	Bathed		1	1	1
1	1	1	1	4	Shaved		1	1	1
1	1	1	1	5	Tooth care	Personal hygiene and housekeeping	1	1	1
1	1	1	1	6	Hair care		1	1	1
1	1	1	1	7	Nail care		1	1	1
1	1	1	1	8	Clean clothes		1	1	1
1	1	1	1	9	Zipped/Buttoned		1	1	1
1	1	1	1	10	Shoes/Socks		1	1	1
1	1	1	1	11	Appearance		1	1	1
1	1	1	1	12	Night wear		1	1	1
					Individual treatment program				
2	2	2	2	+	Individual prescriptions	+	2	2	2
1	1	1	1	+		+	1	1	1
1	1	1	1	+		+	1	1	1
					Total earnings				
					Purchases				
3	3	3	3	Breakfast	Meals		3	3	3
3	3	3	3	Lunch			3	3	3
3	3	3	3	Dinner			3	3	3
4	4	4	4	Private	Room rent		4	4	4
3	3	3	3	Semi-private			3	3	3
2	2	2	2	Ward			2	2	2
0	0	0	0	Mattress			0	0	0
2	2	2	2		Beverages		2	2	2
3	3	3	3		Games/Radio/TV		3	3	3
3	3	3	3		Grounds		3	3	3
5	5	5	5		Town		5	5	5
2	2	2	2		Lobby		2	2	2
2	2	2	2		Naps		2	2	2
4	4	4	4		Appt with professional		4	4	4
2	2	2	2		Money draw		2	2	2
2	2	2	2		Individual spendings		2	2	2
					Individual treatment program				
2	2	2	2	–	Individual prescriptions	–	2	2	2
1	1	1	1	–		–	1	1	1
1	1	1	1	–		–	1	1	1
					Inappropriate behaviors				
5	5	5	5		Fighting/Stealing		5	5	5
2	2	2	2		Begging/Bumming/Bugging		2	2	2
2	2	2	2		Creating disturbance		2	2	2
5	5	5	5		Destroying property/Throwing things		5	5	5
2	2	2	2		Lying		2	2	2
3	3	3	3		Vulgarity		3	3	3
5	5	5	5		Not signing out		5	5	5
3	3	3	3		Illegal smoking		3	3	3
2	2	2	2		Missing medication		2	2	2
3	3	3	3		Unpaid privilege		3	3	3
1	1	1	1		Missing second meal		1	1	1
2	2	2	2		Unusual inappropriate behaviors		2	2	2
1	1	1	1		Littering		1	1	1
2	2	2	2		Ignoring instructions		2	2	2
					Total spending				

Figure 7–4 Sample token card.

tokens have also been known to occur. Consequently the therapist has to become both the economist and the banker to avoid these problems and to guard against inflation.

The key variable in the success of token economy programs is the training and morale of the staff. Unfortunately, hospital personnel often resist this type of program because it may violate their beliefs; and, from a practical viewpoint, implementing

Training and morale of staff as the key to success

such a system requires an increase in the workload during the initial stages. Even when nurses and nurse assistants are trained in operant procedures, they may not be motivated to cooperate fully and may still reinforce much inappropriate behavior (Trudel et al. 1974). One solution to this problem is an incentive or token economy program for staff personnel (Ayllon and Azrin 1968).

Behavior Therapy in Groups

Group therapy has been applied mostly in psychodynamic and humanistic approaches, which emphasize the therapeutic relationship. Behavior therapists focus more on specific problems and on the application of specific techniques tailored to the treatment of those problems, and consequently find group therapy generally less useful than individual therapy, with the exception of such small groups as the couple and the family. Furthermore, behavior therapists have found great individual differences even among people with similar diagnoses.

Groups limit specificity

Nevertheless, behavior therapy techniques have sometimes been used in group situations. For example, Hauserman, Zwebach, and Plotkin (1972) used social reinforcement to increase appropriate verbalization in groups of institutionalized adolescents. They found that once silly, off-topic verbalizations had decreased, peer pressures caused an increase of verbalizations that were appropriate and relevant to the group's interests. Systematic desensitization has also been used in groups for treatment of anxiety (Paul and Shannon 1966; Meichenbaum, Gilmore, and Fedoravicius 1971). Other techniques that have been used in groups are assertiveness training (Bellack and Hersen 1977), rational-emotive therapy (Meichenbaum, Gilmore, and Fedoravicius 1971), and self-control procedures in treating smoking (Ober 1968) and obesity (Wollersheim 1970). Although behavioral principles can be applied to groups, such applications have obvious limitations because of their specificity, and group treatment will probably never achieve the popularity among behavior therapists that it has enjoyed with other forms of treatment.

Analogue subjects, not clinical cases, were studied

Evaluation of Behavior Therapy

Because behavior therapy techniques are numerous and often designed for specific types of abnormal patterns of behavior, the overall effectiveness of behavior therapy is difficult to evaluate. Some have proven to be quite effective and some quite ineffective, but most behavior therapies, like other therapies, have not been adequately evaluated. Four types of studies are relevant to this issue: *case studies, controlled case studies, uncontrolled group studies,* and *controlled group studies.* Our discussion will be restricted to controlled and uncontrolled group studies concerned with the overall effectiveness of behavior therapy. We shall discuss studies that evaluate the effectiveness of a particular technique when we discuss the appropriate disorder.

In an uncontrolled group study Wolpe (1958) found an 89 percent improvement rate in a group of 210 mixed neurotic patients. Only one of 45 patients contacted several years later had relapsed. Lazarus (1963) reported an improvement rate of 78 percent with 408 neurotic patients; even with severely neurotic cases, the improvement rate was 62 percent. These individuals were seen only for an average of fourteen sessions, and at a two-year follow-up Lazarus reported no relapses or symptom substitutions. Hussain (1963) found a 95 percent improvement rate with 126 neurotics. However, these were uncontrolled studies and must be viewed with caution.

Paul (1969a, 1969b) reviewed approximately seventy-five studies of systematic desensitization of which twenty were controlled group studies. He indicates that the results of systematic desensitization are overwhelmingly positive. However, many of these studies were conducted with analogue clinical subjects rather than actual clients.

The best example of such a study was conducted by Paul (1966). With college students who had a fear of public speaking, Paul evaluated systematic desensitization, an insight-oriented treatment group, a bogus treatment control group who received a placebo pill described as an anxiety-reducing agent, and a no-treatment control group. On a complex index of improvement based on behavioral, physiological, and self-

scientific approaches to the study of abnormal behavior

report measures, 100 percent of the desensitization group, 47 percent of the insight-oriented group, 47 percent of the placebo group, and 17 percent of the no-treatment group showed improvement. These effects were maintained at six-month and two-year follow-ups.

A similar study was conducted by Di-Lareto (1971), who compared systematic desensitization, rational-emotive therapy, and client-centered therapy in college students with interpersonal anxiety. These active treatment groups were compared to a placebo therapy group and a no-treatment control group. While all of the treatment groups showed more improvement than the control groups, individuals treated with systematic desensitization improved significantly more than rational-emotive or client-centered therapy groups. He noted that client-centered therapy was more effective with extroverted subjects, while rational-emotive therapy was more effective with introverted subjects. Systematic desensitization, however, seems to be effective regardless of the personality and characteristics of the client. The major problem with analogue studies like these is that if they had been conducted with actual clinical cases the results might have been completely different.

Comparison of Behavior Therapy and Psychotherapy

In general, comparative studies of psychotherapy and behavior therapy have been confusing because of the different goals of treatments in these two approaches. While the main emphasis of self-actualization and psychodynamic and client-centered therapy is on changing the personality structure, the purpose of behavior therapy is to decrease or increase specific target behaviors. Consequently, the effects of psychotherapy are more legitimately evaluated with global measures, such as personality tests, while behavioral assessment of specific target behavior is more relevant to behavior therapy. Nevertheless, several major studies address this question.

Smith and Glass (1977) discussed the results of 375 studies of psychotherapy and behavior therapy. In evaluating these studies they used an *effect size*, or the mean

difference between the treated subjects and the control subjects, divided by the standard deviation. Their results indicate that, regardless of the type of therapy, 75 percent of the therapy clients are functioning more effectively than untreated individuals. They found that only 12 percent of the 375 studies indicated that there was no difference between the active treatment groups and the control groups. In addition, they compared ten types of psychological therapies. If these therapies are ranked in terms of effectiveness, *systematic desensitization* is number one, *rational-emotive* therapy and *behavior modification* are tied for second, and the least effective intervention method is *Gestalt therapy*. When compared with other types of psychological interventions, the behavioral therapies are clearly superior, in spite of the fact that rational-emotive therapy was considered a type of nonbehavioral treatment. However, Smith and Glass noted that this superiority may be an artifact due to the briefer follow-up in the behavioral therapy studies and the greater susceptibility to bias of the behavioral measures (which may or may not be the case). When they corrected for these biases, behavior therapies were still superior but not significantly so. Nevertheless, the study by Smith and Glass is encouraging, as it does indicate that psychological interventions are effective.

A better controlled study that more adequately evaluated this question was conducted by Sloan et al. (1975). They compared behavior therapy, psychotherapy, and no-treatment control in a clinical population of ninety-four patients, two-thirds of whom were neurotic and one-third of whom had personality disorders. This study had the following features:

1. The subjects were randomly assigned to behavior therapy, psychotherapy, or a waiting list.
2. The therapists were either three experienced practitioners of psychoanalytic therapy or three experienced practitioners of behavior therapy.
3. Independent assessment teams were used, who had no direct knowledge of the patient's treatment group.

Different goals make comparative study difficult

Therapy is effective

4. Clients were suffering from a variety of neurotic and personality disorders and received four months of treatment.
5. The study made use of information from friends and relatives as well as various outcome measures, including target behaviors and global functioning, obtained from therapists, patients, assessors, and psychological tests.
6. There was a follow-up at one year and a partial follow-up at two years.

The investigators found that on specific target symptoms 80 percent of the patients in each of the active treatment groups were considered either improved or recovered, while only 40 percent were improved or recovered in the no-treatment control group. Global measures of adjustment tended to be higher, and 93 percent of the patients treated by behavior therapy were considered improved; 77 percent of both psychotherapy and control patients were considered improved or recovered. Patients treated by behavior therapy showed significant improvement in both work and social adjustment, while psychotherapy patients showed only marginal improvement in work and no change in social adjustment. The authors state:

Behavior therapy was more effective . . .

but not significantly more effective

> It would be tempting to argue that behavior therapy was somewhat more effective than psychotherapy. At four months, behavior therapy patients had significantly improved on all three measures, while psychotherapy patients had not improved on social adjustment. At one year, patients who were originally treated by behavior therapy, but not those originally treated by psychotherapy, showed a greater improvement than waiting list patients in reduction of severity of target symptoms. (pp. 137–38)

Accounting for the high rate of spontaneous recovery

This conclusion is probably not justified, as the authors state, because many of these differences were not significant.

Several other findings are important in this study. No symptom substitutions were found. The deterioration effect, discussed in Chapter 6, was observed only in one patient in the waiting control list. Interestingly enough, the 77 percent improvement in the waiting list control was much closer to Eysenck's original figure of spontaneous

The question remains unresolved

recovery than to Bergin's (see Chapter 6). Two major factors can be cited to explain this high figure for spontaneous recovery. In the first place, people usually seek psychological intervention when crises occur. Since crises tend to be temporary, people are likely to consider themselves "improved" when their subjective distress passes.

In the second place, such global measures as improvement versus no improvement are not very accurate reflections of an individual's adjustment, as they are highly reactive to patient and therapist expectations and other contaminating variables. More objective evaluations of an individual's adjustment, either in terms of change in personality structure or functioning or in terms of change in specific target behaviors, would probably yield more conservative estimates of spontaneous recovery.

In two later publications these researchers further clarify their findings (Sloan et al. 1976; Staples et al. 1976). In evaluating process variables, they conclude that substantial differences exist between the two types of therapists. Behavior therapists tended to be much more active and authoritarian, while psychotherapists encouraged greater independence. Even though both approaches provided a warm and accepting atmosphere, behavior therapists offered higher levels of accurate empathy, interpersonal contact, and therapist self-congruence. This is rather curious, since psychotherapists tend to place much more emphasis on the therapeutic relationship. They also found both treatments apparently equally effective with the classic stereotype of the good patient: a verbal, intelligent, well-educated woman of reasonably high income who is not severely disturbed and whose disorder tends more toward neurosis and introversion than personality disturbances or acting-out behavior. On the other hand, the effectiveness of behavior therapy was not particularly related to the diagnosis or to personality characteristics of the individual—which caused the authors to conclude that behavior therapy may be the treatment of choice for patients with acting-out tendencies and more severe pathology. Nevertheless, they suggest that the "temple of truth" may be approached by different pathways. In defense of psychotherapy, it should be noted that this study was brief, consisting of four months of treatment or an average of about fourteen sessions, which is considerably shorter than the number of sessions commonly used in psychotherapy. Thus, it seems the question of the relative effectiveness of psychotherapy and behavior therapy needs further examination.

Summary

Behavior therapy is an application of the principles of psychology to the modification of abnormal behavior. It makes four major assumptions about the nature of abnormal behavior: (1) most abnormal behavior is acquired in the same manner as normal behavior; (2) a scientific approach to abnormal behavior is both feasible and productive; (3) insight is not a necessary prerequisite for behavior change; and (4) the goal of behavior therapy is to modify specific patterns of behavior that have been labeled as deviant.

Behavior therapy is a very active form of treatment that has five major phases of intervention: (1) the problem behavior is carefully defined in assessment; (2) the factors leading to development and maintenance of the behavior patterns are carefully considered, and a formulation of the problem behavior is developed; (3) a suitable treatment technique is selected for the specific problem; (4) the behavior therapist discusses the assessment, formulation, and treatment plan with the client or, in the case of children, with their legal guardians; and (5) the treatment program is implemented with continuous monitoring of the target behavior.

There are a wide variety of behavioral techniques, and the number is growing. Generally, these techniques can be classified as operant conditioning, classical conditioning, modeling, cognitive procedures, biofeedback training, aversion techniques, token economies, and group methods.

Operant techniques make systematic use of environmental contingencies to alter directly the subject's response to specific situations by making reinforcement contingent on specific responses. These techniques include contingent reinforcement, feedback, extinction, shaping, fading and prompting, the Premack principle, and contingency contracting.

Classical conditioning techniques, based on the work of Pavlov, use stimulus substitution, counter-conditioning, and extinction as their primary strategies. The techniques used include systematic desensitization, assertiveness training, flooding, and implosion.

Modeling is a procedure in which an individual observes another individual, often the therapist, engage in some behavior, which the client then imitates in order to control undesired responses or to acquire, or increase the frequency of, desired behavior. Modeling is an element in almost every behavior therapy technique, but the primary techniques of modeling are behavioral rehearsal, participant modeling, and vicarious extinction. The full range of possible treatment techniques derived from modeling has not yet been developed.

In the last few years techniques derived from cognitive psychology have been developed and used to modify both overt behavior and internal mediating processes. These techniques are the behavior therapist's attempt to deal with the mind. Although a number of cognitive treatment strategies are used, the major ones are cognitive restructuring and self-control procedures. Rational-emotive therapy has been the most frequently used cognitive technique.

Biofeedback training is actually an operant conditioning technique in which biological signals are monitored. This information is then provided to the individual, who uses the feedback to modify internal processes. The initial step is learning to discriminate internal sensations so that the individual can self-monitor these responses and in this manner calibrate control in internal events, such as heart rate, blood pressure, skin temperature, muscle tension, or electrical activity of the brain.

Aversion techniques are used primarily when no other alternatives are available or with behaviors considered socially reprehensible or dangerous. These techniques are also used when individuals find their behavior so disturbing that they specifically request the use of such techniques. The procedures involved are noxious stimulation (including punishment and avoidance learning), time-out, response cost, and cognitive aversion techniques.

The major purpose of token economies, used in institutional settings, is to elicit appropriate social and self-care behavior. Token economies require complete cooperation of the staff, or they are not successful. Behavior changes shaped by token economies do not always generalize to the individual's life situation.

Behavioral techniques have been used in groups with problems such as anxiety, smoking, and obesity. The nature of behavior therapy makes it less amenable to group approaches than psychodynamic or humanistic therapy. The prime difficulty is that behavior therapy techniques are usually designed for specific problems and are often modified to fit particular circumstances of a given case.

Some behavior therapy techniques, such as systematic desensitization, have been extensively evaluated and are promising. Other techniques have not received extensive evaluation. Most of the studies indicate that behavior therapy is somewhat more effective than traditional forms of psychotherapy and applicable to a wider range of problems.

Review Questions

1. What four assumptions do behavior therapists make about the nature of abnormal behavior?

2. What are the five major phases of behavioral intervention?

3. Describe one technique to illustrate each of the following:
   a. Operant conditioning
   b. Respondent conditioning
   c. Modeling
   d. Cognitive approaches

4. How does biofeedback change behavior?

5. Under what conditions are aversion techniques used? What are their disadvantages?

6. How does a token economy work?

Key Concepts

assertiveness training

aversion therapy

behavioral rehearsal

behavior therapy (behavior modification)

biofeedback training

cognitive restructuring

contingent reinforcement

extinction

fading

feedback

flooding

implosive therapy

in vivo desensitization

participant modeling

Premack principle

prompts

shaping

systematic desensitization

token economy

scientific approaches to the study of abnormal behavior

neuroses, personality disorders, and special symptoms

Feeling, sensing, knowing, and moving are the four most basic functions of humans. It is therefore not surprising that the four systems involved are subject to a variety of disorders, many of which are classified as **neuroses.** In Chapter 8 we shall discuss neuroses that affect primarily the emotional response system. In Chapter 9 we shall discuss *special symptoms* that affect the sensory, cognitive, and motor response systems. And, since humans are social animals, disorders involving the *socialization process* are also quite common, and we shall discuss some of these in Chapter 10.

neuroses I
disorders of the emotional response system

8

Key Topics

The effects that classifying people instead of behavior has on the diagnosis of neuroses

Roles of the hypothalamus, limbic system, autonomic nervous system, adrenal gland, and cognitive factors in the subjective experience of emotions

Distinctions between fear, phobia, and anxiety

Causative and maintaining factors of phobias

Main characteristics of anxiety neurosis

Role of autonomic reactivity in anxiety neurosis

Anger-affection continuum

Neuroses, the most common of all forms of abnormal behavior, are a heterogeneous assortment of disorders that have little in common with one another. While they appear to be exaggerations of behavior we all experience, they can, when persistent, handicap the individual and interfere with his or her psychological adjustment.

Most neuroses are situational

The major difference between neuroses and more severe behavior disorders, such as psychoses, is that most neuroses seem to be *situational* and do not permeate all aspects of an individual's life. Typically, people with neuroses have good *reality testing:* they hear, see, feel, and evaluate life experiences in much the same way as other individuals. Only rarely do they experience gross distortions of cognition.

Although Kramer (1968) estimated that the prevalence of neuroses had increased 165 percent in the previous two decades, determining the actual prevalence is difficult. The reason for this difficulty is that the label neurosis is quite confusing—any person who is unhappy may be labeled neurotic, thereby inflating the prevalence estimates. Furthermore, people with neurotic behavior patterns rarely require hospitalization, and thus do not often come into contact with agencies that gather prevalence data. They are also less likely to be seen as patients of federal, state, or county agencies, since they often are middle-class individuals who are able to obtain psychotherapy from professionals in private practice.

Is anxiety really the chief characteristic of neurosis?

The Neurotic Constellation: Fact or Fancy?

The neurotic personality as an implicit assumption

As we pointed out earlier, the DSM II description of neuroses fails to adhere to the single classification principle—some categories are based on descriptions of observed behavior, others on assumptions about the causes of abnormal behavior. To avoid being blinded by clinical myths and theoretical preconceptions, we need to take a closer look at this classification. DSM II describes neuroses as follows:

Anxiety is the chief characteristic of neuroses. It may be felt and expressed directly, or it may be controlled unconsciously and automatically by conversion, displacement, and various other psychological mechanisms. Generally, these mechanisms produce symptoms experienced as subjective distress from which the patient desires relief.

The proposition that anxiety is the chief or even the most common characteristic of neuroses is a doubtful one. In some neurotic patterns of behavior, anxiety is a major feature, but in others it is not. For example, a person experiencing a conversion reaction in which the use of a limb has been lost because of psychological factors may have little anxiety. In fact, some theorists claim that *la belle indifférence,* a lack of concern about the malfunction, is a major characteristic of conversion reactions. Only by necessarily complex theoretical schemes, such as the psychoanalytic concept of defense mechanisms, can anxiety be viewed as playing a major role in conversion reactions or several other neurotic disorders.

Furthermore, many behavior patterns labeled neurotic are acquired through positive reinforcement rather than through the aversive experiences ordinarily associated with anxiety. For example, if repeated complaints about aches and pains elicit attention and concern from others, the result may be a behavior pattern labeled *hypochondriacal neurosis.* Such patterns, in turn, cause difficulties in coping with life, possibly leading to anxiety. In such cases the neurotic behavior is the cause, not the result, of anxiety.

Implicit in the diagnosis of neuroses is the assumption that individuals with neurotic patterns of behavior share a **neurotic personality.** This assumption results from the fact that DSM II classifies people rather than response patterns, and it is reinforced by trait approaches to personality. For example, Coleman (1976) claims that individuals with neurotic problems have as a common core a maladaptive lifestyle characterized by anxiety and defense-oriented avoidance behavior. In other words, the neurosis supposedly permeates all aspects of the individual's life and affects most of the individual's activities. There is, however, very little support for this notion (Buss 1966). Like other behavior patterns, neurotic ones are likely to be a function of situations (Mischel 1968). The individual

neuroses, personality disorders, and special symptoms

who has a severe fear of flying may function quite well in other aspects of life and be well adjusted in vocational, marital, sexual, and social relationships. How much a neurotic behavior pattern pervades all aspects of an individual's life depends, instead, on the type of disorder as well as the specific case. For example, depression interferes with many aspects of the individual's life, whereas simple phobias usually do not.

It is also important to differentiate between causal factors (events important in the acquisition of the behavior) and maintaining factors (events facilitating the persistence of the behavior—secondary gains). The classification scheme of DSM II often assumes that the individual does not have insight into the causes of the behavior and that the reasons for the behavior are unconscious. Defense mechanisms prevent self-knowledge in order to reduce anxiety and consequently cause the individual to persist in maladaptive behavior (Dollard and Miller 1950). This apparently self-defeating cycle is labeled the *neurotic paradox.* Yet, this hypothesis too is highly questionable. Many individuals suffering from neurotic behavior patterns can accurately describe events that led to those behavior patterns. Knowledge or insight, furthermore, does not automatically lead to extinction. Besides casting doubt on the practical utility of concepts such as insight and the unconscious, this fact also demonstrates that the causes of a particular behavior pattern may not be responsible for its continuing occurrence. It is thus important to differentiate between *causal* and *maintaining* factors. For example, an individual who received a head injury on the job may continue to experience pain even though that pain no longer has any physiologic basis. However, the person may be receiving disability payments or other reinforcers that cause the pain to persist. No amount of insight is likely to change this behavior until reinforcement is terminated.

In some cases where an individual shows several deviant behavior patterns or types of neuroses, it is commonly assumed that they are produced by a common unconscious conflict. This assumption is questionable logically and clinically. It is quite possible that an individual may be exposed to circumstances that cause a phobia, a different set of circumstances that cause

depression, and perhaps a third set of circumstances that cause a memory loss. The most advisable approach is to empirically establish the independent or dependent causes of the various behaviors, as all three may well be independent.

Typically, neuroses are specific patterns of behavior that cause malfunction primarily in only one response system. For example, anxiety, phobias, and depression are *emotional disorders,* whereas depersonalization and fugue states are *cognitive disorders.* Even in *hysterical neuroses* in which conversion reaction may involve motor or sensory disorders, usually only one response system is involved in any one case. For example, the individual who loses the use of a limb (motor system) rarely, if ever, has sensory disorders such as a loss of vision or exaggerated sensitivity to pain stimuli. The dissociative reactions, assumed to be a form of hysterical neuroses, involve largely either memory or the cognitive system. Even in *obsessive-compulsive neuroses,* usually only one response system is primarily involved. Obsessions are cognitive disorders that can and do occur without compulsions (motor disorders) (Rimm and Somervill 1977). Furthermore, whether obsessions are always precursors of motor rituals is questionable. Meyer and Levy (1973) indicated that some rituals may occur very rapidly, almost involuntarily, without conscious thought. Consequently, obsessional thoughts may not be a defining attribute of a compulsion, but rather an extra-classificatory attribute (see Chapter 2).

Aside from the question of the validity of traditional hypotheses, the preconceptions engendered can cause confusion in the classification of neurotic disorders. It is quite possible and even likely that these heterogeneous disorders have different causes, require different treatment methods, and may be completely different types of disorders. Consequently, the concept of neuroses may not be useful in the classification of psychiatric disorders. We shall use the concept here, however, because it is useful as an index of the disorder's severity.

Causal vs. maintaining factors

Multiple symptoms do not necessarily point to a single cause

A neurosis usually involves only one response system

Emotions and Abnormal Behavior

Emotion, an aspect of behavior that has fascinated people throughout history, is a pervasive phenomenon that stubbornly resists definition. The Greeks discussed emotion much as we do today. For example, Plato in his theory of emotion used the terms *pain* and *pleasure*. In turn, Aristotle provided the first extensive classification of emotions.

Most people identify emotions subjectively by introspection and intuitively know what constitutes rage, love, depression, and other emotional behavior in themselves. However, they have much more difficulty in attempting to identify these reactions in others. Psychologists have similar problems, and the psychological literature is filled with such inadequately defined terms as feelings, affect, mood, temperament, and so on.

Since emotion often appears to be a disruptive experience, it is frequently associated with abnormal behavior. Terms such as an *emotionally unstable personality* and *emotionally disturbed* are often used to characterize this behavior. Consequently, many individuals view abnormal behavior in general as an emotional disorder; however, only certain types are emotional.

Theoretical Aspects of Emotions

Emotional behavior appears to arise from a variety of internal and external cues. In the newborn infant, excitement appears to be the only emotion present (Bridges 1932). By two years of age, the child exhibits emotions that are typical of adults, such as elation, anger, fear, affection, and anxiety. The development and the differentiation of emotions occur as *biological needs* associated with *environmental events*. For example, a parent, who relieves the discomfort of hunger or wet diapers and who provides pleasant experiences such as

a full stomach and physical caresses, rapidly acquires the ability to elicit pleasant emotional states whether the child's biological needs are gratified or not. Such emotional responses may then generalize to other adults.

On the other hand, the child learns to associate certain stimuli with noxious states. For example, wet diapers frequently elicit frowns, scolding, and perhaps physical punishment. Eventually, a frown, a gruff voice, or other evidence of displeasure can elicit in the child anticipation of noxious states. Thus, we observe love developing out of pleasant states and anxiety developing out of noxious ones. As the process of cue discrimination continues, the child soon acquires specific emotional reactions to specific stimulus situations. Emotions are thus acquired by learning and are based on biological needs. Obviously, these conditioning processes have many opportunities to go awry and thereby cause later emotional problems. Furthermore, the conditioning of emotional responses to various internal and external cues can continue throughout the individual's life.

Physiology of Emotions

The physiological aspects of emotion are mediated centrally by the **hypothalamus,** the *limbic system,* and other central nervous system structures, as well as, peripherally, by the *endocrine* and *autonomic nervous systems.* The hypothalamus has been called the "seat" of the emotions, since it exerts direct influence over other groups of autonomic and somatic neurons in the brain stem and other regions of the central nervous system. It appears to organize various components of emotional reaction into definite patterns.

The *limbic (motor) system,* in conjunction with the hypothalamus, appears to mediate emotional experiences and their expression. If specific areas of the hypothalamus are stimulated by small electrical or chemical stimuli, rage, fear, or similar types of emotional behavior are produced (Thompson 1967). Stimulation of the lim-

neuroses, personality disorders, and special symptoms

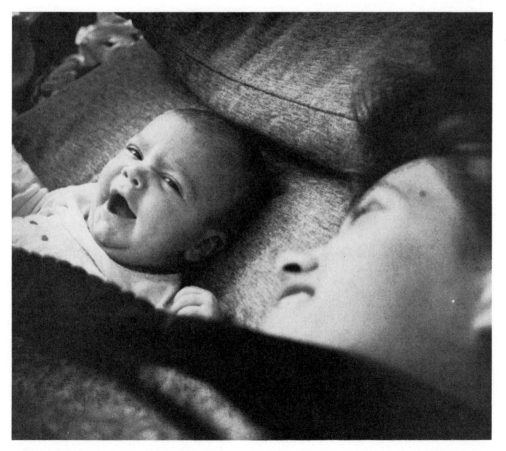

These children have learned different emotional responses: displeasure because of wet diapers and happiness because of closeness and warmth.

bic system by implanted electrodes in the brain of experimental animals is associated with sensations of pleasure or punishment (Olds 1956, 1960).

The hypothalamus directly releases hormones into the bloodstream and also acts on the major nerve control mechanism of the *pituitary gland*. It exerts control over the peripheral autonomic responses, such as those mediated by the *sympathetic nervous system* (increased blood pressure, sweating, dilation of the pupils) as well as those of the *parasympathetic nervous system* (decreased blood pressure, contraction

Role of the adrenal gland

of the bladder); see Figure 8–1. The activity of the autonomic nervous system is obviously an important index of emotional responses. The reactions of the two subdivisions of the autonomic nervous system are listed in Table 8–1.

Changes that occur in the *medulla* of the *adrenal gland,* also innervated (supplied with nerves) by the autonomic nervous system, are also important, since this structure secretes *adrenalin* and *noradrenalin.*

Adrenalin has an effect similar to the effects of the sympathetic nervous system.

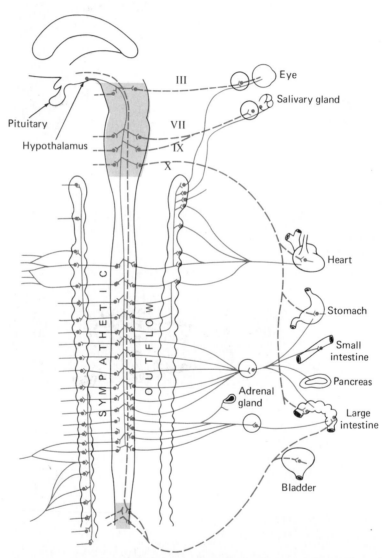

Figure 8–1 The autonomic nervous system. The solid lines show the sympathetic system, which is in the middle section, while the broken lines show the parasympathetic system, which has a cranal (above) and a sacral (below) division. The majority of the organs are innervated by both subsystems.

neuroses, personality disorders, and special symptoms

Noradrenalin has more of a restricted effect that includes the constriction of the small blood vessels, which in turn causes an increased resistance to blood flow. With prolonged stress, the adrenal cortex and its hormones are stimulated by the *adrenocorticotrophic hormone (ACTH)* of the pituitary gland, which, in turn, has been stimulated by the hypothalamus. The secretions of the adrenal cortex, caused in this manner, play an active role in the psychophysiological disorders, which we shall discuss in Chapter 16. All of these physiological reactions are influenced by centers of the cerebral cortex, which mediates cognitive activities. As noted in Chapter 6, chemotherapy of behavioral disorders is often based on the effects various drugs have on these physiological functions.

Situations and Emotions

Situational factors are also important in eliciting and modulating emotional states. Maranon (1924) injected human subjects with adrenalin and asked them to report their reactions. Most subjects did not report emotional experiences, although a few did report "as if . . ." emotions. Consequently, an explanation of emotion that is centered strictly on the physiology of the organism seems insufficient to explain emotion.

The research of Schachter and Singer (1962) and Schachter and Wheeler (1962) sheds some light on this confusion. In their research they gave individuals adrenalin and told some what to expect but misinformed the others (so that the subjects would not attribute tremors and other side effects of the drug to the injection and thereby discount cues that might elicit an emotional experience). Another group of control subjects received saline (saltwater) injections. Schachter and his colleagues then manipulated the social situations to which the subjects were exposed.

This aspect of the experiments was designed to test the hypothesis that stimuli in the subjects' environment could determine the perceived emotion resulting from a given visceral experience. Consequently, some of the subjects were placed in a set-up social situation in which the stooge was high-spirited and euphoric. In another condition the stooge was disagreeable and angry.

Role of situational factors

Table 8–1 Functions of the Autonomic Nervous System

Organ	Function	
	Sympathetic	Parasympathetic
Heart	Acceleration	Inhibition
Blood vessels		
In skin	Constriction	None
In striate muscle	Dilation, constriction	None
In heart	Dilation	Constriction
In abnominal viscera	Constriction	None
Pupils of eye	Dilation	Constriction
Tear glands	(Possibly a secretory function)	Secretion
Sweat glands	Secretion	None
Hair on skin	Hairs erected	None
Adrenal glands	Secretion	None
Liver	Sugar liberated	None
Salivary glands	Secretion (?)	None
Stomach	Inhibition of secretion and peristalsis (some excitation)	Secretion, peristalsis (some inhibition)
Intestines	Inhibition	Increased tone and motility
Rectum	Inhibition	Feces expelled
Bladder	Inhibition	Urine expelled
Genital organs (male)	Ejaculation	Erection

The environmental situation of the subject plays a role in determining the particular emotion experienced. A New York rush hour can lead to irritability and anger, while meeting an old friend probably elicits a pleasant emotional response. The winning of a race may create feelings of euphoria and triumph.

neuroses, personality disorders, and special symptoms

The results indicated that the emotional responses of the misinformed subjects, who could not account for their emotional experiences in terms of side effects, were more in line with the stooges' behavior than the responses of the correctly informed subjects. These differences included both the behavior of the subjects (observed through a one-way mirror) and their moods (indicated in a self-report questionnaire). The control subjects, given saline, were less likely than the adrenaline-injected and misinformed subjects to experience emotions similar to those shown by the stooges. These results suggest that internal visceral cues do play a role in emotions, but the particular emotion experienced is influenced by the environmental situation of the subject. Schachter and Wheeler (1962) obtained similar results in a study investigating humor. These and similar recent studies are important because they illustrate the role of *cognitive mediation* in emotions.

Cognition and Emotions

Mandler (1962), in what he calls the **jukebox theory of emotion,** suggests that the production of an emotion has two stages resembling the two stages in the selection of a tune in a jukebox. The first step in the jukebox process is the insertion of a coin to activate the machine. This step corresponds to the visceral arousal of the individual. The second step is the selection of the melody, which is analogous to the stimulus situation that facilitates the particular emotion. The same stimulus situation can produce both steps simultaneously, as is shown in Figure 8–2. In other words, *arousal* is a necessary but not a sufficient condition for emotion. The *social* situation, *cognitive* activity, and *physiological* responses interact to determine the emotions exhibited or experienced by the individual.

Anxiety

In any discussion of anxiety, we must differentiate between **fear** and **anxiety.** Freud (1917) distinguished between *realistic*

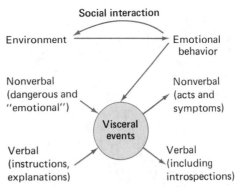

Figure 8–2 Mandler's schematic diagram of the variables implicated in emotion. Arrows refer to possible relations among antecedent and consequent variables. Environmental stimuli elicit an autonomic nervous system reaction that causes emotional behavior. This emotional behavior then serves as feedback to the individual to further enhance emotional behavior and the interpretation of it.

fears and *unrealistic* fears, the latter he called anxiety. Beck (1976) states that fear is an appraisal of an actual or potential danger, which is a cognitive process, while anxiety is an unpleasant emotion that the individual experiences. We shall make a similar distinction here: *Fear* is a psychological reaction to stimulus conditions in the internal or external environment that threatens physical well-being. These stimulus conditions are considered dangerous by external observers and are associated with a high probability of physical injuries (for example, cancer, combat, threats of violence). In short, fear is an example of a biological need—namely, *harm-avoidance.* *Anxiety* is a similar psychological and physiological reaction, but the cues are considered by independent observers, and even by the individual, as relatively mild events. Both fear and anxiety are characterized by subjective reports of discomfort, activation of the sympathetic nervous system, and fight-or-flight behavior. Anxiety is presumably a learned fear reaction.

Since fear is derived from a biological drive (harm-avoidance), defining related anxiety as an emotion rather than an acquired biological need may seem strange. However, most human behavior (for example, cognitions, social behaviors, and emotions) develops from basic biological needs through the socialization process:

Role of internal visceral cues

Jukebox theory of emotion

Difference between fear and anxiety

Phobic reaction: specific
fear, expectation of panic

Agoraphobia—fear of
leaving familiar settings

Social phobias—fear of
criticism or embarrassment

Simple phobia—fear of
specific animals, events,
situations

There is little evidence for instinctual behavior in humans. In addition, acquired biological needs may be defined in terms of changes in the physiological functions of individuals as well as association with biological needs. Drug addiction is a good example of an acquired biological need.

There are two types of anxiety disorders: *phobias* and *pervasive anxiety*. Although we shall discuss these disorders separately, it is, as yet, unclear as to how they are different types of abnormal behavior. We shall explore this question in the following sections.

Phobic Neurosis

A **phobia** is an intense learned fear of specific objects, situations, or living organisms (including humans) as defined by subjective reports, behavioral observations, and autonomic responses to relatively innocuous stimuli. Phobic neuroses include expectations of panic by the individual whenever the relevant stimulus situation is encountered, active avoidance of these cues, and a reaction of the sympathetic nervous system upon encountering the threatening situation. The individual will also attempt to regulate the environment so that the phobic stimulus is avoided. These anxieties are out of proportion to the demands of reality, seem inexplicable, and are beyond voluntary control. Almost any object or event can

serve as a phobic stimulus. Some of the more common phobias are certain animals, surgical and dental procedures, heights, open places, dirt or germs, and other somewhat innocuous stimuli.

DSM III lists three types of phobic disorders: agoraphobia, social phobia, and simple phobia. **Agoraphobia** is anxiety associated with leaving familiar settings such as home. The individual develops an anticipatory, irrational fear of being helpless. Thus, the person is reluctant to be alone; has a fear of unfamiliar situations, such as stores, crowded buses, bridges, tunnels, or similar close, crowded, or even open places; and fears travel. In severe cases the individual may have *panic attacks* and become housebound. **Social phobia** is anxiety associated with exposure to and scrutiny by other people in situations in which the individual may be criticized or embarrassed. Consequently, the social phobic avoids public speaking, eating in public, strangers, cocktail parties, or other social situations. **Simple phobias** are phobias of specific animals, events, or situations.

In differentiating phobias from normal fears, which are associated with realistic dangers, we must first determine whether the emotional response is inappropriate. For example, anxiety about flying is not unusual, but is inappropriate if it arises upon arrival at an airport and causes one to totally avoid flying.

The grasshopper, snake, rat, turtle, or frog can all be phobic objects or simple phobias.

neuroses, personality disorders, and special symptoms

Phobic reactions may also include disorders not usually classified as phobias. As Bandura (1969) has noted, in many individuals' racial attitudes or prejudices are examples of phobic behavior and have all of the characteristics of phobias. Sexual dysfunctions such as impotence, premature ejaculation, and orgasmic dysfunction can also be classified as phobic reactions. These disorders too show all the characteristics of phobias, including avoidance of the sexual situation, negative emotions when exposed to it, and a subjective evaluation by the individual that the reaction is unrealistic. Sexual dysfunctions will be discussed in Chapter 12.

The claim has also been made that phobias arise in pathological personalities and are caused by a pervasive underlying "personality" disorder (Millon 1969). This theory implies that an individual with a fear of flying, for example, would also show behavioral dysfunctions in other areas. However, this position has little supporting evidence. To the contrary, in phobic reactions, particularly cases labeled *monosymptomatic* phobias (single phobias), the possibility that the affected individual will function effectively in other areas of life seems to be as good as for most normal individuals. If the individual has multiple phobias, such as fear of death, fear of flying, and similar phobias, then the probability of normal functioning is reduced. Yet, the fact that an individual has two or more phobias or a phobia and other behavioral disorders is not evidence of a common cause.

The extent to which the phobic disorders interfere with other areas of the individual's life is a rather direct function of the nature of the phobic stimuli. An individual who has a fear of snakes and lives in a large city is unlikely to be handicapped by the snake phobia. On the other hand, a university professor with a speech phobia or any individual with a social phobia (fear of people) is likely to be severely handicapped regardless of location.

In some cases phobias generalize and become progressively broader and more inclusive. For example, an individual who has a specific fear of high places may in time, as the phobia generalizes and intensifies, become unable to stand on a stepladder or even to discuss skyscrapers.

Racism and sexual dysfunctions can also be phobias

Phobias are not symptoms of underlying personality disorders

Phobias in Children

Phobic reactions are quite common in children. Although fears are also quite common in early childhood, normal fears are differentiated from childhood phobias by the fact

A person with a social phobia could never tolerate this happy crowd.

that in the phobic reaction the child is preoccupied with the phobic object or situation, demonstrates a state of anticipatory anxiety, and avoids situations in which the phobic object or event may be encountered, even though the object of the phobic reaction is not dangerous. As in adults, any event can become a cue for the phobic reaction. The most common phobias in children are school phobias, separation anxiety, and fear of animals. **Separation anxiety** is actually a fear of being separated from the parents and occurs in children who are highly dependent and usually overprotected by their parents. When separated from their parents, such children show signs of anxiety and highly intense emotional behavior. In a sense this disorder has features similar to both agoraphobia and social phobia that, when it occurs in children or adolescents, is labeled a *shyness disorder* by DSM III.

Childhood phobias: separation, animals, school

School phobias are a specific type of separation anxiety. Weiss and Burke (1970) state that many children, when they look back upon their resistance to attending school, interpret it as concern for their mothers' well-being and a desire to stay at home rather than a fear of school. There is little doubt that the parents of such children often do not know how to handle this behavior and alternate between begging, bribing, and punishing while the children alternate between feeling helpless about the fear and angry about the parents' lack of understanding. We had one case in which the child left school to return home almost every day. The mother was unable to correct the situation. After several visits, it finally occurred to us that the child's home was several miles from the school, so we asked the mother if, when the child left school, he walked all the way home. "No, the mother replied, I go and pick him up." We insisted that the mother do the obvious, and she reluctantly agreed after expressing some real concern about our judgment and the child's welfare. The child walked home once, and his practice of leaving school ceased.

Childhood phobias are easy to treat

Active avoidance of phobic cues as the major criterion

In general, childhood phobias are easy to treat. Kennedy (1965) recorded 100 percent success in treating fifty cases with a three-day rapid treatment program based on learning concepts. These results should,

Behavioral indices and . . . .

however, be interpreted cautiously, especially in light of a study by Miller, et al. (1972), who treated a group of children with school phobias and separation anxiety. One group was treated with a *desensitization* in fantasy, another group received *play therapy,* and a third group was put on a waiting list. At the end of three months the children in all three conditions were significantly improved and doing equally well. The point is that these types of disorders do tend to disappear with time. However, in order to alleviate the parents' anxiety and solve the problem as rapidly as possible, simple and quick behavior therapy similar to the procedure used by Kennedy is warranted.

Assessment of Phobias

The subject's self-evaulation of phobic reaction usually centers on the terror and apprehension aroused by the phobic stimuli, but it also includes the realization that the fear is unwarranted or inappropriate. Inventories or ratings such as the Wolpe and Lang Inventory (1964) can be used to identify these subjective fears. The Wolpe and Lang Inventory consists of a large list of objects and events by which the individual rates the extent of his or her fear. When the individual is placed in the phobic situation, the fear intensity can be rated on an instrument such as the Fear Thermometer, shown in Figure 8–3.

The major criterion in behavioral assessment of a phobia is the active avoidance of phobic cues. When clinical assessment is necessary to evaluate phobias, an analogue situation is used. In the analogue situation the clinician measures nearness of approach, duration of contact with the phobic stimulus, or some similar index of approach behavior. This assessment may include observing actual motor behavior (such as how closely an individual will approach a snake), or it may require skilled observers to watch for indications of anxiety, such as sweating, pacing, and similar signs of autonomic reactivity in the phobic situation. Behavioral indices are important in assessing phobic reactions because they help determine the nature of the arousing stimuli, an identification that is important in planning for treatment and later for evaluating the effectiveness of the treatment program.

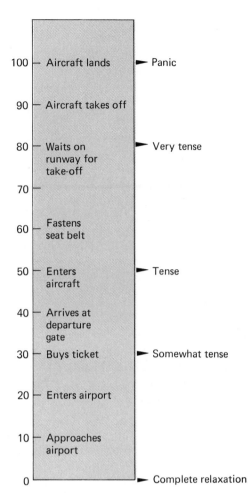

Figure 8–3 A fear thermometer for a flight phobia. The subject simply marks a line through the thermometer to indicate the degree of his or her anxiety or tension.

Psychophysiological indices are becoming more important for clinicians in evaluating phobic reactions. For example, heart rate, galvanic skin response (GSR), and other indices of autonomic nervous system activity in the phobic situation are crucial in the evaluation of the extent and nature of the phobic reaction. The use of telemetric equipment using transducers designed to measure autonomic responses and transmit them to a receiver allows the clinician to place the individual in the actual phobic situation and obtain an index of fear in the natural environment.

Theory and Research

An early explanation of the phobic reaction, suggested by Watson and Rayner in 1920, was that phobias are *conditioned fear responses*. Watson and Rayner's classic demonstration involved the presentation of a white rat to an eleven-month-old boy. Whenever the child played with the rat, a loud noise (UCS) was sounded, which elicited a startle reaction (UCR) in the child. After a few trials, the child began showing signs of anxiety in the presence of the white rat (CR); the anxiety reaction subsequently generalized to similar stimuli, such as furry objects, cotton, wool, and white rabbits. What Watson and Rayner demonstrated was that phobias may well be learned responses. Neutral stimuli can develop phobic qualities when they are associated, temporally and spacially, with fear-provoking stimuli.

Psychophysical indices

Phobias may be learned responses

Eysenck and Rachman (1965) noted that stimuli relevant to fear-provoking situations or that make an impact on the person in the situation are more likely to develop phobic qualities than weak or irrelevant stimuli. Seligman (1971) has suggested that humans may be *biologically prepared* or predisposed to respond to certain stimuli. He states that a CS that bears a biologically significant relationship to a certain UCS will condition rapidly when the two are paired. For example, taste as a CS may become rapidly aversive when paired with gastrointestinal illnesses. Yet, tones or other neutral cues do not condition as rapidly, or at all, when paired with such gastrointestinal tract illnesses. In phobias, objects that were once actually dangerous to the species become threatening more readily than objects that have played little part in natural selection. Such dangerous objects are things that threaten survival—potential predators, unfamiliar places, and the dark. Thus, snakes, spiders, blood, and heights should more rapidly condition phobic responses than flowers or leaves.

Some neutral stimuli are less suitable for conditioning than others

Some support for this hypothesis has been found by Öhmann, Erixon, and Lofbert (1975), who demonstrated that emotional responses as measured by a GSR elicited by a mild shock may be more rapidly conditioned to *prepared stimuli* (such as pictures of snakes and spiders) than to unprepared stimuli (such as pictures of houses and mushrooms). This finding does not mean that anxiety responses cannot be conditioned to unprepared stimuli but suggests that a phobia is more likely to occur when the stimuli is a prepared one.

This white-power group exemplifies Bandura's theory that racial attitudes are an example of phobic behavior.

Repetition of the association between an aversive situation and phobic stimulus strengthens the reaction; but Eysenck (1967) has noted that a single pairing of a neutral stimulus in a highly intense fear situation can elicit a conditioned fear reaction, and the intensity of this reaction may increase over time (called an *incubation effect*). Generalization from the original phobic stimulus to stimuli of a similar nature tends to occur, and responses that allow avoidance of phobic stimuli are reinforced. Eysenck and Rachman (1965) further indicate that phobic reactions are more likely to occur under conditions of excessive restraint, either physical or psychological.

Psychologists have often observed that the causes of many phobias in clinical cases are not clear and cannot be determined from the past history of the individual. For example, a white person who is racially prejudiced may feel uncomfortable, tense, and nervous around blacks. This individual may avoid blacks but may not have had any aversive experiences with black individuals. Bandura (1969) offered a reasonable explanation of the development of phobic reactions in individuals who have had little contact with the phobic stimuli. He explained that many phobic behaviors are not caused by direct experience with the phobic

A conditioned fear response can incubate and grow more intense. . . .

and can occur with little contact with the feared stimulus

In vivo desensitization uses real instead of imagined events

object but by witnessing others respond fearfully to these objects or events. This means that the acquisition of phobias may be mediated by cognitive factors. Thus, the phobic reactions may be acquired either by vicarious emotional conditioning (that is, modeling) or by direct experience.

Modification Techniques

The most successful treatment techniques used to modify phobic reactions attempt to extinguish the anxiety reaction to the phobic stimuli. The most common and effective treatment technique for phobic reactions is *systematic desensitization,* originally developed by Wolpe (1958, 1969), which we described in Chapter 7.

A variation of this technique, *in vivo desensitization,* first used by Meyer (1957), actually exposes the individual to increasingly fear-provoking environmental stimuli. It involves procedures similar to those used in systematic desensitization: The individual is taught relaxation responses, a hierarchy is constructed of real events in the environment, and the individual is then exposed to them in hierarchical order. For example, an agoraphobic individual (a person who fears open space) may be gradually required to go farther and farther out into the environment so that eventually he or

neuroses, personality disorders, and special symptoms

box 8-1
Flying Phobia in a
28-Year-Old Female

My fear of flying and aircraft began seven years ago when I was a passenger on a 707 jet. While in flight, we encountered a brief period of severe air turbulence. Things fell from the racks into the aisle and onto my fellow passengers, the flight attendants lost their footing, and the seat-belt sign flashed on and off. Although the choppy period lasted no longer than five minutes, I was nauseated until we landed. Since that time, I have either avoided flying or made the few flights I had to make with extreme fear and physical discomfort. I knew I was being unreasonable, and I even began to wonder if there might be something wrong with me.

When I entered therapy, the therapist explained that the goal of my treatment program would be to teach me to control or tolerate the "natural" anxieties associated with rough plane rides. First, my therapist trained me in deep muscle relaxation. After I learned how to relax and had practiced at home, my therapist helped me construct a list of hierarchy of my fears. We included things like thinking about an airplane, looking at a picture of a plane in a magazine, looking at a passing plane, preparing for a trip, buying tickets, and driving to the airport. Each week I would meet with my therapist and we would go through the hierarchy together. I would imagine each scene on the list until I could do so without any anxiety. Whenever a scene did make me anxious, I was to signal my therapist and then instruct myself

to relax by saying something like "Relax," "Calm yourself," "You can handle it." When I felt relaxed, I would signal again, and we would go on to the next scene. Between sessions, I practiced going through the scenes and relaxing at home.

After I mastered the imagined drive to the airport (the last item on my hierarchy), I progressed rapidly. I even made a real drive to the airport. My therapist praised me for this early move and suggested that next time I take a tape recorder along and record in detail whatever made me afraid or anxious and my reactions to these things. Soon I was relaxing to my tapes rather than to imagined scenes.

For the next two weeks I made short stays in the airport terminal and on the observation decks. Then, at my next appointment, I could report having taken a short ride in a small four-seater even though I had been somewhat fearful and anxious during the flight. My therapist encouraged me to take my recorder along on these flights and then relax to my recordings of real in-flight experiences. After only six rides in small planes I felt comfortable, confident, and even exhilarated by my flights. Finally, I made a three-hour flight in a 727 commercial jet. While in flight I was able to master my anxiety with self-directed relaxation. My therapist checked with me six months later and was glad to find that I continued to fly fearlessly aboard commercial aircraft whenever I had the chance.

Karoby, 1974

---

she can travel without experiencing any anxiety. In many of these procedures, the response is shaped so that the individual eventually learns to approach the phobic stimuli and endure it. After each response is made, the individual is reinforced.

The procedure used in systematic desensitization may differ somewhat for phobic children. For example, Lazarus and Abramovitz (1962) have used a technique called *emotive imagery*. With this technique the child is taught to imagine a pleasant scene while simultaneously being exposed to phobic cues.

Anxiety Neurosis

Whereas specific cues will elicit a phobic reaction, the environmental or internal cues that elicit or maintain the pervasive anxiety reaction are unclear. An individual with **anxiety neurosis,** which is labeled a **generalized anxiety disorder** by DSM III, shows chronic anxiety with periodic acute attacks that last from a few minutes to hours. These acute panic attacks, which may include hyperventilation and fainting, vary in frequency from several a day to one or two a month. Generalized anxiety can be defined

Chronic anxiety and periodic acute attacks of panic

as a subjective experience of apprehension, anxiety, and tension associated with behavioral and physiological indices, such as motor tremors, rapid eyeblinks, urinary frequency, loss of appetite, shortness of breath, difficulty in concentrating, restlessness, and other indices of increased activity of the sympathetic nervous system. The individual is frequently unable to specify why he or she is tense and remains in a chronic state of anxiety. Because anxiety is always present, the individual may be handicapped in interpersonal relationships and other aspects of life.

Anxiety in Children

Generalized anxiety reactions also occur in children and are labeled by DSM II and DSM III as overanxious reactions of childhood or adolescence. These disorders take essentially the same form as adult reactions and are characterized by chronic anxiety, unrealistic fears, and exaggerated autonomic nervous system reactions. They are often associated with sleeplessness and nightmares.

While the source of generalized anxiety is usually difficult to pinpoint in adults, it is often obvious in children. Anthony (1967) describes three types of childhood anxiety. The first type is **contagious anxiety**, in which the child is exposed to extremely anxious adults, and through the process of modeling, imitates their behavior. The second type is **traumatic anxiety**, in which the reaction is provoked by an unexpected frightening event that the child cannot handle. Severity and permanence of the pervasive anxiety reaction are determined by the seriousness of the event as well as the parents' reaction to the child's fear. The third type of anxiety is **conflict anxiety**, which supposedly results from deep-seated intrapsychic conflicts. A more parsimonious description of this type of anxiety would be that the source of the anxiety is not known; this is commonly true of pervasive anxiety in adults.

Assessment of Anxiety Neurosis

Upon clinical examination, individuals exhibiting anxiety neurosis report feelings of tension, anxiety, and impending catastrophe without the ability to specify the cause of their anxiety. A number of self-report inventories are available to assess such anxiety. One such scale is the Taylor Manifest Anxiety Scale in which the individual responds to such items as "My sleep is restless and disturbed" (True), or "I am usually calm and not easily upset" (False), and similar statements designed to assess anxiety. The individual exhibits remorse, sweating, pacing, and other signs of anxiety. Psychophysiological indices, such as heart rate, GSR, and blood pressure, typically show a pattern of autonomic arousal.

Theory and Research

The first question to be asked about the pervasive anxiety reaction is whether in fact there is evidence for an increased tonic (resting) level of the autonomic nervous system. A number of studies have drawn comparisons between the individual with a pervasive anxiety reaction and normal subjects or individuals with other disorders.

In general, research demonstrates that individuals with generalized anxiety reactions are likely to show greater physiological arousal to stress, slower habituation to repeated stress, and slower recovery from stress situations (Martin 1971). Consequently, the results of studies of physiological arousal of individuals with anxiety neuroses confirm their subjective reports. These data also indicate that the amount of anxiety present in cases of phobias is a direct function of the specificity of phobic cues and the ability of the individual to avoid them. Social phobics, who are constantly exposed to phobic cues and have little opportunity for escape, show arousal patterns similar to those shown in the generalized anxiety disorder. These data suggest that generalized anxiety and phobic reactions may differ only in terms of the ease of avoidance of phobic cues.

Generalized anxiety disorders may develop in the same manner as phobic disorders. In other words, a neutral stimulus of one type or another is associated with an unpleasant experience that elicits a fear response. Following this association, the individual exhibits anxiety or a *conditioned emotional reaction (CER)* when exposed to formerly neutral cues. In phobic reactions, this cue elicits a *conditioned avoidance response (CAR),* which eliminates the CER. However, in generalized anxiety disorders,

Contagious anxiety: exposure to extremely anxious adults

Traumatic anxiety: an unexpected frightening event

Conflict anxiety: source of anxiety unknown

Anxiety and reaction to stress

Generalized anxiety

Phobia

neuroses, personality disorders, and special symptoms

the individual demonstrates only the CER either because specifying the phobic cues is difficult or because the cues are so pervasive that escape is impossible. This is the crucial difference between a phobic reaction and a generalized anxiety disorder. We are dealing in one case with a conditioned avoidance response and in the other case with a conditioned emotional reaction.

Why does the generalized anxiety disorder not extinguish when an association no longer exists between the original aversive stimulus (UCS) and the neutral stimulus? It does not extinguish because conditioning and extinction in the autonomic nervous system are somewhat different from the same phenomena in the skeletal motor system. In the phobia, the phobic cue elicits anxiety while the avoidance response reduces anxiety, thus strengthening the phobic behavior. In generalized anxiety, certain cues may elicit anxiety, and the anxiety itself may serve as a UCS that, through higher order conditioning, maintains the response (Eysenck 1968). In fact, over a period of time an incubation effect may occur during which the strength of the CER actually increases. This situation implies that the original conditioning may have occurred to minimally noxious cues that were not particularly noticeable or annoying to the individual. However, with the incubation effect, the degree of arousal increases, and the anxiety response generalizes to other stimuli until a pervasive anxiety reaction results.

Two other theories attempt to explain the differences between generalized anxiety disorders and phobic reactions. The first explanation, offered by Wolpe (1969), suggests that generalized anxiety responses are conditioned to a wide range of stimuli that the individual cannot escape. An example might be a noxious state associated with a variable interval schedule. Thus, the only stimulus involved would be time, and the variable interval schedule should produce a consistent state of arousal. Here, generalized anxiety would be similar to "superstitious" behavior in which the anxiety response occurred because of an accidental pairing of neutral cues, such as time and anxiety-provoking stimuli. Similar types of neutral stimuli might be social cues, open places, and other pervasive forces. However, an alternative explanation is that the

original conditioning situation involved a highly noxious cue, resulting in an intense emotional experience that caused generalization to many cues in the environment. With incubation, this condition could easily become worse. This is sometimes referred to as the *Napalkov effect* (Eysenck 1967). Eysenck has also suggested that this phenomenon is more likely to occur in individuals who display a consistently high state of arousal than in individuals who have lower states of arousal.

That individual differences exist in the reactivity and basal arousal level of the autonomic nervous systems has been well demonstrated. With this fact in mind, Martin (1971) posited a hereditary component in degree of autonomic reactivity whose existence would imply that a similar factor functions in anxiety disorders. Slater and Shields (1969) found an agreement rate of 41 percent in identical but 4 percent in fraternal twins who were labeled with anxiety neuroses. Therefore, individuals with an inherited tendency to be more autonomically reactive may possibly be more susceptible than others to the development of pervasive anxiety reactions.

In the generalized anxiety reaction, the individual experiences a constant high level of arousal and tension with intermittent periods of panic. Lader and Mathews (1968) provide a plausible hypothesis for these panic attacks. They state that the initial arousal level is higher in generalized anxiety disorders than in normal conditions and that the habituation to stress stimuli is slower. Consequently, repetitive stress stimuli, even if minimal, cause increased arousal in individuals with pervasive anxiety disorders; a "positive feedback mechanism" occurs; the arousal level is augmented; and the result may be a panic attack. This process is illustrated in Figure 8–4, which shows the way an initial high level or arousal may develop into a panic attack.

Modification Techniques

Anxiety neurosis is a difficult condition to modify. In general, systematic desensitization is less effective than it is with phobias because of the high level of arousal (which interferes with teaching relaxation)

For five years I'd been real nervous. If I was in a crowd or around people I didn't know, I'd feel dizzy—like I was going to faint. I couldn't go in a store without shaking, not even if the store was almost empty. If I had to stop at a light, I'd get so scared I'd want to run out of my car. I couldn't finish anything I started. I felt like a real failure. I really resented my wife too because she said my fears were all in my head. She said if I was a strong man, I wouldn't be so afraid all the time. She could get along with people real well. How could she know how I felt? Then I changed jobs just to suit her. I gave up being a janitor and went to being an inspector on the assembly line in my plant. My wife said I needed to make more money and besides being a janitor wasn't good enough. Well, after I changed jobs, I really got nervous, so I went to the nurse at the plant. She said I ought to try therapy.

For two years I saw this doctor, and we talked about what caused my fears and about how my mother had always run me down. She was always screaming at us kids. We never could please her. The doctor said I was running myself down now just like she used to do. Well, I got over being nervous in crowds and stores. I could even go to town with my wife and enjoy it. I wasn't afraid of lights anymore either. But I was still scared to go to work. I got back my old job as janitor, but that didn't help. I was still scared my foreman would run me down for something or ask me to do something a janitor didn't have to. I was scared too that some of the fellows at the plant might find out how nervous I was and take advantage of me.

Then my doctor sent me to somebody for what he called learning therapy. I learned how to relax first. Then I learned how to suggest things to myself while I was relaxed, what the new doctor called autosuggestion. After I'd relax, the doctor would tell me to imagine I was in the plant and think about how good it felt to be there. I was supposed to smile when I felt comfortable. Then I was supposed to pretend that my foreman came up to me and talked friendly to me. When I was comfortable, I was supposed to smile again. I did the same thing for the other fellows I worked with.

Next time I saw the doctor, he made me do the same thing for about half an hour. Then he asked me to pretend like my foreman or some of the fellows were running me down or making fun of me even though they really liked me. I was supposed to see myself taking it all without getting nervous or scared. We did this kind of thing for four weeks. I had to practice at home too.

The doctor also told me, when I was at work and felt nervous, to eat a candy bar. I like candy, and there was a machine on every floor so I could get some real easy. The doctor said that doing something I liked like that would help me feel good when I usually felt scared. He said that I shouldn't start eating candy bars all the time, just when I was relaxing and suggesting things to myself at work.

After the first week, I didn't feel much different, but by the middle of the second week, I noticed I wasn't so tight on the way to work. About the third week, I'd almost stopped shaking when I talked to my foreman or the fellows. After six weeks, I'd go whole days without feeling nervous. Once my boss even called me down for something, and I kept calm so we could talk about it. Then my doctor asked me to take over on my own. He checked on me in two weeks, and I told him I wasn't nervous much anymore. I had even decided to change jobs again because I knew I could handle things this time. The doctor checked with me again in six months, and I was doing pretty well, not scared or nervous, or anything.

Cautela, 1965

Anger/affection—
emotional states
or emotional disorders?

and because of the difficulty of obtaining a stimulus hierarchy. As a method of treatment, Wolpe (1958) suggests carbon dioxide inhalation therapy, since inhaling carbon dioxide does reduce anxiety. Cautela (1966) reported treating three cases of

neuroses, personality disorders, and special symptoms

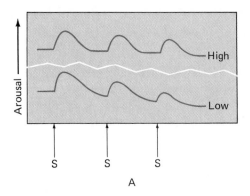

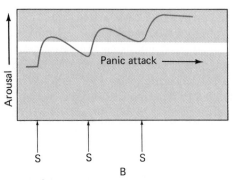

Figure 8-4 Development of a panic attack. *A* shows the relationships found between level of arousal (in terms of spontaneous skin conductance fluctuations) and habituation to repeated stimuli (*S*). The top line illustrates the responses of a highly aroused individual, and the bottom line shows the responses of a normal subject. *B* shows the development of a panic attack in a highly aroused individual after being exposed to three threatening stimulus events.

generalized anxiety with assertiveness training. Another technique used by Marks (1972) is **CS flooding**: The individual is flooded in imagination with aversive stimuli, which increase his or her level of arousal. Ideally, the response to the aversive stimuli will eventually habituate and result in lower arousal levels. Interestingly enough, Marks has suggested that flooding was more effective than systematic desensitization with generalized anxiety cases, while systematic desensitization seemed to be the treatment of choice with specific phobias. However, we do not yet have a highly effective treatment method for use with generalized anxiety.

Anger-Affection Continuum

The emotions variously labeled love, affection, fondness, rage, anger, and similar terms that indicate approach or avoidance

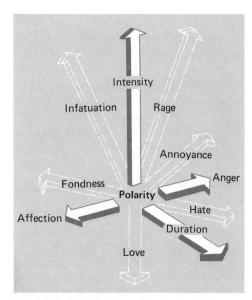

Figure 8-5 Three-dimensional schematic visualization of anger/affection coordinates.

behavior toward other individuals have not been as extensively researched as anxiety nor do they receive much attention in the clinical literature. Some confusion exists over whether these terms denote emotional states or emotional disorders.

Behaviors labeled by these terms can be imagined as existing on a bipolar **anger-affection continuum** that has love on one end, hate on the other end, with fondness, irritability, and similar terms located in between. This love-hate dimension can be described as the subjective experience of the degree of *attraction* or *repulsion* toward an organism, object, or situation; positive or negative behavioral interaction (emitting rewards or punishment) with the organism, object, or situation; and changes in the activity of the individual's autonomic nervous system. The midpoint of this bipolar continuum is defined by a neutral subjective reaction or indifferent behavior toward the organism, object, or situation in question and no concomitant change in autonomic nervous system activity.

Usage of the adjectives describing this dimension varies as a function of the duration of the response or the intensity of the response, or both (see Figure 8-5). For example, a brief intense emotional response on this dimension is usually referred to as rage, while a long-term, intense negative emotional response is called hatred. Infatuation is thus defined as an intense affective response of short duration, while love may differ only in terms of the duration of the response. Similarly, the difference between being annoyed and being angry may be the intensity of the response.

Anger-affection responses always have an object or are elicited by stimulus factors in the environment, usually other individuals. In this way, they are highly similar to anxiety responses. For example, anger may be a response to a threatening situation that is not perceived as being dangerous enough to cause a flight reaction. On the other hand, resentment and anger responses are not always associated with attack behavior or aggression, and the clinician must be careful to differentiate between aggression that is a function of an emotional state of anger and aggression that is an instrumental act to obtain other rewards, such as money. A careful description of the behavior can determine whether aggression is a function of hostility or is instrumental in achieving other rewards by coercive behavior. When injury to another person seems to be the primary objective, it is likely that hostility caused the aggression. These distinctions will be discussed in greater detail in Chapter 10.

Assessment and Research

In terms of assessment, little systematic evaluation has been made of these emotions, and few procedures have been developed to measure anger-affection. The clinician can usually differentiate to some degree between these responses and other emotional responses, such as depression or anxiety, by using observations of the client's behavior, such as social interaction, subjective reports, and psychophysiological indices. There is some evidence, as we noted earlier, that anger can be different from fear or anxiety on the basis of physiological responses (Ax 1953; Schachter 1957; Funkenstein, King, and Drolette 1957). Diastolic blood pressure increases in anger but decreases in fear or anxiety; heart rate increases in both but somewhat more in fear and anxiety. Estimates of cardiac output (blood volume per unit of time) increase in fear and anxiety but remain about the same or decrease in anger. Blood vessel constriction decreases in fear and anxiety but increases in anger.

Physiological indices for different emotions

Explosive Personality or Disorder of Impulse Control

A disorder of emotion characterized by a low rage threshold or "temper tantrum" is similar to the **explosive personality** described in DSM II. Listed as a personality disorder, its primary defining characteristic is outbursts of rage associated with gross verbal or physical aggressiveness. Such outbursts are different from the individual's usual behavior and may be followed by intense remorse. DSM II describes "explosive" individuals as generally excitable and overly responsive to environmental stress and claims that the intensity of the outbursts and the individual's inability to control his or her emotions are distinguishing characteristics. In other words, these individuals' threshold for emotional responses is lowered, and their reaction to provoking stimuli increases in intensity. DSM III calls this a disorder of impulse control rather than personality, but notes that these are affective or autonomic symptoms.

Mandler (1966) has noted that one type of antecedent condition that produces anger is the interruption of goal-oriented behavior. It seems reasonable to assume that the threshold for anger responses is lowered in individuals exhibiting "temper tantrums" in situations in which interruption of goal-directed behavior occurs.

Modification Procedures

As with other emotional responses, an attempt is usually made to eliminate extreme anger responses by teaching the individual self-control procedures. Systematic desensitization has been used with some success (Rimm et al. 1971). However, this technique is difficult if the individual is not able to relax or does not seem to have a hierarchy of responses. In such cases, Wilson and Smith (1968) have used variations of systematic desensitization in which the individual is relaxed and then told to freely associate until he or she begins to feel tense or angry. The individual is then instructed to stop and begin to relax again. In some cases humor has been used as a method of counterconditioning. Humor does appear to counteract anger or fear and has been fairly successful as a method of controlling rage (Smith 1973).

When I finally decided to get professional help, I was on the point of suicide. I couldn't seem to control my temper, no matter what I did. My family and friends said that I'd always had a real problem with my temper, but since I got married and had my little boy, things had gotten a lot worse. My son is a very active child who constantly misbehaved just to get my attention. He would make me so mad that I'd end up screaming at him or even jumping up and down and throwing things. Sometimes I'd even attack him. The same things happened when I got angry with my husband. I'd yell at him, call him names, and sometimes throw things at him. What I did was so automatic that I couldn't seem to control it. My temper was making everyone, including me, miserable.

First, the therapist taught me how to really relax. Then we made up two lists of things that made me angry, one list for my husband and one list for my son. During each visit, we'd go through the lists, and I would try to imagine a scene without feeling angry. But after seven sessions, I wasn't making much progress. Even though I could relax well, I would still get very angry imagining even the most

innocent scenes. Then the doctor told me that humor can help reduce anger, so we tried making each scene funny somehow. Mostly, we added old-fashioned slapstick.

Whenever I would signal the doctor that I was feeling angry, he'd emphasize the humor in the scene. During the first humor session, I could imagine all the scenes in both lists without getting angry. During the next eight sessions, I felt amused by the scenes. Sometimes I even laughed, but I seldom got angry. As treatment continued, I found myself getting angry at my husband and son less and less. I also found myself better able to deal effectively with my son's misbehavior. My depression went away, and I forgot all thoughts of suicide.

My therapist showed me some charts he had made of my heart and what he called my skin resistance while I listened to a tape of our lists. The first chart was made after I had learned to relax but before real treatment had begun. The second chart was made after we used humor in the lists. The difference in the two really showed how I had learned to react to the scenes without getting angry. The therapist also told me that my MMPI scores also showed the changes.

Smith, 1973

box 8–3
Explosive Personality in a 22-Year-Old Female

Summary

Neuroses, the most common of all deviant patterns of behavior, are usually assumed to be a function of anxiety. However, many neurotic conditions are not caused by anxiety, but anxiety may be a consequence of the deviant response pattern. Furthermore, there is little support for the belief that all individuals with neurotic behavior patterns share a neurotic personality. Different types of neurotic behavior often have little in common. The "neurosis" does not necessarily pervade all aspects of the individual's life; for example, an individual with a phobia may function quite well in other aspects of life. It is also important to differentiate between factors that cause a neurotic behavior pattern and factors that are responsible for its continuance.

In general, neurotic behavior patterns are quite heterogeneous, have little in common with another, and are usually exaggerations of behavior patterns exhibited by all individuals. The major differences between neuroses and more severe forms of behavior pathology are that neuroses tend to be situational and do not pervade all aspects of an individual's life. Moreover, the individual with a neurotic behavior pattern has good reality testing and can evaluate life experiences in much the same way as other individuals. Neuroses are specific behavior patterns that cause malfunctioning primarily of one response system. For example, anxiety, phobias, and depression are disorders of emotion, while depersonalization, fugue states, and memory losses are cognitive disorders. Conversion reactions may be either motor or sensory disorders.

Emotions are specific patterns of autonomic nervous system activity, behavior, and subjective experience that occur as a function of rather subtle internal or external cues. The physiological aspects of emotion are mediated essentially by the hypothalamus, the limbic system, and other central nervous system structures as well as peripherally by the hormones and the autonomic nervous system. The relationship among physiology, learning, and cues from the environment is crucial in understanding both normal and abnormal emotional states. While physiologic activity is necessary for the occurrence of a particular emotion, situational factors or cues from the environment are important in determining how individuals interpret their physiological responses and the labels they give to emotional experiences. Nevertheless, there is some evidence that a specific emotion may elicit specific patterns of central and autonomic nervous system reaction.

Anxiety can be defined as a conditioned fear response to relatively mild events, and may take either of two forms: phobias and generalized anxiety. A phobia is a learned fear of a specific object, situation, or organism, as indicated by a subjective report of anxiety and an avoidance of the phobic object. Usually, the individual with a phobic response attempts to avoid the phobic stimuli. Reactions to these stimuli are out of proportion to the demands of reality, seem inexplicable to the individual, and are beyond voluntary control. Almost any object can serve as a phobic stimulus. Depending on the nature of the phobic stimuli, phobic disorders can be severely handicapping. For example, an individual with a social phobia is likely to be severely handicapped in many areas of life. Phobias should be assessed by the individual's subjective reports; by psychophysiologic indices of emotion such as heart rate, GSR, and other autonomic nervous system indices; and by the individual's behavioral avoidance of the fear situation.

Phobias appear to be learned. Stimuli that have evolutionary significance may facilitate the development of the phobic reaction, but a single pairing of a neutral stimulus with a highly intense fear situation can also produce a conditioned fear

response, and the intensity of this reaction may increase over time, through an incubation effect. A number of different behavioral techniques are highly successful in eliminating phobias. They include systematic desensitization, *in vivo* desensitization, flooding, emotive imagery with phobic children, and other techniques.

Although phobic reactions are elicited by specific cues in the anxiety neuroses, the causes of generalized anxiety reactions are unclear. Individuals show chronic anxiety and periodic acute panic attacks that may last from a few minutes to hours. These acute attacks may include hyperventilation and fainting. The individual is usually unable to specify the cause of the anxiety, has difficulty in concentrating, is restless, and shows other indices of increased sympathetic nervous system reaction. Research has demonstrated that individuals with generalized anxiety attacks show increased tonic levels of autonomic nervous system arousal, have slower habituation to stimuli that cause even more anxiety, and show slower recovery from stress situations. It is possible that generalized anxiety develops in the same manner as phobic disorders. The major difference may be that the cues that produce anxiety are so pervasive that the individual cannot avoid them and therefore remains in a chronic aroused state. The generalized anxiety disorder is similar to that of the individual with a social phobia, who also tends to be chronically overaroused. Cues causing the generalized anxiety are not clear, but they may come from internal as well as external stimuli. There is also some indication that, in the case of generalized anxiety, incubation of the fear occurs, and through generalization almost any environmental or internal event may cause anxiety.

Anxiety neuroses are difficult conditions to modify or treat. Typically, the methods used with phobic disorders have not been as successful with generalized anxiety reactions.

Disorders of other emotions, such as anger, are also quite common. One example of this type of disorder is the explosive personality, which is usually described as a personality or impulse disorder but is more appropriately labeled a neurotic condition in which the individual is unable to control his or her temper. Individuals with this problem are overly responsive to environmental stress and exhibit outbursts of rage associated with gross verbal and, occasionally, physical aggressiveness. After the episode these individuals usually feel remorse. Behavior therapy techniques that are used with other emotional disorders and designed to teach the individual self-control of emotional behavior are usually effective with these disorders.

Key Concepts

agoraphobia

anger-affection continuum

anxiety

anxiety neurosis (generalized anxiety disorder)

conflict anxiety

contagious anxiety

emotion

explosive personality

fear

flooding

hypothalamus

jukebox theory of emotion

neuroses

neurotic personality

phobia

separation anxiety (school phobia)

simple phobia

social phobia

traumatic anxiety

Review Questions

1. What effect has the practice of classifying people instead of behavior had on the diagnosis of neurosis?

2. Describe the part that each of the following plays in the subjective experience of emotions:
   a. The hypothalamus and the limbic system
   b. The autonomic nervous system
   c. The adrenal gland
   d. Cognitive factors

3. What are the differences between anxiety, fear, and phobia?

4. What mechanism may be involved in the learning of phobias? What kinds of information are needed in assessing a phobia? What technique has been used successfully to modify phobias?

5. What are the characteristics of anxiety neurosis?

6. What is the possible role that autonomic reactivity may have in anxiety neurosis?

7. What is the anger-affection continuum?

neuroses II 9

special symptoms—disorders of the sensory, cognitive, and motor response systems

Key Topics

Motor disorders: tics and stuttering

Compulsive behaviors: washers and checkers

Avoidance responses and the development of repetitive maladaptive responses

Meyer and the modification of compulsive behaviors

Sensory and motor conversion reactions

Conversion reactions and malingering

Obsessions: doubts and irrational impulses

Dissociative neurosis: amnesia, fugue, and multiple personality

Depersonalization disorders and hypochondriacal and neurasthenic neuroses

Humans experience as well as act. We selectively attend to certain cues in our environment, encode the information, recall other needed information, organize and process the information, choose an option for action, and finally act—either overtly or covertly. In this sequence we use three main response systems: *sensory, cognitive,* and *motor;* that is, we sense, perceive, remember, think, plan, solve problems, and finally take some action—whether it is perceivable by others or not. At any point in this chain of complex processes, psychological malfunctioning can and does occur. In this chapter we shall consider the disorders or *neurotic symptoms* of the motor, sensory, and cognitive systems.

Motor disorder: all requirements are met, but the appropriate response does not occur

The less severe forms of motor disorders, including speech disturbances and other dysfunctions, were originally described in DSM I as neuroses; DSM II designated them as special symptoms; DSM III classifies them as disorders arising in childhood or adolescence. For our purposes, they will be included in this chapter, since these disorders are malfunctions of motor behavior, as are conversion reactions, in which losses of motor function occur.

Motor Disorders

An irresistible impulse precedes a tic

The classification of an abnormal pattern of behavior as a *motor disorder* involves determining first, whether the individual is adequately attending to and *perceiving* appropriate internal and external stimulation; second, whether the individual is adequately *processing* this information received from these sources; and third, whether the individual's resultant motor response is exaggerated, minimized, poorly modulated, or absent. General disorders of motor behavior cause both theoretical and practical problems for the clinician in that all the requirements for effective action, in terms of sensory and cognitive processing, are present, but an adequate motor response still does not occur. Consequently, the research dealing with these disorders has been minimal, and most introductions to abnormal psychology tend to ignore them although their incidence is quite high.

Tics

A **tic** is an involuntary, repetitive muscle spasm usually limited to a single muscle group. Tics tend to occur or increase in frequency whenever the individual feels anxious or tense; the individual may even be unaware of the occurrence of the response. Meige and Feindel (1907) originally suggested that a tic is a coordinated, purposeful act caused by some external stimulus or idea. It becomes habitual through repetition and eventually becomes involuntary (occurring without apparent cause or purpose). At the same time, its intensity and frequency are exaggerated. Execution of the tic is often preceded by an irresistible impulse, and suppression of the tic causes anxiety. Distraction or voluntary effort diminishes the occurrence of the tic, and in sleep it is usually absent. Tics can occur in various parts of the body, including the face, the eyes, the neck, the nose, the arms, the stomach, and the feet. Many tics may occur in a few minutes.

A more specific form of tic is **spasmodic torticollis.** In spasmodic torticollis, the neck muscles are contracted so that the head is held in either a laterally or a vertically deviant position. Torticollis can be either recurrent or constant; if it is constant, the head remains in the deviant position. The sternomastoid muscles are particularly involved, and either the left or the right of these muscles may hypertrophy (increase in size).

A complex form of tic is the **Gilles de la Tourette syndrome.** This disorder is characterized by a compulsive jerking of the voluntary musculature. The effect is widespread, but the face, neck, and extremities are particularly affected. In contrast to other complex tics, this disorder is accompanied by *coprolalia* (compulsive obscene utterances), *echolalia* (repetition of other persons' words and phrases), and *echokinesis* (repetition of other persons' acts). While the spasmodic movements and the obscene utterances always characterize this disorder, the mimicking may or may not be present.

Ticlike movements may occur in many organic conditions involving brain injury and other physiological malfunctioning. Such movements include spasms, choreas, and cerebellar and cerebello-rubrospinal tremor. In general, distinguishing between tics and organic conditions by neurological examination is fairly easy, but the two kinds of disorders may also be distinguished by the fact that tics are subject to voluntary control, usually disappear during sleep, and presumably bring tension reduction upon their execution.

Research and Theory

Tics and ticlike movements are common phenomena in childhood. It has been estimated that the vast majority of children demonstrate one or more persistent movements of a repetitive type and that 72 percent show two or more of these movements (Blatz and Ringland 1935). Another estimate asserts that 15 percent of all children exhibit tics and that these diminish and disappear during adolescence. Only about 6 percent of these childhood tics persist until adulthood (Bakwin and Bakwin 1972). The gradual decline of these movements with increasing age can presumably be attributed to the increased maturation of the nervous system. Whether all tics are simply the persistence of involuntary movements developed in childhood or whether they can develop independently in adults is an important question to which there is no present answer (Yates 1974).

A number of explanations exist for the development of tics, but the majority of them lack real support. Kanner (1957) suggested that tics were once purposeful actions, imitations of the actions of others, or customary gestures that became habitual. A tic is also, according to Kanner, a symptom that may directly represent a psychological conflict (for example, head shaking may represent a negative attitude) or indirectly express generalized emotional upset. Taking a psychodynamic approach, Kessler (1966) stresses the symbolic nature of tics and interprets them as hysterical conversion reactions. According to Kessler, involuntary eye-blinking should be interpreted in the same way as hysterical blindness: as an attempt to deny or repress an image that has been seen. Other evidence indicates that children, such as young Russians, who live in a culture with high regimentation and restriction of free motor behavior may eventually develop tics (Mahler 1944).

Yates (1958) theorizes that tics develop as drive- or anxiety-reducing avoidance responses under highly traumatic circumstances. He suggests that in the situation in which the tic was originally produced, intense fear was aroused, prompting withdrawal. If the withdrawal movement (which later becomes the tic) produced, or coincided with, the cessation or removal of the fear-inducing stimulus, it would then acquire the ability to reduce anxiety. Through stimulus generalization, including internal symbolization, the conditioned fear may be reduced whenever it is aroused by the performance of the movement, which has by now become a tic.

Some evidence indicates that tics are acquired during a traumatic incident, but in many cases identifying any specific trauma with the onset of a tic is impossible. Moreover, because the tic rate increases under stress or anxiety, tics have been thought to reduce anxiety. However, since many tics appear very rapidly, it is difficult to see how they are associated with anxiety reduction. Furthermore, tics do occur when the individual is calm, although they tend to disappear during sleep in most cases. Complicating the problem even further is the fact that the evocation of the tic usually *increases* the general level of anxiety, a result that may, in turn, increase the tic rate. At present no adequate explanation of tics is supported by empirical evidence.

Assessment and Modification

Since tics are viewed as maladaptive motor habits, their elimination has usually focused on techniques designed to break the habit or cause extinction. One technique frequently used with tics is **negative practice,** as delineated by Dunlap (1932). During negative practice, the individual has to mass-practice the tic or greatly increase the frequency of the response. The theory is that mass practice results in fatigue, which causes **reactive inhibition,** preventing the individual from physically responding and compelling the person to rest. Thus, the maladaptive response extinguishes. This technique is generally effective in modifying tics, but not all individuals are responsive to it (Rafi 1962).

Tics are subject to voluntary control

Tics usually disappear in adolescence

Most explanations lack support

Tics may be acquired through trauma

Increasing the tic frequency may extinguish the response

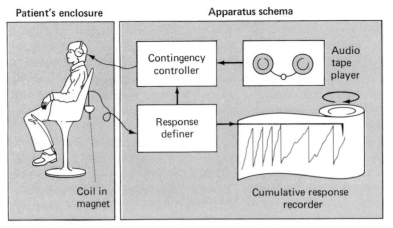

Figure 9-1 Barrett's chair.

In behavior therapy, assessment is often tailored to the particular problem, a practice that, in turn, may lead to the development of innovative treatment methods. This has certainly been the case with tics. For example, to obtain an operant measure of an individual's tics, Barrett (1962) designed an apparatus to record and amplify, via electroencephalograph (EEG) recordings, any spasmodic movements that occurred while the individual was seated in a swivel chair (see Figure 9-1). If the client made a spasmodic movement while in the chair, that movement induced a current, which, amplified by an EEG recorder, operated a relay. Barrett found that her patient—who had contractions of the neck, shoulder, chest, and abdominal muscles, as well as bilateral eye blinking, opening of the mouth, and other mild facial movements—produced a base rate of 64 to 166 tics per minute. Once she had obtained this baseline measurement, Barrett used several procedures to decrease the rate. When she instructed the individual to control the tics, they diminished to a frequency of 50 to 60 per minute. She then tried the application of aversive white noise, contingent upon emission of the tics. This procedure further reduced the frequency to 40 per minute. Finally, she made the interruption of pleasant music contingent upon the occurrence of tics, further reducing the rate to 15 to 30 per minute.

In another case in which mass practice had failed to effect a change in the tic rate, Rafi (1962) devised an apparatus (foot-treadle) that both measured the frequency of the toe-tapping or heel tic and sounded a buzzer whenever the tic occurred. The individual was instructed to decrease the sound of the buzzer by maintaining her foot at rest and thus preventing the closure of a circuit. This procedure was successful in decreasing the frequency of the tic to the point at which its appearance seemed normal.

Brierly (1967) also devised a novel assessment technique for measuring spasmodic torticollis. He designed headgear consisting of a mercury switch on a calibrated band that indicated when the patient's head was in a normal position. After a base rate was obtained, closing the mercury switch resulted in the administration of a mild electric shock. This procedure was successful with two cases, and follow-up reports indicate that both patients were symptom-free after one year.

In another novel treatment-assessment technique, Bernhardt, Hersen, and Barlow (1972) videotaped an individual with torticollis movements. They then placed a piece of clear plastic over a TV monitor and taped horizontal and vertical lines on it. By noticing when the individual's head passed certain intersecting lines, they could determine when the deviant response occurred, as well as how long the head was in a normal position. The base rate of torticollis movement was 74 to 79 percent of the time. The therapists then instructed the individual to hold his head in a normal position. When no changes occurred in his behavior, they added negative feedback consisting of

neuroses, personality disorders, and special symptoms

a white light presented to the patient to indicate the presence of torticollis movement. Later they combined this with verbal instruction. The result was a decrease of the response rate to about 21 to 30 percent of the time.

Stuttering

Stuttering is the inappropriate movement of the speech musculature that produces speech dysfluencies: repetition of speech sounds; prolongation of speech sounds; blocks or periods of silence during which the individual cannot utter a desired sound despite strenuous effort; and motor abnormalities, which include a variety of grimaces and other irrelevant motor behavior, mainly affecting the face but possibly involving also the trunk and limbs. Consonants present particular difficulty, and vowels may be drawn out. Blocks are most frequently associated with initial words, phrases, or sentences and evoke considerable stress. The individual may begin to avoid specific words and may become extremely adept at circumlocution. One of the common characteristics of individuals with these problems is that they tend to avoid situations that elicit or aggravate their stuttering.

Stuttering is associated with a number of stimulus situations. For example, most stutterers do not stutter when they speak to animals, whisper, or sing. Speech problems can result from a number of different sources, including neurological damage and psychological problems. Moreover, stuttering has to be differentiated from poor articulation, a common speech deficit that results from the omission, substitution, or distortion of speech sounds; delayed speech; and aphasia.

Stuttering occurs in 4 to 5 percent of children, but most outgrow it. The incidence of stuttering in the population is approximately 1 percent, 50 percent of stutterers being children (Barber 1959). The disorder is much more common in males than in females, the ratio being variously estimated at from 2.5:1 to 5:1. The onset of stuttering is usually before the age of five, but it can develop later.

As is evident from Mel Tillis's success, the stutterer can often sing normally.

Research and Theory

Most of the research in stuttering has focused on the conditions under which stuttering can be made to increase or decrease. A variety of experiments have shown that if an individual's perception of his or her own speech is delayed, the stuttering rate increases in normally fluent individuals and decreases in stutterers (Webster 1974). As a matter of fact, almost any situation that attenuates or eliminates auditory feedback to a stutterer, such as white noise, can affect a marked decrease in stuttering. In terms of treatment, an even more important finding is that **rhythmic speaking** produces fluency in individuals with stuttering problems. In other words, if the individual speaks in time with a metronome, finger taps, arm swings, or the like, stuttering disappears.

A series of studies have shown that the frequency of stuttering decreases as the individual continues to reread material. This adaptation phenomenon may cause a reduction of as much as 50 percent in the stuttering (Jones 1970). Moreover, individuals with stuttering problems can predict

Stuttering is affected by situational variables

Rhythmic speaking produces fluency

with considerable accuracy the words they are likely to have trouble with, and, by eliminating them, eliminate the stuttering.

Evidence also shows that while stutterers give unfavorable descriptions of stutterers in general, just as normal individuals do, they do not see themselves as sharing these characteristics (Fransella 1965). Furthermore, little objective support exists for the notion that stuttering is a manifestation of a more basic neurotic disorder or even that stutterers have a characteristic personality (Jones 1970).

The genetic basis of stuttering

Some evidence does, however, suggest a genetic basis for stuttering (Andrews and Harris 1974). Approximately 30 percent of stutterers have relatives who stutter, as opposed to less than 0.05 percent of fluent control subjects. Furthermore, the risk increases among first-degree relatives. Some evidence indicates that this relationship may be sex-specific, since the male relatives of female stutterers suffer the greatest risk of developing stuttering, while the risk is least among female relatives of male stutterers. Nevertheless, speech patterns are obviously acquired to a large extent by modeling. Thus, the possibility of cultural transmission is very likely and could account for the increased incidence among relatives.

Labeling and punishing stuttering may make it permanent

A particularly popular theory is that stuttering develops as a function of anxiety (Sheehan 1958). This hypothesis is appealing because it is consistent with the clinical observation that when stutterers are placed in stress situations, they increase their stuttering rate. Johnson (1959), on the other hand, has suggested that faulty training is the cause. He claims that certain parents become alarmed at normal dysfluencies in their children's speech and express disapproval or even punish the children. Consequently, the children become anxious about their speech and develop avoidance responses. In other words, when an individual is labeled as a stutterer and punished for it, the deviant speech pattern is likely to become permanent (Beech and Fransella 1968).

The faulty feedback hypothesis

Desensitization to inhibit anxiety

A completely different approach to the cause of stuttering has been taken by Webster (1974). He emphasizes a *servo-system model* of speech control and suggests that stuttering is due to aberrations of the auditory feedback signals normally involved in speech guidance. He theorizes that the faulty feedback is due to the muscle mechanisms located in the stutterer's middle ear canal. Considerable evidence supports this hypothesis since the disruption of auditory feedback causes stuttering in normally fluent individuals and fluency in stutterers. The well-known fact that many stutterers have much more difficulty while talking on the telephone may be due to the fact that the only feedback involved is auditory. This approach does not account for the social anxiety of stutterers, but Webster has implied that anxiety may be a product rather than a cause of the disorder.

Modification Procedures

The specialists who assess and devise remedial programs for speech problems are speech therapists who study fluencies and dysfluencies in stuttering and other speech conditions. Their therapeutic efforts are focused on such problems as the child's breathing habits, the self-image created by poor speech, and the inability to make certain sounds. The speech therapist is often the key person in integrating psychological, educational, medical, and dental contributions in solving speech problems.

Most contemporary speech-therapy clinics are influenced by Van Riper's (1971) *expressive and dynamic symptomatic therapy.* This approach involves general psychotherapeutic procedures aimed at enabling stutterers to understand themselves and the nature of their disorder, to increase tolerance for their own stuttering and the subsequent reactions of listeners, and to become more independent and tough-minded. This therapy also involves graduated desensitization during which practice is given in progressively more difficult situations in an attempt to inhibit anxiety even though stuttering may continue to occur. In addition, more direct forms of speech therapy are employed, including differential relaxation of the speech musculature, rhythmic speaking games, and voluntary stuttering during which the individual stutters not only on feared words but on words that are not expected to cause difficulty. Speech therapists also use *cancellation,* a procedure during which the individual stops after a stuttered word and

neuroses, personality disorders, and special symptoms

repeats it. The therapist may also stop the individual after a stuttered word, single it out, and have the individual repeat it slowly, syllable by syllable, until it can be produced without stuttering. Or the therapist may attempt a modification of speech before the stuttered word is completed. In a five-year follow-up of this method, Van Riper reports that 50 percent of stutterers no longer stutter or that their dysfluency is so mild that it does not constitute a handicap.

A somewhat different approach has been taken by Meyer and Mair (1963). Two major aspects of their program are important. First, they use a variation of systematic desensitization in which the individual constructs a hierarchy of situations that provoke anxiety and stuttering. They then teach the client progressive muscle relaxation, after which they present the first situation in imagination. If the individual is completely comfortable and experiences no anxiety, he or she is asked to imagine speaking in the situation. Next, the individual imagines the situation and whispers. Finally, the individual speaks out loud while imagining being in the situation. The stutterer is taken through the rest of the hierarchy in the same manner. This procedure supposedly eliminates social anxiety and teaches the individual fluency in particular situations.

The second aspect of the program is based on the fact that stuttering decreases when speech is rhythmic. At the beginning of the program, the individual is given a Pacemaster, an instrument that produces a rhythmic sound and is worn like a hearing aid (Brady, 1971). The individual wears this metronome at all times. When the individual's speech becomes completely fluent, the metronome is gradually faded, first by turning it off in difficult situations and then by removing it and speaking without it. This process is fairly effective, but it is also complex and time consuming.

Webster (1974) uses a fluency-shaping program that requires forty to sixty laboratory hours per individual. In it, he teaches three basic skills. First, the subject learns to gently initiate phonation (produce speech sounds). Second, the subject learns to produce unvoiced consonants in such a way that the correct phonetic activities can occur following these sounds. Third, the stutterer is taught how to increase slightly the duration of most speech sounds. Speech is broken down into rather simple small response units of sounds and syllables, and only gradually is the difficulty of the verbal unit increased. In a follow-up study of his fluency program, Webster found that nineteen out of twenty former stutterers remained fluent.

A simpler technique has been used by Resick, et al. (1978). They simply teach stutterers to slow their speech, which produces fluency. After the stutterers have learned to speak at a certain rate per minute, they gradually increase their speaking rate. This program has much promise—it is simple, easily administered, and apparently effective.

Obsessive-Compulsive Neuroses: Compulsions

A **compulsion** is a stereotyped, repetitive motor act that appears to be irrational and beyond the control of the individual. Its defining characteristic is the individual's internal resistance. The individual with **compulsive behaviors** often attempts to resist the act and considers it disgusting, repulsive, or aversive. Compulsive behaviors can involve almost any activity, such as repetitive counting, handwashing, checking of activities, or almost any stereotyped motor act. It is often a complex sequence that, if not performed precisely, can cause the individual to abort the whole process and start again.

The chain of events in compulsive behaviors is typically the following:

1. The urge to perform the behavior. This urge is not always present, since these behaviors often occur so rapidly that the individual engages in them without thought (Meyer and Levy 1973).
2. A feeling of anxiety associated with the idea that the act is unacceptable, undesirable, and uncontrollable. The irrationality of the compulsion is obvious to the individual.
3. An attempt to resist the behavior.
4. The performance of the behavior.
5. A subsequent reduction of anxiety.

Use of a metronome to aid rhythmic speech

Shaping fluency

Internal resistance to compulsive behavior as a feature of the behavior

Compulsive behaviors, which consist of repetitive overt motor acts, and **obsessions,** which consist of repetitive cognitive activity, are often assumed to be a single syndrome because they consist of repetitive activity (Carr 1974). Whereas assuming that a thought always precedes a motor act ("My hands are contaminated: I must wash them") is logical, it does not necessarily follow that the thoughts preceding a compulsive behavior are the same type seen in an obsessional neurosis (Rimm and Somervill 1976). Furthermore, obsessional thinking often occurs without compulsive behavior, the two disorders respond differently to different treatment methods, and the causes of the two types of behavior are probably different. Obsessions will be considered in the section of this chapter covering cognitive disorders.

Compulsions and obsessions are two different disorders

Washers and checkers

Individuals with compulsive behaviors usually come from upper-income, highly intelligent groups (Nemiah 1967). Typically, most of those who exhibit compulsive disorders can be divided into two categories: **washers** and **checkers** (Hodgson and Rackman 1972). The individual with a washing compulsion usually perceives certain objects as contaminated, and exposure to those objects increases anxiety and activates the urge to ritualize. Relief comes only when the behavior occurs. Checkers, on the other hand, have to make sure they have not done something potentially dangerous. For example, they must repeatedly make sure a door is locked or a stove is not lit. Checkers seem to be flooded with indecisiveness (Roper, Rachman, and Hodgson 1973). Contrary to Wolpe's belief (1973), compulsive behaviors do not seem to produce anxiety; or, if they do, they do so very infrequently (Rachman, DeSilva, and Roper 1976).

Little evidence of a compulsive personality

The doubtful role of anxiety

Psychoanalytic theory assumes that compulsive behaviors develop in individuals who have difficulty at the anal stage of development and exhibit character traits that have been called the **anal triad** (frugality, orderliness, and pedantry). The question is whether the individual who engages in a compulsive behavior displays any characteristics that might constitute a compulsive

Punishing a successful avoidance response may make it fixated, stereotyped, or repetitive

personality and that might be shared by other so-called compulsive personalities. As Buss (1966) points out, little evidence supports this hypothesis, and it appears quite likely that compulsive behaviors could occur in almost any individual, given the proper circumstances.

A major question is how stereotyped compulsive behaviors are acquired and how they become so resistant to extinction. A rather obvious explanation—and the first one always cited for any unusual behavior—is that the behavior reduces anxiety. While anxiety is doubtless associated with compulsive behavior, little evidence exists that either anxiety or anxiety reduction maintains this type of behavior, in spite of the subjective report of the afflicted individual (Hodgson and Rackman 1972). Moreover, techniques designed to reduce anxiety, such as systematic desensitization, are not highly effective with compulsive behavior (Meyer and Levy 1973).

Compulsive behaviors tend to be complicated, but four obvious situations lead to the development of repetitive maladaptive responses:

1. **Double reinforcement** occurs when response functions as an avoidance response and also generates positive reinforcement, resulting in anxiety reduction. An example is compulsive masturbation in an individual who has been punished for sexual behavior. Increase in sexual tension is a cue for anxiety. Masturbation reduces sexual tension and is, therefore, positively reinforcing, but it also reduces anxiety by eliminating the stimuli that elicit anxiety. This type of situation causes a response pattern to become repetitive.

2. **A punished instrumental avoidance response** tends to become fixated, stereotyped, or repetitive. For example, Solomon, Kamin, and Wynne (1953) found that if dogs who had learned to avoid shock by jumping a hurdle were then shocked after jumping, they acquired a faster and more stereotyped response.

3. **Reappearance of previously successful avoidance response under stress** will also lead to stereotyped response. In a study conducted by Fonsberg and quoted by Wolpe (1958), one group

neuroses, personality disorders, and special symptoms

of dogs was trained to perform a leg-lifting response as a method of avoiding a strong electric shock in the right foreleg, while another group was trained to perform a head-shaking response to avoid a strong puff of air to the ear. When the animals were exposed to an insoluble discrimination, leg-lifting appeared in the dogs for whom it had previously been a successful response, while head-shaking appeared in the dogs for whom that response had been successful. In other words, the compulsive behavior may consist of responses that were previously successful in reducing anxiety and that reappear in the individual's behavior when the individual is exposed to new and unresolvable stresses.

4. **Adjunctive behavior** occurs when reinforcement is delivered on an intermittent schedule, where targeted responses are accompanied by behaviors that are not correlated with the reinforcement and appear to be unique to the individual. These responses are labeled as *adjunctive behaviors* and are induced by certain schedules of reinforcement. In rats, intermittent schedules induce a variety of nonreinforced behaviors, such as air licking, excessive drinking (polydipsia), and grooming. Children placed on an extinction schedule exhibit various types of aggressive behavior (Frederiksen and Peterson 1974). Noncontingent reinforcement elicits a variety of behaviors, some of which are odd and are labeled *superstitious behavior*; they are also a type of adjunctive behavior. Patients labeled schizophrenic, when placed on an intermittent schedule of pulling a cord for pennies, develop adjunctive behavior that consists of pacing and drinking (Kachanoff et al. 1973). Normal subjects, placed on a variety of schedules while playing slot machines, developed an assortment of behaviors, including various movements, playing, and bizarre behaviors (Wallace et al. 1975). Compulsive behavior may thus be adjunctive behavior induced by

intermittent reinforcement schedules. This would explain why it is so difficult to determine how compulsive behaviors are learned and why they are difficult to modify. It could be that compulsive behavior is not directly shaped or reinforced but is induced by the acquisition and maintenance of other, almost independent, patterns of behavior. Furthermore, this hypothesis would imply that the most efficient way to eliminate compulsive behavior would be to modify the correlated behavior pattern that induced the rituals rather than directly attempting to eliminate the behaviors.

A related question is why the behavior persists in spite of strong criticism. Taylor (1963) points out that the behavior itself produces immediate reinforcement, and criticism follows a short time later. Because of the delay, the criticism does not eliminate or suppress the behavior but does cause an emotional response. Consequently, after a number of experiences with this situation, the individual persists in the motor response, but the act now elicits guilt and emotional behavior. Therefore, attempts to deal with the emotional aspects of the behavior as a way of eliminating it are doomed to failure because the emotion is the consequence rather than the cause of the compulsive behavior.

Modification Procedures

Compulsive behaviors are among the most resistant to modification of all neurotic behavior. In a study that followed patients with compulsive disorders for ten to twenty years, Kringlen (1970) found that 75 percent of them remained unchanged. The failures of psychodynamic therapy and many forms of behavior therapy to modify these disorders are legend. Fortunately, in the last ten years Victor Meyer and his colleagues (Meyer 1966; Meyer and Levy 1973) have developed a treatment technique that seems to be highly effective. Although Meyer calls it a means of modifying the patient's expectation that a catastrophe

Stress may evoke a stereotyped response

Intermittent reinforcement can produce superstitious behavior

My wife's problems began about three years ago, right after the birth of our daughter. A few months after the baby was born, C began to wash and wash the diapers so that the baby wouldn't get diaper rash—or so she said. Before I knew it, she had started worrying about anything that might be dirty—doorknobs, blankets, clothes, trashcans, meat, animals, men, even me! She wouldn't touch much of anything unless she had tissue paper to protect her hand. She wouldn't even let me or our daughter touch her unless we were "clean." Needless to say, she stopped having sex with me. She spent more and more of her time cleaning and scrubbing. She washed her hands over and over until she got a bad skin irritation on them. Finally, she just stayed inside all day for fear of getting contaminated or infected with dirt. She wouldn't even go shopping or walking.

We tried everything, it seemed like. We'd been to three different hospitals where she'd had electric shock treatment, supportive psychotherapy, drugs, and behavior therapy. We were ready to give up when we went to see Dr. Meyer. He decided to readmit her to the hospital and try to modify her expectations that a catastrophe would occur if she did not wash. After she entered the hospital, Dr. Meyer took her off all drugs and made sure a nurse was with her at all times to prevent her from washing. They even turned off the taps in her room and watched her to see that she didn't get more than a certain amount of cleansers.

Every time she felt like washing, the nurse would try to keep her from it. She would try to persuade C not to, reassure her, encourage her—whatever it took to keep her from washing. Meanwhile, the doctor made her do the things that worried her most. He made her touch doorknobs,

handle trashcans, pick up the baby's toys and milk bottles, use public transportation, and go shopping. At first C would get very upset. She'd cry sometimes and get very worried about being contaminated or getting sick; then again, she'd be resentful and angry and shout about the poor standards of cleanliness in the hospital. After a while, though, the reassurance and encouragement helped, and she started to cooperate better.

All the time she was in the hospital, she had to keep a record of the number of times she'd wash every day and the number of times she wanted to but didn't. During the first four weeks, when the nurse was with her all the time, she didn't wash much at all. When the doctor allowed her to be by herself more, she started washing again, but not nearly as much as usual—maybe only four or five times a day. After about nine weeks, C got to come home on weekends. Even though she still washed pretty often, she didn't complain so much about getting contaminated, and when she did, she didn't sound as serious about it as she used to.

It's been fourteen months now since C was discharged. She still washes more than most people, but she spends only about a fourth of what she spent for a while on cleaners. She still hates to touch anything she thinks might be dirty; she can if she has to. She goes out walking and shopping now, too, even though she still gets nervous if dogs come around. But most important, our family life has improved. She's not nearly as worried as she was about me and our daughter getting dirty or getting her dirty. She and I are having sex again too. In all, we're more than pleased with the progress. We're a family again, enjoying each other's company.

Meyer 1966

---

will occur if the ritual is not performed, the principal ingredient in the technique seems to be **response prevention** (Rackman, Hodgson, and Marks 1971).

The procedure is fairly simple. The behavior is first well delineated. The individual must then agree to allow professionals to prevent any engagement in the behavior. The individual, who is usually hospitalized, is observed twenty four hours a day and prevented from engaging in the behavior by persuasion, distraction, and other techniques for ten to fourteen days. When the

neuroses, personality disorders, and special symptoms

behavior is a naturally occurring behavior, such as hand washing, that has increased in frequency, the individual is allowed to engage in only a normal amount of the activity. Initially, the individual may become quite emotional, but this behavior disappears after several days, and the patient seems to take the attitude that any catastrophe that occurs is the therapist's responsibility. This change in expectation is what Meyer thinks is the active ingredient in the program. After a number of days, supervision is gradually faded out, and the individual may be flooded with the stimuli that caused the ritual. This is a highly successful treatment technique that worked in over 90 percent of the cases in the Meyer series. These results have also been replicated by Mills et al. (1973).

Sensory or Motor Disorders: The Conversion Reactions

Hysteria, a disorder that mimics a physical illness and is characterized by an involuntary, psychogenic loss or disorder of function, has had a long and controversial history. Hippocrates, following the suggestion of Egyptian physicians, attributed emotional instability in women to a wandering uterus. Consequently, hysteria, from the Greek word *hustera* meaning *womb*, was assumed to be a disorder of women only. This assumption has, however, proved erroneous.

DSM II calls one type of hysteria Hysterical neurosis, conversion type. This label again illustrates the influence of psychodynamic theory on diagnosis and classification in DSM II. Freud originally used the term to denote a transformation of underlying psychosexual conflicts into physical disorders. According to Freud's theory, the symptom expressed is seen as somatic and assumed to symbolize underlying or repressed sexual thoughts, ideas, or impulses (Fenichel 1945). DSM III calls these disorders **Somatoform disorders** of the conversion disorder type (physical symptoms suggesting psychological disorders), which avoids this problem.

An enormous variety of deviant response patterns are labeled **conversion reactions.** Their common denominator is an involuntary disturbance of physical functions that are normally under voluntary control. These behavior patterns usually mimic physical disorders, but upon examination no physical basis for their occurrence can be found. Conversion reactions may be classified into two major kinds of disturbances: sensory and motor. Usually, individuals have either one kind or the other, but rarely both.

Sensory Disorders

Conversion reactions can afflict almost any one of the senses—vision, taste, touch, smell, or hearing—in any of three ways. They may produce **anesthesia** (total loss of sensation), **hypoesthesia** (reduced sensitivity), or **paresthesia** (unusual sensation, such as distorted vision or tingling). Visual symptoms may consist of blindness in one or both eyes or in half of each eye; or double vision (diplopia) or tunnel vision, in which the individual sees straight ahead as if wearing blinders. Or objects may appear too dim or too bright, or too small (micropsia) or too large (macropsia). Deafness is the most common auditory symptom, but ringing of the ears may also occur. "Stocking" or "glove" anesthesias sometimes affect the sense of touch. In these anesthesias the individual does not respond to touch or pain stimuli in the area normally covered by these articles of clothing. The most common sensory symptom, however, is vague pain in various areas of the body, especially when the area is stimulated. This type of pain behavior is labeled as **psycholgia** by DSM III. If the individual is distracted during stimulation, the pain response is much reduced, indicating the pain may not have a physiological basis. A sensation of a lump in the throat, called *globus hystericus*, has been a particularly interesting sensory disorder to psychoanalysts who assumed it represented some underlying conflict about fellatio, making it a prime symptom of hysteria (Fenichel 1945).

Motor Symptoms

The variety of *motor symptoms* are legion. In all of them, however, the individual's ability to perform voluntary movements is either diminished or lost. The fingers, the knees, the elbows, and most other motor

Confronting the catastrophic expectation

Conversion reactions: involuntary disturbance of physical functions normally under voluntary control

Vague pain as the most common sensory symptom

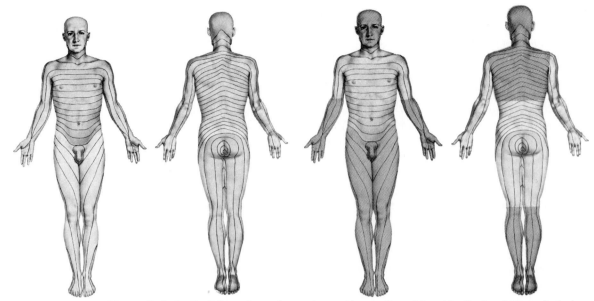

Figure 9-2 On the left are the patterns of neural innervation of the skin. On the right are typical areas of conversion reactions such as pain or loss of function.

systems of the body can be affected. Paralysis may occur in either or both limbs. Loss of verbal motor behavior may affect the patient, who may then be unable to speak aloud, yet still be able to whisper. An even more unusual disorder is **astasia-abasia.** Patients affected by this disorder cannot stand or walk but have complete control of their limbs when sitting or lying down.

Stress as a precipitating factor

Conversion reactions are usually precipitated by a stress situation and are rapid in onset. Since many physical conditions can produce similar symptoms, thorough physical and neurological examinations are required to differentiate conversion reactions from physical illness. Some of the signs of a conversion reaction are obvious, since the resemblance between the response pattern and organic disease is fairly superficial. Most conversion reactions are physiological nonsense. For example, as Figure 9–2 shows, the sensory or motor losses associated with conversion reactions do not make sense physiologically or anatomically because of the way in which the body is innervated.

The selectivity of conversion reactions

Conversion reactions are usually selective. For example, a "blind" person may avoid obstacles. Hysterical fainting, or hysterical convulsions, which are quite rare, can be differentiated from true convulsions by their selectivity. During an attack the individual does not completely lose consciousness; never falls in an injurious manner; does not bite the tongue; is not incontinent; becomes red in the face rather than blue or white; retains coronary, pupillary, and other reflexes; and resists attempts to force open the eyes. Moreover, conversion reactions are usually purposeful: they usually do not occur unless there is reinforcement involved, such as attention or concern from an audience. In some cases **la belle indifference** is present, and the individual is apparently unconcerned about the symptoms. Other symptoms may be **iatrogenic** (physician-caused); that is, symptoms inadvertently suggested by a physician during examination may be present on the next examination.

Conversion reactions are often confused with hypochondriacal neuroses and psychophysiological disorders, conditions we shall discuss later. Here, we briefly note that hypochondriacal neuroses differ from conversion reactions in that they are generally preoccupied with health than with disorders of function.

A careful and complete physical examination is always required in cases of conversion reaction. In a nine-year follow-up of individuals initially diagnosed as exhibiting conversion reactions, Slater and Glithero (1965) found that 60 percent had either died from, or developed signs of, physical

neuroses, personality disorders, and special symptoms

diseases related to the central nervous system. Whitlock (1967) compared the incidence of organic brain disorder in fifty-six patients diagnosed as exhibiting conversion reactions with fifty-six diagnosed as displaying other neurotic conditions. He found that 62.5 percent of the conversion reaction cases suggested organic brain disorder, but such evidence appeared in only 5.3 percent of the other neurotic cases. Rather than indicating an organic basis for conversion reactions, these studies probably show careless diagnostic practices. Unfortunately, there is a tendency to explain physical symptoms as psychological in nature when tests for physical disorders are negative.

A chronic, unresolved problem in conversion reactions is determining whether an individual is faking the symptoms, or **malingering.** The rule-of-thumb in differentiating between conversion reaction and malingering is that malingering is considered a conscious behavior for which the individual is responsible, while conversion reactions are considered unconscious behavior for which the individual is not responsible. This rule is of little help, however, since it is based upon the idea of the unconscious, a psychoanalytic concept that, on a practical level, tells us nothing more than whether an individual can or will account for specific behavior. Thus, deciding whether motivation is conscious or unconscious is not much simpler than deciding in the first place whether the individual's disorder is a conversion reaction or malingering.

Research and Theory

Despite the traditional classification of conversion reactions and hysteria as disorders of females, the classic research studies cited in most abnormal psychology textbooks suggest that they are much more prevalent in males. For example, the Chodoff and Lyons (1958) study considered fifteen men and two women, all VA patients; the Mucha and Reinhardt (1970) study reported on fifty-six male student naval aviators; and the Kiersch (1962) study included ninety-two male and six female military personnel. The obvious reason for the prevalence of males in these studies is that military and veteran populations are traditionally male majorities. But it is also obvious that clinical myths tend to persist when they reinforce a stereotype. Chodoff and Lyons spoke cogently about this problem over twenty years ago:

Thus what has resulted in the case of hysterical personality is a picture of women in the words of men, and, as a perusal of these traits will show, what the description sounds like amounts to a caricature of femininity! The truth of this can be seen if one attempts, as we have done, to apply the criterion for the hysterical personality to male patients, when one comes to the realization that the male who would most closely fit the description would be a passive homosexual. (p. 739)

They liken the process to the analagous situation in which female psychiatrists would spend generations coolly observing and labeling the least attractive traits of males and then formulating them into a "characteristic" male personality. Although it is still unknown whether conversion reactions are more frequent in women than in men, there is little doubt that men are susceptible to developing this deviant behavior pattern.

In terms of theoretical explanation, psychoanalytic theory assumes that conversion reactions are associated with an unresolved Oedipal or Electra complex. The child is attracted to the parent of the opposite sex but represses these incestuous wishes. Later in life, environmental stress reactivates the conflict, which is then converted into symptoms. Fenichel (1945) listed four determinants of the site of the symptoms. The first is the *stage of fixation.* Although all conversion reactions are assumed to fixate primarily at the phallic stage, they are also thought to vary in *secondary fixations.* For example, if the secondary fixation occurs at the oral stage, symptoms related to the mouth and digestive tract will result. The second determinant is the presence of a *weak organ system,* which is susceptible to disease and stress. The third determinant is *timing.* Body parts most active during the crucial conflicts and ensuing repression are most likely to be affected at a later date when the conflict is re-elicited. For example, if rage toward the same sex parent were involved, a chronic, uncontrollably clenched fist might be the resulting symptom. The

Organic disorders are often misdiagnosed as conversion reactions

Distinguishing between conversion reaction and malingering

Conversion reactions do occur in men

When L was first referred to me, she had had a history of grand mal seizures, which had been partially controlled with diphenylhydantoin (Dilantin) and phenobarbital. Six months previously, however, she had married a man a year younger than herself, and shortly thereafter she had suffered a fall that had allegedly left her paralyzed in the legs. She had spent a month in the hospital during which time a laminectomy (spinal surgery) was performed, the result being an apparently complete cure. About three months prior to seeing me, she had begun to have a second kind of seizure in which she experienced blackouts, slumped to the ground, and was unresponsive, but did not bite her tongue, become incontinent, or suffer amnesia.

Examination of L's history revealed that these new seizures had begun at the same time as the following incidents in her life: (1) her husband had been forced to leave his job because of a foot injury and debts had accumulated; (2) L had been forced to change jobs and then terminate because of the new seizures; (3) she and her husband had begun to quarrel more frequently. Examination also revealed that L's family, including her husband, responded to these seizures in what might best be called a nurturant fashion.

After a neurological examination showed no physiological cause for the seizures, I decided to hospitalize L. During the first three days, the nurses were instructed merely to observe her in order to obtain baseline frequency for the seizures and various somatic complaints. When a seizure occurred, the nurses were to check vital signs and look for indications of a grand mal episode. A general attitude of concern was to be shown, but L was to be returned to her room and put to bed if she fell in public areas of the ward. During the first day, L had four seizures; during the second day, two; and during the third, three.

Following baseline, I instituted a behavior modification program. I based the program primarily on extinction and the use of time-out. I told L that her seizures had no organic base and that whenever she exhibited "seizurelike" behavior, she would be put to bed and expected to remain there alone for thirty minutes. I also told her that I would be very happy to see her after her enforced "rest." I further instructed the nurses to ignore somatic complaints. On the first day of the program, L had two seizures. Subsequently, none were noticed. After three days her somatic complaints had ceased also.

Conversion reactions may occur after a physical disability has been cured . . .

fourth determinant is *symbolism.* Some organs are thought to be better suited to represent the underlying conflict than others. This sort of symbolism is referred to as *somatic* or *body language.* Thus, incorporative tendencies may be represented by the mouth, or hostility by the paralyzed clenched hand.

In a behavioral approach to conversion reaction, Ullmann and Krasner (1975) indicate that two main questions are pertinent. The first is whether the individual is capable of such behavior. The second is, if the individual is capable of the behavior, under what conditions will it be emitted. Two situations seem to be conducive to conversion reactions. In many cases, a conver-

sion reaction begins after an individual has actually experienced a physical disability and that disability has been cured. Instead of resuming normal functioning, the individual continues in the behavior pattern associated with the illness. For example, in the classic case reported by Brady and Lind (1961), hysterical blindness occurred after the individual developed dendritic keratitis (ulcerated cornea) resulting from surgery. Although the corneal scarring that had caused the loss of vision cleared, the blindness remained. Whiplash injuries are also good examples of this problem. Initially, back pain results from stress to neck and back, but after the physical difficulty clears, pain often persists. Blanchard and Hersen (1976) reported such a case in which an

neuroses, personality disorders, and special symptoms

Eight days after the start of the program, I talked to L's family and told them that her seizures were not organic and should be ignored. Unfortunately, the family did not ignore them when I let her go home for a four-day pass, and the seizures returned dramatically. I was called at least five times during this period by her husband who sounded panic-stricken. Thus, following her readmittance to the hospital, extinction procedures had to be reintroduced. One week later, after another family conference, I again let her go home on pass.

Four days later L was readmitted, claiming that her legs were paralyzed so that she could neither stand nor walk. Examination revealed that she had had no trouble until she and her husband quarrelled, and he admitted that he was involved with another woman. At this point, L had taken an overdose of phenobarbital and then informed her family of her actions. She was taken to a hospital, and her stomach was pumped. She then announced that her legs were paralyzed.

Extinction and time-out programs were reinstated for the seizures and somatic complaints, and a shaping program was implemented for gradually reinstating standing and walking. Initially, L was required only to stand unassisted for increasing periods of time (two seconds,

seven seconds, fifteen seconds). Reinforcement in the form of meals, access to public areas of the ward, and therapy time was given whenever she succeeded in meeting the criteria during each of four brief daily sessions. Usually, L failed on the first trial of each session but succeeded on the second. Her success was liberally praised. Walking was reinstated in the same way, the criteria for success being the number of steps taken. In nine days, L was fully ambulatory. Only one recurrence of a seizure was reported. This occurred at the foot of the stairs to the recreation room. When she claimed paralysis, L was allowed to lie on the floor unaided, while staff and patients walked around her. After eighty minutes, she got up and stalked angrily to her room.

Daily therapy sessions focused on allowing L to ventilate her disappointment about her marriage, helping her to make realistic plans about divorce, and helping her cope with problems in general. After another family conference, L was released. She was referred to a local mental health center for follow-up. A check with the center after four months revealed no recurrence of problem behavior. L was involved in getting a divorce and participating in a vocational rehabilitation program.

Blanchard and Hersen, 1976

individual who had undergone surgery for disc fusion underwent additional orthopedic surgery seven years later for pain. Five years after the second operation, the individual suffered stooping episodes and was unable to walk. No physical basis was ever established for the condition.

The second method of acquiring conversion behavior is through either modeling or avoidance conditioning. Under certain circumstances, an individual may imitate a sick role, usually when contingent reinforcement is present. This reinforcement is a secondary gain, which we discussed earlier.

Because of secondary gains, some of these cases are called **compensation neuroses.** Secondary gain, originally a psychodynamic concept, means, in effect, that the

behavior is "paying off." One of the main ways it can pay off is in allowing the individual to avoid unpleasant or potentially threatening events; that is, it facilitates avoidance conditioning. Ironside and Batchelor (1945), in a study of World War II airmen, found that the airmen's conversion symptoms were closely related to their duties. The airmen were experiencing visual problems such as blurring and night blindness, which made flying impossible. Their fears of flying were causing behaviors that allowed them to avoid flying—that is, avoidance conditioning was taking place.

Mucha and Rhinehardt (1970) confirmed this observation when they found that 73 percent of their student aviators

or through modeling or avoidance conditioning

Fear of flying can produce symptoms that make flying impossible

displayed visual impairment, such as blurred vision, diplopia, accommodation problems, transit blind spots, visual scotoma, difficulty in focusing, depression of visual acuity, and other similar symptoms. Interestingly enough, they also found that 70 percent of the patients' parents had had previous significant illnesses in the organ system involved in the conversion reaction and that most of the aviators had had multiple physical symptoms before enlistment. These data support both the modeling and the previous-experience hypotheses. Thus, we may conclude that conversion reactions occur not only because of monetary, social, or positive reinforcers but also because they allow individuals to avoid unpleasant or potentially threatening situations.

Assessment and Modification

Although the first procedure in identifying a conversion reaction is always a complete physical examination, psychological measures are also used to determine conversion reactions. For example, the MMPI criterion for conversion reaction is as follows: Hs (Hypochondriasis Scale) and Hy (Hysterical Scale) must be equal to or greater than a T-score of 70, and D (Depression Scale) must be at least 10 T-score points less than Hs and Hy, provided that no other clinical scales are equal to or greater than a score of 70. Mucha and Rhinehardt (1970) found that this stringent criterion was not particularly successful in identifying their conversion reaction cases. When they modified the criterion, however, they could correctly identify approximately 95 percent of their patients.

A rather interesting and novel finding by Hernandez-Peon, (1963) suggests some of the neuropsychological mechanisms in the development of hysterical analgesia. The subject, a fifteen-year-old girl, developed a partial paralysis of her left hand and seven days later developed analgesia of the entire left arm from fingers to shoulder with a loss of the sense of hot and cold in the lower left arm. A single pinprick caused no pain, but repeated pricks evoked a report of normal pinprick pain. No physical or neurological abnormalities could be found. The investigators attached electrodes to the patient's scalp to detect sensory potentials evoked by incoming sensory signals (a type of EEG). (Environmental stimuli usually evoke electrical activity in the brain.) They found that the subject's right, nonanalgesic arm produced normal evoked potentials; but her left, analgesic arm produced no evoked potentials. These results suggest that an inhibitory mechanism may be involved in many conversion reactions; that is, the individual may learn in some way to block or inhibit incoming pain stimuli. Interestingly enough, this same study found that, when the subject was under a light, barbiturate-induced sleep, an evoked potential could be obtained from the left arm. This procedure may be useful in assessing conversion reactions, particularly in terms of differentiating them from malingering, since the evoked potential may be absent in conscious states but present in altered states of consciousness, such as those induced by hypnosis or barbiturate drugs.

A variety of techniques have been used in attempts to modify conversion. Hypnoanalysis has often been used since, when the subject is under hypnosis, the conversion symptom can be modified; for example, to move a paralysis from one arm to the other. If the maintaining factors (secondary gains) are not eliminated, however, relapse may occur, or some other form of behavior may occur (Blanchard and Hersen 1976). Blanchard and Hersen have shown that if a conversion symptom is eliminated but the reinforcement for the behavior is not eliminated, another symptom may occur to replace the original one, a sort of symptom substitution.

A common procedure has been to treat the behavioral deficit by gradually shaping the desired behavior through contingent reinforcement. For example, an individual whose conversion reaction is psychological blindness may be reinforced for seeing (Brady and Lind 1961). Eventually, the individual may be shaped to see.

Cognitive Disorders

All complex behavior involves cognitive processes since the organization of behavior patterns cannot occur without the operation of the central nervous system. As for behavior disorders, some are primarily a function of aberrant cognitive processes, while others are not. Thus, *cognitive disorders* are established largely by the process of elimination; that is, no disorder of sensory input is evident, the motor behavior is intact, and emotional arousal and social interaction are not the primary problems. By necessity, assessment of cognitive behavior involves verbal reports and indirect indices of private events. Consequently, much confusion appears in the clinical and research evidence concerning the classification of these disorders, their possible causes, and their modification. Moreover, if the disruption of the cognitive processes is extremely severe and the form as well as the content of the verbal behavior is so grossly altered that the individual appears confused and bizarre, the condition is more likely to be labeled a *psychosis*.

Obsessional Neuroses

An **obsession** may be defined as a thought, wish, plan, or admonishment that intrudes persistently into an individual's conscious awareness and that the individual considers irrational. Occasionally, we all have obsessions: We dwell continuously on a song lyric, concerns about a decision, aspects of a given situation, or similar topics that seem difficult to ignore. When neurotic, such obsessions are much more intense, persistent, will torment the individual, and will usually involve ideas the individual considers strange or repulsive. The individual is unable to terminate this cognitive activity in spite of strong and even desperate attempts to do so. In contrast to compulsions, which typically relieve anxiety, obsessional thinking causes an increase in autonomic arousal and subjective distress.

There are two major types of obsessional thoughts: (1) *obsessional doubting* and (2) *irrational impulses* or *ideas*. The central feature of obsessional doubting is rumination about a topic or problem of a personal, religious, or philosophical nature. Pros and cons of the question are repetitively considered, or the various aspects of the situation are debated in a prolonged, fruitless, and inconclusive internal dialogue. Far from relieving the individual's

doubts, this continuous debate fills the individual with still more doubt and may lead to despair. Obsessional doubters have real difficulty making decisions in their lives.

Irrational, repetitive thoughts usually consist of ideas that are completely repugnant to the individual. A mother may be obsessed with the idea of strangling her baby; or a man may have irresistible urges that he considers repulsive and horrifying, such as exhibiting himself in public or shouting obscene words. Other frequent obsessional thoughts include wishing the death of a close relative or friend, committing suicide, or going insane. The individual may actively attempt to resist these ideas, be unable to control them, and then become highly emotional.

Research and Theory

As previously mentioned, obsessional thinking, a cognitive activity, has been traditionally thought of as a type of a neurotic compulsive motor activity, even though obsessions can and do occur without compulsive motor rituals. Whether an obsessional neurosis is equivalent to or different from a compulsive neurosis is a question rarely considered (Rimm and Sommervill 1977). Although little research is available on this question, assessment and treatment approaches indicate, as Buss (1966) noted, that little basis exists for linking obsessions and compulsions as the same disorder.

Psychoanalytic theory views the individual with an obsessional neurosis as being fixated at the anal-sadistic stage of development. The major conflict of this phase is supposedly the expression of aggressive and hostile impulses. The ego is thought to utilize four major defense mechanisms against these impulses.

The first defense is *isolation,* whereby the individual tries to protect against the anxiety-provoking effects or impulses by separating them from their ideational component. The result is that the emotional component is totally repressed and the individual is aware only of the idea.

Undoing, the second major defense mechanism, is an attempt at restitution, whereby the individual tries to counteract

Obsessions persistently intrude into awareness

Two types of obsession: doubting . . .

and irrational impulses or ideas

Defense mechanisms as a factor in obsessions

the occurrence of forbidden thoughts or action and thus produces a sequence of two responses that cancel each other out. For example, a mother may decide to treat her child firmly, be beset by obsessional doubting of the correctness of her action, and change her mind and decide to be supportive and reinforcing.

The third defense mechanism is *reaction formation,* in which anger and rage are replaced by affection and tenderness.

The fourth mechanism is *displacement,* in which a similar but remote object replaces the original object of the anger. Since psychoanalytic theory does not differentiate between obsessions and compulsions, it is not clear whether this explanation is satisfactory for one or both of the disorders. Similarly, behavioral formulations of obsessive thoughts have not been well-delineated, probably because obsessions are not differentiated from compulsions.

The continued persistence of obsessive thoughts is, from the behavioral viewpoint, a paradox. If a thought is unpleasant or distressing, why does the person not learn to avoid the thought? After all, reinforcement should be associated with the removal of the aversive stimulus. Martin (1971) has suggested three possible reasons:

1. The individual has learned to experience the thought without emotional response so that the negative effect is minimized. In other words, the individual has managed to split apart the cognitive and the emotional components (isolation by intellectualization). Lazarus and Alferd (1964) have found that when individuals are shown a film of an industrial accident that causes stress to most people, if they are asked to observe the film in a calm, detached manner, their emotional response to the aversive situation is reduced. This process they call *intellectualization,* but it can also be viewed as *isolation.* This explanation is not completely satisfactory because it does not realize that most obsessional thoughts increase the individual's degree of discomfort.

2. The obsessional thought persists because it is a strong response being continuously elicited by prevailing stimuli. Obsessional thoughts of murder and injury may continue to occur because their object may continue to evoke such responses in the individual.

3. An individual may ruminate repeatedly because exposure to the obsessional cognitions may, on occasion, reduce anxiety, especially if some displacement is involved. In other words, the individual with strong conflicts about aggression may become preoccupied with philosophical issues so that enemies can be demolished in a safe, intellectual manner. If some degree of anxiety relief occasionally results, the obsessional thoughts then produce reinforcement on a partial schedule, one that makes responses notoriously resistant to extinction.

Assessment and Modification

A major method of treating obsessive thoughts has been the **thought-stopping technique** (Wolpe 1958). This procedure consists of three phases. In the first phase the individual is instructed to engage in the obsessional thinking. At some point, the therapist yells loudly "Stop!" which interrupts and stops the obsessional thought. In the second phase, the individual is again instructed to engage the obsessional activity, but this time it is the individual who yells "Stop!" In the third phase, the individual is instructed to nonverbally think "Stop!" each time the obsessional activity occurs. While this technique has occasionally proved successful, its effects are short-lived. Once the individual habituates to the technique and "Stop!" no longer elicits a startle reaction, the obsessional ideation continues at a high rate. Similarly, a variety of other behavioral techniques, such as systematic desensitization, have not been highly successful.

A technique that has been somewhat effective is aversion therapy. The individual is instructed to engage in the obsessional ideation while aversive stimuli, such as electric shock to the fingers, are administered. The rationale is that the obsessional

Separating emotion from cognition as a factor

Prevalence of stimuli as a factor

Anxiety reduction as a factor

The individual may habituate to thought-stopping

Use of aversion therapy

neuroses, personality disorders, and special symptoms

When Mrs. G was referred to me, she had been suffering for seven years with recurring thoughts concerned with temptations to carry out aggressive or sexual acts which she described as "horrific." She had tried drug therapy and prolonged psychotherapy without improvement. I decided to try faradic disruption to interrupt her patterns of obsessive ideation. First, we made a list of her twelve most distressing thoughts. These included "I am going to yell that I'm going insane"; "I am going to strangle my children"; and "I am going to have sex with my dog." During each session, Mrs. G sat with her back to me. I attached a finger electrode and determined her shock pain threshold. I then asked Mrs. G to repeat one of the obsessional phrases to herself. When she had done so, she raised her finger, and I administered an electric shock at pain intensity for 0.5 second. After a pause of 30 seconds, we repeated the procedure with the next phrase until all the phrases had been completed. Each session lasted forty minutes, and each phrase was repeated three or four times during the session. I scheduled sessions three to five times a week so that she could not easily rehearse the obsessional behavior between sessions. After the third session, I introduced a variable ratio schedule (60 percent). I also monitored the latency of phrase repetition during each session.

After three sessions, Mrs. G reported that her obsessive thoughts were less frequent. I scheduled four more sessions in order to stabilize the therapeutic effect.

I checked again with Mrs. G six months later and found that most of her obsessional temptations had disappeared. She no longer had the urge to strangle someone when she saw a tie or a belt in a shop window, nor did she fear insanity. The temptations she did have no longer presented real threats to her. For example, she no longer feared the urge to jump from a high place. Generally, she appeared less anxious, and her improvement was maintained even when her son was admitted to the hospital for surgery. For the first time since her marriage, she thought, though she didn't feel, that sex was for more than procreation. At eight months, her improvement was still maintained.

Kenny, Solyom, and Solyom, 1973

box 9-3
Obsessive Ideation in a 33-Year-Old Female

thought serves as a CS and the aversive stimulus as a UCS. After a few trials the individual can escape or avoid the aversive stimulus by not thinking the thought.

Dissociative Disorders

In DSM II, the dissociative type of hysterical neurosis is marked by alterations in the patient's consciousness or identity that produce symptoms such as amnesia, fugue, multiple personality, and somnambulism. Somnambulism, or sleepwalking, is a disorder of the sleep state, and since it bears little resemblance to other dissociative neuroses (Borkovec, Slama, and Grayson 1977), we shall describe it later, in Chapter 11. (DSM III also lists somnambulism as a sleep disorder.) In DSM III these behavior patterns are *dissociative disorders* and have four types: *psychogenic amnesia, psychogenic fugues, multiple personalities,* and *depersonalization disorders*.

Dissociative phenomena are examples of memory disorders and may, therefore, indicate dysfunction in *registration, retention,* or *retrieval* of events. Registration is the encoding of events or learning, while retention is the storage of events, either short or long term. Since in most cases individuals do eventually recover their memory, the main difficulty in this type of disorder would appear to be with the retrieval of past events rather than with learning or complete loss of memory. Since depersonalization disorders do not involve a memory loss, we shall discuss them in the next section.

Dissociative disorders are memory disorders

The three major types of dissociative neuroses are as follows:

1. **Psychogenic amnesia** is characterized by an extensive memory loss that may endure for a few hours, days, or months. Typically, the loss involves knowledge of identity, residence, occupational skill, and past experiences. The forgetting may be partial or total. Typically, the individual does not know who or where he or she is, does not recognize friends or family, and cannot recall a home address or other personal information. However, there is rarely a loss of basic learned abilities, such as speaking, reading, adding, subtracting, or other common skills in the individual's life. Although a similar partial or total loss of past experiences often occurs in organic brain syndromes, hysterical amnesia differs in several ways: (a) it tends to appear and disappear rapidly; (b) it is often selective, and the blank periods usually include traumatic events; (c) under certain circumstances, such as hypnotic trance, memory can be recovered; and (d) there is no evidence of organic brain disease or a traumatic head injury that could cause such loss.

2. **Fugue states** are not much different from hysterical amnesia except that the individual literally leaves real life circumstances and flees to another environment. The fugue may last for a number of days or as long as several years. While in this state, behavior may appear normal. A few fugue cases may seek a different environment, remarry, take another job or occupation, and assume a completely different identity. When the individual recovers, however, recall of behavior performed in the fugue state is rare. Thus, we may identify at least three criteria for diagnosing a fugue state: (a) the person has wandered away from the usual environment; (b) the person is at least partially amnesic for events leading up to and including the wandering; and (c) the person seems to be in a conflict situation (Laughlin 1967).

3. **Multiple personality** is a relatively rare condition in which separate and distinct personalities supposedly exist within a single individual. The various personalities appear alternately, and each seems to possess different or contrasting traits. Usually, one of the personalities is dominant. The various personalities may be completely unaware of the existence of one another, or one personality may be fully aware of all the others. Since such cases are dramatic, they are interesting to both writers and the public. As a result, they have received more public exposure than is justified by their rare occurrence.

Amnesia usually does not include loss of basic learned abilities

After recovery, the individual rarely remembers behavior in the fugue state

Multiple personalities are often sharply contrasting

The mime illustrates how the individual exhibiting multiple personalities can adopt different characters or social roles.

neuroses, personality disorders, and special symptoms

An early twentieth-century case, reported by Morton Prince, was that of Miss Beauchamp, in whom three different personalities appeared: the saint—idealistic, inhibited, self-righteous; the woman—aggressive, realistic, capable of sexual feeling; and Sally—impish, immature, childish. The saint and the woman shared many memories, but Sally made fun of the saint. The saint remained unaware of Sally. A more recent, well-known case appeared in **Three Faces of Eve** (Thigpen and Cleckley 1957). Eve White, the dominant personality, had no knowledge of a second personality, Eve Black, although they had been alternating in control for some years. Whenever Eve Black surfaced, all Eve White could report was that she had blackouts. Eve White was bland, quiet, and serious, a rather dull personality; while Eve Black, on the other hand, was carefree, mischievous, and uninhibited. During treatment, a third personality, Jane, emerged. Jane was co-conscious of both Eves and eventually merged them as a result of therapy. However, in a later report, the client claimed she had as many as twenty-one different personalities, an assertion that certainly weakens the credibility of the case report.

In general, such a dissociation reaction is extremely rare. With the exception of sleepwalking, Abse (1966) could find only 200 documented cases in the literature. Often multiple personality is confused with **split personality,** a term sometimes used to describe schizophrenia. Split personality, however, refers to the splitting of fantasy from reality or thoughts from emotions rather than the division of the personality into two or more identities.

Research and Theory

Because of the rarity of the disorder, little research has been done on it. However, a study by Kiersch (1962) that investigated malingering in amnesia might be appropriately considered here. Malingering is a chronic problem in amnesia cases, since memory loss is one of the easiest symptoms to simulate and one of the hardest to disprove. Kiersch studied ninety-eight military personnel who had been admitted to one of two army general hospitals and diagnosed as amnesiac. Kiersch used both hypnotic and sodium amytol ("truth serum") interviews to evaluate the amnesiac syndrome. Of these cases, forty-one admitted either consciously or under the influence of hypnosis or sodium amytol that they had faked the symptoms. Of the remaining cases, twenty-four were found to be due to organic brain syndrome or acute alcoholism, and thirteen to mixed causes, which included eight cases of alcohol-induced amnesia with

box 9-4
Multiple Personality
in a 31-Year-Old
Female

When Gina first came to me for therapy, I was reluctant to arrive at the diagnosis of multiple personality. In fact, it took some four months from the start of therapy for me to do so. Since cases of multiple personality are thought to be rare at best and even nonexistent by some psychologists, I was uneasy with the diagnosis and initially considered milder forms of dissociative reaction. We all hate to be gullible, and in the beginning all I had to go on were the reports of Gina and her friends that she suffered some somnambulism, episodic amnesia, and behavior that at times seemed quite out-of-keeping with what she and her friends thought of as her "normal" personality. As therapy progressed, however, the diagnosis of multiple personality seemed inescapable.

When Gina began therapy, she was thirty-one years old, single, and employed as a writer by a large educational publishing firm from which she earned a good salary. The youngest of nine siblings, Gina had been born to Italian protestant immigrants, who had settled on a farm in West Virginia. She was a child of her parents' later years, her father being eighty-five and her mother seventy-four at the time of the initial interview. According to Gina, she was never close to her father whom she saw as passive and weak and who, she felt, had largely ignored her. Her mother had been the most domineering person Gina had ever known. Early in life, Gina had learned to be obedient out of fear and felt she had been well-treated because she did what her parents wanted her to do.

Although she had eight brothers and sisters, she had never been very close to them. Her oldest sister was, Gina said, completely dominated by her mother, and her oldest brother, who was given to temper tantrums, had had numerous "nervous breakdowns." Marilyn, the sister who had been most involved in mothering Gina and to whom she had been closest, left to get married when Gina was two. Jenny, the sister whom Gina had replaced as the "baby" of the family, was particularly disliked.

Gina herself was intelligent and well-educated, holding her M.A. degree and being pushed by her mother to pursue the Ph.D. degree. In bearing, Gina was rather masculine. Her friends had told her she walked like a coal miner—the way, Gina noted, that her father really walked. In therapy Gina and I had a good working relationship. Although she was "tough" and acted in as masculine a manner as she could, she was far from hostile.

Gina had suffered some somnabulism since her early teens. She said that the sound of her mother's name awakened her. The lights in her bedroom were usually on when she woke. According to her roommate, Gina herself was the one who screamed her mother's name. Gina later recalled that her sleepwalking had begun at age twelve after a particularly disturbing incident with her sister Jenny. Jenny had incurred the wrath of their mother when she announced that she wanted to get married. Every night for two weeks, the mother had flown into a rage and beat Jenny, while the father sat passively by. One night, Gina heard her mother storming upstairs to kill Jenny and ran upstairs to save her sister.

At the time of therapy, Gina was involved with a rather passive, warm, but befuddled married man, TC. It was he who during a session brought out the second of Gina's feminine selves, Mary Sunshine, for what proved to be the only glimpse I was to have of her. Several previous incidents had, however, indicated the emergence of Mary, the most childish, petulant, and troublesome of the three feminine personalities. Although neither Gina nor her roommate liked hot chocolate, cups that had contained chocolate were found in the sink in the morning. Moreover, in spite of Gina's earning a high income, she found herself with a depleted bank account at the end of each month. Once she found herself on the phone ordering a sewing machine even though she did not know how to sew or care to do so. Finally, she gave in and bought Mary the material she desired and a few weeks later came into the office attired in an attractive dress Mary had made from it.

In spite of Gina's willingness, two sessions of hypnosis failed to unravel her string of personalities. It took the presence of Gina's erstwhile boyfriend TC to bring out Mary for me to see and hear. Because TC continually procrastinated about getting a divorce to marry Gina as he had promised, Gina had become disgusted with him. Mary reacted differently, however. When Gina entered my office with TC, she was her tough, sarcastic self. But as TC talked, her posture, facial expression, tone of voice, and the content of her conversation changed markedly. She seemed deeply sympathetic toward her suitor and assured him that she knew he cared for her. After the session, Gina could not remember much of what happened. She remembered being angry with TC at the first, but after that, she drew a blank.

When TC did not show up for their date the next week, Mary became angry and chewed off Gina's fingernails. Gina, in turn, had started cleaning her gun and planning Mary's death. Finally, she forgave Mary and started talking to her—and getting replies! Mary did not like Gina because Gina was mean to her, and she did not like me because I had lied to her about TC. Mary had even begun by saying, "Hello, Gina" at meetings and embarrassing Gina quite a bit. When Mary came out, Gina reported that she felt very warm, uncomfortably so, as if she had a fever.

With just a little simplification, we might say that Mary represented the opposite of most of what was Gina. Where Gina was masculine, Mary was feminine. Where Gina was sarcastic and rather moralistic, Mary was flirtatious. Where Gina was reserved and impatient, Mary was full of love and accepting of others. Where Gina seemed seriously interested in working on her problem, Mary had no use for me at all. Mary Sunshine was obviously fighting for her independent existence against all the other personalities and against me. Therapy was bringing to light complications and realities which the childish Mary could not handle.

Particularly interesting at this time were a series of warning dreams in which Mary threatened that she and the others were going to kill Gina. According to Mary, Gina had kept her locked up so long that she could never have TC now. Gina accepted the verdict of the others, and after the date on which the killing was to take place, she came back much changed. She had lost much of her previous interest and motivation. From dream reports and conversations, we learned that Mary was preparing for her wedding to TC and Gina was suffering from exhaustion and becoming very, very weak. At this point, an attempt to talk to Mary via "inner conversation" resulted in the emergence of Evelyn. Gina reported that Evelyn came out only once a day then—until she got used to the world—but promised to talk to me when she felt stronger. During this time, the tape recorder we had set up to record Gina's nocturnal adventures began to reveal some interesting information. Different and distinct voices, both feminine and masculine, were discernible. We now learned that Gina had at least three main personalities and seven minor ones.

After the emergence of Evelyn, therapy progressed rapidly. Evelyn appeared to be a neutral personality who wanted only to "do the job"—that is, reintegrate her personality. This goal took precedence over her job, her love life, anything else. Evelyn seemed to possess the integrative functions of the ego. Through inner conversations she mediated between the rather childish, impulsive Mary and the more moralistic, sarcastic Gina. Both Mary and Gina, it seemed, were in their own way exaggerations. I must admit it took me a while to realize that Gina was not merely exaggerating: she herself *was* the exaggeration. Toward the end of therapy, Evelyn appeared more frequently and more consistently. She tended to denigrate both of the other personalities and mental illness as well. I believe that Evelyn existed before therapy, but was submerged. Therapy probably helped to bring her out, but it did not create her. It gave her the opportunity to appear as the more-or-less "happy medium" between the two extremes of Mary and Gina and to integrate them into a personality that could function well in her environment. Once this complex of behaviors that constituted the "personality" of Evelyn began to be reinforced, the behaviors that had constituted the other personalities could be dropped. That Evelyn was indeed a fortunate outcome for therapy is evident from two results: (1) Evelyn never again suffered any of the sleepwalking difficulties or periods of amnesia that had plagued Gina, an indication that conflicts were now resolved in a satisfactory way; and (2) Evelyn is at this time happily married to a physician and functioning well in family life.

Osgood, Luria, Jeans, and Smith, 1976

exaggerated memory loss and five cases of psychogenic amnesia. Of the ninety-eight cases, thirty-two were under court martial charges or were being investigated for alleged offenses. Of these thirty-two, twenty-one fell into the faking group, and nine fell into the mixed or questionable group. While caution is necessary with verbal report data obtained by hypnosis and amytol interviews, such figures imply quite strongly that anyone in serious legal difficulty who claims amnesia may be faking the symptoms or at least be suffering from a questionable amnesia. Kiersch's study found no real relationship between personality types and amnesia, except in the faking group, which exhibited a high percentage of personality disorders.

To explain multiple personality, psychoanalytic theory heavily emphasizes repression. Supposedly, multiple personalities result from successive reawakenings of repressed ego states—impulses or patterns of behavior that existed previously but were repressed because they were threatening to the individual (Jeans 1976). Under stress, they reappear.

In terms of behavioral formulations, Ullmann and Krasner (1975) have focused on role playing and the limits of the attention span as crucial elements in explaining multiple personality. They argue that when individuals are playing specific roles, their awareness or consciousness of other roles is limited. In normal subjects, other behavior patterns or roles can be brought to awareness by various cues that facilitate the retrieval of these patterns of behavior. In individuals displaying dissociative reactions, however, either the attention span or the events that can facilitate retrieval are highly restricted.

Multiple personalities may have limited attention spans

Assessment and Modification

In terms of evaluation and treatment, knowledge of appropriate methods is limited. Typically, these cases are usually treated by psychoanalytic psychotherapy and hypnosis, both because of their rarity and because behavioral clinicians are skeptical of the disorder's existence. However, Kohlenberg (1973) used behavioral techniques in a case of multiple personality in which the patient had also been diagnosed as schizophrenic. When the individual received reinforcement for the behaviors of the relatively normal personality, this personality became more dominant.

Depersonalization Disorder

According to DSM II and DSM III, **depersonalization** is characterized by a feeling of unreality and estrangement from the self, the body, or the environment. A brief experience of depersonalization is not necessarily a symptom of the disorder, and the diagnosis should not be used if it is an aspect of another mental disorder such as an acute situational reaction. The difficulty with depersonalization, as with other cognitive disorders, is that it refers to private events in the individual's experience. Ackner (1954), however, stated that this syndrome can be distinguished by four principal characteristics:

1. **A feeling of change** where the individual feels completely different from the normal state and notes that a profound change has taken place.
2. **A feeling of unreality** where the self and the body appear unreal as if the individual were dreaming. This experience is often called *derealization* and denotes loss of specific feelings and accompanying action (sometimes considered a prime symptom of depersonalization).
3. **The unpleasant quality of the experience** distinguishes true depersonalization from a feeling of change and detachment that occurs occasionally in alcoholic and drug states, especially those produced by the hallucinogens. This unpleasant feeling is often associated with a fear of going insane or dying.
4. **The nondelusional quality of the experience** differentiates depersonalization neurosis from that which often occurs in psychosis. The individual reports an "as if . . ." quality to the experience; that is, the individual is well aware that the external world is real and that it only appears to be unreal.

Other symptoms that often occur with depersonalization are distortion of body image, alteration of self-concept, changes in time and space perception, altered perception of form, feelings of déjà vu (already been seen) or jamais vu (never seen before), and similar phenomena (Weckowicz 1970). The data on the incidence of depersonalization as a behavioral disorder are minimal, probably because it is rare as a pathological state.

Research and Theory

Depersonalization experiences occur frequently. For example, Dixon (1963) found that between one-third and one-half of college students questioned had had depersonalization experiences. Moreover, the incidence seems to be greater in women, and the most frequently reported age of onset is in the twenties (Weckowicz 1970).

A number of events can stimulate or precipitate depersonalization episodes. Roth (1959) mentioned as precipitating causes personal calamity, physical illness, exhaustion, and anesthesia, all conditions that constitute an acute threat to the individual and cause acute fear. A similar factor was discovered by Lader and Wing (1964) in their study of habituation in a patient with an anxiety neurosis. At the beginning of the session, the patient's skin resistance soared upward, but the spontaneous fluctuations of the response then diminished greatly in number, and the response habituated almost to zero. On being questioned afterward, the patient reported that she had felt a panic attack coming on about two-thirds of the way through the session. Her feelings of panic increased until she wanted to ask that the recording be stopped. The feelings of panic suddenly subsided, however, and she felt as if her surroundings were no longer real. The walls of the room seemed to have disappeared, and the recording electrodes seemed to be no longer attached to her arm. Experimental induction of depersonalization by means of sensory deprivation, auditory feedback of white noise, and weightlessness like that encountered in space travel can also produce such experiences (Weckowicz 1970).

In explaining depersonalization, psychoanalytic theorists primarily emphasize the ego defense of denial. That is, the in-

dividual supposedly defends against forbidden impulses by saying, "This is only a dream; it is not real." Depersonalization is thought to alleviate the anxiety caused by forbidden impulses, anal exhibitionist wishes, fears of castration, or similar threats because it assures the individual that there is no danger. Existential theorists stress a lack of ego activity, a lack of active integration of experience, a split between the self and the external world, and the fragmenting of experience with a disruption of its continuity (Weckowicz 1970). As yet, no behavioral explanations of the disorder have been formulated.

Assessment and Modification

Because depersonalization lasts such a short time and usually clears up spontaneously, very little has been done to develop assessment or treatment methods for it. It does tend to recur, however, and many cases have been resistant to treatment. Roth (1959) stated that depersonalization does not respond to ECT and that some patients with depression even develop the disorder following this treatment. A variety of treatments, both biological and psychoanalytical, have been tried with varying degrees of success.

Hypochondriacal and Neurasthenic Neuroses

In **hypochondriasis,** the individual is preoccupied with the body and with fears of presumed diseases. The concern with health is so exaggerated that it usurps all other interests. The individual may chronically check heartbeat or attend to muscle twitches, stomach disturbances, or other indications of possible lack of health. Kenyon (1965) records a description of hypochondriacs from *The Anatomy of Melancholy* by Robert Burton (1628):

. . . fear and sorrow, sharp belchings, fulsome crudities, heat in the bowels, wind and rumblings in the gut, vehement gripings, pain in the belly and stomach, . . . cold sweat, . . . cold joints, indigestion. They cannot endure their own fulsome belching . . . midriff and bowels pulled up, and the veins about their eyes look red and swell from vapours and winds. (pp. 308–309)

Many college students have depersonalization experiences

Sensory deprivation, weightlessness, and white noise can also produce depersonalization

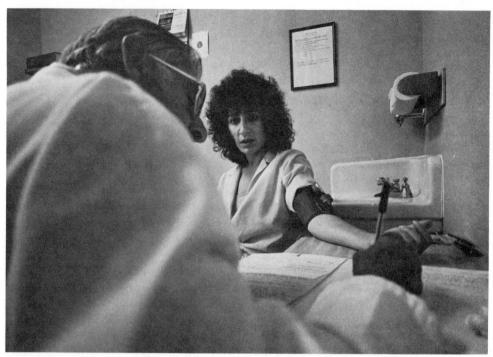

A hypochondriac is preoccupied with the body and with fears of physical illness.

Notably, the vast majority of these descriptions are concerned with the viscera, which are largely controlled by the parasympathetic nervous system.

At the slightest provocation, these individuals will consult a physician. It has been claimed that this type of patient constitutes a large portion of the physician's workload. When the physician finally realizes the nature of the disorder, the individual goes shopping for another physician who will be more understanding. Most of these individuals resent suggestions that their condition may be due to psychological factors. For drug and health-food firms, hypochondriacs are big business. Many are walking encyclopedias of health information, particularly when the topic relates to disease. As Suinn (1975) has noted, they seem to be enjoying poor health.

In many ways the hypochondriacal neuroses are similar to the obsessional neuroses. The crucial difference is that the hypochondriac seems to enjoy the disorder, while individuals with obsessions recognize that the thoughts that plague them are irrational and experience anxiety whenever the thoughts occur. Hypochondriasis is relatively rare, according to Coleman (1972),

occurring in only five percent of the neurotic population. However, this statistic may be inaccurate because many of these individuals do not view their problems as psychological. Because aspects of the disorder are very similar to delusions, it is often classified as a psychosis, from which it must be differentiated (Kenyon 1965). Much more frequent than other types of hypochondriacal neuroses are the cardiac neuroses, in which the focus of attention centers on cardiovascular disorders or heart attacks (Rifkin 1968). These disorders are described by DSM III either as somatization or as atypical somatoform disorders.

Neurasthenic neurosis is a disorder characterized by complaints of chronic weakness, quick fatigue, and exhaustion. It differs from hysterical neurosis in that the complaints are genuinely distressing to the individual, yet no physical symptoms are found. Often, the individual can go to bed tired and wake up even more tired. This disorder is usually rather selective in that the individual may be too exhausted to mow the lawn, but have plenty of energy to play golf. The only real difference between neurasthenic neurosis and asthenic personality disorder is that in the former condition the individual feels distressed about the condition.

neuroses, personality disorders, and special symptoms

© 1979 United Feature Syndicate, Inc.

The person with neurasthenic neurosis complains of chronic weakness, quick fatigue, and exhaustion.

Neurasthenic neurosis has had a long history in the psychiatric literature and has been described since 1869 (Slade 1968). However, some real skepticism exists over whether this disorder is a meaningful pattern of neurotic behavior. Chatel and Peele (1970) have noted that the scope of neurasthenia is like an accordion, expanding and contracting in relation to the rise and fall of diagnostic fads. They surveyed St. Elizabeth Hospital, one of the largest psychiatric institutes in the United States, for the frequency of the use of neurasthenia as a diagnostic label. They found that from 1885 to 1901 the term was never used. From 1902 onward, it was not used more than four times in any one year, and during many years it was not used at all. For all the admissions to St. Elizabeth Hospital in the past 114 years, the term has been used fewer than fifty times. Rimm and Sommervill (1977) also believe, as do Ullmann and Krasner (1975), that this diagnosis denotes no identifiable behavior disorder. It is perhaps best considered as a specific form of hypochondriasis or as an aspect of other disorders.

Research, Theory, and Modification

Hypochondriacal behavior is a serious difficulty for physicians, since the hypochondriac's psychogenic pain and somatic preoccupation not only waste their time but may also lead to unnecessary operations or medical treatment (Binchi 1973). It seems fairly evident that the hypochondriacal individual is more sensitive to internal stimuli produced by the bodily apparatus. Some evidence to support this theory emerged from a study of somatic complainers by Dickinson and Smith (1973). They measured the GSR of both somatic complainers and control subjects under stress and nonstress conditions and found that the complainers showed rapid habituation of the basic components of orienting responses, an indication that they were more parasympathetically aroused. This result suggests that somatic complainers should show a heightened sensitivity to stimuli, particularly painful stimuli, from the viscera.

According to Freud, hypochondriasis and neurasthenia are actual neuroses; that is, they are not the result of mental conflicts but are rather the product of a damming up of sexual energy. Masturbation was seen as one cause of neurasthenia because through masturbation libidinal energy had been withdrawn from the outer world and focused on the self. Other writers note that displacement is important because anxieties are displaced upon bodily functions rather than upon other objects or situations (Kleinmuntz 1974).

Behavioral formulations of this disorder are primitive. Certainly, the reinforcement and secondary gains derived from this type of disorder are obvious.

Modification of these disorders can be difficult, since most individuals exhibiting them are not likely to seek psychological assistance because they do not see their problems as psychological. A number of individuals who have anxiety for various illnesses have been treated with behavioral techniques (Ullmann and Krasner 1975); however, a number of these cases can best be described as phobias.

Hypochondriasis may lead to unnecessary operations and treatments

Summary

Psychological malfunction can occur in the motor, sensory, or cognitive response systems. This chapter describes the less severe forms of these malfunctions, which DSM II labels as neuroses or special symptoms.

The classification of an abnormal behavior pattern as a motor disorder involves determining (1) whether the individual is adequately attending to or perceiving appropriate internal and external stimulation; (2) whether the individual is adequately processing information from these sources; and (3) whether the resultant motor response is exaggerated, minimized, poorly modulated, or absent. The major types of motor disorders are tics, stuttering, and compulsive rituals.

A tic is an involuntary repetitive muscle spasm, usually limited to a single muscle group. Two special forms of tics are spasmodic torticollis, a disorder in which the head is held constantly or recurrently in a deviant lateral or vertical position, and the Gilles de la Tourette syndrome, a complex tic accompanied by compulsive obscene utterances. Tics are very common in children but decline in frequency with increasing age. Various theories have been offered for the development of tics. Psychodynamic theorists have interpreted tics as hysterical reactions, and behaviorists have viewed them as drive- or anxiety-reducing avoidance responses acquired under highly dramatic conditions. Various other theories have received little support. In general, there is no well-accepted method for eliminating tics, although mass practice has been used with some success. In most cases, treatment techniques are innovative and adapted to the particular form of tic.

Stuttering is an inappropriate movement of the speech musculature. The frequency of the resulting dysfluencies varies with a number of conditions. For example, individuals do not stutter when they speak to animals, whisper, or sing. Experimentally, a number of conditions result in increases or decreases in stuttering. These include delayed auditory feedback, adaptation, and rhythmic speaking. Explanations of stuttering have focused on anxiety and reduction or disruption of auditory feedback. A number of treatment procedures have been used, often quite effectively. These include expressive and dynamic symptomatic therapy, systematic desensitization, combined rhythmic speaking, fluency-shaping programs, and slowed speech.

A compulsion is a stereotyped, ritualistic motor act that appears irrational and out of the individual's control. Its defining characteristic is the individual's attempt to resist the motor act. Typically, individuals with ritualistic disorders come from upper-income, highly intelligent groups. Individuals with compulsive behavior may be classified as either "washers" or "checkers."

Psychoanalytic theory suggests that rituals develop in individuals who have had difficulty at the anal stage of development and consequently exhibit the character traits of the anal triad (frugality, orderliness, and pedantry). Evidence for this hypothesis is weak at best, however, and rituals apparently can occur in individuals with almost any personality type. Behaviorist formulations have focused on (1) double reinforcement, (2) a punished instrumental avoidance response, (3) reappearance of a previously successful avoidance response under stress, and (4) adjunctive responses.

Although rituals have been very difficult to modify, a promising procedure is response prevention, during which the individual is prevented from engaging in the rituals by persuasion, distraction, and other techniques for ten to fourteen days. This procedure is highly effective and apparently works in over 90 percent of the cases.

The conversion reactions consist of both sensory and motor disorders. These disorders tend to mimic physical illnesses, but careful medical examination reveals no physical basis for their occurrence. The sensory disorders can affect any of the senses—vision, taste, touch, smell, or hearing—in any of three ways: (1) a total loss of sensation, (2) reduced sensitivity, or (3) unusual sensitivity. Motor symptoms can affect a wide variety of motor functions, all of which involve the individual's ability to produce voluntary movement. Conversion reactions are usually precipitated by stress situations and are rapid in onset.

Psychodynamic theorists assume that conversion symptoms develop in hysterical personalities. However, research evidence does not support this conclusion. Furthermore, in spite of common beliefs, conversion reactions often occur in males. Behaviorist explanations focus on whether the individual is capable of producing such behavior and, if so, under what conditions. In the typical case, the individual initially experiences an actual physical disability, which is reinforced by secondary gains so that the behavior continues even after its physiological basis has been removed, hence the term compensation neuroses for these disorders.

The cognitive disorders include obsessional neuroses, dissociative neuroses, hypochondriacal neuroses, and neurasthenic neuroses. The obsessional disorders involve obsessional doubting and irrational impulses or ideas. Obsessional thinking has been assumed to be associated with compulsive neuroses in spite of the fact that obsessions can and do occur without motor rituals. Obsessional thoughts have been treated by thought-stopping and aversion therapy.

The dissociative disorders involve an alteration in the patient's state of consciousness or identity, which produces such symptoms as amnesia, fugue, and multiple personality. Dissociative phenomena are memory disorders and indicate dysfunction in the registration, retention, or retrieval of events. Hysterical amnesia involves memory losses for a few hours, days, or months. Typically, the loss includes knowledge of identity, residence, occupational skills, and past experiences. It may be partial or total. Fugue states are not very different from psychogenic amnesia except that the individual literally leaves present life circumstances and flees to another environment. Multiple personality is a rare disorder in which the individual exhibits several different personalities. A chronic problem with these disorders is determining whether the individual is malingering or faking the symptoms. In explanation of multiple personality, psychoanalytic theory heavily emphasizes repression, while behavioral theories emphasize role playing and the limits of attention span. A variety of treatments have been used with this disorder.

Depersonalization disorders are characterized by a feeling of unreality and estrangement from the self, the body, or the environment. Such experiences are quite common in normal individuals and can only be considered deviant if they cause panic in the individual.

Hypochondriasis and neurasthenic neuroses involve preoccupation with the body and fear of presumed diseases of various organs. In neurasthenia the individual has chronic fatigue reactions.

Key Concepts

anal triad

anesthesia

astasia abasia

"checkers"

compensation neuroses

compulsion

compulsive behaviors

conversion reactions

depersonalization

fugue state

Gilles de la Tourette syndrome

hypochondriasis

hypoesthesia

hysteria

iatrogenic effect

la belle indifference

malingering

multiple personality (split personality)

negative practice

neurasthenic neurosis

obsessions

paraesthesia

psychogenic amnesia

psycholgia

reactive inhibition

response prevention

rhythmic speaking

somatoform disorders

spasmodic torticollis

stuttering

thought stopping technique

"washers"

tics

Review Questions

1. What are tics? Describe a technique that has been used to modify tics.

2. List two factors that can affect a person's stuttering rate. Describe a technique that has been used to modify stuttering.

3. What is the chain of events that produces a compulsive behavior?

4. What four situations can lead to the development of repetitive maladaptive responses?

5. What technique did Meyer and his associates use to modify compulsive behavior?

6. What would be an example of a sensory conversion reaction? What would be an example of a motor conversion reaction?

7. What two situations are conducive to conversion reactions?

8. What is an obsession? Describe two types of obsessional thought.

9. What are the three major types of dissociative neurosis?

10. What would a depersonalization experience feel like?

11. How does a hypochondriacal neurosis differ from an obsessional neurosis?

12. What are the characteristics of neurasthenic neurosis?

neuroses, personality disorders, and special symptoms

personality disorders
the disorders of social behavior

10

Key Topics

Contrast between state models and
    trait models

Four criteria of personality
    disorders

Cleckley's characteristics of the
    antisocial personality

Roles of EEG abnormalities,
    autonomic reactivity, and
    avoidance learning in antisocial
    behavior

Four obstacles to modifying
    antisocial behavior

Ethical concerns of compulsory
    therapy

Hysterical personalities

Obsessive-compulsive personalities

Schizoid personalities

Personality is one of the most controversial concepts in psychology, largely because psychologists are unable to agree on what the term means. Gordon Allport (1937), a pioneer in the study of personality, argued that the term is one of the most abstract in our vocabulary and that it "like any abstract word suffers from excess use" (p. 25). Allport presented fifty different definitions of personality, including those based on external appearances, on distinct personal qualities, on self-concept, on the living human being in its entirety, on an individual's social stimulus value, on the way one really is, on the system of habits representing characteristic adjustment to the environment, and on an individual's life-style. By Allport's own definition, **personality** "is the dynamic organization within the individual of those psychophysical systems that determine his unique adjustment to the environment" (p. 48).

What characteristics persist across situations? How are they related?

Modern *personologists* define personality in a similar manner. For example, "personality is a stable set of characteristics and tendencies that determine those commonalities and differences in the psychological behavior (thoughts, feelings, and actions) of people that have continuity in time and that may or may not be easily understood in terms of the social and biological pressures of the immediate stimulus situation" (Maddi 1972 p. 9).

What changes in situation variables produce changes in behavior?

Trait and State Models

Perhaps the most common assumption in personality theory is that the essence of an individual's personality is stable across time and situations. This assumption developed because psychologists interested in personality have generally been **trait** or dynamic theorists who use two approaches. First, they determine specific characteristics that an individual exhibits in all or at least most situations. For example, an individual who may be described as dependent should appear so in almost every situation. Second, they determine how these characteristics are related to one another. An example might be the relation between intelligence and grade-point average; or, in abnormal

Interactionism: behavior as a function of both trait and situation

psychology, order of birth and neuroticism, or introversion and neuroticism. The regularities observed in human behavior derived from this approach are called *response-response (R-R) laws.*

In contrast to the trait approach, many psychologists, particularly behaviorists, maintain that behavior is a function of situations and will change as situations change. This approach, called **situationalism,** tends to ignore organismic factors, regarding them as secondary to the impact of external stimuli. Psychologists interested in this approach typically manipulate various external stimulus factors to observe changes in behavior. They study behavior in terms of stimulus and response and generate what have been known as *stimulus-response (S-R) laws.* Certainly the differences between S-R and R-R approaches are going to generate different types of information, but the fundamental question remains: Is behavior a function of a stable organization of traits or is it a function of situations?

In a comprehensive review of the literature, Mischel (1968) concluded that behavior is a function of situations and that little support exists for the notion of traits or habits that are stable across situations. This conclusion has naturally met with opposition from trait theorists. As frequently happens in such disagreements among psychologists, both sides are partially right (Bowers 1973). This controversy has resulted in the realization that a third position is possible that might be called **interactionism.** According to this position, behavior observed in various situations may be a function of both the type of situation and the individual's predisposition or traits (Bower 1973). Bowers reviewed a number of studies in which it was possible to determine whether the behavior observed was a function of the individual's predispositions, the situation, or an interaction between the two. In general, his data indicated that situational variables explain some behavior and traits explain others, but that more frequently an interaction of the two accounts for the observed behavior.

We shall take more of an *operational approach* to personality, even though to do so might seem arbitrary. What most people refer to as personality is usually observed

neuroses, personality disorders, and special symptoms

in human interactions, and our judgment of whether people are aggressive, dependent, or whatever, usually depends upon the way they interact socially with us or others. For our purposes, personality will refer to an individual's social skills or the ability to elicit social and other types of reinforcement from others (Libet and Levinsohn 1973). We shall define *personality disorders* as deficits in social skills and social interactions with other individuals. Furthermore, we shall assume that the situations in which these interactions occur can enhance or aggravate these deficits (Bem and Funder 1978).

Criteria of Personality Disorders

Sometimes, individuals exhibit deviant response patterns in social situations even when no specific neurotic symptoms, such as conversion reactions, are apparent. Such maladaptive patterns of social behavior are labeled personality disorders and are described by DSM II as a "group of disorders . . . characterized by deeply ingrained maladaptive patterns of behavior that are perceptively different in quality from psychotic and neurotic symptoms." The DSM III description of personality disorders is similar.

In contrast to the neuroses, which cause subjective distress, a personality disorder may be quite acceptable to the individual even though it produces negative reactions from other people. In other words, the behavior pattern itself does not cause discomfort or subjective distress; on the contrary, other people's reactions to the behavior, which may include avoiding or chastising the individual, produce the distress.

DSM II further characterizes personality disorders as "generally . . . life-long patterns often recognizable by the time of adolescence or earlier." Some recent studies indicate that in some individuals personality behavior patterns tend to be stable across time and situations (Bowers 1973; Endler 1973; Mischel 1973). Significantly, this stability of behavior occurs largely in individuals who are labeled as maladjusted (Bowers 1973). As a matter of fact, one indication of abnormal behavior may be that it does not change or vary as a function of the stimulus situation.

From this discussion, we can infer that four criteria distinguish a personality disorder:

1. The behavior is stable over time and generally is acquired in childhood or adolescence.
2. The behavior tends to be stable across situations.
3. The behavior pattern is not distressing to the individual. However, the *consequences* of the behavior are distressing to the individual, since others react negatively to it and either avoid, punish, or take other adverse action toward the individual.
4. Personality disorders are maladaptive patterns or deficits in social skills. Although other target behaviors or symptoms may be present on occasion in the emotional, sensory, biological, or cognitive response systems, personality disorders can be consistently identified by observing the individual's pattern of social interaction.

In this chapter we shall cover disorders that consist of stable but deviant patterns of social interaction. Episodic disorders, such as the explosive or cyclothymic personalities, and disorders that appear to be independent of social interaction (that is, the behavior may or may not occur in social situations), will be covered elsewhere in this book. Likewise, it seems appropriate to discuss the paranoid personality in Chapter 15, when we discuss paranoid disorders, since this disorder may be a less severe form of paranoia.

Antisocial Personality and Juvenile Delinquency

According to DSM II and DSM III, **antisocial personalities** have basically unsocialized behavior patterns that bring the individual repeatedly into conflict with society. Such individuals are incapable of significant loyalty to other individuals, groups, or social values. They are grossly selfish,

Personality as social skills and ability to obtain reinforcement from others

Personality disorders are not always distressing to the individual

Abnormal behavior may be extremely stable

Antisocial personalities: unsocialized people whose behavior brings them into conflict with society

Both Machiavelli and Charles Manson could be labelled antisocial personalities.

callous, irresponsible, impulsive, and unable to experience guilt or to learn from experience or punishment. Their frustration tolerance is low, and they tend to blame others or rationalize their behavior. The antisocial personality has been given many labels, including **psychopath** and **sociopath,** and the condition has been given various labels, including *moral insanity* and *constitutional psychopathic inferiority*. Although antisocial personalities are often involved in criminal activity, they are not necessarily so, nor are all crimes committed by antisocial personalities. On the contrary, crimes are committed by a variety of individuals, some of whom might be labeled normal. The sociopath's behavior, though it may not always be criminal, is nevertheless consistently viewed by other people as immoral and reprehensible.

A variety of behavioral characteristics have been cited as essential features of the antisocial personality (Cleckley 1959; Hare 1970; McCord and McCord 1964). While some variation has occurred, agreement on the principal characteristics has been fairly consistent. Some of these characteristics

may be absent in certain types of antisocial personalities, but the following are generally believed to occur in most sociopathic disorders (Cleckley 1959):

1. **Lack of anxiety and guilt** is notable in sociopaths who violate moral or legal standards, physically or emotionally harm others, or anticipate some obnoxious event, like being caught. Because sociopathic personalities do not have these characteristics, they are often assumed to lack a conscience.

2. An **inability to profit or learn from experience** marks sociopathic individuals who may be otherwise quite intelligent. For example, they may deliberately continue to commit the same crime in the same way, often even in the same place, even though they have previously been apprehended.

3. **Impulsiveness and difficulty in delaying gratification** is typical of sociopaths, who have particular difficulty in controlling their hostility and sexual impulses. They are oriented almost exclusively to the

neuroses, personality disorders, and special symptoms

box 10-1
Antisocial
Personality in a
24-Year-Old Male

The patient was referred for psychiatric examination by a court social worker after he had been arrested four times in one year for corrupting the morals of a minor. On this occasion, the father of a sixteen-year-old girl had pressed charges when he found them together. His previous arrests had resulted in release when he had evaded conviction, mainly through his charming demeanor. The only child of an unstable couple, he was a school problem by age nine. By sixteen he had organized a schoolyard drug and theft ring. At eighteen he enlisted in the Marines but was discharged after going AWOL thirteen times. He next established sexual relationships with a number of waitresses and persuaded several to become prostitutes while acting as their pimp. He flourished in this occupation, winning a reputation as a hustler and seeming well on his way to a stable street career, until he began impulsively seducing young girls from middle-class families and began to run afoul of the police.

Pasternack, 1974

present, and if they want to do something, they usually do it, regardless of the consequences.

4. **Lack of emotional ties and inability to form meaningful relationships with other individuals** identifies the sociopathic individual's behavior as shallow and often callous and self-centered, even toward spouse, children, parents, and other individuals most people feel concern for. Moreover, sociopaths seem incapable of loyalties to other people and often behave as if other people were objects to be manipulated for their personal pleasure.

5. **Inability to adjust to the boredom of everyday life** has the sociopath constantly seeking stimulation. If nothing exciting is happening, the sociopath is likely to create trouble just for the thrill. The individual may be thus motivated to try dangerous drugs, exploitive forms of sexual behavior, or numerous other immoral or asocial acts.

6. **Ability to make a good impression on others** allows sociopathic individuals to be quite charming, appear intelligent, seem sincere, and have what looks superficially like good social skills. These characteristics allow them to "con" people, to manipulate their way out of tight spots, and to convince others (frequently legal authorities or clinicians) of their good intentions.

Types of Antisocial Personality

In general there are two major types of antisocial personalities. The first is the **primary** or **classic sociopath,** who is considered the true sociopath (Hare 1970). The chief characteristic of the primary sociopath is a lack of anxiety or guilt. The second type is the **neurotic sociopath,** who engages in antisocial or aggressive acts and shares many of the characteristics of primary sociopathy but does feel guilt or remorse, or exhibits emotional disturbances that indicate frustration and inner conflict. Other terms that have been used to designate this type of individual are *acting-out neurotic, neurotic delinquent,* and *neurotic character disorder.*

In addition to these two generally recognized types of sociopathic disorder, a third, described by many authors and included as a separate diagnostic category in the earlier version of the DSM, is the **dissocial reaction** or, as it is called in children, **subcultural delinquency.** Individuals of this type are people who have grown up in a subculture whose values and norms are at variance with society's standards. Consequently, these individuals violate society's standards and laws but are considered normal within their own subculture. Unlike the primary or neurotic sociopath, they have strong loyalties and emotional ties within their own group. DSM II calls this sort of behavior the *group delinquent reaction.*

Neurotic sociopaths feel guilt, primary sociopaths do not

Dissocial sociopaths are normal within their own subculture

box 10–2
Primary or Classic
Sociopathy in a
30-Year-Old Male

Donald S., thirty years old, has just completed a three-year prison term for fraud, bigamy, false pretenses, and escaping lawful custody. The circumstances leading up to these offenses are interesting and consistent with his past behavior. With less than a month left to serve on an earlier eighteen-month term for fraud, he faked illness and escaped from the prison hospital. During the ten months of freedom that followed, he engaged in a variety of illegal enterprises; the activity that resulted in his recapture was typical of his method of operation. By passing himself off as the "field executive" of an international philanthropic foundation, he was able to enlist the aid of several religious organizations in a fund-raising campaign. The campaign moved slowly at first, and in an attempt to speed things up, he arranged an interview with the local TV station. His performance during the interview was so impressive that funds started to pour in. However, unfortunately for Donald, the interview was also carried on a national news network. He was recognized and quickly arrested. During the ensuing trial, it became evident that he experienced no sense of wrongdoing for his activities. He maintained, for example, that his passionate plea for funds "primed the pump"—that is, induced people to give to other charities as well as to the one he professed to represent. At the same time, he stated that most donations to charity are made by those who feel guilty about something and who therefore deserve to be bilked. This ability to rationalize his behavior and his lack of self-criticism were also evident in his attempts to solicit aid from the very people he had misled. Perhaps it is a tribute to his persuasiveness that a number of individuals actually did come to his support. During his three-year prison term, Donald spent much time searching for legal loopholes and writing to outside authorities, including local lawyers, the Prime Minister of Canada, and a Canadian representative to the United Nations. In each case he verbally attacked them for representing the authority and injustice responsible for his predicament. At the same time he requested them to intercede on his behalf

and in the name of the justice they professed to represent.

While in prison he was used as a subject in some of the author's research. On his release he applied for admission to a university and, by way of reference, told the registrar that he had been one of the author's research colleagues! Several months later the author received a letter from him requesting a letter of recommendation on behalf of Donald's application for a job.

Donald was the youngest of three boys born to middle-class parents. Both of his brothers led normal, productive lives. His father spent a great deal of time with his business; when he was home, he tended to be moody and to drink heavily when things were not going right. Donald's mother was a gentle, timid woman who tried to please her husband and to maintain a semblance of family harmony. When she discovered her children engaged in some mischief, she would threaten to tell their father. However, she seldom carried out these threats because she did not want to disturb her husband and because his reactions were likely to be dependent on his mood at the time; on some occasions he would fly into a rage and beat the children and on others he would administer a verbal reprimand, sometimes mild and sometimes severe.

By all accounts Donald was considered a willful and difficult child. When his desire for candy or toys was frustrated, he would begin with a show of affection, and if this failed, he would throw a temper tantrum; the latter was seldom necessary because his angelic appearance and artful ways usually got him what he wanted. Similar tactics were used to avoid punishment for his numerous misdeeds. At first he would attempt to cover up with an elaborate facade of lies, often shifting the blame to his brothers. If this did not work, he would give a convincing display of remorse and contrition. When punishment was unavoidable, he would become sullenly defiant, regarding it as an unjustifiable tax on his pleasures.

Although he was obviously very intelligent, his school years were academically undistinguished. He was restless, easily bored, and frequently truant. His behavior in the presence of the teacher or some other authority was usually quite good, but when he was on his own he generally got himself or others into trouble. Although he was often suspected of being the culprit, he was adept at talking his way out of difficulty.

Donald's misbehavior as a child took many forms, including lying, cheating, petty theft, and the bullying of smaller children. As he grew older, he became more and more interested in sex, gambling, and alcohol. When he was fourteen he made crude sexual advances toward a younger girl, and when she threatened to tell her parents, he locked her in a shed. It was about sixteen hours before she was found. Donald at first denied knowledge of the incident, later stating that she had seduced him and that the door must have locked itself. He expressed no concern for the anguish experienced by the girl and her parents, nor did he give any indication that he felt morally culpable for what he had done. His parents were able to prevent charges being brought against him. Nevertheless, incidents of this sort were becoming more frequent and, in an attempt to prevent further embarrassment to the family, he was sent away to a private boarding school. His academic work there was of uneven quality, being dependent on his momentary interests. Nevertheless, he did well at individual competitive sports and public debating. He was a source of excitement for many of the other boys, and was able to think up interesting and unusual things to do. Rules and regulations were considered a meaningless hindrance to his self-expression, but he violated them so skillfully that it was often difficult to prove that he had actually done so. The teachers described him as an ''operator'' whose behavior was determined entirely by the possibility of attaining what he wanted—in most cases something that was concrete, immediate, and personally relevant.

When he was seventeen, Donald left the boarding school, forged his father's name to a large check, and spent about a year traveling around the world. He apparently lived well, using a combination of charm, physical attractiveness, and false pretences to finance his way. During subsequent years he held a succession of jobs, never staying at any one for more than a few months. Throughout this period he was charged with a variety of crimes, including theft, drunkenness in a public place, assault, and many traffic violations. In most cases he was either fined or given a light sentence.

His sexual experiences were frequent, casual, and callous. When he was twenty-two he married a forty-one-year-old woman whom he had met in a bar. Several other marriages followed, all bigamous. In each case the pattern was the same: he would marry someone on impulse, let her support him for several months, and then leave. One marriage was particularly interesting. After being charged with fraud, Donald was sent to a psychiatric institution for a period of observation. While there he came to the attention of a female member of the professional staff. His charm, physical attractiveness, and convincing promises to reform led her to intervene on his behalf. He was given a suspended sentence, and they were married a week later. At first things went reasonably well, but when she refused to pay some of his gambling debts, he forged her name to a check and left. He was soon caught and given an eighteen-month prison term. As mentioned earlier, he escaped with less than a month left to serve.

It is interesting to note that Donald sees nothing particularly wrong with his behavior, nor does he express remorse or guilt for using others and causing them grief. Although his behavior is self-defeating in the long run, he considers it to be practical and possessed of good sense. Periodic punishments do nothing to decrease his egotism and confidence in his own abilities, nor do they offset the often considerable short-term gains of which he is capable. However, these short-term gains are invariably obtained at the expense of someone else. In this respect his behavior is entirely egocentric, and his needs are satisfied without any concern for the feelings and welfare of others.

Hare, 1970

These Ku Klux Klan members have strong loyalties to each other characteristic of the dyssocial reaction.

Some examples of this type of antisocial personality would be members of the Mafia, the Ku Klux Klan, or revoluntionary or terrorist groups.

Juvenile Delinquency

Jenkins and his associates (1964, 1966) have repeatedly isolated several types of personality characteristics that occur in delinquent children. The three most common clusters have been labeled as the **unsocialized-aggressive syndrome** (assaultive tendencies, proclivity for starting fights, cruelty, defiance of authority, inadequate guilt feelings, and a penchant for malicious mischief); the **overanxious syndrome** (seclusiveness, shyness, apathy, tendency to worry, sensitivity, submissiveness, and neurotic tendencies); and the **socialized delinquency syndrome** (association with bad companions, participation in gang activities such as cooperative stealing, and habitual truancy from school and home). Numerous other studies have consistently identified the same three main subgroups of delinquency, although they might use somewhat different labels (Hare 1970). These descriptions are very similar to the types of sociopathic behavior. Consequently, there is little reason to believe that any fundamental difference exists between juvenile delin-

The three types of delinquency resemble the three types of sociopathy

quency and antisocial reactions except in terms of age. The causes of these behavior patterns are likely to be similar in both cases. DSM III labels these disorders of children and adolescents as conduct disorders and notes that, if they continue into adulthood, they should be classified as antisocial personality disorders.

Research and Theory

As contrasted with other personality disorders, sociopathy and juvenile delinquency have been the subject of hundreds of studies. Consequently, in this section we shall try to give an overview and a general indication of the principal findings. These will be organized into physiological aspects, learning characteristics, and results of socialization.

Constitutional and Genetic Models

In the late nineteenth century, Cesare Lombrosi, an Italian criminologist, stated that criminality was genetically transmitted and that criminals could be recognized by certain physical features, such as a low forehead and protruding ears. (As we have noted, not all antisocial personalities are criminals and vice versa, but a sizable portion of them do engage in criminal activities.) However, evidence for the genetic transmission of criminal behavior or sociopathic personality characteristics is scant.

neuroses, personality disorders, and special symptoms

Habitual truancy from school and home is behavior associated with the socialized delinquency syndrome.

A sizeable portion of antisocial personalities engage in criminal activities.

In evaluating studies of this issue, Rosenthal (1970) concluded that environmental factors in antisocial behavior and crime were of overriding importance. Rosenthal also found that the concordance rate was consistently high for identical twins, often running over 90 percent, but that the concordance rate for nonidentical twins was also high and not significantly different from that for identical twins. This finding further emphasizes the importance of environmental factors in the acquisition of criminal and antisocial behavior.

Evidence also shows that antisocial behavior occurs in a much higher proportion of males than females. This finding parallels what we know about crime in general: criminal activity is much more common among males than among females, although more women have become criminals in recent years. Perhaps this frequency has lent support to the rather tenuous hypothesis linking genetic or chromosomal makeup and criminal activity. As we have said previously, the human being has forty-six chromosomes, two of which—the X and the Y chromosomes—determine the sex of the individual. Normally, a female has two X chromosomes and a male has one X and one Y chromosome. Occasionally, however, a male is born with an extra Y chromosome (XYY). This genotype results in a so-called "super male," supposedly possessing unusual height, borderline intelligence, and an abnormal susceptibility to aggressive outbursts. The incidence of this genotype is about 1 in every 1,500 people in a normal population, but has been found to be higher among inmates of penal institutions (Borgaonkar and Shah 1975; Hook 1973). Consequently, some researchers have therefore speculated that a relationship exists between **XYY males** and violent crime. The belief is that the XYY type confers a double dose of male aggressiveness and thus predisposes its bearer toward brutal crimes. However, this hypothesis has not been generally supported, since studies that assess the aggressiveness of XYY males have not consistently found them to be more aggressive than other groups (Borgaonkar and Shah 1975). The incidence of the XYY genotype among all criminals is very low, on the order of 1 percent or less, and many XYY males appear normal in every respect and do not engage in violent crime.

Neurological Models

The electroencephalogram (EEG) is another method of assessing biological malfunction in antisocial personality disorders and is a recording of the phasic or transit fluctuations of the brain's electrical activity. In the average awake subject, the dominant rhythm, taken from the back of the head, has a frequency of 8–13 hertz (H.) (cycles per second) and an amplitude of about 40–50 microvolts. This pattern is called the *alpha* rhythm. Attentiveness caused by novel stimulation, anxiety, or other forms of mental activity generally results in *desynchronization* or blocking of the alpha rhythm, which is replaced by a high-frequency (14–25 H.), low-voltage rhythm known as *beta* rhythm. In normal subjects, several very low frequencies are also found, which in excessive amounts are considered abnormal. These slow waves are the *theta* waves (4–7 H.) and the *delta* waves (less than 4 H.). During sleep the alpha rhythm is gradually replaced by irregular low-voltage activity and by an increase in theta and delta activity, as well as by 12–14 H. waves known as sleep spindles. In very deep sleep the EEG consists of generalized high-voltage delta activity with a frequency as low as 1 H. See Figure 10.1.

Brain-wave activity in infants consists primarily of slow and irregular low-voltage waves. As the child matures, the slow waves are gradually replaced by the faster alpha waves, except in about 10 to 15 percent of the normal population, in whom excessive amounts of slow waves (theta activity) persist into childhood. The persistence of such activity is described as immature.

The evaluation of the EEG is often used in many areas of psychology and medicine to evaluate various disorders, particularly in neurological examinations to determine the possibility of central nervous system damage. Evidence shows that between 31 and 58 percent of all antisocial personalities show some form of EEG abnormality (Ellington 1954). Other studies have consistently shown the same high incidence of EEG abnormalities in antisocial personalities (Hare 1970). These abnormalities are of two major types. The first type is the occasional occurrence of positive spikes,

neuroses, personality disorders, and special symptoms

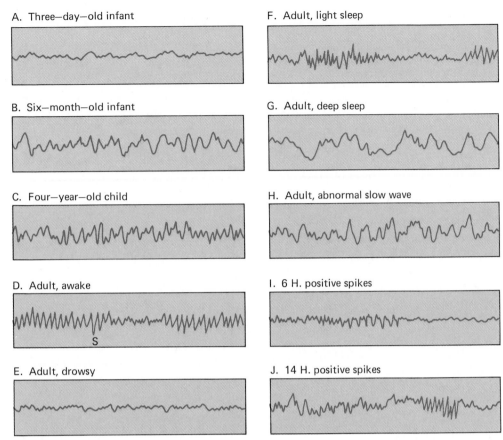

A. Three—day—old infant

B. Six—month—old infant

C. Four—year—old child

D. Adult, awake
S

E. Adult, drowsy

F. Adult, light sleep

G. Adult, deep sleep

H. Adult, abnormal slow wave

I. 6 H. positive spikes

J. 14 H. positive spikes

Figure 10–1 Some EEG waveforms. The record in *D* shows alpha waves being blocked at point S and temporarily replaced by beta waves.

bursts of 6–8 H. and/or 14–16 H. activity, which occurs primarily in the temporal area of the brain. The second type of EEG abnormality is abnormally slow wave activity in the temporal lobes (Hare 1970). Since this kind of activity is present in young children, Hare hypothesizes that the asocial activity of antisocial personalities and delinquents may be due to cortical immaturity.

More consistent relationships have been found between the autonomic nervous system, avoidance learning, and antisocial behavior. As Table 10.1 shows, a definite relationship exists between arousal and behavior. Levels of arousal vary across different states of the individual, from deep sleep to strong, excited states. These levels of arousal, as shown in Figure 10.2, are directly related to behavioral efficiency and to affective experiences. Because the level of arousal has motivational properties, an individual will probably seek to increase arousal if the arousal level is too low. Likewise, an individual will attempt to decrease

the arousal level if it is too high. The general goal seems to be finding and maintaining some optimal level of arousal. We can thus assume that changes in arousal toward the more optimal level ought to be rewarding, while changes away from the optimal level should be punishing.

A group of studies has yielded rather good evidence that the sociopathic individual demonstrates a low level of autonomic arousal in terms of a number of indices (Hare 1970). These findings—which are consistent with the generally held clinical belief concerning the antisocial personality's lack of anxiety, guilt, and emotional tension—have two implications. The major implication is that antisocial personalities perform poorly on tests that are tedious, seek excitement, and cannot tolerate routine boredom. That antisocial personalities show **stimulus hunger** and tend to engage in activity often of an immoral or illegal nature may be a function of their need to increase the stimulation in their environment and thereby increase their optimal level of arousal.

Antisocial personalities have a low level of ANS arousal

Illegal or immoral activities may be an effort to satisfy a stimulus hunger

Table 10-1 Levels of Arousal and Their EEG, Psychological, and Behavioral Correlates

Level of arousal	Behavioral continuum	EEG	State of awareness	Behavioral efficiency
High	Strong, excited emotion (fear, rage, anxiety)	Desynchronized: low to moderate amplitude; fast, mixed frequencies	Restricted awareness: divided attention; diffused, hazy; "confusion"	Poor (lack of control, freezing-up, disorganized)
	Alert attentiveness	Partially synchronized: mainly fast, low amplitude waves	Selective attention, but may vary or shift, "concentration" anticipation, "set"	Good (efficient, selective, quick, reactions)
	Relaxed wakefulness	Synchronized: optimal alpha rhythm	Attention wanders—not forced; favors free association	Good (routine reactions and creative thought)
	Drowsiness	Reduced alpha and occasional low amplitude slow waves	Borderline, partial awareness; imagery and reverie; "dreamlike states"	Poor (uncoordinated, sporadic, lacking sequential timing)
	Light sleep	Spindle bursts and slow waves (larger), loss of alphas	Markedly reduced consciousness (loss of consciousness); dream state	Absent
Low	Deep sleep	Large and very slow waves	Complete loss of awareness (no memory for stimulation or for dreams)	Absent

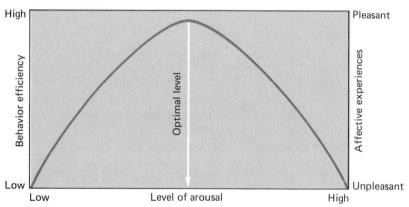

Figure 10-2 Hypothetical curve relating level of arousal to behavioral efficiency and affective experiences.

Learning Models

The other major implication of these data is in terms of learning, particularly avoidance conditioning in which the level of anxiety or arousal determines the rate of learning. A number of studies have shown that antisocial personalities appear to be deficient in avoidance conditioning but not particularly different from normals in terms of learning associated with positive

Sociopaths showed less avoidance learning than normals

reinforcement. A study conducted by Schmauk (1970) is relevant here. Schmauk used three different punishing stimuli in an avoidance learning task: physical punishment (electric shock), material punishment (losing a quarter from an initial pile of forty), and social punishment (experimenter calling the subject "wrong"). As Figure 10.3 shows, both neurotic and primary sociopaths showed less avoidance learning for electric shock than normal controls. Mild social punishment was no more effective

neuroses, personality disorders, and special symptoms

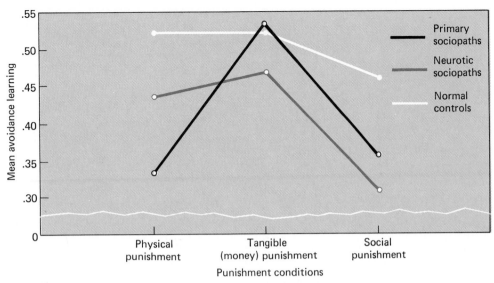

Figure 10-3 Mean avoidance learning scores plotted for three groups across three punishment conditions.

than electric shock. On the other hand, when money was at stake, sociopaths did not differ significantly from normals.

The evidence collected in these studies has begun to yield some indication of what may occur in the development of antisocial patterns of behavior. As noted earlier and as described by Bandura (1977), acquisition of social behavior is dependent on being reinforced directly, or observing a model's positive reinforcement for appropriate behavior, and directly learning to avoid transgressions because of anticipatory fear. A rather consistent finding about antisocial personalities is that they often have parents (models) who themselves are antisocial or who exhibit other abnormal kinds of behavior. In a study of antisocial behavior in children, Robins (1966) found, for example, that only 36 percent had both parents at home, while 32 percent lived in foster homes. In 60 percent of the cases, one or both parents had died, the parents were divorced, or the mother was unmarried. Abnormal behavior in the fathers ranged from excessive drinking (32 percent) to arrest and illegal occupations (11 percent). Abnormal behavior in the mothers ranged from nonsupport and neglect of the home (20 percent) to illicit sexual behavior (19 percent). This study essentially duplicates other studies and shows that models observed by sociopathic individuals are often seriously lacking in appropriate social behavior. Furthermore, it is less likely that

these parents consistently reinforced their children for appropriate social behavior.

As we mentioned in Chapter 4, the acquisition of social controls is directly related to avoidance conditioning. The child learns quite early in life that certain behavior is followed by punishment and consequently begins to demonstrate anticipatory anxiety or fear when exposed to temptation. If transgression does occur, the fear of punishment, or guilt, or both, results. This process of socialization gives rise to entities such as conscience, superego, and internalized social control. The research evidence, however, consistently indicates a deficit of fear conditioning in antisocial personalities. It would be predictable, then, that these individuals would show a real deficit in those aspects of behavior that we call conscience.

Another way of looking at this phenomenon is that, since many types of social constraints are aimed at activities that are psychologically and often physically pleasant, we may expect many social transgressions to have both positive and negative aspects. When confronted with the temptation to transgress, the individual faces an *approach-avoidance* conflict. The closer the individual gets to the pleasant activity (the approach gradient), either in time or distance, the more rewarding the experience becomes, and the greater the anticipatory

Sociopaths may lack the anticipatory fear needed for acquiring social behavior

Antisocial role models may also be a factor

personality disorders: the disorders of social behavior

263

This child is learning social control through the mother's scolding behavior. The antisocial personality often fails to respond to such conditioning.

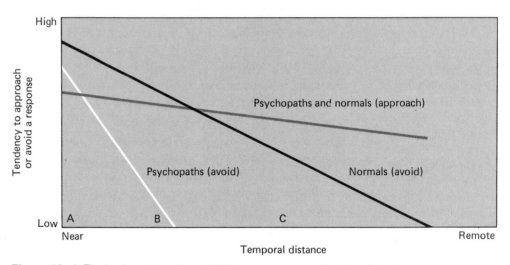

Figure 10–4 The tendency to make or inhibit a response as a function of the temporal remoteness of anticipated reward and punishment.

fear (the avoidance gradient) becomes. Empirical evidence shows that the avoidance gradient is much steeper than the approach gradient, as Figure 10–4 illustrates. However, antisocial personalities have a much lower avoidance gradient than normals because they show less anticipatory fear (Hare 1970). Consequently, their tendency to inhibit socially disapproved behavior is weaker than that of normals.

It is rather interesting that the tendency to approach is about the same for both nor-

mals and antisocial personalities. This similarity results from the fact that antisocial personalities exhibit little or no deficit in learning under conditions of positive reinforcement and are, therefore, in most cases well aware of what is appropriate behavior. Their difficulty comes in inhibiting inappropriate behavior or in avoiding social transgression, most probably because of their deficiency in avoidance and fear conditioning.

neuroses, personality disorders, and special symptoms

Assessment and Modification

In the detection of antisocial personalities, the most frequently used self-report index is the MMPI. On the MMPI, antisocial personalities exhibit a 4–9 pattern with elevations on the P_d scale, which contains such items as, "I am sure I get a raw deal from life" or "I use alcohol excessively." They also exhibit elevations on the M_a scale, which contains such items as, "When I get bored, I like to stir up some excitement" or "Something exciting will pull me out of it when I am feeling low." Behavioral assessment techniques for this disorder have not been specifically developed, but a history of sociopathic behavior can be easily detected. Although psychophysiological assessment techniques have not at present been developed as assessment devices, they may be the chief instruments in the future for diagnosing sociopaths.

The results of most empirical studies of the modifications of antisocial behavior, particularly in adults, are discouraging (McCord and McCord 1964). Various forms of individual and group therapies as well as the biological therapies have been almost equally ineffective. As Hare (1970) has observed, this situation is not particularly surprising because, as Patterson (1966) pointed out, various modification techniques share several common premises:

1. Most therapies are based on the assumption that abnormal behavior is personally distressing and painful and that the individual is therefore motivated to alter the behavior. Sociopaths, however, rarely see anything wrong with their behavior and are therefore unlikely to be motivated to change it. Their behavior distresses other people, not themselves.
2. It is usually recognized that an individual's present behavior is influenced by expectations about its future consequences. A number of studies indicate, however, that sociopaths are concerned only with the present, not with what may happen in the future.

3. It is also recognized that psychotherapy involves a complex interpersonal relationship between therapist and patient and that this relationship is affective as well as cognitive and intellectual. As previously noted, however, sociopathic personalities rarely form deep personal relationships and are therefore unlikely to become any more deeply or personally involved in the therapeutic process than they are in other relationships.
4. Finally, both patients and therapists normally expect therapy to produce beneficial results. Since much skepticism exists about the possibility of modifying sociopathic behavior, this negative attitude quite possibly decreases the chances that therapy will be effective.

Most forms of therapy have been ineffective in treating sociopathy

Low motivation

Some spontaneous improvement does seem to occur in sociopathic behavior, perhaps in as much as 57 percent of those who receive no treatment (Robins 1966). More specifically, Robins has shown that these individuals show a reduction in both the range and the severity of antisocial behavior as they age, with improvement most often occurring between the ages of thirty and forty. They seem to experience less trouble with the police, and their relationships with other people improve. Nevertheless, these individuals represent only a part of the population. Consequently, effective treatment methods are still badly needed.

Disinterest in the future

Inability to form a deep relationship

Milieu Therapy

Most of the treatment studies done with sociopathic individuals have been conducted in institutional settings using some sort of therapeutic community or **milieu therapy.** In general, the results of these studies have been fairly consistent. For example, in a study of sociopathic males, Craft, Stephenson, and Granger (1964) compared one treatment program that was essentially self-governing and included intensive group therapy with tolerant staff members to another program that was more authoritarian and included a firm but sympathetic form of discipline and only superficial individual therapy. A follow-up one year after release found that those treated

Low expectations

under the more authoritarian program had been convicted of significantly fewer offenses than those in the self-governing regimen. The results of this study indicate that work training in a friendly but disciplined setting is probably more effective in treating sociopathy than work training combined with psychotherapy in a permissive setting. Hare (1970) has reviewed a number of studies that essentially came to the same conclusion.

Achievement Place

Attempts to resocialize juvenile delinquents have yielded more encouraging results. One such program is *Achievement Place,* a group home for boys twelve to fourteen years old who have committed minor offenses but seem to be on the road to more serious crime (Fixsen, Phillips, and Wolf 1973). Six to eight delinquent or predelinquent youths lived together in a family-style arrangement supervised by a couple known as the teaching parents. The intervention program has four main features: a token economy, a self-government system, a comprehensive behavioral skills training curriculum, and the development of a mutually reinforcing relationship with the teaching parents. In the token economy the youths exchange points for privileges, but this arrangement is usually faded out after a few weeks, at which time the youngsters go on a merit system in which all privileges are free. Modeling, role playing, and reinforcement are used to teach both social skills, such as responding appropriately to criticism, and academic skills, such as completing homework assignments.

This approach to treating sociopathic or delinquent youths seems fairly effective. Wolf, Phillips, and Fixsen (1974) compared eight subjects from Achievement Place with eighteen similar subjects and found that during the two years following the initial assignment, 56 percent of the control group were institutionalized as compared with only 12 percent of the Achievement Place group. Furthermore, the cost per youth per day at Achievement Place averaged fifteen dollars, while the cost at a state institution averaged forty-five dollars. Thus, the Achievement Place

approach seems quite promising and is now being implemented in a number of places throughout the United States.

Ethical Issues

Because sociopaths do not appear to be motivated toward or amenable to the usual forms of treatment and because the data suggest that they respond better to more discipline-oriented forms of treatment, behavior modification would seem to be the most desirable method of rehabilitating these individuals. Unfortunately, the answer is not that simple. The crucial legal and ethical issue in the use of any rehabilitation procedure with criminals is voluntary consent. If juvenile delinquents or individuals institutionalized for crime do not want rehabilitation services, does society have the right to force such services upon them?

Unfortunately, the ethical issues have become even more confused by critics who lump brain surgery, drug treatment, and electroconvulsive shock treatment together under the general heading of behavior modification. Their criticisms and the increased activism among prisoners themselves (who often have good reason for their objections) have threatened rehabilitation programs in prisons and institutions for criminals and delinquents alike.

Perhaps one solution to this problem is to build in safeguards for the prisoners' rights by having a committee pass on both the goals and the methods of the proposed treatment programs and monitor the programs when they are put into effect (Brown, Wienckowski, and Stolz 1975). This committee would include prisoner-representatives and at least one lawyer knowledgeable in civil liberties. Each potential participant in a program should be offered a choice among several kinds of programs and the right to decline. Such an approach would represent a reasonable compromise between using undue coercion to force inmates into rehabilitation programs and abandoning rehabilitation efforts altogether. The clash between the rights of individuals and the rights of society remains a lively—and confusing—controversy.

neuroses, personality disorders, and special symptoms

Hysterical Personality

The **hysterical** or **histrionic personality** is a disorder characterized by excitability, emotional instability, overreactivity, and self-dramatization. This self-dramatization is usually attention seeking and sometimes seductive, whether or not the individual is aware of its purpose. Hysterical or histrionic individuals are also presumed to be immature, self-centered, often vain, and usually dependent on others. All of us know people who tend to make a performance out of every situation, who use exaggerated gestures and make histrionic remarks, or who use other flamboyant means of gaining attention.

Alarcon (1973) surveyed a number of studies of this disorder and concluded that seven main features characterize this pattern of behavior:

1. **Histrionic response patterns** include dramatic, theatrical appearances, demonstrativeness, and an air of superiority for the purpose of gaining attention, sympathy, or even admiration.
2. **Emotional lability** is evident in hysterical personalities, who are given to outbursts of laughter or crying—often in an uncontrolled manner—which may be precipitated by a seemingly insufficient cause.
3. **Dependency** on others is often unduly present and the individual gives at least the pretense of being weak and of being in need of someone to care for him or her.
4. **Excitability** in these individuals reflects a *chameleon reaction* or a proneness to be strongly influenced by changes in the environment. They may be simply impressionable or they may, at the other extreme, have a greater sensory awareness.
5. **Egocentricity** marks histrionic individuals, who seem to have an exaggerated tendency to serve and gratify their own needs, regardless of any other consideration. For this reason, these self-engrossed and self-

centered people have often been called narcissistic and seem to have a compulsive need to be loved and to be the center of attention.

6. **Suggestibility** is high in hysterical personalities, who often appear innocent or naive and tend to take other people's word for anything, so long as doing so serves their purposes. As previously noted, one indication of suggestibility in hysterical personalities is the ease with which they are hypnotized.
7. **Seductiveness** among histrionic personalities constitutes an attempt to manipulate other people. Such individuals may make a constant display of charm, clothing, gestures, or other attempts to impress and amuse others. Occasionally, this seductiveness may become an overtly sexual activity whose aim is not the expression of love or the desire for sexual gratification but rather an attempt to control.

The hysterical personality is often described as being sexually provocative but actually quite frightened and cold in possible or actual sexual encounters. O'Neill and Kempler (1969) tested this hypothesis by comparing females with characteristics of hysteria to normal females under neutral and sexually provocative conditions. In the neutral condition they found that hysterical females were much more sensitive to stimuli with possible sexual connotations, but under sexually provocative conditions, these females avoided or were selectively inattentive to sexual stimuli. This study lends support to the clinical belief that the seductiveness of hysterical personalities is an attempt to control others.

The seductiveness may be merely a device for controlling others

Research and Theory

Like other personality disorders, the hysterical or histrionic personality is differentiated from neurotic conditions by the

box 10–3
Hysterical
Personality in
a 22-Year-Old
Female

Why did I take all those pills? Because of Randy, that's why. He drove me to it, the way he was acting. When we first started seeing each other, he seemed attentive enough, but then he started finding excuses to be away from me—going hunting, fishing, playing cards with his friends while I sat home alone. I knew he liked them better than me even though he said he didn't. And not only that! He started seeing another woman too. Of course, all he wanted was sex. That's all men want anyway. Say "no" once, and they run off after some tramp. Oh, he said I led him on, made him think I'd go to bed with him and then wouldn't. Men are such idiots, all of them. They're just like children they're so gullible. Give them any attention at all, and they immediately think you're seducing them. Why, a woman with any sense can wrap them around her little finger. But they're really animals at heart, just looking for sex, sex, sex. That's all they want.

I told Randy I wasn't well. I never have been strong, but lately my nerves have been a wreck. My stomach, too. I have to be very careful of what I eat. Sometimes, especially in the middle of the night, I just have to have a Coke, the kind from the drugstore with all the ice. At first Randy didn't mind my calling him to go get me one. I told him how my family didn't love me enough to do little things like that for me. If people really love you, they'll do anything for you. But not my family, oh no; they couldn't care less if I lived or died. It turned out that Randy didn't either. He stopped going, told me I was being unreasonable. He stopped coming over when I couldn't sleep too. Of course, my not being able to sleep is my doctor's fault because he won't give me sleeping pills strong enough to do any good. So I just lie there and get lonely and scared. So much can happen to a woman alone at night! Sometimes, I get really panicky all by

myself. It's terrible how women are really so dependent on men. But Randy doesn't care. He says it's all in my head.

He says I sulk and pout too. Well, why should I be nice to him, the way he treats me sometimes. Men think they can be completely thoughtless and still have a woman bow to their every whim. I told him he was going to drive me to something desperate. I told him several times, but he didn't listen. You know what he told me? He told me he thought I needed "help," like I was crazy or something. Then he left me. That was just too much. I was so angry! I'd told him and told him I'd be forced to kill myself. Well, there was only one thing to do: take the pills.

My sister found me and called the ambulance that took me to the hospital. Oh, I called Randy right after I took the pills and told him what I'd done, but he said he didn't believe me. Then he called my sister just to check on me. He came to the hospital, but he wouldn't even come in my room. He talked to my family, told them it was best if he didn't see me any more. They told him I'd been through this "routine," as they call it, with other men! Those creeps!

So, now, here I am "committed" to a mental hospital. That's how much they care. If they only cared, I wouldn't be forced to take pills and things. It's all their fault. And now that so-called psychologist who sees me—he doesn't really care either. He won't help me make them see how mean they've been to me. He says he can teach me to be more assertive in a relationship, to stop acting so self-destructive and self-defeating. Well, he's just a man like all the rest, just an idiot, just a child waiting for me to wrap him around my finger. He'll be no problem, no problem at all. But these nurses! What bitches! They won't even bring my meals to my room when I'm not well. If anybody really cared. . . .

Dramatization based on similar cases reported by Kass, Silvers, and Abroms, 1972

individual's lack of distress over the behavior in question and by the fact that the behavior represents response patterns acquired through maturation and socialization. Eysenck and Claridge (1962) have found that most hysterical personalities are extroverts as measured by the Maudsley Personality Inventory and that the hysterical attitudes or traits are associated with the hysterical personality, but not with conversion reactions. Thus, hysteria seems to fall into two categories, one based on *personality patterns* and one based on *symptomology*, as noted in Chapter 9.

Although the exact incidence of hysterical personality disorders is not known, Tupin (1974) states that it is rather high among females. This frequency of occurrence probably reflects the feminine role expectation in American society, which produces a continuum from normal femininity to pathological exaggerations of these characteristics. While this disorder is assumed to be relatively rare in men, it does occur.

Slavney and McHugh (1974) compared individuals who had hysterical personality disorders with control psychiatric patients also requiring hospitalization and made several rather interesting observations. Approximately 50 percent of those diagnosed as hysterical personalities were admitted after a suicide attempt, which was usually superficial, as compared to 28 percent of the control patients, most of whom were admitted for depression. Furthermore, the majority of those diagnosed as hysterical personalities (72 percent as compared to 37 percent of control patients) came from unhappy homes, had unhappy marriages (75 percent as compared to 20 percent of the control patients), or both. Other researchers have noted a high incidence of alcoholism and sociopathy among male relatives of hysterical personalities and a high incidence of hysteria among their female relatives.

Assessment and Modification

Perhaps because psychoanalysis was based on the treatment of a similar disorder, hysteria in general and the hysterical personality in particular have been favorite candidates for psychodynamic psychotherapy. Even so, no systematic evaluation of the effectiveness of this approach with such cases has been made. One may conjecture that psychodynamic therapy is probably effective with these disorders because the patient-therapist relationship is aimed at attempting to resolve problems of dependency, manipulation of others, and similar interpersonal interactions that manifest themselves in close relationships such as that established in psychotherapy.

Behavior modification of hysterical personality disorders would require a complex approach that focused on modifying the social skills. One example of such a treatment approach was that of Kass, Silvers, and Abroms (1972). They used a behavioral group approach in treating five young women diagnosed as hysterical personalities and admitted to the hospital for suicide attempts. The patients were given the responsibility for specifying each other's hysterical behaviors and providing the rewards and penalties required for behavior change. They were placed on a tight daily schedule of activities, and target behaviors, such as manipulation of others, suicide threats and gestures, histrionic behavior, and similar responses, were singled out. The behavioral techniques used included positive and negative feedback, assertiveness training, negative practice, discrimination, and operant conditioning by rewards and punishments. Role playing and psychodrama were also used both in conjunction with behavioral techniques and as a means of rehearsing real-life encounters. The researchers also used videotaping as a means of self-observation and feedback, which seemed to be particularly effective in spotting covert hostility, histrionics, and shallow affect.

During the one-month treatment program, all five patients underwent a crisis in which suicidal thoughts increased. This period occurred most frequently after about two weeks, probably when the individuals realized that their former behavior patterns of social interaction were not working. A similar burst of responding is often encountered in individuals placed on an extinction schedule. The outcome of this treatment program indicated that four of the five women showed systematic improvement and enhanced social behavioral repertoires at discharge. Their improvement continued during an eighteen-month follow-up.

Hysterical personality shows an exaggeration of feminine role characteristics

Psychodynamic therapist-patient relationship geared to treating hysterical personality symptoms

Target behaviors singled out

Obsessive-Compulsive Personality

The **obsessive-compulsive personality,** or the **anankastic personality** as it is sometimes called, is characterized by excessive concern with detail, organization, punctuality, and routine. As DSM II and DSM III state, individuals of this type are overly concerned with conformity and adherence to standards of conscience. Consequently, they may be rigid, excessively inhibited, overly conscientious, overly dutiful, and unable to relax easily. They can be exasperating in their attentiveness to details and their demand for unusually high moral standards for themselves and others. They are almost at the other end of the continuum from the sociopathic personality and take their responsibilities and social obligations very seriously.

Determining the frequency and the demographical characteristics of this disorder is difficult because of a failure in most clinical and research studies to differentiate between obsessional and compulsive neuroses and the obsessive-compulsive personality. However, according to Black (1974), we can assume (1) that there is little difference in the proportion of men and women exhibiting the disorder; (2) that compulsive personalities are more frequently found in the upper and middle classes; (3) that they tend to be quite intelligent, on the average; and (4) that they show a lower marriage rate than the general population. Moreover, the adjective obsessive may in itself be misleading, since no evidence indicates that the cognitive activities of these individuals have the characteristics of obsessional thinking. For this reason, DSM III labels individuals with these characteristics as *compulsive personalities,* omitting the term obsessive. The response pattern that characterizes the compulsive personality is identified primarily by social behavior, since it is concerned mainly with responsibility, conformity, and obedience to society's regulations. However, it does bear some relationship to obsessive behavior in that if one interferes with the compulsive personality's routine, anxiety or other negative emotions are likely to result.

Research and Theory

Research indicates that the clinical description of the characteristics of the obsessive-compulsive personality is fairly accurate. For example, Asch (1958) found that compulsive personalities tend to demonstrate negative response sets on personality inventories, a pattern that may be related to the frequent negativism and critical attitudes of these individuals. In comparing clinical cases of compulsive personality with matched normals in a psychiatric control group, Reed (1969a, 1969b) found that compulsive personalities exhibit reduced conceptional flexibility and tend to overdefine or overspecify both verbal and nonverbal concepts. In general, available research indicates that this classification represents a meaningful and consistent personality disorder.

An important question that has received much attention in the research literature is whether obsessional and compulsive neuroses are the same disorder as the obsessive-compulsive personality. In answering this question, Foulds (1965) distinguished between symptoms and signs of maladjustment on the one hand and personality traits and attitudes on the other. This distinction is fairly similar to that between personality disorders and other disorders made earlier in this chapter. The three criteria Foulds used for making distinctions are:

1. Traits and attitudes are universal; symptoms and signs are not.
2. Traits and attitudes are relatively *ego-syntonic* (congruent, or consistent, with one's self-image); symptoms and signs are distressful to the individual.
3. Traits and attitudes, particularly traits, are relatively enduring.

A related question is whether, when placed under stress, the individual with a compulsive personality will develop obses-

Rigid; overly conscientious, inhibited, dutiful; unable to relax easily

The "obsessive" label may be misleading

Reduced conceptional flexibility

sive or compulsive symptoms as opposed to other types of psychological disorders. Again, the answer seems fairly clear (Black 1974). The neurotic symptoms of compulsive personalities, when and if they develop, may be anxiety reactions, depersonalization neuroses, anorexia nervosa, migraines, or duodenal ulceration. Once more, there is no evidence of a relationship between personality types and neurotic symptoms.

A similar question is whether the compulsive personality should be considered a psychological disorder, since its distinguishing features appear to be acceptable to the individual exhibiting them. If we ignore the opinion of the afflicted individual, evidence suggests that the compulsive personality is emotionally unstable compared to normal individuals (Orne 1965). Davies and Demonchoux (1973) studied young men with obsessive personalities and compared them in terms of their moods with other young men with hysterical personalities for a year at an Antarctic base, an obviously stressful situation because of the isolation. They found obsessive-compulsive personalities did show more unpleasant moods and more direct responses to emotional stimuli than the hysterical personalities.

In terms of theoretical formulation, the obsessive-compulsive personality has received relatively little attention. Psychodynamic theorists focus on what the British call the "battle of the chamber pot." That is, they seldom differentiate between obsessive-compulsive symptoms and obsessive-compulsive traits. When they do distinguish between the two, they note that the pathological character traits are ego-syntonic, while the symptoms are "ego-alien" (apart from the self). In other words, individuals with obsessive-compulsive symptoms are likely to seek help, while those with compulsive personality traits are not. Behavioral formulations of the disorder offer little specific theory. However, were a behavioral theory to be formulated, it would probably center around the acquisition of patterns of compulsive behavior as a function of the socialization process and society's reinforcement of compulsive traits. In obsessive-compulsive personali-

ties, the socializing process has worked all too well, the result being that these individuals are oversocialized.

Assessment and Modification

A number of personality inventories and rating devices have been developed for the subjective assessment of obsessive-compulsive personality disorders. Sandler and Hazari (1960) developed an instrument in which Type A items represent a set of compulsive personality characteristics and Type B items represent obsessive-compulsive symptoms. A similar instrument is the Leyton Obsessional Inventory (Cooper 1970), which consists of forty-six symptom and twenty-three trait items. These scales seem to be related to the dimension of extraversion-introversion as tapped by a number of personality inventories and thus seem to confirm Eysenck's hypothesis that hysteria and sociopathy are disorders characteristic of extraverted individuals, while obsessive-compulsive symptoms and the obsessive-compulsive personality are characteristic of introverted individuals. In terms of behavioral assessment, standardized procedures have not been developed, although doing so would obviously be easy. The simple observation of an individual's time schedule and how well it was kept, the office or home arrangement, and other indications of concern with detail or form could probably be easily developed.

At present, there is little evidence to suggest what might be an acceptable method of modifying the obsessive-compulsive personality. Whether treatment is required or not probably depends on the degree of the disability and the extent of the character rigidity as well as the individual's desire for treatment. Obsessive-compulsive personalities rarely seek treatment, as Weintraub (1974) states, because, even though their lives are often drab and devoid of pleasure, they are generally successful in their careers and may experience little discomfort. Probably the most feasible goal for most treatment procedures for these disorders would be to increase spontaneity and flexibility of action.

No evidence of a relationship between personality types and neurotic symptoms

Obsessive-compulsive personalities are oversocialized

Most feasible therapy goal: more spontaneity and flexibility

The twenty-five-year-old patient sought treatment after physically assaulting his girl friend. This was the first time he had ever struck a woman, and his lack of control frightened him. According to the patient, he had led an extremely orderly adult life. He prided himself on his self-control and his control of others. He did not entertain in his apartment because he feared disarranging the very precisely arranged furniture, nor did he allow anyone to touch the carefully arranged contents of his glove compartment. His present girl friend, a psychiatric nurse, had become disgusted

with his meticulous and controlling behavior and had accused him of being unable to change if he wanted to. This challenge angered the patient so that he tried to become more flexible, but found that doing so caused great stress. He became preoccupied with the fear that his anus was dirty after defecation and washed it repeatedly. He also became extremely worried that the needle on his stereo was pressing too hard on his records and damaging them. In addition to this stress, he was still confronted with the "wild analysis" of his girl friend. Finally, he lost control and hit her.

Weintraub, 1974

Schizoid Personality

Schizoid personality: shyness, oversensitivity, avoidance of close or competitive relationships, eccentricity

According to DSM II, the behavior pattern known as the **schizoid personality** is characterized by shyness, oversensitivity, seclusiveness, avoidance of close or competitive relationships, and eccentricity. Autistic thinking without loss of capacity to recognize reality may also be present in the form of excessive daydreaming and the inability to express hostile and ordinary aggressive feelings.

DSM III has subdivided the schizoid personality into two categories of personality disorders. If the individual has a family history of schizophrenia and peculiarities of cognitive processes, then the label used is **schizotypal personality disorder.** If these characteristics are not present, then the individual is labeled as exhibiting an **introverted personality disorder.**

Schizoid personality manifests early in childhood

To confuse the matter further, DSM III described a third type of personality disorder, the **avoidant personality disorder,** which is characterized by social isolation and is quite similar to the schizoid personality. The avoidant personality apparently differs from the introverted personality disorder by exhibiting hypersensitivity to criticism and from the schizotypical personality disorders by not exhibiting a family history of schizophrenia or oddities of thinking, perception, communication, or behavior.

Only time and research will determine whether these distinctions of types of schizoid or "socially withdrawn" personality disorders are valid.

As Jenkins (1950) noted, most individuals are attuned to the feelings and motives of other people by being sensitive to the verbal and nonverbal cues of others in social situations. The schizoid personality, however, apparently misses or is not sensitive to the nonverbal cues of others. Schizoid personalities are often described as being in another world. Frequently, they seem to be unaware of what someone is trying to tell them or even of the other person's existence. Consequently, this behavior pattern may be identified in terms of both deficiencies in social interaction and autistic behavior, a cognitive disorder.

The schizoid personality pattern apparently is manifested quite early in childhood. As Jenkins (1950) noted, the schizoid youngster is typically an underachiever, characterized by oversensitivity, an unstable alternation of inhibited behavior and impulsiveness, an absence of interest, and a poverty of techniques for obtaining satisfaction in the real world. In terms of intellectual performance, such youngsters may be intellectually superior but scholastically retarded. For example, Jenkins and Glickman (1947) found that the performance IQs of schizoid children were ten or more points below their verbal IQs, an indication that the practical components of their intelligence are relatively low.

neuroses, personality disorders, and special symptoms

The schizoid personality is characterized by isolation and withdrawal.

Research and Theory

A major problem in research with the schizoid personality is differentiating this condition from social phobias and less severe forms of schizophrenia. The individual with a social phobia also tends to avoid social interaction, and even the anticipation of a social encounter is likely to elicit anxiety. Because avoiding social interaction is almost impossible, the level of arousal in people with this problem may be chronically high. Nevertheless, the social phobic may have adequate social skills and be capable of appropriate behavior in a social situation in spite of high anxiety. Schizoid individuals, on the other hand, appear, if anything, emotionally underaroused in social situations. They seem not to know appropriate social behavior or to be aware of cues eliciting certain forms of interpersonal interactions.

Thus, in the social phobic we are apparently dealing with a dwindling performance due to anxiety, while in the schizoid individual we are dealing with a basic skills deficit. In other words, schizoid individuals may not have learned the appropriate skills of social interaction and are therefore avoided or shunned by their peers, which results in further social isolation. When social interaction does occur, ineptness may elicit social criticism, which in turn results in anxiety and avoidance as a function of social interaction. Thus, social phobias and the schizoid personality appear to be two completely different conditions, although discriminating between them may occasionally be difficult.

A more confusing issue is whether the schizoid personality is a less severe form of schizophrenia or is a precursor to the development of schizophrenic reactions (Rosenthal 1970). Rosenthal states that children who later become schizophrenic have the traits of the schizoid personality. They appear apathetic, dreamy, listless, shy, and seclusive. Often, they are friendless, socially maladaptive, shut-in, and disinterested. Klein (1972) distinguishes the schizoid with an early childhood history of asocial development, learning deficits, poor peer relationships, and emotional eccentricity from the shy, socially backward, but obedient person who is fearful and therefore isolated. It has also been claimed that the schizoid personality, when it is a precursor to schizophrenia, results in a process type

The schizoid individual has a skill deficit

of psychosis, which is slow in onset and involves psychological and emotional deterioration and chronicity.

Labeling schizoid personality as latent schizophrenia is unsound and inappropriate

While there is little doubt that some schizoid personalities do develop schizophrenia, it is also highly likely that many do not. Thus, labeling these individuals as exhibiting latent schizophrenia is methodologically unsound and ethically inappropriate. Mellsop (1973) tested the validity of regarding a schizoid personality as a common precursor of schizophrenia by examining published longitudinal studies of adult patients with schizophrenia on whom information had been collected during their childhood, and found the evidence linking the two to be only tenuous. Because of the catastrophic results of labeling an individual potentially schizophrenic, we should probably regard these individuals as distinct from schizophrenics until research recommends we do otherwise.

Autism may be a result, not a cause, of social isolation

Evidence suggests, furthermore, that the commonly reported autism that causes many clinicians to conclude that the schizoid personality is a type of schizophrenia may be a consequence and not a cause of the social isolation of these individuals. For example, Leef and Hirsch (1972) found that when normal male medical students were subject to a period of sensory deprivation, their deviant scores on the Rorshach increased significantly, as did the schizoid factor of the 16 PF, which indicates autism. It seems obvious that if individuals have little interpersonal contact, daydreaming and fantasy—both forms of autistic behavior—will occupy a greater part of their time.

In theorizing about the causes of the schizoid personality, psychodynamic hypotheses focus on the fact that this behavior develops early in life as a result of a disturbed primary parent-child relationship,

Schizoid personalities daydream and avoid social interaction.

neuroses, personality disorders, and special symptoms

typically at the oral stage, which leads the child to turn inward for safety and to rely more and more on fantasy and withdrawal. The notion is that the ego is threatened on all sides in an unresponsive universe, the result being that the individual oscillates between clinging to objects and expelling them (Appel 1974). Behavioral formulations would probably focus on the individual's lack of assertiveness and deficits in social skills, which probably develop early in life.

Assessment and Modification

Regardless of theoretical orientations, it is clear that the most appropriate method of assessing and diagnosing schizoid personalities would be in terms of social skills. The assessment of social skills involves measurement of an individual's emotional expressions, posture, facial expression, nonverbal speech characteristics, and socially appropriate speech content as described by subjective reports, behavioral assessment, and occasionally by psychophysiological assessment (Hersen and Bellack 1977). Self-report techniques include such scales as the Social Anxiety and Distress Scale (SAD), which measures the tendency to experience negative affect in interpersonal situations and therefore avoid them (Watson and Friend 1969). Representative items designed to test for this tendency include, "I feel relaxed even in unfamiliar situations" (False), and "I try to avoid talking to people unless I know them well" (True). A similar scale developed by the same authors is the Fear of Negative Evaluation Scale (FNE), which assesses negative affect and discomfort in social situations as well as the fear of receiving negative evaluations from others. A number of other self-report inventories also attempt to tap social skills deficits in various situations.

In terms of behavior assessment, the typical method is to place individuals in analogue situations in which they are given specific tasks or social skills to perform and then have them graded on various aspects of social interaction, such as appropriate content, voice quality, response latency, and other measures of adequate social interaction. Typically, role playing is also used. Each person is asked to imagine a particular situation and then to interact with a confederate. A representative example is, "You are on a date and have just come out of a theater after seeing a movie. You ask your date what she would like to do since it is early, and she replies, 'Oh, I don't know; it's up to you.'" The individual must then respond and interact. In the process the behavior may be tape-recorded or video-recorded for later scoring analysis and feedback. Some behavioral clinicians also use *in vivo* interactions, which require the individual to interact with a live confederate in a face-to-face situation in which the person may or may not be given a preparatory set. Individuals are then rated on their social skills along such dimensions as initiation of conversation, number of silences, verbal reinforcement of the partner, head nods, smiles, time spent gazing at the partner, and contents of the response.

Analogue situations and role plays used for behavioral assessment

In modification or treatment of the schizoid personality, it is fairly obvious that assessment or identification of the social skills deficit is one of the major steps in initiating a comprehensive treatment program. It is also fairly obvious that passivity and withdrawal are the principal problems and are highly related to unassertive behavior. For this reason, a great deal of attention in social skills training has focused on the teaching of assertive responses.

Assertiveness training originally developed as a treatment for persons with a passive or inhibited life-style, and has been used successfully in the treatment of various clinical problems, including sexual deviation, depression, marital conflict, and the interpersonal functioning of schizophrenics (Wolpe 1969). Assertive behavior is rather complex, involving the many components of socially acceptable expressions of personal rights and feelings as well as the expression of positive emotions, such as affection, empathy, admiration, and appreciation (Wolpe 1969). Teaching appropriate assertive behavior usually involves role playing, instructions, coaching, feedback, behavioral rehearsal, and modeling. When the individual learns appropriate social skills, the stage is set for appropriate interpersonal functioning, for either child or adult.

Assertiveness training has been used successfully

box 10-5
A Schizoid Child

Jane was an eight-year-old third-grader referred to treatment because of her difficulty in relating to peers. She was described as passive, and she experienced difficulty expressing anger when appropriate, was unable to refuse unreasonable requests, was overly sensitive to criticism, and rarely volunteered in class. The behavior assessment and training sessions were conducted in a video studio in which three chairs were arranged in a triangle to accommodate the subject and two role models. Male and female role models sat next to the subject and provided predetermined prompts to facilitate the responses. Role-played scenes were narrated over an intercom from a control room where directions, instructions, and feedback were given.

Jane was given nine scenes, five involving a same-sex role model and four involving an opposite-sex role model. An attempt was made to include situations in which the subject was likely to engage each day with other children. This similarity between the scenes and the typical daily encounters was expected to facilitate her ability to respond as she might in the natural environment. Six of the scenes randomly selected from the pool of nine were used as training items for her, while the remaining three scenes (4, 5, and 9) comprised the generalization series. These nine scenes were as follows:

Female Model

1. **Narrator** You're part of a small group in science class. Your group is trying to come up with an idea for a project to present to the class. You start to give your idea when Amy begins to tell hers also.

   Prompt "Hey, listen to my idea."

2. **Narrator** Imagine you need to use a pair of scissors for a science project. Betty is using them but promises to let you have them next. But when Betty is done, she gives them to Ellen.

   Prompt "Here are the scissors, Ellen."

3. **Narrator** Pretend you loaned your pencil to Joanie. She comes over to give it back to you and says that she broke the point.

   Prompt "I broke the point."

4. **Narrator** Imagine you're about to go to art class when Cindy asks you if she can use your desk while you're gone. You agree to let her use it, but tell her that you'll need it when you get back. When you come back from art, Cindy says she still needs to use your desk.

   Prompt "I still need to use your desk."

5. **Narrator** Your class is going to put on a play. Your teacher lists the parts, asking for volunteers. She reads a part you like, and you raise your hand. But Sue raises her hand after you and says that she would like to get the part.

   Prompt "I want to play this part."

Male Model

6. **Narrator** You're playing a game of kickball in school, and it's your turn to get up. But Bobby decides he wants to get up first.

   Prompt "I want to get up."

7. **Narrator** Imagine you're playing a game of four squares in gym. You make a good serve into Barry's square. But he says that it was out and keeps the ball to serve.

   Prompt "It's my time to serve."

8. **Narrator** You're in school, and you brought your chair to another classroom to watch a movie. You go out to get a drink of water. When you come back, Mike is sitting in your seat.

   Prompt "I'm sitting here."

9. **Narrator** Imagine you're standing in line for lunch. Jon comes over and cuts in front of you.

   Prompt "Let me cut in front of you."

In the initial assessment there were three administrations of the entire behavioral assertiveness test for children. In general, Jane was instructed to respond as realistically as possible to the situations. She was given the following instructions:

Narrator Hi. I'm next door. Can you hear me? See that box on the floor? Well, my voice comes through there. You must imagine things sometimes. You probably pretend a lot of things. For instance, maybe you pretend that you're doing something with someone else. Well, we're going to imagine a lot of different things with you. At times we will pretend that you are doing something in your classroom, in gym, or in the lunchroom. Each imaginary situation will be about you doing something with someone from school. When I describe each situation, I want you to really try to pretend that you are part of the situation.

To make it even more real, John and Susan (the role models), who are in the room with you, will pretend that they are the other people in the situations. They will be someone from school in the different situations. They will say something to you, and you try really hard to imagine that they are those people. When they are finished talking, you say what you would say if you were really doing something with that person. Do you know what I mean?

O.K., why don't we try a situation. Let's imagine you're with your friend in an ice-cream store. She wants to know what kind of ice cream you want.

Role model prompt What kind of ice cream do you want? *(Subject responds.)*

Narrator Can you taste it? Is it good? . . . . O.K., now remember you pretend that John or Susan is someone from school in the different situations. When either he or she is done talking, you say what you would say if you were really doing something with that person.

Following the practice scene, probe sessions then proceeded as follows: (1) the narrator presented the scene; (2) the role model delivered the prompt; and (3) the subject then responded to the role model.

Jane's responses to the nine scenes were videotaped on three separate occasions for the four weeks and retrospectively rated on three verbal and nonverbal components of assertive behavior and for overall assertiveness. An evaluation of her behavioral deficits was then conducted. It was found that she was deficient in eye contact, loudness of speech, and requests for new behaviors. In addition, the measure of overall assertiveness on a scale of one to five showed that she was very unassertive, as may be seen in Figure A.

Following baseline assessment Jane received three weeks of social-skills training consisting of three thirty-minute sessions per week. A multiple baseline design was used where training was applied sequentially and cumulatively to the three target behaviors over the three-week period. During the first week she received training for increasing eye contact, during the second week she received training for increasing loudness of speech, and during the final week she was trained on increasing the number of requests. Social skills training involved specifically the following:

1. The therapist presented one of the scenes from the behavioral assertiveness test for children, the model delivered a prompt, and Jane responded.
2. The therapist provided the subject with feedback on her performance with reference to the specific target behavior.
3. The therapist then discussed feedback with Jane to ensure that she understood.
4. The role model then modeled responses with specific attention to the target behavior.
5. The therapist then gave specific instructions concerning the target behavior. Jane then responded a second time.
6. Rehearsal continued for a scene until

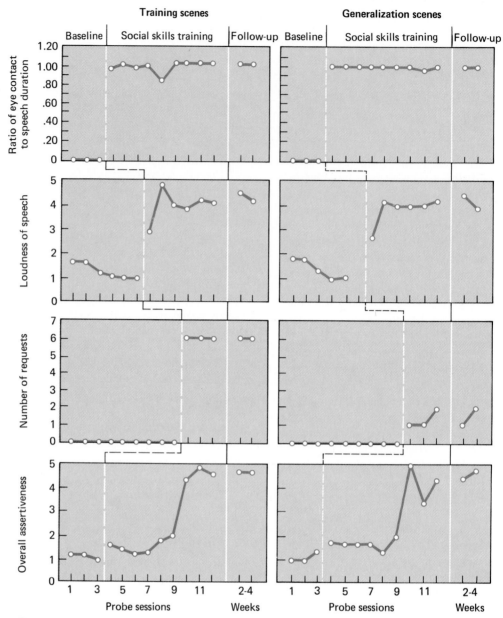

Figure A Probe sessions during baseline, social-skills treatment, and follow-up for training scenes and generalization scenes for Jane. The multiple baseline analysis is of ratio of eye contact while speaking to speech duration, loudness of speech, number of requests, and overall assertiveness.

the therapist felt that the criterion for that target behavior had been reached.

7. Training then advanced to a new interpersonal situation and proceeded in a similar fashion through all of the training scenes. Generalization on the three scenes for which she had not been trained was then determined.

Figure A shows the results for Jane, in terms of her assertiveness, for both the training scenes and the generalization scenes, and also her performance at a two-week and at a four-week follow-up. While there was no check of generalization in the natural environment, or with other children, this type of treatment methodology is extremely promising in treating both children and adults with severe social skills deficits.

Bornstein, Bellack, and Hersen, 1977

neuroses, personality disorders, and special symptoms

Other Personality Disorders

A number of other personality disorders have been delineated, but little research has been done on the characteristics, assessment, causes, or modification of these disorders. Consequently, their description is largely a function of clinical lore, and their importance as types of clinical disorders remains to be demonstrated.

Passive-Aggressive Personality

The pattern of behavior known as the **passive-aggressive personality** is, as the name implies, characterized by both passivity and aggressiveness. The aggressiveness may be expressed passively, for example, by obstructionism, pouting, procrastination, intentional inefficiency, or stubbornness.

The three principal characteristics of this disorder are direct aggressiveness, indirect aggressiveness (such as stubbornness and pouting), and dependency. Passive-aggressive individuals are a virtual "thorn in the flesh" of other people because they constantly test one's patience. They may be passive, clinging, and helpless on occasions, yet they may sabotage any project with which they do not agree, or feel bitter and pout when they finally provoke another individual into an unreasonable act. They are typically unpopular with other people because they arouse an especially annoying sort of anger. The hidden resentments, the subtle undermining of common goals, and the inability to be honest about their basic hostility are enough to try the patience of a saint.

DSM III, noting that the passive-aggressive personality disorder is a controversial diagnostic category, has introduced another type of personality disorder, the **dependent personality disorder,** which is characterized by passivity and dependency but no aggressive tendencies. A similar distinction between passive-aggressive personality types was made in DSM I, which described the subtypes of the passive-aggressive personality disorder as aggressive, passive-aggressive, and passive-dependent types.

Despite the scarcity of scientific studies of this syndrome, mental health officials frequently encounter it. It was listed in 3.1 percent of patients hospitalized in public mental institutions and in over 9 percent of patients in an outpatient clinic in 1966 (Pasternack 1974). In a long-term follow-up of 100 passive-aggressive personalities for a period of seven to fourteen years, Small and Small (1971) found that:

1. The psychiatric difficulties of these individuals usually start in adolescence.
2. Their family background frequently includes alcoholism.
3. The likelihood of the disorder is equal for males and females.
4. The lives of these individuals are commonly characterized by interpersonal strife, emotionalism, and impulsive behavior.
5. Other disturbances include frequent suicidal gestures, neglect of responsibility, disturbance of affect, and, quite commonly, somatic complaints of all kinds.

Small and Small note, however, as did Pasternack (1974), that the most salient characteristic is the individual's maladaptive social relationships.

Asthenic Personality

Individuals diagnosed as **asthenic personalities** are easily fatigued and display a low energy level, lack of enthusiasm, marked incapacity for enjoyment, and oversensitivity to physical and emotional stress. Although DSM II states that this condition should be differentiated from the neurasthenic neuroses, descriptions of the two conditions are essentially the same. Perhaps the only distinguishing feature is that in the neurotic condition the fatigue reaction is distressing to the individual, while in the personality disorder it is not. This disorder does not appear in DSM III.

Inadequate Personality and Borderline Personality Disorders

Individuals diagnosed as **inadequate personalities** are characterized by ineffectual response to emotional, social, intellectual,

Aggressiveness may be expressed passively

Passive-aggressives are unpopular

Fatigue is not distressing to the asthenic personality

and physical demands. Although these individuals seem neither physically nor mentally deficient, they do manifest inability to adapt, ineptness, poor judgment, social instability, and lack of physical and emotional stamina. A similar personality disorder, the **borderline personality,** is described by DSM III, which emphasizes the instability of these people. Borderline probably refers to the fact that some of these individuals have occasional brief psychotic episodes. These conditions are difficult to assess and describe because meaningful scientific investigations have not been done.

Narcissistic Personality Disorder

Self-importance, preoccupation with their success and power, self-centeredness, lack of concern about others, lack of empathy, tendency to exploit others, self-absorption

Individuals diagnosed by DSM III as exhibiting **narcissistic personality disorders** are characterized by a grandiose sense of self-importance, exhibitionism, preoccupation with their success and power, self-centeredness, and lack of concern for others. Their insensitivity to the feelings of others, lack of empathy, tendency to exploit others, and self-absorption cause disturbed interpersonal relationships. This disorder is easily confused with the histrionic personality disorder. Although clinical lore on this disturbance is plentiful, empirical information about it is not.

Summary

Personality has always been a controversial concept in psychology. Although most theorists assume that personality is stable across time and situations, others believe behavior is a function of situations. This disagreement seems to be due largely to the different approaches to the study of behavior. Situationalists see behavior in terms of change (S-R laws), while trait theorists look at it in relation to other responses or environmental conditions (R-R laws). The most appropriate solution, however, seems to be interactionalism, a compromise between these two positions. According to this theory, behavior may be a function of the situation, the individual, or both.

For our purposes, we shall define personality as behaviors resulting from social interaction with others. Personality disorders may then be defined as deficits in social skills or maladaptive patterns of social interaction. Four criteria may be used to distinguish personality disorders from other types of disorders: (1) the behavior is acquired early in life; (2) the behavior is stable across situations; (3) the behavior is not distressing to the individual; and (4) the behaviors are maladaptive patterns or deficits in social skills.

Antisocial personalities or sociopaths are individuals who are basically unsocialized and whose behavior patterns bring them into conflict with society. They do not experience anxiety, are impulsive and unable to learn from their experience, do not form emotional ties with others, and cannot tolerate boredom. They are often able to make a good impression on others, however.

Three major types of antisocial personalities may be observed among adolescents and adults. Primary sociopaths or psychopaths are distinguished by a lack of anxiety or guilt. Neurotic sociopaths repeatedly engage in antisocial behavior but experience guilt and remorse. Individuals having dissocial reactions are those who have grown up in a subculture whose values and norms are at variance with society's standards.

The main criterion for distinguishing between sociopathy and juvenile delinquency is age. Although a number of causes have been suggested for sociopathy, including heredity and chromosomal abnormalities, the most convincing hypothesis is that the sociopathic individual demonstrates a low level of arousal of the autonomic nervous system, which results in poor avoidance conditioning, the type of learning most important in the acquisition of conscience. Moreover, evidence also suggests that sociopaths have had inadequate models in their childhood. In terms of treatment, most psychological and medical techniques have achieved little success with antisocial individuals, although these people do appear to respond to highly structured, authoritarian treatment procedures.

The hysterical personality is characterized by histrionic behavior, emotional lability, dependency, excitability, egocentricity, suggestibility, and seductiveness. This disorder was once assumed to occur primarily in females, but evidence now shows that it occurs in males as well. Evidence further indicates little,

neuroses, personality disorders, and special symptoms

if any, consistent relationship between hysterical symptoms (conversion reactions) and hysterical personalities. Explanations for the hysterical personality are vague except for psychoanalytic theory, but it is obviously a disorder acquired in early childhood or adolescence. Hysteria in general has been a favorite candidate for psychodynamic therapies, but the effectiveness of these techniques is largely a matter of conjecture. Behavioral techniques usually focus on modifying the social skills of the hysterical individual, but there has been little evaluation of the effectiveness of these techniques.

Obsessive-compulsive personalities are characterized by concern with details, organization, punctuality, and routine. These individuals seem to be overly concerned with conformity to the standards of society and can be called oversocialized. In contrast to those having obsessive-compulsive neuroses, obsessive-compulsive personalities do not find their behavior distressing. In general, research supports the clinical conception of this disorder but does not support the belief that the obsessive-compulsive personality will develop ritualistic behavior or obsessional thinking when placed under stress. Psychodynamic theorists conjecture that stress in the anal stage of development is responsible for this disorder. Other explanations for this type of personality are lacking. As with other personality disorders, treatment procedures are only vaguely conceptualized, and the effectiveness of psychological intervention has not been demonstrated.

The schizoid personality is characterized by shyness, excessive sensitivity, seclusiveness, avoidance of close or competitive relationships, and eccentricity. This personality pattern apparently is manifested quite early in childhood, the schizoid youngster being typically an underachiever, overly sensitive, and more concerned with fantasy than with the real world. A major problem is differentiating the schizoid personality from the social phobic on the one hand, and the less severe forms of schizophrenia on the other. Evidence suggests that the schizoid personality is probably not a common precursor of schizophrenia. Explanations for the schizoid personality have been minimal and inadequate. Treatment procedures focus on teaching assertive behavior and social skills.

The passive-aggressive personality is characterized by both passivity and aggressiveness. In other words, the aggressiveness may be expressed in a passive manner through deliberately obstructive behavior, pouting, procrastination, intentional inefficiency, and stubbornness. Although this disorder is observed frequently in both mental hospitals and outpatient clinics, little systematic research has been done on its modification or treatment.

Asthenic personalities have low energy levels, lack of enthusiasm, incapacity for enjoyment, and extreme sensitivity to physical and emotional stress. As in the neurotic pattern of behavior labeled neurasthenia, the meaningfulness and clinical usefulness of a diagnosis of asthenic personality remains to be demonstrated. Similarly, the diagnostic category of inadequate or borderline personality, which consists of individuals characterized by ineffectual responses to emotional, social, intellectual, and physical demands, is another vague description that seems to be of little use in diagnosing personality disorders. Narcissistic personality disorder is another vague disorder for which few factual data are available.

Key Concepts

anankastic personality

antisocial personality (psychopath, sociopath)

assertiveness training

asthenic personality disorder

avoidant personality disorder

borderline personality disorder

dependent personality disorder

dissocial reaction

hysterical (or histrionic) personality disorder

inadequate personality disorder

interactionism

introverted personality disorder

milieu therapy

narcissistic personality disorder

neurotic sociopath (acting-out neurotic)

obsessive-compulsive personality disorder

overanxious syndrome

passive-aggressive personality disorder

personality

primary (classic) sociopath

schizoid personality disorder

schizotypal personality disorder

situationalism

socialized delinquency syndrome

stimulus hunger

subcultural delinquency

traits

unsocialized-aggressive syndrome

XYY males

Review Questions

1. How do state models differ from trait models?

2. What four criteria can be used to label a pattern of behavior as a personality disorder?

3. According to Cleckley, what are the six main characteristics of the antisocial personality?

4. What roles appear to be played in antisocial behavior by EEG abnormalities, autonomic reactivity, and avoidance learning?

5. What are four major obstacles to the modification of antisocial behavior?

6. What are the ethical concerns involved in the use of behavior modification programs to treat juvenile delinquents and institutionalized sociopaths?

7. What behavior pattern typifies the hysterical personality?

8. What behavior pattern typifies the obsessive-compulsive personality?

9. What behavior pattern typifies the schizoid personality?

neuroses, personality disorders, and special symptoms

disorders of biological needs

Several behavior disorders arise either from failure to meet one's biological needs or from meeting those needs in maladaptive ways. In Chapter 11 we shall discuss disorders that affect the basic processes of eating, eliminating, and sleeping. In Chapter 12 we shall discuss disorders that arise in the attempt to meet sexual needs (or that prevent such attempts). And in Chapter 13 we shall examine disorders involving needs that have been created by the ingestion of various substances—in other words, drug and alcohol abuse.

disorders of biological needs
basic processes

11

Key Topics

Primary and secondary motives

Food scarcity and obesity

External vs. internal cues in obesity

Stuart's behavior modification
    program for obesity

Anorexia nervosa

Treatment for encopresis

Bell-and-pad method and the dry-
    bed method of treating
    enuresis

Effects of sleep deprivation

Behaviors involved in
    pseudoinsomnia, insomnia,
    narcolepsy, hypersomnia,
    sleep apnea, and night terrors

Scientific approaches to the study of human behavior, as we noted earlier, begin with an assumption of determinism—if we ask the right questions, we can discover cause-and-effect processes that explain the behavior. "Why does this person behave in this way?" is in fact such a basic question in psychology that the attempt to answer it has generated an entire branch of the discipline—**motivation.** The study of motivation is the study of *needs* and *drives,* the forces that impel people toward specific goals or away from specific threats.

The search for motives is a complex and often confusing undertaking, involving almost every aspect of behavior. We can simplify that search somewhat by dividing motives into two types: **primary motives,** which involve physiological, unlearned states such as hunger, and **secondary or acquired motives,** which are learned behaviors, such as anxiety or jealousy, that we assume are acquired by association with primary motives and that vary greatly among individuals and societies.

Maslow (1954) believed that needs operate in a hierarchy (see Figure 11-1), in which the higher needs can only be felt or learned when the lower, more basic ones

Primary motives are mainly physiological; secondary motives are acquired through learning

Metabolic changes increase arousal, which energizes motivation

have been satisfied. The needs at the bottom of the hierarchy are physiological needs, and the behaviors they motivate are those necessary for maintaining life—eating, breathing, and sleeping, for example. The person gasping for air or suffering acute hunger pangs is hardly in a position to care about esteem needs, but once the basic needs are satisfied, the higher order needs emerge through learning. The disorders we shall discuss in this chapter involve the basic physiological needs—specifically, food, elimination, and sleep.

A **need** is an energizing condition of the organism that moves it toward a certain goal. The process involved might be visualized as follows:

Need $\rightarrow$ Drive $\rightarrow$ Behavior $\rightarrow$ Satiation

Primary needs arise most frequently from metabolic changes in tissue that increase *arousal,* the energizing function of motivation. The **drive** states or drive stimuli that are energized—such as hunger pangs—instigate behavior patterns that are both selective and directional. For example, the hungry organism becomes more sensitive to food odors and approaches places where its hunger may be satisfied. This is

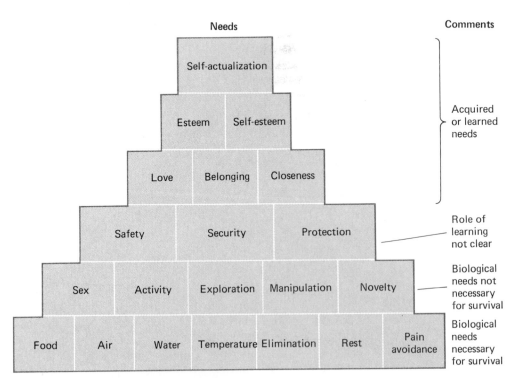

Figure 11-1 Maslow's hierarchy of needs.

disorders of biological needs

Overeating is a national pastime.

the guiding function of drive stimuli, which affect both the attention and the perception of the organism by making it more sensitive to cues that will lead to satisfaction of the need. The final behavior in this sequence is a *satiety* cue that emerges after the need has been satisfied.

Most physiological motives appear to operate by **homeostatic mechanisms,** which attempt to maintain constancy of internal states regardless of environmental conditions. Any biochemical imbalance provides negative feedback, activating physiological and psychological mechanisms that in turn effect the changes necessary to restore the organism to its former state. Primary motives can be seen as states of living organisms that are caused by internal and external conditions and that function to maintain a constant internal balance.

Feeding Disturbances

Hunger may be general or specific. When it is general, foodstuffs are interchangeable to a degree in supplying the body's energy requirements. When hunger is specific; the body needs certain kinds of substances, such as carbohydrates, proteins, fats, minerals, or vitamins.

Obesity

According to the United States Department of Health, Education, and Welfare (1967), there are between forty and eighty million obese Americans. Obesity is a major health hazard, since it increases vulnerability to a wide range of physical illnesses, particularly cardiovascular and adrenal diseases, that profoundly affect an individual's social, sexual, and occupational adjustment. It can also be emotionally painful because it inhibits participation in many kinds of useful or pleasurable activities and leads to self-hatred and rejection.

Obesity can be defined as body weight that is greater than 20 percent of standard weight as determined by standard height and weight charts. It results from ingesting more calories than the body can use for energy and is directly related to particular patterns of eating. Obese individuals, on the

Homeostasis functions to keep internal states constant

Obesity is a major health hazard

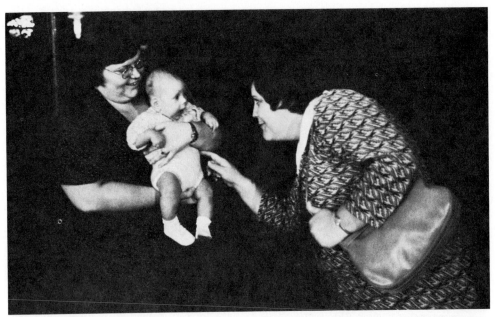

Here the pattern of overeating has extended over three generations. This baby probably will be an overweight adult.

Obese people are less active than normal-weight people

average, eat only slightly more than normal individuals. Though they eat fewer meals per day, they eat more per meal, and eat more rapidly than individuals with normal weight. The increase in weight is probably related to the fact that obese individuals are less active than people of normal weight (Rodin 1977). For example, Chirico and Stunkard (1960) used a pedometer to measure the distance walked each day by obese and normal individuals and found that normal individuals walked nearly six miles a day, while the obese walked slightly less than four miles.

Obese people are no more neurotic than others

Interestingly enough, a similar pattern of behavior appears in animals who have lesions in the **ventromedial hypothalamus (VMH)**, the center that influences satiety by signaling that enough has been eaten. This coincidence does not mean that the hypothalamus of the obese human has sustained any structural damage, but it does indicate that the parallel in animals and humans may be quite useful in studying obesity in humans. Our knowledge of the parameters of obesity in animals actually has contributed greatly to our knowledge of obesity in humans.

A genetic factor in obesity is likely

Research and Theory

Perhaps the first question to be asked about obesity is its relationship to personality fac-

tors and other forms of abnormal behavior. Rodin (1977) has reviewed a number of studies that have concluded that no consistent relationship exists between obesity and neurotic symptoms. Obese individuals seem to have their share of abnormal behavior patterns, but these patterns are not consistently associated with being overweight. Furthermore, no consistent personality type, such as the oral character, seems to be associated with weight problems.

As a matter of fact, Stunkard and Mendelson (1967) have stated that only two factors consistently relate to obesity: overeating and body image. They further state that the disturbed body image does not occur in emotionally healthy obese persons and is found only in a minority of neurotic obese people. These disturbances in body image seem to be a consequence, rather than a cause, of obesity because they occur primarily in people for whom obesity began in childhood and for whom there is real evidence of emotional disturbances. The evidence seems clear that most overweight people are psychologically normal in other respects.

It is also quite likely that, in some way, obesity is related to genetic predisposition. For example, 60 percent of individuals who are overweight have at least one overweight parent. In addition, a high correlation appears between the weights of obese children and their parents, but a low correlation exists between the weights of adopted children and their adoptive parents. Furthermore, identical twins are much more similar in weight than fraternal twins (Rodin 1977).

This evidence does not necessarily indicate a genetic malfunction but may, as Nisbett (1972) has noted, show that some individuals are biologically programmed to be fat. According to Nisbett, the quantity an individual eats is a function of the number and size of his **adipocytes,** the fat cells in the body. The number of adipocytes in an individual is essentially fixed and stable and presumably results from genetic endowment but can also be affected by early nutritional experiences. The hypothalamus then adjusts food intake to maintain adipose (fat) tissue cells at a baseline or set point. These baselines are different in different people and result in a normal distribution of weight in the population. Perhaps, as Nisbett's hypothesis suggests, being overweight is normal for some individuals, and requiring those individuals to diet or to reduce is like asking an individual of normal weight to reduce, which can cause emotional depression and loss of sex drive. If Nisbett's hypothesis is correct, it could explain why obesity is often such a difficult condition to modify.

There is also excellent evidence that obesity is related to environmental factors. For example, it appears to be directly related to socioeconomic class, since obesity is seven times more common in lower socioeconomic groups than in higher ones, this difference being particularly marked among women (Rodin 1977). Furthermore, almost twice as many women in the upper social classes as in the lower classes are dieting to lose weight. Although such factors as variations in social attitudes and the high caloric value of cheaper food could explain these differences, another important factor is the history of eating behavior in these groups. It has been well documented that eating patterns established early in infancy and childhood are important in the development of obesity. Gross (1968) directly investigated the effects of scarcity and unpredictability of food supply by exposing rats to conditions of both constant and random deprivation and found

that his randomly deprived animals showed an interest in food independent of hunger or satiety. Bruch (1961) found similar evidence in humans, indicating that exposure to prolonged food deprivation often results in a persistent tendency to overeat. In both studies, when sufficient food was available, obese individuals would glut themselves, which could result in a higher baseline. Since it has been demonstrated that critical adipose tissue development occurs between birth and age two in obese children (overfeeding an infant increases the *number* of fat cells, making obesity very difficult to reverse), and that patterns of eating are directly related to the scarcity and regularity of food supply, it is not particularly surprising that obesity is more common in the lower socioeconomic classes (Knittle 1975).

A crucial question is how these factors are related to the control of food intake. It has been demonstrated that scarcity and unpredictability of food supply, family size, and similar factors influence not only the amount of eating but also the significance of the external cues that affect the eating response. Thus, one hypothesis might be that obese individuals are more sensitive to external than internal cues. Stunkard and Koch (1964) had food-deprived subjects swallow an intragastic balloon that continuously recorded stomach contractions, as shown in Figure 11–2. Every fifteen minutes the subjects were asked whether they were hungry. For normal weight subjects a strong correlation appeared between stomach contractions and self-reported hunger. For overweight subjects the correlation was far less. These and other data led Schachter and his colleagues to a **stimulus-bound theory of obesity:** Eating behavior of obese individuals is extremely responsive to external cues. For example, Schachter, Goldman, and Gordon (1968) had subjects refrain from eating for several hours before an experiment. Immediately before being tested, half of them were fed two roast beef sandwiches, while the others remained hungry. All of the subjects were then asked to complete a lengthy taste questionnaire evaluating a variety of crackers for quality, such as "cheesiness" and "saltiness." During this tasting session normal-weight subjects who were hungry ate

Environmental factors are also indicated

Prolonged food deprivation produces a tendency to overeat

Obese people are more sensitive to external cues

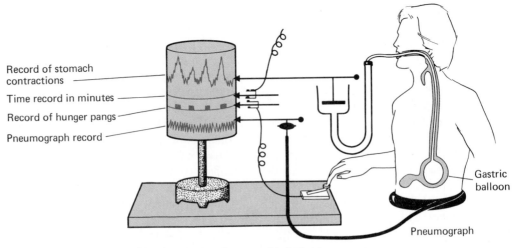

Record of stomach contractions
Time record in minutes
Record of hunger pangs
Pneumograph record

Gastric balloon
Pneumograph

Figure 11-2 Recording of hunger pangs using a gastric balloon.

far more crackers than those who were filled. Overweight subjects ate slightly more if they had just eaten than if they had not. Thus, loading the stomach had little effect on the eating behavior of obese subjects.

The external cues hypothesis was also supported by a study (Nisbett 1968) in which each subject, after completing an experiment, was given a form to fill out and left alone in a room containing a refrigerator and a table and chair. The subject was invited to eat the sandwiches placed on a plate on the table and, if desired, to eat more sandwiches from the refrigerator. Obese subjects ate whatever was on the plate, whether it was one sandwich or three, and did not take any from the refrigerator. "Normals" ate until they were full, even if that meant leaving uneaten sandwiches on the plate or going to the refrigerator for more. Nisbett concluded that the obese subjects were "plate-cleaners."

Time, another external cue that should influence eating, was manipulated in an experiment by Schachter and Gross (1968). By rigging a clock to run slow or fast, they were able to convince subjects, at the conclusion of an experiment, that it was either dinner time or an hour earlier. The actual elapsed time was thirty minutes in each trial, but in some trials the clock indicated the passage of an hour, and in other trials it indicated the passage of fifteen minutes. The experimenters returned to the room, nibbling crackers from a box, asked subjects

to complete a final questionnaire, and offered them crackers, which were left on a table. Obese subjects who thought an hour had elapsed ate twice as many crackers as obese subjects who thought fifteen minutes had elapsed. Normal-weight subjects who thought an hour had elapsed ate fewer crackers than other normals, many saying that they did not want to spoil their meal. Once again the eating behavior of obese individuals was controlled to a greater extent than that of normals by external rather than internal cues.

The above studies appear to confirm that obese people are strongly influenced by external cues. Surprisingly, however, obese individuals may eat little more than normals. Schachter and Robin (1974) have shown that eating behavior in the obese is triggered only when food cues are highly salient or potent. In other words, if food stimuli are weak or entirely absent, obese people will eat less than normal individuals. Goldman, Jaffa, and Schachter (1968) found that on Yom Kippur—the Jewish day of atonement, a time of fasting and prayer during which external food cues are extremely sparse for those who remain in a synagogue—obese Jews were more likely to fast than equally religious Jews of normal weight. Normal-weight Jews, responsive to their internal deprivation state, found fasting painful whether they remained in the synagogue or not. Further

Obese people may be plate-cleaners

Time is another external cue that influences the eating behavior of obese individuals

Obese people evidently respond more readily to salient external cues

disorders of biological needs

Literally thousands of books have tackled the fat problem.

evidence on this question comes from Nisbett (1968), who had subjects taste one of two ice creams, an excellent and expensive French vanilla and a vanilla that had been adulterated with quinine. Obese subjects ate more of the tastier and less of the bad-tasting ice cream than normal subjects. The taste of the ice cream determined the amount consumed in obese individuals, who appeared to be more reactive to taste than to hunger.

In summary, early experience seems to play a crucial role in obesity, especially when it involves a scarcity of food. Furthermore, such early experiences apparently cause an individual's eating behavior to be more responsive to external than to internal cues. Obesity developed during childhood seems to be the most resistant to treatment, the odds against successful reduction being twenty-eight to one (Bray 1970). To complicate the situation further, obesity appears to be related not only to overeating but also to physical inactivity. These facts lead us to the conclusion that

obesity is not simply a function of overeating but may be complexly related to genetic factors, early experience, lack of exercise, and oversensitivity to external cues.

Assessment and Modification

Since obesity is relatively easy to assess and the goal of modification procedures (weight reduction) is fairly simple, one would expect the remedy for this condition to be fairly simple: all the individual has to do is restrict food intake. This is not the case, however. While almost any obese person can lose weight, few can keep it off. Because of this fact and because obesity is a major health hazard, techniques designed to control weight have proliferated.

A rather obvious answer to the problem is dieting, and a great variety of diet programs are available. Individuals do lose weight when placed on a strict diet, particularly if they are in a controlled environment, such as a hospital. Moreover, dieting seems to be more efficient if the individual

Early experience plays a crucial role in obesity

Dieting is more efficient if the individual eats 5 or 6 small meals a day

disorders of biological needs: basic processes

Perhaps one of the most heartbreaking ironies of our land of plenty is that we are the most overfed and undernourished people on earth. Nowhere is our preoccupation with food more evident than in the recent explosion of diet fads. While millions all over the world are dying of starvation, Americans are constantly fighting the battle of the bulge. Even if we ignore accusations that we are a nation of junk-food addicts, sugar junkies, and people pickled in our own preservatives, we cannot deny that we are diet-crazy. Fashion almost dictates that one be dieting or at least following some exotic regimen. And true to our American way, we have a host of souls, some serious and some outright quacks, waiting in the wings to recommend ever new means of shedding unwanted pounds or developing healthier bodies.

Compounding the problem, however, is the undeniable fact that most of these fashionable diet fads we find so alluring are at best useless, at worst downright deadly. Like biblical devils, the alternatives are legion: There are diets high in protein and low in carbohydrates, diets allowing vegetables but no animal products, diets recommending only organic foods, diets high in fiber and low in salt, diets consisting mainly of grapefruit or rice, and the diet to end all diets—no food at all. While each regimen may have its staunch supporters, each is also haunted by the spectre of those who have become its victims. Emaciation, enlarged livers, scurvy, protein deficiencies, constipation, diarrhea, clogged arteries, faintness, heart attacks, and death itself are some of the grim side effects of many diet crazes.

To complicate even further the horrors of our diet mania, we are a nation of pill-poppers. We have ultimate faith in anything in pill or capsule form, anything we can swallow. Choosing to ignore what must be blatantly obvious symbolism to anyone who seriously considers our pill-religion, we spend fortunes daily on vitamin supplements. Indeed, our faith in vitamins is growing at such a pace that we now believe we can cure everything from brittle nails to hyperactivity to impotence to cancer and outright insanity with ever larger doses of vitamins. Instead of megatons, we are now concerned with mega-vitamins.

It is a pity we do not have a great satirist like Jonathan Swift alive today to expose our nutritional madness to the ridicule it well deserves. Unfortunately, like good Swiftian satire, our story has its tragic side too. In our desperate attempt to have life and have it more abundantly, we are killing ourselves. Only the richest nation on earth could afford to be so faddish and so terminally ridiculous. What is the ultimate dietary formula? Perhaps, in a word, balance. Perhaps also moderation, simplicity, and wholeness. Perhaps we need to reconsider our entire attitude toward eating. Whatever the answer, let us not immortalize ourselves in some nerve-chilling parody of Swiftian satire: "I saw a woman dying from scurvy, a surfeit of protein, and an enlarged liver the other day, and you would be surprised how it altered her appearance for the worse."

Mary Baine

---

is taught to consume five to six small meals per day (Leon 1976). Glennon (1966) reported on a follow-up, ranging from twelve to twenty-four months, on persons who had been hospitalized and placed on an 800- to 1,200-calorie reducing diet. All of these individuals lost weight in the hospital, but at follow-up, only 23 percent were able to achieve and maintain a twenty-pound

Prolonged fasting is quicker but may lead to complications

weight loss, and only 6 percent a forty-pound weight loss. Other studies of dieting reveal similar results.

Another method of dieting is prolonged fasting. The advantage of this method is that hunger sensations are not experienced after the first two to four days. Weight loss from fasting is rapid, but unfortunately, in some cases therapeutic fasting may result in serious physical complications and a decrease in the individual's overall adjustment (Leon 1976). The efficiency of this technique is difficult to determine. Possible complications aside, individuals tend to regain the weight they lost on the fast. Because of the difficulty of maintaining weight loss and the number of serious physical complications associated with prolonged starvation, this technique should be used only in extreme situations.

Drug therapy has also been used to effect weight loss. Commonly used drugs include a variety of anorexigenics (drugs that decrease appetite or hunger), and metabolic stimulators. In general, surveys of the drug literature indicate that the long-term results of appetite suppressant drugs were uniformly poor and that with extended use or abuse these drugs may create their own problems due to drug dependency and personality changes (Edicon 1971).

A more recent medical procedure is **intestinal bypass surgery,** in which a major portion of the small intestine is bypassed, thus drastically reducing the absorptive capacity of that organ and causing weight loss. This procedure has been found to produce marked weight loss, but in many cases serious problems have occurred, such as electrolyte imbalance, nutritional deficits, severe diarrhea, and in some cases, death (Leon 1976). For this reason it has been suggested that the procedure be discontinued or used with caution only in cases of intractable massive obesity (Welch 1973).

Hypnosis, individual psychotherapy, and group psychotherapy have all been used to control weight problems with little success. Lately, national organizations such as Weight Watchers International, Inc., and its competitors, such as Lean Line, Inc., have prospered so that they are now multimillion-dollar concerns. Other groups, such as TOPS (Take Off Pounds Sensibly), have also developed.

In 1958 Stunkard came to three conclusions about the treatment of obesity that he did not alter until much later. These conclusions were that (1) Most obese people will not stay in treatment for obesity; (2) Of those who stay in treatment, most will not lose weight; and (3) Of those who do lose weight, most will regain it.

Later, however, Stunkard (1972) altered his earlier verdict and concluded that behavior modification is the most effective treatment for obesity, a conclusion generally supported by Leon (1976) in her review of various methods of treating obesity. A typical behavior modification program is the self-directed behavior change procedure described by Stuart (1967), which has the following components:

1. **Description of the behavior to be controlled**   Clients are required to keep detailed daily records of the amount, nature, time, and circumstances of their eating. They also must monitor and graph their daily body weight. These data help the client to identify the discriminative, eliciting, and reinforcing stimuli that are maintaining inappropriate eating behavior and give the therapist a continuous source of feedback about how effective the program is and how it might be improved. A typical example of the self-monitoring and graphing of behavior is shown in Figure 11–3.

2. **Modification of the stimulus control of eating**   Obese clients are taught to narrow the inevitably wide range of discriminative stimuli that prompt eating. Meals are eaten only at predetermined times, in specific rooms, and at a specific table with distinctively colored napkins and tablecloths. Eating in other situations and being exposed to other salient cues that may initiate eating are prohibited.

3. **Modification of actual eating behavior**   The clients are instructed to eat more slowly, to finish chewing and swallowing the last bite before putting any more food on the fork, to pay close attention to the food in their mouth, and to introduce short breaks during a meal by laying utensils down and sitting at the table for a prescribed time without eating.

Drugs and surgery can have serious side effects

Behavior modification may be the most effective treatment for obesity

Narrowing the range of eating stimuli

Eating slowly

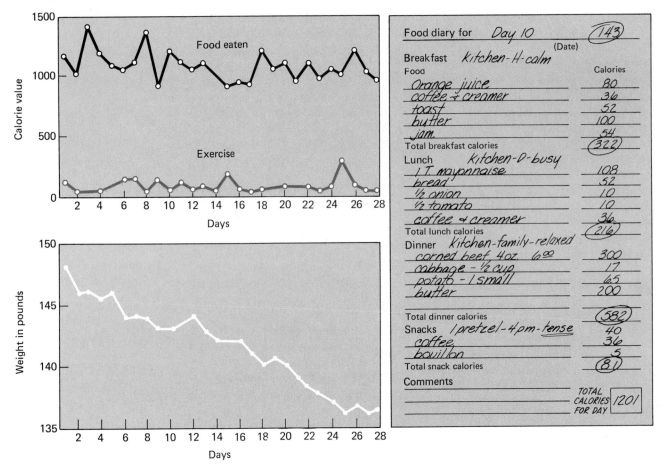

Figure 11-3 Self-monitoring of eating behavior.

4. **Reinforcement of self-controlling behavior** This aspect of the program is essentially an attempt to encourage clients to reinforce themselves for noneating behavior and to engage in some positive, competing activity when the urge to eat is strong. Tension, depression, and anger caused either by dieting or by other events that trigger eating can be managed by training in relaxation skills and other competing responses.

A number of controlled studies have compared the effectiveness of behavioral techniques with competing treatment methods and placebo treatment. For example, Wollersheim (1970) compared a positive-expectation, social-pressure group, a nonspecific therapy condition, and a delayed-treatment control group with a multifaceted behavioral program modeled after Stuart's program. The procedures used in the positive-expectation, social-pressure group were similar to those used in the TOPS weight reduction program. The subjects made a commitment to lose weight and were checked in at weekly weigh-ins before the group, a procedure that provided appropriate positive reinforcement for weight loss or punishment (social censure) for weight gain. Group discussions centered on providing factual information about obesity, health, nutrition, and weight loss without emphasizing specific ways to decrease eating. The nonspecific therapy group was designed to control for factors such as placebo, expectancy of therapeutic gain, and therapeutic contact. Subjects received relaxation training with the rationale that this would help them to develop insight, discuss hypothetical underlying causes of their weight problem, and participate in psychoanalytically oriented groups.

Reinforcing noneating behavior

disorders of biological needs

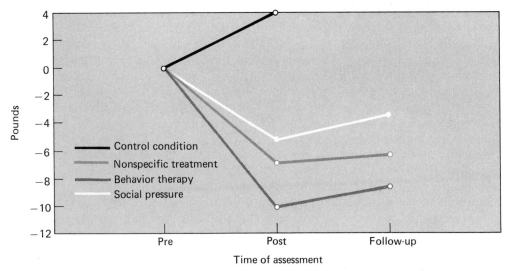

Figure 11-4 Mean changes in weight at posttreatment and follow-up measurements.

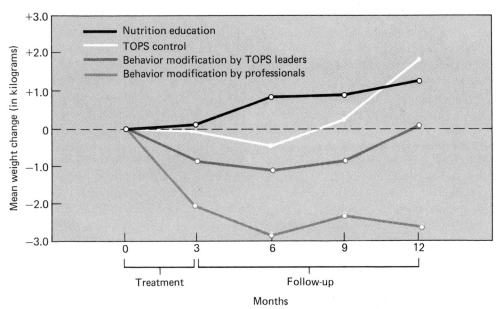

Figure 11-5 Mean weight change during treatment and at follow-up for four groups.

The results of the study are shown in Figure 11-4. At posttreatment and at an eight-week follow-up, the greatest weight loss and reduction of reported overeating occurred in the behavioral treatment group.

Levitz and Stunkard (1974) compared behavior modification programs conducted by either professional behavior therapists or leaders from different TOPS chapters with standard TOPS procedures with and without the addition of nutritional education programs. Their results are shown in Figure 11-5. Notably, the professional behavior therapists produced greater weight

loss in their subjects than the TOPS chapter leaders even though the same behavioral programs were used, an indication of the superiority of professional over nonprofessional therapists in dealing with this problem. These and a number of similar studies hint at the potential of behavioral techniques for dealing with obesity.

Anorexia Nervosa

Undereating is also a problem in our culture, although seemingly less prevalent

Behavioral treatment was most effective

than obesity. Kanner (1972) states that one-fourth of all children have feeding difficulties. He indicates also that food refusal is rare—almost nonexistent—among primitive cultures and is peculiar to our modern civilization. This difference probably exists because our culture requires far more of children during eating periods than simply ingestion of food. Children are told that they must eat neither too slowly nor too fast, chew with their mouths closed, avoid touching the food with their hands, use eating utensils in a proper manner, suppress burps and belches, and never vomit. When these social expectations are also combined with other stresses and with other excessive demands, it is not surprising that eating problems are so frequently reported for both young children and adults.

One such eating disorder is **anorexia nervosa.** Sir William Gull, a British physician, first described the condition in 1868 and conjectured that the loss of appetite—anorexia—was due to disordered mental processes related to a disturbance in CNS (central nervous system) activity—nervosa. Most often, this condition is observed in young women between the ages of sixteen and twenty-three. In a review of 473 published cases, Bliss and Branch (1960) found, in fact, that females outnumbered males nine to one.

The disorder is characterized by severe reduction of food intake, extreme weight loss and emaciation, amenorrhea (absence of menstruation), slow pulse, dryness of skin, brittle nails, intolerance to cold, low metabolic rate, reduced blood pressure, gastrointestinal syndromes with hyperacidity, and abnormal (usually flat) blood sugar curves. The definition of anorexia nervosa has varied because there is no well-defined distinction between a transient loss of appetite and the diminished appetite of true anorexia. Nevertheless, the typical pattern is a sudden reduction of food intake during adolescence. When starvation becomes advanced, physiological changes associated with malnutrition make the process difficult to reverse.

Anorexic individuals often have a real aversion to food and may resist forced feeding. They may wear bulky clothes to conceal the amount of weight loss and may induce vomiting or take a laxative to rid their system of food. This restriction of nourishment is often accomplished painstakingly with detailed attention to caloric intake so that it often resembles dieting "gone wild." Fatal physiological complications sometimes occur. The range of mortality rates is from 10 to 23 percent, the most frequently cited figure being 15 percent (Van Buskirk 1977). There does seem to be some waxing and waning of the condition with periodic remissions and relapses. Even with the severity of the emaciation and the possible threat of death, anorexic patients are difficult to manage.

A disorder similar to anorexia nervosa is **chronic rumination** in infants. Kanner (1957) defines this disorder as the bringing up of food without nausea, retching, or disgust. The food is ejected into the mouth, reswallowed, or, if it is liquid, allowed to run out. This type of behavior appears to be voluntary: that is, children actively engage in behavior that induces rumination and are observed to strain vigorously to bring food back into their mouths. The incidence of this type of disorder is unknown, since it is often confused with food allergies, especially to milk (Sajwaj, Libet, and Agras 1974). However, it has severe clinical complications similar to those of anorexia nervosa, including malnutrition, dehydration, lowered resistance to disease, and weight loss. The fatality rate with this type of disorder is close to 20 percent (Kanner 1957; Sajwaj, Libet, and Agras 1974). A variety of treatments have been used for this disorder, including surgery, drugs, mechanical devices (chin straps, esophagus blocks), feedings thickened with farina, social reinforcement with attention, mild electric contingent shock, contingent Tabasco sauce, and lemon juice (Sajwaj, Libet, and Agras 1974). At present, the causes of this disorder are unknown, but fairly adequate modification techniques have been developed.

Food refusal is peculiar to our modern civilization

Anorexia (loss of appetite) nervosa (central nervous system disturbance) . . .

resembles dieting gone wild

Chronic rumination appears to be voluntary

disorders of biological needs

Research and Theory

Little systematic research has been done with anorexia nervosa and chronic rumination, but environmental factors are assumed to be important. Kanner (1972) claims that anorexia nervosa is always a manifestation of a severe emotional conflict. Others suggest that social reinforcement occurring because of the failure to eat may maintain noneating behaviors (Leitenberg, Agras, and Thompson 1968). In one study of fifteen anorexic girls, self-starvation was related to concern about obesity, distress, and self-punishment (Lesser et al. 1960).

A definite relationship does seem to exist between sex roles, obesity, and anorexia nervosa. Bakwin and Bakwin (1972) maintain that anxiety about sex roles is prominent in most anorexic individuals and that their parents are often emotionally unstable. Kessler (1966) lists four factors associated with anorexia:

1. One or both parents drink or eat too much or exhibit some type of gastrointestinal symptoms.
2. Food has some special significance to the parents and has been uniquely important to the patients themselves long before the onset of anorexia. Anorexic individuals often have a past history of overeating and problems associated with excessive weight.
3. The patients show resistance to growing up and assuming a mature heterosexual role. Excessive weight often leads to the disappearance of secondary sex characteristics and interrupts menstruation as well.
4. The patients tend to regress emotionally.

Ross (1974) suggested a more behavioral explanation. He assumes that individuals must learn appropriate labels for various bodily sensations that eventually come to guide or direct behavior that is relevant to those sensations. In this case, individuals must learn to label correctly the sensations that normally precede eating behavior. If they do not, they fail to learn the appropriate labels for those sensations or to know when they are hungry or satisfied. Parents take primary responsibility for determining what and how much a child should eat. Consequently, if the child has not learned the internal cues indicating satiation or hunger, the child is likely to overeat if the parent insists on plate cleaning. During adolescence the responsibility for controlling eating behavior shifts to the child, but because the child has not learned to respond to internal hunger cues, he or she may cease to eat. In addition, because of the overemphasis on eating, which may itself be stressful, food may acquire noxious properties and elicit food refusal, which is a form of avoidance behavior (Ross 1974). Consequently, some types of anorexia nervosa can be seen as a phobia of eating or of gaining weight.

Modification Procedures

Since immediate weight gain is necessary to eliminate the physiological dangers in anorexia nervosa, the primary concern is with how effective the treatment is in restoring weight to a minimal level in a short period. In addition, the technique should maintain a safe weight and ensure adequate adjustment (Van Buskirk 1977). A number of techniques have been used. In the initial phase, most treatments focus on bed rest, high-calorie diets, and when necessary, tube feeding. Occasionally, the patient is given chlorpromazine, insulin, or other drug therapies. A variety of psychological treatments are used, from psychotherapy and family therapy to behavior modification. Several different behavioral techniques can be used, including systematic desensitization and contingent reinforcement for eating. It has been generally agreed that behavioral approaches are somewhat effective in rapidly solving this problem (Rimm and Somervill 1977).

Concern about obesity, distress, and self-punishment as factors in anorexia nervosa

Other factors include anxiety about sex role . . .

parental eating behavior, special significance of food, and emotional regression

But Ross suggests failure to learn internal cues (hunger and satiety) and overemphasis on eating, making it stressful

Sandra was born at home to a rather poor rural family after an unplanned but uncomplicated pregnancy. The day after her birth, she was admitted to the hospital for feeding difficulties associated with a cleft palate and lip. These difficulties were corrected, and Sandra was discharged nine days later. During the next four months, weight gain was below average although her mother reported no further feeding difficulties. There were, however, some indications of neglect, and Sandra was cared for by a number of different people, including some neighborhood children.

At age six months, she was readmitted to the hospital because of a failure to gain weight due to rumination. She was emaciated and unresponsive to her environment. There was no grasping of objects, no smiling, no babbling, no gross movements, and some crying. Exhaustive medical examination and laboratory analysis revealed no organic cause for her difficulties. Her weight was falling rapidly, however, and was below her birth weight and below the third percentile for infant girls. Malnutrition and dehydration were pressing problems, and death was a distinct possibility.

Feeding of a commercially prepared formula every four hours was immediately followed by ruminative behavior. Sandra would open her mouth, elevate and fold her tongue, and then vigorously thrust her tongue backward and forward until milk began to appear at the back of her mouth and slowly flow out. This behavior continued for twenty to forty minutes until she had apparently lost all the milk she had just consumed. No crying or evidence of pain occurred during the rumination, which could be interrupted by touches, mild slaps, or pokes. The behavior would resume immediately, however.

Baseline was obtained by having several observers watch Sandra for twenty minutes after each feeding. Ruminative behavior was defined as tongue thrusting with her mouth open. Milk did not have to be visible, nor did the tongue have to be folded or elevated. Sandra was weighed daily on the same scale while she was clad only in a diaper.

Lemon juice therapy was then begun. This consisted of squirting about five to ten cubic centimeters of unsweetened lemon juice into the side of her mouth as soon as vigorous tongue movements were detected. For the next thirty to sixty seconds, no more was administered. If ruminative tongue movement persisted or a new episode began, the juice was reapplied. After eight weeks of lemon juice therapy, Sandra was discharged into the care of foster parents who were carefully instructed in the use of the lemon juice.

Results indicated that the initial use of the lemon juice reduced the ruminative movements to below 10 percent of baseline. Weight ceased to fall and stabilized at just under eight pounds. A brief omission of the lemon juice led to a return to high levels of rumination, but the resumption of the treatment again reduced the behavior. After the twelfth day, no regurgitated milk was ever observed in her mouth. Weight began to increase and did so until discharge. Follow-up checks confirmed a continued weight increase. The foster parents reported only two occurrences of ruminative behavior, which were immediately followed by the lemon juice. Concurrent with the weight gain were changes in other behaviors. Sandra became more attentive, began to smile and to grasp objects, and even began to babble for the first time.

After five months, Sandra was returned to her biological parents. She was then seen at seven follow-up visits over a period of twelve months. During the follow-up visits, it was evident that her motor, social, and speech developments were continuing. At the one-year follow-up, her weight was just over twenty-four pounds.

Sajwaj, Libet, and Agras, 1974

disorders of biological needs

box 11–3
Anorexia Nervosa
in a 20-Year-Old
Female

At first I thought I'd lose just a few pounds before graduation, but then I started having problems with my roommates and just didn't feel like eating much, especially not with the terrible food the school cafeteria served. Before I knew what had happened, I weighed only 95 pounds. I left school and went home to live with my parents and brothers, but I was really scared to start eating again. My mother was 40 pounds overweight, and I'd been kind of chubby myself at about fourteen or fifteen. I was afraid I'd just blow up like a balloon if I started eating.

When I hit 80 pounds, I went to my family doctor. He examined me thoroughly and decided there was nothing physically wrong with me, so he sent me to a psychiatrist. After the psychiatrist talked to me awhile, he said he thought I had two phobias: one about gaining weight and the other about the way my looks would change if I did. He told me he was going to put me in a hospital for awhile and show me how to get over my fears by learning how to relax and think about the things that scared me most about gaining weight. After I got to the hospital we made two lists of scary thoughts, one about gaining weight and the other about changes in my appearance. Then we ranked them according to how scary they were. Next, I learned to relax deeply by learning to tense my muscles and then relax them. Pretty soon I could relax completely whenever I wanted to.

After I had learned how to relax, the doctor would have me get comfortable, close my eyes, and relax. Then he would describe the least scary scene in one of the lists. If I felt the least bit anxious about it, I would raise my finger. Then I'd stop and relax again. When I was relaxed, the doctor would try the scene again. We went through both lists this way. One day I told him I was afraid the treatment wasn't going to work because the scenes were beginning to bore me. He said he thought that meant I was getting over my fears.

And he was right. Gradually, I began to eat a little more every day. The doctor never forced me to eat, but if I went for twenty-four hours without any stomach pain or other discomfort from what I had eaten one day, he'd increase the number of calories I'd get the next day. When I first got to the hospital, the doctor had the nurses just watch me for a few days. They said I was eating about 600 calories a day. But after I'd been there a little over a month and worked through my lists many times, they told me I was eating 3600 calories a day. I even had viral pneumonia while I was in the hospital, but I didn't stop gaining weight. By then I was also seeing a psychotherapist just to talk about my problems too.

By the time I went home after about two and a half months, I weighed nearly 90 pounds. A month later I weighed 96 pounds. When the doctor saw me again after six months, I weighed 105 and was holding my weight. I wasn't afraid of being fat anymore, and I had learned how to be a lot more relaxed about life in general, too.

Schnurer, Rubin, and Ray, 1973

Other Feeding Problems

Several other types of eating and appetite disorders have been identified. One specific type is **pica,** a craving for nonfood, nonnutritional substances (Kanner 1957). All children go through a stage in which they experiment with ingesting various types of materials but rapidly learn what is and is not appropriate. However, the child with pica systematically seeks out and eats substances such as rubber, dirt, feces, polish, and clay. This disturbance also occurs in some adults who have particular cravings for unusual substances such as white clay, as often occurs in the southeastern United States. This reaction may be a response to specific nutritional deficiency, especially

Pica may be a response to a nutritional deficiency

calcium; therefore, a complete medical examination and laboratory tests are necessary for assessment. The danger with this disorder is that the individual may ingest poisons or toxic substances, with fatal results. The reasons for this disorder are not known, but Kessler (1966) indicates that this type of unusual feeding pattern usually occurs in an uninteresting environment that constrains a child and is devoid of affection and fun.

Another fairly common feeding problem sometimes assumed to be associated with psychological factors is **colic.** Colicky babies usually experience sharp intestinal pains and cry for hours at a time. This disorder tends to disappear by six months of age and is not physically dangerous. It does, however, have an important impact on the child's psychological adjustment. Colic, which seldom occurs in hospital nurseries, is especially common among firstborn infants. Lakin (1957) found that the mothers of colicky babies were generally more tense and anxious during pregnancy than mothers of noncolicky babies. Apparently, tension and ambivalence in the mother may be related to colic in children.

Colic may be due to tension and ambivalence in the mother

Elimination Disturbances

Toilet training in Western civilization is a major developmental task for children and a major concern of parents. The age at which toilet training is initiated varies markedly among various cultures. Some primitive African tribes using imitation training have children who are not trained until they are almost six years of age; while in London mothers have initiated training as early as the first two weeks of life (O'Leary and Wilson 1975). Although two weeks of age is clearly too early to begin toilet training, the exact age in which it should be undertaken is not clear. Our beliefs about when toilet training should be initiated have vastly changed as various theories of child development have been put forth. Wolfenstein (1951) has given an interesting account of governmental advice to parents regarding toilet training during the years 1914 to 1951. In 1914 a mother was

Advice to parents on toilet training has varied considerably over the years

advised to begin toilet training by the third month and was warned against scolding or punishing the child while toilet training was in process. By 1921 the advice was even more severe. Parents were to begin toilet training by the end of the first month and to finish by the end of the first year. In 1942 the trend was reversed and mothers were advised to begin by the eighth month; and in 1951 mothers were being told to begin training at eighteen months to two years.

This change resulted from the belief that children's cognitive and affective development would be harmed if they were not allowed to acquire toilet habits in a relaxed manner. This belief stems from Freud's theory that an adult's personality is in part determined by the manner in which the child is toilet trained, since toilet training is the child's first significant contact with the rules and regulations of society. While an extremely stressful interaction between the parent and the child can have a later effect on adjustment, there is probably nothing sacred about toilet training per se. Any stress-filled interaction between parent and child could cause later emotional difficulties.

The only real criterion for determining when to begin toilet training is that the child must be sufficiently maturated for the training to be successful (MacFarlane, Allen, and Honzik 1954). An extensive study with normal children evaluating the effectiveness of various toilet-training techniques gives some indication of the age at which this training should occur (Madsen et al. 1969). Seventy children were divided into four separate age groups: (1) twelve- to fourteen-month-old children, (2) sixteen- to eighteen-month-old children, (3) twenty- to twenty-two-month-old children, and (4) children over twenty-four months old. These children were then randomly assigned to five different training conditions, as follows:

1. **Maturational control group** Mothers were asked to make no attempt at toilet training.
2. **Parents' method control group** Mothers were told to do as they planned to do before they heard of the project.

disorders of biological needs

The atmosphere around toilet training is very important. The child should be taught that all body functions are normal.

3. **Reward group** The mothers were given instructions on how to shape the child to spend time on the potty by using M&M candies or caramels and then to slowly increase the amount of time spent on the potty. In the next phase they were asked to give candy to the children only when they had eliminated successfully. They were instructed never to reprimand the child for accidents or refusals.

4. **Buzzer pants** Mothers were asked to use, sewn into the child's training pants, a transistorized signal package that emitted a low-intensity buzzing sound whenever liquid touched it. The buzzer was the mother's cue to take the child to the bathroom as quickly as possible, remove the pants, put the child on the potty, and disconnect the buzzer.

5. **Reward and buzzer pants** In this group, procedures for both the reward group and the buzzer-pants group were used.

The three treatment groups—the reward group, the buzzer-pants group, and the reward-plus-buzzer-pants group—were significantly more effective in establishing toilet habits than the two control groups, but their results were not significantly different from one another. The buzzer pants did add to the efficiency of the reward technique, although the increase was not statistically significant. The mothers reported general satisfaction with the buzzer pants, since it eliminated the need for scheduling toilet time. Although the study does not specifically answer the question of when a child can best be toilet trained, it does indicate that all three of the older groups performed better than the twelve- to fourteen-month-old group. This result suggests what many child-rearing manuals advocate: A child in the sixteen- to eighteen-month-old range is better prepared than a younger one for toilet training.

Bowel and bladder training differ somewhat in the manner in which they are taught and the rate at which the response can be acquired. Generally, in boys as well as girls bladder training is more easily accomplished with the child sitting down. Bladder control begins somewhat earlier in girls, and while some children can train themselves almost instantly, the process is usually gradual. Waking bladder control appears around two years of age, but sleeping bladder control occurs somewhat later. Nighttime bladder control usually follows daytime control automatically (O'Leary and Wilson 1975). Failure to develop nighttime bladder control is called nocturnal en-

uresis. At early ages stress and novel situations can cause children to revert to bedwetting.

If control of bladder and bowel functions is not acquired after two or three years of life, the conditions are considered clinically significant and are labeled as enuresis and encopresis, respectively.

Encopresis

Encopresis is involuntary defecation after the second year of life that is not due to gross disease of the muscles (Bakwin and Bakwin 1966). At two years of age approximately 50 percent of children have bowel control, whereas by four over 90 percent have control. At eight years of age only 2 to 3 percent of boys and 0.7 percent of girls have not achieved control. Bowel control usually occurs before bladder control and, in contrast to bladder control, nighttime control is typically acquired before daytime control.

Encopresis is rarer than enuresis and is considered more serious, particularly in its effects on children. Soiling is unclean, and the child who soils is frequently referred to as "dirty" or "stinky," epithets that can seriously undermine the self-concept of some children and harm their relationship with their parents. Soiling is likely to elicit an extremely emotional reaction in parents, which occasionally causes them to employ some questionable training techniques. Kanner (1972) gives an example of a mother who whipped her child, rubbed his face in the feces, and then made him wash his clothes. Even this procedure was not successful.

There are two types of encopresis—retentive and nonretentive. In **nonretentive encopresis,** which accounts for only a small percentage of the cases, the child produces a soft, fully formed stool. This condition has often been called *soiling* and can develop from a variety of causes, including lax parental training methods or coercive methods that have led to anxiety surrounding the toilet-training situation. Clinically, the use of coercive methods is always suspected if the child refuses to sit on the toilet or displays highly emotional negative reactions to the toilet situation. In general,

disorders of biological needs

the strategy of treatment for this type of disorder should be either to extinguish the anxiety associated with the toilet situation and to make it rewarding to go to the toilet, or to provide more precise methods of training. Since soiling may be due to a variety of organic problems, including *spina bifida* (a deficit of the spinal canal), perforated anus, inflammation of the spinal cord following an injury to the cord, or some similar disorder, encopretic children should undergo a thorough physical examination to determine whether the problem is organic.

In **retentive encopresis,** the soiling consists primarily of a constant leakage of fecal stain fluid from the rectum. In this case, retention of the stool eventually leads to an accumulation of mucoid material which flows around the fecal mass and gradually leaks out of the rectum (Bakwin and Bakwin 1966). As a result of this retention, the rectum becomes distended by the hard fecal materials that may persist until the normal defecatory reflex extinguishes. This fecal material may become so impacted that medical intervention is required to cause evacuation. Retention over an extended period can lead to an enlarged colon and can be a serious medical problem.

Retentive encopresis is a form of constipation, which may develop in infancy because of painful defecation during which retention becomes a means of pain avoidance. Psychoanalytic theory might stress disturbances during the anal-retentive phase of psychosexual development or disturbances in parent-child relationships as a cause of this problem. Kessler (1966) conjectures that the child retains the feces as personal property in defiance of the parent's wish to take it away. She further states that this reaction is readily linked with unconscious and aggressive wishes toward the parents and is a weapon the child uses. Evidence for this hypothesis is lacking, but there is reason to believe that difficulties in parent-child relationships are often associated with this disorder.

Ross (1974) suggests that the child may have learned only the "hold" part of the chain of responses called the "hold-wait-seek toilet-defecate" sequence. This behav-

ioral explanation is particularly appropriate if there is painful defecation, which would cause avoidance conditioning. In retentive encopresis, medical treatment involving enemas and laxatives appears to be successful in 80 to 90 percent of the cases (Rimm and Somervill 1977). Systematic reinforcement for appropriate toilet training facilitates the acquisition of bowel control in cases in which it is necessary.

Enuresis

Enuresis is defined as frequent, accidental urination after the age most children in our culture have been bladder-trained. Although as many as 20 percent of the children below school age may have occasional wetting accidents, persistent enuresis after the age of three or four can be considered a clinical problem. Most enuretic problems occur in males, perhaps as much as two-thirds of all cases. Typically, enuretics wet only at night (63 percent). Thirty percent wet during both the day and the night; and only seven percent wet only during the day. A major question is whether enuresis is the primary problem or merely a symptom of a more deeply rooted psychological problem. If it is a symptom of deeper psychological problems, one would expect to find that enuretic children have other kinds of psychological problems that persist even if the enuresis is eliminated. If enuresis is the main difficulty, other kinds of problems may still exist, but these problems are either independent of the enuresis or a consequence of it. The evidence seems to indicate that the correlation between other forms of psychopathology and enuresis is small and that most of these children do not have any readily apparent emotional disturbances (Rimm and Somervill 1977). There is no evidence that in those who do have problems that the problems are causally related to enuresis. There is some evidence that enuretic children do have lower self-concepts than normals, but following successful treatment, scores on self-concept measures rise to those of normal controls (Ross 1974).

Retentive encopresis: constant leakage

Most enuretic children do not have other psychological problems

box 11–4
Encopresis in a
6-Year-Old Male

Jerry, a first-grader of average intelligence, was referred to me because, although he had previously been toilet trained and continent, he was now encopretic. Examination revealed that Jerry had suffered an illness four months prior to our meeting which was correlated with the beginning of soiling. During the illness, soiling of his underwear and trousers occurred both at home and at school about twice a day, his parents told me. Their attempts to correct the problem included ignoring it, having Jerry wash his clothing as punishment, spanking Jerry, and finally obtaining medical advice. When medical examination revealed no organic problem, Jerry was referred to me.

Because high anxiety and fear normally accompany encopresis, I first focused on parental response to the soiling in order to reduce fear of punishment. I instructed Jerry's parents to ignore the unpleasant aspects of Jerry's soiling; continue to have him wash his clothes, not as punishment but rather as a means of accepting responsibility for his actions; and follow an instrumental scheduling program under their control. With Jerry and his parents, I agreed upon a verbal contract, the terms of which were as follows: Four times each day (morning, noon, after school, and at bedtime) Jerry was to go to the toilet and try to eliminate. Each ten-minute attempt would be rewarded with a penny; each success would receive a nickel. I placed emphasis on trusting Jerry to report accurately.

During the first week, Jerry had only two accidents, both of which occurred as a result of his forgetting to try to eliminate at noon. I told Jerry I thought he needed a cue to remind him to try to eliminate. With dramatic appropriateness, he pasted a picture of a toilet on his lunchbox! During the second week, Jerry soiled eight times. Examination revealed that in view of the previous week's success, Jerry's father had lessened attention to him and begun to devote it on his other children. Thus, I revised the treatment program so that parental praise would be paired with financial reinforcement. I also gave Jerry colored paper and crayons to make a progress chart. For each day free of soiling, he could paste a star on his chart.

During weeks three and four, Jerry soiled only once. His parents reported that Jerry was proud of his chart. During the fifth week, Jerry had influenza and soiled twice. But weeks six through eight were free of soiling. During this last three-week period, Jerry himself gradually phased out the money and the chart saying, "I don't have to be paid to go to the toilet." I supplemented Jerry's own treatment by counseling his parents in ways to relieve tension and pressure on the children at home and advised them on child-rearing practices in general. At a three-month follow-up, Jerry remained entirely free of soiling.

Plachetta, 1976

---

*Enuretic children show
exceptional arousal
when being awakened
from deep sleep*

*Frequency and urgency
of daytime urination
and bladder capacity
are also factors*

A relationship between sleeping pattern and bladder functioning does seem to exist. Although bedwetting can occur at any stage of sleep, EEG studies indicate that it typically occurs during deep sleep. Although enuretic children seem to have no difficulty in going to sleep and do not seem to be extremely deep sleepers, there is evidence that they show more extreme physiological arousal when being awakened from deep sleep. One of these reactions appears to be larger and more frequent contractions of the bladder.

Relationships also exist between **nocturnal enuresis** and the following factors: frequency of urination during the day, urgency of urination (some children must go to the bathroom immediately), and a small bladder capacity (Werry 1972). However, as Werry has concluded, enuresis appears to be related to a number of other factors, such as social disorganization occurring in broken homes and mother-child separation.

If untreated, all but about 2 percent of enuretic children will cease to have problems by the age of fourteen. The most successful treatment method has been the bell-

disorders of biological needs

box 11-5
Nocturnal Enuresis
in an Adolescent
Male

When fourteen-year-old David was referred to me, he was described as suffering from chronic nocturnal enuresis. Although he had achieved daytime control at an early age, he had always been enuretic at night. Medical examination revealed no organic problems. David's parents had already tried a number of solutions, including psychotherapy, family therapy, and participation in an adolescent socialization group, all without success.

After interviewing David and his parents, I instructed him to record whether he was wet or dry each night. While I gave David full responsibility for the records, I also instructed both him and his parents that the parents were to serve as consultants. The family was given an appointment to return in two months. Data collected during this time served as my baseline information.

During the second visit, I told David that he was to continue to maintain his own records and return to see me once a week. During these weekly visits David received one coupon for each dry night during the week. In addition, David and I kept a chart on my office wall to record his progress. After he had collected fifteen coupons, he could turn them in for five dollars. The coupon requirement was gradually raised from fifteen to twenty and then to thirty-five. At all times David maintained complete control over the records, the chart, and the money.

During the pretreatment period, David averaged one dry night per week. From weeks one through six, the number gradually increased from two to five. Then David went to spend a week with his married sister. During this time, he was completely dry for the first time in his life. Upon his return, his parents lavished much attention on him to maintain the previous week's success, but in spite of the attention, he wet every night. During weeks nine through thirteen, the number of dry nights gradually increased to seven. From weeks thirteen through twenty, the number alternated between six and seven.

At week twenty, the token program was interrupted by my vacation. Upon my return (week twenty-three) the visits were resumed but not the tokens. David's parents were encouraged to increase verbal reinforcement at home, and David still maintained his chart. From week twenty-four to twenty-eight (the end of treatment) David was completely dry at night. A six-month follow-up revealed that David remained free of nocturnal enuresis.

Popler, 1976

and-pad technique, which is based on the assumption that the child has not learned to respond by waking to internal cues associated with bladder pressure. Thus, the desired response—waking up—is conditioned to bladder pressure cues. To condition the response, a loud buzzer is connected to a pad on which the child sleeps. Bladder pressure (CS) precedes urination, which dampens the sheet, activates the buzzer (UCS), and awakens the child (UCR). After a number of trials the child should wake up (CR) to the bladder pressure preceding urination (Mowrer and Mowrer 1938). This technique has been effective in 90 percent of the cases, but relapse, perhaps as much as 35 percent, has been a problem (Lovibond and Coote 1970).

A number of drugs have been used in an attempt to control enuresis, but in general the effects have been disappointing (Lovibond and Coote 1970). The most promising drug seems to be the antidepressant imipramine (Tofranil). This drug seems to be fairly effective, but the withdrawal of medication is usually followed by a return to earlier levels of wetting. However, a study by Poussant and Ditman (1965) in which a high dosage of imipramine was used and then followed by a slow withdrawal has suggested that imipramine may be much more effective than placebo.

Another technique used by Muellner (1960), who believed that limited bladder capacity was the major cause of enuresis, is **diurnal bladder training.** This technique, which requires the bedwetter to practice retaining the urine during the day after drinking large quantities of fluid, has had some success.

disorders of biological needs: basic processes

A more recent procedure, based on operant conditioning, is the **dry-bed procedure**, which requires one night of intensive training followed by the use of a urine alarm or the **bell-and-pad procedure** for about a week (Azrin, Sneed, and Foxx 1973). The major features of this intensive training procedure are:

1. A large fluid intake to increase the desire to urinate
2. Hourly awakenings
3. Teaching the child to awake to mild prompts
4. Practice in going to the toilet
5. Reinforcement for urinating in the toilet at home
6. Use of a urine-alarm apparatus to signal bedwetting

7. Training for the awareness of dry versus wet conditions in the bed

Azrin, Sneed, and Foxx (1974) found that the dry-bed procedure was significantly superior to the bell-and-pad method in twenty-four children with an average age of eight who had been wetting the bed every night since infancy. Furthermore, a major advantage was that after a six-month follow-up no relapses had occurred. Thus, at present, the dry-bed procedure seems to be the most promising technique in treating enuresis.

Disorders of Sleep

We spend approximately one-third of our lives asleep. For most of us, sleeping is both restful and pleasant. We awake, our bodies refreshed. However, for millions of individuals whose sleep is disturbed, sleep may be anxiety provoking and represent a serious problem in their lives. If individuals are under stress, they may have difficulty dropping off to sleep and trouble maintaining normal sleep patterns during sleep. Or, if deprived of sleep, they may feel groggy and drowsy and have difficulty concentrating.

Essentially, four stages of sleep have been identified, as shown in Figure 11–6 (Dement 1965). As a person lies quietly with eyes closed, EEG records show low voltage (about 50 microvolts), mixed-frequency brain waves accompanied by the alpha pattern (about 10H.). When the individual enters stage 1 sleep, usually after one to seven minutes, alpha disappears, the muscles begin to relax, and the EEG is characterized solely by low voltage mixed-frequency waves. In this stage, sensory perception ceases, and the eyes begin to roll slowly from side to side. Stage 2 is distinguished by the appearance of sleep spindles (bursts of 12 to 14 H. waves) and K-complexes on the EEG. In stage 3, moderate random delta (1 to 2 H. waves) occur with some superimposed spindling, while in stage 4 delta waves increase in amplitude or voltage with no spindling. Because they involve the largest and slowest wave form, these last two stages are called **slow-wave sleep.** As the sleeper passes from stage to stage, heart rate, respiration rate, body temperature, and muscle tone decrease, while the number of GSRs increases. The deeper the sleep, the more difficult it is to awaken the individual, and when aroused the individual seldom recalls imagery or thoughts. Any material recalled during slow-wave sleep is usually quite vague and does not incorporate recently presented external stimuli. Approximately 50 percent of adult sleep time is spent in stage 2, and about 5, 7, and 16 percent are spent in stages 1, 3, and 4, respectively (Johnson 1973). If there has been physical exertion during the day, a higher proportion of slow-wave sleep occurs (Baekeland and Laskey 1966).

Aserinsky and Kleitman (1953) discovered a second sleep phenomenon—**rapid eye movement, (REM)**. The interesting aspect of REM sleep is that the EEG resembles either an awake or a stage 1 record. However, the skeletal muscles have almost no tone, spontaneous GSR and spinal reflexes disappear, heart rate and respiration become regular, twitches appear in many muscles, and penile erection in males is common. During REM sleep, oxygen use in the brain becomes very high, and the pituitary gland is activated. In humans a sawtooth wave appears just before the onset of REM and continues throughout the REM period. In other words, even though the EEG indicates light sleep, relaxation is complete, reflexes are lost, and the individ-

disorders of biological needs

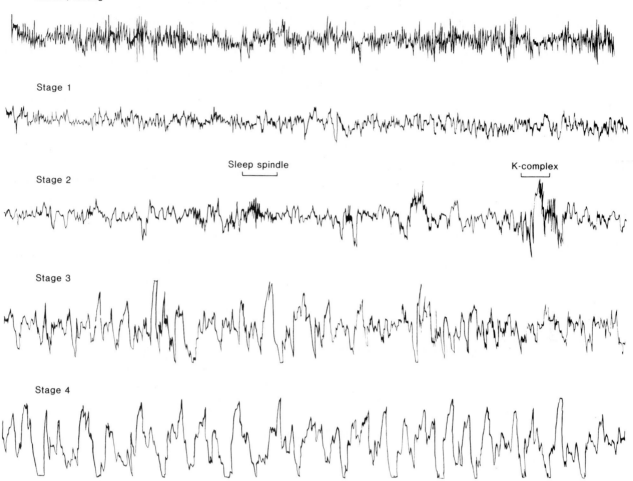

Awake, resting

Stage 1

Sleep spindle | K-complex

Stage 2

Stage 3

Stage 4

Figure 11–6 EEG activity during resting state and during four stages of sleep.

ual is very difficult to awaken, all indications that REM is a very deep sleep. For this reason, the REM stage is also known as **paradoxical sleep.** Adults spend about 25 percent of their sleeping time in REM sleep every night. Most drugs, including sleeping pills, decrease REM sleep and may block it out entirely (Kales and Kales 1973).

Typically, in adults there are four to six nonREM-REM (NREM-REM) cycles during the night, each cycle averaging about 90 minutes, with the first REM period occurring about one and one-half hours after the individual falls asleep (Borkovec, Slama, and Grayson 1977). Infants average about sixteen to eighteen hours of sleep; this amount decreases to the seven or eight hours in the normal adult, but may increase again in old age. In addition, the soundness

or depth of sleep decreases throughout life. Infants experience a much higher proportion of REM sleep. In fact, slow wave sleep is not fully present in the infant until about three months; then it remains at a fairly constant level until the age of thirty and then begins to decrease to such an extent that many older people show no stage 3 or 4 sleep at all (Feinberg, Korosko, and Heller 1967).

If an individual is deprived of sleep, both behavioral and physiological changes occur. The individual may feel fatigued, irritable, or even persecuted; he or she may be unable to concentrate, become disoriented, and if deprivation is severe, experience visual and tactile hallucinations. Physiological changes include drooping eyelids, mild eye muscle dysfunction after three days, and after seven to eight days

Adults usually have 4 to 6 NREM-REM cycles during the night

Sleep deprivation produces behavioral and physiological changes

disorders of biological needs: basic processes

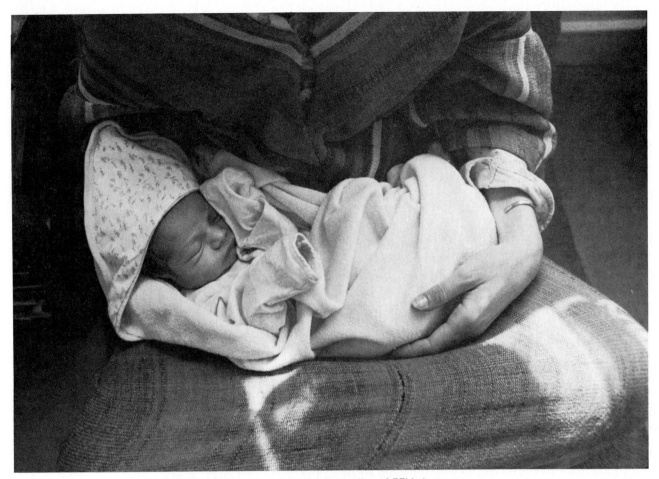

Infants experience a much higher proportion of REM sleep.

slurring of speech, mild tremors, and EEG changes indicating an increase in discharges associated with convulsive seizures. After being subjected to a long period of sleep deprivation, individuals display a tremendous increase in stage 4 and REM sleep (Berg and Osward 1962). The first night shows largely a stage 4 rebound, but this activity is normal thereafter. The next two or three nights show large proportions of REM sleep. Interestingly enough, if the individual is deprived only of REM sleep by being awakened during that stage of sleep, the characteristic rebound effect occurs even if the amount of sleep is sufficient (Agnew, Webb, and Williams 1967).

Sleep may involve physical restoration

Although the need for sleep varies widely across individuals in different environmental conditions, it appears to be a complex function of several variables, including (1) genetic-constitutional factors; (2) early experiences, especially parental attitudes and behavior controls; (3) physiological differences, such as nutrition, endocrine functions, and blood system factors; and (4) psychological and physical stress (Webb 1969). Although it is rather obvious that sleeping involves a physiological restoration process, the exact function of sleep is still a mystery. Jouvet (1969) has suggested that NREM sleep allows some form of physical restoration process to occur as well as being a preparatory stage for the occurrence of REM sleep. It might be assumed, particularly from the high incidence of REM sleep in premature and newborn infants, that REM sleep provides stimulation necessary for the development of certain cortical functions.

Most dreaming occurs during REM sleep. If individuals are awakened from REM sleep, they usually report that they were experiencing vivid dreams. Freud

310   disorders of biological needs

(1950) presumed dreams to be the guardians of sleep—outside stimuli are incorporated into a dream story and thus prevented from awakening the sleeper. However, in view of EEG research, recent opinion tends to regard Freud's theory as erroneous (Borkovec, Slama, and Grayson 1977). As previously mentioned, Freud also thought that dreams served the purpose of allowing repressed psychic material to be expressed in disguised and acceptable symbolic form—hence the emphasis on dream analysis in psychoanalytic theory.

A number of psychological and physiological disorders can cause disturbances of sleep. Some disorders, such as depression, mania, and anxiety, are rather consistently associated with disturbances in sleep patterns. However, sleep disturbances are secondary to the basic disorder. For example, in depression the relationship between sleep disorders and alteration in mood is almost always present. In these cases, assessment and modification focus on the primary disorder, and sleep disturbances are of secondary interest. In primary sleep disorders, other complaints either are not present or are a consequence of the sleep disturbances. It is these disorders that we shall discuss in the remaining sections of this chapter.

Pseudoinsomnia

Verbal reports are rarely sufficient for diagnosis of sleep disturbances (Mitler et al. 1975). Many individuals complain of difficulty in getting to sleep, fatigue during the day, loss of sleep, waking up several times during the night, and early awakening. However, when these individuals are observed in a sleep clinic, their sleep records often do not confirm their subjective reports (Mitler et al. 1975). In other words, the individual's belief about the sleep pattern and the actual pattern may be quite different, a phenomenon that is a consistent problem in the use of verbal report as an assessment technique. This discrepancy may be due to any number of problems, including a phobia of insomnia. A letter to the sleep clinic at Stanford University School of Medicine is a good example of this problem:

Dear Sleep Clinic:

Now that I know that I get a normal amount of sleep, I don't fret and worry about sleeping. I seem to awaken less frequently during the night. It is a relief not to use sleeping tablets anymore, as they make me dopey and depressed. I find that nowadays I am not particularly depressed. . . .(Mitler et al. 1975, pp. 45–46)

This individual recovered after being confronted with the fact of his **pseudoinsomnia.** The real danger in this and other sleep disorders is that the victim may resort to tranquilizers or barbiturates, which may aggravate the problem by causing the more lasting medical problem of drug-related insomnia, which we shall discuss in the next section.

Insomnia

Insomnia is the most common sleep disturbance and may occur in as much as 10 percent of the normal population, although as many as half of the adults who complain of insomnia show a normal sleep record as measured by the polygraph (Schwartz, Guilbaud, and Fishgood 1963). Insomnia is an inability to get to sleep in a short period of time, frequent awakenings, an inability to go back to sleep after nighttime or early morning awakenings, and short sleep cycles. A commonly used research criterion is less than six hours of sleep per night and drowsiness during the daytime, indicating a need for sleep.

A major problem with insomnia is that many physicians tend to rely on tranquilizers or barbiturates to deal with the problem. This approach starts a vicious cycle of chemical dependency in which the individual builds up a tolerance to sleeping pills so that even large doses do not give normal sleep. This problem tends to occur with all the sleep-inducing drugs prescribed by most doctors for insomnia, with the possible exception of Dalmane (Kales and Kales 1973). Although the occasional use of a pill to get sleep at difficult times is probably harmless, the automatic bedtime sedative, if used regularly, may cause dependency on the drug for sleep and aggravate the insomnia it is intended to cure. Unfortunately,

Dreaming occurs in REM sleep

Some people believe erroneously that they suffer from insomnia

Less than six hours sleep per night, and daytime drowsiness

Drug-dependent insomnia is the most serious type

most of these drugs eliminate or interfere with REM and stage 4 sleep, which is the type of sleep most required for restoration processes. Consequently, the individual becomes more dependent on the drug. If withdrawal from the pills is abrupt, the result may be vivid nightmares caused by REM rebound. As a result, drug-dependent insomnia is recognized by most sleep researchers as the most serious of all types of insomnia. At best, withdrawal must be very gradual—in some cases as long as eighteen months (Mitler et al. 1975).

Because of the numerous problems associated with drug therapy for insomnia, much attention has been focused on psychological methods of modifying sleep disturbances. Two major, fairly effective techniques have been developed: relaxation training and stimulus-control procedures. Relaxation training, as used by Borkovec and his colleagues, is a variation of progressive muscular relaxation, in which the individual is taught to reduce heightened physiological activity and to focus attention on pleasant, monotonous internal sensations, thus precluding intrusive and sleep-preventing thoughts (Borkovec, Kaloupek, and Slama 1975). This technique allows for the reduction of sleep-onset time and may enhance the depth of sleep.

Stimulus-control procedures are based on the assumption that sleep is a conditioned behavior that occurs if the sleeping quarters are associated with behavior compatible with sleep (Bootzin 1973). If behaviors occurring in sleeping quarters are incompatible with sleep, insomnia results. Therefore, the individual is instructed to observe a regular sleep schedule, such as retiring and awaking at the same time each day and avoiding daytime naps and bed behavior that is incompatible with sleep; such as watching television, eating, or studying. Occasionally, individuals are also instructed to leave the bedroom within ten minutes after retiring if they are unable to fall asleep and to return only when drowsy. This program guarantees that only sleep-compatible behaviors are occurring and assures rapid sleep onset. Although these techniques appear to be highly effective

with primary insomnia, additional evaluation is needed. Where the sleep disturbances are secondary to other problems, it is often necessary to treat the primary problem, such as depression, but this procedure may also be combined with treatment for insomnia.

Narcolepsy

Narcolepsy is profound difficulty in staying awake, with consistent daytime attacks of irresistible drowsiness and fatigue while at work, driving, making love, or engaging in other activities. Individuals with this problem may doze off in the midst of a conversation, but narcolepsy is most likely to occur during boring, monotonous, and unstimulating activities (Yoss and Daly 1960). Three major symptoms occur with narcolepsy:

1. **Cataplexy,** which is a complete loss of muscle tone, often occurring when the individual gets excited or angry
2. **Hypnagogic hallucinations,** which are often like vivid and terrifying nightmares
3. **Sleep paralysis,** an inability to move while conscious at the beginning or ending of a sleep period

The incidence of narcolepsy in the population is generally believed to be under 1 percent, and some researchers claim it is primarily a male disorder (Kanner 1972; Sours 1963).

Studies of the sleep sequence with a polygraph have given some insight into the cause of this disorder. Individuals with narcolepsy seem to enter immediately into full-blown REM sleep, as opposed to normals who require approximately ninety minutes to do so. Consequently, while there is consciousness, there is also a tremendous decrease in control of motor activity, resulting in the loss of motor movement. The hallucinations are probably REM dreams. Sleep paralysis is characteristic of REM sleep, during which the central nervous system blocks the transmission of motor impulses, and occurs in all of us occasionally when we wake up and find that our arms, legs, or trunks are partially to totally paralyzed.

disorders of biological needs

Narcolepsy was once viewed as a neurotic or psychotic process, but most clinicians and researchers now view it as being due to an injury or some abnormality of the brain's REM sleep system. This disorder typically appears in late adolescence, and though it may remit occasionally, it never entirely disappears. At present the disorder is assumed to be incurable (Borkovec, Slama, and Grayson 1977), but methylphenidate hydrochloride (Ritalin), a stimulant, does decrease the frequency of the attacks. Tricyclic antidepressants are often effective in controlling the catalepsy and hallucinations (Mitler et al. 1975).

Hypersomnia

Hypersomnia is extreme sleepiness that may last several days and is rather common in teenagers. When the disorder is chronic, individuals tend to have marked confusion on awakening, absence of REM periods, and occasionally narcoleptic symptoms (Rechtschaffen and Dement 1969). One form of this disorder, called *Kleine-Levin syndrome,* occurs in young men and consists of episodes of excessive sleeping lasting several days and involving eighteen to twenty hours of sleep per day. This sleep pattern is associated with tremendous hunger, overeating, and occasionally hypersexuality. Sleep seems normal in every respect except duration. Mitler et al. (1975) found a similar sleep problem among psychologically normal female adolescents, usually just before the onset of an irregular menstrual cycle. When menstruation became regular, either spontaneously or by the use of hormonal supplements, the daytime somnolence tended to disappear. Controversy exists over whether this disorder in males is associated with other psychological abnormalities. Gallinek (1967) reports psychological symptoms, such as decreased sensory awareness, amnesia episodes, and the classic depressive syndrome; Mitler et al. (1975) report that the disorder occurs mainly in young men who are schizoid; and Fresco (1971) claims that these cases present no psychological abnormalities. At present the disorder is assumed to be biologically caused and there is no consistent modification procedure.

Sleep Apnea

An apnea is an inability to breathe. **Sleep apnea** is breath stoppage during sleep, which occurs in about one out of every twenty individuals who have sleep disturbances. These individuals may complain of too little sleep or too much, but the consistent finding is that the body's automatic control of breathing breaks down in the shift from wakefulness to sleep (Mitler et al. 1975). Apparently, patients stop breathing as soon as they fall asleep because their diaphragms and the respiration muscles between their ribs become immobilized. Relaxation of the throat muscles also occurs, cutting off the flow of air, decreasing the amount of oxygen in the blood, and upsetting the normal pH balance. This imbalance causes the brain to wake up and the respiration muscles to begin functioning again, although the lungs may not be filled because the throat has collapsed. Victims then struggle further until tone returns to the throat muscles, gulp for air, snore loudly, and then return to sleep. Many extremely loud snorers suffer from this disturbance.

Sleep apneas can lead to chronic high blood pressure and may predispose the victim to cardiovascular crises. There are drugs that may slightly improve the symptoms, but most hypnotic drugs aggravate the basic ailment because they retard respiratory activity and may, if taken in large doses, increase the risk of the victim's death. One treatment is tracheotomy, in which the upper airway just below the larynx is opened and a breathing tube is inserted. This tube can be closed during the daytime and the individual can breathe normally. Mitler et al. (1975) suggest that this procedure may be quite useful with these disorders.

Nightmares and Night Terror

Nightmares are vivid, horrifying dreams that take place during REM sleep (Jacobson, Kales, and Kales 1969). These dreams occur most often in children but may continue to torment an individual throughout

Extreme sleepiness

Loss of automatic breathing control during transition from wakefulness to sleep

Children's nightmares can be very frightening experiences.

adult life. The reasons for nightmares are not clear, although it has been suggested that they may result from fairly normal childhood fears (Kessler 1966), poor home environments, or emotional stress (Bakwin and Bakwin 1972). It is known that extremely stressful experiences, such as combat conditions, can cause nightmares.

In a similar fashion, **night terror** can also occur in both children and adults. In night terror, apparent arousal during sleep is accompanied by expressions of intense fear and emotion (Kales and Kales 1970). Individuals often wake screaming, but have no recall of the experience other than a feeling of intense fear. Lack of recall is a major factor in distinguishing night terror from nightmares.

Drugs that eliminate REM sleep can be used with these disorders, but there is also a possibility that the disorders may be intensified when the drug is withdrawn because of the REM rebound effect. Behavioral treatment, particularly with nightmares, appears to be promising.

Lack of recall distinguishes night terrors from nightmares

disorders of biological needs

Sleepwalking

DSM II views **sleepwalking,** or somnambulism, as a conversion reaction, dissociative type. However, this disorder is more accurately described as a sleep disturbance, and it is so labeled in DSM III. Sleepwalking folklore abounds. For example, it is believed that a full moon can cause sleepwalking and that a woman ceases sleepwalking once she has conceived her first child. It is also believed that sleepwalkers can perform amazing feats, such as walking tightropes, climbing walls, and similar unusual acts.

Typically, sleepwalking takes place in the early hours of sleep and occurs with open eyes, a bland expression, and an unsteady gait. The sleepwalker's movements are rigid and generally appear quite purposeless, although the person may avoid obstacles. Sleepwalkers seldom awaken of their own accord and generally return to bed or lie down in some other place. Sleepwalking probably occurs in most children some time in their lives. Contrary to popular belief, sleepwalkers can harm themselves during these episodes.

Sleep researchers have found that sleepwalkers show more slow-wave activity throughout the night, as well as more body movement. These individuals are typically deep sleepers or difficult to arouse, regardless of the sleep stage. Standing an individual up during sleep may induce sleepwalking if the individual is in stage 3 or 4 (Mitler et al. 1975). Nonsleepwalkers, however, are not affected by the process. Psychoanalysts believed at one time that sleepwalking was caused by childhood sexual experiences, but later investigations indicated that it is probably the motor enactment of a dream. No differential frequency of its occurrence appears between normals or neurotics; and sleepwalking is less frequent in psychotics than in normals (Winokur, Guze, and Pfeiffer 1959). Drugs that suppress stage 4 sleep have been found effective in reducing sleepwalking, although at present most authorities discourage the use of drugs, and few recommend psychotherapy. Generally, it is recommended that sleepwalkers be locked in their rooms and dangerous objects

be removed at night. In treating a young sleepwalker, a strain gauge was attached from his mattress to the floor. When the individual got off the bed, the decrease in weight on the mattress activated a loud bell and awoke the child. After a few nights, awakening was conditioned to the movement of arising from the bed.

Sleepwalkers are typically deep sleepers

Other Sleep Disorders

Sleeptalking, or **somniloquy,** is the utterance of speech or other meaningful sounds during sleep without the subject's awareness of the event (Arkin 1966). Although the phenomenon is especially common in childhood, almost everyone occasionally talks during sleep. Arkin found that sleeptalking occurred in as many as 40 percent of college students. Typically, the speech is unclear and garbled, and the lighter the sleep the better the articulation. In general, the content tends to be concerned with the previous day's experience, and communication with the sleeptalker is occasionally possible to a degree. It is doubtful that deep dark secrets are revealed in this way. Most of the EEG studies show that the most sleeptalk occurs during stage 2, although about 33 percent appears in stage 4 and 7 percent in REM sleep (Rechtschaffen, Goodenough, and Shapiro 1962). In the Rechtschaffen experiment, rather than revealing embarrassing personal secrets, most of the sleeptalk related to the experiment itself, again an indication of the importance of environmental stimuli in instigating this activity. When subjects are awakened immediately after sleeptalk, about three-fourths of them have some recall, although it is rather vague. Most authorities agree that sleeptalk is a fairly normal phenomenon.

Sleeptalkers may sometimes be engaged in conversation

Bruxism, the inappropriate grinding or clenching of teeth typically occurs during sleep. This disorder occurs in about 15 to 20 percent of children and decreases with age. Apparently associated with tension and stress, bruxism is a problem because it can cause a variety of dental problems, facial pain, muscle sensitivity, and headache

Bruxism seems to be a response to stress

box 11–6

Sleepwalking in a
24-Year-Old Male

Bill had walked in his sleep for nine years, he told me when we got married. I really didn't mind until one night he took down the shotgun and prepared to fire at imaginary burglars. Luckily, my screaming woke him before he fired. I was so scared I insisted he see someone about his problem the very next day.

While the doctor was talking to Bill, Bill casually remarked that ever since high school, he had suffered a whole lot from being nervous right before a test. He'd tried tranquilizers, but they didn't help very much. Now he was beginning to get real nervous because his bar exam was coming up in a month. The doctor said he thought that there might be some relationship between the gun incident and the worry over the test, so he decided to work on Bill's nervousness as well as his sleepwalking.

At the office, Bill and the doctor made up a list of scenes that made Bill nervous when he thought about them, like "hearing about a friend who has a test," "trying to study several days before a test," and "receiving the test paper and looking it over." That was the scariest. At home, we moved our beds together so Bill would have to crawl over me to get out of his bed. Then I bought a loud whistle. The doctor told me to blow it as hard as I could every time Bill started to walk in his sleep. I also had to write down how many times Bill walked and how long it took him to hear the whistle.

During the first week, Bill walked four times, but he'd wake immediately when I blew the whistle. The second week, he walked five times, and the third week, he walked twice. After the fourth week, he didn't walk anymore. He was finding studying easier too. The first week he didn't do much better, but after that he found it easier and easier. The doctor was seeing him twice a week to help him get ready for the bar exam. By the time the exam came up, he was ready for it and passed with a better score than he had hoped for.

The doctor checked with us again in three months to see how Bill was doing. We were happy to report that he had walked in his sleep only twice in that time and that he was having no trouble concentrating on his work.

Meyer, 1975

(Glaros and Rao 1977). It tends to occur during stage 2 sleep and is associated with body movement that does not awaken the sleeper. Most researchers tend to agree that bruxism occurs in individuals who are under a significant amount of stress, both from situational conditions and from interpersonal sources. Apparently this disorder occurs when there is a shift from deep sleep to light sleep during which teethgrinding is triggered by internal or external, physical or emotional sleep-disturbing stimuli. Thus, it appears that bruxism is an arousal disorder and that teethgrinding can be experimentally induced by using arousal stimuli (Glaros and Rao 1977).

In general, treatment of bruxism must be aimed both toward correcting factors that lead to bruxism and toward attempting to prevent further damage to the teeth and the supporting tissue. Occlusal adjustments have been used and appear to be successful in eliminating bruxism in some patients. A number of behavioral techniques have also been used. These include classical or avoidance conditioning programs—similar to the Mowrer and Mowrer technique for the treatment of enuresis—in which grinding sounds cause the occurrence of a sound blast and thus condition awakening; tension reduction techniques such as muscular relaxation; and biofeedback. The effectiveness of these techniques has not been determined, but they appear promising.

A similar disorder is **nocturnal head-banging**, which involves a rhythmic rolling of the head from side to side on the pillow while going to sleep or during stage 4 sleep. This disorder is quite rare and occurs largely in young children. Presumably, this

disorders of biological needs

unusual activity may be the result of three factors: (1) positive reinforcement after awakening, (2) the reinforcing values of the rhythmic activity itself, or (3) escape behavior in the form of awakening from a nightmare or other unpleasant mental activity (Ross, Meichenbaum, and Humphrey 1971). This type of disorder has received little attention in the literature, and the treatment methods consist largely of ignoring the behavior and desensitization for repetitive dream content (Ross, Meichenbaum, and Humphrey 1971).

Summary

Primary motives, such as hunger and thirst, arise from unlearned physiological needs, while secondary motives, such as anxiety and jealousy, arise from learned needs. The degree to which socialization influences the primary needs depends on the variety and number of environmental stimuli that will satisfy the need, and also on the maximum possible duration of the deprivation cycle.

Feeding disturbances include obesity, anorexia nervosa, pica, and colic. Obesity can be defined as body weight that is greater than 20 percent above standard weight as given in height and weight charts. Obese individuals eat only slightly more than normal individuals. They eat fewer meals per day, but eat more per meal, and eat more rapidly than individuals with normal weight. They are also less active. Only two factors seem to be consistently related to obesity: overeating and body image. Although some evidence suggests that obesity is related to genetic factors, eating patterns established in infancy and childhood are also important in its development. Apparently, scarcity of food supplies and irregularity of eating lead to a tendency to overeat. In obese individuals, eating behavior is relatively unrelated to internal hunger cues but strongly influenced by external cues. A number of weight-loss programs have been developed, but the loss is not usually maintained. Dieting, fasting, drug therapy, and surgical techniques have all been used, but these procedures are either ineffective or, in some cases, dangerous. Hypnosis, individual psychotherapy, group psychotherapy, and national organizations such as Weight Watchers have also had limited success. The most effective procedure for treating obesity seems to be behavior modification.

Undereating is also a problem in our culture. Anorexia nervosa and chronic rumination in children are severe disorders leading to a significant number of fatalities. Like obese persons, individuals with these disorders seem to be responding to external rather than internal hunger cues. Eating behavior acquires noxious properties that results in food refusal and excessive weight loss. A variety of medical and psychological treatment methods have been only partially successful with these disorders. Two other eating problems, pica and colic, also appear to be associated with psychological factors.

Our society's intense concern with bladder and bowel training has resulted in swings from very strict early toilet training to very permissive toilet training, depending on current theoretical beliefs. Both the age at which toilet training is initiated and the precision of training appear to be important in acquiring toilet habits. Bladder control, which appears earlier in girls, is somewhat gradual, and waking bladder control appears before sleeping bladder control. Enuresis is defined as frequent accidental urination after the age at which most children in our culture have been bladder-trained. It appears to be related to a number of stress factors. If untreated, all but about 2 percent of enuretic children will cease to be problems by the age of fourteen. Encopresis, or involuntary defecation, is significant only if it persists beyond the age of four. There are two types of encopresis: retentive and nonretentive. A number of behavioral techniques have been quite successful with encopresis and enuresis, including the bell-and-pad method, diurnal bladder training, and the dry bed procedure.

Although the exact function of sleep is something of a mystery, it is necessary for all individuals. Sleep occurs in four major stages: stage 1, during which alpha waves disappear, the muscles begin to relax, and the EEG is characterized by a low voltage, mixed-frequency waves; stage 2, which is distinguished by the appearance of sleep spindles and K-complexes; stage 3, during which moderate random delta waves occur with some superimposed spindling; and stage 4, in which delta waves increase in amplitude with no spindling. Stage 4 is called "slow wave sleep." In addition to the four stages of sleep, there is a second type of sleep characterized by rapid movement of the eyes and resembling either an awake or stage 1 record. This type of sleep is called REM (rapid eye movement) sleep. In REM sleep the skeletal muscles have almost no tone, spontaneous GSR and spinal reflexes disappear, heart rate and respiration become regular, twitches appear in many muscles, and penile erection in males is common. Even though EEG records indicate light sleep, relaxation is complete, and reflexes are lost in REM sleep. For this reason REM sleep is called paradoxical sleep.

Although disturbance of sleep can be a function of other disorders, there are primary sleep disorders. Pseudoinsomnia occurs when individuals believe they have a sleep disorder, but their sleep records do not confirm their beliefs. This discrepancy between subjective belief and actual sleep behavior can be due to a number of problems. Insomnia is the most common of all sleep disorders and may be aggravated by reliance on tranquilizers or barbiturates to produce sleep. Stimulus control procedures and progressive muscular relaxation are highly effective with this disorder. Narcolepsy is difficulty in staying awake, with persistent daytime attacks of irresistible drowsiness and fatigue while at work, driving, making love, or engaging in other activities. This disturbance is related to disorders of REM sleep. Hypersomnia is extreme sleepiness, which may produce sleep that lasts for several days. Sleep apnea, nightmares, night terror, sleepwalking, sleeptalking, and bruxism (teeth grinding) are other sleep disorders.

Key Concepts

adipocytes

anorexia nervosa

bell-and-pad procedure

bruxism

buzzer pants

cataplexy

chronic rumination

colic

diurnal bladder training

dry-bed procedure

encopresis

enuresis

homeostatic mechanisms

hypersomnia

hypnagogic hallucinations

insomnia

intestinal bypass surgery

motivation

narcolepsy

needs and drives

nightmares

night terror

nocturnal enuresis

nocturnal headbanging

nonretentive encopresis

paradoxical sleep

pica

primary motives

pseudoinsomnia

rapid eye movement (REM) sleep

retentive encopresis

secondary (acquired) motives

sleep apnea

sleepwalking

slow-wave sleep

somniloquy

stimulus-bound theory of obesity

ventromedial hypothalamus (VMH)

Review Questions

1. How do primary motives differ from secondary motives?

2. What effect does food scarcity appear to have on obesity?

3. What role do external cues play in obesity?

4. What are the four components of Stuart's behavior modification program for obese individuals?

5. What is anorexia nervosa?

6. What is the strategy of treatment for encopresis?

7. What is the bell-and-pad method of treating enuresis? What is the dry-bed method?

8. What are the effects of sleep deprivation?

9. Describe each of the following:
   a. Pseudoinsomnia
   b. Insomnia
   c. Narcolepsy
   d. Hypersomnia
   e. Sleep apnea
   f. Night terror

disorders of biological needs

disorders of biological needs
sexual behavior

12

Key Topics

Four stages of the human sexual
response

Sexual arousal and the wide range
of stimuli

Sexual preference and sexual
behavior

Acquisition of sexual orientation and
gender identification

Importance of heterosocial and
heterosexual skills

Acquisition of sexual dysfunctions

Four major types of sexual
dysfunctions in males

Three major types of sexual
dysfunction in females

Sensate focus and the modification
of sexual dysfunctions

Transvestism, transsexualism,
fetishism, exhibitionism,
voyeurism, pedophilia, sadism,
masochism, and incest

Counseling for rape victims

Support for one of our main themes in this book—that behavior labeled abnormal cannot be understood without also understanding the vast heterogeneity and variability of behavior labeled normal—is especially abundant in the study of sexual behavior. Sexual behavior is incredibly diverse, and what constitutes sexual behavior labeled normal is influenced by a great many variables, including physiology, biochemistry, social class, culture, religion, and laws. Although the role of the sex drive in human behavior has probably been exaggerated, we can have little doubt that restrictive religious beliefs, prohibitive customs, and legal sanctions against a great variety of sexual behaviors are factors in an amazing number of sexual disorders in our society.

X   X = XX

X   Y = XY

Sexual differentiation is complete three months after conception

To understand the disorders that affect sexual behavior, it is necessary to understand the normal processes of sexual development, sexual identification, and sexual arousal. We shall therefore begin with a summary of those processes.

Sexual Differentiation and Sexual Development

Socialization is the major factor in gender identity, sexual orientation, and other sex-linked behavior

Sexual differentiation begins at conception: if the egg, which contains an X-chromosome, is fertilized by a sperm cell that also carries an X-chromosome, the embryo's genetic sex will be female (XX); if it is fertilized by a sperm cell that carries a Y-chromosome, the embryo's genetic sex will be male (XY). These events initiate but do not entirely determine sexual morphology. Except for the gonads, the male and female sexual structures of the fetus depend for their development on the presence or absence of testicular hormones. Under the influence of the sexual hormones, the gonads begin to function early in the prenatal period and produce male hormones (**androgens**). In males, these hormones circulating in the blood stream at critical times sensitize target tissues. The effect on the internal duct system is to develop the vas deferens and the seminal vesicles and to suppress differentiation of the uterus and fallopian tubes. Slightly later, the external morphology becomes a penis and scrotum rather than a clitoris and labia majora and vagina.

Similarity of male and female sexual responses

If, on the other hand, the gonads become ovaries, only small amounts of hormones are released during fetal life, resulting in the absence of the testicular hormones and consequent development of the female anatomy. This process is relatively complete by the third month of prenatal life. These developments continue until pubescence, when following the sudden increase of sex hormones, the individual develops secondary sex characteristics and sexual differentiation becomes more pronounced.

Even though genetic factors and hormone production largely determine the sexual morphology of males and females, gender identity, sexual orientation, and other sex-linked aspects of behavior are very greatly influenced by environmental factors and the socialization process. The tremendous impact of these factors often overrides the genetic and morphological influences. For example, an individual who is morphologically and genetically a male may identify himself with and exhibit the characteristics of females, or vice versa. No other biological drive is as heavily influenced by the socialization process.

We shall examine four major components of sexual behavior: *sexual arousal, gender identification, heterosocial skills*, and *heterosexual skills* (Barlow 1974).

Sexual Arousal

Sexual arousal consists of a variety of physiological and psychological states varying in intensity from mild excitement to orgasm. Masters and Johnson (1966), who first clearly described the human sexual response, found the responses of men and women surprisingly similar. The response cycle appears to have four stages (see Figure 12–1). In the **excitement stage** the sexual response is initiated by whatever is sexually stimulating to the individual. As we suggested earlier, learning plays a big part in arousal, and the stimulus could be as direct as fondling of the genital area or as indirect as the sight of a woman's shoe.

If stimulation is allowed to continue, sexual tension increases to the **plateau stage**. If stimulation is uninterrupted and

disorders of biological needs

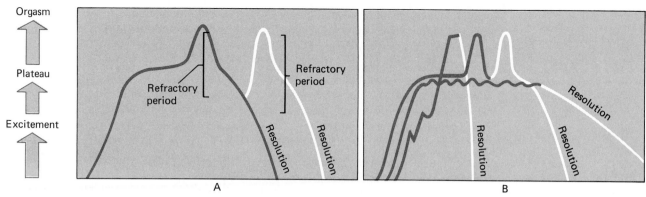

Figure 12-1 *A* (male) and *B* (female) sexual response cycles. The colored lines indicate the most common patterns of response; the white lines indicate variations.

continues to be effective, the plateau stage is followed by the **orgasm stage,** a totally involuntary and sudden discharge of tension that occurs when stimulation reaches maximum intensity. The orgasm stage is followed by the **resolution stage,** a gradual decrease of remaining sexual tension to the unstimulated state. Some women are capable of having multiple orgasms if sufficient stimulation is continued during this stage, but for all but a few men restimulation is impossible; this is called a **refractory** period.

In both sexes the basic body responses to sexual stimulation are **myotonia** (increased muscular tension in the genital area) and **vasocongestion** (engorgement of tissues in the genitals and surrounding areas with blood, producing penile erection in the male and clitoral erection and vaginal lubrication in the female). These physiological responses result from *parasympathetic nervous system* impulses that pass through the sacral portion of the spinal cord to the genitals. As we shall see later, these responses are the basis for the psychophysiological assessment of sexual arousal.

Men and women have the same basic physiological responses to sexual stimulation whether that stimulation is coital, manipulative, or fantasy induced. Intensity and duration of response do, however, vary with the method of stimulation used. In the laboratory setting Masters and Johnson found that masturbation produces the most intense response, manipulation by a partner's hand the next most intense response, and intercourse the least intense response.

In other animals sexual behavior is almost entirely determined by genetic and hormonal influence, but in humans, sexual arousal and behavior are largely determined by postnatal environmental influences. This seems to be especially true of sexual arousal and the stimuli that elicit sexual responses. Consequently, a tremendous range of possible stimuli can acquire the capacity to arouse people sexually—small breasts or large; long legs or barrel chests; blondes, brunettes, or redheads; shoes, panties, or leather boots; extreme youth or extreme age; a partner's resistance or a partner's submissiveness; spanking; enemas; horseback riding—the list is endless. For any one individual, however, the possible range is likely to be much narrower.

The claim has been made that sexual arousal, attraction, and behavior occur in children who have not reached puberty. While this belief may have some validity, it is doubtful that prepubescent children experience sexual arousal in the same manner as adults. The differences between the child's behavior and the adult's are that children are not capable of experiencing orgasm, nor are they physiologically capable of a sexual response. This development occurs at puberty.

The confusion is probably due to two factors: (1) the practice of defining a sexual response as any activity that is pleasant and that superficially resembles adult sexual behavior, and (2) the confusion of gender identification and heterosocial behavior with sexual arousal. The first factor has caused people to erroneously identify as

Some females have multiple orgasms; males cannot be restimulated during a refractory period after ejaculation

Sexual arousal: myotonia *(muscular tautness) and* vasocongestion *(blood engorgement) in genitals, felt as penile erection in males; as clitoral erection and vaginal lubrication in females*

Human sexual arousal is shaped largely by environmental stimuli

disorders of biological needs: sexual behavior

sexual such behaviors as manipulation of the genitalia, which may be simply an expression of curiosity, or erections in male children, which can occur without sexual arousal. As for the second factor, gender identification may or may not be consistent with sexual arousal or preference, as we shall see later in this chapter.

It is probably true that the acquisition of gender identification and heterosocial behavior begins in infancy and that they are important influences on the development of sexual arousal to specific stimuli, but they appear to be modulating or predisposing rather than determining factors in the development of sexual preferences, and the development of mature sexual arousal patterns is probably initiated and stabilized during puberty.

Orgasm increases the reinforcing value of the experience or fantasy that precedes it

In males the crucial variable in determining sexual preferences seems to be the nature of the first few sexual experiences. If these experiences are pleasurable or are then used as material for fantasy during masturbation, or both, conditioning occurs. As McGuire et al. (1965) pointed out, any stimulus that regularly precedes ejaculation by the correct time interval can become sexually exciting. This rule applies to specific experiences as well as to specific fantasies. Thus fantasy during masturbation plays a crucial role in the development of sexual preferences. One individual, for example, first became intensely aroused while his broken leg was being put in a cast. He later masturbated to the fantasy and ultimately could only be aroused with a cast on his leg. While this can be considered a deviant response, normal responses are acquired through the same conditioning process.

Males see more of the environment in an erotic light; females believe in an emotionally charged relationship

A person's sexual behavior does not necessarily reflect a sexual preference

How sexual preferences are acquired by females is less clear. In males masturbation plays a key role, since any fantasy reinforced by orgasm establishes a pattern of arousal—people want to do what they masturbate to. But fewer females masturbate— 62 percent at some time in their lives, as opposed to 92 percent for males (Kinsey et al. 1948, 1953), and females typically begin later in life. Sexual arousal in females tra-

ditionally occurs more in the context of romantic love and marriage or the expectation of marriage, or at least a long-term relationship.

These and other differences in the patterns of sexual arousal learned by males and females have some important implications. Males are more likely than females to engage in sexual activity in which the sustaining motive is sexual. They tend to fantasize more, to see large parts of the environment in an erotic light, and to have the capacity to be turned on by a greater variety of stimuli, all of which may help explain why sexual *deviations* are more common in males. Even homosexuality appears to have a much smaller prevalence in women than in men. In contrast, women are more sensitive to the language of love and are taught to believe in a capacity for an intense, emotionally charged relationship. Whether or not any of this contributes to the high prevalence of sexual *dysfunction* in females is uncertain. That prevalence is at least as high as it is for males, if not higher (Masters and Johnson 1970).

An individual's sexual preferences do not always coincide with his or her sexual behavior, and this important distinction is all too often overlooked. For example, one individual may consciously choose celibacy or masturbation as a sexual lifestyle even though a willing and attractive partner is available, whereas another individual who practices celibacy or masturbation might strongly prefer heterosexual coitus but be blocked by physical isolation, social phobias, or some other obstacle. Similarly, many individuals whose sexual preference is heterosexual sometimes engage in homosexual behavior, and vice versa. Men in prison are a classic example—their homosexual behavior is an adaptive strategy that does not belie or reverse their heterosexual orientation. In a similar vein, homosexuals often enter into heterosexual marriages in response to social expectations. In such situations people are often able to function in the less preferred behavior by fantasizing the more preferred behavior.

An obvious corollary of the distinction between preference and behavior is that an individual's sexual preferences should be

disorders of biological needs

assessed in terms of arousal rather than behavior. For example, the prostitute who whips a masochistic customer is not necessarily a sadist—her behavior is only a job to her, no matter how exciting it may be to her client. Likewise, a stripper cannot legitimately be called an exhibitionist, since her motive is money, not pleasure.

Gender Identity and Sexual Orientation

The critical factors in the acquisition of sexual orientation and preference are initial sexual experiences, but subsequent fantasies or masturbation, as well as early experiences during childhood, do facilitate the development of specific sexual orientation.

Gender Identification and Behavior

A major component of sexual behavior is **gender role identification**, the enactment of roles typically labeled as male or female. These behaviors are usually associated with an individual's **sexual orientation**: whether one identifies oneself as male or female. However, in some cases, a male may exhibit effeminate behavior, yet label himself as a male and identify with males. This illustrates the point that genetic (XX or XY) or physiological gender does not completely determine gender identification or sexual orientation. Those two variables are also influenced by environmental factors. A lack of congruence between genetic sex, sexual orientation, and gender identity can be the basis for the development of sexual disorders (Green and Money 1969).

Training in appropriate gender role behavior and identification begins at birth: male infants are dressed in blue and female infants in pink. This learning process continues into early childhood during which time boys are expected to engage in certain activities and demonstrate certain personality traits, such as aggressiveness, while girls are rewarded for feminine behavior. Sexual identity is probably developed through *modeling*. That is, children model their behavior after the behavior of the same-sex parent and other adults of the same sex, and in most cases this modeling is consistently reinforced.

The learning of sex roles begins at birth

The boy's body position and turned-up cap indicate male gender identification. The girl has established female gender identification and behavior by dressing appropriately as a female.

The school cafeteria is one place for children to develop basic heterosocial skills.

Heterosocial Behavior

Heterosocial skills are the social skills necessary to initiate and maintain casual or intimate relationships with the other sex. Such behavior includes initiating and maintaining relationships with potential sexual partners, other-sex family members, casual or intimate opposite-sex friends, and opposite-sex colleagues. Although heterosocial behavior is part of the general package of social skills, so that on most occasions one behaves toward opposite-sex persons in the same way one behaves toward same-sex individuals, some occasions do require different skills with opposite-sex individuals. Difficulty in relating to the other sex is a problem that can be related either to a deficit in heterosocial skills or to heterosocial phobias. These disorders of heterosocial relationships are not necessarily associated with gender role behavior, identification, appropriate arousal, or heterosexual skills. Some individuals have quite appropriate sexual arousal and perform quite well sexually but have inadequate heterosocial skills.

An individual can be normal in terms of gender identity, sexual arousal, and sexual performance but lacking in heterosocial skills

Heterosexual Behavior

The acquisition of **heterosexual skill** probably begins just before or at the same time as the development of sexual orientation and preferences. Heterosexual skill is the ability to initiate and maintain a satisfactory and gratifying sexual relationship with an other-sex partner. This type of behavior is often independent of sexual arousal, gender identification, and heterosocial skills. Individuals who are quite talented in those

disorders of biological needs

areas may still have difficulty in initiating such a relationship, may be inept or fearful in such encounters, or may be disinterested. These difficulties come from a variety of sources and are sometimes associated with sexual dysfunctions. The deficit may be due to naiveté, a lack of training in heterosexual behavior, disgust and fear because of various situations in the heterosexual interaction, a bad experience that has resulted in the loss of pleasure in sexual situations, or the avoidance of heterosexual encounters. The last two conditions can be labeled as *heterosexual phobias* and may develop as a result of rape or other painful or degrading experiences.

Assessment of Sexual Behavior

An adequate assessment of sexual behavior, for either clinical or research purposes, requires evaluation of all four components of sexual behavior (sexual arousal, gender identification, heterosocial skills, and heterosexual skills). As noted before, difficulties can and do occur in any of these areas or in various combinations of them. Indices of subjective report, behavioral observation, and physiological recording of all four components of sexual behavior are required when possible because there may be discrepancies among these three indices (Tollison and Adams 1979). Such discrepancies give an indication of the accuracy of the assessment procedure and, on occasion, important clues to the proplem under investigation.

Until recent years researchers and clinicians relied almost exclusively on interviews as a method of obtaining information about sexual behavior. If the interviewee was assured of confidentiality, the interview could be an important source of data. It was the principal technique used by Kinsey and his colleagues. The validity of such interviews is dependent on a number of factors such as motivation to report accurately, how well interviewees understand their problems, the skills with which the interview is conducted, and similar factors.

Nevertheless, the interview should be considered only as the preliminary step in conducting an actual sexual assessment.

Until recently, self-report was about the only index of sexual orientation and arousal. In the past a number of questionnaires, such as the MMPI MF scale, have purported to measure sexual orientation, but these scales tended to be too global, often detecting factors other than sexual orientation or arousal. For example, the MMPI MF scale can be elevated in highly educated males because they tend to have cultural interests that cause them to score in the feminine range. As Kinsey and his colleagues have demonstrated, more direct questioning about sexual behavior often yields more pertinent data. In spite of criticism, it has been demonstrated that sexual behavior questionnaires are a reliable source of information (Udry and Morris 1967).

A number of questionnaires are available, such as the Sexual Orientation Method (SOM), which is designed to measure heterosexual and homosexual arousal patterns in males (Feldman and MacCulloch 1971). Obler (1973) has developed a scale designed to assess cognitively experienced social and sexual anxiety in males (SAS). This scale contains twenty-two items that cover a range from anxiety experienced during nonsexual contact with a member of the opposite sex to anxiety experienced during vaginal penetration. Hoon, Hoon, and Wincze (1976) devised a scale designed to measure female sexual arousal (SAI) that consists of twenty-eight items describing erotic experiences, which the individual rates along a seven-point scale of arousal. It is applicable to single, married, or homosexual women.

A rather different approach is the card-sorting technique devised by Barlow, Leitenberg, and Agras (1969). Various sexual scenes are typed on cards, which the individual then has to sort into five envelopes to represent a hierarchy of sexual arousal, with zero representing no arousal and four representing very strong arousal. An example might be, "You are alone in a room

Heterosexual phobias can interfere with heterosexual skills

Discrepancies between subjective report, behavioral observation, and physiological recordings can provide important clues

More direct questioning yields more pertinent data

with a very sexy-looking ten-year-old girl with long blond hair." This technique is useful with males and females of various sexual orientations. Unfortunately, individuals respond in unique ways, making this procedure difficult to evaluate in terms of reliability and validity.

A very useful self-report technique in the assessment of sexual disorders is self-monitoring (Ciminero, Nelson, and Lipinski 1977). This technique requires the individual to keep a daily record of all sexual urges. For example, an exhibitionist might be asked to count the number of urges to expose himself. In addition, the antecedents and the consequences of each urge are usually described. An example might be, "I saw this attractive woman leave the theater, so I followed her home and later exposed myself to her through her window." Self-monitoring can be used in a variety of ways so that the individual can record all incidents of sexual activity, incidents of masturbation and the fantasy employed, and other incidents of sexual arousal and behavior.

Behavioral assessment of sexual arousal and behavior has been minimal for obvious reasons. For this reason the work of Masters and Johnson (1966, 1970) has been dramatic, since they pioneered in directly observing and recording sexual behavior in their own laboratory under well-controlled conditions. In their initial work they observed over 690 couples engaging in intercourse or masturbation under laboratory conditions, and these observations provided the most comprehensive and accurate information ever compiled about the human sexual response. Their methods of direct observation combined with physiological recordings have proved to be the most objectively accurate procedure for collecting data on the sexual response. This information has added immeasurably to our knowledge of heterosexual skills and of the physiology of sexual behavior.

More recently, Barlow and his colleagues (1977) et al. developed an observational checklist for assessing heterosocial skills in males. They attempted to pinpoint the social behaviors that are unique to the

heterosocial situations necessary to initiate and maintain relationships with the other sex. Individuals were rated on voice, form of conversation, affect, and motor behavior. Users of this scale can differentiate between heterosocially adequate and inadequate males. Unfortunately, a similar scale has not been developed for females.

Gender identification has been largely assessed by self-report. However, behavioral assessment of gender role behaviors has recently been developed for both children and adults (Barlow 1977; Rekers 1977). These observational techniques have relied on the fact that some motor behaviors of males and females, even from a young age, are different. With children, the procedure consists of taking time samples, from behind a one-way mirror, of a child playing with toys considered appropriate for boys or girls (Rekers 1977). In addition, Rekers and his colleagues (Rekers, Amoro-Plotkin, and Lowe 1977) indicate that motor mannerisms also reliably distinguish among normal male, normal female, and gender-disturbed male children.

In a similar fashion, Barlow, Reynolds, and Agras (1973) directly assessed gender role by observing the motor behaviors of sitting, standing, and walking. They claim that the modes of sitting, standing, and walking are specific to traditional learned male and female gender role behaviors (see Table 12–1). According to Barlow (1977), the checklist demonstrates that females have a much greater variety of behavior while sitting, standing, and walking than males, who tend to fall into a very narrow range of characteristically masculine behavior. He also notes that transsexual males score consistently more feminine than the female sample and suggests that there may be a measurable difference between females and effeminate males.

Largely because of the work of Masters and Johnson, in the last ten years increased emphasis has been placed on psychophysiological assessment of sexual arousal. A number of nongenital physiological measures change as a function of sexual arousal, including blood pressure, heart rate, respiration, skin conductance, and pupillary dilation. Since assessing physiological

disorders of biological needs

Table 12-1   Masculine and Feminine Gender Role Behaviors

Gender role behavior	Masculine	Feminine
Sitting		
Buttocks: position from back of chair	Distant	Close
Legs uncrossed, knees	Apart	Close
Legs crossed	Foot on knee	Knee on knee
Arm movement from	Shoulder	Elbow
Fingers	Together and straight	Relaxed
Wrist action	Firm	Limp
Standing		
Feet apart	Greater than three inches	Less than three inches
Arm movement from	Shoulder	Elbow
Hand motion	Minimal or in pocket	Greater than four movements per minute
Wrist action	Firm	Limp
Walking		
Strides	Long	Short
Hip "swish"	Absent	Present
Arm movement from	Shoulder	Elbow
Wrist action	Firm	Limp
Arm to trunk relationship	Free and swinging	Close and nonswinging

responses during coitus or other sexual activities for clinical purposes is rather difficult, clinical and research work has relied largely on measuring antecedents of sexual performance, such as various sexual fantasies. Fortunately, this type of assessment may be more appropriate in any case, since sexual difficulties typically occur in the antecedents of sexual behavior rather than during actual coitus or other sexual activity. A major problem in the use of these autonomic indices of sexual arousal is that the same responses also occur in other emotional states. For this reason more direct measures of genital responses have evolved.

Modern sexual assessment procedures have successfully removed sexual behavior in normal, dysfunction, and deviant individuals from the realm of armchair speculation and have contributed greatly to the development of adequate modification techniques for these disorders.

In males, the most direct index of sexual arousal is penile erection. Two techniques of measuring penile erection are *volumetric measures* and *measures of penile circumference*. In the volumetric technique the penis is placed in a glass cylinder. As penile tumescence occurs, air in the chamber is displaced and the volume of air displaced can be measured (Freund, Sedlacek, and Knob 1970). A less cumbersome and perhaps as accurate a device is the penile strain gauge, which yields an indication of penile circumference (Barlow et al. 1970). As the aroused penis increases in circumference, the resistance in the strain gauge is changed, which can then be recorded on a polygraph.

In the typical sexual assessment procedure using these devices, the individual is placed in a chamber, the device is attached, and he is given various erotic stimuli from

Sexual problems typically occur before rather than during coitus

Penile erection can be measured with a penile strain gauge

his own fantasy, audio tape recordings, slides, videotapes, or films. The erotic stimuli may appeal to heterosexual, homosexual, pedophiliac, or various other sexual preferences. From this procedure or variations of it, very subtle questions of sexual preferences and orientation can be answered (Abel et al. 1975). Interestingly enough, although an individual may know generally that a situation is sexually exciting to him, it may be difficult for him to specify the exact stimulus within the situation that arouses him. In some cases the individual's self-reported arousal and even his estimate of penile erection are not highly correlated with objectively measured penile erection.

Recently, devices for the psychophysiological assessment of arousal in females have also been developed. These techniques are based on the fact that the principal physiological response during female sexual arousal is genital vasocongestion (Masters and Johnson 1966). The most useful and accurate of these devices is the **vaginal photophethysmograph**, developed by Geer, Morokoff, and Greenwood (1974). It is a clear acrylic probe, approximately one-half inch in diameter and one- and three-fourths inches in length, with an incandescent light source on one side and a selenium photocell detector on the other. Essentially, the probe measures the amount of light reflected from the tissue of the vaginal wall and thus indicates the degree of vasocongestion. This device has been improved sufficiently to be an accurate measure of sexual arousal in females (Hoon, Wincze, and Hoon 1976).

Social and Legal Issues in Sexual Behavior

Many naive individuals believe that sexual laws are aimed primarily at the promiscuous, the perverted, or the financially enterprising, but such is not the case. As a matter of fact, if sexual laws were rigorously enforced, 75 percent of the population would be in jail in most states. Although progress has been made in some states in liberalizing legal codes regulating sexual contact, such laws are still mostly archaic and repressive.

Laws regulating sexual behavior are extremely vague in many areas, and the greatest number of violations are labeled crimes against nature or sodomy. **Sodomy** is a term that specifically refers to anal intercourse (either heterosexual or homosexual), but in most states the sodomy laws are more encompassing and include fellatio, cunnilingus, or even pedophilia. The law does not usually differentiate between homosexual and heterosexual relationships but prohibits specific acts whether between same- or opposite-sex partners (Hoffman 1968). Many sexual offenders such as homosexuals are prosecuted on such charges as outrageous conduct, lewd and lascivious behavior, or vagrancy, rather than for the nature of their sexual acts. About 95 percent of all arrests of homosexuals in California, for example, are for disorderly conduct (Davison and Neale 1974).

Primarily to protect the constitutional right of privacy, a number of states (Colorado, Illinois, Delaware, Oregon, Hawaii, Ohio, California, and Connecticut) have decriminalized all forms of sexual behavior between consenting adults in private. However, the Supreme Court has ruled (Doe v. Commonwealth Attorney of the City of Richmond) that there is no right to privacy where criminal behavior is involved. In other words, this decision did not find any inherent criminality in homosexuality or other behavior, but it did affirm that the right to privacy does not apply in situations involving what society labels criminal behavior—including extramarital intercourse and homosexuality.

Hoffman (1968) made the interesting observation that changes in the law based on the right to privacy have not improved the legal situation for homosexuals, since the police still make arrests but base the charges on laws against "public" conduct. Even if states pass a right-to-privacy law with regard to sexual behavior, it will not prevent harassment of deviant sexual behavior by police using statutes dealing with public conduct. Acceptance by law enforcement authorities and by the public that in most cases sexual deviation is a psychological rather than a legal problem is the only real solution to the dilemma.

disorders of biological needs

What constitutes abnormality of sexual behavior is no less complex a question for behavioral scientists than it is for lawmakers. DSM II states that sexual deviants are "individuals whose sexual interests are directed primarily towards objects other than people of the opposite sex, toward sexual acts not usually associated with coitus, or toward coitus performed under bizarre circumstances as in necrophilia, pedophilia, sexual sadism and fetishism." It further indicates that these individuals may find their sexual practices distasteful but be unable to substitute normal sexual behavior. It limits this definition by stating that individuals who perform deviant sexual acts because normal sexual objects are not available to them are not considered sexual deviants. The manual then lists a number of terms, such as homosexuality, fetishism, pedophilia, and the like, without any further description. DSM III's descriptions of psychosexual disorders, with exceptions noted later, are essentially the same.

In a hearing held in New York on February 8, 1973, before the Nomenclature Committee of the American Psychiatric Association, the gay liberation movement succeeded in having homosexuality dropped from DSM II, on the grounds that the behavior of homosexuals is no more maladaptive in other areas than that of heterosexuals. DSM II lists sexual dysfunctions as psychophysiological, genitourinary (pertaining to genital organs) disorders and includes them with such disorders as disturbances in menstruation and micturition (urination). This has been corrected in DSM III, which classifies sexual dysfunctions as psychosexual dysfunctions.

Compounding the confusion are labels such as pedophilia (sexual activity with children) that are not particularly descriptive. A pedophiliac may be a homosexual or a heterosexual, may or may not be a rapist, and may or may not be a sadist or a masochist. A major problem in determining the causes of, or deciding upon methods of assessing or modifying, sexual dysfunctions and deviations is the definition and classification of such disorders.

Sexual Dysfunctions

The most common of all sexual disorders are the **sexual dysfunctions**, behavior patterns usually learned early in life that prevent a satisfactory sex life. Our knowledge of the causes and treatment of these disorders has increased tremendously in the last twenty years, largely because of the growing liberal attitudes toward sexual behavior and the pioneering work of Masters and Johnson. There is little doubt that our sexual mores and expectations are changing. Women in particular have become more concerned about the development and free expression of their sexuality and have objected to the passive role they have been taught to assume. The feminist movement has been instrumental in changing these attitudes. Regardless of the cause, many women are unwilling to suffer in silence any longer and want a more active and cooperative partnership in sexual activities.

DSM II labeled sexual dysfunctions as psychophysiological disorders. This label has some logic, since most of these disorders are caused by malfunctions of the autonomic nervous system. They are also quite similar to phobic reactions, since, in most cases, they involve avoidance behaviors aimed at reducing anxiety. DSM III labels these conditions as psychosexual dysfunctions.

Sexual Dysfunctions in Males

Four major types of sexual dysfunctions occur in males:

1. **Primary impotence** The individual has never been able to achieve an erection sufficient for successful intercourse, either heterosexual or homosexual. When he has been unable to obtain erection on any occasion, even during masturbation or while asleep, the cause may be physical illness.
2. **Secondary impotence** The individual has difficulty achieving an erection in coitus but not during fantasy or masturbation.

DSM II: Deviance defined in terms of act, object, or circumstance

Homosexuality no longer listed as a sexual disorder

Sexual dysfunctions as psychophysiological disorders

disorders of biological needs: sexual behavior

3. **Premature ejaculation** The individual is unable to delay ejaculation long enough for the female partner to have orgasm in at least 50 percent of their contacts. This definition, derived from Masters and Johnson, has problems because one person's dysfunction is defined in terms of a partner's satisfaction. A more accurate definition is that of Kaplan (1974), who defines premature ejaculation as the absence of voluntary control of ejaculation, whether it occurs after two or after five thrusts, or whether it occurs before the female partner's orgasm or not. In other words, this difficulty is an inability to sustain high levels of sexual arousal without reflexive ejaculation.

4. **Ejaculatory incompetence** The individual can achieve and sustain an erection, achieve intromission, and sustain intercourse, but is unable to ejaculate intravaginally. In most of these cases, the individual is able to ejaculate with masturbation. A similar disorder is defined when the individual is able to maintain an erection, sustain penetration, and ejaculate, but ejaculates without pleasure.

Primary disorders are not affected by changing the partner or the situation

Note that some of these problems are labeled as either primary or secondary. The *primary* condition is not related to a particular partner or situation and is usually of long duration. In *secondary* sexual dysfunctions, the disorder is usually related to the circumstances: for example, being turned off to the sexual partner or having ingested too much alcohol or drugs. Under the proper circumstances and with a desirable sexual partner, these individuals have no sexual problem. In either case a complete physical examination is required to rule out a variety of illnesses from diabetes to local genital infections that can cause

No apparent connection between sexual dysfunctions and general maladjustment

such disorders. Furthermore, drug abuse—whether of alcohol, heroin, barbiturates, tranquilizers, or other pharmacological agents—can cause sexual dysfunctions. The vast majority of these conditions, however, are psychogenic in origin. Only 5 to 15 percent of all cases of sexual dysfunctions are attributed to known organic and physiological causes, including deformities, obesity, rheumatic fever, hepatic cirrhosis, urethritis, pernicious anemia, mumps, spinal cord lesions, diabetes, and the effects of alcohol and drugs.

The incidence of male disorders is not known precisely, but Kinsey et al. (1948) indicated that by the age of thirty-five approximately 6 percent of the white male population are sexually impotent, and as many as 25 percent are impotent by the age of sixty-five. Despite the seeming correlation, impotence is not a function of aging, although the belief that it is could contribute to some cases.

Research and Theory

According to one estimate, approximately one-half of the male population have had occasional episodes in which they experienced difficulty in achieving or maintaining an erection (Masters and Johnson 1970). Sexual dysfunctions do not seem to be associated with general maladjustment, and individuals exhibiting such behavior are typically normal or at least not severely disturbed psychologically. In terms of the distress it causes, however, as Kaplan has noted, no medical condition is more frustrating and humiliating for a male than impotence. In almost all cultures and socioeconomic groups a great deal of male esteem is invested in the erection.

Explanations of sexual dysfunctions come from clinical case histories, interview surveys, and questionnaire studies that have serious methodological weaknesses (Faulk 1973), but there does seem to be consistency among theorists in the explanation of sexual dysfunctions.

Determinants of sexual inadequacy can be divided into two types, *predisposing* and *precipitating* factors. Predisposing factors are usually learned behaviors or attitudes acquired early in life. One of the most common predisposing factors, by virtue of its message that sexual behavior is sinful, is religious orthodoxy. Furthermore, the male whose early training includes both religious orthodoxy and the prevailing values of our culture, which identify masculinity with sexual activity, faces a conflict arising from the double message—to be sexually active is sinful and therefore shameful, whereas to be sexually inactive is unmasculine and therefore shameful.

This conflict is often aggravated by ignorance, especially for anyone raised by parents who could not discuss or acknowledge sex without discomfort or embarrassment, or were secretive about their own sexuality, or were not knowledgeable about sex.

The major precipitating factor in male sexual dysfunctions appears to be an initial failure, which can result from any of a variety of causes, such as excessive alcohol or drug intake, which lowers inhibitions but also suppresses the sexual response, or unpleasant or frightening circumstances. If the initial attempt is made in the back seat of a car or in the parents' home, fear of discovery can put a premium on rapid completion of the act, and the resulting haste is especially conducive to premature ejaculation or impotence. Other factors include feelings of inadequacy in terms of sexual performance or penile size, as well as lack of sexual attraction toward the partner or declining sexual interest due to habituation over a long period of time.

Since these problems occur in most males at one time or another, it is not the failure itself that is crucial but the performance anxiety that may occur during a later episode. Such anxiety inhibits arousal and produces a self-fulfilling prophecy. This conditioned or performance anxiety may become so devastating to the individual that he begins to avoid sexual encounters. Why an individual develops a specific type of sexual dysfunction—such as impo-

tence—rather than another type—such as premature ejaculation or delayed ejaculation—is not clear. Either the individual's past sexual history or factors in the present situation can be seen as causal. One plausible explanation is that anxiety affects individuals differently, causing erectile failure in some and accelerating ejaculation in others. At the present time, no real evidence is available to explain these differences, although it has been suggested that premature ejaculation may be associated with a sexual history in which rapid sexual performance was demanded.

Modification

The early work of behavior therapists, including Wolpe (1958) and Masters and Johnson (1970), has caused a major revolution in the treatment of sexual dysfunctions. Consequently, humanistic or psychodynamic approaches are used only infrequently since behavior therapy has been highly successful and relatively fast. While there are many variations, the two major therapies focus on anxiety elimination and sexual education.

Masters and Johnson work as a sex therapy team and treat only couples, even though one member of the couple is previously identified as dysfunctional and the other is not. The use of male and female cotherapists guards against the possibility of a client feeling intimidated by two members of the opposite sex. Furthermore, a cotherapist of the same sex may understand more fully the unique problems of the client and decrease the possibility of any special relationship developing between therapist and a client.

The program typically requires two weeks and is focused on demonstrating that sexual difficulties are a function of performance-related fear. The couple is encouraged to proceed slowly. All sexual contacts are to progress to a more intimate stage only when the male feels perfectly confident. For example, a male may achieve

Initial failure as the major precipitating factor

Role of performance anxiety

Masters and Johnson treat the couple

erection while his wife gently strokes his body, but intercourse should not be attempted until the erection can also be achieved while the penis itself is stimulated. Individuals are also taught to avoid the spectator role—worrying about performing adequately or about satisfying their partners—which may distract them from the sensate pleasure that produces sexual arousal.

The spectator role is avoided by the focus on sensate pleasure

To eliminate performance anxiety, the therapist prohibits the individual from any sexual activity not specifically sanctioned by the therapist or outlined in a carefully graduated program of mutually pleasurable sensual and sexual intimacies between the partners. Called **sensate focus**, the procedure involves learning to think and feel sensuously by giving and receiving bodily pleasure, first by nongenital contact and then by specific genital stimulation. The use of moisturizing lotions has been found to facilitate these feelings. During these

Sensate focus: learning to think and feel sensuously by giving and receiving bodily pleasure

homework assignments, increased verbal and nonverbal communication between the partners about what they find sexually gratifying is encouraged.

With problems of premature ejaculation, the squeeze technique is also used. The male acquires an erection and focuses on sensations experienced preceding ejaculation. Just before ejaculation the female, using her thumb and the first two fingers of the same hand, firmly squeezes the penis on each side of the coronal ridge for three or four seconds, as shown in Figure 12–2. This pressure eliminates the urge to ejaculate, and the procedure is repeated until the male is able to maintain an erection for longer periods of time. The woman then straddles the man and inserts the penis into her vagina while remaining motionless in response to a gradual build-up of vigorous pelvic thrusting (see Figure 12–3). If at any time the male feels he is going to ejaculate too quickly, the woman dismounts, repeats

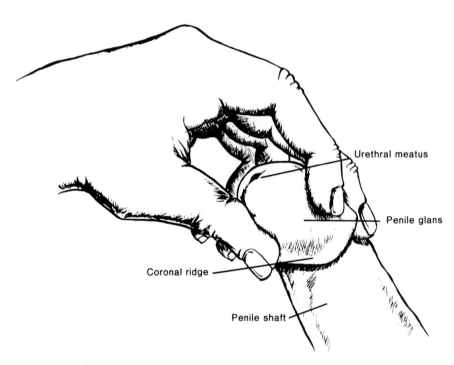

Figure 12–2 Demonstration of the squeeze technique.

disorders of biological needs

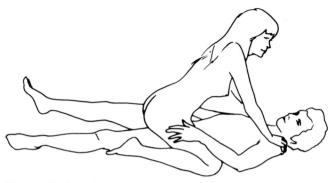

Figure 12-3 The female superior coital position.

Table 12-2   Systematic Desensitization Hierarchy for Anxiety in Male Sexual Dysfunction

Item

1. You are dancing with your wife/girl friend while fully clothed.
2. She is sitting on your lap, fully clothed.
3. She kisses your cheeks and forehead tenderly.
4. You are at home alone with her, and she gives you a warm, suggestive look or comment.
5. She kisses you in a warm, suggestive way on your lips.
6. You caress her shoulders and back (vice versa).
7. You caress her buttocks and thighs (vice versa).
8. She French-kisses you, with tongue contact.
9. You embrace and hug while clothed and are aware of your partner's desire for sexual relations.
10. You caress your partner's genitals while you are clothed.
11. You are lying in bed clothed, are hugging and cuddling, and she is aware of your erection and desire for intercourse.
12. You are lying in bed unclothed, hugging and holding your partner prior to her arousal, and aware of the feeling of her body against yours, and of her desire for sex.
13. You are in bed unclothed, hugging her, and aware of your erection as you feel her body against yours.
14. You caress her breasts while you are naked.
15. You orally stimulate her breasts and nipples.
16. You are lying in bed unclothed, and she runs her hands over your nude body (vice versa).
17. You caress your partner's genitals while she is nude.
18. You manually stimulate her clitoral area.
19. You insert your finger into her vagina during foreplay.
20. You penetrate her for the initiation of intercourse, with her in the superior position.
21. You are engaged in active sexual intercourse.
22. You are engaged in sexual intercourse, using a new position.

---

the squeeze technique, and then reinserts the penis.

Other behavioral treatments of male sexual dysfunctions proceed along somewhat similar lines. However, the usual emphasis is on systematic desensitization during which the therapist teaches the individual progressive muscular relaxation and obtains a hierarchy of anxiety in the sexual situation. In addition, many behavior therapists insist that the couple refrain from sexual intercourse during treatment in order to diminish performance anxiety.

Often, the no-coitus rule is so effective in reducing performance fears that the resulting high levels of sexual arousal lead to violation of the rule. Some behavior therapists expect the rule to be violated before therapy is concluded and take that as a sign that the rule has done its job. A typical hierarchy is shown in Table 12-2. The individual may then be led through the hierarchy in imagination by the therapist,

The no-coitus-yet rule reduces performance fears

disorders of biological needs: sexual behavior

and in some cases by the partner as instructed by the therapist. When an item has been mastered, the client is instructed to practice it at home. The squeeze technique, sensate focus, or other methods of enhancing sexual arousal, such as warning the individual to refrain from masturbation, are used in conjunction with home practice. The final item in the hierarchy is usually penetration without thrusting, which, if the program has been successful, the patient finds difficult to do.

Flexibility of the behavioral approach

The behavioral approach offers two major advantages. First, the individual is taught direct skills for controlling anxiety (that is, progressive muscular relaxation), and the emphasis is on his never experiencing anxiety during sexual contacts. The second advantage is flexibility—the program can be devised for an individual's specific problems. For example, an individual in his midforties had begun to be impotent with his wife. He was extremely religious, a deacon in his church. On assessment, the problem seemed to be that he had become habituated to his wife, since they had been married twenty-five years, and it was difficult for them to introduce any excitement into their sex life.

This is not an uncommon problem among individuals who have been married a long time and is usually resolved by the use of fantasy during intercourse. Sexual fantasy of other individuals or activities during intercourse is a common practice of both males and females, particularly if they have had a long history of sexual relationships with each other. In this case, the individual was unable to employ such fantasies because of his strict religious rearing. Furthermore, the wife had already exhausted all of the usual tricks for making herself more sexually desirable. Since the usual program for impotence evidently would not work for this individual, a variation was used in which he was trained in sexual fantasies during masturbation, using illustrated magazines and images of attractive women he had met during the day. He was soon able to arouse himself sexually by fantasy and, in a short time, was maintaining a satisfactory and enjoyable sexual relationship with his wife.

Sexual Dysfunctions in Females

The term frigidity, once an all-encompassing label for sexual dysfunction in women, has come to be perceived as archaic in recent years. Masters and Johnson have suggested instead the term **orgasmic dysfunction**. In general, three different categories of sexual dysfunction occur in women:

1. **Orgasmic dysfunction**   Included in this category are general inhibition of sexual arousal, a lack of erotic feelings, and, on occasion, absence of the vasocongestion that typically prepares a woman for intercourse (Kaplan 1974). Some women do not experience orgasm even in the presence of erotic feeling. In *primary orgasmic dysfunction* the female reports no history of orgasmic experience whether through intercourse, noncoital stimulation by a partner, or masturbation. In *situational orgasmic dysfunction*, the female is able to achieve orgasm in some ways but not in others, such as by masturbation but not through intercourse, or with some partners but not with others. In some cases, the woman may experience disgust, anxiety, or absence of pleasure during foreplay or intercourse, which DSM III labels as *psychosexual dysfunction with inhibited excitement*. If there is only a failure to achieve orgasm after normal sexual excitement and activity, DMS III diagnoses the condition as *psychosexual dysfunction with inhibited orgasm.*

2. **Vaginismus**   This is an involuntary spasm of the muscles surrounding the vaginal entrance whenever vaginal penetration is attempted. In many cases women exhibiting vaginismus do not lack general sexual responsiveness or the ability to achieve orgasm through either self- or partner-stimulation. Vaginismus is painful and often prevents intercourse. It is usually diagnosed during a pelvic examination.

disorders of biological needs

3. **Dyspareunia** This is pain or discomfort during and following intercourse. It also occurs in some males.

Kinsey et al. (1953) stated that approximately one-half of all married women have not experienced orgasm by their first anniversary, but this figure decreases until, after twenty years of marriage, approximately 65 percent of women report regular orgasm and more than 90 percent report at least some orgasmic experiences. In terms of the prevalence of various sexual problems, *primary orgasmic dysfunction* accounts for more than half of all female sexual difficulties, *situational orgasmic dysfunction* for another 40 percent, and *vaginismus* for about 7 percent (Masters and Johnson 1970). These figures are only estimates, however, since with the exception of vaginismus, it is relatively easy for a female to conceal her sexual problems, a refuge not usually available for males.

Research and Theory
The predisposing factors in female sexual dysfunctions are similar to those found in males. They include physical causes, restrictive moral or religious teaching, and ignorance or fear associated with sexual behavior. The precipitating factors, however, are somewhat different. Probably the most common precipitating factor is an initial experience with a clumsy or inept sexual partner who is either ignorant or unconcerned with the fact that many females require more foreplay and preparation for sexual intercourse. A painful or disgusting experience for the female may result, and in time it may cause anxiety and negative emotions about sexual activity. *Sexual trauma*, such as rape, incest, and other physically or mentally painful sexual experiences can also cause difficulties in females who, before the experience, may have been sexually responsive.

Sexual ignorance can cause or aggravate these disorders. One husband who complained of his wife's frigidity brought her for treatment. A careful sexual history revealed that she was quite sexually responsive, but the husband penetrated for only four or five strokes—the problem was premature ejaculation. In another case a very young newlywed couple came to the psychology clinic complaining of painful intercourse. Examination revealed that they engaged in almost no foreplay, and the husband was penetrating before the wife lubricated sufficiently to avoid pain. An hour or two of sexual counseling is often sufficient to eliminate these problems.

Modification
The treatment of female sexual dysfunction is usually required when any or all of the following problems are present: (1) arousal dysfunction or lack of sexual arousal, (2) anxiety reactions associated with sexual interactions, (3) orgasmic dysfunctions, and (4) dyspareunia and vaginismus (Wincze 1977).

When there is an arousal dysfunction, the female usually describes herself as being bored with or uninterested in sex. She is not necessarily anxious about sex but views it as a waste of time even though she achieves orgasm during intercourse. Generally, this problem is extremely difficult to treat. Simply exposing these individuals to sex manuals or trying to enhance their sexual responses by reading erotic literature, masturbation, performing coitus in new and interesting ways, and engaging in fantasy may not be sufficient. As Wincze (1977) has suggested, much more research and information into the physiological and cognitive development of sexual arousal is needed before really effective techniques of treating this disorder can be devised.

Where a phobic or anxiety reaction to sex occurs, the female may enjoy nonsexual interaction with males, but when sexual behavior is initiated, she may become uncomfortable and engage in maneuvers to avoid sexual activity. Typically, her anxiety and disgust increase as sexual foreplay and activity progress until she simply wants the partner to get it over with. With this type of problem, variations of the Masters and Johnson technique and systematic desensitization as described earlier for males are

Predisposing factors in females are similar to those in males

Sexual trauma and sexual ignorance are both common factors

Arousal dysfunction usually takes the form of boredom or disinterest

A phobic or anxiety reaction may lead to avoidance maneuvers

disorders of biological needs: sexual behavior

usually very successful. The goal is usually to eliminate anxiety while enhancing sexual responsiveness and arousal.

In treating primary orgasmic dysfunction, the initial step is a discussion of the female orgasm with the woman and her partner. Masters and Johnson have demonstrated that orgasm in women are obtained from stimulation of the clitoris and do not necessarily require an erect penis in the vagina. The initial counseling session also allows the therapist to develop a program for the specific problem. A general program that seems to be somewhat successful is the one developed by Lobitz and LoPiccolo (1972).

The Lobitz and LoPiccolo 9-step Masturbation Desensitization Program

This program involves a step-by-step procedure for orgasmic training through progressive genital stimulation and masturbation. In general, the individual increases her awareness of her body by exploring it visually and tactilely. She is then instructed to locate sensitive spots that produce erotic pleasure when stimulated. Next, she manually stimulates the pleasure areas and continues until orgasm occurs. Once she has experienced orgasm through masturbation, her partner is introduced into the procedure: first he observes her in her masturbation practice, and eventually he stimulates her himself. This procedure desensitizes the female to displaying arousal and orgasm. The final step is for the couple to engage in intercourse while the male stimulates the female's genitals, either manually or with a vibrator.

Dyspareunia and vaginismus can occur independently of each other

A woman with dyspareunia may develop vaginismus, but the two conditions can also exist independently. A woman experiencing vaginismus often can tolerate the insertion of tampons or her finger, but goes into spasm when penile insertion is attempted. In some cases, women are unable to tolerate any insertion and must be anesthetized even for a routine pap smear. Masters and Johnson have used a procedure that consists of an extensive explanation of the nature of the condition, including demonstration of muscle spasms by attempting digital insertions during a pelvic examination. In their homework, the couple is encouraged to attempt digital and penile insertion gradually

Behavior therapy has been extremely successful in treating sexual dysfunctions

and for longer periods of time until full thrusting of the erect penis can be tolerated. Relaxation training may also be helpful.

Effectiveness of Treatment Procedures for Sexual Dysfunctions

In general, the programs devised by behavior therapists and by Masters and Johnson (who also use essentially behavioral techniques such as sensate focus, which resembles systematic desensitization) have proved extremely successful. Masters and Johnson (1970) report, for example, 74 percent success in treating secondary impotence, 80 percent for situational orgasmic dysfunction, 82 percent for ejaculatory incompetence, 83 percent for primary orgasmic dysfunction, 89 percent for premature ejaculation, and 100 percent for vaginismus. Similar results have been obtained by Lobitz and LoPiccolo (1972), Wolpe (1973), and a number of others. Using thirty-seven females and twenty-seven males who had a variety of problems of sexual dysfunction, Obler (1973) compared behavior therapy with both traditional group therapy and no treatment. He found that behavior therapy was highly effective, while group therapy was no more effective than no treatment.

Enhancing Sexual Functioning: Public Entertainment or Public Nuisance?

With the success of modern sex therapies and the resulting publicity, a multitude of sex clinics and sex therapists have sprung up all over the country. This phenomenon is similar to the one that occurred when the public became enchanted with encounter and marathon groups and the one that is beginning to occur with biofeedback or mind control. Most of these centers and therapists are moneymaking operations that capitalize on the public's continuing interest in male-female relationships and its fascination with sexual behavior. Unfortunately, most of these sex therapists are

disorders of biological needs

poorly trained, if trained at all. Many of the procedures they use or recommend are untested or ill-advised and can sometimes do serious harm. In most cases, these amateur sex therapists probably do not harm the sexually normal individual, but they probably provide little assistance beyond entertainment. The treatment of sexual problems requires extensive knowledge of psychology and medicine, since sexual deviations and dysfunctions can arise from a variety of sources or can be secondary to other psychological or medical problems. Sexual problems require professional expertise and people who need assistance for sexual problems should seek help from therapists or sexual treatment clinics connected with hospitals or universities. If there is any doubt about the legitimacy of a therapist or a clinic, one should ask a local medical society or state psychological association. In a similar fashion, guidebooks for self-treatment may facilitate enhanced sexual pleasure in normally functioning couples but are probably useless or disastrous when used by individuals who have sexual problems.

Sexual Deviations

Sexual deviations differ from conventional sexual behavior in terms of either the sexual object or the sexual activity. In the first category of deviance the object may be a member of the same sex (*homosexuality*), a relative (*incest*), a child (*pedophilia*), an animal (*zoophilia*), or an inanimate object or a part of the body (*fetishism*). The second type of activity may involve watching others undress or engage in sexual behavior (*voyeurism*), exposing the genitals (*exhibitionism*), using force (*rape*), inflicting pain (*sadism*), or enduring pain (*masochism*). Except for homosexuality, these conditions are labeled as *paraphilias* by DSM III. As noted earlier, the human sex drive is extremely plastic, and any activity or object may at one time or another be sexually exciting for someone.

It has been often stated that what constitutes normal or deviant sexual behavior is directly related to social class and culture, and that a wide variety of sexual practices are acceptable in various societies. While true, this statement is probably misleading, since it pertains largely to legal sanctions and social intervention rather than approval or encouragement by members of the society of these deviant forms of sexual practices. If the latter definition of acceptability is used, the variety of acceptable sexual practices is greatly reduced. Conversely, it should not be automatically assumed that, since a society does not have legal sanctions or methods of intervention against it, a sexual practice is acceptable to most members of that society.

Sexual deviations are practices that are unacceptable to society, and these practicing individuals are regarded by the public as perverted, mentally ill, or even criminal. The majority of individuals who engage in deviant sexual practices agree with this assessment, but many do not and consider the reaction of society unwarranted. Child molesters, for example, often believe that their relationships are as good as or better than those of other people and that they are engaging in an activity the child enjoys. One exhibitionist told us he was contributing to the education of women. Some rapists may believe that women enjoy being forcibly raped. The discrepancy between society's attitude toward sexual deviation and the sexual deviant's attitude toward the deviant practice causes great confusion when we try to determine scientifically what constitutes a normal or an abnormal sexual practice.

Since most of the statistics on sexual practices are obtained when an individual commits a sexual offense or volunteers for treatment, the exact prevalence of these disorders is a matter of conjecture. For example, it is well known that rape is one of the most unreported crimes; many rape victims hesitate to report these offenses for fear of the embarrassing, humiliating experiences that often follow. The same is true of other sexual offenses.

Some sexual deviants consider society's reaction unwarranted

Homosexuality

Homosexuality is a sexual and affectional preference for members of the same sex. Although the term homosexuality is derived from the Greek word homo, meaning "the same as," in popular usage it usually applies to male homosexuality, and female homosexuality is called **lesbianism**, from the Greek Island of Lesbos, home of the presumably homosexual poet Sappho. Homosexual activities are similar to those of heterosexuals. Like heterosexuals, homosexuals engage in foreplay, including kissing, fondling, and tactile stimulation of the genitals. For males, orgasm is usually accomplished by mutual masturbation, **fellatio** (oral stimulation of the penis), or, less commonly, anal coitus. Lesbians typically achieve orgasm through mutual masturbation or **cunnilingus** (oral stimulation of the female genitals). A small number of lesbian couples also imitate heterosexual intercourse by using an artificial penis, or dildo.

DSM III: Homosexuality is a disorder only when the person's sexual behavior and values are in conflict

DSM III calls homosexuality a psychosexual disorder only if the individual's sex behavior is not consistent with the individual's values, causing subjective distress and maladjustment. These individuals, labeled by the DSM III as *ego-dystonic* homosexuals, have very weak or no heterosexual arousal but desire a heterosexual lifestyle. DSM III notes that homosexuality *per se* does not necessarily imply subjective distress or an inherent disability in terms of affectionate sexual activity between adults, which is characteristic of paraphilias.

Myths about homosexuals

Many of the beliefs about homosexuality are myths. For example, male homosexuals are often assumed to be "swishy," limp-wristed, effeminate types, while lesbians are assumed to be tough, masculine "dykes." However, gender confusion or opposite-sex gender behavior occurs only in a small minority of homosexuals. Most homosexuals cannot be distinguished outwardly from heterosexuals. Another common assumption is that homosexuals have a distinct personality type. However, this is not the case,

No evidence that homosexuals are more maladjusted in general than heterosexuals

and homosexuals vary as much in personality makeup as heterosexuals (Hooker 1957). Furthermore, the common belief that homosexuals tend to take either an active or a passive role in their sexual relationships is also false. Surveys have consistently shown that both male and female homosexuals usually alternate between passive and active roles (Saghir and Robins 1969).

Saghir and his colleagues (Saghir and Robins 1969; Saghir, Robins, and Walbran 1969) conducted interviews with male and female members of gay groups and found that the sexual behavior of homosexual men is more like that of heterosexual men, while homosexual women are more like heterosexual women. In other words, the males were more promiscuous, enjoyed more "one-night stands," and were able to separate sex easily from emotional involvement. Lesbians, on the other hand, tended to have more long-term relationships, which were not as explicitly sexual as those of males. In general, lesbians apparently opt for relationships in which caring, love, and emotional support are more important than sexual gratification (Simon and Gagnon 1970).

The major controversy over homosexuality in the research literature is whether homosexuals are more maladjusted in general than heterosexuals. Currently the data offer no real support for the assumption that the two groups differ in adjustment (Davison 1977). The belief that homosexuality indicates general maladjustment is derived from trait or psychodynamic theory and is no more justified than the belief that an individual with a flight phobia is also maladjusted in other areas of life (Sturgis and Adams 1978). However, this conclusion does not resolve the issue of whether homosexual behaviors, in and of themselves, should be considered abnormal. As Sturgis and Adams have indicated, this is an empirical issue that should be resolved scientifically rather than through opinion or political pressure.

In their surveys of sexual behavior, Kinsey et al. (1948, 1953) found that 37 percent of all males had had at least one

disorders of biological needs

homosexual experience, 18 percent had had as many homosexual as heterosexual experiences, and, for at least three years between the ages of sixteen and fifty-five, 4 percent were exclusive homosexual. For women a somewhat different picture emerges, with only 13 percent of women experiencing homosexual orgasm after the onset of adolescence and only 3 percent having been primarily or exclusively homosexual at any age. As Terman (1948) indicated, the Kinsey survey presents a number of problems, including the fact that an exclusively white, highly educated population was used. However, Gebhard (1972), in a similar survey, tended to confirm Kinsey's findings.

Research and Theory

A number of biological theories have been proposed to explain homosexuality, but there has been little evidence to support them. For example, Rosenthal (1971) surveyed the literature, including twin studies, and found little evidence of a genetic basis for homosexuality. A more convincing biological theory is the hormonal hypothesis, which focuses on the role of *testosterone*, a hormone that is responsible for sperm production and male secondary sex characteristics, such as a deep voice and beard growth. This theory assumes that there is less testosterone in homosexual than in heterosexual males, and more testosterone in lesbians than in heterosexual females. Several studies have found support for this hypothesis (Loraine, et al. 1971; Kolodny et al. 1971), but more recent studies have found few if any significant differences (Brodie et al. 1974; Tourney, Petrilli, and Hatfield 1975). These results should not be surprising, since few homosexuals have gender identification or behavior problems. As a matter of fact, Evans (1969) found in a survey of male homosexuals that 95 percent of them rated themselves moderately or strongly masculine.

The major psychoanalytic explanation of homosexuality focuses on an unresolved Oedipal conflict or heterophobia: The male homosexual is unable to overcome his attachment to his mother or identify with his father and therefore unable to proceed to mature genital sexuality. Because of intense conflict, he has castration anxiety and avoids contact with female genitals for fear of loss of or injury to his penis. There is some support for this theory. Bieber (1962) asked his psychiatric colleagues to complete questionnaires on the family histories of their homosexual patients. He found that these histories revealed disturbed relationships between parents: often the mother transferred her love to the son while at the same time being overprotective, so that the father withdrew and became resentful of or hostile toward his son. Mothers tended to be seductive with the son and to communicate their contempt of the male role. However, it should be noted that this pattern is present in the history of some heterosexual males but not in the history of all homosexual males.

In a similar study Evans (1969) surveyed forty-three male homosexuals and found that during childhood these individuals described themselves as frail, clumsy, and less athletic. Most were afraid of physical injury, tended to play with girls rather than boys, and thought of themselves as loners who seldom entered into competitive games. His data also indicated a relationship with mother and father similar to that found by Bieber.

Feldman and MacCulloch (1971) distinguished between primary and secondary homosexuals. Primary homosexuals are individuals who have never had any sexual arousal or experiences with the other sex, whereas secondary homosexuals are those who have had a history of some heterosexual behavior. They propose that biological variables cause primary homosexuality and that social learning determines secondary homosexuality. They believe, furthermore, that the biological variables causing primary homosexuality preclude successful behavioral treatment to reverse sexual orientation. However, as they admit, this hypothesis is sheer speculation. And evidence suggests that behavioral sexual reorientation programs are successful in some cases of primary homosexuality (Adams and Sturgis 1977).

Primary homosexuals: Those who have had no heterosexual arousal or experience

Early experiences do play an important role in facilitating the development of homosexual behavior. The relationship between the child and the mother and/or the father, the early identification with the male role, and puritanical attitudes toward sex may serve as important predisposing factors in the development of homosexuality. However, the crucial factor in the development of most homosexual preferences, at least in males, is early sexual arousal experiences (Gagnon and Simon 1973). As in the development of any sexual preference, the individual uses the memory of an initial sexual experience, usually around the age of puberty, to stimulate sexual arousal, usually in masturbation or other sexual experiences. As a consequence of such pairing of a same-sex partner or homosexual activity with sexual arousal and orgasm, a stable pattern of sexual preference develops. The development of sexual preferences is based on positive reinforcement. A homosexual may or may not have negative experiences with the other sex and may develop a phobia of heterosexual contact. However, it is doubtful that aversive experience with the other sex is in itself a necessary or sufficient cause for the development of homosexuality (Tollison and Adams, 1979).

Assessment and Modification

The goal of therapy may be sexual reorientation . . .

The primary question in the initial assessment of homosexuals who seek professional treatment for sexual reorientation is whether they really want to change their sexual orientation. Although about 68 percent of homosexuals hide their sexual orientation, only about 28 percent would prefer to be heterosexual, and only 14 percent want treatment for their condition (Weinberg and Williams 1974). Evidence also suggests that lesbians have less desire than male homosexuals for sexual reorientation programs (Adams and Sturgis 1977).

or adjustment to a gay lifestyle

The conscientious clinician will carefully explore this problem, recommending to clients that they consult with various people or groups, such as the gay liberation group, before coming to any decision about trying to change their sexual preferences. Furthermore, many homosexual clients may have other problems that require intervention in addition to difficulty in their homosexual relationships. The clinician should not automatically assume that any problem a homosexual has is due to homosexuality or insist on treating the individual for sexual preferences alone (Sturgis and Adams 1978). Many clinicians, if the homosexual desires it, will help the individual in adjusting to homosexual relationships and a gay life-style.

If it can be established that the individual is sincere in the attempt to change sexual preference, four areas become important. First, the individual's sexual arousal to homosexual stimuli must be reduced. A number of techniques are available to accomplish this goal, including various forms of aversion therapy, such as covert sensitization or aversive shock therapy. The procedure used by Feldman and MacCulloch involved the individual's selecting stimulus materials, such as pictures, reading materials, or fantasies that elicit a sexual response, and then pairing these stimuli with noxious stimuli. These techniques cause disturbing emotions such as anxiety to compete with sexual arousal and are fairly successful in eliminating sexual arousal to homosexual objects.

The second aspect of sexual reorientation is facilitating the development of heterosexual arousal. This step is crucial, since, if the heterosexual response is not learned, the individual may relapse. A number of techniques are available, including fading (Barlow 1974), masturbation training, and if a partner is available, procedures similar to the Masters and Johnson program or other behavioral programs used with impotent males. In masturbation training individuals are instructed to masturbate to heterosexual stimuli. If they are unable to arouse themselves to heterosexual stimuli, they are instructed to use homosexual stimuli first, and then just before ejaculation substitute the heterosexual stimuli. The heterosexual stimuli are introduced earlier and earlier in the sequence until the homosexual stimuli are eliminated entirely.

disorders of biological needs

The third major area of assessment is heterosexual and heterosocial skills. In some cases, male homosexuals have a heterosexual phobia; that is, they experience anxiety in heterosexual contacts. If this is the case, then this aspect of their behavior is treated in the same manner as any phobic reaction with such techniques as systematic desensitization. In some cases these individuals do not know how to initiate or maintain a heterosexual relationship. Their heterosocial skills are assessed, and programs using social skills training are instituted to help overcome these difficulties.

The final aspect of assessment and modification is gender identity. In other words, does the individual have masculine behaviors that will facilitate a heterosexual adjustment? If he does not, he may be taught to lower his voice, acquire more masculine motor behavior, or engage in various other types of masculine gender behavior (Barlow 1974).

The complexity of a behavior reorientation program depends primarily on whether the homosexual individual has deficits in only one or in most of these areas. Consequently, treatment of individuals who are labeled as primary homosexuals becomes very complex, because all four components of sexual behavior must be modified, and the individual must be adjusted to a heterosexual lifestyle. Modifying sexual arousal while ignoring the individual's other problems in life increases the probability of failure and may actually aggravate the individual's problems (Adams and Sturgis 1977).

Most of the data on the causes and the treatment of homosexuality are derived from male subjects. Very little information is available about lesbians. For example, in the last twenty years only four cases of sexual reorientation treatment with female homosexuals have been reported (Adams and Sturgis 1977). Our knowledge about the causes of lesbianism and its treatment, when it is desired, is extremely primitive.

Civil Rights of Homosexuals

Because of social and legal oppression, many homosexuals have banded together in organizations such as the Daughters of Bilitis, the Mattachine Society, and the gay liberation movement to establish rights for homosexuals. The primary goals of most of these organizations are to encourage homosexuals to declare openly, and take pride in, their sexual orientation. They view their members' problems as analogous to the struggles of blacks for civil rights. Homosexuals undoubtedly have been, in many instances, oppressed and denied basic civil rights. Obviously, there is little justice in discriminating against individuals in employment because of their sexual orientation. Their sexual orientation does not interfere with the performance of their trade or profession. There is no basis for expecting that individuals who happen to be homosexuals will allow their sexual preferences to interfere with their job performance any more than heterosexuals would. It is doubtful that homosexuals are any less professional in teaching or other careers. Furthermore, the fear that children will model their behavior on that of a homosexual teacher or superior and facilitate the development of homosexuality is groundless.

Another major issue is whether homosexuality should be considered a form of abnormal behavior. Under pressure from the gay liberation movement and other groups, the American Psychiatric Association modified the diagnosis of homosexuality as a mental illness to include only those who wished to change their sexual orientation. In other words, homosexuality was removed from the official list of mental disorders. Certainly, as we observed earlier, no evidence can be found that homosexuals are more maladjusted than heterosexuals if their sexual behavior is ignored. Whether homosexuality *per se* is abnormal is an issue that can be resolved only through empirical research.

A related issue is the opposition by the gay liberation movement to the attempts of psychiatrists and clinical psychologists to

Reorientation of primary homosexuals must include all four components of sexual behavior

Homosexuals have become politically active.

Should homosexuals be denied reorientation therapy?

treat homosexuals with sexual reorientation procedures. The extreme position, as taken by Davison (1977), is that all sexual reorientation programs for homosexuals should be stopped because they are immoral and unethical. In other words, even if an individual is homosexual and sincerely wants to become heterosexual, the person should be denied treatment. Davison (1978) maintains that such individuals should be denied treatment even if denial of treatment will cause them severe suffering, as in the case of married persons whose homosexual behavior is disrupting their marriages and their lives. Although the position taken by most mental health professionals a few years ago, (that all homosexuals are deviant and should be treated) was doubtless a violation of civil rights, the denial of sexual reorientation treatment programs to individuals who sincerely want them is also an obvious violation of basic rights (Sturgis and Adams 1978). It would be interesting to see what position proponents of this position would take on the rights of transsexuals to sex-change operations.

The decision for treatment, regardless of the particular behavior problem, should be made by the individual with the best possible advice from mental health professionals if the individual is not in serious legal difficulties and is competent to make such decisions. If the individual with phobias or compulsive rituals decides against treatment, that is the individual's right. The same applies to homosexuals. However, if they desire treatment, it is their right to undergo such treatment.

disorders of biological needs

Transvestism is the preference for dressing in the clothes of the opposite sex.

Transvestism

Transvestism is the preference for dressing in the clothes of the opposite sex in order to obtain sexual arousal or gratification. Transvestites are usually heterosexuals who find cross-dressing necessary for sexual arousal or as a prerequisite to coitus. Homosexuals may also cross-dress, but their purpose is to attract partners, and the act of cross-dressing in itself does not sexually arouse them.

When they wear opposite-sex clothing, transvestites to some degree enter the social role of the opposite sex. Transvestism is almost exclusively a male behavior. Most transvestite males believe they have a female side that is seeking expression, and they often consider themselves as different personalities when they are cross-dressed.

Transvestites do not usually have conflicts with the law, and social attitudes toward transvestism seem to range from indifference to curiosity as contrasted with the negative opinion of homosexuality. For example, transvestite performers have been popular in the last several decades. (Whether these performers are actually transvestites is questionable and depends on whether they are sexually aroused by cross-dressing. Their motive may simply be to earn money.)

Research and Theory

Very little research has been conducted on transvestism, although the incidence of the disorder is estimated at 1 to 3 percent of the population. Transvestites see themselves as an oppressed minority, and have

Transvestites are usually heterosexuals who cross-dress to obtain sexual arousal

formed clubs, held conventions, and publish a magazine, *Transvestia*. Prince and Bentler (1972) administered questionnaires to readers of *Transvestia* and found that 86 percent of the readers had heterosexual interests, 28 percent had had some homosexual experiences, and 78 percent were married. Among the respondents who had been married and were divorced, approximately one-third of the divorces were believed to have resulted from cross-dressing. Interestingly enough, the statistics on homosexual experiences among transvestites are similar to those Kinsey found in the general male population. With the assistance of the National Transvestite Organization, standardized personality tests have been administered to a large sample of male transvestites and have indicated that as a group transvestites appear to be no more neurotic or psychotic than the population at large (Bentler and Prince 1969, 1970; Bentler, Shearman, and Prince 1970).

The exact reason for this disorder is not apparent, but strong evidence points to family support and reinforcement for cross-dressing behavior (Stoller 1967). In some cases, members of the family openly encourage a child to dress in clothing of the opposite sex.

Modification
Modification techniques for individuals desiring treatment have not been extensively developed or evaluated, but some variation of behavior therapy tailored to this behavior would seem to be the most appropriate treatment.

Transsexualism

Transsexualism is a rare disorder characterized by an intense denial of one's biological sex, usually associated with a history of cross-dressing. Strictly speaking, this is a disorder of gender identification rather than of sexual arousal: transsexuals believe they were born with a body of the wrong sex and have an intense desire to be a member of the opposite sex. This disorder appears quite early in life, often as early as

age two and always before age five (Green 1974). Transsexual individuals often describe themselves as being a female trapped in a male body, or vice versa.

In children, there are apparently two basic types of gender disorders: **gender behavior disturbance** and **cross-gender identification** (Rosen, Rekers, and Fraiar 1977). These disorders have been studied almost exclusively in males because they are more frequent in males than in females and because parents are more concerned over female sex-role behaviors in their sons than they are over masculine behavior in their daughters (Green and Money 1969). The boy with gender behavior disturbance adopts female behavior to some degree but does not identify with the opposite sex. This disorder involves cross-gender clothing preferences; the use of feminine cosmetic articles; the presence of feminine gestures, mannerisms, voice inflection, and speech content; and an aversion to masculine sex-typed activities. The boy with cross-gender identification not only behaves in a feminine way, but wishes to be, or believes that he is, a girl. The first disorder is similar to transvestism, while the second is similar to transsexualism. At present we do not know what percentage of boys outgrow these gender disturbances or what percentage become adult transsexuals or transvestites.

Transsexualism is quite different from transvestism. Although the transsexual is often interested in female clothing, the purpose is not strictly sexual arousal and gratification. Furthermore, cross-gender activity is not limited to specific occasions as it is in the transvestite. In a similar manner, some transsexuals desire sex with the same biological sex, but they see this as natural and do not see themselves as homosexuals.

The incidence of transsexualism is apparently about 1 in 37,000 males and 1 in 103,000 females. These figures have been found in Sweden (Walinder 1968), and about the same figure has been found in England and Wales (Hoenig and Kenna 1973).

Transvestites appear to be no more neurotic or psychotic than other people

Transsexuals believe they were born with a body of the wrong sex

disorders of biological needs

The similarity between transsexualism and homosexuality is quite superficial (Money and Brennan 1968), although homosexuals usually identify themselves as males even in sexual interaction. The audio descriptions that follow and the response graph in Figure A show how a careful sexual assessment can differentiate between the two conditions.

It's in the evening time and you're with George. You're a woman, you're a woman and you're in bed with him and you're having intercourse. He really loves you and he's right on top of you there. You can feel the weight of his body. George is right on top of you. You see his face, beard. He's right on top of you and he's got a stiff erection. You can feel his erection, it's right in your vagina. He's moving up and down on top of you. He's whispering that he loves you, whispering that he loves you and you can feel his penis right in you. Deep in you, he's got his penis deep into your vagina, he's really excited and just losing control of his sexual arousal. He's really stimulated. You can

feel his penis right in your vagina. [End of first minute of audio description with patient as a woman.]

Now you're a man, he's having intercourse with you, you're a man and he's having anal intercourse with you. He has his arms around you. He really loves you and cares for you and is really excited by your body. You're a man and he's having anal intercourse with you. You can feel his penis in you. You can feel his penis in you, deep in you, and he's really penetrated you deep. You're a man and he's holding on to you, he has his arms around you. You can feel his arms around you. He's holding you very closely, he really cares about you. He's a man. He's really attracted by your body. He says he loves you, you can hear him, he says he loves you. His arms around you, he has penetrated you deep, deep into your rectum. He's having intercourse with you. He's really enjoying you, he's really excited. [End of second minute of description with patient as a homosexual.]

box 12-1
Differentiating Transsexual and Homosexual Arousal

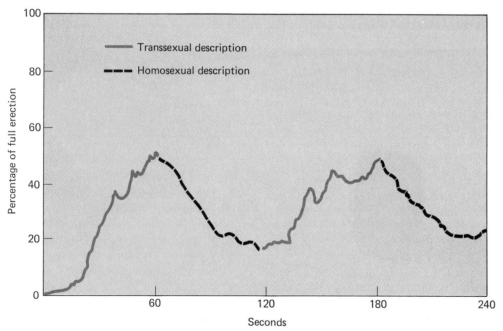

Figure A Erections to transsexual and homosexual audio descriptions.

Barlow and Abel, 1976

box 12–2
Identity Change in
a 21-Year-Old Male
Transsexual

Ever since his birth in 1952 John had thought of himself as a girl. By the time he was four, he was dressing in his older sister's clothes and applying makeup. His favorite activities were staying home alone to dress in his sister's clothes and doing housework. He envied his mother and sister for their femaleness and loathed his maleness. During his childhood, he slept in the bed with his mother, his father having left the family when John was eight.

During his teens, he read about transsexualism and began estrogen treatment on his own. At sixteen he was involved in an automobile accident, and in the aftermath, his cross-gender identity was discovered when the examining physicians noted the effects of the estrogen (his thinning body hair and breast enlargement). His mother was very upset at this discovery and insisted that he seek psychiatric help. Examination revealed no psychosis but a mild situational depression, presumably due to family pressures.

At this point he was working as manager of a fried chicken stand and reported that he was enjoying his work. He was saving his money for sex-reassignment surgery and had moved into his own apartment because of continuing trouble with his mother. He started once again on full estrogen therapy and began to prepare for surgery. He had started to cross-dress and reported that he was extremely comfortable and relaxed. His breasts had enlarged to bra size 36-B and electrolysis had removed most of his facial hair.

As a preparation for surgery, a number of assessment procedures were administered to measure gender identity, gender role behavior, and sexual arousal patterns. All assessment measures remained consistent with the diagnosis of transsexualism although sexual arousal, as measured by rating scales and penile circumferences, was relatively low and consistent with his expressed lack of interest in sex. John had, in fact, had no sexual contact and masturbated very infrequently due to disgust with his male genitalia. A behavioral checklist of gender-role behavior was filled out surreptitiously by a secretary as John walked into the office, stood, and sat while waiting for his appointment. Feminine gender motor behavior was emitted consistently.

Research and Theory

What etiological factors play a role in transsexualism is not clear, but probably neither a purely hereditary nor a purely environmental explanation of the origin of gender roles and orientation will prove adequate (Money, Hampson, and Hampson 1957). According to Green (1974), the following environmental variables appear to be important in the background of transsexual boys:

1. Parental indifference to feminine behavior in a boy during his first years
2. Parental encouragement of feminine behavior in a boy during his first years
3. Repeated cross-dressing of a young boy by a female
4. Maternal overprotection and inhibition of boyish or rough-and-tumble play during his first years
5. Excessive maternal attention expressed in physical contact and resulting in a lack of separation or individualization of a boy from his mother
6. Absence of an older male as an identity model during the boy's first years, or parental rejection of a young boy
7. Physical beauty of a boy that influences adults to treat him as they would a girl
8. Lack of male friends during the boy's first years of socialization

Cross-living began uneventfully. John changed his name to Judy and explained the situation to his employer with great maturity. She straightened out her legal affairs with relative ease and then departed for surgery. She sent us a card saying she had arrived. That was the last we heard from her until late fall when a research assistant involved in the case came running back from a half-finished lunch shouting, "Judy's back, but she's not Judy any more; she's John!"

John was invited back to our offices for a session which occurred in early January. He enthusiastically related his story. After journeying to the identity clinic, he had kept a promise he had made to the owner of the fried chicken stand to visit her private physician in that city before entering the hospital. After examining him, the physician, who was a member of a fundamentalist Protestant sect, announced that John was perfectly healthy but that he was possessed by devils and proceeded to carry out a laying on of hands by which he exorcised no less than twenty-two devils. John reported that he fainted and revived repeatedly as the doctor drew forth one devil after another, calling each by name as he did so. A letter to us from the physician confirmed the account.

Immediately after the session, John announced that he was indeed a man. He went to the barber shop and had his hair and nails cut short. Hiding his breasts as well as he could, he discarded his female clothing for three-piece suits and well-polished shoes. After the session, he returned home and lived with his mother for awhile, but when he felt some doubts about his conversion and some recurrence of feminine feelings, he visited a well-known faith healer in another state, who reaffirmed his faith and performed another laying on of hands. After this session, John noticed that his breasts were gone.

Several months later he had started dating. He had dated approximately ten girls intermittently and one for an extended period. He had had no sexual contact nor did he masturbate because such behaviors were not consistent with his new religion. He did report some sexual arousal to these girls, however. Card sorts and gender identity checklists revealed consistently masculine role behavior with no trace remaining of his former feminine behaviors. At this point, John reported that he was doing very well in his business and looking forward to getting married.

Barlow, Abel, and Blanchard, 1977

9. Maternal dominance in a family in which the father is relatively powerless
10. Castration fears

Modification

Most transsexuals seeking treatment request sex change operations. The usual procedure is extensive counseling, hormone therapy, and a trial period during which the individual is encouraged to live as a member of the opposite sex before surgery. A sex change operation is then performed only if it is still indicated. Surgery for a male involves removing the penis and testes and creating a vaginal opening and breasts. In the female the operation involves removing the ovaries, uterus, and breasts and creating a penis. The creation of a penis is much more difficult and also less satisfactory than the surgical creation of a vagina. After the operation there is extensive psychotherapeutic counseling to help the individual adapt to a new sex role. Hormones to stimulate development of opposite gender characteristics are also administered. Sex reassignment surgery has been discontinued at Johns Hopkins Hospital on the grounds that it has been no more effective than other methods in producing therapeutic psychological adjustment.

Therapeutic interventions in which individuals are encouraged to accept their biological gender have been largely unsuccessful. However, behavioral treatment has been used successfully in one case (Barlow, Reynolds, and Agras 1973).

Sex reassignment surgery is only part of the process

Fetishism

The habitual use of part of the body or of an inanimate object to produce sexual arousal or gratification is called **fetishism.** The object of a fetish can be almost anything, including feet, hands, panties, stockings, shoes, gloves, or similar objects. The sexual activity usually consists of kissing, rubbing, and smelling the fetish object while masturbating. Individuals with fetishes spend time collecting new examples of their favorite sex objects and may illegally enter homes to steal objects that are sexually arousing to them. As we noted previously, all individuals respond to special stimuli that produce sexual arousal: some men prefer women with large breasts, and some women prefer men with large penises. However, the true fetish is defined by the following characteristics: (1) sexual arousal occurs only when the fetish object is present; (2) the fetish object serves as a primary means of sexual gratification rather than as a prelude to coitus; (3) the desire to possess the fetish object or article is compulsive. Like most other sexual deviations, fetishism is a predominantly male disorder.

Classically conditioning a fetish

Our knowledge of this condition is based largely on clinical case studies. In an experimental analogue of this condition, Rackman (1956) demonstrated how the development of a fetish may occur. He asked male subjects to sit passively while they were first shown boots (CS) and then pictures of nude females (UCS) in a classical conditioning paradigm. Over a series of trials, the subjects began to experience sexual arousal to the boots alone, although the boots had previously been nonarousing. Even though a number of other factors influence the development of fetishism, this study indicates that the major cause may be classical conditioning in which objects rather than people are associated with sexual excitation and gratification. In one case a seventeen-year-old male had looked into a window and seen a girl dressed only in her panties. He was so sexually aroused

that he later masturbated repeatedly to the memory, and gradually his masturbation fantasies fixated on female underwear (McGuire et al. 1965). Behavior therapy has been used rather successfully in modifying fetishisms (Mark, Gelder, and Bancroft 1970).

Exhibitionism and Voyeurism

Undressing and watching a partner undress are usually part of the normal sequence of events in foreplay, which enhances arousal and serves as a prelude to coitus. These two activities can be considered deviant when, as a source of arousal and gratification, they replace coitus or when one party does not consent. In both disorders, in fact, the crucial element for sexual arousal appears to be the other person's lack of consent. Voyeurs could easily visit topless clubs, watch sex films, or find a willing partner, but these stimuli do not arouse them. Exhibitionists, likewise, could visit a nude beach or a nudist camp, or find a willing partner.

Lack of consent as the crucial element in voyeurism and exhibitionism

Exhibitionism is almost exclusively a male disorder. Strippers, or topless or bottomless entertainers, for example, are seldom sexually aroused by stripping and do so mainly for economic gain (Skipper and McCaghy 1969). In a similar fashion, the fad of streaking among college students was designed to shock observers and did not usually elicit sexual arousal in the pranksters. The exhibitionist usually exposes himself in a public place and is sexually aroused by the response of the victim, which is generally fear or disgust. The individual may or may not have an erection during the exposure. The exposure itself can cause ejaculation, or it may serve as an arousal stimulus for masturbation. The obscene phone caller who describes sexual activities over the telephone while masturbating is also an exhibitionist. The female who is indifferent or shows scorn usually cheats the exhibitionist of his sexual gratification. Exhibitionists are rarely dangerous, although they are often reported to law enforcement agencies and may have a history of convictions for this offense.

disorders of biological needs

The patient sought treatment for a long-standing trousers fetish. Fetishistic behavior consisted primarily of masturbation carried out by rubbing a pair of young men's trousers against his penis. But trousers also provided fantasy material for masturbation and for fetishistic thoughts that occurred at odd times, such as during lectures. The patient had a rather large collection of trousers that he would wear once and then use for masturbation. He also engaged in behaviors designed to procure trousers for masturbation, such as raiding locker rooms at hockey games and summer camps.

Thus, the subject sought help for three fetish-related behaviors: (1) the use of trousers in physical contact during masturbation, (2) fantasies that occurred during and apart from masturbation, and (3) overt behavior aimed at procuring trousers for masturbation. The treatment program was designed to consist of three phases. During the first part, aversive conditioning was used to decrease arousal to deviant stimuli. The subject was asked to bring to the sessions various favorite pairs of trousers and was then punished for such behaviors as reaching for the trousers, picking up the trousers, feeling them, smelling them, and rubbing them against his body. In addition, the subject was also punished for imagining his most recurrent fantasies. Punishment consisted

of electric shock accompanied and slightly preceded by the therapist's shouting "Stop that!" or simply by the command itself.

In the second phase, masturbation was used to recondition arousal to heterosexual stimuli. The subject was provided with heterosexual material and instructed to make use of it during masturbation by substituting it for deviant fantasies earlier and earlier in the process of masturbation. Since he was not very knowledgeable about heterosexual activities, the subject was also instructed to read widely in sex manuals and related material.

In the third phase of the program, the subject was provided with a small bottle of smelling salts, which he was to keep with him at all times and inhale from whenever he began to indulge in trousers fantasies at odd times.

The subject was seen at one-, two-, three-, and six-month intervals. Response to deviant stimuli, as measured by a penometer, had decreased markedly, while arousal to heterosexual stimuli had increased. The smelling salts had also served the purpose of decreasing fantasies at odd times. The subject reported his only difficulty to be in maintaining heterosexual fantasy during masturbation between initiation and ejaculation, but he assured us that he was improving all the time. The subject had not engaged in any more trousers-procuring behavior.

Marshall, 1974

box 12–3
Multiple Fetish-Related Behaviors in a 21-Year-Old Male

Voyeurs, or peeping Toms, obtain sexual excitement and gratification from observing others without their consent. Typically, the voyeur is a male who observes a female undressing, but some voyeurs may try to observe couples engaging in coitus. In either case, the crucial element for sexual excitation is lack of consent in the individual or individuals being observed. Like exhibitionists, voyeurs may also take advantage of modern technology to enhance their sexual enjoyment. The individual who calls

on the phone, breathes deeply, and says nothing while the victim talks is usually a voyeur. Like the exhibitionist-caller who "exhibits" verbally, the voyeur-caller "looks" by listening. Like the exhibitionist, this kind of caller usually masturbates during the call.

Although voyeurs may frighten or anger their victims, they are not likely to be dangerous. Voyeurism is often the only sexual behavior in which these individuals participate. Furthermore, there is no indication of any progression from mild offenses such as voyeurism to more serious sexual offenses such as rape.

Research and Theory

These two disorders usually occur in socially withdrawn and sexually anxious males who may be impotent during intercourse. These shy and immature males often have highly puritanical attitudes toward sex and often remain attached to a very passive mother (Witzig 1968). Apparently, exhibitionists display their genitals in order to convince themselves of their masculine prowess, a theory that provides some support for Freud's belief that this disorder is related to castration fears (Blane and Roth 1967). Possibly, voyeurism has a similar explanation.

McGuire et al. (1965) gave several examples of how a preference for exhibiting may develop. They discuss two exhibitionists who reported similar experiences in which they were urinating in a semipublic place when they were surprised by a passing female. Although they were embarrassed at the time, the sexual significance of the encounter later became apparent to them, and each then masturbated frequently to the memory of the incident. Eventually, the thought of self-exposure became so sexually arousing that each acted upon the idea.

Modification

Use of behavior therapy

As with other sexual disorders, behavior therapy seems to be the treatment of choice. Treatment procedures that include aversive escape conditioning for deviant fantasies seem to be especially successful (Evans 1967). The success of such treatments provides support for the hypothesis proposed by McGuire et al. that deviant sexual patterns are developed through masturbatory conditioning, at least in males. As a matter of fact, Evans (1968, 1970) found that exhibitionists who masturbated to normal fantasies before and between treatment sessions responded significantly more rapidly and successfully to approximately twenty-four weeks of aversion therapy than pa-

Pedophiliacs usually do not harm their victims

tients using deviant fantasies during genital arousal. Success was measured in terms of the absences of exposure during a six-month follow-up.

Pedophilia

Pedophilia is the abuse of a child by an adult for sexual gratification. It is a very heterogeneous disorder and covers a range of activities that may be either homosexual or heterosexual. Common pedophiliac practices include openly or secretly masturbating while talking to a child, fondling a child, manipulation of a child's sexual organs, masturbation between a child's thighs, having a child masturbate the individual or perform fellatio, or actual intromission.

Child molesters are the most horrifying sex deviants in the eyes of the public and the law, although they usually do not harm their victim. In a study of individuals convicted of pedophilia, Cohen, Seghorn, and Calmas (1969) suggested that there are three major types of pedophiliacs:

1. **Fixated type** This individual has never been able to develop or maintain a mature interpersonal relationship with either male or female peers. Typically, the individual is comfortable only with children and seeks them out as companions. Sex play occurs only after a period of developing friendship.

2. **Regressed type** This individual has usually had a normal adolescent heterosexual development preceding the pedophiliac period. Under stress, often of a sexual nature, such as discovering that one's wife or girl friend is having an affair with another man, the individual begins to engage in sex acts with children. Characteristically, the children who are victims of this type of offender are not known to the offender, and the act is often impulsive.

3. **Aggressive type** The primary aim of this type is aggression towards young boys, and the act may be cruel and vicious assault on the genital or anal areas. This type is rare.

disorders of biological needs

box 12-4
A 34-Year-Old
Homosexual
Pedophiliac

When the patient sought treatment, he had been arrested twice in the last eight years for child molesting. He considered his sexual orientation to be homosexual, but he was aroused only by boys between the ages of six and twelve. About twice each week, he would prowl for sexual contacts with male children at playgrounds or swimming pools. These episodes did not always result in contacts, but they did result in arousal and subsequent frustration. The patient also complained of "thoughts" about children whom he found sexually attractive. These occurred two or three times a day. Such thoughts also provided the material for masturbation fantasies, masturbation occurring several times a week.

The treatment plan consisted of two phases. During the first phase, aversive conditioning was used to reduce arousal to children. The patient described a number of scenes of prowling and sexual contacts with children which he found arousing. He was then instructed to imagine these in detail, one at a time. When each scene was vividly in his mind, he received an electric shock at a level he had previously determined as painful. Eleven such pairings were made during the first aversive-conditioning session, and six were made during the second. The patient reported that these pairings seemed to be effective, and his self-reports confirmed this by showing fewer incidents of prowling or "thoughts."

During the third and fourth weeks, the procedures for aversive conditioning were similar to those of the two previous weeks. The effect of the shock, however, did not seem to reduce the number of incidents any further. Therefore, the second phase of the treatment was initiated. During this phase, the patient was taught to respond sexually to an adult male through a modified Masters-and-Johnson-type therapy program. The patient's partner was a male friend (thirty-two years old), who was willing to participate out of friendship for the patient. Encounters between the two men, which were to occur twice a week with both men naked in bed, were graded as follows:

1. Touching for sensate pleasure, no genital involvement
2. Touching for sensate pleasure, some exploratory genital touching
3. Simultaneous genital touching, orgasm not permitted
4. Simultaneous genital touching and belly rubbing with genital contact, no orgasm
5. No restrictions, orgasm permitted

During the first session, the patient reported, he was very anxious and sweated profusely. However, after the goals of the session were reviewed and the patient's partner assured him that it was all right if the patient did not become aroused, the patient reported the second session to be quite pleasant and mildly arousing. After this session, progress was rapid, the last step being reached during the thirteenth treatment week.

At a six-month follow-up, the patient reported that he had become less preoccupied with children and had ceased prowling. Moreover, he reported that he found adult men sexually attractive and had had sexual contacts with adult males.

Kohlenberg, 1974

Research and Theory

Usually, pedophiliacs tend to be religious, moralistic, and Victorian in their attitudes toward sex. Although they are often uncomfortable with adult females, most male pedophiliacs are married. However, the discomfort seems to vary considerably with the age of the offender (Mohr, Turner, and Jerry 1965). Adolescent pedophiles tend to be sexually inhibited and inexperienced boys. Those in their mid-thirties have developed serious mental and social maladjustments, including alcoholism, which is often associated with the act. Older pedophiles, those in their late fifties, tend to be more normal psychologically, at least earlier in life, but suffer from loneliness and isolation, which the relationship with the child relieves. In most cases, pedophiliacs know the child they molest, since they are often a next-door neighbor, an uncle, a grandfather, or someone who has routine contact with the child (Gebhard et al. 1965).

Contrary to popular belief, most pedophiliacs do not use force or violence, and the child is seldom psychologically traumatized. In most cases, the negative effect on the child is caused or facilitated by the hysterical reaction of others, which serves to define the experience as disastrous and shameful. In fact, the child may even be rather nonchalant about the whole affair.

Modification

Modification is sometimes difficult, since it often involves not only changing sexual arousal patterns, but also teaching the individual how to relate to members of his own age group. This problem is aggravated by the fact that many of these individuals are referred by courts and enter treatment under protest, since they often view their act as part of their friendship with the child. Many pedophiliacs see their activity as harmless and resent the interference of society.

Sadism and Masochism

Sadism, named after the Marquis de Sade (1740–1814), is achieving sexual gratification by inflicting pain on the partner. **Masochism,** named after nineteenth-century novelist, Leopold von Sacher-Masoch, is obtaining sexual gratification from receiving pain, punishment, or psychological humiliation. Giving and receiving a certain amount of pain is sometimes a prelude to or a part of normal coitus, during which individuals may bite, scratch, or slap; for the sadist and masochist, however, inflicting or receiving pain is often in itself sufficient to trigger orgasm. It is not uncommon, furthermore, to find both sadistic and masochistic behavior occurring

in the same individual, and the behavior may be heterosexual or homosexual. Often sadomasochistic activities involve the use or presence of such traditional paraphernalia as whips, chains, and other instruments, which are sometimes important in sexual arousal. Many sadomasochistic activities also involve bondage. In most cases, these activities are harmless, and the pain inflicted is mild or feigned. In many situations, in fact, the sadism and masochism are restricted to fantasy associated with masturbation.

In a small number of cases, sadism may be extreme. In these cases individuals may commit horrifying acts of murder and mutilation during which they bind, whip, bite, or cut their victims. These acts of cruelty intensify arousal, and the sight of blood or the victim's cry of pain is often sufficient to trigger ejaculation.

Sadism is explained by psychodynamic theorists as a means of relieving anxiety associated with sexual pleasure. That individuals are able to do to others what they fear may be done to them allows them to overcome their fears and to increase their power or prestige, or both, since the victim is helpless. Psychodynamic theorists also believe that masochism may develop from sadism, since they view masochism simply as obtaining sexual excitement and gratification by inflicting self-injury. In other words, masochism is merely sadism turned inward.

Behaviorists theorize that sadism and masochism develop when sexual excitation and orgasm become associated with viewing or participating in painful behavior. For example, Hirschfeld (1948) describes a masochistic man who reported the following experience at age thirteen. He and two older sisters were in the care of a sadistic governess who beat the girls almost daily. He would view these beatings through a keyhole and later in the evening masturbate to the memory of them. The governess caught him in the act of masturbation and spanked him with a stick on his bare bottom during which time he experienced sexual arousal. He reported also that during the beating one of the hands of the governess was between her legs and stayed there.

disorders of biological needs

Such early experiences in which pain and sexual excitation are paired and later used as fantasy material for masturbation are apparently sufficient to foster the development of these disorders. Very little is known about the effectiveness of various techniques in modifying them.

Rape

There are two legal categories of **rape**: statutory rape, which involves sexual intercourse or activity with a minor in the absence of force; and forcible rape, in which the victim is coerced. Homosexual rapes also occur and are particularly a problem in prisons. However, most homosexual rape is usually ignored unless the victim is a minor. The exact prevalence of rape is difficult to estimate, since most of these crimes are not reported, and legal definitions of what constitutes rape vary from state to state.

Like pedophilia, rape is a heterogeneous collection of disorders and can be classified according to the relationship between sex and aggression involved in the rape. In a study of convicted rapists, Cohen and his colleagues (1969) described four different categories of rape:

1. **Displaced aggression** In this type of rape the intent of the act is primarily aggressive: the rapist wants to physically harm, degrade, or defile the victim. Sexual feelings are usually minimal, and sexual intercourse is used only as an instrument of aggression. Rapists of this type are usually angry at a wife, a girl friend, or a mother. In most of these cases the victim is unknown to the attacker.

2. **Compensatory** In these cases the primary motive is sexual. Force is used to gain submission so the individual can gratify his sexual desires. The offender is usually in a state of intense sexual arousal and may have an orgasm in the simple pursuit of the victim or upon first contact. Typically, the victim's resistance is sexually arousing to the rapist. In many cases these

individuals have feelings of sexual inadequacy and may have difficulty in performing with a consenting female.

3. **Mixed sex-aggression** In this type of rape, which is similar to the second category, sex and aggression have become so strongly associated that the rapist is unable to experience or even imagine sexual desires without the use of aggressive thoughts and feelings. At the extreme are sexual sadists who viciously assault, and even murder, their victims. According to Cohen and his colleagues, these individuals are usually loud and assertive.

4. **Impulsive** In these cases the act is often performed in the context of some other social behavior, such as a robbery or burglary. The individual sees a chance for sexual intercourse with little force and thinks, "Why not?" Typically, in this type of rape the individual is a sociopath who would probably desist with resistance, since persisting would be too much trouble.

A major concern of psychologists who work with rapes is their impact on the victim. Two aspects of this situation are extremely important. First is the obvious psychological and physical trauma to the victim, which, as Masters and Johnson (1970) indicated, can leave a mark on a woman for many years afterwards, giving her a very negative attitude toward her sexual relationships with other males. Some form of counseling or behavior therapy is usually necessary to help rape victims overcome the reactions to this stressful event, such as shame, embarrassment, humiliation, depression, and sexual fear.

The second major aspect of this problem, and one in which the feminist movement has been concerned and helpful, is ensuring that the victim is treated as a victim and not further harassed by social or judicial attitudes that commonly aggravate rather than relieve her distress. Feminists have

Most rapes are not reported

The rape victim needs the opportunity to verbalize her feelings about the attack to another woman, since it is often difficult for her to discuss the incident with a man.

been instrumental not only in helping establish centers for counseling rape victims but also in demanding the inclusion of policewomen on vice squads responsible for investigating rape reports, promoting the repeal of many laws that seem designed to protect the rapist, and establishing rape crisis centers, which offer immediate aid to the victims.

In terms of research and theory very few data are available. Working with convicted rapists, Abel, et al. (1975) were able to demonstrate that rapists are sexually aroused (as measured by penile erection) by scenes involving resistance. This study has implications for distinguishing rapists from nonrapists, and it also indicates that behavioral techniques that focus on eliminating deviant fantasies may be useful in the treatment of rapists. Unfortunately, there are no specific programs for the treatment of rapists, and this problem is aggravated by the fact that mental health

Resistance may be sexually arousing to rapists

professionals are unlikely to see the individuals sexually aroused by rape until they have been convicted of the crime.

Incest

Almost all human societies have a taboo on **incest.** In spite of this, incest is more common than usually suspected. Kinsey and his colleagues (1953) reported that 0.5 percent of males interviewed in the study admitted to acts of incest. By far the most common pattern is brother-sister incest; father-daughter incest is about one-fifth as common; and mother-son incest is apparently quite rare. Homosexual acts between relatives can also be considered incest.

Research indicates that brother-sister incest seems to occur almost accidentally in lower-class families in which brothers and sisters share the same bed and is difficult to label as pathological (Bagley 1969). In father-daughter incest, the pathology seems to be much clearer. Although

disorders of biological needs

Rape crisis centers work to ensure that the rape victim is treated as a victim and not further harassed by social or judicial attitudes.

it is generally assumed that fathers in these situations are simply psychopathic, promiscuous individuals who take advantage of their daughters, this is not the case. As a matter of fact, the typically incestuous father tends to confine his extramarital sexual contact to his daughter or daughters (Cavallin 1966). Moreover, these fathers are likely to be highly moralistic and de-

voutly attached to a fundamental religious doctrine (Gebhard et al. 1965). Often these relationships occur in connection with a disturbed marital sex relationship and may even be tacitly encouraged by the mother. Our knowledge about the prevalence, causes, and treatment of these disorders is minimal.

Incestuous fathers are likely to be moralistic and fundamentalist

box 12-5
Incestuous Behavior
in a 52-Year-Old
Male

The patient sought treatment for a five-year history of incestuous behavior with his oldest daughter, who was twenty-two at the time treatment was requested. Incestuous activity had consisted of kissing, fondling, and mutual masturbation. The patient's first wife had learned of the relationship when the daughter was sixteen, and her discovery resulted in separation and eventual divorce. Prior to his request for treatment, the patient had remarried and visited his daughter for the first time in five years. When a second visit led to recurrence of incestuous behavior, he apprised his second wife of this difficulty and sought help.

The treatment plan consisted of covert sensitization to be accomplished by pairing noxious scenes with scenes of incestuous behavior. The subject was first trained in deep muscle relaxation. He was then presented with each of ten scenes of incestuous behavior that he had previously sorted according to how strong his desire would be to indulge in the depicted activity. After the presentation of each scene, a noxious scene was immediately presented. For the first five treatment days, this scene was one of severe nausea. However, the patient reported that this scene was not particularly aversive to him, so for the remainder of the treatment period, the scene was changed to one describing the patient and his daughter being discovered by his wife, his father-in-law, and the family priest.

One of the scenes was presented as follows:

You are alone with your daughter in your trailer and decide you want to caress her breasts. You put your arm around her and your hand down her blouse when the door opens and in walk your wife and Father X. Your daughter begins to cry and runs out the door. Your wife follows her. You are left alone with Father X, who looks at you in disbelief. He wants some explanation of what he's just seen. You know what he must think of you. You fumble for words. Finally, you begin to cry. You realize that you may have lost the respect of Father X and the love of your wife. Then you hear your daughter crying hysterically. Father X says, "Do you know what this may have done to your daughter?" You want to run, but you can't. You feel miserable and disgusted with yourself.

The description of the aversive scene lasted from thirty to ninety seconds with a sixty-second period between trials. These scenes were followed by a series of neutral scenes in which the patient was described as feeling happy, relaxed, and secure. The daughter's feelings toward her father during these scenes were presented as loving, respectful, admiring, and the like.

Since the goal of the treatment was not merely the suppression of incestuous behavior but the development of acceptable father-daughter interactions, scenes depicting fatherly behavior were also presented. These were followed by reinforcing consequences, such as respect and love not only from the daughter but also from the people in the aversive scenes as well. It was hoped that the strengthening of nondeviant behaviors would help in the suppression of the deviant behaviors.

Posttreatment indices of arousal as measured by penile circumference changes in response to slides and audiotapes of incestuous activity showed significant decreases when compared with pretreatment indices of the same measures. Moreover, arousal to nondeviant material increased in comparison to pretreatment measures.

Harbert et al., 1974

Other Sexual Disorders

As stated earlier in the chapter, almost any kind of activity can become sexually arousing simply because the necessary condition for the development of a sexual disorder is the pairing of some neutral object or activity with sexual gratification, which then is often used in masturbatory fantasies. As described by McCary (1967), other sexual disorders include the following:

1. **Troilism** Having sexual relationships with or in the presence of more than one person. Whether such acts should be considered pathological or not is questionable.

disorders of biological needs

2. **Sexual oralism** The exclusive reliance on oral-genital contact for sexual gratification.
3. **Sexual analism** The exclusive reliance on the anus instead of the vagina for penile insertion and gratification.
4. **Zoophilia (bestiality)** Sexual contacts with animals for either intercourse or masturbation.
5. **Frottage** The achievement of sexual satisfaction by rubbing, pressing, or pinching another person, typically without engaging in sexual intercourse.
6. **Saliromania** Obtaining sexual gratification from soiling or mutilating female bodies or clothing.
7. **Gerontosexuality** The preference for older people as sexual partners.
8. **Mate swapping** Exchange of marital partners.
9. **Coprophilia** Obtaining sexual gratification from handling feces.
10. **Necrophilia** Sexual relationships with corpses.

In general, these disorders are rare and their causes are quite different. Little research has actually been done on them. However, these sexual disorders are also learned or conditioned and illustrate our thesis that almost any activity or object can become sexually arousing and be used as a method of obtaining sexual gratification.

Summary

Genetic and prenatal hormonal factors determine the morphology of males and females, but sexual orientation and differentiation are largely determined by environmental influence. Of all the biological drives, the sex drive is the most susceptible to the influence of socialization.

Sexual behavior can be divided into four major components: sexual arousal, gender identification, heterosocial skills, and heterosexual skills. Sexual arousal is a function of stimuli that elicit a variety of physiological and psychological states, from mild excitement to orgasm. A four-stage cycle of sexual arousal occurs for both sexes, consisting of excitement, plateau, orgasm, and resolution.

Stimuli that elicit a sexual response can come from a variety of sources. Sexual arousal in sexual deviations is learned in the same manner as normal sexual arousal.

The modulating factors in the acquisition and maintenance of sexual orientation are gender identification, heterosocial behavior, and heterosexual behavior. Gender identification appears to be learned quite early and includes the behaviors we identify as masculine or feminine. Heterosocial skills are the social skills necessary to initiate and maintain casual and intimate relationships with the opposite sex. Heterosexual skills are the skills required to initiate and maintain a satisfactory and gratifying sexual relationship with an opposite-sex partner. Both heterosexual and heterosocial skills are probably acquired in early adolescence and developed throughout life.

Methods of assessing sexual behavior include self-reports of sexual urges and behavior; behavioral assessment of sexual arousal, heterosocial skills, heterosexual skills and gender identification, and physiological measures of sexual arousal. Physiological assessment of sexual arousal uses penile strain gauges to measure erection in males and vaginal probes to assess lubrication in females.

There are two types of sexual disorders: sexual dysfunctions and sexual deviations. The most common of all sexual problems are the sexual dysfunctions, which usually involve negative emotions associated with sexual performance. Four major types of sexual dysfunctions occur in males: primary impotence, secondary impotence, premature ejaculation, and ejaculatory incompetence. In males the secondary dysfunctions can be related to not being attracted to the sex partner, overindulgence in alcohol or drugs, or anxiety in the sexual situation. Predisposing factors in these disorders include ignorance about sexual behavior and rigid, moralistic rearing. The Masters and Johnson programs and other behavior therapy programs are very effective in treating these disorders.

Three major sexual disorders occur in women: orgasmic dysfunction, vaginismus, and dysparenuia. These dysfunctions result from physical factors, restrictive moral or religious teaching, ignorance, and fear of sexual behavior. The initial sexual experience is often important in precipitating these disorders. In general, the Masters and Johnson program and other behavioral techniques are extremely effective with these disorders.

The sexual deviations differ from conventional sexual behavior in terms of either the sex object or the type of sexual activities. Sexual deviations are largely the province of males: even the incidence of homosexuality is estimated to be lower in females. Homosexuality is sexual behavior between members of the same sex. Homosexual behavior is similar to heterosexual behavior, including foreplay, mutual masturbation, fellatio, or anal intercourse. Lesbians typically achieve orgasm from mutual masturbation or cunnilingus or imitate heterosexual intercourse by using a dildo. Most of the common beliefs about homosexuals' appearance and behavior are myths. There are no indications that homosexuals are any more maladjusted in nonsexual areas of their lives than heterosexuals, and there seems to be little evidence of biological causes for homosexuality. On the contrary, early sexual experiences appear to be most important in the development of this behavior. For individuals who desire sexual reorientation, behavior therapy has been fairly successful. Treatment has focused on modification of heterosocial skills and heterosexual skills, gender identification problems, and deviant sexual arousal. Techniques include fading, masturbation training, aversion therapy, and programs similar to that of Masters and Johnson.

Transvestism is dressing in clothes of the opposite sex in order to obtain sexual arousal or gratification. Most transvestites are heterosexual and find cross-dressing necessary for sexual arousal or as a prerequisite for coitus. Transvestism is almost exclusively a male problem. The exact causes of this disorder are not evident, although strong evidence suggests that cross-dressing encouraged early in life plays a major role. Transsexualism is a rare disorder involving intense denial of one's biological sex, usually associated with a history of cross-dressing. This is a disorder of gender identification rather than sexual arousal and is initiated quite early in life. The only major successful technique for transsexual disorders has been surgery resulting in sex change. Fetishism is the habitual use of a part of the body or an inanimate object to produce sexual arousal or gratification. Again, this disorder appears to be acquired through classical conditioning and is responsive to behavior therapy.

Exhibitionism and voyeurism are superficially similar to events that are normally part of foreplay, but these activities may be classified as disorders when gratification requires a nonconsenting partner and when the activities in themselves are sufficient for gratification. Pedophilia is the abuse of a child by an adult for sexual gratification. This is a complex disorder that may be homosexual or heterosexual and usually involves a number of activities, such as openly or secretly masturbating while interacting with a child, fondling a child, manipulating a child's sexual organs, and other sexual activities. The child molester is usually not violent. Sadism and masochism are sexual deviations in which sexual gratification depends on receiving or giving pain or humiliation.

Rape can be homosexual or heterosexual and may be statutory or forcible. Unfortunately, there are no specific programs for the treatment of rapists. Incest typically occurs between brother and sister or father and daughter; mother-son incest is rare. Although a variety of other types of sexual disorders exist, they are much less common than the ones already listed.

Key Concepts

androgens

cross-gender
  identification

cunnilingus

dyspareunia

ejaculatory
  incompetence

excitement stage

exhibitionism

fellatio

fetishism

gender behavior
  disturbance

gender role
  identification

heterosexual
  skills

heterosocial
  skills

homosexuality

incest

lesbianism

masochism

myotonia

orgasm stage

orgasmic
  dysfunction

pedophilia

plateau stage

premature
  ejaculation

primary
  impotence

rape

refractory period

resolution stage

sadism

secondary
  impotence

sensate focus

sexual deviation

sexual
  dysfunction

sexual
  orientation

sodomy

transsexualism

transvestism

vaginal
  photophethys-
  mograph

vaginismus

vasocongestion

voyeurism

Review Questions

1. What are the four stages of the human sexual response?

2. Why are humans able to be aroused by such a wide range of possible stimuli?

3. Can a person's sexual preferences be assessed by observing that person's sexual behavior? Why or why not?

4. What are the critical factors in acquisition of sexual orientation and preference?

5. How is gender identification acquired?

6. Name four major types of sexual dysfunction in males and three types in females, and define each type.

7. How are sexual dysfunctions acquired?

8. How does sensate focus help to modify sexual dysfunctions?

9. On what issue relating to the nature of homosexuality do psychologists disagree? What is the issue psychologists disagree on that relates to the modification of homosexual behavior?

10. Define each of the following:

    transvestism   pedophilia
    transsexualism   sadism
    fetishism   masochism
    exhibitionism   incest
    voyeurism

11. Why is counseling useful and perhaps necessary for a woman who has been raped?

disorders of biological needs
drug abuse

13

Key Topics

Addiction and psychological
dependency

Tolerance, withdrawal, and cross-
tolerance

Short- and long-term physiological
effects of alcohol

Controversy regarding alcoholism
and moderate drinking

Effect of family and cultural
attitudes on drinking behavior

Antabuse and aversion therapy in
treating alcoholism

Physiological and subjective effects
of depressants

Physiological and subjective effects
of stimulants

Physiological and subjective effects
of nicotine, hallucinogens, and
marijuana

Methadone maintenance

For almost every problem, the solution is simple: take a drug.

Free advice for the person troubled by arthritis, rheumatism, tension, drowsiness, insomnia, indigestion, a common cold, or a headache is never any farther away than the nearest television set. Too tense? Take a tranquilizer. Too drowsy? Take a pep pill. Headache? Take a pain reliever. For almost every problem, the solution is simple: take a drug. From time to time this stream of friendly counsel is interrupted by program material in which the solution to every problem is violence. Only occasionally are we treated to a public service message warning about the dangers of drug abuse.

Drugs are the usual device, in our society, not only for coping, but also for recreation, as attested by the countless billboard and magazine ads for cigarettes,

bourbon, and beer. How then does one define drug abuse? If we use legality as a criterion, we are faced with the contradiction that two of the most dangerous drugs—alcohol and tobacco—are legal, that some illegal drugs, such as marijuana, have not been shown to be dangerous, and that many drugs, such as amphetamines and barbiturates, are overprescribed by physicians and widely abused, often with tragic results. And then some of the abused substances are not even ordinarily considered drugs—for example, airplane glue, which is harmful, and hair spray, which is lethal.

DSM II classifies drug dependencies and addictions as personality disorders and assumes that addictions stem from underlying personality disturbances. **Drug dependency** is defined as habitual use of a drug, frequently out of perceived need, and the term is often used interchangeably with the term **addiction**. However, many professionals make a distinction between the two terms and define addiction as a physiological or biochemical change that, over time, necessitates greater amounts of the drug to produce the desired effect (**tolerance**). When the individual is deprived of the drug, the body may exhibit *withdrawal* symptoms, which may be minor or catastrophic to the person's health, depending on the drug. *Psychological dependency* is when no evidence of physiologic withdrawal symptoms occur upon withdrawal, but the individual experiences subjective distress and drug-seeking behavior when deprived of the drug. Individuals deprived of sex often exhibit similar behavior—distress and gratification-seeking behavior. Whether the drug is physically addicting or causes psychological dependency, deprivation produces effects opposite to those of the drug, particularly with the depressants and narcotics.

DSM III labels any undesirable, excessive indulgence in drugs as a **substance use disorder** without implying any personality disorder. The substance use disorders are subdivided into *substance abuse* and *substance dependency*. In substance abuse the individual develops psychological dependency on the drug, sometimes with unusual patterns of use, such as staying intoxicated for a week or more. The individual also exhibits disruptions of social behavior associated with drug use. Substance dependency involves substance abuse as well as tolerance and withdrawal (physiological addiction). If excessive use of the substance causes a physical disorder of the central nervous system, DSM III labels this reaction a *substance-induced organic mental disorder*.

If two or more drugs are taken, such as alcohol and barbiturates, the development of tolerance to one drug may transfer to the other drug(s). This is called **cross-tolerance** and occurs when physical dependency has developed for one drug, which is withdrawn and replaced by a second drug, and the second drug prevents the withdrawal syndrome. Cross-dependency occurs only when the two drugs belong to the same class.

Drugs may also have a *potentiating effect*: that is, one drug taken in combination with another drug may potentiate or increase the effect of the first drug. Potentiation may result in an **overdose (OD)**, which can cause extreme physiological reactions or even death. This is particularly a problem with street drugs, since the strength of the drug is usually unknown. OD deaths may be caused directly by the drug or by a factor associated with it. At present, deaths associated with overdose, particularly in the case of heroin, are a mystery, since no real evidence has been found that the drug overdose by itself is responsible for the death (Brecher 1972).

Although several systems of drug classification have been suggested, there is little agreement among mental health professionals on a classification system. For our purposes, we shall focus on alcoholism and then discuss other drugs under the headings of depressant, stimulant, narcotic, and hallucinogenic.

Alcohol

Of all drugs, alcohol poses the most serious health hazard to the public. It accounts for over 50 percent of first admissions to mental hospitals, is associated with more than half of all automobile accidents, and increases the suicide rate among users. Alcoholism is associated with a shortened life span because of its contribution to brain damage, liver disease, cancer, and heart failure. It is estimated that 10 million Americans are alcoholics, and the impact of alcoholism is even greater as it causes distress to other individuals—family, employers, and friends. In terms of employee absenteeism, alcohol costs employers billions of dollars each year. Moreover, 31 percent of all arrests in the United States are for public drunkenness.

The World Health Organization has defined alcoholism as excessive drinking in which individuals are dependent on alcohol to such a degree that they show noticeable disturbances in their mental and bodily health, their interpersonal relationships,

Tolerance and withdrawal

Abuse and dependency

Cross-tolerance

Potentiation and overdose

Prevalence of alcoholism

About 10 million people are addicted to alcohol in the United States.

and their social and economic functioning; or show the prodromal (beginning) signs of such disturbances (Kessel and Walton 1965). The two major factors in this definition are that the individual has lost *control* of consumption and that alcohol *interferes* with the individual's life.

Although alcohol is not usually regarded as a drug, it is a *depressant,* first acting on the higher brain centers, which have a primarily inhibiting effect on behavior. Thus, the initial effect of alcoholism seems to be stimulating: the individual becomes more animated as he or she becomes less inhibited.

Alcohol passes rapidly into the bloodstream through the stomach walls and from the small intestines. It must then be metabolized by a process called *oxidation.* In this process alcohol fuses with oxygen and is broken down so that its basic components leave the body as carbon dioxide and water. The primary site of this breakdown is the liver, which can break down about one ounce of 100 proof (50 percent) alcohol per hour in most individuals. Excesses of this amount remain in the bloodstream.

The effects of alcohol vary directly with the concentration of the drug in the bloodstream (blood alcohol level), which is dependent on the amount ingested in a given time, the absorption rate, and the efficiency of the liver. Tables 13–1 and 13–2 show these effects. Larger amounts interfere with complex thought processes, motor coordination, balance, speech, and vision. In large dosages, alcohol is capable of decreasing pain and causing sedation and sleep. As a matter of fact, before modern drugs, alcohol was used to prepare patients for surgery.

Development of Alcoholism

Though the causes of alcoholism have not been clearly determined, Jellinek (1952), in a study of the life history of alcoholics, has stereotyped four stages in the development of alcohol addiction:

Table 13-1 Relationships among Sex, Weight, Oral Alcohol Consumption, and Blood Alcohol Level

Absolute alcohol (ounces)	Beverage intake*	Blood alcohol levels (mg/100ml)					
		Female (100 lbs.)	Male (100 lbs.)	Females (150 lbs.)	Male (150 lbs.)	Female (200 lbs.)	Male (200 lbs.)
½	1 oz. spirits† 1 glass wine 1 can beer	0.045	0.037	0.03	0.025	0.022	0.019
1	2 oz. spirits 2 glasses wine 2 cans beer	0.09	0.075	0.06	0.05	0.045	0.037
2	4 oz. spirits 4 glasses wine 4 cans beer	0.18	0.15	0.12	0.10	0.09	0.07
3	6 oz. spirits 6 glasses wine 6 cans beer	0.27	0.22	0.18	0.15	0.13	0.11
4	8 oz. spirits 8 glasses wine 8 cans beer	0.36	0.30	0.24	0.20	0.18	0.15
5	10 oz. spirits 10 glasses wine 10 cans beer	0.45	0.37	0.30	0.25	0.22	0.18

*In one hour.
† 100 proof spirits.

Table 13-2 Blood Alcohol Level: Physiological and Psychological Results

Blood alcohol level	Effect	Blood alcohol level	Behavior
0.05%	Lowered alertness; usually good feeling, release of inhibitions, impaired judgment	0.03%	Dull and dignified
0.10%	Slowed reaction times and impaired motor function; less caution	0.05%	Dashing and debonair
0.15%	Large, consistent increases in reaction time	0.10%	May become dangerous and devilish
0.20%	Marked depression in sensory and motor capability, decidedly intoxicated	0.20%	Likely to be dizzy and disturbing
0.25%	Severe motor disturbance, staggering; sensory perceptions greatly impaired, smashed!	0.25%	May be disgusting and disheveled
0.30%	Stuporous but conscious—no comprehension of the world around them	0.30%	Delirious and disoriented and surely drunk
0.35%	Surgical anesthesia; about LD (lethal dose) 1, minimal level causing death	0.35%	Dead drunk
0.40%	About LD 50	0.60%	Chances are that the individual is dead

1. **The prealcoholic symptomatic phase** The prealcoholic starts drinking in conventional social situations but soon learns that alcohol relieves tension. The individual then begins to rely on alcohol as a tranquilizer, but heavy drinking is still infrequent, occurring only in times of crisis. However, the tolerance for tension decreases, and the rate of drinking increases until the individual is drinking almost daily. This phase usually lasts from several months to several years.

2. **The prodromal phase** This phase is marked by an onset of *blackouts,* after which the individual cannot remember the events occurring during the drinking, even though he or she may show few if any signs of intoxication during this period and carry on normal drinking activities. Jellinek believes that this amnesia without loss of consciousness (sometimes even without intake of excessive amounts of alcohol) indicates a heightened susceptibility to alcohol. In addition, other behaviors begin to make their appearance. Among these are surreptitious drinking, a preoccupation with alcohol that often takes the form of worrying about whether there will be enough to drink at a social gathering, having several drinks ahead of time in anticipation of a possible shortage, avid drinking in which the individual gulps the first two or three drinks, guilt feelings about drinking behavior with the realization that intake cannot be controlled, and avoidance of reference to alcohol in conversation.

3. **The crucial stage** In this stage alcohol begins to control the individual's life. After one drink, drinking cannot be stopped. The individual's social adjustment begins to deteriorate, and the person may begin to drink early in the morning or throughout the day. Soon, social and business obligations are neglected. In an attempt to fight the addiction, the individual may try to abstain for various periods of time. Episodic drinking or benders begin to occur at this stage, and hallucinations and delirium tremors may occur when drinking is stopped. Often the individual begins to rationalize the drinking, blaming it on others. At this stage the individual is usually drinking without regard to schedule, is chronically tense, and often begins to neglect good nutrition, which may aggravate the problem.

4. **Chronic stage** In this stage the individual loses complete control. Drinking is continuous, and benders are frequent. It is as if the individual lives only to drink. The bodily system becomes so adjusted to alcohol that abstinence causes withdrawal symptoms. At this stage the individual's life begins to deteriorate, and he or she may lose job, family, and self-respect. If liquor is not available, the individual may consume any liquid that contains alcohol, such as shaving lotion, hair tonic, or flavoring extracts. Malnutrition and physiological changes begin to occur.

These stages do not occur in all alcoholics. There is evidence that modest drinking does not cause blackouts in the prodromal stage, as Jellinek has suggested (Goodwin, Crane, and Guze 1969). Furthermore, the belief that the individual cannot control drinking once a single drink is taken in the crucial stage is not warranted (Marlatt, Demming, and Reid 1973).

Types of Alcoholism

Patterns of drinking seem to vary with a number of factors, including cultural and social differences, as well as individual differences in the acquisition of drinking behavior. A major question is whether there are one or several types of alcoholism. Jellinek (1960) claims there are four types or patterns of drinking behavior:

1. **Alpha** In this pattern of drinking, alcohol is used as a means of alleviating tension or pain. The drinking is then uncontrolled only in the sense that it violates society's rules about drinking, such as those of time, occasion, locale, amounts, and effects of drinking. The individual seems to have control of the drinking behavior and does have an ability to abstain. The principal difficulty of **alpha alcoholism** is disturbed interpersonal relationships. There are no signs that the alcoholism becomes progressive, and this pattern may persist for many years.

Onset of blackouts

Alcohol takes control

Loss of control

Tension relief by drinking

disorders of biological needs

The chronic stage of alcoholism leads to social isolation and deteriorating physical health.

2. **Beta** This drinking pattern is characterized by physical complications, such as gastritis or cirrhosis of the liver, which may occur with or without addiction or physiological dependence. With **beta alcoholism** the nutritional damage is a major effect, which causes a shorter life span and lower vocational productivity.

3. **Gamma** **Gamma alcoholism** affects the tissue tolerance for alcohol, demonstrating an increase in the amounts necessary to have an effect. The classic symptoms of this pattern include withdrawal symptoms, compulsion, and loss of control. Furthermore, a marked deterioration occurs in the individual's life circumstances.

4. **Delta** This pattern of drinking is also associated with an increased tolerance for alcohol and withdrawal symptoms. The major difference between delta and gamma alcoholism is that, in **delta alcoholism,** the individual is unable to abstain for even a short period of time, although the person may be able to control the amount of intake at any given time. The delta type dominates in wine-drinking countries such as France, while gamma alcoholism is much more frequent in the United States. These types of alcoholism have been largely accepted by clinicians, but they have not been validated by research evidence.

Physical complications

Tolerance

Inability to abstain for even a short time

disorders of biological needs: drug abuse   367

Consequences
of Chronic Alcoholism

When an individual has been drinking excessively for a long time or has a reduced tolerance for alcohol (because of various factors such as brain lesions), either alcohol intake or alcohol abstinence can cause serious acute psychological and physiological reactions—confusion, excitement, and delirium that are labeled acute or chronic brain disorders.

Pathological Intoxication

Pathological intoxication is an acute reaction that occurs in individuals whose tolerance to alcohol is chronically low or whose tolerance has been reduced by exhaustion, emotional stress, or other conditions. Following the consumption of small amounts of alcohol, these individuals may become disoriented, confused, and occasionally violent. This state is usually followed by deep sleep with complete amnesia afterwards. Amnesia for the episode and extreme unacceptable social behavior are usually the prime characteristics of this disorder.

Delirium

Delirium tremens (DTs) is a common reaction among those who drink excessively for long periods of time. DTs may occur after a prolonged alcoholic bout followed by a period of abstinence. Usually the delirium is preceded by a period of restlessness or insomnia during which the individual feels quite tense. The situational context (for example, a sterile hospital room or other sensory-deprived situation) may enhance the probability of DTs. When DTs occur, they include:

1. Disorientation for time and place
2. Vivid hallucinations, such as snakes, elephants, or small animals
3. Acute panic
4. Extreme suggestibility (the individual can be induced to see almost any form or animal simply by having them suggested)
5. Marked tremors of the hand, tongue, and lips, a prime symptom of this disorder

Korsakoff's psychosis and Wernicke's syndrome

6. Physiological symptoms, such as perspiration, fever, and a rapid and weak heartbeat.

The delirium may last from three to six days and usually is followed by deep sleep. After recovery the individual is rather badly scared and may not resume drinking for a short period of time. However, drinking usually recurs, followed by a return to the hospital and more DTs. The death rate from delirium tremors in alcoholics has been estimated to be as high as 10 percent (Tavel 1962). However, some of the newer tranquilizing drugs have reduced the death rate and have ameliorated many of the symptoms of this disorder. Drugs such as chlordiazepoxide are fairly effective in controlling DTs.

Acute Alcoholic Hallucinosis

In **acute alcoholic hallucinosis** the main symptoms are auditory hallucinations. The individual hears voices, usually making critical and sarcastic remarks about personal weaknesses. The voices may evaluate these weaknesses for the individual and may suggest that the person is going to be punished. Panic may occur when the individual hears footsteps approaching in a threatening manner, gunshots, sharpening of knives, or similar possible threats, and may scream or attempt suicide. This condition continues for several days or even weeks, during which the individual is depressed but fairly well oriented and coherent except for the hallucinations. This disorder may be precipitated by alcohol or, in some cases, by other drugs in an individual who is already maladjusted.

Cerebral Beri Beri

One of the consequences of alcoholism is a form of malnutrition, called **cerebral beri beri**. Because of its high caloric content, alcohol provides most of the individual's calories. Consequently, the alcoholic eats less because of poor appetite or lack of money to buy food. This malnutrition may be associated with a shortage of water-soluble vitamins, particularly vitamin B—a shortage that causes beri beri. Beri beri can cause either **Korsakoff's psychosis** or **Wernicke's syndrome.**

The gradual loss of memory in chronic alcoholics can be permanent if the disease

disorders of biological needs

has progressed sufficiently. The loss affects recent memory first, and progresses. Korsakoff's psychosis is marked by confusion, disorientation, and amnesia, and is distinguished from other aspects of alcoholism by a tendency to fill in the memory gaps by making up answers to questions, or **confabulation.** This confabulation is an attempt to maintain self-esteem rather than admit the frightening amount of confusion and memory loss.

Whereas Korsakoff's psychosis is a disorder primarily of behavior and thought processes, Wernicke's syndrome is diagnosed primarily in terms of neurological symptoms (Levitt 1976). Wernicke's syndrome is manifested by sudden paralysis of the muscles controlling eye movement, by an inability to maintain balance when walking (ataxia), and by disturbances of consciousness (amnesia and disorientation for time, place, and situation). The individual with Wernicke's syndrome finds concentrating very difficult and answers questions very slowly.

The development of physical dependency on alcohol causes other physiological changes as well. Perhaps the best known is cirrhosis of the liver, a disorder characterized by an inflammation and hardening of the liver tissue. Chronic alcoholics develop three types of liver disease: fatty livers, alcoholic hepatitis, and cirrhosis (Gall and Mostof 1973). The consequences of chronic alcohol consumption can obviously be quite unpleasant.

Research and Theory

One assumption about alcohol is that once the alcoholic takes a drink, a compulsion is set off that cannot be stopped until the person is completely inebriated. This belief was based on the hypothesis that alcoholism is a disease that the individual is powerless to control. However, the assumption of "first drink, then drunk" has been seriously questioned in recent years. Sobell, Sobell, and Christelman (1972) evaluated this hypothesis with a population of over 200 alcoholics. They found that most alcoholics also believed this myth. However, in a series of studies conducted at Patton State Hospital with chronic gamma alcoholics who were asked to ingest between one and six ounces of 80 proof liquor, Sobel et al. found that only between 2 and 5 percent left the hospital to obtain more alcohol.

A similar study comparing alcoholics and social drinkers also tested the belief that one drink leads to uncontrolled drinking (Marlatt, Demming, and Reid 1973). Subjects were told that the experiment was a study of taste preference. Before the actual taste comparison began, subjects were given either vodka and tonic or a glass of tonic water. Half of the subjects were told that they were drinking alcohol, while the other half were told that they were receiving a nonalcoholic beverage.

Three different decanters were then prepared from three different brands of vodka with four ounces in each decanter and were filled with twenty ounces of tonic water. Half of the group that expected to taste alcohol and half of the group that expected to taste tonic water were then allowed to drink as much as they wanted from each decanter and asked to rate each one with an adjective such as bitter, strong, watery, and sweet, while the experimenter excused himself to set up another study. The rest of the subjects were allowed to drink as much as they wanted from three similarly filled decanters that contained no alcohol.

Cirrhosis of the liver

If the loss-of-control hypothesis were correct, the alcoholics given the vodka should have consumed more alcohol than those initially given only tonic water, whether or not they believed they were drinking alcohol. Furthermore, they should have consumed more than social drinkers in this situation. They did not. Their drinking behavior was not affected by the presence or absence of alcohol in the drinks they were served during the waiting and testing periods. Instead, the relevant variable was expectation: subjects who expected alcohol, whether they actually received it or not, drank more than those who expected tonic. Clearly, the loss-of-control hypothesis is questionable.

The myth of one drink

As for the role of personality patterns in alcoholism, the most impressive data result from a longitudinal study conducted by Jones (1968). From his Oakland growth study, which started about thirty-five years

Expectation as the relevant variable

ago when the subjects were approximately ten years of age, Jones interviewed men in their midforties about current drinking patterns to classify them as either problem or nonproblem drinkers. He found that problem drinkers tended to be rebellious, compulsive, and hostile as children, while the nonproblem drinkers were often more productive and ambitious, with a wide range of interests. The traits of the future problem drinkers caused social difficulty even in early years. In women, however, the pattern was less clear. Among women, the problem drinkers and those who abstained from alcohol altogether in adulthood were very similar. Both groups were characterized in high school as vulnerable, withdrawn, dependent, irritable, and sensitive to criticism. In other words, the patterns of poor social adaptation that correlated with heavy drinking in men were in women associated with either problem drinking or total abstinence. Other studies of the alcoholic personality have been confusing at best (Franks 1970).

Similarity of problem drinkers and total abstainers

Another important aspect of drinking patterns is the ethnic or cultural background of alcoholics. A high prevalence of alcoholism occurs in northern France, the United States, Sweden, Switzerland, Poland, and northern Russia. A low prevalence is found in Greece, Italy, and Spain. The reasons for these differences are complex and cannot be attributed simply to abstinence in various cultural groups. For example, Moslems do not drink because of their religious beliefs and their alcoholism rates are low, but a large percentage of Jews do drink, yet their alcoholism rates are also low. Overindulgence in alcohol appears to be a function of the way drinking is viewed relative to customs, values, and sanctions. The National Institute on Alcohol Abuse and Alcoholism (NIAAA) (1974) has listed eight conditions that are associated with a low incidence of alcoholism among groups who use alcohol freely:

NIAAA's 8 conditions

Genetic differences in sensitivity to alcohol

1. A child is exposed to alcohol early in life but within a strong family or religious setting. When the beverage is served, it is usually diluted in small quantities, the result being a low blood alcohol level.

2. The beverages commonly consumed, such as beer and wine, usually contain relatively large amounts of nonalcoholic components per volume, which also results in low blood alcohol levels.
3. The alcoholic beverage is considered primarily a food and is usually consumed with meals.
4. The model presented by parents is one of moderate drinking.
5. No moral importance is attached to drinking, and it is not considered either a virtue or a sin. Drinking is not viewed as proof of adulthood or virility.
6. Abstinence is socially accepted. Declining a drink is not considered rude or ungracious.
7. Excessive drinking or intoxication is not socially expected nor considered stylish, comic, or tolerable. It is not viewed as proof of adulthood or virility.
8. There is wide and usually complete agreement among members of the group on what might be called the ground rules of drinking.

The evidence for biological explanations of alcoholism has been mixed. Clear differences have been shown between Orientals and Caucasians at birth in sensitivity to alcohol: Japanese, Korean, and Taiwanese respond with obvious facial flush and clear signs of intoxication after being given small amounts of alcohol that have no detectable effects on Caucasians. Such ethnic differences indicate that sensitivity to alcohol is related to genetic factors, possibly affecting the autonomic nervous system (Wolff 1972).

Further support for the genetic basis of alcoholism comes from a study by Goodwin and his colleagues (Goodwin et al. 1973; Goodwin et al. 1974), who found that sons of alcoholics placed in foster homes early in life were four times more likely to develop alcoholism than adoptees without known alcoholism in their biological parents. In a second study they compared rates of alcoholism for sons of alcoholic parents adopted in infancy with brothers who remained with their alcoholic parents. No significant differences appeared in the high

disorders of biological needs

rate of alcoholism in these two groups. However, the data on twin studies evaluated by Rosenthal (1970) are much less convincing.

Psychodynamic and psychoanalytic theories focus on the role of oral fixation and unsatisfied dependency needs. There is some evidence for this theory, since it has been demonstrated both that alcoholics are more likely than nonalcoholics to have intense oral needs, as reflected in heavy cigarette smoking (Maletzky and Kotter 1974), and to be dependent (McCord, McCord, and Gudeman 1960).

Originally, behavioral explanations centered on alcoholism as a learned response that occurred because alcohol reduces the tension arising from social frustration and anxiety. This assumption is based on Conger's earlier work (1951) with lower organisms, which demonstrated that alcohol reduced fear. That assumption was buttressed when Freed (1971) demonstrated that conflict and anxiety increase alcohol consumption.

These results also support a hypothesis long popular among many mental health professionals—that alcoholism develops in individuals who are neurotic, maladjusted, unable to relate to others, and low in frustration tolerance because alcohol acts as a sedative to reduce their ambivalence and conflict. That hypothesis has a major flaw, however. Studies have demonstrated that in alcoholics the initial few drinks increase rather than decrease negative emotions, a response that does not occur in nonalcoholics (Mendelson 1964; Nathan et al. 1970). One explanation may be that this reaction develops after drinking has begun to cause negative consequences, but another explanation is that the hypothesis is too simplistic.

The alcoholics-as-neurotics hypothesis has to be considered in light of two possibilities. The first, described in detail by Davidson (1974), is that alcoholism can develop in individuals, adjusted or maladjusted, as a function of positive reinforcement *per se*. In other words, alcohol consumption persists because alcohol intake is pleasant. The rate of drinking increases because it is reinforcing, and after a period of time a high rate of drinking

behavior stabilizes. The second is that the individual's difficulties in social adjustment and negative emotion are possibly a consequence rather than a cause of the high rate of drinking.

A pertinent question in this type of analysis is why some individuals become problem drinkers and others do not. This question may best be answered in terms of the individual's acquisition of appropriate drinking skills. For example, studies have demonstrated that alcoholics are less sensitive to internal cues of intoxication, tend to take larger sips, tend to drink more rapidly, are more likely to drink straight rather than mixed drinks, and exhibit other behaviors that result in rather rapid inebriation (Schaefer, Sobell, and Mills 1971). Appropriate drinking skills are probably acquired both by observation of others (modeling) and by direct reinforcement for controlled drinking. Furthermore, these skills are probably acquired as a function of the eight factors delineated by the NIAAA (1974). Thus, while variation might occur in individual cases, the three factors that are crucial in behavioral explanations are (1) the anxiety-reducing effect of alcohol, (2) positive reinforcement for drinking or nondrinking, and (3) failure to acquire appropriate drinking skills through modeling or direct experience. It is also probable that biological factors may play a role in the development of alcoholic disorders.

Another important aspect of alcoholic disorders is the blackout or amnesia that occurs in alcoholic states. This phenomenon may be explained by **state-dependent learning:** learning that occurs in the drug states is often not accessible when the individual is in the normal state (Storm and Smart 1965). In other words, this is a form of learned discrimination in which behavior acquired in the drinking state is dissociated from behavior in the sober state. This lack of transfer or stimulus generalization decrement increases as the dose rate of alcohol increases. As a result, memory for events in the drunken state should diminish in the sober state and eventually disappear, a phenomenon that accounts for blackouts.

Oral fixation and dependency

The alcoholics-as-neurotics hypothesis

Which came first: alcoholism or social maladjustment?

Blackouts and state-dependent learning

The negative experiences and sanctions against drinking learned while a person is sober have little or no effect once the individual is drunk.

Therefore, the negative experiences and injunctions against drinking that a person learns while sober have little or no effect once drunk, and uncontrolled drinking may occur. State-dependent learning also explains why students who use stimulants to keep awake while studying may have difficulty recalling material for an exam unless they also use the stimulants before taking the exam.

Assessment

Despite the wide use of self-report in assessing alcohol abuse, most clinicians question the validity of this procedure. Attempts have nonetheless been made to help alcoholics evaluate their drinking behavior. Sobell and Sobell (1973) have developed an alcoholic intake sheet to be used by individuals for monitoring and recording their own daily alcohol consumption in terms of time, type of drink, percentage of alcohol content, number of sips per drink, total amount consumed, and the environment in which the drinking occurred. It is fairly obvious that the accuracy of this self-monitoring procedure is directly related to the motivation of individuals to give an accurate estimate of their drinking patterns.

disorders of biological needs

In cases of suspected intoxication or "drinking under the influence," the breathalizer test is used to evaluate the presence of alcohol.

Since many individuals with drinking problems are motivated to conceal their drinking rate, valid assessments of their problems also require either behavioral observation or monitoring with physiological techniques.

Self-monitoring can also be used to regulate one's blood alcohol level. For example, Huber, Karlin, and Nathan (1976) taught subjects how to estimate their blood alcohol level by teaching them the relationship between their weight and dose rate. They taught another group of subjects to estimate their blood-alcohol level by focusing on internal cues, such as muscle states, subjective feeling, clarity of thinking, and other internal sensory cues related to blood alcohol level. They found that attending to a combination of internal and external cues improved the accuracy of their estimates of inebriation. Such a technique would be useful in teaching individuals to estimate their state of inebriation and control it (Huber, Karlin, and Nathan 1976).

In behavioral assessment, the best method seems to be to observe drinking behavior as it occurs in the natural setting by recording (1) the number of drinks ordered,

(2) the kind of drinks ordered, and (3) the size of sips. Using this method, one can easily determine not only the sip length and the interval between sips and drinks but also whether the individual sips or gulps, and whether mixed rather than straight drinks are ordered. With this technique alcoholics can be differentiated from social drinkers (Schaefer, Sobell, and Mills 1971). The same technique has also been used by Kessler and Gromberg (1974) to observe and record components of drinking behavior in various bars in the community. By observing how individuals drink, one may determine whether they are alcoholic. Some investigators have also set up bars or other analogues in institutions to observe drinking behavior (Miller 1976). If a surreptitious drinking measure is required, a taste-rating task similar to the one we discussed previously used by Marlatt, Demming, and Reed (1973) can be used.

In physiological assessment, two major methods of analyzing blood alcohol concentration are the *breathalyzer* and urine surveillance. The small portable device consisting of a glass tube connected to a balloonlike collection bag (breathalyzer) is well known to those who fear being arrested for drinking while driving. Such devices

Observing drinking behavior in the natural setting

range from simple screening instruments that provide crude but immediate estimates to more complex types that provide accurate estimates by means of chromatography. Urinalysis and blood tests also can be used to determine ethanol levels.

Modification of Alcoholism

The treatment of chronic alcoholism generally begins with a **detoxification** program that consists of eliminating alcohol from the individual's system and treating the withdrawal symptoms. The person is usually hospitalized and often tranquilized for five to seven days to control withdrawal symptoms. The individual is also given massive doses of vitamins, especially B-complex, to counter alcohol-caused nutritional deficits, and a high liquid intake to combat dehydration, which is common in withdrawal. On occasions, anticonvulsive drugs, such as Dilantin, may be administered to eliminate the possibility of seizure. Detoxification is often necessary before other programs can be administered.

Pharmacological treatment of alcoholism usually consists of administration of **disulfiram (Antabuse).** This is a drug that, after ingestion, causes nausea and vomiting when the individual drinks alcohol. Disulfiram is merely a deterrent to alcohol intake and is rarely used as a sole treatment approach. Its function is to allow a period of time during which the individual cannot drink. If disulfiram is not combined with other approaches after release from the hospital or clinic, however, the individual may discontinue the disulfiram and return to former drinking habits. If the individual is not motivated to stop drinking, this procedure, like others, is useless.

Perhaps the best known treatment of alcoholism is that provided by **Alcoholics Anonymous** (AA). This is group therapy in a loosely knit voluntary fellowship of alcoholics who meet regularly to help each other stay sober. It is based on the assumption that alcoholism is a mental, physical, and spiritual problem, and that alcoholics cannot stop drinking without external help.

AA sees alcoholism as a lifelong disease, much like diabetes, and recommends total abstinence as the way to recovery. The three-fold recovery program is outlined in twelve suggested steps that begin with the alcoholic's acceptance of his or her powerlessness over alcohol. The effectiveness of the AA program is difficult to determine because AA keeps no formal records and because many problem drinkers either refuse to join AA or quit. However, if the individual's goal is total abstinence and if the individual can follow the simple program, AA is an effective procedure (Leach 1973).

In general, psychotherapeutic approaches have been ineffective, as have a variety of other treatment modalities. For example, Gerard, Saenger, and Wile (1962) state that only 19 percent of alcoholics from a variety of clinics and treatment programs were abstinent after one year. Other studies of the effects of psychotherapy have also shown that its value in modifying alcoholism is questionable (Hill and Blanc 1967; Wallgren and Berry 1970).

Aversion therapy has long been used in the treatment of alcoholism and was originally used with nausea-inducing drugs (Voegtlin 1947; Lemere and Voegtlin 1950). In essence, treatment consisted of four to seven sessions over a period of ten days during which the individual was given a dose of oral emetine followed by an injection of emetine-pilocarpine-ephedrine mixture as a predisposing factor to vomiting. The individual was then given an ounce of alcohol and instructed to concentrate on the sight, smell, and thought of alcohol, then to taste and swallow it. Additional amounts of alcohol, usually with water, were given until vomiting occurred. The client would then be given a glass of beer containing a tartar emetic to prolong vomiting, and the procedure was repeated. During subsequent sessions, the doses of emetine were increased and the range of beverages ingested was broadened. The latter aspect of the program was important in view of the finding by Lemere and Voegtlin that establishing aversion to these beverages was difficult because the reaction was

disorders of biological needs

An Alcoholics Anonymous meeting. Group therapy sessions with sharing of alcoholic experiences is the method of coping with alcoholism used in AA meetings.

fairly specific and did not generalize from one beverage to another. In a follow-up of over 4,000 cases, Lemere and Voegtlin reported an overall abstinence rate of 51 percent over a one- to ten-year period. However, it should be noted that booster aversion conditioning sessions were often necessary and that this procedure was counter-indicated on medical grounds in about 40 percent of the cases.

Some researchers have suggested that electrical aversion conditioning may be a more effective behavioral treatment for alcoholism than nausea-inducing drugs (Eysenck and Beech 1971; Franks 1966). Taste stimuli such as alcohol are, however, more readily conditioned to gastrointestinal responses such as nausea than to pain responses produced by shock (Garcia, McGoward, and Green 1962). But chemically produced aversion often violates the parameters of traditional S-R conditioning since

the alcohol (CS) follows the aversive stimulus (UCS). Controlling the parameters of the aversive stimuli is easier with electrical aversion. Furthermore, mild electric shock is probably less repulsive than vomiting both to the client and the therapist. An example of this procedure is a study by Blake (1965) who used an escape conditioning design in which individuals were asked to sip but not swallow their preferred beverage. A shock of increasing intensity, starting randomly above a perceptible pain threshhold was then contingently paired with sips on a random 50 percent reinforcement schedule, and the response of spitting out the alcohol immediately terminated the shock. Conditioning sessions lasted four to eight days. Another group of subjects in this particular study received relaxation

box 13-1
Institutional
Treatment of an
Alcohol Addicted
Physician

At the time of admission, the patient was a forty-year-old, successful general practitioner with a long history of alcohol abuse. He was the only son of a prominent family. The patient's father was in his late sixties at the time the patient was born. He died when the patient was twelve. First use of alcohol started at about this time.

Patient reported use of alcohol throughout school, including medical school. He first began to experience blackouts at age twenty-seven. Patient drank each day, with the first drink taken upon arising and the last drink at bedtime. His medical practice, although quite successful, began to suffer from his increased alcohol dependence. Marital and family problems resulted from the patient's assaultive behavior while intoxicated.

Previous to admission for long-term treatment of alcohol abuse, the patient had entered several short-term treatment programs. The longest period of sobriety upon completion of these programs was two months. The patient came to the hospital following an unsuccessful suicide attempt. He tried to shoot himself, but the gun misfired. At the time, the patient was estranged from his wife and four children. He had been unable to practice for a month prior to admission.

The patient was voluntarily admitted to in-patient care at a mental health facility specializing in the long-term treatment of addictive disorders. He had been detoxified at home by a local physician previous to admission. Treatment consisted of a one-year period of hospitalization, including a program of increasing privilege based on abstinence from the addicting substance. Daily group therapy sessions conducted by various mental health professionals, including psychiatrists; psychologists; psychiatric social workers; recreational, music and occupational therapists; and nurse practitioners; and recovered addicts were a key part of treatment. Alcoholics Anonymous sessions were held twice weekly in the unit and antabuse therapy was also available to the patients.

Upon admission, the patient was confined to the treatment building for the first two weeks. Treatment included mileu therapy with the patient being responsible for various ward duties. Various psychological and physical tests were administered to help evaluate the patient's case.

Covert desensitization

training in addition to the aversion conditioning. In a one-year follow-up of individuals given aversion therapy alone, 23 percent were abstinent, 27 percent were improved (their drinking was now social and in no danger of escalation), 27 percent had relapsed, and 23 percent could not be found. Of those treated with relaxation and aversion conditioning, 45 percent were abstinent, 12 percent were improved, 30 percent relapsed, and 13 percent were missing. In electrical aversion therapy, as in the use of nausea-inducing drugs, booster sessions are often required. The above estimate seems to be fairly representative of results of electrical aversion with alcoholics (O'Leary and Wilson 1975). However, the effects of electrical aversion conditioning with alcoholics may be more related to general therapeutic factors such as placebo than to any specific conditioning process (Miller et al. 1973).

Because of the objections to mild electric shock and nausea-inducing drugs, covert desensitization is often considered a reasonable alternative (Cautela 1970). This approach involves the pairing of aversive images and fantasies with alcohol. A possible fantasy script might be as follows:

You are walking into a bar; you decide to have a glass of beer; you are now walking toward the bar. As you approach the bar, you have a funny feeling in the pit of your stomach. Your stomach feels all queasy and nauseous. Some liquid comes up in your throat and is very sour. You try to swallow it back down; but, as you do, food particles start coming up your throat to your mouth. You are now reaching the bar, and you order a beer.

Based on abstinence from alcohol and attendance at group sessions, the patient earned grounds privileges within one month of hospital admission. Since he was a licensed practitioner, the patient began a work assignment in the operating room of the medical hospital nearby. Treatment was uneventful until the patient's first overnight home visit. He returned to the building intoxicated and abusive. He had to be detoxified again at the time.

Work and home visit privileges were denied for a two-week period. Following this episode the patient expressed a desire to enter a residency offered in neurology by the treating facility. He was highly qualified for the program and therefore began his residency with the next class about two months after his slip.

He remained in treatment until the end of his residency, decreasing therapy sessions as he began to function in his new professional capacity as a staff neurologist.

The patient was followed up yearly for a twelve-year period following his hospitalization for alcohol addiction. In addition, he was also informally contacted from time to time as he remained on the staff of the treating facility. Two years after completing treatment, he reported reconciling with his wife, and the marriage has remained stable since then.

Patient reports no incidents of alcohol use. At the time of admission, he was severely dehydrated and undernourished due to prolonged alcohol abuse. He gained thirty pounds during the treatment period, and now reports he must be very careful not to "abuse" food. When he feels pressures in his professional or family situation, he eats ice cream instead of taking a drink. Because of this he has gained another thirty pounds over a twelve-year follow-up period.

In the interim, the patient has built a very successful private practice, conducted research into the neurological implications of alcohol addiction, and started a group therapy session for drug addicts with two of his colleagues. He reports that he feels he can never again touch alcohol because even one drink will lead to a return to the destructive behavior he exhibited on admission. He no longer attends therapy sessions himself but feels the therapy group he conducts twice a week for drug addicts helps him maintain his sobriety.

As the bartender is pouring the beer, puke comes into your mouth. . . . As soon as your hand touches the glass, you can't hold the vomit down any more. You have to open your mouth, and you puke. It goes all over your hand, all over the glass and the beer. You can see it floating around in the beer. . . (Cautela 1970, p. 87).

The effectiveness of this technique is similar to that of other aversion procedures.

Perhaps the most promising type of behavior therapy with alcoholism is the *multi-modal approach* in which the modes of treatment are selected by the individual (Sobell and Sobell 1973). For example, an individual may choose to be abstinent or may choose to modify drinking behavior and acquire appropriate social drinking patterns. Such comprehensive treatment programs have been devised by Sobell and Sobell, and include self-management training, social skills training, video feedback of drunk and sober behavior, a programmed failure experience, and aversive conditioning. The interesting aspect of such programs is that individuals can be trained in appropriate drinking skills. Training involves punishment by mild electric shock for inappropriate drinking behavior, such as ordering a straight drink, taking a sip larger than one-sixth of the total volume of a mixed drink or one-twelfth of a beer, ordering a drink within twenty minutes of a previous drink, or ordering any more than three drinks. The goal was to teach individuals how to monitor their drinking and pace themselves. Individuals were also shown a

Acquisition of appropriate drinking behavior

videotape of themselves while drunk, another powerfully aversive experience. At a six-months follow-up, 78 percent were abstinent in the social drinking group, and 75 percent were abstaining in the group who chose to abstain. These results demonstrate that controlled drinking may be taught. Furthermore, when alcoholic patients are trained to accurately discriminate differences in their blood alcohol levels as well, the effects of these procedures are likely to be enhanced (Lovibond and Caddy 1970).

Other Depressant Drugs

A wide variety of legal and illegal drugs—depressants, stimulants, hallucinogens, tranquilizers—can be as destructive as alcohol. Many of these drugs, such as opium, have been known throughout human history, while others, such as LSD, have only recently been discovered. Until the turn of the century, many of these drugs were sold legally. For example, Laudanum, a form of opium, was widely dispensed before the twentieth century to aid sleep. Morphine was commonly administered as a cure for dysentery and other ailments during the Civil War. The major ingredient in the best-selling cough syrups at the turn of the century was a newly discovered miracle drug called heroin. Cocaine was a widely used drug taken by such famous people as Freud and even the legendary Sherlock Holmes. However, in 1914 the Harrison Narcotic Act was passed, and since that time most drugs have been subject to state and federal regulations.

Central nervous system depressants

Depressants act on the central nervous system to reduce pain, tension, and anxiety; to relax and disinhibit; and to slow down intellectual and motor reactivity. Alcohol, the narcotics, tranquilizers, and barbiturates are the major types of depressants and account for the majority of all drug abuse, both legal and illegal. Depressants have a number of important effects in common: physiological addiction occurs, tolerance develops, and excessive doses depress the functioning of vital systems such as respiration and may result in death.

Rapid action of heroin

Narcotics

Narcotics induce relaxation, produce euphoria, and provide relief from pain. They have both sedative and analgesic properties. The major narcotics, such as morphine and codeine, are derived from the opium poppy. Morphine was widely used as a pain reliever during the mid-nineteenth century, but after it became apparent that morphine was addictive, attempts were made to find a narcotic that would relieve pain without causing addiction. Subsequently, Heinrick Dreser transformed morphine into heroin, a supposedly nonaddictive drug that was much stronger than morphine. Interestingly enough, heroin was originally considered useful in treating addiction to morphine.

Morphine
Morphine is frequently used for the relief of pain and is administered by injection because, when taken orally, it is deactivated by the enzymes of the stomach and intestines. Rather than acting on the pain receptors themselves, morphine inhibits systems in the brain that mediate the effect of adverse stimuli. In normal subjects only about 10 percent find the effects of an injection of morphine pleasant, 50 percent find it neutral, and 40 percent find it unpleasant (Levitt 1976). One reason for unpleasant effects is that morphine consistently produces nausea, constricts the pupils of the eyes, and has a constipating effect on the stomach and intestines. The main reason for overdose deaths with morphine is an inhibition of mechanisms in the brain stem that maintain respiration.

Heroin
Because of the nature of the blood-brain barrier, **heroin** enters the brain more rapidly and in greater concentration than morphine and thus produces a much more powerful effect. This faster action results in the rush, which is described as being similar to sexual orgasm and lasting about one or two minutes, followed by euphoria. Not

disorders of biological needs

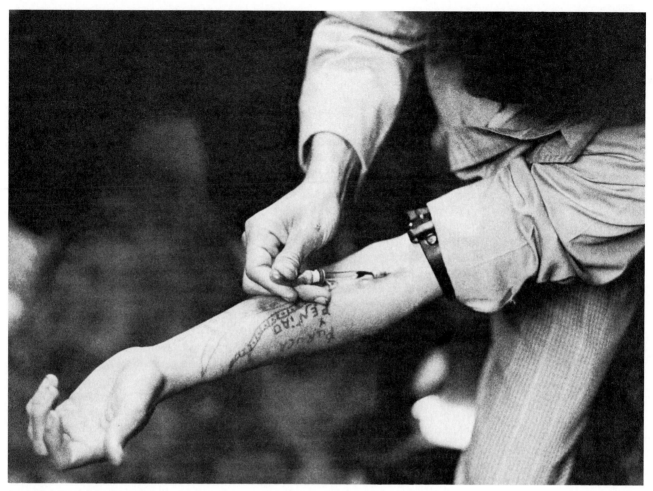

An addict "mainlining" heroin.

all individuals have this euphoric experience the first time, but all do respond initially with nausea, which in some cases counteracts the euphoric effects. Heroin can be sniffed, smoked, injected into a vein ("mainlined"), or injected beneath the skin ("skin popping"), and its effects last from four to six hours. Bodily needs, including those for food and sex, markedly diminish, and pleasant feelings of relaxation, euphoria, and well-being arise during this time. Afterward, the addict begins to crave the drug. Apparently, when heroin is sniffed or smoked and is of high purity, it is not highly addictive, since only about 7 percent of the soldiers in Vietnam who had

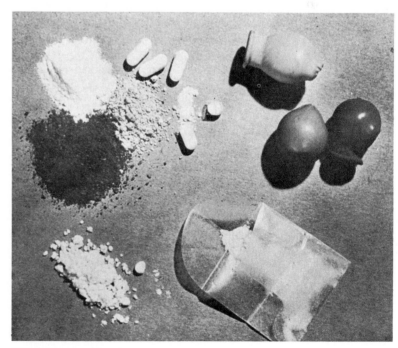

Different forms of heroin.

smoked heroin were addicted after returning to the United States (Robins 1974). For mainliners, the story is entirely different: about 75 percent of them remain addicted.

Codeine

Codeine is similar to morphine, but differs in that it is only about one-twelfth as powerful. However, codeine retains about two-thirds of its effectiveness when taken orally as compared to injection, while morphine retains only about one-thirtieth of its potency. Although codeine has been claimed to be less addictive than morphine, it is not if equal analgesic dosages are used (Jaffe 1975). Consequently, morphine is used if injection is called for, and codeine is used for oral ingestion. Examples are orally administered analgesics and antitussives (cough suppressants). Since relatively small amounts of codeine are effective and create little danger of addiction, it is often combined with other nonnarcotic analgesics such as aspirin. The combination of codeine and aspirin has a potentiating effect and produces an even greater analgesic effect than either drug alone.

Methadone

Methadone is a synthetic narcotic analgesic that is similar to morphine but can be administered either orally or by injection. It is about twice as potent by injection as by mouth, but the onset of action is slow, with peak analgesia occurring after about two hours. Because of the high ratio of oral to injective effectiveness, methadone can be given orally for the control of moderate to severe pain.

In recent years methadone has been used in the treatment of heroin addiction. Transferring dependency from heroin to methadone is desirable because methadone produces milder withdrawal symptoms than heroin and allows oral administration. Theoretically, the goal, then, is to withdraw addicted individuals from methadone, but in actual practice they are usually maintained on methadone. Furthermore, this may be simply a case of cross-tolerance.

Although narcotics, particularly heroin, are often associated with deaths, there is little evidence of elevated levels of heroin or morphine in the blood of overdose victims (Levitt 1976). Autopsies have revealed that *syndrome "X,"*—cardiovascular collapse and pulmonary edema (fluid in the air sacs of the lungs)—can occur with a relatively small dose of injected heroin. The mechanism of syndrome X is not known, but it has been suggested that an allergic reaction occurs to the heroin or to the adulterants commonly mixed with heroin sold on the streets. Death is so rapid that victims are often found with the needle still in the arm. Evidence also suggests that many apparent heroin suicides may have been the unexpected consequences of normal dosage of heroin (Brecher 1972).

Tolerance to narcotics develops quite rapidly, often in less than a month, and may last as long as fifteen months after a single large injection of morphine (Murphree 1971). As tolerance increases, problems arise for the illegal user because the amount of narcotic intake necessary to produce an effect and avoid withdrawal greatly increases, and the habit becomes extremely expensive. Addicts have been known to go through withdrawal or enter treatment centers just to reduce their tolerance and thus reduce the cost of their habit.

As tolerance increases, physical dependence results, and withdrawal symptoms occur when the drug is discontinued. Although the speed of onset of the **withdrawal syndrome** may vary with the type of narcotic, the symptoms are about the same. If an adequate dose of the drug is not received within four to twelve hours, the individual begins to experience muscle pains, sneezes, sweats, become tearful, yawns a great deal, and has an uncontrollable craving for the drug. After thirty-six hours severe cramps, uncontrollable muscle twitches, restlessness, an increase in blood pressure and heart rate, inability to sleep, nausea and vomiting, and diarrhea also appear. Five to ten days are necessary for this reaction to subside completely, and death can occur if the individual has cardiovascular problems. Associated problems are the prolonged effects of malnutrition from poor eating hab-

What causes overdose deaths?

Withdrawal symptoms

disorders of biological needs

its; loss of sexual interests; respiratory difficulties; and the danger of abscesses, infections, tetanus, and hepatitis from unsterile needles.

The rate of narcotic addiction is about one in 3,000 members of the population, and males outnumber females eight to one (Richard and Carroll 1970). The cost of addiction may run more than $100 per day, and many addicts resort to illegal activities to meet the expense. Typically, such activities involve theft and prostitution. In England, in order to eliminate criminal sale and distribution of narcotics, addiction has been legalized and the addicted individuals placed under the care of a physician. Besides eliminating the profit for criminals, this procedure may also decrease addiction because addicts no longer need to sell drugs and initiate new members to pay for their own habit.

Barbiturates

New chemical compounds known as **bromides** were introduced during the mid-nineteenth century and became immediately popular as sedatives. Abuse often resulted in a *toxic psychosis* involving delusions, hallucinations, and a variety of neurological disturbances, that, for a time, was the leading cause of admission to mental hospitals (Jarvik 1967). In the 1930s bromides were replaced by more powerful sedatives called **barbiturates,** which were also used in the treatment of insomnia, anxiety, epilepsy, and in anesthesia. Many different drugs fall into this category, but the most common ones are *phenobarbital* (Nembutal), *secobarbital* (Seconal), and *butabarbital* (Butiserpine). These drugs are usually prescribed by physicians as sleeping pills or combined with diphenylhydantoin (Dilantin) to control seizures. On the street, they are known as downers, red devils, or rainbows. Their effects are similar to those of alcohol and include the possibility of a hangover the next day. Methatualone (Quaalude or Sopor), a sedative very similar to the barbiturates, has become unusually popular as a street drug.

Social side effects of heroin addiction

The long-acting barbiturates such as phenobarbital are usually used for sedation and are rarely abused. The short-acting barbiturates are used for prompt sedation and sleep and produce a euphoric state as well as muscle relaxation. In large doses they produce restlessness and weight loss and impair cognitive functions. Large doses can also cause death, as the diaphragm relaxes and the individual suffocates. Barbiturates are particularly dangerous, since they potentiate the effects of alcohol. Besides being very addictive, these drugs can cause internal bleeding, coma, and death from overdose.

Barbiturates potentiate alcohol

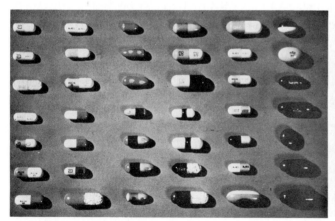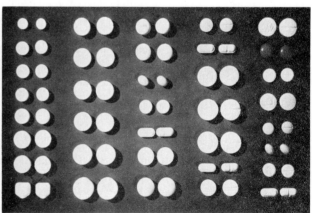

Different forms of barbiturates.

Excessive use of barbiturates can lead to the development of tolerance, including psychological as well as physiological dependency. Cross-dependency occurs between alcohol and barbiturates and the administration of barbiturates such as phenobarbital will terminate alcohol DTs. Approximately 3,000 deaths from overdoses of barbiturates occur per year and have claimed such unfortunates as Judy Garland and Marilyn Monroe (Bayh 1971).

Withdrawal from barbiturates is very similar to alcohol DTs and includes hallucinations, sweating, agitation, confusion, and insomnia. This reaction commences after about fifteen hours of abstinence and peaks at about thirty hours. Convulsions similar to grand mal seizures are common and may continue for a forty-seven-hour period. These symptoms last about five days, after which the individual sleeps and, upon waking, is much improved. However, insomnia or severe nightmares follow withdrawal and often last for many months. Occasionally, the abuser will use barbiturates (downers) to counteract the effects of stimulant drugs (uppers) such as amphetamines, and a cyclic pattern then emerges in which the individual is alternately stimulated and sedated. This amphetamine-barbiturate abuse cycle can cause a variety of medical complaints and is often lethal. An example of such a cycle is one in which amphetamines are used in dieting and barbiturates are used as sleeping pills or to control anxiety; the individual rapidly increases the intake of both and becomes addicted to both (Kunnes 1973).

In many cases, withdrawal from barbiturates is more severe than withdrawal from the opiates. However, the craving and the psychological dependency are probably less.

Mixing uppers and downers is often lethal

Although the individual addicted to barbiturates is usually middle-aged and older, Seconal has become a favorite barbiturate of the young. Adolescents can often ensure their supply with relative ease by simply going to the family medicine cabinet. A relationship does seem to exist between these drugs and aggression in young men arrested for assault. Some younger offenders reported that they expected to be more aggressive when they used "reds" and often took Seconal when they wanted to "have a party" (Tinklenberg and Woodrow 1974).

Stimulants

The **stimulants** are drugs whose major effects produce energy, alertness, and feelings of confidence. Stimulants include caffeine consumed in coffee, tea, or cola drinks; nicotine from tobacco; amphetamines; and cocaine.

Amphetamines

The **amphetamines** are synthetic stimulants, the most common being amphetamine (Benzedrine), dextroamphetamine (Dexedrine), and methamphetamine (Methedrine). These are ordinarily referred to as speed or pep pills and produce an effect similar to that of norepinephrine, a synaptic transmitter. When these drugs are ingested, the individual feels alert, energetic, euphoric, and outgoing. Very large doses make the individual nervous, agitated, and confused, and may result in heart palpitations, headache, dizziness, and sleeplessness. Large doses can also cause delusions of persecution similar to paranoia. Because of their effects on gastrointestinal functions, they often reduce appetite. They also increase heart rate and blood pressure and dilate the blood vessels and mucous membranes.

Therapeutically, the amphetamines are used in the treatment of depressed states and narcolepsy (to keep the individual awake) and to relieve symptoms associated with poisoning by depressant drugs such as barbiturates and alcohol. They are also used to treat children diagnosed as hyperkinetic.

Perhaps the most common use for amphetamines has been to depress appetite in individuals with weight problems. Many doctors have specialized in administering amphetamines to obese people to cause weight loss, often with unfortunate results. College students and truck drivers often use amphetamines to stay awake. Unfortunately, amphetamines also produce such a feeling of euphoria that individuals believe they perform better on tests when they are on amphetamines. However, there is good reason to believe that the reverse is true (Tinkelenberg 1971). Athletes use pep pills to improve their motor coordination and combat fatigue. In spite of common beliefs, amphetamines are not a magical source of extra energy but simply push users to a greater expenditure of their own resources and often produce a hazardous peak. Many gifted athletes have damaged their careers by using speed to try to improve their stamina and performance (Furlong 1971).

"Speed freaks" often inject methedrine, the strongest of the amphetamines, directly into their veins, feel euphoric for a few days without eating or sleeping, then crash for several days, and then start the cycle again. Such behavior can often result in *amphetamine psychosis*. When taken in regular low dosages, amphetamines do not appear to cause any behavioral or physiological problems. As with other psychoactive drugs, the problems occur with high dosages and habitual use.

Tolerance does develop in higher dosages. Generally, withdrawal symptoms are not severe, but on occasion they include cramping, nausea, diarrhea, and convulsions (Kunnes 1973). In typical withdrawal from these drugs, weariness and depression peak after forty-eight to seventy-two hours, but milder feelings of depression and lassitude may persist for months. Extreme abuse of amphetamines can cause amphetamine psychosis, occasionally with homicidal or suicidal acts. Chronic abuse of amphetamines can result in brain damage, the residual effects of which may also include impaired ability to concentrate, learn, and remember, as well as being associated with social, economic, and personality deterioration.

Cocaine

Cocaine, a plant product derived from coca leaves, has been used since ancient times. Like opium, cocaine can be ingested by sniffing, swallowing, or injection. Slang names include coke, snow, and nose candy. The most important medical application of cocaine is its use as a local anesthetic that blocks nerve conduction on local application. Its most important systemic effect is its use as a general CNS stimulant. It appears to act on the cortex to produce a state of euphoria, restlessness, and excitation. Cognitive abilities do not seem to diminish, and motor activity is usually well coordinated until higher dosages are reached. Cocaine is sometimes a stimulant for sexual arousal. Overdosage often produces a state resembling schizophrenia and is characterized by paranoid ideation; persecutory delusions; and visual, auditory, and tactile hallucinations. The *cocaine bug* in toxic states is the hallucination that insects or snakes are crawling under the skin. Chronic sniffing of cocaine can cause severe and irreversible damage to the mucous membranes of the nostrils.

The pep pill myth

Cocaine is so rapidly metabolized by the body that no tolerance develops nor does it show any cross-tolerance with other stimulants. There are few, if any, physiological withdrawal effects; the psychological effects of withdrawal, however, usually involve a pronounced depression that is alleviated only by another dose of cocaine. The euphoria produced by the cocaine and the depression following its use cause the user to increase dosage, often to toxic levels. Rather than physiological addiction, cocaine causes psychological dependency and a habit that is difficult to break.

Euphoria/depression and psychological dependency

Nicotine

Nicotine, a chemical obtained from the tobacco plant, was first used by the American Indians and then exported to Europe in the fifteenth century. Nicotine has no therapeutic use and in large doses can cause toxic effects and death (Aviado 1971).

Nicotine can be sniffed, chewed, or smoked. In the vast majority of cases, smoking is the major problem. The person usually absorbs about 2.5 to 3.5 mg of nicotine from a single cigarette, the observed effect of this dose being similar to a 1 mg dose injected intraveneously (Volle and Koelle 1970). Typically, a nonsmoker gets sick from smoking only one cigarette, but experienced smokers smoke considerably more than this. They develop a tolerance that includes tolerance to the lethal effect of tobacco smoke. Heat from the burning tobacco vaporizes the nicotine, and about 10 percent of the available nicotine is inhaled. Of this amount, 90 percent goes into the bloodstream along with other compounds produced during smoking. Apparently, the carcinogenic (cancer-producing) effect of tobacco does not directly involve nicotine but results from other substances ingested in the smoke (Levitt 1976).

The buildup of tolerance to nicotine is obvious, since the novice may be sick after one cigarette, while heavy smokers may consume as many as sixty cigarettes per day. Withdrawal from nicotine produces drowsiness, headache, digestive disorders, sweating, cramps, insomnia, and nervousness (Brecher 1972). Chronic nicotine addiction is not usually associated with antisocial behavior commonly observed with addiction to other drugs. In general, theories of tobacco addiction, as well as techniques for modifying smoking behavior, have not been productive. Still, there is little doubt that smoking is a major health hazard. Public campaigns to decrease the rate and initiation of nicotine addiction have had a noticeable effect, and the Department of Health and Human Services has begun to emphasize the socially undesirable aspects of smoking.

Smoking is a major health hazard. Public campaigns to decrease the rate and initiation of nicotine addiction have had noticeable effects.

disorders of biological needs

Psychedelic Drugs

The **psychedelic drugs** produce marked changes in sensory, perceptual, and cognitive functioning. They have a variety of labels, of which *psychedelic* emphasizes their mind-expanding properties; *psychomimetic* refers to the psychoticlike behavior they supposedly produce; and *hallucinogenic* refers to the hallucinatory sensory experiences they produce. Usually, neither dependence nor withdrawal results from use of these drugs. Tolerance and cross-tolerance do develop, but death attributed directly to their use is extremely rare in the literature.

LSD

Lysergic acid diethylamide, or LSD, the most potent of the hallucinogens, was discovered accidentally by Dr. Albert Hoffman, a chemist of the Sandoz Pharmaceutical Laboratories in Switzerland in 1943. When he accidentally ingested some of the substance, he initiated a chain of events almost as bizarre as the drug's effects. LSD has been viewed as the source of a model psychosis resembling schizophrenia, as a mind-expanding drug that enhances creativity and insight, and as a therapuetic drug useful in the treatment of certain behavior disorders. It appears to be none of these.

The physiological effects of LSD include increased heart rate, elevated blood pressure, augmented muscle tone, and increased rate and rhythm of breathing. It also has major effects on the central nervous system. The reaction to an LSD trip typically lasts about eight hours, during which time changes occur in sensory perception, personalization, and detachment. Objects seem to become clearer, sharper, and brighter. Individuals may lose themselves in contemplation of an object, seeing and hearing aspects of it that they have never experienced or noticed before. In addition, they may feel a "cosmic consciousness" during which they seem to be empathetically joined with all humankind in experiencing such universal emotions as love, loneliness, or grief.

Originally, the LSD trip was viewed as unpleasant because of the altered sensory experiences and emotional effects. However, when LSD became a popular drug among college students, the experience was viewed differently. Nevertheless, bad trips are not unusual, and individuals under the influence of bad trips have "freaked out" as did the young British law student who tried to "continue time" by using a dental drill to bore a hole in his head (Rorvik 1970). These reactions can become quite severe. Of 114 subjects admitted to Bellevue Hospital in New York City with acute psychosis induced by LSD, 13 percent showed overwhelming fear, and another 12 percent experienced uncontrollable violent urges with suicide or homicide being attempted by approximately 9 percent (Rorvik 1970). Typically, bad trips start when the individual takes the drug while emotionally upset. These panic states are frequent among younger and inexperienced users, but a bummer can happen even to the most veteran tripper (Brecher 1972).

An unusual phenomenon that may occur following the use of LSD is the *flashback,* an involuntary recurrence of perceptual distortion or hallucinations weeks or even months after the drug was ingested. Flashbacks are more likely to occur in individuals who have had a number of trips but can occur among individuals who have taken only one LSD trip. It has been estimated that about one in twenty consistent users experiences such a flashback (Horowitz 1969).

So far, the exact physiological effects of LSD are unknown, but it probably does not cause chromosomal damage as had been reported earlier. It is also unlikely that it makes the user more creative or insightful. Some have suggested that LSD may be useful as a therapeutic drug for behavioral disorders, but this has not been verified because of legal restriction.

The 8-hour acid trip

Bummers . . .

and flashbacks

Bad trips on LSD are not unusual and may involve overwhelming fear or uncontrollable violent urges.

Mescaline and Psilocybin

Mescaline, derived from the small disklike growth button on the top of the peyote cactus, and **psilocybin,** obtained from a variety of sacred Mexican mushrooms, have been used for centuries among Indians in Central and South America and have hallucinogenic properties. As with LSD, no conclusive evidence has been produced that mescaline or psylocybin actually expands the consciousness or improves creativity.

Marijuana

Marijuana comes from the dried and ground leaves and stems of the female hemp plant, *Cannabis sativa.* Its colloquial names include grass, reefer, joints, dope, or maryjane. Marijuana is ordinarily smoked but can also be baked in brownies or other foods. In some cultures, the leaves are soaked in hot water, and the liquid is then drunk as a tea. Hashish is a much stronger drug derived from the resin exuded by the plant and is made into a gummy powder.

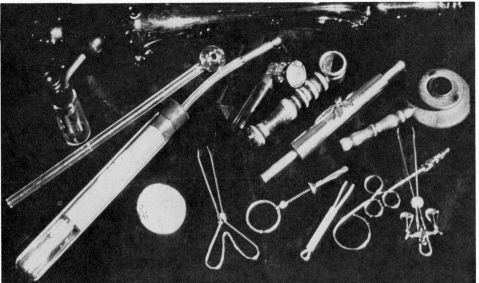

Marijuana paraphernalia.

The marijuana plant.

Hashish may be smoked, chewed, or drunk. In the nineteenth century, hashish was recommended for use with rheumatism, gout, depression, cholera, and neuralgia.

The specific effects of marijuana vary greatly, depending upon quality and dosage, mood of the user, situation, and the user's expectation. In general, regular users experience mild euphoria, heightened perceptual acuity, and pleasant relaxation. Sensory inputs are enhanced, and trivial events may seem important. Occasionally, like alcohol, marijuana may induce unpleasant states, including anxiety, depression, delusions, hallucinations, and other psychosislike behavior. The physiological effects of marijuana include a moderate increase in heart rate, a slowing of reaction time, bloodshot and itchy eyes, a dry mouth, and an increased appetite. High doses tend to produce lethargy and passivity. Interestingly, a reverse tolerance seems to occur with marijuana—with habitual use, very small doses can induce the effect. This may be in part due to learning the proper method of smoking and, to a large extent, the subjective influences of the anticipated effects. There is some evidence that individuals can turn off the effects of marijuana if necessary (Cappell and Pliner 1973). Marijuana does not lead to physiological dependency and is not similar to the

narcotics, as has been suggested. For example, discontinuing the drug does not cause withdrawal symptoms. As with cigarettes and other drugs, however, the individual can develop a psychological dependency and feel a strong need whenever anxious or tense.

A number of beliefs prevail about marijuana, most of then untrue. The National Commission on Marijuana and Drug Abuse (1972) has indicated that marijuana smoking does not lead to antisocial and criminal behavior, is not a stepping-stone to more harmful drugs, does not cause psychotic behavior, and does not cause genetic damage. Marijuana appears to be a substitute for alcohol in the youth culture, although its use is also increasing among older individuals.

Effects of marijuana

Marijuana myths

Research and Theory in Drug Abuse

Who uses drugs? Studies show that those who most frequently use legal, medically prescribed drugs also tend to show a higher incidence of nonmedical drug use (Blum, Braunstein, and Stone 1969). This fact seems to be related to the reduction of inhibitions about self-experimentation with drugs and adopting recreational drug use as a part of a life-style. Some cultural and social factors also seem to be involved in patterns of drug use. The poor and culturally deprived tend to show a higher incidence of problems with narcotics, while the upper middle class and educated tend to use the major hallucinogens, such as LSD, more frequently (Levitt 1976). Although it is probably more in vogue among the young, the educated, and the avant-garde, marijuana use seems to occur at all levels of society.

Relationships between specific personalities and specific drugs, or drugs in general, are not evident. Furthermore, no single behavioral disorder seems to be predictive of recreational or abusive drug use (Levitt 1977), with the possible exception of the antisocial personality (Sutker 1971). The major precipitating factor in drug use seems to be peer pressure, although drug use by parents also seems to facilitate use (Rohr and Densen-Gerber 1971; Kandel 1973).

The primacy of oral cravings

Psychoanalytic explanations of addictions are not particularly helpful because they draw little distinction between addicts and other individuals with deviant behavior (Mensh 1965). These theories view addicts as individuals whose psychosexual development has been arrested or who have regressed to infantile oral stages of development because early parent-child interactions caused frustrated dependency needs. Since these intense oral needs are never fulfilled in reality, the orally dependent individual is frustrated and reacts with hostility toward the typically overindulgent but rejecting mother. Drug use is interpreted as a manifestation of this conflict (Wilner and Kassebaum 1965).

Drug use as an acquired drive

A number of conditioning explanations of addiction have been suggested, since it is obvious that drugs produce positive reinforcement. Basing his model on opiate addiction, Wikler (1965, 1971) views each injection of a drug as a reinforcement of drug-seeking behavior, since the injection results in drive reduction. An acquired drive is then developed from early changes in feeling or sensation produced by previous injections of the drug. The preoccupation of addicts with hustling for drugs becomes reinforcing, in and of itself, even during

A-processes arouse B-processes

periods of nonaddiction, because it has been associated with drive reduction. Other secondary reinforcers, such as members of the drug culture, are also associated with the acquisition of the drug during addiction.

Wikler views relapse after withdrawal as the result of incomplete extinction of these behaviors. He notes that the development of physical dependency on drugs creates a new biological need comparable to hunger or thirst and views the addiction as an acquired drive. However, the major innovation in Wikler's theory is the suggestion that specific classes of drugs affect specific types of motivation. For example, opiates suppress the primary drives of pain, sex, hunger, and thirst. Consequently, an individual whose chief source of anxiety is related to pain, sexuality, or repression of aggressive drives will obtain specific relief from morphine. Alcohol, on the other hand, disinhibits sexual and aggressive drives by its effect on the cerebral cortex. Consequently, individuals who act out in anxiety-provoking situations prefer alcohol.

A more recent theory by Solomon (1977) emphasizes the *opponent process theory* of acquired motivation. Solomon notes that all primary affective processes (pleasure, anger, fear) are elicited by stimulus onset. These primary stimulus-induced states are phasic and sensitive to small stimulus changes and rarely show much sensitization or habituation. For example, a feeling of well-being is elicited by a few drinks of alcohol or by smoking marijuana. These are the *A-processes,* which can be either negative or positive. Termination of drinking or smoking, however, causes the individual to come down. Thus the A-processes arouse the *B-processes*—those associated with the cessation of the stimulus, which oppose and suppress the affective strength of the A-processes. The B-processes (such as hangovers) are sluggish, characterized by a relatively long latency or reaction time. They are slow to build up to maximum amplitude and slow to decay after the stimulus input (UCS) is terminated and the A-processes (UCR) have ceased. As shown in Figure 13–1, the affect and hedonistic qualities of the B-processes are opposite to the qualities of the A-pro-

disorders of biological needs

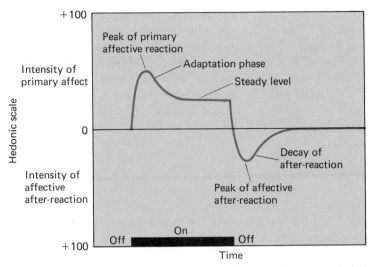

Figure 13–1 The five distinctive features of affect resulting from a typical input or stimulus in opponent process theory. For example, if the input is alcohol, the reaction will be a nice high (A-state) that will decay and result in a "high over" (B-state). The B-state occurs after the A-state and is the reverse of A. If the input causes fear (A), then the termination of the stimulus causes relief (B).

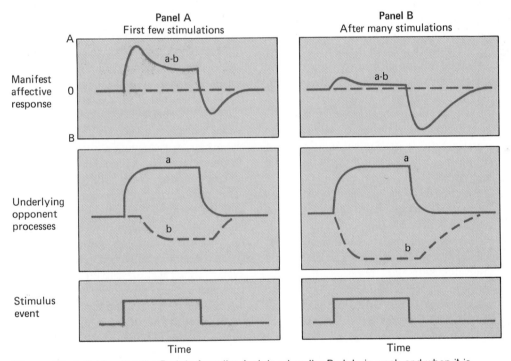

Figure 13–2 Subtracting the B-state from the A-state when the B-state is weak and when it is strengthened by repeated use. After the B-state is strengthened, it is more intense and longer lasting, while the A-state is diluted. A good example is opiate addiction, where the drug no longer gives a pleasant reaction (A), but withdrawal is severe (B).

cesses. The interesting aspect of these processes is that the B-processes are strengthened with repeated pairing, while little change occurs in the A-processes, as Figure 13–2 shows. Thus, for the individual initially "shooting up" with heroin, much pleasure (A-process) would be followed by a B-process of some negative emotions and craving. Over time the B-process would strengthen and thereby decrease the pleasure in the A-process and increase the craving and negative emotion associated with the nondrug state.

disorders of biological needs: drug abuse

With these basic parameters in mind, we can begin to understand drug addiction. Addiction begins when the hedonic, affective, and behavioral phenomenona of drug addiction emerge slowly during repeated self-dosing and in the interval between them. The first self-dosing is often a blend of several kinds of aversive and pleasurable feelings. For example, the first cigarette or injection of heroin often causes nausea. However, if the pleasurable components outweigh the aversive ones, sufficient craving may ensue for the user to repeat the self-dosing. This effect is likely if the drug has an instrumental *escape feature,* such as the alleviation of anxiety or frustration.

An aversive state of craving as the defining criterion of addiction

The use of the drug does not make an individual an addict, since many people use drugs casually. The defining criterion for addiction in opponent process theory is the psychological feature common to all abstinence syndromes with all drugs—an aversive state of craving.

The addiction cycle is instituted if the individual self-doses during B-process. In other words, there is a critical delay duration. If the individual suffers the agony of the withdrawal process and does not self-dose during this interval to alleviate the aversive state, addiction will not result. If self-dosing does occur, the addictive cycle is initiated.

Cross-tolerance as stimulus generalization

As this cycle starts, the intensity and duration of the withdrawal agony gradually increase, since the B-process is strengthened by repeated use. Furthermore, the positively reinforcing pleasurable state associated with later doses gradually declines in quality and intensity. In opiate users, this pattern is called the *loss of euphoria.* The user has developed tolerance and requires increasing amounts of the drug to induce a pleasurable A-process.

In addition, tolerance develops to drugs whose affective or hedonistic qualities are similar to those of the one the individual is using. This relationship has some practical implications. For example, if one uses heroin or aspirin to alleviate an alcohol hangover, an addictive cycle for alcoholism is not initiated. However, if one uses barbiturates to alleviate an alcohol hangover, tolerance to both barbiturates and alcoholism develops and begins an addictive cycle.

Once the cycle is initiated, it is extremely difficult to break, since both withdrawal from the drug and exposure to CSs associated with A- and B-processes increase craving. Thus, if an individual's addiction is treated with abrupt and absolute withdrawal ("cold turkey") in a socially unfamiliar environment, no extinction of exposure to CS-A or CS-B events occurs. After the prolonged, enforced, physiological extinction is successfully completed, addicts are returned to their own environment. When they are exposed again to CS-A and CS-B cues that have not been extinguished, the possibility of relapse is greatly enhanced. Thus, the relapse of various drug addiction is extremely high, as Figure 13–3 shows.

Another phenomenon making it difficult to break the addiction cycle is *cross-tolerance*—the generalization of addiction across aversive or pleasant processes. Solomon found that if an aversive A-process such as influenza generalizes to a different aversive B-process such as heroin craving, relapse in an abstaining addict would then be potentiated by influenza because it intensifies craving. Or, if an aversive A-process 1 generalizes to B-process 2 (assuming that B-2 is heroin craving, and A-1 is the addict's estranged spouse), relapse will then be potentiated by the presence of the spouse. A similar situation can occur if an aversive B-1 generalizes to an aversive B-2. If aversive B-1 is nicotine craving and B-2 is loneliness, then nicotine abstinence might increase loneliness, which in turn would increase nicotine craving. Thus, smoking will reduce craving and loneliness. Moreover, if an aversive B-1 (nicotine craving) generalizes to an aversive A-2 (some painful experience, such as toothache, headache, gastritis), abstinence from nicotine will enhance the aversiveness of the painful experience. With cross-tolerance, or generalization from one aversive state to another, the strength of the addictive cycle grows phenomenally. Craving can be increased by illness, loneliness, guilt, anger, jealousy, or

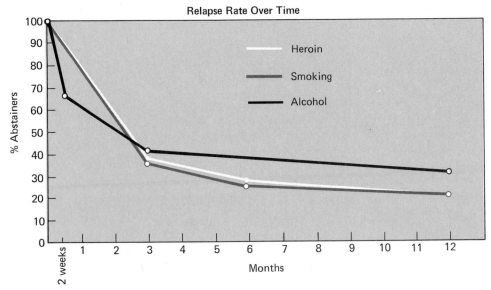

Figure 13-3 The relapse curve for nicotine, heroin, and alcohol addicts, as a function of months after "cure." These data cover those subjects who were "cured" during treatment.

similar states, and relapse can be potentiated by seemingly irrelevant, hedonic, and affective processes that seem almost independent of the drug process, which explains why many alcohol and drug treatment programs claim the addict can never feel completely recovered.

Assessment and Modification of Drug Abuse

Many methods can be used to assess drug addiction, including subjective reports, behavioral observations, and physiological indices taken in both natural and contrived settings. A number of self-report indices are available, but in general they have been poorly standardized and are highly subject to purposeful distortion by the client.

A number of behavioral indices have also been developed to measure a drug state. For example, as Figure 13–4 shows, pupillary reactions can generally indicate whether the individual is taking a stimulant or a depressant drug.

Physiological indices of drug states include a number of biochemical methods for analysis of the blood or urine. In contrast, no physiological method is available for assessing some drugs such as marijuana.

In an attempt to modify addiction, a variety of medical and psychological techniques have been used, largely without noticeable success. If a particular type of drug addiction causes withdrawal syndrome, the first step is detoxification so that a modification program can be instituted. Once the individual is clean, a wide variety of possible treatment methods are available, depending on the case and the type of addiction.

Chemotherapy is used in a variety of ways to treat addictions. For example, tranquilizers may be administered to alleviate withdrawal symptoms. The individual may then be given different drugs, such as Antabuse, to maintain the drug-free condition. Methadone has been used in a similar fashion with narcotic addicts. Methadone is also a narcotic but can be administered orally, appears to block the urge to return to heroin, and allows the individual to return to the community and become self-supporting. In other words, it has cross-tolerance with heroin, but it seems to maintain an even high (Dole and Nyswander 1965). Supporters of the methadone maintenance approach have noted that diabetics are just as dependent upon insulin as addicts are

The methadone maintenance controversy

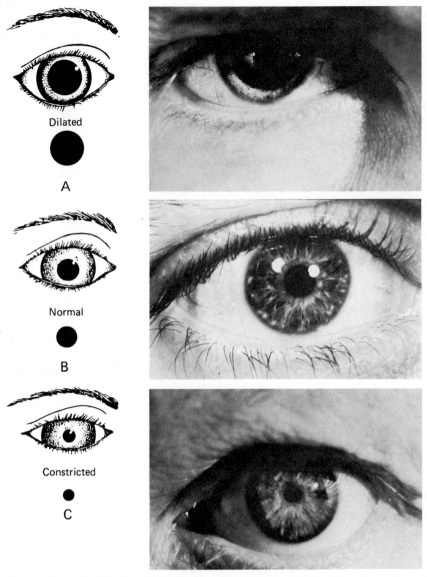

Figure 13–4 *A.* Dilated pupil reaction to a stimulant drug. *B.* Normal pupil reaction in light of average intensity. *C.* Constricted pupil reaction to a depressant drug.

upon methadone (Levitt 1976). However, it has been criticized as merely the substitution of one addictive drug for another, and methadone is rapidly becoming a black market product. Thus, methadone is both a solution and a problem (Arehart 1972; Bazell 1973).

Self-help groups similar to AA are available to drug addicts who are willing to change their behavior. Synanon, the best-known of these groups, requires the individual to accept the addiction ("I'm a dope fiend"), to refrain from drug use, and to take part in a form of group therapy—the "square" games. Rationalizations and other defenses are attacked and ridiculed by group members, many of whom once used the same defenses. Because 90 percent of those who leave the Synanon communities have relapsed (Brecher 1972), Synanon now tries to emphasize alternative lifestyles. Unfortunately, Synanon leaders have recently been accused of violent acts, which is not uncommon in self-help groups. Nevertheless, several such groups seem to be succeeding, including Delancey Street, Phoenix House, Gateway House, and Daytop Village.

disorders of biological needs

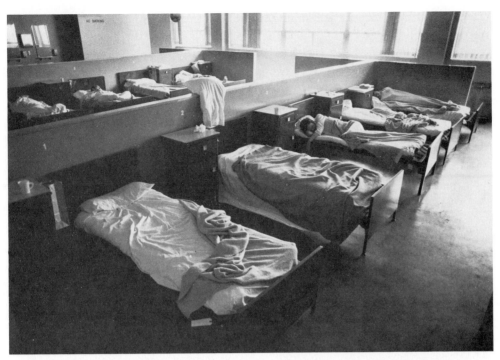

The first step in modifying addiction is detoxification, or supervised withdrawal of the drug.

The use of psychotherapy, whether group or individual, has been of limited value for drug addiction (Hill and Blanc 1967; Neuman and Tamerin 1971). Behavior therapy, which directly attacks the offending behavior, has been somewhat more promising, although its effectiveness remains to be demonstrated. A variety of techniques have been utilized, depending on the type of drug problem. These procedures usually involve the use of aversion therapy and an assortment of other techniques in multifaceted programs for a variety of addictions, including heroin, Demerol, amphetamines, and nicotine (O'Leary and Wilson 1975).

An example of such a program has been described by Copeman (1973), who uses a multifaceted behavioral approach for heroin addicts, incorporating both individual and group therapy within a residential treatment program. All addicts are initially detoxified and then subjected to electrical aversion conditioning, which usually includes a wide range of external and internal cues spanning the full range of drug-related behaviors. For example, shock is paired with anticipatory thoughts about heroin,

perceived physiological sensations related to craving, traveling to obtain the drug from a contact, preparing the "spike," and injection. Often the electrical aversion conditioning is supplemented with aversive imagery procedures.

Group therapy emphasizes role-playing methods directed toward the development and reinforcement of prosocial behavior. Each individual progresses through four levels of increasingly more complex group development. Level one consists of basic social restructuring and retraining. Level two involves the use of rational-emotive therapy and other procedures aimed at modifying distorted and irrational thinking. Level three involves training in solving real problems, such as how to get a job. Level four is the phase-out period prior to discharge in which the individual is carefully observed by staff members for signs of continuing maladaptive behavior.

The goals of this program are to establish an effective behavioral repertoire for dealing with problems of daily living and

box 13-2
Behavior Therapy
Use with a
Morphine Addict

The subject was a twenty-one-year-old college senior at the time of initial contact. There was a history of morphine use two or three times a week, and the patient reported that use of the drug was becoming increasingly important to him. The drug was readily available at home since the patient's father was a physician. Patient complained of long-standing anxiety and feelings that he was a "junkie." He had successfully "kicked the habit" once before by leaving school and locking himself in a hotel room until the withdrawal symptoms subsided. When he came for treatment, he feared that he was again becoming dependent on the drug. Classroom work was deteriorating, and he reported a number of incomplete grades from earlier semesters. Patient had had a six-month course of weekly sessions with a psychoanalytically trained psychologist who was no longer in practice. He was referred for treatment and agreed to twice weekly behavioral therapy.

A behavioral modification program was outlined that included two types of training: (1) training in relaxation to overcome tension and as a substitute for drug-induced relaxation; and (2) training in self-assertion to overcome the need for drugs. Since the patient had a poor opinion of himself, this second method was also aimed at increasing self-esteem. The patient was discouraged from his associations with drug users because the temptation to use drugs would be a strong counterbalance to the treatment program, especially in initial phases.

A modified Jacobson technique as described by Wolpe (1958) was used. The patient was also asked to read Salter's *Conditioned Reflex Therapy* (1949). Methods of self-assertion were discussed after the patient finished this text.

The patient was able to relax his whole body after only four sessions. In fact, he reported that the tingling in his relaxed fingers was very similar to that felt when he used narcotics. Following the seventh session, the patient was able to attend his first college dance. He reported that he had enjoyed this social experience and also that he had refused two offers of free narcotics.

Therapy was interrupted by the school vacation. While at home, the patient reported using some narcotics that were readily available in the home. He also reported visiting some of his addicted friends on return to campus and using narcotics once.

It became apparent that another step had to be added to the treatment process to help the patient avoid drugs. He had to learn to associate anxiety, instead of pleasure, with drug use. Aversive conditioning was initiated, pairing a painful electric shock to the patient's enactment of drug injection. The shock was discontinued when the patient said "Stop." At the same time he was instructed to stop visualizing the injection process. This process had been broken down into five phases, or steps, and the patient actually had to drop the injection equipment during aversive conditioning.

Aversive therapy was done twice a week—three times at each session. After eight weeks of conditioning, it was done only once a week. After sixteen sessions, a partial reinforcement schedule was gradually decreased until the twenty-fourth or last session.

The patient did use morphine after the eighth aversive session, but he reported that the pleasant sensation previously associated with its use was no longer present. He felt he would not use the drug again.

The patient began to express feelings of self-confidence. He began to look for a job and his schoolwork improved. He graduated from college and got a job in a field related to his college major. The patient's parents remarked at the time of graduation that he seemed like a different person. He was now able to relate to them and others successfully.

The patient was interviewed seven and ten months after the end of treatment. He reported successful job adjustment. Letters to the therapist during the period showed him to be a bright sensitive individual involved in the world around him. The patient did still smoke marijuana occasionally, but he did not feel this was a problem. Treatment appeared to be successful with this highly motivated, mildly addicted morphine user.

to create a sense of individual responsibility. However, this program also reveals some of the problems of treating the addict. For example, of fifty heroin addicts who entered the program, twenty-three dropped out before or immediately after treatment had started. Of the fourteen who completed treatment, 50 percent remained drug free for a period of twenty months, while the other 50 percent were drug free for only one year.

Public and Legal Aspects of Drug Abuse

Clearly, people will continue to use psychologically active drugs for recreational purposes. It is interesting that abuse of legal drugs, such as alcohol and nicotine, may present more serious health hazards than the use of illegal drugs. Unfortunately, the public policies of federal and state governments have rarely been consistent with scientific facts and often have resulted in misinforming the public about drug abuse. This attitude on the part of government only aggravates the personal and the societal problems of drug abuse. The recommendations of *Consumer Reports* (Brecher 1972) go to the heart of the problem:

1. Stop emphasizing measures designed to keep drugs away from people. This aggravates the problem since prohibition does not work. What prohibition does do is increase prices, stimulate a black market, and force addicts to resort to crimes to finance their purchases. Further, it results in more hazardous concentrates of drugs, which are often contaminated.
2. Stop publicizing the horrors of "drug menace." This publicity often backfires and popularizes drugs or serves as a lure to recreational drug use.
3. Stop increasing the damage done by drugs. The emphasis should be directed at minimizing the damage. For example, the laws which make possession and sale of hypodermic paraphernalia illegal force the addict to use nonsterile and shared

equipment. The addict who obtains illegal drugs often uses adulterated, impure, and mislabeled drugs. The results are severe health hazards for the people involved.
4. Stop misclassifying drugs. Alcohol and nicotine, two of the most dangerous drugs, are classified essentially as nondrugs, while marijuana is equated with heroin. This stupidity damages the credibility of any government-sponsored program.
5. Stop viewing the drug problem as a national problem to be solved on a national scale. It is quite possible that a solution that works in one part of the country like New York may not work in another part.
6. Stop pursuing the goal of stamping out illegal drug use. Such attempts tend to increase both drug use and drug damage and shift the drug user to another, often more dangerous, drug.

In addition, Consumer's Union (CU) offers these solutions to the black market problem:

1. Devise drug policies and practices that ensure that no narcotic addict need get drugs from the black market.
2. Place methadone maintenance programs under medical supervision available to every narcotic addict.
3. Make other forms of narcotic maintenance, including opium, morphine, and heroin, available along with methadone maintenance under medical supervision on a carefully planned experimental basis.

CU further recommends the immediate repeal of all federal laws governing the growing, processing, transportation, sale, possession, and use of marijuana. They advocate that each of the fifty states similarly repeal its existing marijuana laws and pass new laws legalizing the cultivation, processing, and orderly marketing of marijuana.

Summary

Most Americans indulge in drugs, usually to alter their physiological state. Addiction is a physiological process of biochemical changes that over time requires a greater amount of the drug to produce the desired effect (tolerance). If an individual is deprived of an addicting drug, withdrawal symptoms occur. Psychological dependency occurs when there are no withdrawal symptoms but the individual feels subjective distress when deprived of the drug. Cross-tolerance is tolerance for one drug that may also occur when a similar drug is taken.

Alcoholism is defined by the individual's loss of control of consumption and alcohol's interference with the individual's life. Alcohol is a depressant drug that first acts on higher brain centers and creates a feeling of well-being. There are four stages of the development of alcoholism addiction: the prealcoholic symptomatic phase, the prodromal phase, the crucial stage, and a chronic stage. There are four different types of alcoholism: alpha, beta, gamma, and delta. Excessive drinking can cause pathological intoxication, delirium tremens, acute alcoholic hallucinosis, and cerebral beri beri. Beri beri causes both Korsakoff's and Wernicke's syndromes.

No strong evidence exists for a purely biological basis of alcoholism. Behavioral explanations focus on the fact that alcohol reduces anxiety and stress, and that alcohol intake is positively reinforcing.

Assessment of alcoholism is usually by means of subjective reports, self-monitoring, observation of drinking behavior, and physiological assessments that analyze the blood alcohol concentration.

Detoxification is the first step in modification. Pharmacological treatment usually consists of administration of disulfiram (Antabuse), which temporarily makes drinking highly aversive, but does not solve the drinking problem. AA and various forms of individual or group psychotherapy have had moderate success with alcoholism. Aversion therapy has been fairly successful. Among some behavior therapists, the goal of treatment for alcoholism has recently shifted from abstinence to the acquisition of appropriate drinking skills.

The depressant drugs have a number of important effects in common: physiological addiction occurs, tolerance develops, and high doses depress the functioning of vital systems. The narcotics induce relaxation, induce euphoria, and provide relief from pain. The major types of narcotics are derived from the opium poppy and include morphine, codeine, and heroin. Although codeine is similar to morphine, it is about one-twelfth as powerful, but its ratio of oral to injected effectiveness is much higher. Heroin has no real medical use and is strictly a street drug. Methadone is a synthetic narcotic similar to morphine that has been used in the treatment of heroin addiction. Syndrome "X" is death associated with heroin addiction, but the cause does not seem to be an overdose. Tolerance to narcotics develops rapidly. Withdrawal symptoms with narcotics are usually severe.

The barbiturates have a number of medical uses and are also a popular street drug. Unfortunately, barbiturates are highly dangerous drugs that have cross-tolerance with alcohol. Withdrawal from barbiturates is similar to alcohol withdrawal symptoms. Occasionally, barbiturates are used to counteract the effects of stimulant drugs, and a cyclic pattern emerges in which the individual is alternately stimulated and sedated. This amphetamine/barbiturate abuse cycle is often lethal.

The stimulants are classes of drugs whose major effects are increased energy, alertness, and confidence. The amphetamines are synthetic stimulants that have some therapeutic uses. They are also often used by college students and others to stay awake and by many individuals to control weight or as "pep pills." Withdrawal symptoms from amphetamines are usually not severe but extreme abuse can cause amphetamine psychosis.

The most important medical application of cocaine is its use as a local anesthetic, but it also acts on the cortex to produce a state of euphoria. Because it is so rapidly metabolized, there is no tolerance or cross-tolerance with other stimulants. Furthermore, there seem to be no withdrawal effects. Nicotine is another stimulant that has no therapeutic effect but that causes a variety of health problems, primarily from the smoke.

The psychedelic and hallucinogenic drugs produce marked changes in sen-

disorders of biological needs

sory perception and cognitive function. Tolerance and withdrawal do not occur. The most potent of the hallucinogenics is LSD, which produces drastic psychological effects that may result in psychotic behavior. Flashbacks can occur long after an individual has terminated the use of LSD. Mescaline and psilocybin produce milder but similar effects.

Marijuana is a drug that has attained great popularity, particularly among adolescents, in the last few years. It apparently is becoming a substitute for alcohol among many individuals. It is one of the few drugs that show reverse tolerance.

The major precipitating factor in drug use seems to be peer pressure, although the type of drug used depends upon cultural and social factors. Psychodynamic theory focuses on oral fixation and frustrated dependency needs, while behavioral explanations emphasize the positive reinforcement or drive-reduction properties of drugs. The opponent process theory of acquired motivation emphasizes the difference between the onset of the drug effect, which is primarily pleasant (A-process) and the reaction to cessation of the drug which is primarily negative (B-process). Cross-tolerance, or generalization, among emotional and drug states, as well as conditioning factors to these states, make it difficult to treat these disorders. Treatment includes detoxification, chemotherapy, self-help groups, and various types of psychotherapy and behavior therapy. The results of these approaches are not impressive.

Key Concepts

acute alcoholic hallucinosis

addiction

Alcoholics Anonymous

alpha alcoholism

amphetamines

barbiturates

beta alcoholism

bromides

cerebral beri beri

cocaine

codeine

confabulation

cross-tolerance

delirium tremens (DTs)

delta alcoholism

depressants

detoxification

disulfiram (Antabuse)

drug dependency

gamma alcoholism

heroin

Korsakoff's psychosis

lysergic acid diethylamide (LSD)

marijuana

mescaline

methadone

morphine

narcotics

nicotine

overdose (OD)

pathological intoxication

psilocybin

psychedelic drugs

state dependent learning

stimulants

substance use disorder

tolerance

Wernicke's syndrome

withdrawal syndrome

Review Questions

1. What is the difference between addiction and dependency?

2. Define (a) tolerance, (b) withdrawal, and (c) cross-tolerance.

3. What are the short-term effects of alcohol? What are the long-term effects?

4. Why do some researchers not agree that alcoholics cannot drink in moderation?

5. What are the ways in which family and cultural attitudes influence drinking behavior?

6. What purpose does disulfiram (Antabuse) serve in treatment of alcoholism?

7. What is the goal of aversion therapy in treating alcoholism?

8. What are the physiological and subjective effects of depressant drugs?

9. What are the physiological and subjective effects of stimulant drugs?

10. What are the physiological and subjective effects of (a) hallucinogens such as LSD; and (b) marijuana?

11. How does methadone maintenance work? What is the main objection to such programs?

psychotic behavior ^{unit}4

If human behavior can be viewed as being distributed along a continuum, psychotic behavior would be represented at the extreme end, opposite normal behavior. In Chapter 14 we shall briefly summarize the kinds of **psychotic behavior** and then examine psychotic behaviors that appear primarily as disorders of the emotional response system—the *affective* disorders. We shall also discuss *suicide*, which is a major problem in the affective disorders. In Chapter 15 we shall examine *schizophrenia*, a loosely defined category of psychotic behaviors that produce disturbances in communication, speech, social behavior, cognitive behavior, and sometimes motor behavior. *Paranoia*, discussed next, is a more narrowly defined disorder that seems to affect primarily the cognitive response system. We conclude our discussion of the psychoses by examining *infantile autism* and *childhood schizophrenia*, each of which differs in some degree from adult schizophrenia, although the differences are still a matter of debate.

the affective disorders and suicide 14

Key Topics

Classification of psychoses

Psychotic hallucinations

Mania and depression

Primary and secondary depressions

Exogenous and endogenous
depressions, and

Unipolar and bipolar depressions

Three stages of anaclitic
depression

Genetic factors in bipolar
depression

Electrolyte hypothesis

Norepinephrine hypothesis

Psychodynamic theories of
depression

Cognitive triad

Learned helplessness hypothesis

Cognitive theories of depression

Learning theories of depression

Difficulties in assessing depression

Advantages and drawbacks of ECT
and chemotherapy

Major goals of behavior therapy in
treating depression

Four major reasons for committing
suicide

Some people experience extremes of depression or elation that interfere with their ability to function and that may even lead them to take their own lives. Although most of us have felt elated or depressed at times, relatively few have known the runaway activity of true mania or the utter despair of psychotic depression. Because this is the first chapter in this book to deal with specific psychoses, we shall begin with a general description of psychotic behaviors.

Types of Psychotic Behaviors

The psychotic disorders differ from other forms of abnormal behavior in two major respects. The first distinguishing feature of **psychosis** is a gross distortion of reality. In psychotic states a malfunction of cognition typically occurs that may or may not involve other response systems. The second characteristic is a severe disorganization of behavior that, in contrast to other forms of abnormal behavior, may pervade all aspects of the individual's life. Individuals exhibiting psychotic behavior may not perceive, reason, or act as other individuals do, and their behavior may be obviously bizarre.

Gross distortion of reality

Psychotic reactions may be long-term or short-term episodes. In long-term psychotic disorders, syndromes may wax and wane, new bizarre behavior may appear, and the individual may deteriorate over time with intellectual, emotional, and social functioning becoming even more unstable and bizarre.

Psychoses may be organic or functional

A distinction is made between the **functional psychoses** and the **organic psychoses**. In the functional psychoses, no physiological disorders are apparent, whereas organic psychoses are caused by physiological events that, in some cases, may be life-threatening. Organic disorders will be discussed in Chapter 17.

Distinction between psychotic and nonpsychotic hallucinations

Unlike other forms of abnormal behavior, psychotic behavior often involves more than one response symptom. Psychotic symptoms often cluster in such a way that they are used to distinguish the subtypes of psychotic reactions. The types of *psychotic symptoms* may be classified according to the response systems affected.

Sensory and Perceptual Response System

The major type of perceptual disorder is the report of sensory experiences that cannot be validated by external observers. Such experiences are called **hallucinations**. Hallucinations are assumed to differ from misperceptions, such as illusions and hypnagogic (drowsiness) experiences, in that the individual assumes they are produced by external stimuli. A number of different agents, such as drugs, sensory deprivation, lack of sleep, physiological malfunctions, and fevers or other pathological conditions, can produce hallucinations.

In general, auditory hallucinations are the most frequent types of misperception, but visual hallucinations are not unusual. Hallucinations of touch, taste, and smell are relatively rare. In functional psychoses, auditory hallucinations are predominant, while other types of hallucinations are more common in organic psychoses. If hallucinations are viewed as reflecting the individual's social needs and distress, the predominance of auditory hallucinations should be expected, since speech is the major method of communication between people (Al-Issa 1977).

Three major factors are important in evaluating hallucinations for diagnostic purposes:

1. The belief that the sensory percept is real usually differentiates psychotic from other types of hallucinations. For example, if the individual treats the experience as mental imagery rather than stimuli from the external environment, it is generally assumed that reality testing is good. However, this criterion does not always differentiate between psychosis and other conditions. For example, some cultures consider hallucinations to be religious experiences and to be normal and real.

2. The situational context of hallucinations must be evaluated. If individuals are taking drugs, have fevers, are deprived of sleep, are suffering sensory deprivation, or the like, the ensuing hallucinations are not usually considered psychotic. In psychotic conditions no obvious stimuli are apparent to account for the hallucinations. In the absence of external stimuli, internal sensory cues are often associated with psychotic hallucinations. For example, McGuigan (1966) found that behavioral correlates of speech, such as muscle activity in the vocal apparatus, increased just before auditory hallucinations—a finding that indicates that auditory hallucinations may consist of hearing one's own voice (subvocalization).

3. Social and cultural factors are also important in differentiating between psychotic and other hallucinatory experiences. While hallucinations are not generally an accepted experience in Western societies and are viewed as signs of a psychosis, many non-Western and nontechnological cultures view them in a positive or neutral fashion. In some cultures hallucinations are even considered normal. Apparently, when hallucinations are socially sanctioned, they tend to be similar from individual to individual but different between societies (Al-Issa 1977).

For clinical assessment, an important sign is the individual's reaction to the hallucinations. In most cases involving psychosis the individual is extremely upset and distressed by the experience (Shean 1978).

Cognitive Response System

The prime characteristic of all psychotic disorders is the disturbance of reasoning, thinking, and communication. One type of such disorders are **delusions**—beliefs that are contrary to the facts of the situation and highly resistant to change. Delusions can be fragmentary and unorganized or systematic and logical.

Sometimes delusion and fact are difficult to differentiate, particularly if a delusion is well organized and logical. In some highly systematic delusions, acceptance of the first premise is crucial, for the subsequent beliefs are often consistent with it. Delusions often develop from **ideas of reference**: that is, people believe that everyday experience has some personal meaning for them. An example would be to see several people talking in the hall and conclude that they are discussing you.

Delusions may be classified into a number of types. The most common is the *delusion of persecution*, during which an individual believes that someone is trying to cause personal injury. The persecutors may be neighbors, competitors, political groups, the FBI, the CIA, or just "they." Delusions are easily confirmed by misinterpreting everyday experiences, such as seeing the same individual every day in the same location and concluding that the FBI is spying on you. Trivial events, such as the way a TV news commentator gestures or the content of the news message itself, can be interpreted as subtle threats or warnings. When both hallucinations and delusions occur in functional psychoses, the hallucinations are usually consistent with the delusional system.

Delusions of influence involve the belief of being controlled by external agents. Suicidal impulses, wild sexual fantasies, homicidal urges, or even sensations such as feeling electricity in the body are believed to be imposed from the outside. The external agent may use any number of techniques to control the individual, such as hypnosis, extrasensory perception, machines like television or radio, or other devices. For example, a patient got into a barroom brawl and was arrested after receiving a cut on the scalp. The cut was subsequently sewn up by a physician. Shortly afterwards the patient began to hear voices and accused the physician of implanting a radio that was broadcasting thoughts to him, as well as reading his thoughts.

the affective disorders and suicide   403

box 14–1
A Case of
"Normal"
Hallucinations

A young woman was referred to the mental health consultant. She had been sneaking out of the family home at night, when she visited on weekends, to see her new boyfriend, of whom the family did not approve. As punishment, she was to sleep downstairs in the living room. She reported that at midnight the image of her dead brother appeared in the most minute detail: His face was streaming tears as he looked at her with unbearable grief. She described his coat, shirt, tie, and shoes in detail. She related this to her parents, who were shocked because the description fit her brother, who had died fourteen years earlier when the girl was three years old. The clothes were his favorite garb and were the ones in which he had been buried. The young sister had not been permitted to go to the funeral or to view the body.

On those nights when the hallucination appeared she was unable to sleep because she was upset by the grief on his face. Her adjustment at the center began to suffer. She began to lose interest in her classes and was increasingly absent at bed check.

The familiar pattern again appeared. The young woman appealed for help, but the only problem she identified was being bothered by the image of her brother. After the relaxation failed, she was instructed to communicate with her *aumakua*[1] and find out what made him sad. She reported that the vision revealed to her that seeing the forbidden boyfriend and staying out late against her parents' wishes made her *aumakua* very sad. She spontaneously suggested she might "go along with his request" in much the same manner one might humor the peculiar desires of a respected elder. Immediately, she began to sleep better, her adjustment at the center improved, and she did not again report seeing the vision. A two-month follow-up revealed that she was abiding by the wishes of her parents and that her favorable adjustment continued. It should be noted that she didn't again have to sleep in the living room (a possible cue for the vision).

aumakua—friendly spirit

Delusion of grandeur involves the belief that one has some special talent, has been selected for some special purpose, or is an agent of God. *Self-deprecatory delusions* occur in individuals who believe that they have committed a horrible sin; such delusions are associated with guilt and a desire for punishment.

Delusions of body change involve erroneous beliefs about the appearance or condition of the body. One may believe, for example, that the body has changed from male to female, that one's insides are rotting, or that one's head has become smaller.

Disorders of the *structure of thought processes* occur mainly in schizophrenia and cause severe communication difficulties. They are characterized by disconnected sequences of ideas that often seem fragmented and incoherent, even to the individuals themselves. People with these behavior patterns often say that their thoughts become jumbled or that they wander off in different directions.

Several types of *psychotic thought processes* and disorders of cognitive association may be distinguished. *Concreteness* is said to occur when the individual does not see beyond the obvious. For example, if asked the meaning of a proverb such as "People who live in glass houses should not throw stones," the individual might reply, "That's obvious: If a stone hits glass, the glass will break." *Overgeneralization* or *over-inclusion* is also a common type of psychotic thought process. In this disorder irrelevant items are included in thinking processes and make verbal production appear strange and incoherent, as Table 14–1 shows. The individual with a thought disorder often has difficulty in filtering out irrelevant and intruding responses. For instance, *cognitive*

Table 14-1   Schizophrenic Verbalizations

Type	Example
General	"Why do you think people believe in God?" Patient: "Uh, let's, I don't know why, let's see, balloon travel. He holds it up for you, the balloon. He don't let you fall out, your little legs sticking out down through the clouds. He's down to the smokestack, looking through the smoke trying to get the balloon gassed up you know. Way they're flyin on top that way, legs sticking out, I don't know, looking down on the ground, heck, that'd make you so dizzy you just stay and sleep you know, hold down and sleep there. The balloon's His home you know up there. I used to sleep out doors, you know, sleep out doors instead of going home. He's had a home but His not tell where it's at, you know." (Chapman and Chapman 1973)
Neologisms (coining new words)	"I am here from a foreign university . . . and you have to have a 'plausity' of all acts of amendment to go through for the children's code . . . and it is no mental disturbance or 'puterience' . . . it is an 'amorition' law . . . there is nothing to disturb me . . . it is like their 'privatilinia' . . . and the children have to have this 'accentuative' law so they don't go into the 'mortite' law of the church." (Vetter 1969, p. 189)
Word salad	"The house burnt the cow horrendously always." (Vetter 1969, p. 147)
Flight of ideas	"Yesterday I went downtown to buy $50,000 worth of real estate but they wouldn't believe me when I said that I would earn enough in the next month to pay them for it. You know my father is a big man in the city. You wear nice clothes and how much does the watch cost?" (Sherman 1938, p. 637)
Clang associations	"Have you a sister? I have three and they are all very fine girls—'girls, curls, furls,' isn't that funny?" (Sherman 1938, p. 637)
Perseveration	In response to *cruel*: "To try and believe what you really are. It's cruel sometimes to be kind." In response to *near*: "To cure kindness you've got to be keen on kindness. Sometimes it's cruel." In response to *chivalry*: "It's sometimes more cruel to act age instead of beauty." (Vetter 1969, p. 14)
Opposite speech	In response to *disgust*: "Disgusted, when you're feeling good, happy, and contented." In response to *stammer*: "Stutter, when the words come out easier and you have trouble." In response to *limp*: "Limping around, able to walk." (Laffal 1965, p. 31)

ambivalence occurs when the individual is unable to reject one of two contradictory or competing ideas. Another phenomenon is *blocking*, in which the individual's thought processes appear to stop suddenly (McGhie and Chapman 1961). These unusual and bizarre thought patterns are often referred to as *autistic* because the individual appears to be responding only to internal cues and ignores external stimuli. Some clinicians believe that these responses are similar to early stages of thought processes seen in children or reflect what psychoanalysts call primary process thinking.

The speech of individuals with cognitive disorders may seem almost incoherent. *Incoherent speech* *Flight of ideas* may occur, during which the individual changes rapidly from one topic to another, often leaving the listener confused. *Clang associations* are somewhat similar to flight of ideas in that the individual connects ideas by rhyming. For example, "She said her name was Joy; perhaps she is a boy; should I buy her a toy?" *Word salads* are strings of unrelated words that

the affective disorders and suicide   405

make no sense to the listener. *Neologisms* are ordinary words that are condensed and combined into new words. An example is "spectroautorotation," which a patient stated was meant to convey circling in every way as with checkers or a bat in baseball (Forrest 1969). *Verbigeration* is a senseless repetition of the same word or phrase. *Echolalia* occurs when the individual repeats what a previous speaker just has said. *Perseveration* occurs when the individual continues to give the same response to a series of different questions or other stimuli.

Individuals exhibiting psychotic behavior also show disorders of memory. One of the most frequent memory disorders is *loss of orientation*, during which individuals do not know what day it is, who they are, or what situation they are in. Such disorientation for time, place, and situation may be an example of both short-term and long-term memory deficits.

Motor Response System

Individuals whose behavior is labeled psychotic often exhibit extreme disturbances in motor behavior. Their motor behavior may be greatly accelerated as in the frantic activity of manic behavior or can be completely retarded so that the individual becomes immobile, as in some cases of catatonia and stuporous depression. These individuals may exhibit **catalepsy**, during

Catatonic individuals can exhibit catalepsy, during which they may remain in a fixed posture for hours.

psychotic behavior

which they remain in a fixed position until someone changes it. Catalepsy is often called *waxy flexibility*, since the individual's arms and legs can be placed easily in any position and will retain that position for hours. On the other hand, *negativism* may be exhibited, meaning that the individual resists any change in posture. People may also exhibit strange mannerisms, such as weird facial expressions, unusual gestures, or sequences of movements of fingers, arms, and hands that seem completely bizarre. *Echopraxia* or the imitation of motor movements of others is seen in some cases.

Emotional Response System

Bizarre changes in mood are often a common characteristic of these disorders. This may be a gross exaggeration of mood—extreme elation or depression—or affect inappropriate to the individual's surroundings. In some cases, the individual's affect is labeled as flat, since virtually no situation or event elicits an emotional response. This blunting of affect is usually observed in schizophrenia and makes the individual appear completely apathetic and *anhedonic* (unable to feel pleasure). Other individuals who display inappropriate affect may giggle or laugh in situations that normally elicit sadness or despair.

Social Response System

One of the major indications of a psychotic reaction is grossly inappropriate social behavior. This may be exhibited as a loss of the usual social inhibitions or concerns. Individuals classified as psychotic may be unable or unwilling to dress, undress, feed themselves, or attend to hygienic needs. They may lose ordinary inhibitions so that they urinate, defecate, or masturbate in public. They may discontinue social communication and may become mute. They

Waxy flexibility in catatonic schizophrenia

Flat affect

Riding a bicycle in the nude down a crowded street is an example of antisocial behavior.

may also withdraw from social activity in favor of fantasy, daydreaming, and autistic activity. Consequently, these individuals may have few friends and may be labeled as "out of contact with reality," since they seem to be involved in their own inner world, to lack interest in external events, and to withdraw from interpersonal activity.

Most of these unusual behaviors are assumed to occur in schizophrenia, but they also occur in other types of psychoses (Pope and Lipsinski 1978). A few of these behaviors, such as delusions, are common to most psychotic disorders. The prime characteristic of a psychosis is a disorder of the cognitive processes that is associated with disorders of other response systems. The exception is the affective disorders, which we shall discuss in the remainder of this chapter. Affective disorders include both the neurotic and psychotic disorders. In Chapter 15 we shall discuss the four other types of psychotic disorders—schizophrenia, paranoia, childhood schizophrenia, and infantile autism.

Affective Disorders

Affect is a term that has been used as roughly equivalent to emotion but it has a much more restrictive meaning. For our purposes, we shall define affect as a particular type of emotion that has as its opposite poles elation and depression. **Affective disorders** are abnormal states of *mania* (elation) or *depression* and can be considered specific types of emotional disorders. Although many clinicians have emphasized the cognitive aspects of affective disorders and pointed to the central role of irrational or self-defeating thoughts, it is also logical to assume that the prime characteristic of affective disorders is arousal of the autonomic nervous system. Even though cognition plays a major role in all behavior, it is doubtful that affective disorders are merely disturbances in thinking or reasoning similar to the cognitive disorders. DSM

III, for example, defines affective disorders as a primary disturbance of mood accompanied by related symptoms.

In 1917 Freud pointed out the similarity between grief or mourning and depression in his classic piece *Mourning and Melancholia*. Grief is a normal response associated with loss or other stressful events, such as the death of a friend or a relative, the loss of a limb, a terminal illness, and the like, which would be distressing to anyone. However, grief reactions are usually brief and time-related to an event, and only rarely do they require the intervention of a professional clinician. **Depression** is similar in that it too is often precipitated by some loss in the individual's life, but is distinguished by its depth, duration, and the extent of associated guilt, feelings of worthlessness, delusions, hallucinations, and somatic changes.

The major signs of depression are emotional, cognitive, and somatic. The emotional reaction is sadness, unhappiness, and grief, which may be accompanied by crying, wringing of the hands, and other motor symptoms of pathological depression. The cognitive symptoms are related primarily to the individual's self-concept and self-appraisal. Depressed individuals often see themselves as unworthy, inadequate, incompetent, and sinful. They often have severe guilt feelings because of their perceived inadequacies, and these feelings result in the erosion of motivation and ambition. Their thought processes are characterized by pessimism and self-deprecating moods. At times these cognitive reactions can become so severe and have so little basis in reality that they can be called delusional. If hallucinations occur in severe depression, they are usually of a self-deprecating type. The somatic features include constipation, loss of weight, poor appetite, insomnia, menstrual changes, and disturbances in sex drive.

In terms of observable behaviors, depression may take two different forms. In one kind depressed individuals may show motor retardation or engage in slow, deliberate, painful movements. These individuals typically withdraw, engage in very little activity, and may not speak. Other depressed

Table 14–2   Signs and Symptoms of Depression

Mood	Somatic
Sad, unhappy, blue	Loss of appetite
Crying	Loss of weight
	Constipation
Thought	Poor sleep
Pessimism	Aches and pains
Ideas of guilt	Menstrual changes
Self-denigration	Loss of libido
Loss of interest and motivation	
Decrease in efficiency and concentration	**Anxiety features**
	Suicidal behavior
Behavior and appearance	
Neglect of personal appearance	Thoughts
Psychomotor retardation	Threats
Agitation	Attempts

individuals become highly agitated and restless, exhibiting signs of anxiety and panic. Table 14–2 summarizes these behaviors.

Mania seems similar to happiness or euphoria, but, like depression, seems exaggerated. Three prime signs are *imperturbability* (not being easily influenced by others), *amorality*, and *acceleration of activities*. As in depression, changes in emotional, cognitive, and somatic responses occur. The emotional changes include exaggerated feelings of well-being and happiness, even though life circumstances might not justify this reaction. Manic individuals may seem to be happy-go-lucky, carefree, and elated. If stressed, they may become wildly angry, aggressive, and irritable. In terms of cognitive changes, these individuals feel effective, overconfident, and excessively positive about themselves. Flight of ideas (rapid jumping from one topic to another), *logorrhea* (rapid outpouring of words), and ideas of grandiosity, including great potency, wealth, power, and perceptiveness, may also occur. Somatic changes are often very similar to those in depression in that individuals do not eat, do not sleep, and lose weight. Table 14–3 shows some of the more common symptoms of manic states.

A major question is whether elation and depression are polar opposites along some continuum designated by such terms as elation-depression, euphoria-dysphoria, or happiness-sadness. In this sense the intensity of the experience is an important consideration, in that happiness may be a less intense experience than extreme elation, while sadness is a less intense experience than depression. On the other hand, as Mendels (1970) has mentioned, it is quite possible that mania and depression are the same disorder, since some features of extreme elation are similar rather than opposite to those of depression. This hypothesis is consistent with the assumption of some psychologists that mania actually represents a defense against an underlying depression. This notion is supported by the fact that depressive reactions and manic reactions show similarities in terms of sleep patterns, some clinical features such as spontaneous crying, and the high activity level that characterizes both the manic and the agitated depressive reaction. However, one explanation of this paradox is the curvilinear relationship of mood with arousal. In other words, extreme states of both depression and elation reflect increased arousal, while normal mood states reflect appropriate arousal, as shown in Figure 14–1. Consequently, the similarity of sleep patterns and activity levels could be explained by a higher arousal level and would eliminate the necessity for seeing mania and depression as separate types of emotional disorders. Nevertheless, the issue of whether various types of depressive and manic reactions are distinct disorders rather than behavior patterns that represent opposite ends of the same continuum remains a lively and confusing issue in clinical literature.

Are mania and depression opposites?

Table 14-3 Classical and "Atypical" Symptoms in Twenty Manic Patients

Symptoms	Patients manifesting symptoms (%)
Hyperactivity	100
Extreme verbosity	100
Pressure of speech	100
Grandiosity	100
Manipulativeness	100
Irritability	100
Euphoria	90
Mood lability	90
Hypersexuality	80
Flight of ideas	75
Delusions	75
Sexual	(25)
Persecutory	(65)
Passive	(20)
Religious	(15)
Assaultiveness or threatening behavior	75
Distractibility	70
Loosened associations	70
Fear of dying	70
Intrusiveness	60
Somatic complaints	55
Some depression	55
Religiosity	50
Telephone abuse	45
Regressive behavior (urinating or defecating inappropriately, exposing self)	45
Symbolization or gesturing	40
Hallucinations (auditory and visual)	40
Confused	35
Ideas of reference	20

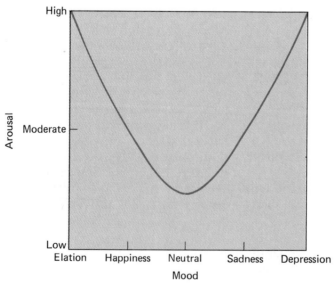

Figure 14-1 The relationship between mood states and arousal level or intensity of reaction.

psychotic behavior

This young woman is exhibiting the downcast countenance associated with depressive disorders.

Depression is a common disorder. It is claimed that about 15 percent of a random sample of adults display significant depressive features (Becker 1977). Although depression has been viewed predominantly as a disorder of middle age, recent data indicate that the highest incidence of depression occurs in the eighteen to twenty-nine age range. Women are diagnosed as depressed two to three times more frequently than men (Weissman and Paykel 1974). Twenty-five percent of hospitalized depressives and 10 percent of diagnosed depressives are considered psychotic by rigorous criteria (Becker 1977). Mania, on the other hand, appears to be much less common than depression (Silverman 1968).

Types of Affective Disorders

In DSM II, affective disorders were classified into a variety of categories, including the *neuroses, personality disorders,* and *psychoses.* However, current beliefs about affective disorders are undergoing a revolution, reflected in DSM III. These changes seem to have been prompted by recent research, a decline in the popularity of the psychodynamic models, and an increased interest in more empirical bases for classification. To illustrate the impact of research on clinical issues and beliefs, we shall discuss the subcategories described in DSM II, the research on the factors involved in these distinctions, and the new subtypes in DSM III. In DSM II the various subtypes of affective disorders were as follows:

1. **Depressive neurosis** This disorder was assumed to be due to an internal conflict or to an identifiable event, such as the loss of a loved object or cherished possession. Individuals diagnosed as suffering from this disorder looked depressed and

dejected and subjectively reported being "blue" or "down." Agitation, extreme restlessness, sleep disturbances, and other signs of distress were often present. This type of depression was differentiated from other affective disorders by the presence of a distinct precipitating event and by the absence of reality distortion or interference with the cognitive process.

2. **The cyclothymic personality (affective personality)** This affective disorder was assumed to be a stable aspect of an individual's personality, and was marked by recurring and alternating periods of depression and elation. As in manic-depressive psychosis, presumably no external circumstances caused these alterations of mood. Diagnosis was supposed to specify whether the mood was characteristically depressed, hypomanic, or alternating.

3. **Psychotic depressive reaction** In this disorder the depression was supposedly precipitated by an external event, but the individual had no history of repeated depression or mood swings. It was distinguished from depressive neurosis by its severity and the distinct impairment of cognitive functioning or reality testing.

4. **Involutional melancholia** Involutional melancholia occurred in the involutional period from the midforties to age sixty. Impaired reality testing is due to the mood disorder. Worry, anxiety, agitation, severe insomnia, guilt, and somatic preoccupation were believed to be the most frequent symptoms. This disorder was differentiated from manic-depressive illness by the lack of previous depressive episodes, and by a lack of external precipitating factors. It was assumed to be two or three times as common in women than in men and was assumed to be related to menopause in women and reduced sexual potency in males. As a matter of fact, in DSM I this disorder was

classified as a result of a disturbance of hormonal function, but recent evidence has shown no relationship between hormonal changes and involutional melancholia. Obviously, this period of life is related to developmental crises and is a landmark in the process of aging. Individuals are losing their sexual attractiveness and their youth, their children are leaving home, and the accomplishment of life goals has or has not occurred. Nevertheless, it is doubtful that involutional melancholia is different from depression occurring in younger patients (Beck 1967). Consequently, the only difference between this disorder and other depressions seems to be age, which is rarely a meaningful basis for classification.

5. **Manic depressive illnesses (manic depressive psychosis)** Whereas the other affective disorders were usually referred to as reactions, the manic depressive disorders were called illnesses. This classification was due to the presumption that since there were no precipitating events eliciting this behavior, it was a biological disorder. The disorder was divided into three major subtypes: *manic types, depressive types,* and *circular types.*

The manic types were largely characterized by extreme elation, irritability, talkativeness, flight of ideas, and accelerated speech and motor activities. It was assumed that in this type, real depressive episodes never occurred.

The depressed type supposedly consisted exclusively of depressive episodes characterized by severely depressed moods and by mental and motor retardation (retarded rather than agitated depression), which occasionally progressed to stupor. In this type of disorder, hallucinations and delusions occurred and were attributed to the mood disorder. Depressive illness was differentiated from psychotic depressive reaction by a lack of external precipitating events.

psychotic behavior

Depression may be due to developmental crises associated with aging.

The cyclic type of manic depressive illnesses were characterized by at least one attack of a depressive episode and a manic episode. It was often assumed that cyclic disorders followed a regular course, with manic episodes alternating with depressive episodes. This timing was assumed to be associated with biological regularity. However, the evidence indicates that in some individuals alternation of mood seems almost random, while in other individuals a cyclic regularity occurs. The reason for this difference is not clear.

Issues in the Classification of Affective Disorders

The distinction between what Akiskal and McKinney (1975) call *primary* and *secondary* depressions seems meaningful, but other distinctions between subtypes of affective disorders are not so clear. Secondary depression is caused by another disorder, either behavioral or physical, while primary depression is not. However, the distinction between *neurotic* and *psychotic* depressions, assumed to be different types of disorders, may not be valid and may merely

Secondary depression is caused by another disorder; primary is not

the affective disorders and suicide   413

A thirty-five-year-old biochemist was brought to the clinic by his frightened wife. To his psychiatrist the patient explained, "I discovered that I had been drifting, broke the bonds, and suddenly found myself doing things and doing them by telegraph. I was dead tired and decided to go on a vacation, but even there it wasn't long before I was sending more telegrams. I got into high gear and started to buzz. Then a gentle hint from a friend took effect, and I decided to come here and see if the changes in my personality were real." He entered the ward in high spirits, went about greeting the patients, insisted that the place was "swell," and made quick puns on the names of doctors to whom he was introduced. Meanwhile his wife said she was "scared to death." "His friends used to call him 'Crazy Charley,' " she said, "but I haven't seen this streak in him for years."

When his wife had left, the patient soon demonstrated what he meant by "high gear." He bounded down the hall, threw his medication on the floor, leaped up on a window ledge and dared any one to get him down. When he was put in a room alone where he could be free, he promptly dismantled the bed, pounded on the walls, yelled, and sang. He made a sudden sally into the hall and did a kind of hula-hula dance before he could be returned to his room. His shouting continued throughout the night, and betrayed in its content the ambivalent attitudes which the patient maintained toward his hospitalization: "What the hell kind of a place is this? A swell place? I'm not staying here. I'm having a hell of a good time. Oh, I'm so happy. I have to get going. My gray suit please, my gray coat please, my gray socks, all gray on their way, going to be gay. I'm going out as fast as I came in, only faster. I'm happier than I have ever been in my life. I'm 100 percent better than normal."

Cameron and Margaret, 1951

reflect a difference in intensity. In an investigation of fifty patients diagnosed as psychotic depressives and fifty patients diagnosed as neurotic depressives, Beck (1967) found that the same behaviors appeared in both neurotic and psychotic depression but that the psychotic patients showed the symptoms to a greater degree. This relationship is shown in Table 14–4.

A related question is the distinction between endogenous and exogenous depression. **Endogenous depression** is supposedly associated with behavioral retardation, deep depression, low reactivity to environmental changes, loss of interest in life, somatic complaints, self-pity, insomnia, and a lack of precipitating stress. **Exogenous depression** is characterized by high reactivity to the environment, precipitating stress, agitation and irritability, and personality disturbances (Depue and Evans 1976). This is the same distinction that has been made between *agitated* and *retarded* depression and is based on the assumption that endogenous depression results primarily from internal physiological or biological determinants, while exogenous depression is caused by environmental stresses.

A clear distinction does exist between *bipolar* and *unipolar* depression (Perris 1966). **Bipolar depression** is diagnosed when both depressive and manic episodes occur, while **unipolar depression** is diagnosed when manic episodes do not occur. Good evidence indicates that differences do exist between bipolar and unipolar depression and that these subtypes can be consistently identified (Schuyler 1974; Winokur 1973).

Because of these controversies and the evidence that the various distinctions between major affective disorders could not be established according to the previously mentioned criteria, DSM III classifies these disorders generally as affective disorders, with three major subcategories: *manic disorders, depressive disorders*, and *bipolar affective disorders*, which show a history of both mania and depression. These subcategories are based on observable behavior

Exogenous depressions are highly reactive to the environment

DSM III improvements

Table 14–4 Frequency of Clinical Features in Fifty Patients Diagnosed as Neurotically Depressed (ND) and Fifty Patients Diagnosed as Psychotically Depressed (PD)

Clinical feature	Feature present ND (percentage)	Feature present PD (percentage)	Present to severe degree ND (percentage)	Present to severe degree PD (percentage)
Sad faces	86	94	4	24
Stooped posture	58	76	4	20
Speech: slow, etc.	66	70	8	22
Low mood	84	80	8	44
Diurnal variation of mood	22	48	2	10
Hopelessness	78	68	6	34
Conscious guilt	64	44	6	12
Feeling inadequate	68	70	10	42
Somatic preoccupation	58	66	6	24
Suicidal wishes	58	76	14	40
Indecisiveness	56	70	6	28
Loss of motivation	70	82	8	48
Loss of interest	64	78	10	44
Fatigability	80	74	8	48
Loss of appetite	48	76	2	40
Sleep disturbance	66	80	12	52
Constipation	28	56	2	16

rather than assumed etiology and avoid many of the questionable distinctions that impair the reliability and validity of diagnoses according to DSM II. However, the distinction between personality and psychotic disorders is continued with the DSM III, and includes chronic hypomanic disorder (hypomanic personality), chronic depressive disorder (depressive personality), and cyclothymic disorders (cyclothymic personality).

Affective Disorders in Children

Although the exact prevalence of affective disorders in children is unknown, such disorders have been estimated to occur in approximately 20 percent of children (Lefkowitz 1977). However, depression in children is probably a transitory developmental phenomenon that largely dissipates with age.

The major problem in determining the incidence of depression in children and adolescents, as well as the parameters of the disorders, is that serious controversy has occurred over what constitutes depression in children. The concept of **masked depression**, which has developed from psychoanalytic theorizing, is partially responsible for this confusion. Because of this concept, a child who is hyperactive, disobedient, or phobic, or who has psychophysiological reactions can be identified as having an underlying depression that manifests itself in these symptoms. The consequence of such a position is that nearly all childhood behavioral disorders exhibit these *depressive equivalents*, and can be labeled as depression. As Kovacs and Beck (1977) have noted, this concept is counterproductive since it does not differentiate between primary and secondary depression. In other words, a number of conditions, such as enuresis or phobias, instigate depression and loss of self-esteem among children. It would be more fruitful to view these secondary depressions as consequences of enuresis or phobia rather than interpreting enuresis and phobias as types of depression.

The most useful criteria have been developed by the subcommittee on criteria for diagnosis of depression in children (Dweck et al. 1977). According to these criteria, the two essential features of depression are *dysphoria* and a *generalized impairment response* to previously reinforcing experiences without the introduction of new sources of reinforcement. This impairment is manifested by reduction in instrumental self-initiated activities across a broad class of behavior. Previously pleasant events often

Problems due to masked depression model

Anaclitic depression, or dependency depression, occurs primarily in children between six months and six years of age.

are no longer effective in regulating behavior. Furthermore, this reaction must be present for a minimum of four weeks. The characteristics of dysphoria and reduced response to reinforcement are somewhat different at different ages, but they include guilt, personal and general pessimism, blaming others, and changes in self-esteem. Interestingly enough, mania in children has not been discussed and is rarely if ever observed in early childhood.

Anaclitic depression or dependency depression occurs primarily in children between six months and six years of age and has been well documented (Bowlby 1973; Spitz 1946). Pediatricians often refer to this disorder as **marasmus**. It has also been described as "hospitalism," since it frequently occurs in children maintained in emotionally sterile, institutional settings.

psychotic behavior

This disorder occurs as a consequence of a child's prolonged separation from its mother and has three distinct phases (Bowlby 1973). In the first stage, the child displays severe temper tantrums with crying and screaming, random activity, occasionally stereotyped behavior, and other behavioral indices of stress. This is the *protest stage*, which rarely lasts longer than a few days. It is followed by the *stage of despair*, which can be described as a rejection of the environment, increasing loss of contact with others, retardation of development, retardation of reaction to stimuli, slowness of movement, dejection, stupor, and the outward expressions that in adults would be described as depression. Withdrawal and reduction of activity continue during the despair phase. This phase persists until the child is reunited with its mother. The third stage, which may or may not occur, is the *detachment phase* in which indifference and hostility toward parents after reunion may persist for several months.

The drastic effects of separation from parents have been confirmed with monkeys by Harry Harlow and his colleagues (Seay, Hansen, and Harlow 1962; Seay and Harlow 1965; Suomi and Harlow 1977). These investigators separated infant monkeys from their mothers and found the same protest and despair stages described by Spitz and Bowlby. The young monkeys first exhibited high levels of vocalization and motor activity followed by inactivity, social withdrawal, and a lack of social play. However, as with humans, the nature of the infant's attachment relationship affected the nature of the response to removal from the mother. For example, those infants most active in maintaining proximity to the mother and least likely to leave her to explore the environment tended to exhibit the greatest disturbance following separation (Hinds and Spencer-Booth 1970). However, the offspring of permissive mothers who neither punished their infants for approach nor restrained them from interacting with other monkeys were unlikely to exhibit depression following separation if they had access to other monkeys. Ainsworth (1976) reported similar findings with

human mothers and infants. These investigators also found that the longer the separation between the mother and the infant and the younger the infant, the more severe the immediate and the long-term consequences. This finding is similar to Spitz's original finding that recovery from anaclitic depression became poorer as the separation of infants from their mothers increased. In adolescent and adult monkeys subject to peer and maternal separations, such grief reactions do not seem to occur, a finding that suggests that the factors that induce depression later in life are perhaps different in monkeys and humans.

As Suomi and Harlow (1977) state, three factors are associated with the depressive reaction as a consequence of separation. These factors are (1) loss of a salient portion of the environment, (2) lack of anything in the separated environment that can replace what is lost, and (3) the individual's powerlessness or inability to change its current social situation. The subject in these situations is thus helpless and hopeless, a state consistent with both Beck's (1967) negative cognitive set and the learned helplessness explanations of depression (Seligman 1975). Thus, it may be possible to induce depression in monkeys if the individual is placed in a situation in which helplessness occurs.

Research and Theory

Biological Theories

When viewed overall, the evidence for a genetic basis for affective disorders is more impressive than that for any other type of abnormal behavior. However, a distinct difference seems to exist where unipolar and bipolar disorders are concerned. Perris (1966) found that relatives of bipolar depressed individuals developed bipolar depression, while relatives of unipolar depressed individuals developed unipolar depression. Genetic studies that largely used bipolar depression came to a similar conclusion. Price (1968), in reviewing the genetic studies, found that 66 of 97 monozygotic pairs of twins were concordant for manic-depressive psychosis, but only 27 of 119 dizygotic pairs were concordant. On the other hand, in a study of 8 identical and

Anaclitic depression: first protest . . .

Then despair . . .

Then detachment

Helplessness and hopelessness

16 fraternal same-sex twins who had been diagnosed as neurotic or unipolar depressive, Slater and Shields (1969) found that none of the twins received the same diagnosis—the concordance rate was essentially zero in identical as well as fraternal twins. These studies support the validity of the unipolar-bipolar dimension as well as implying that genetic factors play a greater role in bipolar than in unipolar affective disorders.

Role of genetic factors greater in bipolar affective disorders

Genes exert their influence by altering or modifying biochemical activity. Consequently, a direct relationship between genetic endowment and biochemical functioning is necessary for a viable genetic theory of affective disorders. A variety of biochemical theories have been proposed, of which only the major ones will be discussed here.

The Electrolyte Hypothesis

Neural impulses are caused by electrolytes that change into electrically charged particles and move along the neurons. *Sodium* and *potassium* chlorides are the two electrolytes involved in this reaction. Positively charged sodium particles are distributed on either side of the membrane of the nerve cell. There is a high concentration of sodium outside the cell wall and a high concentration of potassium within it, maintaining what is known as the resting potential of the nerve cell. A change in the distribution of sodium and potassium ions produces changes in the resting potential that affect the excitability of the neuron so that it is readily fired by an impulse transmitted from another neuron. The **electrolyte hypothesis** suggests a disturbance in the balance of sodium and potassium in depressed patients. Psychotic depression is often accompanied by abnormally high sodium levels, which return to normal after recovery (Shaw 1966; Coppen 1967). There is also evidence of higher retention of both sodium and potassium in depressed patients (Depue and Evans 1976). Other evidence comes from the fact that lithium salts and electroconvulsive shock, both of which result in a decrease in sodium levels, are

Sodium-potassium balance and depression

Norepinephrine depletion and depression

effective in the treatment of affective disorders (Coppen 1967). Nevertheless, the relationship of sodium balance to affective disorders is still controversial (Becker 1977).

The Catecholamine Hypothesis

A related biological hypothesis is concerned with *neurotransmitters*. There are two major classes of neurotransmitters: *cholinergic* and *adrenergic*. The biogenic amines of the adrenergic system include the catecholamines (norepinephrine and dopamine) and the idolamines (serotonin). The **catecholamine** or **norepinephrine hypothesis** of depression assumes that depression is associated with a deficiency of norepinephrine in certain parts of the brain, particularly the hypothalamus, a structure critical in all manifestations of emotion and motivation. Mania, on the other hand, is assumed to be associated with an excess of this neurotransmitter. It has been shown that drugs that deplete the brain of norepinephrine and related substances produce behavioral states similar to depression (Bunney and Davis 1965). On the other hand, drugs that increase the supply of brain norepinephrine are the two principal classes of drugs used to treat depression in humans: The MAO inhibitors and the tricyclics. Furthermore, the hypothalamus, which has been thought to be the location of reward centers (Boles 1975), has the largest concentration of norepinephrine in the central nervous system. As is obvious from a clinical description of depression, a marked loss of reinforcement or reward value is associated with the disorder. Thus, it is plausible to postulate a fundamental malfunction of the brain reward center associated with the depletion of norepinephrine in the hypothalamus in depression.

Bunney and his colleagues (Bunney, Goodwin, and Murphy 1972a; Bunney, et al. 1972b) have suggested that in bipolar depression the switch from depression to mania is associated with changes in norepinephrine, which can be determined by urine tests. They followed the transition from depression to mania and from mania to depression in ten patients. During the depressed state these individuals conformed

psychotic behavior

more to the retarded than to the agitated depressive pattern and tended to be seclusive, unresponsive, and dozing most of the day. For all these patients the transition to the manic state was preceded by a normal phase lasting from one to four days during which they began to initiate conversation, become more physically active, and be more concerned about their relationships with others.

This normal period was followed by a somewhat slow onset of the manic phase during which the individuals in the first day began to show a marked increase in the amount of talking and physical activity over that of the previous period. This activity level increased until within several days the individuals' behavior was characterized by excessive talking, shouting, movement, poor judgment, sexual preoccupation, anger, and aggression. In the more intense phase the individuals showed grandiose ideas, delusions, flight of ideas, rhyming and punning, and physical combativeness. As is typical, the patients slept little at night during the manic period.

Bunney and his colleagues found that levels of norepinephrine were extremely high during the manic phase and low during the depressive phase. Every one of their patients showed an increase in norepinephrine levels on the day preceding the onset of mania. Bunney and his colleagues thus suggest that bipolar depression may be a genetically transmitted defect in enzymes that affects the reuptake of norepinephrine at the presynaptic neural membrane. However, as noted before in discussion of the electrolyte balance hypothesis, an unusually high concentration of sodium inside the neural cell may block normal reuptake of norepinephrine, and as a result excessive amounts accumulate. As previously mentioned, there is some indirect evidence for high levels of intracellular sodium in manic patients.

Other evidence supports the catecholamine hypothesis. For example, affective disorders, particularly bipolar depression, have sometimes been classed as sleep disorders. Both extreme mania and depression interfere with sleep activity, and the reuptake or absorption of neurotransmitters is one of the functions of sleep. Furthermore,

evidence suggests an increase in blood level of a substance called cortisol in depressive states (Beck 1967). Cortisol, a hormone produced by the adrenal cortex, is released when an individual is stressed, and it plays a major role in the metabolism of norepinephrine. Unfortunately, elevated cortisol is a general consequence of stress or anxiety and is not specific to depression.

Although the evidence is largely circumstantial, the biological hypothesis of affective disorders, particularly bipolar depression, is appealing—even convincing. However, a number of problems remain. For example, changes in amine levels are responses to stress and are not specific to depression (Bliss, Wilson, and Zwanziger 1966). Furthermore, that agents alter biogenic amine levels, such as the antidepressants and lithium substances, and are effective in modifying affective states does not necessarily mean these disorders were caused by malfunction of the biological systems. In addition, drugs that alter the level of the biogenic amines in normals produce reactions similar to depressed states that may or may not be "true" depressions.

In summary, the major problem of all the biochemical theories of abnormal behavior is that an environmental factor causes biochemical changes. The demonstration of abnormal states of biochemical functioning in depression, mania, and other abnormal states becomes a chicken and egg question. Do the abnormal biochemical states produce the behavior disorders or vice versa? No obvious answer to this question has been found. One solution would be to demonstrate that differences in biochemical factors exist between normals and individuals who exhibit affective disorders when they are not in the abnormal state. If such a difference could be shown, it would clearly demonstrate a difference in biochemical functioning.

Increased norepinephrine and mania

Which comes first: behavior disorder or biochemical disorder?

Psychodynamic Theories
Psychoanalytic theory has had a major influence on theories of depression with the major emphasis being on regression to earlier stages of psychosexual development, particularly the oral and the anal stages. In

other words, the severely depressed person has regressed to modes of coping with the external world that are characteristic of a child two or three years old. As Fenichel (1945) has noted, dependency is the major factor when there is a desire to receive gratification of needs passively, and a tendency to react violently often results when such needs are frustrated. The sequence appears to be frustration of dependency needs, rage, fear of further loss, turning of hostility inward, and loss of self-esteem associated with guilt and self-punishment. Freud believed that mania is a reaction formation against this self-hate wherein the individual engages in childlike self-admiration.

The major theme in psychodynamic theory—that depressive individuals are very dependent—has become common to all theories of depression. Depressive individuals interact with others in a passive, clinging, or helpless way that induces others to take care of them. As will be seen subsequently, childlike dependency or the helpless-and-hopeless syndrome that follows an object loss is the major postulate in most psychological theories of depression.

Cognitive Theories

Cognitive theories of depression usually take the position that depression is a cognitive disorder and that the affect and motivational disturbances are the results of this fundamental cognitive disorder. Beck (1967), for example, has theorized that depression centers around a **cognitive triad** consisting of a negative view of the *world*, a negative concept of *self*, and a negative appraisal of the *future*. These schemata develop from a number of situations including (1) biased conclusions drawn from neutral situations, (2) selection of wrong aspects of situations, (3) overgeneralization of single experiences to one's whole life, (4) distortion of the importance of events, and (5) inexact labeling of experiences resulting in misconceptions.

These distorted attitudes cause *faulty perception*, which results in responses that lead to negative feedback, which in turn perpetuates the cycle. Therefore, the depressive individual exaggerates minor setbacks as total failures, accepts the re-

sponsibility for such failure, and may be reluctant to accept responsibility for any success. This pattern results in a tendency to interpret experiences in a negative way and view life in terms of defeat, deprivation, or disparagement. A second pattern is *low self-esteem*, in which the individual tends to view the self as inadequate, unworthy of love, or otherwise defective. The third pattern, one that is often central in cognitive theories, is *helplessness and hopelessness*, a tendency to view suffering as uncontrollable and the future as a life of unending hardship and failure. Consequently, minor stresses in the depressed individual's life cause motivational changes, which in turn cause the individual to withdraw toward a state of inactivity and to exhibit emotional paralysis. Furthermore, the behavioral manifestations of depression, such as low mood, hopelessness, fatigability, and agitation, as well as the physiological signs of depression, such as loss of appetite, constipation, and sleep disturbances, are thought to be consequences of negative cognitions. Predictably, Beck (1967) suggests that therapeutic intervention should focus on helping the patient to reformulate cognitions and thus help eliminate depressive behaviors.

A second major cognitive theory of depression is **learned helplessness** (Miller, Rosellini, and Seligman 1977; Abramson, Seligman, and Teasdale 1978; Seligman 1975). Learned helplessness, conceptually developed from animal research, was extended to depression theory and later modified to incorporate cognitive factors. In the typical experiment in which learned helplessness is induced in animals, a two-phase sequence occurs. First, the animal undergoes numerous painful experiences from which it cannot escape. For example, a dog may be placed in a harness and lifted above the floor. Shock electrodes are then placed on its legs, and numerous painful electric shocks are administered which the dog is completely helpless to escape. In the second phase of the procedure the animal is placed in an avoidance situation from which it can escape. For example, it is placed in a hurdle box in which one compartment contains a shock grid and a second compartment contains no grid. As soon as the animal hears a warning signal, it can jump to the second compartment and escape the shock. In the normal animal this response is learned rapidly. Animals who have been exposed to an inescapable shock, however, do not acquire this avoidance response rapidly and often take the shock passively.

Seligman and his colleagues suggest that the animal has acquired a sense of helplessness that comes from the animal's experience of reality: responding and reinforcement are not correlated. In other words, organisms exposed to inescapable aversive situations develop the belief that their behavior will not alter a situation, and consequently they feel helpless and hopeless. When stressful events occur, the individual feels helpless, a feeling that elicits the symptoms of helplessness. These symptoms are defined by two types of behavior: (1) a failure to initiate responses to alleviate the noxious situation, and (2) difficulty in learning that responding *is* effective in controlling the stressor. These behaviors initiate other symptoms of helplessness, including anorexia, weight loss, sleeplessness,

withdrawal, sexual problems, and perhaps depletion of norepinephrine. These symptoms are assumed to be present in depression as well as learned helplessness (Miller, Rosellini, and Seligman 1977).

Seligman and his colleagues (Abramson, Seligman, and Teasdale 1978) have reformulated the learned helplessness model by incorporating attribution theory to account for cases in which outcomes are uncontrollable for all people—*universal helplessness*—or cases in which they are uncontrollable only for some people—*personal helplessness*—as well as to explain when helplessness is general or specific, and when it is chronic or acute. In other words, when something stressful happens, but the individual believes that under the circumstances no one could do anything about the situation (universal helplessness due to external events), the person is not as likely to demonstrate symptoms of helplessness or depression. On the other hand, if the individual believes that he or she cannot, but perhaps others could, solve the problem (personal helplessness due to internal factors), the individual is apt to feel helpless, to exhibit low self-esteem, and to feel like a failure (see Table 14–5). Whether the

The two symptoms of helplessness

Personal versus universal helplessness

Table 14–5 Formal Characteristics of Attribution and Some Examples

| Dimension | Internal | | External | |
	Stable	Unstable	Stable	Unstable
Global				
Failing student	Lack of intelligence	Exhaustion	ETS gives unfair tests	Today is Friday the thirteenth.
	(Laziness)	(Having a cold, which makes me stupid)	(People are usually unlucky on the GRE.)	(ETS gave experimental tests this time which were too hard for everyone.)
Rejected woman	I'm unattractive to men.	My conversation sometimes bores men.	Men are overly competitive with intelligent women.	Men get into rejecting moods.
Specific				
Failing student	Lack of mathematical ability	Fed up with math problems	ETS gives unfair math tests.	The math test was from No. 13.
	(Math always bores me.)	(Having a cold, which ruins my arithmetic)	(People are usually unlucky on math tests.)	(Everyone's copy of the math test was blurred.)
Rejected woman	I'm unattractive to him.	My conversation bores him.	He's overly competitive with women.	He was in a rejecting mood.

Note: ETS = Educational Testing Service, the maker of graduate record examinations (GRE).

depression is chronic and how general it is depends upon whether the individual attributes the deficit to a global or a specific cause, whether the cause is internal (personal) or external (universal), and whether the factor is stable ("I am stupid") or unstable ("I am doing badly because I have a cold") (see Table 14–5). Thus, it is rather obvious that if the individual attributes helplessness to factors that are internal, stable, and global, the intensity of the depression is likely to be severe and chronic.

Limitations of learned helplessness theory

A number of general and specific criticisms apply to cognitive theories of depression. In the first place, some real questions arise about whether learned helplessness or Beck's cognitive theory adequately accounts for the symptoms observed in affective disorders. For example, the learned helplessness theory appears to predict the passivity and psychomotor retardation found in bipolar depression but is also offered as a model for unipolar depression, a condition in which passivity and psychomotor retardation seldom occur (Huesmann 1978).

Which came first: distorted cognitions or depressive symptoms

Furthermore, the occurrence of mania is rarely considered in cognitive and behavioral explanations of depression. The lack of correspondence between symptoms of affective disorders and those observed in learned helplessness is often explained by asserting that affective disorders are a heterogeneous group of disorders and that cognitive explanations may account for only specific types. For example, Seligman (1978) states that his hypothesis may account only for a subclass of depression called "helplessness depression." This type

High aversion/ low reinforcement in depression

of reasoning also occurs in other approaches to explanations of depression, such as that of Depue and Monroe (1978) for bipolar disorders. According to this theory, one type has a family history of these episodes (genetic basis for disorders) and another type does not (environmental causes). But, as we showed in Chapter 3, this type of reasoning confuses classification with explanation. This is a classic example of "begging the question," in which the concern is whether the affective disorders were viewed as heterogeneous before or after the model of depression did not fit. It is questionable to attempt to search for depressive types that fit certain theoretical models of etiology and treatment rather than to develop models that account for the facts.

A second major problem of cognitive theories that is difficult to resolve is whether depressive behaviors are a function of distorted cognitions or whether distorted cognitions are developed as a result of the individual's behavioral deficits (or depressive symptoms). For example, the individual who feels inadequate handles situations poorly and consequently has lower self-esteem, a negative perception of the self, the world, and the future, and may be accurately perceiving the situation. As a matter of fact, the individual may not handle interactions with others very well, may have deficits in social skills, and be perceived by others as inept. Beliefs about oneself and the world can develop from accurately perceiving one's inadequacies and can then lead to depression. In this case, the cognitions are a function of behavior and the solution to the problem would be to shape appropriate coping behaviors and interpersonal skills that would increase self-esteem.

Behavioral Theories

As noted by Ferster (1973), a behavioral explanation of depression starts with a functional analysis of depressive responses as related to environmental events. Depression can be elicited by any of the following events: (1) a high level of exposure to aversive events and the need to avoid aversive situations; (2) a low level of positive reinforcement; (3) a sudden change in the environment resulting from the loss of a discriminative stimulus that has controlled a large amount of behavior, such as retirement or the death of a loved one; (4) exposure to reinforcement schedules that require much effort to earn reinforcement; and (5) the expression of anger that annoys other people and thus deprives one of positive reinforcement.

The **reinforcement theory of depression** has been elaborated and expanded by Lewinsohn (1974). His behavior theory is based on three major assumptions.

Often, the depressed individual does not have a wide circle of friends. Like this man, much of the depressed person's time is spent alone.

1. A low rate of response-contingent positive reinforcement acts as an eliciting stimulus for some depressive behavior such as dysphoria, fatigue, and other somatic complaints.

2. A low rate of response-contingent positive reinforcement often constitutes an explanation for depression and low rates of behavior. The individual is assumed to be on a prolonged extinction schedule.

3. The total amount of response-contingent reinforcement an individual receives is presumed to be a function of three sets of variables: (a) the number of potentially reinforcing events for the individual (this variable is assumed to be subject to individual differences and influenced by biological and experiential variables); (b) the number of potentially reinforcing events that can be provided by the environment; and (c) the instrumental behavior of the individual (the skills needed to emit behaviors that will elicit reinforcement from the environment). These relationships are shown in Figure 14–2. Low self-esteem, pessimism, guilt feelings, and similar cognitive changes are assumed to be secondary elaborations of the low rate of reinforcement rather than causal factors. Furthermore, the hostility often exhibited by depressive individuals is fairly characteristic of organisms on extinction schedules. Factors that commonly precipitate depression, such as loss of a loved one, are viewed as events that cause a drastic change in the rate of reinforcement.

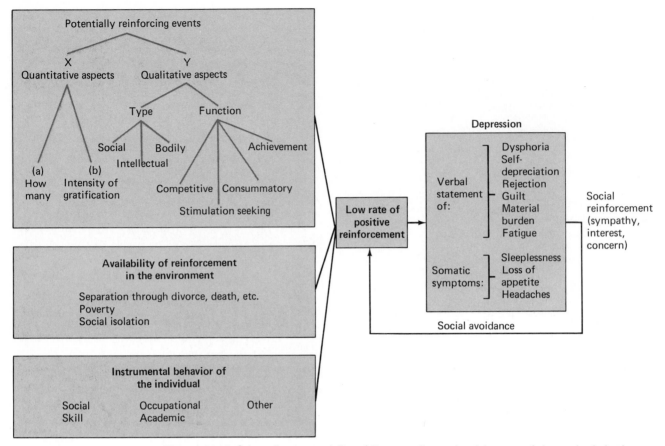

Figure 14-2 Schematic representation of the causation and maintenance of depressive behavior.

Depressed individuals are more sensitive to noxious stimuli and more reactive to stress . . .

and have poor social skills

Which came first: inadequate reinforcement or inadequate response to reinforcement

Lewinsohn and his colleagues have conducted a number of studies attempting to demonstrate the relationship between reinforcement and dysphoric (depressive) reactions. They have found that depressed individuals elicit fewer behaviors from other people than control subjects (Shaffer and Lewinsohn 1971; Libet and Lewinsohn 1971). Furthermore, they found that mood is determined by the number of pleasant activities in the subject's life (Lewinsohn and Libet 1973). As a matter of fact, the total amount of positive reinforcement appears to be less for depressed than for nondepressed people (MacPhillamy and Lewinsohn 1972).

The two major reasons for the above cycle of depressive behaviors appear to be related to two characteristics of depressed individuals. First, the depressed individual appears to be more sensitive to noxious stimuli than other individuals (Lewinsohn, Lobitz, and Wilson 1973). Individuals prone to depression tend to react more to stress than other people.

The second major factor is that the individual prone to depressive behaviors has poor social skills (Lewinsohn and Shaffer 1971). This observation is consistent with clinical lore that the depressed individual is a highly dependent person whose social behavior and relationships are characterized by tension and frustration. In support of this hypothesis Suárez, Adams, and Crowe (1978) noted that depressed individuals seem to be characterized by a passive avoidance response set rather than by learned helplessness. In other words, depressed individuals tend to show behavior characteristic of passive avoidance, such as withdrawing and becoming passive and highly emotional. This tendency to become immobilized in stressful situations results in a loss of reinforcement and initiates the depressive cycle, particularly since depressed individuals are extremely sensitive to noxious stimuli and may respond even to minor social stresses. At present the behavioral theory of depression is promising, but here too we have a chicken or the egg question. Depressive individuals may not, for whatever reasons, be able to respond to appropriate reinforcement.

Assessment of Affective Disorders

Since depression can occur as a consequence of other disorders and the types of behaviors observed may vary as a function of the severity of the condition, depression has been a difficult phenomenon to describe and assess. One solution to this problem is to assess depression *per se*, assess other problem behaviors if they are present, and then determine whether depression is primary or secondary to these other conditions. The assessment of bipolar depression, particularly mania, is another problem, because very little work has been conducted on the assessment of mania.

Unlike some other conditions, affective disorders are less likely to be situational. They tend to be pervasive and to be exhibited in most situations. However, these disorders do fluctuate in time so that intraindividual observation can be conducted and mood graphed as a function of time. Depression is usually evident in verbal report, can be observed in the individual's overt motor behavior, and does have definite physiological components. These facts play a major role in diagnosing depression as well as allowing an ongoing monitoring of changes in affective behavior.

In obtaining a subjective report, a number of self-report inventories have been used, the most popular being the depression scale of the MMPI, as it taps subjective depression, psychomotor retardation, complaints about physical or psychic malfunctioning, and brooding. Unfortunately, this scale also taps anxiety and tension, which causes it to be a kind of "distress" scale. An additional advantage of the MMPI is that it also contains a scale for mania, which taps the amorality, imperturbability, and acceleration of motor activity present in this condition (Harris and Lingo 1955).

However, the MMPI was not designed to allow continuous monitoring of mood. For this purpose, scales such as the Beck Depression Inventory or the Lubin Depressive Adjective Checklist can be used. The Beck Depression Inventory consists of twenty-one items to reflect different specific *Self-report inventories* manifestations of depression, including self-report of motor, physiological, and cognitive behaviors, as shown in Figure 5.1. The Lubin Depressive Adjective Checklist consists of items (adjectives) that the individual endorses. As contrasted with the Beck scale, the Adjective Checklist tends to target depressed affect (Lubin 1967).

In addition to self-rating scales, there are a number of interviewer rating scales, such as the Hamilton Rating Scales (Hamilton 1967). This scale includes cognitive, behavioral, and physiological symptoms usually associated with depression, as well as correlated behavior, such as derealization, depersonalization, paranoid behaviors, and obsessive behavior.

In terms of overt motor behavior, depression and mania are sometimes obvious and can be clearly observed even by the untrained observer. A sad demeanor, a hanging head, drooping shoulders, crying, decreased motor activity, and a variety of other motor behaviors are obvious in depression. In mania, the individual may be unreasonably happy with smiling, laughing, and other signs of elation being exaggerated, while motor activity is tremendously increased.

Lewinsohn (1974) has used a behavioral *Behavioral coding system* coding system for assessing depressed behavior. This system measures the following variables: (1) total amount of behavior, (2) the use of positive and negative reactions, (3) interpersonal verbal efficiency, and (4) the range of interaction with others. This system directly taps the social skills of the individual as well as the activity level. Lewinsohn and his colleagues have found with this assessment technique that depressed individuals emit fewer positive reactions to others but do not differ on negative reactions. The interpersonal range tends to be narrow; moreover, depressed subjects have lower total activity levels and low rates of mutual reinforcement with others. An additional measure, *action latency,* indicates that depressed subjects are significantly

Depression also is characterized by lethargy, feelings of fatigue, and poor appetite.

slower in response to another's reaction (Libet and Lewinsohn 1973). This coding system usually requires well-trained observers in home or group settings, but is quite sensitive to behaviors associated with depression.

To determine the number of events that are reinforcing to the individual, Lewinsohn (1974) generated a list of positive events that individuals rate on a scale of one to five from not pleasant to very pleasant. In addition, individuals indicate how frequently they have experienced these events during the day. This schedule then measures activity level defined as the sum of the frequency rating, the reinforcement potential defined as the sum of the pleasantness ratings, and the obtained reinforcement defined as the sum of the products of the frequency and pleasantness rating of the items. This scale seems to differentiate very well between depressed individuals and other groups. Items from this scale that the individual rates as very pleasant can also be used as a basis for daily logs of ongoing behavior. An example of this activity schedule is shown in Figure 14–3.

The association of depression and mania with somatic or physiological changes has been well established. Particularly evident are the changes in the autonomic nervous system. For example, Gatchel and his colleagues (1977), as well as Suárez, Adams, and Crowe (1978), have shown that depression is associated with increases in GSR responses, which indicate an overall increase in the arousal level of the individual. Unfortunately, it is generally not possible with autonomic indices such as GSR and heart rate to differentiate between depression and other aroused states, such as anxiety. Recent research does indicate, however, a possibility that patterns of facial and postural muscle activity can be used to differentiate between various emotions, including depression. These data were discussed in Chapter 8.

Modification of Affective Disorders

The cyclic nature of most affective disorders makes it difficult to determine the effectiveness of any single treatment approach. The likelihood of spontaneous remissions

| Name_____ | Date_____ | Raw Score_____ | Weighted Score_____ |

Instructions: Place check marks in the frequency column to correspond to the number of times an activity takes place during the day. For example, if you go for a walk two times during the day, place two check marks in the frequency column. Only activities that were at least a little pleasant during the day being considered should be checked. If an activity differs in pleasantness from your initial ratings, write in how pleasant the activity was for that particular day, using the following rating system: 2 means a little, 3 means a fair amount, 4 means much, and 5 means very much.

Activity	How pleasant		
	Initially	Today	Frequency
Talking with other teachers	3		
Developing own teaching materials	4		
Talking with students			
Teaching students	4		
Cleaning house	3		
Carrying on conversation with daughter	4		
Taking a trip (to)	5		
Going on a date			
Hearing a lecture	3		
Attending class	3		
Going to a play	4		
Going to a concert	2		
Attending a church discussion group	4		
Playing a game	2		
Eating at home	2		
Dining out	3		
Having a drink with a friend			
Solving mathematical problems	4		
Solving crossword puzzles	2		
Listening to music	3		
Watching animals	3		
Watching sports	1		
Reading for teaching purposes	3		
Reading for entertainment	4		
Looking at interesting buildings	2		
Looking at beautiful scenery	4		
Watching TV	2		
Singing alone			
Singing with others	3		
Dancing	2		
Performing on a musical instrument	1		

Figure 14–3 Pleasant events schedule.

makes it necessary to determine whether the technique in question prevents relapse or recurrence and also whether the technique eliminates the disturbed affect state.

The major physical or medical techniques for treating affective disorders are electroconvulsive shock therapy (ECT) and chemotherapy. ECT is often used with patients when a rapid and effective treatment technique is required, as in stuporous depression, and when the individual poses an immediate and serious suicide risk (Hurwitz 1974). A complete remission of symptoms may occur after about four to ten convulsive treatments in as many as 90 percent of patients with affective disorders. Furthermore, when drug treatment has failed, there is a 50 percent chance that the person will respond favorably to ECT (Davis 1975). The two major side effects of ECT are temporary amnesia and confusion. While the amnesia and confusion can be viewed as undesirable side effects, these effects may also be responsible for the remission of the depression, since the individual has difficulty in recalling events precipitating or maintaining the depression.

Use of ECT

How ECT works is not clear. Some psychodynamic theorists speculate that it provides an individual with punishment, which reduces guilt, and thus causes the depression to subside. Others theorize that the therapeutic effect occurs because ECT causes changes in the cholinergic and the adrenergic neurotransmitters, assumed by some theorists to be disturbed in affective disorders (Adams, Reynolds, and Sutker 1969). Ethical issues have been raised with regard to the use of this procedure, however, since numerous ECT treatments may cause central nervous system impairment and the treatment procedure is unpleasant.

Antidepressant drugs

The two major antidepressant drugs effective in alleviating depression are the tricyclic antidepressants and the MAO inhibitors. Generally, it is believed that tricyclic antidepressives, particularly imipramine, are more effective than the MAO inhibitors, and they tend to have fewer side effects. Whereas these drugs increase norepinephrine (see the norepinephrine hypothesis), lithium carbonate decreases it. *Lithium* is assumed to be highly effective, has become extremely popular, and is often regarded as a wonder drug for manic reactions. The blood concentration of Lithium has to be monitored regularly, since excessive amounts of lithium may interfere with the body's ability to use sodium, and this can be fatal. The evidence of the effectiveness of lithium as compared to placebo has been much more conservative than the enthusiastic response it has received from medical clinicians. However, most studies indicate that lithium is somewhat more effective than placebo with bipolar depression, particularly in preventing relapses (Prien, Caffey, and Klett 1973).

The applicability and effectiveness of psychological interventions depend on the severity of the disorder. Milder cases of affective disorders have been popular choices for psychological intervention procedures. Two types of therapy will be described, *cognitive therapy* and *behavior therapy*. Beck (1976) has presented evidence that cognitive therapy is quite effective, superior to behavior therapy and antidepressant medication (imipramine). Beck's (1976) cognitive therapy is based on his theory of depression. While Beck uses many techniques that can be labeled as behavior therapy, the principal goal of his approach is cognitive modification, since he believes the core of depression is the individual's negative cognitions. The first step in treatment with cognitive therapy is separating the syndrome of depression into its specific components and then selecting one of these components for change. Various techniques are used with various symptoms. These techniques include:

1. **Graded task assignments** The therapist starts with a simple assignment that the individual is able to complete. Gradually the activities are increased in complexity and duration. This procedure is designed to give depressed individuals a chance to be successful and thus enhance their self-esteem.

2. **Mastery and pleasure therapy (M & P therapy)** This procedure is designed to penetrate the blindness of depressed patients to situations in which they are successful. It includes keeping a running account of their activities and marking down *M* for each mastery experience and *P* for each pleasant experience.

3. **Cognitive reappraisal** This is a major technique since it is designed to modify faulty patterns of thinking. It has seven steps: (a) identification of sequences between depressed cognition and sadness; (b) identification of sequences between cognitions and motivation, such as avoidance of social activities and suicidal impulses; (c) exploration of depressive cognitions; (d) examination, evaluation, and modification of these cognitions; (e) identification of overgeneralization, arbitrary inferences, and dichotomous thinking; (f) identification of underlying assumptions; (g)

examination, evaluation, and modification of basic premises and assumptions.

4. **Alternative therapy** This procedure consists of considering alternative explanations for experiences and considering alternative ways of dealing with personal and situational problems. This allows the individual to find and act on solutions to problems considered unsolvable.

5. **Cognitive rehearsal** This technique requires the individual to imagine going through the steps involved in some specific activity that has caused problems. Thus, the individual is able to anticipate obstacles and resolve conflicts in imagination before entering a situation.

6. **Triple columns** In this procedure the individual uses three columns to write down (a) the situation that elicits unpleasant feeling, (b) the negative automatic thought, and (c) the corrective response to the negative thought.

7. **Homework assignment** Here the individual is required to do, outside the therapy session, a substantial amount of work that is assumed to counteract depressive symptoms.

Behavior therapy usually has two major goals in the treatment of depression. The first is to eliminate the extreme sensitivity of depressed individuals to aversive stimuli, and the second is to increase the rate of positive reinforcement in their lives.

The first goal has been approached by using techniques such as systematic desensitization and flooding (Hannie and Adams 1974). The purpose is to extinguish the overactivity of the autonomic nervous system when the individual has negative thoughts or cognition. Everyone has had negative thoughts about personal failures, ineptness, and inadequacies. The difference between the normal individual and the individual prone to depression is that the latter overreacts emotionally to such thoughts in a way that encourages the reaction to persist.

The usual purpose of the second goal is to have the individual increase rates of activity and thereby generate more positive reinforcement (Lewinsohn 1974). Unfortunately, it has been shown that when the rate of activities increases in depressive individuals, they often become more depressed (Hammen and Glass 1976). This result is not surprising because an individual with deficits in social skills may, as Lewinsohn has proposed, find that increasing interaction with people will result in exposure to more social criticism and ostracism. The obvious solution to this problem is first to teach the individual social skills so as to acquire a repertoire of responses that enhance positive reinforcement and reduce negative reinforcement in social interactions. When some level of proficiency and social skills has been achieved, the individual can be reinforced for increasing the rate of social interaction.

The major difference between behavior therapy and cognitive therapy is one of emphasis. Cognitive therapists believe that if one can correct distortion in thinking, the behavior will change toward a more meaningful social interaction. (This assumption is similar to the belief that insight causes behavior change.) Behavior therapists, on the other hand, emphasize elimination of the emotional states, acquisition of adequate social skills, and direct alteration of the behavior to generate fewer negative and more positive consequences. The result will be a change in the individual's attitudes and cognitions.

Unfortunately, few if any specific psychological interventions have been attempted with manic reactions. This dearth may be due to the fact that mania is rarely treated in outpatient settings and is somewhat rare and that people with manic reactions are usually not cooperative. Furthermore, mild and moderate cases of mania may be perceived positively in our society.

Behavior therapy goals: reduce extreme sensitivity to aversive stimuli; increase positive reinforcement

box 14–3
Neurotic Depression
in a Twenty-Two-
Year-Old Female

For the past two years I'd felt so depressed I didn't know what to do. I felt worthless and criticized myself for everything I did. I just couldn't seem to please myself. I didn't have much energy either. I just sat around most of the time. I tried several therapists. They tried to find out why I felt like I did. They asked me about my childhood. I told them I was an only child, but that I never pleased my mother much. She would always lecture me about how other kids my age loved and respected their mothers more than I did her. My father was a kind man, but he never made much effort to defend me from my mother. In school I always did pretty well, better than most of my friends, I guess. I got my B.A. in sociology with a B average, but I never really felt like I was doing the best I could. My husband told the doctors I was a great housekeeper, but that I was always ready to criticize myself. When the doctors asked me to look at myself and my work objectively, I had to admit that I did better than most girls my age. But that didn't help the depression. It would always come back.

Then I went to a different therapist. He asked me about what kinds of rewards or praise I gave myself. I told him that I had been taught not to think too highly of myself or indulge myself too much. I told him I used to compliment myself sometimes, but not very often. Recently, I hadn't done it at all. Every time people said something nice to me, I'd feel funny and say something bad about myself right away.

The doctor told me to pick something I did often and thought was important. I took housekeeping. Then he told me to write down at the same time every day the time I spent doing dishes and dusting. I also had to rate how depressed I felt on a ten-point scale with ten being very depressed. Last I had to write down the number of rewards I gave myself for housework every day. He said a reward

was praising myself, doing something I liked, or just feeling contented for doing my housework. I kept these records for ten days.

During my second appointment, the doctor explained self-reinforcement to me. He said it was important to reinforce ourselves for what we do when others aren't around to reinforce us all the time. He told me to take each chore by itself and decide exactly what I wanted to accomplish and how much time I wanted to spend on it. He helped me lower my goals at first so it would be easier for me to succeed. Before I started a job, I'd write down my goals; when I finished, I'd see how close I came to my goal. If I thought I'd done well or better than I planned, I was supposed to reward myself immediately by doing something pleasant. I could compliment myself, smoke a cigarette, or call a friend. The doctor also gave me a box of poker chips and told me to take out as many as I thought I deserved, up to ten. During the visit, he showed me what to do, and I rehearsed it until I got it right.

I started rewarding myself on the eleventh day. Pretty soon, I began to feel depressed less of the time and better about rewarding myself. I felt easier about my work too, and even spent less time on it. On my own, I started doing the same sort of thing with my duties as hostess. I'd decide what things to watch and then reward myself. The doctor liked the idea.

During my fourth visit, I could report that my depression was almost all gone. The doctor told me then that I could stop rating my depression and recording my time and goals, but I should keep rewarding myself. About two months later, he asked me to start recording again. When we checked my records, I could easily see how I'd stopped feeling that what I did wasn't good enough and had started feeling happy and satisfied about what I did.

Jackson, 1972

Suicide

It is generally assumed that individuals who take their own lives are seriously depressed. As a matter of fact, it has been estimated that approximately 75 percent are depressed at the time of the suicidal act (Leonard 1974). However, depression is only one of the many factors in **suicide** and may be relatively absent in some cases. Crucial facts about suicide are difficult to generate because the targeted population is deceased. Furthermore, people who attempt suicide may not be representative of this population. Seiden (1974) found that less than 10 percent of individuals who make a suicidal attempt kill themselves later. For this reason, the ingenuity of clinical researchers has been taxed to devise methods to gather clues about self-destructive behavior.

Facts about Suicide

Suicide ranks among the first causes of deaths in most countries, including the United States. In the United States over 200,000 attempts to commit suicide occur each year, and about 25,000 of these attempts are successful. This rate is about 12 persons per 100,000, but despite popular opinion to the contrary, the rate is not increasing and is about the same as it was in 1900 (Pokorny 1968).

Suicide does fluctuate with environmental conditions. For example, it has been noted that suicide rates tend to increase during economic slumps, such as the Great Depression in the thirties, and decrease during periods of prosperity or when social cohesion is high, such as during a war (Coleman 1976).

Suicide also varies considerably from one society or country to another. For example, Hungary has an annual index of 33 per 100,000, the world's highest suicide rate. High rates are also present in Czechoslovakia, Finland, Austria, and Sweden, all over 20 per 100,000. This rate drops drastically in Mexico, New Guinea, and the Phillipine Islands to less than 1 in 100,000. As a matter of fact, among certain non-technological societies the rate of suicide is almost zero (Kidson and Jones 1968). Ap-

parently the attitudes of a society, including religious taboos, are important in the rate of suicide. Some societies, such as Japan, have socially approved reasons for suicide, usually associated with disgrace to the individual or the group.

Environmental factors in suicide

In general, the peak age for suicide is between twenty-four and forty-four, but the greatest increase in recent years has been in the fifteen to twenty-four age group, in which the rate has almost doubled. In this group college students and nonwhites are particularly vulnerable. For example, among black youths the rate is about twice the national average, and among youths of some American-Indian groups it is about five times the national average (Frederick 1973). Three times as many men as women commit suicide, but more women make suicide attempts. Depressed persons, the elderly, alcoholics, individuals living alone, and migrants have high rates. Professionals, such as physicians, lawyers, dentists, and psychologists, have extremely high rates, with female physicians and psychologists committing suicide at a rate three times that of women in the general population. Male physicians have a suicide rate about twice that of men in the general population, with psychiatrists having the highest rate of suicide in the professional group (Ross 1974; Schaar 1974).

Demographic factors in suicide

Among males the methods of committing suicide tend to be more violent, such as the use of firearms and hanging; while among females there is a great tendency to use drugs, such as the barbiturates. However, the use of prescription drugs like the barbiturates as a method for suicide is definitely increasing.

Indicators of Suicide

The prediction of suicide is a necessary prerequisite to its control. Unfortunately, very little success has been achieved in this area. The results of personality tests are quite discouraging (Lester 1970). Demographic variables, such as age, sex, marital status, and living arrangement, have also been tried. Shneidman (1975) devised a scale of lethality that yields ratings (from 1 to 9) of absent, low, medium, and high, which supposedly indicate the probability of an individual's committing suicide. This scale focuses on changes in the individual's life for determining lethality, including changes in interests, habits, attitudes, eating patterns, and similar events. Unfortunately, its validity has not been well established.

Litman and Wold (1974) have posited three features characteristic of the depressed individual who commits suicide: somatic problems, such as disturbed appetite and fatigue; disturbed affect (feeling of helplessness and worthlessness); and social isolation. They found that a previous attempt is particularly indicative of a possible future attempt. In depression the greatest period of danger appears to be shortly after discharge from treatment (Shneidman and Farberow 1957; Wheat 1960). Individuals who intend to commit suicide do usually give some signal of their intent (Litman and Wold 1974; Seiden 1966). These messages usually include a "cry for help" or some form of suicide threat.

Three features: somatic problems, disturbed affect, social isolation

Causes of Suicide

Depression is often cited as a major cause of suicide, but the motivation for the act may come from a number of sources. Shneidman and Farberow (1970) have developed a procedure they call the *psychological autopsy* in which they try to gather information that allows an investigator to evaluate the motives for suicide. This information may come from suicide notes, telephone calls made prior to suicide, interviews with relatives and friends, and other data. Approximately 24 percent of suicides leave notes, the content of which varies from very positive (51 percent) to neutral (18 percent) to mixed (18 percent) to hostile (6 percent), as reported by Tuckman, Kleiner, and Lavell (1959). In analyzing over 800 of these notes left by actual suicides, Shneidman and Farberow (1957) found that they could be sorted into three types—logical, psychotic, and confused. Unfortunately, as Cohen and Fiedler (1974) have noted, suicide notes have not given any great insight into the causes of suicide.

Three types of suicide notes

Some of the reasons for suicide are as follows:

1. **Escape from suffering** Beck (1976) suggests that suicidal thoughts and their intention are related to helplessness. The individual who is depressed because of overwhelming emotional or physical problems may become apathetic, feel hopeless, and see suicide as a method of solving a problem. This is often the case in individuals with terminal diseases and in older males for whom the future looks dim. Schuyler (1974) suggests that a feeling of helplessness may be the best predictor of suicide.

   Seiden (1966) has claimed that college students have a significantly higher rate of suicide than their noncollege peers because the stress in college is severe. In a study of suicidal cases at the University of California at Berkeley during a ten-year period, Seiden (1966) found that the suicide rate was greater for graduate students than for undergraduates and that three times as many male students as female students committed suicide. Approximately 50 percent of those who committed suicide had some previous psychiatric or mental health contact. Furthermore, they tended to give warnings of their intent and saw their problems as hopelessly unsolvable and stressful.

2. **Retaliation against others** Some people seem to commit suicide to make others feel guilty for their death. These irrational guilt processes often take the form, "I'll kill myself and then you'll be sorry." In this sense, suicide is a hostile act towards others.

3. **Attention seeking** Some individuals commit or attempt suicide to make themselves famous or immortal. The dramatic gestures of suicide for a cause can be included here as can committing suicide in public. An example of this type is the Buddhist monks who burned themselves in public places to protest the actions of the South Vietnamese government in the late 1960s and early 1970s.

During World War II, Japanese kamikaze pilots would commit culturally accepted suicide by dive-bombing their planes into enemy ships.

4. **Altruism** There are two variations of this type of suicide. The first is that an individual feels death can solve a problem. A good example is the person who self-inflicts death so that the family can collect the insurance policy. The second may be illustrated by the Kamikaze pilot during World War II. Such individuals view society's goals and values as more important than their own lives.

Colson (1973), using sophisticated statistical procedures in a population he assumed to be strongly suicidal, found five clusters of suicide intent due to: (1) loneliness and interpersonal failure, (2) health problems, (3) fear of failure and a dim future,

(4) manipulation of someone else, and (5) a fear of going insane. To some extent this categorizing of motivation fits the factors previously discussed.

Prevention of Suicide

One answer to the extremely difficult problem of suicide prevention is the *crisis intervention center,* where individuals can call someone and discuss their problems. In this manner, suicide attempts may be diverted. The purpose of these centers is to help individuals consider other alternatives and to direct them to resources for psychotherapeutic or other forms of help. These centers have widely publicized telephone numbers and are usually staffed by both professionals and volunteers.

The crisis intervention center selects people because of their ability to relate to others and gives special training in the nature of suicide and how to talk to potential suicides on the phone. Rapid intervention, reversal of despair, and the eliciting of hope are the main goals. It is important to maintain contact with potential suicides and tell them exactly how to handle their problems. It does seem that these centers handle high-risk suicide groups, since Wold and Litman (1973) attempted to reinterview a random sample of 417 people who had made calls to a suicide prevention center two years earlier and found that nine of them were dead from suicide, a rate almost 100 times greater than that of the general population.

Importance of maintaining contact

How successful crisis centers are is not clear. Farberow and Litman (1970) have reported that the estimated suicide rate among people who are judged to be high risks for suicide is 6 percent, while the rate is slightly less than 2 percent among the high-risk individuals who use the crisis intervention center services. On the other hand, in Los Angeles, where these centers were initiated and pioneered, the suicide rates have significantly increased since their opening. Perhaps, the suicide rate in Los Angeles would have increased even more during this period of time if there had not been suicide prevention centers. In any case, the problem of suicide remains an enigma, and the solutions to it are not readily apparent.

Summary

The affective disorders include both neurotic and psychotic patterns of behavior. The psychotic disorders differ from other forms of abnormal behavior in that they cause a gross distortion of reality and a severe disorganization of behavior patterns. Bizarre behavior patterns can occur in the following:

1. **The sensory and perceptional response system** Disorders of this response system are usually called hallucinations.
2. **The cognitive response system** The primary system disturbed in all psychotic disorders except for the affective psychoses. Disorders of reasoning, thinking, and communication are common in psychotic behavior patterns.
3. **The motor response system** Motor behavior may be retarded, accelerated, or simply bizarre.
4. **The emotional response system** The individual exhibits unusual changes in mood or gross exaggeration of affect.
5. **The social response system** Disturbance is usually indicated by a loss of usual social inhibitions or skills. Various types of these behavior patterns cluster in such a way as to define schizophrenia, affective psychoses, and other psychotic disorders.

Affective disorders are abnormal states of elation (mania or depression) that can be considered specific types of emotional disorders. However, many clinicians point to the central role of irrational, self-defeating thoughts. The major signs of depression are emotional, cognitive, and somatic, all reflecting dysphoric moods. Manic behavior reflects a euphoric mood but has many similarities to depression. The types of depressive disorders defined in DMS-II include (1) depressive neuroses, (2) cyclothymic personality, (3) psychotic depressive reaction, (4) involutional melancholia, and (5) manic depressive reaction. However, differentiating between these types of disorders is difficult, and in DSM-III the affective disorders are manic disorders, depressive disorders, and bipolar affective disorders.

Affective disorders in children have caused much controversy. This controversy centers around masked depression, the theory that a child who is hyperactive, disobedient, or phobic or who exhibits other such behaviors is depressed. The two essential features of depression in children are dysphoria and a generalizing impairment in response to previously reinforcing experiences without the introduction of new sources of reinforcement. Anaclitic depression occurs in children between six months and six years of age and has three stages: protest, despair, and detachment. That separation of an infant from its parents causes this reaction has been confirmed with monkeys by Harlow and his colleagues.

The genetic hypothesis of affective disorders has strong support for bipolar depression but little support for unipolar depression. Furthermore, some evidence suggests that depression and mania may be caused by alterations of biochemical functioning. Two such hypotheses have been the electrolyte hypothesis and the catecholamine hypothesis. It has been shown that in the transition from depression to mania or vice versa, changes in mood are associated with changes in biochemical functioning. In general, the biochemical hypotheses of affective disorders are viable.

Psychoanalytic theory, which has had a strong influence on theories of depression, focuses on the individual's oral dependency needs and a tendency to react to frustration with hostility directed inward. Mania is supposedly a defense against this reaction and thus results in grandiose and self-adulatory attitudes.

Cognitive theories of depression take the position that depression is a cognitive disorder and that the affective and motivational disturbances are the result of disordered cognitions. Beck states that depression centers around a cognitive triad of a negative view of the world, a negative concept of self, and a negative appraisal of the future. These distorted attitudes cause faulty perceptions, which result in negative feedback that, in turn, perpetuates the depressive cycle. The individual also has low self-esteem and a feeling of helplessness and hopelessness. A major cognitive approach to depression is the learned helplessness hypothesis—that depressed individuals have been subjected to aversive experiences in their lives that they could not control. Consequently, they tend to view their responding as independent of reinforcement and believe that they cannot control their destiny. Two major criticisms of cognitive theo-

ries are that they do not adequately account for depressive behavior patterns, and that it is not clear whether distorted cognitions produce an individual's behavioral deficits or vice versa.

Behavioral explanations of depression have centered on a high level of exposure to aversive events, a low level of positive reinforcement, a sudden change in the environment, reinforcement schedules in which much effort is required to earn reinforcement, and the theory that expression of anger annoying to other people deprives one of further positive reinforcement. Lewinsohn, in elaborating this hypothesis, has pointed to the fact that depressive individuals are very sensitive to aversive events and often have deficits in social skills.

A number of methods have been used to test affect disorders, including subjective reports, self-monitoring procedures, observation of motor behavior, and physiological indices. Lewinsohn has used a behavioral coding system for tapping depressive behaviors that can be used in social situations by observing the interaction of the depressed individual with other people.

The major medical techniques for treating affective disorders have been ECT and chemotherapy. Both have been fairly effective, particularly when rapid changes in behavior are required. Beck has developed a cognitive therapy based on his theory of depression that seems also to be effective when compared to behavioral therapy and medical treatment. Behavior therapy usually centers on the elimination of the extreme sensitivity of depressed individuals to aversive situations and the teaching of social skills, which generate more appropriate reinforcement schedules.

Suicide occurs largely among individuals who are depressed, although suicide can occur for other reasons. The reasons for suicide include (1) escape from suffering, (2) retaliation against others, (3) attention seeking, and (4) altruism. Suicide varies greatly with social or cultural milieu, economic conditions, professional status, and racial groups. Attempts at predicting and preventing suicide have not been highly successful. Prevention of suicide is extremely difficult, but crisis intervention centers appear to have been fairly useful.

Key Concepts

affective disorders

anaclitic depression

bipolar depression

catalepsy

catecholamine hypothesis (norepinephrine hypothesis)

cognitive triad

cyclothymic personality

delusions

depression

depressive neurosis

electrolyte hypothesis

endogenous depression

exogenous depression

functional psychoses

hallucinations

ideas of reference

involutional melancholia

learned helplessness

mania

manic depressive illnesses

marasmus

masked depression

organic psychoses

psychosis

psychotic depressive reaction

reinforcement theory of depression

suicide

unipolar depression

Review Questions

1. How do psychoses differ from other behavior disorders?

2. How do psychotic hallucinations differ from other hallucinations?

3. How do mania and depression differ from each other? How do they differ from ordinary emotional states?

4. What is the difference between primary and secondary depressions? Exogenous and endogenous depressions? Unipolar and bipolar depressions?

5. What are the three stages of anaclitic depression?

6. What part do genetic factors play in bipolar depression? In unipolar depression?

7. What is the electrolyte hypothesis? What is the norepinephrine hypothesis?

8. What is the major problem in evaluating biochemical theories of abnormal behavior?

9. What is the major theme in psychodynamic theories of depression?

10. What is the cognitive triad?

11. What is the learned helplessness hypothesis?

12. State two major criticisms of cognitive theories of depression.

13. What factors are cited in learning theories of depression?

14. Why is assessment of depression difficult?

15. What are the major advantages and drawbacks of using ECT and chemotherapy to treat depression?

16. What are the two major goals of behavioral approaches to treating depression?

17. What are the four major reasons for which people commit suicide?

psychotic behavior

schizophrenia, paranoia, and childhood psychoses

15

Key Topics

Four fundamental symptoms of schizophrenia

Five main subtypes of schizophrenia

Three major research-based dimensions of schizophrenia

Problems in diagnosing schizophrenia

Attention, information processing, and arousal disturbances of schizophrenics

Problems in discriminating contextual cues by schizophrenics

Hypothesis of self-produced stimuli in the hallucinations of schizophrenics

Perseveration chaining model of schizophrenic speech

Problem in evaluating evidence of genetic factors in schizophrenia

Meehl's diathesis-stress model of schizophrenia

Transmethylation and dopamine hypotheses of schizophrenia

Hypothesis of the "schizogenic mother"

Three conditions present in a double-bind

Laing's mystification of experience

"Social drift" hypothesis and alternative explanations

Universality of schizophrenia

Ullmann and Krasner's sociopsychological model of schizophrenia

Antipsychotic drugs and schizophrenia

Milieu therapy and token economies for institutionalized schizophrenics

The paranoid personality

Differences between paranoia and schizophrenia

Five different theories of paranoia

Childhood schizophrenia and infantile autism

Psychodynamic and behavioral approaches to autistic children

The behavior patterns we shall discuss in this chapter seem, on the surface at least, further removed from most of our everyday experiences than any behavior we have discussed thus far. Severe deficits in reality testing, orientation, and social interaction with others are common. Extreme social withdrawal and bizarre behavior patterns may also occur. Children with these psychoses indulge in hours-long sessions of headbanging. But most frustrating, none of the many explanations for these behavior patterns have been supported by enough evidence to make them convincing, and clinicians have not been able to agree on definitions, classifications, or assessments.

Schizophrenia

The revolving door pattern in treatment

Approximately one-half of all patients in mental hospitals in this country are diagnosed as schizophrenic. The admission rate for both sexes is concentrated between the ages of twenty and forty, most frequently between twenty-five and thirty-four. Schizophrenia appears early in life and continues to handicap most sufferers throughout their lives (Shean 1978). It has been estimated that up to 6 percent of the population could be diagnosed as schizophrenic at any given time. The actual prevalence of schizophrenia, particularly in the United States, is difficult to determine because the diagnosis has proved hightly variable and unreliable (Bellak, Hurrich, and Gediman 1973).

Fundamental and accessory symptoms

The pattern of treatment of the disorders designated as schizophrenia has changed drastically in the last twenty-five years. In 1955, 77 percent of all patients under care were in inpatient settings (hospitals). In 1973 this had dropped to 32 percent (Taube and Redick 1976). The present trend in the treatment of schizophrenia is toward brief hospitalization followed by discharge to home or sheltered care with outpatient treatment. This trend has been made possible by the use of major tranquilizers, which has also led to a revolving-door pattern of admission-release-readmission in hospital treatment.

Schizophrenia has been present throughout history. Galen and others described it with terms such as madness, lunacy, and insanity, but the first clear description of schizophrenia was given by Emil Kraepelin. Kraepelin believed the disorder was due to an underlying organic disease of the central nervous system that he thought was progressive and irreversible. He called the disorder **dementia praecox** because the mental deterioration (dementia) was first evident during adolescense (praecox). He classified schizophrenia into a number of different types, such as *paranoia, catatonia, hebephrenia,* and *simple schizophrenia.* His theory of schizophrenia, particularly his classification and his belief that schizophrenia was a cognitive disorder, still influences modern theories of schizophrenia.

Eugen Bleuler first introduced the term **schizophrenia.** He believed that the common ingredient of these disorders was a split (*schism*) within the mind (*phrenos*) and particularly emphasized the split between the cognitive processes and the emotions. He divided symptoms into *fundamental symptoms,* which were present in every case, and *accessory symptoms,* which may or may not be present in a given case. The four fundamental symptoms (sometimes called the four A's) of schizophrenia are as follows:

1. **Altered associations** Cognitive or thought disturbances are the prime disorders in schizophrenia. Normal associative processes are weakened, ideas are condensed and displaced into symbols, thoughts are generalized broadly, and reasoning or logic is greatly impaired. Because of the associative disturbance or what Meehl (1962) calls cognitive slippage, thinking becomes illogical, unclear, and often incoherent.

2. **Altered affect** Bleuler believed that affective disturbances were perhaps the most striking symptoms of schizophrenia. The emotional responses of affected individuals do not fit their circumstances and may be exaggerated, inappropriate, or absent. For this reason, many individuals classified as schizophrenic appear apathetic or anhedonic, since they do not seem to experience pleasure.

3. **Ambivalence** Bleuler defined ambivalence as entertaining completely contradictory ideas without resolving the contradictions. An individual could experience love and hate toward the same person at the same time. Or one might believe that he or she is in New York and San Francisco at the same time (*double orientation*).
4. **Autism** Autism is a loss of contact with reality and a withdrawal from social interaction. Schizophrenic individuals lose contact with reality; withdraw from involvement with the external world; and live in a world of fantasy, wish-fulfillment, and daydreaming.

The accessory symptoms, discussed in Chapter 14, include delusions, hallucinations, and bizarre social or motor behavior. Bleuler believed that these symptoms are given undue weight in the diagnosis of schizophrenia, since they may or may not be present in a given case. Bleuler also differentiated between **primary symptoms,** which he thought resulted directly from underlying organic disease processes, and **secondary symptoms,** which he believed resulted from the interaction of the organic disease with factors in the individual's environment. Unfortunately, his list of fundamental and accessory symptoms does not correspond exactly with his list of primary and secondary symptoms. As a matter of fact, the only symptom he viewed as both fundamental and primary was altered associations, which reflected the organic disease process and was present in every case of schizophrenia. Most theorists agree with Bleuler in assuming that cognitive disturbance is the prime characteristic of schizophrenia.

As will become evident, the concept of schizophrenia is controversial and, on occasions, very confusing. Some clinicians believe that schizophrenia results from a disease process or is fundamentally biochemical and genetic in nature. Others claim schizophrenia is a type of adjustment: individuals enter a hospital as a refuge from the world in which they are reluctant, or unable, to be effective social participants. In fact, schizophrenic behavior is perfectly comprehensible on this basis (Braginsky, Braginsky, and Ring 1969). Szasz (1960) says mental illness and schizophrenia are like ether or ghosts—they do not exist. He believes people have problems in living that have been labeled as illness. Laing and Esterson (1964) contend that behavior patterns such as those labeled schizophrenia are merely attempts at sanity in an insane society.

One practical approach to clarifying this issue would be to ask three major questions. First, what is schizophrenia? Can we describe it or recognize it as a distinct pattern of behavior? At issue here are diagnostic labels in terms of clinical classification as well as characteristics of the disorder that can be demonstrated by empirical evidence. Second, what causes schizophrenia? What are the theories of schizophrenia and what evidence exists to support such theories? Third, if schizophrenia exists, can it be modified or treated? If schizophrenia does not exist—a distinct possibility for some theorists—then how do we eliminate the myth?

Cognitive disturbance as the prime characteristic of schizophrenia

Different concepts of schizophrenia

Clinical Classification of Subtypes of Schizophrenia

DSM II defines schizophrenia as a disturbance in thinking, mood, and behavior. Disturbances in thinking are marked by alterations of concept formation. Such alterations may lead to misinterpretation of reality and sometimes to delusions and hallucinations, which frequently appear psychologically self-protective. Mood changes include ambivalence, constricted and inappropriate emotional responsiveness, and a lack of empathy with others. Behavior may be withdrawn, regressed, or bizarre, or all of these. The mental status is attributed primarily to a thought disorder.

The subcategories of schizophrenia have been fairly consistent in DSM throughout its three editions. The first four types are consistent with Kraepelin's subcategories of schizophrenia. However, simple schizophrenia has been dropped from DSM III.

Simple schizophrenia is presumed to be most frequent among such individuals as prostitutes.

The other subtypes have developed because, presumably, some types of schizophrenic behavior did not fit the first four subcategories.

Simple Type

Simple schizophrenics or social misfits?

Simple schizophrenia is characterized by slow onset, oddities of conduct, difficulties in social relationships, unreasonableness, and a decline in social behavior and performance. It is presumed to be most frequent among prostitutes, drifters, vagrants, petty criminals, and the like (Rimm and Somervill 1977). These individuals usually exist on a very low social-biological level. They usually have minimal motivation and are apathetic, withdrawn, and autistic. They may appear to be mentally retarded but are not. They rarely exhibit florid psychotic symptoms, such as delusions and hallucinations. The difficulty with this subcategory, as noted by Rimm and Somervill (1977), is that it is quite readily used to label social misfits.

psychotic behavior

Catatonic Type

Catatonic schizophrenia is characterized by severe disturbances in motor behavior. Individuals classified as catatonic can be wildly excited and agitated or, when in a stuporous state, may assume an unusual posture for hours. Their muscles may be rigid or they may show catalepsy, or waxy flexibility. In the stuporous phase, catatonic individuals may show negativistic behavior, refusing to comply with requests and sometimes doing the opposite of what is requested. Typically, catatonic individuals show both types of behavior—and, on occasion, may be lucid when not exhibiting either type of bizarre motor behavior. From the self-report of individuals who have experienced this state, we may conclude that it is marked by weird hallucinations and delusional thinking. For example, one such individual stated he could not move because atoms were dropping from him and movement would cause disintegration.

Hebephrenic Type

Hebephrenic schizophrenia is characterized by disorganized thinking; shallow and inappropriate affect; unpredictable giggling; silly, regressed behavior and mannerisms; and bizarre hypochondriacal complaints. Hebephrenia means mind of a child. It is one of the more blatant forms of schizophrenia and fits the public's conception of a lunatic. The hebephrenic individual may show incoherent babbling, impulsiveness, inexplicable mood shifts, and regressive behavior, such as smearing feces. In most cases, these individuals begin to exhibit seclusiveness and preoccupation with philosophy or religion at a very early age—at which time their behavior begins to deteriorate. Because of their behavioral deterioration, hebephrenics lend some support to the psychoanalytic belief that schizophrenia is a regressive phenomenon. This disorder is rare, and London (1968), for example, reported that not one case of catatonia or hebephrenia had appeared in the first-admission records of one large mental hospital for a period of over five years.

Paranoid Type

Paranoid schizophrenia is usually characterized primarily by the presence of persecutory or grandiose delusions, which are sometimes associated with hallucinations. Excessive religiosity appears in some cases, and the individual's attitude is frequently hostile and aggressive. However, behavior is usually consistent with the delusions. The gross personality disorganization seen in other types of schizophrenia does not appear in this type. DSM II states that paranoid individuals rely on projection—they ascribe to others characteristics they cannot accept in themselves. The major characteristic of this disorder is delusion. Persecutory and grandiose delusions often occur together, a logical phenomenon, since individuals who believe they are persecuted often ascribe the persecution to the fact that they are someone special. The paranoid type of schizophrenic tends to be more intelligent, show less deterioration of behavior, and present well-organized delusions. The majority of schizophrenics are labeled paranoid (Maher 1966).

Whether paranoid schizophrenia is a different disorder from paranoia is a difficult question to resolve. An individual having the fundamental symptoms of schizophrenia and showing delusions is usually labeled a paranoid schizophrenic. However, it may be that those individuals who are better integrated, whose disorder is less severe, who do not require institutionalization, and who come from a higher socioeconomic class are labeled as exhibiting paranoia.

Schizo-Affective Type

Although schizophrenia is primarily viewed as a thought or cognitive disorder and the affective disorders are viewed as basically disorders of mood, the **schizo-affective type** of schizophrenia is believed to reflect a mixture of the two. Thus, this category is used for individuals who have schizophrenic symptoms but who also show pronounced elation or depression. Nevertheless, the cognitive disorder is considered the major difficulty.

Other Schizophrenia Types

A number of other diagnostic subcategories are also labeled schizophrenia even though the behavior patterns are not clear-cut or special circumstances are present. For example, the diagnosis of *acute schizophrenic*

Waxy flexibility in catatonics

Hebephrenics as the prototypical lunatics

Persecutory and grandiose delusions in paranoid schizophrenia

episode is used for a rapid onset of schizophrenic symptoms associated with confusion; perplexity; ideas of reference; emotional turmoil; dreamlike states; and excitement, depression, or fear. The speed of onset of this condition distinguishes it from simple schizophrenia, and it is assumed that in time individuals who display acute schizophrenic reactions will take on the characteristics of catatonic, hebephrenic, or paranoid types of schizophrenia if the condition becomes stable. *Schizophrenia, latent type,* is reserved for individuals having the fundamental symptoms of schizophrenia but no history of a psychotic episode. This type is also sometimes designated as incipient, prepsychotic, pseudoneurotic, pseudopsychopathic, or borderline schizophrenia. *Schizophrenia, residual type,* describes individuals who have had a psychotic, schizophrenic episode and are no longer psychotic but show residual signs of schizophrenia. *Schizophrenia, chronic undifferentiated type,* is used for individuals who show mixed schizophrenic symptoms but who present definite schizophrenic thoughts, affect, and behavior as well as a long history of the disorder. In essence, this category becomes a catch-all of chronic schizophrenics whose subtype is not clearly defined.

Absence of a clear
precipitating event in
process schizophrenia

Research-Based Dimensions of Schizophrenic Behavior

Although the above subcategories have been used clinically, research evidence has yielded little support for them. Research has shown three major but somewhat overlapping dimensions of schizophrenic behavior that may contribute to understanding and classification of schizophrenia.

Reactive and Process Schizophrenia

One variable which has consistently been associated with a number of characteristics of schizophrenia is the rate of onset of the disorder, or *premorbid adjustment.* This is called the *process-reactive* dimension and

was first described by Bleuler (1923). Wiener (1958) described individuals with **reactive schizophrenia** as showing fairly normal development. Their maturational and developmental histories show few deficits, and their physical health is generally good. These individuals usually have a good relationship with their parents and develop normal heterosexual relationships. The reactive patient has had friends and appears to be coping fairly well before the onset of the disorder, which is sudden with a clear precipitating event. Aggression is usually expressed verbally, and there is usually little deterioration in social behavior. This type of disorder is marked by massive hallucinatory experiences, ideas of reference, paranoid trends, and sensory impairment. A thought disorder is present but response to treatment is good.

In contrast, **process schizophrenia** reveals a prepsychotic history of markedly inadequate behavior in the sexual, social, and occupational areas, as well as social isolation or withdrawal. There is no clear stressful event that precipitates the psychotic reaction. Instead, the onset usually begins in adolescence and is insidious without a recognizable or consensually validated cause. In terms of behavior there is a gradual onset of emotional blunting, a withdrawal from life's daily activities, apathy and indifference, and somatic delusions. Marked disturbances in thinking are present and persist for long periods of time (Garmezy 1970).

Phillips (1953) developed a scale that rates the individual's premorbid history. Scale items pertain to recent sexual adjustment, social aspects of recent sexual life, past history and recent adjustment in personal relationships, and precipitating factors. Actually, asking a single question such as "Has the individual ever been married" seems to be highly predictive of premorbid adjustment, at least of male schizophrenics (Held and Cromwell 1968). Nevertheless, other indices of social adjustment are also important. Harris (1975) has recently revised the Phillips Scale of Premorbid Adjustment (see Table 15–1) and reduced it to two sections: premorbid sexual adjustment and premorbid personal-social adjustment.

Table 15-1 Abbreviated Form of Premorbid Adjustment Scale

Abbreviated scale of premorbid sexual adjustment

Category	Score
I. Married, presently or formerly.	
A. Married, only one marriage (or remarried only one time as a consequence of death of spouse), living as a unit.	
1. Adequate heterosexual relations achieved.	0
2. Low sexual drive, difficult sexual relations, or extramarital affairs, either partner.	1
B. Married, more than one time, maintained a home in one marriage for at least five years.	
1. Adequate sexual relations during at least one marriage.	1
2. Chronically inadequate sexual life.	2
C. Married and apparently permanently separated or divorced without remarriage, but maintained a home in one marriage for at least five years.	2
D. Same as *C*, but maintained a home in one marriage for *less than* five years.	3
II. Single (thirty years or over).	
A. Has been engaged one or more times or has had a long-term relationship (at least two years) involving heterosexual relations or apparent evidence for a "love affair" with one person, but unable to achieve marriage.	3
B. Brief or short-term heterosexual or social dating experiences with one or more partners, but no long-lasting sexual experiences with a single partner.	4
C. Sexual and/or social relationships primarily with the same sex, but may have had occasional heterosexual contacts or dating experiences.	5
D. Minimal sexual or social interest in either men or women.	6
III. Single (under thirty years, Age twenty to twenty-nine)[1]	
A. Has had at least one long-term "love affair" (minimum of six months to one year), or engagement, even though religious or other prohibitions or inhibitions may have prevented actual sexual union.	
1. If ever actually engaged.	1
2. Otherwise.	2
B. Brief or short-term heterosexual or social dating experiences, "love affairs," with one or more partners, but no long-lasting sexual experiences with a single partner.	3
C. Casual sexual or social relationships with persons of either sex, with no deep emotional meaning.	4
D. Sexual and/or social relationships primarily with the same sex, but may have had occasional heterosexual contacts or dating experiences.	5
E. Minimal sexual or social interest in either men or women.	6

The scoring category 0 has been eliminated in the absence of evidence that the single person, age twenty to twenty-nine, will ever achieve marriage. Although a significant percentage of such subjects may eventually marry, no serious scoring error is made by assigning these subjects a conservative score of 1.

Abbreviated scale of premorbid social-personal adjustment

Category	Score
A. A leader or officer in formally designated groups, clubs, organizations, or athletic teams in senior high school, vocational school, college, or in young adulthood.	0
B. An active and interested participant, but did not play a leading role in groups of friends, clubs, organizations, or athletic teams in senior high school, vocational school, college, or in young adulthood.	1
C. A nominal member, but had no involvement in, or commitment to, groups of friends, clubs, organizations, or athletic teams in senior high school, vocational school, college, or in young adulthood.	2
D. From adolescence through early adulthood, had only a few casual or close friends.	3
E. From adolescence through early adulthood, had no real friends, only a few superficial relationships or attachments to others.	4
F. From adolescence through early adulthood, (i.e., after childhood) quiet, seclusive, preferred to be by self; minimal efforts to maintain any contact at all with others.	5
G. No desire to be with playmates, peers, or others, from early childhood. Either asocial or antisocial	6

Note: This scale should prove to be of particular value in cases (e.g., single persons) in which formal marital status or sexual adjustment is viewed as an unfair or inadequate estimate of premorbid adjustment.
—Adapted from Harris, 1975

One of the major values of the process-reactive distinction is that it has predictive value. In other words, individuals labeled good premorbids or reactive schizophrenics show less psychological disorganization at first hospitalization than poor premorbids (Higgins 1969). They have a higher probability of discharge, require a briefer hospitalization, and are unlikely to be re-hospitalized (Strauss 1973). In general, good premorbids are more likely to benefit from psychological prevention than poor premorbids, who are more likely to benefit from the antipsychotic drugs (Goldstein et al. 1969).

Process-reactive distinction has predictive value

Reactive schizophrenia is often assumed to be induced by environmental events, while **process schizophrenia** is assumed to be true schizophrenia, caused largely by genetic factors (Garmezy 1970). Some theorists view the process-reactive dimension as a continuum with the majority of patients falling at the midpoint and not well described by either extreme (Freeman 1969). On the other hand, those interested in the biological basis of schizophrenia view the process and reactive categories as two distinct types of schizophrenia (Chapman and Chapman 1973).

Acute and Chronic Schizophrenia

Acute schizophrenia describes the initial or early stages of schizophrenia and is often operationally defined as less than three years of hospitalization, while **chronic schizophrenia** indicates institutionalization for more than six years; the gap avoids overlap of categories (Shean 1978). The major use of the acute-chronic distinction is in investigating behavior as a function of length of hospitalization. For example, chronicity in schizophrenics is associated with growing detachment from external and internal stimulation as well as changes on measures of cognition, intellectual functioning, and perception (Broen 1968). It is not clear whether these differences are due to deterioration, which was at one time considered characteristic of schizophrenia, or whether they are the effects of long-term institutionalization.

Paranoid and Nonparanoid Schizophrenia

The **paranoid** and **nonparanoid schizophrenias** involve determining whether paranoid behaviors are present or not. Researchers have demonstrated that paranoid schizophrenics differ from nonparanoid schizophrenics on a number of factors, including intelligence, reaction type, distractibility, length of hospitalization, and behavioral deterioration (Shean 1978). Paranoids tend to be superior on all these measures. In other words, deficits associated with paranoid schizophrenics tend to be less severe, and the individuals' adjustment tends to be better.

The paranoid-nonparanoid dimension is measured by overt behavior, the process-reactive dimension by development history, and the acute-chronic dimension by the length of time the disorder has been diagnosed. A definite overlap occurs between these dimensions, and there is little doubt that it renders the acute-chronic distinction almost meaningless. For example, acute schizophrenics tend to have a better premorbid adjustment and are more likely to exhibit paranoid behaviors. Quite possibly, these dimensions can be reduced to the *acute reactive paranoid* type versus the *chronic process nonparanoid* type. Nevertheless, the distinctions have been useful in investigating the behavior of schizophrenic individuals, the role of premorbid history in the disorder, and the course or development of the behavior. Moreover, the acute-chronic distinction is important in detecting the effects of the course of schizophrenia, particularly as it is influenced by hospitalization, using cross-sectional methods.

Clinical Identification of Types of Schizophrenia

Can clinicians reliably identify schizophrenia? Can they agree on specific subtypes? Obviously, the definition of schizophrenia is vague. Consequently, reliability of the diagnosis of schizophrenia is low, rater agreement being typically around 60 percent. Beck et al. (1962) reported rater agreement of 53 percent; Kaelbling and Volpe (1963) reported a figure of 60 percent; and Sandifer, Pettus, and Quade (1964) reported an agreement of 74 percent.

However, when clinicians are asked to rate specific behavior patterns in contrast to the vaguely defined diagnostic syndrome of schizophrenia, agreement is quite high. For example, Yusin, Nihira, and Mortashed (1974) found that when raters were asked to indicate the presence or absence of twenty-seven specific symptoms associated with schizophrenia, the average agreement was 93 percent. For this reason, identification of schizophrenia using the criteria shown in Table 15–2 from DSM III will probably be more accurate.

Less than three years hospitalization: acute schizophrenia

More than six years hospitalization: chronic schizophrenia

Superiority of the paranoids

Acute-reactive-paranoid versus chronic-process-nonparanoid

Table 15-2 Diagnostic Criteria for a Schizophrenic Disorder

A. Characteristic schizophrenic symptoms

At least one symptom from any of the following ten symptoms was present during an active phase of the illness (because a single symptom is given such diagnostic significance, its presence should be clearly established):

Characteristic delusions

1. Delusions of being controlled: Individual experiences thoughts, actions, or feelings as imposed on him by some external force.
2. Thought broadcasting: Individual experiences thoughts, as they occur, as being broadcast from his or her head into the external world so that others can hear them.
3. Thought insertion: Individual experiences thoughts, which are not his or her own, being inserted into his or her mind (other than by God).
4. Thought withdrawal: Individual believes that thoughts have been removed from his or her head, resulting in a diminished number of thoughts remaining.
5. Other bizarre delusions (patently absurd, fantastic, or implausible).
6. Somatic, grandiose, religious, nihilistic, or other delusions without persecutory or jealous content.
7. Delusions of any type if accompanied by hallucinations of any type.

Characteristic hallucinations

8. Auditory hallucinations in which either a voice keeps up a running commentary on the individual's behaviors or thoughts as they occur, or two or more voices converse with each other.
9. Auditory hallucinations on several occasions with content having no apparent relation to depression or elation, and not limited to one or two words.

Other characteristic symptoms

10. Either incoherence, derailment (loosening of associations), marked illogicality, or marked poverty of content of speech—if accompanied by either blunted, flat, or inappropriate affect, delusions, or hallucinations, or behavior that is grossly disorganized or catatonic.

B. During the active phase of the illness, the symptoms in A have been associated with significant impairment in two or more areas of routine daily functioning, e.g., work, social relations, self-care.

C. Chronicity

Signs of the illness have lasted continuously for at least six months at some time during the person's life and the individual now has some signs of the illness. The six-month period must include an active phase during which there were symptoms from A with or without a prodromal or residual phase, as defined below.

Prodromal phase

A clear deterioration in functioning not due to a primary disturbance in mood or to substance abuse, and involving at least *two* of the symptoms noted below.

Residual phase

Following the active phase of the illness, at least *two* of the symptoms noted below, not due to a primary disturbance in mood or to substance abuse.

Prodromal or Residual Symptoms

1. Social isolation or withdrawl.
2. Marked impairment in role functioning as wage-earner, student, homemaker.
3. Markedly eccentric, odd, or peculiar behavior (e.g., collecting garbage, talking to self in cornfield or subway, hoarding food).
4. Impairment in personal hygiene and grooming.
5. Blunted, flat, or inappropriate affect.
6. Speech that is tangential, digressive, vague, overelaborate, circumstantial, or metaphorical.
7. Odd or bizarre ideation, or magical thinking, e.g., superstitiousness, clairvoyance, telepathy, "sixth sense," "others can feel my feelings," overvalued ideas, ideas of reference, or suspected delusions.
8. Unusual perceptual experiences, e.g., recurrent illusions, sensing the presence of a force or person not actually present, suspected hallucinations.

Examples

Six months of prodromal symptoms with one week of symptoms from A; no prodromal symptoms with six months of symptoms from A; no prodromal symptoms with two weeks of symptoms from A and six months of residual symptoms; six months of symptoms from A, apparently followed by several years of complete remission, with one week of symptoms in A in current episode.

D. The full depressive or manic syndrome (criteria A and B of Depressive or Manic Episode) is either not present, or if present, developed after any psychotic symptoms.

E. Not due to any organic mental disorder.

Rater agreement on subcategories of schizophrenia is even more dismal. Blashfield (1973) had fifty-five judges, all clinical psychologists, rate descriptions of various patients whose symptoms were described so as to coincide with the various subcategories of schizophrenia. Of the ten subtypes listed in DSM–I, only four yielded significant agreement among raters. Agreement for the paranoid type was 24 percent; schizo-affective type, 15 percent; hebephrenic type, 13 percent; and catatonic type, 12 percent—disappointing figures, to say the least.

Rater agreement is high when schizophrenia is broadly defined, low when narrowly defined

Even more alarming, the labeling of an individual as schizophrenic is likely to depend on time and location. Chapman and Chapman (1973) identified, in first-admission diagnoses in public mental health institutions, an increasing trend to use the label schizophrenic and a decreasing trend to use the label manic-depressive. More recently, however, they also found this trend to be reversing. A resurgence in manic-depressive diagnoses has begun, presumably because of the efficacy of lithium in treatment of this disorder. Furthermore, the Chapmans note that the percentage of psychotics labeled manic-depressive varies from 1.1 percent in North Dakota to 21.8 percent in Vermont.

Any schizophrenic symptom justifies the label

Kramer (1965) noted that the use of the label schizophrenia in England and Wales was 33 percent lower than in the United States, but the manic depressive label was used nine times as often in England and Wales. Katz, Cole, et al. and Lowery (1969) further illustrated this problem by having a large number of American and British psychiatrists witness a film of a psychiatric interview. One-third of the forty-two Americans labeled the patient schizophrenic, but not one of the thirty-two British psychiatrists did. A similar study was conducted by Kendall et al. (1971). They had British and American psychiatrists rate a videotaped case and found that 69 percent of American psychiatrists rated the patient schizophrenic, but only 2 percent of the British psychiatrists did so. In a second case, the comparative figures were 85 percent versus 7 percent.

Is schizophrenia a disease or a hypothesis?

Such differences in diagnosis result from beliefs about, and definitions of, schizophrenia. For this reason, Fitzgibbons and Shearn (1972) have suggested that the concept of schizophrenia is no longer useful because theoretical orientation and professional discipline rather than the individual's behavior determine diagnosis of the disorder.

The major reason for the usual diagnosis of schizophrenia is the assumption that if any of the many symptoms of schizophrenia are present, the individual should be labeled schizophrenic, which insures a *disjunctive* category. The diagnosis of other behavioral disorders is discouraged unless there is a clear absence of schizophrenic symptoms. Pope and Lipinski (1978), in a comprehensive evaluation of this procedure, have shown that classic schizophrenic symptoms with the exception of flat affect do not differentiate between true schizophrenia and various other types of psychoses including manic-depressive psychosis. They proposed that the label schizophrenia should be used only if manic or depressive symptoms are not present and only if the disorder is *not* episodic. They note that reactive or acute schizophrenia is more similar to affective disorders of psychotic types than process or true schizophrenia and may constitute a third type of psychosis that can be labeled as *atypical psychosis* according to DSM III. If their suggestion is followed, then it is possible that the reliability of the diagnosis of schizophrenia will increase and that the incidence of the disorder in the United States will be similar to its incidence in England and Wales.

As we have noted, the diagnosis of schizophrenia is confounded by many variables, including the socioeconomic class of the patient, the effects of institutionalization, and the geographical location in which the diagnosis takes place. But the major cause of the confusion is the lack of a precise definition of schizophrenia. With a more rigorous definition, most of the superficial findings will vanish, and the actual parameters and causes of the disorder will be established, if indeed schizophrenia exists as a real entity rather than—as R. D. Laing (1967) claims—a mere construct in the minds of clinicians. Hopefully, the di-

psychotic behavior

agnostic criteria proposed by DSM III and shown in Table 15–2, will partially solve this problem.

Characteristics of Schizophrenia

Before the causes of schizophrenia can be established and precise treatment programs designed, an attempt must be made to make sense of the vast array of bizarre behaviors called schizophrenic. In general, schizophrenia appears to be a disorder of *attention* associated with disorders of information processing and, perhaps, arousal. Attention involves alertness, readiness to respond, and a selective process by which the individual ignores irrelevant cues, both internal and external. Shakow (1977) calls this the *generalized set* and notes that it requires appropriate integration of cognitive-conative (motivational)-affective components. He suggests that schizophrenia is characterized by *segmental sets* that produce a lack of integration of these components.

The disturbance in readiness to respond can be demonstrated quite simply. If you ask individuals seated before an apparatus that looks like a telegrapher's key to press the key as rapidly as they can when signalled to do so, the total amount of time taken to perform this task is called a *reaction time*. Consistently, the reaction of schizophrenic subjects is slower despite the fact that they do not differ on measures of concentration, motor reflexes, or steadiness (Shakow 1962).

If a preparatory cue such as a tone is given just before the signal occurs, so that the subject has a short period of time to prepare to respond, the difference between schizophrenic and normal subjects disappears. If this preparatory interval is long, eight seconds or more, schizophrenic subjects are no longer aided by the preparatory cues, and their reaction again becomes quite slow. The explanation for this behavior seems to be that schizophrenic subjects have difficulty in maintaining alertness to a specific cue and are easily distracted by irrelevant stimuli either from the environment or their own internal responding.

This difficulty in maintaining alertness and filtering out irrelevant cues can be demonstrated in several other ways. For example, suppose that the subject is asked to respond to the following, or similar, statement (Chapman, Chapman, and Miller 1964):

When the farmer bought a herd of cattle, he needed a new pen. This means:
  a. He needed a new writing implement (incorrect response in this context, but the usual definition of the word).
  b. He needed a new fenced enclosure (the correct response in this context, but a less used definition of the word).
  c. He needed a new pick-up truck (irrelevant response).

When schizophrenic persons, as compared to normal ones, are given a test composed of items such as these they tend to make more mistakes because they select responses that are correct but not within the item context. Chapman and Chapman (1973) referred to this as an *excessive yielding to normal biases*. In this sense, the responses of schizophrenic individuals are not qualitatively but quantitatively different from those of normals: they simply make more mistakes than normal individuals because they appear to be unable to discriminate or use the contextual cues of the situation. The reason schizophrenic persons ignore such cues is not readily obvious, but various investigators have suggested that schizophrenic individuals are overaroused, presumably because of high levels of anxiety (Broen 1968; Mednick and Schulsinger 1968; Venables 1964). High levels of arousal interfere with discrimination and thus cause difficulty in responding to appropriate contextual cues.

This deficit in responding to appropriate contextual cues is also observed in perception. For example, Weckowicz (1957) has noted that schizophrenics tend to underestimate the size of distant objects, presumably because they do not use spatial cues that are necessary in order to judge that an object has the same actual size at different distances despite changes in apparent size. Another perception disturbance is hallucinations in which generally the same variables appear to be operating. Mintz and Alpert (1972) administered two tests to

Schizophrenia as a disorder of attention, information processing, and arousal

Yielding to normal biases / failing to use contextual cues

hallucinating schizophrenics, nonhallucinating schizophrenics, and nonpsychiatric subjects. The first test asked them to assess the vividness of their auditory imagery by closing their eyes and imagining hearing a phonograph record playing "White Christmas" with both words and music. After thirty seconds, subjects rated the vividness of the image they were able to produce on a scale ranging from "I heard a phonograph record of 'White Christmas' clearly and believed that it was actually playing" to "I did not hear the record." In the second test, earphones were placed on the subjects so that they were able to hear a set of twenty-four sentences, each with an intelligibility level of about 50 percent. After each sentence was completed, the individuals tried to repeat exactly what they had heard and rate their confidence in the accuracy of their reproduction on a scale ranging from positively correct to positively incorrect.

Eighty-five percent of the hallucinating schizophrenic patients reported that they heard "White Christmas" and believed it was actually playing or that they had heard the record clearly but knew that a record was not playing. Only 5 percent of the nonhallucinating schizophrenic subjects reported having heard the record with any vividness. On the sentence reproduction test the hallucinating schizophrenic subjects also appeared much poorer at judging how accurate their reproduction had been. The investigators concluded that hallucinating schizophrenics show a vivid imagination and a defective capacity for perceiving the environment (discriminating relevant cues).

Hallucinations as self-produced stimuli

Thus, hallucinations may reflect a failure to discriminate between self-produced stimuli and stimulation from the external world. A study by McGuigan (1966) supports this belief. He instructed patients to press a key whenever they experienced an auditory hallucination and at the same time took EMG (electromyograph) measures from the individuals' larynxes. He found that when an individual reported a hallucination, an increase in muscular activity in the larynx occurred simultaneously. Auditory hallucinations, then, seemed to occur when the individuals were talking to themselves, but they failed to discriminate that the sensory input was internal rather than external.

Another aspect of this question is why schizophrenic individuals are so difficult to understand and why their speech appears bizarre. Again, similar processes seem to be operating. For example, Cohen and Camhi (1967) used schizophrenics and normal individuals in a word association game similar to the television game "Password." In this game the speaker is shown, one at a time, a series of word-pairs such as "car-automobile." The experimenter designates one of these words as the target and the speaker has to provide a one-word clue that helps the listener distinguish the target word from the other. For example, if the target was "car" clues might be "sports," "hop," or "railroad." A clue such as "crash" would not be as accurate. Four groups were used: schizophrenic speakers with schizophrenic listeners, schizophrenic speakers with normal listeners, normal speakers with schizophrenic listeners, and normal speakers with normal listeners. The results indicated that the schizophrenics did not differ from normals in listening ability but were very poor as speakers.

If schizophrenic thought and speech are qualitatively different from normal speech and thought, then schizophrenics should perform poorly both as listeners and speakers in this experiment. Such is not the case. Their associative hierarchies are apparently the same as those of normal individuals, and they respond well when they are being given clues. Perhaps as speakers they are again yielding to normal biases as the Chapmans have stated. In other words, their clues are correct, but their associations to the clues are more remote and therefore result in poor performance.

A further example of such communication difficulties is illustrated by Nachmani, Rosenbert, and Cohen (1974). Schizophrenic individuals and medical center employees were shown a series of two or more colored disks that they were asked to describe so that a listener could identify the correct color disk. Later they served as listeners. For example, the speaker might say the "red one" if the other disks were not red. Essentially, this requires two stages: the first stage (*sampling stage*) involves selecting possible labels for describing the disk (for example, red), and the second stage (*comparison stage*) involves editing the labels to determine whether they discriminate between the target disk and the other disks. For example, if the other disks are some variation of red, the individual has to edit out the word red, since it does not discriminate between the disks. When the colors are quite dissimilar, editing is an easy task. However, suppose there were two red disks. The responses of normal subjects might be "They are both red; this one, however, has more pink." On the other hand, descriptions by schizophrenic subjects might be something like this: "This one's blood-colored, looks like someone's bled on it, like a menstrual cycle."

As might be expected, schizophrenic subjects were poorer than control subjects at devising useful descriptions. Moreover, when following their own tape-recorded descriptions, they were also less accurate than control subjects in choosing the correct disks. In explaining these results, the experimenter noted that it is possible to have three different models of schizophrenic speech. The first is the *Tower of Babel* model, which suggests that schizophrenic subjects sample from a repertoire of idiosyncratic phrases. Thus, they should be poor describers but should be able to respond accurately to their own descriptions. This result did not occur.

The second model, the *Impulsive Speaker* model, suggests that schizophrenic subjects sample from a nondeviate repertoire of responses but fail to self-edit or go through the comparison stage. Thus, the failure to self-edit should lessen the effectiveness of the schizophrenics' description for listeners and for themselves when they serve as listeners. This prediction was supported, but if this model is correct, the schizophrenic subjects should spend less time editing and therefore the reaction time should not change when the number of disks in a display is increased or when the colors are more similar. The data indicate that the reaction times of both groups were longer when there were more disks and the

disks were similar. Furthermore, the reaction time of the schizophrenic subjects was slower. Thus, this model does not seem to be accurate either.

A *Perseveration Chaining* model seems to describe the data more accurately. This model states that schizophrenic subjects are unable to ignore a descriptive phrase that occurs to them even when they recognize it as a poor describer. Thus, the schizophrenic subject may (1) sample a label (such as red) from a normal repertoire of descriptions (2) edit and reject it because other items are similar and then (3) sample a second label based on associations to the rejected item rather the stimulus to be described (that is, the individual samples *associations* to red—such as lipstick—rather than the disk, and edits accordingly). Thus, the sampling-editing process continues until a describer phrase is selected, but the sampling is based on *associations* to the last item sampled rather than to the object itself. The schizophrenic subjects seem to lose sight of the task or relevant cues and, consequently, give odd responses.

In describing *segmental set,* Shakow (1977) has noted a similar ignoring of relevant cues that results from distraction elicited by internal or external stimuli or both. For instance, if one asks, "Where were you yesterday evening?" segmentation occurs and the schizophrenic individual selects one element or fragment of the question, such as "eve" from "evening," and gives a response based on the association to Adam and Eve. The resulting answer is, "In the Garden of Eden." This type of response appears strange, even though the association is logical.

Although most studies have consistently reported the already mentioned characteristics of schizophrenic subjects, some have not. This discrepancy may be due to the confusion caused by vague definitions of schizophrenia. The importance of a rigorous definition of schizophrenia has been shown by Oltmanns, O'Hayon, and Neale (1978), who found that subjects diagnosed as schizophrenic by a mental hospital were no more distractible than controls and

Inability to ignore a descriptive phrase that comes to mind even if it is a poor one

The schizophrenic samples associations to the last item rather than to the original object

showed no attention deficits. If these subjects were rediagnosed using the more stringent European diagnostic rules developed by Spitzer, Endicott, and Robins (1975), they would be considered quite distractible, significantly more so than normal control subjects. The remaining patients who, under these criteria are now judged not to be schizophrenic, would be not significantly different from the normal control subjects.

Diagnostic precision as a crucial factor in the wide range of results from twin studies

Theories of Schizophrenia

A variety of explanations of *schizophrenia* have been proposed—ranging from an organic disease process to an epiphenomenon (that is, that it does not exist). In this section, a sample of the most representative theories based on the medical, phenomenological, or environmental models will be covered.

Biological Basis of Schizophrenia: Genetic Factors

The belief that schizophrenia is a disease process has been a prominent and compelling explanation for many decades. Kraepelin (1904, p. 219) stated that "The disease apparently develops on the basis of a severe disease process in the cerebral cortex. . . ." In the medical model the most obvious explanation for schizophrenia is genetic. Four types of evidence support the genetic hypothesis: twin studies, family morbidity studies, adoption studies, and high-risk-of-schizophrenia studies.

Twin Studies

In the twin study, the general method is to identify schizophrenic subjects who have monozygotic or dizygotic twins and then calculate the concordance rate. If schizophrenia is strictly a genetic disorder, identical twins should show a 100 percent concordance because of identical genetic makeup. On the other hand, fraternal twins should show much lower concordance, probably no more than other siblings but higher than the general population.

Studies of identical twins have been summarized by Kringlen (1966) and Rosenthal (1971). Concordance rates have varied from 0 to almost 100 percent among monozygotic pairs and from 0 to approximately 20 percent among dizygotic pairs. Earlier studies, such as Kallman's (1938), show a much higher concordance than later studies. There seem to be three reasons for such discrepancies: First, what constitutes schizophrenia is a crucial factor. For example, individuals who are somewhat shy and withdrawn may be regarded as falling within the *schizophrenic spectrum* (that is, having one or more but not all of the symptoms) and thus inflate concordance rates. When schizophrenia is defined more precisely, as it is in the European and Scandinavian countries, concordance rates are much lower.

A second problem is that in a number of studies the raters know that the proband or the affected twin has been identified as schizophrenic. The lack of blind raters inflates concordance rates, particularly if the experimenter is biased toward a genetic basis for schizophrenia.

The third problem is a sampling problem due to base rates of schizophrenic and nonschizophrenic individuals. For example, in twin studies, if a matched control group is used, it is obvious to the rater that 50 percent of the probands are schizophrenic. On the other hand, if the rater were evaluating a random sample of the normal population of twins, the occurrence of schizophrenia in the probands would be around 1 percent. The role of experimenter expectancy and bias cannot be underestimated in any study, but because of this different rate of occurrence of schizophrenia in a normal population and in twin studies, rater agreement is especially likely to be inflated.

The better studies that control for some of these factors are shown in Table 15–3. The concordance for monozygotic twins varies from 6 to 42 percent with an average concordance of about 23 percent, while the average concordance in dizygotic twins is approximately 6 percent. Interestingly enough, in these better controlled studies, the concordance rate for dizygotic twins is approximately the same as for full siblings, whereas in the less controlled studies the rate for dizygotic twins has been much higher. Since the similarity of genetic background of the dizygotic twins is not greater

psychotic behavior

Table 15-3 Concordance Rates for Schizophrenia in Monozygotic and Dizygotic Twins in Well-Controlled Studies

Study	Country of study	Percentage concordant in monozygotic twins	Percentage concordant in dyzygotic twins
Gottesman and Shields (1966)	England	42	9
Kringlen (1967)	Norway	25	8
Tienari (1968)	Finland	6	5
Fischer et al. (1969)	Denmark	19	6
Hoffer et al. (1968)	U.S. veterans	16	5
Allen et al. (1972)	U.S. veterans	27	5
Average concordance rates		23	6

than that of full siblings, the large discrepancy in the earlier studies indicates that the concordance rate was inflated. The conclusion that can be drawn from twin studies is that there may be a genetic predisposition in schizophrenia causing vulnerability to the disorder, but genetic factors are not the sole cause of schizophrenia.

Family Morbidity Studies

Another method for evaluating this question is to assume that the closer the blood kinship, the more similar the genetic background and the greater the possibility of schizophrenia. This is called the *family morbidity risk method*. The prevalence of schizophrenia in the general population is usually estimated to be around 0.8 percent (Shields 1967). Zerbin-Rudin (1972) has compiled an average estimate of morbidity risk for schizophrenia among relatives. These estimates indicate risk factors of 9 to 16 percent for children with schizophrenic parents, 8 to 14 percent for siblings, 1 to 4 percent for nieces and nephews, 3 to 5 percent for grandparents. The prevalence of schizophrenia is higher in first-order relatives such as siblings and children and parents of schizophrenic patients than in the second-order relatives such as aunts, uncles, nieces, and nephews. This rate in turn is higher than the prevalence in the general population. However, these morbidity studies suffer from the same methodological flaws described for twin studies, and no clear-cut conclusions can be derived from them.

Adoption Studies

A third method for investigating the role of genetics in schizophrenia is *adoption studies*. Again, the logic is fairly simple. If schizophrenia is due to environmental causes, then the child of schizophrenic parents placed in a foster or adopted home with a normal family should not exhibit the disorder. Likewise, if a child with normal parents is adopted or placed in a home with schizophrenic foster parents, the child should exhibit the disorder. The genetic hypothesis would predict that schizophrenia would be exhibited regardless of environmental conditions.

Heston (1966) followed up forty-seven individuals who had been born to schizophrenic mothers while they were in a state mental hospital. These infants were taken away from the mother after birth and given either to relatives or to a foundling home. Fifty control subjects were selected from among the residents of the same foundling home. A rather complete assessment was conducted on all of these cases. If abnormal behavior were present, the individual was judged as either schizophrenic, mental defective, sociopathic, or neurotic. It was found that the control subjects were less disabled than the children of the schizophrenic mothers. Sixty-six percent of the children of schizophrenic mothers were diagnosed as exhibiting abnormal behavior, as compared to 18 percent of the control subjects. None of these control subjects were diagnosed as schizophrenic, while 16.6 percent of the offspring of schizophrenic mothers were so diagnosed.

Kety et al. (1968) surveyed a sample of over 5,000 adults who had been adopted early in life by persons not biologically related to them. Thirty-three had been admitted to mental hospitals and were diagnosed as schizophrenic. A matched control subject who had never been admitted to the hospital was then picked for each schizophrenic index patient. Both the adoptive and the biological parents as well as the siblings and foster siblings of the two groups were then identified, interviewed, and rated independently by three experienced clinicians who were not aware of which interviewees were relatives of schizophrenic or normal probands.

Of 365 interviewees, 24 individuals, or 7 percent, were rated by all three clinicians as having diagnoses within the schizophrenic spectrum. The prevalence of diagnoses of schizophrenic illness in those genetically related to the schizophrenic index cases was 13.9 percent, as compared with 2.7 percent in adopted relatives and 3.8 percent in subjects not genetically related to the index cases. However, Shean (1978) noted that the biological relatives of index and control subjects were significantly different only when the concept of schizophrenia was broadened to include the controversial concept of a schizophrenic spectrum of genetically related disorders. Kety and his associates found no significant difference between index and control subjects with regard to true schizophrenia.

In a similar study by Rosenthal (1974), not one of the adopted offspring of thirty process schizophrenics was hospitalized for schizophrenia. This figure compares with 16.6 percent reported by Heston and a median rate of 10 percent for offspring of schizophrenics.

There is one study by Wender and his associates (1974) with children born to nonschizophrenic parents but adopted and reared by families in which one of the parents was schizophrenic or borderline schizophrenic. This type of study should gauge

The broad versus narrow definition problem again . . . and again

the effects of being reared by a schizophrenic parent. Approximately 10.7 percent of these individuals were judged schizophrenic or near schizophrenic on the basis of interviews. Two other groups served as controls: (1) people with normal biological parents who were adopted at an early age and reared by normal individuals and (2) people with schizophrenic biological parents who were adopted at an early age and reared by normal foster parents. The prevalence of schizophrenia or near schizophrenia in these control groups was 10.1 percent and 18.8 percent, respectively. However, it should be noted that this estimate of schizophrenia or near schizophrenia in the group with biologically schizophrenic parents is higher than other estimates previously quoted. Again, the use of a broad schizophrenic spectrum greatly confuses the issue.

High-Risk Studies
The last type of evidence is concerned with high-risk research. In this procedure a child is identified who might be vulnerable to the development of schizophrenia. (Vulnerability is usually identified in terms of having a schizophrenic parent.) This method entails a longitudinal study but is quite useful, since it may be possible to identify the stimulus situations created by the schizophrenic parent that enable acquisition of a less adaptive response repertoire. In these studies about 15 percent of the children of schizophrenic mothers become schizophrenic, but the prevalence of schizophrenia in families in which the mother was not schizophrenic is much lower (Offord and Cross 1969).

In a similar longitudinal study of high-risk children, S. A. Mednick (1970, 1971) found that high-risk children who developed schizophrenia had mothers who were hospitalized much earlier in the child's life than either low-risk children or high-risk children who did not develop schizophrenia. Their mothers were also more severely disturbed than mothers of high-risk subjects who did not show a breakdown. Moreover, 70 percent of the sick mothers were found to suffer one or more serious pregnancy or delivery complications, more than double

psychotic behavior

the percentage for the mothers of other subjects. Both the mother's psychiatric history and her complications with pregnancy or delivery were related to the prevalence of sick cases. This finding would indicate that both genetic background and prenatal factors are important in the development of schizophrenia. Although it has been demonstrated that the mother's adjustment has a much greater effect than the father's on the child's adjustment, if both parents exhibit a severe psychological disorder, the child is even more likely to show abnormal behaviors (Mednick 1973; Rutter 1966).

Diathesis-Stress Hypotheses

When the results of these studies are evaluated, conclusions are mixed. Even though some evidence points to a genetic basis for schizophrenia, it is by no means overwhelming. Because of this fact, **diathesis** (predisposition)-**stress hypotheses** have been suggested (Meehl 1962; Rosenthl 1974). These theories postulate an inherited predisposition to develop schizophrenia, which develops only under sufficient environmental stress, implying an interaction between heredity and environment. Meehl's model is probably the best known of the diathesis models. It states that diathesis must interact with social learning to produce a schizotype or a mild degree of cognitive and affective disturbance. If an individual with a schizotype is subjected to social-environmental stress such as a schizophrenogenic family, schizophrenia is likely to develop.

The diathesis theory is probably more accurate than genetic theories which minimize the role of environmental variables, but it is not unique to schizophrenia. For example, it may be that, if given the proper environmental experiences, individuals born with an overreactive autonomic nervous system will develop pervasive anxiety. Likewise, those born with an under-reactive autonomic nervous system may show a deficit in avoidance conditioning in the acquisition of social control and may, if placed in the proper environment, develop sociopathy. There seems to be little doubt that any pattern of behavior, normal or abnormal, is influenced by both heredity and environment. Suppose the same studies covered in this section were conducted to determine the genetic basis for being a basketball player. The conclusions would probably be the same. If a professional basketball player had an identical twin, the twin would be more likely to be a professional basketball player than a fraternal twin, and thus the concordance rate would be high. Furthermore, there would probably be more professional athletes in the family. As kinship increases the morbidity rate, the risk of developing this talent would be greater for one having an affected relative. Furthermore, the individual's athletic ability would probably be more similar to that of the biological parents than that of any adoptive parents the individual might have.

The conclusions are obvious. Genetics and environment both play a role in most of our behavior patterns. Genetic endowment probably limits the range of our behavioral patterns (for example, males who are 5 ft. 5 in. tall do not become professional basketball players), while the environment determines behavior patterns within those limits. Genetic endowment may have a clear determining role in physical diseases that cause structural changes, but in functional disorders the role of genetic endowment is usually much more complex.

Meehl's diathesis-stress model

Biological Basis of Schizophrenia: Biochemical Factors

Biochemical hypotheses of schizophrenia assume that the disorder is caused by aberrant enzymatic or metabolic processes, particularly in the neural transmitters. Whereas genetic theories of schizophrenia require biochemical aberrations, the reverse is not necessarily true. Biochemical aberrations that result in behavioral deviations may be due to such nongenetic factors as environmental stress, trauma, or infections. We shall discuss two of the most prominent biochemical hypotheses of schizophrenia.

Transmethylation Hypothesis

The **transmethylation hypothesis** assumes that schizophrenia results from an accumulation of certain hallucination-producing matabolites. Neural transmitters have

Do metabolic deficits produce hallucinogenic substances in the body?

a chemical structure similar to that of LSD or mescaline. Thus, a deficit in the metabolic processes that normally produce these neural transmitters could instead result in the production of hallucinogenic substances. For example, Osmond and Smythies (1952) have postulated that abnormal methylation of dophymine could lead to the symptoms of catatonic schizophrenia. Furthermore, Friedhoff and Van Winkle (1962) report finding a substance in the urine of schizophrenics that could conceivably reflect such abnormal dophymine methylation, namely DPEA (3, 4-dimethoxyphenethylamine). This substance is commonly referred to as the *pink spot* because, when excreted and treated with certain chemicals, it takes on a pink color. Whether this substance exists in the urine of schizophrenics but not nonschizophrenics is still a matter of controversy (Wyatt, Termini, and Davis 1971).

On the basis of theory closely related to the transmethylation hypothesis, Hoffer and Osmond (1962, 1964, 1968) predict that the treatment of schizophrenia with massive doses of nicotinic acid (niacin, Vitamin B$_3$) should result in a reduction of schizophrenic symptoms, a result they have reported achieving. However, others have not been able to produce such an effect (Wyatt, Termini, and Davis 1971; Ban and Lehmann 1971).

Dopamine Hypothesis

Excessive dopamine activity as a possible explanation for schizophrenia

The **dopamine hypothesis**, which holds that schizophrenia may be a result of excessive dopamine activity, was derived from two major findings. The first is suggested in the literature on amphetamine psychosis and the effects of the major tranquilizing drugs on dopamine receptors. Amphetamines produce a state closely resembling paranoid or acute schizophrenia and their effects center largely on dopamine receptors (Kety 1972). Furthermore, amphetamines tend to aggravate symptoms in persons already labeled schizophrenic (Angrist, Lee, and Gershon 1974), while antipsychotic drugs are effective in controlling both amphetamine

Failure to convert dopamine into norepinephrine leads to a pleasure deficit

psychosis and schizophrenia. The antipsychotic drugs (phenothiazines and butyrophenones) also tend to produce Parkinson-like symptoms, an indication of a deficit of dopamine.

A variation of the dopamine theory has been proposed by Stein and Wise (1971). They argue that schizophrenic behavior stems from a genetic abnormality associated with the brain's reward center (the hypothalamus and limbic system). Specifically, this reward center is activated by the neural transmitter norepinephrine. In schizophrenic individuals Stein and Weiss suggest that this reward center is malfunctioning because of a deficiency of a certain enzyme—dopamine hydroxylase. The result is that dopamine is not converted into norepinephrine, and the individual is therefore unable to experience pleasure or reinforcement. The pleasure-deficit notion of schizophrenia is consistent with earlier hypotheses of schizophrenia. For example, Bishop, Elder, and Heath (1964) found that when electrodes were implanted in the brain reward centers of schizophrenic subjects, stimulation did not result in behavior indicating that they were experiencing reinforcement. However, the Stein-Weiss hypothesis has difficulty in accounting for the cognitive disorders on the basis of reduced ability to experience reward (Levitt and Lonowski 1975). A number of similar dopamine hypotheses have been suggested, but none of them have been consistently supported (Shean 1978).

Evaluating the biochemical literature on schizophrenia is rather difficult because of a number of factors that influence the chemistry of the body. A consistent difficulty, particularly in earlier studies, is that the biochemical composition of blood and urine can be attributed to differences in the diet of schizophrenics, particularly if the individual had been hospitalized for a long time. Stress and other situational factors can also cause changes in body chemistry. Furthermore, a major difficulty in most biochemical hypotheses of schizophrenia is that the disorder may have caused the malfunction in biochemistry rather than the reverse. All behavior has a biochemical basis, and biochemical investigations are crucial to our understanding of schizophrenia. Nevertheless, biochemical theories of schizophrenia are still confusing and controversial.

Psychological Theories of Schizophrenia

Many of the psychological theories of schizophrenia evolve from psychoanalytic theory. They emphasize the role of developmental environmental factors and the relationship between the schizophrenic individual and the family.

Psychodynamic Theories

The key concept in Freud's (1924) explanation of schizophrenia was regression. Freud saw regression in the neuroses as temporary and partial, but he saw it as much more extensive in schizophrenia. In schizophrenia the regression supposedly extends back to the early oral stage in which the ego is just beginning to develop, to a state of *primary narcissism* before the development of reality testing. As a result the individual's thought processes are at the same level as those of a child in the first year or two of life. According to psychoanalytic theory, this regressive phenomenon manifests itself in two major categories of symptoms: *symptoms of regression* and *symptoms of restitution* (Fenichel 1945).

There are four major symptoms of regression. The first is a collapse of reality testing and other ego functions, which causes bizarre symptoms such as fantasies of world destruction. Because the early stages of ego development supposedly occur before differentiation of the boundaries of one's body or development of the body image, the collapse of the ego is also marked by hypochondriacal symptoms and alterations of body sensations.

The second major symptom of regression is a feeling of depersonalization and estrangement from personal experience. This feeling supposedly represents a withdrawal of attachments to reality.

The third symptom is the occurrence of delusions of grandeur or omnipotence, which are similar to the daydreams of nonpsychotic individuals. The schizophrenic individual, however, takes these narcissistic daydreams seriously and believes them to be true.

The fourth symptom is a mode of archaic thinking similar to that of primitives or infants and termed *schizophrenic logic*. Overall, the type of thinking that characterizes this regression is primary process thinking.

Four major symptoms of regression

Restitution symptoms are supposedly attempts to re-establish ego controls and reality contact. Of these symptoms hallucinations are the most important, since they represent an attempt to respond to external percepts after partial or total loss of reality testing. Delusions are interpreted as attempts to reconstruct reality in a way that is less threatening to the individual.

Restitution symptoms: delusions and hallucinations

Questions of concern here are twofold: Is the behavior of schizophrenic individuals similar to that of children, and do their thought processes represent a regressive phenomenon? In general, the answer seems to be no. After reviewing the evidence, Maher (1966) states that the concept of schizophrenia as a psychosis of regression has not been demonstrated and that any such demonstration would probably not be of particular value in the study of the disorder. In an evaluation of cognitive functioning in schizophrenic individuals, Brown (1973) has come essentially to the same conclusion.

Schizogenic Parents

Psychodynamic theories also emphasize the role of the mother in the development of schizophrenia. Fromm-Reichmann (1948) labeled the type of mother who supposedly engenders in her children a predisposition to schizophrenia the **schizogenic mother.** These women are thought to be rejecting, dominating, cold, and unconcerned about their children and the needs of others, but in terms of their overt behavior they may seem quite accepting of their children or possessively overprotective and smothering. Fathers in such situations are generally

The schizogenic mother (and father)

passive. Thus, the children are placed in conflict, not knowing whether they are loved or hated. They are deprived of a sense of identity. Their views of themselves and their world are distorted, and they experience pervasive feelings of inadequacy and helplessness.

What is the evidence for this hypothesis? Using data gathered on a large sample of boys as part of a delinquency prevention project, McCord, Porta, and McCord (1962) found that twelve of these boys eventually became psychotic at a later date. When compared with a control group, 67 percent of the mothers of these psychotic boys were rated as over-controlling or smothering, as compared to only 8 percent in the control group. However, it is quite possible that potentially schizophrenic children elicit more overprotective responses from their mothers than the mothers would otherwise make. This latter hypothesis is consistent with the finding that mothers of schizophrenic children are no more over-possessive than mothers of brain-injured or retarded children (Klenbanoff 1959). A major problem of this theory is that investigators have been unable to establish conclusively that this or any other behavior pattern characterizes the mothers of schizophrenic individuals (Fontana 1966).

Double-Bind Hypothesis

Related to this theory is the **double-bind hypothesis** (Bateson et al. 1956). According to this theory, the double-bind has three conditions:

1. The individual has an intense relationship with another person that makes understanding communications from that other person very important;
2. The other person gives two messages when making a statement, one of which contradicts the other (a double message);
3. The individual cannot comment on the mutually contradictory messages, cannot withdraw from the situation, and cannot ignore the messages.

Bateson et al. (1956) give as an example of a double-bind the tactic used by Zen masters. The master holds a stick over the novice and says: "If you say this stick is real, I will strike you with it. If you say this stick is not real, I will strike you with it. If you fail to say anything, I will strike you with it." While such a double-bind may produce enlightenment in a Zen novice, it may well precipitate a thought disorder in a child.

Again we must ask what is the evidence for this hypothesis? Ringuette and Kennedy (1966) had different groups of judges try to identify double-bind communications in letters written by parents to hospitalized schizophrenic and nonschizophrenic children. These letters were then compared with letters written by volunteers instructed to compose letters as if they were writing to a hospitalized offspring. The judges, experts in detecting double-bind communications, could not agree on which letters contained the double-bind communications nor could they differentiate between the letters written by the parents and those written by the volunteers. As Schuhan (1967) notes, the research literature has failed to support the assumptions and predictions of the double-bind hypothesis.

Role of the Family

Other investigators have focused on the role of the family in fostering the development of schizophrenia. The most widely quoted studies of the families of schizophrenic individuals were conducted by Lidz and his colleagues (Lidz et al. 1957; Fleck 1960). In their intensive studies they found that the families were either *schismatic* or *skewed*. In the schismatic family, one characterized by chronic strife and controversy between the parents, the child has difficulty in identifying with one parent without provoking the wrath of the other. In the skewed family, the parents are able to avoid overt conflict but only at the expense of some disturbance in family relationships such as the creation of a weak, ineffectual father who acquiesces to the demands of a domineering mother. Unfortunately, these studies often had no control group, and in a survey of all the research based on direct observation of family interaction, Jacob (1975) found evidence that families of schizophrenic individuals were not different from the families of normal control individuals except in being less clear and accurate in their communications.

Existential Model

The major *existential* hypothesis of schizophrenia is also centered on the family as a primary locus of craziness. Ronald Laing (1964) believes that schizophrenia is not an illness but a label for an individual reacting to an insane environment. In a sense Laing takes the same position as family theorists in viewing the family as the source of behavior called schizophrenic. His basic thesis is that the behavior and thought processes of people diagnosed as schizophrenic may seem crazy outside of the family context but may be quite rational when viewed from inside the family situation. Laing sees the family as communicating confusing double-bind messages. In particular, these messages require the individual to invalidate the evidence of his or her own senses, a process Laing calls the *mystification of experience* and which, he contends, lead to the strange behavior labeled schizophrenic (Laing and Esterson 1971). Laing further states that the schizophrenic individual is on a journey toward health necessitated by untenable environmental demands and is therefore in need of guidance to ensure that the journey results in enlightenment. Except for a few case histories, there is little evidence to support his theory that the family is a source of difficulty or his contention that a schizophrenic episode is a journey toward health. His view that schizophrenia is not an illness but a label used to solve social problems is, however, consistent with a number of other theories, including that of Ullmann and Krasner (1975).

Sociological Hypothesis

Sociologists emphasize the role of social class in the development of schizophrenia. It has been well demonstrated that the majority of schizophrenic individuals come from the lower socioeconomic classes although this relationship is weaker in rural communities (Kohn 1968). This distribution would suggest that the stresses associated with the extremes of social disorganization and poverty found in the lower socioeconomic levels, especially in urban areas, facilitate or even cause schizophrenia. Another explanation, however, is that because of their cognitive dysfunctions and inadequate coping skills schizophrenic individuals drift into slum areas and the lower socioeconomic classes (Gerrard and Huston 1953).

One way to test between the **social disorganization** and the **social drift hypotheses** is to evaluate social mobility among schizophrenic individuals. A number of studies have been conducted on the social class and economic level of the parents of schizophrenic individuals. These studies have produced good evidence that, although the occupations of schizophrenic sons are concentrated in the lower socioeconomic levels, the occupations of their fathers are not. This finding suggests a downward drift on the part of the sons (Goldberg and Morrison 1963; Turner and Wagonfeld 1967). Although most of the evidence supports the drift hypothesis, the relationship between social class and schizophrenia is quite complex. That the stresses of economic hardships may facilitate the development of schizophrenic reactions is fairly obvious, but it is also obvious that not everyone experiencing severe economic hardships develops schizophrenia.

A related question is the relationship between culture and schizophrenia; that is, does schizophrenia occur in all cultures? Some investigators believe that it does and have studied the geographical concentrations of schizophrenia as well as historical changes and differences in various cultures that seem to have influenced its occurrence. Lehmann (1975) has suggested that paranoid reactions are associated with highly developed cultures while catatonic reactions are more often observed in more primitive cultures. Torrey (1973), on the other hand, argues that there is no valid evidence for the universality of schizophrenia. In his review of the literature he raises questions about methodological issues and diagnoses in many studies. The answer to the question "Is schizophrenia universal?" may again depend on how one defines schizophrenia.

Going crazy as a way out of an insane situation

Mystification of experience: parents invalidate the child's reality by double messages and by reinterpreting the child's world for the child

The downward mobility of schizophrenics

Schizophrenia is universal only if broadly defined

If a broad-spectrum definition is used, the answer is yes. If a narrow operational definition is used, the answer is probably no.

No widely accepted behavioral definition of schizophrenia exists, probably because no good operational definition has yet been proposed. The only major behavioral explanation of schizophrenia is the sociopsychological model of Ullmann and Krasner (1969).

Sociopsychological Hypothesis

The **sociopsychological model** postulates that schizophrenic disorders are learned, maintained, and modified in exactly the same way as any other behavior patterns (Ullmann and Krasner 1975). The two major parameters of this formulation are *attention* and *iatrogenic* (doctor-caused) *effects*. The key assumption is that schizophrenic individuals do not attend to the same stimuli as normal people. Ullmann and Krasner posit that schizophrenic individuals have been extinguished for attending to social stimuli because they have not been reinforced for this behavior. If this theory is correct, then many of the characteristics of schizophrenia are understandable. For example, social withdrawal and lack of emotional responsiveness can be attributed to the fact that schizophrenic individuals cease to react to others because they have not been sufficiently rewarded for such behavior. Indeed, a vicious cycle ensues in which apathy further decreases the likelihood of being reinforced and the individual begins to be labeled odd or weird. The increasingly bizarre actions of the schizophrenic individual may be an attempt to get attention from others. If such behavior elicits the desired attention, the individual's behavior is then shaped into a pattern of craziness. Moreover, since schizophrenic individuals do not attend to relevant cues, they may begin to exhibit cognitive impairment and thought disorders. For example, hallucinations may be talking to oneself, but because of a failure to attend, the individual may be unaware that these voices (or other perceptions) are derived from internally rather than externally generated stimuli.

Attention deficit as a consequence of inadequate reinforcement

The hospital as the source of symptoms

Since such individuals create social problems but may not be dangerous or criminal, one simple solution is to label them schizophrenic or mentally ill. This labeling process usually results in the individual's being hospitalized, a fate that may aggravate the condition because of the iatrogenic nature of hospitalization. The conditions that characterize existence in a psychiatric ward have been described in detail by Goffman (1961) and Rosenhan (1973), discussed earlier. In brief, the individual loses personal legal rights, is severely restricted, and is allowed only minimal privacy. Furthermore, people in the hospital environment respond as if the person had an organic illness, and expect the person to behave as a patient. These conditions breed a sense of powerlessness and depersonalization. But more important, the hospital staff's expectation that an inmate will behave in a disturbed fashion because the person is supposedly schizophrenic inadvertently shapes such behavior and results in a self-fulfilling prophecy (the iatrogenic effect). The direct reinforcement of uncomplaining passivity in a mental hospital has been well described in Kesey's novel *One Flew Over the Cuckoo's Nest*.

Like biological theories of schizophrenia, theories emphasizing environmental influences have also had mixed and confusing support from the research evidence. Environmental models like that of Ullmann and Krasner may have some validity but the role of biological factors cannot be lightly dismissed. Perhaps a moral is involved here: before we can explain a phenomenon, we must first rigorously define it and prove that it exists. Otherwise, the best we can hope for is rampant confusion.

Modification of Schizophrenia

While almost every technique of medical and psychological intervention from classic psychoanalysis to megavitamins has been used to treat schizophrenia, few techniques have been highly successful.

Chemotherapy and Electroconvulsive Therapy

The major tranquilizers introduced during the 1950s have supposedly revolutionized the treatment of schizophrenic and other psychotic individuals (Gellhorn and Kiely 1973). The most important of these drugs are the *phenothiazines* such as Thorazine and Mellaril, which seem to reduce the intensity of the following categories of schizophrenic symptoms: arousal symptoms such as hyperactivity, irritability, aggressiveness, and insomnia; affective symptoms such as anxiety, depression, aggressiveness, and withdrawal; and cognitive-perceptual symptoms such as delusions and hallucinations (Lehmann 1975). The clinical uses of these antipsychotic drugs are for (1) management of acute schizophrenic crises, (2) treatment of chronic schizophrenic conditions, (3) symptomatic treatment of acute psychomotor disorders, and (4) maintenance therapy for patients in remission (Lehmann 1974). However, these drugs do not usually affect the thought disorder or the progressive social deterioration observed in schizophrenia (Dunner and Somervill 1977).

Electroconvulsive therapy (ECT) is also used in the treatment of schizophrenic individuals and has been fairly effective. For instance, May (1968, 1975) compared five groups of schizophrenic subjects who received either (1) individual psychotherapy, (2) antipsychotic drugs, (3) individual psychotherapy plus antipsychotic drugs, (4) ECT, and (5) control conditions (in this case, the social and physical benefits from hospitalization). In general, he found that antipsychotic drugs and ECT were much more effective than psychotherapy and control conditions and that the cost of these treatments was far less. In a five-year follow-up, May further demonstrated that whether they received psychotherapy or not, patients who had received either drugs or ECT spent less time in the hospital during the follow-up period than patients who had received psychotherapy or control conditions.

Not all of the clinical studies have consistently supported the use of ECT or antipsychotic medication, however, and a number of problems occur when these techniques are used. The main problem being, of course, that they do not eliminate the disorder.

The best controlled triple-blind study in the drug literature, that of Paul, Tobias, and Holly (1972), questioned this procedure. Often medication is used for maintenance with schizophrenic patients, the result being that the individual stays on the drug for life. They used a group of chronic schizophrenic patients who had been receiving maintenance antipsychotic drugs for many years and assigned them to treatment programs (to be discussed later). One-half of each group continued to receive the same drugs, in a different capsule, that they had been receiving, while the other half of the group was abruptly withdrawn, with placebo substitution. Neither experimenters, patients, nor physicians knew who was receiving drugs and who was receiving placebo.

It would be expected that when chronic schizophrenic patients were withdrawn from antipsychotic drugs, florid schizophrenic behavior would occur. It did not. As a matter of fact, less bizarre behavior was exhibited in the placebo group. Not one incident of acute psychotic episodes occurred in the placebo group following abrupt withdrawal. Furthermore, individuals continued on drugs did not perform as well in the treatment programs to which they were assigned, a result that might be expected since antipsychotic drugs usually interfere with the acquisition of new responses. This study suggests that the occurrence of psychotic episodes when chronic schizophrenic patients are removed from a medication may be more a function of the therapist's and the patient's expectations than of the discontinuation of the medication. Antipsychotic drugs may be useful in the management of acute psychotic episodes, but the usefulness and the advisability of continuing individuals on maintenance doses of these drugs for a long period of time is questionable.

Major tranquilizers reduce symptoms but do not alter the thought disorder

Expectations as the crucial factor in the effectiveness of medication

R. D. Laing

Therapist's unique talent, not technique, as the crucial factor

Verbal reinforcement

Operant conditioning

Psychodynamic Therapy

Although various types of psychodynamic and humanistic psychotherapy have been attempted with schizophrenic individuals, it is generally agreed that these types of talk therapy are not particularly effective with such patients. This is not to deny that a number of talented and dedicated psychotherapists such as Harry Stack Sullivan, John Rosen, R. D. Laing, and Otto Will, among others, have worked very successfully with schizophrenic individuals. Nevertheless, their success appears to be due more to their unique talents than to their treatment techniques. In general, experimental studies of these procedures, such as the one by May previously quoted, suggest that psychodynamic and humanistic approaches offer little promise as therapeutic procedures in the treatment of schizophrenia. However, group and individual supportive psychotherapy (advice, persuasion, and good human relationships) are commonly used with schizophrenic individuals and have proved valuable in helping these people manage their lives.

Behavior Therapy

No specific technique or group of techniques of behavior therapy has been devised for the modification of schizophrenia. The reason is fairly obvious: behavior therapy devises specific treatment techniques for specific behavior patterns, but schizophrenia is usually an assortment of deviant behaviors that vary from individual to individual. With the exception of token economies, to be discussed later under institutionalization, the behavioral technique used with schizophrenic individuals depends on the type of deviant behavior they are exhibiting.

A relevant question is whether behavioral techniques are capable of modifying some of the more fundamental symptoms or characteristics of schizophrenia, which are often assumed to be biological in origin. The answer to this question is a guarded "yes." For example, behavioral techniques have been successful with at least three of the major problem areas in schizophrenia:

1. **Affective disorders** One of the main signs of schizophrenia is lack of interest in the environment, emotional blunting, and lack of affect. One indication of this symptom is that the individual's speech is devoid of emotional words. Many studies have shown that the number of emotional words emitted by schizophrenic subjects can be drastically increased through the use of verbal reinforcement (Ullmann and Krasner 1975).

   Shafer and Martin (1966) have noted that apathy is a limited responsiveness to the environment; that is, as the environment changes, the patient does not. This failure to change results in the individual's being called withdrawn, apathetic, disinterested, or emotionally flat. In a token economy system, tokens, verbal praise, and at times more direct reinforcers such as cigarettes are used quite successfully to increase the rate of social interactions, adequate working performance, and personal hygiene.

2. **Autism or social withdrawal** A number of studies using a variety of techniques have shown that the social interactions of individuals labeled schizophrenic can be increased. For example, working with psychiatric patients, Gutride, Goldstein, and Hunter (1973) used structured learning therapy consisting of modeling, role playing, and shaping by social reinforcement and found that it was effective in increasing social interaction. Discipio, Glickman, and Hollander (1973) used operant approaches to increase interpersonal awareness and social interaction among individuals labeled schizophrenic.

3. **Cognitive disorders** Associative difficulties or cognitive slippage is assumed to be the primary characteristic of schizophrenia. This type of behavior can be measured in terms of bizarre verbalizations, which are interpreted as disorganization of

thinking. Ullmann and his colleagues (Ullmann et al. 1965) labeled this verbal behavior *sick talk* and then reinforced schizophrenic subjects for *healthy talk,* using reinforcement such as smiling, nodding the head, and showing other signs of approval. They found that they could thus increase the rate of healthy talk and decrease the rate of sick talk. A similar study conducted by Meichenbaum (1969) yielded similar results.

While most of these studies were experimental in nature, they do suggest that the prime problem behaviors of schizophrenia can be modified and that perhaps meaningful, effective techniques can be developed to treat schizophrenia.

Institutional Treatment

Many schizophrenic patients are institutionalized when it is assumed that the disorder can be better managed and treated in a hospital. In general, the routine for psychiatric patients is similar to that of medical patients and involves medication, controlled diet, and planned routines that are assumed to contribute to the individual's rehabilitation. When the individual is discharged from the hospital, follow-up or outpatient treatment is usually continued for some time.

In addition to the usual type of medical care administered in a hospital, two major types of psychological intervention are also employed in the mental hospital: *milieu therapy* and *token economies*. These procedures are particularly applicable to individuals who require long-term care in an attempt to rehabilitate them and prepare them for discharge to outpatient status.

Milieu therapy is based on the concept of the therapeutic community in which the major assumption is that everyone involved with patients should contribute to their adjustment. The main objective is to prepare the individual for returning to the community. Consequently, the basic operations of the hospital must be a model of the community (Schwartz and Swartzburg 1976). In milieu therapy the central theme is that

individuals should take responsibility for their behavior and that of others on the ward. It includes more informal patient status, freedom of movement, and a greater voice in the activities of the hospital. As in the community, the expectations of majorities impose standards on the individual. In short, milieu therapy increases social interaction and group activities with the expectation that group pressure will direct the individual toward more normal functioning. It is reminiscent of the moral model and is, to some extent, a resumption of 19th century moral treatment.

Another approach to institutional treatment is the **token economy, or social learning therapy,** which is an application of the basic principles of learning theory to the modification of deviant behavior. Token-economy programs have several well-delineated aspects: (1) a careful observation of the individual's behavior as well as the antecedents and consequences of that behavior in order to determine what elicits the behavior and how it is maintained; (2) the determination of what is appropriate and what is inappropriate behavior; (3) the determination of what events may serve as reinforcers—these are then used as backup reinforcers for tokens; (4) a medium of exchange—the particular tokens to be used to obtain positive reinforcers; (5) making tokens contingent on behavior—tokens given for appropriate behavior and taken away (fines, or response cost) for inappropriate behavior; and (6) rules of exchange that specify the number of tokens lost or gained for specific behaviors and the number of tokens required to gain specific backup reinforcers. While individual programs can be designed for patients who require an individualized program, the token economy is usually applied to a whole ward. The major problem of the token economy has been a lack of generalization to the community (Bellack and Hersen 1977).

Both milieu therapy and social learning programs actively try to reshape adaptive social behavior. The major difference between these two approaches is that milieu

Reinforcing "healthy talk"

Milieu therapy aims at preparing the individual for return to the community

therapy accomplished this goal by expectations of appropriate behavior and group pressures, while social learning programs shape appropriate social behavior by the use of contingent reinforcement.

Paul and Lentz (1977) conducted an extremely well-controlled, comprehensive outcome experiment over several years that compares social learning programs, milieu therapy, and control conditions (in this case, the usual hospital treatment). The results of these treatment programs were evaluated in terms of (1) resocialization: individuals were expected to learn normal daily habits of self-care and to engage in interpersonal interactions; (2) instrumental role performance: residents were expected to learn vocational and housekeeping skills, and they were also taught how to take personal and financial responsibility for themselves and for a family; and (3) the reduction or elimination of extremely bizarre behavior: the aim was to eliminate crazy behavior including maladaptive cognitions and assaultiveness.

While the data gathered from this project are too complicated to discuss in detail, one conclusion is clear: social learning programs were superior to milieu therapy, which in turn was superior to the usual hospital routine. These results were obtained in spite of the fact that the patients involved in this project were severely psychotic individuals who had been in the institution for an average of 14 years.

Some of the results of this study are shown in Figures 15–1, 15–2, 15–3, and 15–4. Figure 15–1 shows changes in positive behavior from the time the program was introduced, and Figure 15–2 shows

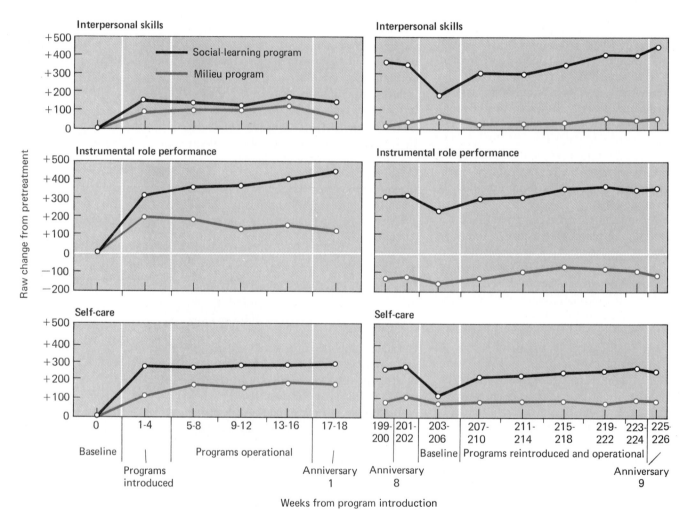

Figure 15–1 The changes in various types of adaptive behavior in the social learning and milieu programs. (Instrumental role behavior is, for example, being on time for a job.) The horizontal axis shows the total number of incidences of the type of behavior after subtracting the number of incidences before the programs were introduced. Thus, a negative score means the group was doing worse.

psychotic behavior

changes in maladaptive behavior. The overall change in adaptive functioning is shown in Figure 15–3. Perhaps the best indication of the effectiveness of the various programs is the percentage of individuals who were discharged to the community. These results are shown in Table 15–4. It should be noted that these effects were achieved in the social learning group and the milieu therapy group even though psychotropic drugs were rarely used (see Table 15–5). In summary, then, the Paul-Lentz study indicates that social learning programs are extremely effective in treating chronic inpatient schizophrenic individuals without resorting to chemotherapy. Moreover, it also suggests that milieu therapy is a reasonable and viable alternative to routine medical treatment given in most state mental hospitals.

As noted before, a major problem with most institutional procedures is a lack of generalization of adaptive skills to the community. Facilitating the transition of the individual from the mental hospital to the community was the major goal of the Fairweather project (Fairweather 1964; Fairweather et al. 1969). In this program, patients were trained in small groups in problem solving, making their own decisions, evaluating their own progress, and regulating their own activities. Privileges such as passes and money were awarded by the group and were made contingent upon the individual's achievement of progressively more complex levels of social and self-directive behavior. These self-directed groups developed pride in group achievement and group identification. After the patients were functioning adequately they were transferred to a semi-autonomous

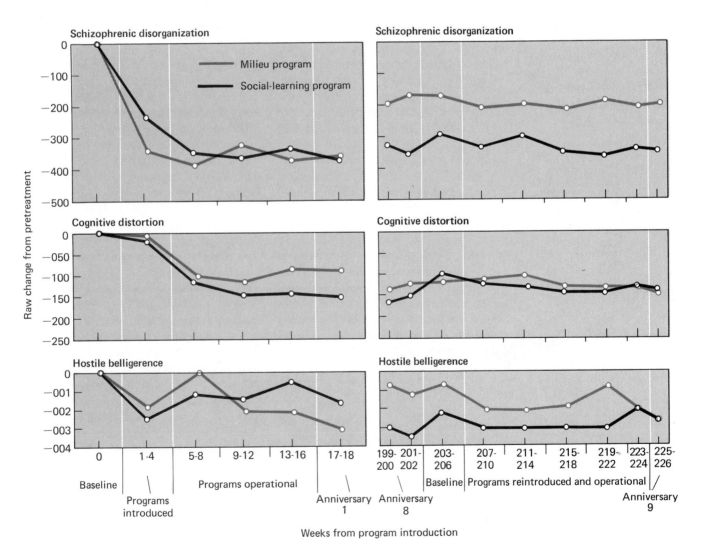

Figure 15–2 This figure should be interpreted in the same way as Figure 15–1 except that it illustrates maladaptive behaviors. Schizophrenic disorganization is bizarre motor behavior. Cognitive distortion is bizarre verbal behavior.

schizophrenia, paranoia, and childhood psychoses

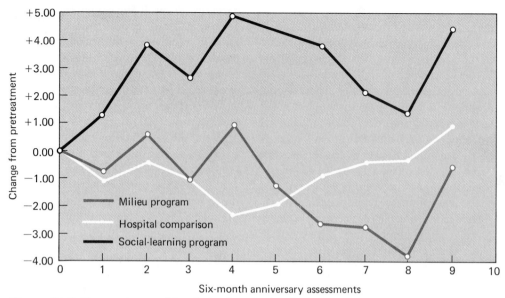

Figure 15–3 Changes in overall functioning from the inpatient assessment battery during the intramural treatment period for the original equated groups (N = 28 each).

The semi-autonomous lodge as a way station from hospital to community

Paranoid personality: suspicion, jealousy, envy, self-importance, blame, and attribution of evil motives to others

The centrality of the delusional system

lodge, which was initially supervised by a hospital staff member and subsequently by a lay person. The patients assumed full responsibility for running the lodge, regulating the administration of drugs, and managing their own financial affairs. The lodge trained patients in activities that earned income, and that income was shared according to each person's productivity and role within the system. The lodge became fully autonomous after thirty-three months. A control group received the same training within the hospital but received the traditional hospital assistance and outpatient care after being discharged. As shown in Figure 15–4, this procedure, which permits a gradual transition to community living, greatly enhances the person's adjustment. Similar programs may help in reducing the transfer of skills problem in hospital treatment programs for chronic patients.

Paranoia

Behavior labeled *paranoid* usually consists of being oversensitive to slights, extremely jealous, suspicious, distrustful, rigidly adhesive to rules, overly critical of others, self-righteous, and socially isolated. In extreme cases delusions of persecution, influence, grandeur, and reference may also be exhibited.

There are several major types of paranoia. The most common of these is the *paranoid personality*. The paranoid personality is characterized by hypersensitivity, rigidity, unwarranted suspicion, jealousy, envy, excessive feelings of self-importance, and a tendency to blame others or ascribe evil motives to them. As might be expected, these characteristics often interfere with the individual's ability to maintain satisfactory interpersonal relationships (DSM II 1968; DSM III 1980). Thus, the paranoid personality is primarily a disorder of social behavior.

Paranoia itself is a rare condition characterized by the gradual onset of an intricate, complex, and elaborate delusional system based on, and often logically proceeding from, misinterpretations of actual events. Frequently, paranoid individuals consider themselves endowed with unique and superior abilities. Thus paranoia delusional beliefs are the essential distinguishing abnormality. If disturbances in mood or cognitive processes (including hallucinations) are present, they are derived from the delusional system, whereas in affective psychoses and schizophrenia, mood and thought disorders, respectively, are themselves the distinguishing abnormalities. The paranoid states differ from paranoia in being more disorganized in their delusional systems, more out of contact

Table 15-4
Comparative Rates of Significant Release at Termination of Intramural Programs

Treatment program	No.	Percent achieving significant release Original equated groups	No.	All residents treated
Social-learning	28	96.4%	40	97.5%
Milieu therapy	28	67.9%	31	71.0%
Hospital comparison	28	46.4%	29	44.8%

Note: Significant release required a minimum continuous community stay of ninety days. Chi-square = 16.90, *df* = 2, *p* < 0.01 for original groups: Chi-square = 24.46, *df* = 2, p < 0.01 for ever-treated groups.

Table 15-5 **Utilization of Psychotropic Drugs during the Last Six Months of the Intramural Period for Original Groups (N = 28 each)**

Treatment program	High dosage[1]	Low dosage	None
Social-learning		10.7%	89.3%
Milieu therapy	3.6%	14.3%	82.1%
Hospital comparison	57.1%	42.9%	

[1] > 400 mg/day chlorpromazine or equivalent for a single drug. Chi-square = 56.28, *df* = 2, *p* < 0.01, drugs versus no drugs.

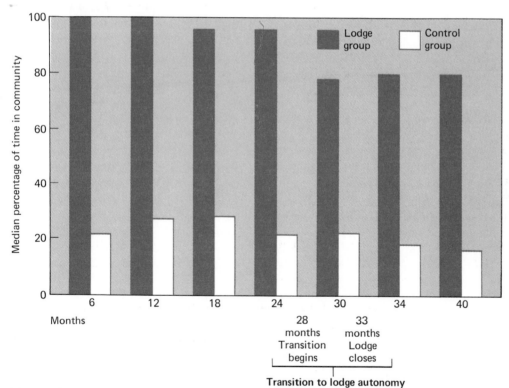

Figure 15-4 Percentage of time that patients in the lodge and hospital programs spent in the community for forty months of follow-up. The lodge program was discontinued after thirty-three months.

schizophrenia, paranoia, and childhood psychoses

box 15–1
Paranoid
Schizophrenia in a
Thirty-Nine-Year-Old
Female

When I first saw the patient, she had just been admitted to our hospital on an involuntary basis. She had had five psychotic breaks within the last four years, and even though there had been some remission of gross psychotic symptoms during this time, she had never been able to function satisfactorily as either wife or mother. Previous treatments had included ECT, chemotherapy, and analytic therapy in private sanitariums. On admission the patient was having auditory hallucinations and was markedly delusional in a persecutory sense.

Her basic problems in living were (1) the feeling that she was being accused of making sexual advances to her six-year-old son; (2) the feeling that she was being accused of sexual advances toward other women, and subsequent refusal to use the ward's shower stall with other female patients; (3) an inability to establish a consistent relationship with her son because of an inclination to vacillate between overindulgence and complete indifference toward him; (4) resistance to sexual intercourse when initiated by her husband; (5) a lack of communication between her and her husband and her husband's withdrawal into hobbies; and (6) a belief that her psychiatrist and her sister-in-law were spying on her in her present hospital location. For treatment purposes, I divided these problems into two major areas: those associated with her husband and those associated with her son. Primary aims of therapy were also divided into two broad areas: (1) teaching the patient to think more clearly about her

problems by helping her learn to label her experiences more appropriately and thus discriminate between them more clearly; and (2) teaching the patient more adaptive motor behavior toward both husband and son.

The first task was to reduce anxiety about the patient's feared sexual responses toward her son. To do so, I used a modified method of counterconditioning and desensitization. During therapy sessions I instructed her to recall and verbalize five specific incidents in relation to her son. When she finished, I would deliberately recall her fears of sexually hurting her son. This technique was used for ten sessions. In addition, she was required to spend twenty-five to thirty minutes per week responding only to the child but in her husband's presence. I explicitly told the patient what games to play and always selected those that involved some sort of physical interaction, such as playing ball. As therapy progressed, the patient was required to play with her son farther and farther away from her husband until she could do so without her husband's presence. At first she was rather anxious, but by the end of therapy she was playing relaxedly and alone with her son. Toward the end of therapy, I discovered that the patient was herself molested sexually when six years old by two boys while playing in a field. I thought that perhaps gross similarities between this incident and her relationship toward her son might be contributing to the problem. I therefore made the patient tell me specific and concrete differences

---

Shared paranoid disorder

with reality, and more transient. DSM III suggests that paranoid states are often induced by changes in the individual's life situation.

When two people share the same delusional system, with the dominant one influencing the more submissive, a rare type of paranoia called **folie à deux** is said to occur

(*à trois, à quatre,* or *en famille* if the delusion is shared by three, by four, or the entire family). Most commonly, this shared paranoid disorder is shared sister to sister when both are spinsters living together. Less frequent are husband to wife and mother to child. Shared paranoia is a rather rare disorder in which the delusional system involves persecution, and the partners cooperate to ward off threats.

psychotic behavior

between the two situations and then list them in a book. I then pointed out to her that some of her fears concerning possible sexual responses to her son were partly a function of stimulus generalization.

The patient's problems with her husband were handled along similar lines. She recalled that her first heterosexual experience had been with a man who had treated her warmly, promised marriage, and forced himself on her. I pointed out that her resistance to sexual intercourse initiated by her husband was similar in some respects to this situation and probably stemmed from it to some extent. I then had her list the differences between the two situations as she had before in regard to her son. She was again able to see that her response was to the gross similarities between the two dissimilar situations and was a result of poor discrimination on her part. I further pointed out that her tendency to indulge her son and to attend to him almost completely at times had alienated her husband even more and caused him to retreat into his hobbies.

Each week I required that the patient spend twenty-five to thirty minutes alone with her husband and to discuss present concerns and future plans. Whenever the patient was granted an off-grounds pass, she was required to sit alone in the front seat of the car with her husband and to let her son sit in the back with his grandmother. My intention was to give the patient and her husband a chance to interact without the presence, interference, and demands of the child.

During home visits, I required that the patient and her husband go alone to a forest preserve where there were cabins for couples. My intention was to give her a chance to respond sexually to her husband in an environment as unlike her home as possible. Moreover, because the patient was hospitalized, she was necessarily on a deprivation schedule for heterosexual responses, and I felt that this fact in itself would enhance her chances for responding to her husband.

As verbal and sexual communication improved between the patient and her husband, she became less preoccupied with homosexual concerns and was able to use the ward shower with no anxiety.

In addition, the patient was required to take part in two social events that took place on her ward. On both occasions, I made sure that other professionals told the patient frequently how well she looked and how competent she was. Because she was a college graduate and a former teacher, I also required that she function as a teacher at least twice a week by teaching other patients basic skills such as reading and writing.

At the end of therapy all delusional matter had dropped out of her speech, her home visits were reported to be extremely satisfactory, and the reports of staff and relatives were all positive. A follow-up questionnaire sent to the patient and her husband one year and four months later showed that there had been no recurrence of symptoms and that the patient had had no further need for outpatient psychiatric care.

Wickramasekera, 1967

Another rare type of paranoid delusion is *Capgras's syndrome*. In this variant, the individual believes that a close acquaintance is an imposter who intends direct harm. This imposter may masquerade as the individual's doctor, mailman, or almost anyone else with whom the individual is acquainted. Obviously, unacceptable attitudes and feelings toward the friend can be displaced to the double or imposter.

Generally, paranoid delusions are usually the only psychotic manifestation, and center around religion, politics, legal processes, or sex. Extreme jealousy of a spouse or a friend of the opposite sex is not unusual in paranoid disorders. One has to be very careful in interpreting aspects of these delusions as unreal, since many paranoid beliefs are true or contain elements of truth.

Paranoid beliefs are not always baseless

As Johnson (1977) has noted, the experience is often real in paranoid cases; it is the individual's interpretation that is questionable. In other words, if one accepts the original erroneous assumptions, the delusion is quite logical.

In interacting with others, individuals with paranoid ideas constantly confirm their beliefs in three major ways. First, they are masters of the double bind. For example, in jealousy, the individual may interpret any warmth or tenderness on the part of the spouse as an attempt to cover up unfaithfulness. On the other hand, if the spouse is hostile and bitter, the individual may interpret this behavior as a result of the spouse's comparing the individual unfavorably with the suspected lover. Second, paranoid individuals are always creating situations in which to test their hypotheses. In jealousy, the individual might continuously expose the spouse to attractive members of the other sex and watch carefully to see if and how the spouse responds. *Paranoia as self-fulfilling prophecy* Third, paranoid individuals engage in self-fulfilling prophecy. For example, if the individual decides that another person does not return affection, the individual may be sarcastic and antagonistic toward this other person, and the other person then reacts with hostility. Thus, the original suspicion is confirmed. Arguments and logic are useless in combating such delusions. In fact, being instructed to decrease delusional behavior actually causes paranoid individuals to increase the rate of such behavior (Wincze, Leitenberg, and Agras 1970). Reinforcement of nondelusional talk can decrease the rate of delusional verbalizations, but generalization across situations does not occur.

Often it is difficult to distinguish between paranoid ideation and false beliefs that can be acquired in any culture and contain an element of truth. In some cases, paranoia differs from common false beliefs only in being an individual's personal, eccentric, stable, and persistent belief system. Cultural paranoia is not an unusual phenomenon, however. An excellent example is the belief of many Germans during World War II that they were a superior race.

Cultural paranoia was exhibited in Nazi Germany by the adulation of Hitler and the belief in a "master race."

Research and Theory

A great deal of theoretical speculation about paranoia has appeared, but relatively little research has been conducted. Indeed, it seems that about all clinicians can agree on is the severity of the paranoid symptoms (Lorr 1964; see Figure 15–5). Recently, Colby (1977) has described four major theories of paranoia.

Psychoanalytic Theory

Freud based his explanation of paranoia on the assumption that paranoia was a consequence of repressed homosexuality against which the major ego defense was projection. According to this theory, the individual with repressed homosexual urges may have the thought "I love him or her" about the person to whom the individual is attracted. But this proposition is also threatening to the individual's self-concept—"I should not love him or her." So a second step occurs in which the individual transforms this idea into the belief "I don't love him or her; I hate him or her." This is also an unacceptable idea and is projected so that the final belief is "He or she hates me." While there is some evidence of a connection between homosexual concerns and paranoid phenomena, it does not account for the cases in which no independent evidence for homosexual wishes can be found. Many paranoid women are good examples of such cases (Colby 1977). Furthermore, many paranoid individuals are openly homosexual, an obvious contradiction to the theory.

Hostility Theory

In *hostility theory,* the first step in the homosexual theory is simply eliminated, the result being a projection of the proposition "I hate" into "I am hated." This theory is simple enough, but it does not explain why the individual is originally hostile.

Paranoia as projection

Homeostatic Theory

Homeostatic theory assumes that any organism seeks equilibrium and that any pronounced change, including feelings of inadequacy, causes disequilibrium, which the organism experiences as a threat. In explanation of this threat, the individual forms the belief that "others threaten me." This conclusion restores equilibrium and achieves security by protecting the self against feelings of inadequacy or guilt about one's own feelings. A major problem of homeostatic theory is that it does not specify the conditions that cause disequilibrium and thus is too general to be testable.

Paranoia as an attempt to restore equilibrium

Shame-Humiliation Theory

Shame-humiliation theory (Colby 1975) assumes that the individual has a model of the self that is used to simulate experiences and try anticipatory responses or react to the future in simulation before situations actually arise. When a belief in the self's inadequacy can be activated by the simulated experience, the paranoid individual uses a cognitive process to avoid the threatened unpleasant affective experience of humiliation and shame. The shame signal evokes a strategy of blaming others, which

Paranoia as a way of blaming others to avoid shame and humiliation

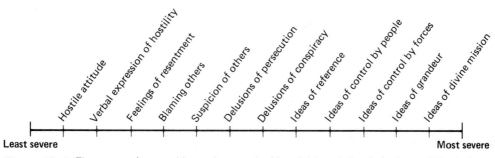

Figure 15–5 The range of paranoid symptoms ranked by clinicians in Lorr's factor analytic study (1964).

After four years at the Matteawan State Hospital for the Criminal Insane, thirty-nine-year-old Victor Rosario became a free man yesterday, largely because he finally got someone to look into a fantastic story that he had tenaciously insisted was true.

The core of the story was that his wife's love had been stolen by another man who drew blood from his arms and drank it in beer to prove his vigor. Mr. Rosario told this story to everyone, including at least eleven psychiatrists, but not until a woman lawyer verified it did anyone believe him. Yesterday charges of assault that had been brought against him in 1958 were dismissed in Bronx Criminal Court.

In 1957 Mr. Rosario had been placidly married for almost eight years. He and his wife, Caen, had two children, Martha and Victor, now nine and seven years old respectively. Then Mr. Rosario introduced a male boarder into their home at 725 Fox Street, the Bronx. It was this man who won Mrs. Rosario's affection. The wife, from whom Mr. Rosario is separated, signed a sworn affidavit in June stating that this was true.

Mr. Rosario, a waiter and longshoreman, ordered the boarder to leave. He refused and the two men lived in the apartment in considerable tension until Mr. Rosario left.

He returned later, however, in a jealous rage and allegedly struck and kicked his wife and threatened her with a bailing hook. She called the police, who said they arrested him on June 22, 1958.

Mr. Rosario was charged with simple assault, resisting arrest, and illegally using a weapon. He was sent to Bellevue Hospital for observation and was committed to Matteawan on October 14, 1958, on the testimony of two psychiatrists. They said that he appeared to be a paranoiac and was incapable of understanding the charges against him.

Matteawan is a large and formidable-looking institution in the Hudson Valley hills at Beacon, about sixty miles north of the city. There Mr. Rosario worked in the kitchen cleaning silverware and paring vegetables, and he began his long campaign to free himself.

He had come to New York in 1946 from Puerto Rico and his English was very limited, but he labored painstakingly with a dictionary and wrote to a great many

When the patient, a thirty-seven-year-old black male with no previous history of psychiatric disturbance, presented himself at the emergency room, he complained that he was experiencing intercourse with "a warm form." While sitting naked on his bed watching television, he felt a warm object press against his genitals and soon after ejaculated. He denied masturbation, saying he thought it an unacceptable form of sexual activity. He said he realized his story sounded strange, but he also insisted it was true.

Examination revealed that the patient had been married twice, his first wife having died and his second marriage ending in divorce. Since his divorce he had been sexually active, abstaining for no

longer than two weeks. Because of the rather unusual nature of the problem, the patient was admitted with a tentative diagnosis of paranoid schizophrenia. Subsequent examination and observation revealed no other problems. The patient seemed interpersonally competent and vocationally adjusted.

My colleagues and I decided that the problem was one of faulty attribution and an attempt at reattribution was instituted. We made every effort to treat the patient's problem as normal rather than abnormal. We told him that the problem was real and that we needed to measure the presence of the warm form. He was instructed to tell a nurse whenever he experienced it. At that time the nurse would give him a penile

government figures, to friends and lawyers. He also drew up six writs of habeas corpus, all of which were dismissed by State Supreme Court in Dutchess County or were ignored.

Mr. Rosario told everyone who interviewed him the story of the drawn blood. 'The doctors told me that if I forgot that story, they might let me go, but the truth is the truth no matter what anyone says,' he said yesterday. So he never changed his story.

Last November he wrote the first of several appeals to Mrs. Sara Halbert of Zapata and Halbert, a New York City law firm. He was told that a relative would have to confer with Mrs. Halbert. At length two cousins flew up from Puerto Rico and prevailed upon the lawyer to visit Mr. Rosario.

After a second visit, Mrs. Halbert went to Mr. Rosarios's wife. She confirmed his story and signed the affidavit, asserting that the boarder had taken the blood in beer and had written on a wall in letters of blood.

Mrs. Halbert said she presented the affidavit to Dr. Cecil Johnston, director of the hospital on Aug. 27. She asked that Mr. Rosario be released immediately. The following day, four psychiatrists interviewed him, and he was shortly declared fit to return to the Bronx to face trial.

Dr. Johnston said by telephone yesterday that more than the affidavit had entered into the decision, but he acknowledged that the new information had caused the staff to look on the patient in a little different manner. He said Mr. Rosario had been interviewed on seventeen occasions by nine psychiatrists in four years.

Mrs. Halbert moved in court yesterday that the case be dismissed. The motion was granted by Judge Ambrose J. Haddock, after Assistant District Attorney Joseph Tiger had agreed.

It seems that poor Mr. Rosario's "delusions" were true, after all. And yet, according to the account in the *Times,* the psychiatric authorities did not feel that a mistake had been made. On the contrary. They implied that whatever the circumstances surrounding Victor Rosario's incarceration might have been, the "fact" of his "mental illness," proved by nine psychiatrists over a period of four years, justified his involuntary "hospitalization."

Szasz, 1963

strain gauge attached to a voltmeter. We told him that this device would verify the form's presence by measuring its arousal effects. After he attached the gauge to his penis, he and a male assistant would monitor the voltage indicator for movement. We also told him that we would try to videotape the session with a special filter to detect the presence of the form.

Shortly after this explanation, the patient signaled the presence of the form, and the gauge was attached. During this time, the assistant observed that the patient lay on his side and executed enough leg movement to produce arousal.

We then discussed the episode with the patient. He was impressed that no recording device detected the presence of the form. He also accepted the explanation of the leg movements, of which he had been completely unaware. He now labeled his problem a *feeling* rather than a form. We further explained that the unusual features of the experience, including its shameful aspects, and his limited contact with male peers caused him to devise the strange explanation for the problem.

Follow-up interviews showed no recurrence of the problem. The patient seemed satisfied with the explanation of his problem and accounted for several spontaneous erections in terms of it. Significantly, he stoutly resisted the suggestions of some members of his family that he was being plagued by demons and spirits.

Johnson, Ross, and Mastria, 1977

schizophrenia, paranoia, and childhood psychoses

Table 15-6 Theory Coverage of Paranoid Phenomena

Phenomena	Theory			
	Homosexual	Hostility	Homeostatic	Shame-Humiliation
Signs and symptoms				
Persecutory delusions	+	+	+	+
Accusatoriness	+	+	+	+
Rigidity	+	+	+	+
Hypersensitivity	+	+	−	+
Excessive fear	+	−	+	+
Excessive anger	−	+	−	+
Concern with homosexuality	+	−	−	+
Precipitating factors				
Social isolation	−	−	+	+
Language difference	−	−	+	+
False arrest	−	−	+	+
Birth of deformed child	−	−	+	+
Increasing deafness	−	−	+	+
Severe accident	−	−	+	+
School or job failure	−	−	−	+
Sexual defeat	−	−	−	+
Assault on self-esteem	−	−	−	+

Note: Plus = accounting for. Minus = not accounting for.

prevents humiliation by relieving the self of responsibility. Chronically humiliating situations such as a job, school, marriage, or a sexual relationship that elicits fears about one's inadequacies result in defense against the threats by paranoid strategies. As Table 15–6 shows, shame-humiliation theory more adequately explains the signs, symptoms, and precipitating factors in paranoia than the other three theories.

Behavioral Theory

Lemert (1962) has proposed yet another theory of paranoid behavior. He argues that the individual's suspiciousness may be a realistic response to the situation and to the feeling that one is being watched or that one is being specially treated or that people are against the individual. These beliefs may indeed be true because the paranoid individual is generally difficult, different from others, or placed in a humiliating situation. Consequently, the paranoid individual may seem more abrupt, lacking in sensitivity, and overly aggressive. Lemert thus suggests that both the individual and those around the individual must be investigated. He goes on to say that calling a person paranoid permits others to disregard their social obligations to the individual,

More about truth in paranoia

isolates the individual from the mainstream of information and responsibility, and removes the individual from the scene through hospitalization. When genuine issues arise from differences of opinion, particularly in stressful situations such as a sudden change in the environment caused by the death of a relative, loss of position, loss of status, age, or other similar stress variables, one person may indeed become the object of attack. The paranoid individual may be right in believing that others are not being accepting.

In formulating a theory of paranoia, Ullmann and Krasner (1975) essentially agree with Lemert's position. They ask two major questions: First, why does a person labeled paranoid develop behaviors threatening to others? Second, why are paranoid individuals so sensitive to threatening stimuli? In answer, they suggest that when an individual is isolated from others, as the paranoid person is, it is difficult to accept another's view of a situation, and thus the individual's information-gathering and evaluation are disrupted. As a result, the paranoid person thinks accurately about a biased sample of information. The core behavior of paranoids is the expression of beliefs so improbable as to be considered false. Consequently, people do not check the paranoid person's stories, but instead label them delusions.

Modification of Paranoid Behavior

As Kleinmuntz (1980) notes, psychotherapy with paranoid individuals is all but impossible because of their suspiciousness of the therapists' motives. Batchelor (1969), Cameron (1967), and many other clinicians believe that paranoia is untreatable. ECT and drug therapies have also proved ineffectual because, in many cases, they provide the individual with evidence that others are engaged in persecution. However, Colby (1977) is much more optimistic. He states that in the management of paranoid individuals, efforts should be made to remove them from chronically humiliating situations, such as their job, school, or sexual relationship. He further indicates that treatment should involve desensitizing individuals to threats of humiliation and influencing their beliefs about their abilities. However, in most cases of paranoia, the usefulness of behavior therapy has not been demonstrated.

Childhood Psychoses

The two major types of childhood psychoses are early infantile autism and childhood schizophrenia. These disorders are differentiated principally by the time of onset: early infantile autism usually appears within the first two years of life, while childhood schizophrenia develops around age five. Since the cognitive processes, particularly speech, have not fully developed in children, the type of psychotic behavior observed in children is different from that observed in adults. Hallucinations, for example, are rare in childhood psychoses. The question of whether the same processes or disorders are responsible for childhood and adult psychoses has not been resolved.

In general, psychosis is rare in children as compared with adults. The rate of autism is approximately two to four per 10,000 children, and the rate for childhood schizophrenia is about six to seven per 10,000. The incidence of adult psychoses, on the other hand, is approximately 100 per 10,000. Whereas the sex ratio in adult psychoses is approximately equal, the ratio for childhood psychoses shows boys outnumbering girls. The ratio has been variously believed to be from 2:1 to 9:1 (Werry 1972). DSM II does not describe autism, but DSM III covers it extensively. Moreover, what has been called childhood schizophrenia is labeled atypical childhood psychosis in DSM III.

Childhood Schizophrenia

Childhood schizophrenia is characterized by marked withdrawal from interpersonal contact, bizarre speech including echolalia, bizarre motor behavior, blunted response to emotional stimuli (flat affect), low frustration tolerance, unusual fears, and withdrawal of interest in one's environment. Some children exhibiting this disorder show sudden and wild outbursts of either aggressive or self-mutilating behavior such as self-biting, self-hitting, or severe headbanging. Their motor behavior may include peculiar motility disturbances such as hyper- or hypoactivity, peculiar posturing, and ritualistic hand or finger movements. Delusional thinking and hallucinations occur but are rare.

Bender (1955) suggested that such children may have physiological as well as psychological disorders. She noted, for example, an upset in physiological rhythms that produces disturbances in sleeping and eating. In addition, she claimed that either the walls of the blood vessels do not constrict or expand in response to heat or cold or they over-respond, the result being excessive pallor or flushing.

Supporting Bender's theory of physiological disturbance is a motor response schizophrenic children exhibit called whirling. If asked to close both eyes and stretch out both arms while an examiner rotates the child's head, a schizophrenic child will turn its body (whirl) to keep it in line with its moving head. Normal children rarely respond this way but try instead to keep the body in the same position.

Another distinguishing characteristic of the schizophrenic child is a sustained resistance to change in the environment. Any alteration in the environment may cause excessive and seemingly illogical anxiety in the child.

Difficulty of treating paranoia

Is childhood schizophrenia a physiological disorder?

box 15–4
A Family Portrait

This is a house the wind blows through

And this is a child
who doesn't speak
as he rocks in a chair
with a wicker seat
but who grunts or shrieks
and can't be reached
who will need years
of costly care
who never leaves
a three-story house
the house the wind blows through

And this is the red
eye of the mother
blurred with love
and rage as she
watches the child
who never speaks
but rocks back
and forth like
a pendulum
or bangs his head
in a rhythmic beat

Here is the father
with bitter mouth
who loves the mother
with reddened eyes
and fears the child
who costs so much
in the house the wind
blows through

This is the drafty heart of the house:
an unspeakable room
the child in a chair
rocking and rocking

away from the man
with blood in his eyes
the woman with bitter-
sweet mouth
not knowing
how far their child
will rock or why

as they love and rage
faster and harder
each day they find less
to say to each other

in the house the wind blows through

Phyllis Janowitz

Childhood schizophrenia supposedly occurs in children whose behavior has been satisfactory until age five, when it begins to deteriorate. Like adult schizophrenia, childhood schizophrenia is assumed to be a regressive phenomenon. DSM-III notes, however, that onset can be as early as thirty months. Moreover, Creak (1968) found that only 31 percent of children labeled schizophrenic showed behavioral regression from a previously higher level of adjustment, while 18 percent showed a plateau or failure to maintain a previous developmental rate, and 50 percent seemed to be profoundly backward even during the early months of life. Another study found that in 80 percent of the cases examined normal development had never occurred, while the remainder showed two or three years of normal development (Rutter and Lockyer 1967). As we shall see, these findings make distinguishing between childhood schizophrenia and infantile autism rather difficult.

Unresponsiveness of autistic children

Infantile Autism

The basic features of **infantile autism** are a lack of responsiveness to other human beings (autism), gross impairment in communication skills, and bizarre responses to various aspects of the environment, all of which develop in the first few months of life. Infants exhibiting this disorder fail to develop interpersonal relationships and skills almost from the beginning. In infancy, for example, they do not tense their bodies or orient their arms when they are lifted from their cribs. They do not maintain eye contact even when attempts are made to force them to do so by holding their heads. They do not initiate or respond to interaction with adults. They ignore others in favor of engaging in persistent, ritualistic activity with toys, particularly those that move in repeated patterns like pinwheels,

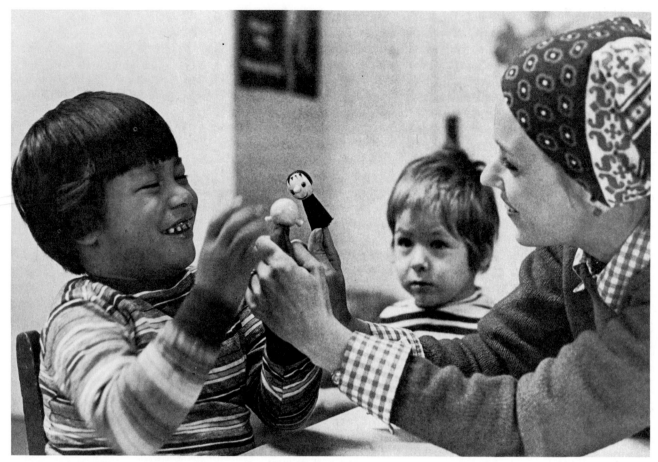

Autistic children have communication deficits and limited attention spans.

doorknobs, and balls. These behavior patterns continue until at later ages autistic children relate more often to objects than to peers and frequently engage in solitary repetitive behaviors (Montgomery 1975).

A major difficulty with autistic children is their deficits in communication. These appear extremely early, often before these children begin to use words. Babbling, the verbal behavior of children that precedes speech, occurs infrequently in autistic children and seems to be far less meaningful than that of normal children. Ricks (1972) played tape recordings of the babbling of both autistic and mentally retarded children to their own mothers and to other mothers. Although mothers best understood the meaning of the noises of their own children, the babbling of autistic children was less meaningful to the other mothers than the babbling of the mentally retarded children.

About 50 percent of older autistic children are mute (Rutter 1966). When speech is present, it is extremely peculiar and may involve repeating the phrases of other people (echolalia) or pronoun reversal in which the self is referred to as "he" or "she" and to others as "I." Even nonverbal communication is deficient; autistic children do not use gestures as substitutes for speech, and teaching them to do so is difficult (Bartak, Rutter, and Cos 1975).

Communication deficit

Other characteristics of autistic children include resistance, even catastrophe reactions, to minor changes in the environment, a reflection of their attempts to maintain the sameness of their environment. In addition, they perform poorly on standardized tests of intellectual functioning. This deficit may be due to their lack of communication skills, which are required in most standardized tests of intelligence. They actually perform better than many normals on tasks requiring manipulative skills, visual-spatial skills, or memory. Occasionally, autistic

Need for sameness

children appear deaf because they seem insensitive to noise and light. The autistic child may also have eating problems, often refusing to eat or eating only one or a few kinds of food. Bowel training is frequently delayed.

The autistic child's failure to relate to other people has been well demonstrated in an experiment by Hutt and Ounstead (1966). These researchers observed autistic children and control children in a room in which five masks had been mounted on the wall (Figure 15–6). Among the five masks were two human faces (one happy and one sad), a blank oval mask, and two animal masks (a monkey and a dog). Hutt and Ounstead found that autistic children spent most of their time looking at environmental stimuli such as furniture, lights, windows, and pictures, while normal children inspected all types of stimuli, including the masks.

The diagnostic criteria for infantile autism given in DSM III reflect all these areas of problem behavior: (1) onset prior to thirty months of age; (2) pervasive lack of responsiveness to other human beings; (3) gross deficits in language development; (4) peculiar speech patterns—if delayed speech does occur—such as metaphorical language, pronominal reversal, and immediate or delayed echolalia (echolalia is said to be delayed when the child does not repeat the sentence or phrase of another until hours or weeks after hearing it); and (5) bizarre responses to various aspects of the environment, including resistance to change and peculiar interest in or attachment to animate or inanimate objects.

One Disorder or Two?

Are infantile autism and childhood schizophrenia different disorders or are they the same psychosis, differing merely in the age of onset? Rimland (1964) and Rutter (1968), among others, contend that they are two distinct disorders and can be differentiated by the following characteristics found in the autistic child but not in the schizophrenic child (Ward 1970):

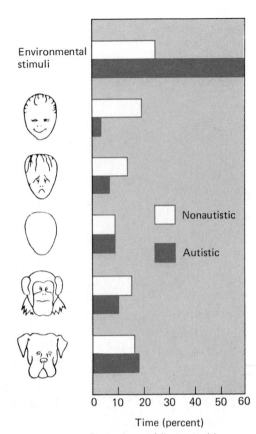

Figure 15–6 Percentage of time spent by autistic and nonautistic children inspecting face models and environmental stimuli such as room fixtures.

1. Lack of object relationships from birth or detachment and isolation from the environment.
2. Lack of the use of speech in communication. Even when speech is present, it is impaired (Rutter 1968).
3. Maintenance of sameness via stereotypical behavior.
4. Lack of neurological or developmental dysfunctions (no organic deficits). Autistic children are physically healthy compared with schizophrenic children, who have many health problems.

Schizophrenic children, on the other hand, have more abnormal emotional dependency than autistic children, often show normal development before the onset of the disorder, and have abnormal speech rather than an absence of speech. The family history of autistic children also seems to be different from that of schizophrenic chil-

Childhood schizophrenia and infantile autism are very difficult to differentiate.

dren, in that autistic children come from higher socioeconomic backgrounds than schizophrenic children (Kolvin et al. 1971). Moreover, the fathers of autistic children have higher than average intelligence (Allen et al. 1971), and there seems to be a lower incidence of mental disorders in the families of autistic children than in the families of schizophrenic children (Lotter 1966; Treffert 1970).

In spite of these differences, distinguishing between childhood schizophrenia and infantile autism is difficult (Margolies 1977). Many children do not conform to the typical description of either childhood schizophrenia or infantile autism. Compounding the problem even further is the fact that these disorders are also confused with or complicated by mental retardation. Thus, the question often becomes: is the basic disorder retardation or psychosis?

Do Psychotic Children Become Psychotic Adults?

One of the fundamental questions concerning psychotic children is their prognosis. In other words, do psychotic children become psychotic adults? Since most psychotic children receive some form of treatment, this question is confounded with the effectiveness of the treatment in eliminating the problem.

In reviewing the prognostic information concerning childhood schizophrenia, Werry (1972) concluded that at least 50 percent of the children labeled schizophrenic have serious social impairment in adulthood. The best predictor of eventual adjustment is the child's intellectual functioning, whether judged by intelligence tests or by language development. Werry further states that no convincing evidence exists to indicate that psychotherapy has a significant long-term effect on children exhibiting childhood schizophrenia. Bender (1973) has reported follow-up information on a hundred psychotic children seen from 1935 to 1952 who were between twenty-two and forty-six years of age at the time of the follow-up. About two-thirds were found to have been placed in institutions for the mentally ill or the mentally retarded. The remaining third were living in the community with various degrees of adjustment. Those individuals with an unfavorable outcome were more likely to have had an associated organic disorder or a predominant picture of infantile autism.

The picture is even more dismal for infantile autism. Kanner, Rodrigues, and Ashendu (1972) found that approximately 10 percent of a sample of ninety-six autistic children diagnosed prior to 1953 were sufficiently integrated into the texture of society to be employable, had no obvious behavior problems, and were acceptable to those around them. The clearest prognosticators of success were the presence of speech before the age of five and being kept out of state institutions. In an earlier article, Kanner (1971) reported on a twenty-eight year follow-up of eleven autistic children. Of the eleven, one could not be located, another had died, five had gone to state institutions, two had gone to live on a farm, one was in a school for brain-damaged children, and one had received intensive schooling at the Devereux School for Children. Kanner concluded from this follow-up that admission to a state institution was a catastrophe for the individual. In contrast, the child who had been placed in the residential school and the two who had gone to live on a farm fared quite well.

Research and Theory

Biological and psychological hypotheses about the causes of childhood schizophrenia are similar to those for other types of schizophrenia. Genetic studies have shown a high degree of concordance between identical twins (86 percent) and a relatively low concordance rate in dizygotic twins. Bender (1955) also found that 40 percent of a sample of schizophrenic children had one schizophrenic parent and 11 percent had two schizophrenic parents. Unfortunately, studies of adoptees and identical twins reared apart have not focused on this disorder.

In infantile autism, the concordance rate also tends to be higher in identical twins than in fraternal twins (Judd and Mandell 1968). The rate of autism in siblings has been found to be about 2 percent, a figure that is higher than that in the general population but that does not approximate the rate found in siblings of schizophrenic children (Rutter 1965). Furthermore, Kanner (1954) found that only about 1.3 percent of the parents, grandparents, uncles, and aunts of autistic children could be diagnosed as psychotic. Consequently, a genetic basis for infantile autism does not appear very likely, and the data for childhood schizophrenia seem to suffer most of the deficits found in the data for other studies of schizophrenia.

Intellectual functioning as the best predictor of eventual adjustment

Admission to a state hospital as catastrophic to the individual

psychotic behavior

Another theory about the causes of childhood psychoses is that psychotic children suffer from more complications during pregnancy and birth than normal children. Such problems would be likely to cause early damage to the central nervous system either in utero or at birth. Although the rate of pregnancy and birth complications does not seem to differ between autistic and normal children, these complications do seem to occur more often in the histories of schizophrenic children (Kanner and Lasser 1958; Gittleman and Birch 1967). However, even these complications among schizophrenic children are not particularly frequent.

A rather interesting theory has been proposed by Moore and Shiek (1971), who suggest that autistic children tend to be delivered late and are thus more physically developed at birth than other children. Since these children have longer prenatal periods or develop at a faster rate, Moore and Sheik suggest that during the time most children are developing initial perceptual or communication skills (normally the first week or two after birth) these children have not been delivered and thus suffer sensory deprivations that result in atypical behavior repertoires. Attractive as this hypothesis may sound, however, no real evidence exists to support it.

A number of theories point to neurological deficits in autism and childhood schizophrenia, primarily because about 80 percent of children who exhibit these disorders are reported to have abnormal EEGs (Taterkis and Kety 1955). Lotter (1974), for example, reported that about one-third of autistic children appear to have neurological deficits exhibited either in seizures or in abnormal EEGs. Rutter and Lockyer (1967) also reported that 14 to 20 percent of autistic children later develop seizures. Harper and Williams (1975) divided 131 autistic children into two groups on the basis of the age of onset. They called these two groups *natal* (when onset was from birth) and *acquired* (when a period of seemingly normal development preceded the onset of the pathological process—before age three in all cases). As Table 15–7 shows, mothers of the natal group showed significantly more physical and psychological strains during pregnancy than the mothers of the acquired group. Moreover, the children in the acquired group showed significantly higher percentages of injuries and psychological stress than normal children during the first three years of postnatal development. These researchers suggest that postnatal environmental stresses do not necessarily cause the autistic disorder in the acquired group but may be simply imposed on a group already predisposed to develop such a disorder. Rimland (1973) has recently suggested that metabolic weaknesses of the adrenal glands, vitamin deficiencies, and an inability to tolerate certain foods may also be related to the development of autistic behavior in children.

Possible neurological deficits

Table 15–7   Variables Distinguishing Natal and Acquired Groups of Autistic Children

| | Percent occurrence | | |
Variable	Natal (N = 37)	Acquired (N = 94)	P
Child variables			
Neurological signs	68	38	.01
Birth difficulties	22	4	.01
Physical abnormalities	14	1	.01
Mother variables (during pregnancy)			
Rubella (measles)	22	4	.01
Physical strain or accident	19	2	.01
Severe emotional strain	51	30	.01
Postnatal environmental stresses			
Injuries and accidents	0	12	.05
Reaction to separation from parents	5	22	.05
Reaction to birth of sibling	3	29	.05

Thus, the data seem to suggest that biological factors may be involved in childhood psychoses.

Psychological explanations of childhood schizophrenia are much like the psychological explanations of adult schizophrenia. Typically, these explanations have focused on the schizogenic mother as the main cause of the disorder (Despert 1947). Block et al. (1958) have cast doubt on the importance of the mother, however, on the basis of pyschological tests that showed that the parents of schizophrenic children were not significantly different from the parents of neurotic children. On the other hand, Bender (1973) found that three-fourths of 100 families with a schizophrenic child were severely pathological. Mothers or fathers or sometimes both either were psychotic or had an inadequate adjustment. However, the criterion for abnormality was poorly defined.

What kind of parents foster autistic children?

Kanner (1957) noted that the relationship between autistic children and their parents appeared rather cool and distant. He noted that the parents as a group were strongly preoccupied with artistic, scientific, or literary abstractions and limited in genuine contact with people. Singer and Wynne (1963) gave projective tests to parents and then had psychologists sort these protocols into two groups: the parents of autistic children and the parents of neurotic children. The psychologists correctly identified seventeen out of twenty couples in

The benign setting

each group. The test protocols indicated that the parents of autistic children were cynical, passive, apathetic about interaction with other people, superficial, and obsessional.

On the other hand, in comparing child-rearing behavior, DeMyer and her colleagues (DeMyer et al. 1972) matched samples of the parents of autistic, brain-injured, and normal children and found that all three groups of parents provided at least average amounts of warmth, attention, and stimulation to their children during infancy. Furthermore, Kanner et al. noted that parental aloofness, when present, may be due to a lack of responsiveness in the child. It is difficult to explain how such profound symptoms as appear in au-

tism could appear so early in life and yet be caused by parental styles of child rearing or interaction. For childhood schizophrenia, an interaction between biological and environmental factors—the diathesis-stress model—is feasible; but its value for explaining the causes of autism is questionable. Consequently, the causes of childhood psychoses, particularly those of infantile autism (if it does differ from childhood schizophrenia), are largely a mystery.

Modification

As previously noted, the treatment of childhood psychoses, particularly infantile autism, has been a failure (O'Leary and Wilson 1975; Werry 1972). Institutionalization of psychotic children is often little better than custodial care (Kanner 1971). While chemotherapy is sometimes useful in the control of extreme behaviors such as assaultiveness or violence, it has little remedial effect on these disorders. For our purposes, we shall discuss two types of treatment: the psychodynamic approach of Bettelheim (1955) at the Orthogenic School of the University of Chicago, and behavior modification.

Bettelheim's Strategy

Bettelheim's approach to the residential treatment of children is somewhat representative of other psychodynamic approaches. Bettelheim's strategy is to provide a benign setting in which children have an opportunity to relax their defenses, fully express their troubled emotions, and develop a more adaptive personality pattern. An example is Mary, an 8½-year-old girl who was allowed to scream, express hostile emotions, masturbate as much as she wished, or engage in almost any sort of aberrant behavior. Counselors provided generous amounts of affection and support. The structure of the treatment program involved schooling, play and recreational activities, and special play or talk therapy. Mary remained at the Orthogenic School for about four years and at age fifteen—three years after leaving—was doing relatively well in a foster home as well as performing adequately at school. Bettelheim (1973) claims that over 85 percent of the

psychotic behavior

children at the Orthogenic School have returned to full participation in life. However, these data are somewhat subjective because no real assessment procedure and no control group of equally disturbed children were used.

Behavior Modification

The behavioral training approach to childhood psychoses was instigated largely by Ferster (1961), who proposed that the basic problem of autistic children was that the environment failed to acquire secondary reinforcing values for them. Although the social learning approach was and still is primitive in explaining infantile autism and childhood schizophrenia, Lovass (1973) has indicated that no real evidence exists of a unitary disorder that warrants either diagnostic label. He goes on to say that the psychotic child has experienced so many disturbing events that seeking a fundamental cause is futile, that the causal factors may be different from the maintaining factors, and that psychotic children can be treated without knowledge of the initial causes of their disorders by treating overt behaviors directly.

In the behavioral approach, specific target behaviors are identified in an attempt to modify them (Margolies 1977). Generally, behavior therapy has two major goals: eliminating the maladaptive behavior and expanding the behavior repertoire of the child. Maladaptive behaviors that have been treated by behavior therapists include self-destructive behavior, tantrums, aggressive and disruptive behavior directed toward others, and self-stimulation. In attempting to expand the behavior repertoire, behavior therapists have shaped toilet training, eye contact, imitation, verbal behavior, language skills, peer and classroom interactions, and prosocial behavior.

A real problem in the use of behavior therapy with psychotic children is finding appropriate reinforcers and eliminating distraction during training. As Ferster and DeMyer (1961) have noted, these children do not respond to secondary reinforcers, such as attention and praise. Thus, primary reinforcers such as food and candy must often be used. Through pairing with primary reinforcers, secondary reinforcers are developed as soon as possible.

The use of contingent shock to eliminate maladaptive behaviors is still a controversial practice. The question often boils down to whether it is ethical or moral to use contingent mild shock to prevent a child from picking out hunks of flesh, banging its head until it loses an eye or suffers brain damage, or engaging in other violent and destructive behavior toward itself or others. The issue is not a simple one. For example, Lovass and Simmons (1969) immediately slapped a child on her buttocks after she hit her head on the wall. Each successive head bang was punished with a hard swat. The girl soon stopped the behavior. Lovass and his colleagues note that showering sympathy and love on autistic children often increases the frequency of destructive behaviors. Thus, people working with autistic or schizophrenic children may unwittingly reinforce the destructive behavior they are trying to eliminate.

Necessity for using primary reinforcers

Perhaps the most important aspect of a behavioral treatment program for psychotic children is teaching appropriate language skills. This involves three stages: (1) the formation of words from *phonemes* (Da + De = Daddy), (2) the proper use of words in labeling objects, and (3) the meaningful (semantic) use of the words in sentences (syntax). Sentences are built up from words and phrases by the method of successive approximation or shaping. Although some children develop rather stereotyped and mechanistic speech and affective responses after behavior therapy, many attain fairly adequate skills in verbal and emotional communication. In spite of these imperfections, behavior therapy has been the most successful method of initiating and maintaining speech in psychotic children.

Ney, Palvesky, and Markley (1971) compared the effectiveness of play therapy (a psychodynamic approach) with that of operant conditioning in the treatment of matched groups of children diagnosed as exhibiting childhood schizophrenia. These children were aggressive, self-abusive, and functioning at a retarded level. Operant conditioning was shown to be the more effective treatment method. Lovass and his colleagues (Lovass et al. 1973) evaluated

Effectiveness of operant conditioning

box 15-5
A "Psychotic"
Child

When Quincy wasn't talking or even communicating with us by the time he was four, I decided to have him tested. I got various diagnoses—autistic, schizophrenic, retarded—and none of them pleased me at all. I was convinced Quincy had normal intelligence and was only discouraged, *not* retarded or psychotic. So I started enrolling him in school. At first all he did was shred paper in mounds around his desk and laugh out loud sometimes. But other than that, he was well-behaved, so the school authorities let him stay. Finally, one principal expelled him after I enrolled him in second grade. At this point, I decided to get professional help, especially since my mother who is a teacher of retarded children had been able to teach him only five words and I knew that he had to have communication skills of some sort.

The doctors and I agreed that Quincy would not see them, that all his training would be done at home, and that I would be the trainer. We set up a program for me to follow. During the first week, all I did was record Quincy's number of relevant and irrelevant responses during certain defined periods of time so that we'd have something to measure progress against. During the second week I began rewarding appropriate responses, especially verbal ones, with candy. I also set aside five-minute periods during which I would ask Quincy direct questions and reward relevant responses. This program worked all right until Quincy tired of it. At that point, we agreed that I should start showing him pictures and asking questions about the pictures. Correct or apt answers were rewarded as before except that I changed the reward to raisins and sweets other than candy because he seemed to have tired of the candy. I also rewarded him with smiles and pats and hugs. Pretty

soon the doctors had me pairing simple stories with the pictures and then with words written on cards. Before I knew it Quincy could read three words and then five and so on.

When Quincy seemed to get tired of our sessions and refused to participate, the doctors and I reviewed my approach. They suggested that I be very regular in the time and length of the sessions and that I choose the content rather than let Quincy choose what he'd like to do. We also agreed that I should vary the rewards and give food sometimes and privileges, like singing with me into a tape recorder, at other times. With these changes Quincy's interest revived.

Pretty soon he was naming objects outside the room and even out of sight. He was also talking about the pictures after I showed them and then put them away. As I looked back over the contents of our sessions, I noticed that he no longer made irrelevant responses or remarks and that his rate of reading had really increased. At last we were playing a simple but important game: I'd hide the reward, and to find it Quincy had to ask the right questions. We started slowly at first, but he caught on quickly.

As I look back over these last few months of training, I am very glad I did not accept any of the labels a few professionals wanted to attach to my son. If I had, he would probably be doomed to a life of isolation or institutionalization as a retardate or a psychotic, instead of reading at a second-grade level and taking an active part in family life. Instead of watching my son deteriorate into a chronic problem case, I watched him increase his self-esteem and begin to enjoy the world as only a child can.

Mathis, 1971

their behavioral treatment of a number of psychotic children in a follow-up study. They measured the frequency of two undesirable behaviors and three appropriate behaviors (Figure 15–7) and found improvement in all five areas after treatment. They also found that these improvements were lost after treatment if the children were returned to a state institution rather than to a parent. This finding confirms Kanner's (1971) hypothesis concerning the effects of institutionalization on psychotic children.

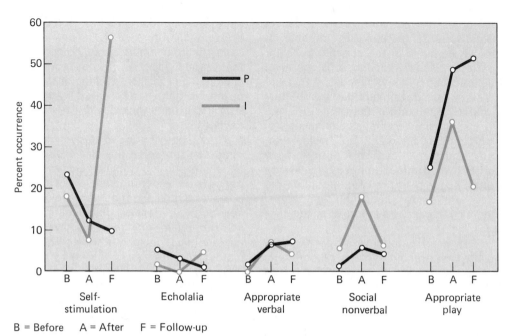

B = Before   A = After   F = Follow-up

Figure 15–7 Percent occurrence of the various behaviors is plotted on the ordinate for before (B) and after (A) treatment, and for the latest follow-up (F) measures. *I* refers to the average results for the four children who were institutionalized, and *P* refers to the average results for the nine children who were discharged to their parents' care. Percent occurrence of the behaviors is presented on the ordinate.

Summary

The fundamental symptoms of schizophrenia are altered associations, altered affect, ambivalence, and autism. Accessory symptoms include delusions, hallucinations, and bizarre social or motor behavior.

The concept of schizophrenia is confusing because it is poorly defined. The types of schizophrenia include simple, catatonic, hebephrenic, paranoid, schizoaffective, and other mixed types. Schizophrenia can be classified according to three major overlapping dimensions: process-reactive, acute-chronic, and paranoid-nonparanoid types. The clinical identification of schizophrenia is unreliable unless specific behavior patterns are used. More rigorous definitions result in higher rater agreement.

The major characteristic of schizophrenia appears to be a disorder of attention associated with disorders of information processing and arousal. Individuals labeled schizophrenic have difficulty ignoring irrelevant cues, both internal and external, and thus have problems in maintaining alertness and filtering out irrelevant information.

Twin studies, family morbidity studies, adoption studies, and high-risk studies suggest the influence of genetic factors in the development of schizophrenia. Numerous biochemical hypotheses of schizophrenia have also been proposed, but the evidence is mixed. Psychological theories of schizophrenia focus on the role of developmental and environmental factors. Psychoanalytic theory focuses on regression. Other psychodynamic theories emphasize the family, the double-bind hypothesis, and the role of social class. There is little evidence for any of these hypotheses, however.

In the modification of schizophrenia almost every conceivable medical and psychological technique has been used, most with little success. The antipsychotic medications are fairly successful in managing acute psychotic episodes, but the value of maintenance therapy for chronically institutionalized individuals has been questioned. The effect of ECT on schizophrenia has also been controversial. It is generally agreed that psychodynamic and humanistic psychotherapies are not particularly effective. Behavioral techniques are capable of modifying some of the specific behavior patterns associated with schizophrenia, but because of the vagueness of this disorder, it is impossible to say that behavioral therapies are effective.

Institutional treatment consists of medical and custodial care, milieu therapy, and social learning therapy. These latter two approaches have been shown to be superior to the usual hospital routine with some suggestion that social learning therapy is superior to milieu therapy.

The major categories of paranoia include the paranoid personality, paranoia, and paranoid states. Several minor types such as *folie a deux* and Capgras syndrome also occur. The prime symptom of paranoia is delusions, which is extremely resistant to change and sometimes difficult to differentiate from fact. The four major theories of paranoia are psychoanalytic, hostility, homeostatic, and shame-humiliation. It has also been argued that paranoid behavior is a realistic response to a situation in which calling a person paranoid permits others to disregard their social obligations to that person and to solve thereby the problems the individual presents. Paranoid disorders are generally believed to be untreatable with drugs, ECT, and psychotherapy. However, behavioral techniques appear to be promising.

The major childhood psychoses are early infantile autism and childhood schizophrenia. The difference between these two disorders is primarily time of onset: early infantile autism appears within the first two years of life, while childhood schizophrenia develops around age five. Childhood schizophrenia is marked by withdrawal, bizarre speech and motor behavior, and blunted emotional responses. Infantile autism is basically a lack of responsiveness to other people, gross impairment in communication skills, and bizarre responses to various aspects of the environment. About 50 percent of older autistic children are mute. At present some controversy exists over whether childhood schizophrenia and infantile autism are different disorders or variations of the same disorder. Some evidence suggests that the individual who is psychotic as a child has an excellent chance of showing psychotic behavior as an adult, particularly if the early disorder is infantile autism.

The results of genetic studies of childhood schizophrenia are similar to those of schizophrenic adults. Genetic evidence is not as strong for infantile autism, however. Other theories have pointed to neurological deficits in autistic and schizophrenic children. Psychological explanations include the schizogenic mother and the role of the family in producing this disorder. While the causes of childhood psychoses are not clear, it is apparent that both biological and environmental factors play a role.

Treatment of childhood psychoses, particularly infantile autism, has been generally unsuccessful. Institutionalization is often little better than custodial care, and chemotherapy only controls extreme behavior. At present, the behavioral approach, which attempts to eliminate specific patterns of deviant behavior and teach social and communication skills, appears to be the most effective method of modifying this problem, especially in teaching language skills.

Key Concepts

acute schizophrenia	diathesis-stress hypotheses
altered affect	dopamine hypothesis
altered associations	double-bind hypothesis
ambivalence	*folie à deux*
autism	hebephrenic schizophrenia
catatonic schizophrenia	infantile autism
childhood schizophrenia	milieu therapy
chronic schizophrenia	nonparanoid schizophrenia
dementia praecox	paranoia

paranoid
  schizophrenia

primary
  symptoms

process
  schizophrenia

reactive
  schizophrenia

schizo-affective
  type

schizophrenia

schizogenic
  mother

secondary
  symptoms

simple
  schizophrenia

social
  disorganization
  hypothesis

social drift
  hypothesis

sociopsychologi-
  cal model

token economy
  (social learning
  therapy)

transmethylation
  hypothesis

Review Questions

1. What are the four fundamental symptoms of schizophrenia?

2. What are the five main subtypes of schizophrenia? Describe each briefly.

3. What are the three major research-based dimensions of schizophrenia?

4. What is the main problem in diagnosing schizophrenia?

5. What attention, information processing, and arousal disturbances occur in schizophrenia?

6. What problem do schizophrenics have in discriminating contextual cues?

7. How do self-produced stimuli presumably figure in schizophrenic hallucinations?

8. What is the perseveration chaining model of schizophrenic speech?

9. What is the major problem in evaluating evidence of genetic factors in schizophrenia?

10. What is Meehl's diathesis-stress model?

11. What are the transmethylation and dopamine hypotheses?

12. According to psychoanalytic theory, what are the two major symptoms of regression in schizophrenics?

13. Describe the "schizogenic mother."

14. What are the three conditions present in a double-bind, according to Bateson?

15. What is the "mystification of experience," as described by Laing?

16. What is the "social drift" hypothesis? What alternative explanation can be given for the evidence presumably supporting that hypothesis?

17. Why are there two answers to the question, "Is schizophrenia universal?"?

18. What are the two major parameters of Ullmann and Krasner's sociopsychological model of schizophrenia?

19. What are the uses and limitations of antipsychotic drugs in treating schizophrenia?

20. How are milieu therapy and token economies used in treating institutionalized schizophrenics?

21. What sort of person fits the description of the paranoid personality?

22. What are the differences between paranoia and schizophrenia?

23. Name and describe five different theories of paranoia.

24. Why is paranoia all but impossible to treat? What can be done to make it easier?

25. What are the symptoms of childhood schizophrenia? What are the symptoms of infantile autism?

26. Why is therapy especially difficult with autistic children?

27. Describe (a) a psychodynamic approach and (b) a behavioral approach to treating autistic children.

disorders having
organic causes or results

Mind and body are traditionally differentiated in Western thought, although we also customarily acknowledge the artificiality of the distinction. In Chapter 16 we shall discuss the *psychophysiological disorders*, ailments such as ulcers, asthma, hypertension, and headaches that often are precipitated by stress, tension, or other psychological factors. In Chapter 17 we discuss *mental retardation*, which in most cases involves cognitive deficits that are assumed to be physiological. And in Chapter 18 we shall discuss the *organic brain disorders*, which also involve physiologically caused disorders of the cognitive response system.

psychophysiological disorders 16

Key Topics

Definition of psychophysiological
disorders

Three stages of Selye's general
adaptation syndrome

The specific emotion hypothesis
and specific attitude
hypothesis

Type A and type B personalities
and the relation to
psychophysiological disorders

The somatic weakness hypothesis

Learning model of
psychophysiological disorders

Brady's study of executive monkeys

Physiological and emotional factors
associated with peptic ulcers

Three categories of asthma

Personality and essential
hypertension

Two major types of headaches

Major factors in muscle contraction
headaches

Biofeedback techniques and
migraine headaches

A common Western belief is that humans are divided into a mind or soul, which is nonphysical, and a body and its behavior, which are physical. This belief, called **dualism,** was stated by René Descartes (among others), who attempted to show the mind and the body as separate but interacting entities. The mind/body problem caused great difficulty for science because "physical" usually implied something observable and potentially measurable, while "mental" implied something unobservable and not measurable. Through necessity scientists rejected this belief and have assumed that mind/body, internal/external, and physiological/psychological events are all physical. In a sense, science has replaced the mind with the concept of *cognitive processes,* which, while internal, are the operations of the central nervous system and related structures.

The mind/body problem

A more scientifically meaningful distinction can be made between *structure* and *function.* Structure usually refers to the morphological characteristics of humans and function to the specific activities of the individual. Thus, human disorders can be divided into two major types: disorders of *structure* (physiology) and disorders of *function* (behavior). These disorders can be caused either by biological events that damage the physiological apparatus or by psychological events that disrupt behavioral activity. Generally, disorders caused by biological events fall within the scope of medicine and disorders caused by psychological events fall within the scope of the behavioral sciences. However, it has also been shown that psychological events can alter physiological structure and function. Such disorders are called **psychophysiological disorders.** Biological events that cause behavioral disruption as well as physiological damage usually involve central nervous system disorders and some forms of mental retardation, and will be discussed in Chapters 17 and 18.

Structure versus function

Role of the autonomic nervous system

The relationships between psychological and physiological events are shown in Table 16–1. From this analysis it is easy to see that distinguishing among psychological causes and disorders and biological causes and disorders is no simple matter. Rather, these conditions appear to overlap, since all physical disorders involve some psychological problems and psychological disorders may induce physiological disorders. For this reason, there has been increasing interest in medical psychology, or **behavioral medicine,** which studies the relationship between physiology and behavior in terms of causes, assessment, and modification by both physiological and psychological methods.

Psychophysiological disorders are those in which undesirable structural and functional changes are assumed to be caused by psychological factors. These disorders are associated with the autonomic nervous system and related organ systems. DSM II defines these disorders as physical symptoms caused by psychological factors and involving a single organ system, usually under autonomic nervous system innervation. Subcategories include:

1. **Psychophysiological skin disorders:** eczema, urticarica (hives), and neurodermatitis.
2. **Psychophysiological musculoskeletal disorders:** muscle cramps, backache, and tension headaches.
3. **Psychophysiological respiratory disorders:** respiratory disorders such as bronchial asthma, hyperventilation syndrome, sighing, and hiccups.

Table 16–1   Classification of Types of Human Malfunction

Type of Causes	Type of Disorder	
	Behavioral	Physiological
Psychological	Behavioral disorders	Psychophysiological disorders
Biological	Central nervous system disorders and some forms of mental retardation	Medical disorders

disorders having organic causes or results

4. **Psychophysiological cardiovascular disorders:** hypertension, paroxysmal tachycardia, vascular spasms, and migraine headaches.
5. **Psychophysiological gastro-intestinal disorders:** gastritis, peptic or duodenal ulcers, colitis, hyperacidity of the stomach, heartburn, spastic colon, and chronic constipation.
6. **Psychophysiological genito-urinary disorders:** menstrual disorders such as amenorrhea, menorrhagia, polymenorrhea; urinary disorders such as dysurea (painful or difficult urination), polyurea, (passing of excessive amounts of urine), and enuresis. DSM II includes the sexual dysfunctions in this subcategory, but DSM III categorizes them as psychosexual disorders, which is more accurate.
7. **Psychophysiological endocrine disorders:** diabetes mellitus, hyperthyroidism, and myxedema.

Other psychophysiological disorders include disorders of the hemic and lymphatic systems and disorders of special senses. Because of space limitations and the specialized nature of these disorders, this chapter will be limited to a general overview of research and theory in psychophysiological disorders and selective illustrations of research, theory, and modification of well-researched and common types.

Theories of Psychophysiological Disorders

The psychophysiological disorders appear to be a heterogenous collection of physiological malfunctions. Some disorders such as peptic ulcers involve a change in structure, or tissue damage, which may be life threatening. Other disorders such as muscle contraction headaches involve a change in function that is painful but not life threatening. Still other disorders, such as essential hypertension, involve an initial change in functioning (increased blood pressure)

that over time may cause changes in structure or actual damage to physiological systems. In this section the focus will be on the similarities among these diverse disorders and the general psychosomatic theories that attempt to explain all of these disorders. In subsequent sections the focus will be on description and theories of specific types of psychophysiological disorders.

Three major questions that must be addressed by a general theory of psychophysiological disorders are (1) what causes the disorder, (2) what precipitates the specific reaction, and (3) why is one organ system rather than another affected? Although it is generally agreed that **stress** induces changes in the autonomic nervous system that affect other organ systems, stress cannot be clearly identified as a causal or precipitating factor in some disorders. Migraine headaches, for instance, are likely to occur when the individual is relaxed and happy, perhaps on a weekend or on vacation. Furthermore, with a few exceptions, no clear precipitating factor can be identified in migraine (Adams, Feuerstein, and Fowler 1980). One possible explanation for these apparent discrepancies is that what constitutes stress for one individual may not be so for others. An example is the individual who experiences panic attacks when promoted and given a raise in pay, a situation most people would see as positive. However, for this individual, the promotion may involve more responsibility, greater risk of failure, and an increased workload. A more likely explanation is that these disorders are precipitated by a release from stress, as with the individual who develops an ulcer attack only after resolving a particularly stressful situation. In any case, the role of stress in psychophysiological disorders is not as clear-cut as people once assumed.

Stress as a precipitating factor

Selye's General Adaptation Syndrome

Whenever stress is encountered, the individual reacts with a **fight or flight reaction,** which serves as a protective adaptive function, as we have noted several times in previous chapters. However, when stress is prolonged so that the body cannot recover its equilibrium, malfunctions are likely to occur. Selye (1956) calls this reaction the **general adaptation syndrome** and divides it into three stages. The first stage is an *alarm* reaction, which produces both hormonal and autonomic nervous system reactions. The second stage is *resistance,* during which the organism defends against the stressor with processes that restore physiological balance or homeostasis. The third state is *exhaustion,* during which prolonged exposure to stress depletes physiological resources and lowers the organism's capacity to resist. When these reactions occur, a breakdown in one of the organ systems follows. Although it is not clear why one organ rather than another breaks down in a given individual, Selye (1974) has stated that both general and specific reactions occur in stress and notes that every stressful event produces nonspecific reactions in addition to the specific effects characteristic of each of the stressors. Thus, the type of stress may determine the disorder.

Life Stress

The fact that even pleasant events in one's life can be stressful has also been noted by Holmes and Rahe (1967). They defined **life stress** as a change in one's life situation. These changes may be negative, such as the death of a loved one, or positive, such as marriage. These life situations can be ranked on a scale of 1 to 100 as shown in Table 16–2. If these changes in life are summed up over a given period of time, such as a year, to produce a life-change unit and correlated to an individual's health, a relationship does seem to exist between life stress and physical illness. For example, Marx, Garridy, and Bowers (1975) used a similar scale and found a high relationship between life changes and increased illness. This relationship was greater in females than in males, as shown in Table 16–3. Such a relationship has also been observed by Rahe and Lind (1971), who studied the life changes of thirty-nine Swedish men who were sudden victims of heart diseases.

Marriage, although a positive event, is a very stressful change in one's life situation.

disorders having organic causes or results

Table 16–2 Social Readjustment Rating Scale

Rank	Life event	Mean value
1	Death of spouse	100
2	Divorce	73
3	Marital separation	65
4	Jail term	63
5	Death of close family member	63
6	Personal injury or illness	53
7	Marriage	50[1]
8	Fired at work	47
9	Marital reconciliation	45
10	Retirement	45
11	Change in health of family member	44
12	Pregnancy	40
13	Sex difficulties	39
14	Gain of new family member	39
15	Business readjustment	39
16	Change in financial state	38
17	Death of close friend	37
18	Change to different line of work	36
19	Change in number of arguments with spouse	35
20	Mortgage over $10,000	31
21	Foreclosure of mortgage or loan	30
22	Change in responsibilities at work	29
23	Son or daughter leaving home	29
24	Trouble with in-laws	29
25	Outstanding personal achievement	28
26	Wife begins or stops work	26
27	Begin or end school	26
28	Change in living conditions	25
29	Revision of personal habits	24
30	Trouble with boss	23
31	Change in work hours or conditions	20
32	Change in residence	20
33	Change in schools	20
34	Change in recreation	19
35	Change in church activities	19
36	Change in social activities	18
37	Mortgage or loan less than $10,000	17
38	Change in sleeping habits	16
39	Change in number of family get-togethers	15
40	Change in eating habits	15
41	Vacation	13
42	Christmas	12
43	Minor violations of the law	11

[1]Marriage was arbitrarily assigned a stress value of 500; no event was found to be any more than twice as stressful. Here the values are reduced proportionally and range up to 100.

Table 16–3 Life Changes and Illness

Life change category	Mean number of illness days	
	Males	Females
High	40.96	55.14
Medium	24.60	34.23
Low	19.10	23.39
Mean value	27.80	37.25

This group included some individuals who had a history of prior coronary heart disease and others who did not. As Figure 16–1 shows, life stress increased greatly just before death in both types of subjects. Furthermore, the authors compared their findings to those of another study of survivors of heart attacks and found that the survivors experienced considerably fewer life changes.

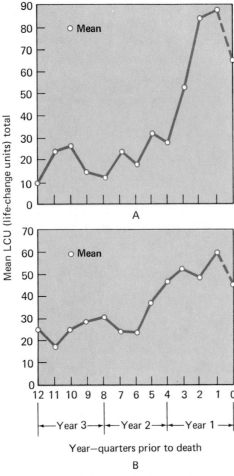

Figure 16-1 *A.* Sudden-death subjects without a history of coronary heart disease. *B.* Sudden-death subjects with a prior heart disease.

Psychoanalytic Models: The Specific Personality Hypothesis

Specific personalities associated with specific disorders

Why do some people respond to stress with disorganized behavior patterns and others with maladaptive physiological responses? A possible answer is that the type of reaction is determined by the individual's personality or attitude. Dunbar (1943) was one of the first to note a relationship between personality types and psychophysiological disorders. For example, the individual who is rigid, highly sensitive to threat, and prone to chronic underlying hostility tends to develop hypertension, while the achievement-oriented perfectionist usually develops migraine headaches. Psychoanalytic theorists like Alexander (1950) have suggested that

Specific emotions associated with specific disorders

Specific attitudes associated with specific disorders

psychophysiological disorders are products of unconscious emotional conflicts. For each disorder psychoanalytic theory posits a specific typical conflict. An example might be in peptic ulcers a repressed need for love and protection. According to psychoanalytic theory, this need is equated with the need for food so that stomach activity is stimulated by what is essentially a need for affection. This excessive stomach activity produces the gastric secretions that cause the ulcer. This theory is one version of the **specific emotion hypothesis,** which states that each type of emotional response causes specific psychophysiological activity. However, as we noted earlier, the evidence for this belief is meager.

Specific Attitude Hypothesis

A similar hypothesis developed by Grace and Graham (1952), the **specific attitude hypothesis,** suggests that particular attitudes are associated with particular patterns of physiological change and hence with specific psychophysiological disorders. Grace and Graham interviewed a number of patients with psychophysiological disorders to determine their characteristic reactions. Some of the disorders and their attitudes are shown in Table 16–4. Graham, Stern, and Winokur (1958) took this hypothesis a step further by hypnotizing a group of normal young male subjects and giving them suggestions designed to produce the attitudes specific either to (1) urticaria (hives) or (2) Raynaud's disease. These two disorders were selected because a clear difference appears in the skin temperature responses associated with them: hives produces high skin temperature, while individuals suffering from Raynaud's disease have lower-than-normal skin temperatures. These researchers found that when their subjects were given the hives attitude, skin temperature rose, while the Raynaud's disease attitude caused it to fall.

A later study by Peters and Stern (1971), however, questioned these findings. These investigators had several sessions with each subject during which either the Raynaud's disease or the hives attitude was

disorders having organic causes or results

Table 16–4 Psychophysiological Disorders and Their Characteristic Attitude

Symptom	Number of patients	Attitude
Urticaria	31	Sees himself as being mistreated and is preoccupied with what is happening to him, not with retaliation. *Ex:* "The boss cracked a whip on me."
Eczema	27	Feels that he is being interfered with or prevented from doing something and cannot overcome frustration; is concerned with the obstacle rather than the goal. *Ex:* "I want to make my mother understand but I can't."
Cold, moist hands (Raynaud's disease)	10	Feels need to undertake some activity but may not know what to do. *Ex:* "Something had to be done."
	(4)	(Included in previous group.) The contemplated action was hostile. *Ex:* "I wanted to put a knife through him."
Vasomotor rhinitis	12	Facing a situation that he would rather avoid or escape. Essential feature was desire to have nothing to do with it. *Ex:* "I wanted to go to bed and pull the sheets over my head."
Asthma	7	Same as in vasomotor rhinitis.
Diarrhea	27	Desired to get a situation over with, to get rid of something or somebody. *Ex:* (Patient had bought a defective car.) "If only I could get rid of it."
Constipation	17	Individual grimly determined to carry on with a situation but with no expectation of improvement or success. *Ex:* "It's a lousy job, but it's the best I can do."
Nausea and vomiting	11	Preoccupied with a past mistake, something he wished he hadn't done or that hadn't happened. *Ex:* "I wish things were the way they were before."
Duodenal ulcer	9	Individual seeking revenge, wishing to injure a person or thing that had injured him. *Ex:* "He hurt me, so I wanted to hurt him."
Migraine headache	14	When individual had been making an intense effort to carry out a planned program and was now relaxing. It made no difference whether or not the project had succeeded. *Ex:* "I had to meet a deadline."
Arterial hypertension	7	Individual feels that he must be constantly prepared for threat. *Ex:* "Nobody is ever going to beat me. I'm ready for anything."
Low back pain	11	Individual thinking of walking or running away from something; physical movement involved. *Ex:* "I just wanted to walk out of the house."

induced with or without hypnosis. They found that the temperature of the finger showed a decline when the individual was hypnotized, whatever disease attitude was suggested, while the temperature increased when the subject was not hypnotized, regardless of the attitude induced.

Type A and Type B Personalities

Another popular hypothesis of this sort is the one that relates the **type A personality,** whose characteristics appear in Table 16–5, with heart disease. This hypothesis is simply a refinement of Dunbar's (1943) suggestion that executive personality types are

Table 16–5 Characteristic Behaviors of a Type A Person

1. Speaks explosively, hurriedly, uses limited vocabulary. Impatient with discursive or slow speech in others.
2. Walks, eats, moves rapidly.
3. Gets impatient at the rate at which events occur, such as the movement of traffic. Sets unnecessary deadlines.
4. Strives to do two or more things at once (such as drinking coffee while dictating letters).
5. Always strives to bring conversations around to preferred topics; often only pretends to listen to others.
6. Feels guilty for relaxing. *Very* competitive in sports.
7. Does not notice interesting or lovely things in the environment (for instance, would not stop to look at a beautiful scene).
8. Is preoccupied with getting things (*having*) rather than becoming something worth *being*.
9. Attempts to schedule more and more activities in less and less time.
10. Challenges other Type A persons aggressively.
11. Has certain nervous gestures such as fist clenching, table-banging, or facial tics.
12. Attributes success to speed.
13. Evaluates people on the basis of numbers, such as amount of sales, number of publications, or appendectomies performed.

The Type A personality tends to be excessively competitive, aggressive, impatient, and plagued by a sense of urgency.

disorders having organic causes or results

the most vulnerable to coronary or heart disease. The type A personality tends to be excessively competitive, aggressive, impatient, and plagued by a harrying sense of urgency (Friedman and Rosenman 1974). The **type B personality** is the reverse. Friedman and Rosenman (1975) have found that type A personalities have higher serum cholesterol levels (in spite of highly similar diets), smoke more cigarettes, and exhibit higher rates of heart disease than type B personalities. Such typical studies have classified groups of healthy men into A and B personalities and then followed them over a long period of time. Type As have been found to have from 1.4 to as high as 6.5 times as many heart attacks as type Bs. Furthermore, type As have a higher risk for recurrence and fatal heart attacks (House 1974).

This hypothesis is greatly oversimplified, however. Jenkins (1974) identified what he called the type A person in a group of 2,700 men. During a four-year follow-up period, he found that the men who scored high on type A behaviors had twice as many heart attacks as those who scored low. However, the majority of high scorers did not have heart attacks, and some of the low scorers did. In other words, individuals with highly similar personality types may or may not develop the same disorder. Furthermore, having a type B personality does not necessarily protect the individual from a heart attack.

Most challenging to this hypothesis is that in some psychophysiological disorders the personality type may be a result of the disorder rather than its cause. This relationship has been strongly suggested in a study of people with rheumatoid arthritis (Robertson et al. 1972). This belief receives further support from the fact that Crown and Crown (1972) failed to find a definite personality type in cases of early rheumatoid arthritis. Rheumatoid arthritis and other such disorders do cause suffering and handicaps, which could cause changes in personality.

Response Specificity

If the type of personality does not explain why a given individual develops a specific psychosomatic disorder, what is the explanation? Wolff (1950) has argued that each individual responds to stress of any type with a typical preferred pattern of autonomic responses. In other words, some individuals are muscle reactors, others are stomach reactors, pulse reactors, or skin temperature reactors. The individual who characteristically responds to stressful situations with an increase in blood pressure will be particularly vulnerable to hypertension, while those who react with increased secretion of stomach acids will be likely to develop peptic ulcers. This individual **response specificity** or **stereotypy** has had good support from the research evidence (Malmo 1967).

It has been shown consistently that individuals have the same characteristic physiological response patterns to all types of emotionally arousing stimuli (Lacey, Bateman, and VanLehn 1953). For example, Malmo and Shagass (1949) have shown that patients with cardiovascular symptoms are more likely to react to stress with increased cardiovascular activity than with increased muscle tension, while tension headache patients are inclined to react with increased muscle tension rather than with cardiovascular responses. This symptom specificity or the consistent tendency for a person to react to stress more with one organ system than with another is a widely observed phenomenon (Malmo, Shagass, and Davis 1950).

Why does such response specificity occur? Several answers seem likely. First, these response patterns appear to be present at birth. In studies of the autonomic responses of neonates (newborns), different patterns of autonomic reactivity have been identified at an age when social learning could not have occurred (Richmond, Lipton, and Steinschneider 1962). Grossman

Type A: competitive, aggressive, impatient, harried

Do different individuals have different autonomic reactions to stress?

Response specificity exists at birth

and Greenberg (1957) have found that, using any single index of the autonomic nervous system, such as heart rate, a given group of newborn infants shows a normal distribution of responsiveness from slight to extreme. Moreover, the same individual may show a reversed degree of responsivity when some other autonomic response is measured. In other words, some degree of autonomic patterning or specificity is present in newborn infants. Research by Mirsky (1958) supports this theory. Mirsky found that some infants showed gastric hypersecretion, which led to the inference of a genetic susceptibility to peptic ulcers. Response specificity may thus be largely determined by genetic endowment.

Somatic Weakness Hypothesis

Secondary gain can reinforce a psychophysiological disorder

Nevertheless, considerable evidence suggests that environmental influences are also important in determining what specific organ system will be susceptible to psychophysiological disorders. For example, the **somatic weakness hypothesis** suggests that the kind of disorder that may occur in an individual is determined by the weakest organ. This view suggests an interaction of environmental stresses with a genetic predisposition, resulting in vulnerability in a particular organ system, which is reflected in a history of early illnesses in that system. For example, a history of respiratory infections has been found in the histories of most asthmatic patients (Rees 1964; Bulatov 1967). Thus, the individual who has had a respiratory infection may have especially vulnerable lungs because of genetic influences or prior illness, or both, and emotional stress may bring on attacks of bronchitis or asthma.

Learning Models

Another important factor in the acquisition of a specific type of psychophysiological disorder is *learning*. It has been demonstrated that changes in the responses of the autonomic nervous system and related organs—heart rate, blood pressure, intestinal activity, urine production, respiration responses, and similar activities—can be produced both by operant and by classical conditioning (Miller 1969). From this finding, it is fairly logical to assume that psychophysiological disorders may arise through accidental conditioning and reinforcement of such behavior patterns. For example, Lang (1970, p. 86) stated that "A child who is repeatedly allowed to stay home from school when he has an upset stomach may be learning the visceral responses of chronic indigestion." In support of this notion, Turnbull (1962) demonstrated that by reinforcing certain breathing behaviors an experimenter can induce respiratory patterns that are progressively closer approximations of asthmatic breathing. Furthermore, a psychophysiological disorder can be maintained regardless of what instigated it by the fact that it generates reinforcement (secondary gain). A number of investigators have supported this theory.

The role of suggestion or cognitive mediation also appears to be important. For example, in a study of forty volunteer asthmatic subjects, Bleeker (1968) found that nineteen subjects developed asthmatic symptoms after breathing the mist of a salt solution that they were told contained allergens such as dust and pollen. Twelve of the subjects had full-fledged asthmatic attacks. When these subjects then took what they thought was a drug to combat asthma, actually the same salt mist, their symptoms disappeared. There is obviously little doubt that suggestion and reinforcement for the disorder can aggravate psychophysiological problems.

In summary, psychophysiological disorders seem to develop as a function of stress when stress is broadly defined as a change in life situation. The specific type of psychophysiological disorder that an individual develops appears to be determined by that person's unique physiological patterns of response to stress. This response specificity is influenced by genetic endowment and environmental factors, such as previous illnesses and learning experiences.

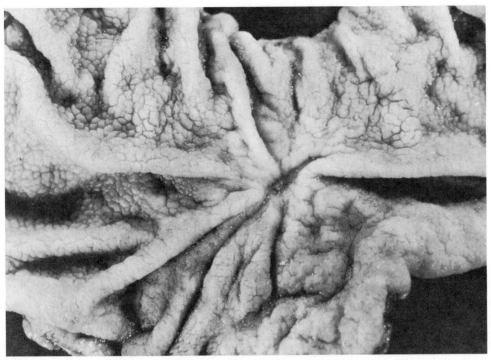

A peptic ulcer. The erosion of the mucous membrane has resulted in a craterlike wound.

Peptic Ulcer

Disorders of digestion, which are among the most common psychophysiological disorders, include erosion of the mucous membrane of either the duodenum (a portion of the small intestine) or the stomach. When an individual is subjected to prolonged stress or emotional arousal, the vagus nerve is activated and intestinal contractions and secretions of gastric juices stimulated. This excessive flow of digestive or peptic acids eats away the lining of the stomach or duodenum and leaves a craterlike wound, an **ulcer**. In the normal individual, acid secretion occurs when food enters the stomach and stops when digestion has been completed. In the ulcer patient, acid activity occurs when the stomach is empty and consequently damages the stomach tissue. Ulcer patients are reported to secrete four to twenty times more acid than normal individuals when the stomach is comparatively empty (Dragstedt 1958). This overactivity can be cut nearly in half by severing the vagus nerve, an intervention that alleviates the ulcers. The parasympathetic branch of the autonomic nervous system controls the secretion of gastric acids, a fact that may explain why most ulcer attacks occur at night or during periods of rest.

Approximately 10 percent of the American people are expected to develop ulcers sometime in their lives (Nechelas 1970). Duodenal ulcers are more prevalent in men than in women, the ratio being somewhere between 3 to 1 and 6 to 1 (Pflanze 1971).

Stress activates the vagus nerve, stimulating intestinal contractions and gastric secretions

Research and Theory

The role of stress and conflict has been well demonstrated in the production of ulcers. For example, Sawrey and his colleagues (Sawrey, Conger, and Turrell 1956; Sawrey and Weisz 1956) exposed rats to shock whenever they approached food or water. By the end of two weeks of exposure to this approach-avoidance conflict situation, many of the rats had developed ulcers or died from gastrointestinal hemorrhages. Control animals deprived of food and water but not shocked did not show this reaction. This result demonstrates that environmental stress, whether due to conflict or to the shock itself, can cause ulcers to develop.

Approach-avoidance conflict produces ulcers in rats

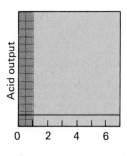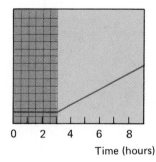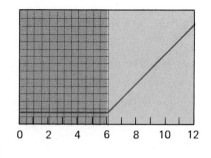

Acid output

Time (hours)

Figure 16–2 Stomach acidity of executive monkeys did not increase during avoidance sessions, but rather during the subsequent rest periods. The greatest increase followed a six-hour session; no rise followed a one-hour session.

Brady's executive monkeys developed ulcers. . . .

Brady et al. (1958) showed that a similar reaction occurs in primates. They also demonstrated that the effect was due to *conflict* rather than to shock *per se*. They placed monkeys in restraining chairs and subjected them to a series of shocks that might be avoided by pressing a lever at least once every twenty seconds. These monkeys were run in pairs. One of them (the executive) was responsible for pressing the lever and preventing shock to itself and the control partner. The number of shocks was the same for both animals, but the executive monkey was subjected to the additional psychological stress involved in the avoidance learning situation. The executive monkeys developed ulcers, but the control monkeys did not. To assess gastric activity, Brady (1958) made a surgical opening (or fistula) in the abdomen, thereby permitting a sampling of the stomach contents as required. He then observed the effects of various periods of work and rest on acid output. He found, as shown in Figure 16–2, that a one-hour work session had no effect on acid secretion, but a three-hour work session produced a significant amount of acidity. Notably, the gastric secretion began after the session was over rather than during the actual avoidance conditioning period. This finding is consistent with the reports of ulcer patients who awaken in the middle of the night with an attack.

A methodological problem in the Brady studies was that the monkeys placed on the executive training schedule were those who

but they may have been more anxious than control monkeys initially

Weiss found that ulcers were more likely when the animal felt helpless

made the first avoidance response. This rapidity of response has been shown to be related to the level of anxiety (Sines, Cleeland, and Adkin 1963). Thus, the executive monkeys may have developed ulcers because they were highly anxious rather than because they made coping responses. The Brady studies have been clarified by Weiss (1971a, 1971b, 1971c), who found that the availability of coping responses decreases the probability of ulceration and other signs of stress. In other words, if the subject is able to make a controlling response, the probability of ulceration is reduced, provided that feedback is available about the effectiveness of the response. If the animal performs a coping response but receives no feedback about the effectiveness of the response, it becomes a prime candidate for ulcer formation. The greater the feedback, the less likely the ulceration, weight loss, and increased emotionality. These findings contradict the Brady studies and suggest that ulcer formation is particularly likely when the individual is stressed and feels helpless.

It is fairly obvious that not all individuals placed in the situation described above develop ulcers. Why do some individuals develop ulcers when others do not? This difference seems to be due to the fact that some individuals have higher pepsinogen levels or gastric activity than others (Ader, Beels, and Tatum 1960). Mirsky (1958) stated that this difference in gastric activity is found reliably between patients suffering from duodenal ulcers and normal controls but not between patients with gastric ulcers

disorders having organic causes or results

and normal controls. However, a study by Weiner et al. (1957) found that high pepsinogen levels predict the development of ulcers. They measured serum pepsinogen for over 2,000 draftees and selected 63 who had values in the upper 15 percent of the total distribution and 57 who fell in the lower 90 percent. A total of nine peptic ulcer cases were reported, all of them in the high pepsinogen group. Their assessment also included psychological tests. They claimed that the presence of a peptic ulcer was correlated with the presence of persistent oral-dependent wishes that conflicted with environmental sources of oral gratification and resulted in unexpressed reactive hostility toward environmental sources. This finding is consistent with the hypothesis of Engel (1975), who stated that the psychological makeup of ulcer patients centered around strong needs to be taken care of, to lean on others, to be fed, and to be nurtured. He stated that, although developmental influences determine the precise expression of these personality characteristics, three basic patterns emerge:

1. **Pseudoindependence** The individual hides the dependency under a facade of aggressive, controlling self-reliance.
2. **Passive dependency** The individual's dependency needs are conscious and are overtly expressed by passivity, compliance, and eagerness to please.
3. **Acting-out dependency** The individual is infantile and exhibits behavior marked by insistent and demanding attitudes, often expressed in antisocial and even criminal acts.

The common denominator of all these patterns of behaviors is *dependency*. However, the strong influence of genetic and biological factors in ulcers must be emphasized: Mirsky (1958) demonstrated that individual differences in pepsinogen levels are present even in newborns.

Clinically, the relationship between gastric activity and emotional reaction has been well demonstrated. For example, Figure 16–3 shows measures of gastric activity taken from an ulcer patient during an interview. At the beginning of the interview,

the patient was discussing his resentment toward his wife who had been sexually promiscuous. He stated:

I'd come home nights and she would be out— no supper was ready—she was running around with another man—I found them accidentally in another house. She went to her mother. I felt downhearted and wanted to leave altogether. . . . I got a decent supper only on Saturday or Sunday. I do not want to believe the neighbors' gossip about her. . . . Pain started when I discovered she was running around. . . . She threatened to poison me (Mittelmann and Wolfe 1972, pp. 34–35).

As the figure shows, much gastric activity occured during this conversation. Stomach contractions were frequent and intense in the initial period of the interview. The level of hydrochloric acid (free HCL) in the stomach, and the total acid activity were high at the beginning of the conversation. At the midpoint of the interview, these measures reached a peak and declined as the patient's attitude changed to one of acceptance and rapport with the interviewer. It is interesting that this patient's resentment toward his wife resulted not only from her neglect of him but also from her failure to feed him. This connection between food and ulcers has been noted previously.

High pepsinogen levels and a strong need for nurturing are also factors

Again, the connection between food and ulcers

Assessment and Modification

Medical treatment of ulcers usually consists of a bland diet that restricts intake of the high-protein foods that stimulate the secretion of hydrochloric acid. Drug therapy consists of administration of anticholinergic and antacid drugs. Individuals are also instructed to decrease any heavy use of alcohol, coffee, tea, and cigarettes.

Some physicians have questioned this treatment procedure. Palmer (1967) found that thirty ulcer patients placed on a diet of water, multivitamins, pancakes, and small capsules containing minimal amounts of shaving cream did as well as those on the classic diet and medication for ulcers. Moreover, he also allowed 230 ulcer patients to choose between a solution containing two ounces of diluted hydrochloric acid

The shaving cream diet and other placebo effects

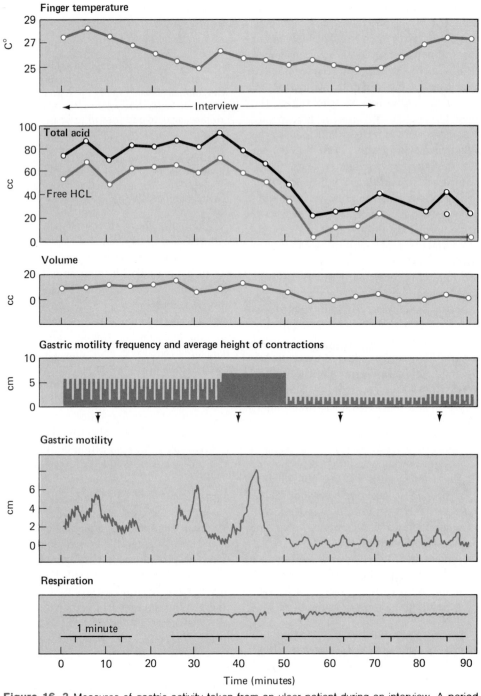

Figure 16-3 Measures of gastric activity taken from an ulcer patient during an interview. A period of resentment with high acidity and peristaltic activity is followed by a decrease in both with induced feelings of security and relaxation.

(equivalent to gastric acid) which should aggravate the ulcer condition and two ounces of aluminum hydroxide, an antacid that should have a beneficial effect. The patients were encouraged to try each one and then determine which worked the best. No significant difference appeared in their selection of the two solutions or their determination of which was most helpful. Palmer concluded that antacid and special diets were simply a gesture.

disorders having organic causes or results

Similar results have been found in studies of psychotherapeutic interventions. For example, Orgel (1958) examined the results of psychoanalytic therapy with ten clients, five of whom had stomach ulcers and five of whom had duodenal ulcers. He found that all who completed analysis were free of symptoms at follow-up periods ten to twenty-two years later. Five other ulcer patients who started analysis but did not complete it continued to have ulcers.

However, Baron and Wastell (1972) noted that research on the effects of psychotherapy for ulcer patients has lacked appropriate controls, particularly for the effects of placebo. Bockman, Kalliola, and Ostling (1960) found that 71 percent of ulcer patients reported symptomatic relief after being given an antacid drug, and 73 percent reported similar relief after being given a placebo. This study illustrates the need for control groups for placebo before the effectiveness of techniques for these disorders can be determined.

Biofeedback training has also been explored with ulcer patients. In one method the individual swallows a tube so that some of the stomach content can be sucked out with a drainage pump and the stomach content thus monitored continuously (Welgan 1974). This technique has shown that biofeedback can be used to alter or control gastric acid secretion. Another technique involves inserting a nasogastric tube that contains an electrode to measure the pH balance in the stomach rather than the pH balance of aspirated stomach content (Blanchard and Epstein 1978; Whitehead, Renault, and Goldiamond 1975). Unfortunately, a relatively low correlation appears between these measures of stomach content. Nevertheless, evidence suggests that ulcer patients and normals show some change in stomach acid with the help of biofeedback and instructions. The major problem with biofeedback techniques at present is that the techniques themselves (electrode swallowing and nasal insertions) cause distress that most individuals are unable to tolerate. Although biofeedback techniques are promising, much further work is needed before their usefulness in ulcer disorders can be determined.

Bronchial Asthma

Bronchial asthma is a respiratory disorder characterized by wheezing, coughing, shortness of breath, gasping, and thoracic constriction. The subjective reaction may include panic, fear, irritability, and fatigue. Physiologically, increased responsiveness to various stimuli occurs in the trachea, major bronchi, and peripheral bronchioles and is manifested by intensive narrowing of the airways, which impairs air exchange, primarily in expiration, and thus induces wheezing (Purcell and Weiss 1970). The asthma sufferer takes a longer time than normal to expire air, and whistling sounds called *rales* can be detected throughout the chest. Air seems to be trapped within the lungs.

The prevalence of asthma in the United States has been estimated at 2.5 to 5 percent of the population. This disorder usually affects children, 60 percent of asthmatics being sixteen years of age or less. Males are about twice as likely to suffer from asthma as females (Graham et al. 1967).

Research and Theory

Although breathing is a voluntary activity, excessive parasympathetic activity of the autonomic nervous system is usually accompanied by asthmatic difficulty in breathing. Activation of the parasympathetic nerves can occur either by a reflex response to local irritation of the bronchial tissues or direct innervation from autonomic centers in the CNS, especially the hypothalamus. Consequently, emotional states can cause an asthmatic response through the mediation of the hypothalamus.

Emotional states can cause an asthmatic response

A number of irritations of the bronchi will produce asthmatic attacks without the mediation of any psychological factor. Many people are allergic to substances such as household dust, tobacco smoke, cold air, flower and weed pollens, and certain food proteins, which are usually inhaled from the atmosphere and produce an asthmatic response.

Psychological factors, primary emotional stress, and suggestion can induce asthmatic attacks. Masuda, Notske, and Holmes (1966) subjected asthmatic patients to a stressful interview and found that the interview induced wheezing in seven of the seventeen patients. Kleeman (1967) interviewed twenty-six asthmatic patients over an eighteen-month-period and found that 69 percent of their attacks began with an emotional disturbance. The role of suggestion has been investigated by Luparello et al. (1971). They told a group of asthmatic and control subjects that they wanted to determine what concentration of various substances would induce wheezing. The asthmatic subjects were further told that they would inhale different concentrations of an irritant or allergen that had been previously established as a contributing cause of their asthmatic attacks. They were given five nonallergenic saline solutions to inhale but were told that each successive sample would have a high concentration of the allergen. The control subjects were given similar instructions. Fourteen of forty asthmatic patients reacted with a significant airway obstruction and twelve went into a full-fledged asthmatic attack. None of the control subjects showed this reaction. The twelve subjects who developed asthmatic attacks were then given the same saline solution to inhale but were told that the solution was a bronchodilator. Every one of the twelve subjects improved. This study confirms the role of suggestion and other forms of cognitive mediation in precipitating attacks in some asthmatic individuals.

Suggestion can also cause an asthmatic response

Rees (1964) stated that asthma can be divided into three different categories: *allergic, infective,* and *psychological*. In the allergic reaction it is quite possible that the cells in the respiratory tract may be especially sensitive to one or more substances such as pollen or dust that elicit the asthmatic attack. Respiratory infections, typically acute bronchitis, can also cause asthma. However, the functioning of the respiratory system is influenced by the autonomic nervous system, and therefore

Three categories of asthma: allergic, infective, psychological

Moving a child from home to hospital may reduce asthmatic symptoms

anxiety, frustration, anger, depression, and even pleasure are psychological factors that can also induce asthma. In a sample of psychological and medical information on 441 asthmatic patients, Rees found that the major cause of asthma was psychological in 37 percent of the cases, infectious in 38 percent of the cases, and allergic in 23 percent of the cases. However, Ellis (1970) claimed that the most common cause of asthma is an allergic reaction in which the individual has become sensitized to certain substances such as ragweed and pollen.

Personality variables, particularly dependency needs, have been hypothesized as important in the etiology of asthma. Alexander (1950) stated that asthma is a consequence of neurotic dependency-striving in which the individual wants to be protected by the mother. These dependency strivings are believed to be heightened in situations involving or suggesting a threat from the mother. Some psychoanalysts have suggested that the asthmatic attack is itself a substitute for crying and that wheezing resembles sobbing without tears (Weiss and Englis 1957). A relationship between asthma and the removal of the child from its home to a hospital has been fairly well demonstrated (Purcell 1963; Purcell et al. 1969). In one investigation, Purcell et al. (1969) selected a group of twenty-two children whom they divided into two groups. The first contained thirteen children in whom psychological factors were considered the principal cause of asthma; the second contained those for whom allergic or infectious factors were considered more significant. Figure 16–4 shows that, in those children for whom psychological factors were important, separation from the home caused a great improvement in the asthmatic disorder in terms of decreased wheezing, attacks, and medication, while reunion renewed the difficulty.

Learning clearly plays a significant role in the development of asthmatic attacks in some individuals. For example, Turnbull (1962) demonstrated that asthmaticlike breathing can be shaped in animals via conditioning procedures. However, similar results have not been consistently demonstrated with humans.

disorders having organic causes or results

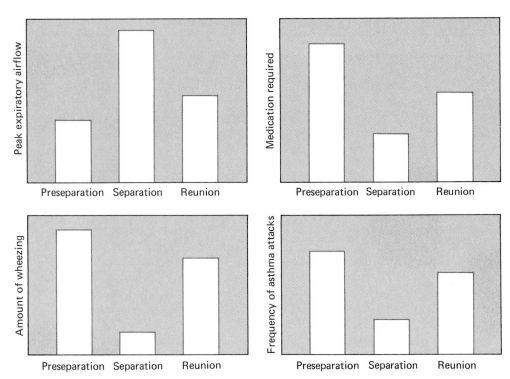

Figure 16-4 Improvement on several measures of asthma among children who were predicted to do well after being separated from their parents.

The existence of a physiological predisposition to asthma has been deduced from the finding that asthmatic individuals have underresponsive sympathetic nervous systems (Miklich et al. 1973). This low-level arousal of the autonomic nervous system is further verified by the fact that activation of the sympathetic nervous system is known to reduce the intensity of an asthmatic attack.

Assessment and Modification

A variety of techniques have been used to treat asthma. Honsberger and Wilson (1973) used transcendental meditation (TM) with a group of asthmatic patients and reported that 94 percent of them could breathe more freely after practicing TM. Autogenic training, which emphasizes relaxation and meditation exercises has also been assumed to be useful. In this technique, a series of physiological exercises are practiced to develop feelings of body heaviness and warmth, focus concentration on heart beat and respiration mechanisms, and produce warmth in the solar plexus area

and coolness in the forehead. However, the exact effectiveness of this technique with asthmatics has not yet been demonstrated with a controlled outcome study.

Behavior therapy, particularly systematic desensitization, has had a long history of use with asthmatic cases. For example, Walton (1960) reported conditioning an incompatible response of relaxation to relevant environmental stimuli that previously evoked asthma attacks. In a more systematic study Yorkston and his colleagues (Yorkston et al. 1974) compared relaxation instructions alone with systematic desensitization to symptoms of asthma attacks as methods for treating patients with bronchial asthma. The desensitization procedure consisted of teaching the patients to relax and then exposing them to a hierarchy consisting of the anxiety-provoking aspects of an asthmatic attack and varying from mildly uncomfortable items ("My chest feels tight") to quite terrifying items ("I am choking to death"). Relaxation by itself

Transcendental meditation and other meditation or relaxation techniques can be helpful in treating asthma

Systematic desensitization combined with relaxation is more effective than asthmatic medication

Ever since he was six months old, our son had had asthma. The attacks began when we were living in Japan and required that he be hospitalized for periods of one to four weeks. The doctors told us that the attacks would probably diminish when we returned to the United States. They didn't. Instead, we were continually making trips to the emergency room for relief. In addition, our son was getting more and more nervous, and the more nervous he got, the more frequent the attacks became. Finally, we sought psychological assistance.

After reviewing the situation, the doctors decided that the extra attention and medication we were giving our son, especially during the night, were prolonging the attacks and even encouraging their occurrence. Thus, we were told to put the boy to bed at night with all our usual love and attention and then leave him alone. If he coughed or wheezed, we were to listen for any real danger but otherwise ignore him till morning. Also we were instructed to make lunch money contingent upon decreases in coughing and wheezing

during the night. Any night that he coughed or wheezed less than he had the night before, we gave him money to buy his lunch at school the next day. This way, the doctors said, we could reward even the slightest improvement and make the lack of attention somewhat less painful.

Improvement was quick and dramatic. We could hardly believe the results came so fast. When the doctors suggested we try reversing the procedure, we were very reluctant but agreed to do so. We started giving the boy attention again in the night and gave him lunch money regardless of the amount of coughing and wheezing the night before. Before we knew it, the old problem was back. We asked the doctors to please let us begin the treatment program again, and they agreed. Again, we were amazed and pleased to see how fast the asthma disappeared.

It has been eleven months now since we stopped seeing the doctors, and our son has continued to improve. His daytime coughing and wheezing have decreased too, and he doesn't seem so nervous anymore either.

Neisworth and Moore, 1972

---

was somewhat effective, but verbal desensitization was more effective in improving air flow and decreasing the use of asthmatic medication. This effect was still present two years later for the desensitization group, but not for the group given only relaxation training.

Hyposensitization is also effective

Herxheimer and Prior (1952) used a technique similar to systematic desensitization with allergic forms of asthma. Called *hyposensitization,* the technique uses a styrometer to record a stable ideal breathing capacity while the individual receives through a breathing apparatus an aerosol allergen extract that the individual is suspected of being sensitive to. If no asthmatic attack occurs, the inhalation time for the next test is increased by 50 percent. If a mild attack occurs, inhalation time on the next occasion is increased by 20 to 30 per-

Biofeedback can also be used

cent. If the attack is moderate or severe, inhalation time is drastically reduced. This procedure is repeated until the allergen produces no attack or a mild attack. These experimenters used this technique with seventy-two patients who had monovariant (one allergy) and polyvariant allergies. They found a five-fold increase in tolerance by 27 percent of the patients, who remained symptom-free in spite of exposure to the allergen. An additional 27 percent showed increased tolerance and relative freedom from attack. Hyposensitization appears to be a promising technique but has not been followed up.

Biofeedback training is also a promising technique for treatment of asthma. Usually, biofeedback procedures focus on producing dilation of the bronchi and bronchioles as a means of alleviating problems in inspiration and expiration of air. Kahn, Staerk, and Bonk (1973) treated twenty

disorders having organic causes or results

asthmatic children with biofeedback by teaching them to do substitute bronchial dilation for bronchial constriction when exposed to stimuli that had previously elicited an asthmatic attack. During a one-year follow-up period these children showed a significant reduction in the frequency and severity of asthmatic attacks. Vachon and Rich (1976) decreased respiratory resistence with biofeedback in thirteen individuals. These studies and a number of single case studies indicated that biofeedback may be extremely useful in modifying asthma (Blanchard and Epstein 1978).

Essential Hypertension

Essential hypertension is an increase of systolic and diastolic blood pressure due to unknown causes. Blood pressure can be elevated by increased cardiac output or by the amount of blood leaving the left ventricle of the heart per minute, by increased resistance to the passage of blood through the arteries because of vasoconstriction, or by an increase in blood volume. Quite possibly, the kidneys and the adrenal glands, which are highly susceptible to stress, also play a significant role in cases of hypertension.

Chronic hyperactivity of the sympathetic division of the autonomic nervous system accelerates cardiac activity and functions to maintain certain blood vessels in a constricted state. This situation requires more blood than normal to be pumped through narrow vessels and results in high blood pressure. Prolonged elevation of blood pressure may cause heart failure, kidney disease, atherosclerosis (clogging of the arteries), heart attacks, and strokes. Individuals with high blood pressure are more likely to die at an early age. The age of onset in essential hypertension varies from fifteen to fifty years with a peak occurrence at age thirty-five. It has been estimated that the prevalence of hypertension in the general population may be as high as 6 percent (Wolf et al. 1955). This estimate may be low, since one survey found that 59 percent of hypertensives had not been previously diagnosed (Schoenberger, Stamler, and Shekelle 1972). The prevalence of essential hypertension is higher among blacks.

Subjective indices of hypertension are mild anxiety, insomnia, fatigue, dizziness, sweating, and headaches (Lyght 1966). The disorder seems to develop in two stages (Maher, 1966). In the initial stage frequent but temporary bursts of high blood pressure occur, presumably because of psychological factors. During this stage essential hypertension is reversible. After a number of years a second stage begins that seems to be the consequence of the organic changes produced by the first stage and is presumably irreversible. A long-term essential hypertensive disorder can cause a diffused thickening or hardening of the arteries (atherosclerosis), which, by cutting off the supply of blood, may eventually lead to heart disease, kidney destruction, and cerebral hemorrhage.

Chronic hyperactivity of the sympathetic nervous system results in essential hypertension

Research and Theory

Can psychological factors as well as disease of the kidneys, drugs, and dietary factors cause an increase in blood pressure? It has been well demonstrated that under stress the heart works faster (rate) and harder (pressure). It has also been demonstrated that a number of stressful events including stressful interviews, anger, anxiety, and natural disasters produce profound elevations in blood pressure (Innes, Millar, and Valentine 1959; Ruskin, Board, and Schaffer 1948; Ax 1953; Lachman 1972). The most widely quoted study of this phenomenon was conducted by Kasl and Cobb (1970). This study was initiated upon the closing of a plant, a time when many individuals faced the loss of their jobs.

Stress as a factor in essential hypertension

Measures of blood pressure were taken two months before and two years after the subjects were terminated. The experimental subjects were married, males, aged thirty-five to sixty, with at least three years of seniority. A comparable group of men employed in a similar work setting served as a control group. Blood pressure was higher for the experimental subjects during periods of anticipation of job loss, unemployment, or probationary reemployment than for later periods of stable employment in new jobs. Blood pressure changes were also higher among men who were relatively rigid and had higher overall mean blood pressures. These findings clearly indicate a relationship between environmental stress and high blood pressure.

A similar study by Liljefors and Rahe (1970) further verified the role of life stress in coronary heart disease by examining twins. The subjects of this study were thirty-two pairs of identical twins between forty-two and sixty-seven years of age in which only one twin in each pair suffered from a coronary heart disease. Liljefors and Rahe found that the twins suffering heart diseases were more work-oriented, took less leisure time, had more home problems, and experienced general dissatisfaction in their lives.

Genetic variables may also play a part

A relation between physiological and genetic variables and essential hypertension has also been shown. Weight problems and small increases in sodium intake can have significant effects on blood pressure. Obese individuals tend to show high blood pressure because with each extra pound of weight the heart must pump harder to supply the fatty cells, thereby increasing blood pressure. Schachter et al. (1974) found that heart rate during sleep was significantly higher among black newborns than among white newborns. These authors speculated that this elevated heart rate, one of the predictors of hypertension in later life, may be related to the fact that hypertension is more common among blacks than whites.

Hypertensive individuals are less likely to express hostility openly

As previously noted in our discussion of type A versus type B personalities in cardiovascular problems, personality factors do play a role in essential hypertension. Alexander hypothesized that essential hypertension is caused by repressed anger and hostility (Alexander 1950; Alexander, French, and Pollack 1968). Matarazzo

Response specificity in hypertensives

(1954) demonstrated that, compared to normals, hypertensive patients express less direct hostility when harshly criticized by an experimenter.

Kaplan et al. (1961) found a significantly greater hostile content in the speech of hypertensives as compared to normals when they are allowed to engage in uninterrupted speech about a personal experience. Another experiment that lends some support to this hypothesis was conducted by Sapira et al. (1971). They suggested that hypertensive individuals screen out potentially noxious stimuli as a response to their hyperreactive pressor (vasoconstrictive) system. They showed two films involving an interaction between a doctor and a patient to nineteen hypertensive and fifteen normatensive individuals. In the first film the doctor appeared rude, disinterested, irritable, and curt. In the second film, the same doctor was relaxed, pleasant, courteous, and friendly. The hypertensive group denied perceiving any difference between the doctor's behavior in the first and second films, while the control group readily identified the differences in the doctor's behavior. These studies suggest that hypertensive individuals have difficulty handling situations involving anger.

Why do some individuals develop essential hypertension rather than other types of psychophysiological disorders? Two reasons are possible. Engel and Bickford (1961) reported that patients with essential hypertension react to many different types of stimuli in terms of increased systolic blood pressure rather than in terms of other response modalities such as skin temperature or muscle activity. This pattern of reaction, as we mentioned previously, may have a genetic basis. On the other hand, Miller (1969) demonstrated that increases and decreases in blood pressure can be learned. Consequently, the specific learning history of the individual may yield clues to the development of essential hypertension. However, a more plausible hypothesis is that vulnerability to high blood pressure results from the interaction of genetic predisposition, stress in an individual's life, and learning.

disorders having organic causes or results

Modification

The medical treatment of essential hypertension consists of the use of various drugs known to be effective in lowering both systolic and diastolic blood pressure. Monosulfamyl diuretic (Chlorthalidon) increases the excretion of sodium chloride through the kidneys and thus reduces arterial pressure. Reserpine reduces arterial pressure and produces a sedative effect. However, drug treatment only controls the problem. It does not eliminate it. Weight control, diet, and reduction of salt intake have also been used as methods for controlling essential hypertension.

The effectiveness of psychological techniques in treating essential hypertension has not been convincingly demonstrated. Although psychotherapy has been used to treat this disorder, its effectiveness is generally unknown. Behavioral approaches have used biofeedback training with a variety of cardiovascular disorders including essential hypertension. Most of this research has centered on teaching patients with essential hypertension to lower their blood pressure. Two major strategies have been used for achieving this goal: direct attempts to lower blood pressure and indirect attempts in which the individual is taught a response, such as muscle relaxation, that is correlated with lower blood pressure.

Direct control of blood pressure is difficult because of problems in continuously monitoring blood pressure, a necessary procedure for the use of biofeedback. The most accurate way to measure blood pressure would be to insert a small tube called a cannula directly into an artery and connect it to a pressure-measuring device. However, this procedure is uncomfortable, often dangerous, and quite impractical as a research or clinical technique. Another technique is to inflate a cuff on a subject's arm to a pressure just above the systolic blood pressure so that no Korotkoff sounds (sounds of heart pulse) are detected in the artery distally (away) from the cuff but the pulse can be detected proximally (near) to the cuff. The pressure is then gradually released until sound appears (systolic blood pressure) and then disappears (diastolic blood pressure). Unfortunately, this procedure poses problems because one cannot leave an inflated cuff on the individual. Periodic inflation and deflation of the cuff have been used, but even this method is not completely satisfactory (Blanchard and Epstein 1978). Nevertheless, it has been shown in a controlled study that hypertensive patients could significantly reduce diastolic pressure (Elder et al. 1973). Another study of four patients with hypertension by Blanchard et al. (1975) illustrates this procedure. They used intermittent visual feedback of blood pressure over twelve sessions to teach these individuals to lower their systolic blood pressure. The results for one patient are shown in Figure 16–5. However, whether direct feedback of blood pressure as a method of controlling hypertension is a feasible treatment technique remains to be demonstrated.

Attempts to teach individuals to lower their blood pressure indirectly have used techniques such as progressive muscular relaxation or GSR (galvanic skin response) and EMG (electromyograph) biofeedback. For example, over a three-month period Patel (1973) treated twenty hypertensive patients with a combination of passive relaxation training and GSR biofeedback. She found that sixteen of twenty patients produced decreases in their blood pressure. The systolic pressure decreased an average of 25 mm Hg, while the average decrease in diastolic pressure measured 14 mm Hg. Five of these patients discontinued antihypertensive medication altogether, and eight others had reductions of at least 33 percent. In a second study, Patel (1975) replicated these results and was able to demonstrate that the reduction in blood pressure continued throughout a twelve-month follow-up period. In a third study Patel and North (1975) combined passive relaxation training, yoga, and GSR biofeedback and found similar results.

Monitoring blood pressure continuously is difficult

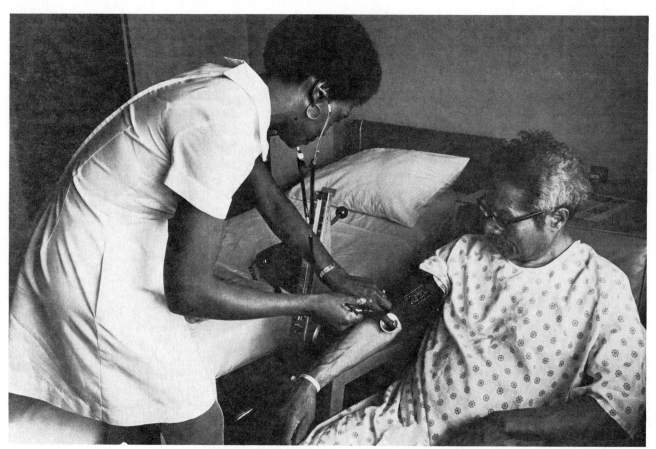

Hypertensive patients can be taught to significantly reduce blood pressure.

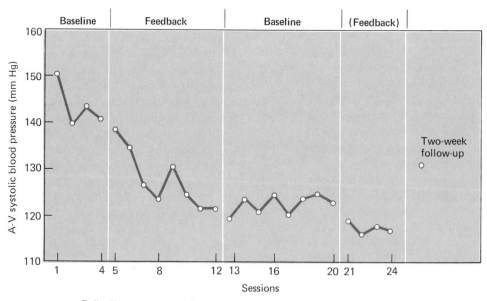

Figure 16–5 Patient's average systolic blood pressure for each session of the experiment.

disorders having organic causes or results

Head pain, or headache, has been divided into four major types: muscle contraction (tension), migraine, combined muscle contraction and migraine, and hypochondriacal headache.

Headaches

Head pain, like fever, can occur as a function of a number of physiological or psychological disorders, including lesions or tumors of the central nervous system, cerebral vascular abnormalities, or any other of a wide variety of physical or psychological factors. However, in most headaches, the pain is *psychogenic* and not associated with a structural alteration of the anatomy or with physical illness. In general, psychological factors are implicated in four major types of head pain: *muscle contraction (tension), migraine, combined migraine and muscle contraction,* and *conversion or hypochondriacal headaches.*

Muscle contraction headaches (tension headaches) are characterized by a sensation of tightness and pressure in the cephalic (head) or neck area. They vary widely in intensity, frequency, and duration. This type of headache is generally assumed to be a function of the individual's cephalic and neck muscles reacting during stress by sustained contractions. Pain is usually bilateral (two-sided), occipital (rear), frontal, facial, or *hatband* (circular) in distribution. These headaches are nonpulsative with a duration of hours or days. Everyone has tension headaches occasionally, and clinical cases differ from normal headache activity only in terms of increased frequency, duration, and severity of the head or neck pain.

Five variants of vascular headaches of the **migraine** type have been identified: *classic, common, cluster, hemiplegic,* and *lower-half.* The classic migraine occurs in

Muscle contraction headaches are due to tension in the head and neck muscles

Five variants of migraine headache: classic, common, cluster, hemiplegic, and lower-half

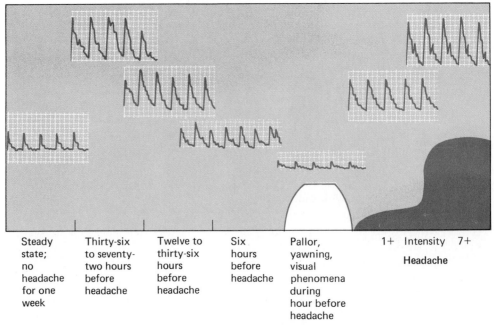

Steady state; no headache for one week	Thirty-six to seventy-two hours before headache	Twelve to thirty-six hours before headache	Six hours before headache	Pallor, yawning, visual phenomena during hour before headache	1+ Intensity 7+ Headache

Figure 16–6 Representative record of the sequence of temporal–artery pulse-wave changes prior to and during a migraine headache. The variability of the pulse waves obtained seventy-two hours prior to the headache continues until the headache is gone.

approximately 10 percent of migraine patients and consists of a sharply defined transit sensory (frequently visual or motor) prodrome (preliminary symptom) and unilateral pain with a throbbing sensation. Subjectively, in the sensory prodrome of this pain the individual may experience an *aura*: numbness, visual disturbances, and other signals that a headache will shortly occur. This phase is followed by unilateral pain of a throbbing nature. The individual also experiences extreme sensitivity to sound and light, which may be associated with nausea and vomiting. The pain may last from two to twenty-four hours and become so intense that medication such as Demerol is required. These headaches occur on an average of every week or ten days, but, in individual cases, they vary from daily to once every two or three months.

Two stages of migraine attack

In classic work done during the 1940s, Wolff demonstrated a **two-phase theory** of the physiological mechanism for migraines (Dalessio 1972). In the first phase a constriction of the intra- and extracranial arteries occurs that is associated with the transit sensory or motor aura. These symptoms are apparently due to the reduction

of the blood supply to the cephalic region. The second phase is initiated by a rebound dilation of these arteries which is associated with the onset of pain. Biochemically, it has been suggested that *neurokinin,* a pain substance, is secreted just prior to the rebound dilation. These effects may be seen in Figure 16–6.

The common migraine differs from the classic migraine primarily in the absence of the sharply defined aura (Ad Hoc Committee on the Classification of Headaches 1962). The duration of the common migraine is usually greater than that of the classic migraine and the pain more frequently bilateral. The common migraine occurs in approximately 85 percent of those experiencing migraine headaches. There is some controversy over whether the initial phase of vasoconstriction occurs in common migraines or whether individuals with this disorder do not discriminate the sensations of cephalic vasoconstriction (Adams, Feuerstein, and Fowler 1980).

The cluster migraine is similar to the common type in the absence of an aura and similar to the classic migraine in that the pain tends to be unilateral (Friedman 1973). Only about 4 percent of migraine patients experience the cluster variant. Pain

disorders having organic causes or results

in this disorder is extremely severe. The onset is associated with nose and nasal stuffiness, tearing, and unilateral facial flushing. The major difference between the cluster migraine and other variants is that the cluster migraine occurs for eight to twelve weeks every two or three years. Another characteristic of the cluster migraine is that the pain may terminate abruptly within a twenty- to ninety-minute interval and occur as frequently as two or three times every day.

The hemiplegic and lower-half headaches are extremely rare, and the role of psychological factors in these disorders has not been established. Headaches of a delusional, conversion, or hypochondriacal nature are those in which the characteristic clinical disorder is similar to a delusional or conversion mechanism and peripheral pain mechanisms are not present. Consequently, these headaches are often referred to as *psychogenic headaches* and have not been well delineated (Packard 1976). It is doubtful that the psychogenic headache is a psychophysiological disorder, since no change in the function or structure of the physiology has been documented in these cases.

It has been estimated that approximately twelve million individuals in the United States suffer from some form of migraine headache. Approximately thirty million people report having tension headaches, a figure that suggests that headaches are almost as prevalent as the common cold. Sex differences in the incidence of migraines has been a subject of controversy. The estimate has varied from no differences between sexes to 60 to 80 percent of the cases being females (Adams, Feuerstein, and Fowler 1980). Onset has been recorded as early as eighteen months, but the typical age of onset is approximately twenty years. Migraines can become relatively frequent as early as ten years of age. After thirty the probability of developing vascular headaches decreases and continues to decline until the age of sixty (Walter 1971). Tension headaches tend to develop at a later age.

The precipitating factor in migraines is unclear. They commonly occur when the individual is relaxing (during vacations or on weekends) or during the middle of the night. Certain events such as eating various foods, visual stimulation, and negative emotions have been suggested as precipitators of migraines, but little evidence exists to support this notion. In women, oral contraceptives, pregnancy, and the menstrual cycle do appear to be related to the onset of migraines in approximately 40 to 50 percent of the cases (Adams, Feuerstein, and Fowler 1980). Tension headaches, on the other hand, are directly related to stress.

Muscle contraction headaches appear to be the consequence of emotional stress. Muscles surrounding the skull contract as a function of stress and result in the individual's experiencing a band of pain that seems to circle the head. The exact cause for this disorder is not clear, but individuals who experience this sort of headache are probably muscle responders and have a high resting level of muscle activity. It should also be noted that the individual who has muscle contraction headaches can also have migraines (combined muscle contraction-migraine cases).

Research and Theory

The etiology of migraines is not clear. Genetic factors do seem to be important, since a family history of migraines appears in approximately 50 percent of the cases. However, family histories are usually obtained from the patient. When family members are directly questioned, the prevalence of migraines drops to 10 percent, not much more than the prevalence of migraines in the general population (Adams, Feuerstein, and Fowler 1980). It has been fairly well documented that migraines occur in individuals who have cephalic arteries that are dilated in the resting state or who tend to have an overreactive autonomic nervous system. These two characteristics may precipitate the two-phase pain sequence.

What causes migraine headaches is not clear. . .

but tension headaches appear to be caused by stress

Genetic factors may play a part in migraine headaches. . .

Two common psychological explanations are given: personality types and emotional specificity. The emotional specificity hypothesis states that specific emotional responses elicit specific types of physiological response patterns. As a consequence of continual emotional stimulation, an overreactive and eventually disruptive organ system develops (Alexander 1950). As Harrison (1975) indicated, most studies implicate unexpressed anger as the critical emotion in migraines. The presence of the unexpressed anger results in an overreactive cephalic vasomotor system that eventually becomes dysfunctional. Unfortunately, most research in psychophysiology appears to support the notion that no specific pattern of physiological responses is associated with a given emotion (Greenfield and Steinback 1972). Consequently, this hypothesis does not seem feasible.

and personality factors may also be involved

Another hypothesis suggests that individuals who have certain personality traits develop migraines. The individual with migraines is described as having excessive compulsive traits including perfectionism, orderliness, moralistic preoccupations, and rigidity (Friedman, Storck, and Merritt 1954). The victim is also supposedly more intelligent than average. Recent reviews by Harrison (1975), Bakal (1975), and Adams, Feuerstein, and Fowler (1980) have not supported any of these hypotheses. Moreover, Harrison states that no relationship between inability to express hostility and migraine headaches has been demonstrated.

Psychological techniques have had varying results

Wolff (Dalessio 1972) hypothesized a susceptibility to migraines determined by genetic factors. This predisposition manifested itself in headaches when the individual was placed under stress, although personality factors and attitudes modulated the appearance of the disorder. While the exact cause of migraine headaches is still not clear, it is likely that an interaction between biological and psychological variables will eventually be demonstrated in these disorders.

Behavioral techniques are somewhat effective. . .

and biofeedback is the most promising treatment

Modification

Medical treatment of various types of headaches has been the major method. With muscle contraction headaches, analgesics such as aspirin are fairly effective. Treatment for migraines includes the use of vasoconstrictors, such as ergotamine tartrates; drugs that inhibit serotonin activity, such as methysergide maleate; beta adrenergic blocking agents, such as propranolol HCL; and drugs directed at preventing depletion of vasoactive amines, such as the antidepressive drugs. These drugs, in most cases, give symptomatic relief or may be used for prophylactic purposes in preventing vasoconstriction and rebound dilation. In a high percentage of patients a specific drug program is usually successful in controlling the migraines.

Psychological techniques have been used to treat headaches with varying results. Psychoanalysis and other variations of psychodynamic therapy have been of limited value (Adams, Feuerstein, and Fowler 1980). For muscle contraction headaches, behavior therapy techniques—particularly those emphasizing progressive muscular relaxation, assertiveness training, desensitization, and stress inoculation—have been quite successful. Some evidence also suggests that systematic desensitization, assertiveness training, and progressive muscular relaxation are somewhat effective with migraines (Adams, Feuerstein, and Fowler, 1980). Mitchell and Mitchell (1971) have had good success in treating migraines with behavioral approaches.

The most promising treatment for headaches, particularly of the muscle contraction types, has been biofeedback training. Blanchard and Epstein (1978) reviewed a number of studies using EMG (electromyograph, a device that measures muscle tension) biofeedback with muscle contraction headaches and concluded that EMG biofeedback has been highly effective, although they question the specific role of biofeedback as the active ingredient of the treatment procedure. They suggest that progressive muscular relaxation may be as effective as EMG biofeedback.

disorders having organic causes or results

The major biofeedback procedure used with migraine headaches has been a combination of autogenic and *temperature training* (Sargent, Green, and Walters 1972). In this procedure, temperature is monitored from both the finger tip and the forehead. Feedback is given for raising temperature in the hands and lowering it in the forehead. It was once assumed that this procedure caused vasoconstriction in the cephalic area and vasodilation in the hands. This relationship has not been confirmed, however, and the effects of temperature training may be due to the fact that this response is also associated with relaxation. Nevertheless, the results of the Sargent et al. procedure indicated that 63 percent of migraine patients showed improvement, according to clinical evaluation and the patients' daily record of headache intensity and medication use.

The value of temperature training as a treatment technique was confirmed in a later control group outcome study (Blanchard et al. 1977). This study used three groups: (1) a combination of temperature training, autogenic training, and regular home practice; (2) progressive muscular relaxation with regular home practice; and (3) a no-treatment, waiting list control group. The treatment groups received training sessions twice a week for six weeks. As Figure 16–7 shows, a reduction occurred in total headache activity, headache intensity, and medication use in the two treated groups. However, there was no difference between progressive muscular relaxation training and temperature biofeedback combined with autogenic training. The crucial variable in these procedures may be the relaxation response.

Another biofeedback procedure used to treat migraine headaches is training individuals to directly control the vasomotor activity of the temporal branch of the cephalic arteries. This technique consists of placing a photoelectric transducer on the artery on the pain site. This transducer gives the amplitude of the *blood volume pulse,* a measure of vasodilation. Then the individual is given feedback either to dilate

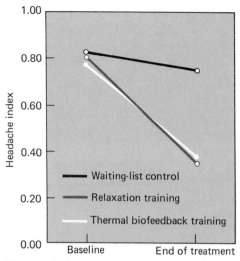

Figure 16–7 Changes in headache index (average intensity of headaches per week) for all three experimental groups as a result of treatment.

or to constrict the affected arteries (BVP feedback). After a number of sessions the individual is taught voluntary control of the response by either dilating or constricting the arteries on instruction. Friar and Beatty (1976) used this procedure, as did Feuerstein and Adams (1975). In all these studies experimental subjects have fewer headache attacks than a control group. Bild and Adams (1980) compared BVP feedback with EMG feedback and a waiting-list control group. The BVP and EMG biofeedback subjects were given ten one-hour sessions. With improvement defined as one-half the frequency of headaches per week as well as one-half the hours of headache activity per week, 86 percent of the BVP group, 50 percent of the EMG group, and 17 percent of the waiting-list group showed improvement. A drastic decrease in drug intake appeared with the BVP, a moderate decrease in the EMG group, but no increase in the waiting-list control group. This study also indicates that relaxation is somewhat effective in controlling migraines. It further indicates that direct acquisition of vasoconstriction is a promising technique.

Temperature training may really be another form of relaxation training

Blood volume pulse is another measure that can be used in biofeedback treatment of migraine headaches

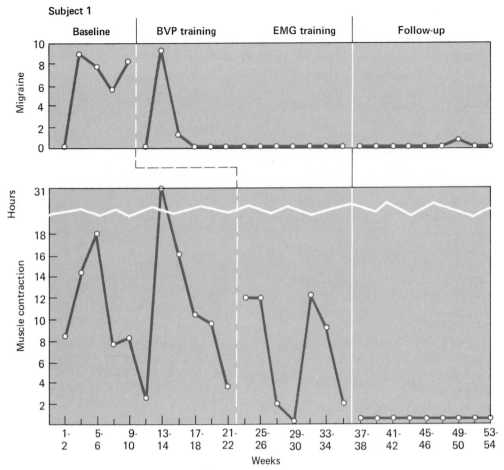

Figure 16-8 Biweekly mean duration per headache (Subjects 1 and 2).

Sturgis, Tollison, and Adams (1978), using a multiple-baseline single-case design with combined muscle contraction-migraine headaches, illustrated the effectiveness of EMG feedback with tension headache and BVP feedback with migraine headaches. In two cases, shown in Figure 16–8, both types of headaches and medication intake were completely eliminated.

Summary

Psychophysiological disorders are disorders in which psychological factors presumably cause structural and functional changes in physiology. These disorders are associated with the autonomic nervous system and related organ systems. They include skin, musculoskeletal, respiratory, cardiovascular, gastrointestinal, genito-urinary, endocrine, hemic, lymphatic, and special-sense disorders.

In some psychophysiological disorders a change in the function of physiological activities occurs, while in others a change in anatomical structure results. Muscle contraction headaches are an example of the former type, and ulcers are an example of the latter. It is generally agreed that stress induces many of these disorders because they appear after the individual has been exposed to stress. According to Selye, stress apparently involves three stages. The first stage is alarm, the second is resistance, and the third is exhaustion. Selye has indicated that the type of stress may determine the type of disorder. Stress may be a function of any change in a person's life situation.

A number of theories have been suggested to explain psychophysiological disorders. Psychoanalytic theories have suggested that specific types of conflict cause specific psychophysiological dis-

disorders having organic causes or results

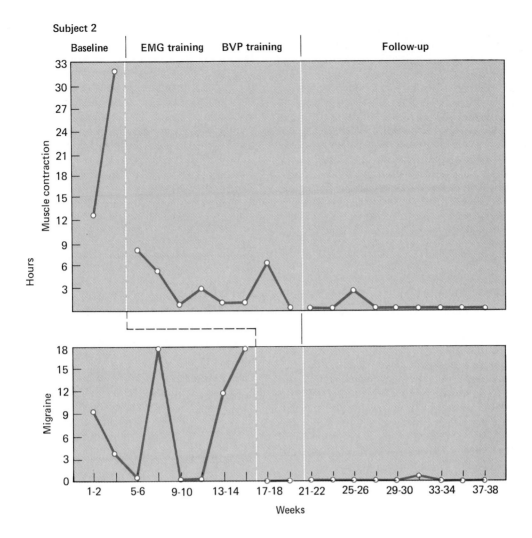

Subject 2

Baseline | EMG training | BVP training | Follow-up

orders. Other theories have suggested that the attitude of the individual is associated with particular patterns of physiological changes and is therefore associated with specific disorders. Another popular hypothesis relates personality characteristics and types of psychophysiological disorder, such as the type A personality and heart disease. None of these theories have been strongly supported by the data.

Perhaps the most plausible explanation is that each individual has a unique psychophysiological response to stress, some reacting with muscle tension, others with gastric secretions, others with changes in the cardiovascular system. These individual patterns of response predispose the individual to develop specific types of psychophysiological disorders. For example, patients with cardiovascular symptoms are more likely to

react to stress with increased cardiovascular activity. Response stereotypy seems to be due to both genetic and environmental factors.

Gastro-intestinal disorders are among the most common psychophysiological diseases. If an individual is subject to prolonged stress, the vagus nerve is activated and stimulates intestinal contraction and the secretion of gastric juices. The result is an erosion of the duodenum lining—an ulcer. Ulcers can be experimentally induced in animals, particularly if the organism is helpless. A predisposition to ulcers seems to be due to the fact that some individuals have higher pepsogin levels or gastric activity than others. Treatment of ulcer patients by diet, medication, and psychotherapeutic intervention has not been more effective than placebo. Biofeedback techniques for these disorders have been explored but are in the early stages of development.

psychophysiological disorders 517

In bronchial asthma an increased responsiveness to various stimuli occurs in the trachea, the major bronchi, and the peripheral bronchials. The resulting narrowing of the air-ways impairs air exchange. Allergens, emotional factors, and infections of the respiratory tract can induce the asthmatic attack. Dependency needs have also been hypothesized as important in the etiology of asthma. Behavior therapy, biofeedback, and TM (transcendental meditation) have shown promise in treating these disorders.

Essential hypertension is an increase in the systolic and diastolic blood pressure due to unknown causes. However, it is known that the kidneys and adrenal glands, both highly active in stress reactions, are important in producing increased blood pressure. In the initial stages frequent but temporary bursts of high blood pressure occur. After a number of years, organic changes occur, such as a thickening or hardening of the arteries, which may eventually lead to heart disease. Stress and other environmental factors, as well as physiological variables such as weight problems and salt intake can cause increases in blood pressure. The type A personality (competitive, aggressive, impatient, harried) has been associated with hypertension. Weight control, diet, and pharmacological treatment have been used to control hypertension. Biofeedback is another promising procedure.

Headache of a psychological origin can occur because of either tension or vascular mechanisms. There are five types of migraine headaches: classic, common, cluster, hemiplegic, and lower half. Migraines begin with a constriction of the temporal, cephalic arteries for a short period of time, which is associated with prodromal symptoms in some patients. This is followed by a dilation of these arteries, associated with intense, pulsating pain. These headaches are often unilateral, last from two to twenty-four hours, and occur on an average of two to four times per month.

In most cases, what precipitates migraine headaches is unclear. Genetic factors may be important. As with other psychophysiological disorders, personality traits have also been suggested as a factor, but the evidence has not supported this hypothesis.

Tension, or muscle contraction, headaches are usually precipitated by emotional stress. They occur as often as six or seven times a week and are less painful than migraines. Muscle contraction headaches appear to be induced in individuals who are "muscle responders."

A variety of medical procedures have been used to treat both types of headaches. Psychotherapeutic procedures have not been particularly successful, especially with migraines. However, biofeedback training and behavior therapy are promising.

Key Concepts

behavioral medicine

bronchial asthma

dualism

essential hypertension

fight or flight reaction

general adaptation syndrome

life stress

migraines

muscle contraction headaches

psychophysiological disorders

response specificity or stereotypy

somatic weakness hypothesis

specific attitude hypothesis

specific emotion hypothesis

stress

two-phase theory of migraine

type A personality

type B personality

ulcers

Review Questions

1. What is a psychophysiological disorder?

2. Describe the three stages in Selye's general adaptation syndrome.

3. What is the specific personality hypothesis? What is the specific attitude hypothesis?

4. How do type A personalities differ from type B personalities? What is the significance of this difference in terms of specific psychophysiological disorders?

disorders having organic causes or results

5. What is the somatic weakness hypothesis?

6. Describe one learning model of psychophysiological disorders.

7. What methodological problem in Brady's study of executive monkeys led to a reversal of his conclusions?

8. What physiological and emotional factors are associated with peptic ulcers?

9. What are the three categories of asthma? What are the major predisposing and precipitating factors in asthma?

10. What personality factors are associated with essential hypertension?

11. What are two major types of headaches and how do they differ?

12. What is the major factor in muscle contraction headaches?

13. How is biofeedback training used to treat migraine headaches?

Key Topics

Three criteria used to define mental
retardation

Four levels of mental retardation

Two major types of mental
retardation

Genetic hypothesis of intelligence

Environmental hypothesis of
intelligence

The Milwaukee project and shaping
the intellectual environment

Down's syndrome

PKU, cretinism, microcephaly, and
hydrocephaly

Ayllon's modification of disruptive
classroom behavior

A person's effectiveness in coping with the world is influenced by three types of characteristics: *cognitive, affective,* and *conative* (Burt 1955). Cognitive characteristics include such intellectual processes as reasoning, judgment, and memory—the abilities that largely determine scores on standardized tests of intelligence. Affective or emotional processes are also important in determining an individual's effectiveness. A bright person, for example, may behave stupidly when anxious or angry, or may be insensitive to important emotional responses in others. Conative characteristics, the motivational aspects of behavior, are also obviously important in determining an individual's effectiveness. A person highly capable of abstract reasoning may be completely ineffective if not motivated to use that talent. Moreover, the individual with modest cognitive ability may prove to be a surprisingly effective person because of high motivation, persistence, and high energy level.

Rate and ultimate level of intellectual development are lower in retardates

We shall define *intelligence* as a hypothetical construct that describes cognitive processes such as thought, memory, concept formation, and reasoning. We shall define **mental retardation** as substandard performance on measures of these cognitive processes. As Zigler (1971) and Inhelder (1968) have noted, the retarded individual progresses through the same sequence of early cognitive development as other individuals but at a slower rate. The essential characteristic of the retarded individual is this difference in the rate of cognitive development, coupled with the ultimate or final level of intellectual functioning achieved. Another important characteristic is **social competence**, which measures how effectively the retarded individual adjusts to the environment. Although intelligence influences the behaviors that demonstrate social competence, social competence does not invariably reflect intellectual functioning any more than the relative absence of such behaviors in the emotionally unstable, the criminal, or the social misfit inevitably reflects intellectual subnormality (Zigler 1971). As we shall show, clear differentiation between the two concepts *intelligence*

Intelligence and social competence are different concepts

DSM and AAMD definitions differ

and *social competence* is necessary to understand the origin and the nature of the behavior of individuals labeled retarded and particularly to avoid the error of attributing all maladaptive behavior of the retarded individual to deficits in cognitive functioning.

Classification of Mental Retardation

Many terms have been used to describe the individual with deficits in intellectual functioning: feebleminded, idiot, moron, imbecile. These terms have been discarded because they have acquired negative connotations. Unfortunately, any term used to describe individuals of subnormal intelligence rapidly acquires a negative meaning. For example, at present it is not unusual to hear school children refer to someone who makes a mistake as an "EMR," an abbreviation for the emotionally and mentally retarded. This labeling reflects society's negative attitude toward mental retardation. Mental retardation was defined by DSM II as "subnormal general intellectual functioning which originates during the developmental period and is associated with impairment of either learning and social adjustment or maturation or both." DSM III uses a similar definition. The American Association on Mental Deficiency (AAMD) in its manual on terminology and classification of mental retardation (1973) states that mental retardation "denotes significantly subaverage general intellectual functioning existing concurrently with defects in adaptive behavior and manifest during the developmental period."

All of these definitions use a combination of three criteria:

1. **Lowered intellectual functioning** as measured by standardized tests of intelligence such as the Stanford-Binet or the Wechsler Scale
2. **Defects in adaptive behavior,** which are usually measured by the Cain-Levine Social Competency Scale, the Vineline Social Maturity Scale, and the American Association on Mental Deficiency Adaptive Behavior Scale.

disorders having organic causes or results

Table 17-1 Level of Severity of Mental Retardation

Level	Percentage of retarded individuals	IQ scales Stanford-Binet (SD = 16)	Wechsler (SD = 15)
Mild	75.0	68–52	69–55
Moderate	20.0	51–36	54–40
Severe	3.5	35–20	29–25
Profound	1.5	19 and below	24 and below

Since none of these scales are accepted as being sufficiently reliable and valid, clinical judgment is also used for the assessment of adaptive behavior.

3. **Early onset of the disorder** Mental retardation is seen as a developmental disorder, and deficits in intelligence that occur after adolescence as a result of central nervous system impairments are not viewed as mental retardation.

As Table 17-1 shows, there are four general levels of mental retardation:

1. **Mild mental retardation** This group constitutes the largest number of those labeled mentally retarded: approximately 75 percent. These individuals develop social and communication skills during the preschool period, have minimal retardation in sensory-motor areas, and are often not distinguished from normal children until a later age. They can learn academic skills up to the sixth-grade level by their late teens, and their intellectual level as adults is comparable to that of the average eight- to twelve-year-old child. They often need special education but are generally educable. They rarely show signs of brain pathology or other physical anomalies. Their social adjustment is similar to that of an adolescent, although they may lack the normal adolescent's imagination, inventiveness, and judgment. With early diagnosis, parental assistance, and special education programs, most of these individuals can adjust

socially and achieve vocational skills adequate for minimal self-support. They may need guidance and assistance when under unusual social or economic stress, but to some extent they can become self-supporting citizens.

2. **Moderate mental retardation** Individuals in this category can usually learn to talk and communicate during the preschool years but may have poor social awareness. As adults, they attain an intellectual level similar to that of an average four- to seven-year-old child, although some of them can be taught to read and write. The rate of learning for academic material is rarely beyond the second-grade level, and the level of conceptualization is extremely limited. Physically, they may appear clumsy, and they occasionally suffer from structural deformity and poor motor coordination. During school age they do profit from training in social and occupational skills. In some cases during their adult years they achieve self-maintenance under sheltered conditions in which they can receive supervision and guidance when under mild social or economic stress. They may be capable of holding semi- or unskilled jobs.

3. **Severe mental retardation** Motor and speech development is severely retarded in these individuals, and they commonly have physical handicaps. During school age they can learn to talk or otherwise communicate, can be trained in

Victims of mild retardation are educable

Victims of moderate retardation are trainable

Victims of severe retardation can learn communication, self-care and some self-maintenance

Table 17-2 AAMD Adaptive Behavior Classification

	Preschool age (0–5) Maturation and development	**School age (6–21)** Training and education	**Adult (21)** Social and vocational adequacy
Level I	Gross retardation; minimal capacity for functioning in sensorimotor areas; needs nursing care	Some motor development present; cannot profit from training in self-help; needs total care.	Some motor and speech development; totally incapable of self-maintenance; needs complete care and supervision.
Level II	Poor motor development; speech is minimal; generally unable to profit from training in self-help; little or no communication skills.	Can talk or learn to communicate; can be trained in elemental health habits; cannot learn functional academic skills; profits from systematic habit training. ("Trainable")	Can contribute partially to self-support under complete supervision; can develop self-protection skills to a minimal useful level in controlled environment.
Level III	Can talk or learn to communicate; poor social awareness; fair motor development; may profit from self-help; can be managed with moderate supervision.	Can learn functional academic skills to approximately fourth-grade level by late teens if given special education. ("Educable")	Capable of self-maintenance in unskilled or semiskilled occupation; needs supervision and guidance when under mild social or economic stress.
Level IV	Can develop social and communication skills; minimal retardation in sensorimotor areas; rarely distinguished from normal until later age.	Can learn academic skills to approximately sixth-grade level by late teens. Cannot learn general high school subjects. Needs special education, particularly at secondary school-age levels. ("Educable")	Capable of social and vocational adequacy with proper education and training. Frequently needs supervision and guidance under serious social or economic stress.

elementary health habits, and may profit from self-care training. During their adult years they can contribute partly to self-maintenance under complete supervision, but they will be dependent on others all of their lives. This group constitutes approximately 3.5 percent of retarded individuals.

4. **Profound mental retardation** These individuals are severely deficient in adaptive behavior and unable to master any but the simplest tasks. Useful speech is rudimentary, if developed at all. During school age some further motor development may occur, and they may respond to minimal or limited training in self-help skills. Severe physical deformities, central nervous system pathology, and retarded growth are typical. Convulsions, seizures, mutism, deafness, and other physical anomalies are common. Health and resistance to disease are poor, a short life expectancy is common, and custodial care is required.

Victims of profound retardation may achieve minimal self-help skills

Causes may be either organic or cultural-familial

Another method of classifying retarded individuals is in terms of adaptive behavior at various ages, as Table 17–2 shows.

Occasionally, a retarded individual may have exceptional ability in some specific area. These individuals are called **idiot savants**. Typically, the idiot savant's special skill does not require abstract reasoning. For example, Hill (1975) described a retardate with a diagnosed IQ of 54 who could play eleven different musical instruments by ear and had outstanding skill in calculating dates. Morishima (1975) has described a famous Japanese painter with an assessed IQ of 47. These cases are rare.

Two major types of mental retardation are known. The first type is associated with a variety of *pathological physical* conditions that interfere with the individual's psychological and physiological functioning. In these cases the individual's retardation is secondary or is a by-product of physical injuries or diseases. The second type is **cultural-familial retardation.** The cause of cultural-familial retardation is not

disorders having organic causes or results

known, though some combination of environmental and genetic influences is probably involved, as the name suggests.

Cultural-Familial Mental Retardation

In this type of mental retardation neither physical symptoms nor any evidence of physical causes for lowered intellectual functioning are apparent. It is the most common type, numbering some 75 percent of retardates. Many psychologists view this disorder as reflecting the 2 or 3 percent of the general population that fall at the lower end of the distribution of intelligence (mild retardation). These individuals are not usually diagnosed as mentally retarded until they enter school and have serious difficulty in academic achievement. Most of these children are from poverty-stricken, unstable, and often disruptive family backgrounds. Their homes may be characterized by lack of intellectual stimulation, poor social interaction with others, and environmental deprivation (Braginsky and Braginsky 1974; Heber 1970). The probability is high that other family members will also be retarded or below normal in intelligence.

A relation between cultural-familial retardation and poverty has been consistently demonstrated. The frequency of mental retardation, though it is less than 3 percent in the general population, has been estimated at between 10 and 30 percent among the poor (Cytryn and Lourie 1967). A sizable portion of cultural-familial retardates come from stable lower-class families in which employment is steady and the child's physical needs are met (Robinson and Robinson 1976). The intellectual and educational level, even in these homes, is low, however, with few of the parents having IQs above the borderline range (Heber 1970). The tendency for the cultural-familial retarded child to come from lower socioeconomic classes and from families with lower IQs is even more pronounced among children who are institutionalized. In a sample of institutionalized mentally retarded children who had IQs above 50 (moderately retarded) and no obvious neurological symptoms, Benda et al. (1963) found that only 13 of 205 cases came from homes in which no apparent retardation was present in the immediate family. Only one-fourth of these families were intact and able to provide even minimal food, shelter, and clothing for the child.

These figures do not mean, however, that all children reared in deprived economic environments are retarded. Heber (1970) investigated the intellectual functioning of eighty-eight mothers and their offspring in a city slum and found that a minority of mothers gave birth to the majority of children whose IQs were in the mild mentally retarded range. Seventeen percent of the mothers with IQs of less than 68 reared 64.5 percent of the children in that range and 32.9 percent of the children with IQs of 68 to 83.

These findings seem to be restricted to cultural-familial retardation, since severely retarded individuals appear to be equally distributed in all classes (Penrose 1946). Furthermore, it has been demonstrated that the greater the mental retardation (the lower the IQ), the less likely it is that one or both parents are retarded (Gruensberg 1966).

Two possible interpretations of these data have resulted in a conflict similar to the Jensen (1969)-Kamin (1974) controversy over the determinants of intelligence. The first explanation is that intelligence is inherited and that the cultural-familial retardates and their families represent the lower end of the normal distribution of intelligence, as Figure 17–1 suggests. However, this distribution is not a smooth bell-shaped curve; it has a bump on the lower end. This bump may represent individuals whose retardation results from specific organic deficits.

The evidence for the genetic hypothesis is appealing. Samples of identical twins show them to be uniformly more similar than fraternal twins on intelligence tests. Furthermore, identical twins reared apart are more alike than fraternal twins reared together (Scarr 1975). An evaluation of the studies of adopted children also seems to support the genetic hypothesis. Munzinger (1975) found five studies, involving 351 families, in which adequate methodology

Cultural-familial retardation is related to poverty. . .

but severe retardation is not

Genetic hypothesis, the bump in the bell-shaped curve

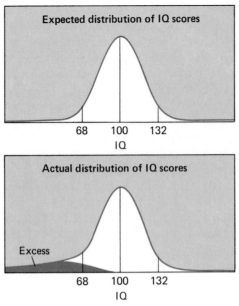

Figure 17-1 Expected and actual distribution of IQ scores.

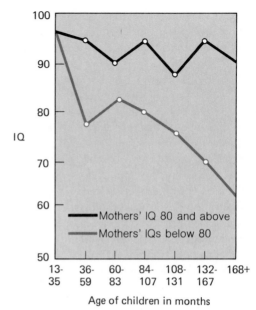

Age of children in months

Figure 17-2 Mean IQs of 586 children of eighty-eight mothers as a function of age of children.

(1) Uncertainty about what intelligence tests measure

(2) Poorly designed studies supporting the genetic hypothesis

(3) Environment affects intelligence

The environmental hypothesis: the more early stimulation, the higher the child's intelligence

Socioeconomic differences in child-rearing practices

was used. These studies revealed that the IQ of adopted children correlated more closely with the mental age of the biological parents (.48) than with that of the adoptive parents (.19).

For a number of reasons, scientific as well as humanistic, the genetic hypothesis of intelligence has been controversial. First, determining exactly what intelligence tests measure is difficult. Furthermore, they do not measure all aspects of what can be conceptualized as intelligence. Second, the studies supporting the genetic hypothesis were poorly designed and executed (Kamin 1973). Third, there is little doubt that environment does affect intelligence. Identical twins reared apart are clearly less alike in IQ than those reared together (Erlenmeyer-Kimling and Jarvik 1963). Furthermore, environmental conditions can alter IQs in both directions, as we shall see later in this chapter. Perhaps Dobzhansky's (1955) conclusion is the most appropriate. He suggests that all healthy children are born with a wide potential of performance, even though genetic endowment places certain constraints or limits on such potential. The level achieved within those limits is largely determined by the environment.

The second explanation states that intelligence is a function of environmental factors. This position assumes essentially that the richer the environment is in terms of cognitive stimulation, the higher the intellectual functioning will be. As noted earlier in the discussion of other abnormal conditions, early environmental deprivation is consistently associated with maladaptive behavior, including lowered intellectual functioning. It has been shown, for example, that the children of mothers whose IQs are near average have IQs that remain fairly stable as they grow older. The IQs of children whose mothers have IQs below 80, however, tend to decrease as the children grow older (Heber, Dever, and Conry 1968), as may be seen in Figure 17-2.

A deprived economic background can influence intellectual functioning in a number of ways. For instance, in mother-child interaction in which mothers are asked to teach their children how to solve standard problems, middle-class mothers tend to give more verbal explanation with their instructions, more positive feedback in terms of praise, and more specific feedback or suggestions in the form of questions than lower-class mothers. Conversely, lower-class mothers make nonverbal intrusions and give more negative feedback in the form of criticism (Bee et al. 1969; Hess and Shipman 1965).

disorders having organic causes or results

The more apathetic the mother, the lower the child's IQ. Disadvantaged parents are often apathetic.

Polansky, Bergman, and DeSaix (1972) shed further light on this problem in their study of impoverished families in rural Appalachia. They found that the mother-child interaction in impoverished families is characterized by an **apathy-futility pattern** of behavior. This pattern manifests itself in the feeling that nothing is worth doing, in the absence of meaningful personal relationships, in a generalized incompetence, and in a lack of motivation to acquire competence. Moreover, those raised in such a pattern tend to infect those who try to help them with the same feeling of futility. In a sample of sixty-five mother-child pairs, these authors found a negative correlation between ratings of the mother's apathy-futility feelings and the child's IQ. The more apathetic the mother, the lower the child's IQ. This maternal apathy-futility was also associated with lethargic, withdrawn, dependent, and clinging children. This evidence is consistent with the hypothesis that children from disadvantaged homes tend to have poor self-concepts, a low sense of mastery, and a high expectation of failure (Kagan 1970). Children from deprived families perform very poorly on intellectual tasks *because they expect to fail.* Both the mothers and the children demonstrate behavior similar to what Seligman (1975) called learned helplessness.

Good evidence suggests that enriching a child's environment can enhance intellectual functioning. An early study by Skeels and Dye (1939)—even though it suffers from methodological deficits—suggests that cultural enrichment may enhance intellectual functioning. Twenty-five individuals who had been classified as mentally retarded at a very young age in an orphanage were either allowed to remain in the orphanage (twelve individuals) or placed in an institution for the mentally retarded. In the institution for the mentally retarded they were placed in a ward with older retarded girls who had relatively high IQs. These children received much love and attention from the older girls. Two years after the children were placed, intelligence tests were readministered, and the group placed in the care of the girls showed an average increase in IQ of twenty-seven points, while the other children in the orphanage showed an average decrease of twenty-six points. Twenty years later, another follow-up was conducted to assess the intellectual performance of these individuals. The experimental group, cared for by the retarded girls, had reached a striking level of adult adaptation compared to the group that remained in the orphanage (Skeels 1966). Another study came to a similar conclusion. Kirk (1958) studied children living in their own homes and in public institutions. Some were given preschool enrichment from one to three years before entering the first grade, while others were not. Seventy percent of the children given experiences in mental and social development improved their intelligence and social maturity scores by ten points and held these gains during a five-year follow-up period. The control children who lived in adequate homes tended to catch up within the first year or two, but control children living in deprived homes and institutions suffered a consistent decline in ability.

Heber and his colleagues (Heber and Garber 1975; Heber et al. 1976) conducted an even more enlightening experiment in which children of mothers whose IQs were less than 75 were randomly assigned to experimental and control groups (twenty in each group). At three years of age the children in the experimental group began to attend a special enrichment program that continued all day, five days a week, twelve months a year until the children entered school at age six. These children were provided with a variety of experiences appropriate to their age level. In the meantime, their mothers were given remedial academics, homemaking and child-rearing instructions, and vocational training. Measures of intelligence were obtained at six-month intervals for both groups and showed that the experimental children averaged over twenty IQ points higher than the control groups between two and six years of age. The average IQ at age six was 121 for the experimental group and 87 for the control group. The Milwaukee project, as this study was called, provides convincing evidence that intellectual functioning can be modified. This type of approach is more humane than the eugenics procedure of voluntary sterilization for retardates that was proposed by Reed and Reed (1965) on the basis of their research. The latter suggestion is based on the belief that retardation is genetic and that voluntary sterilization would elevate the average intellectual level of the general population. A more humane procedure would be to provide children with social and intellectual enrichment to enhance their level of intellectual functioning.

Mental Retardation Associated with Organic Causes

Any factor that interferes with the physiological integrity of the central nervous system can cause mental retardation. In these cases, mental retardation is the by-product of an organic disease or illness. The American Medical Association (1965) has identified over 200 different causes of mental retardation. These include genetic factors, chromosomal disorders, infections, toxic agents, Rh-factor, malnutrition, radiation exposure, and numerous others. Mental retardation associated with organic causes accounts for the majority of the

disorders having organic causes or results

more severely retarded cases, particularly individuals labeled profoundly retarded. In contrast to cultural-familial retardation, which is usually detected when the child enters school, retardation associated with organic factors is usually detected in preschool years.

We shall discuss the more common clinical types of organic mental retardation in the next section. Many of these clinical types are identified by their physical appearance. In some cases the disorder is caused by a specific factor, while in other cases a variety of physical agents can cause similar physical symptoms such as hydrocephaly.

Down's Syndrome

Down's syndrome, first described by Langdon Down in 1886, is the most common of the clinical conditions associated with moderate and severe mental retardation. About one in every 600 children born in the United States is diagnosed as having Down's syndrome, although the incidence varies depending on the population from which the statistics are gathered (newborns, mental defectives, or the total population) (Gustavson 1964). Down's syndrome is commonly called *mongolism* because of the physical features it produces, particularly the almond-shaped, slanted eyes. However, the similarity between these features and true Oriental or Mongolian features is superficial, as the condition is easily recognizable in Oriental as well as Caucasian children (Kramm 1963).

Other physical symptoms common in children with Down's syndrome include abnormally thick skin on the eyelids; a protruding stomach; smaller than normal extremities; a broad, flat face, nose, and back of the head; a tongue too large for the mouth or deeply fissured; a speckled iris; a short, broad neck; stubby fingers; and a little finger often more noticeably curved than the other fingers. Instead of the whorls found in the fingerprints of others who are mentally retarded, individuals with Down's syndrome show loops. Their adult height is rarely over five feet. While the diagnosis of Down's syndrome may be difficult with infants, it is relatively clear with older children. Most individuals with this disorder have IQs of less than 50 and are usually classed as moderately retarded. These children are often described as extremely placid, cheerful, and cooperative.

Approximately 10 percent of these cases show an associated congenital heart defect. They may also be predisposed to leukemia (Miller 1970) and are particularly susceptible to circulatory, gastrointestinal, and respiratory disorders. About 25 percent of these children will not survive the first few years, and mortality after age forty is abnormally high. With advances in medicine, better medical care, and a more healthful environment, however, the life expectancy of these individuals is increasing.

Until approximately twenty years ago, it had been assumed that the cause of mongolism was faulty heredity in spite of the fact that more than one case of Down's syndrome in a family was very infrequent. In 1959 Lejeune, Turpin, and Cautier found that forty-seven chromosomes rather than the usual forty-six were present in the cells of individuals with Down's syndrome. This condition is called *standard trisomy-21* because the twenty-first set of chromosomes contains three rather than two chromosomes as a result of nondisjunction (failure of one pair of chromosomes to separate) during mitosis. Trisomy-21 can be detected by a chromosomal analysis in which a tissue culture is made and enlarged photographs of a cell are taken with a microscope. The silhouettes of the individual chromosomes in the cell are then cut out and assembled by hand in pairs according to size and shape. This results in a *karyogram* such as the one that was shown in Figure 4–1. The reason for this chromosomal abnormality is not known, although it does not seem to be an inherited disorder (Dunn 1973). One factor associated with this disorder is the age of the mother. The incidence of Down's syndrome increases with the age of the mother from about 1 in 1500 during the twenties to about 1 in 85 during ages of forty to forty-four (Karp et al. 1974). One suggestion has been that progressive deterioration of the egg cells due to aging may increase the chance of a chromosomal error (Lilienfield and Benesch 1964).

It is now possible to detect Down's syndrome after the thirteenth week of pregnancy by **amniocentesis,** a painless pro-

Lower life expectancy of children with Down's syndrome

Standard trisomy-21: three instead of two chromosomes in the 21st set

cedure in which a small amount of fluid is drawn from the amniotic sac into a hollow needle passed through the abdomen. These cells are then cultured and scanned for chromosomal irregularity or broken down for other chromosomal tests. This procedure involves very little risk, and recent advances in computer-assisted chromosomal analysis have yielded a more rapid, less expensive procedure (Dunn 1973). In the future many mothers will be advised early in their pregnancies about the risk of Down's syndrome as well as other chromosomal abnormalities so that they can decide whether to continue or terminate the pregnancy.

Phenylketonuria

Phenylketonuria (PKU) is a rare metabolic disease occurring in about 1 in 20,000 births and accounting for about 1 in 100 institutionalized retardates (Schild 1972). This disorder is assumed to be caused by a pair of recessive genes that result in a metabolic disturbance. This particular combination produces a deficiency of a liver enzyme, phenylalanine-hydroxylase, which is needed to convert phenylalanine, an amino acid, to tyrosine. Consequently, phenylalanine and its derivative, phenylpyruvic acid, accumulate in the body fluid and ultimately cause irreversible brain damage. These unmetabolized amino acids interfere with the process of myelination (sheathing of neuron axons that are involved in the rapid transmission of impulses and information in the nervous system). The neurons of the frontal lobes are particularly affected.

The child may appear normal at birth but the disorder becomes apparent between six and twelve months when the signs of mental retardation become apparent. Early symptoms such as vomiting, a peculiar odor, infantile eczema, and seizures may be present in some children during the first few weeks of life. Motor incoordination and other neurological manifestations are common as the disease progresses. About one-third of PKU individuals cannot walk, and over 60 percent never learn to talk. More than half of them have IQs less than 20. Their behavioral characteristics have been described as fearful, restless, and occasionally destructive.

About one in seventy persons is thought to be a carrier of the recessive gene associated with PKU. Varying degrees of PKU seem to exist, and the effects of this disorder on intelligence are variable, perhaps an indication that other genetic factors may ameliorate the destructive effects of the enzyme (Burns 1972). State laws require a laboratory test of the infant's blood to determine if excess phenylalanine is present within four or five days after birth. If PKU is detected, a diet low in phenylalanine is prescribed. If this restricted diet is administered from as early as three months until the age of six when brain development is fairly adequate, the deterioration process can be arrested. In these cases, the range of possible intellectual functioning is from borderline intelligence to normal functioning. In some cases, however, children suffer mental retardation despite restricted phenylalanine intake and other treatment measures.

The role of genetic counseling is important in prevention of this disease. When an individual with PKU is present in the family, it is important to determine whether other prospective parents carry the recessive gene.

Cretinism

Cretinism is due to an endocrine imbalance resulting from a malfunctioning thyroid gland. Cretinism, once the most common type of retardation, was more frequent in certain parts of the world such as the Himalayas, the Andes, the Rocky Mountains, and the Swiss Alps. An iodine deficiency was soon discovered in the soil in these areas and in the food grown in it. This deficiency resulted in the birth of infants with defective thyroid glands that remained underdeveloped or that atrophied later. As with many disorders, while the cause of cretinism was unknown, it was assumed to be genetic. After cretinism was found to be due to an insufficiency in iodine, the use of iodized salt and other preventive measures became widespread and greatly reduced the incidence of the disorder. However, thyroid deficiences may also occur as a result of birth injuries and infectious diseases such as measles, whooping cough, or diphtheria. The age at which the thyroid deficiency occurs determines the degree and duration of the deficiency that results. Today, because

disorders having organic causes or results

of modern treatment methods cretins constitute less than 5 percent of the retarded in institutions in the United States.

The physical symptoms associated with cretinism usually do not begin to attract attention until about the sixth month of life. If the thyroid deficiency has been severe from an early age, the cretin has a dwarflike, thickset body and short, stubby extremities. The cretin's height is rarely over three feet and is accentuated by slightly bent legs and curvature of the spine. The gait is shuffling. Wiry black hair is abundant in these individuals; their eyelids are thick and give the cretin a sleepy appearance; the skin is dry, thickened, and cold to the touch. The nose is thick and flat; the eyes are wide set; the lips are puffy; and the teeth are pegshaped. Cretins tend to suffer from respiratory difficulty, impaired motor coordination, and general muscular weakness. Measures of their metabolic rate are helpful in a diagnostic examination.

Cretinism is associated with severe to moderate levels of intellectual functioning, depending on the severity of the brain damage following the endocrine imbalance. A high correlation exists between the severity of the physical symptoms and the severity of the mental defect. In terms of personality characteristics cretins are described as placid, quiet, good tempered, and affectionate. They are considered to have fewer behavior problems than other retardates.

Detection of the condition and preventive measures are crucial in this condition. If early treatment is initiated with a synthetic form of thyroid hormone, many of the anomalies associated with the condition do not occur, and normal intellectual functioning may be achieved.

Microcephaly

The distinguishing characteristic of **microcephaly** is an extremely small head that is associated with the failure of the brain to grow to normal size. Alteration in brain size may vary from only a slight degree of arrested growth to a marked decrease. Individuals with this disorder were once referred to as pinheads. One criterion for the diagnosis of microcephaly is a head circumference smaller than three standard deviations below the mean for age and sex, but this diagnosis should never be based on head size alone (Warkeny and Dignan

1973). Usually the microcephalic is extremely retarded. Fortunately, this is a rare condition, occurring in only about one percent of retarded persons in institutions.

Two forms of microcephaly, primary and secondary, are presumed to exist. Primary microcephaly is an inherited condition transmitted in autosomal recessive genes (Grossman 1973). Secondary microcephaly results from a number of conditions, including maternal rubella (German measles), X-ray exposure during pregnancy, and birth injuries (Grossman 1973). Once the growth of the brain is arrested, there is no effective cure or treatment. Genetic counseling may permit preventive measures. Avoidance of exposure to radiation and infection during pregmancy, as well as other preventive measures, are necessary to reduce the incidence of this disorder.

Primary microcephaly is inherited; secondary microcephaly is due to disease or injury

Hydrocephaly

Hydrocephaly is a relatively rare condition in which an abnormal amount of cerebrospinal fluid accumulates within the cranium, causing damage to the brain tissue and enlargement of the head. The excessive cerebrospinal fluid results from a disturbance in the formation, absorption, or circulation of this fluid. The buildup of fluids occurs in the lateral third and fourth ventricles of the brain and causes pressure that pushes the surrounding brain tissue outward against the skull. The result is the abnormal expansion of the cranium in the fetus or the newborn child. The head may already be enlarged at birth or it may begin to enlarge soon after, and thus the condition can be diagnosed before twelve months of age (Wortis 1973). This condition may also develop in infancy or early childhood following disease, injury, or infection that produces a blockage of the cerebrospinal fluid pathways and an accumulation of fluid in the brain area. No real evidence exists to support a genetic basis for hydrocephaly (Pratt 1967). However, in some families, if the mother has had one hydrocephalic child, the risk of a second may be greater than in the general population. The risk of having a hydrocephalic child increases with maternal age. A number of factors can cause hydrocephaly, including brain injuries, tumors, diseases such as meningitis,

Hydrocephaly is due to excess cerebrospinal fluid in the brain

Table 17–3   Some Other Physical Disorders Causing Mental Retardation

Clinical type	Symptoms	Causes
Bilirubin encephalopathy	Abnormal levels of bilirubin usually released by red blood cell destruction; choreoathelosis frequently occurs.	Usually Rh, ABO blood type incompatibility between fetus and mother
Hurler's Syndrome (Gargoylism)	Metabolic disorder resulting in deformed stunted growth, deterioration of vision, coarse facial features, enlarged head, and swollen abdomen. Onset occurs from birth to five or six years of age, causing severe retardation in most cases.	Autosomal recessive genes
Klinefelter's syndrome	Presence of small testes after puberty; development of feminine secondary sex characteristics; only 25 percent retarded.	Sex chromosome anomaly
Niemann-Pick's disease	Onset in infancy with dehydration, weight loss, and progressive paralysis.	Disorder of lipoid metabolism
No. 18 Trisomy syndrome	Multiple congenital anomalies usually low set, malformed ears, small mandible and heart defects	Autosomal anomaly of chromosome set 18
Tay-Sach's diseases	Hypertonicity, listlessness, blindness, progressive paralysis, and convulsion. Death usually occurs by third year. Similar disorders are late infantile cerebral lysordosis (Beilschowsky-Jansky disease), early juvenile cerebral lysordosis (Spielmeyer-Vogt disease), and late juvenile cerebral lysordosis (Kuf's disease) which occurs at later ages	Disorder of lipoid metabolism caused by a set of recessive genes
Turner's syndrome	Sexual infantilism, webbing of neck, and increased carrying angle of forearm	Anomaly of sex chromosomes

encephalitis, and toxoplasmosis. Some evidence also suggests that hydrocephaly increases in frequency if the mother has been exposed to the Asian flu during the first trimester of the pregnancy. In many cases, the causes are not known (Carter 1966).

There is no real cure for hydrocephaly, but the most successful type of treatment is surgery. A shunt or hollow tube is inserted into the brain to drain away excess cerebrospinal fluid. If performed early, this procedure minimizes nervous system damage and head enlargement. The mortality rate associated with surgical intervention is fairly high (Carter 1966).

A variety of other conditions can cause mental retardation. Some of these conditions can be seen in Table 17–3.

Prevention of Mental Retardation

Since biological forms of mental retardation cannot be effectively treated, prevention of mental retardation is essential. Advances in biological screening for various disorders (for example, amniocentosis, the reading of the genetic structure of the fetus in the uterus) are now being used. Detection of Rh factor and PKU is now possible. Genetic counseling is also becoming widely available to provide parents with information about the possibility of having a child who may be mentally retarded, particularly in cases showing a history of a genetic disorder. Public education can also decrease mental retardation caused by toxic substances such as lead-containing paint (Byers 1959).

Prevention of cultural-familial retardation is a quite different problem. Since it

disorders having organic causes or results

has been demonstrated that enrichment programs such as the Milwaukee project do enhance the intellectual functioning of individuals from the lower socioeconomic classes, expansion of such programs should be beneficial in reducing this type of retardation. The answer, ultimately, is in enhancing the standard of living for all citizens, including facilitating educational opportunities and cognitive development for the underprivileged.

The Family and Mental Retardation

Mental retardation causes severe problems for the parents and the family because it is often poorly understood and considered a social stigma. The parents may suffer overwhelming feelings of guilt, minimize the child's deficits, or frantically search for miracle cures. Some parents have severe adjustment problems because of their attitudes of disbelief, shame, guilt, self-pity, and often anger toward the child or even the clinician for not being able to produce magical results. Others, particularly some poorly educated parents, are unable to recognize their child's handicap and may thus aggravate the child's condition.

Parents must face several issues if they choose to raise the child. First, they should be aware of, and prepared for, the fact that intellectually subnormal children develop feelings of worthlessness, depression, and helplessness. These reactions can become worse as the retarded individuals grow older because they fall behind their friends and may be excluded from social groups. The frustration of being rejected, difficulty in competing intellectually, and feelings of worthlessness may cause the individual to act out and rebel. The retarded individual's adjustment may be complicated by parental guilt, particularly if the parents try to overprotect the child and thus impede development of the child's ability to cope with the world. Informed parents who are sensitive to their own reactions and the needs of the child are essential in assisting the retarded individual to adjust to the environment.

In some cases of severe retardation, medical care is required or the family is unable to take care of the individual and institutionalization is necessary. Parents must be advised about the type of residential institutions available, such as state-supported institutions and private and nonprofit organizations. In some cases, institutionalization seems to be the best arrangement, and the family should be prepared for this separation.

Institutions

Only about four percent of mentally retarded individuals require institutional care. Many institutions for the mentally retarded suffer from the same deficits as those for psychotic patients and are characterized by overcrowded wards and sterile environments. In the last few years, repeated exposés by the press have aroused concern over institutions that have a repressive and demoralizing effect on their inmates. There is little doubt, as Braginsky and Braginsky (1971) noted, that the retarded person is forced to act stupid in many institutions in order to satisfy the staff. Many of these institutions teach the retarded persons to be patients rather than prepare them to function in the community.

The effects of institutionalization are not always deleterious. Institutions vary considerably, and the effects of institutionalization vary with the individual's pre-institutional life experiences, the environment of the institution, and the sex and diagnosis of the individual (Balla, Butterfield, and Zigler 1971). In more modern institutions, such as the development centers in California, training methods are used to improve the function of even the profoundly retarded (Rivera 1972). The trend toward smaller regional centers in the community, sheltered workshops, and programs for subsidized employment of the retarded have been extremely helpful.

Child may feel worthless, depressed, and helpless

Many institutions force the retarded person to act stupid

Teachers of special education classes must have a positive attitude toward the "retarded" child's capacity to learn.

Modification of Retardate Behavior

Although it may not be feasible to eliminate completely the cognitive deficits in severely or moderately retarded individuals, their skills can be enhanced, and they can be taught many social-interaction and self-help skills. It should not be automatically assumed that all of the deviant behavior exhibited by retarded persons is due to their cognitive deficits. Deviant behavior in retarded individuals comes from a variety of sources. As Zigler (1971) noted, much of

it is a product of emotional and motivational states. Consequently, treatment programs aimed at both facilitating academic performance and adjusting retarded people to their environment are crucial.

One method of achieving these goals has been the creation of self-contained special education classes. In general, the theory of these classes is that, since retardates learn at a slower rate, they should not be subjected to the demands of a regular classroom situation. Because of their special problems, special curricular materials and techniques are needed and are best implemented in small classes by specially trained teachers. These classes are provided in res-

disorders having organic causes or results

idential schools for the retarded, in special schools in the community, and in special classes in public schools. In some cases, the teaching methods used in special education classes follow behavior modification principles and use specific techniques to handle deviant behavior.

The desirability of special classes, as found in most schools, has been questioned. The individual placed in a self-contained special education class is labeled retarded and is clearly identified as such by peers. This labeling often encourages stigmatization and rejection of the child by peers. Consequently, the retarded person and the normal peer may view attendance in a special class as degrading. Moreover, teachers may regard the child attending a special education class as incapable of significant learning, and the child may fall further behind in academic skills. Because of such factors, special educators are advocating returning the retarded individual to regular classes.

With severely and moderately retarded individuals who have minimal verbal and social-interaction skills, special methods of behavior change are required. In particular, behavior modification has focused on self-help skills, toilet training, mealtime behavior, verbal behavior, social interaction, and classroom behavior.

The acquisition of very simple skills, such as dressing and feeding, are crucial for severely retarded children. Minge and Ball (1967) have devised a detailed step-by-step program for shaping dressing behavior. The steps include behavior such as attending, coming to the technician, sitting down, remaining seated, and removing and putting on various articles of clothing. Using food as a reinforcing stimuli, these authors were successful in teaching six girls with an average IQ of 16 to dress themselves.

Watson (1973) has also described in detail how to teach children to dress. They are taught in a backward fashion in very small steps at their own pace. They are first taught to complete the last sequence in the chain of behavior; for example, in taking off a shirt they first learn how to take it off the wrist. In successive sessions the child is taught to add, one at a time, each step preceding the step already learned. For example, the child may be completely dressed except for shoes. The child is then asked to put on the shoes and reinforced for doing so. Later, the child is required to put on socks and shoes before reinforcement. Next, the child is dressed in pants and underclothes and required to put on a shirt followed by socks and shoes before reinforcement. Other self-help skills, such as making a bed, taking a shower, and being on time, can also be shaped (Spradlin and Girartheau 1966).

We discussed the acquisition of appropriate toilet training in Chapter 12. Use of these techniques with retardates has been illustrated by Mahoney, Van Wagenen and Myerson (1971). Each child wore a pair of pants equipped with a transistor that signaled the child with a buzzer to go to the toilet whenever urine flowed. The children were taught the following sequence of toileting behavior: (1) walking to the commode in response to the signal (2) lowering their pants (3) sitting on the toilet or taking the male stance facing the toilet (4) pulling up their pants and (5) practicing the behavioral sequence without the aid of the auditory signal.

Messy table manners and eating behavior often cause a retardate to be viewed as an animal rather than a child. Therefore, teaching desirable mealtime behavior is also necessary. Using a natural punishment contingency (interruption of the behavior as soon as it begins), Hendrickson and Doughty (1967) eliminated five types of undesirable mealtime behavior in four profoundly retarded children. These behaviors were (1) eating too fast, (2) eating with the hands, (3) stealing food from others' trays, (4) hitting each other at mealtime, and (5) throwing food and trays or deliberately spilling food. The frequency of undesirable eating behavior was drastically reduced in thirteen weeks.

Whitman, Mercurio, and Caponigri (1970) used behavioral principles to increase social interaction with two severely retarded, withdrawn children. In training sessions conducted by two undergraduates,

EMR classes tend to stigmatize the child

Dressing behavior can be shaped

Undesirable eating behavior can be reduced

the boy and the girl sat three feet from each other to roll a ball back and forth between them. Initially, they had to be passively shaped or guided in the motion of rolling the ball. They were then taught to pass a block from one to another and later to two children who were brought into the training session after about six weeks. (Both of these children had increased their rate of social interaction.) In a similar manner, verbal behavior can also be increased in children who either are mute or engage in bizarre or unintelligible speech. Cook and Adams (1966) used a procedure in which the child was first taught to attend, then to emit any verbal behavior. Gradually words and sentences were shaped in the retarded child.

A major prerequisite for the acquisition of academic skills is appropriate classroom behavior. The child has to be taught to engage in behavior that allows learning. These behaviors involve attention, self-control, and cooperation. Disruptive behaviors in the classroom have been the focus of much attention for behavior modifiers who have used time-out, tangible reinforcers, and tokens to shape appropriate classroom behavior. Unfortunately, eliminating disruptive behavior may not facilitate the acquisition of academic skills, which takes a second place in these programs. However, in their work with four highly disruptive but educable retarded boys, ages twelve to thirteen, Ayllon, Layman, and Burk (1972) have shown that reinforcement of academic behavior alone may result in reducing disruptive behavior. In their program tokens were given to the children immediately after they engaged in the desired academic behavior. Tokens could be exchanged for candy, puzzles, conversation with a friend, and similar rewards. The boys were not given rewards for good behavior in class but for being *on target* with the assigned academic task. Not only did disruptive behavior decrease, but within nineteen hours of reinforcement contingent upon academic performance, reading comprehension improved from a preprimer to a second-grade level for two boys and from a first-grade to a fourth-grade level for the other two. Thus, rewarding a child for being *on task* with academic work may be sufficient to eliminate disruptive classroom behavior.

When academic learning behavior is reinforced, disruptive behavior is not a problem

Summary

The prime characteristics of retarded individuals are a slower rate of cognitive development and a lower ultimate level of intellectual achievement. How these individuals adjust to their environment is determined by intellectual functioning and social competence. Mental retardation is defined by the combination of three criteria: (1) lowered intellectual functioning, (2) deficits in adaptive behavior, and (3) early onset of the disorder. There are four levels of mental retardation: mild, moderate, severe, and profound. There are two major types of mental retardation: that caused by physical diseases or injuries and that associated with no known organic cause (cultural-familial retardation).

In cultural-familial mental retardation the major evidence of the disorder is lowered intellectual functioning. Cases of this kind include 75 percent of mental retardates and may not be diagnosed until they enter school. This disorder has been consistently shown to be associated with poverty. However, a minority among lower socioeconomic class individuals give birth to the majority of retarded children. The explanations for this disorder have aroused controversy similar to that concerning the determinants of intelligence. Although a genetic basis for cultural-familial retardation has received support from many studies, most of these studies are scientifically unsound. Furthermore, environmental conditions can either suppress or enhance intellectual functioning. For example, the Milwaukee project, which enriched the environment of the experimental group, resulted in children from lower-class families increasing their IQs, on an average, twenty to thirty points over the no-treatment control group.

Any factor that interferes with the physiological integrity of the central nervous system can cause mental retardation. This type of mental retardation is a by-product of an organic disease or illness. There are over 200 different physical factors that can cause mental retardation. The mental retardation associated with organic causes accounts for the majority of the more severely and profoundly retarded cases. It is usually detected shortly after birth.

Down's syndrome is the most common type of mental retardation associated

disorders having organic causes or results

with organic condition. It has been called mongolism because of the physical features it produces. Individuals with this condition are highly susceptible to diseases and infections and often have congenital heart defects and a short life expectancy. This condition is due to a chromosomal abnormality, called trisomy-21, in which the twenty-first set of chromosomes contains three rather than two chromosomes. The cause of this chromosomal abnormality is not known, but the incidence of Down's syndrome increases with the age of the mother. The condition can now be detected prenatally by amniocentesis.

Phenylketonuria (PKU) is a rare metabolic disease associated with a deficiency of phenylalanine-hydroxylase that causes phenylalanine and its derivitive, phenylpyruvic acid, to accumulate and produce irreversible brain damage. If this condition is detected early, a diet low in phenylalanine can be prescribed, and the deterioration process can be arrested.

Cretinism results from an endocrine imbalance resulting from a malfunction of the thyroid gland associated primarily with iodine deficiency. Preventive measures such as the use of iodized salt have greatly reduced the incidence of cretinism. Early treatment with synthetic thyroid hormones is also useful in alleviating this condition.

Microcephaly is caused by a variety of conditions including recessive genes, X-ray exposure, and birth injuries. Hydrocephaly is a rare condition in which an abnormal amount of cerebrospinal fluid accumulates within the cranium and causes damage to the brain tissue and enlargement of the head. This condition may develop in infancy, early childhood, or even prenatally. Any number of factors can cause hydrocephaly. The most successful type of treatment is surgery, which allows the brain fluid to be drained.

Prevention is of prime importance in mental retardation, particularly the avoidance of environmental conditions that increase the possibility of intellectual malfunction. Enrichment programs such as the Milwaukee project for socially deprived individuals could be helpful in reducing the incidence of cultural-familial retardation.

Mental retardation causes severe problems for the family because of guilt, denial, and the social stigma associated with the condition. Family counseling to help the family adjust to the retardate's condition as well as handle their own emotional reactions is extremely important in these cases. Occasionally, institutionalization is required. Institutions for retarded individuals vary widely in their effect on the retarded person's adjustment.

Cognitive functioning, even in severely and moderately retarded individuals, can be enhanced. Many can be taught social interaction and self-help skills. Not all deviant behavior in these individuals is a function of their cognitive deficits. Treatment programs of various types, including special education classes, have been aimed at facilitating the academic and social adjustment of these individuals. Specific target behaviors such as self-help skills, toilet training, mealtime behavior, verbal behavior, social interaction, and classroom behavior have been enhanced with behavior modification techniques that consist of breaking the behavior down into small components and teaching the individual the desired behavior in a detailed, step-by-step program supplemented by tangible as well as social reinforcers.

Key Concepts

amniocentesis

apathy-futility pattern

cretinism

cultural-familial retardation

Down's syndrome (mongolism)

hydrocephaly

idiot savant

mental retardation

microcephaly

phenylketonuria

social competence

1. What are the three criteria of lowered intellectual functioning used to define mental retardation?

2. What are the four levels of mental retardation? How do they differ?

3. What is the distinction between the two major types of mental retardation?

4. What is the scientific objection to the genetic hypothesis of intelligence?

5. What is the environmental hypothesis of intelligence?

6. How does enriching a child's environment affect the child's intellectual functioning?

7. What is Down's syndrome? What causes it?

8. What are the causes of PKU? Cretinism? Microcephaly? Hydrocephaly?

9. How did Ayllon reduce disruptive classroom behavior in educable retarded boys?

disorders having organic causes or results

organic brain disorders 18

Key Topics

Primary symptoms of organic brain
    disorders

Localization hypothesis of brain
    function

Three types of aphasia

Grand mal and petit mal epilepsy

Syphilis

Concussions, contusions,
    lacerations, and hematomas

Toxic causes of organic brain
    disorders

Thyroid and adrenal gland
    disturbances and brain tumors

Atherosclerosis

Alzheimer's disease, Pick's
    disease, Parkinson's disease,
    and Huntington's chorea

Organic etiology of senile dementia

Well-organized patterns of behavior that deal efficiently with the demands of an ever-changing environment require a healthy, normally functioning central nervous system. Diseases or injury to the brain usually produce temporary or permanent disruption of these behavior patterns, particularly the cognitive functions. Obviously all behavior, normal or not, depends on brain function. The difference between *organic brain syndromes* and other types of behavioral disorders is that the organic brain syndromes occur as a result of change in the *structure* of or alterations in normal physiological processes in the brain.

The type of behavior observed in organic brain syndromes depends on the location, the rate of onset, the progression, and the duration of the brain pathology. When the injury or disease is *focal* or restricted to one area of the brain, the behavioral deficit may be quite specific, perhaps a motor disorder or loss of speech, and the type of abnormal behavior that occurs will depend on where the lesion is. When the damage is *generalized*, a much more pervasive pattern of deviant behavior may occur.

A brain disorder may also be either **acute** or **chronic**. If the disorder is acute, the impaired brain functioning is reversible and usually has a rapid onset. If it is chronic, the damage is irreversible and often slow in onset.

The extent of behavioral disorganization caused by an organic brain disorder is directly affected by the premorbid adjustment of the individual. Minor brain damage can cause severe maladjustment in the psychologically fragile individual, but major damage may have little impact on the well-integrated person.

Primary Symptoms of Organic Brain Disorders

The organic brain disorders can be viewed in two ways: either in terms of the causes of the disorder—such as infection, neoplasms, brain trauma, or other conditions—or in terms of patterns of behavior that indicate brain damage. DSM II used the first

Local injury leads to a specific behavioral deficit

Delirium is a disorder of attention

Memory disturbances also occur . . .

method of classification, while DSM III emphasizes the second. For our purposes we shall describe the patterns of behaviors indicating organic brain syndromes and then, later in the chapter, give examples of disorders caused by specific pathological agents. In general, the symptoms of brain damage involve an impairment of orientation, memory, intellectual functioning, and emotions, as well as loss of control of primitive impulses.

Delirium

Delirium is the rapid onset of disturbances of attention, memory, and orientation. Reduced wakefulness or insomnia, perceptual disturbances, and increases or decreases of psychomotor activity also appear. This syndrome is often an acute brain syndrome caused by agents such as toxic substances but may result from a variety of organic causes whose principal effect is a disorder of attention.

The disorder of attention in delirium is manifested by an inability to sustain attention to various stimuli or to engage in goal-directed thinking or goal-directed behavior. Very simple activities or tasks may not be continued for any length of time because attention wanders. In severe cases, attention cannot be maintained for more than a few moments. Consequently, thinking may appear fragmented and disjointed. Speech may become incoherent as the individual *perseverates* or switches from one subject to another and loses the train of thought and reasoning. Reasoning and goal-directed behavior of any complexity are thus impossible.

Disturbances of memory that result from the short attention span may also occur. A difficulty in registering new information and an inability to retain it may also occur and cause a short-term-memory deficit. The individual may be unable to remember information after a few minutes. Long-term-memory deficits may also be present, since the individual cannot focus on the cues necessary to retrieve information. These memory deficits may be *retrograde* (impairment of recall or memories of events prior to onset of delirium) or *anterograde* (deficits in information registra-

disorders having organic causes or results

tion following the onset of delirium), or both. The individual usually has difficulty recalling any of the experiences during the delirium. Because of inattentiveness to environmental events, the individual may be confused and suffer a time, place, or person disorientation.

Frequently, disturbances in arousal result in reduced wakefulness varying from simple drowsiness to coma. In other individuals, delirium may be manifest in an excessively alert state and difficulty in sleeping. Fluctuation of arousal or alternating from one state to the other is not unusual. During sleep vivid dreams and nightmares may occur.

Perceptual disorders are common, and the individual may experience a variety of misinterpretations, illusions, or hallucinations. The sensory misperceptions or hallucinations are often visual but can occur in other sensory modalities as well. Other disorders of higher cortical function that are commonly observed in delirium include difficulty in naming objects (*dysnomia*) and impaired writing ability (*dysgraphia*).

The onset of a delirium is rapid, usually within hours or days. The symptoms of cognitive impairment may fluctuate unpredictably, and individuals may experience lucid intervals during which they are more attentive and rational. Any number of factors can cause delirium, including systemic infections, metabolic disturbances, substance abuse, drug withdrawal, postoperative states, and brain trauma. The duration of the disorder is usually brief but varies with the causal agent. Individual reaction to this disorder varies from anxiety and depression to suicide attempts.

Dementia

Dementia, as contrasted to delirium, is relatively slow in onset. But with some causal agents such as head trauma, it may appear quite suddenly. It is associated with a chronic brain syndrome in which there is a clear deterioration of previously acquired intellectual abilities that interferes with social or occupational functioning, memory, abstract thinking, judgment, and impulse control. Dementia may be progressive, static, or reversible, although the term implies a progressive and irreversible condition. Reversibility depends on the pathological condition and the timely application of effective treatment.

The most obvious feature of dementia is a disruption of memory. The memory losses can be for ongoing events and new learning (**anterograde amnesia**) or past events (**retrograde amnesia**). In the early stages, the individual may hesitate in response to questions or have to have questions repeated several times to facilitate memory. Forgetting telephone numbers, names, directions, events of past days, and plans for the future are typical. The individual may leave tasks unfinished because of failure to remember to return if the chore is interrupted. In advanced stages of deterioration even remote memory is severely impaired and only birth dates and knowledge of immediate family members can be recalled.

Disruption of memory

Impairment of abstract reasoning is also common. The individual has difficulty in generalizing, synthesizing, and differentiating, and thus, in logical reasoning and concept formation. These deficits are particularly evident in coping with novel tasks under time pressure. Consequently, individuals with this disorder may avoid situations and tasks that involve processing of novel or complex information and respond to such situations with anxiety and irritability. The individual's responses to situations tend to be controlled by specific environmental stimuli (concrete events) rather than more abstract cognitive processes (Goldstein 1939).

Impairment of abstract reasoning

Other major features of this disorder are impairment in judgment and loss of control of impulses. Individuals with this disorder may neglect personal appearance and hygiene and disregard conventional rules of social conduct. For example, they may engage in use of crude language, may attempt overt sexual contact with strangers, or may manifest asocial behavior such as shoplifting. Such behavior may represent a real change in personality characteristics for the individual who goes from being extremely cautious to extremely reckless. This type of impairment of judgment and impulse control is characteristic in dementias caused by frontal lobe lesions.

Impairment of judgment and impulse control

A number of associated features of dementia such as vague, stereotyped speech with frequent naming errors may, if extreme, make the individual almost totally incomprehensible. The performance of complex motor tasks and gestures may also be difficult. If this deficit is severe, *apraxia* (impairment of motor abilities) may result, and the individual may be unable to dress unaided or perform other motor functions.

Personality changes

The personality changes occurring in dementia may be either an accentuation or alteration of premorbid personality traits. Thus, individuals may become apathetic when previously they had been active or they may display more marked compulsive, histrionic, or paranoid traits than before. Individuals may react adversely to these deficits. They may become anxious and depressed. They may attempt to conceal or compensate for perceived intellectual deficits by social withdrawal, excessive orderliness, or the tendency to tell the same stories with endless details to avoid exposure of memory gaps. In some cases, they may attempt to blame others for their deficits and become extremely paranoid. In severe dementia, individuals become less aware of and less concerned about their handicaps. These individuals are particularly responsive to physical and social stress, which may aggravate their intellectual and emotional deficits.

This type of disorder can occur at almost any age of life, but before the age of three or four a child so affected is usually diagnosed as mentally retarded. Dementias in childhood are relatively rare; they are far more common among the elderly. This disorder can be caused by neurological diseases, head trauma, presenile and senile dementias, brain tumor, and various other physical diseases and injuries.

Amnestic Syndrome

Delusions may be poorly formed or highly organized

Amnestic syndrome is diagnosed in the absence of a dementia or delirium and is characterized primarily by short-term memory disturbances. These disturbances are assumed to occur because the individual is unable to consolidate memory into permanent memory storage or is unable to retrieve

Short-term memory disturbance

memory from storage. Therefore, new information cannot be retained for more than a very brief interval, usually less than twenty-five minutes, and events that occurred prior to this time cannot be recalled. However, the individual is able to remember events immediately after they occur. The best test for this memory malfunction is a digit-span task in which the individual is instructed to listen closely while the examiner gives a series of numbers, which the individual must then repeat. Individuals with this disorder can usually perform the task adequately. However, if they are asked to recall three names of objects presented to them twenty-five or thirty minutes previously, they cannot.

Memory for events that occurred before the onset of the symptom may also be impaired (retrograde amnesia), but usually remote memories are better preserved than more recent ones. If the degree of amnesia is severe, it may result in disorientation and confusion. **Confabulation**, filling in the memory gaps with invented stories, is sometimes resorted to. Occasionally, the individual denies the memory deficits, despite evidence of their existence. Individuals with amnesia may be apathetic, lack initiative, and be emotionally bland.

Amnestic syndrome is rare. It occurs when any pathological process causes bilateral damage to the limbic structure located in the diencephalon and temporal lobe. These pathological processes may include head trauma, surgical interventions, anoxia, thiamine deficiency, and chronic alcoholism (APA 1980).

Organic Delusional Syndrome

Organic delusional syndrome is diagnosed only when there is clear evidence of a particular organic etiology and the individual does not exhibit the behavior associated with organic hallucinosis, delirium, or dementia. The delusions occur in a state of full wakefulness or alertness and vary from simple, poorly formed paranoid delusions, as are sometimes seen with brain tumors, to highly organized paranoid delusional states similar to those seen in an acute schizophrenic disorder caused by amphetamines (*amphetamine psychosis*). The associated features are mild cognitive impairment; language or communication disorders such as incoherence and tangentiality; perplexity; abnormality of psychomotor activity such as pacing, rocking, or immobility; or ritualistic or stereotyped behavior. Depression is also common.

Organic Hallucinosis

Organic hallucinosis is diagnosed when there is clear evidence for an organic basis for hallucinations that occur in a state of wakefulness and alertness and when there is no reason to suspect other organic brain syndromes. The type of hallucinations varies with the etiological agent, individual differences, and social surroundings. Hallucinogenic drugs and alcoholism are common causes, but sensory deprivation produced by deafness, blindness, or experimental situations can also produce hallucinations, as can seizures focused in the temporal and occipital lobes. Any sense modality may be involved, although auditory hallucinations are most common. Hallucinogenic drugs usually cause visual hallucinations, while the reaction to alcohol is more commonly auditory hallucinations. The duration of these hallucinations depends on causal agents and may be from hours to years. The hallucinations may be pleasant or frightening with anxiety and depression. The individual may be firmly convinced that these hallucinations are real.

Organic Affective Syndrome

Organic affective syndrome is diagnosed when the behavior resembles a depressive or manic episode but has a clearly defined organic factor and does not meet the criteria for other organic brain syndromes. The severity of this syndrome ranges from mild forms of affective syndromes to severe or psychotic states. If delusions or hallucinations are present, they resemble those associated with the affective disorders.

This reaction is often caused by toxic or metabolic factors. Some drugs such as the hallucinogens, reserpine, and methyldopa can cause a depressive reaction. Hormonal disorders, carcinoma of the pancreas, viral illness, and direct damage to the brain by trauma or tumor may all cause this reaction.

Organic Personality Syndrome

The major characteristic of the **organic personality syndrome** is a marked change in personality characteristics that is clearly associated with an organic cause in the absence of behaviors observed in other organic brain syndromes. The particular alteration of behavior patterns depends on the nature and the location of the pathological process. A common reaction is increased emotional lability, impairment in social judgment, and difficulty in controlling primitive impulses. The individual may become belligerent, have temper outbursts, indulge in sudden episodes of crying with little or no provocation, or display socially inappropriate behavior or marked apathy and indifference. The individual may lose interest in usual hobbies and appear unconcerned with events occurring in the immediate environment. These latter two symptoms are associated with damage to the frontal lobes and have sometimes been referred to as the *frontal lobe syndrome*. Some individuals may become very suspicious and show paranoidlike behavior. Associated features include irritability and mild cognitive impairment. This disorder can result from almost any pathological process such as tumors, trauma, vascular accidents, or any similar event. A less common cause is temporal lobe epilepsy. Drugs such as steroids or an endocrine disorder may also cause this type of reaction.

These patterns of behavior are associated with impairment of the brain's integrity. Once a physiological malfunction has been clearly established, an attempt must be made to determine the type of causal agent so as to predict duration, course, and remedial procedures.

Secondary Symptoms of Organic Brain Disorders

In addition to the direct deficits organic brain syndromes produce, there may also be severe emotional reactions to the personal and socioeconomic consequences. It

Different agents may produce hallucinations of different sense modalities

Frontal lobe syndrome

Secondary symptoms
are reactions
to the consequences
of the cognitive deficits

is very difficult to distinguish symptoms that are directly due to the brain disorder from those that are *secondary* or are a reaction to it. This distinction may not be important when the disorder is extremely severe or terminal, but assessment of the reactive features in individuals who have relatively mild deficits is important in terms of rehabilitation.

How individuals respond to their deficits depends on their previous pattern of adjustment, educational level, interpersonal relationships, and other factors as well as the type and severity of the brain syndrome. Individuals with extreme damage to brain tissue may show little disorganization of behavior, while those with minor injuries may show complete behavior decompensation. It is not unusual for the individual with a brain syndrome to become depressed, anxious, irritable, or suicidal. Compulsive individuals tend to be particularly disturbed by their reduced cognitive capacity or their perceptual anomalies because they fear loss of control. With pronounced memory losses, some individuals may respond by marked orderliness, which helps them to maintain some degree of control of their lives. In individuals who are already suspicious and distrustful, cognitive impairment may cause paranoid attitudes and delusions. These individuals may accuse others of stealing their possessions, blame external agents for their intellectual or perceptual deficits, and physically attack others. Some display euphoria and jocularity, but others display apathy. *Circumstantiality* (talking around the point) and confabulation are often used as attempts to conceal gaps in memory. Withdrawal and decreased social activity out of fear that someone will discover their deficits is not unusual in some individuals. Again, previous adjustment and behavior patterns are crucial variables in the kind of behavior displayed in brain syndromes. These secondary features often require psychological interventions.

Relation of brain structures
and functions determines
evaluation

Assessment of Brain Disorders

When a brain syndrome is suspected, a complete physical and neurological examination is required. Neurological examinations consist of checking various reflexes, examining the retina for any blood vessel damage, and evaluating motor coordination and perception. Other procedures include skull X rays, which often detect tumors; brain scans for similar purposes; and electroencephalographs (EEG) to detect abnormalities in the brain's electrical activity. If the brain damage is severe or generalized, detecting and diagnosing the individual's condition is not usually difficult. However, if the alteration in brain functioning and structure is subtle, the brain injury may be difficult to detect by direct measurements. In these cases it is often helpful to have the individual examined by a clinical psychologist using a neuropsychological battery of tests.

One such test used to detect organic brain damage is the Bender Visual Motor Gestalt Test, which may be seen in Figure 18–1. This test involves sequentially copying nine geometric designs. Inability to reproduce the gestalt of the Bender is a useful indication of organic brain syndromes, particularly those that involve the right parietal lobes, but normal performance does not insure the absence of cerebral disease (Garron, Cheifetz, and Garron 1965).

A more elaborate neuropsychological evaluation has been developed by Reitan (1966) on the basis of a battery of tests originally developed by Halstead (1947). This battery taps a number of different functions. Evaluation of performance on the battery is determined by knowledge of the relationship between certain brain structures and their functions, as illustrated in Figures 18–2 and 18–3. For example, control of speech and language tends to be localized in the left cerebral hemisphere. A deficit in the aphasia screening test suggests a lesion in this area. Another test, finger tapping, is controlled by a brain area just in front of the central sulcus. With this battery the clinical psychologist is able, in

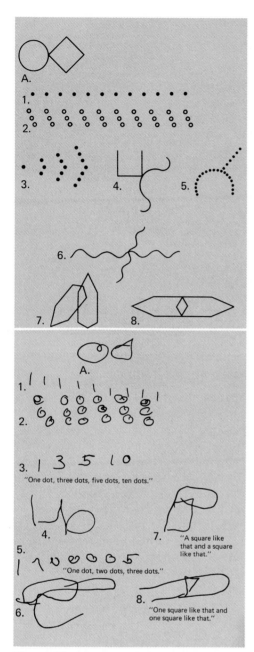

Figure 18–1 Bender Gestalt Test and test results of a thirty-year-old male with dementia paralytica.

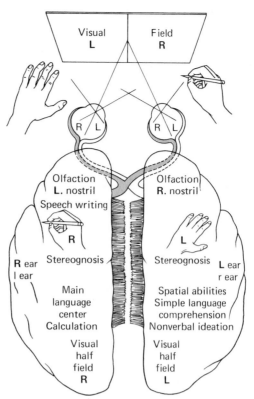

Figure 18–2 Schematic diagram of visual fields, optic tracts, and associated brain areas, showing left and right lateralization of functions in humans. Note that each hemisphere specializes in certain functions.

successfully than any single laboratory test such as the EEG, X ray, or brain scan. As a supplementary diagnostic procedure in cases of subtle brain injury, neuropsychological examinations are often useful.

Focal Lesions and Localization of Function

Experts agree that sensory and motor functions are controlled by specific areas of the brain, but they disagree over other psychological functions. Certain scientists believe in a strict **localization of function** and attempt to discover the areas of the brain that are responsible for specific behaviors, or map the brain in terms of behavioral functions (Kleist 1962). Other theorists believe that there is very little localization of function outside the primary sensory and motor

some cases, to locate the area of the brain that has been affected by injury. Reitan (1964), for example, identified the location of a lesion in about 70 percent of his attempts with sixty-four brain-damaged patients. Filskov and Goldstein (1974) used the Reitan test battery in a study of eighty-nine patients who had various types of cerebral disorders. The battery predicted both the location and the type of pathology more

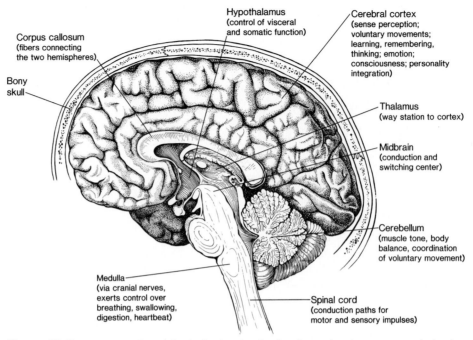

Figure 18–3 A cross section of the brain showing the functions of various areas and structures.

Mass action hypothesis: little localization of function outside primary sensory and motor areas

areas (the *mass action hypothesis*) (Goldstein 1939). The implication of the two positions for evaluation and treatment of brain injury is obvious. The mass action hypothesis states that deficits in behavior associated with brain damage are determined by the *extent* of the damage rather than the specific *locus* of damage. On the other hand, the localization of function theory assumes that a specific behavioral deficit indicates that a specific area of the brain had been injured.

Localization theory: specific behavioral deficit indicates injury of a specific brain area

As is often the case, the truth is somewhat complex. Some functions like memory and reasoning seem to have little or no localization, while other functions such as language are a function of specific areas of the brain. For example, damage to the parietal area can cause left/right disorientation and a dressing apraxia in which the individual has difficulty matching left and right sides of clothing to correspondent body parts. Individuals with this type of damage often exhibit disturbed spatial orientation and get lost trying to find their way around a hospital ward or to a specific location (Benson and Geschwind 1973). Posterior parietal cortex damage, on the other hand, can cause difficulty with the compre-

One hemisphere is usually dominant

hension of words and thus result in difficulty in the acquisition of reading skills. It has also been suggested that damage to the frontal and prefrontal lobes causes difficulty with recent memory or delayed response and also with planning functions (Morgan 1965). These disorders will be further elucidated in our discussion of aphasia.

In formation, the brain is symmetrical with left hemisphere being very much like the right. However, most of us have a major and a minor hemisphere. The obvious example is handedness: most of us are right-handed. Ambidextrous individuals are rare. Some behavioral functions are lateralized; that is, one hemisphere is responsible for the behavior. For example, voluntary motor behavior is executed through the pyramidal nerve tracts, which cross from one side of the body to the opposite side of the brain. In other words, for a right-handed individual, the *left* motor cortex is the major or dominant hemisphere. In other functions such as the speech musculature, the activities are bilateral. That is, the tongue, the lips, and the vocal cords are controlled by both sides of the brain. In such functions, the sensory and motor nerve tracts do not cross over. With other functions, it is not clear whether both sides of the brain are used or only one.

The evidence suggests that control of psychological functions depends more on one hemisphere than on the other but that cerebral dominance varies with the type of function (Zangwill 1960). For example, the side that is dominant for speech may or may not be the side that is dominant for handedness. In general, the left hemisphere tends to be dominant in speech and verbal intelligence as it is for handedness. Thus, adults with left hemisphere damage experience difficulty with language behavior, but such difficulty is rare when damage is restricted to the right hemisphere, especially in right-handed people. However, the control of language functions is primarily in the left hemisphere even for about 65 percent of left-handed people.

The right hemisphere is usually dominant for nonverbal intellection. Damage restricted to the right hemisphere results in deficits in spatial ability with the result that individuals with right hemisphere damage have difficulty copying geometric designs and recognizing pictures they have been shown previously. Thus, individuals with right-side lesions do more poorly on tests like the Wechsler Block Designs because these tests require visual-spatial abilities.

Such findings have important implications for brain injuries. For example, they show that individuals with a lesion in the nondominant side are less likely to show a verbal deficit than those with a lesion in the dominant side. Moreover, research also shows that if the dominant side for speech is injured, the formerly nondominant side can begin to mediate speech patterns, particularly if the damage occurs in childhood (Roberts 1958). Table 18-1 shows the relative strengths of the brain hemispheres.

Aphasia

Aphasia is impairment in speech, language, and communication as a result of specific lesions in the language areas of the brain,

Table 18-1 Relative Strengths of the Brain's Hemispheres

Right hemisphere (left hand)	Left hemisphere (right hand)
Intuitive	Rational
Spatial	Verbal
Wholistic	Analytic
Sensuous	Intellectual
Diffuse	Focal
Simultaneous	Sequential
Experience	Argument
Space	Time
Yin: The receptive	Yang: The creative
Eternity	History
Dark	Light
Night	Day
Left	Right

although massive damage can also cause aphasia. The location of the lesions will determine the exact language deficit, although aphasia is almost always related to damage to the dominant hemisphere, typically the parietotemporal area. There are fairly specific language and related sensory-motor disorders in most cases. Some of the more common are as follows:

1. **Acalculia** Loss of the ability to do simple arithmetic.
2. **Agraphia** Loss of the ability to express thoughts in writing.
3. **Apraxia** Loss of the ability to perform simple voluntary motor acts.
4. **Auditory aphasia** Loss of the ability to understand spoken words.
5. **Dyslexia** Loss of the ability to read.
6. **Expressive aphasia** Loss of the ability to speak required names.
7. **Formulation aphasia** Loss of the ability to formulate sentences.
8. **Nominal aphasia** Loss of the ability to recall the names of objects.
9. **Paraphasia** Garbled speech, marked by inappropriate word use, transposed sound, and ungrammatical sentences.

Cerebral dominance varies with the type of function

Left hemisphere: language ability

Right hemisphere: spatial ability

Aphasia related to dominant hemisphere

These syndromes can be grouped into three types of aphasia: *expressive, receptive,* and *amnesic.* In expressive aphasia a disturbance occurs in the ability to express oneself because of difficulty in the production of written or spoken symbols. Individuals with expressive aphasia may know what they want to say but be unable to say it. Included in this group is *apraxia,* since apraxia is the inability to guide muscle groups so that they execute a motor response. This condition does not involve a specific motor deficit but rather an impairment of the CNS (central nervous system) that causes loss of control over voluntary muscle groups. Generally, these disturbances of expressive behavior are thought to be a result of damage to the frontal or anterior portion of the brain (Osgood and Miron 1963).

Receptive aphasia is a disturbance of the reception of auditory and visual stimuli that renders the individual incapable of recognizing written or spoken words, familiar sounds, or common objects. Although the individual may perceive an object such as a book clearly, it may not have any significance. Receptive aphasias are assumed to result from damage to the posterior portion of the brain, including the auditory and visual projection system in the posterior occipital lobes (Osgood and Miron 1963).

Amnesic aphasia involves a disturbance in language patterns resulting from memory losses for names of objects. In this case, the individual may not be able to think of the right word for a common object such as a table or a chair. Amnesic aphasia rarely occurs in isolation, and both expressive and receptive aphasia usually involve some form of memory loss. It has been assumed that amnesic loss is associated with lesions in the frontal, temporal, or parietal lobes (Longerich and Bordeaux 1954).

Schuell (1974) has not found the distinction between various types of aphasia useful. She indicates that almost all aphasic persons show deficits in expressive, sensory, and memory functions. She also indicates that the basic deficit is a loss of access to words and their meaning as well as an inability to retain more than a few words at a time in a given thought sequence.

If damage to the dominant hemisphere occurs near birth, language functions can often be taken over by the other hemisphere. Aphasias resulting from damage to the dominant hemisphere during infancy or early childhood are likely to be more transitory than those resulting from similar damage occurring during later years (Osgood and Miron 1963).

Epilepsy

Epilepsy, a term derived from the Greek word epilipsia meaning seizure, denotes a disorder characterized by periodic convulsions that are due to a spontaneous discharge of neurons in one area of the brain and spreading to other areas. In epilepsy a hyperexcitable aggregate of neurons in the brain randomly discharges and causes abnormal electrical activity (Pincus and Tucker 1974). Epilepsy is actually a disorder caused by a variety of events. Two major types are *symptomatic epilepsy,* which develops following brain injury or disease, and *idiopathic epilepsy,* in which alterations of consciousness are due to unknown causes. The prevalence of epilepsy has been estimated at 29.8 cases per 100,000 (Ervin 1967); it is somewhat higher in males than in females.

Many epileptic attacks appear to occur spontaneously, but a variety of events in some cases can trigger an attack and an alteration of consciousness. Bright flickering lights such as those that can be provided by photic stimulation during an EEG examination or by a defective television can induce seizures (Livingston 1963).

Seizures are more likely to occur during sleep or drowsy states. For this reason, EEG diagnostic procedures use a sleep record to detect abnormal electrical brain activity.

disorders having organic causes or results

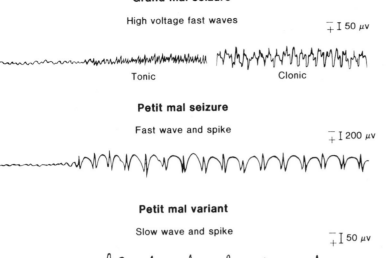

Grand mal seizure

High voltage fast waves

$\mp\ I\ 50\ \mu v$

Tonic   Clonic

Petit mal seizure

Fast wave and spike

$\mp\ I\ 200\ \mu v$

Petit mal variant

Slow wave and spike

$\mp\ I\ 50\ \mu v$

Psychomotor attack

High voltage square and six per second waves

$\mp\ I\ 50\ \mu v$

A   B   1 SEC.

Figure 18-4 EEG patterns of various types of epileptic seizures.

Alexander the Great as well as other historic leaders, such as Julius Caesar, suffered from epilepsy.

Other precipitating factors include hyperventilation, menstruation, withdrawal from anticonvulsant drugs, and emotional stress.

In some forms of epilepsy, sensations or auras such as abdominal pain, headaches, dizziness, spots before the eyes, humming or buzzing sensations, musical sounds, peculiar odors, and peculiar tastes warn of an impending attack. The aura often allows the person time to take precautions, such as lying down before the seizure activity spreads.

Most epileptic disorders (three of the four major types) can be detected by an EEG examination, since they represent abnormal changes in the electrical activity of the brain, as shown in Figure 18-4.

Grand Mal

Of the four major types of epilepsy, the **grand mal** is the most common. This is the one that typifies epilepsy to the general public, since it is the most dramatic form. In most cases, the seizure is preceded by an aura during which the individual experiences sensations such as numbness, tingling, or other unusual sensory or motor activity. The individual may then give a low cry or shriek and, if standing, become very rigid and fall in the direction he or she is leaning. The convulsions begin with the *tonic phase,* a period of ten to twenty seconds during which the muscles of the entire body become rigid, the jaw clinches, and breathing stops. This is followed by violent, rapid jerking movements of the arms, legs, and trunk (*clonic phase*). During the seizure the individual may bite the tongue and lose voluntary control over bladder and

Auras may precede epilepsy

Tonic phase and clonic phase

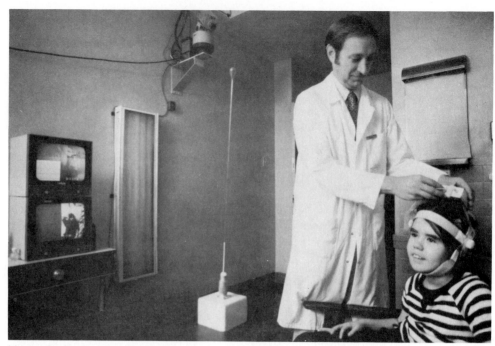

Most epileptic disorders can be detected by an electroencephalograph (EEG).

Petit mal common in children

bowel; breathing often becomes jerky or is temporarily suspended, and the face turns blue. The duration of the seizure may vary from less than a minute to thirty minutes or more. The frequency of these attacks varies from many times a day to once every several years. If the seizure is brief, the individual may return to normal functioning within minutes; but if it is long, the individual may pass into deep sleep, after which confusion, fatigue, headache, and nausea may occur. Upon awakening, the individual usually has no memory of the attack.

Petit Mal

A **petit mal seizure** involves a loss or alteration of consciousness lasting only a few seconds, after which the individual resumes normal activity. There are no obvious convulsions and, in some cases, the individual may not know that the attack occurred. The only apparent changes in behavior may be simply staring with a momentary loss of consciousness, rhythmic eye blinking, head nodding, jerking of the arms, or a sudden loss of posture. This disorder is most common in children between the ages of four and eight and usually disappears in pubescence. Children with petit mal attacks may also develop grand mal or other types of seizures in adolescence or adulthood (Boshes and Gibbs 1972).

Jacksonian

Jacksonian epilepsy begins in one part of the body, such as the face or the hand, and spreads to other parts of the body, causing seizure activity and a loss of consciousness. This effect, sometimes known as Jacksonian march, is caused by the spread of electrical disturbances from the focus of the hyperexcitable neurons in the cortex to neighboring neurons within the sensory or motor areas of the cortex (Penfield and Rasmussen 1950). In a few cases, there is a restriction in focus with seizures in that particular motor area. These seizures are typically related to tumor, vascular disease, or trauma in the side of the brain opposite the affected area of the body (Pincus and Tucker 1974).

disorders having organic causes or results

Psychomotor

Psychomotor seizures are caused by abnormal electrical discharges originating in the temporal lobes. It is characterized by a period of automatic behavior during which the individual may repetitively engage in a highly complex behavior sequence (Monroe 1970). During a psychomotor attack individuals appear to be in a kind of trance, after which they report distinct subjective experiences including alteration of mood, anxiety, compulsive thoughts of a disturbing nature, *déjà vu* experiences, visual distortion, dreamlike states or sensations, hallucinations of taste or smell, and abdominal pain (Pincus and Tucker 1974). In some cases they may show evidence of fearfulness or belligerence accompanied by temper outbursts. In rare cases, the belligerence is associated with violent crimes including murder. It is speculated that Vincent Van Gogh was having a psychomotor seizure when he cut off his ear.

As contrasted with other epileptic individuals, the person with psychomotor epilepsy tends to have a marginal adjustment. As a matter of fact, Boshse and Gibbs (1972) state that the majority of patients labeled as epileptic personalities are psychomotor epileptics, while individuals with other types of epilepsy usually have normal personalities.

Treatment of epilepsy usually consists of the administration of anticonvulsive drugs such as Dilantin and Phenobarbital. (The two drugs taken together are more effective than either taken separately.) If a tumor causes the seizures, surgery is indicated. In other cases of intractible seizures, surgical separation of the left and the right hemispheres has been performed in an effort to prevent abnormal electrical activity in one hemisphere from spreading to the other (Bogen and Vogel 1962). In cases in which emotional factors play a major role in precipitating the seizures, psychological intervention is warranted. Most individuals with epilepsy can live a normal life.

Recently, biofeedback techniques have been developed in an attempt to control seizures (Sterman 1973; Lubar and Bahler 1976; Seifert and Lubar 1975). The objective is to teach epileptic individuals to increase the occurrence of sensorimotor rhythm, a 12- to 14-Hz rhythm recorded over the sensorimotor cortex (the part of the cortex that lies roughly in a band across the top of the head between the ears and is associated with control of voluntary movement). Normally, individuals suffering from seizure disorders have very little of this activity present in the EEG. By using biofeedback to increase this activity, these individuals have been able in a number of cases to decrease seizure activity. Reduced seizure frequency is also associated with significant decreases in abnormal EEG activity and increases in the density of sensorimotor rhythm. Seizure activity does, however, seem to return gradually after biofeedback training (Finley 1976; Sterman, McDonald, and Stone 1974). Nevertheless, the initial work with biofeedback appears promising and suggests that alternative treatments for epilepsy may be developed in the future.

Biofeedback shows promise in controlling seizures

Brain Disorders Associated with Infections

Bacteria or viruses that invade the brain and destroy or damage nerve tissue can cause severe behavior disorders as a result of CNS dysfunction. These infectious diseases include *meningitis* (an infection of the covering of the brain); *encephalitis* (a direct invasion of the brain by infections); *acute viral encephalitis* (viral encephalitis with a sudden onset of symptoms); and *chronic encephalitis* (usually caused by a bacterial infection such as syphilis). Cerebral syphilis will be described as an example of these disorders.

Syphilis

Syphilis is almost always spread from person to person through forms of sexual intercourse, whether penile/vaginal coitus, fellatio, cunnilingus, or anogenital coitus.

Syphilis has decreased but is now increasing

First stage: chancre

Second stage: rash

Third stage: symptoms disappear

In rare cases, it may be contracted through kissing or from direct contact with open syphilitic sores or lesions. It can also be transmitted from mother to child during fetal development, the result being *congenital syphilis*. Before the discovery of penicillin, syphilis accounted for 10 to 20 percent of admissions to state hospitals for the mentally ill (Friedman, Kaplan, and Sadock 1972). The use of penicillin decreased this figure to less than 1 percent. However, in recent years, the number of reported cases of syphilis has doubled in the United States, and it is now estimated that there are 1,000,000 untreated cases in this country (Ford 1970).

The *spirochetes* (bacteria) of syphilis enter the body through breaks or scratches in the skin or through a mucous membrane such as the lining of the mouth or the genital tract. They systematically destroy internal organs in four well-defined stages. In the first stage, they multiply rapidly and in ten to twenty days cause a hard chancre or sore to appear at the point of infection. This usually takes the form of a pimple that feels hard to the touch or an open, ulcerated sore. If untreated, this sore, which may be so insignificant the person is unaware of its existence, disappears in four to six weeks. In the second stage, three to six weeks later, a copper-colored skin rash, which may be mild and transitory or more severe, covers the whole body. This rash looks like measles or smallpox and is responsible for the term *the great pox*. During this stage the individual may also have fever, headache, indigestion, loss of appetite, loss of hair in spots over the scalp, or other symptoms not usually associated with syphilis. In the third stage, or latent period, all symptoms disappear and the individual may feel cured. In actuality, the spirochetes have bored their way into the bloodstream where they multiply and spread throughout the body, attacking various internal organs and causing permanent degeneration. Attacked areas include the brain, bone marrow, spleen, lymph glands, or almost any organ tissue of the body. Blood vessels and nerve cells are favorite targets.

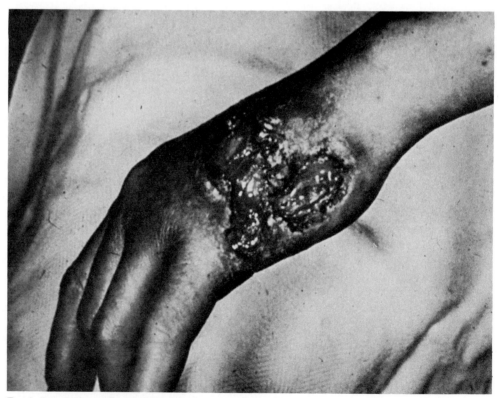

Ten to twenty days after syphilitic infection, a small chancre or open ulcerated sore appears.

disorders having organic causes or results

In the fourth stage the damage produced during the latent period begins to be manifested ten, twenty, or even thirty years after the infection. The degeneration caused by the spirochetes may become apparent in sudden heart failure, failure of vision, loss of motor coordination, or behavioral disturbances. For this reason, syphilis has been called the *great imitator* because it may produce a wide range of organic or behavioral symptoms.

There are three major types of cerebral syphilis: *general paresis, juvenile paresis,* and *meningovascular paresis.* Approximately 5 percent of untreated cases of syphilis eventually develop general paresis. The first symptom of **paresis** appears ten to fifteen years after the infection, although the time interval may be as short as two years or as long as forty. Unless the individual receives treatment, the outcome is always fatal, death occurring within two to three years after the initial symptoms.

Behaviorally, general paresis is associated with a wide range of symptoms. In the early stages the individual may become careless and inattentive, personal habits may show deterioration, concentration and judgment show marked change, and a blunting of affect may occur. As the disorder progresses, physical symptoms begin to appear. The pupils are irregular in size, and the pupillary reflex to light is sluggish or absent. Speech functions become disturbed with a stuttering and slurring of words. The individual may mispronounce a word such as "methodist episcopal" in a variety of ways. Tremors may be noted when the individual is writing, and other difficulties may occur in motor coordination. One symptom is a shuffling, unsteady walk referred to as *locomotor ataxia.* In addition to the motor symptoms and tremors, convulsive seizures may also appear. Memory deficits and a deterioration of general personality patterns may be progressive. The personality deterioration may appear as emotional reactions or marked euphoria, depression, or apathy. For this reason, clinical types of paresis are some-times called *expansive, depressed,* or *demented.* Why only one in twenty cases of untreated syphilis develops general paresis is not clear.

Juvenile paresis occurs in childhood or adolescence. This disorder is no longer a very common problem in the United States but is relatively common in other countries and contributes to a high infant mortality rate. The symptoms of juvenile paresis are similar to those in general paresis with progressive physical and psychological deterioration. The course of the disorder is around five years between the appearance of the initial symptoms and death. At one time syphilis accounted for more than half of all blindness in children at birth and was a primary cause of death for many infants during the first year of life.

Meningovascular syphilis differs from general paresis in that the syphilitic damage centers in the blood vessels and meninges of the brain rather than in the neural tissue. This disorder is rare. The major symptoms are persistent headaches, dizziness, blurring or doubling of vision, lethargy, confusion, and difficulty in concentration. The pupillary reflexes to light are diminished, and the knee-jerk reflex is accentuated. While speech and writing are usually not affected, convulsive seizures are common.

If the disorder is caught early before extensive cerebral damage, medical treatment is effective. The crucial factor is the prevention of infection or the early detection and treatment when infection has taken place. In this country facilities are provided for free diagnosis and treatment of syphilis. Physical examination before marriage and mandatory reporting of cases of syphilis by physicians to local health authorities are also helpful in detecting and preventing syphilis. Unfortunately, many individuals do not seek treatment, either out of ignorance or because of the stigma attached to venereal disease. Thus, one person can infect a multitude of others.

Fourth stage: permanent degeneration

Clinical types: expansive, depressed, demented

Early treatment is effective

Brain Disorders Associated with Trauma

The skull protects the brain and is capable of withstanding minor to moderate injuries with no discernible effects other than lacerations of the skin. However, a severe blow or injury does have acute and chronic effects on physiological and behavioral functions. There are four major types of trauma injuries: concussions, contusions, lacerations, and hematomas.

Concussion: disruption of circulatory and other functions

A *concussion* is caused by a sudden hard blow to the head that jars the brain and causes a disruption in circulatory and other physiological functions. The blow may also cause a loss of consciousness. On regaining consciousness, the individual may be confused and disoriented, show a loss of memory of the accident, and have a headache. If the injury is minor, the individual will recover within a few hours or days, but on occasion a transitory postconcussion syndrome occurs that consists of headaches, dizziness, fatigue, and inability to concentrate. Partial or total amnesia for the circumstances of the accident sometimes remains. The best example is the football player who is knocked unconscious during a game.

Contusion: brain is bruised

Cerebral *contusions* result from a blow so severe that the brain is pushed against the skull and bruised. The brain is usually pressed against the side of the skull opposite to the side receiving the blow. In addition to the symptoms that follow a concussion, there may be prolonged unconsciousness that lasts for hours, days, or even weeks and may involve more severe symptoms including delirium. When consciousness is regained, the individual complains of severe headaches, sensitivity to noise and light, dizziness, nausea, and weakness. While many of these symptoms disappear within a few days, others such as irritability may persist for longer periods and may be associated with impairment of intellectual and motor functions. This injury is common among boxers, who are constantly taking blows to the head that cause intracerebral

Laceration: rupture or tearing of brain tissue

Hematoma: collection of blood enclosed in a fibrous membrane

hemorrhaging or bleeding at the site of the damage. As a result of accumulated damage, boxers may become punch drunk and suffer from impaired memory, inability to concentrate, involuntary movements, and loss of body balance or equilibrium.

Cerebral *lacerations* are actual ruptures or tearing of the brain tissue that occurs in skull fractures or injuries by missiles such as bullets that penetrate the cranium. The immediate symptoms of cerebral lacerations are identical to those of contusion, although residual impairment of intellectual and motor functions may also occur. The effects of such injuries largely depend upon the extent and location of the damage. Some individuals may survive massive injury to cortical areas, but penetration of the brain stem systems can cause sudden death.

A *hematoma* is a collection of blood that becomes enclosed with a fibrous membrane. Hematoma occurs when the injury results in the rupture of a small vessel, causing gradual bleeding and the accumulation of a mass of blood. The hematoma may take days or weeks to develop. With some head injuries, a form of hematoma called a *subdural hematoma* (between the dura and the subarachnoid space or the linings of the brain) can occur with a buildup of blood that causes compression of brain tissue, resulting in pressure and intense headaches. If these subdural hematomas are not corrected by surgery, drowsiness, periods of unconsciousness, and coma may result.

Head injuries may cause chronic brain syndromes if the brain damage is extensive. The individual's general intellectual level may be reduced, especially if severe frontal lobe lesions occur. Very specific neurological and psychological deficits may follow localized brain damage to various brain systems, as mentioned before. For example, lesions in the occipital lobes may cause impaired vision, lesions in the parietal lobes may result in sensory aphasia, and so forth. In some cases, the individual may develop convulsive seizures and exhibit marked personality changes.

disorders having organic causes or results

Brain Disorders Associated with Toxic and Metabolic States

The brain is partially protected from toxic substances by a mechanism known as the *blood brain barrier*, which screens the flow of substances from the brain to the central nervous system. The blood brain barrier permits entry to substances essential for health and proper functioning, but a period of oxygen deprivation as well as certain toxins may impair the functioning of the barrier and result in brain disorders.

Many drugs, gases, or metals can produce brain damage, a common example being the bromide psychosis (Arena 1963). Bromides affect the functioning of the CNS by replacing chloride in the fluid surrounding nerve cells. Bromides are a common ingredient in many nonprescription sedatives such as sleeping pills or in medications used to alleviate headaches or the effects of excessive alcohol consumption. Symptoms of chronic bromide poisoning include weakness, coarse tremors of the hands, incoordination, headache, staggering gait, disturbed speech, mania, delirium, hallucinations, and coma. Unfortunately, many victims take medication containing bromides to relieve symptoms produced by the drug itself. Since behavioral changes accompanying bromide intoxication may simulate and be mistaken for schizophrenia, many of these individuals are admitted to mental hospitals (Arena 1963). Many different medications can cause similar results.

Lead is probably the most common heavy metal that has adverse effects on the central nervous system. The average individual is exposed daily to a minimal amount of lead in food, drink, and air. The average intake is around 0.33 milligram per person, but lead from exhaust fumes of automobiles has been increasing this daily intake (Derman 1970). Although a minimal amount of lead in the human system may not be harmful, high concentrations of lead can produce severe and sometimes permanent damage. In children the most common source of lead poisoning is eating paint flakes that contain lead. (These paints are now outlawed.) This exposure may lead to inflammatory and degenerative lesions in the brain.

Other toxic substances causing brain damage are mercury, found in many compounds used in medicine and agriculture, manganese, carbon monoxide, copper, and arsenic. Overexposure to X rays can also be dangerous, particularly in early pregnancy when X rays are dangerous to the developing organism, as we noted in Chapter 17.

Acute and chronic nutritional deficits can also cause brain dysfunction. These disorders, particularly deficiency of certain vitamins, cause degenerative changes similar to those observed in the degenerative diseases of the central nervous system. One example is pellagra, which is caused by a nicotinic acid deficiency. The result is neuron degeneration in the brain, which manifests itself behaviorally by irrational fear, depression, agitation, hallucination, disorientation, and intellectual deterioration. Beri beri is caused by a thiamin deficiency and treated by administration of this vitamin. This syndrome, associated with fatigue, weakened muscles, extreme lassitude, irritability, and insomnia, was once common in the Far East because of an exclusive diet of polished (white) rice.

Two other disorders associated with nutritional deficits are **Wernicke's syndrome**, caused by a severe deficit of thiamin and marked by a sudden onset of drowsiness, paralysis of eye movements, and an inability to walk (Brody and Wilkins 1968) and **Korsakoff's psychosis**, which is primarily a memory disorder associated with a deficit in the vitamin B complex. The latter disorder is commonly observed in chronic alcoholics who develop lesions within the limbic system (Victor, Adams, and Collins 1971). The individual with Korsakoff's psychosis may retain normal abilities as well as established skills, but memory will be impaired, particularly for recent events. These deficits in memory may be concealed by confabulation.

Impairment of blood brain barrier leads to brain disorders

Bromides can lead to a vicious cycle

Nutritional defects can also cause brain dysfunction

Brain Disorders Associated with Endocrine Disturbances

Brain malfunction can be caused by underactivity or overactivity of the endocrine glands, resulting in a variety of symptoms. For example, developmental disorders of the pituitary gland can cause unusual acceleration or retardation of growth, resulting in giants or midgets. Thyroid dysfunctions, either oversecretion or undersecretion of the hormone thyroxin, produce physical pathologies and abnormal behaviors. For example, **hyperthyroidism** causes weight loss, tremor, tenseness, insomnia, emotional excitability, or impairment in concentration and other cognitive processes. Because of the intense anxiety and agitation common in this condition, it is often mistaken for an anxiety disorder. In severe cases, it causes a toxic reaction with delirium. **Hypothyroidism** is usually associated with iodine deficiency and leads to a condition commonly called **myxedema**. In myxedema the individual gains weight, becomes sluggish in action and thought, has difficulty in concentrating, and may show impairment for recent memory. Severe depression can result. Usually, these disorders are easily detected and early treatment eliminates the severe reactions.

Hyperthyroidism can be mistaken for an anxiety disorder

The *adrenal glands* consist of the *adrenal cortex*, which secretes steroids, and the *adrenal medulla*, which secretes adrenalin, a hormone important to emotions and stress reactions. Obviously, dysfunction of these glands will cause severe behavioral disorders. One example is **Addison's disease**, which is produced by a deficiency in the adrenal cortex and characterized by a variety of physiological disturbances including lowering of blood pressure, body temperature, and basic metabolic rate. Psychological symptoms include a lack of vigor, easy fatigability, depressed sexual functioning, headaches, irritability, lassitude, and lack of ambition. Another example is **Cushing's syndrome**, often caused by a tumor or abnormal growth on the adrenal cortex and resulting in oversecretion of cortisone. This syndrome is relatively

Adrenalin plays an important part in emotions and stress reactions

Brain tumor can cause absence of spontaneity, disinhibition and lability of affect, forced emotions

rare, occurring more often among young women. Symptoms include muscle weakness, fatigue, reduced sex drive, and headaches. A number of disfiguring body changes also occur, such as obesity, changes in skin color and texture, and spinal deformity. Adrenal disorders are usually treated with drugs. With early detection and treatment, the prognosis in adrenal disorders is highly favorable.

A number of other disorders that disturb endocrine balance and metabolic rate can produce behavioral pathology. These conditions include starvation, exhaustion, postpartum (post-childbirth) disorders, and postoperative surgical procedures.

Brain Disorders Associated with Brain Tumors

Neoplasms or new growth in the brain are composed of cells, fibers, and blood vessels. There are two major types of neoplasms: (1) *benign* brain tumors whose growth is slow, partially contained by surrounding brain tissue, and not likely to recur if surgically removed; and (2) *malignant* brain tumors, which show rapid growth, are likely to recur in spite of surgery, and are usually terminal. The effect of a brain tumor depends on its location, size, and rapidity of growth. Typical symptoms (which increase in severity as the tumor growth increases intracranial pressure) include persistent headache, vomiting, memory impairment, depression, and disorientation. Convulsive seizures, vomiting, sensorymotor losses, hallucinations, and an impairment of intellectual functioning are seen in later stages. If the growth of the tumor is not retarded, the individual is reduced to a vegetative stupor and dies. Three forms of emotional disturbances are common: (1) the absence of spontaneity, (2) disinhibition and lability of affect, often with euphoria, and (3) forced emotions, which are abruptly expressed and then terminated (Dobrokhotova 1968).

disorders having organic causes or results

Tumors in the special sensory areas of the brain may result in hallucinations of sight, hearing, taste, and smell. Visual hallucinations may involve vividly colored lights or various animals or other objects. In temporal lobe tumor, Lilliputian hallucinations in which the individual sees small figures are sometimes observed. Tumors of the olfactory pathways result in perception of peculiar odors such as that of rubber burning. Frontal lobe tumors often produce subtle peculiarities such as jocularity, punning, inability to concentrate, and a loss of inhibitions.

Brain Disorders Associated with Cerebrovascular Disorders

The brain is dependent on a continuous flow of blood to supply glucose and oxygen that enable brain cells to function. This requires a normal healthy cardiovascular system, and any changes in the blood supply may result in an acute or chronic brain syndrome. The brain is particularly sensitive to decreases in the supply of oxygen and requires about 20 percent of the oxygen used by the body in a resting state. If oxygen deprivation to the brain exceeds two minutes, the brain cells are damaged.

A number of brain disorders associated with the cardiovascular system originate in a process called **atherosclerosis.** This process is the result of two types of changes in the arteries, the first being *atheroma* or the depositing of fatty substances containing a large amount of cholesterol along the interior walls of the arteries. These deposits hinder the normal flow of blood. The second change is *thrombosis,* or the forming of blood clots inside the arteries. The effects of this process depend on which area of the brain has clogged arteries and whether it is also being supplied by nonaffected blood vessels. In *cerebral thrombosis,* a blood clot forms at the site narrowed by atherosclerosis, and the blocked circulation decreases

oxygen, builds up carbon dioxide, and damages neural tissues. The result may be a loss of consciousness or a stroke (*cerebral ischemia*). Temporary impairment of normal functioning occurs but permanent impairment may occur in prolonged episodes during which the affected neurons die. This type of cerebrovascular problem has the highest incidence.

If the process of atherosclerosis is progressive, surrounding tissues are increasingly deprived of blood, and degeneration occurs. This process is aggravated by other disorders such as diabetes or hypertension (Irving, Bagnall, and Smith 1970). The result is a series of minor cerebrovascular accidents until clinical signs of a chronic brain syndrome lead to a diagnosis of atherosclerotic dementia. In atherosclerosis the individual shows disturbances in speech, vision, recent memory, and in intellectual ability. Personality and emotional changes include frequent outbursts of crying, childlike demands, moodiness, depression, and other disturbances of emotion. This disorder usually occurs after age fifty, and the loss of memory is one of the earliest and most consistent signs. It is more common among men than among women (Agate 1970). There is no effective treatment, and the condition becomes progressively worse until a terminal cerebrovascular accident occurs.

Other types of cerebrovascular disorders include *cerebral embolisms* and *intracerebral hemorrhages.* In cerebral embolisms, a bloodclot becomes detached from a larger thrombus within the heart and travels in the bloodstream until it reaches a point at which the diameter of the blood vessel is smaller than the clot. A blockage of blood flow and consequent brain damage ensues. Intracerebral hemorrhages occur as a result of a circulatory disorder such as leukemia through rupture of an *aneurysm* (a weak point in the blood vessel), or as a consequence of repetitive and sudden changes in blood pressure in which the vessels are weakened and eventually burst. When hemorrhaging does occur, it may be at the base of the brain, which is concerned with vital

Atherosclerosis can cause crying, childlike demands, moodiness, depression

functionings such as breathing. In these cases, death occurs in 15 to 20 percent of patients with a first episode and almost 80 percent of those patients who suffer a second hemorrhage (McKissock, Richardson, and Walsh 1962). The physiological and psychological effects of these disorders vary with the extent and location of the trauma.

Brain Disorders Associated with Degenerative Diseases

Degenerative diseases involve a slow progressive physical deterioration of cells within the nervous system. Genetic factors seem to play an important role in the development of these diseases. When they begin in the forty-to-fifty age range, they are called presenile dementias. There are four major types of these presenile dementias: Alzheimer's disease, Pick's disease, Parkinson's disease, and Huntington's Chorea.

Alzheimer's Disease

Alzheimer's disease can resemble neurotic disorders

Alzheimer's disease is a degenerative disease in which cells in all areas of the cerebral cortex die. The frontal and temporal lobes are most often affected. The disorder is more common among women than among men and usually begins between forty and sixty-five; deterioration is progressive, and the disease is terminal. The initial symptoms resemble those found in neurotic disorders including anxiety, depression, restlessness, and sleep difficulties. Memory for recent events deteriorates, and as the disease progresses, all intellectual functioning deteriorates. The cause of the disease is apparently genetic (Pratt 1967). Since the pathological changes in the brain are similar to those in senile dementias (to be discussed later) there is a question whether Alzheimer's disease is a distinct disorder or an early onset of senile dementias.

Pick's disease involves typically the frontal lobes

Parkinson's disease leads to tremor and "pillrolling"

Pick's Disease

Pick's disease is a rare disorder that is very similar to Alzheimer's disease and occurs in the same age range. However, only a circumscribed area of the brain is usually involved, typically the frontal lobes. It is equally common in both men and women. Unlike other senile and presenile disorders, it involves little impairment of memory of recent events, perhaps because very little pathological change occurs in the *hippocampus*, a subcortical structure assumed to be important in memory of recent events. The disorders of behavior and emotions are similar to those that occur with other degenerative diseases.

Parkinson's Disease

Parkinson's disease may be caused by several different factors. It may occur at any time during the adult years but is more frequent between forty and sixty. The basic pathology of this disease appears to be a loss of neurons within the basal ganglia. Onset is marked by a tremor that appears first in one hand and progresses until both sides of the body are affected. Muscles in the limbs are particularly affected. One of the most frequent characteristics is the rhythmic "pillrolling" motion of the thumb and fingers which occurs in conjunction with pronounced tremors (three to five per second) of the hands. Muscular weakness and rigidity are associated with a slowness of movement (*akinesia*). The face of the afflicted individual is often described as masklike. Although this disease is assumed to be a disorder of movement without intellectual deterioration, some evidence suggests general intellectual impairment (Pollock and Hornabrook 1966).

The motor disorders associated with Parkinson's disease seem to be caused primarily by a deficit in dopamine. Therefore, the treatment of choice is a precursor of dopamine called L-Dopa, which decreases tremors and muscular rigidity and reduces symptoms of slow movement. Although behavioral side effects, probably caused by an

disorders having organic causes or results

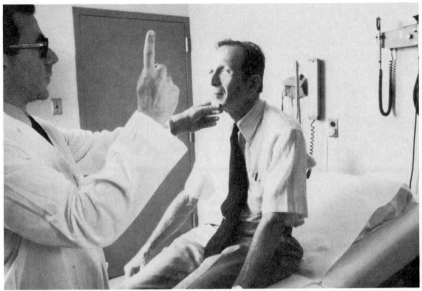

Parkinson's disease is most frequently diagnosed between the ages of forty to sixty. Representative Morris Udall of Arizona is afflicted with Parkinson's disease.

increase in arousal, are reported in 10 to 15 percent of the individuals treated with L-Dopa, drug therapy is rapidly replacing surgical intervention (Riklan 1973).

Huntington's Chorea

Huntington's chorea is determined by a single dominant gene, the presence of which means that 50 percent of the offspring of an afflicted individual will inherit the disease (Pratt 1967). The development of the disease is slow, symptoms appearing first in the 30s or 40s; degeneration is progressive; and death occurs within fifteen years following the onset of the symptoms (Haase 1971). The initial symptoms are usually motoric and include involuntary jerky movements of the face, tongue, and extremities. Intellectual impairment, particularly of memory for recent events, and severe emotional disturbances also occur. Part of the emotional lability and behavior pathology associated with Huntington's Chorea is the reaction of the individual to the disorder (Pearson 1973). Huntington's Chorea appears to be a disorder of the midbrain, particularly the basal ganglia. At present there is no cure for Huntington's Chorea.

The abnormal involuntary movements may be alleviated by several types of drugs, and the emotional reactions controlled with psychotropic drugs.

Senile Dementia: Chronic Brain Syndrome or Psychological Disorder?

Senescence, the process of aging, affects all parts of the body. It is evident in the wasting of muscles, easy fatigability, and an unsteady gait. Some individuals age more rapidly than others, however, and this condition is called **senile dementia**. In senile dementia, the individual may first show a gradual deterioration in behavioral functions, becoming careless in personal hygiene, and exhibiting explosive outbursts of irritability, depression, and memory impairment, particularly for recent events. Confusion, impaired judgment, blunting of emotions, and distortion of the truth or confabulation are common. If severe, psychosis of the aged can have paranoid, manic, depressive, or schizophrenic features.

Huntington's chorea leads to jerky movements, intellectual impairment, and severe emotional disturbances

The cause of senile dementia is poorly understood. Many of these cases show marked atherosclerotic brain conditions with thickening and hardening of the arterial walls, resulting in reduction of the supply of oxygen and other materials to the brain. Other factors, such as heredity and endocrine disorders, are also assumed to contribute to the condition. On autopsy, many cases of senile dementia show generalized brain atrophy, especially of the frontal lobes.

Senile dementia involves a slowing down of performance

Psychologically, the most significant change in behavior is a slowing of performance on speed tasks, which results in immediate and short-term memory losses as well as declines in sensory and perceptual abilities (Jarvik and Cohen 1973). This slowed reaction time would be expected as biological changes occur, but when speed factors are eliminated, performance on cognitive tasks shows no change or even slight improvement up to the eighth decade (Jarvik and Cohen 1973).

Expectations may play the major role in senile dementia

Is all senility caused by organic changes? At one time, diminished flow of blood and lowered oxygen consumption were thought to be the main reasons for this disorder, but this is no longer the case (Terry and Wisniewski 1974). A number of studies have investigated the relationship between behavioral deterioration in the aged and brain pathology. Gal (1959) conducted postmortem studies of over 100 patients between sixty-five and ninety-four and found a lack of correlation between brain damage and behavior. Raskin and Ehrenberg (1956) also conducted a postmortem study of 270 patients between sixty and ninety-seven years and found that the presence of atherosclerosis and brain damage was much more frequent in normal individuals than had been previously suspected. They concluded that there was no significant relationship between brain damage and senility. Carp (1969) has noted that senility is an ill-defined term much like schizophrenia, which has no scientific meaning. He compared a group of normal older people with a group of college students on traits usually associated with

senility such as depression, anxiety, and rigidity and found that the older people were less senile than the students.

The evidence indicates that there may be a basis for considering senility a psychological, sociological, and cultural disorder as well as an organic one. In a study of people known for their amazing longevity, including the Vilcabamba of Ecuador, the Hunza of West Pakistan, and the Georgians of the Soviet Union, Leaf (1973) indicated that it was possible for people to live a vigorous, active life involving physical activity for at least 100 years or even longer. The typical traits of senility were not present in these individuals.

The aged person is subject to sufficient environmental stress to account for the disintegration of coping behavior. Cultural attitudes and the expectations of society are extremely relevant. The end of a career and forced retirement is a noxious life event for most individuals. While the percentage of the population age sixty-five and over has risen steadily from 2.7 in 1860 to 9.1 in 1970, the proportion of aged males gainfully employed in the labor market has dropped from 68 percent in 1890 to 26 percent in 1969 (Zubin 1973). These problems are expected to be aggravated by increased longevity. For example, an estimated 700,000 older people in the United States were institutionalized for psychosis of the aged in 1970, and the figure was projected to climb to over a million by 1980 (Jarvik, Yen, and Goldstein 1974).

The standard retirement age of sixty-five is a product of the 1930s Depression. Numerous studies have shown that sixty-five-year-olds are productive workers and that many would prefer to keep working when they reach retirement age (Offir 1974). Furthermore, retirement is accompanied by losses of social reinforcement, professional status, and financial stability that can induce feelings of inferiority, reduce motivation, and spur withdrawal from society. As a matter of fact, retirement may be the cause of sudden aging rather than the result (Barrett 1972). Associated with this period of age are also increased feelings of isolation and loneliness. People in this age bracket suffer the loss of friends from

disorders having organic causes or results

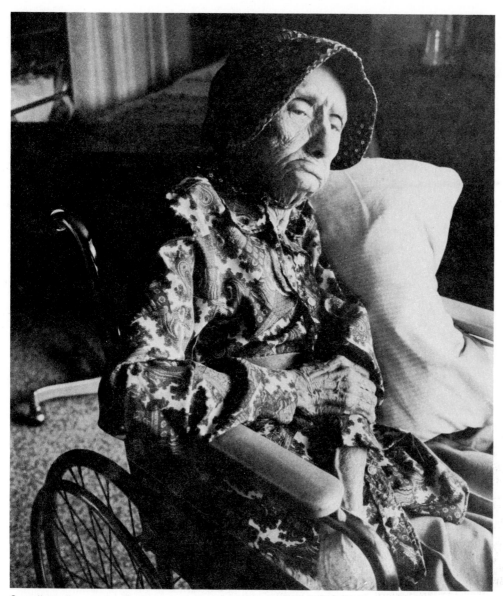
Sometimes the aged suffer increased stress due to invalidism. They no longer can care for themselves.

death, decreased interaction with younger individuals, and decreased contact with children as the children develop their own lives. This problem is especially common among women, who tend to outlive their spouses in the United States by some seven years.

Other stress factors are due to invalidism and impending death. With a gradual deterioration of one's body, the possibility of chronic and debilitating diseases, impairment of vision and hearing, and a restriction of physical activity are distinct possibilities.

Enforced limitations of activities may enhance physical as well as psychological deterioration (MacDonald 1973).

For the family and society, one solution to the problem of aged individuals is to place them in a nursing home. Nursing homes are custodial care facilities established on the expectation that individuals who enter them will never regain the capacity to care for themselves. Individuals

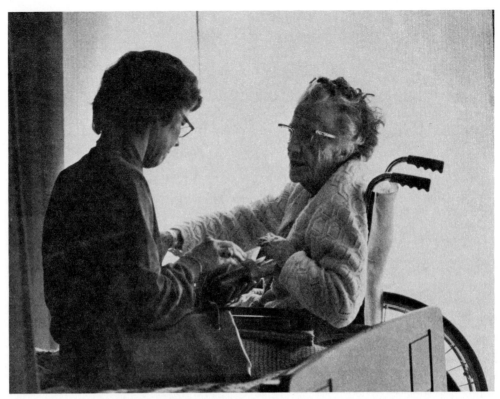

The nursing home itself may be responsible for an increase of senility in the aged because of stereotyping, illness, and environmental deprivation.

The sick role may be a self-fulfilling prophecy

are thus forced into sick roles in an institution that exists to give medical and custodial care. In any disorder, institutionalization of the individual is usually undesirable, but it is especially so for elderly people. Studies comparing the death rate among elderly people admitted to nursing homes or similar institutions with the death rate among those who are not have shown a higher rate among the institutionalized during the first year of relocation and particularly in the first three months (Botwinich 1973). Moreover, programs that provide the most extensive service in the protected environment are associated with higher patient mortality rate than limited service programs (Blankner 1967). The orientation of nursing homes and their effects are illustrated by the fact that 20 to 80 percent of their residents are considered senile, but in the general population of elderly people only 1 to 2 percent are considered senile (MacDonald 1973). MacDonald has argued that the nursing home itself is responsible for the apparent increase of sen-

ility in the aged because (1) the staff of nursing homes expects the aged individual to become senile and fosters such behavior; (2) various somatic illnesses may produce signs often indicating senility, but these illnesses could be reversed if properly treated; and (3) the environmental deprivation experienced by some nursing home residents may enhance or bring on senility.

A classic study by Volpe and Kastenbaum (1967) has shown what can be done with aged individuals who do require institutionalization. They worked with men whose mean age was seventy-eight and who were so physically and psychologically impaired that they required twenty-four-hour nursing care. These individuals performed no services for themselves, were agitated and incontinent, and had a history of assaultiveness. The investigators introduced some very simple innovations. They provided a record player, a decorated bulletin board, games, and cards; dressed the patients in white shirts and ties; and served beer in 12 oz. bottles with crackers and cheese at 2 p.m. each day. In less than a month a noticeable change occurred in the

disorders having organic causes or results

Old age does not have to be associated with social withdrawal and inactivity.

behavior of these men. The amount of medication given dropped sharply and there was a decrease in incontinence and jacket restraint. There were requests for, and participation in, dances and parties as well as marked improvement in orientation. Chien (1971) and Becker and Cesar (1973) have confirmed these results. If mutual gratification is expected by patients and staff and if the individual is treated as a normal human being, many bizarre behaviors disappear. Studies like this illustrate the possibility of a variety of psychological techniques that can be utilized in modifying behaviors associated with senility and enhancing the life of the aged.

Summary

Diseases or injuries to the brain induce disruption of well-organized patterns of behavior, particularly the cognitive functions. The degree to which the person's capabilities are disrupted depends upon location, rate of onset, progression, and duration of the brain pathology. These disorders may be focal or generalized. When the injury is focal—restricted to a specific area of the brain—the behavioral deficits may be quite specific.

Organic brain disorders can be described in terms of the causes of the disorder or in terms of the patterns of behavior that indicate brain damage. A number of specific patterns of behavior are associated with brain damage. Delirium is rapid in onset and marked by disturbances of attention, memory, and orientation with the result that the individual has difficulty in maintaining attention to various stimuli. Disturbance of arousal associated with delirium results in loss of wakefulness, varying from drowsiness to stupor or coma. Dementia is relatively slow in onset and is marked by a disruption of memory and an impairment of abstract reasoning. Frequently, impairments in judgment and loss of control of impulses also occur. Organic delusional syndromes vary from poorly formed paranoid delusions to highly organized paranoid delusional states. Organic hallucinosis is a disorder in which clear evidence points to an organic basis for hallucinations that occur in a state of full wakefulness. Organic affective syndrome occurs when a clearly defined organic disorder causes behavior that resembles bipolar depression. An organic personality syndrome is a marked change in personality characteristics associated with an organic cause. Often secondary symptoms or organic brain syndrome occur. These include severe emotional reactions to the personal and socioeconomic consequences of the cognitive deficits.

Assessment of brain syndromes include complete physical and neurological examinations, skull X rays, brain scans, EEG, and, occasionally, neuropsychological examinations. Neuropsychological examinations are particularly useful when lesions are focal and the disorder can be pinpointed.

Specific areas of the brain seem to be associated with specific psychological functioning. Damage to these particular areas causes specific deficits in behavior. Generally, the two hemispheres seem to be lateralized in function, that is, each hemisphere is responsible for a particular type of behavior. In some functions, however, both hemispheres are equally important.

Aphasia is the impairment of speech, language, and communication as a result of a specific lesion in the language area of the brain. The various types of aphasia can be grouped into three principal types: expressive, receptive, and amnesic. Epilepsy is a spontaneous discharge of neurons that occurs in one area of the brain and spreads to other areas, thus causing a state of abnormal electrical activity in the brain. The major types of epilepsy are grand mal, petit mal, Jacksonian, and psychomotor.

Some disorders result from a number of different bacteria or viruses that invade the brain and destroy or damage nerve tissue. Syphilis, an example of such disorders, has four well-defined stages. These stages develop over a period of years, and the last stage causes a variety of physical disorders as well as behavioral disturbances. The three major types of cerebral syphilis are general paresis, juvenile paresis, and meningovascular paresis. Only about 5 percent of untreated cases of syphilis develop general paresis.

A blow or severe injury to the skull can cause acute or chronic brain damage, or both. There are four major types of traumatic injuries: concussions, contusions, lacerations, and hematomas, as well as a number of brain disorders associated with toxic and metabolic states. Such toxic substances as drugs, gases, or metals may cross the blood-brain barrier and cause damage. Bromides are a common cause of such disorders. Similarly, endocrine disturbances including those of the pituitary gland and the adrenal gland can produce deficits in the functioning of the brain as well as other physical conditions. New growths in the brain are also associated with brain damage.

disorders having organic causes or results

These neoplasms can be either slow- or rapid-growing. The symptoms associated with brain tumors are dependent on the severity and size of the tumor.

The brain also requires a continuous flow of blood to supply glucose and oxygen so that brain cells can function. If a disruption of the cardiovascular system causes a change in the blood supply to the brain, an acute or chronic brain syndrome may result. One such disorder is atherosclerosis.

A number of degenerative diseases are associated with chronic brain syndromes. These disorders usually start in the forties and fifties and are sometimes referred to as presenile dementias. They include Alzheimer's disease, Parkinson's disease, Huntington's chorea, and Pick's disease.

Whether senile dementia is due to physical aging or is produced by psychological factors associated with aging is still not certain. A number of factors including retirement, the expectations of society, and stress associated with age are sufficient to account for the disintegration of behavior seen in aged individuals. For this reason both medical and psychological treatment are necessary with the aged.

Key Concepts

acute and chronic brain syndromes

Addison's disease

Alzheimer's disease

amnestic syndrome

anterograde amnesia

aphasia

atherosclerosis

confabulation

Cushing's syndrome

delirium

dementia

epilepsy

grand mal seizure

Huntington's chorea

hyperthyroidism

hypothyroidism (myxedema)

Jacksonian epilepsy

Korsakoff's psychosis

localization of function

neoplasms

organic affective syndrome

organic delusional syndrome

organic hallucinosis

organic personality syndrome

paresis

Parkinson's disease

petit mal seizure

Pick's disease

psychomotor seizure

retrograde amnesia

senile dementia

syphilis

Wernicke's syndrome

Review Questions

1. What are the primary symptoms of organic brain disorders?

2. What are the opposing positions of scientists in the disagreement over localization of brain function?

3. What are the three types of aphasia?

4. What is the difference between grand mal and petit mal epilepsy?

5. What are the stages in the development of general paresis?

6. What is a concussion? a contusion? a cerebral laceration? a cerebral hematoma?

7. Name three different toxic substances that can cause organic brain disorders.

8. How do thyroid and adrenal gland disturbances affect behavior? How does a brain tumor affect behavior?

9. What happens to the brain in atherosclerosis?

10. What is Alzheimer's disease? Pick's disease? Parkinson's disease? Huntington's chorea?

11. Why have some scientists begun to doubt the organic explanation of senile dementia?

Glossary

acquisition A new response that has been added to the organism's repertory of responses through learning.

acute alcoholic hallucinosis Auditory hallucinations that may be precipitated by alcohol or other drugs.

acute brain syndrome A brain disorder with reversible impairment of functioning usually having a rapid onset; due to drugs, injury, or organic disease.

acute schizophrenia A term defining schizophrenia as a function of length of hospitalization; operationally defined as less than three years of hospitalization.

addiction Physiological or biochemical change resulting in dependence on a drug.

Addison's disease A brain disorder associated with an endocrine dysfunction characterized by a deficiency in the adrenal cortex producing a variety of physiological and psychological symptoms.

adipocytes (adipose tissue) The fat cells in the body; their number is essentially fixed and stable, presumably resulting from genetic endowment, but the number can also be affected by early nutritional experiences.

affective disorders Abnormal states of manic elation or depression.

aging process Changes that occur naturally as the body ages; specific problems are related to each stage of life.

agoraphobia Anxiety associated with leaving familiar settings such as home.

Alcoholics Anonymous A loosely knit voluntary fellowship of alcoholics; provides group therapy for one another.

alpha alcoholism The use of alcohol as a means of alleviating tension or pain.

altered affect Inappropriate emotional responses that do not fit circumstances; may be exaggerated, inappropriate, or absent.

altered associations Cognitive or thought disturbances characteristic of schizophrenia, including illogical, unclear, and often incoherent thinking.

Alzheimer's disease A terminal degenerative disease in which cells in all areas of the cerebral cortex die; initial symptoms resemble those found in neurotic disorders; onset is usually between the ages of forty and sixty-five.

ambivalence Entertaining completely contradictory ideas simultaneously; for example, experiencing love and hatred toward the same individual at the same time.

amnestic syndrome A memory disorder characterized by short-term memory disturbances; diagnosed in the absence of dementia or delirium.

amniocentesis A screening procedure used to detect the presence of hereditary disorders during the thirteenth week of pregnancy by extracting and analyzing a small amount of amniotic fluid.

amphetamine A synthetic stimulant, including Benezedrine, Dexedrine, and Methedrine; ordinarily referred to as speed or pep pills.

anaclitic depression Depression or dependency occurring primarily in children between the ages of six months and six years.

anakastic personality Obsessive-compulsive personality characterized by excessive concern for detail, organizing, punctuality, and routine.

anal triad Frugality, orderliness, and pedantry; according to psychoanalytic theory these attributes are characteristic of individuals exhibiting compulsive behavior because of difficulties at the anal stage of development.

analytic psychology Jungian psychology; any system of psychology that attempts to reduce phenomena to their basic elements.

androgens Male hormones that operate before birth on the internal duct system to develop the vas deferens and the seminal vesicles, the penis, and the scrotum.

anesthesia Total loss of sensation; sometimes associated with conversion reaction, can occur in any of the five senses.

animism The belief that spirits, gods, or demons animate natural forces, objects, animals, and humans.

anorexia nervosa An eating disorder, first described by Sir William Gull, characterized by loss of appetite (anorexia); thought to be due to disordered mental processes related to a disturbance in CNS activity (nervosa); most often observed in young women between the ages of sixteen and twenty-three.

anterograde amnesia Memory loss of new learning and ongoing events.

antianxiety drugs Drugs used to alleviate or suppress anxiety, nervousness, or neurotic behavior.

antidepressive drugs Tricyclic compounds and monoamine oxidase inhibitors that are used as mood elevators.

antimanic drugs Drugs such as lithium carbonate that suppress or alleviate confused, hyperactive behaviors that are associated with mania.

antipsychotic drugs Drugs that are effective in the treatment of various psychotic disorders; assumed to eliminate agitation, hallucinations, hyperactivity, and delusions.

antisocial personality (psychopath, sociopath) An individual who exhibits basically unsocialized behavior patterns; characterized by lack of anxiety or guilt, inability to learn from experience, impulsiveness, lack of emotional ties, inability to adjust to boredom, and the ability to make a good impression on others.

anxiety A similar psychological and physiological reaction to fear but in response to relatively nonthreatening events as evaluated by others and the individual.

anxiety neurosis (generalized anxiety) Chronic anxiety with periodic acute attacks that include a subjective experience of apprehension, anxiety, tension, and an inability to specify the specific eliciting stimuli.

apathy-futility pattern A pattern characteristic of the mother/child interaction in impoverished families; characterized by the feeling that nothing is worth doing, a lack of meaningful personal relationships, generalized incompetence, and a lack of motivation.

aphasia Impairment in speech, language, and communication as a result of specific lesions in language areas of the brain.

archetypes According to Jung, universal and primordial ideas or images that are so basic they pervade every culture.

assertiveness training A behavioral technique aimed at improving the ability for self-expression and insistence on one's rights.

astasia abasia A conversion disorder in which the patient cannot stand or walk but has complete control of the limbs when sitting or lying down.

asthenic personality disorder A personality disorder characterized by easy fatigability, low energy level, lack of enthusiasm, marked incapacity for enjoyment, and oversensitivity to stress.

asthma A respiratory disorder characterized by wheezing, coughing, shortness of breath, gasping, and thoracic constriction.

atherosclerosis A brain disorder resulting from the depositing of fatty substances containing a large amount of cholesterol along the interior walls of the arteries and the formation of blood clots within the arteries.

autism A loss of contact with reality and withdrawal from social interaction.

aversion therapy Various techniques, including noxious stimulation, punishment, avoidance training, escape training, and time out, where the correct response allows the client to escape aversive consequences or punishment.

avoidant personality disorder A personality disorder characterized by social isolation; similar to schizoid personality but exhibiting hypersensitivity to criticism.

barbiturate A powerful sedative that replaced bromides (phenobarbital, secobarbital, butabarbital).

behavior analogues An attempt to construct a situation as similar to real life as possible to allow accurate assessment of target behavior.

behavior therapy (behavior modification) The application of classical conditioning and operant learning methods to the modification of problem behaviors.

behavioral assessment Evaluation of behavior to select, devise, and evaluate individuals to select, devise, and evaluate behavior modification procedures.

behavioral classification system A classification system of abnormal behavior based on normal behavior; classifying on the basis of responses that are overt, measurable, and based on current behavior.

behavioral interviews Verbal interaction to obtain information for devising a behavioral assessment program.

behavioral medicine (medical psychology) The study of the relationship between physiology and behavior in terms of causes, assessment, and modification of both physiological and psychological methods.

behavioral observation Observation and recording of target behaviors that are clearly defined.

behavioral questionnaires Questionnaires devised to report the status of current problem behaviors.

behavioral rehearsal A modeling technique in which the client describes a difficult situation and then discusses the appropriate behavioral response with the therapist.

behaviorist position A theoretical position assuming that symptoms of abnormal behavior are learned habits.

bell and pad procedure A procedure for curing enuretics that conditions the waking-up response to bladder pressure cues; a loud buzzer is connected to a pad on which the individual sleeps, bladder pressure precedes urination and dampens the pad, activating the buzzer and awakening the child; after a number of trials the child should awaken to bladder pressure.

beta alcoholism A drinking pattern characterized by physical complications, such as gastritis or cirrhosis of the liver, with or without addiction or physiological dependence.

biofeedback training An operant conditioning technique in which an individual monitors biological signals from the CNS, the ANS, the musculoskeletal system, and the cardiovascular system in order to acquire control of these responses.

biogenic approach A theoretical approach that assumes that mental illness is caused by systemic diseases, by the individual's genetic endowment.

bipolar depression The diagnosis when both depressive and manic episodes occur.

borderline personality disorder A personality disorder characterized by occasional brief psychotic episodes and marginal adjustment to life.

bromides A sedative introduced during the mid-nineteenth century; ingestion often resulted in a toxic psychosis.

bruxism The inappropriate grinding or clenching of the teeth that typically occurs during sleep; can lead to dental problems, facial pain, muscle sensitivity, and headache.

buzzer pants A potty-training method that involves a transistorized signal package that is sewn into the training pants and that emits a low-intensity buzzing sound when the pants are wet.

case history design A single-case design in which an individual's behavior is observed and then a treatment applied.

catalepsy A trancelike state in which the muscles are held rigid for long periods of time.

cataplexy The complete loss of muscle tone, which is one of the three major symptoms of narcolepsy; loss of tone often occurs when the individual is angry or excited.

catatonic schizophrenia The schizophrenic process characterized by severe disturbances in motor behavior, including the extremes of wild excitement or stupor.

catecholamine hypothesis (norepinephrine hypothesis) A hypothesis associating depression with a deficiency of norepinephrine in certain parts of the brain, particularly the hypothalamus.

catharsis The apparent therapeutic value of discussing the origin of symptoms according to Breuer and Freud; the talking cure associated with psychoanalysis.

cause-and-effect relationships A given event, the cause, leads to a given event, the effect; demonstration of this relationship is a major purpose of science.

cerebral beri beri A form of malnutrition associated with a shortage of vitamin B.

chaining A sequential form of conditioning in which a sequence of behaviors is taught with one response providing a cue for the next.

"checkers" Individual with a compulsion to make sure that he or she has not done something potentially dangerous.

chemical shock therapy The treatment of severe mental disorders by chemically induced convulsions; chemicals such as insulin or Metrazol are used.

childhood schizophrenia A childhood psychosis that develops about the age of five.

chromosomal analysis Examination of photomicrographs of chromosomes to evaluate the presence of certain physical abnormalities.

chronic brain syndrome Irreversible brain impairment, often with slow onset, due to drugs, injury, or organic disease.

chronic rumination The bringing up of food without nausea, retching, or disgust; an apparently voluntary disorder found in infants.

chronic schizophrenia A term defining schizophrenia as a function of length of hospitalization; operationally defined as more than six years of hospitalization.

circular reasoning Thinking in which one conclusion builds upon another which in turn refers back to the first conclusion; for example, Jack is schizoid because he is shy. He is shy because he is schizoid.

cocaine A plant product derived from coca leaves; used as local anesthetic and general central nervous system stimulant; produces euphoria, restlessness, and excitation.

codeine An opium derivative one-twelfth as powerful as morphine; an effective oral analgesic.

cognitive restructuring The identification and elimination of misguided or irrational beliefs.

cognitive triad of depression According to Beck, three ideas around which depression centers—a negative view of the world, a negative concept of self, and a negative appraisal of the future.

colic A feeding disorder, especially common among firstborn infants, characterized by sharp intestinal pains and crying.

collective unconscious A concept introduced by Jung postulating a shared unconscious that contains memories retained from previous generations and the archetypes of myths, dreams, and symbols.

compensation neurosis Conversion disorder that provides secondary gains, such as allowing the individual to avoid unpleasant or potentially threatening events.

compulsion A stereotyped, repetitive motor act that appears to be irrational and beyond the control of the individual.

concordance rate In twin studies of some trait, illness, or behavior, the proportion of a representative sample of affected twins whose co-twins are or will be similarly affected.

concurrent validity The degree to which a measuring instrument yields results consistent with other measurements of the same behavior.

conditioned avoidance response (CAR) A conditioned response that prevents the presentation of a noxious or painful stimulus.

conditioned emotional response (CER) An emotional response that has been associated with a certain stimulus pattern through conditioning techniques.

conditioned response In classical or respondent conditioning, the response to the conditioned stimulus; for example, in Pavlov's experiment, the response of salivation that came before receiving the food powder.

conditioned stimuli A neutral stimuli that has been paired with an unconditioned stimuli eventually evoking a conditioned response.

confabulation Compensation for loss of memory by fabrication of missing details; filling in the gaps in memory with invented stories.

conflict anxiety Childhood anxiety of unknown source; similar to pervasive anxiety in adults.

conjunctive categories In defining abnormal behavior, categories in which symptoms or behavior patterns included in the definition are necessary and sufficient for membership in that category or diagnosis; the absence of one or more of these symptoms disqualifies a behavior from that category.

constitution The physical appearance as it influences behavior patterns and personality characteristics.

construct validity The degree of fit between a hypothetical notion or theory and actual behavior in the test situation.

contagious anxiety An anxiety disorder in children that results from modeling anxious adult behavior.

content validity The degree to which a test or assessment technique samples the behavior it is designed to measure.

contingent reinforcement Reinforcement schedule based on the performance of the desired response.

conversion reactions Involuntary disturbance of physical functions that are normally under voluntary control.

correlational studies A study that measures the degree of relationship between two or more variables.

counterbalancing An experimental procedure for eliminating the effect of irrelevant variables by presenting them in a different order along with the independent variable.

cretinism Dwarfism and severe mental retardation due to thyroid insufficiency during early life.

criterion of adjustment The labeling of abnormal behavior based on how well an individual copes with his or her environment; the concept is, within limits, culture free.

criterion of labeling The labeling of abnormal behavior as a function of local conventions that vary from society to society, from time to time, and from place to place.

cross-gender identification The exhibiting of behavior characteristic of the opposite sex; the wish or belief that one is a member of the opposite sex.

cross-tolerance The transference of tolerance from one drug to another drug, making it necessary to take more of both drugs to obtain the desired effect.

cultural-familial retardation The most common type of retardation; mental retardation without physical symptoms or any evidence of physical causes; associated with impoverishment and unstable family background; probably the result of a combination of genetic and environmental influences.

cultural relativism A proposition of environmental models that states that what constitutes acceptable or abnormal behavior varies from culture to culture.

cunnilingus Oral stimulation of the female genitalia.

Cushing's syndrome A brain disorder associated with endocrine dysfunction as a result of a tumor or abnormal growth on the adrenal cortex causing an oversecretion of cortisone.

cyclothymic personality A depressive disorder supposed to be a stable aspect of an individual's personality.

DSM II Diagnostic and Statistical Manual of Mental Disorders II; the system of classifying abnormal behavior formulated by the American Psychiatric Association; traditionally based on the medical model assumptions.

DSM III Diagnostic and Statistical Manual of Mental Disorders III; the newest revision of the American Psychiatric Association's system of classification of abnormal behavior; the medical model bias has been somewhat eliminated.

defense mechanisms The means by which the organism protects itself against impulses and affects, including repression, displacement, denial, intellectualization, projection, fixation, regression, sublimation, and reaction formation as formulated by Freud.

delirium A state of mental confusion; a rapid onset of disturbances of attention, memory, and orientation that may result from fever, drugs, or shock; associated with acute brain syndrome.

delirium tremens (DTs) An acute alcoholic condition characterized by tremors, anxiety, hallucinations, and delusions following alcohol withdrawal.

delta alcoholism A pattern of alcoholism associated with increased tolerance and withdrawal symptoms; the individual is unable to abstain for even a short period of time.

delusions Beliefs that are contrary to the facts of the situation and highly resistant to change.

dementia A deterioration, usually gradual, of intellectual, judgmental, and emotional processes associated with chronic brain syndrome.

dementia praecox According to Kraepelin, a mental disorder due to underlying organic disease of the central nervous system; mental deterioration (dementia) first evident during adolescence (praecox).

dependent personality disorder A personality disorder characterized by passivity and dependency without aggressive tendencies.

dependent variable An experimental variable in which changes are consequent upon changes in the independent variable.

depersonalization A neurotic disorder characterized by a feeling of unreality and estrangement from self, body, or the environment.

depressants Drugs that act on the central nervous system to relax or disinhibit, to slow down intellectual and motor reactivity, and to reduce pain, tension, and anxiety; includes alcohol, narcotics, tranquilizers, and barbiturates.

depression An extreme state of unresponsiveness with self-depreciation, delusions of inadequacy and hopelessness, hallucinations, and somatic changes.

depressive neurosis A depressive disorder due to an internal conflict or identifiable event, such as loss of love object.

determinism The belief that the universe is orderly and that all events occur within the framework of cause and effect.

detoxification The elimination of alcohol from the system and the treatment for withdrawal symptoms.

deviation In determining intelligence, individuals are compared to others of their own age group in terms of how they perform on intellectual tasks.

diathesis-stress hypotheses Theories that postulate an inherited predisposition (diathesis) to develop schizophrenia which is activated only under sufficient environmental stress.

different group method Another name for the *ex post facto* method; the experimenter begins with groups that are initially different in some ways and then treats them identically.

differential reinforcement for other behavior (DRO) Reinforcement of competing or other responses; used in conjunction with extinction or punishment in behavioral treatment programs.

disjunctive categories Categories in which any number of symptoms define a specific abnormal behavior; the appearance of one or some of the designated symptoms allows use of that category or diagnosis.

dissocial reaction A personality disorder exhibited by individuals who have grown up in subcultures whose values and norms are at variance with society's standards.

disulfiram (antabuse) A drug used to treat alcoholism; causes nausea and vomiting when an individual ingests alcohol.

diurnal bladder training A technique to stop enuresis that requires the bedwetter to practice retaining the urine during the day after drinking large quantities of fluid.

dopamine hypothesis The hypothesis that postulates that schizophrenia results from excessive dopamine activity in the brain.

double-bind hypothesis A psychodynamic theory that schizophrenia may develop from a situation in which a hostile significant other reacts on one level of communication in one way and on another level in another way; thus, the individual is placed in a no-win situation that ultimately leads to schizophrenia.

Down's syndrome (mongolism) A genetic disorder associated with moderate or severe mental retardation; commonly called mongolism because it produces almond-shaped slanted eyes.

dream interpretation A major technique in psychoanalysis in which dream material is analyzed in terms of manifest (or reported) content and latent content (unconscious material expressed in symbolic ways).

drive A state resulting from metabolic changes in tissue that increases arousal and instigates selective and directional behavior patterns.

drug dependency Habitual use of a drug, frequently out of perceived need.

dry-bed procedure An operant conditioning procedure used to correct bedwetting; requires one night of intensive training followed by the use of a urine alarm or the bell-and-pad procedure for about one week.

dualism A philosophical belief stated by René Descartes postulating the mind and body as separate but interacting entities.

dyspareunia In women, pain or discomfort during or following intercourse.

ego In psychoanalytic theory, the second of the three major components of personality; consists of the reality-testing functions of problem solving, thinking, memory, and other higher level cognitive processes.

ejaculatory incompetence The inability to ejaculate intravaginally.

electroconvulsive therapy (ECT) A form of antidepressive or antipsychotic therapy consisting of application of weak electrical currents to the head to induce convulsions and unconsciousness.

electrolyte hypothesis A hypothesis suggesting an imbalance in sodium and potassium levels in depressed patients.

emotion A complex reaction involving a high level of activation and visceral change accompanied by strong feelings or affects.

empiricism A philosophical school that asserts that the only source of knowledge is observable fact or objective experience.

encopresis Involuntary defecation after the second year of life that is not due to gross disease of the muscles.

encounter groups A group process aimed at increasing the social effectiveness and growth of essentially normal individuals.

endogenous depression Depression supposedly associated with behavioral retardation, deep depression, low reactivity to environmental changes, loss of interest in life, somatic complaints, self pity, insomnia, and lack of precipitating stress.

enuresis Frequent accidental urination after the age most children in our culture have been bladder trained.

environmental models A model of behavior that assumes that behavior is learned, that it is determined by environmental factors, and that scientific laws require observable demonstration.

epilepsy A periodic convulsive disorder due to spontaneous discharge of neurons in one area of the brain and spreading to other areas.

equivalent group method An experimental method in which the groups selected are chosen to be as alike as possible and then treated differently.

essential hypertension An increase of systolic and diastolic blood pressure due to unknown causes.

ex post facto study A method in which the experimental groups are selected "after the fact" or without direct experimental manipulation.

excitement stage One of the four stages of sexual arousal; the stage in which the sexual response is initiated by whatever is sexually stimulating to the individual.

exhibitionism A compulsive tendency to expose parts of the body, especially sex organs, to achieve sexual arousal.

exogenous depression A depression characterized by high reactivity to the environment, precipitating stress, agitation, irritability, and personality disturbance.

experimental methods The techniques used for discovering information by means of experimentation; manipulation of variables to investigate causal relationships.

experimenter bias Distortion or error in an experimental design or interpretation due to experimenter prejudice.

explosive personality A disorder of impulse control with accompanying anger and temper tantrums.

extinction The decrease in the probability or magnitude of a conditioned response that occurs when the conditioned stimulus is no longer paired with the unconditioned stimulus.

extraclassificatory attributes Symptoms or behaviors that do not empirically correlate with essential attributes.

fading Gradual reduction of a prompt following successful performance of the desired behavior.

family therapy A psychodynamic group therapy approach that treats the client and family members as a unit.

fear A psychological reaction to stimulus conditions in the internal or external environment that threaten the organism's physical well-being.

feedback Any kind of return information that is useful in regulating behavior.

fellatio Oral stimulation of the male genitalia.

fetishism The habitual use of part of the body or of an inanimate object to produce sexual arousal or gratification.

fight or flight reaction The protective response of an organism to stress.

flooding A procedure for extinguishing anxiety by overexposing the client, usually in the imagination, to anxiety-provoking stimuli.

folie a deux A rare type of paranoia in which two people share the same delusional system with the dominant person influencing the more submissive one.

free association In traditional psychoanalysis, the basic rule that a patient must say anything that comes to mind on the theory that mental wandering will facilitate recall of repressed material.

fugue state A dissociative disorder similar to hysterical amnesia except that the individual literally leaves real life circumstances and flees to another environment.

functional psychosis A psychosis for which there is no organic basis.

gamma alcoholism A drinking pattern with increased tissue tolerance; an increase in the amount of alcohol is necessary to have an effect.

gender behavior disturbance Adoption of opposite sex behavior to some degree without identifying with the opposite sex.

gender role identification The enactment of roles typically labeled as male or female.

general adaptation syndrome (GAS) A three-stage process (alarm, resistance, exhaustion) resulting from stress and involving profound physiological changes in the endocrine and other organ systems.

genetic inheritance The hereditary characteristics, such as height, that result from genes.

genotype The actual genetic constitution; a trait or the totality of traits that can be transmitted by an individual.

Gilles de la Tourette syndrome A complex tic characterized by compulsive jerking of the voluntary musculature with obscene utterances and/or echolalia.

grand mal seizure One of the four major types of epilepsy; characterized by generalized convulsions and loss of consciousness.

group comparison designs An experimental method in which two or more groups are treated identically in all respects except one.

hallucinations Sensory experiences that cannot be validated by external observers; a false perception.

hebephrenic schizophrenia The schizophrenic process characterized by disorganized thinking, shallow and inappropriate affect, unpredictable giggling, silly, regressed behavior, and bizarre hypochondriacal complaints.

heroin A morphine derivative; one of the most widely used addictive drugs.

heterosexual skills The ability to initiate and maintain a satisfactory and gratifying sexual relationship with a member of the opposite sex.

heterosocial skills The social skills necessary to initiate and maintain causal or intimate relationships with members of the other sex.

homeostatic mechanisms Physiological mechanisms that attempt to maintain constancy of internal states regardless of environmental conditions; any biochemical imbalance provides negative feedback, activating these mechanisms that in turn effect the changes necessary to restore the organism to its former state.

homosexuality A sexual and affectional preference for members of the same sex.

hospitalism Spit's theory that claims that infants who are not cuddled, fondled, or involved in the usual mother-child caring relationship will show serious behavioral and developmental abnormalities.

Huntington's chorea A genetic disorder determined by a single dominant gene; symptoms first appear between the ages of thirty and fifty; progressive deterioration of the midbrain results in motor and intellectual impairment and death.

hydrocephaly Retardation due to an abnormal amount of cerebrospinal fluid accumulating within the cranium, causing tissue damage and an enlarged head.

hypersomnia Extreme sleepiness that may last several days and is rather common in teenagers; if chronic, there is marked confusion upon awakening, absence of REM periods, and occasionally narcoleptic symptoms.

hyperthyroidism A disorder due to oversecretion of thyroxin, causing weight loss, emotional excitability and other symptoms; often mistaken for anxiety disorder.

hypnagogic hallucinations Vivid or terrifying nightmares that are symptomatic of narcolepsy; these nightmares occur in the region between sleeping and wakefulness.

hypnosis A temporary condition of altered attention; may be induced by another person; includes alterations in consciousness, increased susceptibility to suggestion, and production of responses and ideas unfamiliar in the usual state of consciousness.

hypochondriasis A neurotic disorder in which the individual is preoccupied with the body and with fears of presumed diseases.

hypoesthesia Reduced sensitivity or sensation in any of the senses.

hypothesis A scientific assumption that serves as a tentative explanation.

hypothetical construct An intervening variable that is assumed to have meaning beyond its function as scientific shorthand; the operationalization of a theoretical construct.

hypothyroidism A disorder due to undersecretion of thyroxin, causing weight gain, difficulty in concentration, and, possibly, impairment of recent memory.

hysteria A disorder that mimics a physical illness and is characterized by involuntary psychogenic loss or disorder of function.

hysterical personality disorder A disorder characterized by excitability, emotional instability, overreactivity, and self-dramatization.

iatrogenic effect Physician-caused symptoms; symptoms inadvertently suggested by a physician during examination that may appear on the next examination.

id In psychoanalytic psychology, one of the three parts of the personality; the only personality structure present at birth and the reservoir of psychic energy.

ideas of reference The belief that everyday experience has some personal meaning.

idiot savant A mentally retarded individual with a highly specialized talent in one area, such as rapid calculation, memory, or execution of music.

implosive therapy A variation of flooding; a combination of learning and psychodynamic therapies based on the theory that neurotic behavior consists of avoidance responses.

in vivo **desensitization** Gradual exposure to anxiety-provoking stimuli in a real-life setting.

inadequate personality disorder A personality disorder characterized by ineffectual response to emotional, social, intellectual, and physical demands.

incest Sexual relations between persons closely related by blood; degree of relationship is set by law and social custom.

independent variable The scientific variable that is controlled and manipulated by the experimenter and that is applied to determine its effect on the dependent variables.

infantile autism A childhood psychosis differentiated from childhood schizophrenia by onset within the first two years of life.

insomnia The most common sleep disturbance; may occur in as much as ten percent of the normal population; characterized by an inability to get to sleep in a short time, frequent awakenings, an inability to go back to sleep after awakening, and short sleep cycles.

intelligence quotients (IQ) An index of the relative level of intelligence of an individual as compared with others older, younger, or the same age; obtained by dividing the mental age by the chronological age and multiplying by 100.

intelligence tests Tests that sample behaviors that are indices of intellectual performance; for example, Stanford Binet, Wechsler.

interactionism A theoretic position that holds that behavior is a function of both the type of situation and the individual's predisposition or traits.

intervening variable Scientific shorthand for the relation between two or more operationally defined variables; not physical constructs but processes defined and measured by appropriate instruments and techniques.

interview Verbal interaction between two or more people to gather firsthand information about the client.

intestinal bypass surgery A weight-loss method in which a major portion of the small intestine is bypassed, drastically reducing the absorptive capacity of the organ and causing weight loss.

introverted personality disorder A schizoid personality disorder without a family history of schizophrenia or peculiarities of cognitive processes.

involutional melancholia A depressive disorder occurring in the involutional period (mid-forties to age sixty) and characterized by impaired reality testing due to the mood disorder.

isolated populations A method used for investigating inbreeding in humans; isolated populations often intermarry because of a lack of other alternatives.

Jacksonian epilepsy A type of epilepsy characterized by localized convulsions usually limited to one limb.

"jukebox" theory of emotion The theory that postulates the production of emotion as a two-stage process—visceral arousal and labeling of the appropriate affective response.

kindreds A method used for determining the influence of heredity on a specific characteristic by assuming that as the degree of kinship or blood relationship decreases, the similarity of genetic endowment also decreases.

Kleine-Levin syndrome A form of hypersomnia that occurs in young men and consists of episodes of excessive sleeping (eighteen to twenty hours per day) for several days, tremendous hunger, and, occasionally, hypersexuality.

Klinefelter's syndrome An hereditary disorder of males that is characterized by the superficial appearance of a male—usually a normal-size penis but very small testicles; may also include developed breasts and little body hair.

Korsakoff's psychosis Primarily a memory disorder associated with a deficit in the vitamin B complex.

la belle indifference A seemingly unconcerned attitude about the presence of physical symptoms.

law of effect The basis of instrumental learning formulated by Edward Lee Thorndike; asserts that responses that are followed by positive consequence are more likely to recur when the stimulus patterns that elicited them are repeated; or the converse.

learned helplessness The learning theory that postulates that depression is caused by exposure to inescapable aversive situations, leading to a belief that personal behavior will not alter a situation; feelings of helplessness and hopelessness about one's capacity to avoid punishment.

learning The acquisition of any relatively permanent change in behavior as a result of practice or experience.

lesbianism Female homosexuality.

life stress According to Holmes and Rahe, a positive or negative change in one's life situation; life situations are ranked on a 1 to 100 scale and summed for a given period of time.

localization of function The scientific belief that various functions are specific to particular places in the cerebral cortex or other parts of the nervous system.

locus of control The place or location of control; in behavior control, the locus can come from within the person (self control) or from others (social control) or both.

lysergic acid diethylamide (LSD) The most powerful psychedelic drug; has major side effects on the central nervous system.

malingering Faking of physical symptoms.

mania Violent, uncontrollable behavior characterized by excessive motor activity, excitement, impulsiveness, imperturability, amorality, and acceleration of activities.

manic depressive illness A severe mental disorder characterized by cyclic swings in emotion or mood; divided into three major subtypes—manic type, depressive type, and circular type.

marasmus A progressive malnutrition in infants believed to be due to lack of mothering; see *hospitalism*.

marijuana Dried and ground leaves and stems of the female hemp plant that usually induce mild euphoria, heightened perceptual activity, and pleasant relaxation when smoked or ingested.

masked depression According to psychoanalytic theory, hyperactive, disobedient, or phobic behavior as symptoms of an underlying depression in children.

masochism Obtaining sexual gratification from receiving pain, punishment, or psychological humiliation.

maturation The developmental process that constitutes the biological contributions to behavior.

medical models Models that define deviant behavior as mental illness; the most popular models of abnormal behavior based on the medical model of physical illness.

mental retardation Substandard performance on measures of cognitive processes, such as thought, memory, concept formation, and reasoning; can be mild, moderate, severe, or profound depending on the degree of impairment.

mescaline A hallucinogen derived from the small disklike growth button on top of the peyote cactus; induces hallucinations when chewed.

methadone A synthetic narcotic analgesic similar to morphine; about twice as effective by injection.

method of agreement The principle that states that when condition X is present, condition Y will also be present (John Stuart Mill).

method of difference The principle that states that if condition X is not present, condition Y will not be either (John Stuart Mill).

microcephaly Retardation associated with an extremely small head and failure of the brain to grow to normal size.

migraine A headache disorder characterized by severe, usually unilateral, head pain accompanied by nausea and visual disturbances.

milieu therapy Institutional treatment of mental disorders in which the major assumption is that everyone involved with the patients contributes to their adjustment.

modeling A behavior modification technique that is based on observation of a model performing the fear-evoking behavior (or other desired behavior).

moral models A model of abnormal behavior that postulates that abnormal individuals were once normal but "lost their reason" due to exposure to psychologically or socially stressful environments that they could not manage because they had deviated from contemporary moral or social standards.

morphine An opium derivative frequently used for relief from pain.

motivation The study of needs and drives; the forces that impel people toward specific goals or away from specific threats.

multiaxial classification The innovative classification system used in DSM III that allows classification along five different axes: Axis I—Clinical Psychiatric Syndrome and Other Conditions; Axis II—Personality Disorders and Specific Developmental Disorders; Axis III—Severity of Physical Disorders and Conditions; Axis IV—Severity of Psychological Stressors; and Axis V—Highest Level of Adaptive Functioning (in the past year).

multiple baseline design An experimental design in which another response, another situation, or another subject serves as a control.

multiple personality (split personality) A relatively rare dissociative disorder in which separate and distinct personalities supposedly exist in one person.

muscle contraction headaches Head pain characterized by a sensation of tightness and pressure in the head and neck area.

myatonia A response to sexual stimulation resulting in increased muscular tension in the genital area.

narcissistic personality disorder A personality disorder characterized by a grandiose sense of self-importance, exhibitionism, preoccupation with success and power, self-centeredness, and lack of concern for others.

narcolepsy Profound difficulty in staying awake, with consistent daytime attacks of irresistable drowsiness and fatigue; symptoms include cataplexy, hypnagogic hallucinations, and sleep paralysis.

narcotics Depressant drugs that induce relaxation, produce euphoria, and provide relief from pain; for example, morphine, codeine.

naturalistic observation The collection of behavioral data in real-life situations with as little interference from the researcher as possible.

need An energizing condition of the organism that moves it toward a certain goal.

neoplasms New growth or tumors.

neurasthenic neurosis A disorder characterized by complaints of chronic weakness, quick fatigue, and exhaustion.

neuroses A heterogeneous assortment of disorders that are less severe than psychoses, do not permeate all aspects of the person's life, do not typically impair reality testing, and rarely result in gross cognitive distortion.

neurotic personality The assumption that individuals who exhibit neurotic patterns of behavior share a common personality pattern.

neurotic sociopath (acting out neurotic) An antisocial individual who exhibits antisocial and aggressive acts; shares many of the characteristics of the primary sociopath but feels guilt or remorse for these acts.

nicotine A chemical obtained from the tobacco plant; can cause toxic effects and death in large doses.

night terror Apparent arousal during sleep accompanied by expressions of intense fear and emotion; individuals often awake screaming but have no recall of the experience other than a feeling of intense fear.

nightmares Vivid, horrifying dreams that take place during REM sleep; occur most often in children.

nocturnal enuresis Frequent accidental urination at night or bedwetting.

nocturnal headbanging A sleep disorder that involves a rhythmic rolling of the head from side to side while going to sleep or during stage 4 sleep.

nonparanoid schizophrenia A psychosis usually characterized by greater impairment in intelligence, reaction time, and behavior; longer hospitalization; and greater distractibility; poor premorbid adjustment and prognosis.

nonretentive encopresis Involuntary defecation in which the individual produces a soft, fully formed stool; often called soiling.

norms Any pattern, standard, or representative performance for a group.

obsession A thought, wish, plan, or admonishment that intrudes persistently into consciousness and that the individual considers irrational.

obsessive-compulsive personality disorder A personality disorder characterized by excessive concern with detail, organization, punctuality, and routine.

operant conditioning Instrumental learning; consequent-governed behavior; the process of reinforcing a person's spontaneous activities.

operational definition A definition formulated in terms of the way a behavior is measured or assessed; a definition made in terms of measurement operations.

organic affective syndrome A disorder characterized by behavior similar to depressive or manic episodes with a clearly defined organic factor.

organic delusional syndrome An organic disorder occurring when there is clear evidence of organic etiology; characterized by delusions occurring in a full state of wakefulness, mild cognitive impairment, language or communication disorder, perplexity, abnormal psychomotor activity, or stereotyped behavior.

organic hallucinosis Hallucinations occurring in a state of wakefulness and alertness; clear evidence of organic etiology without evidence of other organic brain syndrome.

organic personality syndrome A disorder characterized by marked change in personality characteristics; clearly associated with organic cause without evidence of other organic brain syndrome.

organic psychosis A psychosis that is caused by a physiological dysfunction.

orgasm stage The third stage of sexual arousal; characterized by a totally involuntary and sudden discharge of tension that occurs when stimulation reaches maximum intensity.

orgasmic dysfunction In females, the general inhibition of sexual arousal, a lack of erotic feelings, and/or an absence of vasocongestion that typically prepares a woman for intercourse.

overanxious syndrome One pattern of personality characteristics seen in delinquent children; includes seclusiveness, shyness, apathy, tendency to worry, sensitivity, submissiveness, and neurotic tendencies.

overdose (OD) Too large an intake or ingestion of a drug; can cause extreme physiological reactions or even death.

paradigm clash Use of a paradigm both guides and limits observation; the more a model is used, the more it forces the scientist to recognize events that fail to fit the model.

paradoxical sleep Another name for rapid eye movement (REM) sleep; paradoxical because of its conflicting characteristics—EEG similar to Stage 1 sleep with deep relaxation and difficulty in arousal.

paraesthesia Unusual sensation, such as distorted vision or tingling; can affect any of the five senses.

paranoia A rare condition characterized by the gradual onset of an intricate, complex, and elaborate delusional system that is based on and often logically proceeds from misinterpretations of actual events.

paranoid schizophrenia The schizophrenic process usually characterized by the presence of persecutory or grandiose delusions, sometimes associated with hallucinations; usually characterized by less intellectual and behavioral impairment and shorter hospitalization than nonparanoid schizophrenia.

paresis A disorder associated with gross behavioral and physiological deterioration caused by syphilitic infections.

Parkinson's disease A disorder that appears to be due to a loss of neurons within the basal ganglia with characteristic tremor.

participant modeling Observation of a skillful individual performing the desired response, followed by imitation of this model.

passive-aggressive personality disorder A personality disorder characterized by both passivity and aggressiveness.

pathological intoxication An acute reaction occurring in individual's whose tolerance to alcohol is chronically low or reduced; characterized by drunkenness after a small intake of alcohol.

pedigrees A scientific method for determining, by the use of a single family history, whether heredity influences a given characteristic.

pedophilia Abuse of a child by an adult for sexual gratification.

personality According to Allport, the dynamic organization within the individual of those psychophysical systems that determine unique adjustment to the environment.

petit mal seizures One of the four major types of epilepsy; characterized by loss or alteration of consciousness lasting only a few seconds.

phenomenological models Models or paradigms of abnormal behavior based on the belief that a person's behavior is best understood in terms of that person's consciousness; the explanation of abnormal behavior in terms of blocked feelings, negative self-image, and loss of authenticity.

phenotype The physical expression of the genotype; the visible physical characteristics that express the underlying hereditary characteristics.

phenylketonuria A rare genetic metabolic disease resulting in mental retardation due to a malfunction in amino-acid metabolism.

phobia An intense learned fear of specific objects, situations, or living organisms as defined by subjective report, behavioral observation, and autonomic response to relatively innocuous stimuli.

physiological assessment The quantification of physiological events as they are related to psychological variables.

pica A craving for nonfood, nonnutritional substances; may be due to a specific nutritional deficiency.

Pick's disease A rare disorder similar to Alzheimer's disease with same age of onset; typically only frontal lobe involvement.

plateau stage The second stage of sexual arousal; sexual tension increases if stimulation is uninterrupted.

potentiating effect Effect created when one drug is taken in combination with another; combination may potentiate or increase the effect of the first drug.

predictive validity The degree to which a testing or assessment technique predicts future performance.

Premack principle A principle of operant conditioning that states that a behavior of low probability can be reinforced and thus increased by making the privilege of engaging in another preferred or more probable behavior contingent upon the performance of the low probability behavior.

premature ejaculation The absence of voluntary control of ejaculation.

primary (classic) sociopath An antisocial individual whose chief characteristic is a lack of anxiety or guilt.

primary impotence An inability to achieve erection on any occasion, including during masturbation and sleep.

primary motives States that involve physiological, unlearned motives, such as hunger; states that are caused by internal and external conditions and that function to maintain a constant internal balance.

primary process According to Freud, the thinking that consists largely of unrestrained sexual and aggressive fantasies.

primary symptoms According to Bleuler, symptoms of schizophrenia resulting directly from underlying organic disease processes.

proband In genetic studies, the original case constituting the starting point of a family study.

process schizophrenia A schizophrenia characterized by poor premorbid adjustment, gradual onset, nonparanoid symptomatology, and poor prognosis.

projective techniques The use of vague, unstructured stimulus items to elicit the individual's characteristic methods of perceiving the world; for example TAT, Rorschach test.

prompts Cues, instructions, gestures, directions, examples, and models that facilitate the probability of the desired behavioral response.

pseudoinsomnia A sleep disturbance characterized by reports of the symptoms associated with insomnia but with the inability to confirm such a pattern in the sleep lab.

psilocybin A hallucinogenic substance obtained from a variety of sacred Mexican mushrooms.

psychedelic drugs Drugs that produce marked changes in sensory, perceptual, and cognitive functioning following ingestion.

psychic determinism The belief that every aspect of human behavior has a cause and that even seemingly trivial events are significant in understanding the individual's behavior; a major premise of psychoanalysis.

psychic trauma Any painful event that causes serious and lasting damage to the personality or self.

psychoanalysis A system of psychology derived by Sigmund Freud that seeks the roots of human behavior in unconscious processes.

psychodrama A group therapy approach in which the clients act out their feelings as if they were in a play; group members assume various roles in these dramas.

psychogenic amnesia A dissociative disorder characterized by extensive memory loss that may endure for a few hours, days, or months; memory loss may be partial or total.

psychogenic approach The assumption that the causes of mental illness involve psychic trauma, such as Oedipal conflicts or sibling rivalry.

psycholgia Vague pain in various parts of the body, especially when an area is stimulated.

psychomotor seizure A type of epilepsy characterized by abnormal electrical discharges in the temporal lobe, results in periods of automatic behavior often associated with aggressive outbursts.

psychophysiological disorders Physical ailments, such as ulcers, asthma, hypertension, and headaches, often precipitated by stress, tension, or other psychological factors.

psychosis A severe mental disorder characterized by disorganization of thought processes and bizarre behavior that may pervade all aspects of the individual's life.

psychosurgery A brain operation aimed at alleviating a mental disorder; for example, prefrontal lobotomy.

psychotic depressive reaction A depressive disorder precipitated by an external event with no previous history of repeated depression or mood swings.

public verification In terms of scientific discovery, a principle or a set of results must be able to provide enough information to allow other researchers to use the same methods to repeat or replicate the results.

rape Sexual intercourse or activity with a minor in the absence of force (statutory rape) or sexual relations with the use of coercion (forcible rape).

rapid eye movement (REM) sleep The sleep phase characterized by an EEG indicating light sleep, complete relaxation, absence of reflexes, and difficulty in awakening; also referred to as paradoxical sleep.

rating scales A test consisting of a series of items that have been assigned ranks or values to assess various attitudes, traits, or behaviors.

rationalism The belief that humans can understand and explain the universe solely by applying correct logic without direct observation of the natural world.

reactive schizophrenia A schizophrenic process characterized by good premorbid adjustment, rapid onset, paranoid symptomatology, and good prognosis.

reality principle The reality-testing function of the ego that is used to mediate between the id and the outside world.

reciprocal determinism The belief that control of behavior operates between the individual and society.

refractory period The resolution stage of sexual arousal; in men, restimulation is impossible during this stage.

reification Treating an abstraction as if it were real or alive.

reinforcement theories of depression Theories of depression that relate the incidence of depression to absent or low levels of reinforcement due to internal or external causes.

reinforcing stimulus (S) Any stimulus that increases the probability of a response.

reliability The degree to which an assessment procedure gives the same reading at different times and with different examiners; in diagnosis, the consistency of diagnosis and agreement among classifiers.

resistance According to psychoanalysis, the attempt to avoid having unconscious material become conscious.

respondent conditioning Classical conditioning; the linking of the conditioned stimulus with the unconditioned stimulus that originally evoked the unconditioned response, followed by the conditioned response that begins to be evoked by the conditioned stimulus; for example, Pavlov's dog.

response prevention A behavioral technique used to modify compulsive behaviors by persuasion, distraction, or other techniques preventing completion of the ritual.

response specificity (stereotypy) The theory that each individual responds to stress of any kind with a typical preferred pattern of autonomic responses.

response systems The units of classification used in a behavioral response system differentiating, for example, the following systems— emotional, sensory, cognitive, motor, biological needs, acquired biological needs, and social behavior.

retentive encopresis Involuntary defecation in which the soiling consists primarily of a constant leakage of fecal stain fluid from the rectum.

retrograde amnesia Memory loss of past events.

rhythmic speaking A treatment for stuttering involving speaking in time with a metronome or finger taps.

sadism Achievement of sexual gratification by inflicting pain on a partner.

schizo-affective type. A psychotic disorder that is a mixture of schizophrenia and manic-depressive psychosis.

schizogenic mother A psychodynamic conceptualization of a rejecting, cold, dominating, overprotective, and smothering mother who precipitates the development of schizophrenia in her children.

schizoid personality disorder A personality disorder characterized by shyness, oversensitivity, seclusiveness, avoidance of close or competitive relationships, and eccentricity.

schizophrenia According to Bleuler, a severe mental disorder characterized by a split (schism) within the mind (phrenos) emphasizing the split between cognitive processes and emotion.

schizotypal personality disorder A schizoid personality disorder characterized by a family history of schizophrenia and peculiarities of cognitive processes.

school phobia (separation anxiety) A specific separation anxiety involving refusal to leave the home to attend school.

scientific inquiry A method of investigating causality that emphasizes methodology.

scientific terminology The proper use of language that defines measurable qualities; the use of language that differentiates between observations and inferences.

secondary gains Another name for maintaining factors; the gain or compensation one experiences by being ill.

secondary impotence Difficulty in achieving erection in coitus but not during fantasy or masturbation.

secondary motives (acquired motives) Learned behavior, such as anxiety or jealousy, that is assumed to be acquired by association with primary motives; varies greatly among individuals and societies.

secondary symptoms According to Bleuler, symptoms of schizophrenia resulting from the interaction of organic disease with factors in the individual's environment.

selective breeding A method to determine the influence of genetics on specified behavior patterns; inbreeding of individuals possessing a particular trait and comparison of their offspring with the offspring of those who do not possess the trait.

self-actualization According to Carl Rogers, the tendency to develop one's own capacities and talents.

self-monitoring Self-observation of the target behavior by the client.

self-report inventories rating instruments or judgments made by the individual about himself or herself.

senile dementia A gradual deterioration in intellectual, judgmental, and memory processes found in some persons in old age.

sensate focus Treatment to eliminate sexual performance anxiety involving learning to think and feel sensuously by giving and receiving bodily pleasure, first by nongenital contact and then by specific genital stimulation.

sensory deprivation An experimental or natural situation wherein the intensity of stimulus patterns is much reduced.

sex chromosomes The chromosome responsible for determining an individual's sex.

sexual deviation Sexual practices that differ from conventional sexual behavior in terms of sexual object or activity.

sexual dysfunction Behavior patterns, usually learned early in life, that prevent a satisfactory sex life.

sexual orientation Whether one identifies oneself as male or female.

sexual trauma Physically or mentally painful experiences that cause sexual difficulties; for example, rape, incest.

shaping An operant conditioning technique used to teach very complex behavior by teaching a sequence of responses so that the individual gradually approximates the desired behavior; also called successive approximation.

simple phobia Irrational fears of specific animals, events, or situations.

simple schizophrenia The schizophrenic process characterized by slow onset, oddities of conduct, difficulties in social relationships, unreasonableness, and decline in social behavior and performance.

single case design A sophisticated investigation of one individual in which interest centers on how a particular variable affects that individual.

single classification principle The classification of abnormal behavior based on one principle, either on behavior or etiology, but not on both.

situationalism The point of view that maintains that situational or environmental factors determine behavior.

sleep apnea Breath stoppage during sleep; the breakdown of the body's automatic control of breathing in the shift from wakefulness to sleep.

sleepwalking (somnambulism) A sleep disorder associated with walking during the early hours of sleep; occurs with open eyes, bland expression, and an unsteady gait.

slow-wave sleep The last two stages of sleep involving the largest and slowest EEG wave forms.

social competence Measurement of how effectively the retarded individual adjusts to the environment.

social-cultural model The second proposition of environmental models: any culture's success in creating conformity to its standard of normal behavior is limited.

social deprivation The relative loss or removal of social privilege due to socioeconomic class.

social disorganization hypothesis The sociological hypothesis that states that schizophrenia is prevalent in the lower socioeconomic classes because of disorganization, deprivation, and poverty.

social drift hypothesis The social hypothesis that postulates that schizophrenia is more prevalent in lower socioeconomic classes because cognitive dysfunctions and inadequate coping skills cause schizophrenic individuals to drift into the lower classes and slum areas.

social phobia Anxiety associated with exposure to scrutiny by other people in situations that could lead to criticism or embarrassment.

social psychological model The paradigm that assumes that no intrinsic difference exists between normal and abnormal behavior.

social stratification The level of location of an individual's roles in the social strata or levels.

socialization The act or process of producing uniform patterns of behavior, beliefs, and attitudes in society's members.

socialized delinquency syndrome A cluster of behaviors seen in one pattern of delinquent children; characteristics include association with bad companions, participation in gang activities, and habitual truancy from school and home.

somatic weakness hypothesis The theory that suggests that the type of psychophysiological disorder developed is determined by the weakest organ.

somatoform disorders The DMS III category that includes conversion disorder type syndromes (physical symptoms suggesting psychological disorders).

somatotypes Sheldon's classification of people or personalities according to three body types; endomorph, mesomorph, and ectomorph.

somniloquy Sleeptalking; the utterance of speech or other meaningful sounds during sleep without the subject's awareness of the event.

spasmodic torticollis A tic in which the neck muscles are contracted so that the head is held either in a laterally or vertically deviant position.

specific attitude hypothesis A theory developed by Grace and Gram stating that particular attitudes are associated with particular patterns of physiological change or psychophysiological disorder.

specific emotion hypothesis A belief regarding psychophysiological disorders stating that each emotional response causes specific psychophysiological activity.

stages of psychosexual development In psychoanalytic theory, the sequence through which socialization proceeds, linked to the body's erogenous zones; stages include oral stage (birth to two years), anal stage (concurrent with toilet training), phallic stage (three to five years), latent period (six to twelve years), and genital period.

standardization In test procedures, the degree to which different examiners can administer a test in the same manner and thereby, presumably, achieve the same results.

state dependent learning Learning that occurs in drug states and is often inaccessible in normal states; a possible explanation for alcoholic blackouts.

stimulants Drugs that produce energy, alertness, and feelings of confidence.

stimulus-bound theory of obesity The belief that the eating behavior of obese individuals is extremely responsive to external cues, for example, the sight of food.

stimulus discrimination The process by which a subject learns to discriminate or differentiate between similar stimuli.

stimulus generalization The principle that proposes that when a subject has been conditioned to respond to a specific stimulus, similar stimuli will evoke the same response.

stimulus hunger A tendency for antisocial individuals to engage in activity of an immoral or illegal nature as a function of their need to increase the stimulation in their environment, thus increasing their optimal level of arousal.

stimulus substitution The process by which any neutral stimulus paired with a stimulus that regularly evokes the desired response will acquire the properties of that stimulus.

stress A state of physical or psychological strain.

stuttering Inappropriate movement of the speech masculature that produces speech dysfluencies, including repetition and prolongation of speech sounds.

subcultural delinquent Dissocial reaction of childhood that results from membership in a subculture whose values and norms are at variance with society's standards.

substance-induced mental disorders According to DSM III, excessive use of substances that cause a physical disorder of the central nervous system.

successive approximation An operant conditioning technique used to teach very complex behavior by teaching a sequence of response so that the individual gradually approximates the desired behavior; also called shaping.

suicide Intentional taking of one's own life.

superego In psychoanalysis, the part of the personality is representative of society; the moral arm of the personality.

symptom substitution A psychoanalytic principle that assumes that other symptoms will develop in some cases if the basic underlying conflicts have not been resolved.

syndrome Specific cluster of symptoms.

syphilis An infectious venereal disease caused by spirochetes which systematically destroy internal organs in four well-defined stages.

systematic desensitization A behavioral technique developed by Joseph Wolpe used to deal with maladaptive anxiety reactions; the technique includes deep muscle relaxation, and gradual or gradient presentation of the anxiety stimuli.

taxonomy The classification of data according to their natural relationships.

T-groups Therapy groups utilizing group dynamics to develop self-awareness and interpersonal skills; sensitivity training.

thought stopping A three-stage procedure developed by Wolpe for treating obsessive thoughts; the individual thinks the thought and the therapist yells "Stop!", the individual thinks the thought and personally yells "Stop!", and finally, the individual nonverbally thinks "Stop!"

tic An involuntary, repetitive muscle spasm usually limited to a single muscle group.

time out A withdrawal of reinforcement; a behavioral technique used in shaping the behavior of children.

token economy (social learning therapy) An application of learning theory to the modification of deviant behavior through the use of tokens or rewards for appropriate behavior that can be exchanged for desired objects or privileges.

tolerance The necessity over time for greater amounts of a drug to be ingested to produce the desired result.

trait A relatively consistent and persistent behavior pattern manifested over a wide range of circumstances.

transactional analysis A form of psychotherapy based on psychoanalysis, communication theory, and social role theory.

transference In psychoanalysis, displacement of affect or emotion from the parent to the analyst; the development of an extremely positive or negative reaction to the analyst.

transmethylation hypothesis A hypothesis that assumes that schizophrenia results from an accumulation of certain hallucination-producing matabolites in the brain.

transsexualism A rare disorder characterized by an intense denial of one's biological sex; usually associated with a history of cross-dressing.

transvestism The preference for dressing in the clothes of the opposite sex to obtain sexual arousal or gratification.

traumatic anxiety An anxiety reaction in children provoked by an unexpected frightening event the child cannot cope with.

Turner's syndrome An hereditary disorder, similar to Klinefelter's syndrome, characterized by the superficial appearance of a female but with immature sexual development and abnormalities.

two-phase theory of migraine Wolff's two-stage physiological mechanism characterizing migraines—first a constriction of the intro- and intracranial arteries associated with sensory or motor aura followed by a rebound dilation of these arteries associated with onset of pain.

type A personality According to Friedman and Rosenman's theory, a personality type characterized by excessive competition, aggression, impatience, and vulnerability to coronary heart disease.

type B personality According to Friedman and Rosenman's theory, the opposite of the Type A personality.

ulcers An open sore or lesion on some mucous membrane in the lining of the small intestine or stomach due to hypersecretion of gastric acid.

unconditioned response (UCR) A response that is evoked by a stimulus without the need for learning.

unconditioned stimulus (UCS) A stimulus that evokes a response without the need for learning.

unconscious conflicts Conflicts or distressing situations that are not in a person's awareness; underlying mechanisms that are responsible for symptoms of mental illness, as postulated by Freud.

unipolar depression Depression without the occurrence of manic episodes.

unsocialized aggressive syndrome A cluster of behaviors that characterize one type of delinquent children; behaviors include assaultive tendencies, proclivity for starting fights, cruelty, defiance of authority, inadequate guilt feelings, and a penchant for malicious mischief.

vaginal photophethysmograph A clear acrylic probe, approximately one-half inch in diameter and one-and-three-fourths inches in length with an incandescent light source on one side and a selenium photocell detector on the other; used to measure the degree of vasocongestion in the vaginal wall.

vaginismus An involuntary spasm of the muscles surrounding the vaginal entrance whenever vaginal penetration is attempted.

validity In diagnosis, the assurance that labels describe what they are supposed to describe; the degree to which a measure is meaningful, that is, that the information obtained is the information sought.

vasocongestion Engorgement of tissues in the genitals and surrounding areas with blood, producing penile and clitorial erection as well as vaginal lubrication during sexual stimulation.

ventromedial hypothalamus (VMH) The center in the brain that influences satiety by signaling that enough has been eaten.

vicarious extinction The elimination of anxiety by observation of another engaging in anxiety-producing behavior without undue consequence.

voyeurism Achieving sexual arousal and gratification by watching others undress or engage in sexual activity.

"washers" A type of compulsion in which the individual feels that certain objects are contaminated; exposure to these objects increases anxiety and activates the urge to ritualize.

Wernicke's syndrome An organic brain dysfunction associated with a severe deficit of thiamine and marked by a sudden onset of drowsiness, paralysis of eye movements, and inability to walk.

withdrawal design An equivalent time experimental design in which experimenters introduce and then withdraw the independent variable.

withdrawal syndrome Physical and mental symptoms (including anxiety, profuse perspiration, cramps, etc.) associated with loss of dependence on narcotics.

XYY males Males who have an extra Y chromosome; sometimes referred to as "super males"; supposedly possess unusual height, borderline intelligence, and abnormal susceptibility to violence.

References

Abel, G. G.; Barlow, D. H.; Blanchard, E. B.; and Guild, D. *The components of rapist's sexual arousal.* Paper read at 128th Annual Meeting of the American Psychiatric Association, Anaheim, California, May 5, 1975.

Abel, G. G.; Blanchard, E. G.; Barlow, D. H.; and Mavissakalian, M. Measurement of sexual arousal in male homosexuals: Effects of instructions and stimulus modality. *Archives of Sexual Behavior,* 1975, 4:212–17.

Abramson, L. Y.; Seligman, M. E. P.; and Teasdale, J. P. Learned helplessness in humans: Critique and reformation. *Journal of Abnormal Psychology,* 1978, 87:49–74.

Abse, D. W. *Hysteria and related mental disorders.* Baltimore: Williams & Wilkins, 1966.

Achenbach, T. *Developmental psychopathology.* New York: Ronald Press, 1974.

Ad Hoc Committee on Classification of Headaches. Classification of headache. *Neurology,* 1962, 12:378–80.

Adams, H. E., and Calhoun, K. S. Innovations in the treatment of abnormal behavior. In K. S. Calhoun, H. E. Adams, and K. M. Mitchell (eds.), *Innovative treatment methods in psychopathology.* New York: Wiley, 1974.

Adams, H. E.; Doster, J. D.; and Calhoun, K. S. A psychological based system of response clarification. In A. R. Ciminero, K. S. Calhoun, and H. E. Adams (eds.), *A handbook of behavior assessment.* New York: Wiley, 1977.

Adams, H. E.; Feuerstein, M.; and Fowler, J. L. The migraine headache: A review of parameters, theories, and interventions. *Psychological Bulletin,* 1980, 87:217–37.

Adams, H. E.; Heyse, H.; and Meyer, V. Issues in the clinical application of behavior therapy. In H. E. Adams and I. P. Unikel (eds.), *Issues and trends in behavior therapy.* Springfield, Ill.: Charles C Thomas, 1973.

Adams, H. E.; Hoblit, P. R.; and Sutker, P. B. Electroconvulsive shock, brain acetylcholinesterase activity, and memory. *Physiology and Behavior,* 1969, 4:113–16.

Adams, H. E., and Sturgis, E. T. Status of behavioral reorientation techniques in the modification of homosexuality: A review. *Psychological Bulletin,* 1978, 84:1171–88.

Ader, R.; Beels, C. C.; and Tatum, R. Blood pepsinogen and gastric erosions in the rat. *Psychosomatic Medicine,* 1960, 22:1–12.

Adler, A. Compulsion neurosis. *International Journal of Individual Psychology,* 1931, 9:1–16. Reprinted in H. L. Ansbacher and R. R. Ansbacher (eds.), *Superiority and social interest.* New York: Viking Press, 1964.

Agnew, H. W., Jr.; Webb, W. B.; and Williams, R. L. Comparison of stage four and 1-REM sleep deprivation. *Perceptual and Motor Skills,* 1967, 24:851–58.

Ainsworth, M. D. S. Discussion of Suomi and Bowlby by chapters. In G. Serban and A. Kling (eds.), *Animal models in human psychobiology.* New York: Plenum Press, 1976.

Akiskal, H. S., and McKinney, W. T., Jr. Depressive disorders: Toward a unified hypothesis. *Science,* 1973, 182:20–30.

Akiskal, H. S., and McKinney, W. T., Jr. Overview of recent research on depression. *Archives of General Psychiatry,* 1975, 32:285–304.

Alarcon, R. D. Hysteria and hysterical personality: How come one without the other? *Psychiatric Quarterly,* 1973, 47:258–75.

Albin, R. Therapy research: Still a way to go. *APA Monitor,* 1977, 8(9/10): 11–12.

Alexander, F. *Psychosomatic medicine.* New York: Norton, 1950.

Alexander, F.; French, T. M.; and Pollack, G. H. *Psychosomatic specificity.* Chicago: University of Chicago Press, 1968.

Al-Issa, I. Social and cultural aspects of hallucinations. *Psychological Bulletin,* 1977, 84:570–88.

Allen, J.; DeMyer, M.; Norton, J. A.; Pontius, W.; and Young, E. Intellectuality in parents of psychotic, subnormal, and normal children. *Journal of Autism and Childhood Schizophrenia,* 1971, 1:311–26.

Allen, M.; Cohen, S.; and Pollin, W. Schizophrenia in veteran twins: A diagnostic review. *American Journal of Psychiatry,* 1972, 128:939–45.

Allison, J.; Blatt, S. J.; and Zimet, C. N. *The interpretation of psychological tests.* New York: Harper & Row, 1968.

Allport, G. W. *Personality: A psychological interpretation.* New York: Holt, Rinehart & Winston, 1937.

American Association on Mental Deficiency. *Manual on terminology and classification in mental retardation.* Rev. ed. H. J. Grossman (ed.). Special Publication Series No. 2, 1973.

American Medical Association. Mental retardation: A handbook for the primary physician. *Journal of the American Medical Association,* 1965, 191:183–231.

American Psychiatric Association. *Diagnostic and statistical manual of mental disorders.* 1st ed. Washington, D.C.: American Psychiatric Association, 1952.

American Psychiatric Association. *Diagnostic and statistical manual of mental disorders.* 2nd ed. Washington, D.C.: American Psychiatric Association, 1968.

American Psychiatric Association. *Diagnostic and statistical manual of mental disorders.* 3d ed. Washington, D.C.: American Psychiatric Association, 1980.

Andrews, G., and Harris, M. *The syndrome of stuttering.* London: Haneman, 1964.

Angrist, B.; Lee, H. K.; and Gershon, S. The antagonism of amphetamine-induced symptomology by a neuroleptic. *American Journal of Psychiatry,* 1974, 131:817–19.

Anthony, E. J. Psychoneurotic disorder. In A. M. Freedman and H. I. Kaplan (eds.), *Comprehensive textbook of psychiatry.* Baltimore: Williams & Wilkins, 1967.

Anxiety over antianxiety drugs. *Behavior Today,* 1974, 5(21):149.

Appel, C. An approach to the treatment of schizoid phenomena. *Psychoanalytic Review,* 1974, 61:99–113.

Appell, M. J., and Tisdall, W. J. Factors differentiating institutionalized from noninstitutionalized referred retardates. *American Journal of Mental Deficiency,* 1968, 37:424–43.

Arehart, J. L. The search for a heroin "cure." *Science News,* 1972, 101:250–51.

Arena, J. M. *Poisoning: Chemistry, symptoms, treatments.* Springfield, Ill.: Charles C Thomas, 1963.

Arkin, A. M. Sleep-talking: A review. *Journal of Nervous and Mental Disorders,* 1966, 143:101–22.

Aronson, E. *The social animal.* San Francisco: Freeman, 1972.

Asch, M. J. Negative response bias and personality adjustment. *Journal of Counseling Psychology,* 1958, 5:206–10.

Asch, S. E. Effects of group pressure upon modification and distortion of judgements. In E. E. Maccoby, I. M. Newcomb, and E. L. Hartley (eds.), *Readings in social psychology.* 3rd ed. New York: Holt, Rinehart & Winston, 1958.

Aserinsky, E., and Kleitman, N. Regularly occurring periods of eye motility and concomitant phenomena during sleep. *Science,* 1953, 118:273–74.

Atthowe, J. M. Jr., and Krasner, L. A preliminary report on the application of contingent reinforcement procedures (token economy on a "chronic" psychiatric ward). *Journal of Abnormal Psychology,* 1968, 73:37–43.

Averill, J. R. Personal control over aversive stimuli and its relationship to stress. *Psychological Bulletin,* 1973, 80:286–303.

Aviado, D. M. Ganglionic stimulant and blocking drugs. In J. R. DiPalma (ed.), *Drill's pharmacology in medicine.* 4th ed. New York: McGraw-Hill, 1971.

Ax, A. F. The physiological differentiation between fear and anger in humans. *Psychosomatic Medicine,* 1953, 15:433–42.

Ayllon, T., and Azrin, N. H. *The token economy: A motivational system for therapy and rehabilitation.* New York: Appleton-Century-Crofts, 1968.

Ayllon, T.; Layman, D.; and Burk, S. Disruptive behavior and reinforcement of academic performance. *Psychological Record,* 1972, 22:315–23.

Azrin, N. H. Effects of punishment intensity during variable internal reinforcement. *Journal of Experimental Analysis of Behavior,* 1960, 2:123–42.

Azrin, N. H.; Sneed, T. J.; and Foxx, R. M. Dry bed: A rapid method of eliminating bedwetting (enuresis) of the retarded. *Behaviour Research and Therapy,* 1973, 11:435–42.

Babladelis, G., and Adams, S. *The shaping of personality.* Englewood Cliffs, New Jersey: Prentice-Hall, 1967.

Backman, H.; Kallisla, H.; and Ostling, G. Placebo effect in peptic ulcer and other gastrointestinal disorders. *Gastroectenterlogia,* 1960, 94:11–20.

Baekeland, F., and Lasky, R. Exercise and sleep patterns in college athletes. *Perceptual and Motor Skills,* 1966, 23:1203–7.

Bagley, C. Incest behavior and incest taboo. *Social Problems,* 1969, 16:505–19.

Bakal, D. A. Headache: A biopsychological perspective. *Psychological Bulletin,* 1975, 82:369–82.

Bakwin, H., and Bakwin, R. M. *Clinical management of behavior disorders in children.* Philadelphia: Saunders, 1966.

Bakwin, H., and Bakwin, R. M. *Behavior disorders in children.* 4th ed. Philadelphia: Saunders, 1972.

Balla, O. A.; Butterfield, E. C.; and Zigler, E. Effects of institutionalization on retarded children: A longitudinal cross-institutional investigation. *American Journal of Mental Deficiency,* 1971, 78:530–49.

Ban, T. A., and Lehmann, H. E. Nicotinic acid in the treatment of schizophrenics. In *Progress Report 1, Canadian Mental Health Association Study.* Toronto: Canadian Mental Health Association, 1971.

Bandura, A. *Principles of behavior modification.* New York: Holt, Rinehart & Winston, 1969.

Bandura, A. Effecting change through participant modeling. In J. D. Krumboltz and C. E. Thoresen (eds.), *Counseling methods.* New York: Holt, Rinehart & Winston, 1976.

Bandura, A. *Social learning theory.* Englewood Cliffs, N.J.: Prentice-Hall, 1977.

Bandura, A., and Menlove, F. T. Factors determining vicarious extinction of avoidance behavior through symbolic modeling. *Journal of Personality and Social Psychology,* 1968, 8:99–108.

Bannister, D.; Thelman, P.; and Leiberman, D. M. Diagnosis-treatment relationships in psychiatry: A statistical analysis. *British Journal of Psychiatry,* 1964, 110:726–32.

Barber, T. Y. Toward a theory of pain-relief of chronic pain by prefrontal leucotomy, opiates, placebos, and hypnosis. *Psychological Bulletin,* 1959, 56:430–60.

Barlow, D. H. The treatment of sexual deviation: Towards a comprehensive behavioral approach. In K. S. Calhoun, H. E. Adams, and K. M. Mitchell (eds.), *Innovative treatment methods in psychopathology.* New York: Wiley, 1974.

Barlow, D. H. Assessment of sexual behavior. In A. R. Ciminero, K. S. Calhoun, and H. E. Adams (eds.), *Handbook of behavioral assessment.* New York: Wiley, 1977.

Barlow, D. H.; Leitenberg, H.; and Agras, W. S. Experimental control of sexual deviation through manipulation of the noxious scene in covert sensitization. *Journal of Abnormal Psychology,* 1969, 74:596–601.

Barlow, D. H.; Becker, R.; Leitenberg, H.; and Agras, W. S. A mechanical strain gauge for recording penile circumference. *Journal of Applied Behavior Analysis,* 1970, 3:73–76.

Barlow, D. H., and Agras, W. S. Fading to increase heterosexual responsiveness to homosexuals. *Journal of Applied Behavior Analysis,* 1973, 6:355–66.

Barlow, D. H.; Reynolds, J.; and Agras, W. S. Gender identity change in a transsexual. *Archives of General Psychiatry,* 1973, 28:569–76.

Barlow, D. H., and Abel, G. G. Sexual deviation. In W. E. Craighead, A. E. Kazdin, and M. J. Maloney (eds.), *Behavior modification: Principles, issues, and applications.* Boston: Houghton Mifflin, 1976.

Barlow, D. H.; Abel, G. G.; Blanchard, E. B.; Bristow, A. R.; and Young, L. D. A heterosocial skills checklist for males. *Behavior Therapy,* 1977, 8:229–39.

Barlow, D. H.; Abel, G. G.; and Blanchard, E. B. *Gender identity change in a transsexual: An exorcism.* Unpublished manuscript, University of Tennessee Medical School.

Barnes, E. H. The relationship of biased test responses to psychopathology. *Journal of Abnormal Social Psychology,* 1955, 51:286–90.

Baron, J. H., and Wastell, C. Medical treatment. In C. Wastell (ed.), *Chronic duodenal ulcer.* New York: Appleton-Century-Crofts, 1972.

Barrett, B. H. Reduction in rate of multiple tics by free operant conditioning methods. *Journal of Nervous and Mental Disease,* 1962, 135:187–95.

Barrett, J. H. *Gerontological psychology.* Springfield, Ill.: Charles C Thomas, 1972.

Bartak, L.; Rutter, M.; and Cos, A. A comparative study of infantile autism and specific developmental language disorders: The children. *British Journal of Psychiatry,* 1975, 126:127–45.

Batchelor, I. R. C. *Henderson and Gillespie's textbook of psychiatry.* London: Oxford University Press, 1969.

Bateson, G.; Jackson, D.; Haley, J.; and Weakland, J. Towards a theory of schizophrenia. *Behavioral Science,* 1956, 1:251–64.

Bayh, B. *Opening statement on hearing on the abuse of barbiturates.* U.S. Senate, December 15, 1971.

Bazell, R. J. Drug abuse: Methadone becomes the solution and the problem. *Science,* 1973, 179:772–75.

Beck, A. T. *Depression: Clinical, experimental and theoretical aspects.* New York: Harper & Row, 1967.

Beck, A. T. Measuring depression: The depression inventory. In T. W. Williams, M. M. Katz, and J. A. Shields (eds.), *Recent advances in the psychobiology of the depressive illnesses.* Washington, D.C.: U.S. Government Printing Office, 1972.

Beck, A. T. *Cognitive therapy and the emotional disorders.* New York: International Universities Press, 1976.

Beck, A. T.; Ward, C. H.; Mendelson, M.; Mock, J. E.; and Erbaugh, J. K. Reliability in psychiatric diagnoses: 2. A study of consistency in clinical judgments and ratings. *American Journal of Psychiatry,* 1962, 119:351–57.

Becker, J. *Affective disorders.* Morristown, N.J.: General Learning Press, 1977.

Becker, P. W., and Cesar, J. A. Use of beer in geriatric patient groups. *Psychological Reports,* 1973, 33:182.

Bee, H. L.; VanEgern, L. F.; Streissguth, A. P.; Nyman, B. A.; and Leckie, M. S. Social class differences in maternal teaching strategies and speech patterns. *Developmental Psychology,* 1969, 1:726–34.

Beech, H. R., and Fransella, F. *Research and experiment in stuttering.* Oxford: Pergamon Press, 1968.

Bellack, A. S. Behavior therapy for weight reduction: An evaluation review. *Addictive Behaviors,* 1975, 1:73–82.

Bellack, A. S., and Hersen, M. *Behavior modification: An introductory textbook.* Baltimore: Williams & Wilkins, 1977.

Bellak, L.; Hurrich, M.; and Gediman, H. *Ego function in schizophrenics, neurotics, and normals.* New York: Wiley, 1973.

Bem, D. J., and Funder, D. C. Predicting more of the people more of the time: Assessing the personality of situations. *Psychological Review,* 1978, 85:485–501.

Benda, C. E.; Squires, N. D.; Oronik, M. J.; and Wise, R. Personality factors in mild mental retardation: Family background and sociocultural patterns. *American Journal of Mental Deficiency*, 1963, 68:24–40.

Bender, L. *A visual motor gestalt test and its clinical use.* New York: American Orthopsychiatric Association, 1938.

Bender, L. Twenty years of research on schizophrenic children with special reference to those under twenty years of age. In G. Kaplan (ed.), *Emotional problems of early childhood.* New York: Basic Books, 1955.

Bender, L. The life course of children with schizophrenia. *American Journal of Psychiatry*, 1973, 130:783–86.

Benedict, R. Anthropology and the abnormal. *Journal of General Psychology*, 1934, 10:59–82.

Benson, O. F., and Geschwind, N. Psychiatric conditions associated with focal lesions of the central nervous system. In S. Arieti and M. F. Reiser (eds.), *American handbook of psychiatry.* Vol. 4. 2d ed. New York: Basic Books, 1975.

Bentler, P. M., and Prince, C. Personality characteristics of male transvestites. III. *Journal of Abnormal Psychology*, 1969, 74:140–43.

Bentler, P. M.; Shearman, R. W.; and Prince, C. Personality characteristics of male transvestites. *Journal of Clinical Psychology*, 1970, 26:434–35.

Berger, R. J., and Osmond, I. Effects of sleep deprivation on behavior, subsequent sleep and dreaming. *Journal of Mental Science*, 1962, 108:455–65.

Bergin, A. E. Some implications of psychotherapy research for therapeutic practice. *Journal of Abnormal Psychology*, 1966, 71:235–46.

Bergin, A. E. The evaluation of therapeutic outcomes. In A. E. Bergin and S. L. Garfield (eds.), *Handbook of psychotherapy and behavior change: An empirical analysis.* New York: Wiley, 1971.

Berne, E. *Games people play.* New York: Grove, 1964.

Bernhardt, A. J.; Hersen, M.; and Barlow, D. H. Measurement and modification of spasmodic torticollis: An experimental analysis. *Behavior Therapy*, 1972, 3:294–97.

Bernstein, A. The psychoanalytic technique. In B. B. Wolman (ed.), *Handbook of clinical psychology.* New York: McGraw-Hill, 1965.

Bernstein, D. A. Behavioral fear assessment: Anxiety or artifact? In H. E. Adams and I. P. Unikel (eds.), *Issues and trends in behavior therapy.* Springfield, Ill.: Charles C Thomas, 1973.

Berscheid, E., and Graziano, W. The initiation of social relationships and interpersonal attraction. In R. L. Burges and T. L. Huston (eds.), *Social exchange in developing relationships.* New York: Academic Press, forthcoming.

Bettelheim, B. *Truants from life.* Glencoe, Ill.: The Free Press, 1955.

Bettelheim, B. *A home for the heart.* New York: Knopf, 1973.

Bieler, I. *Homosexuality: A psychoanalytic study of male homosexuals.* New York: Basic Books, 1962.

Bielski, R. J., and Friedel, R. O. Prediction of tricyclic antidepressant response. *Archives of General Psychiatry*, 1976, 33:1479–88.

Bijou, S. W.; Peterson, R. F.; Harris, F. R.; Allen, K. E.; and Johnston, M. S. Methodology for experimental studies of young children in natural settings. *Psychological Record*, 1969, 19:177–210.

Bild, R., and Adams, H. E. Modification of migraine headaches by cephalic blood volume pulse and EMG biofeedback. *Journal of Consulting and Clinical Psychology*, 1980, 48:51–57.

Binchi, G. N. Patterns of hypochondriasis: A principle components analysis. *British Journal of Psychiatry*, 1973, 122:541–48.

Binswanger, L. *Being-in-the-world.* Translated by J. Needleman. New York: Basic Books, 1963.

Bishop, M. P.; Elder, S. T.; and Heath, R. G. Attempted control of operant behavior in man with intracranial self-stimulation. In R. G. Heath (ed.), *The role of pleasure in behavior.* New York: Harper & Row, 1964.

Black, A. The natural history of obsessional neurosis. In H. R. Beech (ed.), *Obsessional states.* London: Methuen & Co., 1974.

Blake, B. G. The application of behavior therapy to the treatment of alcoholism. *Behaviour Research and Therapy*, 1965, 3:75–85.

Blanchard, E. B.; Young, L. D.; and Haynes, M. R. A simple feedback system for the treatment of elevated blood pressure. *Behavior Therapy*, 1975, 6:241–45.

Blanchard, E. B., and Hersen, M. Behavioral treatment of hysterical neurosis: Symptom substitution and symptom return reconsidered. *Psychiatry*, 1976, 39:118–29.

Blanchard, E. B., and Epstein, L. H. *A biofeedback primer.* Reading, Mass.: Addison-Wesley Co., 1978.

Blanchard, E. B.; Theobald, D. E.; Brown, D. A.; Silver, B. V.; and Williamson, D. A. Temperature biofeedback in the treatment of migraine headaches. *Archives of General Psychiatry*, 1978, 35:581–88.

Blane, L., and Roth, R. H. Voyerism and exhibitionism. *Perceptual and Motor Skills*, 1967, 24:391–400.

Blashfield, R. An evaluation of the DSM-II classification of schizophrenia as a nomenclature. *Journal of Abnormal Psychology*, 1973, 82:382–89.

Blatz, W. E., and Ringlend, M. C. *The study of tics in preschool children.* University of Toronto Studies (Child Development Series No. 3). Toronto: University of Toronto Press, 1935.

Bleeker, E. Many asthma attacks are psychological. *Science News,* 1968, 93(17):405.

Blenkner, M. Environmental change and the aging individual. *Gerontologist,* 1967, 7:101–5.

Bleuler, E. *Lehrbuch der Psychiatrie.* Berlin: Springer, 1923.

Bleuler, E. *Dementia praecox or the group of schizophrenias.* Translated by J. Ziskin. New York: International University Press, 1950.

Bliss, E. L., and Branch, C. H. *Anorexia nervosa.* New York: Paul B. Hoeker, 1960.

Bliss, E. L.; Wilson, V. B.; and Zwanziger, J. Changes in brain norepinephrine in self-stimulating and "aversive" animals. *Journal of Psychiatric Research,* 1966, 4:59–63.

Block, J. *The challenge of response sets: Unconfounding meaning, acquiescence, and social desirability in the MMPI.* New York: Appleton-Century-Crofts, 1965.

Block, J.; Patterson, V.; Block, J.; and Jackson, D. D. A study of the parents of schizophrenic and neurotic children. *Psychiatry,* 1958, 21:387–97.

Blum, R.; Braunstein, L.; and Stone, A. Normal drug use: An exploratory study of patterns and correlates. In J. Cole and J. Wittenborn (eds.), *Drug abuse.* Springfield, Ill.: Charles C Thomas, 1969.

Bockoven, J. *Moral treatment in American psychiatry.* New York: Springer, 1963.

Bogen, J. E., and Vogel, P. J. Cerebral commissurotomy: A case report. *Bulletin of the Los Angeles Neurological Society,* 1962, 27:169.

Bootzin, R. *Stimulus control of insomnia.* Paper read at 126th Annual Meeting of the American Psychological Association, Montreal, August 1973.

Bord, R. Rejection of the mentally ill: Continuities and further developments. *Social Problems,* 1971, 18:496–509.

Borgaonkar, D. S., and Shah, S. A. The XYY chromosome male—or syndrome. In A. A. Steinberg and A. G. Bearn (eds.), *Progress in medical genetics.* Vol. 10. New York: Grune & Stratton, 1975.

Borkovec, T. D.; Kaloupek, D. G.; and Slama, K. M. The facilitative effect of muscle tension-release in the relaxation treatment of sleep disturbance. *Behavior Therapy,* 1975, 6:301–9.

Borkovec, T. D.; Slama, K. M.; and Grayson, J. B. Sleep, disorders of sleep, and hypnosis. In D. C. Rimm and J. W. Somervill (eds.), *Abnormal psychology.* New York: Academic Press, 1977.

Borstein, M. R.; Bellack, A. S.; and Hersen, M. Social-skills training for unassertive children: A multiple-baseline analysis. *Journal of Applied Behavior Analysis,* 1977, 10:183–95.

Boshes, L. D., and Gibbs, A. *Epilepsy handbook.* 2d ed. Springfield, Ill.: Charles C Thomas, 1972.

Botwinick, J. *Aging and behavior: A comprehensive integration of research findings.* New York: Springer, 1973.

Boulougouris, J.; Marks, I. M.; and Marset, P. Superiority of flooding (implosion) to desensitization for reducing pathological fear. *Behaviour Research and Therapy,* 1971, 9:7–16.

Bowen, M. The use of family theory in clinical practice. *Comparative Psychiatry,* 1966, 7:345–74.

Bowers, K. S. Situationism in psychology: An analysis and a critique. *Psychological Review,* 1973, 80:307–36.

Bowlby, J. *Maternal care and mental health.* Geneva: World Health Organization Monograph Service, No. 2, 1951.

Bowlby, J. *Separation: Anxiety and anger.* New York: Basic Books, 1973.

Brady, J. P. Metronome conditioned speech retraining for stuttering. *Behavior Therapy,* 1971, 2:129–50.

Brady, J. P., and Lind, D. L. Experimental analysis of hysterical blindness. *Archives of General Psychiatry,* 1961, 4:331–39.

Brady, J. V. Ulcers in "executive" monkeys. *Scientific American,* 1958, 199(4):95–100.

Brady, J. V.; Porter, R. W.; Conrad, D. G.; and Mason, J. W. Avoidance behavior and the development of tal gastroduodenal ulcers. *Journal of Experimental Analysis of Behavior,* 1, 1958, 1:69–73.

Braginsky, B. M., and Braginsky, D. D. The mentally retarded: Society's Hansels and Gretels. *Psychology Today,* 1974, 7:18; 20–21; 24; 26; 28–30.

Braginsky, B. M.; Braginsky, D. D.; and Ring, K. *Methods of madness: The mental hospital as a last resort.* New York: Holt, Rinehart & Winston, 1969.

Braginsky, D. D., and Braginsky, B. M. *Hansels and Gretels: Studies of children in institutions for the mentally retarded.* New York: Holt, Rinehart & Winston, 1971.

Braid, J. *Neurypnology, or the rational of nervous sleep.* London: Churchill, 1843.

Bray, G. A. The myth of diet in the management of obesity. *American Journal of Clinical Nutrition,* 1970, 23:114–18.

Brecher, E. M., and the Editors of *Consumer Reports. Licit and illicit drugs.* Boston: Little, Brown, 1972.

Brener, J. A general model of voluntary control applied to the phenomena of learned cardiovascular change. In P. W. Obrist, A. H. Black, J. Brener, and L. V. DiCara (eds.), *Cardiovascular psychophysiology.* Chicago: Aldine, 1974.

Breuer, J., and Freud, S. *Studies in hysteria,* 1895. Reprint. New York: Avon Books, 1966.

Bridges, K. M. B. Emotional development in early infancy. *Child Development,* 1932, 3:324–41.

Brierly, H. The treatment of hysterical spasmodic torticollis by behaviour therapy. *Behaviour Research and Therapy,* 1967, 5:139–42.

Brill, N. G. Gross stress reaction. II: Traumatic war neurosis. In A. M. Freedman and H. I. Kaplan (eds.), *Comprehensive textbook of psychiatry.* Baltimore: Williams & Wilkins, 1967.

Brodie, K. H.; Gartrell, N.; Doering, C.; and Rhue, T. Plasma testosterone levels in heterosexual and homosexual men. *American Journal of Psychiatry,* 1974, 131:82–83.

Brody, I. A., and Wilkins, R. H. Neurological classics IX: Wernicke's encephalopathy. *Archives of Neurology,* 1968, 19:228–32.

Broen, W. E., Jr. *Schizophrenia: Research and theory.* New York: Academic Press, 1968.

Brown, B. S.; Wienckowski, L. A.; and Stolz, S. B. *Behavior modification: Perspective on a current issue.* Washington, D.C.: National Institute of Mental Health, 1975.

Brown, R. *A first language: The early stages.* Cambridge, Mass.: Harvard University Press, 1973.

Browne, E. G. *Arabian medicine.* New York: Macmillan, 1921.

Brownfield, C. A. *Isolation: Clinical and experimental approaches.* New York: Random House, 1965.

Bruch, H. Transformation of oral impulses in eating disorders: A conceptual approach. *Psychiatry Quarterly,* 1961, 35:458–81.

Bruner, J. W.; Goodnow, J. J.; and Austin, G. A. *A study of thinking.* New York: Science Editions, 1965.

Bulatov, P. K. The higher nervous activity in persons suffering from bronchial asthma. In *Problems of interrelationship between psyche and soma in psychoneurology and general medicine. Institute Bechtereva,* 1963, 317–328. Reprint. *International Journal of Psychiatry,* Sept. 1967, 245.

Bunney, W. E., Jr., and Davis, J. M. Norepinephrine in depressive reactions: A review. *Archives of General Psychiatry,* 1965, 13:483–94.

Bunney, W. E., Jr.; Goodwin, F. K.; and Murphy, D. L. The "switch process" in manic-depressive illness. III: Theoretical implication. *Archives of General Psychiatry,* 1972a, 27:312–17.

Bunney, W. E., Jr.; Murphy, D. L.; Goodwin, F. K.; and Borge, G. F. The "switch process" in manic-depressive illness: A systematic study of sequential behavioral changes. *Archives of General Psychiatry,* 1972b, 27:295–302.

Burns, G. W. *The science of genetics.* New York: Macmillan, 1972.

Burt, C. The evidence for the concept of intelligence. *British Journal of Educational Psychology,* 1955, 25:158–77.

Burton, R. *The anatomy of melancholy.* New York: W. J. Middleton, 1867.

Buss, A. H. *Psychopathology.* New York: Wiley, 1966.

Byers, R. K. Lead poisoning: Review of the literature and report on 45 cases. *Pediatrics,* 1959, 23:585.

Cameron, N. A. Paranoid reactions. In A. M. Freedman and H. I. Kaplan, (eds.), *Comprehensive textbook of psychiatry.* Baltimore: Williams & Wilkins, 1967, 665–75.

Cameron, N., and Margaret, A. *Behavior pathology.* Cambridge, Mass.: Riverside Press, 1951.

Campbell, D. *Arabian medicine and its influence on the Middle Ages.* New York: Dutton, 1926.

Cannon, W. B. Hunger and thirst. In C. Murchison (ed.), *Handbook of general experimental psychology.* Worcester, Mass.: Clark University Press, 1934.

Cantril, H. *The invasion from Mars.* Princeton, N.J.: Princeton University Press, 1947.

Cappell, H. D., and Pliner, P. L. Volitional control of marijuana intoxication: A study of the ability to "come down" on command. *Journal of Abnormal Psychology,* 1973, 82:428–34.

Carlson, G. A., and Goodwin, F. K. The stages of mania. *Archives of General Psychiatry,* 1973, 28:221–28.

Carp, F. M. Senility or garden variety maladjustment? *Journal of Gerontology,* 1969, 24:203–8.

Carr, A. T. Compulsive neurosis: A review of the literature. *Psychological Bulletin,* 1974, 81:311–18.

Carter, C. H. *Handbook of mental retardation syndromes.* Springfield, Ill.: Charles C Thomas, 1966.

Cartwright, D. Note on "changes" in psychoneurotic patients with and without psychotherapy. *Journal of Consulting Psychology,* 1956, 20:403–4.

Casler, L. Perceptual deprivation in institutional settings. In G. Newton and S. Levine (eds.), *Early experience and behavior.* Springfield, Ill.: Charles C Thomas, 1968.

Cautela, J. R. The application of learning theory "as a last resort" in the treatment of a case of anxiety neurosis. *Journal of Clinical Psychology,* 1965, 21:448–52.

Cautela, J. R. Treatment of compulsive behavior by covert sensitization. *Psychological Record,* 1966, 16:33–41.

Cautela, J. R. Covert sensitization. *Psychological Reports,* 1967, 20:459–68.

Cautela, J. R. Covert reinforcement. *Behavior Therapy,* 1970, 1:33–50.

Cautela, J. R. *Covert modeling.* Paper read at the 5th Annual Meeting of the Association for the Advancement of Behavior Therapy, Washington, D.C., September 1971.

Cautela, J. R., and Kastenbaum, R. A reinforcement survey schedule for use in therapy training and research. *Psychological Reports,* 1967, 20:1115–30.

Cautela, J. R., and Upper, D. The Behavioral Inventory Battery: The use of self-report measures in behavioral analysis and therapy. In M. Hersen and A. S. Bellack (eds.), *Behavioral assessment: A practical handbook.* New York: Pergamon Press, 1976.

Cavallin, H. Incestuous fathers: A clinical report. *American Journal of Psychiatry,* 1966, 74:249–55.

Cerletti, U., and Bini, L. L'Elettroshock. *Archivo General di Neurologia, Psichiatria e Psicoanalisi,* 1938, 19:266.

Chapman, L. J. Studies of psychodiagnostic errors of observation as a contribution toward a nondynamic psychopathology of everyday life. In H. E. Adams and W. K. Boardman (eds.), *Advances in experimental clinical psychology.* Elmsford, N.Y.: Pergamon, 1971.

Chapman, L. J.; Chapman, J. P.; and Miller, G. A. A theory of verbal behavior in schizophrenia. In B. A. Maher (ed.), *Progress in experimental personality research.* Vol. 1. New York: Academic Press, 1964.

Chapman, L. J., and Chapman, J. P. Genesis of popular but erroneous diagnostic observations. *Journal of Abnormal Psychology,* 1967, 72:193–204.

Chapman, L. J., and Chapman, J. P. Illusory correlations as an obstacle to the use of valid psychodiagnostic signs. *Journal of Abnormal Psychology,* 1969, 74:271–80.

Chapman, L. J., and Chapman, J. P. *Disordered thought in schizophrenia.* New York: Appleton-Century-Crofts, 1973.

Chatel, J. C., and Peele, R. A centennial review of neurasthenia. *American Journal of Psychiatry,* 1970, 126:1404–11.

Chedoff, P., and Lyons, H. Hysteria, the hysterical personality, and hysterical conversion. *American Journal of Psychiatry,* 1958, 114:734–40.

Chess, S. Healthy responses, developmental disturbances, and stress or reactive disorder. I. Infancy and childhood. In A. M. Freedman and H. I. Kaplan (eds.), *Comprehensive textbook of psychiatry.* Baltimore: Williams & Wilkins, 1968.

Chien, C. P. Psychiatric treatment for geriatric patients: "Pub" or drug? *American Journal of Psychiatry,* 1971, 127:1070–75.

Child, I. The relation of somatotype to self-ratings on Sheldon's temperament traits. *Journal of Personality,* 1950, 18:440–53.

Chirico, A., and Stunkard, A. Physical activity and human obesity. *New England Journal of Medicine,* 1960, 263:935–40.

Chorover, S. L. Big brother and psychotechnology. II: The pacification of the brain. *Psychology Today,* 1974, 12:59–69.

Ciminero, A. R. Behavioral assessment: An overview. In A. R. Ciminero, K. S. Calhoun, and H. E. Adams (eds.), *A handbook of behavioral assessment.* New York: Wiley, 1977.

Ciminero, A. R.; Nelson, R. O.; and Lipinski, D. P. Self-monitoring procedures. In A. R. Ciminero, K. S. Calhoun, and H. E. Adams (eds.), *A handbook of behavioral assessment.* New York: Wiley, 1977.

Cleckley, H. M. Psychopathic states. In S. Arieta (ed.), *American handbook of psychiatry.* Vol. 1. New York: Basic Books, 1959.

Cohen, B. D., and Camhi, J. Schizophrenic performance in a work communication task. *Journal of Abnormal Psychology,* 1967, 72:240–46.

Cohen, B. D.; Nachmani, J. G.; and Rosenberg, S. Referent communication disturbances in acute schizophrenia. *Journal of Abnormal Psychology,* 1974, 83:1–14.

Cohen, M. L.; Seghorn, T.; and Calmas, W. Sociometric study of the sex offender. *Journal of Abnormal Psychology,* 1969, 74:249–55.

Cohen, S. L., and Fiedler, J. E. Content analysis of multiple messages in suicide notes. *Life Threatening Behavior,* 1974, 4:75–95.

Colby, K. M. Appraisal of four psychological theories of paranoid phenomena. *Journal of Abnormal Psychology,* 1977, 86:54–59.

Coleman, J. C. *Abnormal psychology and modern life.* 4th ed. Chicago: Scott, Foresman, 1972.

Coleman, J. C. *Abnormal psychology and modern life.* 5th ed. Chicago: Scott, Foresman, 1976.

Colson, C. An objective-analytic approach to the classification of suicidal motivation. *Acta Psychiatrica Scandinavica,* 1973, 49:105–13.

Conger, J. J. The effects of alcohol on conflict behavior in the albino rat. *Quarterly Journal of Studies on Alcohol,* 1951, 12:1–29.

Cook, C., and Adams, H. E. Modification of verbal behavior in speech deficient children. *Behaviour Research and Therapy,* 1966, 4:265–71.

Cooper, J. The Leyton Obsessional Inventory. *Psychological Medicine,* 1970, 1:48–64.

Copeman, C. D. *Aversive counter-conditioning and social retraining: A learning theory approach to drug rehabilitation.* Ph.D. dissertation, State University of New York at Stony Brook, 1973.

Coppen, A. The biochemistry of affective disorders. *British Journal of Psychiatry,* 1967, 113:1237–64.

Costin, F., and Kerr, W. D. The effects of an abnormal psychology course on students' attitudes toward mental illness. *Journal of Educational Psychology,* 1962, 53:214–18.

Craft, M.; Stephenson, G.; and Granger, C. A controlled trial of authoritarian and self-governing regimes with adolescent psychopaths. *American Journal of Orthopsychiatry,* 1964, 34:543–54.

Craighead, W. E.; Kazdin, A. E.; and Mahoney, M. J. *Behavior modification: Principles, issues, and applications.* Boston: Houghton Mifflin, 1976.

Crane, G. E. Persistent dyskinesia. *British Journal of Psychiatry,* 1973, 122:395–405.

Creak, M. Psychosis in childhood. In E. Miller (ed.), *Foundations of child psychiatry.* Oxford, England: Pergamon Press, 1968.

Crown, S., and Crown, J. M. Personality in early rheumatoid disease. *Journal of Psychosomatic Research,* 1973, 17:189–96.

Cunningham, C. E., and Linscheid, T. R. Elimination of chronic infant ruminating by electric shock. *Behavior Therapy,* 1976, 7:231–34.

Cytryn, L., and Lourie, R. D. Mental retardation. In A. M. Freedman and H. I. Kaplan (eds.), *Comprehensive textbook of psychiatry.* Baltimore: Williams & Wilkins, 1967.

Dalessio, D. J. *Wolff's headache and other head pain.* New York: Oxford University Press, 1972.

Davidson, M. A.; McInness, R. G.; and Parnell, R. W. The distribution of personality traits in seven-year-old children. *British Journal of Educational Psychology,* 1957, 27:48–61.

Davidson, W. S. Studies of aversive conditioning for alcoholics: A critical review of theory and research methodology. *Psychological Bulletin,* 1974, 81:571–81.

Davies, T. W., and DeMonchaux, C. Mood changes in relation to personality and the excretion of 3-methoxy-4-hydroxy-mandelic acid. *Psychosomatic Medicine,* 1973, 35:205–13.

Davis, J. M. Trycyclic antidepressants. In L. Simpson (ed.), *Textbook of psychotropic drugs.* New York: Plenum, 1975.

Davison, G. C. The ethical challenge. *Journal of Consulting and Clinical Psychology,* 1976, 44:157–62.

Davison, G. C. Not can but ought: The treatment of homosexuality. *Journal of Consulting and Clinical Psychology,* 1977, 46:170–72.

Davison, G. C., and Neale, J. M. *Abnormal psychology: An experimental clinical approach.* New York: Wiley, 1974.

Davison, J.; McLeod, M.; Lay-Yone, B.; and Linnoila, M. A comparison of electroconvulsive therapy and combined phenelzine-amitriptylene in refractory depression. *Archives of General Psychiatry,* 1978, 35:639–42.

Dement, W. Recent studies on the biological role of rapid eye movement sleep. *American Journal of Psychiatry,* 1965, 122:404–8.

DeMyer, M. K.; Pontius, W.; Norton, J. A.; Barton, S.; Allen, J.; and Steele, R. Parental practices and innate activity in normal, autistic, and brain-damaged infants. *Journal of Autism and Childhood Schizophrenia,* 1972, 2:49–66.

Depue, R. A., and Evans, R. The psychobiology of depressive disorders. In B. H. Maher (ed.), *Progress in experimental personality research.* Vol. 8. New York: Academic Press, 1976.

Depue, R. A., and Monroe, S. M. The unipolar-bipolar distinction in the depressive disorders. *Psychological Bulletin,* 1978, 85:1001–29.

Derman, H. Lead poisoning. In F. W. Sunderman and F. W. Sunderman, Jr., (eds.), *Laboratory diagnosis of diseases caused by toxic agents.* St. Louis: Warren H. Green, 1970.

Despert, J. L. Psychotherapy in childhood schizophrenia. *American Journal of Psychiatry,* 1947, 104:36–43.

Dickinson, J. R., Jr., and Smith, B. D. Nonspecific activity and habituation of tonic and phasic skin conductance in somatic complainers and controls as a function of auditory stimulus intensity. *Journal of Abnormal Psychology,* 1973, 82:404–12.

Dienstbier, R. A.; Hillman, D.; Lehnhoff, J.; Hillman, J.; and Valkenaer, M. C. An emotion attribution approach to moral behavior: Interfacing cognitive and avoidance theories of moral development. *Psychological Review,* 1975, 82:299–315.

DiLareto, A. O. *Comparative psychotherapy: An experimental analysis.* Chicago: Aldine-Atherton, 1971.

Discipio, W. J.; Glickman, H.; and Hollander, M. A. Social learning and operant techniques with hospitalized psychotics. *Proceedings of the 81st Annual Convention of the American Psychological Association,* 1973, 8:453–54.

Dixon, C. R. Courses on psychology and students' attitudes toward mental illness. *Psychological Reports,* 1967, 20:50.

Dixon, J. C. Depersonalization phenomena in a sample population of college students. *Journal of Abnormal and Social Psychology,* 1963, 109:371–75.

Dobrokhotova, T. A. On the pathology of the emotional sphere in tumorous lesion of the frontal lobes of the brain. *Zhurnal Nevropatologii Psikhiartrii,* 1968, 68:418–22.

Dobzhansky, T. *Evolution, genetics, and man.* New York: Wiley, 1955.

Dole, V. P., and Nyswander, M. A. A medical treatment for diacetylmorphine (heroin) addiction—A clinical test with methadone hydro-chloride. *Journal of the American Medical Association,* 1965, 198:646–50.

Dollard, J., and Miller, N. E. *Personality and psychotherapy.* New York: McGraw-Hill, 1950.

Dragstedt, L. R. A concept of the etiology of gastric and duodenal ulcer. *American Journal of Roentgenology,* 1956, 75:219–29.

Duffy, E. An explanation of "emotional" phenomena without the use of the concept "emotion." *Journal of General Psychology,* 1941, 25:283–93.

Dunbar, F. *Psychosomatic diagnosis.* New York: Hoeber, 1943.

Dunham, H. W., and Weinberg, S. K. *The culture of the state mental hospital.* Detroit: Wayne State University Press, 1960.

Dunlap, K. A. *Habits: Their making and unmaking.* New York: Liveright, 1932.

Dunn, L. M. (ed.). *Exceptional children in the schools: Special education in transition.* 2d ed. New York: Holt, Rinehart & Winston, 1973.

Dunner, D. L., and Somervill, J. W. Medical treatments. In D. C. Rimm and J. W. Somervill (eds.), *Abnormal psychology.* New York: Academic Press, 1977.

Dweck, C. S.; Gittelman-Klein, R.; McKinney, W. T., Jr.; and Watson, J. S. Summary of the subcommittee on clinical criteria for the diagnosis of childhood depression. In J. G. Schulterbrandt and A. Raskin (eds.), *Depression in childhood: Diagnosis, treatment, and conceptual models.* New York: Raven, 1977.

Eaton, J. W., and Weil, R. J. *Culture and mental disorders.* Glencoe, Ill.: Free Press, 1955.

Edison, G. R. Amphetamines: A dangerous illusion. *Annals of Internal Medicine,* 1971, 74:605–10.

Edwards, A. T. *The social desirability variable in personality research.* New York: Dryden, 1957.

Elder, S. T.; Ruiz, H. L.; Deabler, R. L.; and Dillenkoffer, R. L. Instrumental conditioning of diastolic blood pressure in essential hypertensive patients. *Journal of Applied Behavior Analysis,* 1973, 6:377–82.

Ellenberger, H. F. *The discovery of consciousness.* New York: Basic Books, 1970.

Ellington, R. J. Incidence of EEG abnormality among patients with mental disorders of apparently nonorganic origin: A criminal review. *American Journal of Psychiatry,* 1954, 111:263–75.

Ellis, A. *Reason and emotion in psychotherapy.* New York: Lyle Stuart, 1962.

Ellis, E. F. Asthma—the demon that thrives on myths. *Today's Health,* 1970, 48:63–64.

Endler, N. S. The person versus the situation:—A pseudo issue? A response to Alker. *Journal of Personality,* 1973, 41:287–303.

Engel, B. T., and Bickford, A. F. Response specificity: Stimulus response and individual response specificity in hypertension. *Archives of General Psychiatry,* 1961, 5:478–89.

Engel, G. L. Psychological aspects of gastrointestinal disorders In S. Arieti and M. F. Reiser (eds.), *American handbook of psychiatry.* Vol. 4. 2d ed. New York: Basic Books, 1975.

Enis, B. *Prisoners of Psychiatry.* New York: Harcourt Brace Jovanovich, 1972.

Erlenmeyer-Kimling, L., and Jarvik, L. F. Genetics and intelligence: A review. *Science,* 1963, 142:1477–79.

Ervin, F. R. Brain disorders. IV.: Associated with convulsions. In A. M. Freedman and H. I. Kaplan (eds.), *Comprehensive textbook of psychiatry.* Baltimore: Williams & Wilkins, 1967.

Escalona, S. *Roots of individuality.* Chicago: Aldine, 1968.

Evans, D. R. An exploratory study of emotive imagery and aversive conditioning. *Canadian Psychologist,* 1967, 8:162.

Evans, D. R. Exhibitionism. In C. G. Costello (ed.), *Symptoms of psychopathology.* New York: Wiley, 1970.

Evans, R. B. Sixteen personality factor questionnaire scores of homosexual men. *Journal of Consulting and Clinical Psychology,* 1968, 34:212–15.

Evans, R. B. Childhood parental relationships of homosexual men. *Journal of Consulting and Clinical Psychology,* 1969, 33:129–35.

Eysenck, H. J. The effects of psychotherapy: An evaluation. *Journal of Consulting Psychology,* 1952, 16:319–24.

Eysenck, H. J. Learning theory and behaviour therapy. *Journal of Mental Science,* 1959, 105:61–75.

Eysenck, H. J. *The effects of psychotherapy.* New York: International Science Press, 1966.

Eysenck, H. J. Single trial conditioning, neurosis, and the Napalkov phenomenon. *Behaviour Research and Therapy,* 1967, 5:63–65.

Eysenck, H. J. *The biological basis for personality.* Springfield, Ill.: Charles C Thomas, 1967.

Eysenck, H. J. (ed.). *Behaviour therapy and the neuroses.* New York: Pergamon Press, 1960.

Eysenck, H. J., and Claridge, G. The position of hysterics and dystymics in a two dimensional framework of personality description. *Journal of Abnormal and Social Psychology,* 1962, 64:46–55.

Eysenck, H. J., and Rachman, S. *The causes and cure of neurosis.* San Diego, Calif.: Knapp, 1965.

Eysenck, H. J., and Beech, H. R. Counterconditioning and related methods. In A. E. Bergin and S. L. Garfield (eds.), *Handbook of psychotherapy and behavior change.* New York: Wiley, 1971.

Fairweather, G. W. *Social psychology in treating mental illness.* New York: Wiley, 1964.

Fairweather, G. W.; Sanders, D. H.; Maynard, H.; and Cressler, D. L. *Community life for the mentally ill: An alternative to institutional care.* Chicago: Aldine, 1969.

Farber, I. E. Sane and insane: Constructions and misconstructions. *Journal of Abnormal Psychology,* 1975, 84:589–620.

Farberow, N. L., and Litman, R. E. *A comprehensive suicide prevention program. Suicide Prevention Center of Los Angeles, 1958–1969.* Unpublished final report of DHEW NIMH Grants No. MH 14946 and MH 00128. Los Angeles, 1970.

Farina, A., and Ring, K. The influence of perceived mental illness on interpersonal relations. *Journal of Abnormal Psychology,* 1965, 70:47–51.

Farina, A.; Holland, C. H.; and Ring, K. Role of stigma and set in interpersonal interaction. *Journal of Abnormal Psychology,* 1966, 71:421–28.

Farley, J.; Woodruff, R. A., Jr.; and Guzer, S. B. The prevalence of hysteria and conversion symptoms. *British Journal of Psychiatry,* 1968, 114:1121–25.

Faulk, M. "Frigidity": A critical review. *Archives of Sexual Behavior,* 1973, 3:257–66.

Feinberg, I.; Koresko, R. L.; and Heller, N. EEG sleep patterns as a function of normal and pathological aging in man. *Journal of Psychiatric Research,* 1967, 5:107–44.

Feinsilver, D. B., and Gunderson, J. G. Psychotherapy for schizophrenics—Is it indicated: A review of the relevant literature. *Schizophrenia Bulletin,* 1972, 6:11–23.

Feldman, M. P., and MacCulloch, M. J. The application of anticipatory avoidance learning to the treatment of homosexuality. I: Theory, technique, and preliminary results. *Behaviour Research and Therapy,* 1965, 2:165–83.

Feldman, M. P., and MacCulloch, M. J. *Homosexual behavior: Therapy and assessment.* Oxford: Pergamon Press, 1971.

Fenichel, O. *The psychoanalytic theory of neurosis.* New York: Norton, 1945.

Ferguson, L. R. Dependency motivation in socialization. In R. A. Hoppe, G. A. Milton, and E. C. Simmel (eds.), *Early experiences and the processes of socialization.* New York: Academic Press, 1970.

Ferster, C. B. Positive reinforcement and behavioral deficits of autistic children. *Child Development,* 1961, 32:437–56.

Ferster, C. B. A functional analysis of depression. *American Psychologist,* 1973, 28:857–70.

Ferster, C. B., and Skinner, B. F. *Schedules of reinforcement.* New York: Appleton-Century-Crofts, 1957.

Ferster, C. B., and DeMyer, M. K. The development of performances in autistic children in an automatically controlled environment. *Journal of Chronic Disease,* 1961, 13:312–45.

Feuerstein, M., and Adams, H. E. *Cephalic vasomotor feedback for the treatment of migraine headache: An alternative therapeutic approach.* Paper read at the 9th Annual Association of Behavior Therapy Convention, San Francisco, 1975.

Filskov, S. B., and Goldstein, S. G. Diagnostic validity of the Halstead-Reitan Neuropsychology Battery. *Journal of Consulting and Clinical Psychology,* 1974, 42:383–88.

Finley, W. W. Effects of sham feedback following successful SMR training in an epileptic: Follow-up study. *Biofeedback and Self-Regulation,* 1976, 1:227–34.

Finney, B. C. Say it again: An active therapy technique. In C. Hatcher and P. Himelstein (eds.), *The handbook of Gestalt therapy.* New York: Jackson Aronson, 1976.

Fischer, M.; Harvald, B.; and Hauge, M. A. Danish twin study of schizophrenia. *British Journal of Psychiatry,* 1969, 115:981–90.

Fisher, S. Projective methodologies. In P. R. Farnsworth (ed.), *Annual Review of Psychology,* 1967, 18:165–90.

Fitzgibbons, D. J., and Shearn, C. R. Concepts of schizophrenia among mental health professionals: A factor-analytic study. *Journal of Consulting and Clinical Psychology,* 1972, 38:288–95.

Fixsen, D. L.; Phillips, E. L.; and Wolf, M. M. Achievement place: Experiments in self-government with predelinquents. *Journal of Applied Behavior Analysis,* 1973, 6:31–47.

Fleck, S. Family dynamics and origin of schizophrenia. *Psychosomatic Medicine,* 1960, 22:337–39.

Fonberg, E. On the manifestation of conditioned defensive reactions in stress. Cited by J. Wolpe, *Psychotherapy by reciprocal inhibition.* Stanford, Calif.: Stanford University Press, 1958.

Fontana, A. F. Familial etiology of schizophrenia: Is a scientific methodology possible? *Psychological Bulletin,* 1966, 66:214–27.

Ford, A. B. Casualties of our time. *Science,* 1970, 167:256–63.

Forrest, D. V. New words and neologisms, with a thesaurus of coinages by schizophrenic savant. *Psychiatry,* 1969, 32:44–73.

Foulds, G. A. *Personality and personal illness.* London: Tavistock Publications, 1965.

Fox, R. G. The XYY offender: A modern myth? *Journal of Criminal Law, Criminology, and Police Science,* 1971, 62:59–73.

Frankl, V. E. Basic concepts of logotherapy. *Journal of Existential Psychiatry,* 1962, 3:111–18.

Franks, C. M. Conditioning and conditioned aversion therapies in the treatment of the alcoholic. *International Journal of the Addictions,* 1966, 1:61–98.

Franks, C. M. Alcoholism. In C. G. Costello (ed.), *Symptoms of psychopathology.* New York: Wiley, 1970.

Frederick, C. J. *Suicide, homicide and alcoholism among American Indians.* U.S. Department of Health, Education, and Welfare Publication No. ADM 74–42. Washington, D.C.: U.S. Government Printing Office, 1973.

Fredericksen, L. W., and Peterson, G. L. Schedule induced aggression in nursery school children. *Psychological Record,* 1974, 24:343–51.

Freed, E. X. Anxiety and conflict: Role of drug-dependent learning in the rat. *Quarterly Journal of Studies on Alcohol,* 1971, 32:13–29.

Freeman, T. Symptomatology, diagnosis, and clinical course. In L. Bellak (ed.), *The schizophrenic syndrome.* New York: Grune & Stratton, 1969.

Freeman, W., and Watts, J. W. *Psychosurgery.* Springfield, Ill.: Charles C Thomas, 1942.

Fresco, R. Le syndrome de Klein-Levin: Hypersomnie recurrenta des adolescents males. *Annales Medico-Psychologiques,* 1971, 1:625–68.

Freud, S. The loss of reality in neurosis and psychosis. 1917. *In Collected papers.* Vol. 2. London: Hogarth Press, 1924.

Freud, S. Mourning and melancholia. 1917. In *Collected papers.* Vol. 4. London: Hogarth Press and the Institute of Psychoanalysis, 1950.

Freund, K.; Sedlacek, F.; and Knob, K. A single transducer for mechanical plethysmography of the male genitalia. *Journal of the Experimental Analysis of Behavior,* 1965, 8:169–70.

Friar, L. R., and Beatty, J. Migraine: Management by a trained control of vasoconstriction. *Journal of Consulting and Clinical Psychology,* 1976, 44:46–53.

Friedhoff, A. J., and Van Winkle, E. Isolation and characterization of a compound from the urine of schizophrenics. *Nature,* 1962, 194:897–98.

Friedman, A. P. *Chronic recurring headache: A multimedia learning system.* East Hanover: Sandox Pharmaceuticals, 1973.

Friedman, A. P.; Von Storck, T. J. C.; and Merritt, H. H. Migraine and tension headaches: A clinical study of two thousand cases. *Neurology,* 1954, 4:773–88.

Friedman, M., and Rosenman, R. H. *Type A behavior and your heart.* New York: Knopf, 1974.

Fromm-Reichmann, F. Notes on the development of treatment of schizophrenics by psychoanalytic psychotherapy, *Psychiatry,* 1948, 11:263–73.

Funkenstein, D. H.; King, S. H.; and Drolette, M. E. The experimental evocation of stress. *Symposium on Stress,* Army Medical Graduate School, Washington, D.C., 1953.

Funkenstein, D. H.; King, S. H.; and Drolette, M. E. *Mastery of stress.* Cambridge, Mass.: Harvard University Press, 1957.

Furlong, W. B. How "speed" kills athletic careers. *Today's Health,* 1971, 49:30–33; 62; 64; 66.

Gagnon, J. H., and Simon, W. *Sexual conduct: The sources of human sexuality.* Chicago: Aldine, 1973.

Gal, P. Mental disorders of advanced years. *Geriatrics,* 1959, 14:224–28.

Gall, E. A., and Mostof, F. K. *The liver.* Baltimore: Williams & Wilkins, 1973.

Gall, F. *Fur les fonctions du cervèau.* Paris: Balliere, 1825.

Gallinek, A. The Klein-Levin syndrome. *Diseases of the Nervous System,* 1967, 28:448–51.

Gantt, W. H. *Experimental basis for neurotic behavior.* New York: Hoeber, 1944.

Garcia, J.; McGoward, B. K.; and Green, K. F. Biological constraints on conditioning. In A. H. Black and W. F. Prokasy (eds.), *Classical conditioning. II: Current research and theory.* New York: Appleton-Century-Crofts, 1972.

Gardner, E. *Fundamentals of neurology.* 4th ed. Philadelphia: Saunders, 1963.

Gardner, E. *Principles of genetics.* New York: Wiley, 1968.

Garfield, S. L., and Bergin, A. E. Personal therapy, outcome, and some therapist variables. *Psychotherapy: Theory, Research and Practice,* 1971, 8:251–53.

Garmezy, N. Process and reactive schizophrenia: Some conceptions and issues. *Schizophrenia Bulletin,* 1970, 2:30–67.

Garron, D. C., and Cheifetz, D. I. Comment on "Bender Gestalt discernment of organic pathology." *Psychological Bulletin,* 1965, 63:197–200.

Gatchel, R. J.; McKinney, M. E.; and Koehernick, L. F. Learned helplessness, depression, and physiological responding. *Psychophysiology*, 1977, 14:25–31.

Gebhard, P. H. Incidence of overt homosexuality in the United States and Western Europe. In J. M. Livingood (ed.), *National Institute of Mental Health Task Force on Homosexuality: Final report and background papers*. Rockville, Md.: National Institute of Mental Health, 1972.

Gebhard, P. H.; Gagnan, J. H.; Pomeroy, W. B.; and Christenson, C. V. *Sex offenders: An analysis of types*. New York: Harper & Row, 1965.

Geer, J. H.; Morokoff, P.; and Greenwood, P. Sexual arousal in women: The development of a measurement device for vaginal blood volume. *Archives of Sexual Behavior*, 1974, 3:559–64.

Gelfand, D. M.; Gelfand, S.; and Dobson, W. R. Unprogrammed reinforcement of patients' behavior in a mental hospital. *Behaviour Research and Therapy*, 1967, 5:201–7.

Gellhorn, E., and Loofbourrow, G. N. *Emotions and emotional disorders*. New York: Hoeber, 1963.

Gellhorn, E., and Kiely, W. F. Autonomic nervous system in psychiatric disorder. In J. Mendels (ed.), *Biological Psychiatry*. New York, Wiley, 1973.

Gerrard, D. L., and Houston, L. G. Family setting and the social ecology of schizophrenia. *Psychiatric Quarterly*, 1953, 27:90–101.

Gerrard, D. L.; Saenger, G.; and Wile, R. The abstinent alcoholic. *Archives of General Psychiatry*, 1962, 6:83–95.

Gibbs, F. A.; Gibbs, E. L.; and Lennox, W. G. Influence of the bloodsugar level on the wave and spike formation in petit mal epilepsy. *Archives of Neurology and Psychiatry*, 1939, 41:1111–16.

Gilmer, B., von H. *Psychology*. 2d ed. New York: Harper & Row, 1973.

Gittelman-Klein, R., and Klein, D. School phobia: Diagnostic considerations in the light of imipramine effects. *Journal of Nervous and Mental Diseases*, 1973, 156:199–215.

Gittleman, M., and Birch, H. G. Childhood schizophrenia: Intellect, neurologic status, perinatal risk, prognosis, and family pathology. *Archives of General Psychiatry*, 1967, 17:16–25.

Glaros, A. G., and Rao, S. M. Bruxism: A critical review. *Psychological Bulletin*, 1977, 84:767–81.

Glennon, J. A. Weight reduction—an enigma. *Archives of Internal Medicine*, 1966, 118:1–2.

Glueck, S., and Glueck, E. *Family environment and delinquency*. Boston: Houghton Mifflin, 1962.

Goffman, E. *Asylums*. Garden City, N.Y.: Anchor Books, 1961.

Goldberg, E. M., and Morrison, S. L. Schizophrenia and social class. *British Journal of Psychiatry*, 1963, 109:785–802.

Goldberg, L. R. Simple models or simple processes? Some research on clinical judgements. *American Psychologist*, 1968, 23:483–96.

Goldfarb, W. W. Psychological privation in infancy and subsequent adjustment. *American Journal of Orthopsychiatry*, 1945, 15:247–55.

Goldfried, M. R., and Sprafkin, J. N. *Behavioral personality assessment*. Morristown, N.J.: General Learning Press, 1974.

Goldfried, M. R., and Davison, G. C. *Clinical Behavior Therapy*. New York: Holt, Rinehart & Winston, 1976.

Goldman, R.; Jaffa, M.; and Schacter, S. Yom Kipper, Air France, dormitory food, and eating behavior of obese and normal persons. *Journal of Personality and Social Psychology*, 1968, 10:117–23.

Goldstein, K. *The organism*. New York: American Book Co., 1939.

Goldstein, K. Prefrontal lobotomy: Analysis and warning. *Scientific American*, 1950, 182:44–47.

Goldstein, M. J.; Judd, L. K.; Rodnick, E. H.; and LaPolla, A. Psycho-physiological and behavioral effects of phenothiazine administration in acute schizophrenics as a function of premorbid states. *Journal of Psychiatric Research*, 1969, 6:271–87.

Goodwin, D. W.; Crane, J. B.; and Guze, S. B. Alcoholic "blackouts": A review and clinical study of 100 alcoholics. *American Journal of Psychiatry*, 1969, 126:77–84.

Goodwin, D. W.; Schulsinger, F.; Hermansen, L.; Guze, S. B.; and Winokur, G. A. Alcohol problems in adoptees raised apart from alcoholic biological parents. *Archives of General Psychiatry*, 1973, 28:238–43.

Goodwin, D. W.; Schulsinger, F.; Moller, N.; Hermansen, L.; and Guze, S. B. Drinking problems in adopted and nonadopted sons of alcoholics. *Archives of General Psychiatry*, 1974, 31:164–69.

Goslin, A. A. (ed.). *Handbook for socialization: Theory and research*. Chicago: Rand McNally, 1969.

Gottesman, I. I., and Shields, J. Schizophrenia in twins: 16 years consecutive admissions to a psychiatric clinic. *British Journal of Psychiatry*, 1966, 112:809–18.

Gough, H. G. *California Psychological Inventory manual*. Palo Alto, Calif.: Consulting Psychologists Press, 1957.

Grace, W. J., and Graham, D. T. Relationship of specific attitudes and emotions to certain bodily diseases. *Psychosomatic Medicine*, 1952, 14:243–51.

Graham, D. T.; Stern, J. A.; and Winokur, G. Experimental investigation of the specificity of attitude hypothesis in psychosomatic disease. *Psychosomatic Medicine*, 1958, 20:446–57.

Graham, G., Jr. Effects of introductory and abnormal psychology courses on students' attitudes toward mental illness. *Psychological Reports,* 1968, 22:448.

Graham, P. J.; Rutter, M. L.; Yule, W.; and Pless, I. B. Childhood asthma: A psychosomatic disorder? Some epidemiological considerations. *British Journal of Preventive Medicine,* 1967, 21:78–85.

Grandison, R. J. *The impact of mental illness stigma on self-monitoring, dispositional attribution, and behavior.* Ph.D. dissertation, University of Georgia, 1980.

Green, R. *Sexual identity conflict in children and adults.* New York: Basic Books, 1974.

Green, R., and Money, J. *Transsexualism and sex reassignment.* Baltimore: Johns Hopkins Press, 1969.

Greenblatt, D. J., and Shader, R. I. Meprobamate: A study of irrational drug use. *American Journal of Psychiatry,* 1971, 127:1297–1303.

Greenfield, N. W., and Sternbach, R. A. (eds.). *Handbook of psychophysiology.* New York: Holt, Rinehart & Winston, 1972.

Gross, L. *The effects of early feeding experience on external responsiveness.* Ph.D. dissertation, Columbia University, 1968.

Grossman, J. (ed.). *Manual on terminology and classification.* Baltimore: Garamond/Pridemark Press, 1973.

Grossman, H. J., and Greenberg, N. H. Psychosomatic differentiation in infancy. I: Autonomic activity in the newborn. *Psychosomatic Medicine,* 1957, 19:213–306.

Gruensberg, E. M. Epidemiology of mental retardation. *International Journal of Psychiatry,* 1966, 2:78–129.

Gull, W. Anorexia nervosa. *Transactions of the Clinical Society of London,* 1874, 7:22.

Gulo, E. V., and Fraser, W. Student attitudes toward mental illness. *College Student Survey,* 1967, 3:61–63.

Gustavson, K. H. *Down's syndrome: A clinical and cytogenetical investigation.* Sweden: Institute for Medical Genetics of the University of Uppsala, 1964.

Guthrie, D. J. *A history of medicine.* Philadelphia: Lippincott, 1946.

Gutride, M. E.; Goldstein, A. P.; and Hunter, G. F. The use of modeling and role playing to increase social interaction among asocial psychiatric patients. *Journal of Consulting and Clinical Psychology,* 1973, 40:408–15.

Haley, J. Whither family therapy? *Family Process,* 1962, 1:69–100.

Hall, C. Emotional behavior in the rat. I. Defecation and urination as measures of individual differences in emotionality. *Journal of Comparative Psychology,* 1934, 18:385–403.

Hall, R. V.; Fox, R.; Willard, D.; Goldsmith, L.; Emerson, M.; Owen, M.; Davis, T.; and Porcia, E. The teacher as observer and experimenter in the modification of disputing and talking-out behaviors. *Journal of Applied Behavior Analysis,* 1971, 4:141–49.

Halleck, S. L. *The politics of therapy.* New York: Science House, 1971.

Halstead, W. *Brain and intelligence: A qualitative study of the frontal lobes.* Chicago: University of Chicago Press, 1947.

Hamilton, M. Development of a rating scale for primary depressive illness. *British Journal of Social and Clinical Psychology,* 1967, 6:278–96.

Hammen, C. L., and Glass, D. R. Depression, activity, and evaluation of reinforcement. *Journal of Abnormal Psychology,* 1976, 85:1–10.

Hannie, T. S., and Adams, H. E. Modification of agitated depression by "flooding." *Journal of Behavior Therapy and Experimental Psychiatry,* 1974, 5:161–66.

Harbert, T. L.; Barlow, D. H.; Hersen, M.; and Austin, J. B. Measurement and modification of incestuous behavior: A case study. *Psychological Reports,* 1974, 34:79–86.

Hare, H. D. *Psychopathy: Theory and research.* New York: Wiley, 1970.

Hare, R. D. Temporal gradient of fear arousal in psychopaths. *Journal of Abnormal Psychology,* 1965, 70:442–45.

Harlow, H. F. The nature of love. *American Psychologist,* 1958, 13:673–85.

Harlow, H. F., and Harlow, M. K. Social deprivation in monkeys. *Scientific American,* 1962, 207:137–46.

Harper, J., and Williams, S. Age and type of onset as critical variables in early infantile autism. *Journal of Autism & Childhood Schizophrenia,* 1975, 5:25–36.

Harris, C. S. A nonautomated but practical rapid delivery point card system for token economies. *Behavior Therapy,* 1977, 8:495–97.

Harris, J. G. Abbreviated form of the Phillips Rating Scale of Premorbid Adjustment in Schizophrenia. *Journal of Abnormal Psychology,* 1975, 84:129–37.

Harris, R. E., and Lingoes, J. C. *Subscales for the MMPI: An aid to profile interpretation.* San Francisco: Department of Psychiatry, University of California, 1955. Mimeographed.

Harrison, R. Psychological testing in headache: A review. *Headache,* 1975, 15:177–85.

Hathaway, S. R., and McKinley, J. C. *The Minnesota Multiphasic Personality Inventory.* Rev. ed. New York: Psychological Corporation, 1951.

Hauserman, N.; Zwebach, S.; and Plotkin, A. Use of concrete reinforcement to facilitate verbal initiations in adolescent group therapy. *Journal of Consulting and Clinical Psychology,* 1972, 38:90–96.

Heber, R. F. *Epidemiology of mental retardation.* Springfield, Ill.: Charles C Thomas, 1970.

Heber, R. F.; Dever, R.; and Conry, J. The influence of environmental and genetic variables of intellectual development. In J. J. Prehm, L. A. Hamerlynck, and J. E. Crossen (eds.), *Behavioral research in mental retardation.* Eugene, Oregon: University of Oregon Press, 1968.

Heber, R. F., and Garber, H. The Milwaukee project: A study of the use of family intervention to prevent cultural-familial mental retardation. In B. Z. Friedlander, G. M. Sterritt, and G. E. Kirk (eds.), *The exceptional infant. III: Assessment and intervention.* New York: Brunner/Mazel, 1975.

Heber, R. F.; Garber, H.; Hoffman, C.; and Harrington, S. Preventing mental retardation through family rehabilitation. *Technical Assistance Delivery System infant education monograph.* Chapel Hill, N.C.: TADS, 1976.

Held, J. M., and Cromwell, R. L. Premorbid adjustment in schizophrenia: An evaluation of a method and some general comments. *Journal of Nervous and Mental Disease,* 1968, 146:264–72.

Hempel, C. G. Introduction to problems of taxonomy. In J. Zubin (ed.), *Field studies in the mental disorders.* New York: Grune & Stratton, 1959.

Hendrickson, K., and Doughty, R. Decelerating undesirable mealtime behavior in a group of profoundly retarded boys. *American Journal of Mental Deficiency,* 1967, 72:40–44.

Hernandez-Peón, R.; Chávez-Ibarra, G.; and Aguilar-Figueroa, E. Somatic evoked potentials in one case of hysterical anesthesia. *EEG and Clinical Neurophysiology,* 1963, 15:889–92.

Heron, W. The pathology of boredom. *Scientific American,* 1957, 196:52–69.

Hersen, M., and Barlow, D. H. *Single case experimental designs: Strategies for studying behavior change.* New York: Pergamon Press, 1976.

Hersen, M., and Bellack, A. S. Assessment of social skills. In A. R. Ciminero, K. S. Calhoun and H. E. Adams, (eds.), *A handbook of behavior assessment.* New York: Wiley, 1977.

Herxheimer, H., and Prior, F. N. Further observations on induced asthma and bronchial hyposensitization. *International Archives of Allergy and Applied Immunology,* 1952, 3:189–207.

Hess, R. D., and Shipman, V. C. Early experiences and the socialization of cognitive modes in children. *Child Development,* 1965, 36:869–86.

Heston, L. Psychiatric disorders in foster home reared children of schizophrenic mothers. *British Journal of Psychiatry,* 1966, 112:819–25.

Higgins, J. Process-reactive schizophrenia: Recent developments. *Journal of Nervous and Mental Disease,* 1969, 149:450–72.

Hill, A. L. Investigation of calendar calculating by an idiot savant. *American Journal of Psychiatry,* 1975, 132:557–59.

Hill, M. J., and Blanc, H. T. Evaluation of psychotherapy with alcoholics: A critical review. *Quarterly Journal of Studies on Alcohol,* 1967, 28:76–104.

Hinde, R. A., and Spencer-Booth, Y. Individual differences in the responses of rhesus monkeys to a period of separation from their mothers. *Journal of Child Psychology and Psychiatry,* 1970, 11:159–76.

Hirschfield, M. *Sexual anomalies.* New York: Emerson Books, 1948.

Hodgson, R. J., and Rachman, S. The effects of contamination and washing in obsessional patients. *Behaviour Research and Therapy,* 1972, 10:111–17.

Hoenig, J., and Kenna, J. Epidemiological aspects of transsexualism. *Psychiatric Clinica,* 1973, 6:65–80.

Hoffer, A., and Osmond, H. Some schizophrenia recoveries. *Diseases of the Nervous System,* 1962, 4:204–10.

Hoffer, A., and Osmond, H. Treatment of schizophrenia with nicotine acid: A 10-year follow-up. *Acta Psychiatrica Scandinavica,* 1964, 40:171–89.

Hoffer, A., and Osmond, H. Nicotinamide adenine dinucleotide in the treatment of chronic schizophrenic patients. *British Journal of Psychiatry,* 1968, 114:915–17.

Hoffer, A.; Pollin, W.; Stabenow, J. R.; Allen, M.; and Hrubec, Z. Schizophrenia in the National Research Council's Register of 15,909 veteran twins pairs. Quoted in Rosenthal, D. *Genetic theory and abnormal behavior.* New York: McGraw-Hill, 1968.

Hoffman, M. *The gay world.* New York: Basic Books, 1968.

Hoffman, M. L. Moral development. In Mussen, P. (ed.), *Carmichael's manual of child psychology.* New York: Wiley, 1970.

Hogan, R. A. The implosive technique. *Behaviour Research and Therapy,* 1968, 6:423–32.

Hogan, R. A. Implosively oriented behavior modification: Therapy considerations. *Behaviour Research and Therapy,* 1969, 7:177–84.

Hogarty, G. E., and Goldberg, S. C. Drug and sociotherapy in aftercare of schizophrenic patients: One-year relapse rates. *Archives of General Psychiatry,* 1973, 28:54–64.

Holden, C. Psychosurgery: Legitimate therapy or laundered lobotomy? *Science,* 1973, 179:1109–12.

Hollingshead, A. B., and Redlich, F. C. *Social class and mental illness: A community study.* New York: Wiley, 1958.

Holmes, T. H., and Rahe, R. H. The social readjustment rating scale. *Journal of Psychosomatic Research*, 1967, 11:213–18.

Honsberger, R., and Wilson, A. F. Transcendental meditation in treating asthma. Respiratory Therapy: *The Journal of Inhalation Technology*, 1973, 3:79–81.

Hook, E. G. Behavioral implications of the human XYY genotype. *Science*, 1973, 179:139–50.

Hooker, E. The adjustment of the male overt homosexual. *Journal of Projective Techniques*, 1957, 21:18–31.

Hoon, E.; Hoon, P.; and Wincze, J. The SAI: An inventory for the measurement of female sexual arousal. *Archives of Sexual Behavior*, 1976, 10:234–40.

Hoon, P.; Wincze, J. P.; and Hoon, E. Physiological assessment of sexual arousal in women. *Psychophysiology*, 1976, 13:196–204.

Horowitz, M. J. Flashbacks: Recurrent intrusive images after the use of LSD. *American Journal of Psychiatry*, 1969, 126:147–51.

House, J. S. Occupational stress and coronary heart disease. A review and theoretical integration. *Journal of Health & Science Behavior*, 1974, 15:12–27.

Huber, H.; Karlin, R.; and Nathan, P. E. Blood alcohol level discrimination by nonalcoholics. *Journal of Studies on Alcohol*, 1976, 37:27–39.

Huesmann, L. R. Cognitive processes and models of depression. *Journal of Abnormal Psychology*, 1978, 87:194–98.

Hunt, W. A., and Matarazzo, J. D. Three years later: Recent developments in the experimental modification of smoking behavior. *Journal of Abnormal Psychology*, 1973, 81:107–14.

Hurst, L. Classification of psychotic disorders from genetic point of view. *Proceedings of the Second International Congress of Human Genetics*. Vol. 3. Rome: Institute G. Mendel, 1963.

Hurwitz, T. D. Electroconvulsive therapy: A review. *Comprehensive Psychiatry*, 1974, 15:303–14.

Hussain, A. Behavior therapy in 105 cases. In J. Wolpe, A. Salter, and L. J. Reyna, (eds.), *The conditioning therapies: The challenge in psychotherapy*. New York: Holt, Rinehart and Winston, 1963.

Hutt, C., and Ounsted, C. The biological significance of gaze aversion with particular reference to the syndrome of infantile autism. *Behavioral Science*, 1966, 11:346–56.

Hutt, C., and Ounsted, C. Gaze aversion and its significance in childhood autism. In Hutt, S. J. and Hutt, C. (eds.), *Behavior studies in psychiatry*. New York: Pergamon Press, 1970.

Inhelder, B. *The diagnosis of reasoning in the mentally retarded*. 2d ed. New York: Chandler, 1968.

Innes, G.; Millar, W. M.; and Valentine, M. Emotion and blood pressure. *Journal of Medical Science*, 1959, 105:840–51.

Ironside, R., and Batchelor, I. R. C. The ocular manifestations of hysteria in relation to flying. *British Journal of Ophthalmology*, 1945, 29:88–98.

Irving, R. E.; Bagnall, M. K.; and Smith, B. J. *The older patient: An introduction to geriatrics*. London: English Universities Press, 1970.

Izard, C. *The face of emotion*. New York: Appleton-Century-Crofts, 1971.

Jackson, B. Treatment of depression by self-reinforcement. *Behavior Therapy*, 1972, 3:298–307.

Jackson, D. N., and Messick, S. Content and style in personality assessment. *Psychological Bulletin*, 1958, 55:243–52.

Jacobs, T. Family interaction in disturbed and normal families: A methodological and substantive review. *Psychological Bulletin*, 1975, 82:33–65.

Jacobson, A.; Kales, J. D.; and Kales, A. Clinical and electrophysiological correlates of sleep disorders in children. In A. Kales (ed.), *Sleep: Physiology and Pathology*. Philadelphia: Lippincott, 1969.

Jacobson, E. *Progressive relaxation*. Chicago: University of Chicago Press, 1938.

Jaffe, J. H. Drug addiction and drug abuse. In L. S. Goodman and A. Gilman (eds.), *The biological basis of therapeutics*. 5th ed. New York: Macmillan, 1975.

Janowitz, P. *Rites of Strangers*. Charlottesville, Va.: University of Virginia Press, 1979.

Jarvik, L. F.; Klodin, V.; and Matsuyama, S. S. Human aggression and the extra Y chromosome: Fact or fantasy? *American Psychologist*, 1973, 28:674–82.

Jarvik, L. F.; Yen, F. S.; and Goldstein, F. Chromosomes and mental status. *Archives of General Psychiatry*, 1974, 30:186–90.

Jarvik, L. K., and Cohen, D. A biobehavioral approach to intellectual changes with aging. In C. Esdorfer and M. P. Lawton (eds.), *The psychology of adult development and aging*. Washington, D.C.: American Psychological Association, 1973.

Jarvik, M. The psychopharmacological revolution: *Psychology Today*, 1967, 1:51–59.

Jaspers, K. *Allegemaine Psychopathologie*. Berlin: Springer, 1913.

Jeans, R. F. I. An independently validated case of multiple personality. *Journal of Abnormal Psychology*, 1976, 85:249–55.

Jellinek, E. M. Phases of alcohol addiction. *Quarterly Journal of Studies on Alcohol,* 1952, 13:673–78.

Jellinek, E. M. *The disease concept of alcoholism.* New Haven: Hill House Press, 1960.

Jenkins, C. D. Behavior that triggers heart attacks. *Science News,* 1974, 105:402.

Jenkins, R. L. Nature of the schizophrenic process. *Archives of Neurology and Psychiatry,* 1950, 64:243–62.

Jenkins, R. L. Diagnosis, dynamics, and treatment in child psychiatry. *Psychiatric Research Reports,* 1964, 18:91–120.

Jenkins, R. L. Psychiatric syndromes in children and their relation to family background. *American Journal of Orthopsychiatry,* 1966, 36:450–57.

Jenkins, R. L., and Glickman, S. Common syndromes in child psychiatry. II: The schizoid child. *American Journal of Orthopsychiatry,* 1946, 16:255–61.

Jenson, A. R. How much can we boost IQ and scholastic achievement? *Harvard Education Review,* 1969, 39:1–123.

Johnson, L. C. Are stages of sleep related to waking behavior? *American Scientist,* 1973, 61:326–38.

Johnson, W. *The onset of stuttering.* Minneapolis: University of Minnesota Press, 1959.

Johnson, W. G.; Ross, J. M.; and Mastria, M. A. Delusional behavior: An attributional analysis of developmental modification. *Journal of Abnormal Psychology,* 1977, 86:421–26.

Jones, H. G. Stuttering. In C. G. Costello (ed.), *Symptoms of psychopathology.* New York: Wiley, 1970.

Jones, K. L.; Shainberg, L. W.; and Byer, C. O. *Health Science.* 2d ed. New York: Harper & Row, 1971.

Jones, M. *The therapeutic community.* New York: Basic Books, 1953.

Jones, M. C. A laboratory study of fear: The case of Peter. *Pedigogical Seminary,* 1924a, 31:308–15.

Jones, M. C. The elimination of children's fears. *Journal of Experimental Psychology,* 1924b, 7:382–90.

Jones, M. C. Personality correlates and antecedents of drinking patterns in adult males. *Journal of Consulting and Clinical Psychology,* 1968, 32:2–11.

Jones, M. C., and Mussen, P. H. Self-conceptions, motivations, and interpersonal attitudes of early and late maturing girls. *Child development,* 1958, 29:491–501.

Jourvet, M. Neurophysiological and biochemical mechanisms of sleep. In A. Keales (ed.), *Sleep: Physiology and pathology.* Philadelphia: Lippincott, 1969.

Judd, L., and Mandell, A. Chromosome studies in early infantile autism. *Archives of General Psychiatry,* 1968, 18:450–57.

Kachanoff, R.; Leveille, R.; McLelland, J. P.; and Wayner, M. J. Schedule induced behavior in humans. *Physiology and Behavior,* 1973, 11:395–98.

Kaelbling, R., and Volpe, P. A. Constancy of psychiatric diagnoses in readmissions. *Comprehensive Psychiatry,* 1963, 4:29–39.

Kagan, J. On class differences and early development. In V. H. Denenberg (ed.), *Education of the infant and young child.* New York: Academic Press, 1970.

Kahn, A. U.; Staerk, M.; and Bonk, C. Role of counterconditioning in the treatment of asthma. *Journal of Psychosomatic Research,* 1973, 17:389–92.

Kales, A., and Kales, J. Evaluation, diagnosis, and treatment of clinical conditions related to sleep. *Journal of the American Medical Association,* 1970, 213:2229–35.

Kales, A., and Kales, J. Recent advances in the diagnosis and treatment of sleep disorders. In G. Usdin (ed.), *Sleep research and clinical practice.* New York: Bruner/Maxel, 1973.

Kallman, F. J. *Heredity in health and mental disorder.* New York: Norton, 1953.

Kallman, F. J. *The genetics of schizophrenia.* Springfield, Ill.: Charles C Thomas, 1966.

Kallman, W. M., and Feuerstein, M. Psychophysiological procedures. In A. R. Ciminero, K. S. Calhoun, and H. E. Adams (eds.), *A handbook of behavioral assessment.* New York: Wiley, 1977.

Kamin, L. J. *Heredity, intelligence, politics, and psychology.* Unpublished manuscript, Princeton University, 1973.

Kamin, L. J. *Science and politics of IQ.* Baltimore: Lawrence Erlbaum Associates, 1974.

Kandel, D. Adolescent marijuana use: Role of parents and peers. *Science,* 1973, 181:1067–69.

Kanfer, F. H. Self-management methods. In F. H. Kanfer and A. P. Goldstein (eds.), *Helping people change: A textbook of methods.* New York: Pergamon, 1975.

Kanfer, F. H., and Saslow, F. Behavioral analysis. *Archives of General Psychiatry,* 1965, 12:529–39.

Kanfer, F. H., and Phillips, J. S. *Learning foundations of behavior therapy.* New York: Wiley, 1970.

Kanner, L. To what extent is early infantile autism determined by constitutional inadequacies? *Association for Research in Nervous and Mental Disease,* 1954, 33:378–85.

Kanner, L. *Child psychiatry.* 3d ed. Springfield, Ill.: Charles C Thomas, 1957.

Kanner, L. Follow-up study of eleven autistic children originally reported in 1943. *Journal of Autism and Childhood Schizophrenia,* 1971, 1:119–45.

Kanner, L. *Child Psychiatry.* 4th ed. Springfield, Ill.: Charles C Thomas, 1972.

Kanner, L., and Lesser, L. Early infantile autism. *Pediatric Clinic of North America,* 1958, 5:711–30.

Kanner, L.; Rodrigues, A.; and Ashendu, B. How far can autistic children go in matters of social adaptation? *Journal of Autism and Childhood schizophrenia,* 1972, 2:9–33.

Kaplan, H. S. No-nonsense therapy for six sexual malfunctions. *Psychology Today,* 1974, 8:76–80; 83–84; 86.

Kaplan, S. M.; Gottschalk, L. A.; Magliocco, E. B.; Rohovit, D. D.; and Ross, W. D. Hostility in verbal productions and hypnotic dreams of hypertensive patients. *Psychosomatic Medicine,* 1961, 23:211–322.

Karoby, P. Multicomponent behavioral treatment of fear of flying: A case report. *Behavior Therapy,* 1974, 5:265–70.

Karp, L. E.; Fialkow, P. J.; Hoehn, H. W.; and Scott, C. R. Prenatal diagnosis of genetic diseases. *University of Washington Medicine,* 1974, 1:5–13.

Kasl, S. V., and Cobb, S. Blood pressure changes in men undergoing job loss: A preliminary report. *Psychosomatic Medicine,* 1970, 32:19–38.

Kass, D. J.; Silvers, F. M.; and Abroms, G. M. Behavioral group treatment of hysteria. *Archives of General Psychiatry,* 1972, 26:42–50.

Katz, M. M.; Cole, J. O.; and Lowery, H. A. Studies of the diagnostic process: The influence of symptom perception, past experience, and ethnic background on diagnostic decisions. *American Journal of Psychiatry,* 1969, 125:937–47.

Kazdin, A. E. Response cost: The removal of conditioned reinforcers for therapeutic change. *Behavior Therapy,* 1972, 3:533–46.

Kazdin, A. E. Self-monitoring and behavior change. In M. J. Mahoney and C. E. Thoresen (eds.), *Self-control: Power to the person.* Monterey, Calif.: Brooks/Cole, 1974.

Kazdin, A. E. *Behavior modification in applied settings.* Homewood, Ill.: Dorsey Press, 1975.

Kazdin, A. E., and Bootzin, R. R. The token economy: An evaluative review. *Journal of Applied Behavior Analysis,* 1972, 5:343–72.

Kelly, D. H., and Walter, C. J. S. The relationship between clinical diagnosis and anxiety assessed by forearm blood flow and other measurements. *British Journal of Psychiatry,* 1968, 114:611–26.

Kendall, E.; Cooper, E.; Gourlay, J.; and Copeland, R. M. Diagnostic criteria of American and British psychiatrists. *Archives of General Psychiatry,* 1971, 25:123–30.

Kennedy, W. A. School phobia: Rapid treatment of 50 cases. *Journal of Abnormal Psychology,* 1965, 70:285–89.

Kenny, F. T.; Solyom, L.; and Solyom, C. Faradic disruption of obsessive ideation in the treatment of obsessive neurosis. *Behavior Therapy,* 1973, 4:448–57.

Kent, R. N., and Foster, S. L. Direct observational procedures: Methodological issues in naturalistic settings. In A. R. Ciminero, K. S. Calhoun, and H. E. Adams (eds.), *A handbook of behavioral assessment.* New York, Wiley, 1977.

Kenyon, F. E. Hypochondriasis: A survey of some historical, clinical, and social aspects. *International Journal of Psychiatry,* 1966, 2:308–25.

Kessel, N., and Walton, A. *Alcoholism.* Baltimore: Penguin, 1965.

Kessler, J. W. *Psychopathology of childhood.* Englewood Cliffs, N.J.: Prentice-Hall, 1966.

Kessler, M., and Gromberg, C. Observation of barroom drinking: Methodology and preliminary results. *Quarterly Journal of Studies on Alcohol,* 1974, 35:1392–96.

Kety, S. S. Problems in psychiatric nosology from the viewpoint of the biological sciences. In M. M. Katz, J. O. Cole, and W. E. Barton (eds.), *The role and methodology of classification in psychiatry and psychopathology.* Chevy Chase, Md.: National Institute of Mental Health, 1965.

Kety, S. S. Toward hypothesis for a biochemical component in the vulnerability to schizophrenia. *Seminars in Psychiatry,* 1972, 4:233–38.

Kety, S. S.; Rosenthal, D.; Wender, P. H.; and Schulsinger, F. The types and prevalence of mental illness in the biological and adoptive families of adopted schizophrenics. In D. Rosenthal and S. S. Kety (eds.), *The transmission of schizophrenia.* Elmsford, N.Y.: Pergamon Press, 1968.

Kidson, M., and Jones, I. Psychiatric disorders among aborigines of the Australian Western Desert. *Archives of General Psychiatry,* 1968, 19:413–22.

Kiersch, T. A. Amnesia: A clinical study of ninety-eight cases. *American Journal of Psychiatry,* 1962, 119:57–60.

Kiesler, D. J. Some myths of psychotherapy research. *Psychological Bulletin,* 1966, 65:110–36.

Kinsey, A.; Pomeroy, W.; and Martin, C. *Sexual behavior in the human male.* Philadelphia: Saunders, 1948.

Kinsey, A.; Pomeroy, W.; Martin, C.; and Gebhard, P. *Sexual behavior in the human female.* Philadelphia: Saunders, 1953.

Kirk, S. *Early education for the mentally retarded*. Champaign-Urbana, Ill.: University of Illinois Press, 1958.

Kleeman, S. T. Psychiatric contributions in the treatment of allergy. *Annals of Allergy*, 1967, 25:611–19.

Klein, D. F. *Psychiatric case studies: Treatment, drugs, and outcome*. Baltimore: Williams & Wilkins, 1972.

Klein, D. F., and Davis, J. M. *Diagnosis and drug treatment of psychiatric disorders*. Baltimore: Williams & Wilkins, 1969.

Kleinmuntz, B. *Essentials of abnormal psychology*. 2d ed. New York: Harper & Row, 1980.

Kleist, K. *Sensory aphasia and amnesia: The myelarchitectonic basis*. New York: Pergamon Press, 1962.

Klenbanoff, L. D. A comparison of parental attitudes of mothers of schizophrenics, brain injured, and normal children. *American Journal of Orthopsychiatry*, 1959, 24:445–54.

Klerman, G.; Davidson, E.; and Kayce, M. Factors influencing the clinical responses of schizophrenic patients to phenothiazine drugs and to placebo. In P. Soloman and B. Glueck (eds.), *Recent research on schizophrenia*. Washington, D.C.: American Psychiatric Association, 1964.

Kline, N. S., and Davis, J. M. Psychotropic drugs. *American Journal of Nursing*, 1973, 73:54–62.

Knittle, J. Consequences of commitment to and disengagement from incentives. *Psychological Review*, 1975, 82:1–25.

Kohlenberg, R. J. Behavioristic approach to multiple personality: A case study. *Behavior Therapy*, 1973, 4:137–40.

Kohlenberg, R. J. Treatment of homosexual pedophiliac using in vivo desensitization. *Journal of Abnormal Psychology*, 1974, 83:192–95.

Kohn, M. L. Social class and schizophrenia: A critical review. In D. Rosenthal and S. S. Kety (eds.), *The transmission of schizophrenia*. Elmsford, N.Y.: Pergamon Press, 1968.

Kolodny, R. C.; Masters, W. H.; Hendryx, J.; and Toro, G. Plasma testosterone and semen analysis in male homosexuals. *New England Journal of Medicine*, 1971, 285:1170–74.

Kolvin, I.; Ounstead, C.; Richardson, L. M.; and Garside, R. F. The family and social background in childhood psychoses. III: *British Journal of Psychiatry*, 1971, 118:396–402.

Korchin, S. J. *Modern clinical psychology: Principles of intervention in the clinic and community*. New York: Basic Books, 1976.

Kovacs, M., and Beck, A. T. An empirical-clinical approach toward a definition of childhood depression. In J. G. Schulterbrandt and A. Raskin (eds.), *Depression in childhood: Diagnosis, treatment, and conceptual models*. New York: Raven Press, 1977.

Kraepelin, E. *Lectures on clinical psychiatry*. Translated, revised, and edited by T. Johnstone. London: Bailliere, Tindall, and Cox, 1904.

Kramer, M. Cross-national study of diagnosis of the mental disorders: Origin of the problem. *American Journal of Psychiatry*, 1965, 125:1–11.

Kramer, M. Introduction: The historical background of ICD-8. In American Psychiatric Association, *Diagnostic and Statistical Manual—II*. Washington, D.C.: American Psychiatric Association, 1968.

Kramer, M.; Ornstein, P.; and Whitman, P. Drug therapy. In E. A. Spiegel (ed.), *Progress in neurology and psychiatry*. Vol. 20. New York: Grune & Stratton, 1964.

Kramm, E. R. *Families of mongoloid children*. Children's Bureau Publication No. 401. Washington, D.C.: United States Department of Health, Education, and Welfare, 1963.

Kringlen, E. Obsessional neurotics: A long-term follow-up. *British Journal of Psychiatry*, 1965, 111:709–22.

Kringlen, E. Schizophrenia in twins: An epidemiological-clinical study. *Psychiatry*, 1966, 29:172–84.

Kringlen, E. Hereditary and social factors in schizophrenic twins: An epidemiological-clinical study. In J. Romano (ed.), *The origins of schizophrenia*. New York: Excerpta Medica Foundation, 1967.

Kroll, J. A reappraisal of psychiatry in the middle ages. *Archives of General Psychiatry*, 1973, 26:276–83.

Kuhn, T. S. *The structure of scientific revolutions*. Chicago: University of Chicago Press, 1962.

Kunnes, R. Double-dealing in dope. *Human Behavior*, 1973, 2:22–7.

Kurland, H. D.; Yeager, C. T.; and Arthur, R. J. Psychophysiologic aspects of severe behavior disorders. *Archives of General Psychiatry*, 1963, 8:599–604.

Kushi, M. *The book of macrobiotics: The universal way of health and happiness*. Tokyo: Japan Publications, 1977.

Lacey, J. I.; Bateman, D. E.; and VanLehn, R. Autonomic response specificity: An experimental study. *Psychosomatic Medicine*, 1953, 15:18–21.

Lachman, S. J. *Psychosomatic disorders: A behavioristic interpretation*. New York: Wiley, 1972.

Lader, M. H. Palmer skin conductance measures in anxiety and phobic states. *Journal of Psychosomatic Research*, 1967, 11:271–81.

Lader, M. H., and Wing, L. Habituation of the psycho-galvanic reflex in patients with anxiety states and in normal subjects. *Journal of Neurology, Neurosurgery, and Psychiatry*, 1964, 27:210–18.

Lader, M. H. and Mathews, A. M. A physiological model of phobic anxiety and desensitization. *Behaviour Research and Therapy,* 1968, 6:411–21.

Laffal, J. *Pathological and normal language.* New York: Atherton, 1965.

Laing, R. D. *The divided self: A study in sanity and madness.* Chicago: Quadrangle Books, 1960.

Laing, R. D. Is schizophrenia a disease? *International Journal of Social Psychiatry,* 1964, 10:184–93.

Laing, R. D. *The politics of experience.* New York: Pantheon, 1967.

Laing, R. D., and Esterson, A. *Sanity, madness, and the family.* London: Tavistock, 1964.

Lakin, M. Assessment of significant role attitudes in primiparous mothers by means of a modification of the TAT. *Psychosomatic Medicine,* 1957, 19:50–60.

Lang, P. Autonomic control. *Psychology Today,* 1970, 4:37–41.

LaPolla, A., and Jones, H. Placebo-control evaluation of desipramine in depression. *American Journal of Psychiatry,* 1970, 127:335–38.

Laughlin, H. P. *The neuroses.* Washington, D.C.: Butterworths, 1967.

Laveter, J. *Physiognomische fragmente zur Bëforderung der Menschenkenntiss und Menschenliebe von Johann Casper Laveter.* Leipsig, 1975.

Lazare, A. The hysterical character in psychoanalytic theory—evaluation and confusion. *Archives of General Psychiatry,* 1971, 25:131–37.

Lazarus, A. A. The treatment of chronic frigidity by systematic desensitization. *Journal of Nervous and Mental Disease,* 1963, 136:272–78.

Lazarus, A. A. *Behavior therapy and beyond.* New York: McGraw-Hill, 1971.

Lazarus, A. A. Some reactions to Costello's paper on depression. *Behavior Therapy,* 1973, 251–53.

Lazarus, A. A., and Abramovitz, A. The use of "emotive imagery" in the treatment of children's phobias. *Journal of Mental Science,* 1962, 108:191–95.

Lazarus, R. S., and Alferd, E. Short-circuiting of threat by experimentally altering cognitive appraisal. *Journal of Abnormal and Social Psychology,* 1964, 69:195–205.

Leach, B. Does Alcoholics Anonymous really work? In P. G. Bourne and R. Fox (eds.), *Alcoholism: Progress in research and treatment.* New York: Academic Press, 1973.

Leaf, A. Getting old. *Scientific American,* 1973, 229:45–52.

Leavitt, E. E. Research in psychotherapy with children. In R. E. Bergin and S. L. Garfield (eds.), *Handbook of psychotherapy and behavior change: An empirical analysis.* New York: Wiley, 1971.

Lee, Dorothy. *Freedom and culture.* Englewood Cliffs, N.J.: Prentice-Hall, 1959.

Leef, J. P., and Hirsch, S. P. The effects of sensory deprivation on verbal communication. *Journal of Psychiatric Research,* 1972, 9:329–36.

Leeper, R. W., and Madison, P. *Toward understanding human personalities.* New York: Appleton-Century-Crofts, 1959.

Lefkowitz, M. M. Discussion of Dr. Gittelman-Klein's chapter: Definitional and methodological issues concerning depressive illness in children. In J. G. Schutterbrandt and A. Rankin (eds.), *Depression in Childhood: Diagnosis, treatment, and conceptual models.* New York: Raven, 1977.

Lehmann, H. E. Physical therapies of schizophrenia. In S. Arieti and E. B. Brody (eds.), *American handbook of psychiatry.* Vol. 3. 2d ed. New York: Basic Books, 1974.

Lehmann, H. E. Schizophrenia: Introduction and history. In A. M. Freedman, H. I. Kaplan, and B. J. Sadock (eds.), *Comprehensive textbook of psychiatry.* Vol. 1. 2d ed. Baltimore: Williams & Wilkins, 1975.

Leighton, A. *My name is legion.* New York: Basic Books, 1959.

Leitenberg, H.; Agras, W. S.; and Thompson, L. E. A sequential analysis of the effect of selective positive reinforcement in modifying anorexia nervosa. *Behaviour Research and Therapy,* 1968, 6:211–18.

Lejeune, J.; Turpin, R.; and Gautier, M. Le mongolisme, premier example d'abberation autosomique humaine. *Annales Genetique,* 1959, 2:41–48.

Lejeune, J.; Gautier, M.; and Turpin, R. Study of somatic chromosomes of nine mongoloid idiot children, 1959. In S. H. Boyer (ed.), *Papers on human genetics.* Englewood Cliffs, N.J.: Prentice-Hall, 1963.

Lemere, F., and Voegtlin, W. L. An evaluation of the aversion treatment of alcoholism. *Quarterly Journal of Studies on Alcoholism,* 1950, 11:199–204.

Lemert, E. M. Paranoia and the dynamics of exclusion. *Sociometry,* 1962, 25:2–25.

Leon, G. R. Current directions in the treatment of obesity. *Psychological Bulletin,* 1976, 83:557–78.

Leonard, C. V. Depression and suicidality. *Journal of Consulting and Clinical Psychology,* 1974, 42:98–104.

Lesser, L.; Ashenden, B. J.; Debuskey, M.; and Eisenberg, L. Anorexia nervosa in children. *American Journal of Orthopsychiatry,* 1960, 30:572–80.

Lester, D. Attempts to predict suicidal risk using psychological tests. *Psychological Bulletin,* 1970, 74:1–17.

Levitt, R. A. Recreational drug use and abuse. In D. C. Rimm and J. W. Somervill (eds.), *Abnormal psychology.* New York: Academic Press, 1977.

Levitt, R. A., and Lonowski, D. J. Adrenergic drugs. In R. A. Levitt (ed.), *Psychopharmacology: A biological approach.* Washington, D.C.: Hemisphere/Wiley, 1975.

Levitz, L. S., and Stunkard, A. J. A therapeutic coalition for obesity: Behavior modification and patient self-help. *American Journal of Psychiatry,* 1974, 131:423–27.

Levy, L. H. *Psychological interpretation.* New York: Holt, Rinehart and Winston, 1963.

Lewinsohn, P. M. Clinical and theoretical aspects of depression. In K. S. Calhoun, H. E. Adams, and K. M. Mitchell (eds.), *Innovative treatment methods in psychopathology.* New York: Wiley, 1974.

Lewinsohn, P. M., and Shaffer, M. Use of home observations as an integral part of the treatment of depression: Preliminary report and case studies. *Journal of Consulting and Clinical Psychology,* 1971, 37:87–95.

Lewinsohn, P. M., and Libet, J. Pleasant activities and depression. *Journal of Consulting and Clinical Psychology,* 1972, 79:291–96.

Lewinsohn, P. M.; Lobitz, W. D.; and Wilson, S. "Sensitivity" of depressed individuals to aversive stimuli. *Journal of Abnormal Psychology,* 1973, 8:259–63.

Lewis, H. *Deprived children.* Oxford: Nuffield and Oxford University Press, 1954.

Liberman, R. P. Behavior modification of schizophrenia: A review. *Schizophrenia Bulletin,* 1972, 6:37–48.

Liberman, R. P., and Smith, V. A multiple baseline study of systematic desensitization in a patient with multiple phobias. *Behavior Therapy,* 1972, 3:597–603.

Libet, J. M., and Lewinsohn, P. M. The concept of social skill with special reference to the behavior of depressed patients. *Journal of Nervous and Mental Disease,* 1973a, 152:106–14.

Libet, J. M., and Lewinsohn, P. M. The concept of social skill with special reference to the behavior of depressed persons. *Journal of Consulting and Clinical Psychology,* 1973b, 40:304–12.

Liddell, H. S. *Emotional hazards in animals and man.* Springfield, Ill.: Charles C Thomas, 1956.

Lidz, T.; Cornelison, A. R.; Fleck, S.; and Terry, D. Intrafamilial environment of the schizophrenic patient. I. Marital schism and marital skew. *American Journal of Psychiatry,* 1957, 114:241–48.

Lilienfield, A. M., and Benesch, C. H. *Epidemiology of mongolism.* Baltimore: Johns Hopkins Press, 1969.

Liljefors, I., and Rahe, R. H. An identical twin study of psychosocial factors in coronary heart diseases in Sweden. *Psychosomatic Medicine,* 1970, 32:523–42.

Lindsley, D. B. Psychological phenomena and the electroencephalogram. *EEG and Clinical Neurophysiology,* 1952, 4:443–50.

Lindzey, G. O. On the classification of projective techniques. *Psychological Bulletin,* 1959, 56:158–68.

Lipinski, D., and Nelson, R. The reactivity and unreliability of self-recording. *Journal of Consulting and Clinical Psychology,* 1974, 42:118–23.

Litman, R. E., and Wold, C. J. Masked depression and suicide. In S. Lesse (ed.), *Masked depression.* New York: Jason Aronson, 1974.

Livingston, S. *Living with epileptic seizures.* Springfield, Ill.: Charles C Thomas, 1963.

Lobitz, W. C., and LoPiccolo, J. New methods in the behavioral treatment of sexual dysfunction. *Journal of Behavior Therapy and Experimental Psychiatry,* 1972, 3:265–71.

London, P. *The modes and morals of psychotherapy.* New York: Holt, Rinehart and Winston, 1964.

London, P. The major psychological disorders. In P. London and D. Rosenthal (eds.), *Foundations of abnormal psychology.* New York: Holt, Rinehart & Winston, 1968.

Longerich, M. C., and Bordeauz, J. *Aphasia therapeutics.* New York: Macmillan, 1954.

LoPiccolo, J., and Lobitz, C. The role of masturbation in the treatment of orgasmic dysfunction. *Archives of Sexual Behavior,* 1972, 2:163–71.

Loraine, J. A.; Adamopoulous, D. A.; Kirkham, K. E.; Ismail, A. A.; and Dore, G. A. Patterns of hormone excretion in male and female homosexuals. *Nature,* 1971, 234:552–54.

Lorr, M. A simplex of paranoid projection. *Journal of Consulting Psychology,* 1964, 28:378–80.

Lotter, V. Epidemiology of autistic conditions in young children. I: Prevalence. *Social Psychiatry,* 1966, 1:124–37.

Lotter, V. Factors related to outcome in autistic children. *Journal of Autism & Childhood Schizophrenia,* 1974, 4:263–77.

Lovass, O. I. *Behavioral treatment of autistic children.* Morristown, N.J.: General Learning Press, 1973.

Lovass, O. I., and Simmons, J. Q. Manipulation of self-destruction in three retarded children. *Journal of Applied Behavior Analysis,* 1969, 2:143–57.

Lovass, O. I.; Koegel, R.; Simmons, J. Q.; and Long, J. S. Some generalization and follow-up measures on autistic children in behavior therapy. *Journal of Applied Behavior Analysis,* 1973, 6:131–66.

Lovibond, S. H., and Caddy, G. Discriminated aversive control in the moderation of alcoholic drinking behavior. *Behavior Therapy,* 1970, 1:437–44.

Lovibond, S. H., and Coote, M. A. Enuresis. In C. G. Costello (ed.), *Symptoms of psychopathology.* New York: Wiley, 1970.

Lubar, J. L., and Bahler, W. W. Behavioral management of epileptic seizures following EEG feedback training of the sensorimotor rhythm. *Biofeedback and Self-Regulation,* 1976, 1:77–104.

Lubin, B. *Manual for the Depression Adjective Checklists.* San Diego: Educational and Industrial Testing Service, 1967.

Luborsky, L.; Singer, B.; and Luborsky L. Comparative studies of psychotherapy. *Archives of General Psychiatry,* 1975, 32:995–1008.

Luparello, T J.; McFadden, E. R.; Lyons, H. A.; and Bleecker, E. R. Psychologic factors and bronchial asthma. *New York State Journal of Medicine,* 1971, 71:2161–65.

Lyght, E. E., (ed.). *The Merck manual of diagnosis and therapy.* 11th ed. Rahway, N.J.: Merck, Sharp and Dohme Research Laboratories, 1966.

Lykken, D. T. Psychology and the lie detector industry. *American Psychologist,* 1974, 29:725–39.

Maccoby, E. E., and Masters, J. C. Attachment and dependency. In P. H. Mussen (ed.), *Carmichael's manual of child psychology.* New York: Wiley, 1970.

MacDonald, M. L. The forgotten Americans: A sociopsychological analysis of aging and nursing homes. *American Journal of Community Psychology,* 1973, 72:311–25.

MacFarlane, J.; Allen, L.; and Honzik, M. *A developmental study of the behavior problems of normal children between twenty-one months and fourteen years.* Berkeley, Calif.: University of California Press, 1954.

MacPhillamy, D. J., and Lewinsohn, P. M. *The Pleasant Events Schedule.* Unpublished manuscript, University of Oregon, 1971.

Maddi, S. R. *Personality theories: A comparative analysis.* Homewood, Ill.: Dorsey, 1972.

Madson, C. H.; Hoffman, M.; Thomas, D. R.; Koropsak, E.; and Madsen, C. K. Comparison of toilet training techniques. In D. M. Gelland (ed.), *Social learning in childhood.* Belmont, Calif.: Brooks Cole, 1969.

Maher, B. *Principles of psychopathology.* New York: McGraw-Hill, 1966.

Mahler, M. S. Tics and impulsions in children: A study of motility. *Psychoanalytic Quarterly,* 1944, 17:430–44.

Mahoney, K.; VanWagenen, R. K.; and Myerson, L. Toilet training of normal and retarded children. *Journal of Applied Behavior Analysis,* 1971, 4:173–81.

Mahoney, M. J. *Cognition and behavior modification.* Cambridge, Mass.: Ballinger, 1974.

Maletzky, B. M., and Kotter, J. Smoking and alcoholism. *American Journal of Psychiatry,* 1974, 131:445–47.

Malmo, R. B. Physiological concomitants of emotion. In A. M. Freedman and H. I. Kaplan (eds.), *Comprehensive textbook of psychiatry.* Baltimore, Md.: Williams & Wilkins, 1967.

Malmo, R. B., and Shagass, C. Physiological studies of reaction to stress in anxiety and early schizophrenia. *Psychosomatic Medicine,* 1949, 11:9–24.

Malmo, R. B.; Shagass, C.; and Davis, F. H. Symptom specificity and bodily reactions during psychiatric interview. *Psychosomatic Medicine,* 1950, 12:276–362.

Mandler, G. Emotion. In R. M. Brown, E. Galonter, E. H. Hess, and G. Mandler (eds.), *New directions in psychology.* Vol. 1. New York: Holt, Rinehart and Winston, 1962.

Mandler, G. Anxiety. In D. L. Sills (ed.), *International encyclopedia of the social sciences.* New York: Crowell, Collier and Macmillan, 1966.

Marañon, G. Contribution à l'étude de l'action émotive de l'àdrénaline. *Revue Francoise Endocrinologie,* 1924, 2:301–25.

Margolies, P. J. Behavioral approaches to the treatment of early infantile autism: A review. *Psychological Bulletin,* 1977, 84:249–64.

Mariotto, M. J., and Paul, G. L. Persons versus situations in the real life functioning of chronically institutionalized mental patients. *Journal of Abnormal Psychology,* 1975, 84:483–93.

Mark, V. H., and Ervin, E. P. *Violence in the brain.* New York: Harper & Row, 1970.

Marks, I. M. Flooding (implosion) and allied treatments. In W. S. Agras (ed.), *Learning theory application of principles and procedures to psychiatry.* New York: Little, Brown, 1972.

Marks, I. M.; Gelder, M.; and Bancroft, J. Sexual deviants two years after electric aversion. *British Journal of Psychiatry,* 1970, 117:173–85.

Marlatt, G. A.; Demming, B.; and Reid, J. B. Loss-of-control drinking in alcoholics: An experimental analogue. *Journal of Abnormal Psychology,* 1973, 81:233–41.

Marmor, J. Psychoanalytic therapy as an educational process. In J. H. Masserman (ed.), *Science and psychoanalysis* (Vol. 5). *Psychoanalytic education.* New York: Grune & Stratton, 1962.

Marshall, W. L. A combined treatment approach to the reduction of multiple fetish-related behaviors. *Journal of Consulting and Clinical Psychology,* 1974, 42:613–16.

Martin, B. *Anxiety and neurotic disorders.* New York: Wiley, 1971.

Marx, M. B.; Garridy, T. F.; and Bowers, F. R. The influence of recent life experience on the health of college freshmen. *Journal of Psychosomatic Research,* 1975, 19:87–98.

Maslow, A. H. *Motivation and personality*. New York: Harper & Row, 1954.

Masserman, J. H. *Behavior and neurosis*. Chicago: University of Chicago Press, 1943.

Masters, W. H., and Johnson, V. E. *Human sexual response*. Boston: Little, Brown, 1966.

Masters, W. H., and Johnson, V. E. *Human sexual inadequacy*. Boston: Little, Brown, 1970.

Masuda, M.; Notske, R. N.; and Holmes, T. H. Catecholamine excretion and asthmatic behavior. *Journal of Psychosomatic Research*, 1966, 10:255–62.

Matarezzo, J. O. An experimental study of aggression in the hypertensive patients. *Journal of Personality*, 1954, 22:423–47.

Mathis, H. I. Training a "disturbed" boy using the mother as therapist: A case study. *Behavior Therapy*, 1971, 2:233–39.

Max, T. W. Breaking up a homosexual fixation by the conditioned reaction technique: A case study. *Psychological Bulletin*, 1935, 32:734.

May, P. R. A. *Treatment of schizophrenia*. New York: Science House, 1968.

May, P. R. A. Psychotherapy and ataraxic drugs. In A. E. Gergin and S. L. Garfield (eds.), *Handbook of psychotherapy and behavior change: An empirical analysis*. New York: Wiley, 1971.

May, P. R. A. A follow-up study of treatment of schizophrenia In R. L. Spitzer and D. F. Klein (eds.), *Evaluation of psychological therapies*. Baltimore: Johns Hopkins, 1975.

McCary, J. L. *Human sexuality*. New York: D. Van Nostrand, 1973.

McCary, J. L., and Sheer, D. E. *Six approaches to psychotherapy*. New York: Dryden Press, 1955.

McCord, W.; McCord, J.; and Gudeman, J. *Origins of alcoholism*. Stanford, Calif.: Stanford University Press, 1960.

McCord, W., and McCord, J. *The psychopath: An essay on the criminal mind*. New York: D. Van Nostrand, 1964.

McCord, W.; Porta, J.; and McCord, J. The familial genesis of psychoses. *Psychiatry*, 1967, 25:60–71.

McCutcheon, B. A., and Adams, H. E. The physiological bases of implosive therapy. *Behaviour Research and Therapy*, 1975, 13:93–100.

McGhie, A., and Chapman, J. Disorders of attention and perception in early schizophrenia. *British Journal of Medical Psychology*, 1961, 34:103–16.

McGuigan, F. J. Covert oral behavior and auditory hallucinations. *Psychophysiology*, 1966, 3:421–28.

McGuire, F. J.; Carlisle, J. M.; and Young, B. G. Sexual deviations as conditioned behavior: A hypothesis. *Behavior Research and Therapy*, 1965, 2:185–90.

McKissock, W.; Richardson, A.; and Walsh, L. Middle cerebral aneurysms: Further results in the controlled trial of conservative and surgical treatment of ruptured intracranial aneurysms. *Lancet*, 1962, 11:417–21.

McReynolds, P. Anxiety, perception, and schizophrenia. In D. D. Jackson (ed.), *The etiology of schizophrenia*. New York: Basic Books, 1960.

Mead, M. *Sex and temperament in three primitive societies*. New York: Morrow, 1935.

Mednick, B. R. Breakdown in high-risk subjects: Familial and early environmental factors. *Journal of Abnormal Psychology*, 1973, 82:469–75.

Mednick, S. A. A learning theory approach to research in schizophrenia: Possible predispositional perinatal factors. *Mental Hygiene*, 1970, 54:50–63.

Mednick, S. A. Birth defects and schizophrenia. *Psychology Today*, April 1971, 4:48–50;80–81.

Mednick, S. A., and Shulsinger, F. Some premorbid characteristics related to breakdown in children with schizophrenic mothers. In D. Rosenthal and S. S. Kety (eds.), *The transmission of schizophrenia*. Oxford: Pergamon, 1968.

Meduna, L. Von. General discussion of the cardiazol therapy. *American Journal of Psychiatry*, 1938, 96:40.

Meehl, P. E. The cognitive activity of the clinician. *American Psychologist*, 1960, 15:19–27.

Meehl, P. E. Schizotaxia, schizotypy, schizophrenia. *American Psychologist*, 1962, 17:827–38.

Meichenbaum, D. H. The effects of instructions and reinforcement on thinking and language behavior of schizophrenics. *Behaviour and Research Therapy*, 1969, 7:101–14.

Meichenbaum, D. H.; Gilmore, J. B.; and Fedoravicius, A. Group insight versus group desensitization in treating speech anxiety. *Journal of Consulting and Clinical Psychology*, 1971, 36:410–21.

Meige, H., and Feindel, E. *Tics and their treatment*. London: Appleton, 1907.

Mellsop, G. Antecedents of schizophrenia: The "schizoid" myth? *Australian and New Zealand Journal of Psychology*, 1973, 7:208–11.

Mendel, W. M., and Rapport, S. Determinants of the decision for psychiatric hospitalization. *Archives of General Psychiatry*, 1969, 20:321–28.

Mendels, J. The prediction of response to electroconvulsive therapy. *American Journal of Psychiatry*, 1967, 124:153–59.

Mendels, J. *Concepts of depression*. New York: Wiley, 1970.

Mendels, J. *Biological Psychiatry*. New York: Wiley, 1973.

Mendelson, J. H. Experimentally induced chronic intoxication and withdrawal in alcoholics. *Quarterly Journal of Studies on Alcohol,* Supplement 2, 1964.

Mensh, I. N. Psychopathic condition, addictions, and sexual deviations. In B. B. Wolman (ed.), *Handbook of clinical psychology.* New York: McGraw-Hill, 1965.

Merton, R. K. Bureaucratic structure and personality. In R. K. Merton, *Social theory and social structure.* Rev. ed. Glencoe, Ill.: Free Press, 1957.

Meyer, R. G. A behavioral treatment of sleepwalking associated with test anxiety. *Journal of Behavior Therapy and Experimental Psychiatry,* 1975, 6:167–68.

Meyer, V. The treatment of two phobic patients on the basis of learning principles. *Journal of Abnormal and Social Psychology,* 1957, 55:261–66.

Meyer, V. Modification of expectancies in cases with obsessional rituals. *Behaviour Research and Therapy,* 1966, 4:273–80.

Meyer, V., and Mair, J. M. M. A new technique to control stammering: A preliminary report. *Behaviour Research and Therapy,* 1963, 1:251–54.

Meyer, V., and Levy, R. Modification of behavior in obsessive-compulsive disorders. In H. E. Adams and I. P. Unikel (eds.), *Issues and trends in behavior therapy.* Springfield, Ill.: Charles C Thomas, 1973.

Miklich, D. R.; Rewey, H. H.; Weiss, J. H.; and Kolton, S. A preliminary investigation of psychophysiological responses to stress among different subgroups of asthmatic children. *Journal of Psychosomatic Research,* 1973, 17:1–8.

Miller, L. C.; Barrett, C. L.; Hampe, E.; and Noble, H. Comparison of reciprocal inhibition, psychotherapy, and waiting list control for phobic children. *Journal of Abnormal Psychology,* 1972, 79:269–79.

Miller, N. E. Learning of visceral and glandular responses. *Science,* 1969, 163:434–45.

Miller, P. M., and Hersen, M. Quantitative changes in alcohol consumption as a function of electrical aversive conditioning. *Journal of Clinical Psychology,* 1972, 28:590–93.

Miller, P. M., Hersen, M.; Eisler, R. M.; and Hemphill, D. P. Effects of faradic aversion therapy on drinking by alcoholics. *Behaviour Research and Therapy,* 1973, 11:491–98.

Miller, P. M., and Hersen, M. *Modification of marital interaction patterns between an alcoholic and his wife.* Unpublished manuscript, 1977.

Miller, R. Does Down's syndrome predispose children to leukemia? *Roche Reports,* 1970, 7:5.

Miller, W. R. Alcoholism scales and objective assessment methods: A review: *Psychological Bulletin,* 1976, 83:649–74.

Miller, W. R.; Rosellini, R. A.; and Seligman, M. E. P. Learned helplessness and depression. In J. D. Maser and M. E. P. Seligman (eds.), *Psychopathology: Experimental models.* San Francisco: W. H. Freeman, 1977.

Millon, T. *Modern psychopathology.* Philadelphia: Saunders, 1969.

Millon, T. Reflections on Rosenhan's "On being sane in insane places." *Journal of Abnormal Psychology,* 1975, 84:456–61.

Mills, H. L.; Agras, W. S.; Mills, J. R.; and Barlow, D. H. Compulsive rituals treated by response prevention. *Archives of General Psychiatry,* 1973, 28:524–29.

Minge, M. R., and Ball, T. S. Teaching of self-help skills to profoundly retarded patients. *American Journal of Mental Deficiency,* 1967, 71:864–68.

Mintz, A. Non-adaptive group behavior. *Journal of Abnormal and Social Psychology,* 1951, 46:150–59.

Mintz, S., and Alpert, M. Imagery vividness, reality testing, and schizophrenic hallucinations. *Journal of Abnormal Psychology,* 1972, 79:310–16.

Mirsky, I. A. Physiologic, psychologic, and social determinants in the etiology of duodenal ulcer. *American Journal of Digestive Diseases,* 1958, 3:285–413.

Mischel, W. *Personality and assessment.* New York: Wiley, 1968.

Mischel, W. Direct vs. indirect personality assessment: Evidence and implications. *Journal of Consulting and Clinical Psychology,* 1972, 38:319–24.

Mischel, W. Toward a cognitive social learning reconceptualism of personality. *Psychological Review,* 1973, 80:252–83.

Mitchell, K. R., and Mitchell, D. M. Migraine: An exploratory treatment application of programmed behavior therapy techniques. *Journal of Psychosomatic Research,* 1971, 15:137–57.

Mitter, M. M.; Guilleminault, C.; Orem, J.; Zarcone, V. P.; and Dement, W. C. Sleeplessness, sleep attacks, and things that go wrong in the night. *Psychology Today,* 1975, 9:45–50.

Mittlemann, B., and Wolfe, H. G. Emotions and the gastroduodenal ulcer. *Psychosomatic Medicine,* 1942, 4:5–61.

Mohr, J.; Turner, E. R.; and Terry, M. *Pedophilia and exhibitionism.* Toronto: Toronto University Press, 1964.

Money, J.; Hampson, J. G.; and Hampson, J. L. Imprinting and the establishment of gender role. *Archives of Neurological Psychiatry,* 1957, 77:333–36.

Money, J., and Brennan, J. G. Sexual dimorphism in the psychology of female transsexuals. *Journal of Nervous and Mental Disease,* 1968, 147:487–99.

Monroe, R. R. *Episodic behavioral disorders; A psychodynamic and neurophysiologic analysis.* Cambridge, Mass.: Harvard University Press, 1970.

Montague, A. Chromosomes and crime. *Psychology Today*, 1968, 2:42–49.

Moore, A. O. Effects of modified maternal care in the sheep and goat. In G. Newton and S. Levine (eds.), *Early experience and behavior.* Springfield, Ill.: Charles C Thomas, 1968.

Moore, D. J., and Shiek, D. A. Toward a theory of early infantile autism. *Psychological Review*, 1971, 78:451–56.

Mora, G. History of Psychiatry. In A. M. Freedman and H. I. Kaplan (eds.), *Comprehensive textbook of psychiatry.* Baltimore: Williams & Wilkins, 1967.

Moreno, J. L., and Kipper, D. A. Group psychodrama and community-centered counseling. In G. M. Gazda (ed.), *Basic approaches to group psychotherapy and group counseling.* Springfield, Ill.: Charles C Thomas, 1968.

Morgan, C. T. *Physiological psychology.* 3d ed. New York: McGraw-Hill, 1965.

Morganstern, K. P. Behavioral interviewing: The initial stages of assessment. In M. Hersen and A. S. Bellack (eds.), *Behavioral assessment: A practical handbook.* New York: Pergamon Press, 1976.

Morishima, A. His spirit raises the ante for retardates. *Psychology Today*, 1975, 9(1):72–73.

Moss, F. (ed.). *Comparative psychology.* Englewood Cliffs, N.J.: Prentice-Hall, 1934.

Mowrer, O. H., and Mowrer, W. M. Enuresis: A method for its study and treatment. *American Journal of Orthopsychiatry*, 1938, 8:436–59.

Mucha, T. F., and Reinhardt, R. F. Conversion reactions in student aviators. *American Journal of Psychiatry*, 1970, 127:493–97.

Muellner, S. R. Development of urinary control in children: A new concept in cause, prevention, and treatment of primary enuresis. *Journal of Urology*, 1960, 84:714–16.

Munzinger, H. The adopted child's IQ: A critical review. *Psychological Bulletin*, 1975, 82:623–29.

Murphree, H. B. Narcotic analgesics: I. Opium alkaloids. In J. R. DiPalma (ed.), *Drill's pharmacology in medicine.* 4th ed. New York: McGraw-Hill, 1971.

Murray, H. A. *Thematic Apperception Test manual.* Cambridge, Mass.: Harvard University Printing Office, 1943. Barron.

Musser, P. H., and Jones, M. C. Self-conceptions of early- and late-maturing boys. *Child Development*, 1957, 28:242–56.

Naranjo, C. Present-centeredness: Technique, prescription, and ideal. In J. Fagan and I. L. Shepherd (eds.), *Gestalt therapy now: Theory, techniques, applications.* Palo Alto, Calif.: Science and Behavior Books, 1970.

Nathan, P. E.; Titler, N. A.; Lowenstein, L. W.; Solomon, P.; and Rossi, A. M. Behavioral analysis of chronic alcoholism. *Archives of General Psychiatry*, 1970, 22:419–30.

National Commission of Marijuana and Drug Abuse. *Marijuana: A signal of misunderstanding.* New York: American Library, 1972.

National Institute on Alcohol Abuse and Alcoholism. *Facts about alcohol and alcoholism.* Washington, D.C. (DHEW Publication No. ADM 75–31) 1974.

Nay, W. R. Analogue measures. In A. R. Ciminero, K. S. Calhoun, and H. E. Adams (eds.), *A handbook of behavioral assessment.* New York: Wiley, 1977.

Necheles, H. A blood factor in peptic ulcers. *The Sciences*, 1970, 10:15–16.

Neisworth, J. T., and Moore, F. Operant treatment of asthmatic responding with the parent as therapist. *Behavior Therapy*, 1972, 3:95–99.

Nemiah, J. C. Obsessive-compulsive reaction. In A. M. Freeman and H. I. Kaplan (eds.), *Comprehensive textbook of psychiatry.* Baltimore: Williams & Wilkins, 1967.

Netter, F. H. *The CIBA collection of medical illustrations.* CIBA Pharmaceutical Company, 1972.

Neuman, C. P., and Tamerin, J. S. The treatment of adult alcoholics and teenage drug addicts in one hospital: A comparison and critical appraisal of factors related to outcome. *Quarterly Journal of Studies on Alcohol*, 1971, 32:82–93.

Ney, P. G.; Palvesky, A. E.; and Markley, J. Relative effectiveness of operant conditioning and play therapy in childhood schizophrenia. *Journal of Autism and Childhood Schizophrenia*, 1971, 1(3):337–49.

Nisbett, R. E. Determinants of food intake in human obesity. *Science*, 1968, 159:1254–55.

Nisbett, R. E. Hunger, obesity, and the ventromedial hypothalamus. *Psychological Reviews*, 1972, 79:433–53.

Nisbett, R. E., and Wilson, T. E. Telling more than we know: Verbal reports on mental processes. *Psychological Review*, 1977, 84:231–59.

Nunnally, J. C. *Popular conceptions of mental health: Their development and change.* New York: Holt, Rinehart and Winston, 1961.

Ober, D. C. Modification of smoking behavior. *Journal of Consulting and Clinical Psychology*, 1968, 32:543–49.

Obler, M. Systematic desensitization in sexual disorders. *Journal of Behavior Therapy and Experimental Psychiatry*, 1973, 4:93–101.

O'Conner, R. D. Modification of social withdrawal through symbolic modeling. *Journal of Applied Behavior Analysis,* 1969, 2:15–22.

Offir, C. Old people's revolt— "At 65, work becomes a four-letter word." *Psychology Today,* 1974, 7:40.

Offord, D. R., and Cross, L. A. Behavioral antecedents of adult schizophrenia: A review. *Archives of General Psychiatry,* 1969, 21:267–83.

Öhmann, A.; Erixon, G.; and Löfberg, I. Phobias and preparedness: Phobic vs. neutral pictures as conditioned stimuli for human autonomic responses. *Journal of Consulting and Clinical Psychology,* 1973, 41:289–93.

Olds, J. Pleasure centers in the brain. *Scientific American,* 1956, 195:105–17.

Olds, J. Differentiation of reward systems in the brain by self-stimulation technics. In E. R. Ramsey and D. S. O'Doherty (eds.), *Electrical studies of the unanesthetized brain.* New York: Harper & Row, 1960.

O'Leary, K. D., and Wilson, G. T. *Behavior therapy: Application and outcome.* Englewood Cliffs, N.J.: Prentice-Hall, 1975.

Oltmanns, T. F.; O'Hayon, J.; and Neale, J. M. The effects of anti-psychotic medication and diagnostic criteria on distractibility in schizophrenia. *Journal of Psychiatric Research,* 1978, 14:81–91.

O'Neill, M., and Kempler, B. Approach and avoidance responses of the hysterical personality to sexual stimuli. *Journal of Abnormal Psychology,* 1969, 74:300–305.

Orgel, S. Z. Effect of psychoanalysis on the course of peptic ulcer. *Psychosomatic Medicine,* 1958, 20:117–23.

Orne, M. T., and Evans, F. J. Social control in the psychological experiment: Antisocial behavior and hypnosis. *Journal of Personality and Social Psychology,* 1965, 1:189–200.

Ornstein, R. E. *The psychology of consciousness.* San Francisco: W. H. Freeman, 1972.

Orwell, G. *1984.* New York: Harcourt, Brace & Jovanovich, 1949.

Osgood, C. E., and Miron, M. S. *Approaches to the study of aphasia.* Urbana: University of Illinois Press, 1963.

Osgood, C. E.; Luria, Z.; Jeans, R. F.; and Smith, S. W. The three faces of Evelyn: A case report. *Journal of Abnormal Psychology,* 1976, 85:247–86.

Osmond, H., and Smythies, J. Schizophrenia: A new approach. *The Journal of Mental Science,* 1952, 98:309–15.

Owen, D. R. The 47, XYY male: A review. *Psychological Bulletin,* 1972, 78:209–33.

Packard, R. C. What is a psychogenic headache? *Headache,* 1976, 16:20–23.

Palmer, E. D. *Functional gastrointestinal disease.* Baltimore: Williams & Wilkins, 1967.

Pasternack, S. A. The explosive, antisocial, and passive-aggressive personalities. In J. R. Lion (ed.), *Personality disorders: Diagnoses and management.* Baltimore: Williams & Wilkins, 1974.

Patel, C. H. Yoga and biofeedback in the managenent of hypertension. *Lancet,* 1973, 2:1053–55.

Patel, C. H. 12-month follow-up of yoga and biofeedback in the management of hypertension. *Lancet,* 1975, 2:93–99.

Patel, C. H., and North, W. R. Randomized controlled trial of yoga and biofeedback in management of hypertension. *Lancet,* 1975, 5:108–13.

Patterson, C. H. *Theories of counseling and psychotherapy.* New York: Harper & Row, 1966.

Paul, G. L. *Insight vs. desensitization in psychotherapy.* Stanford, Calif.: Stanford University Press, 1966.

Paul, G. L. Outcome of systematic desensitization. I: Background, procedures, and uncontrolled reports of individual treatment. In C. M. Franks (ed.), *Behavior therapy: Appraisal and status.* New York: McGraw-Hill, 1969a.

Paul, G. L. Outcome of systematic desensitization. II: Controlled investigation of individual treatment, technique variations, and current status. In C. M. Franks (ed.), *Behavior therapy: Appraisal and status.* New York: McGraw-Hill, 1969b.

Paul, G. L., and Shannon, D. T. Treatment of anxiety through systematic desensitization in therapy groups. *Journal of Abnormal Psychology,* 1966, 71:124–35.

Paul, G. L.; Tobias, L. L.; and Holly, B. L. Maintenance psychotropic drugs in the presence of active treatment programs: A "triple-blind" withdrawal study with long-term mental patients. *Archives of General Psychiatry,* 1972, 27:106–15.

Paul, G. L., and Lentz, R. J. *Psychosocial treatment of chronic mental patients: Milieu vs. social learning programs.* Cambridge, Mass.: Harvard University Press, 1977.

Pearson, J. S. Behavioral aspects of Huntington's Chorea. In A. Barbeau, T. N. Chase, and G. W. Paulson (eds.), *Vol. 1: Advances in neurology: Huntington's Chorea, 1872–1972.* New York: Raven Press, 1973.

Penfield, W., and Rasmussen, T. *The cerebral cortex of man.* New York: Macmillan, 1950.

Penrose, L. *The biology of mental defect.* London: Sidgwick & Jackson, 1946.

Perls, F. S.; Hefferline, R. F.; and Goodman, P. *Gestalt therapy: Excitement and growth in human personality.* New York: Crown, 1951.

Perris, C. A study of bipolar (manic-depressive) and unipolar recurrent depressive psychosis. *Acta Psychiatrica et Neurologica Scandinavica*, 1966, 42 (Supplement No. 194):1–189.

Peters, J. E., and Stern, R. M. Specificity of attitude hypothesis in psychosomatic medicine: A reexamination. *Journal of Psychosomatic Research*, 1971, 15:129–35.

Pflanz, M. Epidemiological and sociocultural factors in the etiology of duodenal ulcer. *Advances in Psychosomatic Medicine*, 1971, 6:121–51.

Phillips, L. Case history data and prognosis in schizophrenia. *Journal of Nervous and Mental Disease*, 1953, 117:515–25.

Pincus, H. H., and Tucker, G. J. *Behavioral neurology*. London: Oxford University Press, 1974.

Plachetta, K. E. Encopresis: A case study utilizing contracting, scheduling, and self-charting. *Journal of Behavior Therapy and Experimental Psychiatry*, 1976, 17:195–96.

Pokorny, A. D. Myths about suicide. In H. L. P. Resnik (ed.), *Suicidal behaviors*. Boston: Little, Brown, 1968.

Polak, P. Patterns of discord: Goals of patients, therapists, and community members. *Archives of General Psychiatry*, 1970, 23:277–83.

Polansky, N. A.; Borgman, R. D.; and DeSaix, C. *Roots of futility*. San Francisco: Jossey-Bass, 1972.

Pollack, R. H., and Brenner, M. W. (eds.). *The experimental psychology of Albert Binet: Selected papers*. New York: Springer, 1969.

Pollock, M., and Hornabrook, R. W. The prevalence, natural history, and dementia of Parkinson's disease. *Brain*, 1966, 89:429–40.

Polvan, N. Historical aspects of mental ills in Middle East discussed. *Roche Reports*, 1969, 6(12):3.

Pope, H. G., and Lipinski, J. F. Diagnosis in schizophrenia and manic-depressive illness. *Archives of General Psychiatry*, 1978, 35:811–28.

Popler, K. Token reinforcement in the treatment of nocturnal enuresis: A case study and six-month follow-up. *Journal of Behavior Therapy and Experimental Psychiatry*, 1976, 7:83–84.

Poussant, A., and Ditman, K. A controlled study of imipramine (tofranil) in the treatment of childhood enuresis. *Journal of Pediatrics*, 1965, 67:283–90.

Pratt, R. T. C. *The genetics of neurological disorders*. New York: Oxford University Press, 1967.

Price, J. S. The genetics of depressive disorder. In A. Coppen and A. Walk (eds.), *Recent developments in affective disorders*. British Journal of Psychiatry, Special Publication 2, 1968.

Prien, R. F.; Caffey, E. M.; and Klett, C. J. Prophylactic efficacy of lithium carbonate in manic-depressive illness. *Archives of General Psychiatry*, 1973, 28:337–41.

Prince, M. *The dissociation of personality*. London: Longmans, Green, 1905.

Prince, V., and Bentler, P. M. Survey of 504 cases of transvestism. *Psychological Reports*, 1972, 31:903–17.

Proctor, J. T. Hysteria in childhood. *American Journal of Orthopsychiatry*, 1958, 28:394–407.

Purcell, K. Distinctions between subgroups of asthmatic children: Children's perceptions of events associated with asthma. *Pediatrics*, 1963, 31:486–94.

Purcell, K.; Brody, K.; Chai, H.; Muser, J.; Molk, L.; Gorden, N.; and Means, J. The effect on asthma in children of experimental separation from the family. *Psychosomatic Medicine*, 1969, 31:144–64.

Purcell, K., and Weiss, J. H. Asthma. In C. G. Costello (ed.), *Symptoms of psychopathology*. New York: Wiley, 1970.

Rachman, S. Sexual fetishism: An experimental analogue. *Psychological Record*, 1966, 16:293–96.

Rachman, S.; Hodgson, R.; and Marks, I. M. The treatment of chronic obsessional-compulsive disorder by modelling. *Behaviour Research and Therapy*, 1970, 8:385–92.

Rachman, S.; DeSilva, P.; and Roper, G. The spontaneous decay of compulsive urges. *Behaviour Research and Therapy*, 1976, 14:445–53.

Rafi, A. A. Learning theory and the treatment of tics. *Journal of Psychosomatic Research*, 1962, 6:71–76.

Rahe, K. H., and Lind, E. Psychosocial factors and sudden cardiac death: A pilot study. *Journal of Psychosomatic Research*, 1971, 15:19–24.

Rapaport, D. The structure of psychoanalytic theory: A systematizing attempt. In S. Koch (ed.), *Psychology: A study of science*. Vol. 3. New York: McGraw-Hill, 1959.

Raskin, N., and Ehrenberg, R. Senescence, senility, and Alzheimer's disease. *American Journal of Psychiatry*, 1956, 113:133–36.

Rathus, S. A. A 30-item schedule for assessing assertive behavior. *Behavior Therapy*, 1973, 4:398–406.

Ray, O. S. *Drugs, society, and human behavior*. St. Louis, Mo.: Mosby, 1974.

Rechtschaffen, A.; Goodenough, D. R.; and Shapiro, A. Patterns of sleeptalking. *Archives of General Psychiatry*, 1962, 7:418–26.

Rechtschaffen, A., and Dement, W. C. Narcolepsy and hyperinsomnia. In A. Kales (ed.), *Sleep: Physiology and pathology*, Philadelphia: Lippincott, 1969.

Reed, E. W., and Reed, S. C. *Mental retardation: A family study*. Philadelphia: Saunders, 1965.

Reed, G. F. Obsessionality and self-appraisal questionnaires. *British Journal of Psychiatry*, 1969a, 115:205–9.

Reed, G. F. "Underinclusion": A characteristic of obsessional personality disorders. *British Journal of Psychiatry*, 1969b, 115:787–90.

Rees, L. Constitutional factors and abnormal behavior. In H. J. Eysenck (ed.), *Handbook of Abnormal Psychology*. New York: Basic Books, 1961.

Rees, L. The importance of psychological, allergic, and infective factors in childhood asthma. *Journal of Psychosomatic Research*, 1964, 7:253–62.

Rees, T. P. Back to moral treatment and community care. *Journal of Mental Science*, 1957, 103:303–13.

Rees, W. Physical characteristics of the schizophrenic patient. In D. Richter (ed.), *Schizophrenia: Somatic aspects*. New York: Macmillan, 1957.

Reid, J. B. Reliability assessment of observational data: A possible methodological problem. *Child Development*, 1970, 41:1143–50.

Reitan, R. M. Psychological deficits resulting from cerebral lesions in man. In J. M. Warren and K. Akert (eds.), *The frontal granular cortex and behavior*. New York: McGraw-Hill, 1964.

Reitan, R. M. A research program on the psychological effects of brain lesions in human beings. In N. R. Ellis (ed.), *International review of research in mental retardation*. Vol. 1. New York: Academic Press, 1966.

Rekers, G. A. Atypical gender development and psychosocial adjustment. *Journal of Applied Behavior Analysis*, 1977, 6:275–77.

Rekers, G. A.; Amoro-Plotkin, H.; and Lowe, B. P. Feminine sex-typed mannerisms in normal boys and girls as a function of sex and age. *Child Development*, 1977, 48:275–78.

Resick, P. A.; Wendiggensen, P.; Ames, S.; and Meyer, V. Systematic slowed speech: A new treatment for stuttering. *Behaviour Research and Therapy*, 1978, 16:161–67.

Richard, L. G., and Carroll, E. E. Illicit drug use and addiction in the United States: Review of available statistics. *Public Health Reports*, 1970, 85:1935–41.

Richmond, J. B., and Lustman, S. L. Autonomic function in the neonate. I: Implications for psychosomatic theory. *Psychosomatic Medicine*, 1955, 17:269–75.

Richmond, J. B.; Lipton, E. L.; and Steinschneider, A. Autonomic function in the neonate: V. Individual homeostatic capacity in cardiac response. *Psychosomatic Medicine*, 1962, 24:66–74.

Ricks, D. M. *The beginning of vocal communication in infants and autistic children*. Ph.D. dissertation, University of London, 1972.

Rifkin, B. O. The treatment of cardiac neurosis using systematic desensitization. *Behaviour Research and Therapy*, 1968, 6:239–41.

Riklan, M. *L-dopa and Parkinsonism*. Springfield, Ill.: Charles C Thomas, 1973.

Rimland, B. *Infantile autism*. New York: Meredith, 1964.

Rimland, B. Progress in research. Autism. *Proceedings of the 4th Annual Meeting of the National Society for Autistic Children*. Rockville, Md.: National Institute of Mental Health, 1973, 21–32.

Rimm, D. C.; DeGroot, J. C.; Board, P.; Heiman, J.; and Dillon, P. V. Systematic desensitization of an anger response. *Behaviour Research and Therapy*, 1971, 9:273–80.

Rimm, D. C., and Somervill, J. W. *Abnormal psychology*. New York: Academic Press, 1977.

Ringuette, E. L., and Kennedy, T. An experimental study of the double-bind hypothesis. *Journal of Abnormal Psychology*, 1966, 71:136–42.

Rivera, G. *Willowbrook*. New York: Random House, 1972.

Roberts, W. W. Both rewarding and punishing effects from stimulation of posterior hypothalamus of cat with same electrode at same intensity. *Journal of Comparative and Physiological Psychology*, 1958, 51:400–407.

Roberts, W. W. Fear-like behavior elicited from the dorsomedial thalamus of cat. *Journal of Comparative and Physiological Psychology*, 1962, 55:191–97.

Robins, L. *The Vietnam drug abuser returns*. New York: McGraw-Hill, 1974.

Robins, L. N. *Deviant children grown up*. Baltimore: Williams & Wilkins, 1964.

Robinson, H.; Kirk, R. F., Jr.; Frye, R. F.; Robertson, J. T.; and Robinson, H. A psychological study of patients with rheumatoid arthritis and other painful diseases. *Journal of Psychosomatic Research*, 1972, 16:53–56.

Robinson, H. B., and Robinson, N. M. Mental retardation. In P. H. Mussen (ed.), *Carmichael's manual of child psychology*. Vol. 2. 3d ed. New York: Wiley, 1970.

Rodin, J. Bidirectional influences of emotionality, stimulus responsivity, and metabolic events in obesity. In J. D. Maser and M. E. P. Seligman (eds.), *Psychopathology: Experimental models*. San Francisco: W. H. Freeman, 1977.

Rogers, C. R. *Client-centered therapy*. Boston: Houghton Mifflin, 1951.

Rogers, C. R. A theory of therapy, personality, and interpersonal relationships. In S. Koch (ed.), *Psychology: A study of a science*. Vol. 3. New York: McGraw-Hill, 1959.

Rogers, C. R. *Carl Rogers on encounter groups*. New York: Harper & Row, 1970.

Rogers, C. R., and Dymond, R. F. (eds.). *Psychotherapy and personality change.* Chicago: University of Chicago Press, 1954.

Rohr, C. C., and Densen-Gerber, J. *Adolescent drug abuse: An evaluation of 800 inpatients in the Odyssey House Program.* Paper read at the Annual Meeting of the American Psychiatric Association, Washington, D.C., May 1971.

Roper, G.; Rachman, S.; and Hodgson, R. An experiment on obsessional checking. *Behaviour Research and Therapy,* 1973, 11:271–77.

Rorvik, D. M. Do drugs lead to violence? *Look,* April 1970, 58–61.

Rosen, A. C.; Rekers, G. A.; and Fraiar, L. R. Theoretical and diagnostic issues in child gender disturbances. *Journal of Sex Research,* 1977, 4:120–28.

Rosen, G. Emotion and sensibility in ages of anxiety. *American Journal of Psychiatry,* 1967, 124:771–84.

Rosenhan, D. L. On being sane in insane places. *Science,* 1973, 179:250–58.

Rosenthal, D. Changes in some moral values following psychotherapy. *Journal of Consulting Psychology,* 1955, 19:431–36.

Rosenthal, D. *Genetic theory and abnormal behavior.* New York: McGraw-Hill, 1970.

Rosenthal, D. *Genetics of psychopathology.* New York: McGraw-Hill, 1971.

Rosenthal, D. The genetics of schizophrenia. In S. Arieti and E. B. Brody (eds.), *American handbook of psychiatry.* Vol. 3. 2d ed. New York: Basic Books, 1974.

Rosenzweig, M. R.; Krech, D.; Bennett, E. L.; and Diamond, M. C. Modifying brain chemistry and anatomy by enrichment or impoverishment of experience. In G. Newton and S. Levine (eds.), *Early experience and behavior.* Springfield, Ill.: Charles C Thomas, 1968.

Ross, A. O. *Psychological disorders of children: A behavioral approach to theory, research and therapy.* New York: McGraw-Hill, 1974.

Ross, L. The intuitive psychologist and his shortcomings: Distortions in the attribution process. In L. Berkowitz (ed.), *Advances in experimental social psychology.* Vol. 10. New York: Academic Press, 1977.

Ross, M. This doctor will self-destruct. . . . *Human Behavior,* 1974, 3:54.

Ross, R. R.; Meichenbaum, D. H.; and Humphrey, C. Treatment of nocturnal headbanging by behavior modification techniques: A case report. *Behaviour Research and Therapy,* 1971, 9:151–54.

Roth, M. The phenomenology of depressive states. *Canadian Psychiatric Association Journal,* 1959, 4:532–54.

Rumbaut, R. D. The first psychiatric hospital of the Western World. *American Journal of Psychiatry,* 1972, 128:1305–9.

Rush, B. *Medical inquiries and observations upon diseases of the mind.* 2d ed. Philadelphia: Thomas Dobson, 1794.

Ruskin, A.; Board, O. W.; and Schaffer, R. L. Blast hypertension: Elevated arterial pressure in victims of the Texas City disaster. *American Journal of Medicine,* 1948, 4:228–36.

Rutter, M. The influence of organic and emotional factors on the origins, nature and outcome of childhood psychosis. *Developmental Medicine and Child Neurology,* 1965, 1:518–28.

Rutter, M. Prognosis: Psychotic children in adolescence and early adult life. In J. K. Wing (ed.), *Childhood autism: Clinical, educational, and social aspects.* Elmsford, N.Y.: Pergamon Press, 1966.

Rutter, M. Concepts of autism: A review of research. *Journal of Child Psychology and Psychiatry,* 1968, 9:1–25.

Rutter, M., and Lockyer, L. A five- to fifteen-year follow-up study of infantile psychosis. I: Description of sample. *British Journal of Psychiatry,* 1967, 113:1169–82.

Saghir, M. T., and Robins, E. Homosexuality. I: Sexual behavior of the female homosexual. *Archives of General Psychiatry,* 1969, 20:192–201.

Saghir, M. T.; Robins, E.; and Walbran, B. Homosexuality. II: Sexual behavior of the male homosexual. *Archives of General Psychiatry,* 1969, 21:219–29.

Sajwaj, T.; Libet, J.; and Agras, S. Lemon juice therapy: The control of life-threatening rumination in a six-month infant. *Journal of Applied Behavior Analysis,* 1974, 7:557–63.

Sakel, M. A new treatment of schizophrenia. *American Journal of Psychiatry,* 1937, 93:829.

Sandifer, M. G., Jr.; Pettus, C.; and Quade, D. A study of psychiatric diagnosis. *Journal of Nervous and Mental Disease,* 1964, 139:350–56.

Sandler, J., and Hazari, A. The "obsessional": On the psychological classification of obsessional character traits and symptoms. *British Journal of Medical Psychology,* 1960, 10:33, 113–22.

Sandler, J., and Davidson, R. S. *Psychopathology: Learning theory, research, and applications.* New York: Harper and Row, 1973.

Sapira, J. D.; Scheib, E. T.; Moriarty, R.; and Shapiro, A. P. Differences in perception between hypertensive and normotensive populations. *Psychosomatic Medicine,* 1971, 33:239–50.

Sarbin, T. R. On the futility of the proposition that some people can be labeled "mentally ill." *Journal of Consulting Psychology,* 1967, 31:447–53.

Sargent, J. D.; Green, E. E.; and Walters, E. L. The use of autogenic feedback training in a pilot study of migraine and tension headaches. *Headache,* 1972, 12:120–25.

Satir, V. M. *Conjoint family therapy.* Palo Alto, Calif.: Science & Behavior Books, 1967.

Sawrey, W. L.; Conger, J. J.; and Turrell, E. S. An experimental investigation of the role of psychological factors in the production of gastric ulcers in the rat. *Journal of Comparative and Physiological Psychology,* 1956, 49:269–70.

Sawrey, W. L., and Weisz, J. D. An experimental method of producing gastric ulcers. *Journal of Comparative and Physiological Psychology,* 1956, 49:269–70.

Scarr, S. Genetics and the development of intelligence. In F. D. Horowitz (ed.), *Child development research.* Vol. 4. Chicago: University of Chicago Press, 1975.

Schaar, K. Suicide rate high among women psychologists. *APA Monitor,* 1974, 5:1–10.

Schachter, J. Pain, fear, and anger in hypertensives and normotensives: A psychophysiologic study. *Psychosomatic Medicine,* 1957, 29:17–29.

Schachter, J.; Kerr, J. L.; Wimberly, F. C.; and Lachin, J. M. Heart rate levels of black and white newborns. *Psychosomatic Medicine,* 1974, 36:513–24.

Schachter, S., and Singer, J. E. Cognitive, social, and physiological determinants of emotional state. *Psychological Review,* 1962, 69:379–99.

Schachter, S., and Wheeler, L. Epinephrine, chlorpromazine, and amusement. *Journal of Abnormal and Social Psychology,* 1962, 65:121–28.

Schachter, S.; Goldman, R.; and Gordon, A. Effects of fear, food deprivation, and obesity on eating. *Journal of Personality and Social Psychology,* 1968, 10:91–97.

Schachter, S., and Gross, L. Manipulated time and eating behavior. *Journal of Personality and Social Psychology,* 1968, 10:98–106.

Schachter, S., and Rodin, J. (eds.). *Obese humans and rats.* Washington, D.C.: Erlbaum, 1974.

Schaefer, H. H.; Nobell, M. R.; and Mills, K. C. Some sobering data on the use of self-confrontation with alcoholics. *Behavior Therapy,* 1971, 2:28–39.

Schaie, K. W., and Gribben, K. The impact of environmental complexity upon adult cognitive development. *Proceedings of Third Biennial Meeting of International Social Studies in Behavior Development.* Guilford, England, 1975.

Schapiro, S. Maturation of the neuroendocrine response to stress in the rat. In G. Newton and S. Levine (eds.), *Early experience and behavior.* Springfield, Ill.: Charles C Thomas, 1968.

Scheff, T. J. Decision roles, types of error, and their consequences in medical diagnosis. *Behavioral Science,* 1963, 8:97–107.

Scheff, T. J. *Being mentally ill.* Chicago: Aldine, 1966.

Schild, S. Parents of children with PKU. *Children Today,* 1972, 1:20–22.

Schmaulk, F. Punishment, arousal and avoidance learning in sociopaths. *Journal of Abnormal Psychology,* 1970, 76:325–35.

Schnurer, A. T.; Rubin, R. R.; and Roy, A. Systematic desensitization of anorexia nervosa seen as a weight phobia. *Journal of Behavior Therapy and Experimental Psychiatry,* 1973, 4:149–53.

Schoenberger, J. A.; Stamler, J.; and Shekelle, R. B. Current status of hypertension control in an industrial population. *Journal of the American Medical Association,* 1972, 22:559–62.

Schuell, H. *Aphasia theory and therapy: Selected lectures and papers of Hildred Schuell.* Baltimore: University Park Press, 1974.

Schuham, A. I. The double-bind hypothesis a decade later. *Psychological Bulletin,* 1967, 68:409–16.

Schuyler, D. *The depressive spectrum.* New York: Jason Aronson, 1974.

Schwartz, A. H., and Swartaburg, M. Hospital care. In B. B. Wolman (ed.), *The therapist's handbook.* New York: Van Nostrand Reinhold, 1976.

Schwartz, B.; Guilbaud, G.; and Fishgood, H. Etudes electro-encephalographiques sue le sommeil de nuit. I. L'insomnie chronique. *Presse Medicale,* 1963, 71:1474–76.

Schwartz, G. Biofeedback, self-regulation, and the patterning of physiological processes. *American Scientist,* 1975, 63:314–24.

Schwartz, G. E.; Faire, P. L.; Salt, P.; Mandel, G. L.; and Klerman, J. L. Facial muscle patterning to affective imagery in depressed and nondepressed subjects. *Science,* 1976, 192:489–91.

Seay, B. M.; Hansen, E. W.; and Harlow, H. F. Mother-infant separation in monkeys. *Journal of Child Psychology and Psychiatry,* 1962, 3:123–32.

Seay, B. M., and Harlow, H. F. Maternal separation in the rhesus monkey. *Journal of Nervous and Mental Disease,* 1965, 140:434–41.

Seiden, R. H. Campus tragedy: A study of student suicide. *Journal of Abnormal Psychology,* 1966, 71:389–99.

Seiden, R. H. Suicide: Preventable death. *Public Affairs Report,* 1974, 15:1–5.

Seifert, A R., and Lubar, J. F. Reduction of epileptic seizures through EEG biofeedback training. *Biological Psychology,* 1975, 3:157–84.

Seligman, M. E. P. Phobias and preparedness. *Behavior Therapy,* 1971, 2:307–20.

Seligman, M. E. P. *Helplessness: On depression, development, and death.* San Francisco: W. H. Freeman, 1975.

Seligman, M. E. P. Comment and integration. *Journal of Abnormal Psychology,* 1978, 87:165–79.

Selye, H. *The stress of life.* New York: McGraw-Hill, 1956.

Selye, H. *Stress without distress.* Philadelephia: Lippincott, 1974.

Serber, M. Shame aversion therapy. *Journal of Behavior Therapy and Experimental Psychiatry,* 1970, 1:213–15.

Shaefer, I. G., and Martin, P. L. Behavioral therapy for "apathy," of hospitalized schizophrenics. *Psychological Reports,* 1966, 19:1147–58.

Shaffer, J. B. P., and Galinsky, M. D. *Models of group therapy and sensitivity training.* Englewood Cliffs, N.J.: Prentice-Hall, 1974.

Shaffer, M., and Lewinsohn, P. M. *Interpersonal behaviors in the home of depressed versus nondepressed psychiatric and normal controls: A test of several hypotheses.* Paper read at the Annual Meeting of the Western Psychological Association, Eugene, Oregon, 1971.

Shakow, D. Segmental set. *Archives of General Psychiatry,* 1962, 6:1–17.

Shakow, D. Segmental set: The adaptive process in schizophrenia. *American Psychologist,* 1977, 32:129–39.

Shaw, D. Mineral metabolism, mania, and melancholia. *British Medical Journal,* 1966, 2:262–67.

Shean, G. *Schizophrenia.* Cambridge, Mass.: Winthrop, 1978.

Sheehan, J. Conflict theory of stuttering. In J. Eisenson (ed.), *Stuttering: A symposium.* New York: Harper & Row, 1958.

Sheldon, W.; Stevens, S.; and Tucker, W. *The varieties of human physique.* New York: Harper & Row, 1940.

Sherman, J. A. Use of reinforcement and imitation to reinstate verbal behavior in mute psychotics. *Journal of Abnormal and Social Psychology,* 1965, 70:155–64.

Sherman, M. Verbalization and language symbols in personality adjustment. *American Journal of Psychiatry,* 1938, 95:621–40.

Shields, J. The genetics of schizophrenia in historical context. In A. Coppin and A. Walk (eds.), *Recent developments in schizophrenia. British Journal of Psychiatry Special Publication No. 1.* Ashford, England: Headley, 1967.

Shields, J., and Slater, E. Heredity and psychological abnormality. In H. Eysenck, (ed.), *A handbook of abnormal psychology.* New York: Pitman Medical Publishing, 1961.

Shneidman, E. S. Suicide. In A. M. Freedman, H. I. Kaplan, and B. J. Sadock (eds.), *Comprehensive textbook of psychiatry. II.* Vol. 2. 2d ed. Baltimore, Md.: Williams & Wilkins, 1975.

Shneidman, E. S., and Farberow, N. L. (eds.). *Clues to suicide.* New York: McGraw-Hill, 1957.

Shneidman, E. S., and Farberow, N. L. A psychological approach to the study of suicide notes. In E. S. Shneidman, N. L. Farberow, and R. E. Litman (eds.), *The psychology of suicide.* New York: Jason Aronson, 1970.

Silverman, C. *The epidemiology of depression.* Baltimore: Johns Hopkins Press, 1968.

Simon, W., and Gagnon, J. H. Psychosexual development. In J. H. Gagnon and W. Simon (eds.), *The sexual scene.* Chicago: Aldine, 1970.

Sines, J. O.; Cleeland, C.; and Adkins, J. The behavior of normal and stomach lesion susceptible rats in several learning situations. *Journal of Genetic Psychology,* 1963, 102:91–94.

Singer, M., and Wynne, L. C. Differentiating characteristics of the parents of childhood schizophrenics, childhood neurotics, and young adult schizophrenics. *American Journal of Psychiatry,* 1963, 120:234–43.

Skeels, H. M. Adult status of children with contrasting early life experiences. *Monographs of the Society for Research in Child Development,* 1966, 31(3).

Skeels, H. M., and Dye, H. B. A study of the effects of differential stimulation on mentally retarded children. *Proceedings and Addresses of the American Association on Mental Deficiency,* 1939, 44:114–36.

Skinner, B. F. *Science and human behavior.* New York: Macmillan, 1953.

Skinner, B. F. *Beyond freedom and dignity.* New York: Knopf, 1971.

Skipper, J., and McCagney, C. Stripteasers: The anatomy and career contingencies of a deviant occupation. *Social Problems,* 1969, 17:391–405.

Slade, H. C. The concept of neurasthenia. *Canadian Psychiatric Association Journal,* 1968, 13:281–82.

Slade, P. D. Psychometric studies of obsessional illness and obsessional personality. In H. R. Beech (ed.), *Obsessional states.* London: Methuen, 1974.

Slater, E., and Glithero, E. A follow-up of patients diagnosed as suffering from hysteria. *Journal of Psychosomatic Research,* 1965, 9:9–13.

Slater, E., and Shields, J. Genetic aspects of anxiety. In M. H. Lader (ed.), *Studies of anxiety.* Ashford, England: Headley Brothers, 1969.

Slavney, P. R., and McHugh, P. R. The hysterical personality. *Archives of General Psychiatry,* 1974, 30:325–29.

Sloan, W., and Birch, J. W. A rationale for degrees of retardation. *American Journal of Mental Deficiency,* 1955–1956, 60:250–64.

Sloane, R. B.; Staples, F. R.; Cristol, A. H.; Yorkston, N. J.; and Whipple, K. *Behavior therapy vs. psychotherapy.* Cambridge, Mass.: Commonwealth Publication of the Harvard University Press, 1975.

Sloane, R. B.; Staples, F. R.; Cristol, A. H.; Yorkston, N. J.; and Whipple, K. Patient characteristics and outcome in psychotherapy and behavior therapy. *Journal of Consulting and Clinical Psychology,* 1976, 44:330–39.

Small, I. F., and Small, J. G. Sex and the passive aggressive personality. *Medical Aspects of Human Sexuality,* 1971, 5:78–89.

Smith, M. L., and Glass, G. V. Meta-analysis of psychotherapy outcome studies. *American Psychologist,* 1977, 32:752–60.

Smith, R. E. The use of humor in the counterconditioning of anger responses: A case study. *Behavior Therapy,* 1973, 4:576–80.

Snyder, M.; Tanke, E. D.; and Berscheid, E. Social perception and interpersonal behavior: On the self-fulfilling nature of social stereotypes. *Journal of Personality and Social Psychology,* 1977, 35:656–66.

Snyder, M., and Swann, W. B., Jr. Hypothesis-testing processes in social interaction. *Journal of Personality and Social Psychology,* 1978, 36:1202–12.

Sobell, L. C.; Sobell, M. P.; and Christelman, W. C. The myth of "one drink." *Behaviour Research and Therapy,* 1972, 10:119–24.

Sobell, M. B., and Sobell, L. C. Individual behavior therapy for alcoholics. *Behavior Therapy,* 1973, 4:49–72.

Solomon, R. L. An opponent-process theory of acquired motivation: The affective dynamics of addiction. In J. D. Maser and M. E. P. Seligman (eds.), *Psychopathology: Experimental models.* San Francisco: W. H. Freeman, 1977.

Solomon, R. L., Kamin, L. J.; and Wynne, L. C. Traumatic avoidance learning: The outcome of several extinction procedures with dogs. *Journal of Abnormal and Social Psychology.* 1953, 48:291–401.

Solomon, R. L., and Corbit, J. D. An opponent-process theory of motivation. I: Temporal dynamics of affect. *Psychological Review,* 1974, 81:119–45.

Sours, J. A. Narcolepsy and other disturbances in the sleep-waking rhythm: A study of 115 cases with review of the literature. *Journal of Nervous and Mental Disease,* 1963, 137:525–42.

Sperry, R. W. Hemisphere deconnection and unity in conscious awareness. *American Psychologist,* 1968, 23:723–33.

Spitz, R. A. Hospitalization: An inquiry into the genesis of psychiatric conditions of early childhood. In R. S. Eissler, A. Freud, H. Hartman, and E. Kris (eds.), *The psychoanalytic study of the child.* Vol. 1. New York: International University Press, 1945.

Spitz, R. A. Anaclitic depression. In P. Goenacke, H. Hartmann, E. B. Jackson, E. Kris, L. S. Kubie, B. D. Lewin, M. C. Putnam, R. M. Loewenstein, and R. A. Spitz (eds.), *The psychoanalytic study of the child.* Vol. 2. New York: International Universities Press, 1946.

Spitzer, R. L. On pseudoscience in science, logic in remission, and psychiatric diagnosis: A critique of Rosenhan's "On being sane in insane places." *Journal of Abnormal Psychology,* 1975, 84:442–52.

Spitzer, R. L.; Endicott, J.; and Robins, E. *Research diagnostic criteria.* New York: Biometrics Research, 1975.

Spradlin, J. E., and Girartheau, F. L. The behavior of moderately and severely retarded persons. In N. R. Ellis (ed.), *International review of research in mental retardation.* Vol. 1. New York: Academic Press, 1966.

Stallone, F.; Shelley, E.; Mendlewicz, J; and Fieve, R. R. The use of lithium in affective disorders. III: A double-blind study of prophylaxis in bipolar illness. *American Journal of Psychiatry,* 1973, 130:1006–10.

Stampfl, T. G., and Levis, D. J. Essentials of implosive therapy: A learning-theory-based psychodynamic behavioral therapy. *Journal of Abnormal Psychology,* 1967, 72:496–503.

Staples, F. R.; Sloan, R. B.; Wipple, R.; Cristol, A. H.; and Yorkston, N. Process and outcome in psychotherapy and behavior therapy. *Journal of Consulting and Clinical Psychology,* 1976, 44:340–50.

Staudt, V., and Zubin, J. A biometric evaluation of the somatotherapies in schizophrenia. *Psychological Bulletin,* 1957, 54:171–96.

Stein, L., and Wise, C. D. Possible etiology of schizophrenia: Progressive damage to the noradrenergic reward system by 6-hydroxydopamine. *Science,* 1971, 171:1032–36.

Stephens, J. H., and Kamp, M. On some aspects of hysteria: A clinical study. *Journal of Nervous and Mental Disorders,* 1962, 134:305–15.

Sterman, H. B. Neurophysiologic and clinical studies of sensorimotor EEG biofeedback training: Some effects on epilepsy. *Seminars on Psychiatry,* 1973, 5:507–25.

Sterman, H. B.; McDonald, L. R.; and Stone, R. K. Biofeedback training of the sensorimotor electroencephalograph in man: Effects of epilepsy. *Epilepsia,* 1974, 15:395–416.

Stoller, F. J. Transvestites' women. *American Journal of Psychiatry*, 1967, 124:333–39.

Storm, T., and Smart, R. O. Dissociation: A possible explanation of some features of alcoholism, and implication for its treatment. *Quarterly Journal of Studies on Alcoholism*, 1965, 26:111–15.

Strange, J. *Abnormal psychology*. New York: McGraw-Hill, 1965.

Strauss, M. E. Behavioral differences between acute and chronic schizophrenics: Course of psychosis, effects of institutionalization, or sampling biases. *Psychological Bulletin*, 1973, 79:271–79.

Stuart, R. B. Behavioral control over eating. *Behaviour Research and Therapy*, 1967, 5:357–65.

Stunkard, A. J. The management of obesity. *New York Journal of Medicine*, 1958, 58:79–87.

Stunkard, A. J. New therapies for the eating disorders. *Archives of General Psychiatry*, 1972, 26:391–98.

Stunkard, A. J., and Koch, C. The interpretation of gastric motility. I: Apparent bias in the reports of hunger by obese persons. *Archives of General Psychiatry*, 1964, 11:74–82.

Stunkard, A. J., and Mendelson, M. Obesity and the body image. *American Journal of Psychiatry*, 1967, 123:1296–1300.

Sturgis, E. T., and Adams, H. E. The right to treatment: Issues in the treatment of homosexuality. *Journal of Consulting and Clinical Psychology*, 1978, 46:165–69.

Sturgis, E. T.; Tollison, C. D.; and Adams, H. E. Modification of combined migraine-muscle contraction headaches using BVP and EMG feedback. *Journal of Applied Behavior Analysis*, 1978, 11:215–23.

Suárez, Y.; Adams, H. E.; and Crowe, M. J. Depression: Avoidance and physiological correlates in clinical and analog populations. *Behaviour Research and Therapy*, 1978, 16:21–31.

Suinn, R. M. *Fundamentals of behavior pathology*. 2d ed. New York: Wiley, 1975.

Sullivan, H. S. *The interpersonal theory of psychiatry*. New York: Norton, 1953.

Suomi, S. J., and Harlow, H. F. Apparatus conceptualization for psychopathological research in monkeys. *Behavior Research Methods and Instrumentation*, 1969, 1:247–50.

Suomi, S. J.; Eisek, C. J.; Grady, S. A.; and Harlow, H. A. Depression in adult monkeys following separation from nuclear family environment. *Journal of Abnormal Psychology*, 1975, 84:576–78.

Suomi, S. J., and Harlow, H. J. Production of depressive behaviors in monkeys. In J. D. Maser and M. E. P. Seligman (eds.), *Psychopathology: Experimental models*. San Francisco: W. H. Freeman, 1977.

Sutker, P. B. Personality differences and sociopathy in heroin addicts and non-addict prisoners. *Journal of Abnormal Psychology*, 1971, 78:247–51.

Szasz, T. S. The myth of mental illness. *American Psychologist*, 1960, 15:113–18.

Szasz, T. S. *Law, liberty, and psychiatry*. New York: Macmillan, 1963.

Szasz, T. S. The psychiatric classification of behavior: A strategy of personal constraint. In L. D. Eron (ed.), *The classification of behavior disorders*. Chicago: Aldine, 1966.

Szasz, T. S. *The manufacture of madness*. New York: Harper & Row, 1970.

Taterks, S., and Kety, S. S. Study of correlation between electroencephalogram and psychological patterns in emotionally disturbed children. *Psychosomatic Medicine*, 1955, 17:62–72.

Taube, C. A., and Rednick, R. W. *Utilization of mental health resources by persons diagnosed with schizophrenia*. Rockville, Md.: National Institute of Mental Health, 1973.

Tavel, M. E. A new look at an old syndrome: Delirium tremens. *Archives of International Medicine*, 1962, 109:129–34.

Taylor, J. G. A behavioral interpretation of obsessive-compulsive neurosis. *Behaviour Research and Therapy*, 1963, 1:237–44.

Temerlin, M. K. Suggestion effects in psychiatric diagnosis. *Journal of Nervous and Mental Disease*, 1968, 147:349–53.

Terman, L. M. Kinsey's Sexual behavior in the human male: Some comments and criticisms. *Psychological Bulletin*, 1948, 45:443–59.

Terman, T. M., and Merrill, M. A. *Measuring intelligence*. Boston: Houghton Mifflin, 1960.

Terry, R., and Wisniewski, H. Sans teeth, sans eyes, sans taste, sans everything. *Behavior Today*, 1974, 5:84.

Thigpen, C. H., and Cleckley, H. M. *Three faces of Eve*. New York: McGraw-Hill, 1957.

Thompson, E. E. *Effectiveness of different techniques in training schizophrenic patients to give common associations*. Paper read at the Annual Meeting of the Midwestern Psychological Association, Chicago, April 1967.

Thoresen, C. E., and Mahoney, M. J. *Behavioral self-control*. New York: Holt, Rinehart and Winston, 1974.

Tienari, P. Schizophrenia in monozygotic male twins. In D. Rosenthal and S. S. Kety (eds.), *The transmission of schizophrenia*. London: Pergamon Press, 1968.

Tinkelenberg, J. R. A clinical view of the amphetamines. *American Family Physician*, 1971, 4:82–86.

Tinkelenberg, J. R., and Woodrow, K. M. Drug use among youthful assaultive and sexual offenders. *The Association for Research in Nervous and Mental Disease: Aggression,* 1974, 52:209–24.

Tollison, C. D., and Adams, H. E. *The sexual disorders: Theory, research, and treatment.* New York: Gardner Press, 1979.

Tollison, C. D.; Adams, H. E.; and Tollison, J. W. Physiological measurement of sexual arousal in homosexual, bisexual, and heterosexual males. *Journal of Behavioral Assessment,* 1979, 1:305–14.

Torrey, E. F. Is schizophrenia universal? An open question. *Schizophrenia Bulletin,* 1973, 7:53–59.

Tourney, G.; Petrilli, A. J.; and Hatfield, L. N. Hormonal relationships in homosexual men. *American Journal of Psychiatry,* 1975, 132:288–90.

Treffert, D. A. The epidemiology of infantile autism. *Archives of General Psychiatry,* 1970, 22:431–38.

Truax, C. B. Effective ingredients in psychotherapy: An approach to unraveling the patient-therapist interaction. *Journal of Counseling Psychology,* 1963, 10:256–63.

Truax, C. B., and Mitchell, K. M. Research on certain therapist interpersonal skills in relation to process and outcome. In A. E. Bergin and S. L. Garfield (eds.), *Handbook of psychotherapy and behavior change.* New York: Wiley, 1971.

Trudel, G.; Boisvert, J. M.; Maruca, F.; and Leroux, P. A. Unprogrammed reinforcement of patients' behavior in ward with and without token economy. *Journal of Behavior Therapy and Experimental Psychiatry,* 1974, 5:147–49.

Tryon, R. C. Individual differences. In F. A. Moss (ed.), *Comparative psychology.* Englewood Cliffs, N.J.: Prentice-Hall, 1972.

Tseng, W. S. The development of psychiatric concepts in traditional Chinese medicine. *Archives of General Psychiatry,* 1973, 29:569–75.

Tuckman, J.; Kleiner, R.; and Lavell, M. Emotional content of suicide notes. *American Journal of Psychiatry,* 1959, 116:59–63.

Tupin, J. P. Hysterical and cyclothymic personalities. In J. R. Lion (ed.), *Personality disorders: Diagnosis and management.* Baltimore: Williams & Wilkins, 1974.

Turnbull, J. W. Asthma conceived as a learned response. *Journal of Psychosomatic Research,* 1962, 6:59–70.

Turner, R. J., and Wagonfeld, M. O. Occupational mobility and schizophrenia. *American Sociological Review,* 1967, 32:104–13.

Udry, J. R., and Morris, N. M. A method for validation of reported sexual data. *Journal of Marriage and the Family,* 1967, 5:442–46.

Ullmann, L. P.; Forsman, R. G.; Kenny, J. W.; McInnes, T. L.; Unikel, I. P.; and Zeisset, R. M. Selective reinforcement of schizophrenic interview responses. *Behaviour Research and Therapy,* 1965, 2:205–12.

Ullmann, L. P., and Krasner, L. *Case studies in behavior modification.* New York: Holt, Rinehart and Winston, 1965.

Ullmann, L. P., and Krasner, L. *A psychological approach to abnormal behavior.* Englewood Cliffs, N.J.: Prentice-Hall, 1969.

Ullmann, L. P., and Krasner, L. *A psychological approach to abnormal behavior.* 2d ed. Englewood Cliffs, N.J.: Prentice-Hall, 1975.

United States Department of Health, Education, and Welfare. *Obesity report.* Washington, D.C.: U.S. Government Printing Office, 1967.

Vachon, L., and Rich, E. S. Visceral learning in asthma. *Psychosomatic Medicine,* 1976, 38:122–30.

Valenstein, E. S. *Brain control.* New York: Wiley, 1973.

Van Buskirk, S. Review of anorexia neuroses. *Psychological Bulletin,* 1977, 84:529–35.

Van Riper, C. *The nature of stuttering.* Englewood Cliffs, N.J.: Prentice-Hall, 1971.

Veith, I. *Hysteria, the history of a disease.* Chicago: University of Chicago Press, 1965.

Venables, P. Input dysfunction in schizophrenia. In B. A. Maher (ed.), *Progress in experimental personality research.* Vol. 1. New York: Academic Press, 1964.

Vetter, H. J. *Language behavior and psychopathology.* Chicago: Rand McNally, 1969.

Victor, M.; Adams, R.; and Collins, G. *The Wernicke-Korsakoff syndrome.* Philadelphia: Davis, 1971.

Vinokur A., and Selzer, M. I. Life events, stress, and mental illness. *Proceedings of the 81st Annual Convention of the American Psychological Association.* Montreal, August 1973.

Voegtlin, W. L. Conditioned reflex therapy in chronic alcoholism: Ten years experience with the method. *Rocky Mountain Medical Journal,* 1947, 44:807–11.

Volkman, F. R., and Greenough, W. T. Rearing complexity affects branching of dendrites in the visual cortex of the rat. *Science,* 1972, 196:1445–46.

Volle, R. L., and Koelle, G. B. Ganglionic stimulating and blocking agents. In L. S. Goodman and A. Gilman (eds.), *The pharmacological basis of therapeutics.* 4th ed. New York: Macmillan, 1970.

Volpe, A., and Kastenbaum, R. TLC. *American Journal of Nursing,* 1967, 67:100–103.

Von Kraft-Ebbing, R. *Psychopathia Sexualis,* 1892. Translated by F. S. Klaf. New York: Putnam, 1965.

Walinder, J. Transsexualism: Definition, prevalence, and sex distribution. *Acta Psychiatrica Scandinavica,* 1968, 203:255–58.

Wallace, M.; Singer, G.; Wayner, M. J.; and Cook, P. A. Adjunctive behavior in humans during game playing. *Physiology and Behavior,* 1975, 14:651–54.

Wallgren, H., and Barry, H. *Actions of alcohol.* Vol. 2. Amsterdam: Elsevier, 1970.

Walton, D. The application of learning theory to the treatment of a case of bronchial asthma. In H. J. Eysenck (ed.), *Behavior therapy and the neuroses.* Oxford: Pergamon Press, 1960.

Ward, A. J. Early infantile autism. *Psychological Bulletin,* 1970, 73:350–62.

Warkeny, J., and Digman, P. St. J. Congenital malformations: Microcephaly. In J. Wortis (ed.), *Mental retardation and developmental disabilities: An annual review.* New York: Brunner/Mazel, 1973.

Waters, W. E. Migraine: Intelligence, social class, and familial prevalence. *British Medical Journal,* 1971, 2:77–78.

Watson, D., and Friend, R. Measurement of social-evaluative anxiety. *Journal of Consulting and Clinical Psychology,* 1969, 33:4:448–57.

Watson, J. B. *Psychology from the standpoint of a behaviorist.* Philadelphia: Lippincott, 1919.

Watson, J. B., and Raynor, R. Conditioned emotional reactions. *Journal of Experimental Psychology,* 1920, 3:1–14.

Watson, L. S. *Child behavior modification: A manual for teachers, nurses, and parents.* New York: Pergamon Press, 1973.

Watts, A. *The supreme identity: An essay on Oriental metaphysic and the Christian religion.* New York: Vintage Books, 1972.

Waxler, N. E. Culture and mental illness: A social labeling perspective. *Journal of Nervous and Mental Disease,* 1974, 159:379–95.

Webb, W. B. Twenty-four hour sleep cycling. In A. Kales (ed.), *Sleep: Physiology and pathology.* Philadelphia, Lippincott, 1969.

Webster, R. L. A behavioral analysis of stuttering. In K. S. Calhoun, H. E. Adams, and K. M. Mitchell (eds.), *Innovative treatment methods in psychopathology.* New York: Wiley, 1974.

Wechsler, D. *Manual for the Wechsler Adult Intelligence Scale.* New York: Psychological Corporation, 1955.

Wechsler, D. *The measurement and appraisal of intelligence.* 4th ed. Baltimore: Williams & Wilkins, 1958.

Weckowicz, T. Depersonalization. In C. G. Costello (ed.), *Symptoms of psychology: A handbook.* New York: Wiley, 1970.

Weckowicz, T. E. Size constancy in schizophrenic patients. *Journal of Mental Science,* 1957, 103:475–86.

Weinberg, M. and Williams, C. J. *Male homosexuals: Their problems and adaptations in three societies.* New York: Oxford University Press, 1974.

Weiner, B. "On being sane in insane places": A process (attributional) analysis and critique. *Journal of Abnormal Psychology,* 1975, 84:433–41.

Weiner, B.; Thaler, M.; Reiser, M. F.; and Mirsky, I. A. Etiology of duodenal ulcer. 1: Relation of specific psychological characteristics to rate of gastric secretion. *Psychosomatic Medicine,* 1957, 17:1–10.

Weintraub, W. Obsessive-compulsive and paranoid personalities. In J. R. Lion (ed.), *Personality disorders: Diagnosis and management.* Baltimore: Williams & Wilkins, 1974.

Weiss, E., and English, S. O. *Psychosomatic Medicine.* Philadelphia: Saunders, 1957.

Weiss, J. M. Effects of coping behavior in different warning-signal conditions in stress pathology in rats. *Journal of Comparative and Physiological Psychology,* 1971a, 77:1–13.

Weiss, J. M. Effects of coping behavior with and without a feedback signal on stress pathology in rats. *Journal of Comparative and Physiological Psychology,* 1971b, 77:22–30.

Weiss, J. M. Effects of punishing the coping response (conflict) on stress pathology in rats. *Journal of Comparative and Physiological Psychology,* 1971c, 77:14–21.

Weiss, M., and Burke, A. A 5- to 10-year follow-up of hospitalized school phobic children and adolescents. *American Journal of Orthopsychiatry,* 1970, 40:672–726.

Weissman, M. M., and Paykel, E.S. *The depressed woman: A study of social relationships.* Chicago: University of Chicago Press, 1974.

Welch, C. E. Abdominal surgery. *New England Journal of Medicine,* 1973, 288:609–16.

Welgan, P. R. Learned control of gastric acid secretion in ulcer patients. *Psychosomatic Medicine,* 1974, 36:411–19.

Wender, Ph. H.; Rosenthal, D.; Kety, S. S.; Schulsinger, F.; and Welner, J. Cross-fostering: A research strategy for clarifying the role of genetic and experiential factors in the etiology of schizophrenia. *Archives of General Psychiatry,* 1974, 30:121–28.

Werry, J. S. Organic factors in childhood psychopathology. In H. C. Quay and J. S. Werry (eds.), *Psychopathological disorders of childhood.* New York: Wiley, 1972a.

Werry, J. S. Childhood psychosis. In H. C. Quay and J. S. Werry (eds.), *Psychopathological disorders of childhood.* New York: Wiley, 1972b.

Wesman, A. G. Intelligent testing. *American Psychologist,* 1968, 23:267–74.

Wheat, W. D. Motivational aspects of suicide in patients during and after psychiatric treatment. *Southern Medical Journal,* 1960, 53:273–78.

Whitehead, W. E. P.; Renault, P. F.; and Goldiamond, I. Modification of human gastric acid secretion with operant-conditioning procedures. *Journal of Applied Behavior Analysis,* 1975, 8:147–56.

Whitlock, F. A. The aetiology of hysteria. *Acta Psychiatrica Scandinavica,* 1967, 43:144–62.

Whitman, T. L.; Mercurio, J. R.; and Caponigri, V. Development of social responses in two severely retarded children. *Journal of Applied Behavior Analysis,* 1970, 3:133–38.

Whitwell, J. R. *Historical notes on psychiatry.* London: H. K. Lewis, 1936.

Wickramasekera, I. The use of some learning theory derived techniques in the treatment of a case of paranoid schizophrenia. *Psychotherapy: Theory, Research, and Practice,* 1967, 4:22–26.

Wiener, H. Diagnosis and symptomatology. In L. Bellack, (ed.), *Schizophrenia: A review of the syndrome.* New York: Logos Press, 1958.

Wikler, A. Conditioning factors in opiate addiction and relapse. In D. M. Wilner and G. C. Kassebaum (eds.), *Narcotics.* New York: McGraw-Hill, 1965.

Wikler, A. Some implications of conditioning theory for problems of drug abuse. *Behavioral Science,* 1971, 16:92–97.

Williams R. L. Danger: Testing and dehumanizing black children. *Clinical Child Psychology Newsletter,* Spring, 1970.

Wilner, D. M., and Kassebaum, G. C. (eds.), *Narcotics.* New York: McGraw-Hill, 1965.

Wilson, A., and Smith, F. J. Counterconditioning therapy using free association: A pilot study. *Journal of Abnormal Psychology,* 1968, 73:474–78.

Wincze, J. Sexual deviance and dysfunction. In Rimm, D. C., and Somervill, J. W. (eds.), *Abnormal Psychology.* New York: Academic Press, 1977.

Wincze, J. P.; Leitenberg, H.; and Agras, W. S. The effects of token reinforcement and feedback on the delusional verbal behavior of chronic paranoid schizophrenics. *Journal of Applied Behavior Analysis,* 1972, 5:247–62.

Winkler, R. C. Management of chronic psychiatric patients by a token reinforcement system. *Journal of Applied Behavior Analysis,* 1970, 3:47–55.

Winokur, G. Depression in the menopause. *American Journal of Psychiatry,* 1973, 130:92–93.

Winokur, G.; Guze, S. G.; and Pfeiffer, E. Developmental and sexual factors in women: A comparison between control, neurotic, and psychotic groups. *American Journal of Psychiatry,* 1959, 115:1097, 1100.

Wittenborn, J. R. *Wittenborn Psychiatric Rating Scales.* New York: Psychological Corporation, 1955.

Witzig, J. S. The group treatment of male exhibitionists. *American Journal of Psychiatry,* 1968, 125:75–81.

Wolberg, L. *The technique of psychotherapy.* 2d ed. New York: Grune & Stratton, 1967.

Wold, C. I., and Litman, R. E. Suicide after contact with a suicide prevention center. *Archives of General Psychiatry,* 1973, 28:735–39.

Wolf, M. M.; Phillips, E. L.; and Fixen, D. L. Achievement place: Phase II. *Final report for grant MH20030, Center for Studies of Crime and Delinquency, National Institute of Mental Health,* May 1, 1971 through April 30, 1974.

Wolf, S.; Cardon, P. V.; Shepard, E. M.; and Wolff, H. G. *Life stress and essential hypertension.* Baltimore: Williams & Wilkins, 1955.

Wolfenstein, M. The emergence of fun morality. *Journal of Sociological Issues,* 1951, 7:15–25.

Wolff, H. G. Life stress and cardiovascular disorders. *Circulation,* 1950, 1:187–203.

Wolff, H. G. *Headache and other pain.* Revised by D. J. Dalessio. New York: Oxford University Press, 1972.

Wollersheim, J. P. Effectiveness of group therapy based on learning principles in the treatment of overweight women. *Journal of Abnormal Psychology,* 1970, 76:462–74.

Wolpe, J. *Psychotherapy by reciprocal inhibition.* Stanford, Calif.: Stanford University Press, 1958.

Wolpe, J. *The practice of behavior therapy.* New York: Pergamon Press, 1969.

Wolpe, J. *The practice of behavior therapy.* 2d ed. New York: Pergamon Press, 1973.

Wolpe, J., and Lang, P. J. A fear survey schedule for use in behavior therapy. *Behaviour Research and Therapy,* 1964, 2:27–30.

Wortis, J. (ed.). *Mental retardation and developmental disabilities: An annual review.* Vol. 5. New York: Brunner/Mazel, 1973.

Wyatt, R. J.; Termini, B. A.; and Davis, J. Biochemical and sleep studies of schizophrenia: A review of the literature—1960–1970. *Schizophrenia Bulletin,* 1971, 4:10–66.

Yablonsky, L. *The tunnel back: Synanon.* New York: Macmillan, 1965.

Yalom, I. D. and Lieberman, M. A. A study of encounter group casualties. *Archives of General Psychiatry,* 1971, 25:16–30.

Yates, A. J. Symptoms and symptom substitution. *Psychological Review,* 1958, 65:371–74.

Yates, A. J. *Behavior therapy.* New York: Wiley, 1972.

Yates, A. J. *Theory and practice in behavior therapy.* New York: Wiley, 1975.

Yorkston, N. J.; McHugh, R. B.; Brady, R.; Serber, M.; and Sargeant, H. G. S. Verbal desensitization in bronchial asthma. *Journal of Psychosomatic Research,* 1974, 18:371–76.

Yoss, R. E., and Daly, D. D. Narcolepsy. *Archives of Internal Medicine,* 1960, 106:168–71.

Yusin, A.; Nihira, K.; and Mortashed, C. Major and minor criteria in schizophrenia. *American Journal of Psychiatry,* 1974, 131:688–92.

Zangwill, O. L. *Cerebral dominance and its relation to psychological function.* Edinburgh: Oliver & Boyd, 1960.

Zerbin-Rudin, F. Genetic research and the theory of schizophrenia. *International Journal of Mental Health,* 1972, 3:46–72.

Zigler, E. The retarded child as a whole person. In H. E. Adams and W. K. Boardman (eds.), *Advances in experimental clinical psychology.* Elmsford, N.Y.: Pergamon Press, 1971.

Zigler, E., and Phillips, L. Psychiatric diagnosis and symptomatology. *Journal of Abnormal and Social Psychology,* 1961a, 63:69–75.

Zigler, E., and Phillips, L. Psychiatric diagnosis: A critique. *Journal of Abnormal and Social Psychology,* 1961b, 63:607–18.

Zubin, J. Classification of the behavioral disorders. *Annual Review of Psychology,* 1967, 18:373–401.

Zubin, J. Foundations of gerontology: History, training, and methodology. In C. Eisdorfer and M. P. Lawton (eds.), *The psychology of adult development and aging.* Washington, D.C.: American Psychological Association, 1973.

Zilboorg, G. and Henry, G. A. *A history of medical psychology.* New York: Norton, 1941.

text and visual credits

Text, Table, and Illustration Credits

Chapter 1

Box 1–2 *Going Crazy.* COPYRIGHT © 1975, 1976 by Otto Friedrich. Reprinted by permission of SIMON & SCHUSTER, a Division of Gulf & Western Corporation.

Chapter 2

Tables 2–1, 2–4, 2–5, and 2–6 Reprinted by permission of the American Psychiatric Association.

Table 2–2 M. K. Termerlin, "Suggestion Effects in Psychiatric Diagnosis," *Journal of Nervous and Mental Disease* 147 (1968): 351. © 1968 The Williams & Wilkins Co., Baltimore.

Table 2–3 "On Being Sane in Insane Places," Rosenhan, D. L., *Science*, vol. 179, pp. 250–58, Table 1, 19 January 1973. Copyright 1973 by the American Association for the Advancement of Science.

Box 2–1 Debbie Spray, "I Was a Teenage Incorrigible," *Madness Network News,* February 1975.

Table 2–7 Anthony R. Ciminero, *Handbook of Behavioral Assessment* (New York: John Wiley & Sons). Used by permission.

Chapter 3

Box 3–1 Alan Watts, *The Supreme Identity: An Essay on Oriental Metaphysics and the Christian Religion* (New York: Pantheon Books, a division of Random House, Inc., 1972). All rights reserved.

Figure 3–1 Reprinted with permission of authors and publisher from: Harbert, T. L.; Barlow, D. H.; Hersen, M.; and Austin, J. B. Measurement and modification of incestuous behavior: a casy study. PSYCHOLOGICAL REPORTS, 1974, 34, 79–86, Figure 1.

Figure 3–2 R. V. Hall, et al., "The Teacher as Observer and Experimenter in the Modification of Disputing and Talking-Out Behaviors," *Journal of Applied Behavior Analysis* 4 (1971): 141–49. Used by permission.

Figure 3–3 R. P. Liberman and V. A. Smith, "A Multiple Baseline Study of Systematic Desensitization in a Patient with Multiple Phobias," *Behavior Therapy* 3 (1972): 597–603. Used by permission.

Chapter 4

Figure 4–1 By permission of the Upjohn Company, Kalamazoo, Michigan; and Margery W. Shaw, M.D., Dept. of Human Genetics, University of Michigan Medical School.

Table 4–1 J. Shields and E. Slater, "Heredity and Psychological Abnormality," from *A Handbook of Abnormal Psychology* (New York: Basic Books, 1961). © 1960, Pitman Medical Publishing Co., Inc. Used by permission.

Figure 4–2 F. Moss (ed.), *Comparative Psychology* (Englewood Cliffs, N.J.: Prentice-Hall, 1934). Reprinted by permission.

Table 4–2 Reprinted from *Heredity in health and mental disorder* by F. J. Kallmann, M.D. By permission of W. W. Norton & Co., Inc. Copyright 1953 by W. W. Norton & Co., Inc.

Figure 4–3 From *Abnormal Psychology* by J. Strange. Copyright © 1965, McGraw-Hill. Used with permission of McGraw-Hill Book Company.

Figure 4–4 S. J. Suomi, *Journal of Abnormal Psychology* 81 (1973). Copyright 1973 by the American Psychological Association. Reprinted by permission.

Figure 4–5 Reprinted with permission from *Behavior Research and Therapy* 4, C. Cook and H. Adams, "Modification of Verbal Behavior in Speech Deficient Children," Copyright 1966, Pergamon Press, Ltd.

Chapter 5

Box 5–1, Table 5–6, Table 5–8, Figure 5–5, Figure 5–6 *Handbook of Behavioral Assessment,* A Ciminero, R. Calhoun, and H. Adams (eds.), Copyright © 1977 John Wiley & Sons. Reprinted by permission of John Wiley & Sons, Inc.

Figure 5–1 Copyright © 1978, Aaron T. Beck, M.D., Center for Cognitive Therapy, Room 602, 133 South 36th Street, Philadelphia, PA 19104. ALL RIGHTS RESERVED.

Box 5–2 MMPI profile reproduced by permission. Copyright 1948 by The Psychological Corporation. All rights reserved as stated in the manual and Catalog. The Psychological Corporation, New York, N.Y.

Box 5–3 From pp. 120–21 in THE INTERPRETATION OF PSYCHOLOGICAL TESTS by Joel Allison et al. Copyright © 1968 by Joel Allison, Sidney J. Blatt, and Carl N. Zimet. Reprinted by permission of Harper & Row, Publishers, Inc.

Box 5–4 Roy Schafer, *Psychoanalytic Interpretation in Rorschach Testing: Theory and Application (New York: Grune & Stratton, 1954). Used by permission.*

Table 5–2 L. J. Chapman and J. P. Chapman, "Illusory Correlations As an Obstacle to the Use of Valid Psychodiagnostic Signs," *Journal of Abnormal Psychology* 74 (1969): 274. Copyright 1969 by the American Psychological Association. Reprinted by permission.

Figure 5–2 Published by The Psychological Corporation, New York, N.Y. All rights reserved.

Table 5–5 Reproduced by permission. Copyright 1955 by The Psychological Corporation, New York, N.Y. All rights reserved.

Table 5–7 S. W. Bijou, R. F. Peterson, F. R. Harris, K. E. Allen, and M. S. Johnston. Methodology for Experimental Studies of Young Children in Natural Settings. *The Psychological Record,* 1969, *19,* 177–210.

Figure 5–4 Reprinted from INSIGHT VS. DESENSITIZATION IN PSYCHOTHERAPY by Gordon L. Paul, with the permission of the publishers, Stanford University Press. © 1966 by the Board of Trustees of the Leland Stanford Junior University.

Chapter 6

Table 6-1 From SIX APPROACHES TO PSYCHOTHERAPY edited by James L. McCary. Copyright © 1955 by The Dryden Press. Reprinted by permission of Holt, Rinehart & Winston.

Box 6-1 L. Wolberg, *The Technique of Psychotherapy,* 3d ed. (New York: Grune & Stratton, 1977). Used by permission.

Table 6-2 Eric Berne, *Games People Play,* 1964. Used by permission of Random House, Inc., Alfred A. Knopf, Inc.

Box 6-2 William H. Snyder, *Casebook of Non-Directive Counseling* (Boston: Houghton Mifflin, 1947). Used by permission.

Box 6-3 B. C. Finney, "Say It Again, An Active Therapy Technique," in *The Handbook of Gestalt Therapy,* C. Hatcher and P. Himelstein (eds.) (New York: Jackson Aronson, 1976). Used by permission.

Figure 6-1 From "Prefrontal Lobotomy: Analysis and Warning" by Kurt Goldstein. Copyright © 1950 by Scientific American, Inc. All rights reserved.

Figure 6-2 From Schlesinger, Kurt, and Philip M. Groves, et al., PSYCHOLOGY: A DYNAMIC SCIENCE, © 1976 Wm. C. Brown Company Publishers, Dubuque, Iowa. Reprinted by permission.

Table 6-4 D. C. Rimm and J. W. Somervill, *Abnormal Psychology* (New York: Academic Press, 1977). Used by permission.

Chapter 7

Cartoon on "Shaping" From Noncontingent Nonsense and the APA Division 25 *Recorder,* John R. Lutzker, Editor; Roger Poppen, Artist.

Figure 7-1 D. H. Barlow and W. S. Agras, *Journal of Applied Behavior Analysis* 6 (1973): 355. Used by permission.

Box 7-1 P. M. Miller, "Alternative Skills Training in Alcoholism Treatment," in *Alcoholism: New Directions in Behavioral Research and Treatment,* P. Nathan, G. A. Marlatt, and T. Lorberg (eds.) (New York: Plenum Publishing Corporation, 1978). Used by permission.

Table 7-1 A. S. Bellack and M. Hersen, *Behavior Modification: An Introductory Textbook* (Baltimore: Williams & Wilkens, 1977). Used by permission.

Box 7-2 From CLINICAL BEHAVIOR THERAPY by Marvin R. Goldfried and Gerald C. Davison. Copyright © 1976 by Holt, Rinehart & Winston. Reprinted by permission of Holt, Rinehart & Winston.

Box 7-3 Reprinted with permission from *Behavior Research and Therapy,* vol. 6, R. A. Hogan, "The Implosive Technique," Copyright 1968, Pergamon Press, Ltd.

Box 7-4 Reprinted with permission from *Behavior Research and Therapy,* vol. 7, R. A. Hogan, "Implosively Oriented Behavior Modification: Therapy Considerations." Copyright 1969, Pergamon Press, Ltd.

Figure 7-2 Reprinted with permission from *Behavior Research and Therapy,* vol. 13, B. A. McCutcheon and H. E. Adams, "The Physiological Basis of Implosive Therapy." Copyright 1975, Pergamon Press, Ltd.

Box 7-5 A. Ellis, *Reason and Emotion in Psychotherapy* (New York: Lyle Stuart, 1962).

Table 7-2 Reprinted with permission from *Addictive Behaviors,* vol. 1, A. S. Bellack, "Behavior Therapy for Weight Reduction." Copyright 1975, Pergamon Press, Ltd.

Figure 7-3 C. E. Cummingham and T. R. Linscheid, "Case Reports and Studies: Elimination of Chronic Infant Rumination by Electric Shock," *Behavior Therapy* 7 (1976): 233. Used by permission.

Box 7-6 Reprinted with permission of author and publisher from: Cautela, J.R. Covert sensitization. PSYCHOLOGICAL REPORTS, 1967, 20, 459–468, 19-line quotation (pages 461–462).

Figure 7-4 C. S. Harris, "A Nonautomated But Practical Rapid Delivery Point Card System for Token Economies," *Behavior Therapy* 8 (1977): 496. Used by permission.

Chapter 8

Figure 8-1 E. Gardner, *Fundamentals of Neurology* (Philadelphia: W. B. Saunders, 1968). Used by permission.

Figure 8-2 G. Mandler, "Emotions," in *New Directions in Psychology,* R. W. Brown, E. Galanter, E. H. Hess, G. Mandler (eds.) (New York: Holt, Rinehart & Winston, 1962). Copyright © 1962 Holt, Rinehart & Winston.

Box 8-1 Paul Karoby, "Multicomponent Behavioral Treatment of Fear of Flying— A Case Report," *Behavior Therapy* 5(2), 1974, pp. 265–67. Used by permission.

Box 8-2 J. Cautela, "The Application of Learning Theory As a Last Resort in the Treatment of a Case of Anxiety Neurosis," *Journal of Clinical Psychology* 21 (1965): 449–51. Used by permission.

Figure 8-4 Reprinted with permission from *Behavior Research and Therapy,* vol. 6, M. H. Lader and A. M. Mathews. Copyright 1968, Pergamon Press, Ltd.

Box 8-3 R. E. Smith, "The Use of Humor in the Counterconditioning of Anger Responses: A Case Study," *Behavior Therapy* 4 (1973): 576–80. Used by permission.

Chapter 9

Figure 9-1 L. P. Ullmann and L. Krasner (Eds.), *Case Studies in Behavior Modification,* (New York: Holt, Rinehart & Winston, 1965). Used by permission.

Box 9-1 Reprinted with permission from *Behavior Research and Therapy,* vol. 4, V. Meyer. Copyright 1966, Pergamon Press, Ltd.

Figure 9-2 From *CIBA Collection of Medical Illustrations* by F. H. Netter, M.D., as adapted in Davison/Neale, ABNORMAL PSYCHOLOGY, 2d ed., p. 159. Copyright © 1978 by John Wiley & Sons, Inc. Used by permission.

Box 9-2 Copyright © 1976 by The William Alanson White Psychiatric Foundation, Inc.

Box 9-3 F. T. Kenny et al., *Behavior Therapy* 4 (1973): 452–53. Used by permission.

Box 9-4 Osgood, Luria, Jeans, and Smith, *Journal of Abnormal Psychology* 85(1976): 247–86. Used by permission.

Chapter 10

Box 10-1 J. R. Lion (ed.), *Personality Disorders: Diagnosis and Management* (Baltimore: Williams and Wilkins Co., 1974). Based on case material presented in "The Explosive, Antisocial, and Passive-Aggressive Personalities" by S. A. Pasternack. Used by permission.

Box 10-2, Figures 10-1 and 10-2 R. D. Hare, *Psychopathy: Theory and Research* (New York: John Wiley & Sons, 1970). Copyright © 1970 John Wiley & Sons. Reprinted by permission of John Wiley & Sons, Inc.

Table 10-1 D. B. Lindsley, *Electroencephalography and Clinical Neurophysiology* 4(1952): 443–56. Used by permission.

Figure 10.3 F. J. Schmauk, *Journal of Abnormal Psychology* 1970, pp. 325–335. Copyright 1970 by the American Psychological Association. Reprinted by permission.

Figure 10-4 R. D. Hare, *Journal of Research in Crime and Delinquency* 2(1965): 12–19. Used by permission.

Box 10-3 D. J. Kass, et al., "Behavioral Group Treatment of Hysteria," *Archives of General Psychiatry* 26 (1972): 42–50. Copyright 1972, American Medical Association.

Box 10–4 J. R. Lion (ed.), *Personality Disorders: Diagnosis and Management* (Baltimore: Williams & Wilkins, 1974). Based on case material presented in "Obsessive-Compulsive and Paranoid Personalities" by G. W. Weintraub. Used by permission.

Box 10–5 M. R. Bornstein, A. S. Bellack, and M. Hersen, *Journal of Applied Behavior Analysis 10(1977): 185–90. Used by permission.*

Chapter 11

Figure 11–2 C. Murchison, ed., *Handbook of General Experimental Psychology* (Worcester, Mass.: Clark University Press, 1934). Used by permission.

Box 11–1 Reprinted by permission of Mary Baine, Ph.D.

Figure 11–3 Courtesy Abbott Laboratories.

Figure 11–4 Janet P. Wollersheim, *Journal of Abnormal Psychology* 76(1970): 496. Copyright 1970 by the American Psychological Association. Reprinted by permission.

Figure 11–5 L. S. Levitz and A. J. Stunkard, *The American Journal of Psychiatry,* vol. 131:4, p. 425, 1974. Copyright 1974, the American Psychiatric Association. Reprinted by permission.

Box 11–2 T. Sajwaj, J. Libet, and S. W. Agras, *Journal of Applied Behavior Analysis,* 1974, pp. 557–63. Used by permission.

Box 11–3 Reprinted with permission from *Journal of Behavior Therapy and Experimental Psychiatry,* vol. 4, A. T. Schnurer, R. P. Rubin, and A. Roy. Copyright 1973, Pergamon Press, Ltd.

Box 11–4 Reprinted with permission from *Journal of Behavior Therapy and Experimental Psychiatry,* vol. 7, K. E. Plachetta. Copyright 1976, Pergamon Press, Ltd.

Figure 11–6 Rimm and Somervill, *Abnormal Psychology* (New York: Academic Press, 1977). Used by permission.

Box 11–5 Reprinted with permission from *Journal of Behavior Therapy and Experimental Psychiatry,* vol. 7, K. Popler. Copyright 1976, Pergamon Press, Ltd.

Box 11–6 Reprinted with permission from *Journal of Behavior Therapy and Experimental Psychiatry,* vol. 6, R. G. Meyer. Copyright 1975, Pergamon Press, Ltd.

Chapter 12

Figure 12–1 Masters and Johnson, *Human Sexual Response* (Boston: Little, Brown & Co., 1966). Used by permission.

Table 12–1 D. L. Barlow et al., *Archives of General Psychiatry* 28(1973): 571. Copyright 1973, American Medical Association.

Figure 12–2 From *Human Sexuality* by Goldstein. Copyright © 1975, McGraw-Hill. Used with the permission of McGraw-Hill Book Co.

Box 12–1 Craighead-Kazdin-Mahoney: BEHAVIOR MODIFICATION: PRINCIPLES, ISSUES, AND APPLICATIONS. Copyright © 1976 by Houghton Mifflin Company. Used by permission.

Box 12–2 D. H. Barlow, G. G. Abel, and E. B. Blanchard, "Gender Identity Change in a Transsexual: An Exorcism," *Archives of Sexual Behavior* 6(5), 1977, pp. 387–95. Used by permission.

Box 12–3 W. L. Marshall, *Journal of Consulting and Clinical Psychology* 42(1974): 613–16. Copyright 1974 by the American Psychological Association. Reprinted by permission.

Box 12–4 R. J. Kohlenberg, *Journal of Abnormal Psychology* 83(1974): 192–95. Copyright 1974 by the American Psychological Association. Reprinted by permission.

Box 12–5 Reprinted with permission of authors and publisher from: Harbert, T. L., Barlow, D. H., Hersen, M., and Austin, J. B. Measurement and modification of incestuous behavior: a case study. PSYCHOLOGICAL REPORTS, 1974, 34, 79–86, (page 82) Opening words: "You are alone with your daughter . . ." Closing words: ". . . miserable and disgusted with yourself."

Chapter 13

Tables 13–1 and 13–2 From Ray, Oakley: Drugs, society, and human behavior, ed. 2, St. Louis, 1978, The C. V. Mosby Co.

Figures 13–1 and 13–2 R. L. Solomon and J. D. Corbit, "An Opponent Process Theory of Motivation," *Psychological Review* 81 (1974): 119–45. Copyright 1974 by the American Psychological Association. Reprinted by permission.

Figure 13–3 W. A. Hunt, *Journal of Clinical Psychology* 27(1973): 455–56. Used by permission.

Figure 13–4 Fig. 8–1 in HEALTH SCIENCE, Fourth Edition by Kenneth L. Jones et al. Copyright © 1978 by Kenneth L. Jones, Louis W. Shainberg, and Curtis O. Byer. Reprinted by permission of Harper & Row, Publishers, Inc.

Box 13–2 Reprinted with permission from *Behavior Research and Therapy,* vol. 5, Erwin Lesser, "Behavior Therapy with a Narcotics User." Copyright 1967, Pergamon Press, Ltd.

Chapter 14

Box 14–1 W. Scott McDonald and Chester W. Oden, Jr., *Journal of Abnormal Psychology* 86 (1977): 189–94. Copyright 1977 by the American Psychological Association.

Table 14–2 Joseph Mendels, *Concepts of Depression* (New York: John Wiley & Sons). Used by permission.

Table 14–3 G. A. Carlson and F. K. Goodwin, "The Stages of Mania," *Archives of General Psychiatry* 28 (1973): 226. Copyright 1973, American Medical Association.

Box 14–2 Cameron-Magaret: BEHAVIOR PATHOLOGY. Copyright © 1951, renewed 1970 by Houghton Mifflin Company. Used by permission.

Table 14–4 A. T. Beck, *Depression: Clinical, Experimental and Theoretical Aspects* (New York: Harper & Row, 1967). Used by permission.

Table 14–5 L. Y. Abramson, M. E. P. Seligman, and J. D. Leasdale, *Journal of Abnormal Psychology* 87(1978): 165–79. Copyright 1978 by the American Psychological Association. Reprinted by permission.

Figures 14–2 and 14–3 K. S. Calhoun, H. E. Adams, and K. M. Mitchell, eds., *Innovative Treatment Methods in Psychopathology* (New York: John Wiley & Sons, 1974). Used by permission.

Box 14–3 B. Jackson, *Behavior Therapy* 3(1972): 302–4. Used by permission.

Chapter 15

Table 15–1 J. G. Harris, Jr., *Journal of Abnormal Psychology* 84(1975): 129–37. Copyright 1975 by the American Psychological Association. Reprinted by permission.

Table 15–2 Reprinted by permission of the American Psychiatric Association.

Photo Credits

Unit Opening photography by Bob Coyle

name index

subject index

and alcoholism, 368
bruxism as response to, 315
as a cause of abnormal behavior, 9
in compulsive behavior, 229
in conversion reactions, 232
diathesis-
    hypothesis, and schizophrenia, 453
    model, Meehl's, 453
and dopamine hypothesis of schizophrenia, 454–55
and essential hypertension, 507
and invalidism, 561
life, 492–93
physical, in sleep variables, 310
psychological, in sleep variables, 310
and psychophysiological disorders, 491
as reaction to anxiety, 212
and tension headaches, 513
and ulcers, 499
Stress inoculation, 95
Stressors
    ratings of psychosocial, from APA DSM III, table, 49
    severity of psychological, axis IV, 49
Stripper, and sexual arousal, 323
Strippers, and exhibitionism, 348
Structure
    in organic brain disorders, 540
    versus function, 490
Structure of thought processes, disorders of, in psychoses, 404
Stubbornness, and passive-aggressive personality, 279
Students, college, and depersonalization disorder, 245
Studies
    adoption, and schizophrenia, 451–52
    animal, 78
    case, 189
        controlled, 189
        controlled group, 189
    correlational, 64–65
    family morbidity, 451
    genetic, in childhood psychosis, 478

high-risk, and schizophrenia, 452–53
human population, 78–80
and stuttering, 225–26
twin, 76
    blind analysis in, 77
    and schizophrenia, table, 451
    and theories of schizophrenia, 450–51
uncontrolled group, 189
Studies in Hysteria, 23
Stuttering, auditory feedback and, 226
Stuttering
    and servo-system model of speech control, 226
    and children, 225
    and fluency, 225
    labeling and punishing in, 226
    main discussion 225–27
Style, life, in Adlerian therapy, 141
Subcultural delinquency, in types of antisocial personality, 255
Subdural hematoma, and trauma, 554
Subject expectancy, table, 66
Subjective reports, 121–22
Subjects
    analogue, 188
    in multiple baseline design, 69
Sublimation, introduced, 25
Substance abuse, and drug use, 363
Substance dependency, and drug use, 363
Substance-induced organic mental disorder, 363
Substance use disorder, and drug use, 363
Substance use disorders, table, 47
Substitution, 87
    symptom, 137
Subtests
    performance, tables, 117, 118
    verbal, table, 118
Subtypes of affective disorders, 411
Success, and narcissistic personality, 280
Successive approximation, 88
Succinylcholine, 158
Succubi, 18
Sudden-death subjects, figure, 494
Suffering, escape from, suicide note, 432

Sufficient conditions, 74
Sufficient qualities, 34, 35
Sufficient requirement, 65
Suggestibility, of hysterical personality, 267
Suggestion, and asthmatic response, 504
Suggestion effects, table, 42
Suggestions, related to hypnosis, 22
Suggestions and advice, table, 135
Suicidal behavior, in depression, 409
Suicide, 431–34
    affective disorders and, 401–36
    causes of, 432–33
    disturbed affect of, 432
    facts about, 431
    indicators of, 431–32
    notes, three kinds of, 432–33
    prevention of, 433–34
    social isolation of, 432
    somatic problems of, 432
    three features of, 432
Sullivanians, in evaluation example, 145
Sullivan's interpersonal relationship therapy, table, 135
Superego, 24, 140
Superimposed spindling, in treatment of sleep disorders, 308
Supernatural, belief in, 9
"Supernormal," man, 42
Superstition, 15
Superstitious behavior
    and generalized anxiety, 213
    related to adjunctive behavior, 229
Supervised withdrawal, of a drug, 393
Supervision, faded, 178
Supportive methods, table, 135
Supreme Court, and sexual behavior, 328
Surgery
    icepick, 156
    intestinal bypass, and obesity, 295
    in medical models, 10
    sex reassignment, 347
    and side effects in treatment of obesity, 295
    and transsexualism, 346, 347
Surrogate mother, 84
Survey Schedule
    Assertive Behavior, 122
    Fear, 122, 126
    Wolpe-Lang Fear, 122

Surveys Schedule, Reinforcement, 122
Susto, type, table, 12
Swapping, mate, and sexual disorders, 357
Symbolic form, 24
Symbolism, and conversion reactions, 234
Symbols, in Jung, 26
Sympathetic nervous system in emotions, 202
    and essential hypertension, 507
Sympathetic outflow, diagram of autonomic nervous system, 202
Symptom, special, neuroses, II, 221–50
Symptomatic epilepsy, 548
Symptomatic phase, prealcoholic, 365
Symptomatic therapy, expressive and dynamic, 226
Symptomology, category of hysteria, 269
Symptom remission, 23
Symptoms, 10, 41
    primary, of schizophrenia, 439
    secondary, of schizophrenia, 439
"Symptoms," 6
Symptoms
    asthmatic, and children, 504
    hospital as source of, in schizophrenia, 458
    motor, in conversion reactions, 231–33
    neurotic
        of motor, sensory, and cognitive systems, 222
        and personality types, 271
    in nomenclature table, 38
    paranoid, and Lorr's factor, 469
    Parkinson-like, and dopamine hypothesis of schizophrenia, 454
    physician-caused, in conversion reactions, 232
    primary, of organic brain disorders, 540–43
    psychotic, types of, 402
    secondary, of organic brain disorders, 543–44
    signs and, of depression, table, 409
    special, 40
        neuroses, personality disorders, and, 195–282